New Perspectives on

Microsoft® Office Excel® 2007

Premium Video Edition

Introductory

Approved Courseware

The material in this book is included as part of the text, *New Perspectives on Microsoft® Office Excel® 2007 Comprehensive*, which meets the certification requirements for the Microsoft Certified Application Specialist exam, "Using Microsoft® Office Excel® 2007."

New Perspectives on

Microsoft® Office Excel® 2007
Premium Video Edition

Introductory

June Jamrich Parsons

Dan Oja

Roy Ageloff

Patrick Carey

Australia • Brazil • Japan • Korea • Mexico • Singapore • Spain • United Kingdom • United States

**New Perspectives on Microsoft Office Excel 2007—
Introductory, Premium Video Edition**

Vice President, Publisher: Nicole Jones Pinard

Executive Editor: Marie L. Lee

Associate Acquisitions Editor: Brandi Shailer

Senior Product Manager: Kathy Finnegan

Product Manager: Leigh Hefferon

Associate Product Manager: Julia Leroux-Lindsey

Editorial Assistant: Zina Kresin

Director of Marketing: Cheryl Costantini

Senior Marketing Manager: Ryan DeGrote

Marketing Coordinator: Kristen Panciocco

Developmental Editor: Robin M. Romer

Senior Content Project Manager: Jennifer Goguen McGrail

Content Project Managers: Daphne Barbas, Danielle Chouhan

Composition: GEX Publishing Services

Text Designer: Steve Deschene

Art Director: Marissa Falco

Cover Designer: Elizabeth Paquin

Cover Art: Bill Brown

© 2011 Course Technology, Cengage Learning

ALL RIGHTS RESERVED. No part of this work covered by the copyright herein may be reproduced, transmitted, stored or used in any form or by any means graphic, electronic, or mechanical, including but not limited to photocopying, recording, scanning, digitizing, taping, Web distribution, information networks, or information storage and retrieval systems, except as permitted under Section 107 or 108 of the 1976 United States Copyright Act, without the prior written permission of the publisher.

For product information and technology assistance, contact us at
Cengage Learning Customer & Sales Support, 1-800-354-9706

For permission to use material from this text or product, submit all requests online at **cengage.com/permissions**
Further permissions questions can be emailed to
permissionrequest@cengage.com

Some of the product names and company names used in this book have been used for identification purposes only and may be trademarks or registered trademarks of their respective manufacturers and sellers.

Microsoft and the Office logo are either registered trademarks or trademarks of Microsoft Corporation in the United States and/or other countries. Course Technology, Cengage Learning is an independent entity from the Microsoft Corporation, and not affiliated with Microsoft in any manner.

Disclaimer: Any fictional data related to persons or companies or URLs used throughout this book is intended for instructional purposes only. At the time this book was printed, any such data was fictional and not belonging to any real persons or companies.

ISBN-13: 978-0-538-47560-0

ISBN-10: 0-538-47560-9

Course Technology
20 Channel Center Street
Boston, Massachusetts 02210
USA

Cengage Learning is a leading provider of customized learning solutions with office locations around the globe, including Singapore, the United Kingdom, Australia, Mexico, Brazil, and Japan. Locate your local office at:
international.cengage.com/global

Cengage Learning products are represented in Canada by Nelson Education, Ltd.

To learn more about Course Technology, visit **www.cengage.com/coursetechnology**
To learn more about Cengage Learning, visit **www.cengage.com**

Purchase any of our products at your local college store or at our preferred online store **www.CengageBrain.com**

Printed in the United States of America
1 2 3 4 5 6 7 8 9 14 13 12 11 10

Preface

The New Perspectives Series' critical-thinking, problem-solving approach is the ideal way to prepare students to transcend point-and-click skills and take advantage of all that Microsoft Office 2007 has to offer.

In developing the New Perspectives Series for Microsoft Office 2007, our goal was to create books that give students the software concepts and practical skills they need to succeed beyond the classroom. We've updated our proven case-based pedagogy with more practical content to make learning skills more meaningful to students.

With the New Perspectives Series, students understand *why* they are learning *what* they are learning, and are fully prepared to apply their skills to real-life situations.

About This Book

This book provides thorough, hands-on coverage of Microsoft Office Excel 2007, and includes the following:

- *New with this Edition:* A Video Companion offering a suite of videos that illustrate the most important and challenging Excel 2007 concepts and skills; **look for the ▶ icon in the Table of Contents to see which topics have associated videos**
- *New with this Edition:* An Appendix presenting the basics of the new Microsoft Windows 7 operating system
- Complete instruction on Excel 2007 basics, including creating and formatting a workbook, working with formulas and functions, and creating charts and graphics
- Expanded and in-depth coverage of higher level skills, including working with Excel tables, PivotTables, and PivotCharts; managing multiple worksheets and workbooks; using advanced functions and filtering; and developing an Excel application
- A solid and thorough presentation of important spreadsheet concepts, including order of precedence, function syntax, absolute and relative cell references, what-if analysis, and data validation
- Coverage of new Excel 2007 features, including table styles, design themes, Live Preview, conditional formats, and new sorting and filtering options

System Requirements

This book assumes a typical installation of Microsoft Office Excel 2007 and Microsoft Windows Vista Ultimate with the Aero feature turned off (or Windows Vista Home Premium or Business edition). Note that you can also complete the tutorials in this book using Windows XP; you will notice only minor differences if you are using Windows XP. Refer to the tutorial "Getting Started with Microsoft Office 2007" for Tips noting these differences. The browser used in this book for any steps that require a browser is Internet Explorer 7.

> *I really love the Margin Tips, which add 'tricks of the trade' to students' skills package. In addition, the Reality Check exercises provide for practical application of students' knowledge. I can't wait to use them in the classroom."*
> —Terry Morse Colucci
> Institute of Technology, Inc.

www.cengage.com/ct/newperspectives

"I appreciate the real-world approach that the New Perspectives Series takes. It enables the transference of knowledge from step-by-step instructions to a far broader application of the software tools."
—Monique Sluymers
Kaplan University

The New Perspectives Approach

Context
Each tutorial begins with a problem presented in a "real-world" case that is meaningful to students. The case sets the scene to help students understand what they will do in the tutorial.

Hands-on Approach
Each tutorial is divided into manageable sessions that combine reading and hands-on, step-by-step work. Colorful screenshots help guide students through the steps. **Trouble?** tips anticipate common mistakes or problems to help students stay on track and continue with the tutorial.

InSight

InSight Boxes
New for Office 2007! InSight boxes offer expert advice and best practices to help students better understand how to work with the software. With the information provided in the InSight boxes, students achieve a deeper understanding of the concepts behind the software features and skills.

Tip

Margin Tips
New for Office 2007! Margin Tips provide helpful hints and shortcuts for more efficient use of the software. The Tips appear in the margin at key points throughout each tutorial, giving students extra information when and where they need it.

Reality Check

Reality Checks
New for Office 2007! Comprehensive, open-ended Reality Check exercises give students the opportunity to practice skills by creating practical, real-world documents, such as resumes and budgets, which they are likely to use in their everyday lives at school, home, or work.

Review

In New Perspectives, retention is a key component to learning. At the end of each session, a series of Quick Check questions helps students test their understanding of the concepts before moving on. Each tutorial also contains an end-of-tutorial summary and a list of key terms for further reinforcement.

Apply

Assessment
Engaging and challenging Review Assignments and Case Problems have always been a hallmark feature of the New Perspectives Series. Colorful icons and brief descriptions accompany the exercises, making it easy to understand, at a glance, both the goal and level of challenge a particular assignment holds.

Reference Window
Task Reference

Reference
While contextual learning is excellent for retention, there are times when students will want a high-level understanding of how to accomplish a task. Within each tutorial, Reference Windows appear before a set of steps to provide a succinct summary and preview of how to perform a task. In addition, a complete Task Reference at the back of the book provides quick access to information on how to carry out common tasks. Finally, each book includes a combination Glossary/Index to promote easy reference of material.

www.cengage.com/ct/newperspectives

Our Complete System of Instruction

Coverage To Meet Your Needs
Whether you're looking for just a small amount of coverage or enough to fill a semester-long class, we can provide you with a textbook that meets your needs.
- Brief books typically cover the essential skills in just 2 to 4 tutorials.
- Introductory books build and expand on those skills and contain an average of 5 to 8 tutorials.
- Comprehensive books are great for a full-semester class, and contain 9 to 12+ tutorials.

So if the book you're holding does not provide the right amount of coverage for you, there's probably another offering available. Visit our Web site or contact your Course Technology sales representative to find out what else we offer.

Student Online Companion
This book has an accompanying online companion Web site designed to enhance learning. This Web site, www.course.com/np/office2007, includes the following:
- Internet Assignments for selected tutorials
- Student Data Files
- PowerPoint presentations

CourseCasts – Learning on the Go. Always available…always relevant.
Want to keep up with the latest technology trends relevant to you? Visit our site to find a library of podcasts, CourseCasts, featuring a "CourseCast of the Week," and download them to your mp3 player at http://coursecasts.course.com.

Our fast-paced world is driven by technology. You know because you're an active participant—always on the go, always keeping up with technological trends, and always learning new ways to embrace technology to power your life.

Ken Baldauf, host of CourseCasts, is a faculty member of the Florida State University Computer Science Department where he is responsible for teaching technology classes to thousands of FSU students each year. Ken is an expert in the latest technology trends; he gathers and sorts through the most pertinent news and information for CourseCasts so your students can spend their time enjoying technology, rather than trying to figure it out. Open or close your lecture with a discussion based on the latest CourseCast.

Visit us at http://coursecasts.course.com to learn on the go!

Instructor Resources
We offer more than just a book. We have all the tools you need to enhance your lectures, check students' work, and generate exams in a new, easier-to-use and completely revised package. This book's Instructor's Manual, ExamView testbank, PowerPoint presentations, data files, solution files, figure files, and a sample syllabus are all available on a single CD-ROM or for downloading at http://www.cengage.com/coursetechnology.

www.cengage.com/ct/newperspectives

SAM: Skills Assessment Manager

SAM 2007 is designed to help bring students from the classroom to the real world. It allows students to train and test on important computer skills in an active, hands-on environment.

SAM's easy-to-use system includes powerful interactive exams, training, and projects on the most commonly used Microsoft Office applications. SAM simulates the Office 2007 application environment, allowing students to demonstrate their knowledge and think through the skills by performing real-world tasks, such as bolding text or setting up slide transitions. Add in live-in-the-application projects, and students are on their way to truly learning and applying skills to business-centric documents.

Designed to be used with the New Perspectives Series, SAM includes handy page references, so students can print helpful study guides that match the New Perspectives textbooks used in class. For instructors, SAM also includes robust scheduling and reporting features.

Content for Online Learning

Course Technology has partnered with the leading distance learning solution providers and class-management platforms today. To access this material, visit www.cengage.com/webtutor and search for your title. Instructor resources include the following: additional case projects, sample syllabi, PowerPoint presentations, and more. For students to access this material, they must have purchased a WebTutor PIN-code specific to this title and your campus platform. The resources for students might include (based on instructor preferences): topic reviews, review questions, practice tests, and more. For additional information, please contact your sales representative.

Acknowledgments

We would like to thank the many people whose invaluable contributions made this book possible. First, sincere thanks go to our reviewers: Earl Belcher, Sinclair Community College; Alan Fisher, Walters State Community College; Ranida B. Harris, Indiana University Southeast; Brian Kovar, Kansas State University; Karleen Nordquist, Rasmussen College; Janet Reckmeyer, Glendale Community College; Kenneth J. Sousa, Bryant University; Martha Taylor, Sinclair Community College; and Cathy Van Landuyt, Missouri State University. At Course Technology we would like to thank Kristina Matthews, Acquisitions Editor; Kathy Finnegan, Senior Product Manager; Brandi Henson, Associate Product Manager; Leigh Robbins, Editorial Assistant; Daphne Barbas and Danielle Chouhan, Content Project Managers; Christian Kunciw, Manuscript Quality Assurance Project Leader; and John Freitas, Serge Palladino, Danielle Shaw, Marianne Snow, and Susan Whalen, MQA Testers. Special thanks to Robin Romer, Developmental Editor, for her exceptional efforts, keeping us focused and providing guidance and encouragement as we worked to complete this text.

–June Jamrich Parsons
–Dan Oja
–Roy Ageloff
–Patrick Carey

www.cengage.com/ct/newperspectives

Brief Contents

Office Getting Started with Microsoft Office 2007 .... OFF 1
Preparing a Meeting Agenda

Excel

Excel—Level I Tutorials

Tutorial 1 Getting Started with Excel............................... EX 1
Creating an Order Report

Tutorial 2 Formatting a Workbook................................ EX 57
Formatting a Financial Report

Tutorial 3 Working with Formulas and Functions..................... EX 113
Developing a Budget

Tutorial 4 Working with Charts and Graphics .... EX 161
Charting Financial Data

Excel—Level II Tutorials

Tutorial 5 Working with Excel Tables, PivotTables, and PivotCharts...... EX 217
Tracking Museum Art Objects

Tutorial 6 Managing Multiple Worksheets and Workbooks .... EX 281
Summarizing Ticket Sales

Tutorial 7 Using Advanced Functions, Conditional Formatting,
and Filtering... EX 337
Reviewing Employee Data

Tutorial 8 Developing an Excel Application.......................... EX 393
Creating an Invoice

Appendix A Working with Text Functions and Creating Custom Formats... EX A1

Appendix B Integrating Excel with Other Windows Programs .... EX B1

Appendix A Introduction to Microsoft Windows 7 .... WIN7 1

Glossary/Index REF 1

Task Reference REF 10

The ▶ icon next to a topic in the Table of Contents indicates the topic has an associated video available on the Video Companion.

Table of Contents

Preface v

Getting Started with Microsoft Office 2007
Preparing a Meeting Agenda .... OFF 1

Exploring Microsoft Office 2007 .... OFF 2
   Integrating Office Programs .... OFF 3
Starting Office Programs .... OFF 3
   Switching Between Open Programs and Files .... OFF 5
▶ Exploring Common Window Elements .... OFF 6
   Resizing the Program Window and Workspace .... OFF 6
   Getting Information from the Status Bar .... OFF 7
   Switching Views .... OFF 8
   Zooming the Workspace .... OFF 8
Using the Ribbon .... OFF 10
   Clicking Button Icons .... OFF 10
   Using Galleries and Live Preview .... OFF 12
   Opening Dialog Boxes and Task Panes .... OFF 13
▶ Using Contextual Tools .... OFF 15
   Displaying Contextual Tabs .... OFF 15
   Accessing the Mini Toolbar .... OFF 15
   Opening Shortcut Menus .... OFF 17
Working with Files .... OFF 18
   Saving a File .... OFF 18
   Closing a File .... OFF 21
   Opening a File .... OFF 21
Getting Help .... OFF 23
   Viewing ScreenTips .... OFF 23
   Using the Help Window .... OFF 23
Printing a File .... OFF 27
Exiting Programs .... OFF 28
Quick Check .... OFF 29
Tutorial Summary .... OFF 29
Key Terms .... OFF 29
Review Assignments .... OFF 30
SAM Assessment and Training .... OFF 30
Quick Check Answers .... OFF 31
Reality Check .... OFF 32

Excel Level I Tutorials

Tutorial 1 Getting Started with Excel
Creating an Order Report .... EX 1

Session 1.1 .... EX 2
Introducing Excel .... EX 2
▶ Understanding Spreadsheets .... EX 2
   Exploring the Excel Window .... EX 3
   Navigating a Worksheet .... EX 6
   Navigating Between Worksheets .... EX 7
▶ Planning a Workbook .... EX 8
Entering Text, Numbers, and Dates in Cells .... EX 9
   Entering Text .... EX 10
   Entering Multiple Lines of Text Within a Cell ...... EX 12
   Entering Dates .... EX 13
   Entering Numbers .... EX 13
Working with Columns and Rows .... EX 15
   Changing Column Width and Row Height .... EX 15
   Inserting a Column or Row .... EX 18
   Deleting and Clearing a Row or Column .... EX 20
Session 1.1 Quick Check .... EX 21
Session 1.2 .... EX 21
Working with Cells and Cell Ranges .... EX 21
   Selecting a Cell Range .... EX 22

Moving and Copying a Cell Range	EX 24
Inserting and Deleting a Cell Range	EX 26
▶ Working with Formulas	EX 27
Entering a Formula	EX 27
Copying and Pasting Formulas	EX 30
▶ Introducing Functions	EX 31
Entering a Function	EX 32
Entering Functions with AutoSum	EX 33
Working with Worksheets	EX 35
Inserting and Deleting a Worksheet	EX 35
Renaming a Worksheet	EX 35
Moving and Copying a Worksheet	EX 36
Editing Your Work	EX 36
Undoing and Redoing an Action	EX 37
Using Find and Replace	EX 38
Using the Spelling Checker	EX 39
Previewing and Printing a Worksheet	EX 40
Changing Worksheet Views	EX 41
Working with Portrait and Landscape Orientation	EX 42
Printing the Workbook	EX 43
Viewing and Printing Worksheet Formulas	EX 44
Session 1.2 Quick Check	EX 46
Tutorial Summary	EX 46
Key Terms	EX 47
Review Assignments	EX 48
Case Problems	EX 49
Internet Assignments	EX 55
SAM Assessment and Training	EX 55
Quick Check Answers	EX 55

Tutorial 2 Formatting a Workbook
Formatting a Financial Report ....EX 57

Session 2.1	**EX 58**
Formatting Workbooks	EX 58
Formatting Text	EX 58
Working with Color	EX 60
Applying Font Color and Fill Color	EX 61
Formatting Text Selections	EX 62
Setting a Background Image	EX 63
▶ Formatting Data	EX 64
Formatting Numbers	EX 65
Formatting Dates and Times	EX 66
▶ Formatting Worksheet Cells	EX 67
Aligning Cell Content	EX 67
Indenting Cell Content	EX 68
Merging Cells	EX 69
Rotating Cell Content	EX 70
Adding Cell Borders	EX 71
Working with the Format Cells Dialog Box	EX 72
Copying and Pasting Formats	EX 74
Copying Formats with the Format Painter	EX 74
Copying Formats with the Paste Options Button	EX 75
Copying Formats with Paste Special	EX 76
Applying Styles	EX 76
Working with Themes	EX 78
Session 2.1 Quick Check	EX 80
Session 2.2	**EX 80**
Formatting the Monthly Sales Worksheet	EX 80
▶ Working with Table Styles	EX 82
Selecting Table Style Options	EX 84
▶ Introducing Conditional Formats	EX 86
Adding Data Bars	EX 87
Clearing a Conditional Format	EX 89
Highlighting Cells	EX 90
Hiding Worksheet Data	EX 94
Formatting the Worksheet for Printing	EX 95
Defining the Print Area	EX 96
Inserting Page Breaks	EX 96
Adding Print Titles	EX 98
Adding Headers and Footers	EX 98

Session 2.2 Quick Check	EX 100
Tutorial Summary	EX 101
Key Terms	EX 101
Review Assignments	EX 102
Case Problems	EX 104
Internet Assignments	EX 111
SAM Assessment and Training	EX 111
Quick Check Answers	EX 111

Tutorial 3 Working with Formulas and Functions
Developing a Budget .... EX 113

Session 3.1	**EX 114**
▶ Understanding Cell References When Copying Formulas	EX 114
Using Relative References	EX 115
Using Absolute References	EX 116
Using Mixed References	EX 118
Working with Functions	EX 120
▶ Understanding Function Syntax	EX 121
Inserting a Function	EX 123
Typing a Function	EX 127
Session 3.1 Quick Check	EX 130
Session 3.2	**EX 131**
▶ Working with AutoFill	EX 131
AutoFilling a Formula	EX 132
Using the AutoFill Options Button	EX 133
Filling a Series	EX 134
Developing a Savings Plan	EX 137
▶ Working with Logical Functions	EX 141
Using the IF Function	EX 141
Working with Date Functions	EX 145
▶ Working with Financial Functions	EX 146
Using the PMT Function to Determine a Monthly Loan Payment	EX 147
Session 3.2 Quick Check	EX 151
Tutorial Summary	EX 151
Key Terms	EX 151

Review Assignments	EX 152
Case Problems	EX 153
Internet Assignments	EX 159
SAM Assessment and Training	EX 160
Quick Check Answers	EX 160

Tutorial 4 Working with Charts and Graphics
Charting Financial Data .... EX 161

Session 4.1	**EX 162**
▶ Creating Charts	EX 162
Selecting a Data Source	EX 163
Selecting a Chart Type	EX 164
Moving and Resizing Charts	EX 166
▶ Working on Chart Design	EX 168
Selecting Chart Elements	EX 168
Choosing a Chart Style and Layout	EX 169
Working with the Chart Title	EX 171
Working with the Chart Legend	EX 172
Formatting a Pie Chart	EX 173
Setting the Pie Slice Colors	EX 175
Creating a 3D Pie Chart	EX 176
Working with 3D Options	EX 177
Editing Chart Data	EX 179
Working with Column Charts	EX 180
▶ Creating a Column Chart	EX 180
Formatting Column Chart Elements	EX 181
Formatting the Chart Axes	EX 183
Formatting the Chart Columns	EX 184
Session 4.1 Quick Check	EX 187
Session 4.2	**EX 187**
▶ Creating a Line Chart	EX 187
Formatting Date Labels	EX 188
Setting Label Units	EX 191
Overlaying a Legend	EX 192
Adding a Data Series to an Existing Chart	EX 194
Creating a Combination Chart	EX 196

Working with Shapes	EX 199
Inserting a Shape	EX 200
Resizing, Moving, and Copying a Shape	EX 200
Aligning and Grouping Shapes	EX 201
Creating a Chart Sheet	EX 202
Session 4.2 Quick Check	EX 205
Tutorial Summary	EX 206
Key Terms	EX 206
Review Assignments	EX 207
Case Problems	EX 208
Internet Assignments	EX 213
SAM Assessment and Training	EX 213
Quick Check Answers	EX 213
Reality Check	EX 215

Excel Level II Tutorials

Tutorial 5 Working with Excel Tables, PivotTables, and PivotCharts
Tracking Museum Art Objects .... EX 217

Session 5.1	**EX 218**
Planning a Structured Range of Data	EX 218
Freezing Rows and Columns	EX 220
▶ Creating an Excel Table	EX 221
Renaming an Excel Table	EX 223
Formatting an Excel Table	EX 224
Maintaining an Excel Table	EX 225
Adding Records	EX 225
Finding and Editing Records	EX 226
Deleting a Record	EX 227
▶ Sorting Data	EX 227
Sorting One Column Using the Sort Buttons	EX 228
Sorting Multiple Columns Using the Sort Dialog Box	EX 228
Sorting Using a Custom List	EX 231
Session 5.1 Quick Check	EX 232
Session 5.2	**EX 233**

▶ Filtering Data	EX 233
Filtering Using One Column	EX 233
Filtering Using Multiple Columns	EX 236
Clearing Filters	EX 237
Selecting Multiple Filter Items	EX 237
Creating Criteria Filters to Specify More Complex Criteria	EX 238
Using the Total Row to Calculate Summary Statistics	EX 240
Inserting Subtotals	EX 242
Using the Subtotal Outline View	EX 245
Session 5.2 Quick Check	EX 246
Session 5.3	**EX 246**
▶ Analyzing Data with PivotTables	EX 246
Creating a PivotTable	EX 248
Adding Fields to a PivotTable	EX 251
Applying PivotTable Styles	EX 253
Formatting PivotTable Value Fields	EX 253
Rearranging a PivotTable	EX 254
Changing the PivotTable Report Layout Options	EX 255
Adding a Report Filter to a PivotTable	EX 257
Filtering PivotTable Fields	EX 258
Collapsing and Expanding Items	EX 259
Sorting PivotTable Fields	EX 260
Adding a Second Value Field to a PivotTable	EX 261
Removing a Field from a PivotTable	EX 262
Refreshing a PivotTable	EX 263
Grouping PivotTable Items	EX 265
Grouping Date Fields	EX 267
Creating a PivotChart	EX 268
Session 5.3 Quick Check	EX 270
Tutorial Summary	EX 271
Key Terms	EX 271
Review Assignments	EX 272
Case Problems	EX 273

Internet Assignments . . . . .EX 279

SAM Assessment and Training . . . . .EX 279

Quick Check Answers . . . . .EX 279

Tutorial 6 Managing Multiple Worksheets and Workbooks
Summarizing Ticket Sales . . . .*EX 281*

Session 6.1 . . . .**EX 282**

Using Multiple Worksheets . . . . .EX 282

▶ Grouping Worksheets . . . . .EX 283

    Entering Formulas in a Worksheet Group . . . . .EX 283

    Formatting a Worksheet Group . . . . .EX 285

    Ungrouping Worksheets . . . . .EX 286

Copying Worksheets . . . . .EX 287

Referencing Cells and Ranges in Other Worksheets . . . . . . .EX 288

▶ Using 3-D References to Add Values Across Worksheets . . . . .EX 289

Printing a Worksheet Group . . . . .EX 293

Session 6.1 Quick Check . . . . .EX 295

Session 6.2 . . . .**EX 295**

▶ Linking Workbooks . . . . .EX 295

    Navigating and Arranging Multiple Workbooks . . . . .EX 297

    Creating External Reference Formulas . . . . .EX 299

Updating Linked Workbooks . . . . .EX 303

Opening Destination Workbooks with Source
Workbooks Closed . . . . .EX 304

    Managing Links . . . . .EX 306

Creating an Excel Workspace . . . . .EX 308

Session 6.2 Quick Check . . . . .EX 310

Session 6.3 . . . .**EX 310**

Creating a Hyperlink . . . . .EX 310

    Inserting a Hyperlink . . . . .EX 310

    Editing a Hyperlink . . . . .EX 312

Creating Templates . . . . .EX 313

    Creating a Workbook Based on an Existing Template . . . . .EX 314

▶ Creating a Custom Workbook Template . . . . .EX 316

    Creating a New Workbook from a Template . . . . .EX 319

Saving a Workbook as a Web Page . . . . .EX 321

    Setting the Page Title . . . . .EX 323

    Setting the Web Page Options .EX 323

Session 6.3 Quick Check . . . . .EX 325

Tutorial Summary . . . . .EX 325

Key Terms . . . . .EX 325

Review Assignments . . . . .EX 326

Case Problems . . . . .EX 327

Internet Assignments . . . . .EX 334

SAM Assessment and Training . . . . .EX 335

Quick Check Answers . . . . .EX 335

Tutorial 7 Using Advanced Functions, Conditional Formatting, and Filtering
Reviewing Employee Data . . . .*EX 337*

Session 7.1 . . . .**EX 338**

Working with Logical Functions . . . . .EX 338

    Using the IF Function . . . . .EX 340

    Using the And Function . . . . .EX 343

    Using Structured References with Excel Tables . . . . .EX 344

▶ Creating Nested IF Functions . . . . .EX 348

    Exploring the OR Function . . . . .EX 352

Session 7.1 Quick Check . . . . .EX 353

Session 7.2 . . . .**EX 353**

▶ Using Lookup Tables and Functions . . . . .EX 353

    Looking Up an Exact Match . . . . .EX 355

    Looking Up an Approximate Match . . . . .EX 358

Checking for Data Entry Errors . . . . .EX 360

    Highlighting Duplicate Values with Conditional
    Formatting . . . . .EX 360

    Using the Conditional Formatting Rules Manager . . . . . .EX 362

    Using the IFERROR Function . . . . .EX 365

▶ Summarizing Data Conditionally . . . . .EX 367

    Using the COUNTIF Function .EX 367

    Using the SUMIF Function . . . . .EX 369

Using the AVERAGEIF Function ....EX 370

Summarizing Data Using the COUNTIFS, SUMIFS, and AVERAGEIFS Functions ....EX 371

Session 7.2 Quick Check ....EX 372

Session 7.3 ....**EX 373**

▶ Using Advanced Filtering ....EX 373

Understanding Criteria Ranges ....EX 375

Creating a Criteria Range ....EX 376

Using Database Functions to Summarize Data ....EX 379

Session 7.3 Quick Check ....EX 383

Tutorial Summary ....EX 383

Key Terms ....EX 383

Review Assignments ....EX 384

Case Problems ....EX 385

Internet Assignments ....EX 391

SAM Assessment and Training ....EX 391

Quick Check Answers ....EX 391

Tutorial 8 Developing an Excel Application

Creating an Invoice ....*EX 393*

Session 8.1 ....**EX 394**

Planning an Excel Application ....EX 394

▶ Naming Cells and Ranges ....EX 396

Creating Defined Names ....EX 396

Entering Formulas with Defined Names ....EX 401

Adding Defined Names to Existing Formulas ....EX 405

Session 8.1 Quick Check ....EX 407

Session 8.2 ....**EX 407**

▶ Validating Data Entry ....EX 407

Specifying a Data Type and Acceptable Values ....EX 408

Specifying an Input Message ....EX 409

Specifying an Error Alert Style and Message ....EX 410

Creating a List Validation Rule ....EX 412

Drawing Circles Around Invalid Data ....EX 414

▶ Protecting a Worksheet and Workbook ....EX 414

Locking and Unlocking Cells ....EX 414

Protecting a Worksheet ....EX 415

Protecting a Workbook ....EX 417

Unprotecting a Worksheet ....EX 418

Adding Worksheet Comments ....EX 418

Session 8.2 Quick Check ....EX 420

Session 8.3 ....**EX 420**

Working with Macros ....EX 420

Protecting Against Macro Viruses ....EX 421

Macro Security Settings ....EX 422

▶ Recording a Macro ....EX 424

Running a Macro ....EX 427

Creating the TransferData Macro ....EX 430

Fixing Macro Errors ....EX 432

Working with the Macro Editor ....EX 432

Understanding the Structure of Macros ....EX 433

Writing a Macro Command ....EX 434

Creating Macro Buttons ....EX 436

Saving Workbooks with Macros ....EX 439

Minimize the Ribbon ....EX 440

Opening a Workbook with Macros ....EX 440

Session 8.3 Quick Check ....EX 442

Tutorial Summary ....EX 442

Key Terms ....EX 442

Review Assignments ....EX 443

Case Problems ....EX 444

Internet Assignments ....EX 452

SAM Assessment and Training ....EX 452

Quick Check Answers ....EX 453

Reality Check ....EX 455

Appendix A Working with Text Functions and Creating Custom Formats
Cleaning Data in a Spreadsheet ....EX A1

Opening and Saving Workbooks Created in Earlier Versions of Excel ....EX A2

Using Text Functions ....EX A3

    Using the LEN function ....EX A4

    Using the LEFT Function ....EX A4

    Using the Proper Function ....EX A6

    Joining Text Using the Concatenation Operator ....EX A6

    Using the Text to Columns Command ....EX A8

    Using the UPPER Function to Convert Case ....EX A9

    Using the SUBSTITUTE Function ....EX A10

Adding Special and Custom Formatting ....EX A11

Using Special Formats ....EX A12

Creating Custom Formats ....EX A12

    Working with Numeric Format Codes ....EX A12

Formatting Dates ....EX A14

    Using the Compatibility Checker ....EX A16

Appendix Summary ....EX A17

Key Terms ....EX A17

Review Assignments ....EX A18

Case Problems ....EX A18

Appendix B Integrating Excel with Other Windows Programs
Creating Integrated Documents ....EX B1

Methods of Integration ....EX B2

    Copying and Pasting Data ....EX B2

    Object Linking and Embedding ....EX B2

Linking Excel and Word Files ....EX B3

Updating a Linked Object ....EX B5

Embedding an Object ....EX B6

Modifying an Embedded Object ....EX B7

Appendix Summary ....EX B9

Key Terms ....EX B9

Review Assignments ....EX B10

Appendix A Introduction to Microsoft Windows 7
Exploring the Basics of Microsoft Windows 7 ....WIN7 3

Session 1 ....**WIN7 4**

Starting Windows 7 ....WIN7 6

Touring the Windows 7 Desktop WIN7 7

    Interacting with the Desktop WIN7 7

Exploring the Start Menu WIN7 11

Running Multiple Programs WIN7 14

    Switching Between Programs WIN7 15

    Closing Programs from the Taskbar WIN7 16

Using Windows and Dialog Boxes WIN7 17

Manipulating Windows WIN7 19

    Using the Ribbon WIN7 21

    Using List Boxes WIN7 23

    Working with Dialog Boxes WIN7 24

Session 2 ....**WIN7 26**

The Computer Window WIN7 27

Exploring Your Computer WIN7 28

    Navigating with the Computer Window WIN7 28

    Changing the View WIN7 30

    Navigating with Windows Explorer WIN7 32

Getting Help WIN7 34

    Viewing Windows Basics Topics WIN7 36

    Selecting a Topic from the Contents List WIN7 36

    Searching the Help Pages WIN7 37

Turning Off Windows 7 ....WIN7 38

Review Assignments WIN7 41

Case Problems WIN7 42

ProSkills Exercise: Problem Solving WIN7 46

Glossary/Index ....**REF 1**

Task Reference ....**REF 10**

Getting Started with Microsoft Office 2007

Preparing a Meeting Agenda

Objectives

- Explore the programs that comprise Microsoft Office
- Start programs and switch between them
- Explore common window elements
- Minimize, maximize, and restore windows
- Use the Ribbon, tabs, and buttons
- Use the contextual tabs, Mini toolbar, and shortcut menus
- Save, close, and open a file
- Use the Help system
- Print a file
- Exit programs

Case | Recycled Palette

Recycled Palette, a company in Oregon founded by Ean Nogella in 2006, sells 100 percent recycled latex paint to both individuals and businesses in the area. The high-quality recycled paint is filtered to industry standards and tested for performance and environmental safety. The paint is available in both 1 gallon cans and 5 gallon pails, and comes in colors ranging from white to shades of brown, blue, green, and red. The demand for affordable recycled paint has been growing each year. Ean and all his employees use Microsoft Office 2007, which provides everyone in the company with the power and flexibility to store a variety of information, create consistent files, and share data. In this tutorial, you'll review how the company's employees use Microsoft Office 2007.

Starting Data Files

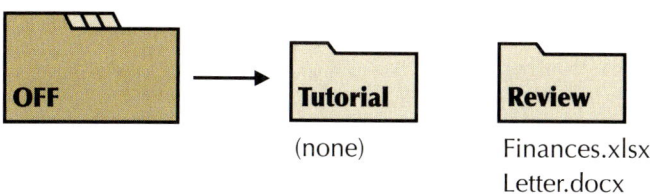

OFF → Tutorial (none)   Review Finances.xlsx Letter.docx

Exploring Microsoft Office 2007

Microsoft Office 2007, or **Office**, is a collection of Microsoft programs. Office is available in many suites, each of which contains a different combination of these programs. For example, the Professional suite includes Word, Excel, PowerPoint, Access, Outlook, and Publisher. Other suites are available and can include more or fewer programs (for additional information about the available suites, go to the Microsoft Web site). Each Office program contains valuable tools to help you accomplish many tasks, such as composing reports, analyzing data, preparing presentations, compiling information, sending e-mail, and planning schedules.

Microsoft Office Word 2007, or **Word**, is a computer program you use to enter, edit, and format text. The files you create in Word are called **documents**, although many people use the term *document* to refer to any file created on a computer. Word, often called a word processing program, offers many special features that help you compose and update all types of documents, ranging from letters and newsletters to reports, brochures, faxes, and even books—all in attractive and readable formats. You can also use Word to create, insert, and position figures, tables, and other graphics to enhance the look of your documents. For example, the Recycled Palette employees create business letters using Word.

Microsoft Office Excel 2007, or **Excel**, is a computer program you use to enter, calculate, analyze, and present numerical data. You can do some of this in Word with tables, but Excel provides many more tools for recording and formatting numbers as well as performing calculations. The graphics capabilities in Excel also enable you to display data visually. You might, for example, generate a pie chart or a bar chart to help people quickly see the significance of and the connections between information. The files you create in Excel are called **workbooks** (commonly referred to as spreadsheets), and Excel is often called a spreadsheet program. The Recycled Palette accounting department uses a line chart in an Excel workbook to visually track the company's financial performance.

Microsoft Office Access 2007, or **Access**, is a computer program used to enter, maintain, and retrieve related information (or data) in a format known as a database. The files you create in Access are called **databases**, and Access is often referred to as a database or relational database program. With Access, you can create forms to make data entry easier, and you can create professional reports to improve the readability of your data. The Recycled Palette operations department tracks the company's inventory in a table in an Access database.

Microsoft Office PowerPoint 2007, or **PowerPoint**, is a computer program you use to create a collection of slides that can contain text, charts, pictures, sound, movies, multimedia, and so on. The files you create in PowerPoint are called **presentations**, and PowerPoint is often called a presentation graphics program. You can show these presentations on your computer monitor, project them onto a screen as a slide show, print them, share them over the Internet, or display them on the World Wide Web. You can also use PowerPoint to generate presentation-related documents such as audience handouts, outlines, and speakers' notes. The Recycled Palette marketing department has created an effective slide presentation with PowerPoint to promote its paints to a wider audience.

Microsoft Office Outlook 2007, or **Outlook**, is a computer program you use to send, receive, and organize e-mail; plan your schedule; arrange meetings; organize contacts; create a to-do list; and jot down notes. You can also use Outlook to print schedules, task lists, phone directories, and other documents. Outlook is often referred to as an information management program. The Recycled Palette staff use Outlook to send and receive e-mail, plan their schedules, and create to-do lists.

Although each Office program individually is a strong tool, their potential is even greater when used together.

Integrating Office Programs

One of the main advantages of Office is **integration**, the ability to share information between programs. Integration ensures consistency and accuracy, and it saves time because you don't have to reenter the same information in several Office programs. The staff at Recycled Palette uses the integration features of Office daily, including the following examples:

- The accounting department created an Excel bar chart on the previous two years' fourth-quarter results, which they inserted into the quarterly financial report created in Word. They included a hyperlink in the Word report that employees can click to open the Excel workbook and view the original data.
- The operations department included an Excel pie chart of sales percentages by paint colors on a PowerPoint slide, which is part of a presentation to stockholders.
- The marketing department produced a mailing to promote its recycled paints to local contractors and designers by combining a form letter created in Word with an Access database that stores the names and addresses of these potential customers.
- A sales representative wrote a letter in Word about an upcoming promotion for new customers and merged the letter with an Outlook contact list containing the names and addresses of prospective customers.

These are just a few examples of how you can take information from one Office program and integrate it with another.

Starting Office Programs

You can start any Office program by clicking the Start button on the Windows taskbar, and then selecting the program you want from the All Programs menu. As soon as the program starts, you can immediately begin to create new files or work with existing ones. If an Office program appears in the most frequently used programs list on the left side of the Start menu, you can click the program name to start the program.

Reference Window | Starting Office Programs

- Click the Start button on the taskbar.
- Click All Programs.
- Click Microsoft Office.
- Click the name of the program you want to start.

or

- Click the name of the program you want to start in the most frequently used programs list on the left side of the Start menu.

You'll start Excel using the Start button.

To start Excel and open a new, blank workbook:

1. Make sure your computer is on and the Windows desktop appears on your screen.

   Trouble? If your screen varies slightly from those shown in the figures, your computer might be set up differently. The figures in this book were created while running Windows Vista with the Aero feature turned off, but how your screen looks depends on the version of Windows you are using, the background settings, and so forth.

> **Windows XP Tip**
>
> The Start button is the green button with the word "start" on it, located at the bottom left of the taskbar.

2. Click the **Start** button on the taskbar, and then click **All Programs** to display the All Programs menu.

3. Click **Microsoft Office** on the All Programs list, and then point to **Microsoft Office Excel 2007**. Depending on how your computer is set up, your desktop and menu might contain different icons and commands.

    Trouble? If you don't see Microsoft Office on the All Programs list, click Microsoft Office Excel 2007 on the All Programs list. If you still don't see Microsoft Office Excel 2007, ask your instructor or technical support person for help.

4. Click **Microsoft Office Excel 2007**. Excel starts, and a new, blank workbook opens. See Figure 1.

Figure 1   New, blank Excel workbook

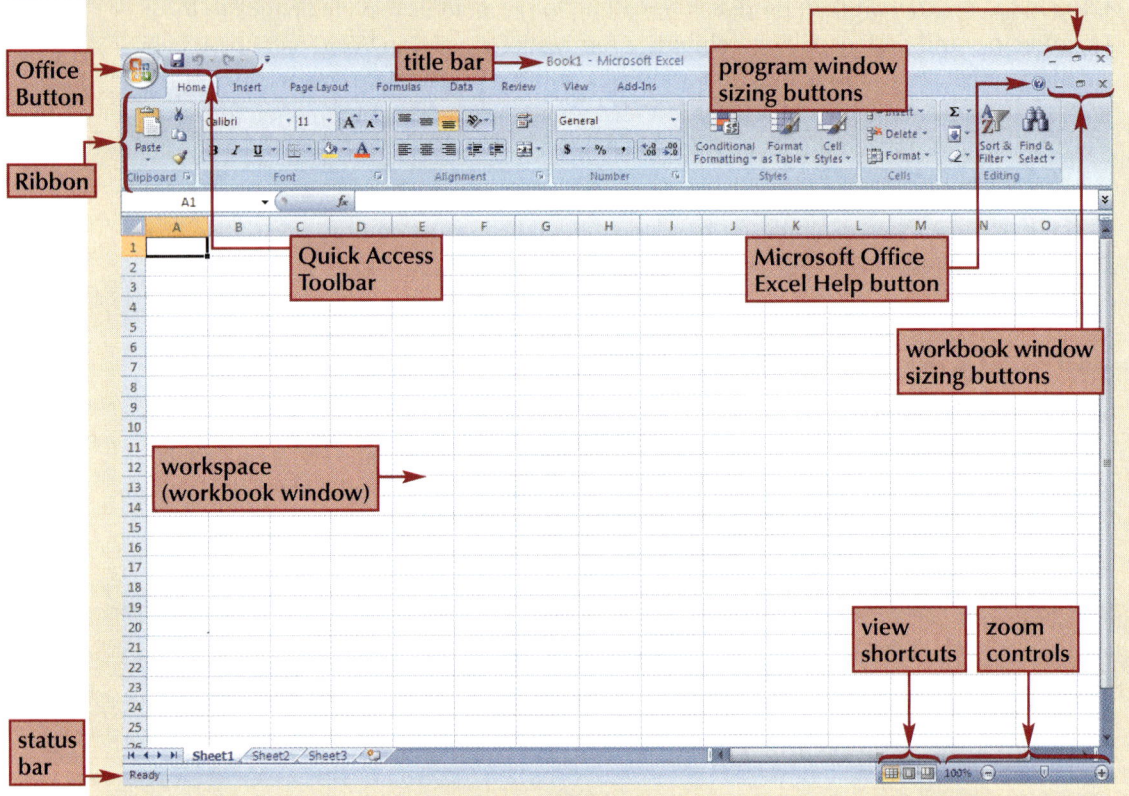

Trouble? If the Excel window doesn't fill your entire screen, the window is not maximized, or expanded to its full size. You'll maximize the window shortly.

You can have more than one Office program open at once. You'll use this same method to start Word and open a new, blank document.

To start Word and open a new, blank document:

1. Click the **Start** button on the taskbar, click **All Programs** to display the All Programs list, and then click **Microsoft Office**.

    Trouble? If you don't see Microsoft Office on the All Programs list, click Microsoft Office Word 2007 on the All Programs list. If you still don't see Microsoft Office Word 2007, ask your instructor or technical support person for help.

2. Click **Microsoft Office Word 2007**. Word starts, and a new, blank document opens. See Figure 2.

Getting Started with Microsoft Office 2007 Office OFF 5

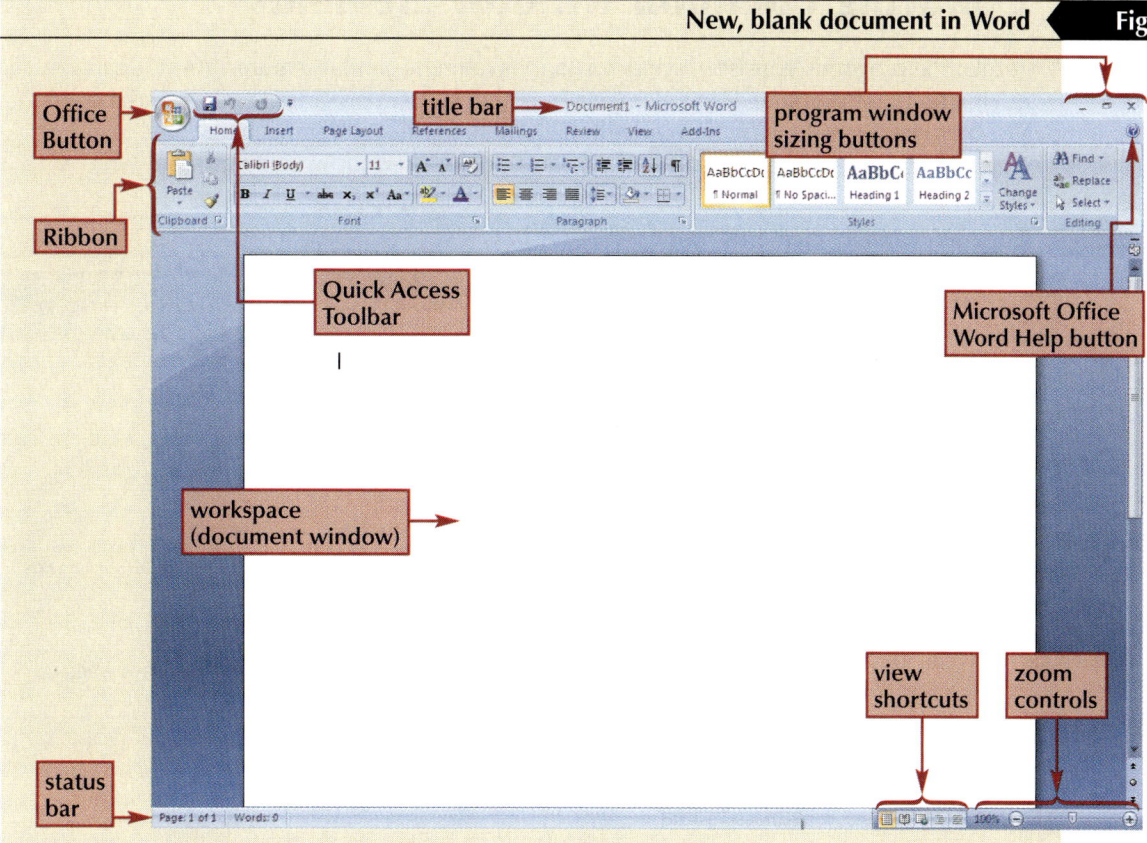

Figure 2 — New, blank document in Word

Trouble? If the Word window doesn't fill your entire screen, the window is not maximized. You'll maximize the window shortly.

Switching Between Open Programs and Files

Two programs are running at the same time—Excel and Word. The taskbar contains buttons for both programs. When you have two or more programs running or two files within the same program open, you can use the taskbar buttons to switch from one program or file to another. The button for the active program or file is darker. The employees at Recycled Palette often work in several programs at once.

To switch between Word and Excel files:

▶ 1. Click the **Microsoft Excel – Book1** button on the taskbar. The active program switches from Word to Excel. See Figure 3.

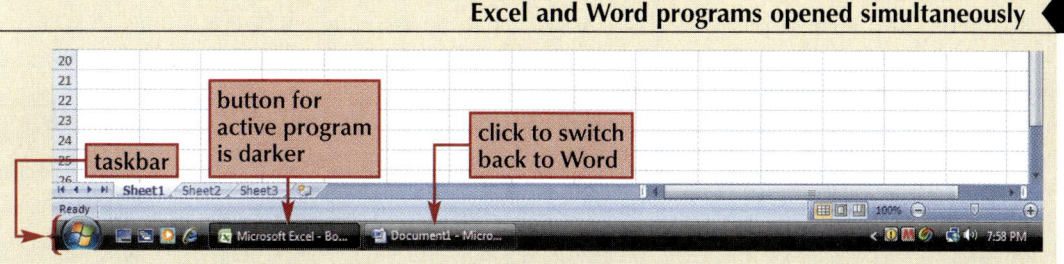

Figure 3 — Excel and Word programs opened simultaneously

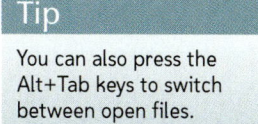

Tip

You can also press the Alt+Tab keys to switch between open files.

▶ 2. Click the **Document1 – Microsoft Word** button on the taskbar to return to Word.

Exploring Common Window Elements

The Office programs consist of windows that have many similar features. As you can see in Figures 1 and 2, many of the elements in both the Excel program window and the Word program window are the same. In fact, all the Office programs have these same elements. Figure 4 describes some of the most common window elements.

Figure 4 — Common window elements

Element	Description
Office Button	Provides access to document-level features and program settings
Quick Access Toolbar	Provides one-click access to commonly used commands, such as Save, Undo, and Repeat
Title bar	Contains the name of the open file, the program name, and the sizing buttons
Sizing buttons	Resize and close the program window or the workspace
Ribbon	Provides access to the main set of commands organized by task into tabs and groups
Microsoft Office Help button	Opens the Help window for that program
Workspace	Displays the file you are working on (Word document, Excel workbook, Access database, or PowerPoint slide)
Status bar	Provides information about the program, open file, or current task as well as the view shortcuts and zoom controls
View shortcuts	Change how a file is displayed in the workspace
Zoom controls	Magnify or shrink the content displayed in the workspace

Because these elements are the same in each program, after you've learned one program, it's easy to learn the others. The next sections explore these common features.

Resizing the Program Window and Workspace

There are three different sizing buttons. The Minimize button, which is the left button, hides a window so that only its program button is visible on the taskbar. The middle button changes name and function depending on the status of the window—the Maximize button expands the window to the full screen size or to the program window size, and the Restore Down button returns the window to a predefined size. The Close button, on the right, exits the program or closes the file. Excel has two sets of sizing buttons. The top set controls the program window and the lower set controls the workspace. The workspace sizing buttons look and function in exactly the same way as the program window sizing buttons, except the button names change to Minimize Window and Restore Window when the workspace is maximized.

Most often, you'll want to maximize the program window and workspace to take advantage of the full screen size you have available. If you have several files open, you might want to restore down their windows so that you can see more than one window at a time, or you might want to minimize programs or files you are not working on at the moment. You'll try minimizing, maximizing, and restoring down windows and workspaces now.

To resize windows and workspaces:

1. Click the **Minimize** button on the Word title bar. The Word program window reduces to a taskbar button. The Excel program window is visible again.

2. If necessary, click the **Maximize** button on the Excel title bar. The Excel program window expands to fill the screen.

3. Click the **Restore Window** button in the lower set of Excel sizing buttons. The workspace is resized and is now smaller than the full program window. See Figure 5.

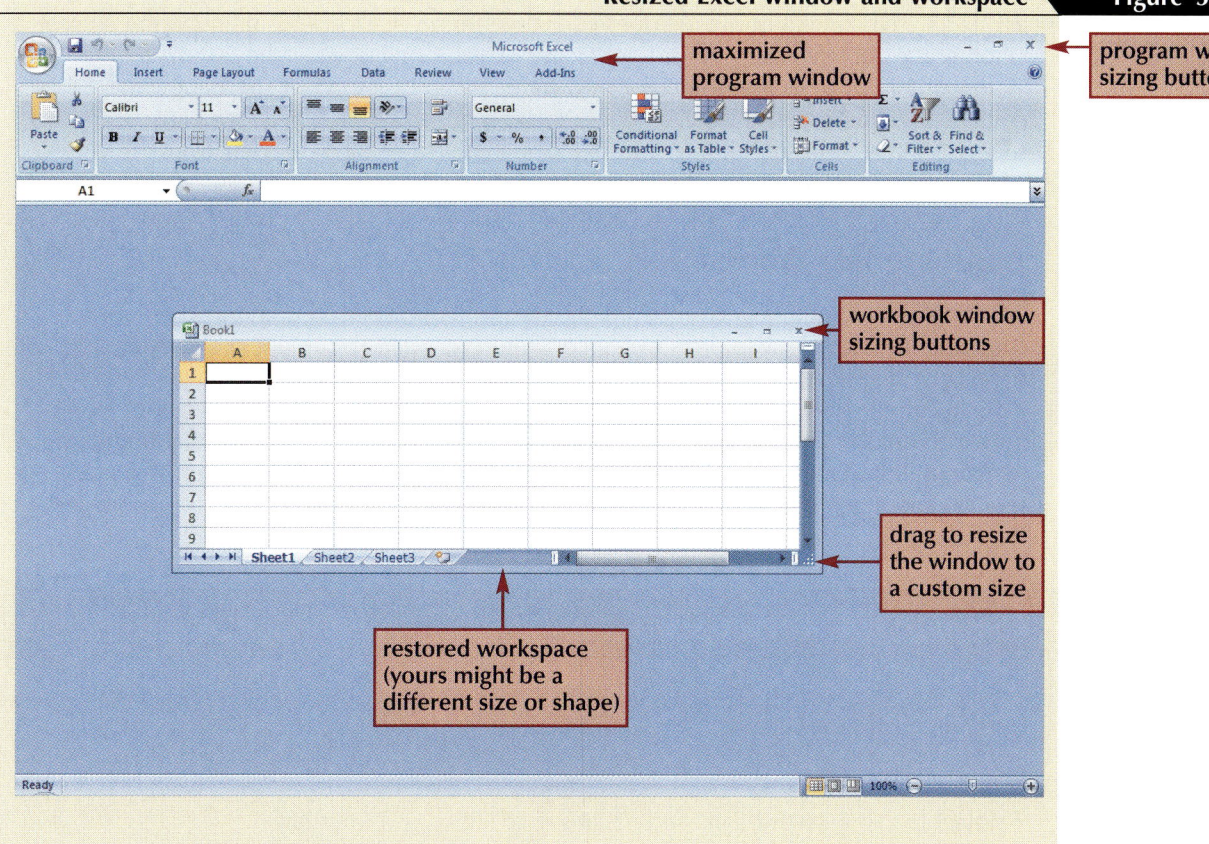

Figure 5 Resized Excel window and workspace

- maximized program window
- program window sizing buttons
- workbook window sizing buttons
- drag to resize the window to a custom size
- restored workspace (yours might be a different size or shape)

4. Click the **Maximize** button on the Excel workbook window title bar. The Excel workspace expands to fill the program window.

5. Click the **Document1 - Microsoft Word** button on the taskbar. The Word program window returns to its previous size.

6. If necessary, click the **Maximize** button on the Word title bar. The Word program window expands to fill the screen.

The sizing buttons give you the flexibility to arrange the program and file windows on your screen to best fit your needs.

Getting Information from the Status Bar

The **status bar** at the bottom of the program window provides information about the open file and current task or selection. It also has buttons and other controls for working with the file and its content. The status bar buttons and information displays are specific to the individual programs. For example, the Excel status bar displays summary information about a selected range of numbers (such as their sum or average), whereas the Word status bar shows the current page number and total number of words in a document. The right side of the status bar includes buttons that enable you to switch the workspace view in Word, Excel, PowerPoint, and Access as well as zoom the workspace in Word, Excel, and PowerPoint. You can customize the status bar to display other information or hide the **default** (original or preset) information.

Switching Views

Each program has a variety of views, or ways to display the file in the workspace. For example, Word has five views: Print Layout, Full Screen Reading, Web Layout, Outline, and Draft. The content of the file doesn't change from view to view, although the presentation of the content will. In Word, for example, Page Layout view shows how a document would appear as the printed page, whereas Web Layout view shows how the document would appear as a Web page. You can quickly switch between views using the shortcuts at the right side of the status bar. You can also change the view from the View tab on the Ribbon. You'll change views in later tutorials.

Zooming the Workspace

Zooming is a way to magnify or shrink the file content displayed in the workspace. You can zoom in to get a closer look at the content of an open document, worksheet, or slide, or you can zoom out to see more of the content at a smaller size. There are several ways to change the zoom percentage. You can use the Zoom slider at the right of the status bar to quickly change the zoom percentage. You can click the Zoom level button to the left of the Zoom slider in the status bar to open the Zoom dialog box and select a specific zoom percentage or size based on your file. You can also change the zoom settings using the Zoom group in the View tab on the Ribbon.

Reference Window | Zooming the Workspace

- Click the Zoom Out or Zoom In button on the status bar (or drag the Zoom slider button left or right) to the desired zoom percentage.

or

- Click the Zoom level button on the status bar.
- Select the appropriate zoom setting, and then click the OK button.

or

- Click the View tab on the Ribbon, and then in the Zoom group, click the zoom setting you want.

The figures shown in these tutorials are zoomed to enhance readability. You'll zoom the Word and Excel workspaces.

To zoom the Word and Excel workspaces:

1. On the Zoom slider on the Word status bar, drag the **slider button** to the left until the Zoom percentage is **10%**. The document reduces to its smallest size, which makes the entire page visible but unreadable. See Figure 6.

Getting Started with Microsoft Office 2007 | Office **OFF 9**

Word document zoomed to 10% Figure 6

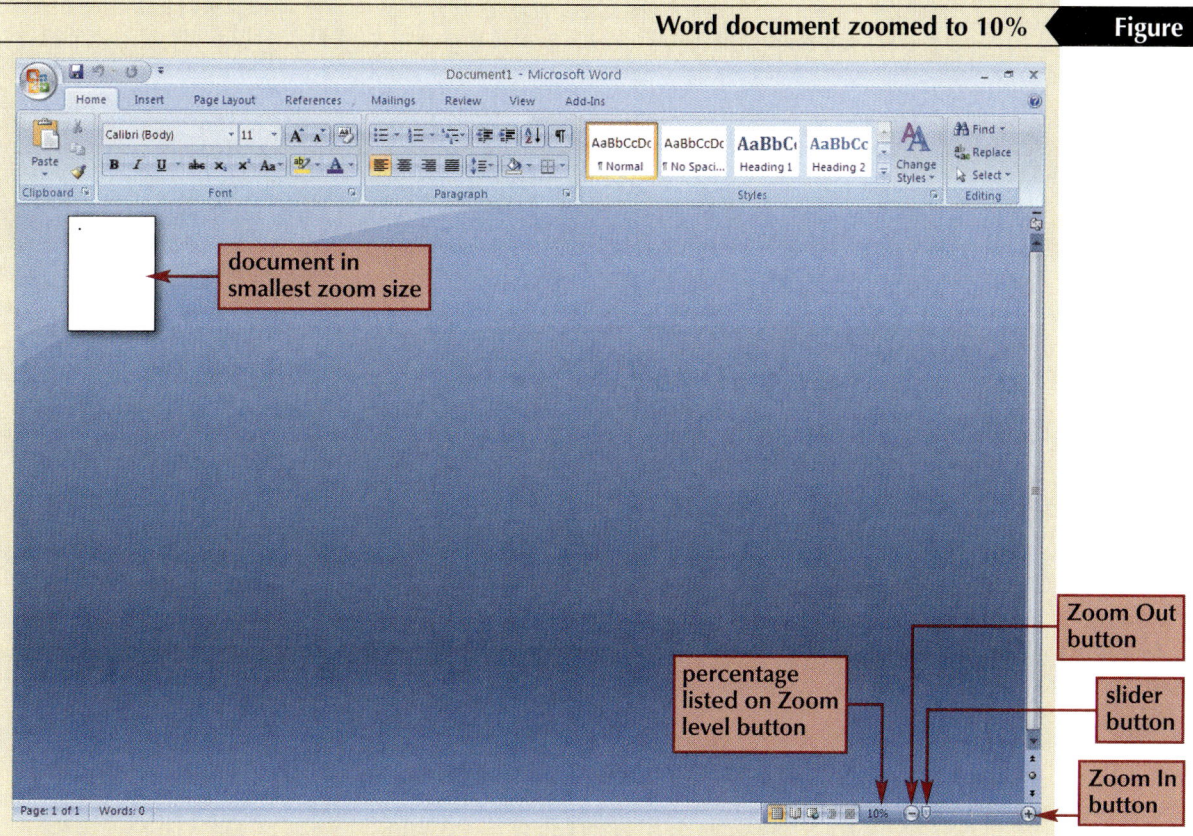

You'll zoom the document so its page width fills the workspace.

▶ **2.** Click the **Zoom level** button 10% on the Word status bar. The Zoom dialog box opens. See Figure 7.

Zoom dialog box Figure 7

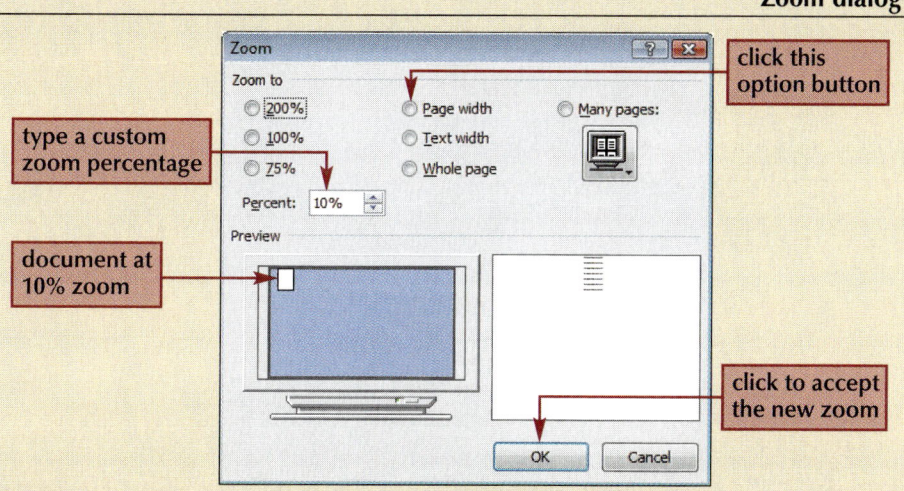

▶ **3.** Click the **Page width** option button, and then click the **OK** button. The Word document magnifies to its page width to match the rest of the Word figures shown in these tutorials.

Now, you'll zoom the workbook to 120%.

4. Click the **Microsoft Excel – Book1** button on the taskbar. The Excel program window is displayed.

5. Click the **Zoom In** button ⊕ on the status bar two times. The workspace magnifies to 120%. This is the zoom percentage that matches the rest of the Excel figures shown in these tutorials.

6. Click the **Document1 – Microsoft Word** button on the taskbar. The Word program window is displayed.

Using the Ribbon

The **Ribbon** at the top of the program window just below the title bar is the main set of commands that you click to execute tasks. The Ribbon is organized into tabs. Each **tab** has commands related to particular activities. For example, in Word, the Insert tab on the Ribbon provides access to all the commands for adding objects such as shapes, pages, tables, illustrations, text, and symbols to a document. Although the tabs differ from program to program, the first tab in each program, called the Home tab, contains the commands for the most frequently performed activities, including cutting and pasting, changing fonts, and using editing tools. In addition, the Insert, Review, View, and Add-Ins tabs appear on the Ribbon in all the Office programs except Access, although the commands they include might differ from program to program. Other tabs are program specific, such as the Design tab in PowerPoint and the Datasheet tab in Access.

To use the Ribbon tabs:

1. In Word, point to the **Insert** tab on the Ribbon. The Insert tab is highlighted, though the Home tab with the options for using the Clipboard and formatting text remains visible.

2. Click the **Insert** tab. The Ribbon displays the Insert tab, which provides access to all the options for adding objects such as shapes, pages, tables, illustrations, text, and symbols to a document. See Figure 8.

| Figure 8 | Insert tab on the Ribbon |

Tip

To view more workspace, you can reduce the Ribbon to a single line by double-clicking any tab on the Ribbon. Double-click any tab again to redisplay the full Ribbon.

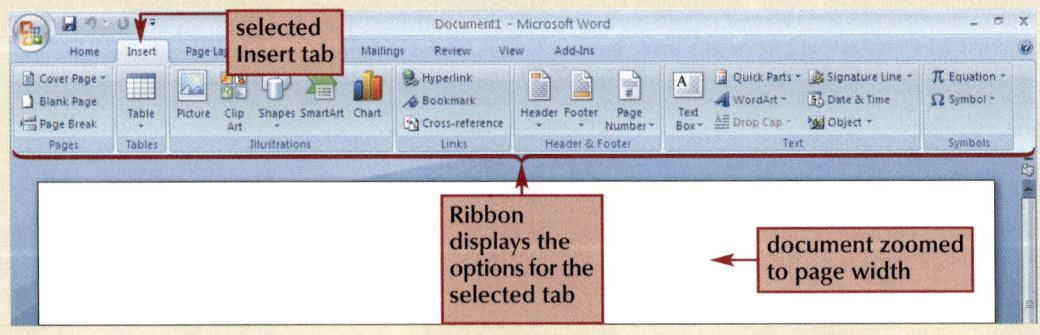

3. Click the **Home** tab on the Ribbon. The Ribbon displays the Home options.

Clicking Button Icons

Each **button**, or icon, on the tabs provides one-click access to a command. Most buttons are labeled so that you can easily find the command you need. For the most part, when you click a button, something happens in your file. If you want to repeat that action, you click the button again. Buttons for related commands are organized on a tab in **groups**. For example, the Clipboard group on the Home tab includes the Cut, Copy, Paste, and Format Painter buttons—the commands for moving or copying text, objects, and formatting.

Buttons can be toggle switches: one click turns on the feature and the next click turns off the feature. While the feature is on, the button remains colored or highlighted to remind you that it is active. For example, in Word, the Show/Hide button on the Home tab in the Paragraph group displays the nonprinting screen characters when toggled on and hides them when toggled off.

Some buttons have two parts: a button that accesses a command and an arrow that opens a menu of all the commands available for that task. For example, the Paste button on the Home tab includes the default Paste command and an arrow that opens the menu of all the Paste commands—Paste, Paste Special, and Paste as Hyperlink. To select a command on the menu, you click the button arrow and then click the command on the menu.

The buttons and groups change based on your monitor size, your screen resolution, and the size of the program window. With smaller monitors, lower screen resolutions, and reduced program windows, buttons can appear as icons without labels and a group can be condensed into a button that you click to display the group options. The figures in these tutorials were created using a screen resolution of 1024 × 768 and, unless otherwise specified, the program and workspace windows are maximized. If you are using a different screen resolution or window size, the button icons on the Ribbon might show more or fewer button names, and some groups might be condensed into buttons.

You'll type text in the Word document, and then use the buttons on the Ribbon.

To use buttons on the Ribbon:

▶ 1. Type **Recycled Palette**, and then press the **Enter** key. The text appears in the first line of the document and the insertion point moves to the second line.

   Trouble? If you make a typing error, press the Backspace key to delete the incorrect letters, and then retype the text.

▶ 2. In the Paragraph group on the Home tab, click the **Show/Hide** button 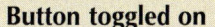. The nonprinting screen characters appear in the document, and the Show/Hide button remains toggled on. See Figure 9.

   Trouble? If the nonprinting characters are removed from your screen, the Show/Hide button 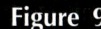 was already selected. Repeat Step 2 to show the nonprinting screen characters.

Figure 9

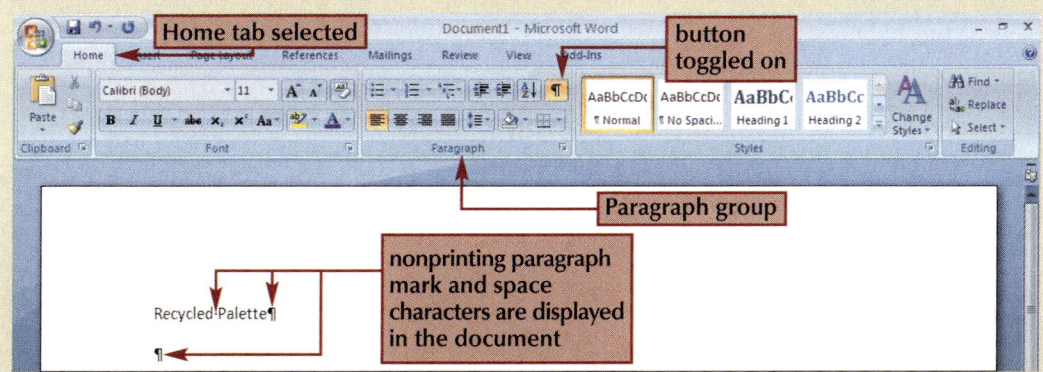

▶ 3. Drag to select all the text in the first line of the document (but not the paragraph mark).

▶ 4. In the Clipboard group on the Home tab, click the **Copy** button. The selected text is copied to the Clipboard.

▶ 5. Press the ↓ key. The text is deselected and the insertion point moves to the second line in the document.

▶ 6. In the Clipboard group on the Home tab, point to the top part of the **Paste** button. Both parts of the Paste button are highlighted, but the icon at top is darker to indicate it will be clicked if you press the mouse button.

▶ 7. Point to the **Paste button arrow**. The button arrow is now darker.

▶ 8. Click the **Paste button arrow**. A menu of paste commands opens. See Figure 10. To select one of the commands on the list, you click it.

Figure 10 | Two-part Paste button

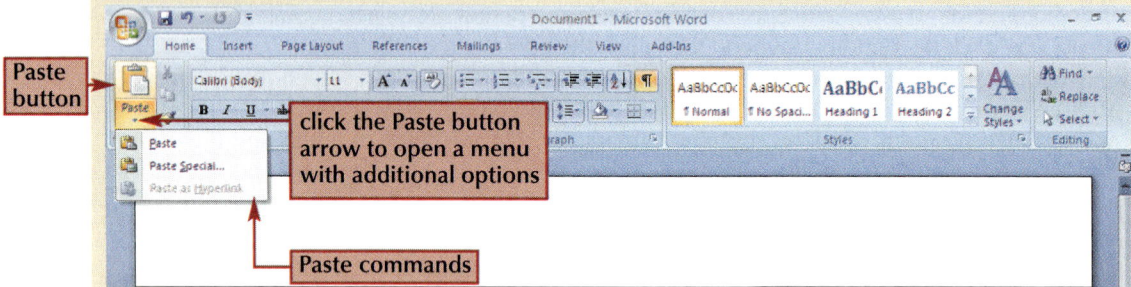

▶ 9. Click **Paste**. The menu closes, and the text is duplicated in the second line of the document.

As you can see, you can quickly access commands and turn features on and off with the buttons on the Ribbon.

InSight | **Using Keyboard Shortcuts and Key Tips**

Keyboard shortcuts can help you work faster and more efficiently. A **keyboard shortcut** is a key or combination of keys you press to access a tool or perform a command. To quickly access options on the Ribbon, the Quick Access Toolbar, and the Office Button without removing your hands from the keyboard:

1. Press the Alt key. Key Tips appear that list the keyboard shortcut for each Ribbon tab, each Quick Access Toolbar button, and the Office Button.
2. Press the key for the tab or button you want to use. An action is performed or Key Tips appear for the buttons on the selected tab or the commands for the selected button.
3. Continue to press the appropriate key listed in the Key Tip until the action you want is performed.

You can also use keyboard shortcuts to perform specific commands. For example, Ctrl+S is the keyboard shortcut for the Save command (you hold down the Ctrl key while you press the S key). This type of keyboard shortcut appears in ScreenTips next to the command's name. Not all commands have this type of keyboard shortcut. Identical commands in each Office program use the same keyboard shortcut.

Using Galleries and Live Preview

A button can also open a **gallery**, which is a grid or menu that shows a visual representation of the options available for that command. For example, the Bullet Library gallery in Word shows an icon of each bullet style you can select. Some galleries include a More button that you click to expand the gallery to see all the options in it. When you hover the pointer over an option in a gallery, **Live Preview** shows the results you would achieve in your file if you clicked that option. To continue the bullets example, when you hover over a bullet style in the Bullet Library gallery, the current paragraph or selected text previews that bullet style. By moving the pointer from option to option, you can quickly see the text set with different bullet styles; you can then select the style that works best for your needs.

To use a gallery and Live Preview:

1. In the Paragraph group on the Home tab, click the **Bullets button arrow**. The Bullet Library gallery opens.

2. Point to the **check mark bullet** style. Live Preview shows the selected bullet style in your document, so you can determine if you like that bullet style. See Figure 11.

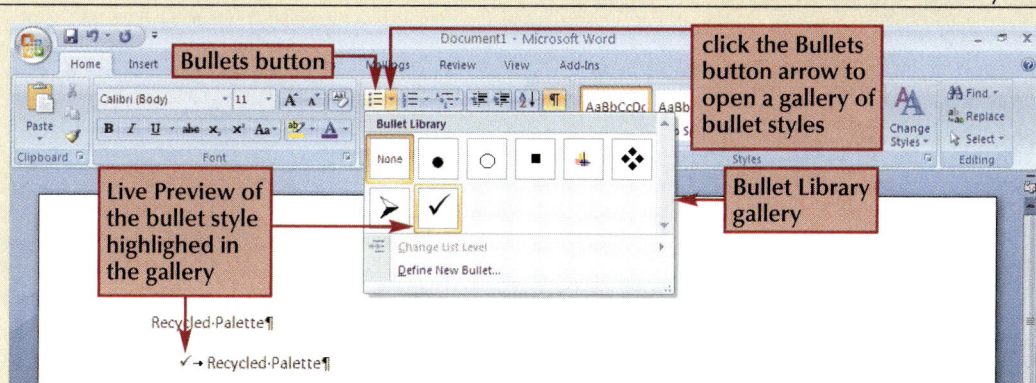

Figure 11 — Live Preview of bullet style

3. Place the pointer over each of the remaining bullet styles and preview them in your document.

   You don't want to add bullets to your document right now, so you'll close the Bullet Library gallery and deselect the Bullets button.

4. Press the **Esc** key on the keyboard. The Bullet Library gallery closes and the Bullets button is deselected.

5. Press the **Backspace** key on the keyboard to delete the text "Recycled Palette" on the second line.

Galleries and Live Preview let you quickly see how your file will be affected by a selection.

Opening Dialog Boxes and Task Panes

The button to the right of the group names is the **Dialog Box Launcher**, which you click to open a task pane or dialog box that provides more advanced functionality for that group of tasks. A **task pane** is a window that helps you navigate through a complex task or feature. For example, the Clipboard task pane allows you to paste some or all of the items that have been cut or copied from any Office program during the current work session and the Research task pane allows you to search a variety of reference resources from within a file. A **dialog box** is a window from which you enter or choose settings for how you want to perform a task. For example, the Page Setup dialog box in Word contains options for how you want a document to look. Some dialog boxes organize related information into tabs, and related options and settings are organized into groups, just as they are on the Ribbon. You select settings in a dialog box using option buttons, check boxes, text boxes, lists, and other controls to collect information about how you want to perform a task.

In Excel, you'll use the Dialog Box Launcher for the Page Setup group to open the Page Setup dialog box.

To open the Page Setup dialog box using the Dialog Box Launcher:

1. Click the **Microsoft Excel – Book1** button on the taskbar to switch from Word to Excel.

2. Click the **Page Layout** tab on the Ribbon.

3. In the Page Setup group, click the **Dialog Box Launcher**, which is the small button to the right of the Page Setup group name. The Page Setup dialog box opens with the Page tab displayed. See Figure 12.

Figure 12   Page tab in the Page Setup dialog box

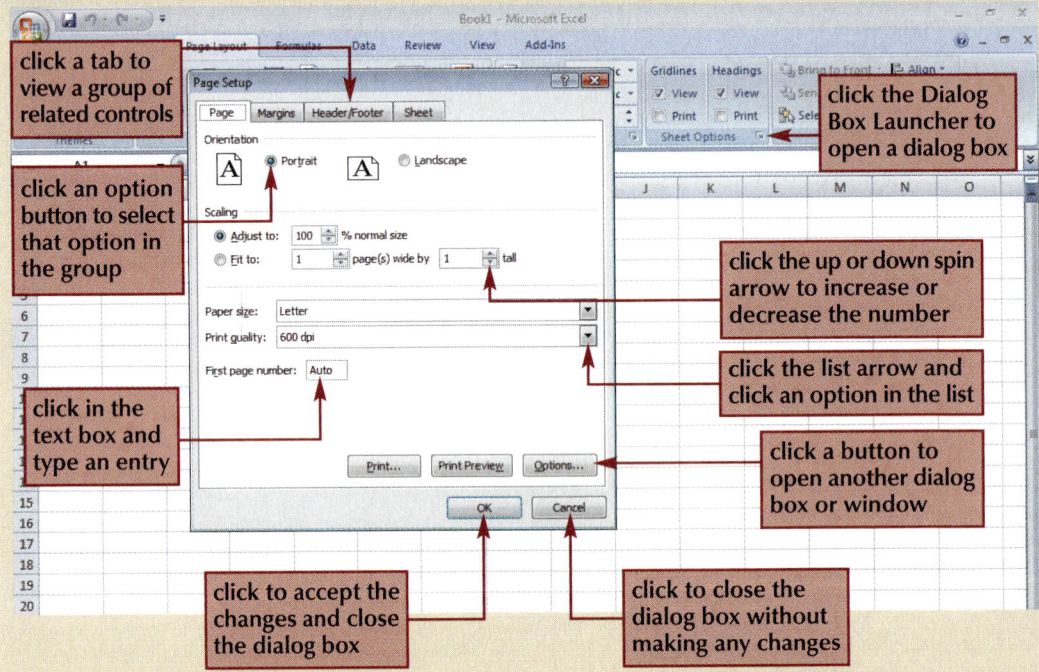

4. Click the **Landscape** option button. The workbook's page orientation changes to a page wider than it is long.

5. Click the **Sheet** tab. The dialog box displays options related to the worksheet. You can click a check box to turn an option on (checked) or off (unchecked). You can check more than one check box in a group, whereas you can select only one option button in a group.

6. In the Print group, click the **Gridlines** check box and the **Row and column headings** check box. Check marks appear in both check boxes, indicating that these options are selected.

You don't want to change the page setup right now, so you'll close the dialog box.

7. Click the **Cancel** button. The dialog box closes without making any changes to the page setup.

Using Contextual Tools

Some tabs, toolbars, and menus come into view as you work. Because these tools become available only as you might need them, the workspace on your screen remains more open and less cluttered. However, tools that appear and disappear as you work can be distracting and take some getting used to.

Displaying Contextual Tabs

Any object that you can select in a file has a related contextual tab. An **object** is anything that appears on your screen that can be selected and manipulated as a whole, such as a table, a picture, a text box, a shape, a chart, WordArt, an equation, a diagram, a header, or a footer. A **contextual tab** is a Ribbon tab that contains commands related to the selected object so you can manipulate, edit, and format that object. Contextual tabs appear to the right of the standard Ribbon tabs just below a title label. For example, Figure 13 shows the Table Tools contextual tabs that appear when you select a table in a Word document. Although the contextual tabs appear only when you select an object, they function in the same way as standard tabs on the Ribbon. Contextual tabs disappear when you click elsewhere on the screen and deselect the object. Contextual tabs can also appear as you switch views. You'll use contextual tabs in later tutorials.

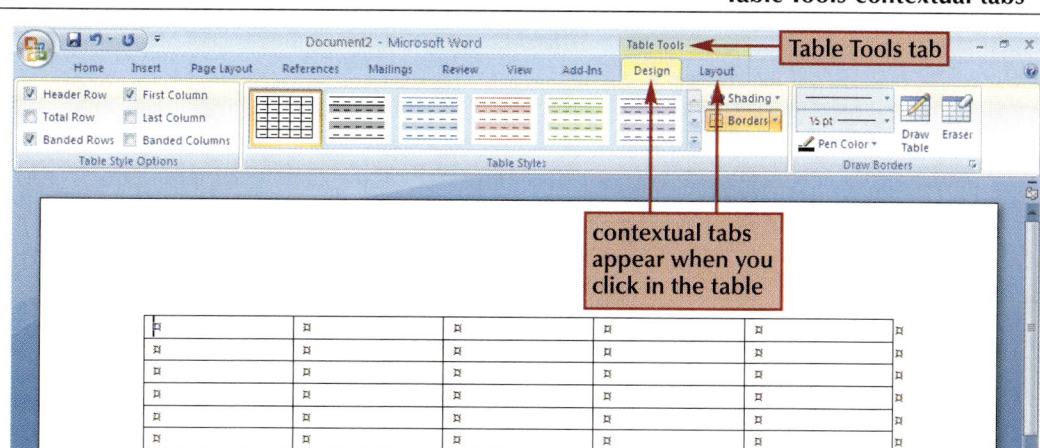

Figure 13 Table Tools contextual tabs

Accessing the Mini Toolbar

The **Mini toolbar** is a toolbar that appears next to the pointer whenever you select text, and it contains buttons for the most commonly used formatting commands, such as font, font size, styles, color, alignment, and indents that may appear in different groups or tabs on the Ribbon. The Mini toolbar buttons differ in each program. A transparent version of the Mini toolbar appears immediately after you select text. When you move the pointer over the Mini toolbar, it comes into full view so you can click the appropriate formatting button or buttons. The Mini toolbar disappears if you move the pointer away from the toolbar, press a key, or press a mouse button. The Mini toolbar can help you format your text faster, but initially you might find that the toolbar disappears unexpectedly. All the commands on the Mini toolbar are also available on the Ribbon. Be aware that Live Preview of selected styles does not work in the Mini toolbar.

You'll use the Mini toolbar to format text you enter in the workbook.

> **Tip**
> You can turn off the Mini toolbar and Live Preview in Word, Excel, and PowerPoint. Click the Office Button, click the Options button at the bottom of the Office menu, uncheck the first two check boxes in the Popular category, and then click the OK button.

To use the Mini toolbar to format text:

1. If necessary, click cell **A1** (the rectangle in the upper-left corner of the worksheet).
2. Type **Budget**. The text appears in the cell.
3. Press the **Enter** key. The text is entered in cell A1 and cell A2 is selected.
4. Type **2008**, and then press the **Enter** key. The year is entered in cell A2 and cell A3 is selected.

   You'll use the Mini toolbar to make the word in cell A1 boldface.

5. Double-click cell **A1** to place the insertion point in the cell. Now you can select the text you typed.
6. Double-click **Budget** in cell A1. The selected text appears white in a black background, and the transparent Mini toolbar appears directly above the selected text. See Figure 14.

Figure 14 | **Transparent Mini toolbar**

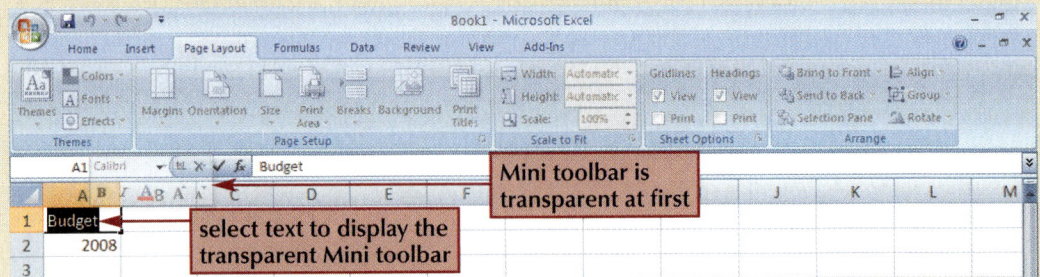

7. Move the pointer over the Mini toolbar. The Mini toolbar is now completely visible, and you can click buttons.

   Trouble? If the Mini toolbar disappears, you probably moved the pointer to another area of the worksheet. To redisplay the Mini toolbar, repeat Steps 5 through 7, being careful to move the pointer directly over the Mini toolbar in Step 7.

8. Click the **Bold** button **B** on the Mini toolbar. The text in cell A1 is bold and the Mini toolbar remains visible so you can continue formatting the selected text. See Figure 15.

Tip

You can redisplay the Mini toolbar if it disappears by right-clicking the selected text.

Figure 15 | **Mini toolbar with the Bold button selected**

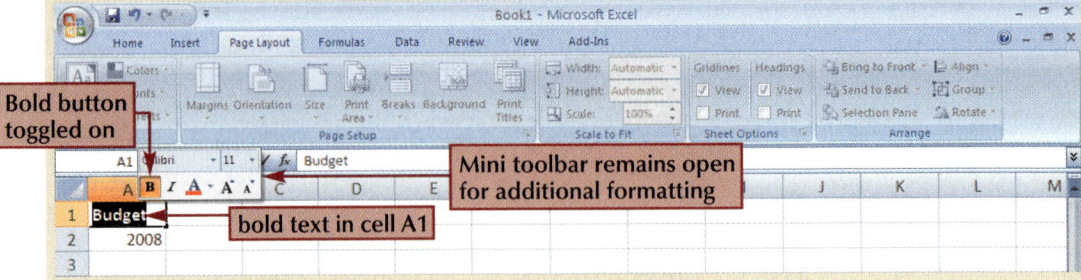

You don't want to make any other changes, so you'll close the Mini toolbar.

9. Press the **Enter** key. The Mini toolbar disappears and cell A2 is selected.

Opening Shortcut Menus

A **shortcut menu** is a list of commands related to a selection that opens when you click the right mouse button. Each shortcut menu provides access to the commands you'll most likely want to use with the object or selection you right-click. The shortcut menu includes commands that perform actions, commands that open dialog boxes, and galleries of options that provide Live Preview. The Mini toolbar also opens when you right-click. If you click a button on the Mini toolbar, the rest of the shortcut menu closes while the Mini toolbar remains open so you can continue formatting the selection. Using a shortcut menu provides quick access to the commands you need without having to access the tabs on the Ribbon. For example, you can right-click selected text to open a shortcut menu with a Mini toolbar, text-related commands, such as Cut, Copy, and Paste, as well as other program-specific commands.

You'll use a shortcut menu in Excel to delete the content you entered in cell A1.

To use a shortcut menu to delete content:

▶ 1. Right-click cell **A1**. A shortcut menu opens, listing commands related to common tasks you'd perform in a cell, along with a Mini toolbar. See Figure 16.

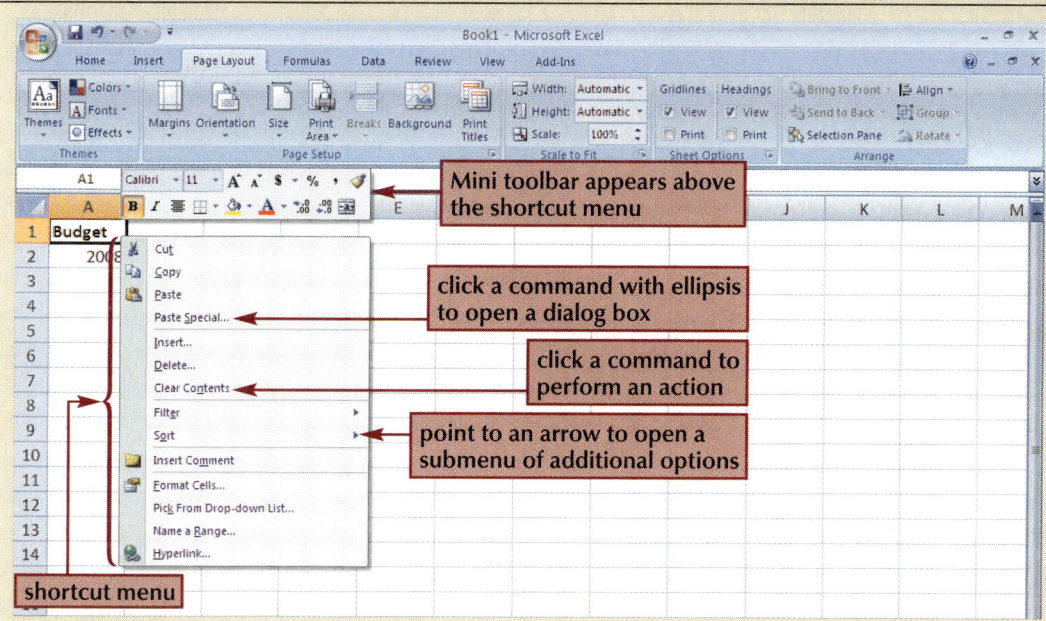

Figure 16 — Shortcut menu with Mini toolbar

You'll use the Clear Contents command to delete the bold text from cell A1.

▶ 2. Click **Clear Contents** on the shortcut menu. The shortcut menu closes, the Mini toolbar disappears, and the formatted text is removed from cell A1.

You'll use the Clear Contents command again to delete the year from cell A2.

▶ 3. Right-click cell **A2**, and then click **Clear Contents** on the shortcut menu. The year is removed from cell A2.

Tip

Press the Esc key to close an open menu, shortcut menu, list, gallery, and so forth without selecting an option.

Shortcut menus enable you to quickly access commands that you're most likely to need in the context of the task you're performing.

Working with Files

The most common tasks you perform in any Office program are to create, open, save, and close files. The processes for these tasks are basically the same in all the Office programs. In addition, there are several methods for performing most tasks in Office. This flexibility enables you to use Office in a way that best fits how you like to work.

The **Office Button** provides access to document-level features, such as creating new files, opening existing files, saving files, printing files, and closing files, as well as the most common program options, called **application settings**. The **Quick Access Toolbar** is a collection of buttons that provide one-click access to commonly used commands, such as Save, Undo, and Repeat.

To begin working in a program, you need to create a new file or open an existing file. When you start Word, Excel, or PowerPoint, the program opens along with a blank file—ready for you to begin working on a new document, workbook, or presentation. When you start Access, the Getting Started with Microsoft Access window opens, displaying options for creating a new database or opening an existing one.

Ean has asked you to continue working on the agenda for the stockholder meeting. You already started typing in the document that opened when you started Word. Next, you will enter more text in the Word document.

> **Tip**
> You can add buttons you use frequently to the Quick Access Toolbar. Click the Customize Quick Access Toolbar button, and then click a button name on the menu.

To enter text in the Word document:

▶ 1. Click the **Document1 – Microsoft Word** button on the taskbar to activate the Word program window.

▶ 2. Type **Meeting Agenda** on the second line of the document, and then press the **Enter** key. The text you typed appears in the document.

   Trouble? If you make a typing error, press the Backspace key to delete the incorrect letters, and then retype the text.

Saving a File

As you create and modify Office files, your work is stored only in the computer's temporary memory, not on a hard disk. If you were to exit the programs without saving, turn off your computer, or experience a power failure, your work would be lost. To prevent losing work, save your file to a disk frequently—at least every 10 minutes. You can save files to the hard disk located inside your computer, a floppy disk, an external hard drive, a network storage drive, or a portable storage disk, such as a USB flash drive.

Reference Window | Saving a File

To save a file the first time or with a new name or location:
- Click the Office Button, and then click Save As (or for an unnamed file, click the Save button on the Quick Access Toolbar or click the Office Button, and then click Save).
- In the Save As dialog box, navigate to the location where you want to save the file.
- Type a descriptive title in the File name box, and then click the Save button.

To resave a named file to the same location:
- Click the Save button on the Quick Access Toolbar (or click the Office Button, and then click Save).

The first time you save a file, you need to name it. This **filename** includes a descriptive title you select and a file extension assigned by Office. You should choose a descriptive title that accurately reflects the content of the document, workbook, presentation, or database, such as "Shipping Options Letter" or "Fourth Quarter Financial Analysis." Your descriptive title can include uppercase and lowercase letters, numbers, hyphens, and spaces in any combination, but not the following special characters: ? " / \ < > * | and :. Each filename ends with a **file extension**, a period followed by several characters that Office adds to your descriptive title to identify the program in which that file was created. The default file extensions for Office 2007 are .docx for Word, .xlsx for Excel, .pptx for PowerPoint, and .accdb for Access. Filenames (the descriptive title and the file extension) can include a maximum of 255 characters. You might see file extensions depending on how Windows is set up on your computer. The figures in these tutorials do not show file extensions.

You also need to decide where to save the file—on which disk and in what folder. A **folder** is a container for your files. Just as you organize paper documents within folders stored in a filing cabinet, you can organize your files within folders stored on your computer's hard disk or a removable disk, such as a USB flash drive. Store each file in a logical location that you will remember whenever you want to use the file again. The default storage location for Office files is the Documents folder; you can create additional storage folders within that folder or navigate to a new storage location.

You can navigate the Save As dialog box by clicking a folder or location on your computer in the Navigation pane along the left side of the dialog box, and then double-clicking folders in the file list until you display the storage location you want. You can also navigate to a storage location with the Address bar, which displays the current file path. Each location in the file path has a corresponding arrow that you can click to quickly select a folder within that location. For example, you can click the Documents arrow in the Address bar to open a list of all the folders in the Documents folder, and then click the folder you want to open. If you want to return to a specific spot in the file hierarchy, you click that folder name in the Address bar. The Back and Forward buttons let you quickly move between folders.

> **Tip**
>
> Office adds the correct file extension when you save a file. Do not type one in the descriptive title, or you will create a duplicate (such as Meeting Agenda.docx.docx).

> **Windows XP Tip**
>
> The default storage location for Office files is the My Documents folder.

Saving and Using Files with Earlier Versions of Office | InSight

The default file types in Office 2007 are different from those used in earlier versions. This means that someone using Office 2003 or earlier cannot open files created in Office 2007. Files you want to share with earlier Office users must be saved in the earlier formats, which use the following extensions: .doc for Word, .xls for Excel, .mdb for Access, and .ppt for PowerPoint. To save a file in an earlier format, open the Save As dialog box, click the Save as type list arrow, and then click the appropriate 97-2003 format. A compatibility checker reports which Office 2007 features or elements are not supported by the earlier version of Office, and you can choose to remove them before saving. You can use Office 2007 to open and work with files created in earlier versions of Office. You can then save the file in its current format or update it to the Office 2007 format.

The lines of text you typed are not yet saved on disk. You'll do that now.

To save a file for the first time:

1. Click the **Save** button on the Quick Access Toolbar. The Save As dialog box opens because you have not yet saved the file and need to specify a storage location and filename. The default location is set to the Documents folder, and the first few words of the first line appear in the File name box as a suggested title.

2. In the Navigation pane, click the link for the location that contains your Data Files, if necessary.

    Trouble? If you don't have the starting Data Files, you need to get them before you can proceed. Your instructor will either give you the Data Files or ask you to obtain them from a specified location (such as a network drive). In either case, make a backup copy of the Data Files before you start so that you will have the original files available in case you need to start over. If you have any questions about the Data Files, see your instructor or technical support person for assistance.

3. Double-click the **OFF** folder in the file list, and then double-click the **Tutorial** folder. This is the location where you want to save the document.

    Next, you'll enter a more descriptive title for the filename.

4. Type **Meeting Agenda** in the File name box. See Figure 17.

> **Windows XP Tip**
>
> To navigate to a location in the Save As dialog box, you use the Save in arrow.

Figure 17 Completed Save As dialog box

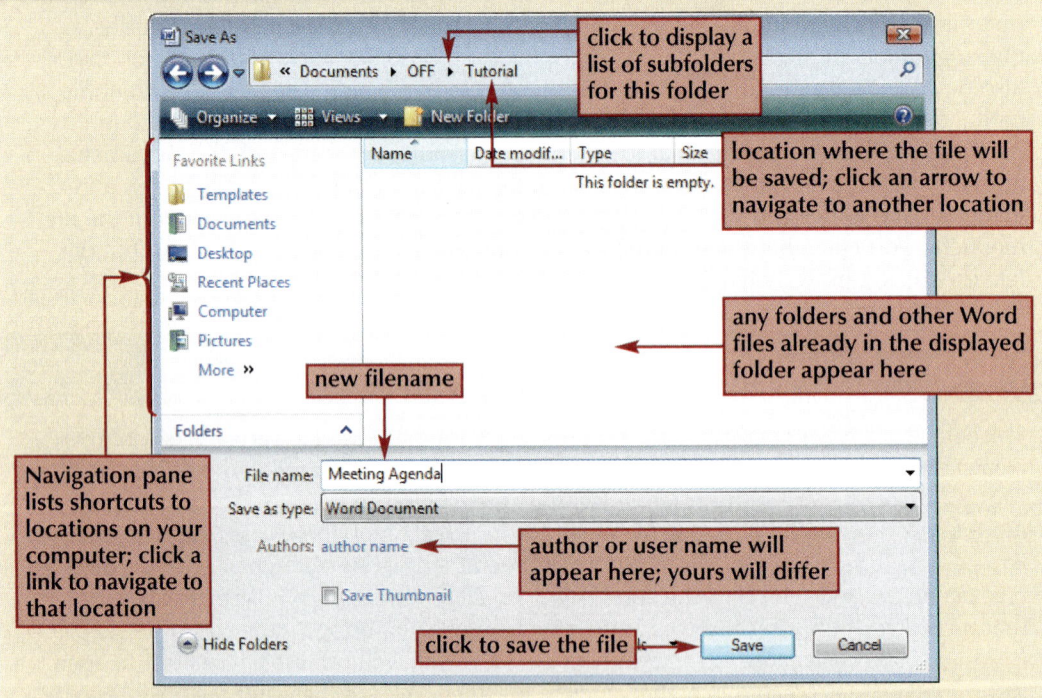

Trouble? If the .docx file extension appears after the filename, your computer is configured to show file extensions. Continue with Step 5.

5. Click the **Save** button. The Save As dialog box closes, and the name of your file appears in the title bar.

The saved file includes everything in the document at the time you last saved it. Any new edits or additions you make to the document exist only in the computer's memory and are not saved in the file on the disk. As you work, remember to save frequently so that the file is updated to reflect the latest content of the document.

Because you already named the document and selected a storage location, the Save As dialog box doesn't open whenever you save the document again. If you want to save a copy of the file with a different filename or to a different location, you reopen the Save As dialog box by clicking the Office Button, and then clicking Save As. The previous version of the file remains on your disk as well.

You need to add your name to the agenda. Then, you'll save your changes.

To modify and save the Word document:

1. Type your name, and then press the **Enter** key. The text you typed appears on the next line.
2. Click the **Save** button on the Quick Access Toolbar to save your changes.

Closing a File

Although you can keep multiple files open at one time, you should close any file you are no longer working on to conserve system resources as well as to ensure that you don't inadvertently make changes to the file. You can close a file by clicking the Office Button and then clicking the Close command. If that's the only file open for the program, the program window remains open and no file appears in the window. You can also close a file by clicking the Close button in the upper-right corner of the title bar or double-clicking the Office Button. If that's the only file open for the program, the program also closes.

As a standard practice, you should save your file before closing it. However, Office has an added safeguard: If you attempt to close a file without saving your changes, a dialog box opens, asking whether you want to save the file. Click the Yes button to save the changes to the file before closing the file and program. Click the No button to close the file and program without saving changes. Click the Cancel button to return to the program window without saving changes or closing the file and program. This feature helps to ensure that you always save the most current version of any file.

You'll add the date to the agenda. Then, you'll attempt to close it without saving.

To modify and close the Word document:

1. Type today's date, and then press the **Enter** key. The text you typed appears below your name in the document.
2. In the upper-left corner of the program window, click the **Office Button**. A menu opens with commands for creating new files, opening existing files, saving files, printing files, and closing files.
3. Click **Close**. A dialog box opens, asking whether you want to save the changes you made to the document.
4. Click the **Yes** button. The current version of the document is saved to the file, and then the document closes. Word is still running.

After you have a program open, you can create additional new files for the open program or you can open previously created and saved files.

Opening a File

When you want to open a blank document, workbook, presentation, or database, you create a new file. When you want to work on a previously created file, you must first open it. Opening a file transfers a copy of the file from the storage disk (either a hard disk or a portable disk) to the computer's memory and displays it on your screen. The file is then in your computer's memory and on the disk.

Reference Window | Opening an Existing File or Creating a New File

- Click the Office Button, and then click Open.
- In the Open dialog box, navigate to the storage location of the file you want to open.
- Click the filename of the file you want to open.
- Click the Open button.

or

- Click the Office Button, and then click a filename in the Recent Documents list.

or

- Click the Office Button, and then click New.
- In the New dialog box, click Blank Document, Blank Workbook, Blank Presentation, or Blank Database (depending on the program).
- Click the Create button.

Ean asks you to print the agenda. To do that, you'll reopen the file.

To open the existing Word document:

1. Click the **Office Button**, and then click **Open**. The Open dialog box, which works similarly to the Save As dialog box, opens.

2. Use the Navigation pane or the Address bar to navigate to the **OFF\Tutorial** folder included with your Data Files. This is the location where you saved the agenda document.

Windows XP Tip
To navigate to a location in the Open dialog box, you use the Look in arrow.

3. Click **Meeting Agenda** in the file list. See Figure 18.

Figure 18 Open dialog box

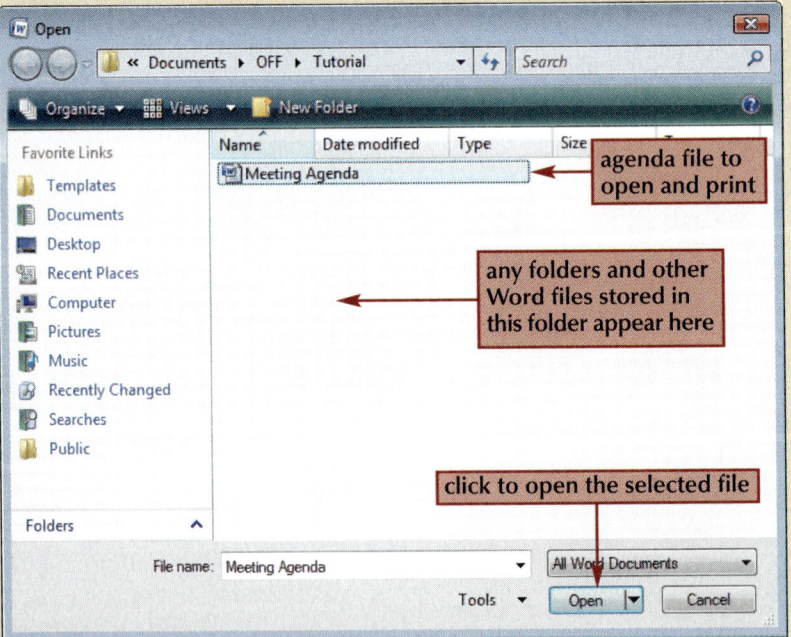

4. Click the **Open** button. The agenda file opens in the Word program window.

Getting Help

If you don't know how to perform a task or want more information about a feature, you can turn to Office itself for information on how to use it. This information, referred to simply as **Help**, is like a huge encyclopedia available from your desktop. You can get Help in ScreenTips, from the Help window, and in Microsoft Office Online.

Viewing ScreenTips

ScreenTips are a fast and simple method you can use to get help about objects you see on the screen. A **ScreenTip** is a box with the button's name, its keyboard shortcut if it has one, a description of the command's function, and, in some cases, a link to more information. Just position the mouse pointer over a button or object to view its ScreenTip. If a link to more information appears in the ScreenTip, press the F1 key while the Screen-Tip is displayed to open the Help window with the appropriate topic displayed.

To view ScreenTips:

1. Point to the **Microsoft Office Word Help** button. The ScreenTip shows the button's name, its keyboard shortcut, and a brief explanation of the button. See Figure 19.

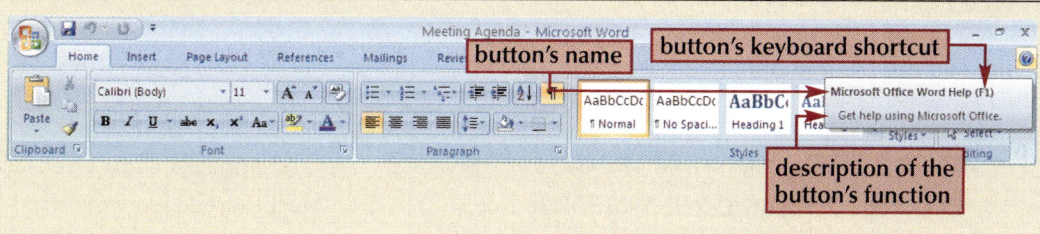

Figure 19 — ScreenTip for the Help button

2. Point to other buttons on the Ribbon to display their ScreenTips.

Using the Help Window

For more detailed information, you can use the **Help window** to access all the Help topics, templates, and training installed on your computer with Office and available on Microsoft Office Online. **Microsoft Office Online** is a Web site maintained by Microsoft that provides access to the latest information and additional Help resources. For example, you can access current Help topics, templates of predesigned files, and training for Office. To connect to Microsoft Office Online, you need Internet access on your computer. Otherwise, you see only those topics stored locally.

Reference Window | Getting Help

- Click the Microsoft Office Help button (the button name depends on the Office program).
- Type a keyword or phrase in the "Type words to search for" box, and then click the Search button.
- Click a Help topic in the search results list.
- Read the information in the Help window. For more information, click other topics or links.
- Click the Close button on the Help window title bar.

You open the Help window by clicking the Microsoft Office Help button located below the sizing buttons in every Office program. Each program has its own Help window from which you can find information about all the Office commands and features as well as step-by-step instructions for using them. You can search for information in the Help window using the "Type words to search for" box and the Table of Contents pane.

The "Type words to search for" box enables you to search the Help system using keywords or phrases. You type a specific word or phrase about a task you want to perform or a topic you need help with, and then click the Search button to search the Help system. A list of Help topics related to the keyword or phrase you entered appears in the Help window. If your computer is connected to the Internet, your search results come from Microsoft Office Online rather than only the Help topics stored locally on your computer. You can click a link to open a Help topic with step-by-step instructions that will guide you through a specific procedure and/or provide explanations of difficult concepts in clear, easy-to-understand language. For example, if you type "format cell" in the Excel Help window, a list of Help topics related to the words you typed appears in the Help window. You can navigate through the topics you've viewed using the buttons on the Help window toolbar. These buttons—including Back, Forward, Stop, Refresh, Home, and Print—are the same as those in the Microsoft Internet Explorer Web browser.

You'll use the "Type words to search for" box in the Help window to obtain more information about printing a document in Word.

To use the "Type words to search for" box:

1. Click the **Microsoft Office Word Help** button . The Word Help window opens.
2. Click the **Type words to search for** box, if necessary, and then type **print document**. You can set where you want to search.
3. Click the **Search button arrow**. The Search menu shows the online and local content available.

4. If your computer is connected to the Internet, click **All Word** in the Content from Office Online list. If your computer is not connected to the Internet, click **Word Help** in the Content from this computer list.

5. Click the **Search** button. The Help window displays a list of topics related to your keywords. See Figure 20.

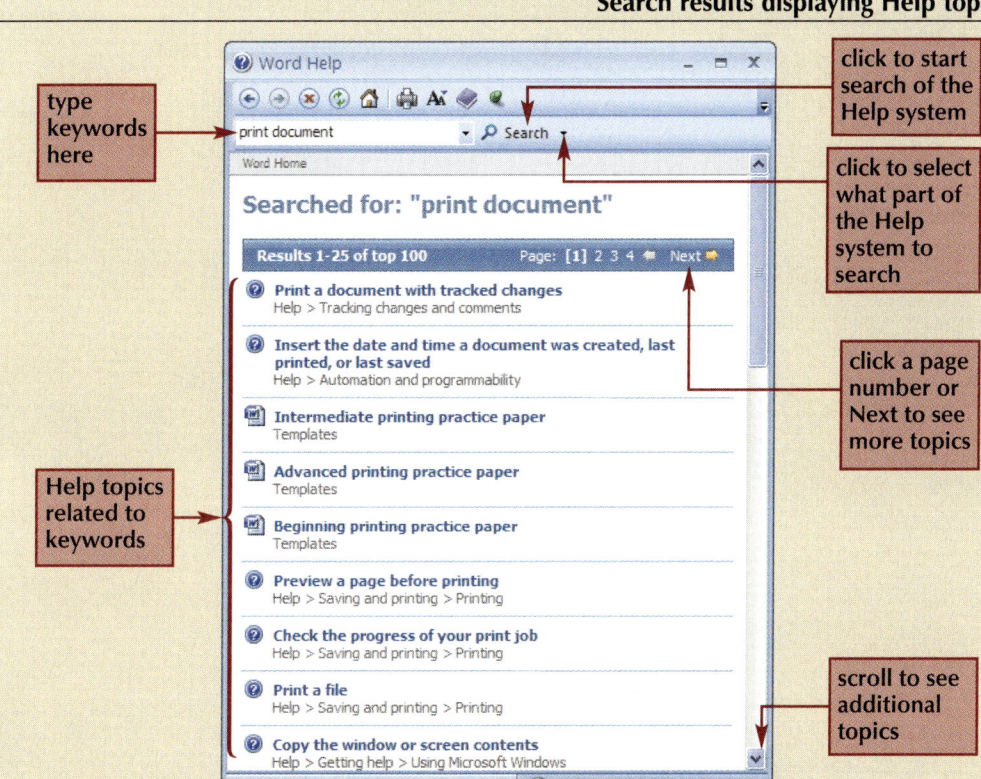

Figure 20 — Search results displaying Help topics

Trouble? If your search results list differs from the one shown in Figure 20, your computer is not connected to the Internet or Microsoft has updated the list of available Help topics since this book was published. Continue with Step 6.

6. Scroll through the list to review the Help topics.

7. Click **Print a file**. The Help topic is displayed in the Help window so you can learn more about how to print a document. See Figure 21.

Figure 21 — Print a file Help topic

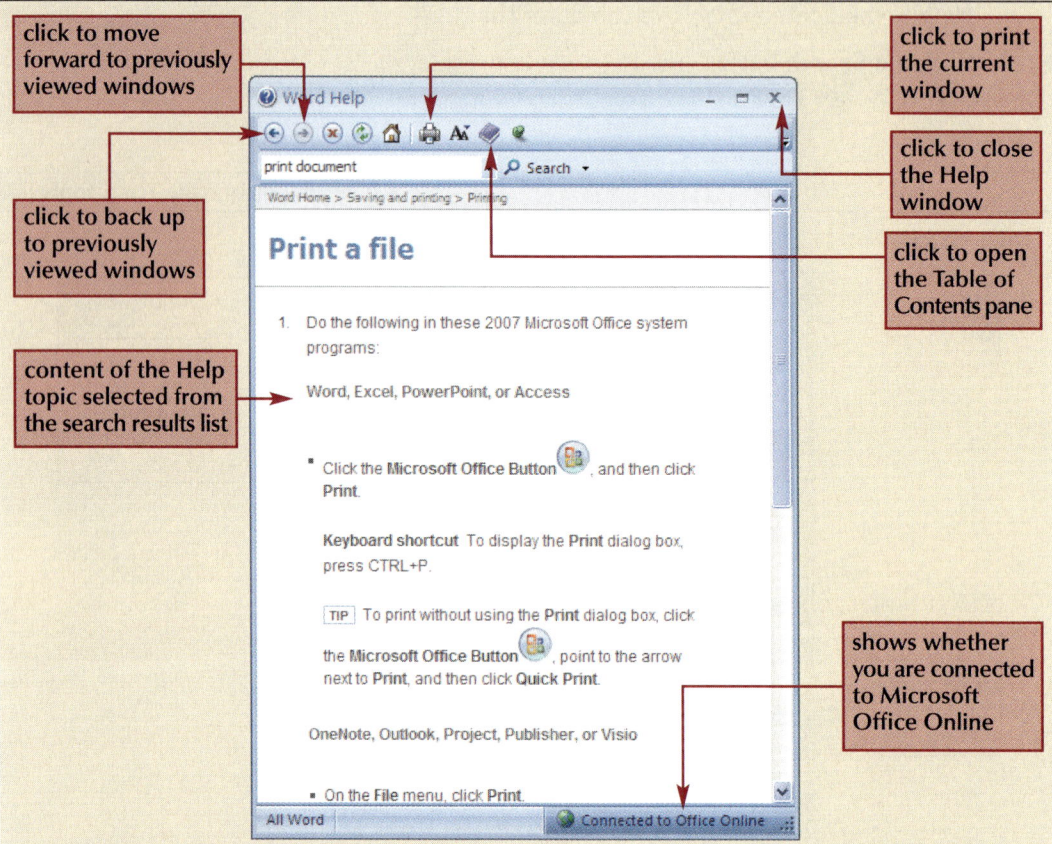

Trouble? If you don't see the Print a file Help topic on page 1, its current location might be on another page. Click the Next link to move to the next page, and then scroll down to find the Print a file topic, repeating to search additional pages until you locate the topic.

▸ **8.** Read the information.

Another way to find information in the Help system is to use the Table of Contents pane. The Show Table of Contents button on the Help window toolbar opens a pane that displays a list of the Help system content organized by subjects and topics, similar to a book's table of contents. You click main subject links to display related topic links. You click a topic link to display that Help topic in the Help window. You'll use the Table of Contents to find information about getting help in Office.

To use the Help window table of contents:

▸ **1.** Click the **Show Table of Contents** button on the Help window toolbar. The Table of Contents pane opens on the left side of the Help window.

▸ **2.** Click **Getting help** in the Table of Contents pane, scrolling up if necessary. The Getting help "book" opens, listing the topics related to that subject.

▸ **3.** Click the **Work with the Help window** topic, and then click the **Maximize** button on the title bar. The Help topic is displayed in the maximized Help window, and you can read the text to learn more about the various ways to obtain help in Word. See Figure 22.

Getting Started with Microsoft Office 2007 | Office **OFF 27**

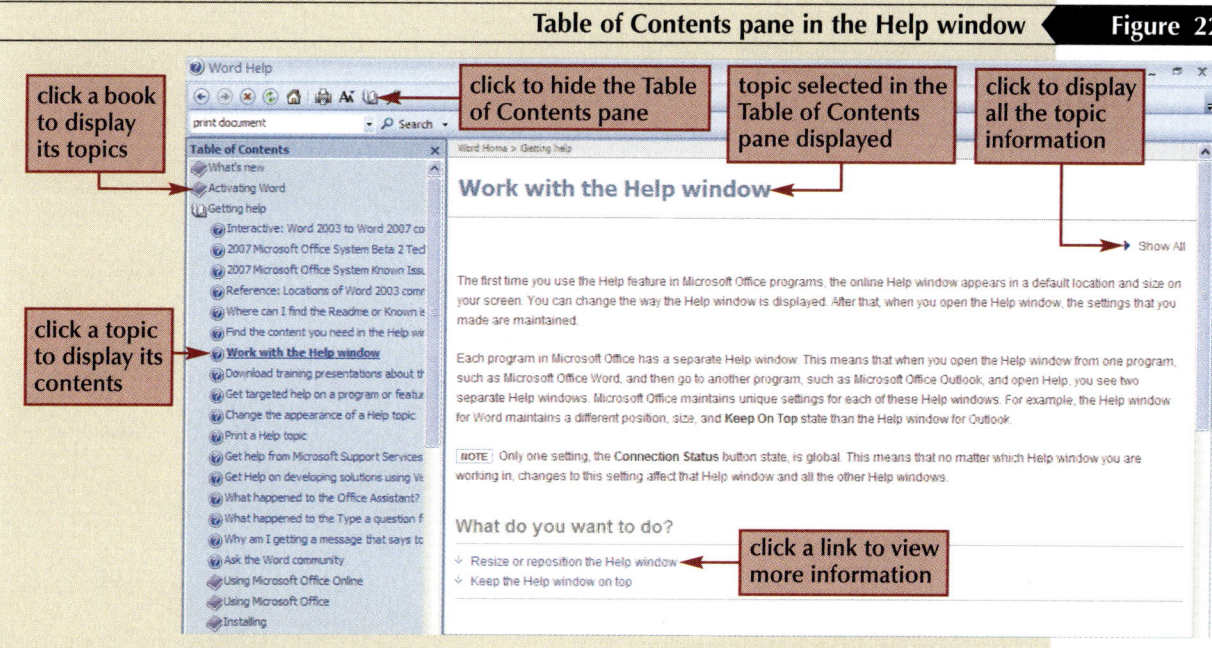

Figure 22 — Table of Contents pane in the Help window

Trouble? If your search results list differs from the one shown in Figure 22, your computer is not connected to the Internet or Microsoft has updated the list of available Help topics since this book was published. Continue with Step 4.

4. Click **Using Microsoft Office Online** in the Table of Contents pane, click the **Get online Help, templates, training, and additional content** topic to display information about that topic, and then read the information.

5. Click the links within this topic and read the information.

6. Click the **Close** button ⊠ on the Help window title bar to close the window.

Printing a File

At times, you'll want a paper copy of your Office file. The first time you print during each session at the computer, you should use the Print command to open the Print dialog box so you can verify or adjust the printing settings. You can select a printer, the number of copies to print, the portion of the file to print, and so forth; the printing settings vary slightly from program to program. If you want to use the same default settings for subsequent print jobs, you can use the Quick Print button to print without opening the dialog box.

Printing a File | Reference Window

- Click the Office Button, and then click Print.
- Verify the print settings in the Print dialog box.
- Click the OK button.

or

- Click the Office Button, point to Print, and then click Quick Print.

Now that you know how to print, you'll print the agenda for Ean.

To print the Word document:

1. Make sure your printer is turned on and contains paper.
2. Click the **Office Button**, and then click **Print**. The Print dialog box opens. See Figure 23.

Figure 23 — Print dialog box

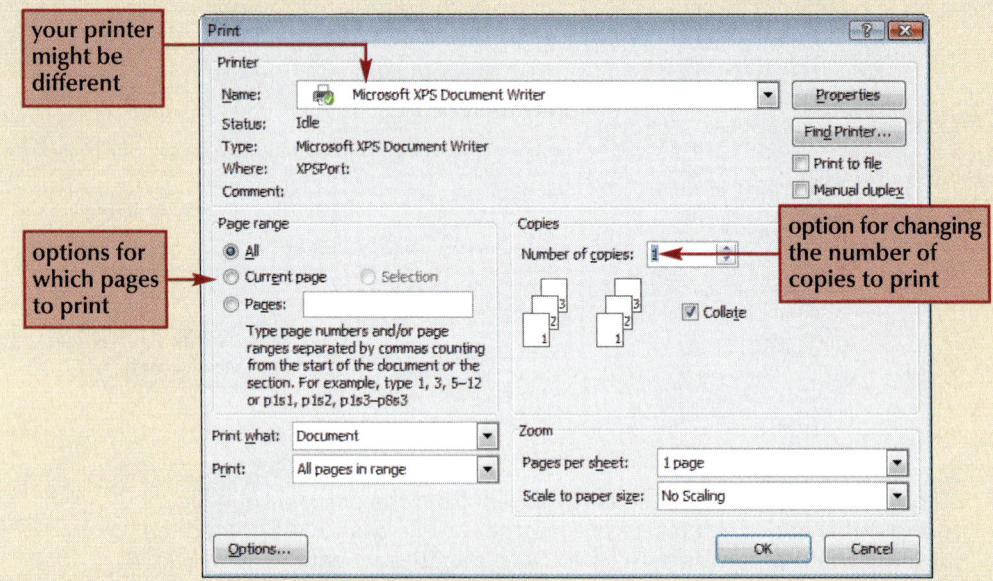

your printer might be different

options for which pages to print

option for changing the number of copies to print

Trouble? If a menu of Print commands opens, you clicked the Print button arrow on the two-part Print button. Click Print on the menu to open the Print dialog box.

3. Verify that the correct printer appears in the Name box in the Printer group. If necessary, click the **Name** arrow, and then click the correct printer from the list of available printers.
4. Verify that **1** appears in the Number of copies box.
5. Click the **OK** button to print the document.

   Trouble? If the document does not print, see your instructor or technical support person for help.

Exiting Programs

When you finish working with a program, you should exit it. As with many other aspects of Office, you can exit programs with a button or a command. You'll use both methods to exit Word and Excel. You can use the Exit command to exit a program and close an open file in one step. If you haven't saved the final version of the open file, a dialog box opens, asking whether you want to save your changes. Clicking the Yes button saves the open file, closes the file, and then exits the program.

To exit the Word and Excel programs:

1. Click the **Close** button on the Word title bar to exit Word. The Word document closes and the Word program exits. The Excel window is visible again.

> **Trouble?** If a dialog box opens, asking if you want to save the document, you might have inadvertently made a change to the document. Click the No button.

▶ 2. Click the **Office Button**, and then click **Exit Excel**. A dialog box opens, asking whether you want to save the changes you made to the workbook. If you click the Yes button, the Save As dialog box opens and Excel exits after you finish saving the workbook. This time, you don't want to save the workbook.

▶ 3. Click the **No** button. The workbook closes without saving a copy, and the Excel program exits.

Exiting programs after you are done using them keeps your Windows desktop uncluttered for the next person using the computer, frees up your system's resources, and prevents data from being lost accidentally.

Quick Check | Review

1. What Office program would be best to use to create a budget?
2. How do you start an Office program?
3. Explain the difference between Save and Save As.
4. How do you open an existing Office file?
5. What happens if you open a file, make edits, and then attempt to close the file or exit the program without saving the current version of the file?
6. What are two ways to get Help in Office?

Tutorial Summary | Review

You have learned how to use features common to all the programs included in Microsoft Office 2007, including starting and exiting programs; resizing windows; using the Ribbon, dialog boxes, shortcut menus, and the Mini toolbar; opening, closing, and printing files; and getting Help.

Key Terms

Access	Help window	Office Button
application settings	integration	Outlook
button	keyboard shortcut	PowerPoint
contextual tab	Live Preview	presentation
database	Microsoft Office 2007	Quick Access Toolbar
default	Microsoft Office Access 2007	Ribbon
dialog box	Microsoft Office Excel 2007	ScreenTip
Dialog Box Launcher	Microsoft Office Online	shortcut menu
document	Microsoft Office Outlook 2007	status bar
Excel	Microsoft Office PowerPoint 2007	tab
file extension		task pane
filename		Word
folder	Microsoft Office Word 2007	workbook
gallery	Mini toolbar	zoom
group	object	
Help	Office	

Practice | Review Assignments

Practice the skills you learned in the tutorial.

Data Files needed for the Review Assignments: Finances.xlsx, Letter.docx

You need to prepare for an upcoming meeting at Recycled Palette. You'll open and print documents for the presentation. Complete the following:

1. Start PowerPoint.
2. Use the Help window to search Office Online for the PowerPoint demo "Demo: Up to Speed with PowerPoint 2007." (*Hint*: Use "demo" as the keyword to search for, and make sure you search All PowerPoint in the Content from Office Online list. If you are not connected to the Internet, continue with Step 3.) Open the Demo topic, and then click the Play Demo link to view it. Close Internet Explorer and the Help window when you're done.
3. Start Excel.
4. Switch to the PowerPoint window using the taskbar, and then close the presentation but leave open the PowerPoint program. (*Hint:* Click the Office Button and then click Close.)
5. Open a new, blank PowerPoint presentation from the New Presentation dialog box.
6. Close the PowerPoint presentation and program using the Close button on the PowerPoint title bar; do not save changes if asked.
7. Open the **Finances** workbook located in the OFF\Review folder included with your Data Files.
8. Use the Save As command to save the workbook as **Recycled Palette Finances** in the OFF\Review folder.
9. Type your name, press the Enter key to insert your name at the top of the worksheet, and then save the workbook.
10. Print one copy of the worksheet using the Print button on the Office Button menu.
11. Exit Excel using the Office Button.
12. Start Word, and then open the **Letter** document located in the OFF\Review folder included with your Data Files.
13. Use the Save As command to save the document with the filename **Recycled Palette Letter** in the OFF\Review folder.
14. Press and hold the Ctrl key, press the End key, and then release both keys to move the insertion point to the end of the letter, and then type your name.
15. Use the Save button on the Quick Access Toolbar to save the change to the Recycled Palette Letter document.
16. Print one copy of the document, and then close the document.
17. Exit the Word program using the Close button on the title bar.

In both cases, Excel adds the values in cells A1 through A10, but the SUM function is faster and simpler to enter and less prone to a typing error. You should always use a function, if one is available, in place of a long, complex formula.

Excel supports over 300 different functions from the fields of finance, business, science, and engineering. Functions are not limited to numbers. Excel also provides functions that work with text and dates.

Entering a Function

Amanda wants to calculate the total number of DVDs she needs to create for her customers. To do that, you'll use the SUM function to add the values in the range F6:F9.

To enter the SUM function:

1. Click cell **E10**, type **TOTAL** as the label, and then press the **Tab** key. The label is entered in cell E10, and cell F10 is the active cell.

2. Type **=SUM(F6:F9** in cell F10. As you begin to type the SUM function, a ScreenTip lists the names of all functions that start with the letter "S." When you type the cell references, Excel highlights all the cells in the specified range to provide a visual reminder of exactly which cells the SUM function is using. See Figure 1-26.

Tip

You can also insert a range reference into a function by selecting the range with your mouse.

Figure 1-26 | **SUM function being entered**

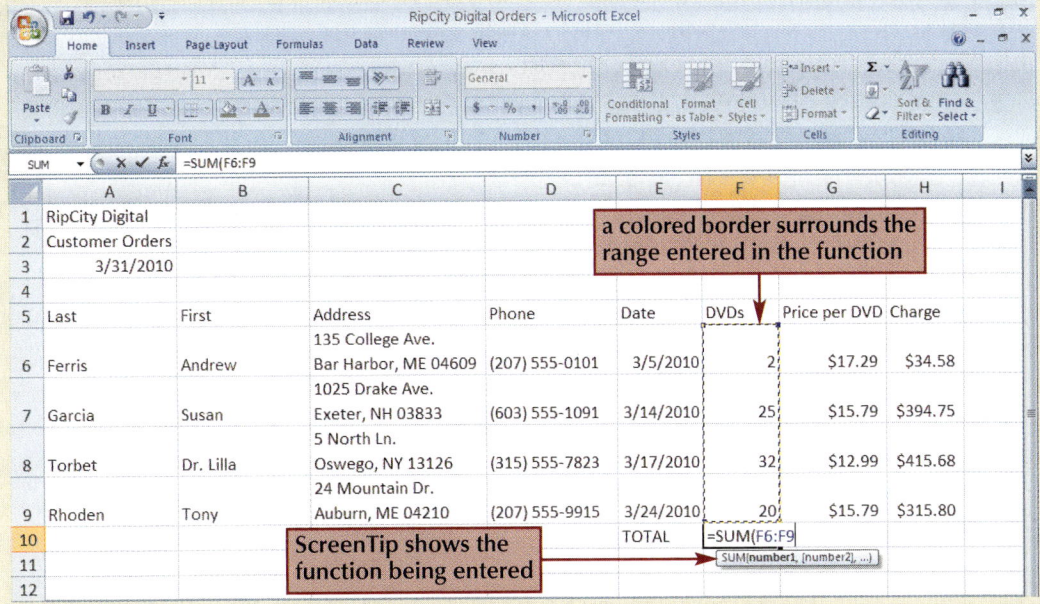

3. Type **)** to complete the function, and then press the **Tab** key. The value of the SUM function appears in cell F10, indicating that Amanda has to create 79 DVDs to meet all of her current orders.

▶ 2. In the Clipboard group on the Home tab, click the **Copy** button. The formula is copied to the Clipboard.

▶ 3. Select the range **H8:H9**, the cells in which you want to paste the formula.

▶ 4. In the Clipboard group, click the **Paste** button. Excel pastes the formula into the selected range. See Figure 1-25.

Figure 1-25   Formula copied and pasted

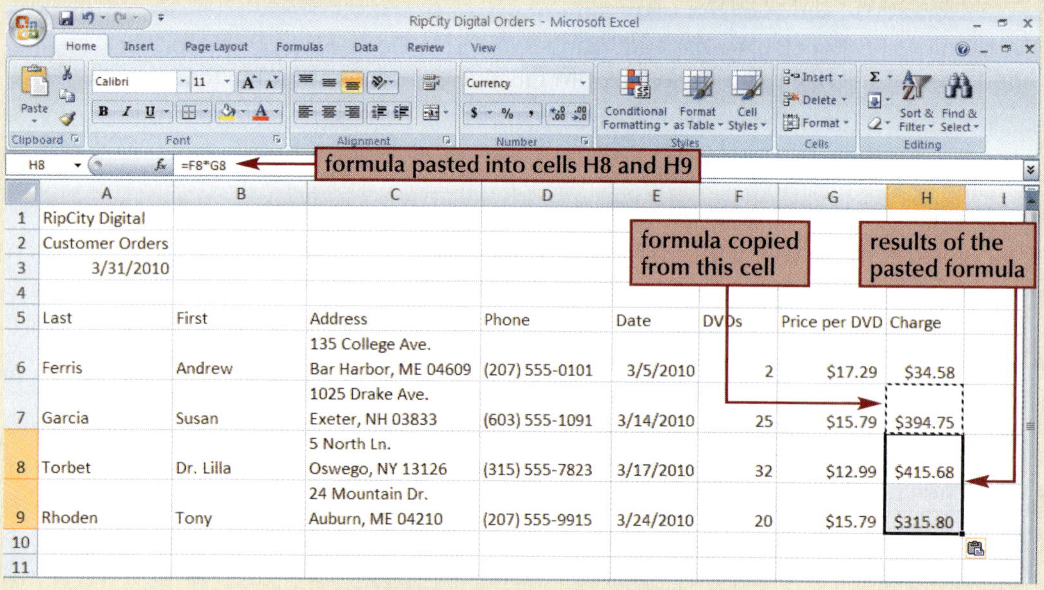

▶ 5. Click cell **H8** and verify that the formula =F8*G8 appears in the formula bar, and then click cell **H9** and verify that the formula =F9*G9 appears in the formula bar.

Pasting a formula is different from pasting a value. With the customer order data, Excel pasted the same values in a new location. With formulas, Excel adjusts the formula's cell references to reflect the new location of the formula in the worksheet. This is because you want to replicate the actions of a formula rather than duplicate the specific value the formula generates. In this case, the formula's action is to multiply the number of DVDs Amanda created for the customer by the price she charged for creating each DVD. By copying and pasting that formula, that action is replicated for every customer in the worksheet.

Introducing Functions

In addition to cell references and operators, formulas can also contain functions. A **function** is a named operation that returns a value. Functions are used to simplify formulas, reducing what might be a long expression into a compact statement. For example, to add the values in the range A1:A10, you could enter the following long formula:

=A1+A2+A3+A4+A5+A6+A7+A8+A9+A10

Or, you could use the SUM function to accomplish the same thing:

=SUM(A1:A10)

Excel EX 1

Tutorial 1

Objectives

Session 1.1
- Understand the use of spreadsheets and Excel
- Learn the parts of the Excel window
- Scroll through a worksheet and navigate between worksheets
- Create and save a workbook file
- Enter text, numbers, and dates into a worksheet
- Resize, insert, and remove columns and rows

Session 1.2
- Select and move cell ranges
- Insert formulas and functions
- Insert, delete, move, and rename worksheets
- Work with editing tools
- Preview and print a workbook

Getting Started with Excel

Creating an Order Report

Case | RipCity Digital

When Amanda Dunn purchased a DVD burner a few years ago, one of her first tasks was to convert her home videos into DVDs. After she saw how simple it was, she upgraded her hardware and software and proceeded to create DVDs from home movies and slides for her parents and friends. Based on her success, Amanda decided to make a business out of her hobby and founded RipCity Digital, an online service specializing in creating DVDs from the home movies, photos, and slides sent to her from customers. Amanda wants to list the weekly orders from her customers, tracking the names and addresses of her clients, the number of DVDs that she creates, and finally the cost of creating and shipping the DVDs.

Amanda is so busy creating DVDs that she asks you to record her orders. You'll do this in **Microsoft Office Excel 2007** (or **Excel**), a computer program used to enter, analyze, and present quantitative data. You'll also enter the latest orders she received for her new business.

Starting Data Files

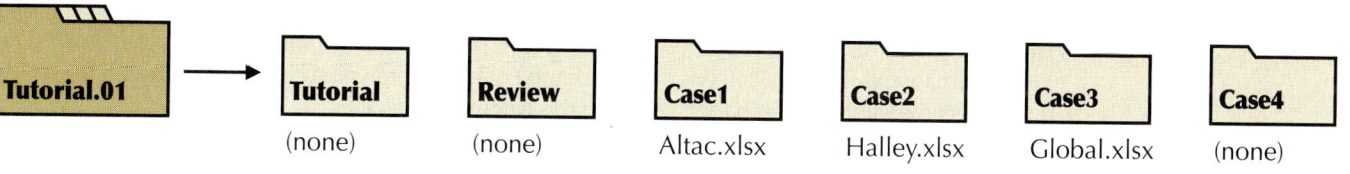

Session 1.1

Introducing Excel

Before you begin working in Excel, Amanda asks you to review some of the features, key terms, and concepts associated with spreadsheets. Understanding spreadsheets and how they work in Excel will help you as you enter RipCity Digital customer orders.

Understanding Spreadsheets

A **spreadsheet** is a collection of text and numbers laid out in a rectangular grid. Spreadsheets are often used in business for budgeting, inventory management, and decision making. They can also be used to manage personal budgets and track household assets. For example, the paper-based spreadsheet shown in Figure 1-1 shows a cash flow report. The spreadsheet records the estimated and actual cash flow for the month of January. Each line, or row, displays a different value, such as the starting cash balance or cash sales for the month. Each column displays the budgeted or actual numbers or text that describes those values. The total cash expenditures, net cash flow, and closing cash balance for the month are not entered directly, but calculated from other numbers in the spreadsheet. For example, the total cash expenditure is equal to the expenditures on advertising, wages, and supplies. For paper spreadsheets, these calculations are done using a hand calculator and then entered into the spreadsheet.

Figure 1-1   Sample paper spreadsheet

Cash Flow Comparison Budgeted vs. Actual		Jan–10
	Budgeted	Actual
Cash balance (start of month)	$4,500.00	$4,500.00
Cash receipts		
Cash sales	12,600.00	14,688.00
Cash expenditures		
Advertising	1,200.00	1,425.00
Wages	7,200.00	7,850.00
Supplies	3,600.00	4,350.00
Total cash expenditures	12,000.00	13,625.00
Net cash flow	600.00	1,063.00
Cash balance (end of month)	$5,100.00	$5,563.00

Excel is a computer program used to create electronic versions of these paper spreadsheets. Figure 1-2 shows the data from Figure 1-1 as it might appear in Excel. As with paper spreadsheets, Excel uses a rectangular grid to lay out the financial information in rows and columns. As you'll see later, values such as total cash expenditures can be calculated automatically rather than entered manually into the spreadsheet. This allows you to use Excel to perform a **what-if analysis** in which you change one or more values in a spreadsheet and then assess the effect those changes have on the calculated values.

Figure 1-2 Spreadsheet data in Excel

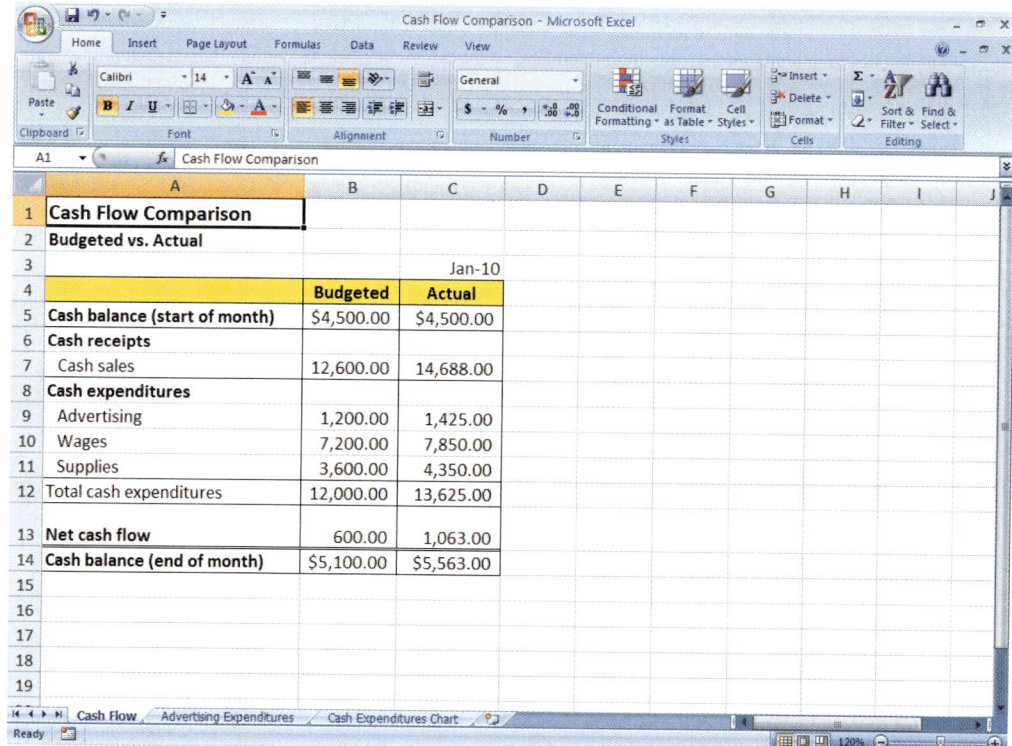

An Excel spreadsheet is more flexible than paper spreadsheets. In fact, it is no longer just an electronic substitute for paper spreadsheets. Excel is now often used for data storage, report generation, and as a tool to access data from the Internet.

Exploring the Excel Window

Before entering Amanda's data, you'll review the different parts of the Excel window. The Excel window contains many of the elements that you find in other Office 2007 programs, including a title bar, the Ribbon, scroll bars, and a status bar. The Excel window also contains features that are unique to Excel. You'll review these features after you start Excel.

To start Excel:

1. Click the **Start** button on the Windows taskbar, click **All Programs**, click **Microsoft Office**, and then point to **Microsoft Office Excel 2007**.

   Trouble? If you don't see Microsoft Office Excel 2007 on the Microsoft Office submenu, look for it on a different submenu or on the All Programs menu. If you still cannot find Microsoft Office Excel 2007, ask your instructor or technical support person for help.

2. Click **Microsoft Office Excel 2007**. The Excel window opens.

   All the figures showing the Excel window in these tutorials are zoomed to 120% for better readability. If you want to zoom your Excel window to match the figures, complete Step 3. If you prefer to work in the default zoom of 100% or at another zoom level, continue with Step 4; you might see more or less of the worksheet on your screen, but this does not affect your work in the tutorials.

3. If you want your Excel window zoomed to match the figures, click the **Zoom In** button on the status bar twice to increase the zoom magnification to **120%**. The worksheet is magnified to 120%, which increases the screen size of each cell, but reduces the number of worksheet cells visible in the workbook window.

4. If necessary, click the **Maximize** button on the Excel window title bar. The Excel window fills the screen, as shown in Figure 1-3. Depending on your installation of Excel and your monitor resolution, your Excel window might look different from the one shown in Figure 1-3.

Figure 1-3   **Parts of the Excel window**

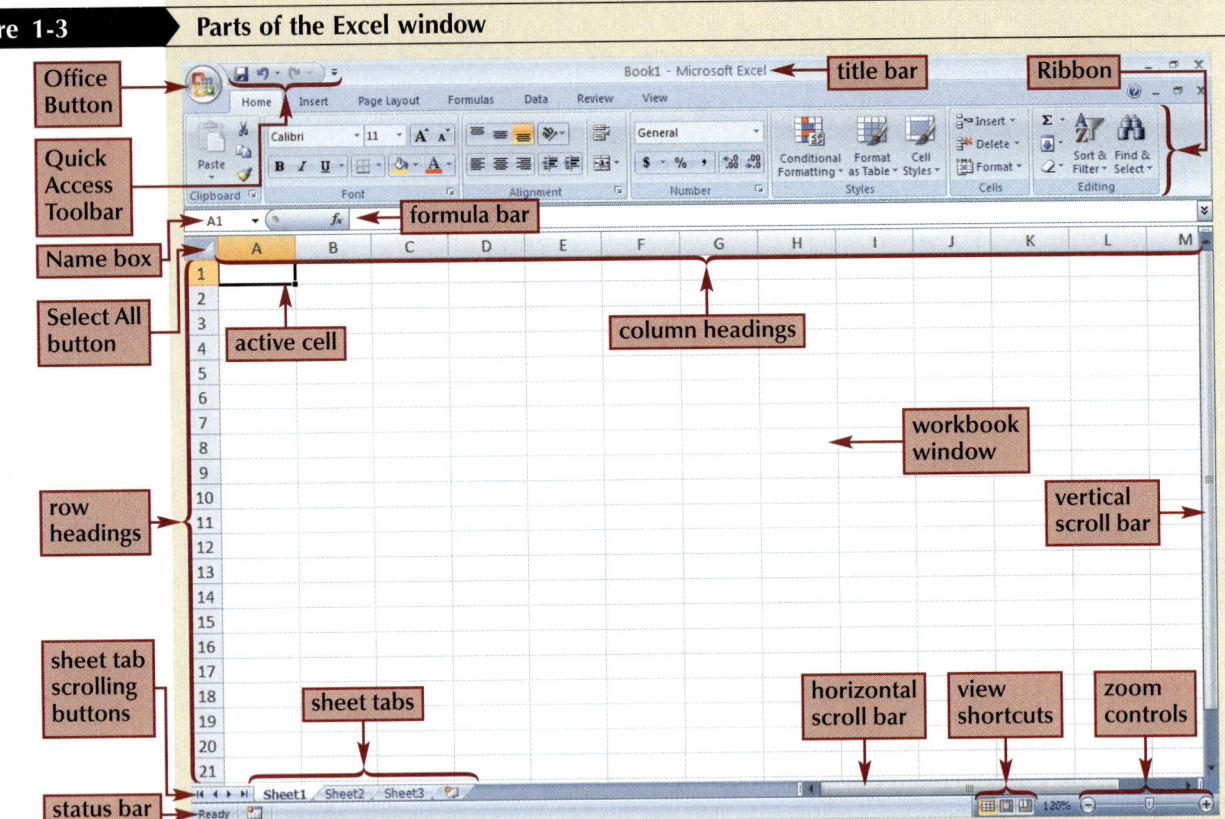

Trouble? If your screen varies slightly from those shown in the figures, your computer might be set up differently. The figures in this book were created while running Windows Vista in the Windows Vista Basic settings, but how your screen looks depends on a variety of things, including the version of Windows, background settings, and so forth.

Excel stores spreadsheets in files called **workbooks**. The contents of a workbook are shown in a **workbook window**. You can open more than one workbook window at a time to display the contents of different workbooks. You can also open multiple workbook windows for one workbook to display different views of the workbook's contents. The workbook that is currently being used is the **active workbook** and is displayed in the **active workbook window**. The name of the active workbook appears in the title bar of the Excel window. By default, Excel starts with a blank workbook named "Book1" in the workbook window, maximized to fill the entire Excel window.

Each workbook is made up of individual **sheets**, just as a notebook an accountant might use is made up of sheets of paper. Excel supports two kinds of sheets: worksheets and chart sheets. A **worksheet** contains data, laid out in rows and columns. A **chart sheet** contains an Excel chart that provides a visual representation of spreadsheet data. Charts can also be embedded within worksheets, allowing you to view both the data and charts in one sheet.

Each sheet is identified by a sheet name. The sheet names are displayed in **sheet tabs** located at the lower-left corner of the workbook window. The sheet currently displayed in the workbook window is the **active sheet**, and its sheet tab is white. In Figure 1-3, the active sheet is named "Sheet1." Other sheets included in the workbook shown in Figure 1-3, but not currently visible, are named "Sheet2" and "Sheet3." The sheet tabs for inactive sheets are gray and stacked behind the Sheet1 tab. An inactive sheet becomes active when you click its worksheet tab. By default, all new Excel workbooks are created with these three worksheets.

Each worksheet is laid out in rows and columns. **Row headings** identify each row by a different number. Row numbers range from 1 to 1,048,576. **Column headings** identify each column by a different letter. The first 26 column letters range in alphabetical order from A to Z. After Z, the next column headings are labeled AA, AB, AC, and so forth. Excel allows a maximum of 16,385 columns in a worksheet (the last column has the heading XFD).

Rows and columns intersect in a single **cell**; all the data entered in a worksheet is placed in different cells. You can have more than 17 billion cells in each worksheet. Each cell is identified by a **cell reference**, which indicates its column and row location. For example, the cell reference B6 indicates the cell located where column B intersects row 6. The column letter always appears before the row number in any cell reference. The cell in which you are working is the **active cell**. Excel distinguishes the active cell by outlining it with a thick border. In Figure 1-3, cell A1 is the active cell. The cell reference for the active cell appears in the **Name box** located in the upper-left corner of the worksheet.

Figure 1-4 describes the different parts of the Excel window, which are labeled in Figure 1-3.

Description of the Excel window elements   Figure 1-4

Feature	Description
Office Button	A button that provides access to workbook-level features and program settings
Quick Access Toolbar	A collection of buttons that provide one-click access to commonly used commands, such as Save, Undo, and Repeat
Title bar	A bar that displays the name of the active workbook and the Excel program name
Ribbon	The main set of commands organized by task into tabs and groups
Column headings	The letters that appear along the top of the worksheet window to identify the different columns in the worksheet
Workbook window	A window that displays an Excel workbook
Vertical scroll bar	A scroll bar used to scroll vertically through the workbook window
Horizontal scroll bar	A scroll bar used to scroll horizontally through the workbook window
Zoom controls	Controls for magnifying and shrinking the content displayed in the active workbook window
View shortcuts	Buttons used to change how the worksheet content is displayed—Normal, Page Layout, or Page Break Preview view
Sheet tabs	Tabs that display the names of the worksheets in the workbook
Sheet tab scrolling buttons	Buttons to scroll the list of sheet tabs in the workbook
Row headings	The numbers that appear along the left of the worksheet window to identify the different rows in the worksheet
Select All button	A button used to select all of the cells in the active worksheet
Active cell	The cell currently selected in the active worksheet
Name box	A box that displays the cell reference of the active cell
Formula bar	A bar that displays the value or formula entered in the active cell

When Excel starts, it opens a blank workbook with Sheet1 as the active sheet and cell A1 as the active cell.

Navigating a Worksheet

Excel provides several ways to navigate a worksheet. You can use your mouse to click a cell to make it the active cell, or you can use the keyboard to move from one cell to another. Figure 1-5 describes some of the default keyboard shortcuts you can use to move between worksheet cells.

Figure 1-5 Excel navigation keys

Press	To move the active cell
↑, ↓, ←, →	Up, down, left, or right one cell
Home	To column A of the current row
Ctrl+Home	To cell A1
Ctrl+End	To the last cell in the worksheet that contains data
Enter	Down one row or to the start of the next row of data
Shift+Enter	Up one row
Tab	One column to the right
Shift+Tab	One column to the left
Page Up, Page Down	Up or down one screen
Ctrl+Page Up, Ctrl+Page Down	To the previous or next sheet in the workbook

You'll use both your mouse and keyboard to change the active cell in Sheet1.

To change the active cell:

1. Move your mouse pointer over cell **A5**, and then click the mouse button. The active cell moves from cell A1 to cell A5, and the cell reference in the Name box changes from A1 to A5. The column heading for column A and the row heading for row 5 are both highlighted.

2. Press the → key on your keyboard. The active cell moves one cell to the right to cell B5.

3. Press the **Page Down** key. The active cell moves down one full screen to cell B25.

    Trouble? If the active cell in your workbook is not cell B25, your monitor size and screen resolution might be different from those used for the figures in these tutorials. Continue with Step 4.

4. Press the **Page Up** key. The active cell moves up one full screen back to cell B5.

5. Press the **Ctrl+Home** keys. The active cell returns to the first cell in the worksheet, cell A1.

The mouse and keyboard provide quick ways to navigate the active worksheet. For larger worksheets that span several screens, you can move directly to a specific cell using the Go To dialog box or by typing a cell reference in the Name box. You'll try both of these methods.

To use the Go To dialog box and Name box:

1. Click the **Home** tab on the Ribbon, if necessary. The button to open the Go To dialog box is in the Editing group.

▶ 2. In the Editing group, click the **Find & Select** button. A menu of options opens.

▶ 3. Click **Go To**. The Go To dialog box opens.

▶ 4. Type **C14** in the Reference text box.

▶ 5. Click the **OK** button. Cell C14 is the active cell and its cell reference appears in the Name box. You'll use the Name box to make a different cell active.

▶ 6. Click in the **Name** box, type **A1**, and then press the **Enter** key. Cell A1 is once again the active cell.

> **Tip**
>
> You can also open the Go To dialog box by pressing the Ctrl+G keys.

To view more of the active worksheet, you can use the horizontal and vertical scroll bars, located at the bottom and right side of the workbook window, respectively, to move through the worksheet horizontally and vertically. Scrolling through the worksheet does not change the location of the active cell.

To scroll the worksheet:

▶ 1. Click the **down arrow** on the vertical scroll bar three times. The worksheet scrolls down three rows, but the active cell remains cell A1.

▶ 2. Click the **right arrow** on the horizontal scroll bar twice. The worksheet scrolls two columns to the right. The active cell still remains cell A1, although that cell is scrolled out of view.

You can scroll several rows and columns by dragging the vertical and horizontal scroll boxes.

▶ 3. Drag the vertical scroll box up until you can see the first row in the worksheet.

▶ 4. Drag the horizontal scroll box to the left until you can see the first column in the worksheet.

Navigating Between Worksheets

Recall that each workbook can contain multiple worksheets and chart sheets. This enables you to better organize data and focus each worksheet on one area of data. For example, a sales report workbook might have a different worksheet for each sales region and another worksheet that summarizes the results from all the regions. A chart sheet might contain a chart that graphically compares the sales results from all of the regions. To move from one sheet to another, you click the sheet tabs at the bottom of the workbook window.

Some workbooks contain so many worksheets and chart sheets that their sheet tabs cannot all be displayed at the same time in the workbook window. For these workbooks, you can scroll through the sheet tabs using the sheet tab scrolling buttons. Similar to the horizontal and vertical scroll bars and the active cell, scrolling through the sheet tabs does not change the active sheet in the workbook window. To change the active worksheet, you must click a sheet tab.

To change the active sheet:

▶ 1. Click the **Sheet2** sheet tab. The Sheet2 worksheet, which is also blank, becomes the active worksheet. The Sheet2 tab is white, indicating that this is the active worksheet.

2. Click the **Sheet3** sheet tab. The Sheet3 worksheet becomes the active worksheet.
3. Click the **Sheet1** sheet tab to return to the first worksheet.

Now that you've had some experience moving around a blank workbook, you are ready to start working on Amanda's workbook.

> **InSight** | **Creating Effective Workbooks**
>
> Effective workbooks are well planned and carefully designed. This helps you avoid errors and makes the workbook readable to others. A well-designed workbook should clearly identify its overall goal, and present information in a well-organized format. The process of developing a good workbook includes the following steps:
> - Determine the workbook's purpose, content, and organization before you start entering data.
> - Create a list of the sheets used in the workbook, making note of each sheet's purpose.
> - Insert a documentation sheet into the workbook that describes the workbook's purpose and organization. Include the name of the workbook author, the date the workbook was created, and any additional information that will help others to track the workbook to its source.
> - Enter all of the data in the workbook. Add text to indicate what the values represent and, if possible, where they originated. Other users might want to view the source of your data.
> - Enter formulas for calculated items rather than entering the calculated values into the workbook. For more complicated calculations, provide documentation explaining them.
> - Test the workbook with a variety of values to weed out any errors in your calculations. Edit the data and formulas to correct any errors.
> - Save the workbook and create a backup copy when the project is completed. Print the workbook's contents if you need a hard-copy version for your files.

Planning a Workbook

Before you begin to enter data into a workbook, you should develop a plan. You can do this by using a **planning analysis sheet**, which includes a series of questions that help you think about the purpose of the workbook and how to achieve your desired results. In the planning analysis sheet, you answer the following questions:

- What problems do you want to solve? The answer defines the goal or purpose of the workbook.
- What data is needed to solve your problem? The answer defines the type of data that you have to collect and enter into the workbook.
- What calculations are required to solve your problem? The answer defines the formulas you need to apply to the data you've collected and entered.
- What form should the solution take? The answer defines the appearance of the workbook content and how it should be presented to others.

Amanda carefully considered these questions and developed the planning analysis sheet shown in Figure 1-6. You'll use this plan to create the workbook for Amanda.

Figure 1-6 Planning analysis sheet

Planning Analysis Sheet
Author: Amanda Dunn
Date: 4/1/2010

<u>What problems do I want to solve?</u>
- I need to have contact information for each RipCity Digital customer.
- I need to track how many DVDs I create for my customers.
- I need to record how much I charge my customers for my service.
- I need to determine how much revenue RipCity Digital is generating.

<u>What data do I need?</u>
- Each customer's name and contact information
- The date each customer order was placed
- The number of DVDs created for each customer
- The cost of creating each DVD

<u>What calculations do I need to enter?</u>
- The total charge for each order
- The total number of DVDs I create for all orders
- The total revenue generated from all orders

<u>What form should my solution take?</u>
- The customer orders should be placed in a grid with each row containing data on a different customer.
- Information about each customer should be placed in separate columns.
- The last column should contain the total charge for each customer.
- The last row should contain the total number of DVDs created and the total revenue from all customer orders.

Entering Text, Numbers, and Dates in Cells

Now that you have Amanda's plan for the workbook, your next step is to enter the data she's collected. You enter data by selecting a cell in the worksheet to make it the active cell, and then typing the content you want to enter in the active cell. When you finish typing, you can press the Enter key or the Tab key to complete the data entry and move to the next cell in the worksheet. As you enter data into the worksheet, the data entry appears in two locations: within the active cell and within the formula bar. The **formula bar** displays the content of the active cell and, as you'll see later, shows any formulas used to create calculated values.

In Excel, data falls into three general categories: text, numbers, and dates and times. **Text data** is a combination of letters, numbers, and some symbols that form words and sentences. Text data is often referred to as a **text string** because it contains a string of text characters. **Number data** is any numerical value that can be used in a mathematical calculation. **Date** and **time data** are commonly recognized formats for date and time values. For example, Excel interprets the cell entry "April 15, 2010" as a date and not as text. By default, text is left-aligned in cells, whereas numbers, dates, and times are right-aligned.

Entering Text

Amanda wants you to enter some of the information from the planning analysis sheet into the first sheet of the workbook. The first sheet will document the purpose and content of the workbook and the sheets that follow. This documentation sheet will contain the name of the workbook, the workbook's author, the date the workbook was created, and a description of the workbook's purpose.

> **Tip**
>
> A documentation sheet reminds you why you created a workbook and what it contains and relays this information to others with whom you share the workbook.

To enter the text for the documentation sheet:

1. Press the **Ctrl+Home** keys to make cell A1 the active cell on the Sheet1 worksheet, if necessary.

2. Type **RipCity Digital Customer Orders** in cell A1. As you type, the text appears both in cell A1 and in the formula bar.

3. Press the **Enter** key twice. Excel enters the text into cell A1 and moves the active cell down two cells to cell A3.

4. Type **Author** in cell A3, and then press the **Tab** key. The text is entered and the active cell moves one cell to the right to cell B3.

5. Type your name in cell B3, and then press the **Enter** key. The text is entered and the active cell moves one cell down and to the left to cell A4.

6. Type **Date** in cell A4, and then press the **Tab** key. The text is entered and the active cell moves one cell to the right to cell B4, where you would enter the date you created the worksheet. For now, you'll leave the cell for the date blank. You'll enter this date soon.

7. Click cell **A5** to make it the active cell, type **Purpose** in the cell, and then press the **Tab** key. The active cell moves one cell to the right to cell B5.

8. Type **To record orders from RipCity Digital customers** in cell B5, and then press the **Enter** key. Figure 1-7 shows the text entered in the Sheet1 worksheet.

Figure 1-7 Documentation sheet

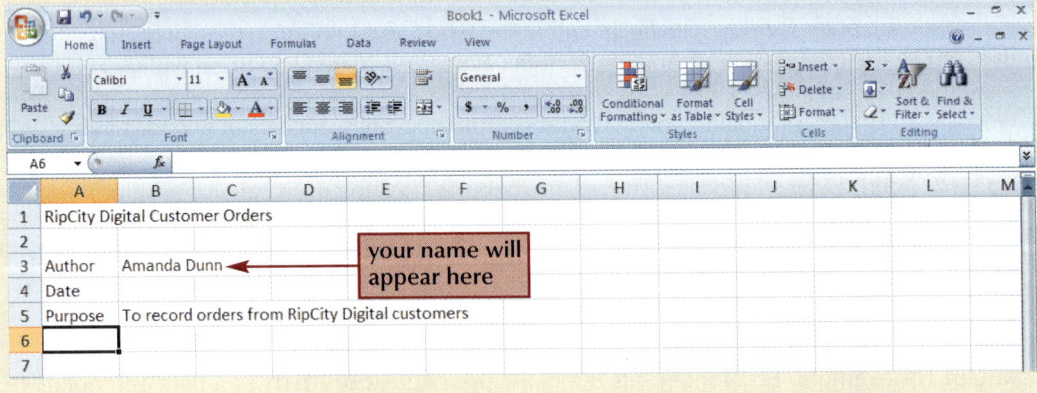

The text you entered in cell A1 is so long that it seems to overflow into cells B1 and C1. The same is true for the text you entered in cells B3 and B5. When you enter more text than can fit in a cell, Excel displays the additional text in the adjacent cells as long as they are empty. If the adjacent cells also contain data, Excel displays only as much text as fits into the cell, cutting off, or **truncating**, the rest of the text entry. The text itself is not affected. The complete text is still entered in the cell, it's just not displayed. To display all of the text, you must increase the cell's width, which you'll learn about in the next session.

Next, you'll enter the RipCity Digital customer orders. As shown in Figure 1-8, the orders will contain the name and address of each customer, the order date, the number of DVDs created from the customer's home videos, and the price per DVD. Amanda's price per DVD decreases for larger orders.

Figure 1-8 Customer orders

Last	First	Address	Date	DVDs	Price per DVD
Dawes	Gregory	402 Elm St. Merrill, MI 48637	3/13/2010	7	$17.29
Garcia	Susan	1025 Drake Ave. Exeter, NH 03833	3/14/2010	25	$15.79
Torbet	Dr. Lilla	5 North Ln. Oswego, NY 13126	3/17/2010	32	$12.99
Rhoden	Tony	24 Mountain Dr. Auburn, ME 04210	3/24/2010	20	$15.79

You'll enter this data in the Sheet2 worksheet.

To enter the text labels and customer names:

1. Click the **Sheet2** sheet tab. Sheet2 becomes the active worksheet. You'll enter the column labels in cells A1, B1, C1, D1, E1, and F1.

2. Type **Last** in cell A1, and then press the **Tab** key. The label is entered in cell A1 and the active cell moves to cell B1.

3. Type **First** in cell B1, and then press the **Tab** key. The label is entered in cell B1 and the active cell moves to cell C1.

4. Type **Address** in cell C1, and then press the **Tab** key.

5. Type **Date** in cell D1, and then press the **Tab** key.

6. Type **DVDs** in cell E1, press the **Tab** key, and then type **Price per DVD** in cell F1. You've typed all the labels for the customer orders.

7. Press the **Enter** key. The active cell moves to cell A2, the start of the next row where you want to begin entering the customer data.

8. Type **Dawes** in cell A2, press the **Tab** key, type **Gregory** in cell B2, and then press the **Tab** key. You've entered the first customer's name and moved the active cell to cell C2. Figure 1-9 shows the text you've entered so far.

Figure 1-9 Text entered for the customer orders

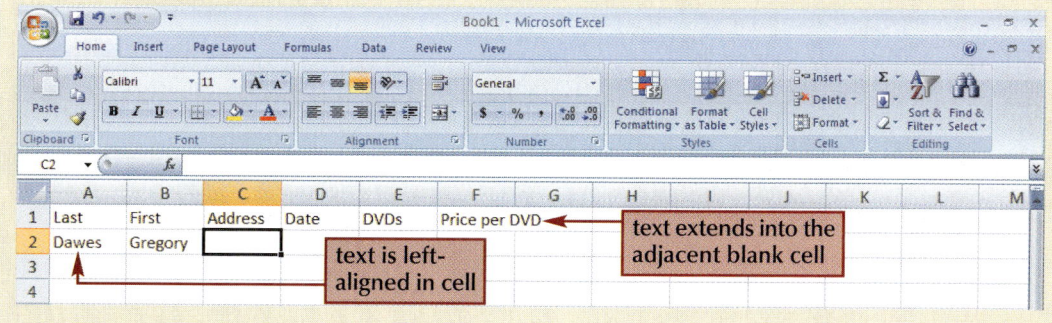

As you enter text in a worksheet, Excel tries to anticipate the text you are about to enter by displaying text that begins with the same letters as a previous entry in the same column. This feature, known as **AutoComplete**, helps make entering repetitive text easier. To accept the suggested text, press the Tab or Enter key. To override the suggested text, continue to type the text you want to enter in the cell. AutoComplete does not work with dates or numbers or when a blank cell is between the previous entry and the text you're typing.

Entering Multiple Lines of Text Within a Cell

The next cell in the Sheet2 worksheet contains the address of the first customer. Addresses are often entered on two or more separate lines. Amanda wants you to follow that convention with her customers' addresses. To place text on separate lines within the same cell, you press and hold the Alt key while you press the Enter key. This creates a line break within the cell.

Reference Window | Entering Multiple Lines of Text Within a Cell

- Click the cell in which you want to enter the text.
- Type the first line of text.
- For each additional line of text, press the Alt+Enter keys (that is, hold down the Alt key as you press the Enter key), and then type the text.

You'll enter the address for the first RipCity Digital customer, which will occupy two lines within the same cell.

To enter two lines of text within a cell:

1. Type **402 Elm St.** in cell C2, but do not press the Tab or Enter key. Instead, you'll insert a new line break.

2. Hold down the **Alt** key and press the **Enter** key, and then release both keys. The insertion point moves to a new line within cell C2.

3. Type **Merrill, MI 48637** on the new line, and then press the **Tab** key. The two lines of text are entered in cell C2, and cell D2 becomes the active cell. See Figure 1-10.

Figure 1-10 | Two lines of text entered within a cell

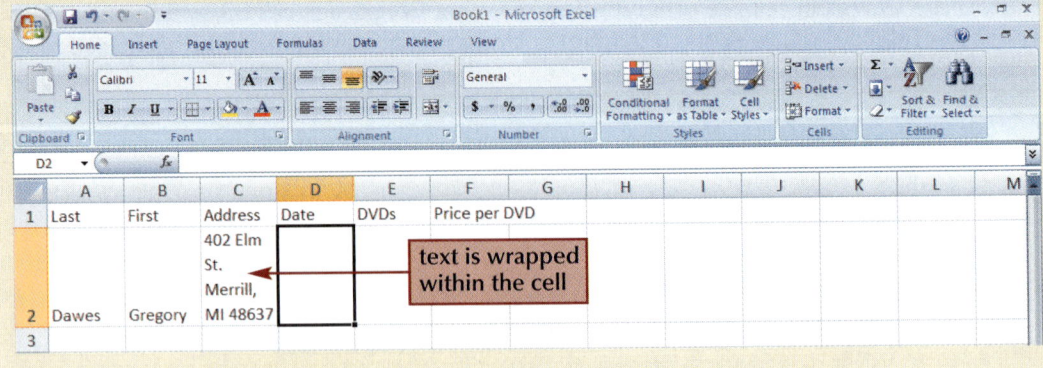

One impact of entering multiple lines of text within a cell is that it changes how text flows within the cell. Excel wraps the text within the cell, increasing the cell's height, if necessary, to show all of the text. As you can see, the text in cell C2 appears on four lines even though you entered the address on two lines. If the cell's width were increased, the text would then appear on two lines as Amanda wants. You'll do this in the next session.

Entering Dates

The next cell will contain the date of the order. You can enter dates in any of the standard formats. For example, you can enter the date April 6, 2010 in any of the following date formats (and many others) and Excel recognizes each format as representing the same date:

- 4/6/2010
- 4/6/10
- 4-6-2010
- April 6, 2010
- 6-Apr-10

In Excel, dates are actually numbers that are formatted to appear as text. This allows you to perform calculations with dates, such as determining the elapsed time between one date and another.

Sometimes Excel alters the date format you've chosen. For example, if you enter the date 4/6/10, Excel displays the date with the four-digit year value, 4/6/2010. Also, if you enter the text April 6, 2010, Excel converts the date format to 6-Apr-10. You'll enter the dates in the format *mm/dd/yyyy*, where *mm* is the month number, *dd* is the day number, and *yyyy* is the four-digit year number.

To enter the dates for the customer orders:

1. Type **3/13/2010** in cell D2, and then press the **Tab** key to move to cell E2. The date of Gregory Dawes's order appears in cell D2 and cell E2 is the active cell.

   You also need to enter the current date in the Sheet1 worksheet so you can document when you started working on this project.

2. Click the **Sheet1** sheet tab. The Sheet1 worksheet is the active worksheet.

3. Click cell **B4** to make it active, type today's date using the format *mm/dd/yyyy*, and then press the **Enter** key.

4. Click the **Sheet2** sheet tab. The Sheet2 worksheet is the active worksheet, and cell E2 is still the active cell.

Entering Numbers

In the next two cells, you'll enter the number of DVDs that Amanda has created for Gregory Dawes and the price she will charge him for making each DVD. In both cases, you'll be entering numbers. In Excel, numbers can be integers such as 378, decimals such as 1.95, or negative such as –5.2. In the case of currency and percentages, you can include the currency symbol and percent sign when you enter the value. Excel treats a currency value such as $87.25 as the number 87.25 and a percentage such as 95% as the decimal number 0.95. Currency and percentages, like dates, are formatted in a convenient way for you to read. Excel right-aligns numbers within cells.

Tip

If a number exceeds its cell size, you see ###### for the truncated numeric value. You can display the entire number by increasing the column width.

You'll complete the information for Gregory Dawes's order by entering the number of DVDs Amanda created for him and the price she charged him for each DVD.

To enter the numbers for the first customer order:

1. Type **7** in cell E2, and then press the **Tab** key. The order quantity for Gregory Dawes is entered and the active cell is cell F2.

2. Type **$17.29** in cell F2, and then press the **Enter** key. The currency value is entered in cell F2, and the active cell moves to cell F3.

3. Click cell **A3**, which is where you want to enter the information for the next customer. See Figure 1-11.

Figure 1-11 **First customer order completed**

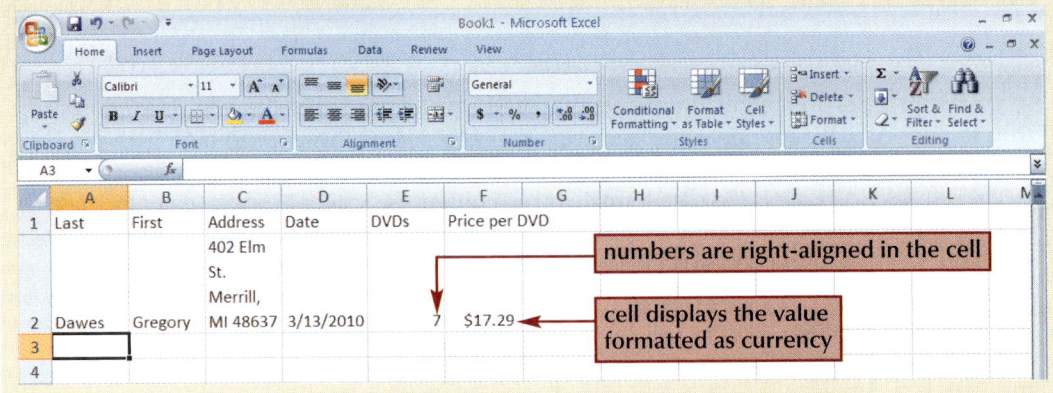

You've completed the data entry for Amanda's first customer. You still need to enter the data for three more customers into the worksheet. You'll use the same techniques you used to enter Gregory Dawes's order to enter their data.

To enter the remaining customer order data:

1. Type **Garcia** in cell A3, press the **Tab** key, type **Susan** in cell B3, and then press the **Tab** key. The second customer name is entered.

2. Type **1025 Drake Ave.** in cell C3, press the **Alt+Enter** keys, type **Exeter, NH 03833** on the next line, and then press the **Tab** key. The second customer's address is entered in the cell on two lines.

3. Type **3/14/2010** in cell D3, press the **Tab** key, type **25** in cell E3, press the **Tab** key, type **$15.79** in cell F3, and then press the **Enter** key. The rest of the second customer's data is entered.

4. Enter the following data for the remaining two customers in rows 4 and 5, making sure that you press the Alt+Enter keys to enter the addresses on two lines. See Figure 1-12.

   Torbet, Dr. Lilla
   5 North Ln.
   Oswego, NY 13126
   3/17/2010, 32, $12.99

   Rhoden, Tony
   24 Mountain Dr.
   Auburn, ME 04210
   3/24/2010, 20, $15.79

Figure 1-12 Customer data for RipCity Digital

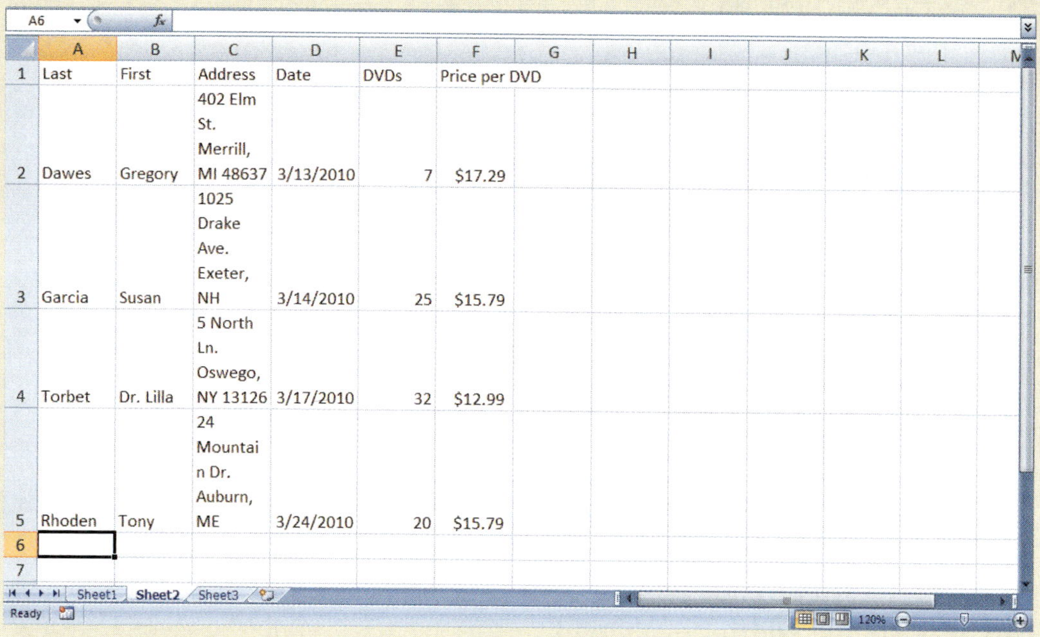

	A	B	C	D	E	F
1	Last	First	Address	Date	DVDs	Price per DVD
2	Dawes	Gregory	402 Elm St. Merrill, MI 48637	3/13/2010	7	$17.29
3	Garcia	Susan	1025 Drake Ave. Exeter, NH	3/14/2010	25	$15.79
4	Torbet	Dr. Lilla	5 North Ln. Oswego, NY 13126	3/17/2010	32	$12.99
5	Rhoden	Tony	24 Mountain Dr. Auburn, ME	3/24/2010	20	$15.79

Working with Columns and Rows

Amanda has reviewed the customer order data you entered in the worksheet. She asks you to modify the worksheet to make it easier to read and include more data. To do this, you'll need to change the column widths and row heights, insert columns and rows, and delete columns and rows.

Changing Column Width and Row Height

The default sizes of the columns and rows in a worksheet might not always accommodate the information you need to enter. For example, the addresses you entered in the worksheet on two lines wrapped within the cell to display all the text. Other times, long cell content might be truncated. To make the cell content easier to read or fully visible, you can resize the columns and rows in the worksheet.

New workbooks use the default sizes for column widths and row heights. Column widths are expressed either in terms of the number of characters the column can contain or the size of the column in pixels. A **pixel** is a single point on a computer monitor or printout. The default column width is 8.38 standard-sized characters. This means that, in general, you can type about 8 or 9 characters in a cell before that entry is either truncated or overlaps the adjacent cell. Of course, if you decrease the font size of characters, you can fit more text within a given cell. Row heights are expressed in points or pixels, where a **point** is 1/72 of an inch. The default row is 15.75 points high.

Setting Column Widths | InSight

You should set column widths based on the maximum number of characters you want to display in the cells rather than pixel size. Pixel size is related to screen resolution and a cell might be too narrow under a different resolution. This might come into play if you work on multiple computers or share your workbooks with others.

| Reference Window | **Changing the Column Width or Row Height** |

- Drag the right border of the column heading left to decrease the column width or right to increase the column width.
- Drag the bottom border of the row heading up to decrease the row height or down to increase the row height.

or

- Double-click the right border of a column heading or the bottom border of a row heading to AutoFit the column or row to the cell contents (or select one or more columns or rows, click the Home tab on the Ribbon, click the Format button in the Cells group, and then click AutoFit Column Width or AutoFit Row Height).

or

- Select one or more columns or rows.
- Click the Home tab on the Ribbon, click the Format button in the Cells group, and then click Column Width or Row Height.
- Enter the column width or row height you want, and then click the OK button.

Amanda suggests you increase the width of the Address column to allow the addresses to appear on two lines in the cells without additional line wrapping.

To increase the width of column C:

1. Move the mouse pointer over the right border of the column C column heading until the pointer changes to ↔.

2. Click and drag to the right until the width of the column heading reaches **20** characters, but do not release the mouse button. The ScreenTip shows the measurements of the new column width first as the numbers of characters and second in parentheses as pixels for the current screen resolution.

3. Release the mouse button. The width of column C expands to 20 characters and all the addresses in column C fit on two lines with no extra line wrapping. See Figure 1-13.

| Figure 1-13 | **Increased column width** |

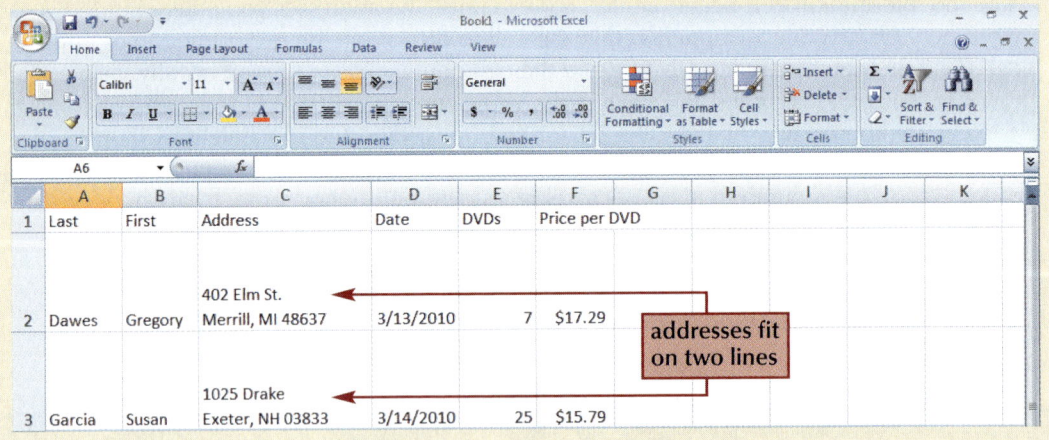

Amanda wants you to increase the widths of columns A and B to 15 characters to accommodate longer names. Rather than resizing each column separately, you can select both columns and adjust their widths at the same time. To select an entire column, you click its column heading. Likewise, to select an entire row, you click its row heading. You can drag across multiple column headings or row headings to select adjacent columns or rows. You can also press the Ctrl key as you click column or row headings to select non-adjacent columns or rows. You can select all the columns and rows in a worksheet by clicking the Select All button in the upper-left corner of the worksheet.

To increase the widths of columns A and B:

1. Click the **column A** column heading. The entire column is selected.
2. Hold down the **Ctrl** key, click the **column B** column heading, and then release the **Ctrl** key. Both columns A and B are selected.
3. Move the mouse pointer to the right border of the column B column heading until the pointer changes to ↔.
4. Drag to the right until the column width changes to **15** characters, and then release the mouse button. Both columns are wide enough to display longer names.

The text in cell F1, "Price per DVD," overflows the cell borders. This column would look better if you increased the width of column F to 12 characters. Rather than use the mouse, you can set the column width using the Format command on the Home tab. The Format command gives you precise control in setting column widths and row heights.

To set the width of column F to 12 characters:

1. Click the **column F** column heading. The entire column is selected.
2. In the Cells group on the Home tab, click the **Format** button, and then click **Column Width**. The Column Width dialog box opens.
3. Type **12** in the Column width box, and then click the **OK** button. The width of column F changes to 12 characters, placing the text in cell F1 entirely within the borders of the cell.

The row heights didn't change after you resized the columns, which leaves a lot of blank space in the four rows of customer data. This extra blank space makes the data difficult to read and extends the content out of view. You'll reduce the heights of all these rows.

Row heights are set in the same way as column widths. You can drag the bottom border of the row or define a specific row height using the Format command on the Home tab. Another option is to autofit a column or row to its content. **Autofitting** eliminates any empty space by matching the column to the width of its longest cell entry or the row to the height of its tallest cell entry. If the column or row is blank, Excel restores the column or row to its default width or height. The simplest way to autofit a row or column is to double-click its border. You can also use the AutoFit commands.

Because you want to remove empty space from the four worksheet rows, you'll autofit the rows to their content rather than specify a particular row height.

To autofit row 2 to its content:

1. Move the mouse pointer over the bottom border of the row 2 row heading until the pointer changes to ╬.

2. Double-click the bottom border of row 2. The height of row 2 shrinks to match the content of cell C2, which is the tallest entry in the row with two lines of text.

You could continue to resize the remaining rows one at a time, but a quicker way is to select the rows you want to resize and then autofit all the selected rows simultaneously. Instead of double-clicking the row border, you'll use the AutoFit Row Height command.

To autofit the height of rows 3 through 5:

1. Drag the pointer across the row headings for rows 3, 4, and 5. The contents of rows 3 through 5 are selected.

2. In the Cells group on the Home tab, click the **Format** button. A menu of commands opens.

3. Click **AutoFit Row Height**. The height of each of the three rows autofits to its contents, and all the empty space is removed.

4. Click cell **A1** to make it the active cell. The other cells in the worksheet are deselected. Figure 1-14 shows the worksheet with the revised row heights.

Figure 1-14 Autofitted row heights

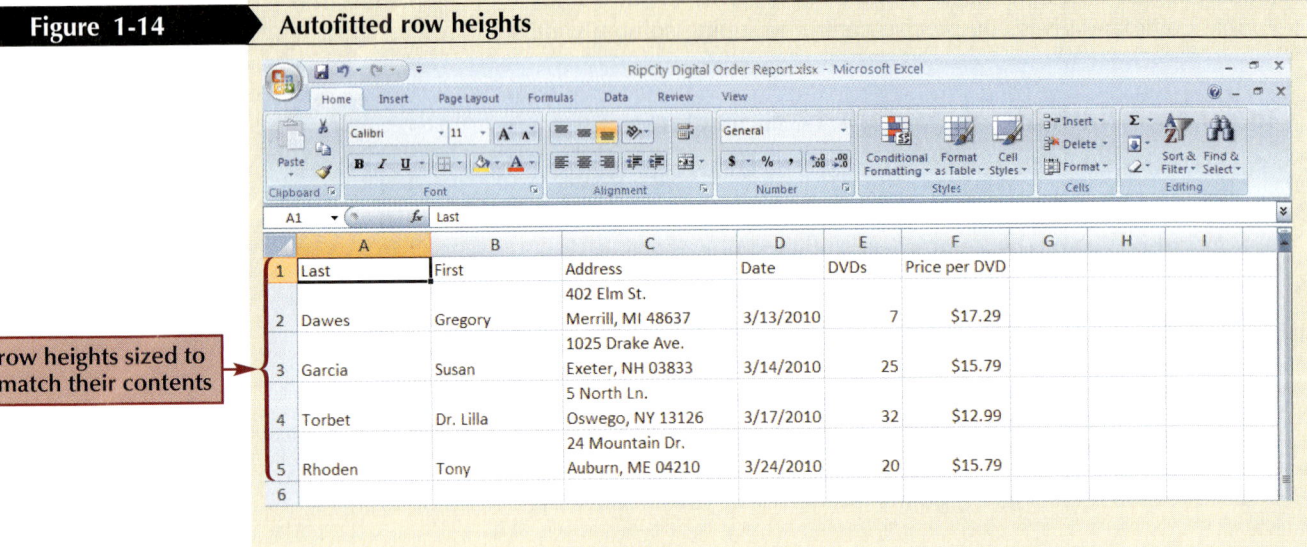

row heights sized to match their contents

Inserting a Column or Row

Amanda notices that the worksheet doesn't include a column containing customer phone numbers. She wants you to insert a column for the customer phone numbers between the Address column and the Date column.

You can insert a new column or row anywhere within a worksheet. When you insert a new column, the existing columns are shifted to the right and the new column has the same width as the column directly to its left. When you insert a new row, the existing rows are shifted down and the new row has the same height as the row above it.

Tutorial 1 Getting Started with Excel   Excel **EX 19**

| Inserting a Column or Row | Reference Window |

- Select the column(s) or row(s) where you want to insert the new column(s) or row(s); Excel will insert the same number of columns or rows as you select.
- In the Cells group on the Home tab, click the Insert button (or right-click a column or row heading or selected column and row headings, and then click Insert on the shortcut menu).

You'll insert a column and enter the customer phone numbers in the new column.

To insert a new column:

1. Click the **column D** column heading to select the entire column.

2. In the Cells group on the Home tab, click the **Insert** button. A new column D is inserted into the worksheet and the rest of the columns shift to the right. The new column has the same width as column C.

3. Reduce the width of column D to **15** characters.

4. Click cell **D1** to make it the active cell, type **Phone** as the label, and then press the **Enter** key. The new column label is entered in cell D1, and cell D2 becomes the active cell.

5. Enter the phone numbers in cells D2, D3, D4, and D5, as shown in Figure 1-15, pressing the **Enter** key after each entry.

New column inserted in the worksheet   Figure 1-15

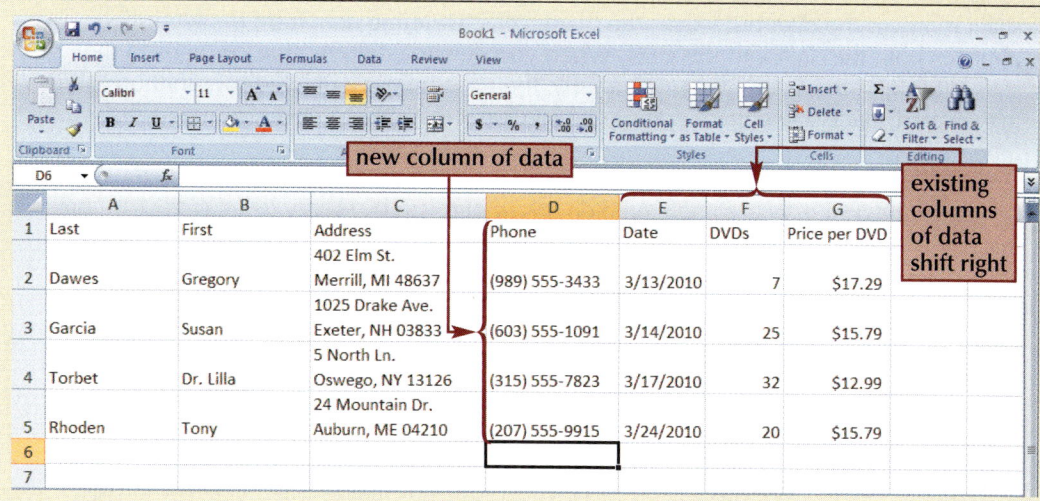

Amanda neglected to include a customer. Because the customer was RipCity Digital's first customer, he should be inserted at the top of the list. To add this new order, you need to insert a new row in the worksheet below the column labels.

To insert a new row:

1. Click the **row 2** row heading. The entire second row is selected.

2. In the Cells group on the Home tab, click the **Insert** button. A new row 2 is inserted, and the remaining rows shift down.

3. Enter the new customer order shown in Figure 1-16 into row 2.

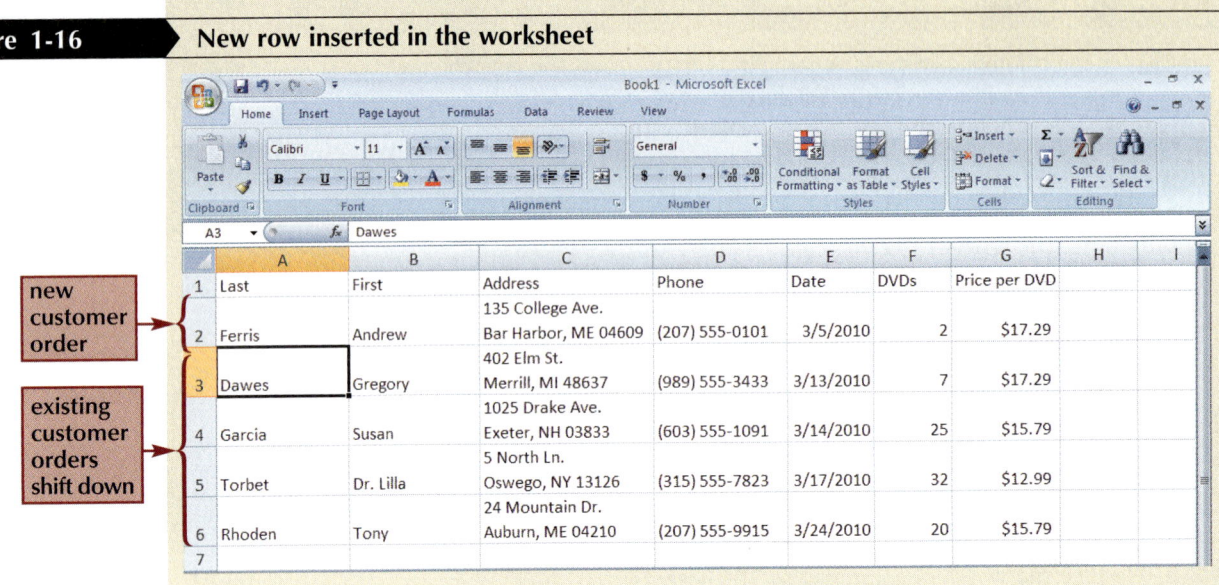

Figure 1-16   New row inserted in the worksheet

Deleting and Clearing a Row or Column

Adding new data to a workbook is common, as is removing old or erroneous data. Amanda just learned that her second customer, Gregory Dawes, canceled his order. She wants you to remove this order from the worksheet.

You can remove data in two ways: clearing and deleting. **Clearing** data from a worksheet removes the data but leaves the blank cells. **Deleting** data from the worksheet removes both the data and the cells. When you delete a column, the columns to the right shift left to fill the vacated space. Similarly, the rows below a deleted row shift up to fill the vacated space. Deleting a column or row has the opposite effect from inserting a column or row.

You'll first clear Gregory Dawes's data from the worksheet and then delete the row that contained the data. Usually, you would do this in one step by simply deleting the row, but this highlights the difference between clearing and deleting.

To clear and delete row 3:

1. Click the **row 3** row heading. The entire row 3 with Gregory Dawes's order is selected.

2. Right-click the **row 3** row heading, and then click **Clear Contents** on the shortcut menu. Excel clears the values in the third row, but leaves the blank row in that space.

3. Verify that the third row is still selected.

4. In the Cells group on the Home tab, click the **Delete** button. The third row is deleted, and the rows below it shift up. Only four customers remain in the worksheet.

Before proceeding, you'll save your workbook with the name "RipCity Digital Orders" in the default Excel workbook format.

To save the current workbook:

1. Click the **Save** button on the Quick Access Toolbar. Because this workbook has not yet been saved, the Save As dialog box opens.

2. Navigate to the **Tutorial.01\Tutorial** folder included with your Data Files. You'll replace the default filename "Book1" with a more descriptive one.

   Trouble? If you don't have the starting Data Files, you need to get them before you can proceed. Your instructor will either give you the Data Files or ask you to obtain them from a specified location (such as a network drive). In either case, make a backup copy of the Data Files before you start so that you will have the original files available in case you need to start over. If you have any questions about the Data Files, see your instructor or technical support person for assistance.

3. Select **Book1** in the File name box, and then type **RipCity Digital Orders**.

4. Verify that **Excel Workbook** appears in the Save as type box.

5. Click the **Save** button. The Save As dialog box closes and the workbook file is saved with its descriptive filename.

> **Tip**
> You can reopen the Save As dialog box to save a workbook with a new filename, to a different location, or in another file format; click the Office Button and then click Save As.

You've entered and saved the customer order data. In the process, you worked with rows and columns. In the next session, you'll learn how to work with individual cells and groups of cells. You will also add calculations to the worksheet to determine how much revenue Amanda will generate from these orders.

Session 1.1 Quick Check | Review

1. What are the two types of sheets used in a workbook?
2. List two ways of identifying the active cell in the worksheet.
3. What is the cell reference for the cell located in the third column and fifth row of a worksheet?
4. What keyboard shortcut moves the active cell to cell A1?
5. What is text data?
6. How do you enter two lines of text within a cell?
7. Cell A4 contains "May 3, 2010"; why doesn't Excel consider this entry a text string?
8. Explain the difference between clearing a row and deleting a row.

Session 1.2

Working with Cells and Cell Ranges

A group of cells is called a **cell range** or **range**. Ranges can be either adjacent or nonadjacent. An **adjacent range** is a single rectangular block of cells. For example, all the customer order data you've entered in cell A1 through cell G5 is an adjacent range because it forms one rectangular block of cells. A **nonadjacent range** consists of two or more distinct adjacent ranges. All the last names in cell A1 through cell A5 and all the numbers in cells F1 through G5 together are a nonadjacent range because they are two distinct blocks of cells. A nonadjacent range can include as many adjacent ranges as you want.

Just as a cell reference indicates the location of an individual worksheet cell, a **range reference** indicates the location and size of a cell range. For adjacent ranges, the range reference specifies the locations of the upper-left and lower-right cells in the rectangular block separated by a colon. For example, the range reference A1:G5 refers to all the cells from cell A1 through cell G5. The range reference for nonadjacent ranges separates each adjacent range reference by a semicolon. For example, A1:A5;F1:G5 is the range reference for cells A1 through A5 and cells F1 through G5.

Selecting a Cell Range

You select adjacent and nonadjacent ranges of cells with your mouse, just as you selected individual cells. Selecting a cell range enables you to work with all of the cells in the range as a group. This means you can do things like move the cells, delete them, or clear all their contents at the same time.

Reference Window | Selecting Cell Ranges

To select an adjacent range:
- Click the cell in the upper-left corner of the adjacent range, drag the pointer to the cell in the lower-right corner of the adjacent range, and then release the mouse button.

or
- Click the cell in the upper-left corner of the adjacent range, press the Shift key as you click the cell in the lower-right corner of the adjacent range, and then release the Shift key.

To select a nonadjacent range of cells:
- Select a cell or an adjacent range, press the Ctrl key as you select each additional cell or adjacent range, and then release the Ctrl key.

To select all the cells in a worksheet:
- Click the Select All button located at the intersection of the row and column headings (or press the Ctrl+A keys).

You'll use the mouse pointer to select the adjacent range A1:G5, which includes all the content you entered in the worksheet so far.

To select the adjacent range A1:G5:

1. If you took a break at the end of the previous session, make sure the RipCity Digital Orders workbook is open and the Sheet2 worksheet is active.

2. Click cell **A1** to select the cell in the upper-left corner of the range A1:G5.

3. Drag the pointer to cell **G5**, which is the cell in the lower-right corner of the range A1:G5.

4. Release the mouse button. As shown in Figure 1-17, all cells in the adjacent range A1:G5 are selected. The selected cells are highlighted with color and surrounded by a black border. The first cell you selected, cell A1, is still the active cell in the worksheet.

Figure 1-17

Adjacent range A1:G5 selected

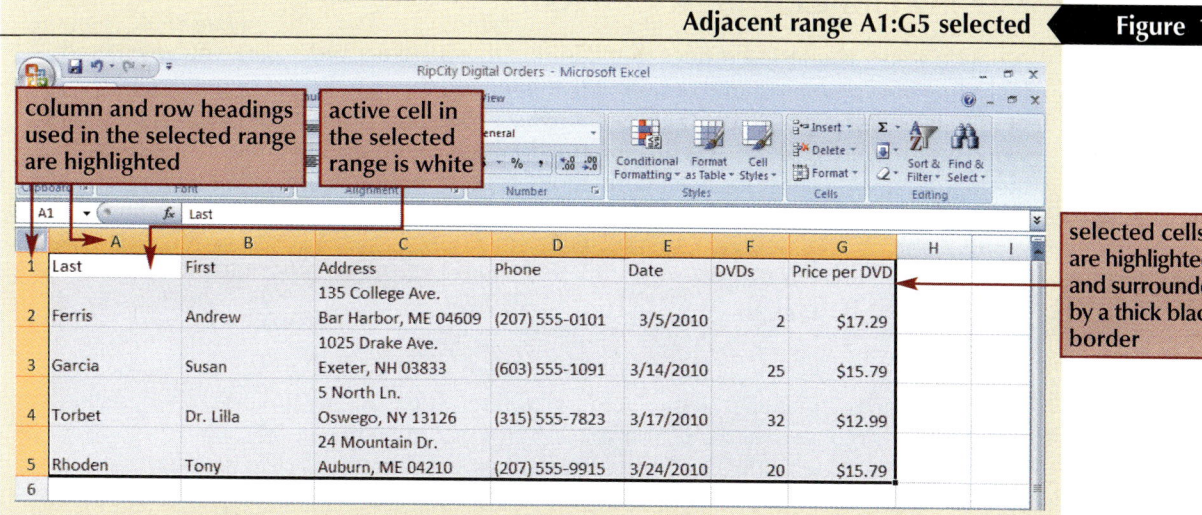

5. Click any cell in the worksheet to deselect the range.

Next, you'll select the nonadjacent range A1:A5;F1:G5.

To select the nonadjacent range A1:A5;F1:G5:

1. Select the adjacent range **A1:A5**.

2. Hold down the **Ctrl** key, and then select the adjacent range **F1:G5**.

3. Release the **Ctrl** key. As shown in Figure 1-18, all the cells in the nonadjacent range A1:A5;F1:G5 are selected.

Figure 1-18

Nonadjacent range A1:A5;F1:G5 selected

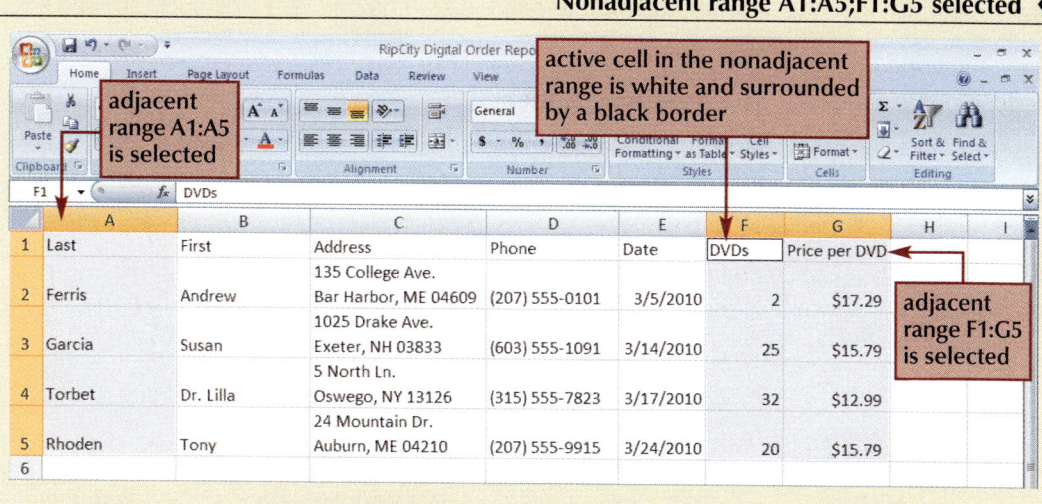

4. Click any cell in the worksheet to deselect the range.

Moving and Copying a Cell Range

Amanda wants you to insert titles that describe the customer order data you've entered. Including the company name, a descriptive title, and the date is part of good worksheet design, enabling others to quickly see the *who*, *what*, and *when* of the data. The current worksheet has no space to add this information. You could insert several blank rows at the top of the worksheet for this information. Another option is to select and then move the customer data lower in the worksheet, freeing up the rows at the top for the new text.

Reference Window | Moving or Copying a Cell or Range

- Select the cell or range you want to move or copy.
- Move the mouse pointer over the border of the selection until the pointer changes shape.
- To move the range, click the border and drag the selection to a new location (or to copy the range, hold down the Ctrl key and drag the selection to a new location).

or

- Select the cell or range you want to move or copy.
- In the Clipboard group on the Home tab, click the Cut button or the Copy button (or right-click the selection, and then click Cut or Copy on the shortcut menu).
- Select the cell or upper-left cell of the range where you want to move or copy the content.
- In the Clipboard group, click the Paste button (or right-click the selection, and then click Paste on the shortcut menu).

Tip
You can drag and drop to a range not currently visible. Drag the selection to the edge of the worksheet in which you want to scroll. When the new location is visible, drop the selection.

One way to move a cell or range is to select it, position the mouse pointer over the bottom border of the selection, and then drag the selection to a new location. This technique is called **drag and drop** because you are dragging the range and dropping it in a new location. You can also use the drag-and-drop technique to copy cells by pressing the Ctrl key as you drag the selected range to its new location. A copy of the original range is placed in the new location without removing the original range from the worksheet.

You'll use the drag-and-drop method to move data.

To drag and drop the customer orders:

1. Select the range **A1:G5**.

2. Move the mouse pointer over the bottom border of the selected range so that the pointer changes to ⇖.

3. Press and hold the mouse button to change the pointer to ▷, and then drag the selection down four rows. Do not release the mouse button. A ScreenTip appears, indicating the new range reference of the selected cells. See Figure 1-19.

Selected range being moved — **Figure 1-19**

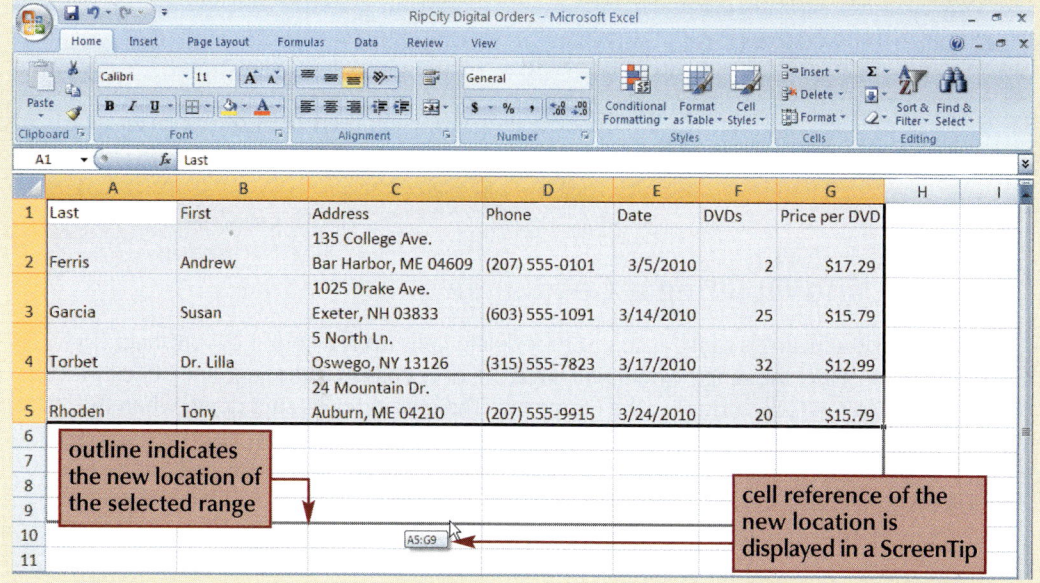

4. When the ScreenTip displays the range A5:G9, release the mouse button. The selected cells move to their new location.

5. Enter the title information shown in Figure 1-20 in the range A1:A3, pressing the **Enter** key after each entry.

Worksheet titles entered — **Figure 1-20**

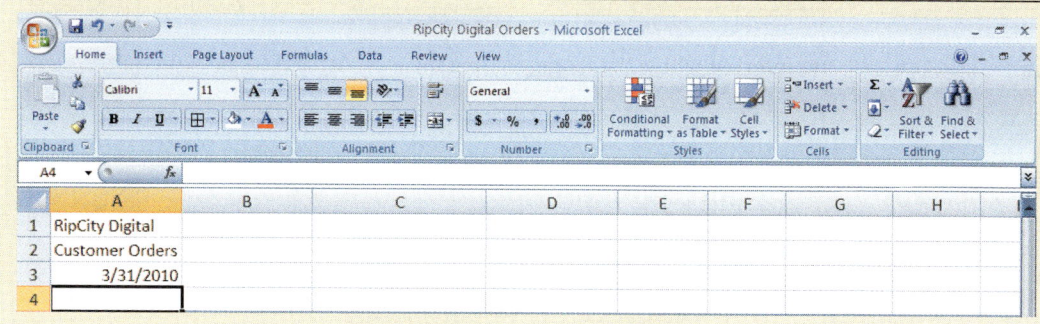

Some people find drag and drop a difficult and awkward way to move a selection, particularly if the worksheet is large and complex. In those situations, it's often more efficient to cut and paste the cell contents. **Cutting** places the cell contents into computer memory or on the Clipboard. The contents can then be pasted from the Clipboard into a new location in the worksheet. You'll cut and paste now.

To cut and paste cell contents:

1. With the range **A5:G9** selected, in the Clipboard group on the Home tab, click the **Cut** button. The selected range is surrounded by a blinking border, which indicates that its contents are stored on the Clipboard.

2. Click cell **A11**. This cell is the upper-left corner of the range where you want to paste the data.

3. In the Clipboard group, click the **Paste** button. Excel pastes the contents of the range A5:G9 into the new range A11:G15. The blinking border disappears as a visual clue that the Clipboard is now empty.

4. Select the range **A11:G15**, and then, in the Clipboard group, click the **Cut** button.

5. Click cell **A5**, and then, in the Clipboard group, click the **Paste** button. The customer order data is pasted into its original location in the range A5:G9.

Inserting and Deleting a Cell Range

Another use of selecting a range is to insert or delete cells from within the worksheet. To insert a range, select the range where you want the new cells inserted, and then click the Insert button in the Cells group on the Home tab. The existing cells shift down when the selected range is wider than it is long, and they shift right when the selected range is longer than it is wide (as illustrated in Figure 1-21). The Insert Cells command located on the Insert button menu lets you specify whether you want to shift the existing cells right or down, or whether to insert an entire row or column into the new range.

Figure 1-21 Cells inserted within a cell range

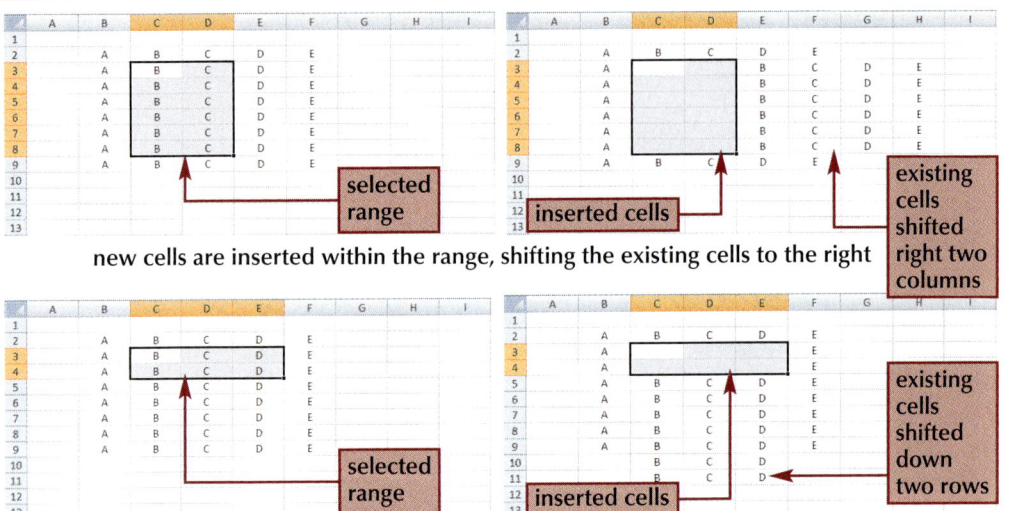

new cells are inserted within the range, shifting the existing cells to the right

new cells are inserted within the range, shifting the existing cells down

If you no longer need a specific cell or range in a worksheet, you can delete those cells and any content they contain. To delete a range, select the range, and then click the Delete button in the Cells group on the Home tab. As with deleting a row or column, cells adjacent to the deleted range either move up or left to fill in the vacancy left by the deleted cells. The Delete Cells command located on the Delete button menu lets you specify whether you want to shift the adjacent cells left or up, or whether to delete the entire column or row.

| Reference Window

Inserting or Deleting a Cell Range

- Select a range that matches the range you want to insert or delete.
- In the Cells group on the Home tab, click the Insert button or the Delete button.

or

- Select the range that matches the range you want to insert or delete.
- In the Cells group, click the Insert button arrow and then click the Insert Cells button or click the Delete button arrow and then click the Delete Cells command (or right-click the selected range, and then click Insert or Delete on the shortcut menu).
- Click the option button for the direction in which you want to shift the cells, columns, or rows.
- Click the OK button.

You do not need to insert or delete any cells in the worksheet at this time.

Working with Formulas

Up to now you have entered only text, numbers, and dates in the worksheet. However, the main reason for using Excel is to perform calculations on data. Amanda wants the workbook to determine the number of DVDs she has to create for her customers and how much revenue will be generated by completing these orders. Such calculations are added to a worksheet using formulas and functions.

Entering a Formula

A **formula** is an expression that returns a value. In most cases, this is a number. You can also create formulas in Excel that return text strings. Every Excel formula begins with an equal sign (=) followed by an expression that describes the operation to be done. A formula is written using **operators** that combine different values, returning a single value that is then displayed in the cell. The most commonly used operators are **arithmetic operators** that perform addition, subtraction, multiplication, division, and exponentiation. For example, the following formula adds 5 and 7, returning a value of 12.

=5+7

However, formulas in Excel most often use numbers stored within cells. For example, the following formula returns the result of adding the values in cells A1 and B2.

=A1+B2

So, if the value 5 is stored in cell A1 and the value 7 is stored in cell B2, this formula would also return a value of 12. Figure 1-22 describes the different arithmetic operators and provides examples of formulas.

Figure 1-22 Arithmetic operators

Operation	Arithmetic Operator	Example	Description
Addition	+	=10+A1	Adds 10 to the value in cell A1
		=B1+B2+B3	Adds the values in cells B1, B2, and B3
Subtraction	–	=C9–B2	Subtracts the value in cell B2 from the value in cell C9
		=1–D2	Subtracts the value in cell D2 from 1
Multiplication	*	=C9*B9	Multiplies the values in cells C9 and B9
		=E5*0.06	Multiplies the value in cell E5 by 0.06
Division	/	=C9/B9	Divides the value in cell C9 by the value in cell B9
		=D15/12	Divides the value in cell D15 by 12
Exponentiation	^	=B5^3	Raises the value of cell B5 to the third power
		=3^B5	Raises 3 to the value in cell B5

If a formula contains more than one arithmetic operator, Excel performs the calculation using the same order of precedence you might have already seen in math classes. The **order of precedence** is a set of predefined rules used to determine the sequence in which operators are applied in a calculation—first exponentiation (^), second multiplication (*) and division (/), and third addition (+) and subtraction (–). For example, consider the formula below:

=3+4*5

This formula returns the value 23 because multiplication (4*5) takes precedence over addition. If a formula contains two or more operators with the same level of precedence, the operators are applied in order from left to right. Note the formula below:

=4*10/8

This formula first calculates the leftmost operation (4*10) and then divides that result of 40 by 8 to return the value 5.

To change the order of operations, you can enclose parts of the formula within parentheses. Any expression within a set of parentheses is calculated before the rest of the formula. Note the following formula:

=(3+4)*5

This formula first calculates the value of the expression (3+4) and then multiplies that total of 7 by 5 to return the value 35. Figure 1-23 shows how slight changes in a formula affect the order of precedence and the result of the formula.

Figure 1-23 Order of precedence rules

Formula (A1=50, B1=10, C1=5)	Order of Precedence Rule	Result
=A1+B1*C1	Multiplication before addition	100
=(A1+B1)*C1	Expression inside parentheses executed before expression outside	300
=A1/B1–C1	Division before subtraction	0
=A1/(B1–C1)	Expression inside parentheses executed before expression outside	10
=A1/B1*C1	Two operators at same precedence level, leftmost operator evaluated first	25
=A1/(B1*C1)	Expression inside parentheses executed before expression outside	1

| Reference Window

Entering a Formula

- Click the cell in which you want the formula results to appear.
- Type = and an expression that calculates a value using cell references and arithmetic operators.
- Press the Enter key or press the Tab key to complete the formula.

Amanda wants the worksheet to include the total amount she charged for creating each customer's DVDs. The charge is equal to the number of DVDs created multiplied by the price per DVD. You've already entered this information for each customer in columns F and G. You'll enter a formula to calculate the charge for each customer in column H.

To enter the formula in column H:

1. Click cell **H5** to make it the active cell, type **Charge** for the column label, and then press the **Enter** key. The column label is entered in cell H5. Cell H6, where you want to enter the formula, is the active cell.

2. Type **=F6*G6** (the number of DVDs created multiplied by the price per DVD). As you type the formula, a list of Excel function names appears in a ScreenTip, which provides a quick method for entering functions. The list will close when you complete the formula. You'll learn more about Excel functions shortly.

3. Press the **Enter** key. The formula is entered in cell H6, which displays the value $34.58. The result is displayed as currency because cell G6 referenced in the formula contains a currency value.

After a formula has been entered into a cell, the cell displays the results of the formula and not the formula itself. If the results are not what you expect, you might have entered the formula incorrectly. You can view the formula by selecting the cell and reviewing the expression displayed in the formula bar. One challenge with formulas, particularly long formulas, is interpreting the cell references. Excel makes this simpler by color coding each cell reference in the formula and its corresponding cell in the worksheet. You'll see this when you view the formula you just entered.

To view the formula:

1. Click cell **H6** to make it the active cell. The formula you entered appears in the formula bar, whereas the value returned by the formula appears in the cell.

2. Click in the formula bar. As shown in Figure 1-24, each cell used in the formula has a different colored border that matches the color of its cell reference in the formula. This provides a visual cue to the formula, enabling you to quickly match cell references with their locations in the worksheet.

Figure 1-24   Formula references color coded

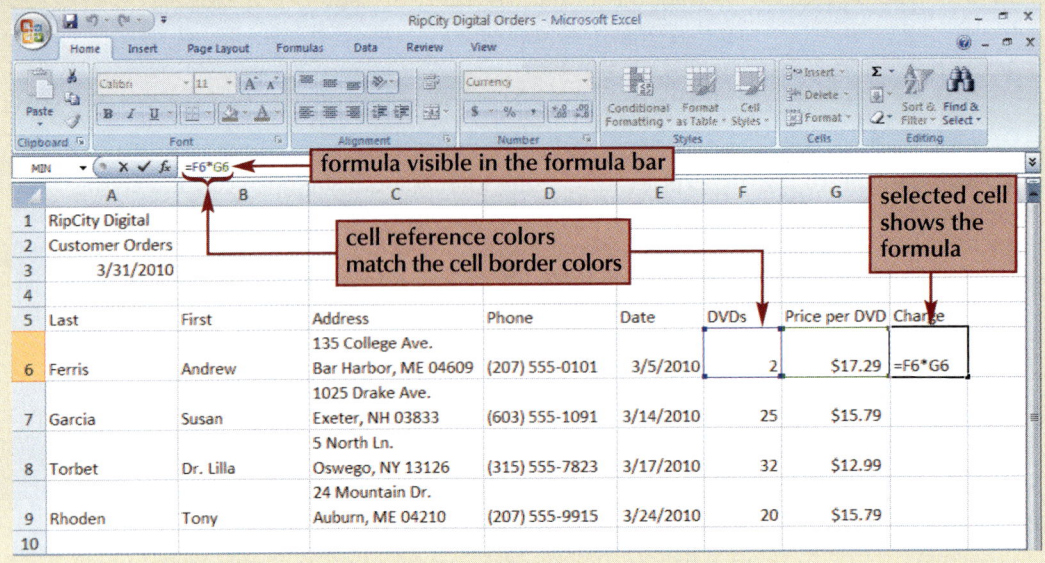

For Amanda's first customer, you entered the formula by typing each cell reference. You can also enter a cell reference by clicking the cell as you enter the formula. This technique reduces the possibility of error caused by typing an incorrect cell reference. You'll use this method to enter the formula to calculate the charge for the second customer.

To enter a cell reference in the formula using the mouse:

1. Click cell **H7** to make it the active cell, and then type **=**. When you type the equal sign, Excel knows that you're entering a formula. Any cell that you click from now on causes Excel to insert the cell reference of the selected cell into the formula until you complete the formula by pressing the Enter or Tab key.

2. Click cell **F7**. The cell reference is inserted into the formula on the formula bar. At this point, any cell you click changes the cell reference used in the formula. The cell reference isn't "locked" until you type an operator.

3. Type ***** to enter the multiplication operator. The cell reference for cell F7 is "locked" in the formula, and the next cell you click will be inserted after the operator.

4. Click cell **G7** to enter its cell reference in the formula, and then press the **Enter** key. Cell H7 displays the value $394.75, which is the total charge for the second customer.

Copying and Pasting Formulas

Sometimes, you'll need to repeat the same formula for several rows of data. Rather than retyping the formula, you can copy the formula and then paste it into the remaining rows. You'll copy the formula you just entered in cell H7 to cells H8 and H9 to calculate the charges for Amanda's two remaining customers.

To copy the formula in cell H7:

1. Click cell **H7** to select the cell that contains the formula you want to copy.

2. In the Clipboard group on the Home tab, click the **Copy** button. The formula is copied to the Clipboard.

3. Select the range **H8:H9**, the cells in which you want to paste the formula.

4. In the Clipboard group, click the **Paste** button. Excel pastes the formula into the selected range. See Figure 1-25.

Figure 1-25 — Formula copied and pasted

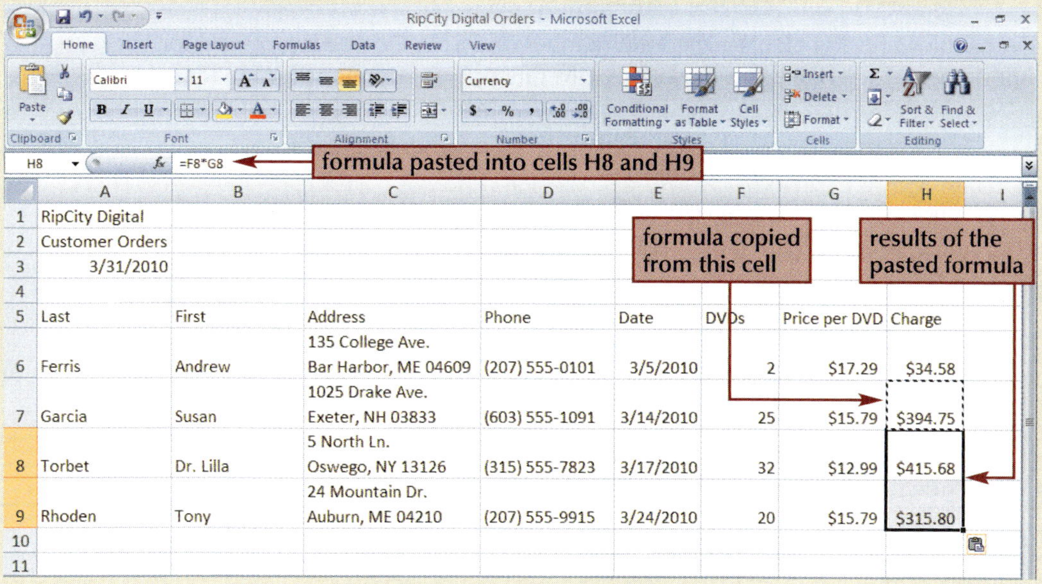

5. Click cell **H8** and verify that the formula =F8*G8 appears in the formula bar, and then click cell **H9** and verify that the formula =F9*G9 appears in the formula bar.

Pasting a formula is different from pasting a value. With the customer order data, Excel pasted the same values in a new location. With formulas, Excel adjusts the formula's cell references to reflect the new location of the formula in the worksheet. This is because you want to replicate the actions of a formula rather than duplicate the specific value the formula generates. In this case, the formula's action is to multiply the number of DVDs Amanda created for the customer by the price she charged for creating each DVD. By copying and pasting that formula, that action is replicated for every customer in the worksheet.

Introducing Functions

In addition to cell references and operators, formulas can also contain functions. A **function** is a named operation that returns a value. Functions are used to simplify formulas, reducing what might be a long expression into a compact statement. For example, to add the values in the range A1:A10, you could enter the following long formula:

=A1+A2+A3+A4+A5+A6+A7+A8+A9+A10

Or, you could use the SUM function to accomplish the same thing:

=SUM(A1:A10)

In both cases, Excel adds the values in cells A1 through A10, but the SUM function is faster and simpler to enter and less prone to a typing error. You should always use a function, if one is available, in place of a long, complex formula.

Excel supports over 300 different functions from the fields of finance, business, science, and engineering. Functions are not limited to numbers. Excel also provides functions that work with text and dates.

Entering a Function

Amanda wants to calculate the total number of DVDs she needs to create for her customers. To do that, you'll use the SUM function to add the values in the range F6:F9.

To enter the SUM function:

1. Click cell **E10**, type **TOTAL** as the label, and then press the **Tab** key. The label is entered in cell E10, and cell F10 is the active cell.

2. Type **=SUM(F6:F9** in cell F10. As you begin to type the SUM function, a ScreenTip lists the names of all functions that start with the letter "S." When you type the cell references, Excel highlights all the cells in the specified range to provide a visual reminder of exactly which cells the SUM function is using. See Figure 1-26.

Tip

You can also insert a range reference into a function by selecting the range with your mouse.

Figure 1-26   **SUM function being entered**

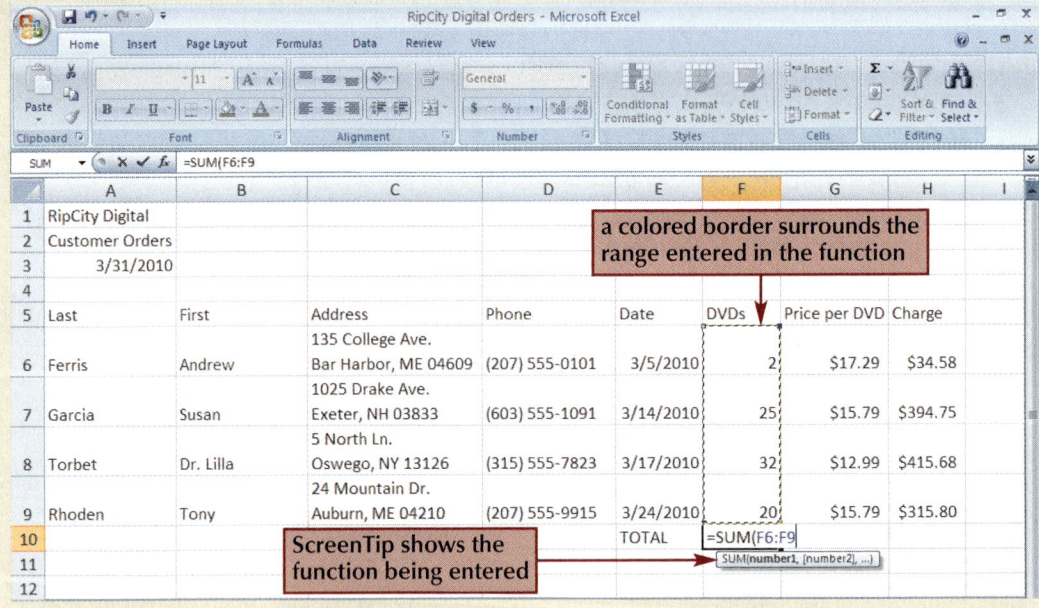

3. Type **)** to complete the function, and then press the **Tab** key. The value of the SUM function appears in cell F10, indicating that Amanda has to create 79 DVDs to meet all of her current orders.

Entering Functions with AutoSum

A fast and convenient way to enter the SUM function is with the Sum button in the Editing group on the Home tab. The **Sum** button (also referred to as the **AutoSum** feature) quickly inserts Excel functions that summarize all the values in a column or row using a single statistic. With the Sum button, you can insert the SUM, AVERAGE, COUNT, MIN, and MAX functions to generate the following:

- Sum of the values in the column or row
- Average value in the column or row
- Total count of numeric values in the column or row
- Minimum value in the column or row
- Maximum value in the column or row

The Sum button inserts both the name of the function and the range reference to the row or column of data to which the summary function is being applied. Excel determines the range reference by examining the layout of the data and choosing what seems to be the most likely cell range. For example, if you use the Sum button in a cell that is below a column of numbers, Excel assumes that you want to summarize the values in the column. Similarly, if you use the Sum button in a cell to the right of a row of values, Excel summarizes the values in that row. When you use the Sum button, Excel highlights the range it "thinks" you want to use. You can change that range by typing a different range reference or selecting a different range with your mouse.

Understanding How the AutoSum Feature Works | InSight

Make sure to always verify the range selected by AutoSum, especially when a worksheet's column or row titles contain numbers. AutoSum cannot differentiate between numbers used as titles (such as years) and numbers used as data for the calculation.

Amanda wants to calculate the total revenue she'll generate by fulfilling her customer orders. You'll use the AutoSum feature to enter the SUM function.

To use AutoSum to calculate the total revenue:

1. Click cell **H10** to make it the active cell.
2. In the Editing group on the Home tab, click the **Sum button arrow** Σ ▼ . The button's menu opens and displays five common summary functions: Sum, Average, Count Numbers, Max (for maximum), and Min (for minimum).
3. Click **Sum** to enter the SUM function. See Figure 1-27.

Figure 1-27 | SUM function entered with AutoSum

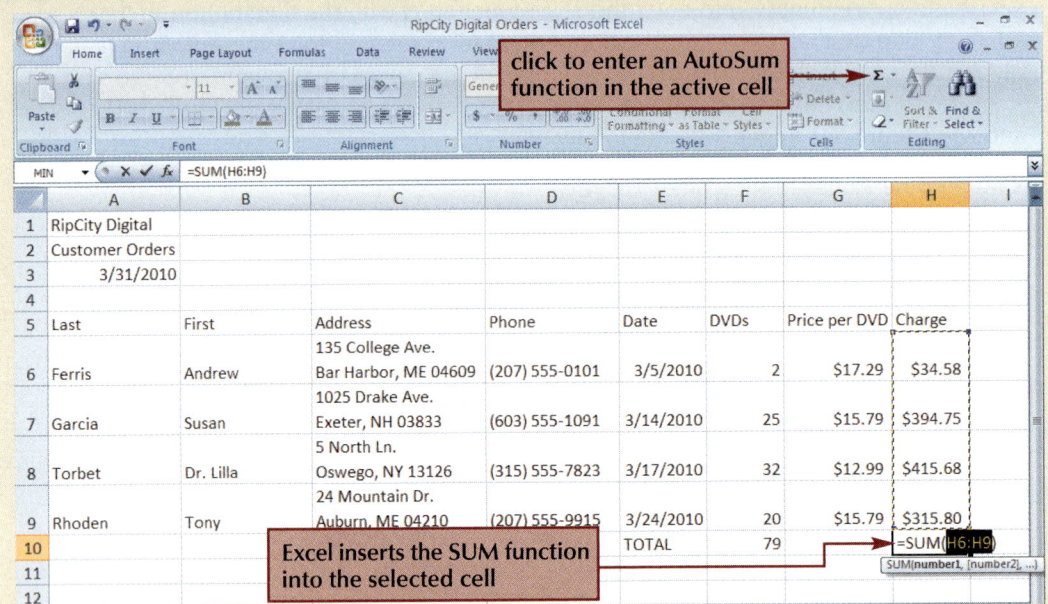

4. Verify that the range H6:H9 appears in the SUM function and is highlighted with a dotted border. The dotted border provides a visual reminder that this is where the SUM function will be applied.

5. Press the **Enter** key to accept the automatically generated formula. The total charge for all of Amanda's customers, shown in cell H10, is $1,160.81.

InSight | Creating Effective Formulas

You can use formulas to quickly perform calculations on business, science, and engineering data. To use formulas effectively:

- Do not place important data in a formula because the worksheet displays the formula result rather than the actual formula. For example, the formula =0.05*A5 calculates a 5% sales tax on a price in cell A5, but hides the 5% tax rate. Instead, enter the tax rate in another cell, such as cell A4, with an appropriate label and use the formula =A4*A5 to calculate the sales tax. Readers can see the tax rate as well as the resulting sales tax.
- Keep formulas simple. Use functions in place of long, complex formulas whenever possible. For example, use the SUM function instead of entering a formula that adds individual cells.
- Break up formulas to show intermediate results. For example, the formula =SUM(A1:A10)/SUM(B1:B10) calculates the ratio of two sums, but hides the two sum values. Instead, enter each SUM function in a separate cell, such as cells A11 and B11, and use the formula =A11/B11 to calculate the ratio. Readers can see both sums and the value of their ratio in the worksheet.

Working with Worksheets

Recall that new workbooks contain three worksheets labeled Sheet1, Sheet2, and Sheet3. You can add new worksheets to the workbook and remove unneeded ones. You can also give worksheets more descriptive and meaningful names. For Amanda's workbook, you'll remove unused worksheets from the workbook, and you'll rename the two worksheets in which you entered data.

Inserting and Deleting a Worksheet

Although each workbook includes three worksheets to start, sometimes you'll need more or fewer worksheets. You can add worksheets or delete unneeded ones. To insert a new worksheet into the workbook, right-click a sheet tab, click Insert on the shortcut menu, select a sheet type, and then click the OK button. Excel inserts the new sheet directly to the left of the active sheet. You can insert a new worksheet at the end of the workbook by clicking the Insert Worksheet tab located to the right of the last sheet tab in the workbook. The new worksheet is named with the next consecutive sheet number, such as Sheet4. You'll insert a new, blank worksheet at the end of your workbook.

To insert a new worksheet:

▶ 1. Click the **Insert Worksheet** tab to the right of the Sheet3 sheet tab. Excel inserts a new worksheet named "Sheet4" at the end of the workbook.

The workbook now includes two empty worksheets: Sheet3 and Sheet4. Because you don't plan to use these sheets, it's a good idea to remove them. You can delete a worksheet from a workbook in two ways. You can right-click the sheet tab of the worksheet you want to delete, and then click Delete on the shortcut menu. You can also click the Delete button arrow in the Cells group on the Home tab, and then click Delete Sheet. You'll use both of these methods to delete the Sheet3 and Sheet4 worksheets.

To delete the Sheet3 and Sheet4 worksheets:

▶ 1. Right-click the **Sheet3** sheet tab, and then click **Delete** on the shortcut menu. Excel removes the Sheet3 worksheet.

▶ 2. If necessary, click the **Sheet4** sheet tab to make it the active sheet.

▶ 3. In the Cells group on the Home tab, click the **Delete button arrow**, and then click **Delete Sheet**. Excel removes Sheet4 from the workbook.

Renaming a Worksheet

The remaining worksheet names, Sheet1 and Sheet2, are not very descriptive. Amanda suggests that you rename Sheet1 as "Documentation" and rename Sheet2 as "Customer Orders." To rename a worksheet, you double-click the sheet tab to select the sheet name, type a new name for the sheet, and then press the Enter key. Sheet names cannot exceed 31 characters in length, including blank spaces. The width of the sheet tab adjusts to the length of the name you enter.

To rename the two worksheets:

1. Double-click the **Sheet2** sheet tab. The sheet name is selected in the sheet tab.

2. Type **Customer Orders**, and then press the **Enter** key. The width of the sheet tab expands to match the longer sheet name.

3. Double-click the **Sheet1** sheet tab, type **Documentation**, and then press the **Enter** key. Both sheets are renamed.

Moving and Copying a Worksheet

You can change the placement of the worksheets in a workbook. A good practice is to place the most important worksheets at the beginning of the workbook (the leftmost sheet tabs), and less important worksheets toward the end (the rightmost tabs). To reposition a worksheet, you click and drag the sheet tab to a new location relative to other worksheets in the workbook. You can use a similar method to copy a worksheet. Just press the Ctrl key as you drag and drop the sheet tab. The new copy appears where you drop the sheet tab, while the original worksheet remains in its initial position. You'll move the Documentation sheet to the end of the workbook and then return it to the beginning.

To move the Documentation worksheet:

1. If necessary, click the **Documentation** sheet tab to make that worksheet active.

2. Press and hold the mouse button so the pointer changes to and a small triangle appears in the upper-left corner of the tab.

3. Drag the pointer to the right of the Customer Orders sheet tab, and then release the mouse button. The Documentation sheet is now the second sheet in the workbook.

4. Drag the Documentation sheet back to be the first sheet in the workbook.

Editing Your Work

As you work, you might make mistakes that you want to correct or undo, or you might need to replace a value based on more current information. Amanda realizes that the price per DVD for Andrew Ferris's order should be $18.29 not $17.29 as entered in cell G6. You could simply clear the value in the cell and then type the correct value. However, sometimes you need to edit only a portion of an entry rather than change the entire contents of a cell, especially if the cell contains a large block of text or a complex formula. To edit the cell contents, you can work in **editing mode**.

You can enter editing mode in several ways: (1) double-clicking the cell, (2) selecting the cell and pressing the F2 key, or (3) selecting the cell and clicking anywhere within the formula bar. When you work in editing mode, some of the keyboard shortcuts you've been using work differently because now they apply only to the text within the selected cell. For example, the Home, End, Backspace, Delete, and arrow keys now move the insertion point to different locations within the cell. The Home key moves the insertion point to the beginning of the cell's content. The End key moves the insertion point to the end of the cell's content. The left and right arrow keys move the insertion point backward and forward through the cell's content. The Backspace key deletes the character immediately to the left of the insertion point, and the Delete key deletes the character to the right of the insertion point. To exit editing mode and accept the changes you made, press the Enter key.

> **Tip**
>
> If you make a mistake as you type in editing mode, you can press the Esc key or click the Cancel button on the formula bar to cancel all of the changes you made while in editing mode.

You'll see how keyboard commands differ when you're in editing mode as you change one digit of the value in cell G6.

To edit the value in cell G6:

▶ 1. Click the **Customer Orders** sheet tab.

▶ 2. Double-click cell **G6**. The mode indicator in the status bar switches from Ready to Edit to indicate that you are in editing mode.

▶ 3. Press the **End** key. The insertion point moves to the end of the cell.

▶ 4. Press the ← key three times. The insertion point moves to the right of the 7.

▶ 5. Press the **Backspace** key to delete the 7, and then type **8**. The value in cell G6 changes to 18.29. See Figure 1-28.

Working in editing mode — Figure 1-28

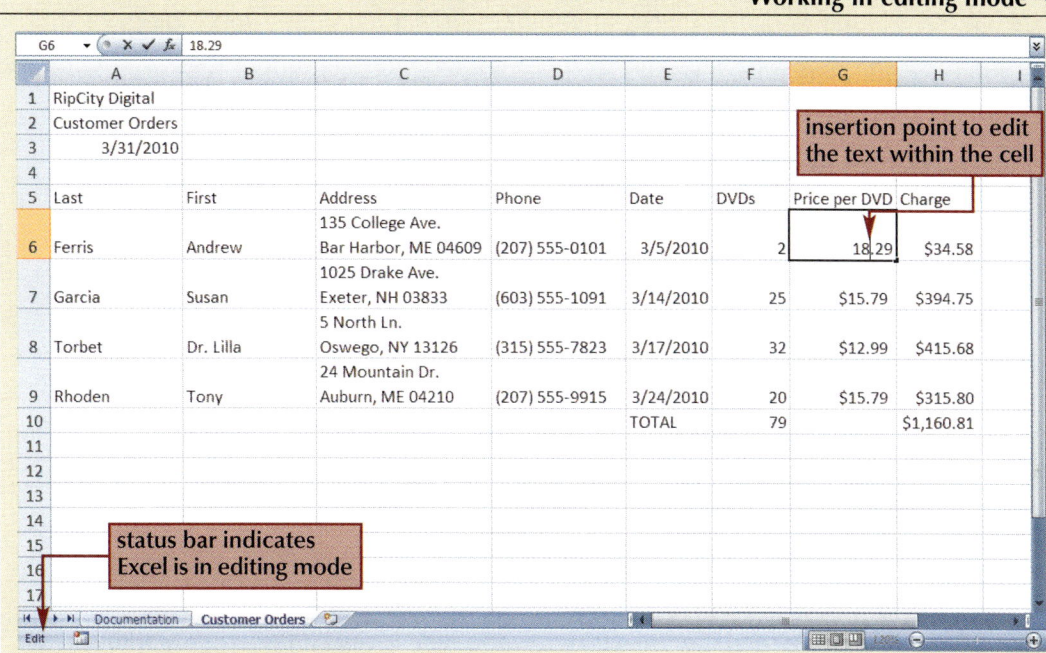

▶ 6. Press the **Enter** key to accept the edit in cell G6. The value $18.29 appears in cell G6, the active cell is cell G7, and the mode indicator in the status bar changes from Edit to Ready to indicate that you are no longer in editing mode.

Undoing and Redoing an Action

As you revise a workbook, you might find that you need to undo one of your previous actions. To undo an action, click the Undo button on the Quick Access Toolbar. As you work, Excel maintains a list of your actions, so you can undo most of the actions you perform in a workbook during the current session. To reverse more than one action, click the Undo button arrow and click the earliest action you want to undo from the list. All actions subsequent to that action will also be undone.

You'll undo the action you just performed, removing the edit to cell G6.

To undo your last action:

1. On the Quick Access Toolbar, click the **Undo** button.
2. Verify that $17.29 appears again in cell G6, indicating that your last action—editing the value of this cell—has been undone.

If you find that you have gone too far in undoing previous actions, you can go forward in the action list and redo those actions. To redo an action, you click the Redo button on the Quick Access Toolbar. As with the Undo button, you can click the Redo button arrow to redo more than one action at a time. You'll use Redo to restore the value of cell G6.

To redo your last action:

1. On the Quick Access Toolbar, click the **Redo** button.
2. Verify that the value in cell G6 returns to $18.29.

Using Find and Replace

Amanda wants to you to replace all the street title abbreviations with their full names. Specifically, she wants you to use "Avenue" in place of "Ave.", "Lane" in place of "Ln.", and "Drive" in place of "Dr." Although you could read through the worksheet to locate each occurrence, this becomes a cumbersome process with larger workbooks. For greater speed and accuracy, you can use the **Find** command to locate numbers and text in the workbook and the **Replace** command to overwrite them. You'll replace each occurrence of a street title abbreviation.

To use the Find and Replace commands:

1. In the Editing group on the Home tab, click the **Find & Select** button, and then click **Replace**. The Find and Replace dialog box opens.
2. Type **Ave.** in the Find what box, press the **Tab** key, and then type **Avenue** in the Replace with box.

   You can limit the search to the current worksheet or search the entire workbook. You can specify whether to match the capitalization in the Find what box and whether the search text should match the entire cell contents or part of the cell contents.

3. Click the **Options** button to display additional Find and Replace options. See Figure 1-29.

Figure 1-29   Find and Replace dialog box

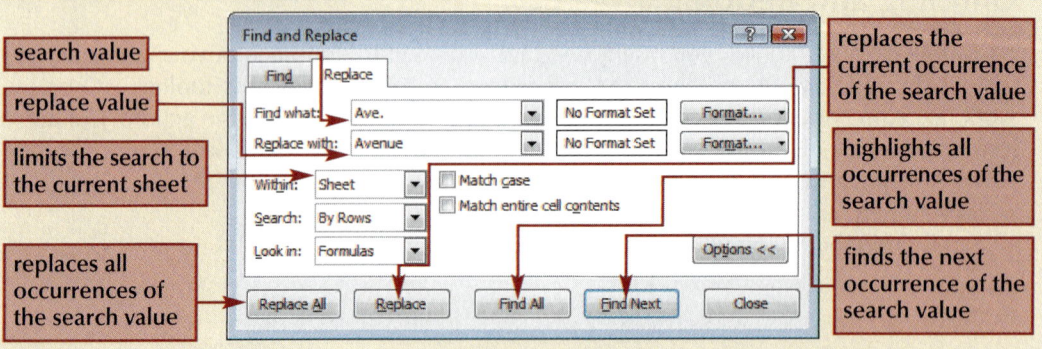

You can choose to review each occurrence of the search value and decide whether to replace it, or you can click the Replace All button to replace all occurrences at once.

4. Click the **Replace All** button. A dialog box opens, indicating that Excel has completed its search and made two replacements.

5. Click the **OK** button to close the dialog box.

6. Type **Ln.** in the Find what box, press the **Tab** key, type **Lane** in the Replace with box, click the **Replace All** button, and then click the **OK** button to close the dialog box that indicates Excel has completed its search and made one replacement.

    Next, you want to replace the street abbreviation "Dr." with "Drive." Because "Dr." is also used as the abbreviation for "Doctor" for one customer, you must review each "Dr." abbreviation and make the replacement only in the addresses.

7. Type **Dr.** in the Find what box, press the **Tab** key, type **Drive** in the Replace with box, and then click the **Find Next** button. The next occurrence of "Dr." in the worksheet occurs in cell B8 with the text, "Dr. Lilla."

8. Click the **Find Next** button to ignore this occurrence. The next occurrence of "Dr." is in the mailing address for Tony Rhoden.

9. Click the **Replace** button to replace this text. You've finished finding and replacing text in the worksheet.

10. Click the **Close** button to close the Find and Replace dialog box. See Figure 1-30.

Revised customer orders   Figure 1-30

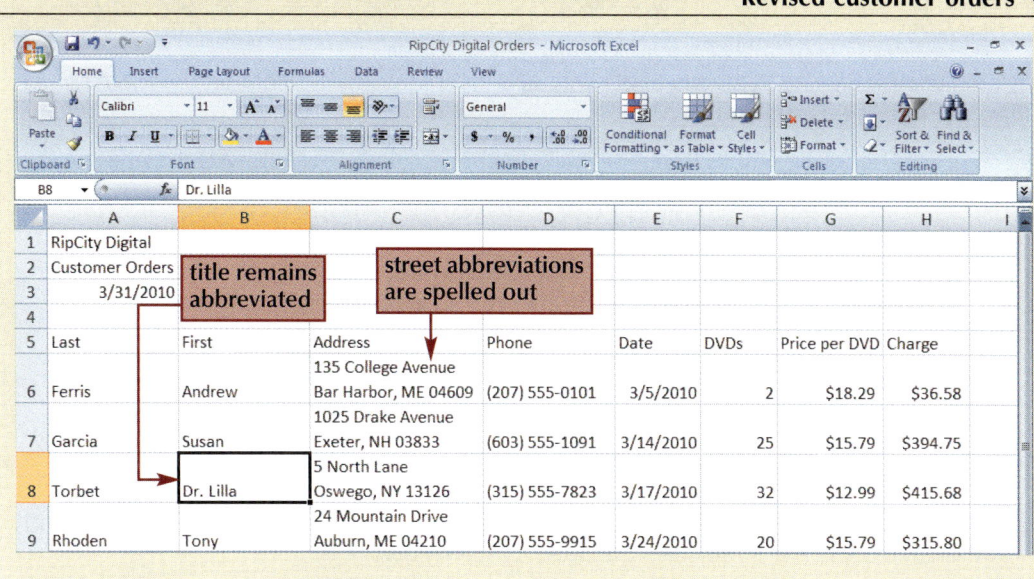

Using the Spelling Checker

Another editing tool is the spelling checker. The **spelling checker** verifies the words in the active worksheet against the program's dictionary. Although the spelling checker's dictionary includes a large number of words, as well as common first and last names and places, many words you use in workbooks might not be included. If the spelling checker finds a word not in its dictionary, the word appears in a dialog box along with a list of suggested replacements. You can replace the word with one from the list, or you can ignore the word and go to the next possible misspelling. You can also add words to the dictionary to prevent them from being flagged as misspellings in the future. Note that the spelling checker will not find a correctly spelled word used incorrectly, such as "there" instead of "their" or "your" instead of "you're." The best way to catch these types of errors is to proofread your worksheets.

Before giving the customer orders workbook to Amanda, you'll check the spelling.

To check the spelling in the worksheet:

1. Click cell **A1**, click the **Review** tab on the Ribbon, and then, in the Proofing group, click the **Spelling** button. The Spelling dialog box opens and flags "RipCity" as a possible spelling error. Excel suggests two alternatives. See Figure 1-31.

Figure 1-31   Spelling dialog box

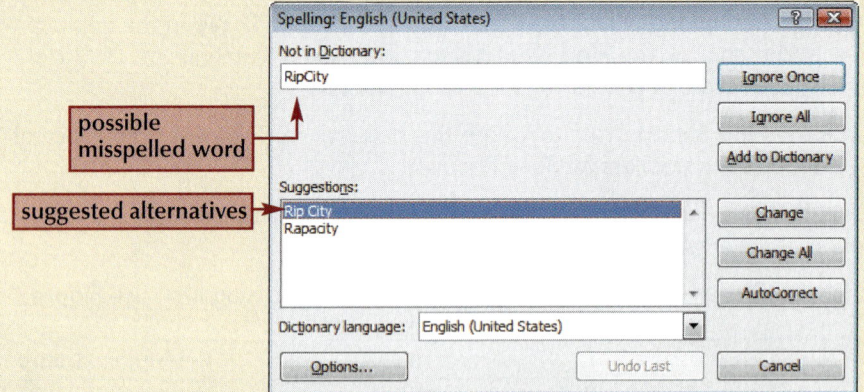

Because RipCity is the name of Amanda's company, you'll ignore all the occurrences of this spelling.

2. Click the **Ignore All** button. The spelling checker flags "Torbet," a last name that is not in the program's dictionary.

3. Click the **Ignore All** button to ignore the spelling of this name. The next potential spelling error is the name "Lilla" in cell B8. Amanda tells you the name should have been entered as "Lila," a first name that the spelling checker recognizes.

4. Click **Lila** in the list of suggestions, if necessary, and then click the **Change** button. The text is changed within the cell. The spelling checker doesn't find any other errors.

   Trouble? If the spelling checker finds another error, you might have another typing error in your worksheet. Use the spelling checker to find and correct any other errors in your workbook, and then continue with Step 5.

5. Click the **OK** button to close the Spelling dialog box.

6. Proofread the worksheet and correct any other spelling errors you find. You do not have to check the spelling in the Documentation worksheet.

Previewing and Printing a Worksheet

Now that you have finished the final edit of the workbook, you are ready to print a hard copy of the customer orders list for Amanda. However, before you print the workbook, you should preview it to ensure that it will print correctly.

Changing Worksheet Views

You can view a worksheet in three ways. **Normal view**, which you've been using throughout this tutorial, simply shows the contents of the worksheet. **Page Layout view** shows how the worksheet will appear on the page or pages sent to the printer. **Page Break Preview** displays the location of the different page breaks within the worksheet. This is particularly useful when a worksheet will span several printed pages.

You'll switch between these views to see how the Customer Orders worksheet will appear on printed pages.

To switch the worksheet views:

▸ 1. Click the **Page Layout** button on the status bar. Excel displays the page layout of the worksheet. You want to see the rest of the data, which extends to a second page.

▸ 2. Reduce the zoom level to **60%**. See Figure 1-32.

Worksheet displayed in Page Layout view Figure 1-32

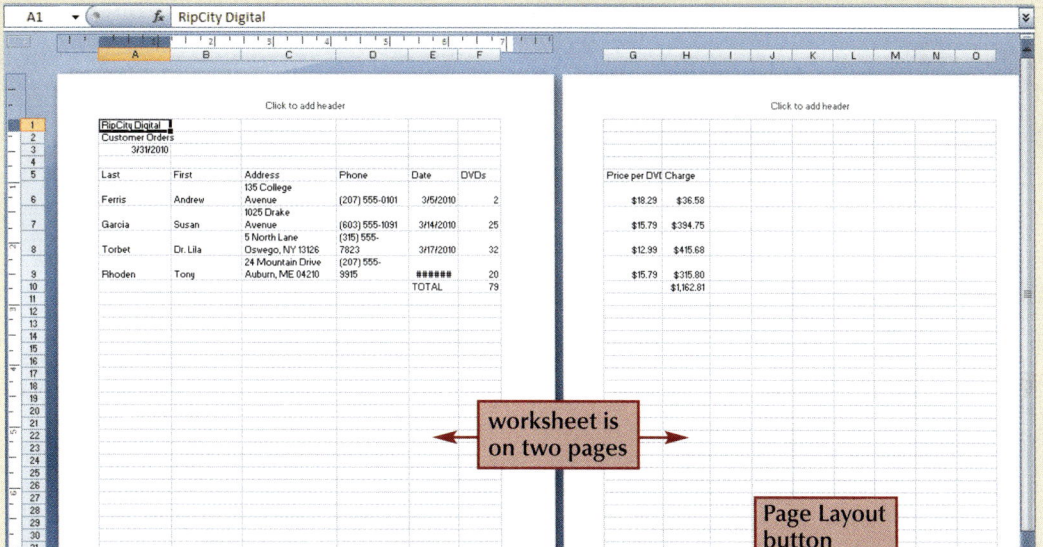

Tip

You can view the workbook in the full screen space (which hides the Ribbon); in the Workbook Views group on the View tab, click Full Screen.

▸ 3. Click the **Page Break Preview** button on the status bar. The view switches to Page Break Preview, which shows only those parts of the current worksheet that will print. A dotted blue border separates one page from another.

Trouble? If the Welcome to Page Break Preview dialog box opens, this is the first time you've switched to Page Break Preview. Click the OK button to close the dialog box and continue with Step 4.

▸ 4. Zoom the worksheet to **120%** so that you can more easily read the contents of the worksheet. See Figure 1-33.

Figure 1-33 Worksheet displayed in Page Break Preview

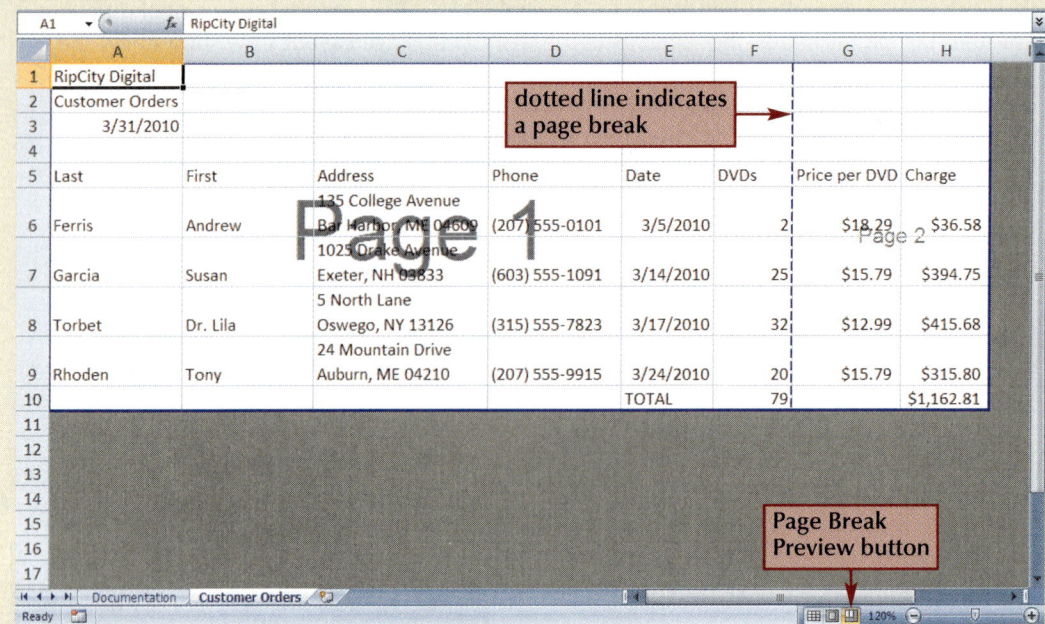

5. Click the **Normal** button on the status bar. The worksheet returns to Normal view. A dotted black line indicates where the page break will be placed when the worksheet is printed.

Working with Portrait and Landscape Orientation

As you saw in Page Layout view and Page Break Preview, the Customer Orders worksheet will print on two pages—columns A through F will print on one page and columns G and H will print on a second page. Amanda wants the entire worksheet printed on a single page. The simplest way to accomplish this is to change the page orientation. In **portrait orientation**, the page is taller than it is wide. In **landscape orientation**, the page is wider than it is tall. By default, Excel displays pages in portrait orientation. In many cases, however, you will want to print the page in landscape orientation.

You'll change the orientation of the Customer Orders worksheet.

To change the page orientation:

1. Click the **Page Layout** tab on the Ribbon.

2. In the Page Setup group, click the **Orientation** button, and then click **Landscape**. The page orientation switches to landscape, and the Customer Orders worksheet contents fit on one page.

3. Click the **Page Layout** button on the status bar, and then verify that all the worksheet contents fit on one page.

Changing the page orientation affects only the active worksheet. The Documentation sheet remains in portrait orientation.

▶ 4. Click the **Documentation** sheet tab, and then click the **Page Layout** button. The entire contents of the Documentation worksheet fit on one page in portrait orientation.

Printing the Workbook

You can print the contents of your workbook by using the Print command on the Office Button. The Print command provides three options. You can open the Print dialog box from which you can specify the printer settings, including which printer to use, which worksheets to include in the printout, and the number of copies to print. You can perform a Quick Print using the print options currently set in the Print dialog box. Finally, you can preview the workbook before you send it to the printer to see exactly how the worksheet will look on the printer you selected with the print settings you've chosen. In general, you should always preview the printout before sending it to the printer.

You'll preview and print Amanda's workbook now.

To preview and print the workbook:

▶ 1. Click the **Office Button**, point to **Print**, and then click **Print**. The Print dialog box opens.

▶ 2. Click the **Name** box, and then click the printer to which you want to print if it is not already selected.

Next, you need to select what to print. You can choose to print only the selected cells, the active sheet (or sheets), or all the worksheets in the workbook that contain data.

▶ 3. If necessary, click the **Entire workbook** option button to print both of the worksheets in the workbook.

▶ 4. Make sure **1** appears in the Number of copies box because you only need to print one copy of the workbook. Next, you'll preview how the worksheet will appear on the printed page with these settings.

▶ 5. Click the **Preview** button. Print Preview displays a preview of the full first page of the printout—the Documentation sheet printed in portrait orientation. The status bar shows that this is the first of two pages that will print.

▶ 6. In the Preview group on the Print Preview tab, click the **Next Page** button. Print Preview shows the second page of the printout.

The printout will include only the data in the worksheet. The other elements in the worksheet, such as the row and column headings and the gridlines around the worksheet cells, will not print.

▶ 7. In the Print group, click the **Print** button. The workbook is sent to the printer and Print Preview closes.

Viewing and Printing Worksheet Formulas

Amanda notices that the printout displays only the worksheet values and none of the formulas. Most of the time, you will be interested in only the final results of the worksheet, not the formulas used to calculate those results. In some cases, you might want to view the formulas used to develop the workbook. This is particularly useful when you encounter unexpected results and you want to examine the underlying formulas. You can view the formulas in a workbook by switching to **formula view**, a view of the workbook contents that displays formulas instead of the resulting values. You'll switch to formula view now.

To view the worksheet formulas:

> **Tip**
> To toggle in and out of formula view, press the Ctrl+` keys. The ` grave accent symbol is usually located above the Tab key on your keyboard.

1. Click the **Customer Orders** sheet tab, if necessary, and then click the **Normal** button on the status bar. The Customer Orders worksheet is active and displayed in Normal view.

2. Press the **Ctrl+`** keys. The worksheet changes to formula view.

3. Scroll the worksheet to the right to view the formulas in columns F and H. The column widths are wider to display the entire formula in each cell. As long as you don't resize the column widths while in formula view, they remain unchanged in other views. See Figure 1-34.

Figure 1-34   Worksheet in formula view

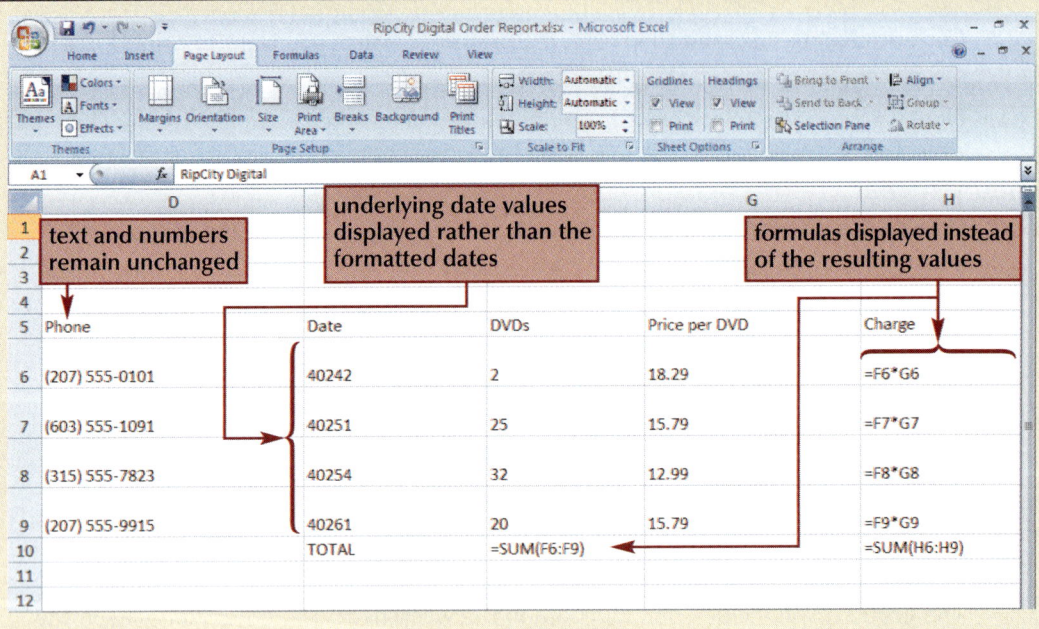

Amanda wants a printout of the formula view. The Customer Orders worksheet will not fit on one page because of the expanded column widths. You can scale the worksheet to force the contents to fit on a single page. **Scaling** a printout reduces the width and the height of the printout to fit the number of pages you specify by shrinking the text size as needed. You can also scale a printout proportionally to a percentage of its actual size. You'll scale the Customer Orders worksheet to a width and height of one page.

To scale the worksheet formulas to print on one page:

1. In the Scale to Fit group on the Page Layout tab, click the **Width arrow**, and then click **1 page**.

2. In the Scale to Fit group, click the **Height arrow**, and then click **1 page**. You'll verify that the worksheet formula view fits on a single page.

3. Click the **Page Layout** button on the status bar, and then zoom the worksheet to **50%**. The formula view of the worksheet fits on one page. See Figure 1-35.

Figure 1-35 — Printout scaled to one page

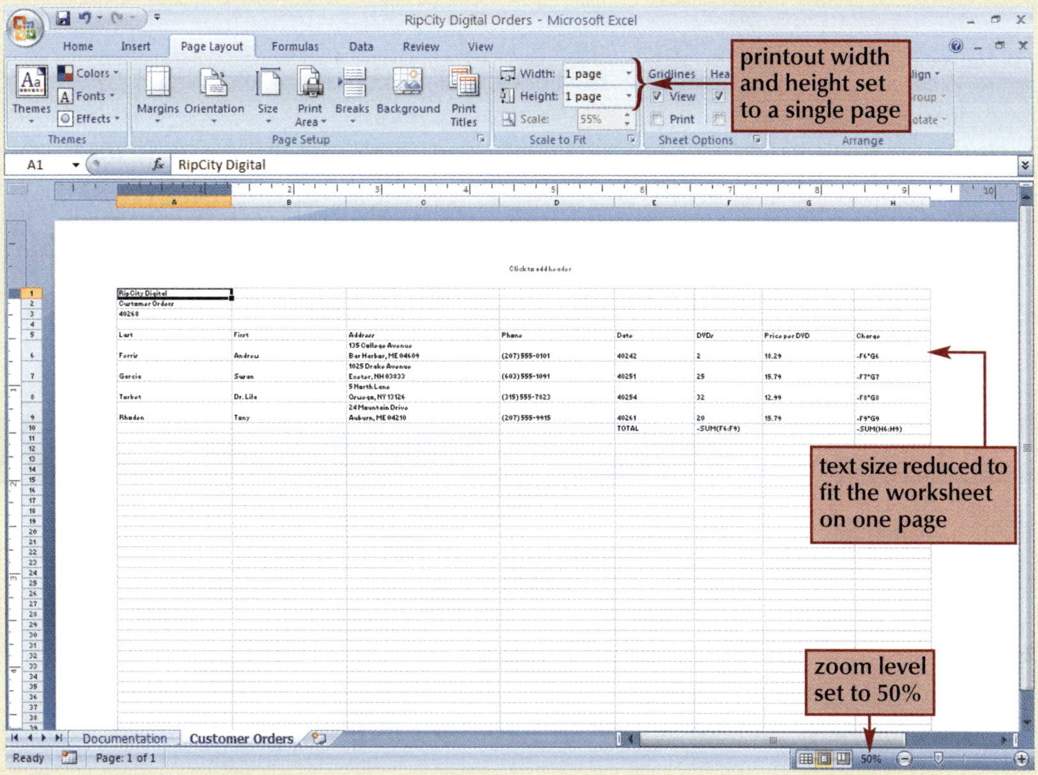

4. Click the **Office Button**, point to **Print**, and then click **Print**. The Print dialog box opens. You'll specify that only the active worksheet will be printed.

5. Click the **Active sheet(s)** option button to print only the Customer Orders worksheet.

6. Click the **Preview** button. Print Preview displays a preview of the one-page printout of the Customer Orders worksheet in formula view.

7. In the Print group on the Print Preview tab, click the **Print** button. The workbook is sent to the printer and Print Preview closes.

At this point, you've completed your work for Amanda. Before closing the workbook, you'll change the view of the workbook contents back to Normal view.

To save and close the workbook:

▶ 1. Press the **Ctrl+`** keys to switch the worksheet back to Normal view.
▶ 2. Save your changes to the workbook, and then close it.

Amanda is pleased with the job you've done for her. She will review the workbook you've created and let you know if she has any changes that she wants you to make.

Review | Session 1.2 Quick Check

1. Describe the two types of cell ranges in Excel.
2. What is the range reference for the block of cells from A3 through G5 and J3 through M5?
3. What formula would you enter to add the values in cells B4, B5, and B6? What function would you enter to achieve the same result?
4. How do you rename a worksheet?
5. Describe four ways of viewing the content of an Excel workbook.
6. Why would you scale a worksheet?
7. How do you display the formulas used in a worksheet?
8. How are page breaks indicated in Page Break Preview?

Review | Tutorial Summary

In this tutorial, you learned the basics of spreadsheets and Excel. After reviewing the major components of the Excel window, you navigated between and within worksheets. You entered text, dates, values, and formulas, and used the AutoSum feature to quickly insert the SUM function. You inserted and deleted rows, columns, and worksheet cells. You selected cell ranges and moved cell contents using drag and drop or cut and paste. You also created new worksheets, renamed worksheets, and moved worksheets within the workbook. You edited your work by using editing mode, finding and replacing text, and using the spelling checker to correct errors. Finally, you previewed and then printed the contents of the workbook.

Key Terms

active cell	editing mode	point
active sheet	Excel	portrait orientation
active workbook	Find	range
active workbook window	formula	range reference
adjacent range	formula bar	Replace
arithmetic operator	formula view	row heading
AutoComplete	function	scale
autofit	landscape orientation	sheet
AutoSum	Microsoft Office Excel 2007	sheet tab
cell	Name box	spelling checker
cell range	nonadjacent range	spreadsheet
cell reference	Normal view	text data
chart sheet	number data	text string
clear	operator	time data
column heading	order of precedence	truncate
cut	Page Break Preview	what-if analysis
date data	Page Layout view	workbook
delete	pixel	workbook window
drag and drop	planning analysis sheet	worksheet

Practice | Review Assignments

Practice the skills you learned in the tutorial using the same case scenario.

There are no Data Files needed for the Review Assignments.

Amanda reviewed your work on the Customer Orders worksheet, and has another set of orders she wants you to enter. The data for the new customer orders is shown in Figure 1-36. In addition to calculating the charge for creating the DVDs, Amanda also wants to include the cost of shipping in the total charged to each customer.

Figure 1-36

Date	Last	First	Address	Phone	DVDs	Price per DVD	Shipping Charge
3/27/2010	Fleming	Doris	25 Lee St. Bedford, VA 24523	(540) 555-5681	7	$18.29	$7.49
4/4/2010	Ortiz	Thomas	28 Ridge Ln. Newfane, VT 05345	(802) 555-7710	13	$16.55	$9.89
4/8/2010	Dexter	Kay	150 Main St. Greenbelt, MD 20770	(301) 555-8823	25	$15.79	$7.23
4/9/2010	Sisk	Norman	250 East Maple Ln. Cranston, RI 02910	(401) 555-3350	15	$16.55	$10.55
4/17/2010	Romano	June	207 Jackston Ave. Westport, IN 47283	(812) 555-2681	22	$15.79	$13.95

Complete the following:

1. Open a blank workbook, and then save the workbook as **Order Report** in the Tutorial.01\Review folder.
2. Rename Sheet1 as **Documentation**, and then enter the following data into the worksheet:

Cell	Data	Cell	Data
A1	**RipCity Digital**		
A3	**Author**	B3	*your name*
A4	**Date**	B4	*the current date*
A5	**Purpose**	B5	**To track customer orders for RipCity Digital**

3. Rename Sheet2 as **Customer Orders**.
4. Delete Sheet3.
5. On the Customer Orders worksheet, in cell A1, enter **RipCity Digital**. In cell A3, enter **Customer Orders Report**. In cell A4, enter **March 27 to April 17, 2010**.
6. In cells A5 through H10, enter the data from Figure 1-36. In column D, enter the address text on two lines within each cell.
7. Set the width of column A to 10 characters, columns B and C to 12 characters, column D to 20 characters, and columns E, G, and H to 16 characters.
8. Autofit all of the rows in the worksheet to the cell contents.
9. In cell I5, enter **Total**. In cell I6, insert a formula that calculates the total charge for the first customer (the number of DVDs created multiplied by the price per DVD and then added to the shipping charge). Increase the width of column I to 11 characters.
10. Copy the formula in cell I6 and paste it into the cell range I7:I10.

11. In cell E11, enter **Total**. In cell F11, use the SUM function to calculate the total number of DVDs created for all customers. In cell I11, use AutoSum to insert the SUM function to calculate the total charges for all of the customer orders.
12. Use editing mode to make the following corrections:
    - In cell D6, change the street address from 25 Lee St. to **2500 Lee St.**
    - In cell F9, change the number of DVDs from 15 to **17**.
    - In cell H8, change the shipping charge from $7.23 to **$8.23**.
13. Use the Find and Replace commands to replace all occurrences of St. with **Street**, Ln. with **Lane**, and Ave. with **Avenue**.
14. Change the page layout of the Customer Orders worksheet to print in landscape orientation on a single page.
15. Preview and print the contents of the entire workbook.
16. Change the Customer Orders worksheet to formula view, landscape orientation, and scaled to fit on a single page. Preview and print the Customer Orders worksheet.
17. Return the view of the Customer Orders worksheet to Normal view, save your changes to the Order Report workbook, and then save the current workbook as **Revised Report** in the Tutorial.01\Review folder. (*Hint:* Use the Save As command on the Office Button to save the existing workbook with a new name.)
18. Kay Dexter has canceled her order with RipCity Digital. Remove her order from the Customer Orders worksheet.
19. Add the following order directly after the order placed by June Romano: date **4/22/2010**; name **Patrick Crawford**; address **200 Valley View Road, Rome, GA 30161**; phone **(706) 555-0998**; DVDs **14**; price per DVD **$16.55**; shipping charge **$12.45**.
20. Verify that Excel automatically updates the formulas and functions used in the workbook so they properly calculate the total charge for this order and for all the orders.
21. Edit the title in cell A4, changing the ending date of the report from April 17 to **April 22**.
22. Save the workbook, preview and print the contents and formulas of the revised Customer Orders worksheet, close the workbook, and then submit the finished workbook and printouts to your instructor.

Apply | Case Problem 1

Use the skills you learned to complete an income statement for a bicycle company.

Data File needed for this Case Problem: Altac.xlsx

Altac Bicycles Deborah York is a financial consultant for Altac Bicycles, an online seller of bicycles and bicycle equipment based in Silver City, New Mexico. She has entered some financial information in an Excel workbook for an income statement she is preparing for the company. She asks you to enter the remaining data and formulas.

Complete the following:

1. Open the **Altac** workbook located in the Tutorial.01\Case1 folder, and then save the workbook as **Altac Bicycles** in the same folder.
2. Insert three new rows at the top of the Sheet1 worksheet, and then enter the following text on two lines within cell A1:
   Altac Bicycles
   Income Statement*
3. In cell A2, enter **For the Years Ended December 31, 2007 through December 31, 2009**.

4. In the range C6:E7, enter the following net sales and cost of sales figures:

	2009	2008	2007
Net Sales	12,510	10,981	9,004
Cost of Sales	4,140	3,810	3,011

5. In the range C11:E14, enter the following expense figures:

	2009	2008	2007
Salaries and Wages	1,602	1,481	1,392
Sales and Marketing	2,631	2,012	1,840
Administrative	521	410	324
Research and Development	491	404	281

6. Select the nonadjacent range C18:E18;C20:E20;C24:E24, and then enter the following values for Other Income, Income Taxes, and Shares, pressing the Enter or Tab key to navigate from cell to cell in the selected range:

	2009	2008	2007
Other Income	341	302	239
Income Taxes	1,225	1,008	781
Shares	3,581	3,001	2,844

7. In the range C8:E8, enter a formula to calculate the gross margin for each year, where the gross margin is equal to the net sales minus the cost of sales.

8. In the range C15:E15, enter the SUM function to calculate the total operating expenses for each year, where the total operating expenses is the sum of the four expense categories.

9. In the range C17:E17, enter a formula to calculate the operating income for each year, where operating income is equal to the gross margin minus the total operating expenses.

10. In the range C19:E19, enter a formula to calculate the pretax income for each year, where pretax income is equal to the operating income plus other income.

11. In the range C22:E22, enter a formula to calculate the company's net income for each year, where net income is equal to the pretax income minus income taxes.

12. In the range C25:E25, enter a formula to calculate the earnings per share for each year, where earnings per share is equal to the net income divided by the number of shares outstanding.

13. Use the spelling checker to correct and replace any spelling errors in the worksheet. Ignore the spelling of Altac.

14. In cell A18, use editing mode to capitalize the word *income*.

15. Increase the width of column A to 18 characters and increase the width of column B to 25 characters. Autofit the height of row 1.

16. Rename Sheet1 as **Income Statement**; rename Sheet2 as **Documentation** and move it to the beginning of the workbook; and then delete the Sheet3 worksheet.

17. In the Documentation worksheet, enter the following text and values:

Cell	Data	Cell	Data
A1	**Altac Bicycles**		
A3	**Author**	B3	your name
A4	**Date**	B4	the current date
A5	**Purpose**	B5	Income statement for Altac Bicycles for 2007 through 2009

18. Save the workbook, preview the workbook and make sure each worksheet in portrait orientation fits on one page in the printout, and then print the entire workbook. Close the workbook, and then submit the finished workbook and printouts to your instructor.

Apply | Case Problem 2

Use the skills you learned to complete a balance sheet for a food retailer.

Data File needed for this Case Problem: Halley.xlsx

Halley Foods Michael Li is working on the annual financial report for Halley Foods of Norman, Oklahoma. One part of the financial report will be the company's balance sheet for the previous three years. Michael has entered some of the labels for the balance sheet but wants you to finish the job by entering the actual values and formulas.

Complete the following:

1. Open the **Halley** workbook located in the Tutorial.01\Case2 folder, and then save the workbook as **Halley Foods** in the same folder.
2. Rename the Sheet1 worksheet as **Balance Sheet**, and then delete the Sheet2 and Sheet3 worksheets.
3. Insert three new rows at the top of the sheet, and then enter the following text on four lines within cell A1:
   Halley Foods
   Balance Sheet
   As of December 31
   For the Years 2007 through 2009
4. Change the width of column A to 30 characters, the width of column B to 20 characters, and the width of column C to 26 characters. Autofit the height of row 1.
5. Enter the assets and liability values shown in Figure 1-37 into the corresponding cells in the Balance Sheet worksheet for each of the last three years.

Figure 1-37

		2009	2008	2007
Current Assets	Cash and equivalents	796	589	423
	Short-term investments	1,194	1,029	738
	Accounts receivable	1,283	1,151	847
	Net inventories	683	563	463
	Deferred taxes	510	366	332
	Other current assets	162	137	103
Other Assets	Investments	7,077	5,811	4,330
	Restricted investments	910	797	681
	Property and equipment	779	696	420
	Other assets	1,178	484	485
Current Liabilities	Accounts payable	350	293	182
	Income taxes payable	608	442	342
	Accrued payroll	661	564	384
	Other accrued liabilities	1,397	1,250	775
Minority Interest		44	43	36
Shareholders' Equity	Preferred and common stock	5,557	4,821	3,515
	Retained earnings	5,666	4,007	3,401
	Other comprehensive income	289	203	187

6. Use AutoSum to calculate the total current assets, other assets, current liabilities, and shareholders' equity in the ranges D11:F11, D17:F17, D25:F25, and D33:F33, respectively, for each of the previous three years.
7. Insert a formula in the range D19:F19 to calculate the total assets (current plus other) for each year.
8. Insert a formula in the range D36:F36 to calculate the value of the total current liabilities plus the minority interest plus the total shareholders' equity for each year.
9. Use the spelling checker to correct any spelling mistakes in the Balance Sheet worksheet, and then proofread the worksheet.
10. Change the zoom level of the Balance Sheet worksheet to 70% in Normal view to view the entire contents of the sheet in the workbook window.
11. View the Balance Sheet worksheet in Page Layout view zoomed to 80%, and then scale the height and width of the worksheet to fit on one page.
12. Insert a new worksheet named **Documentation** at the beginning of the workbook.
13. In the Documentation worksheet, enter the following data:

Cell	Data	Cell	Data
A1	**Halley Foods**		
A3	**Author**	B3	your name
A4	**Date**	B4	the current date
A5	**Purpose**	B5	**Balance sheet for Halley Foods for 2007 through 2009**

14. Save, preview, and then print the entire Halley Foods Balance Sheet workbook.
15. Print the formula view of the Balance Sheet worksheet on two pages in landscape orientation. Return the Balance Sheet worksheet to Page Layout view when you're finished.
16. Save and close the workbook, and then submit the finished workbook and printouts to your instructor.

Challenge | Case Problem 3

Explore using AutoSum to calculate production statistics.

Data File needed for this Case Problem: Global.xlsx

Global Site GPS Kevin Hodge is a production assistant at Global Site GPS, a leading manufacturer of GPS devices located in Crestwood, Missouri. One of Kevin's jobs is to monitor output at the company's five regional plants. He wants to create an Excel workbook that reports the monthly production at the five sites, including the monthly average, minimum, and maximum production and total production for the previous year. He asks you to create the workbook that reports these statistics.

Complete the following:

1. Open the **Global** workbook located in the Tutorial.01\Case3 folder, and then save the workbook as **Global Site** in the same folder.
2. Rename the Sheet1 worksheet as **Production History**, and then insert 12 new rows at the top of the worksheet.
3. Increase the width of column A to 23 characters and the width of columns B through F to 14 characters.
4. In the range B7:F7, enter the titles **Plant1**, **Plant2**, **Plant3**, **Plant4**, and **Plant5**, respectively.

⊕ **EXPLORE**

⊕ **EXPLORE**

⊕ **EXPLORE**

5. In the range A8:A11, enter **Total Units Produced**, **Average per Month**, **Maximum**, and **Minimum**, respectively.
6. Select the range B26:F26, use AutoSum to calculate the sum of the production values for each of the five plants, and then drag and drop the selected cells to the range B8:F8.
7. Select the range B26:F26, use AutoSum to calculate the average of the production values for each of the five plants, and then drag and drop the selected cells to the range B9:F9.
8. Repeat Step 7 to calculate the maximum values for each of the five plants and then move those calculated values to the range B10:F10, and then repeat to calculate the minimum production values and drag and drop those calculated values to the range B11:F11.
9. In the Production History worksheet, enter the following data:

Cell	Data	Cell	Data
A1	Global Site GPS		
A2	Production Report		
A3	Model	B3	MapTracker 201
A4	Year	B4	2010
A5	Total Units Produced		

10. In cell B5, use the SUM function to add the values in the range B8:F8.
11. Insert a new worksheet named **Plant Directory** as the first worksheet in the workbook.
12. In cells A1 and A2, enter **Global Site GPS** and **Plant Directory**, respectively, and then enter the text shown in Figure 1-38 in the range A4:D9, making sure that the address is entered on two lines within the cell.

Figure 1-38

Plant	Plant Manager	Address	Phone
1	Karen Brookers	300 Commerce Avenue Crestwood, MO 63126	(314) 555-3881
2	Daniel Gomez	15 North Main Street Edison, NJ 08837	(732) 555-0012
3	Jody Hetrick	3572 Howard Lane Weston, FL 33326	(954) 555-4817
4	Yong Jo	900 South Street Kirkland, WA 98033	(425) 555-8775
5	Sandy Nisbett	3771 Water Street Helena, MT 59623	(406) 555-4114

13. Set the width of column B to 15 characters, the width of column C to 30 characters, and the width of column D to 16 characters. Autofit the height of each row to its content.
14. Insert a new worksheet named **Documentation** as the first worksheet in the workbook, and then enter the following data:

Cell	Data	Cell	Data
A1	Global Site GPS		
A3	Author	B3	*your name*
A4	Date	B4	*the current date*
A5	Purpose	B5	**Production report for Global Site GPS**

15. Switch the Production History worksheet to Page Layout view, change the orientation to landscape, and then verify that the worksheet fits on a single page.
16. Save your workbook, preview and print the workbook, close the workbook, and then submit the finished workbook and printouts to your instructor.

Create | Case Problem 4

Create an Excel workbook to record service calls for a lawn service agency.

There are no Data Files needed for this Case Problem.

Green Lawns Green Lawns provides yard service and maintenance for homes in and around Mount Vernon, Ohio. Gary Taylor manages the accounts for Green Lawns and wants to use Excel to record weekly service calls made by the company. He asks you to create the workbook for him. Gary provides you the list of service calls made in the first week of August shown in Figure 1-39.

Figure 1-39

Customer	Address	Phone	Last Service	Hours	Base Fee	Hourly Rate
David Lane	391 Country Drive Mount Vernon, OH 43050	(740) 555-4439	8/2/2010	3	$35	$15.50
Robert Gomez	151 Apple Lane Mount Vernon, OH 43051	(740) 555-0988	8/2/2010	3.5	$35	$15.50
Sandra Lee	112 Main Street Mount Vernon, OH 43050	(740) 555-3773	8/3/2010	1.5	$20	$12.50
Gregory Sands	305 Country Drive Mount Vernon, OH 43050	(740) 555-4189	8/3/2010	4	$35	$17.50
Betty Oaks	205 Second Street Mount Vernon, OH 43049	(740) 555-0088	8/3/2010	1	$20	$12.50

Complete the following:

1. Open a blank workbook, and then save it as **Green Lawns** in the Tutorial.01\Case4 folder included with your Data Files.
2. Rename Sheet1 as **Documentation**, and then enter information documenting the workbook. Include the name of the company, your name, the current date, and a brief description of the purpose of the workbook. The layout and appearance of the worksheet is up to you.
3. In Sheet2, enter the service calls shown in Figure 1-39, and then enter appropriate formulas and functions to calculate the service charge for each customer. Green Lawns charges each customer a base fee plus a working fee that is equal to the hourly rate multiplied by the number of hours worked. Also, enter a formula to calculate the total charges for all customer calls. The layout and appearance of the page is up to you.
4. Rename Sheet2 as **Service Calls**, and then delete any unused sheets in the workbook.
5. Check the spelling in the workbook, correcting any spelling errors, and then proofread the workbook.
6. Save your workbook, preview the worksheets to ensure that each fits onto a single page, and then print the entire workbook. Close the workbook, and then submit the finished workbook and printouts to your instructor.

Research | Internet Assignments

Use the Internet to find and work with data related to the topics presented in this tutorial.

The purpose of the Internet Assignments is to challenge you to find information on the Internet that you can use to work effectively with this software. The actual assignments are updated and maintained on the Course Technology Web site. Log on to the Internet and use your Web browser to go to the Student Online Companion for New Perspectives Office 2007 at **www.course.com/np/office2007**. Then navigate to the Internet Assignments for this tutorial.

Assess | SAM Assessment and Training

If you have a SAM user profile, you may have access to hands-on instruction, practice, and assessment of the skills covered in this tutorial. Log in to your SAM account (**http://sam2007.course.com**) to launch any assigned training activities or exams that relate to the skills covered in this tutorial.

Review | Quick Check Answers

Session 1.1

1. chart sheets and worksheets
2. The active cell is surrounded by a thick border and its cell reference appears in the Name box.
3. C5
4. the Ctrl+Home keys
5. a combination of alphanumerical characters that form words and sentences (called a text string)
6. Enter the first line of text, press the Alt+Enter keys, and then type the second line of text.
7. Because it's a date; all dates are numbers formatted to appear in standard date formats.
8. Clearing a row removes only the contents of the row, deleting a row removes the contents and the row.

Session 1.2

1. Adjacent cell ranges contain a rectangular block of cells; nonadjacent cell ranges contain a collection of adjacent cell ranges.
2. A3:G5;J3:M5
3. =B4+B5+B6; =SUM(B4:B6)
4. Double-click the sheet tab, and then type a new name on the sheet tab.
5. Normal view shows the columns and rows of the worksheet. Page Layout view shows the layout of the worksheet as it appears on a page. Page Break Preview shows the page breaks within the worksheet. Formula view shows formulas rather than the values returned by the formulas.
6. to force a worksheet to print on one page
7. Press the Ctrl+` keys to switch to formula view.
8. as dotted lines

Ending Data Files

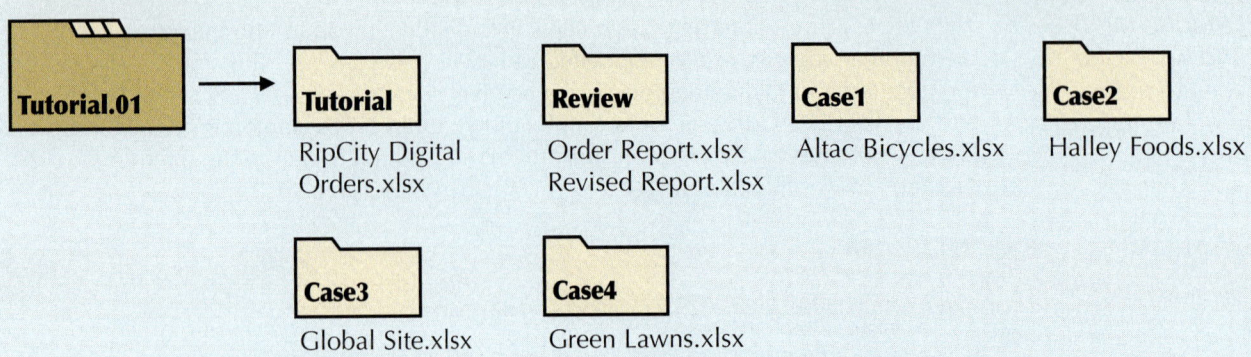

Excel EX 57
Tutorial 2

Objectives

Session 2.1
- Format text, numbers, and dates
- Change font colors and fill colors
- Merge a range into a single cell
- Apply a built-in cell style
- Select a different theme

Session 2.2
- Apply a built-in table style
- Add conditional formats to tables with highlight rules and data bars
- Hide worksheet rows
- Insert print titles, set print areas, and insert page breaks
- Enter headers and footers

Formatting a Workbook

Formatting a Financial Report

Case | ExerComp Exercise Equipment

ExerComp, based in Mason, Ohio, manufactures electronic and computer components for fitness machines and sporting goods. At the upcoming annual sales meeting, sales managers will present reports that detail the sales history of different ExerComp products. Sales manager Tom Uhen will report on the recent sales history of the X310 heart rate monitor.

Tom has already created a workbook and entered the sales figures for the past two years. He wants you to make that data more readable and informative. To do this, you will work with formatting tools to modify the appearance of the data in each cell, the cell itself, and the entire worksheet. Because much of Tom's data has been stored in tables, you will also use some special formatting tools designed for tables.

Starting Data Files

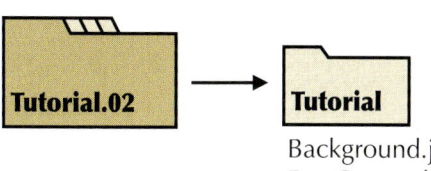

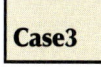

Tutorial.02 → Tutorial
Background.jpg
ExerComp.xlsx

Review
Paper.jpg
X410.xlsx

Case1
Frosti.xlsx

Case2
GrillRite.xlsx

Case3
Iowa.xlsx

Case4
Life.xlsx

Session 2.1

Formatting Workbooks

Tom already entered the data and some formulas in the worksheets, but the workbook is only a rough draft of what he wants to submit to the company. Tom's workbook has three worksheets. The Documentation sheet describes the workbook's purpose and content. The Yearly Sales sheet records the total sales of the X310 heart rate monitor for 2008 and 2009, including the total number of units sold per sales region (labeled R01 through R08) and the total revenue generated by those sales. The Monthly Sales sheet reports the number of X310 units sold in 2008 and 2009 by region and month as well as the corresponding increase in sales. You'll open the workbook and review its content.

To open the workbook:

1. Open the **ExerComp** workbook located in the **Tutorial.02\Tutorial** folder included with your Data Files, and then save the workbook as **ExerComp Sales Report** in the same folder.

2. In the Documentation sheet, enter your name in cell B4 and the current date in cell B5.

3. Review the contents in the three worksheets.

In its current form, the data is difficult to read and interpret. Tom wants you to format the workbook contents to improve its readability and visual appeal. **Formatting** is the process of changing a workbook's appearance by defining the fonts, styles, colors, and decorative features. Formatting changes only the appearance of data—it does not affect the data itself.

InSight	Formatting Workbooks Effectively

A well-formatted workbook can be easier to read, establish a sense of professionalism, help draw attention to the points you want to make, and provide continuity between the worksheets. Too little formatting can make the data hard to understand, whereas too much formatting can overwhelm the data. Proper formatting is a balance between these two extremes. Always remember, the goal of formatting is not simply to make a "pretty workbook," but also to accentuate important trends and relationships in the data.

One goal of formatting is to maintain a consistent look within a workbook. Excel, along with all the Office 2007 programs, uses themes to do this. A **theme** is a collection of formatting that specifies the fonts, colors, and graphical effects used throughout the workbook. The Office theme is the default, although you can choose others or create your own. You can also use fonts and colors that are not part of the current theme.

As you work, **Live Preview** shows the effects of formatting options on the workbook's appearance before you apply them. This lets you see and evaluate different formats as you develop your workbook.

Formatting Text

Tom suggests that you first modify the title in the Documentation sheet. The appearance of text is determined by its **typeface**, which is the specific design used for the characters, including letters, numbers, punctuation marks, and symbols. Typefaces are organized into fonts; a **font** is a set of characters that employ the same typeface. Some commonly used fonts are **Arial**, Times New Roman, and Courier. **Serif fonts**, such as Times New Roman, have extra decorative strokes at the end of each character. **Sans serif fonts**, such as Arial, do not include these decorative strokes. Other fonts are purely decorative, such as a font used for specialized logos.

Fonts are organized into theme and non-theme fonts. A **theme font** is associated with a particular theme and used for headings and body text in the workbook. The Office theme uses the theme font Cambria for headings and the theme font Calibri for body text. When you don't want to associate a font with a particular design, you use a **non-theme font**. Text formatted with a non-theme font retains its appearance no matter what theme is used with the workbook.

Every font can be further formatted with a **font style**, such as *italic*, **bold**, or ***bold italic***, and special effects, such as underline, ~~strikethrough~~, and color to text. Finally, you can set the **font size** to increase or decrease the size of the text. Font sizes are measured in **points** where one point is approximately 1/72 of an inch.

You'll format the company name displayed at the top of each worksheet to appear in large, bold letters using the default heading font from the Office theme. Tom wants the slogan "the Intelligent path to Fitness" displayed below the company name to appear in the heading font, but in smaller, italicized letters.

To format text in the Documentation sheet:

1. Click the **Documentation** sheet tab to make that worksheet active, and then click cell **A1** to make it active.

2. In the Font group on the Home tab, click the **Font arrow** to display a list of fonts available on your computer. The first two fonts are the theme fonts for headings and body text—Cambria and Calibri. See Figure 2-1.

Figure 2-1 Font list

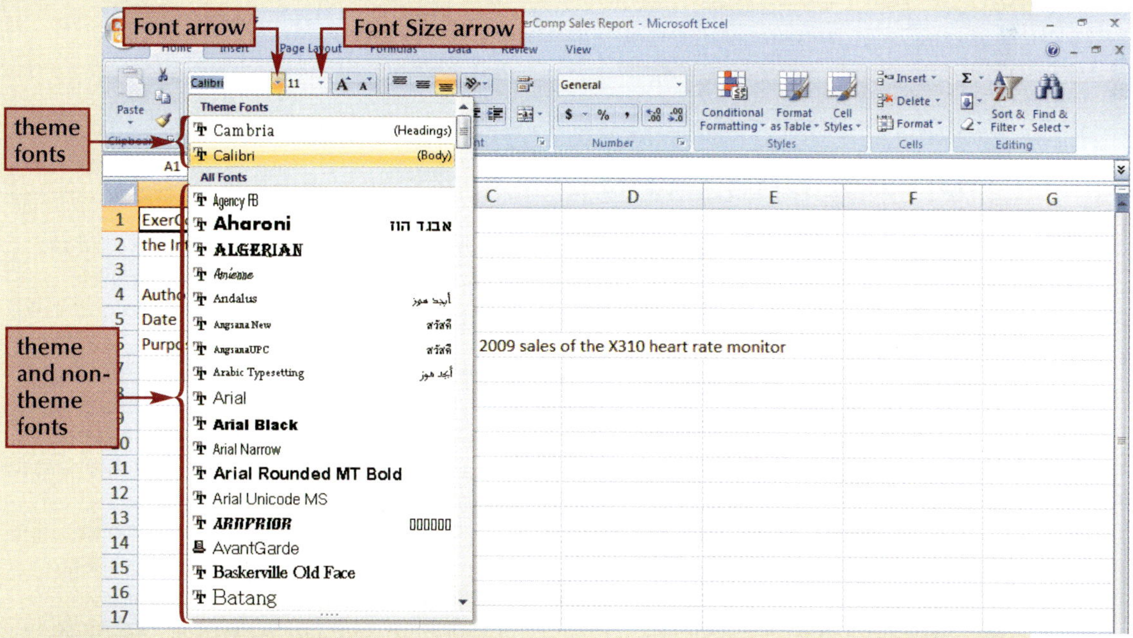

Trouble? If your screen displays more or less of the worksheet, your worksheet is at a different zoom level. If you want your worksheet zoomed to match the figures, click the Zoom In button on the status bar twice to increase the zoom magnification to 120%.

EX 60 Excel | Tutorial 2 Formatting a Workbook

> **Tip**
>
> You can change the font size one point at a time. In the Font group on the Home tab, click the Increase Font Size or Decrease Font Size button.

3. Click **Cambria**. The company name in cell A1 changes to the Cambria font, the default headings font in the current theme.

4. In the Font group, click the **Font Size arrow** to display a list of font sizes, and then click **26**. The company name changes to 26 points.

5. In the Font group, click the **Bold** button **B**. The company name is boldfaced. Next, you'll format the company slogan.

6. Click cell **A2** to make it active. The slogan text is selected.

7. In the Font group, click the **Font arrow**, and then click **Cambria**. The slogan text changes to the Cambria font.

8. In the Font group, click the **Font Size arrow**, and then click **10**. The slogan text changes to 10 points.

9. In the Font group, click the **Italic** button *I*. The slogan is italicized.

10. Select the range **A4:A6**, click the **Bold** button **B** in the Font group, and then click cell **A7**. The column labels are bolded. See Figure 2-2.

Figure 2-2   **Formatted worksheet text**

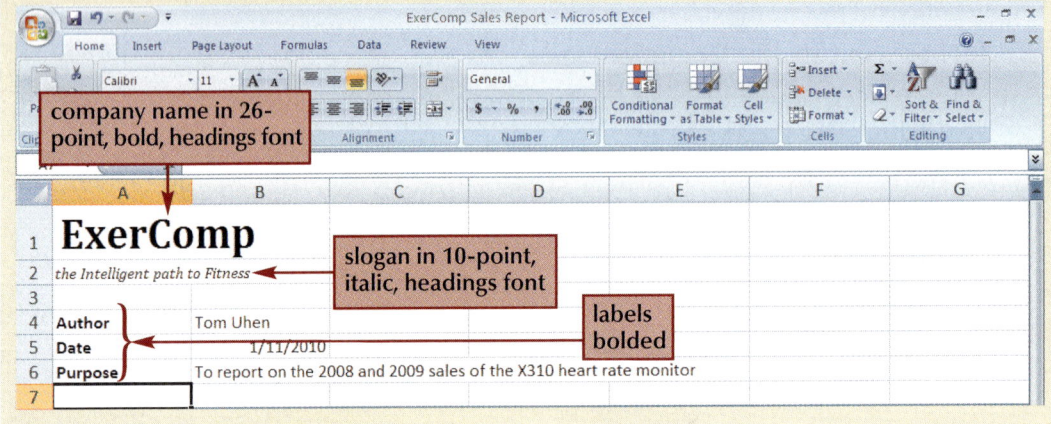

Working with Color

Color can transform a plain workbook filled with numbers and text into a powerful presentation that captures attention and adds visual emphasis to the points you want to make. By default, text is black and cells have no background fill color. You can add color to both the text and the cell background.

Colors are organized into two main categories. **Theme colors** are the 12 colors that belong to the workbook's theme. Four colors are designated for text and backgrounds, six colors are used for accents and highlights, and two colors are used for hyperlinks (followed and not followed links). These 12 colors are designed to work well together and to remain readable in all color combinations.

Ten **standard colors**—dark red, red, orange, yellow, light green, green, light blue, blue, dark blue, and purple—are always available regardless of the workbook's theme. You can also open an extended palette of 134 standard colors. In addition, you can create a **custom color** by specifying a mixture of red, blue, and green color values, making available 16.7 million custom colors—more colors than the human eye can distinguish. Some dialog boxes have an **automatic color** option that uses your Windows default text and background color values, usually black text on a white background.

Applying Font Color and Fill Color

Tom wants the labels in the Documentation sheet to stand out. You will change the ExerComp title and slogan to blue, and then you'll format the other labels in the worksheet with a blue background fill and a white font color.

> **Tip**
> You can add a fill color to a sheet tab. In the Cells group on the Home tab, click the Format button, point to Tab Color, and then click a color.

To change the title and slogan font color and fill color:

1. Select the range **A1:A2**.

2. In the Font group on the Home tab, click the **Font Color button arrow** to display the available theme and standard colors. There are 10 theme colors (the two colors for hyperlinked text are not shown), and each theme color has five variations, or **accents**, in which a different tint or shading is applied to the theme color.

3. Point to the **Blue** color (the eighth color) in the Standard Colors section. The color name appears in a ScreenTip. See Figure 2-3.

Font colors | Figure 2-3

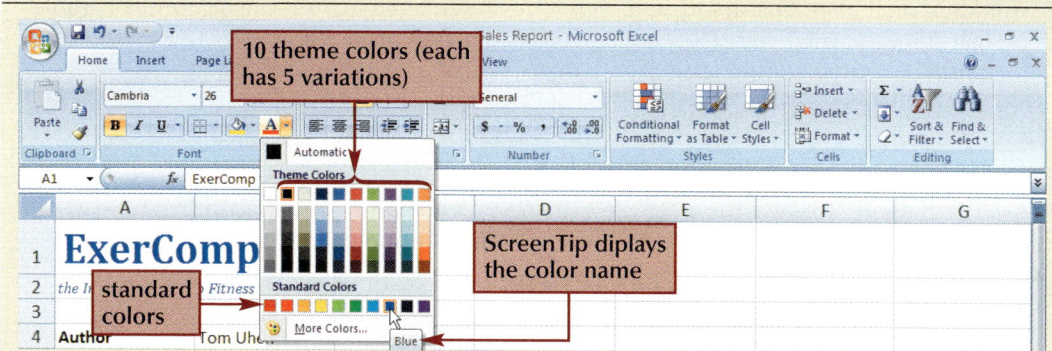

4. Click the **Blue** color. The company name and slogan change to blue.

5. Select the range **A4:A6**. You'll change both the fill and the font colors of these cells.

6. In the Font group, click the **Fill Color button arrow**, and then click the **Blue** color in the Standard Colors section. The cell backgrounds change to blue.

7. In the Font group, click the **Font Color button arrow**, and then click the **white** color (ScreenTip is White, Background1) in the Theme Colors section. The font color changes to white.

8. Click cell **A7** to deselect the range. The white text on a blue background is visible. See Figure 2-4.

Figure 2-4 | Font colors and fill colors applied

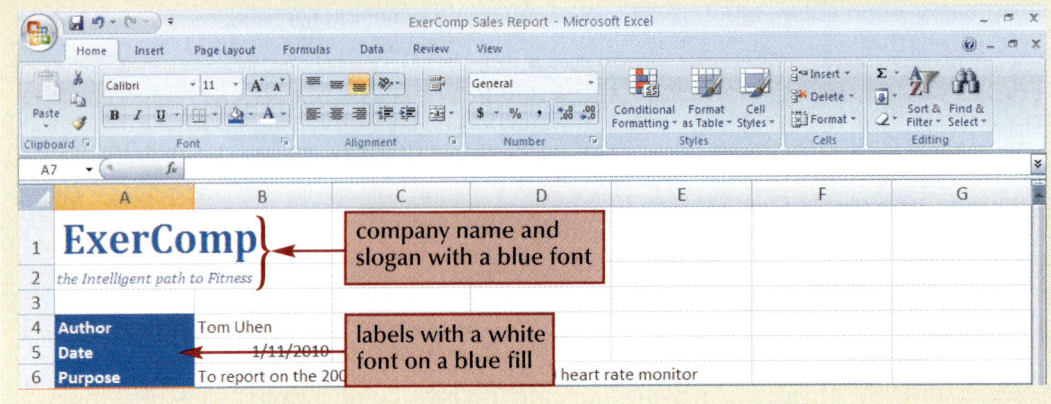

Formatting Text Selections

The ExerComp logo usually appears in two colors—"Exer" in blue and "Comp" in red. Tom asks you to make this change to the text in cell A1. You'll need to format part of the cell content one way and the rest a different way. To do this, you first select the text you want to format in editing mode, and then apply the formatting to the selection. The **Mini toolbar** appears when you select text and contains buttons for commonly used text formats. You'll use the Mini toolbar to format "Comp" in a red font.

To format the "Comp" text selection:

▶ 1. Double-click cell **A1** to select the cell and go into editing mode, and then select **Comp**. A transparent version of the Mini toolbar appears.

▶ 2. Click the **Font Color button arrow** [A▾] on the Mini toolbar, and then click the **Red** color (the second color) in the Standard Colors section. The text color changes and the Mini toolbar remains open for additional formatting. See Figure 2-5.

Figure 2-5 | Mini toolbar used to format text

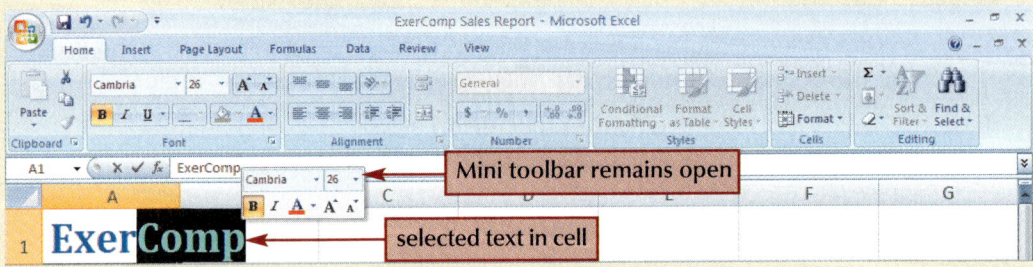

Trouble? If the Mini toolbar disappears before you can click the Font Color button arrow, you probably moved the pointer away from the Mini toolbar, pressed a key, or pressed a mouse button. Right-click the selected text to redisplay the Mini toolbar above a shortcut menu, immediately move your pointer to the Mini toolbar, and then repeat Step 2.

▶ 3. Click cell **A7** to deselect the cell. The text "ExerComp" in cell A1 is blue and red.

Setting a Background Image

You can use a picture or image as the background for all the cells in a worksheet. An image can give the worksheet a textured appearance, like that of granite, wood, or fibered paper. The image is inserted until it fills the entire worksheet. The background image does not affect any cell's format or content. Any cells with a background color display the color on top, hiding that portion of the image. Background images do not print.

Tom has an image that resembles fibered paper that you will use as the background for the Documentation sheet.

To add a background image to the Documentation sheet:

1. Click the **Page Layout** tab on the Ribbon. The page layout options appear on the Ribbon.

2. In the Page Setup group, click the **Background** button. The Sheet Background dialog box opens.

3. Navigate to the **Tutorial.02\Tutorial** folder included with your Data Files, click the **Background.jpg** image file, and then click the **Insert** button. The image file is added to the background of the Documentation sheet.

   Next, you'll change the fill color of the cells with the author's name, the date, and the workbook's purpose to white to highlight them in the worksheet.

4. Select the range **B4:B6**, and then click the **Home** tab on the Ribbon.

5. In the Font group, click the **Fill Color button arrow**, and then click the **white** color in the Theme Colors section.

6. Increase the width of column B to **55** characters, and then click cell **A7** to deselect the range. See Figure 2-6.

Figure 2-6 Background image added to the Documentation sheet

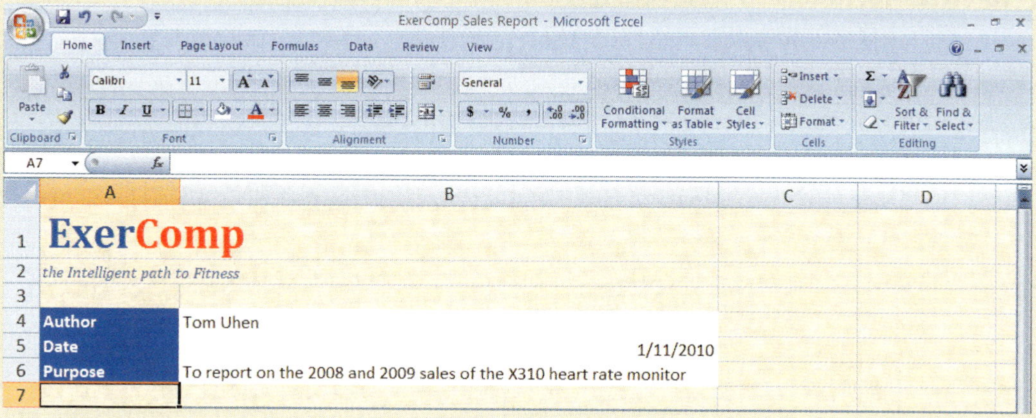

InSight | Enhancing Workbooks with Color

Color, used wisely, can enhance any workbook. Too much color can be just as bad as "not enough" color. An overuse of color can cause readers' eyes to wander around the workbook without focusing on a central point. As you format a workbook, keep in mind the following tips:
- Use colors from the same theme within a workbook to maintain a consistent look and feel across the worksheets. If the built-in themes do not fit your needs, you can create a custom theme.
- Use colors to differentiate types of cell content and to direct users where to enter data. For example, format a worksheet so formula results appear in cells without a fill color and users enter data in cells with a light gray fill color.
- Avoid garish color combinations that can annoy the reader and be difficult to read.
- Print on color and black-and-white printers to ensure that the output is readable in both versions.
- Understand your printer's limitations and features. Colors that look good on your monitor might not print well.
- Be sensitive to your audience. About 8% of all men and 0.5% of all women have some type of color blindness and might not be able to see the text with certain color combinations. Red-green color blindness is the most common color blindness, so avoid using red text on a green background or green text on a red background.

Formatting Data

The Yearly Sales worksheet contains the annual sales figures from 2008 and 2009 for the X310 heart rate monitor. The top of the worksheet displays the number of units sold in each sales region per year, and the bottom displays the sales revenue generated by region per year. You'll add formulas to calculate the total sales for each year as well as the difference and percentage difference in sales from one year to another.

To enter formulas in the Yearly Sales worksheet:

1. Click the **Yearly Sales** sheet tab. The Yearly Sales worksheet becomes active.

2. In cells B15 and B26, enter **Total**; in cells E6 and E17, enter **Increase**; in cells F6 and F17, enter **% Increase**; and then select cell **C15**.

3. In the Editing group on the Home tab, click the **Sum** button Σ, and then press the **Enter** key. The formula =SUM(C7:C14) is entered in the cell, adding the numbers in the range C7:C14.

4. Select cell **C15**, and then, in the Clipboard group, click the **Copy** button. The formula is copied to the Clipboard.

   Next, you'll paste the formula into a nonadjacent range. Remember, to select a nonadjacent range, select the first cell or range, press and hold the Ctrl key as you select other cells or ranges, and then release the Ctrl key.

5. Select the range **D15;C26:D26**, and then, in the Clipboard group, click the **Paste** button. The formula is pasted into cells D15, C26, and D26, adding the values in each column.

6. Select cell **E7**, and then enter the formula **=D7–C7** to calculate the increase in sales from 2008 to 2009 for region R01.

7. Select cell **F7**, and then enter the formula **=E7/C7** to calculate the percentage increase from 2008 to 2009.

8. Select the range **E7:F7**, and then, in the Clipboard group, click the **Copy** button.

9. Select the range **E8:F15;E18:F26**, and then, in the Clipboard group, click the **Paste** button. The formulas are copied into the selected cells.

10. Click cell **A6** to deselect the range. See Figure 2-7.

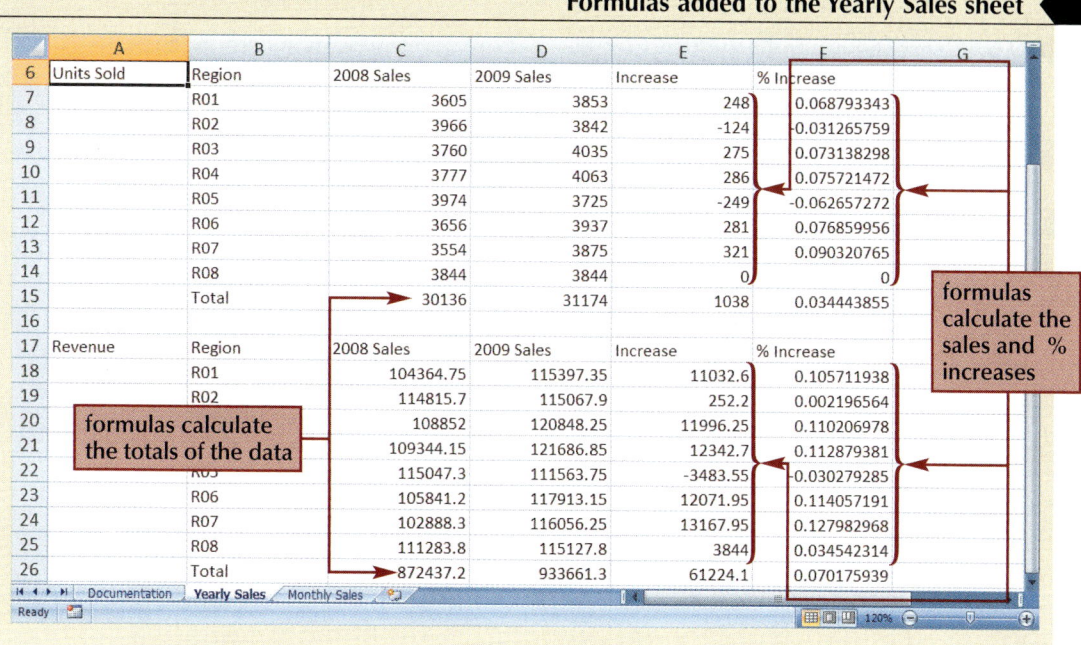

Figure 2-7 Formulas added to the Yearly Sales sheet

The sales figures are hard to read, making them difficult to interpret and understand. By default, values appear in the **General number format**, which, for the most part, displays numbers exactly as you enter them. Calculated values show as many digits after the decimal point as will fit in the cell and the last displayed digit is rounded, as you can see with the percentage increase values in column F. Only the displayed number is rounded; the actual value stored in the cell is not. Calculated values too large to fit into the cell are displayed in scientific notation.

Formatting Numbers

The Number group on the Home tab has buttons for formatting the appearance of numbers. You can select a number format, apply accounting or other currency formats, change a number to a percentage, insert a comma as a thousands separator, and increase or decrease the number of digits displayed to the right of the decimal point.

You'll add a thousands separator to the sales values to make them easier to read and remove the digits shown to the right of the decimal point because the data values for units sold will always be whole numbers. You'll format the percentage difference values as percentages with two decimal places. Tom also wants you to format the revenue values in the range C18:E26 as currency by adding dollar signs. Because applying dollar signs to large columns of numbers often makes them unreadable, standard accounting practice displays currency symbols only in the first and last rows of the range.

To format the units sold, percentage differences, and revenue numbers:

1. Select the range **C7:E15;C18:E26**, and then, in the Number group on the Home tab, click the **Comma Style** button. The numbers include a thousands separator, but still display two digits to the right of the decimal point.

▶ 2. Select the range **C7:E15**, and then, in the Number group, click the **Decrease Decimal** button twice. The two extra digits are removed.

▶ 3. Select the range **F7:F15;F18:F26**, and then, in the Number group, click the **Percent Style** button. The values now include the percentage symbol.

▶ 4. In the Number group, click the **Increase Decimal** button twice. Two digits are added to the right of the decimal point.

▶ 5. Select the range **C18:E18;C26:E26**, and then, in the Number group, click the **Accounting Number Format** button. The first row and the Total row display the currency symbol.

▶ 6. Click cell **A6** to deselect the range. See Figure 2-8.

Figure 2-8   Worksheet after formatting numbers

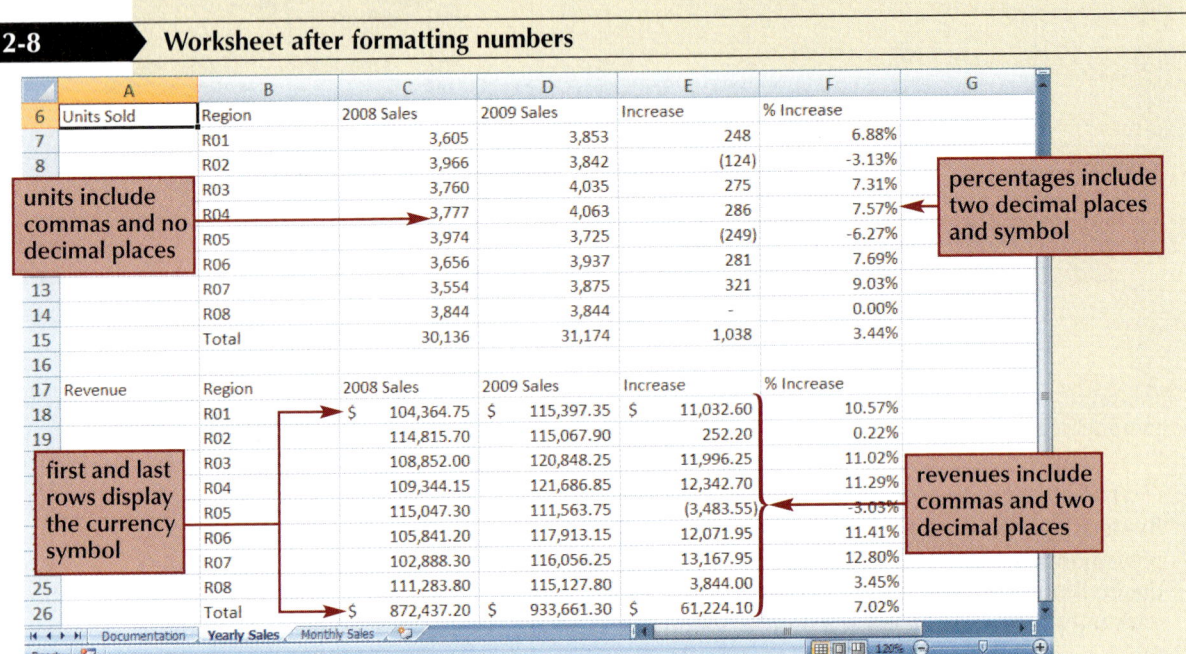

Tom examines this reformatted data and notes that the company sold 1,038 more units in 2009 than in 2008—an increase of 3.44%, which increased revenue by $61,224.10, or 7.02%. This was not uniform across all sales regions. Total sales and revenue for Region R05, for example, decreased from 2008 to 2009.

Formatting Dates and Times

Although dates and times in Excel appear as text, they are actually numbers that measure the interval between the specified date and time and January 1, 1900 at 12:00 a.m. You can then calculate date and time intervals, and you can format a date or time value. For example, you can apply a date format that displays the day of the week for any date value stored in your worksheet.

The date in the Documentation sheet is an abbreviated format, *mm/dd/yyyy*. Tom wants you to use an extended format that includes the day of the week, the full month name, the day, and the year. This Long Date format is a built-in date format.

To format the date in the Long Date format:

1. Click the **Documentation** sheet tab to make that worksheet active, and then select cell **B5**.
2. In the Number group on the Home tab, click the **Number Format arrow** to open a list of built-in number formats.
3. Click **Long Date**. The date format changes to show the weekday name, month name, day, and year. See Figure 2-9.

Figure 2-9 Formatted date

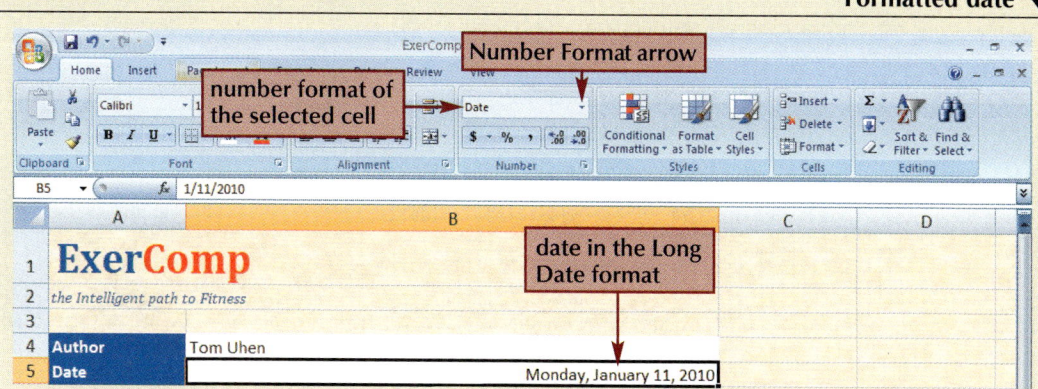

Formatting Dates for International Audiences | InSight

When your workbooks are intended for international audiences, be sure to use a date format that will be clear to everyone, such as November 10, 2010 or 10 November 2010. Many countries use a day/month/year format for dates rather than the month/day/year format commonly used in the United States. For example, the date 10/11/2010 is read as October 11, 2010 by people in the United States but as November 10, 2010 by people in most other countries.

Formatting Worksheet Cells

The date in the Documentation worksheet is formatted to display as text. Because all dates are actually numbers, they are right-aligned in the cell by default, regardless of their date format. Tom asks you to left-align the date to make it easier to read.

Aligning Cell Content

In addition to left and right alignments, you can change the vertical and horizontal alignments of cell content to make a worksheet more readable. You can also increase or decrease the space between the cell content and the cell border. In general, you should center column titles, left-align text, and right-align numbers to keep their decimal places lined up within the column. Figure 2-10 describes the alignment buttons located in the Alignment group on the Home tab.

Figure 2-10 — Alignment buttons

Button	Description
	Aligns the cell content with the cell's top edge
	Vertically centers the cell content within the cell
	Aligns the cell content with the cell's bottom edge
	Aligns the cell content with the cell's left edge
	Horizontally centers the cell content within the cell
	Aligns the cell content with the cell's right edge
	Decreases the size of the indentation used in the cell
	Increases the size of the indentation used in the cell
	Rotates the cell content to an angle within the cell
	Forces the cell text to wrap within the cell borders
	Merges the selected cells into a single cell

You'll left-align the date in the Documentation worksheet and center the column titles in the Yearly Sales worksheet.

To left-align the date and center the column titles:

1. If necessary, select cell **B5**.

2. In the Alignment group on the Home tab, click the **Align Text Left** button. The date shifts to the left edge of the cell.

3. Click the **Yearly Sales** sheet tab to make that worksheet active, and then select the range **C6:F6;C17:F17**.

4. In the Alignment group, click the **Center** button. The column titles in columns C, D, E, and F are centered.

Indenting Cell Content

Sometimes, you want a cell's content moved a few spaces from the cell edge. This is particularly useful for entries that are considered subsections of a worksheet. For example, Tom recorded sales for eight regions and then added the totals. Each region can be considered a subsection, and Tom thinks it would look better if the region labels were indented a few spaces. You increase the indentation by roughly one character each time you click the Increase Indent button in the Alignment group on the Home tab. To decrease or remove an indentation, click the Decrease Indent button. You'll increase the indent for the region labels.

To indent the region labels:

1. Select the range **B7:B14;B18:B25**.

2. In the Alignment group on the Home tab, click the **Increase Indent** button. Each region label indents one space.

3. Click cell **A6** to deselect the range. See Figure 2-11.

Figure 2-11 Centered and indented text

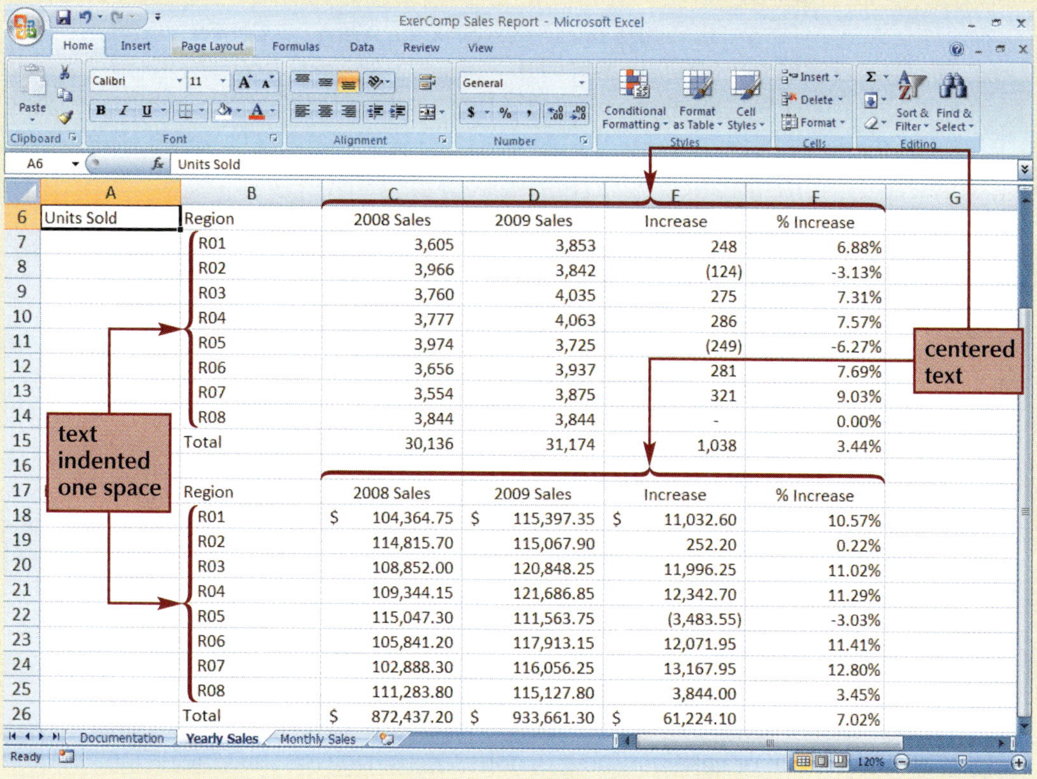

	A	B	C	D	E	F
6	Units Sold	Region	2008 Sales	2009 Sales	Increase	% Increase
7		R01	3,605	3,853	248	6.88%
8		R02	3,966	3,842	(124)	-3.13%
9		R03	3,760	4,035	275	7.31%
10		R04	3,777	4,063	286	7.57%
11		R05	3,974	3,725	(249)	-6.27%
12		R06	3,656	3,937	281	7.69%
13		R07	3,554	3,875	321	9.03%
14		R08	3,844	3,844	-	0.00%
15		Total	30,136	31,174	1,038	3.44%
16						
17		Region	2008 Sales	2009 Sales	Increase	% Increase
18		R01	$ 104,364.75	$ 115,397.35	$ 11,032.60	10.57%
19		R02	114,815.70	115,067.90	252.20	0.22%
20		R03	108,852.00	120,848.25	11,996.25	11.02%
21		R04	109,344.15	121,686.85	12,342.70	11.29%
22		R05	115,047.30	111,563.75	(3,483.55)	-3.03%
23		R06	105,841.20	117,913.15	12,071.95	11.41%
24		R07	102,888.30	116,056.25	13,167.95	12.80%
25		R08	111,283.80	115,127.80	3,844.00	3.45%
26		Total	$ 872,437.20	$ 933,661.30	$ 61,224.10	7.02%

(text indented one space; centered text)

You can make all text visible within a cell rather than extending the text into an adjacent empty cell or truncating it. Just click the Wrap Text button in the Alignment group on the Home tab. The row height increases as needed to wrap all the text within the cell.

Merging Cells

In the Yearly Sales worksheet, Tom wants the title "X310 Yearly Sales Analysis" in cell A4 centered over columns A through F. So far, you've aligned text only *within* a cell. One way to align text over several columns or rows is to **merge**, or combine, several cells into one cell. When you merge cells, only the content from the upper-left cell in the range is retained and the upper-left cell becomes the merged cell reference.

After you merge a range into a single cell, you can realign its content. The Merge button in the Alignment group on the Home tab includes a variety of merge options. Merge & Center merges the range into one cell and horizontally centers the content. Merge Across merges each of the rows in the selected range across the columns in the range. Merge Cells merges the range into a single cell, but does not horizontally center the cell content. Unmerge Cells reverses a merge, returning the merged cell back into a range of individual cells.

Tom wants you to merge and center the title in cell A4 across the range A4:F4.

To merge and center the range with the title:

1. Select the range **A4:F4**.

2. In the Alignment group on the Home tab, click the **Merge & Center** button. The range A4:F4 merges into one cell with a cell reference of A4 and the text is centered within the cell. See Figure 2-12.

Figure 2-12 | Merged range with centered text

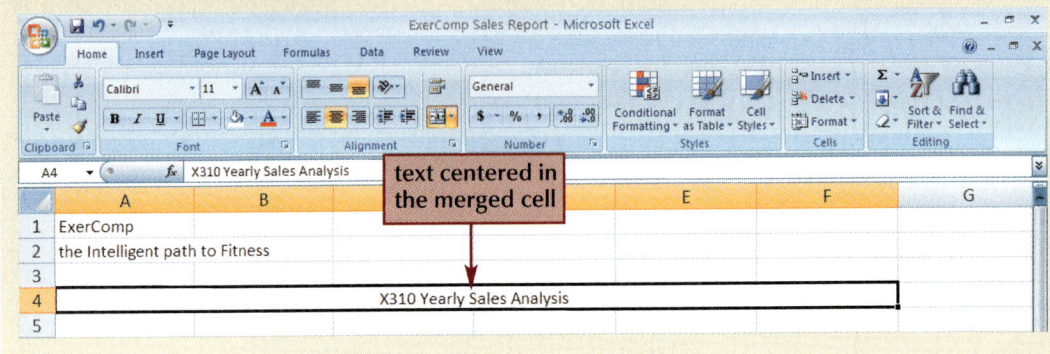

Rotating Cell Content

Text and numbers are oriented within a cell horizontally from left to right. To save space or to provide visual interest to a worksheet, you can rotate the cell contents so that they appear at any angle or orientation. These options are available on the Orientation button in the Alignment group on the Home tab.

Tom wants you to merge and center the ranges with the labels, and then rotate the labels in the merged cells A6 and A17 so they look better and take up less room.

To rotate the labels:

1. Select the range **A6:A15**.

2. In the Alignment group on the Home tab, click the **Merge & Center** button. The text from cell A6 is centered in the merged cell.

3. In the Alignment group, click the **Orientation** button, and then click **Rotate Text Up**. The cell text rotates 90 degrees counterclockwise.

4. In the Alignment group, click the **Middle Align** button. The rotated text vertically aligns within the merged cell.

5. Select the range **A17:A26**, and then repeat Steps 2 through 4 to merge and center, rotate, and align the text.

6. Reduce the width of column A to **5** characters. See Figure 2-13.

Figure 2-13 Merged and rotated cell text

	A	B	C	D	E	F
6		Region	2008 Sales	2009 Sales	Increase	% Increase
7		R01	3,605	3,853	248	6.88%
8		R02	3,966	3,842	(124)	-3.13%
9	Units Sold	R03	3,760	4,035	275	7.31%
10		R04	3,777	4,063	286	7.57%
11		R05	3,974	3,725	(249)	-6.27%
12		R06	3,656	3,937	281	7.69%
13		R07	3,554	3,875	321	9.03%
14		R08	3,844	3,844	-	0.00%
15		Total	30,136	31,174	1,038	3.44%
16						
17		Region	2008 Sales	2009 Sales	Increase	% Increase
18		R01	$ 104,364.75	$ 115,397.35	$ 11,032.60	10.57%
19		R02	114,815.70	115,067.90	252.20	0.22%
20		R03	108,852.00	120,848.25	11,996.25	11.02%
21	Revenue	R04	109,344.15	121,686.85	12,342.70	11.29%
22		R05	115,047.30	111,563.75	(3,483.55)	-3.03%
23		R06	105,841.20	117,913.15	12,071.95	11.41%
24		R07	102,888.30	116,056.25	13,167.95	12.80%
25		R08	111,283.80	115,127.80	3,844.00	3.45%
26		Total	$ 872,437.20	$ 933,661.30	$ 61,224.10	7.02%

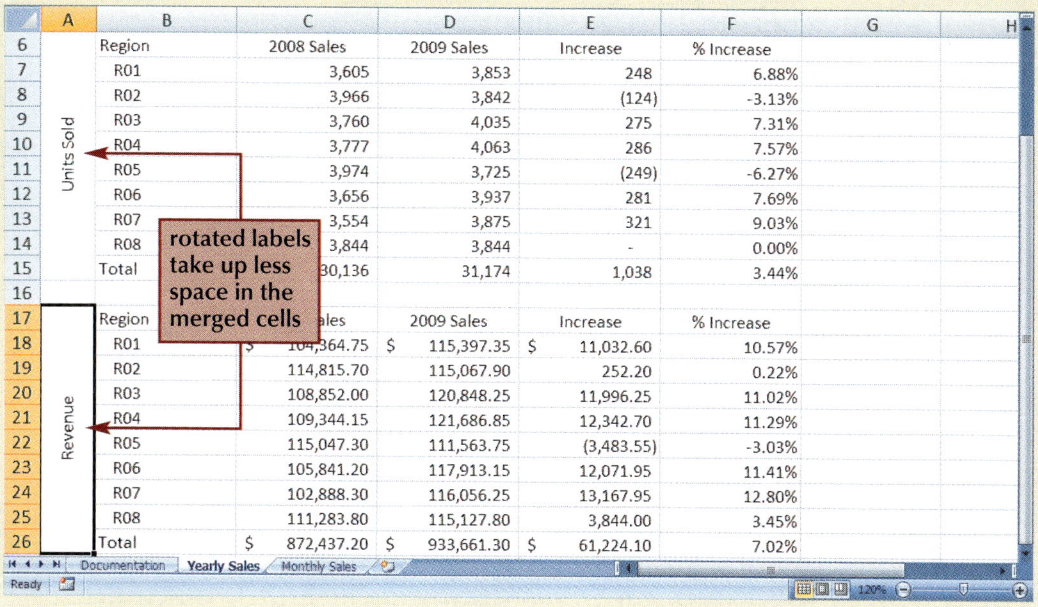

rotated labels take up less space in the merged cells

Adding Cell Borders

When a worksheet is printed, the gridlines that surround the cells are not printed by default. Sometimes you will want to include such lines to enhance the readability of the rows and columns of data. One way to do this is by adding a line, or **border**, around a cell or range. You can add borders to the left, top, right, or bottom of a cell or range, around an entire cell, or around the outside edges of a range. You can also specify the thickness of and the number of lines in the border. To create a border, use the Border button located in the Font group on the Home tab.

Tom wants you to add borders to the column titles and Total rows. Standard accounting practice is to add a single top border and a double bottom border to the Total row to clearly identify a summary row from financial data.

To add cell borders to the column labels and Total rows:

▶ 1. Select the range **B6:F6;B17:F17**. You'll add a bottom border to these column labels.

▶ 2. In the Font group on the Home tab, click the **Border button arrow**, and then click **Bottom Border**. A bottom border is added to the selected cells.

▶ 3. Select the range **B15:F15;B26:F26**. You'll add top and bottom borders to these Total rows.

▶ 4. In the Font group, click the **Border button arrow**, and then click **Top and Double Bottom Border**. The Total rows both have a single top border and a double bottom border, which is standard accounting practice.

▶ 5. Click cell **A5** to deselect the range. See Figure 2-14.

Figure 2-14 — Borders added to cells

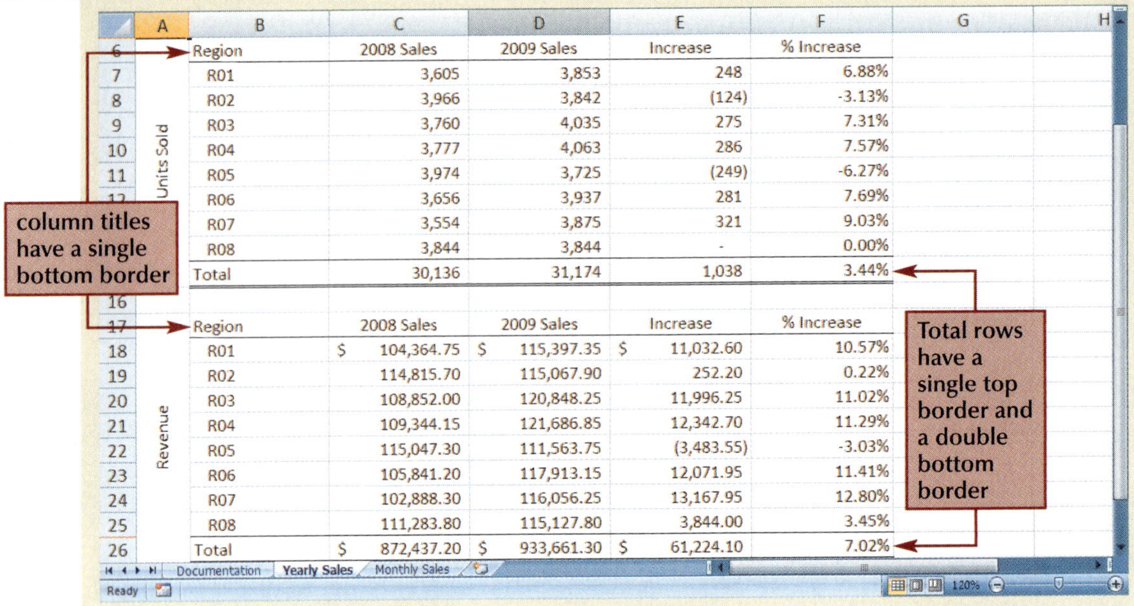

	A	B	C	D	E	F	G
6		Region	2008 Sales	2009 Sales	Increase	% Increase	
7	Units Sold	R01	3,605	3,853	248	6.88%	
8		R02	3,966	3,842	(124)	-3.13%	
9		R03	3,760	4,035	275	7.31%	
10		R04	3,777	4,063	286	7.57%	
11		R05	3,974	3,725	(249)	-6.27%	
12		R06	3,656	3,937	281	7.69%	
13		R07	3,554	3,875	321	9.03%	
14		R08	3,844	3,844	-	0.00%	
15		Total	30,136	31,174	1,038	3.44%	
16							
17		Region	2008 Sales	2009 Sales	Increase	% Increase	
18	Revenue	R01	$ 104,364.75	$ 115,397.35	$ 11,032.60	10.57%	
19		R02	114,815.70	115,067.90	252.20	0.22%	
20		R03	108,852.00	120,848.25	11,996.25	11.02%	
21		R04	109,344.15	121,686.85	12,342.70	11.29%	
22		R05	115,047.30	111,563.75	(3,483.55)	-3.03%	
23		R06	105,841.20	117,913.15	12,071.95	11.41%	
24		R07	102,888.30	116,056.25	13,167.95	12.80%	
25		R08	111,283.80	115,127.80	3,844.00	3.45%	
26		Total	$ 872,437.20	$ 933,661.30	$ 61,224.10	7.02%	

- column titles have a single bottom border
- Total rows have a single top border and a double bottom border

Working with the Format Cells Dialog Box

The buttons on the Home tab provide quick access to the most common formatting choices. For more options, you can use the Format Cells dialog box. For example, the numbers in cells E8 and E11 are displayed in parentheses to indicate that they are negative. Although parentheses are common in accounting to indicate negative currency values, Tom wants you to reformat the units sold numbers to display negative numbers with a minus symbol. You can do this in the Format Cells dialog box.

> **Tip**
> You can also open the Format Cells dialog box by right-clicking a cell or selected range, and then clicking Format Cells on the shortcut menu.

To open the Format Cells dialog box:

1. Select the range **C7:E15**.
2. In the Number group on the Home tab, click the **Dialog Box Launcher**. The Format Cells dialog box opens with the Number tab active.

The Format Cells dialog box has six tabs, each focusing on a different set of formatting options. You can apply the formats in this dialog box to selected worksheet cells. The six tabs are as follows:

- **Number**: Provides options for formatting the appearance of numbers, including dates and numbers treated as text (for example, telephone or Social Security numbers)
- **Alignment**: Provides options for how data is aligned within a cell
- **Font**: Provides options for selecting font types, sizes, styles, and other formatting attributes such as underlining and font colors
- **Border**: Provides options for adding cell borders
- **Fill**: Provides options for creating and applying background colors and patterns to cells
- **Protection**: Provides options for locking or hiding cells to prevent other users from modifying their contents

Although you've applied many of these formats from the Home tab, the Format Cells dialog box presents them in a different way and provides more options. You'll use the Number tab to change the number format for the selected cells. Remember, modifying the number format does not affect the value stored in the workbook.

To set the format for negative numbers of units:

1. In the Category list on the left side of the Format Cells dialog box, click **Number**.
2. Verify that **0** (zero) appears in the Decimal places box.
3. Verify that the **Use 1000 Separator (,)** check box contains a check mark.
4. In the Negative numbers list, verify that **−1,234** (the first option) is selected. See Figure 2-15.

Figure 2-15 Number tab in the Format Cells dialog box

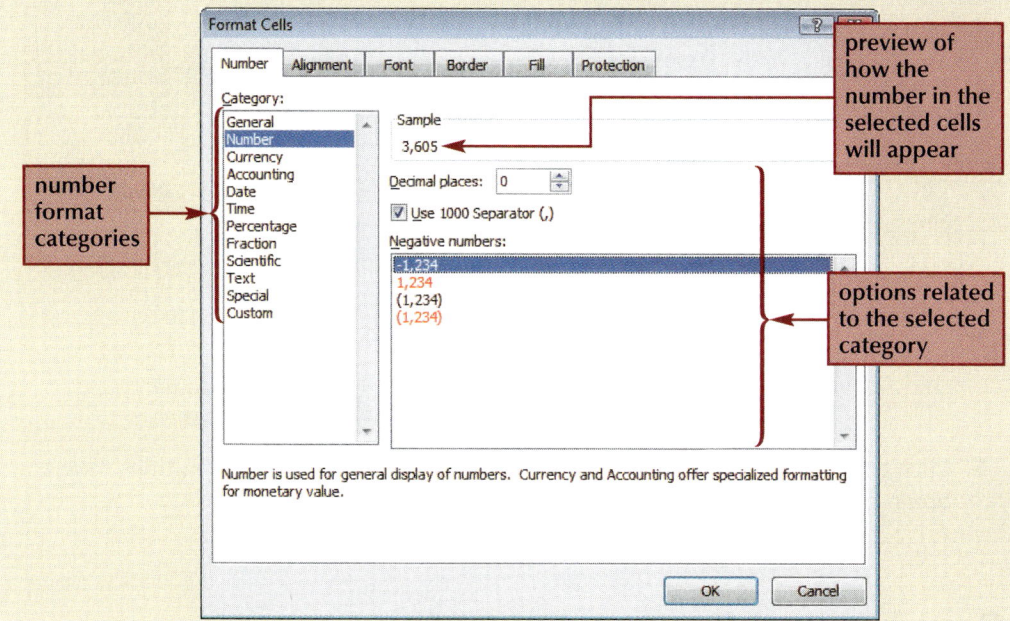

5. Click the **OK** button. The Format Cells dialog box closes and the negative numbers in the range C7:E15 appear with minus symbols, a comma as the thousands separator, and no decimal places.

Tom wants the bottom border color used for the column titles changed from black to green. You'll use the Border tab in the Format Cells dialog box to make this change.

To set the border color for the column title cells:

1. Select the range **B6:F6;B17:F17**.
2. In the Font group on the Home tab, click the **Borders button arrow**, and then click **More Borders**. The Format Cells dialog box opens with the Border tab active.

In the Border tab, you can select a line style ranging from thick to thin, choose double to dotted lines, and place these lines anywhere around the cells in the selected range. Right now, you only want to set the border line color.

▶ 3. In the Line group, click the **Color** arrow to display the color palette, and then click **Green** (the sixth color) in the Standard Colors section.

▶ 4. Click the bottom border of the border preview. A green bottom border is added to the preview. See Figure 2-16.

Figure 2-16   **Border tab in the Format Cells dialog box**

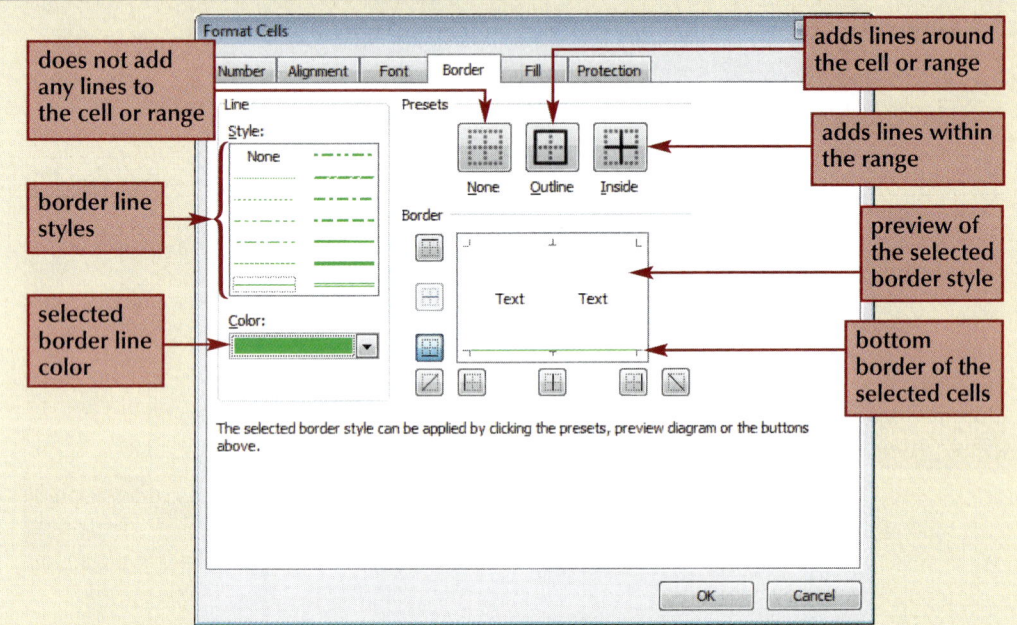

▶ 5. Click the **OK** button. The dialog box closes and the cells with column titles have a green bottom border.

Copying and Pasting Formats

You have not yet formatted the titles in cells A1 and A2 of the Yearly Sales worksheet to match the Documentation sheet. You could repeat the same steps to format these cells, but a quicker method is to copy the formats from the Documentation worksheet into the Yearly Sales worksheet.

Copying Formats with the Format Painter

The **Format Painter** copies the formatting from one cell or range to another cell or range, without duplicating any of the data. Using the Format Painter is a fast and efficient way of maintaining a consistent look and feel throughout a workbook.

You'll use the Format Painter to copy the cell formats from the range A1:A2 in the Documentation sheet into the same range in the Yearly Sales worksheet.

To copy and paste the format:

1. Click the **Documentation** sheet tab to make that worksheet active, and then select the range **A1:A2**.

2. In the Clipboard group on the Home tab, click the **Format Painter** button. The formats from the selected cells are copied to the Clipboard.

3. Click the **Yearly Sales** sheet tab to make that worksheet active, and then select the range **A1:A2**. The formatting from the Documentation sheet is removed from the Clipboard and applied to the selected cells except for the red color you applied to "Comp." Format Painter does not copy formatting applied to text selections.

4. Double-click cell **A1** to go into editing mode, and then select **Comp** in the text string.

5. Click the **Font Color button arrow** on the Mini toolbar, and then click **Red** (the second color) in the Standard Colors section. The selected text changes to red.

6. Press the **Enter** key to exit editing mode.

7. Select the range **A1:A2** in the Yearly Sales worksheet, and then repeat Steps 2 through 6 to copy the formatting to the range A1:A2 in the Monthly Sales worksheet.

> **Tip**
>
> To paste a format to multiple selections, double-click the Format Painter button, select each cell or range to format, and then click the Format Painter button again to turn it off.

Copying Formats with the Paste Options Button

The Format Painter copies and pastes only formatting. When you copy and paste, you can also use the Paste Options button, which lets you choose whether to paste the formatting from a copied range along with its contents. As shown in Figure 2-17, each time you paste, the Paste Options button appears in the lower-right corner of the pasted cell or range. When you click the Paste Options button, you can choose from a list of pasting options, such as pasting only the values or only the formatting.

Figure 2-17 Using the Paste Options button

	A	B	C	D	E	F	G	H	I	J
1										
2			Model	R01	R02	R03	Total			
3		2008 Sales	X310	3,605	3,996	3,760	11,361			
4			X410	1,875	1,924	2,112	5,911			
5			X510	850	912	750	2,512			
6			Total	6,330	6,832	6,622	19,784			
7										
8										
9		2009 Sales	Model	R01	R02	R03	Total			
10			X310	3,853	3,842	4,035	11,730			
11			X410	2,112	1,801	2,304	6,217			
12			X510	1025	1,115	912	3,052			
13			Total	6,990	6,758	7,251	20,999			
14										
15										

pastes only the formats

- Keep Source Formatting
- Use Destination Theme
- Match Destination Formatting
- Values Only
- Values and Number Formatting
- Values and Source Formatting
- Keep Source Column Widths
- ● Formatting Only
- Link Cells

Paste Options button

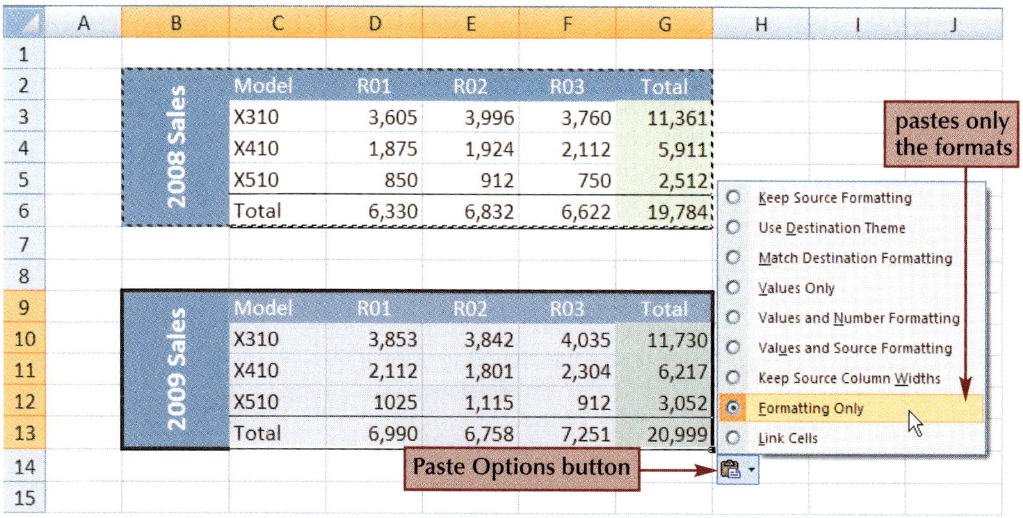

Copying Formats with Paste Special

The Paste Special command is another way to control what you paste from the Clipboard. To use Paste Special, select and copy a range, select the range where you want to paste the Clipboard contents, click the Paste button arrow in the Clipboard group on the Home tab, and then click Paste Special to open the dialog box shown in Figure 2-18. From the Paste Special dialog box, you can specify exactly what you want to paste.

Figure 2-18   Paste Special dialog box

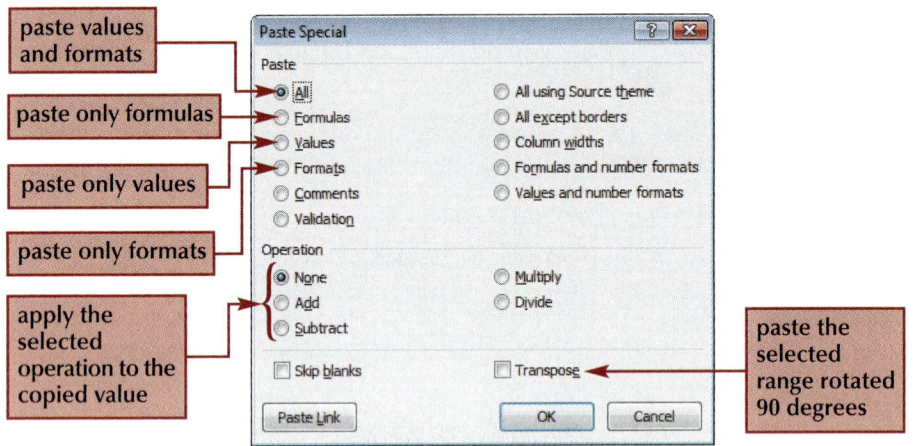

You can use the Transpose option in the Paste Special dialog box to paste a range of numbers cut from a row into a column. You can also use Paste Special to quickly modify all the values in a range. For example, you can copy the value 5 from a cell, select the range, open the Paste Special dialog box, click the Add option button in the Operation group, and then click the OK button. Excel adds 5 to every value in the selected range.

Applying Styles

A workbook often contains several cells that store the same type of data. For example, each worksheet might have a cell displaying the sheet title, or a range of financial data might have several cells containing summary totals. Using the same format on cells storing the same type of data gives your workbook a consistent look. You can do this using the Format Painter or by copying and pasting a format from one cell to another.

The Format Painter is effective, but it can also be time consuming if you have to copy the same format to many cells. Moreover, if you decide to modify the format, you must copy and paste the revised format all over again. Another way to ensure that cells displaying the same type of data use the same format is with styles. A **style** is a collection of formatting. For example, you can create a style to display sheet titles in a bold, white, 20-point Calibri font on a blue background. You can then apply that style to any sheet title in a workbook. If you later revise the style, the appearance of any cell formatted with that style is updated automatically. This saves you the time and effort of reformatting each cell individually.

Excel has a variety of built-in styles to format worksheet titles, column and row totals, and cells with emphasis. You used the built-in Currency and Percent styles when you formatted data in the Yearly Sales worksheet as currency and percentages. Some styles are connected to the workbook's current theme.

Tutorial 2 Formatting a Workbook | Excel | EX 77

Applying Styles | Reference Window

- Select the cell or range to which you want to apply a style.
- In the Styles group on the Home tab, click the Cell Styles button.
- Point to each style in the Cell Styles gallery to see a Live Preview of that style on the selected cell or range.
- Click the style you want to apply to the selected cell or range.

Tom asks you to use some of the built-in styles to add more color and visual interest to the Yearly Sales worksheet.

To apply built-in styles to the Yearly Sales sheet:

1. Click the **Yearly Sales** sheet tab to make that worksheet active, and then select the merged cell **A4**.

2. In the Styles group on the Home tab, click the **Cell Styles** button. The Cell Styles gallery opens.

3. Point to the **Heading 1** style in the Titles and Headings section. Live Preview shows cell A4 in a 15-point, bold font with a solid blue bottom border. See Figure 2-19.

Cell Styles gallery | Figure 2-19

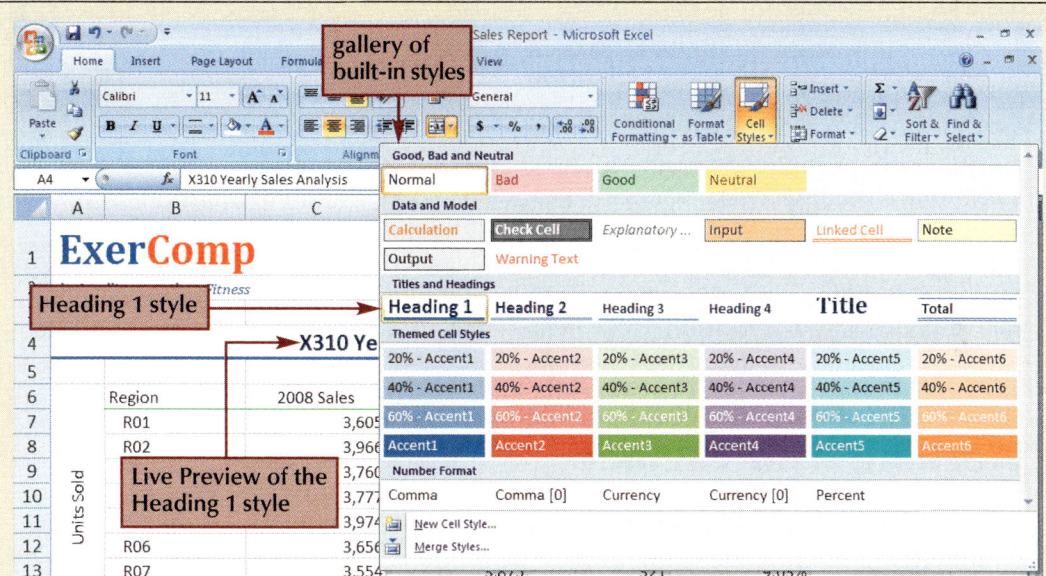

4. Move the pointer over different styles in the Cell Styles gallery to preview cell A4 with each style, and then click the **Heading 1** style. The style is applied to cell A4.

5. Select the range **B6:F6;B17:F17**, click the **Cell Styles** button, and then click the **Accent1** style in the Themed Cell Styles section. Each of the column headings is formatted.

6. Select the range **E7:F15;E18:F26**, click the **Cell Styles** button, and then click the **20% – Accent1** style in the Themed Cell Styles section. The calculated values are formatted differently from the data.

7. Click cell **F1** to deselect the range, and then zoom the worksheet to **90%**. See Figure 2-20.

Figure 2-20   Formatted yearly sales data

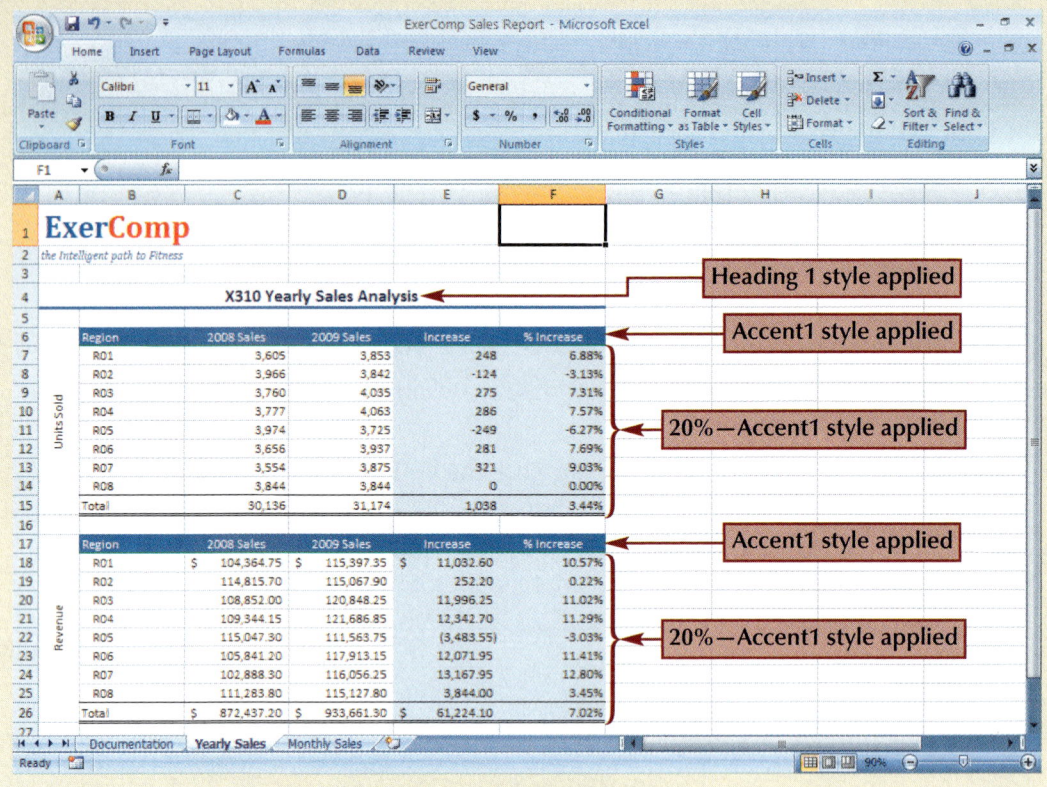

If the built-in styles don't meet your needs, you can modify an existing style or create a new one. To modify a style, right-click the style in the Cell Styles gallery, click Modify on the shortcut menu to open the Style dialog box, and then click the Format button to change the formatting for that style. Any cells formatted with that style are automatically updated. To create a new style, click New Cell Style in the Cell Styles gallery to open the Style dialog box, type a name in the Style name box, and then click the Format button to select the formatting for that style. The new cell style is added to the Cell Styles gallery.

Working with Themes

Most of the formatting you've applied so far is based on the workbook's current theme—the default Office theme. As you've seen, fonts, colors, and cell styles are organized in theme and non-theme categories. The appearance of these fonts, colors, and cell styles depends on the workbook's current theme. If you change the theme, the formatting of these elements also changes.

You'll change the workbook's theme to see its effect on the workbook's appearance.

To change the workbook's theme:

1. Click the **Page Layout** tab on the Ribbon, and then, in the Themes group, click the **Themes** button. The Themes gallery opens. Office—the current theme—is the default.

2. Point to each theme in the Themes gallery. Live Preview shows the impact of each theme on the appearance of the Yearly Sales worksheet.

▶ 3. Click the **Aspect** theme. The Aspect theme is applied to the workbook. See Figure 2-21.

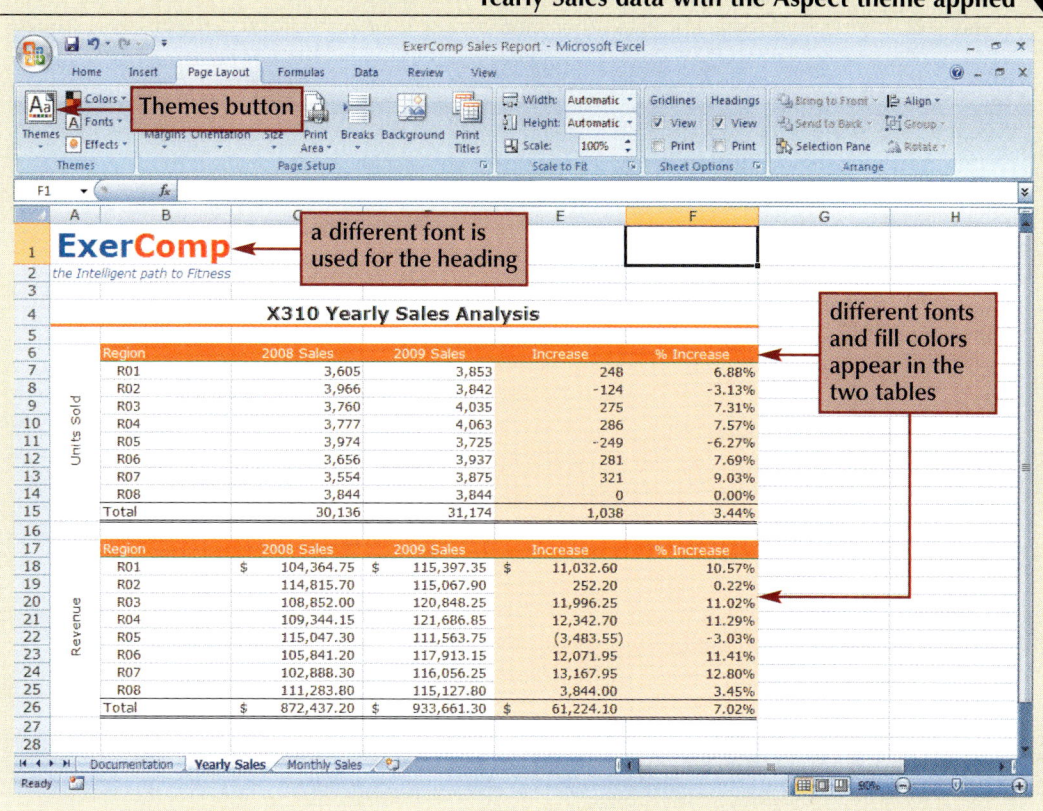

Figure 2-21 Yearly Sales data with the Aspect theme applied

Changing the theme has made a significant difference in the worksheet's appearance. The most obvious changes are the fill colors and the fonts. Only elements directly tied to a theme change when you select a different theme. The cells you formatted with the Accent1 cell style changed because the Accent1 color is blue in the Office theme and orange in the Aspect theme. The Heading 1 style you used for the titles in cells A1 and A2 uses the Cambria typeface in the Office theme and the Verdana typeface in the Aspect theme. The Aspect theme also uses a different font for body text, which is why the rest of the text changed size and appearance.

The logo colors in cell A1 did not change because you used two standard colors, blue and red, which are not part of a theme. Changing the theme does not affect these colors.

Tom prefers the default Office theme, so you'll switch back to that theme and then save the workbook.

To select the Office theme and save the workbook:

▶ 1. In the Themes group on the Page Layout tab, click the **Themes** button, and then click the **Office** theme.

▶ 2. Save your changes to the workbook.

| InSight | Sharing Styles and Themes |

If you're part of a team creating files with Microsoft Office, you might want to use a common style and design theme for all your projects. The easiest way to do this is by saving the styles and themes as permanent files other members of your workgroup can use.

To copy a style from one workbook to another, open the workbook with the styles you want to copy, and then open the workbook in which you want to copy those styles. In the Styles group on the Home tab, click the Cell Styles button, and then click Merge Styles. The Merge Styles dialog box opens, listing the currently open workbooks. Select the workbook with the styles you want to copy, and then click the OK button to copy those styles into the current workbook. If you modify any styles, you must copy the styles to the other workbook; Excel does not update styles between workbooks.

You can save a workbook's theme as a file that can be used in other workbooks or Office files. Microsoft Excel, Word, and PowerPoint use the same file format for their theme files. To save a theme, in the Themes group on the Page Layout tab, click the Themes button, and then click Save Current Theme. The Save Current Theme dialog box opens. Select a save location (in a default Theme folder on your computer or another folder), type a descriptive name in the File name box, and then click the Save button. A Theme file saved in a default Theme folder appears in the Themes gallery, and any changes made to the theme are reflected in any Office file that uses that theme.

You've completed some formatting of Tom's workbook. In the process, you've formatted cells and ranges, applied built-in styles, and applied a new theme. In the next session, you'll work with table styles, conditional formatting, and page layout tools.

| Review | Session 2.1 Quick Check |

1. What is the difference between a serif font and a sans serif font?
2. What is the difference between a standard color and a theme color?
3. What is the General number format?
4. Why are dates right-aligned within a worksheet cell by default?
5. The range A1:C5 is merged into a single cell. What is the cell reference of this merged cell?
6. Where can you access all the formatting options for worksheet cells?
7. You want the range A1:A3 on all the worksheets in your workbook to be formatted the same way. Discuss two methods of applying the same format to different ranges.

Session 2.2

Formatting the Monthly Sales Worksheet

The Monthly Sales worksheet contains the sales results by month for the eight sales regions in 2008 and 2009. Tom's main goal for this data is to identify trends. He's more interested in the "big picture" than in specific numbers. He wants to know which sales regions are performing well, which are underperforming, and, in general, how the sales change throughout the year.

The top of the worksheet contains sales for 2008 and 2009. The bottom of the worksheet displays the increase in sales from 2008 to 2009 for each region and month. You need to calculate the monthly totals and do some basic formatting.

To calculate the monthly totals:

1. If you took a break after the previous session, open the ExerComp Sales Report workbook located in the Tutorial.02\Tutorial folder included with your Data Files.
2. Click the **Monthly Sales** sheet tab to make the worksheet active, and then, in cells B19, B34, B49, K6, K21, and K36, enter **Total**.
3. Select the range **K7:K18;K22:K33;K37:K48**, and then click the **Home** tab on the Ribbon.
4. In the Editing group, click the **Sum** button Σ to add the total of each row.
5. Select the range **C19:K19;C34:K34;C49:K49**, and then, in the Editing group, click the **Sum** button Σ to add the total of each column.

Next, you'll format the row and column titles.

To format the titles:

1. Select the range **A4:K4**, and then, in the Alignment group on the Home tab, click the **Merge & Center** button. The title is centered in the merged cell.
2. In the Styles group, click the **Cell Styles** button, and then click the **Heading 1** style. The Heading 1 style is applied to the title.
3. Select the range **A6:A19;A21:A34;A36:A49**, and then, in the Alignment group, click the **Merge & Center** button. The labels are centered in the merged cells.
4. In the Alignment group, click the **Orientation** button, and then click **Rotate Text Up**. The text in the three cells rotates 90 degrees.
5. In the Alignment group, click the **Middle Align** button. The text is centered both horizontally and vertically in the cells.
6. Reduce the width of column A to **5** characters.
7. Select the range **C7:K19;C22:K34;C37:K49**, and then, in the Number group, click the **Dialog Box Launcher**. The Format Cells dialog box opens with the Number tab displayed.
8. Click **Number** in the Category list, type **0** (a zero) in the Decimal places box, click the **Use 1000 Separator (,)** check box to insert a check mark, verify that the **−1,234** option is selected, and then click the **OK** button. The numbers display a thousands separator and use a minus symbol for negatives.
9. Click cell **A1** to deselect the cells. Figure 2-22 shows the formatted Monthly Sales worksheet for the first range. The other ranges are formatted similarly.

Figure 2-22 — Monthly Sales worksheet with formulas and formatting

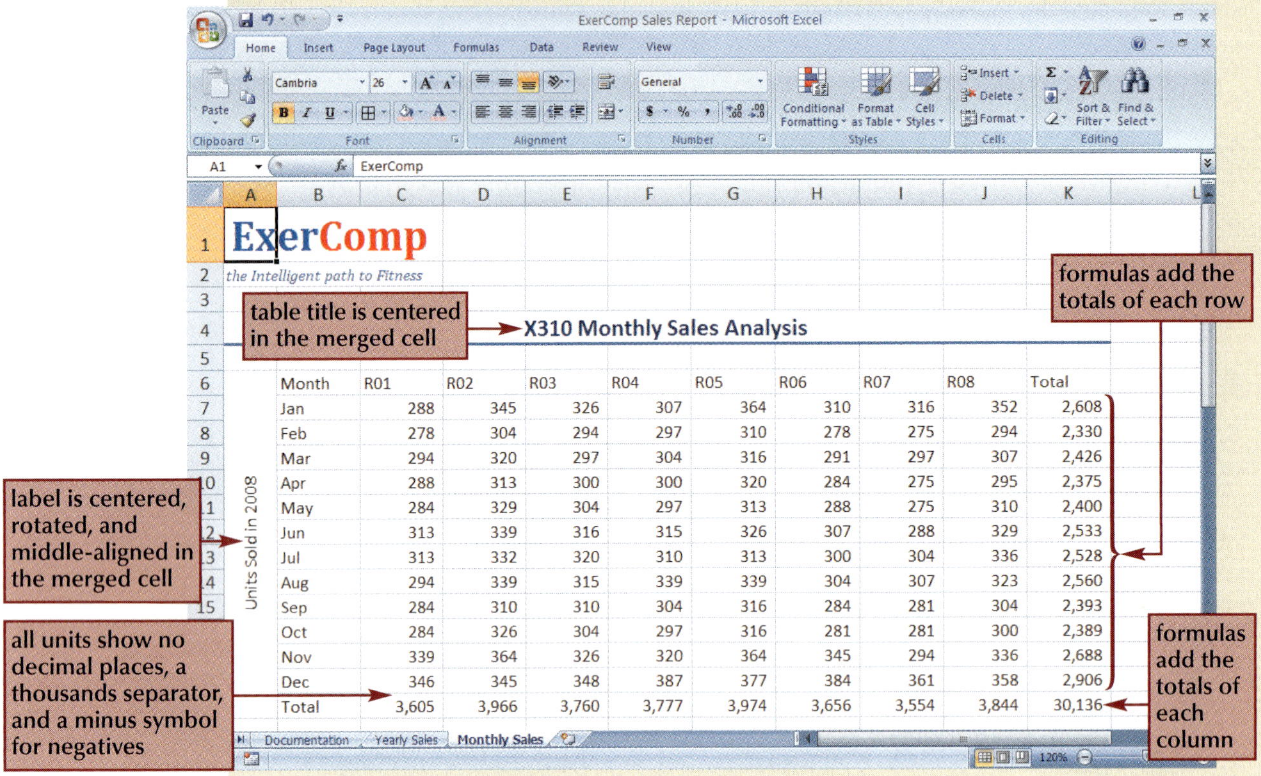

Annotations on the figure:
- table title is centered in the merged cell
- formulas add the totals of each row
- label is centered, rotated, and middle-aligned in the merged cell
- all units show no decimal places, a thousands separator, and a minus symbol for negatives
- formulas add the totals of each column

Worksheet contents:

ExerComp
the Intelligent path to Fitness

X310 Monthly Sales Analysis

Units Sold in 2008

Month	R01	R02	R03	R04	R05	R06	R07	R08	Total
Jan	288	345	326	307	364	310	316	352	2,608
Feb	278	304	294	297	310	278	275	294	2,330
Mar	294	320	297	304	316	291	297	307	2,426
Apr	288	313	300	300	320	284	275	295	2,375
May	284	329	304	297	313	288	275	310	2,400
Jun	313	339	316	315	326	307	288	329	2,533
Jul	313	332	320	310	313	300	304	336	2,528
Aug	294	339	315	339	339	304	307	323	2,560
Sep	284	310	310	304	316	284	281	304	2,393
Oct	284	326	304	297	316	281	281	300	2,389
Nov	339	364	326	320	364	345	294	336	2,688
Dec	346	345	348	387	377	384	361	358	2,906
Total	3,605	3,966	3,760	3,777	3,974	3,656	3,554	3,844	30,136

Working with Table Styles

You can treat a range of data as a distinct object in a worksheet known as an **Excel table**. After you identify a range as an Excel table, you can apply a **table style** that formats the entire table as a single unit. Excel tables can include some common elements, such as a header row that contains titles for the different columns in the table and a total row that contains formulas summarizing the values in the table's data. A table style specifies formats for each of these elements, such as font color, fill color, and so forth. Formatting an entire table with a table style is more efficient than formatting individual cells in the range.

Reference Window | Applying a Table Style to an Existing Table

- Select the range to which you want to apply the table style.
- In the Styles group on the Home tab, click the Format as Table button.
- Click a table style in the Table Style gallery.

A table style will update the table's formatting to reflect changes you make to the table, such as adding or deleting table rows or columns. For example, many tables display alternate rows with different fill colors. This effect, known as **banded rows**, makes the text easier to read, especially in large tables with many rows. You could create the banded rows effect by applying a cell style with a background fill to every other row in the table, but then, if you add or delete a row from the table, the banded rows effect might be lost. A table style, on the other hand, applies alternating row colors to the entire Excel table and adjusts the banded rows effect as needed if you add or delete rows. This is because a table style treats the table as a single object rather than a collection of cells. Figure 2-23 shows the banded rows effect applied both manually and with a table style.

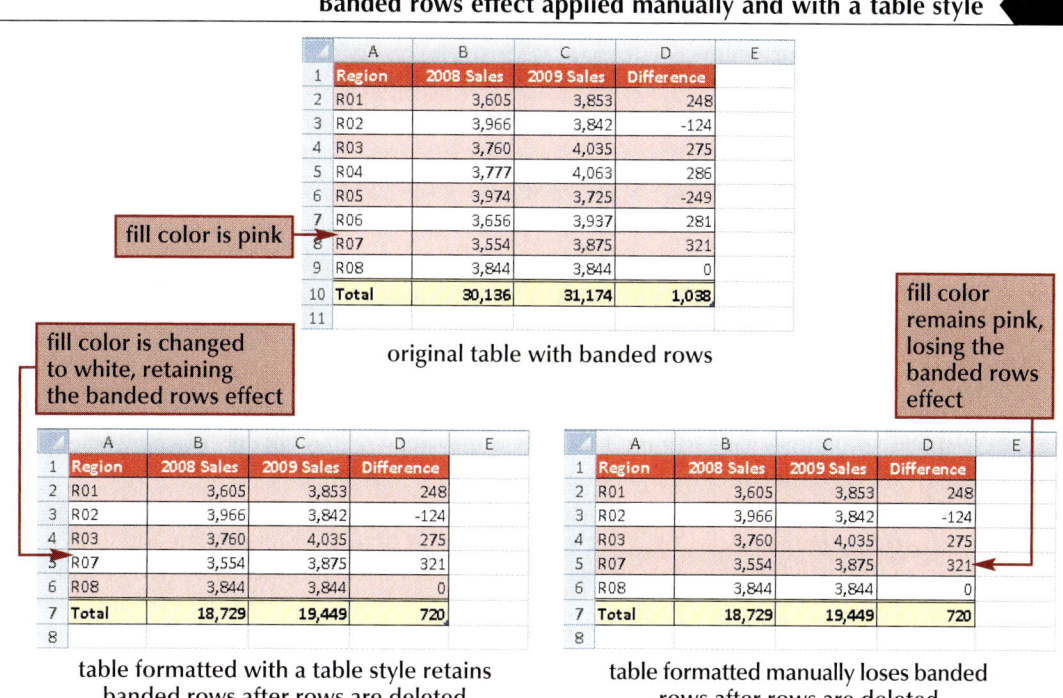

Figure 2-23 Banded rows effect applied manually and with a table style

Tom wants you to format the 2008, 2009, and sales increase data in the Monthly Sales worksheet as Excel tables. First, you'll apply a table style to the units sold in 2008 data.

To apply a table style to the units sold in 2008 data:

1. Select the range **B6:K19**.

2. In the Styles group on the Home tab, click the **Format as Table** button, and then click **Table Style Medium 2** (the second style in the first row in the Medium section). The Format as Table dialog box opens, confirming the range you selected for the table and whether the table includes header rows.

3. Verify that the range is **=$B$6:$K$19**, verify that the **My table has headers** check box contains a check mark, and then click the **OK** button. The table style is applied.

4. Click cell **A5** to deselect the range. See Figure 2-24.

Figure 2-24 | Data formatted with a table style

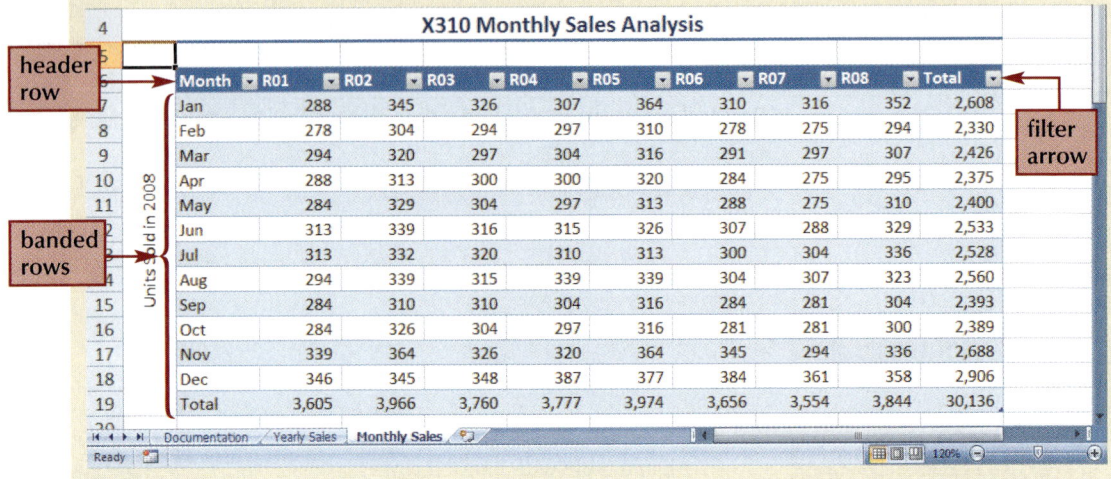

The table style treated the range as a single unit and modified its overall appearance. In this case, Table Style Medium 2 formatted the range so the header row appears in a white font on a blue fill and the remaining rows are formatted as banded rows.

Applying a table style also marks the range as a table, making available tools designed for analyzing tabular data, such as the ability to sort data, transfer data to and from an external file, and filter the data to show only those rows that match specified criteria. The filter arrows next to the column titles in the header row are used for filtering and sorting the table. Tom doesn't want to filter or sort the data right now; he asks you to remove the arrows so he can focus on the table data.

To remove the filter arrows from the table:

▶ 1. Click cell **B6** to make the table active, and then click the **Data** tab on the Ribbon.

▶ 2. In the Sort & Filter group, click the **Filter** button. The filter arrows disappear from the header row.

Selecting Table Style Options

After you apply a table style, you can choose which table elements you want included in the style. Table styles have six elements that can be turned on or off: (1) Header Row, which formats the first row of the table; (2) Total Row, which inserts a new row at the bottom of the table that adds the column values; (3) First Column, which formats the first column of the table; (4) Last Column, which formats the last column of the table; (5) Banded Rows, which formats alternating rows in different colors; and (6) Banded Columns, which formats alternating columns in different colors. For example, if you turn on the Header Row option, you can specify a format for the table's first row, which usually contains text that describes the contents of each table column. If you insert a new row at the top of the table, the new row becomes the header row and is formatted with the table style.

In the table style you just used, only the Header Row and Banded Rows options are turned on. Although the other elements are still part of the table structure, the current style does not format them. Tom wants you to format the table's last column and the header row and remove the banded rows effect.

To select the table style options:

1. If necessary, click cell **B6** to make the table active.
2. Click the **Design** tab on the Ribbon. The table design options appear on the Ribbon.
3. In the Table Style Options group, click the **Last Column** check box to insert a check mark. The last column is formatted.
4. In the Table Style Options group, click the **Banded Rows** check box to remove the check mark. The banded rows are removed from the table.

   Only the Header Row and Last Column elements appear in the table. You'll use a built-in table style to format them.

5. In the Table Styles group, click the **More** button to open the Table Styles gallery, and then, in the Medium section, click **Table Style Medium 20** (the third table style in the sixth column). The table styles in the gallery show the formatting applied to the current table elements. See Figure 2-25.

> **Tip**
> To select a table style option, you can click in the table to make it active. You do not need to select the entire table.

Figure 2-25 Revised table style

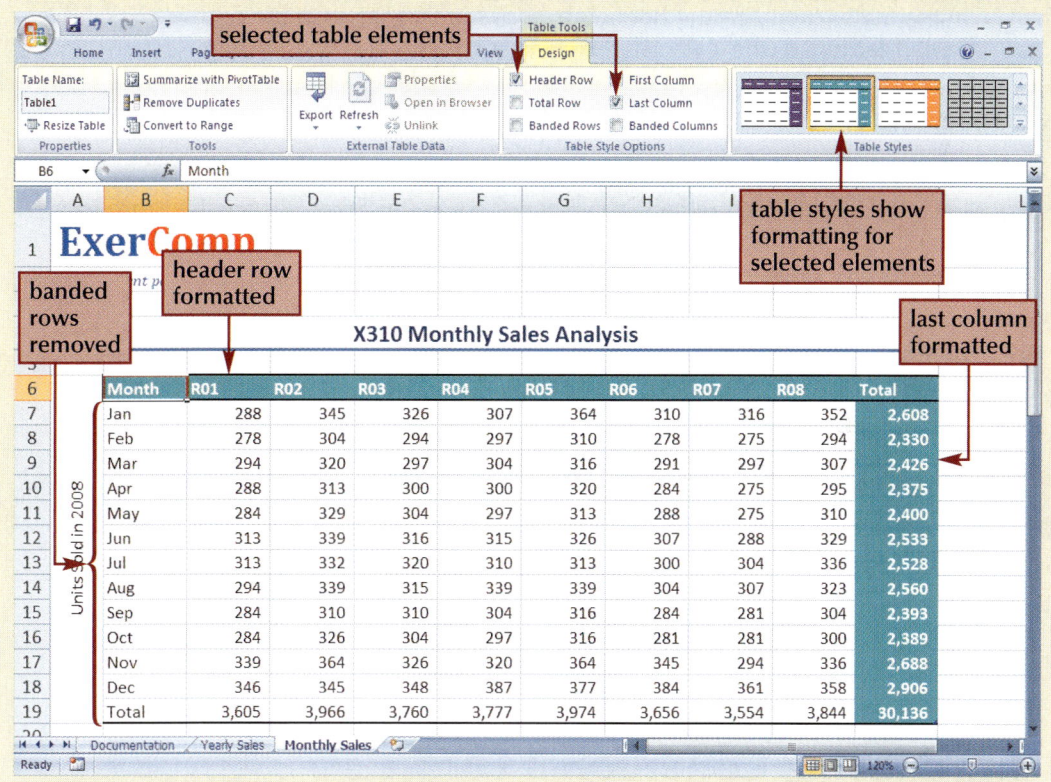

A table style might not format a table exactly the way you want. For example, Tom wants the column titles in the header row to be centered and the Total row to have a single top border and a double bottom border. Because the table style you used does not include either of these formats, you'll add these formats to the table cells. You can use cell styles and the formatting tools you've used with individual cells and ranges to format Excel tables.

To format the header row and the Total row:

1. Select the range **C6:K6**, click the **Home** tab on the Ribbon, and then, in the Alignment group, click the **Center** button. The column titles are centered.

2. Select the range **B19:K19**.

3. In the Styles group, click the **Cell Styles** button, and then, in the Titles and Headings section, click **Total** (the sixth cell style).

4. Click cell **A5** to deselect the range. The Total row is formatted in bold with a single top border and a double bottom border.

Tom likes the formatting of the first table, and wants you to format the other two tables similarly. You cannot use the Format Painter to copy table formats, and you must format each range as a table separately.

To format the other two tables:

1. Select the range **B21:K34**.

2. In the Styles group on the Home tab, click the **Format as Table** button, click **Table Style Medium 6** (the sixth table style in the first row of the Medium section), and then click the **OK** button in the Format as Table dialog box.

3. Click the **Data** tab on the Ribbon, and then, in the Sort & Filter group, click the **Filter** button to turn off the filter arrows.

4. Click the **Design** tab on the Ribbon, and then, in the Table Style Options group, click the **Banded Rows** check box to remove the check mark and click the **Last Column** check box to insert a check mark.

5. In the Table Styles group, click the **More** button, and then click **Table Style Medium 20** (the sixth table style in the third row of the Medium section).

6. Select the range **C21:K21**, click the **Home** tab on the Ribbon, and then, in the Alignment group, click the **Center** button.

7. Select the range **B34:K34**. You'll apply the Total cell style to this range.

8. In the Styles group, click the **Cell Styles** button, and then click **Total** (the sixth cell style in the Titles and Headings section).

9. Select the range **B36:K49** and repeat Steps 2 through 5, select the range **C36:K36** and repeat Step 6, and then select the range **B49:K49** and repeat Step 8.

Introducing Conditional Formats

So far, you have used formatting to make the workbook more readable or visually interesting. Formatting can also help you analyze data by highlighting significant numbers or trends in the data. Tom wants the sales report to highlight sales regions that have performed particularly well or done poorly in the past two years. Tom also wants to show how sales of the X310 heart rate monitor changed during the year. This information can help him plan inventory for the next year as well as project future sales and revenue.

To prepare this kind of report, you can use conditional formatting. A **conditional format** applies formatting only when a cell's value meets a specified condition. For example, a conditional format can make negative numbers red and positive numbers black. Conditional formats are dynamic, so a cell's appearance will change to reflect its current value.

Excel has four conditional formats—data bars, highlighting, color scales, and icon sets. This tutorial looks at data bars and cell highlighting.

| **Applying Conditional Formats (Data Bars and Highlights)** | Reference Window |

- Select the range or ranges to which you want to add data bars.
- In the Styles group on the Home tab, click the Conditional Formatting button, point to Data Bars, and then click a data bar color.

or

- Select the range in which you want to highlight cells that match a specified rule.
- In the Styles group, click the Conditional Formatting button, point to Highlight Cells Rules or Top/Bottom Rules, and then click the appropriate rule.
- Select the appropriate options in the dialog box, and then click the OK button.

Adding Data Bars

A **data bar** is a horizontal bar added to the background of a cell to provide a visual indicator of the cell's value. Larger values are associated with longer data bars; smaller values are associated with shorter data bars. Data bars will help Tom see how the 2008 and 2009 sales totals vary throughout the year.

To format the 2008 monthly sales with data bars:

1. Select the range **K7:K18**.

2. In the Styles group on the Home tab, click the **Conditional Formatting** button, point to **Data Bars** to open the Data Bars gallery, and then click **Purple Data Bar** (the third data bar in the second row of the Data Bars gallery). Data bars appear for the 2008 monthly sales.

3. Click cell **A3** to deselect the range. See Figure 2-26.

Data bars added to the 2008 monthly sales | Figure 2-26

	Month	R01	R02	R03	R04	R05	R06	R07	R08	Total
7	Jan	288	345	326	307	364	310	316	352	2,608
8	Feb	278	304	294	297	310	278	275	294	2,330
9	Mar	294	320	297	304	316	291	297	307	2,426
10	Apr	288	313	300	300	320	284	275	295	2,375
11	May	284	329	304	297	313	288	275	310	2,400
12	Jun	313	339	316	315	326	307	288	329	2,533
13	Jul	313	332	320	310	313	300	304	336	2,528
14	Aug	294	339	315	339	339	304	307	323	2,560
15	Sep	284	310	310	304	316	284	281	304	2,393
16	Oct	284	326	304	297	316	281	281	300	2,389
17	Nov	339	364	326	320	364	345	294	336	2,688
18	Dec	346	345	348	387	377	384	361	358	2,906
19	**Total**	3,605	3,966	3,760	3,777	3,974	3,656	3,554	3,844	30,136

data bar length is based on the cell value

The data bars highlight several important facts that might not be immediately apparent from viewing the cell values. First, the highest sales occurred during the months of November, December, and January—a reflection of heavy shopping during the holiday season. Second, an increase in sales occurred during the summer months. Again, this is expected because customers are more physically active during those months and likely to purchase a heart rate monitor. Third, the periods of lowest sales occurred in the spring and fall. To find out if all of the sales regions reflect this seasonal trend, you'll add data bars to the individual sales region figures.

To add data bars for all sales regions:

1. Select the range **C7:J18**.

2. In the Styles group on the Home tab, click the **Conditional Formatting** button, point to **Data Bars**, and then click **Light Blue Data Bar** (the second data bar in the second row of the Data Bars gallery). Monthly data bars appear for all the sales regions in 2008.

3. Click cell **A3** to deselect the range. See Figure 2-27.

Figure 2-27   Data bars added to the regional monthly sales data

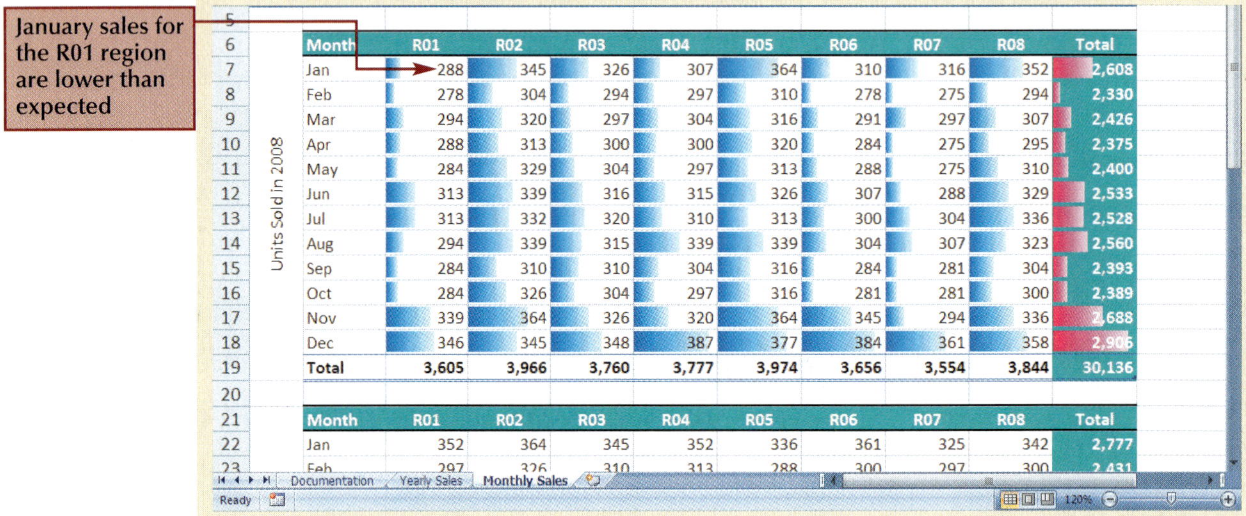

January sales for the R01 region are lower than expected

Month	R01	R02	R03	R04	R05	R06	R07	R08	Total
Jan	288	345	326	307	364	310	316	352	2,608
Feb	278	304	294	297	310	278	275	294	2,330
Mar	294	320	297	304	316	291	297	307	2,426
Apr	288	313	300	300	320	284	275	295	2,375
May	284	329	304	297	313	288	275	310	2,400
Jun	313	339	316	315	326	307	288	329	2,533
Jul	313	332	320	310	313	300	304	336	2,528
Aug	294	339	315	339	339	304	307	323	2,560
Sep	284	310	310	304	316	284	281	304	2,393
Oct	284	326	304	297	316	281	281	300	2,389
Nov	339	364	326	320	364	345	294	336	2,688
Dec	346	345	348	387	377	384	361	358	2,906
Total	3,605	3,966	3,760	3,777	3,974	3,656	3,554	3,844	30,136
Month	R01	R02	R03	R04	R05	R06	R07	R08	Total
Jan	352	364	345	352	336	361	325	342	2,777
Feb	297	326	310	313	288	300	297	300	2,431

For the most part, the seasonal trend is reflected in all the sales regions, with some exceptions. For example, the R01 region had lower-than-expected sales during January 2008. Tom discovers that a distribution problem prevented several stores in the R01 region from receiving its stock of ExerComp heart rate monitors until near the end of January, causing the decreased sales totals. Data bars highlight this important piece of information.

Data bar lengths depend on the values in the selected range. The largest value in the range has the longest data bar; the smallest value has the shortest data bar. For example, in the Total column, the shortest data bar represents the February total of 2,330 and the longest data bar represents the December total of 2,906. You should use different colored data bars to distinguish data bars for different ranges. For example, you used blue data bars for the regional sales and purple data bars for the totals.

Because data bar lengths are based on the values in the range, changing the value of one cell in the range can affect the size of all the other cells' data bars. You'll change the units sold value in cell C7 and see how this affects the data bars.

To see the effect on data bars of changing a units sold value:

1. In cell C7, enter **588**. The lengths of all the data bars in the 2008 sales table change to reflect this increased value.
2. On the Quick Access Toolbar, click the **Undo** button. The value in cell C7 returns to 288, its original value.

Clearing a Conditional Format

Tom wants you to add data bars to the 2009 sales table. You can base the data bars on the values in only the 2009 sales table, or you can base them on the values in both the 2008 and 2009 sales tables. Both approaches have advantages. Basing the data bars on only the 2009 sales allows you to focus on that data and see more detail on the seasonal and regional trends within that year. However, basing the data bars on sales results from both years makes it easier to compare sales trends from one year to another. Tom wants you to base the length of the data bars on the values from both years. First, you need to remove the data bars you created for the 2008 sales table. Then, you can add a new set of data bars based on a different selection of cells.

To clear the data bars from the 2008 sales table:

1. If necessary, click cell **C7** to select it and make the table active.
2. In the Styles group on the Home tab, click the **Conditional Formatting** button, point to **Clear Rules**, and then click **Clear Rules from This Table**. Both sets of data bars are removed from the 2008 sales table.

> **Tip**
>
> To remove all conditional formatting from a worksheet, click Clear Rules from Entire Sheet. To remove it from the selected range, click Clear Rules from Selected Cells.

Next, you'll add data bars for the sales data in both the 2008 and 2009 sales tables.

To add data bars to both the 2008 and 2009 sales tables:

1. Select the range **K7:K18;K22:K33**. This selects the 2008 and 2009 monthly sales totals.
2. In the Styles group on the Home tab, click the **Conditional Formatting** button, point to **Data Bars**, and then click **Purple Data Bar** (the third data bar in the second row of the Data Bars gallery).
3. Select the range **C7:J18;C22:J33**. This selects the 2008 and 2009 monthly sales for each region.
4. In the Styles group, click the **Conditional Formatting** button, point to **Data Bars**, and then click **Light Blue Data Bar** (the second data bar in the second row of the Data Bars gallery).
5. Click cell **A20** to deselect the range. See Figure 2-28.

Figure 2-28 | Data bars added to the 2008 and 2009 sales tables

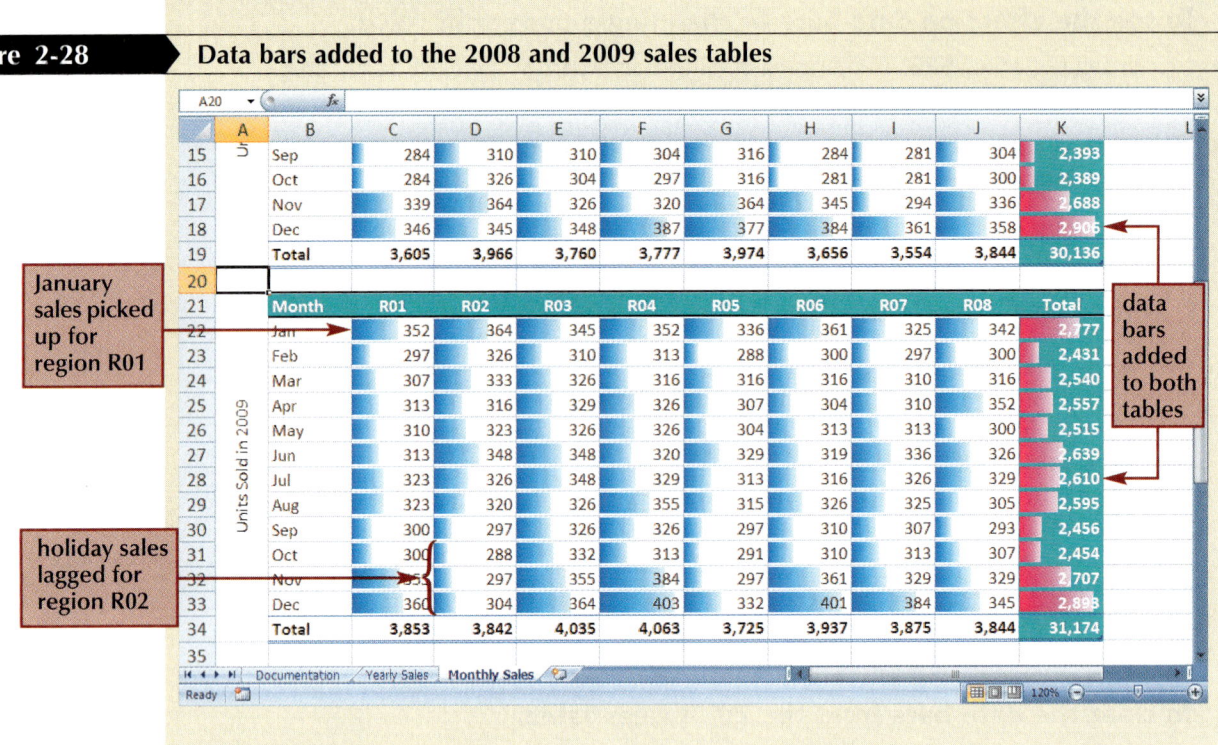

Tom sees some of the same seasonal trends in 2009 as he saw for 2008. He notes that sales in the R01 region did not lag as they did in 2008, but sales in the R02 region were lower than expected during the holiday season. Other than that, it's hard to compare the regional and monthly sales to determine any trends from 2008 to 2009. He knows that, overall, the number of heart rate monitors sold increased in 2009, but he doesn't know if this is true for all regions and for all months. Tom wants to highlight those sales regions and months in which sales increased from 2008 to 2009.

Highlighting Cells

The third table shows the increase in sales from 2008 to 2009, which is the data that Tom wants to analyze. Because Tom wants to highlight those regions and months in 2008 in which the sales increased, you'll highlight only those cells that contain positive values. Highlighting cells based on their values is another type of conditional format. Figure 2-29 describes some of the ways that cells can be highlighted.

Figure 2-29 | Highlighting rules

Rule	Highlights
Greater Than	Cells that are greater than a specified number
Less Than	Cells that are less than a specified number
Between	Cells that are between two specified numbers
Equal To	Cells that are equal to a specified number
Text That Contains	Cells that contain specified text
A Date Occurring	Cells that contain a specified date
Duplicate Values	Cells that contain duplicate or unique values

Tom wants you to highlight all the positive numbers in the third table to show those months and sales regions that increased sales from 2008 to 2009.

To highlight the positive sales numbers:

▶ 1. Select the range **C37:J48**. This selects the difference in sales by region and month for 2008 and 2009.

▶ 2. In the Styles group on the Home tab, click the **Conditional Formatting** button, point to **Highlight Cells Rules**, and then click **Greater Than**. The Greater Than dialog box opens. You want to highlight positive sales numbers, which are numbers greater than zero.

▶ 3. Type **0** (a zero) in the Format cells that are GREATER THAN box, click the **with** arrow, and then click **Green Fill with Dark Green Text**.

▶ 4. Click the **OK** button to apply the highlight rule.

▶ 5. Click cell **A35** to deselect the range. Cells with positive numbers are highlighted in green. See Figure 2-30.

Figure 2-30   Positive cells highlighted

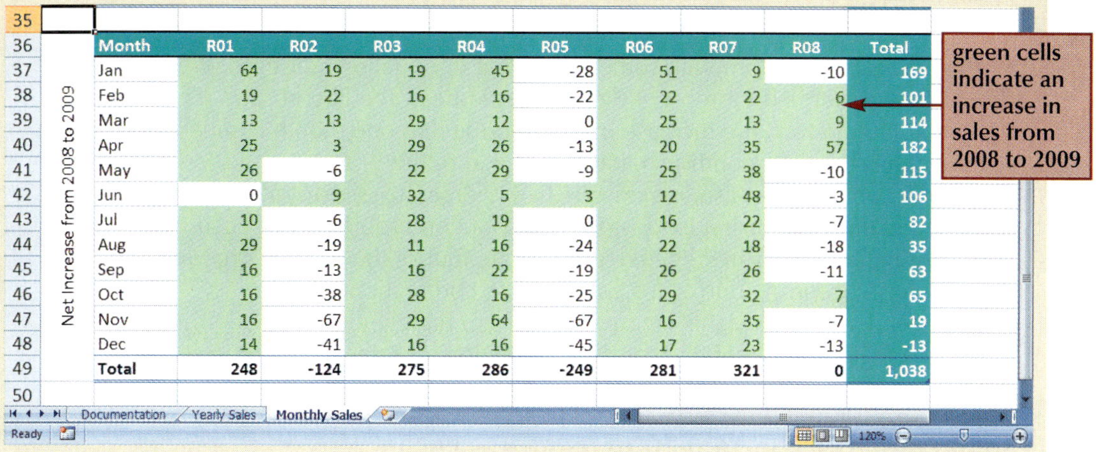

	Month	R01	R02	R03	R04	R05	R06	R07	R08	Total
	Jan	64	19	19	45	-28	51	9	-10	169
	Feb	19	22	16	16	-22	22	22	6	101
	Mar	13	13	29	12	0	25	13	9	114
	Apr	25	3	29	26	-13	20	35	57	182
Net Increase from 2008 to 2009	May	26	-6	22	29	-9	25	38	-10	115
	Jun	0	9	32	5	3	12	48	-3	106
	Jul	10	-6	28	19	0	16	22	-7	82
	Aug	29	-19	11	16	-24	22	18	-18	35
	Sep	16	-13	16	22	-19	26	26	-11	63
	Oct	16	-38	28	16	-25	29	32	7	65
	Nov	16	-67	29	64	-67	16	35	-7	19
	Dec	14	-41	16	16	-45	17	23	-13	-13
	Total	248	-124	275	286	-249	281	321	0	1,038

green cells indicate an increase in sales from 2008 to 2009

From the highlighting, you can tell that most regions and months had increased sales in 2009. Most of the declines occurred in regions R02, R05, and R08. Tom wonders if some months or regions had particularly strong sales increases. You'll remove the current highlighting, and then highlight the top 10% in sales increases.

To highlight the top 10 percent in sales increases:

▶ 1. Select the range **C37:J48**.

▶ 2. In the Styles group on the Home tab, click the **Conditional Formatting** button, point to **Clear Rules**, and then click **Clear Rules from Selected Cells**. The current highlighting is removed.

▶ 3. In the Styles group, click the **Conditional Formatting** button, point to **Top/Bottom Rules**, and then click **Top 10 %**. The Top 10% dialog box opens.

▶ 4. Verify that **10** is entered in the % box, click the **with** arrow, and then click **Green Fill with Dark Green Text**.

▶ 5. Click the **OK** button. Cells whose sales increases for 2008 and 2009 were in the top 10% are highlighted in green.

▶ 6. Click cell **A35** to deselect the range. See Figure 2-31.

Figure 2-31   Top 10% sales increases highlighted

green cells indicate sales increases that were in the top 10%

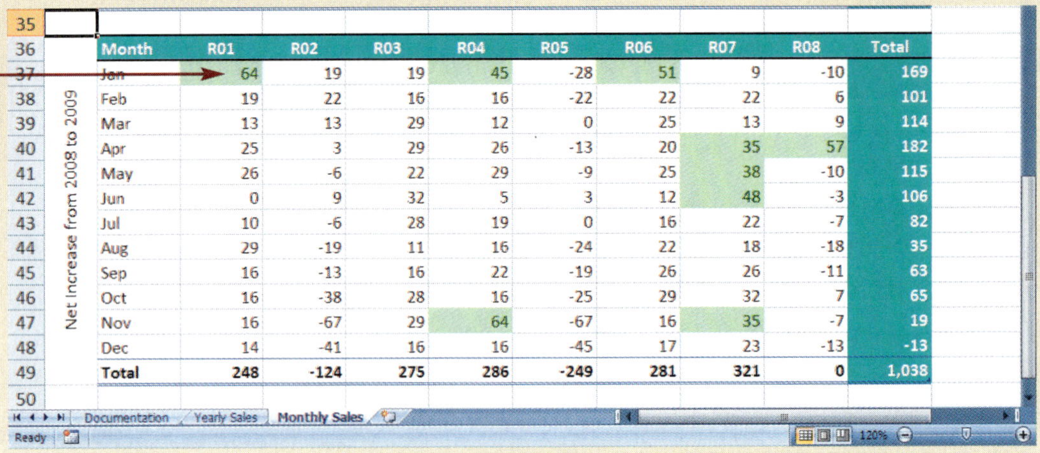

Month	R01	R02	R03	R04	R05	R06	R07	R08	Total
Jan	64	19	19	45	-28	51	9	-10	169
Feb	19	22	16	16	-22	22	22	6	101
Mar	13	13	29	12	0	25	13	9	114
Apr	25	3	29	26	-13	20	35	57	182
May	26	-6	22	29	-9	25	38	-10	115
Jun	0	9	32	5	3	12	48	-3	106
Jul	10	-6	28	19	0	16	22	-7	82
Aug	29	-19	11	16	-24	22	18	-18	35
Sep	16	-13	16	22	-19	26	26	-11	63
Oct	16	-38	28	16	-25	29	32	7	65
Nov	16	-67	29	64	-67	16	35	-7	19
Dec	14	-41	16	16	-45	17	23	-13	-13
Total	248	-124	275	286	-249	281	321	0	1,038

Net increase from 2008 to 2009

    The results provide Tom with some interesting information. For example, region R08, which underperformed for most of the year, had one of the largest sales increases during April (cell J40). In fact, the increase in sales during that one month compensated for the sales declines in other months, so that by the end of the year, region R08 showed no overall decline in sales. Also, region R01 had a large increase in sales during January 2009, indicating that this region fixed the distribution problems that occurred in 2008. Finally, of the nine cells highlighted in the table, four of them come from region R07, three of those occurring during the usually slow spring months.

    Tom wonders what insights he could gain from highlighting the bottom 10% of the table—the regions and months that showed the lowest sales increases in 2009.

To highlight the bottom 10 percent in sales increases:

▶ 1. Select the range **C37:J48**.

▶ 2. In the Styles group on the Home tab, click the **Conditional Formatting** button, point to **Top/Bottom Rules**, and then click **Bottom 10 %**. The Bottom 10% dialog box opens.

▶ 3. Verify that **10** is entered in the % box and **Light Red Fill with Dark Red Text** is selected in the with box, and then click the **OK** button. Red cells highlight the regions and months that placed in the bottom 10% for sales increases from 2008 to 2009.

▶ 4. Click cell **A35** to deselect the range. See Figure 2-32.

Figure 2-32

Bottom 10% of sales increases highlighted

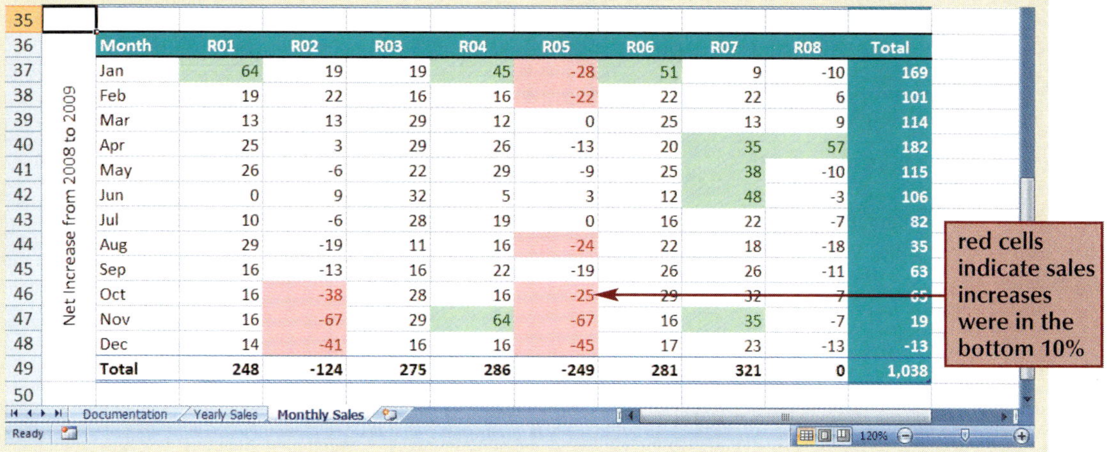

Month	R01	R02	R03	R04	R05	R06	R07	R08	Total
Jan	64	19	19	45	-28	51	9	-10	169
Feb	19	22	16	16	-22	22	22	6	101
Mar	13	13	29	12	0	25	13	9	114
Apr	25	3	29	26	-13	20	35	57	182
May	26	-6	22	29	-9	25	38	-10	115
Jun	0	9	32	5	3	12	48	-3	106
Jul	10	-6	28	19	0	16	22	-7	82
Aug	29	-19	11	16	-24	22	18	-18	35
Sep	16	-13	16	22	-19	26	26	-11	63
Oct	16	-38	28	16	-25	29	32	7	65
Nov	16	-67	29	64	-67	16	35	-7	19
Dec	14	-41	16	16	-45	17	23	-13	-13
Total	248	-124	275	286	-249	281	321	0	1,038

(Net Increase from 2008 to 2009)

red cells indicate sales increases were in the bottom 10%

Tom immediately sees that the bottom 10% come from only regions R02 and R05, and that six of the nine cells highlighted occurred in the most recent months: October, November, and December. Conditional formatting has helped Tom isolate and highlight potential problem areas, which he can investigate further.

When you use conditional formatting to highlight cells in a worksheet, you should always include a **legend**, which is a key that shows each color used in the worksheet and what it means, so others know why certain cells are highlighted. Tom asks you to add a legend to the Monthly Sales worksheet.

To create a conditional formatting legend:

▶ 1. In cell D51, enter **light red**, and then click cell **D51** to select it. You'll use a highlight rule to fill this cell with the light red color used for the bottom 10% sales increases.

▶ 2. In the Styles group on the Home tab, click the **Conditional Formatting** button, point to **Highlight Cells Rules**, and then click **Text that Contains**. The Text That Contains dialog box opens.

▶ 3. Verify that **light red** appears in the Format cells that contain the text box, select **Light Red Fill with Dark Red Text** in the with box, and then click the **OK** button. Cell D51 is filled with the same light red fill color used for the bottom 10% values.

▶ 4. In cell D52, enter **light green**, and then click cell **D52** to select it. You'll use a highlight rule to fill this cell with the green color used for the top 10% sales increases.

▶ 5. In the Styles group on the Home tab, click the **Conditional Formatting** button, point to **Hightlight Cells Rules**, and then click **Text that Contains**. The Text That Contains dialog box opens.

▶ 6. Verify that **light green** appears in the Format cells that contain the text box, select **Green Fill with Dark Green Text** in the with box, and then click the **OK** button. Cell D52 is filled with the same light green fill color used for the top 10% values.

▶ 7. In cell E51, enter **Bottom 10% in terms of sales increase**, and then, in cell E52, enter **Top 10% in terms of sales increase**.

▸ 8. Select the range **E51:E52**. You'll format these cells with a cell style to distinguish them from the rest of the text in the worksheet.

▸ 9. In the Styles group, click the **Cell Styles** button, and then, in the Data and Model group, click **Explanatory** (the third cell style in the first row).

▸ 10. Click cell **A35** to deselect the range. See Figure 2-33.

Figure 2-33 | **Cell highlighting legend**

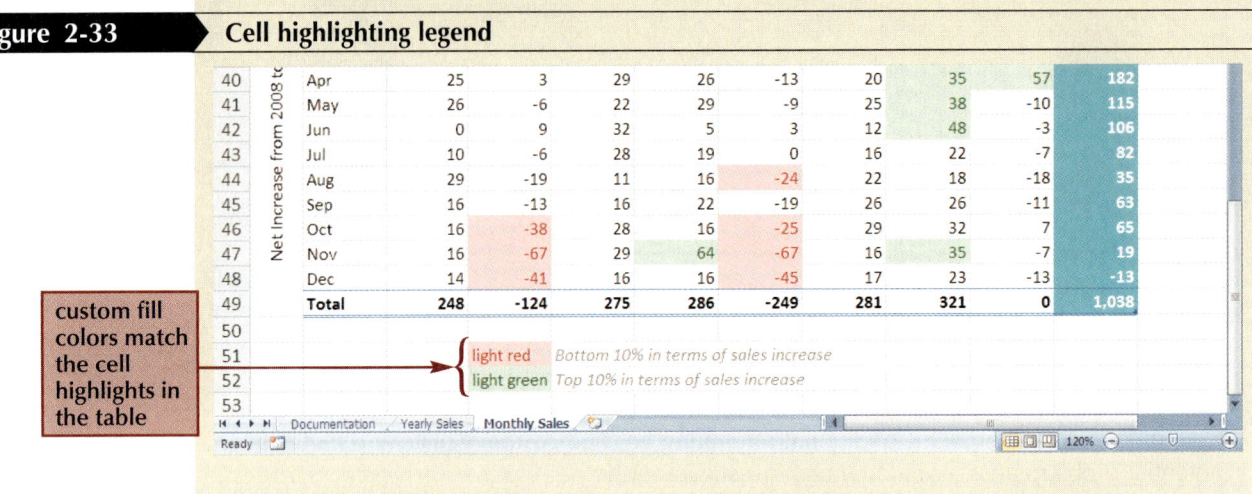

custom fill colors match the cell highlights in the table

The conditional formatting in the Monthly Sales worksheet helps Tom understand how sales of the X310 heart rate monitor changed over the past two years and helps him focus on particular sales regions for additional analysis.

| InSight | **Using Conditional Formatting Effectively** |

Conditional formatting is an excellent way to point out trends and highlight key data values, but it should be used judiciously. An overuse of conditional formatting can sometimes obscure the very data values you want to emphasize. Keep in mind the following tips:

- Document the conditional formats you use. If a bold, green font means that a sales number is in the top 10% of all sales, include that information in a legend in the worksheet.
- Don't clutter data with too much highlighting. Limit highlight rules to one or two per data set. Highlights are designed to draw attention to points of interest. If you use too many, you'll end up highlighting everything—and, therefore, nothing.
- Use color sparingly in worksheets with highlights. It's difficult to tell a highlight color from a regular fill color, especially when fill colors are used in every cell.
- Consider alternatives to conditional formats. If you want to highlight the top 10 sales regions, it might be more effective to simply sort the data with the best-selling regions at the top of the list.
- Don't let data bars overwhelm cell text. Use data bars when you're more interested in the "big picture" rather than specific cell values. If you want to show both, use a chart.

Hiding Worksheet Data

The Monthly Sales worksheet contains too much data to fit into the worksheet window without drastically reducing the zoom level. This would make the contents too small to read easily. Another way to view a large worksheet is by selectively hiding rows or columns (or even entire worksheets in a workbook). Hiding rows, columns, and worksheets is an excellent way to conceal extraneous or distracting information; but you should never hide data that is crucial to understanding a workbook.

Tom wants to view only the third table, which shows the difference in sales between 2008 and 2009, but not the other tables. You'll hide the rows that contain the first two tables and then unhide those rows after Tom has looked at the third table.

To hide and unhide worksheet rows:

1. Select row **6** through row **35** in the Monthly Sales worksheet.

2. In the Cells group on the Home tab, click the **Format** button, point to **Hide & Unhide**, and then click **Hide Rows**. Rows 6 to 35 are hidden, and the row numbers in the worksheet jump from row 5 to row 36. The data in the third table hasn't changed even though its formulas use data from the hidden tables.

3. Select row **5** and row **36**, which are the rows before and after the hidden rows.

4. In the Cells group, click the **Format** button, point to **Hide & Unhide**, and then click **Unhide Rows**. The hidden rows 6 through 35 reappear.

Formatting the Worksheet for Printing

Tom wants you to print this analysis of the monthly sales figures. In preparing the worksheet for the printer, you can select the position of the report on the page, the orientation of the page, and whether the page will include headers or footers. First, you'll look at the Monthly Sales worksheet in Page Layout view to see how it would currently print.

To view the Monthly Sales worksheet in Page Layout view:

1. Click the **Page Layout** button on the status bar. The worksheet switches to Page Layout view.

2. Zoom the worksheet to **60%** to view more of the page layout. See Figure 2-34.

Page Layout view of the Monthly Sales worksheet — Figure 2-34

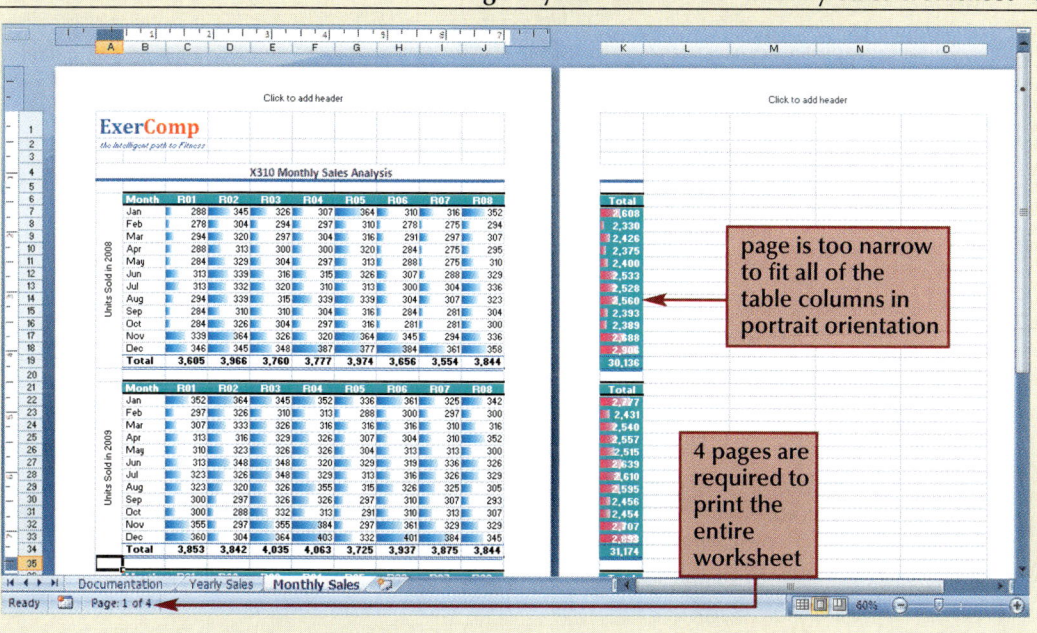

In the worksheet's current orientation, its contents do not fit on a single page and the tables break across pages. You'll change the orientation from portrait to landscape so that the page is wide enough to fit all the table columns on one page.

To change the page orientation to landscape:

▸ 1. Click the **Page Layout** tab on the Ribbon.

▸ 2. In the Page Setup group, click the **Orientation** button, and then click **Landscape**. The page orientation changes to landscape, making each page wide enough to display all of the columns of each table.

Defining the Print Area

By default, all parts of the active worksheet containing text, formulas, or values are printed. You can also select the cells you want to print, and then define them as a **print area**. A print area can cover an adjacent or nonadjacent range.

For his report, Tom wants to print only the first table. You'll set the print area to cover only those cells. It's generally easier to work with the print area in Page Break Preview.

To switch to Page Break Preview and define the print area:

▸ 1. Click the **Page Break Preview** button on the status bar, and then zoom the worksheet to **70%**.

Trouble? If the Welcome to Page Break Preview dialog box opens, click the OK button.

▸ 2. Select the range **A1:K19**, which is the range of the first table.

▸ 3. In the Page Setup group on the Page Layout tab, click the **Print Area** button, and then click **Set Print Area**. The print area changes to cover only the range A1:K19. The rest of the worksheet content is shaded to indicate that it will not be part of the printout.

Tom decides that he wants you to print all the content in the worksheet, so you'll clear the print area you just defined, resetting the print area to the default.

▸ 4. In the Page Setup group, click the **Print Area** button, and then click **Clear Print Area**. The print area again covers the entire contents of the worksheet.

Inserting Page Breaks

Large worksheets often do not fit onto one page unless you scale the printout to fit, but that usually results in text that is too small to read comfortably. When a printout extends to multiple pages, Excel prints as much as fits on a page and then inserts a **page break** to continue printing the remaining worksheet content on the next page. This can result in page breaks that split worksheet content in awkward places, such as within a table.

Instead, you can insert **manual page breaks** that specify exactly where the page breaks occur. A page break is inserted directly above and to the left of a selected cell, directly above a selected row, or to the left of a selected column.

Setting and Removing Page Breaks | Reference Window

To set a page break:
- Select the first cell below the row where you want to insert a page break.
- In the Page Setup group on the Page Layout tab, click the Breaks button, and then click Insert Page Break.

To remove a page break:
- Select any cell below or to the right of the page break you want to remove.
- In the Page Setup group on the Page Layout tab, click the Breaks button, and then click Remove Page Break (or click Reset All Page Breaks to remove all the page breaks from the worksheet).

Tom wants the three tables in the Monthly Sales worksheet to print on separate pages. You'll insert page breaks to accomplish this.

To insert page breaks between the tables:

1. Click cell **A20**.

2. In the Page Setup group on the Page Layout tab, click the **Breaks** button, and then click **Insert Page Break**. A page break separates row 19 from row 20.

3. Click cell **A35**, and then repeat Step 2 to insert a second page break that splits the second table from the third. The printout is now three pages. See Figure 2-35.

Worksheet in Page Break Preview | Figure 2-35

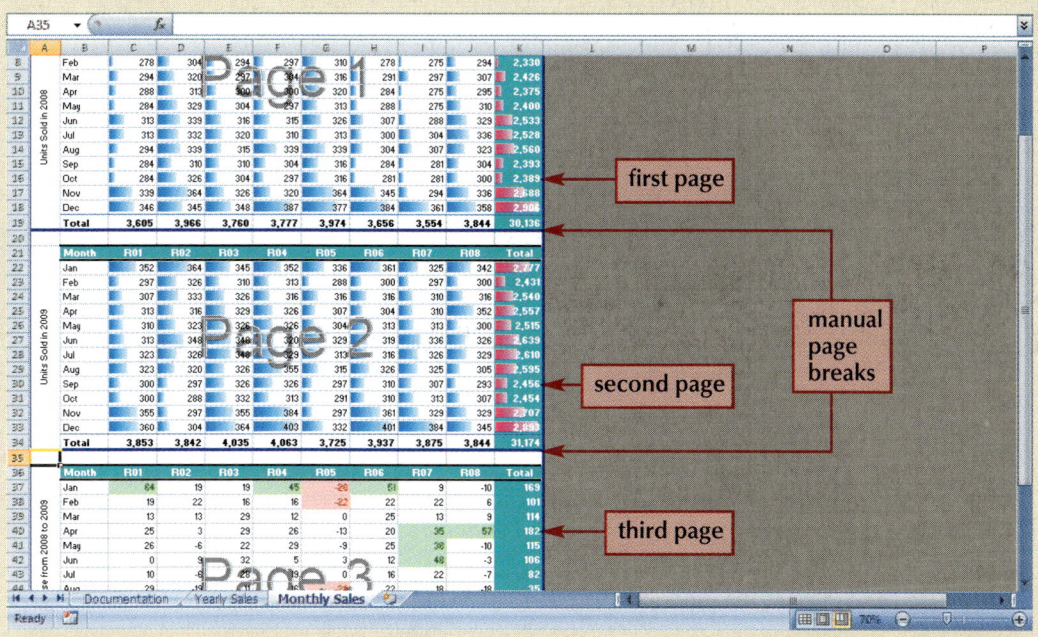

Tip

In Page Break Preview, a dashed blue line indicates an automatic page break and a solid blue line indicates a manual page break.

4. Click the **Page Layout** button on the status bar, and then verify that each table appears on a separate page.

Adding Print Titles

The company name, the slogan, and the worksheet title all appear on the first page of the printout, but do not appear on the other two pages. This is because the range that includes that text is limited to the first page of the printout. It's a good practice to include the company name, logo, and worksheet title on each page of a printout in case a page becomes separated from the other pages. You can repeat information, such as the company name, by specifying which rows or columns in the worksheet act as **print titles**, information that prints on each page.

Tom wants the first four rows of the Monthly Sales worksheet printed on each page.

To define the print titles for the pages:

▶ 1. In the Page Setup group on the Page Layout tab, click the **Print Titles** button. The Page Setup dialog box opens with the Sheet tab displayed.

▶ 2. Click the **Rows to repeat at top** box, move your pointer over the worksheet, and then select the range **A1:A4**. A flashing border appears around the first four rows of the worksheet as a visual indicator that the contents of the first four rows will be repeated on each page of the printout. The cell reference $1:$4 appears in the Rows to repeat at top box.

▶ 3. Click the **OK** button.

▶ 4. Click the **Page Layout** button on the status bar, and then scroll through the second and third pages of the printout in Page Layout view to verify that the company name, slogan, and worksheet title appear on each page. See Figure 2-36.

Figure 2-36 Second page of the printout

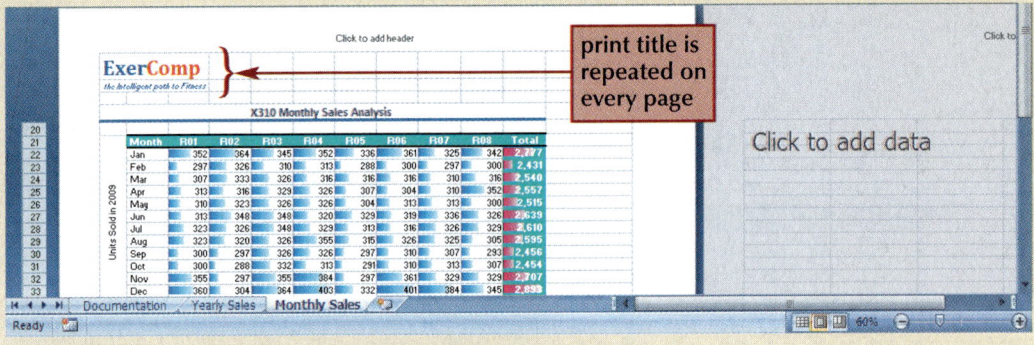

The Sheet tab in the Page Setup dialog box provides other print options, such as printing the gridlines or row and column headings. You can also print the worksheet in black and white or in draft quality. For a multiple page printout, you can specify whether the pages are ordered by first going down the worksheet and then across or across first and then down.

Adding Headers and Footers

Another way to repeat information on each page of a printout is with headers and footers. A **header** is the text printed in the top margin of each page. A **footer** is the text printed in the bottom margin of each page. A **margin** is the space between the page content and the edges of the page. Headers and footers can be used to add information to the printed page that is not found in the worksheet cells, such as the workbook's author, the date the page was printed, or the workbook filename. If the printout covers multiple pages, you can add a footer that displays the page number and the total number of pages in the printout to help ensure you and others have the entire printout.

The header and footer have three sections: a left section, a center section, and a right section. Within each section, you type the text you want to appear or insert elements such as the worksheet name or current date and time. These header and footer elements are dynamic; if you rename the worksheet, for example, the name is automatically updated in the header or footer.

Tom wants his printouts to display the workbook's filename in the header's left section and the current date in the header's right section. He wants the center footer to display the page number and the total number of pages in the printout, and the right footer to display your name as the workbook's author.

To insert the header and footer text:

1. Zoom the worksheet to **90%** in Page Layout view.

2. Scroll to the top of the worksheet, and then click the left section of the header directly above cell A1. The Header & Footer Tools contextual tab appears on the Ribbon.

3. Type **Filename:** in the left section of the header, press the **spacebar**, and then, in the Header & Footer Elements group on the Header & Footer Tools Design tab, click the **File Name** button. The code &[File], which displays the filename of the current workbook, is added into the left section of the header.

4. Press the **Tab** key twice to move to the right section of the header, and then, in the Header & Footer Elements group, click the **Current Date** button. The code &[Date] is added into the right section of the header. See Figure 2-37.

Figure 2-37   Page header

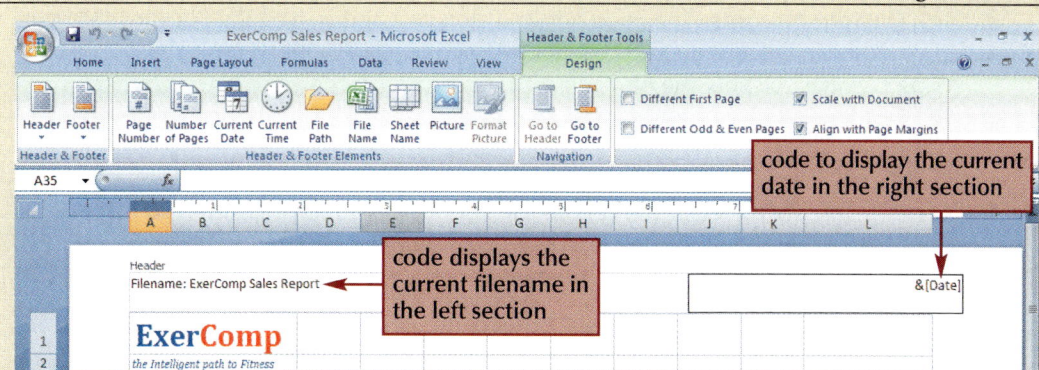

5. In the Navigation group, click the **Go to Footer** button. The right section of the footer is selected.

6. Click the center section of the footer, type **Page**, press the **spacebar**, and then, in the Header & Footer Elements group, click the **Page Number** button.

7. Press the **spacebar**, type **of**, press the **spacebar**, and then, in the Header & Footer Elements group, click the **Number of Pages** button. The text, "Page &[Page] of &[Pages]" appears in the center section of the footer.

8. Press the **Tab** key to move to the right section of the footer, type **Prepared by:**, press the **spacebar**, and then type your name. See Figure 2-38.

Figure 2-38   Page footer

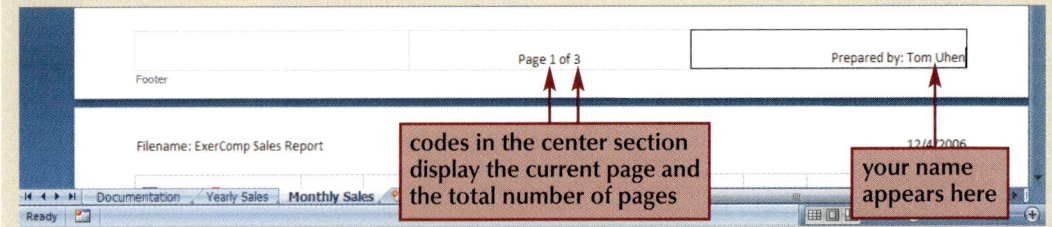

▶ 9. Click cell **A1**, and then scroll through the other two pages of the worksheet to verify that the same header appears for each page and the center section of the footer displays the correct page number and total number of pages.

Adjusting Margins

Tom wants you to try different margins to see the effect on the Monthly Sales worksheet and how it will print. You can use the preset Normal margins, Wide margins, or Narrow margins. Or, you can enter custom settings for each margin in the Page Setup dialog box.

To adjust the worksheet's margins:

▶ 1. In the Page Setup group on the Page Layout tab, click the **Margins** button. The Margins menu opens. The default margin setting, Normal, is selected.

▶ 2. Click **Custom Margins**. The Page Setup dialog box opens, and the Margins tab is active. You can enter the exact margin setting you want in each box. The preview image changes to show the new margins.

▶ 3. Select the text in the Top box, type **2** (you do not need to type the inches symbol), press the **Tab** key to select the text in the Bottom box, and then type **3**.

▶ 4. Press the **Tab** key to select the text in the Left box, type **1**, press the **Tab** key to select the text in the Right box, and then type **1**. The preview image shows the new margins.

▶ 5. Click the **OK** button. The worksheet reflects the new margins.

Tom prefers the default margin settings, so you'll return the margins to their original settings.

▶ 6. In the Page Setup group on the Page Layout tab, click the **Margins** button, and then click **Normal**. The margins change back to their default settings.

Tip

The settings most recently selected in the Page Setup dialog box appear as the Last Custom Setting option in the Margins menu.

The worksheet is formatted for printing. Tom asks you to save and print the Monthly Sales worksheet.

To save the workbook and print the worksheet:

▶ 1. Click the **Normal** button on the status bar to return the Monthly Sales worksheet to Normal view.

▶ 2. Save your changes to the workbook.

▶ **3.** Print the contents of the Monthly Sales worksheet, and then close the workbook. Each table is printed on a separate page and the headers and footers display the filename, current date, page number and total number of pages, and your name.

Tom will analyze the finished report, and distribute it during the upcoming sales meeting.

Session 2.2 Quick Check | Review

1. What is a table style?
2. What are the six table style options you can turn on and off?
3. What is conditional formatting?
4. How is the length of a data bar determined by default?
5. How would you highlight the top five values in the range A1:C20?
6. What are print titles?
7. How do you insert a page break into your worksheet?

Tutorial Summary | Review

In this tutorial, you used formatting tools to create visually appealing and informative workbooks. You formatted text, backgrounds, borders, numbers, and dates, and copied formats from one range into another. You applied built-in styles and themes to the workbook. Next, you looked at how formatting can be helpful for analyzing and interpreting data. You applied a table style to format an Excel table. Then, you used two types of conditional formatting—data bars and highlighting rules—to better understand the data entered into the workbook. Finally, you formatted the worksheet for printing by setting page breaks and page titles, and inserting headers and footers.

Key Terms

accent	Format Painter	points
automatic color	formatting	print area
banded rows	General number format	print title
border	header	sans serif font
conditional format	legend	serif font
custom color	Live Preview	standard color
data bar	manual page break	style
Excel table	margin	table style
font	merge	theme
font size	Mini toolbar	theme color
font style	non-theme font	theme font
footer	page break	typeface

| Excel | Tutorial 2 Formatting a Workbook

Practice | Review Assignments

Practice the skills you learned in the tutorial using the same case scenario.

Data Files needed for the Review Assignments: X410.xlsx, Paper.jpg

ExerComp introduced another heart rate monitor, the X410, two years ago. Tom wants you to format a workbook that compares the sales of the X310 and X410 models during that time. The workbook has a Documentation sheet, a Model Comparison sheet comparing the total units sold for each model in the eight sales regions, and a Monthly Sales sheet reporting the number of units sold per month.

In the Model Comparison sheet, Tom wants you to highlight the sales regions that showed the greatest sales increases from 2008 to 2009. Figure 2-39 shows a preview of the formatted Model Comparison sheet.

Figure 2-39

	A	B	C	D	E	F
1	**ExerComp**					
2	the Intelligent path to Fitness					
3				highest	Highest increase in units sold	
4				highest	Highest % increase in units sold	
5						
6		Region	Units Sold (2008)	Units Sold (2009)	Increase	% Increase
7		R01	3,605	3,853	248	6.88%
8	X310	R02	3,966	3,842	-124	-3.13%
9		R03	3,760	4,035	275	7.31%
10		R04	3,777	4,063	286	7.57%
11		R05	3,974	3,725	-249	-6.27%
12		R06	3,656	3,937	281	7.69%
13		R07	3,554	3,875	321	9.03%
14		R08	3,844	3,844	0	0.00%
15		Total	30,136	31,174	1,038	3.44%
16						
17		Region	Units Sold (2008)	Units Sold (2009)	Increase	% Increase
18		R01	2,488	4,156	1,668	67.04%
19	X410	R02	2,531	4,293	1,762	69.62%
20		R03	2,231	4,292	2,061	92.38%
21		R04	2,613	4,851	2,238	85.65%
22		R05	2,512	4,308	1,796	71.50%
23		R06	2,824	4,689	1,865	66.04%
24		R07	2,355	4,529	2,174	92.31%
25		R08	2,412	4,140	1,728	71.64%
26		Total	19,966	35,258	15,292	76.59%

In the Monthly Sales sheet, Tom wants you to include data bars that show the monthly sales totals for both models during 2008 and 2009. Figure 2-40 shows a preview of the completed Monthly Sales sheet.

Figure 2-40

	A	B	C	D	E	F	G	H	I
1	**ExerComp**								
2	*the Intelligent path to Fitness*								
3									
4		**2008 Sales (Units Sold)**					**2009 Sales (Units Sold)**		
5	Month	X310	X410	All Models		Month	X310	X410	All Models
6	Jan	2,608	-	2,608		Jan	2,777	3,223	6,000
7	Feb	2,330	-	2,330		Feb	2,431	2,612	5,043
8	Mar	2,426	25	2,451		Mar	2,540	2,714	5,254
9	Apr	2,375	75	2,450		Apr	2,557	2,877	5,434
10	May	2,400	1,500	3,900		May	2,515	2,749	5,264
11	Jun	2,533	1,750	4,283		Jun	2,639	2,955	5,594
12	Jul	2,528	2,135	4,663		Jul	2,610	2,839	5,449
13	Aug	2,560	2,620	5,180		Aug	2,595	2,875	5,470
14	Sep	2,393	2,714	5,107		Sep	2,456	2,823	5,279
15	Oct	2,389	2,689	5,078		Oct	2,454	2,791	5,245
16	Nov	2,688	3,144	5,832		Nov	2,707	3,278	5,985
17	Dec	2,906	3,314	6,220		Dec	2,893	3,522	6,415
18	Total	30,136	19,966	50,102		Total	31,174	35,258	66,432

Complete the following. (*Note:* Text you need to enter is shown in bold for ease of reference only; do not bold the text unless otherwise instructed.)

1. Open the **X410** workbook located in the Tutorial.02\Review folder included with your Data Files, and then save the workbook as **X410 Sales Comparison** in the same folder. In the Documentation sheet, enter your name in cell B4 and the current date in cell B5 in the format *mm/dd/yyyy*.
2. In the Documentation sheet, set the font color of cells A1 and A2 to blue, format the text in cell A1 in a 26-point Times New Roman font, and then format the text in cell A2 in a 10-point italicized Times New Roman font. In cell A1, change the font color of the text string "Comp" to red.
3. In the range A4:A6, set the font color to white and set the fill color to blue. In the range B4:B6, set the fill color to white. In the range A4:B6, add border lines around all of the cells.
4. In cell B5, display the date with the Long Date format and left-aligned within the cell.
5. In the Documentation sheet, insert a background image, using the **Paper.jpg** image file located in the Tutorial.02\Review folder included with your Data Files.
6. Use the Format Painter to copy the format from the range A1:A2 in the Documentation sheet to the range A1:A2 in the other two sheets. In cell A1, change the font color of the text string "Comp" to red.
7. In the Model Comparison sheet, merge and center the range A6:A15, center the text vertically, and then rotate the text to a vertical orientation. (*Hint:* In the Alignment group on the Home tab, click the Orientation button, and then click Vertical Text.) Center the text in the range C6:F6, and then indent the region labels in the range B7:B14 one character.
8. In the range C7:E15, format the numbers in a Number format using a thousands separator, no decimal places, and negative numbers displayed with a minus symbol. In the range F7:F15, format the numbers in a Percentage format with two decimal places.
9. Apply the Accent1 cell style to the range B6:F6. Apply the Accent1 cell style to the merged cell A6, and then increase that cell's font size to 18 points and bold. Apply the Total cell style to the range B15:F15.

10. In the range E7:E14, apply a conditional format that adds a Top/Bottom Rule to display the highest number in the range in dark green text with a green fill. In the range F7:F14, apply a conditional format that adds a Top/Bottom Rule to display the highest number in the range in dark red text with a light red fill.
11. Use the Format Painter to copy all of the formats from the range A6:F15 to the range A17:F26.
12. In cell D3, enter **highest**, and then apply a conditional format to cell D3 that adds a Highlight Cells Rule to format the cell that contains the text "highest" with Green Fill with Dark Green Text. In cell D4, enter **highest**, and then apply a conditional format to cell D3 that adds a Highlight Cells Rule to format the cell that contains the text "highest" with Light Red Fill with Dark Red Text.
13. In cell E3, enter **Highest increase in units sold**. In cell E4, enter **Highest % increase in units sold**. Format both cells with the Explanatory Text cell style.
14. In the Monthly Sales sheet, merge and center the range A4:D4, merge and center the range F4:I4, and then apply the Heading 1 style to both merged cells. In the range B5:D5;G5:I5, center the text.
15. In the range B6:D18;G6:I18, format the numbers to show a thousands separator (,) with no decimal places to the right of the decimal point.
16. Select the range A5:D18, and then apply Table Style Light 8 (the first table style in the second row of the Light section in the Table Styles gallery). Turn off the filter arrows, and then turn on only the header row, first column, and last column table style options. In the range A18:D18, apply the Total cell style.
17. Select the range F5:I18, and then repeat Step 16, applying the Total cell style to the range F18:I18.
18. In the range D6:D17, add green data bars. In the range I6:I17, add purple data bars.
19. For the Model Comparison and Monthly Sales worksheets, set the page orientations to landscape, display your name in the center section of the header, display the sheet name in the left section of the footer, display the workbook filename in the center section of the footer, and then display the current date in the right section of the footer.
20. Save and close your workbook. Submit the finished workbook to your instructor, either in printed or electronic form, as requested.

Apply | Case Problem 1

Use the skills you learned to create a sales report for a winter clothing company.

Data File needed for this Case Problem: Frosti.xlsx

FrostiWear Linda Young is a sales manager for FrostiWear, a successful new store based in Hillsboro, Oregon. She's tracking the sales figures for FrostiWear's line of gloves. She created a workbook that contains the sales figures from the past year for three glove models. She wants you to help format the sales report. Figure 2-41 shows a preview of the formatted report.

Figure 2-41

	A	B	C	D	E	F	G	H
1				**FrostiWear**				
2				**2009 Sales Report**				
3		Month	Region 1	Region 2	Region 3	Region 4	Region 5	Total
4		Jan	1,150	1,690	930	2,850	1,210	7,830
5		Feb	1,100	2,200	680	2,340	1,100	7,420
6		Mar	1,070	1,290	960	2,740	1,180	7,240
7	PolyFleece Mitts	Apr	780	1,520	720	2,170	1,180	6,370
8		May	1,070	1,370	700	1,940	1,210	6,290
9		Jun	670	1,300	780	3,430	1,170	7,350
10		Jul	1,390	1,590	1,240	2,230	1,430	7,880
11		Aug	1,310	1,730	610	2,560	960	7,170
12		Sep	1,100	1,820	370	3,040	1,100	7,430
13		Oct	1,350	2,010	750	2,430	1,230	7,770
14		Nov	680	1,620	780	3,210	1,230	7,520
15		Dec	1,120	1,170	670	1,920	1,310	6,190
16		Total	12,790	19,310	9,190	30,860	14,310	86,460
17								
18		Month	Region 1	Region 2	Region 3	Region 4	Region 5	Total
19		Jan	790	1,160	620	2,590	760	5,920
20		Feb	1,010	1,170	610	1,950	1,010	5,750
21		Mar	710	1,270	600	2,050	930	5,560
22	ArcticBlast Gloves	Apr	890	1,190	750	2,030	980	5,840
23		May	990	1,340	660	2,670	1,040	6,700
24		Jun	990	1,280	620	2,330	800	6,020
25		Jul	780	1,180	690	2,260	920	5,830
26		Aug	800	1,220	560	2,460	900	5,940
27		Sep	810	1,150	670	2,500	970	6,100
28		Oct	760	1,070	630	2,350	1,040	5,850
29		Nov	770	1,140	630	2,540	1,080	6,160
30		Dec	850	1,370	590	2,490	1,060	6,360
31		Total	10,150	14,540	7,630	28,220	11,490	72,030
32								
33		Month	Region 1	Region 2	Region 3	Region 4	Region 5	Total
34		Jan	340	780	280	1,670	600	3,670
35		Feb	460	810	280	1,770	480	3,800
36		Mar	410	820	310	1,490	460	3,490
37	Glomitts	Apr	490	890	330	1,610	650	3,970
38		May	470	960	290	1,580	540	3,840
39		Jun	480	740	340	1,780	640	3,980
40		Jul	470	760	320	1,500	640	3,690
41		Aug	490	690	340	1,610	600	3,730
42		Sep	420	780	340	1,660	680	3,880
43		Oct	460	820	350	1,800	660	4,090
44		Nov	550	830	440	1,250	590	3,660
45		Dec	400	790	220	1,620	540	3,570
46		Total	5,440	9,670	3,840	19,340	7,080	45,370

Complete the following. (*Note:* Text you need to enter is shown in bold for ease of reference only; do not bold the text unless otherwise instructed.)

1. Open the **Frosti** workbook located in the Tutorial.02\Case1 folder included with your Data Files, and then save the workbook as **FrostiWear Sales Report** in the same folder.
2. In the Documentation sheet, enter your name in cell B3 and the date in cell B4. Set the background color for all the cells in the worksheet to standard blue, and then set the background color for the range B3:B5 to white. Add a border line around each cell in the range B3:B5.
3. Change the font of cell A1 to the Headings font of the current theme, change the font size to 36 points, change the font color to white, and then bold the text. Change the font size of the range A3:A5 to 16 points, change the font color to white, and then bold the text.

4. In the Glove Sales worksheet, merge and center the range A1:H1, apply the Title cell style, and then increase the font size to 26 points. Merge and center the range A2:H2, apply the Heading 4 cell style, and then increase the font size to 16 points.
5. Merge and center the range A3:A16, set the alignment to Middle Align, rotate the text 90° counterclockwise, apply the Accent1 cell style, increase the font size to 18 points, and then bold the text.
6. Use the Format Painter to copy the format of merged cell A3 into the range A18:A31;A33:A46.
7. Center the text in the range C3:H3. Format the range C4:H16 to include thousands separators (,) and no decimal places. Use the Format Painter to copy the formats in the range C3:H16 to the range C18:H31;C33:H46.
8. In the range B3:H16, apply the Table Style Medium 2 table style. Turn off the filter arrows, and then display the header row, first column, last column, and banded rows. In the range B16:H16, change the fill color of the Total row to standard yellow. In the range H4:H15, change the fill color of the Total column to white.
9. Repeat Step 8 for the other two tables in the worksheet.
10. Increase the width of column H to 25 characters.
11. Add blue data bars to the range H4:H15. Also add blue data bars to the ranges H19:H30 and H34:H45.
12. In the Glove Sales worksheet, set the page orientation to landscape, insert manual page breaks at cells A18 and A33, and then repeat the first two rows of the worksheet on every printed page.
13. Display your name in the center header, display the filename in the left footer, display **Page** *page number* **of** *number of pages* in the center footer, and then display the current date in the right footer.
14. Save and close your workbook. Submit the finished workbook to your instructor, either in printed or electronic form, as requested.

Create | **Case Problem 2**

Create and format a worksheet as a packing slip for GrillRite Grills.

Data File needed for this Case Problem: GrillRite.xlsx

GrillRite Grills Brian Simpko is a shipping manager at GrillRite Grills in Hammond, Indiana. He uses an Excel workbook to provide shipping and order information for customer orders and deliveries. He asks you to help create and format a worksheet that he can use to enter information for packing slips. Figure 2-42 shows the worksheet you'll create for Brian.

Figure 2-42

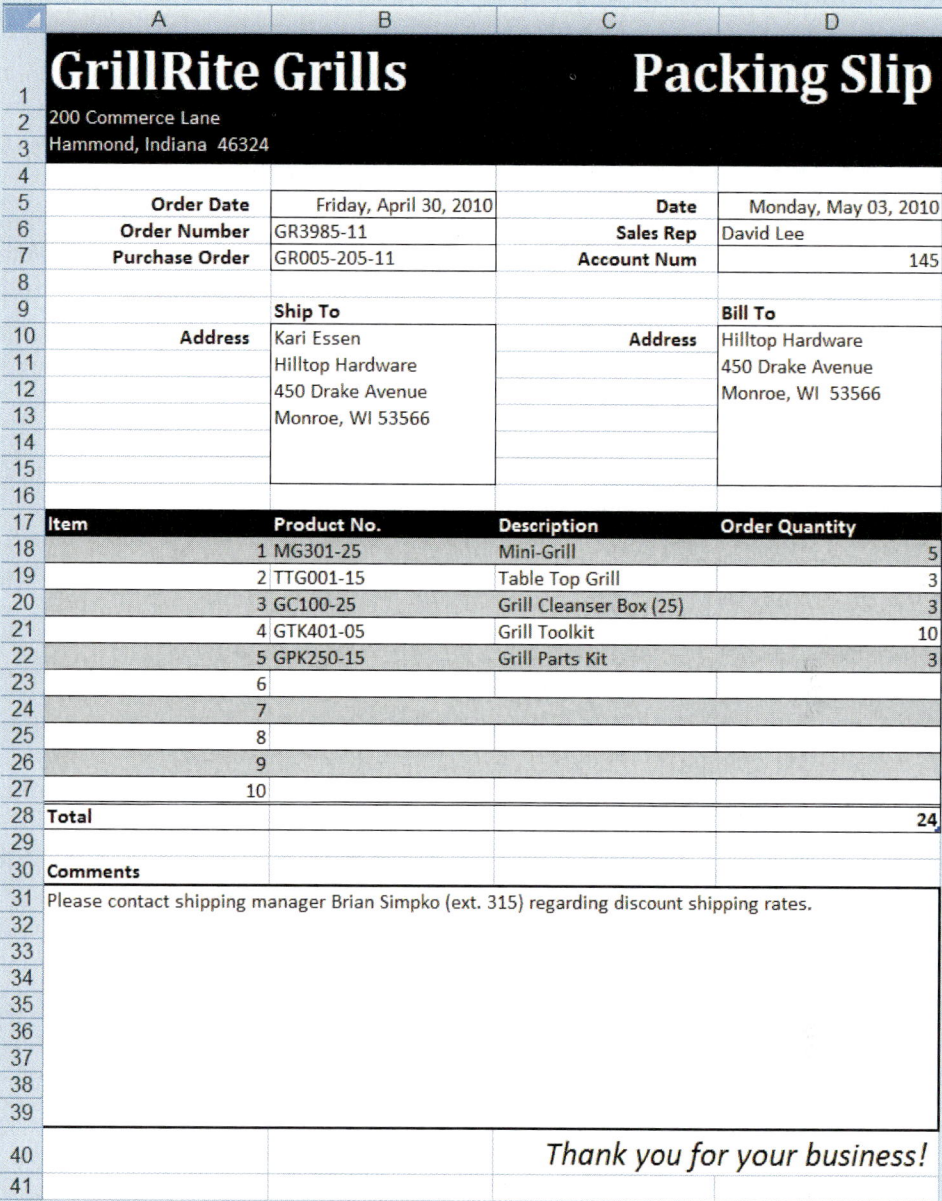

Complete the following. (*Note:* Text you need to enter is shown in bold for ease of reference only; do not bold the text unless otherwise instructed.)

1. Open the **GrillRite** workbook located in the Tutorial.02\Case2 folder included with your Data Files, and then save the workbook as **GrillRite Grills Packing Slip** in the same folder. In the Documentation sheet, enter your name in cell B3 and the date in cell B4.
2. Insert a new worksheet at the end of the document named **Packing Slip**.
3. In the Packing Slip worksheet, select all of the cells in the worksheet. (*Hint:* Click the Select All button at the intersection of the row and column headings.) Change the font to the Body font of the current theme. For the range A1:D3, set the fill color to black and the font color to white.
4. Set the width of columns A through D to 20 characters. Set the height of the first row to 36.

5. Merge the range A1:B3, merge the range C1:D3, and then left- and top-align both merged cells.
6. In cell A1, enter the following three lines of text, and then format the first line in a 26-point bold font using the Headings font of the current theme:
   GrillRite Grills
   200 Commerce Lane
   Hammond, Indiana 46324
7. In cell C1, enter **Packing Slip**, format the text in a 26-point bold font using the Headings font of the current theme, and then right-align the text.
8. In the range A5:A7, enter the following three lines of text in a bold font, and then right-align the text and indent the text one character:
   Order Date
   Order Number
   Purchase Order
9. Format cell B5 in the Long Date format. Insert border lines around each of the cells in the range B5:B7.
10. In the range C5:C7, enter the following three lines of text, and then use the Format Painter to copy the formats from the range A5:B7 to the range C5:D7:
    Date
    Sales Rep
    Account Num
11. In cell B9, enter **Ship To** and in cell D9, enter **Bill To** and then format both in a bold font.
12. In cell A10, enter **Address** in a bold font, right-align the text, and then indent it one character.
13. Merge the cells in the range B10:B15, left- and top-align the cell contents, and then insert a border around the merged cell.
14. In cell C10, enter **Address**. Copy the format from the range A10:B15 into the range C10:D15.
15. Enter the following data into the worksheet:

Cell	Data
A17	**Item**
B17	**Product No.**
C17	**Description**
D17	**Order Quantity**
A18:A27	the numbers from 1 to 10

EXPLORE

16. For the range A17:D27, apply Table Style Medium 1, turn off the filter arrows, and display the header row, total row, and banded rows. In cell D28, select the SUM function from the list.
17. In cell A30, enter **Comments** in a bold font.
18. Merge the range A31:D39, left- and top-align the cell contents, and then add a thick box border around the merged cell.
19. In cell D40, enter **Thank you for your business!** in an italic, 16-point font, and then right-align the cell contents.
20. Enter the packing slip data shown in Figure 2-42.
21. Make sure the worksheet's page orientation is set to portrait, and then add a footer that displays your name in the left section, the filename in the center section, and the current date in the right section.
22. Save and close your workbook. Submit the finished workbook to your instructor, either in printed or electronic form, as requested.

Challenge | Case Problem 3

Explore how to use different Excel formatting features to create an election report.

Data File needed for this Case Problem: Iowa.xlsx

Lewis Reports Kay Lewis is a political columnist, commentator, and blogger. Her Web site, *Lewis Reports*, contains historical information on campaigns and elections. Recently, Kay compiled state-by-state and county-by-county voting totals for the past 15 presidential elections. She wants this information in an Excel workbook so she can analyze voting preferences and trends. Kay has created a workbook that contains the election results from the 2004 presidential election in Iowa. She asks you to format the workbook. She wants formats that quickly show which candidates won at the state and county levels as well as the margin of victory. Counties that went heavily Democratic or Republican should have formats that reflect this fact. Figure 2-43 shows a preview of the worksheet you'll format for Kay.

Figure 2-43

	A	B	C	D	E	F
1	2004 Presidential Election					
2						
3	Iowa Vote Totals					
4	State	Counties	Candidate	Votes		%
5	Iowa	99	George W. Bush (Rep)	746,600		50.46%
6			John F. Kerry (Dem)	733,102		49.54%
7			Total	1,479,702		
8						
9	County-by-County Totals					
10	County	Precincts	Candidate	Votes		%
11	Adair	10	Bush	2,393		56.63%
12			Kerry	1,833		43.37%
13			Total	4,226		
14	Adams	12	Bush	1,313		57.44%
15			Kerry	973		42.56%
16			Total	2,286		
17	Allamakee	23	Bush	3,523		50.62%
18			Kerry	3,437		49.38%
19			Total	6,960		

Complete the following. (*Note:* Text you need to enter is shown in bold for ease of reference only; do not bold the text unless otherwise instructed.)

1. Open the **Iowa** workbook located in the Tutorial.02\Case3 folder included with your Data Files, and then save the workbook as **Iowa Election Results** in the same folder. In the Documentation sheet, enter your name in cell B3 and the date in cell B4.
2. In the Iowa worksheet, apply the Title style to cell A1, and then apply the Heading 1 style to cells A3 and A9.
3. Apply the Accent3 style to the range A4:F4, and then center the heading text in cells D4:F4.
4. In the range D5:D7, format the numbers with a thousands separator (,) and no decimal places. In the range F5:F7, format the numbers as percentages with two decimal places.
5. Merge the range A5:A7, and then left- and top-align the cell contents. Merge the range B5:B7, and then right- and top-align the cell contents. Merge the range E5:E7.
6. Add border lines around each cell in the range A4:F7.

7. Format the range C5:D5 as white text on a standard red background. Format the range C6:D6 as white text on a standard light blue background.
8. Copy the format in the range A4:F7 to the range A10:F13.

EXPLORE
9. Add a double bottom border to the range A11:F13, and then copy the format in the range A11:F13 to the larger range A14:F307. Excel repeats the format until it fills up the larger range.

EXPLORE
10. Select the range E5;E11:E307, which shows the difference in votes between the Republican and Democratic candidates. Create a highlight rule to format cells with values greater than zero (indicating a Republican winner) in red text on a red background (thus, obscuring the text). (*Hint:* In the Greater Than dialog box, click Custom Format in the with list to open the Format Cells dialog box, and then use the Font tab and the Fill tab to select the colors.) Create a second highlight rule to format cells with values less than zero (indicating a Democratic winner) in light blue text on a light blue background. Reduce the width of column E to 3 characters.
11. Select the range F5:F7;F11:F307, which shows the vote percentages for each candidate. Apply green data bars, left-align the cells, and then increase the width of column F to 23 characters.
12. Verify the conditional formatting by entering different totals in column D and checking that the highlights and data bars are changed accurately. Restore the original values to the worksheet.
13. For the Iowa worksheet, make sure the page orientation is set to portrait, and then scale the page so that the width of the printout is one page and the height is automatic. (*Hint:* Use the buttons in the Scale To Fit group on the Page Layout tab.)

EXPLORE
14. Format the printout of the Iowa worksheet to repeat the first 10 rows of the worksheet on every page of the printout. Insert manual page breaks into the rest of the table to keep each county's vote from splitting between two pages.
15. Display your name in the center section of the header, and then display the filename in the left section of the footer, **Page** *page number* **of** *number of pages* in the center section of the footer, and the current date in the right section of the footer.
16. Save and close your workbook. Submit the finished workbook to your instructor, either in printed or electronic form, as requested.

Create | Case Problem 4

Use your creativity to format a meal-planning worksheet that highlights foods with high calorie counts and fat contents.

Data File needed for this Case Problem: Life.xlsx

Life Managers   Kate Dee is a dietician at *Life Managers*, a company in Kleinville, Michigan, that specializes in personal improvement, particularly in areas of health and fitness. Kate wants to create a meal-planning workbook for her clients who want to lose weight and improve their health. One goal of meal planning is to decrease the percentage of fat in the diet. Kate thinks it would be helpful to highlight foods that have a high percentage of fat as well as list their total fat calories. She already created an Excel workbook that contains a few sample food items and lists the number of calories and grams of fat in each item. She wants you to format this workbook.

Complete the following:

1. Open the **Life** workbook located in the Tutorial.02\Case4 folder included with your Data Files, and then save the workbook as **Life Managers Nutrition Table** in the same folder. In the Documentation sheet, enter your name in cell B3 and the date in cell B4.

2. Fat contains nine calories per gram. In the Meal Planner worksheet, add a column that calculates the calories from fat for each food item. The percentage of fat is calculated by dividing the calories from fat by the total number of calories. Enter this calculated value to the table for each food item.
3. Display all calories and grams of fat values with one decimal place. Display the fat percentages as percentages with one decimal place.
4. Design the rest of the Meal Planner worksheet as you'd like, but be sure to include at least one example of each of the following design elements:
   - A range merged into a single cell
   - Text centered and rotated within a cell
   - Cell styles applied to one or more elements
   - Border line styles applied to one or more elements
5. The FDA recommends for good health that the fat percentage should not exceed 30% of the total calories. Apply a rule to the fat percentages to highlight those food items that exceed the FDA recommendations. Include a legend to document the highlighting color you used.
6. Add data bars to the display of calories from fat values to graphically show the relative amounts of fat calories for different food items.
7. Add descriptive headers and footers to the printed document. Also insert page breaks and print titles to ensure that the printout is easily read and interpreted.
8. Save and close your workbook. Submit the finished workbook to your instructor, either in printed or electronic form, as requested.

Research | Internet Assignments

Use the Internet to find and work with data related to the topics presented in this tutorial.

The purpose of the Internet Assignments is to challenge you to find information on the Internet that you can use to work effectively with this software. The actual assignments are updated and maintained on the Course Technology Web site. Log on to the Internet and use your Web browser to go to the Student Online Companion for New Perspectives Office 2007 at **www.course.com/np/office2007**. Then navigate to the Internet Assignments for this tutorial.

Assess | SAM Assessment and Training

If you have a SAM user profile, you may have access to hands-on instruction, practice, and assessment of the skills covered in this tutorial. Log in to your SAM account (**http://sam2007.course.com**) to launch any assigned training activities or exams that relate to the skills covered in this tutorial.

Review | Quick Check Answers

Session 2.1

1. Serif fonts have extra decorative strokes at the end of each character. Sans serif fonts do not include these decorative strokes.
2. Theme colors are the colors that belong to a workbook's basic design, giving the elements in the workbook a uniform appearance. A standard color is always available to every workbook regardless of which themes might be in use.

3. the default Excel number format that displays numbers just as they're entered
4. Dates are formatted numeric values and, as such, are right-aligned in cells.
5. A1
6. Open the Format Cells dialog box.
7. You can use the Format Painter to copy and paste the format from one range into another, or you can define a style for the different ranges.

Session 2.2

1. A style applied to a table allows you to turn on table style options.
2. header row, total row, first column, last column, banded rows, and banded columns
3. A conditional format depends on the cell's value.
4. by the cell's value relative to other cells in the range for which the data bars have been defined
5. Select the range A1:C20, click the Conditional Formatting button in the Styles group on the Home tab, point to Top/Bottom Rules, and then click Top 10%. In the dialog box, enter 5 for the top items to show, and then click the OK button.
6. titles taken from worksheet rows or columns that are repeated on every page of the printed sheet
7. Select the first cell below the row at which you want to insert the page break, click the Breaks button in the Page Setup group on the Page Layout tab, and then click Insert Break.

Ending Data Files

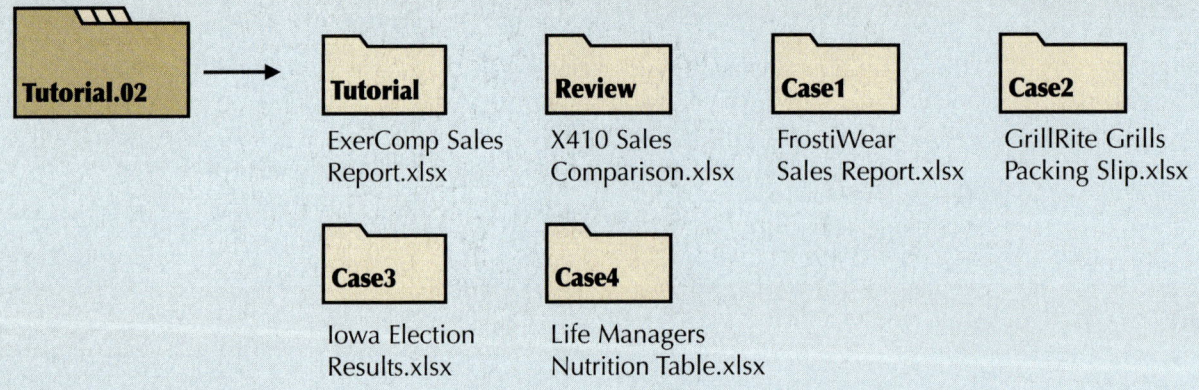

Excel **EX 113**

Tutorial 3

Objectives

Session 3.1
- Copy formulas
- Build formulas containing relative, absolute, and mixed references
- Review function syntax
- Insert a function with the Insert Function dialog box
- Search for a function
- Type a function directly in a cell

Session 3.2
- Use AutoFill to fill in a formula and complete a series
- Enter the IF logical function
- Insert the date with the TODAY function
- Calculate monthly mortgage payments with the PMT financial function

Working with Formulas and Functions

Developing a Budget

Case | Drake Family Budget

Diane and Glenn Drake, newly married, are trying to balance career, school, and family life. Diane works full-time as a legal assistant, and Glenn is in a graduate program at a nearby university where he recently was hired as a lab assistant. In the summer, he does other work that brings additional income to the family. The couple just moved into a new apartment. Although Glenn and Diane's salaries have grown in the past years, the couple seems to have less cash on hand. This financial shortage has prompted them to take a closer look at their finances and figure out how to best manage them.

Diane has set up an Excel workbook and entered the take-home pay from their two jobs. She has identified and entered expenses the family pays on a monthly basis, such as the rent and grocery bill, as well as other expenses that occur only a few times a year, such as Glenn's tuition and vacations. She wants to calculate how much money they are bringing in and how much money they are spending. She also wants to come up with a savings plan for the down payment on a house they hope to buy in a few years.

You'll help Diane complete the workbook. Diane wants you to enter formulas to perform the calculations she needs to get a better overall picture of the family's finances, which, in turn, should help the couple manage their money more effectively.

Starting Data Files

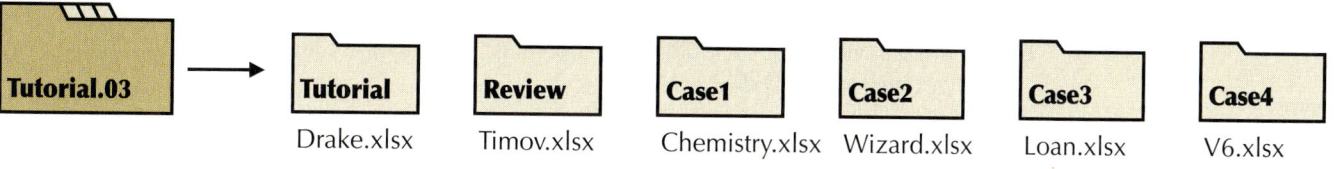

Session 3.1

Understanding Cell References When Copying Formulas

Diane has already done a lot of the work on her family budget. She used data from the past year to estimate the couple's monthly expenses for the upcoming year and she knows their monthly take-home pay. She already entered this data into an Excel workbook. You'll open this workbook now.

To open Diane's workbook:

1. Open the **Drake** workbook located in the **Tutorial.03\Tutorial** folder included with your Data Files, and then save the workbook as **Drake Family Budget** in the same folder.

2. In the Documentation sheet, enter your name in cell B3 and the date in cell B4.

3. Review the contents of the **2010 Proposed Budget** worksheet.

Diane organized the worksheet so the top displays the values that she'll use throughout her budget, such as the family's monthly take-home pay. One of the advantages of placing these values in their own cells in one location is that you can reference them in formulas throughout the worksheets. Then, rather than changing the same value in several locations, you can change it once and any formulas based on that cell are automatically updated to reflect the new value. The top of the worksheet will also include some summary calculations, such as the total take-home pay and expenses for the upcoming year as well as what Diane can expect to earn and spend on average each month. Below that section is a grid in which Diane wants to record how the family's take-home pay and expenses change month by month.

Diane points out a few things about her data. First, she has two possible values for the couple's take-home pay: one for months during the school year and one for months during the summer. Because Glenn works only part-time during the school year as a lab assistant, he earns less during that time than during the summer months. On the other hand, Diane earns the same amount throughout the year. The couple's expenses also vary throughout the year. January and August are particularly expensive months because Glenn has to pay for tuition and books for the upcoming semester. The couple is planning a trip next summer for a family reunion and expenses always seem to add up during the holiday season. With all of these factors in mind, Diane wants to make sure that they will not be caught short in any month. Glenn and Diane hope to purchase a house in about three years, so they need to follow a well-planned budget.

In the range D19:O20, Diane reserved space for entering the couple's monthly take-home pay. You'll enter their projected take-home pay for January through May, using the values at the top of the worksheet.

To insert the monthly take-home pay for January through May:

1. Click cell **D19**, type **=E5**, and then press the **Enter** key. The value 2,000, Diane's take-home pay for January, appears in cell D19.

2. In cell D20, enter the formula **=E6**. The value 950, Glenn's take-home pay for January, appears in cell D20.

3. In cell D21, enter the formula **=D19+D20**. This formula calculates the total take-home pay for the couple in the month of January.

   The couple will have the same take-home pay for the next four months as they did in January, so you can copy the formulas from January into February through May.

4. Select the range **D19:D21**, and then, in the Clipboard group on the Home tab, click the **Copy** button.

5. Select the range **E19:H21**, and then, in the Clipboard group, click the **Paste** button. Figure 3-1 shows the couple's take-home pay for January through May.

Tip

You can also use the SUM function to calculate the total take-home pay by clicking the Sum button in the Editing group on the Home tab.

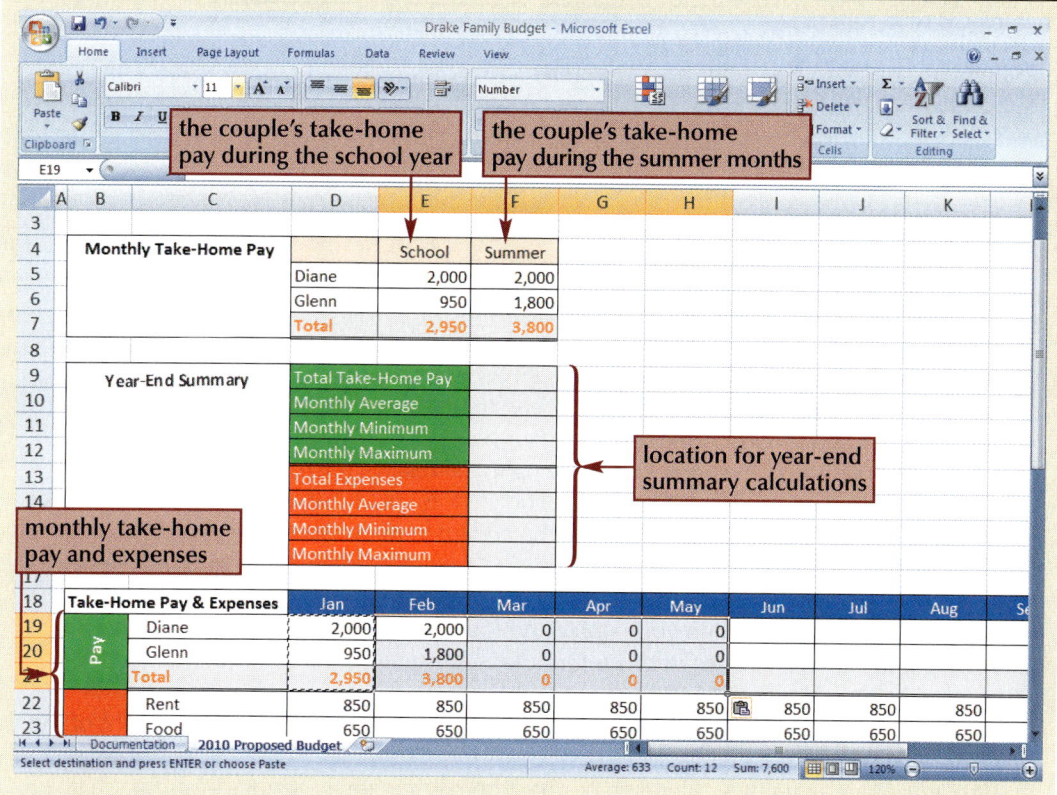

Figure 3-1 Take-home pay values copied through May

Notice that the formulas you copied and pasted from January resulted in incorrect values for February, March, April, and May. Diane's take-home pay of $2,000 is correct for January and February, but incorrectly changed to 0 for March, April, and May. Likewise, Glenn's take-home pay of $950 is correct for January, but incorrectly changed to $1,800 for February and 0 for March, April, and May. You need to investigate why you didn't get the results you expected. You'll examine how formulas change when copied to new locations in the workbook.

Using Relative References

When you enter a formula into a cell, Excel interprets cell references in the formula in relation to the cell's location. For example, the formula =A1 entered into cell A3 tells Excel to insert the value from the cell two rows above cell A3. When you copy the formula into other cells, Excel applies the same interpretation to the formula's new location, always displaying the value from the cell two rows above. Such cell references are called **relative references** because they are always interpreted in relation, or relative, to the location of the cell containing the formula. Figure 3-2 illustrates how a relative reference in a formula changes when the formula is copied to another range.

Figure 3-2 Formula using a relative reference

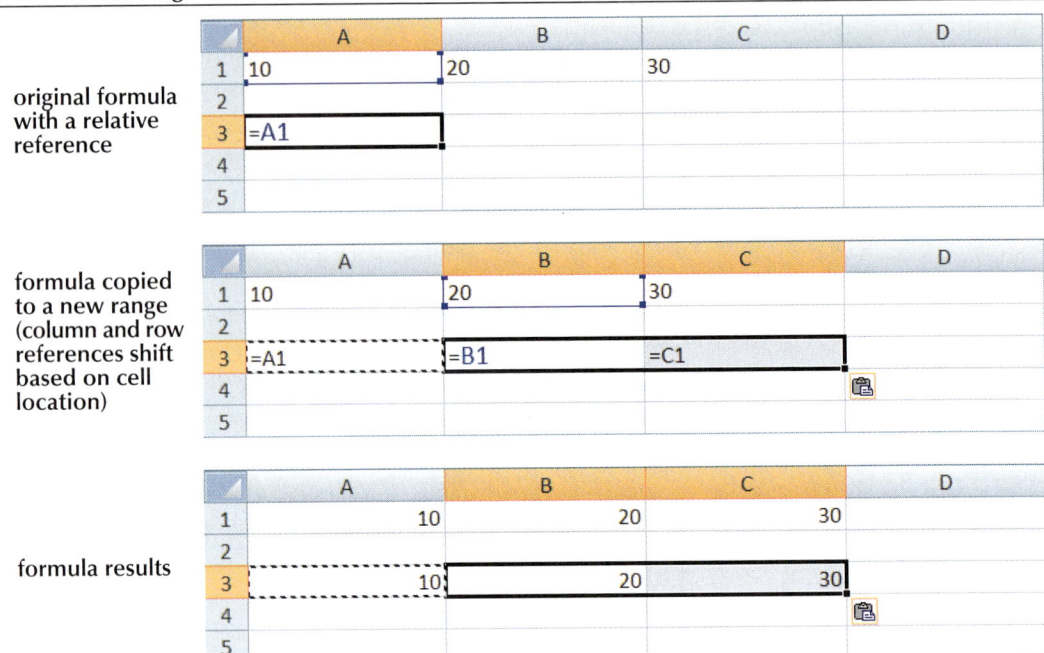

In this figure, the formula =A1 entered in cell A3 produced the result of 10, which is the value in cell A1. After the formula in cell A3 was copied to cell B3, the copied formula changed to =B1 and produced the result of 20, which is the value in cell B1. As you can see, when the formula was copied one cell to the right, the relative reference in the original formula (A1) adjusted one cell to the right to become B1. Similarly, when the formula in cell A3 was copied two cells to the right to cell C3, the copied formula changed to =C1 and produced the result of 30, which is the value in cell C1. In each instance, the formula references the cell two rows above the cell that contains the formula.

In Diane's worksheet, when you copied the formulas in the range D19:D21 into a new range, the cell references in those formulas adjusted to their new cell location. For example, the formula in cell E19 is =F5, the formula in cell F19 is =G5, and so forth. In each case, Excel references the cell that is 14 rows up and one column to the right of the current location.

The advantage of relative references is that you can create a "general" formula that you can use again and again in your worksheet. Relative references free you from having to rewrite a formula each time you copy it to a new location. For example, you can write a formula to add the values in a column of data, and then copy that formula to other columns to quickly add their values. You used this technique in the previous set of steps to calculate the couple's total take-home pay for each of the months from January to May.

Using Absolute References

Sometimes, you want references that are fixed on specific cells in the worksheet. This usually occurs when the referenced cell contains a value that needs to be repeated in different formulas throughout the workbook. In Diane's worksheet, any formulas involving take-home pay should be fixed on those cells that contain those values, which are the range E5:E6 for the school months and the range F5:F6 for the summer months.

References that are fixed are called **absolute references**. In Excel, absolute references are marked with a $ (dollar sign) before each column and row designation. For example, B8 is a relative reference to cell B8, whereas $B$8 is an absolute reference to cell B8. When you copy a formula that contains an absolute reference to a new location, the reference does not change. Figure 3-3 shows an example of how copying a formula with an absolute reference does not change the cell reference.

Formula using an absolute reference   Figure 3-3

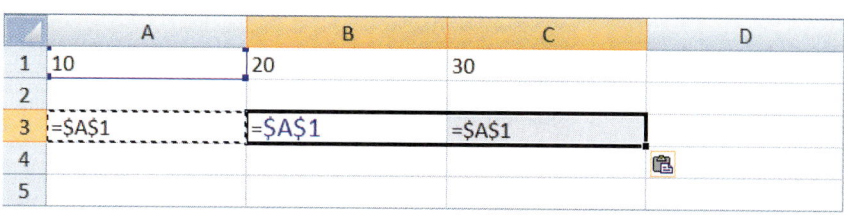

original formula with an absolute reference

formula copied into a new range (column and row references fixed regardless of cell location)

formula results

In this figure, the formula =$A$1 entered in cell A3 produced the result of 10, which is the value in cell A1. After the formula in cell A3 was copied to cell B3, the copied formula remained unchanged and produced the result of 10, which is the value in cell A1. As you can see, when the formula was copied one cell to the right, the absolute reference in the original formula (A1) did not change. Similarly, when the formula in cell A3 was copied two cells to the right to cell C3, the copied formula and the results did not change. In each instance, the formula references the cell A1.

You'll see how absolute references work when you fix the formulas in cells D19 and D20, and then recopy the formulas.

To use absolute references in the take-home pay formulas:

1. In cell D19, enter **=$E$5**. This formula contains an absolute reference to cell E5, which contains Diane's take-home pay during the school months.

2. In cell D20, enter **=$E$6**. This formula contains an absolute reference to cell E6, which contains Glenn's take-home pay during the school months.

3. Copy the corrected formulas in the range **D19:D20**, and then paste them in the range **E19:H20**. As shown in Figure 3-4, the months of February through May now correctly show the take-home pay values that Diane has specified for the school months.

Figure 3-4 — Results of formulas with absolute references

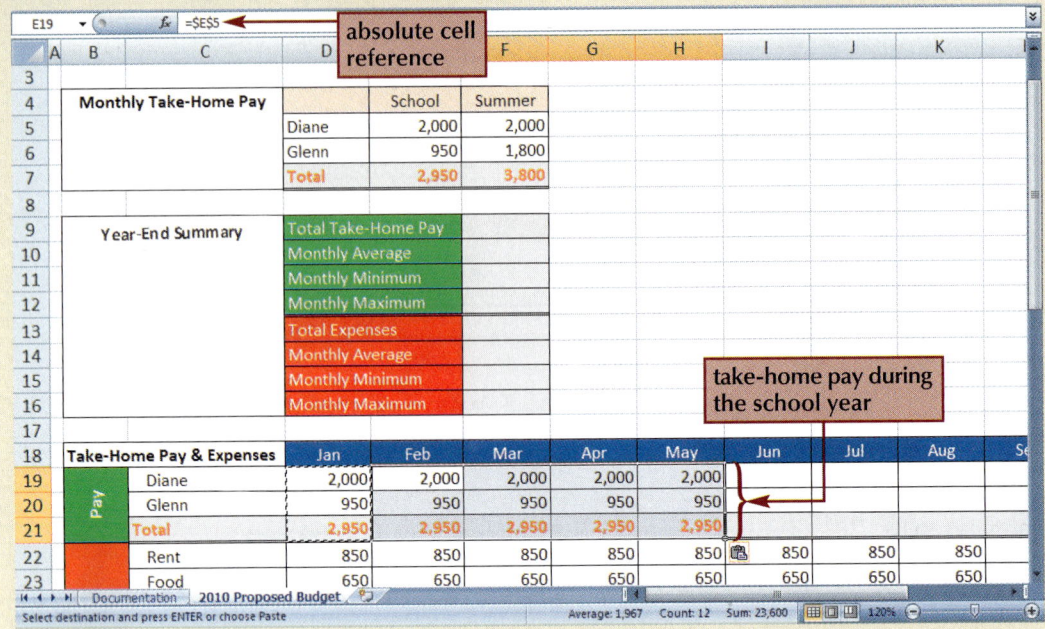

▶ **4.** Click each cell in the range E19:H20 to verify that the formulas =$E$5 and =$E$6 were copied into the appropriate cells.

InSight | Understanding Relative and Absolute References

Part of writing effective formulas is knowing when to use relative and absolute references. Use relative references when you want to repeat the same formula with different cells. For example, in a customer order worksheet, you might need to calculate the cost of an item multiplied by the quantity being purchased. To repeat this formula for all of the items in an order, you would use relative references for the item cost and item quantity. Use absolute references when you want different formulas to refer to the same cell. For example, in a customer order worksheet, you might need to apply the same sales tax percentage to each order. You could store the sales tax percentage in a worksheet cell, and then use an absolute reference to that cell in the formula that multiples the order total with the sales tax percentage.

Using Mixed References

A formula can also contain mixed references. A **mixed reference** contains both relative and absolute references. For example, a mixed reference for cell A2 can be either $A2 or A$2. In the mixed reference $A2, the column reference is fixed on column A and the reference to row 2 is relative. In the mixed reference A$2, the column reference is relative and the row reference is fixed. In other words, a mixed reference "locks" one part of the cell reference while the other part can change. When you copy and paste a formula with a mixed reference to a new location, the absolute portion of the cell reference remains fixed and the relative portion shifts. For example, the mixed reference in the formula =$A2 in cell B2 becomes =$A3 when copied to cell B3, and the mixed reference in the formula =B$1 in cell B2 becomes =C$1 when copied to cell C2.

Figure 3-5 shows an example of using a formula with a mixed reference in which the column is relative and the row is fixed. When you copy and paste the formula from cell A3 into cells A4 and A5, the row reference remains fixed on row 1. In this instance, the column reference, which is relative, doesn't change either, because the formula was copied to the same column. However, when you copy the formula to other columns, the column reference, which is relative, shifts to reflect the new column location. The row reference remains fixed on row 1 and doesn't change no matter where you copy the formula.

Figure 3-5 Formulas using mixed references

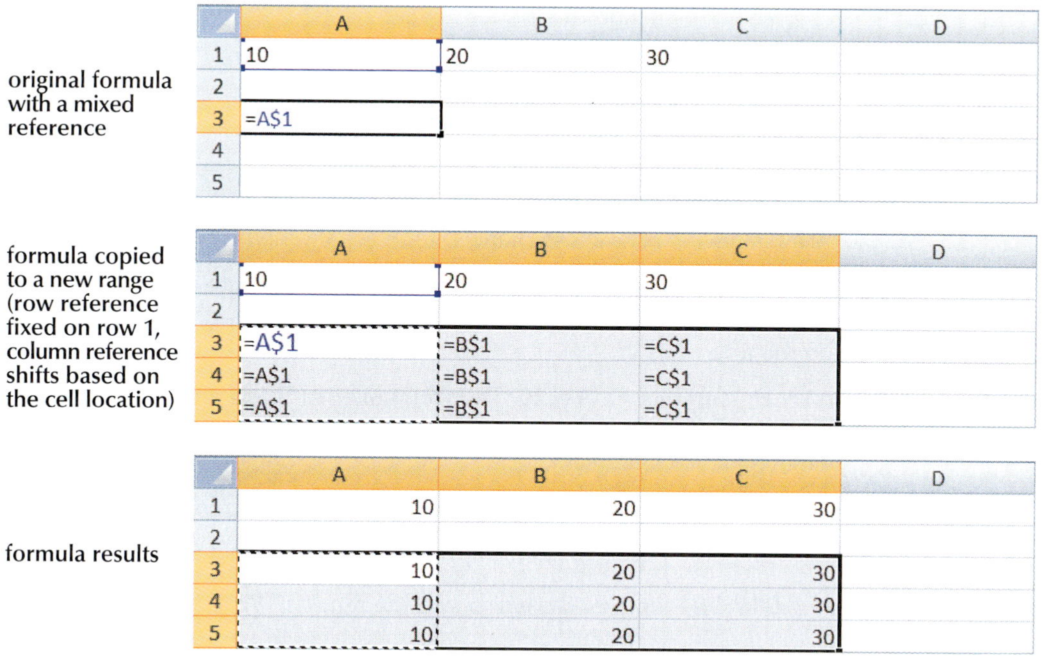

original formula with a mixed reference

	A	B	C	D
1	10	20	30	
2				
3	=A$1			
4				
5				

formula copied to a new range (row reference fixed on row 1, column reference shifts based on the cell location)

	A	B	C	D
1	10	20	30	
2				
3	=A$1	=B$1	=C$1	
4	=A$1	=B$1	=C$1	
5	=A$1	=B$1	=C$1	

formula results

	A	B	C	D
1	10	20	30	
2				
3	10	20	30	
4	10	20	30	
5	10	20	30	

As you develop formulas, you might want to switch a cell reference from relative to absolute or mixed. Rather than retyping the formula, you can switch the reference in editing mode by selecting the cell reference and pressing the **F4 key**. As you press the function key, Excel cycles through the different reference types, starting by changing a relative reference to an absolute reference, then to a mixed reference with the row absolute, then to a mixed reference with the column absolute, and then finally back to a relative reference.

Entering Relative, Absolute, and Mixed References | Reference Window

- To enter a relative reference, type the cell reference as it appears in the worksheet. For example, enter B2 for cell B2.
- To enter an absolute reference, type $ (a dollar sign) before both the row and column references. For example, enter $B$2.
- To enter a mixed reference, type $ before either the row or column reference. For example, enter $B2 or B$2.

or

- Select the cell reference you want to change.
- Press the F4 key to cycle the reference from relative to absolute to mixed and then back to relative.

You'll use the F4 key to cycle through the different types of references as you enter the remaining formulas with the take-home pay for the summer months.

To insert the remaining take-home pay formulas:

▶ 1. Click cell **I19**, type **=**, and then click cell **F5**. The formula =F5 appears in the cell, which remains in editing mode. This formula enters Diane's summer take-home pay for June.

▶ 2. Select the cell reference **F5** in the formula, and then press the **F4** key. The formula changes to =$F$5, which is an absolute reference.

▶ 3. Press the **F4** key again. The formula changes to =F$5, which is a mixed reference with a relative column reference and an absolute row reference.

▶ 4. Press the **F4** key again to change to formula to =$F5, which is a mixed cell reference with an absolute column reference and a relative row reference.

▶ 5. Press the **F4** key again to return to the formula to =F5, which is a relative reference.

▶ 6. Press the **F4** key one more time to change the formula back to =$F$5, and then press the **Enter** key to exit editing mode. You want an absolute reference to cell F5 so that the formula always references Diane's summer take-home pay.

▶ 7. In cell **I20**, enter the formula **=$F$6**. This formula uses an absolute reference to enter Glenn's summer take-home pay for June, and won't change when copied to the rest of the months.

▶ 8. In cell **I21**, enter the formula **=I19+I20**. This formula adds Diane and Glenn's take-home pay for June.

▶ 9. Copy the range **I19:I21**, and then paste the copied formulas into the range **J19:K21**. The summer take-home pay values appear for the months of June through August.

You'll complete the take-home pay values for the remaining school months.

▶ 10. Copy the range **D19:D21**, and then paste it into the range **L19:O21**. The take-home pay for the couple is entered for all twelve months of the year.

Now that you've calculated the monthly take-home pay and expenses for Diane and Glenn, you'll summarize these for the entire year. Diane wants to compare the couple's annual take-home pay to their annual expenses. She also wants to know the average take-home pay and average expenses for a typical month.

Working with Functions

The month-by-month data is too large to see in the workbook window unless you reduce the zoom level, but then the resulting text would be too small to read. Rather than adding another column to this large collection of data, Diane wants to summarize the data at the top of the worksheet. You'll use Excel functions to do these summary calculations.

> ## Summarizing Data | InSight
>
> Statisticians, scientists, and economists often want to reduce a large sample of data into a few easy-to-use statistics. How do they best summarize the data? The most common approach is to average the sample data. You can calculate the average in Excel with the AVERAGE function. However, this is not always the best choice. Averages are susceptible to extremely large or small data values. Imagine calculating the average price of houses on a block that has one mansion and several small homes. The average value is heavily affected by the mansion. When the data includes a few extremely large or extremely small values, it might be best to use the **median**, or middle, value from the sample. You can calculate the median in Excel with the MEDIAN function.
>
> Another approach is to calculate the most common value in the data, otherwise known as the **mode**. The mode is most often used with data that has only a few possible values, such as the number of bedrooms in a house. The most common number of bedrooms per house might provide more relevant information than the average number of bedrooms. You can calculate the mode in Excel using the MODE function.

Understanding Function Syntax

Recall from Tutorial 1 that a function is a named operation that returns a value. Every function has to follow a set of rules, or **syntax**, which specifies how the function should be written. The general syntax of all functions is as follows:

`FUNCTION(argument1, argument2, ...)`

In this syntax, FUNCTION is the name of the function and *argument1*, *argument2*, and so forth are **arguments**, which are the numbers, text, or cell references used by the function to return a value. Arguments are always separated by a comma.

Not all functions have arguments, and some functions have **optional arguments**, which are not required for the function to return a value, but can be included to provide more control over the returned value. If an optional argument is not included, Excel assumes a default value for it. These tutorials show optional arguments within square brackets along with the argument's default value, as follows:

`FUNCTION(argument1, [argument2=value2, ...])`

> **Tip**
> Optional arguments are always placed last in the argument list.

In this function, *argument2* is an optional argument and *value2* is the default value used for this argument. As you learn more about individual functions, you will learn which arguments are required and which are optional, and the default values used for optional arguments.

There are hundreds of Excel functions, which are organized into 11 categories. Figure 3-6 describes these different categories.

Figure 3-6 — Categories of Excel functions

Category	Contains functions that
Cube	Retrieve data from multidimensional databases involving online analytical processing or OLAP
Database	Retrieve and analyze data stored in databases
Date & Time	Analyze or create date and time values and time intervals
Engineering	Analyze engineering problems
Financial	Have financial applications
Information	Return information about the format, location, or contents of worksheet cells
Logical	Return logical (true-false) values
Lookup & Reference	Look up and return data matching a set of specified conditions from a range
Math & Trig	Have math and trigonometry applications
Statistical	Provide statistical analyses of a set of data
Text	Return text values or evaluate text

You can learn about each function using the Help system. Figure 3-7 describes some of the more common Math, Trig, and Statistical functions that you might often use in your workbooks.

Figure 3-7 — Math, Trig, and Statistical functions

Function	Category	Description
AVERAGE(number1 [, number2, number3, ...])	Statistical	Calculates the average of a collection of numbers, where *number1*, *number2*, and so forth are either numbers or cell references. Only *number1* is required. For more than one cell reference or to enter numbers directly into the function, use the optional arguments *number2*, *number3*, and so forth.
COUNT(value1 [, value2, value3, ...])	Statistical	Counts how many cells in a range contain numbers, where *value1*, *value2*, and so forth are text, numbers, or cell references. Only *value1* is required. For more than one cell reference or to enter numbers directly into the function, use the optional arguments *value2*, *value3*, and so forth.
COUNTA(value1 [, value2, value3, ...])	Statistical	Counts how many cells are not empty in ranges *value1*, *value2*, and so forth, or how many numbers are listed within *value1*, *value2*, and so forth.
INT(number)	Math & Trig	Displays the integer portion of a number, *number*.
MAX(number1 [, number2, number3, ...])	Statistical	Calculates the maximum value of a collection of numbers, where *number1*, *number2*, and so forth are either numbers or cell references.
MEDIAN(number1 [, number2, number3, ...])	Statistical	Calculates the median, or middle, value of a collection of numbers, where *number1*, *number2*, and so forth are either numbers or cell references.
MIN(number1 [, number2, number3, ...])	Statistical	Calculates the minimum value of a collection of numbers, where *number1*, *number2*, and so forth are either numbers or cell references.
RAND()	Math & Trig	Returns a random number between 0 and 1.
ROUND(number, num_digits)	Math & Trig	Rounds a number to a specified number of digits, where *number* is the number you want to round and *num_digits* specifies how many digits to which you want to round the number.
SUM(number1 [, number2, number3, ...])	Math & Trig	Adds a collection of numbers, where *number1*, *number2*, and so forth are either numbers or cell references.

For example, the AVERAGE function calculates the average value from a collection of numbers. The syntax of the AVERAGE function is as follows:

`AVERAGE(number1, [number2, number3, ...])`

In this function, *number1*, *number2*, *number3*, and so forth are either numbers or cell references to numbers. For example, the following function calculates the average of 1, 2, 5, and 8:

`AVERAGE(1, 2, 5, 8)`

This function returns the value 4. However, you usually reference values entered in the worksheet. So, if the range A1:A4 contains the values 1, 2, 5, and 8, the following function also returns a value of 4:

`AVERAGE(A1:A4)`

Functions can be incorporated as part of larger formulas. For example, consider the following formula:

`=MAX(A1:A100)/100`

This formula returns the maximum value from the range A1:A100, and then divides that value by 100. Functions can also be placed inside another function, or **nested**. If a formula contains several functions, Excel starts with the innermost function and then moves outward. For example, the following formula first calculates the average of the values in the range A1:A100 using the AVERAGE function, and then extracts the integer portion of that value using the INT function.

`=INT(AVERAGE(A1:A100))`

One challenge of nesting functions is to make sure that you include all of the parentheses. You can check this by counting the number of left parentheses, and making sure that number matches the number of right parentheses. If the numbers don't match, Excel will not accept the formula and offers a suggestion for rewriting the formula so the left and right parentheses do match.

Inserting a Function

Functions are organized in the Function Library group in the Formulas tab on the Ribbon. In the Function Library, you can select a function from a function category or you can open the Insert Function dialog box to search for a particular function.

Inserting a Function | Reference Window

- Click the Formulas tab on the Ribbon.
- To insert a function from a specific category, click the appropriate category button in the Function Library group. To search for a function, click the Insert Function button in the Function Library group, enter a description of the function, and then click the Go button.
- Select the appropriate function from the list of functions.
- Enter the argument values in the Function Arguments dialog box, and then click the OK button.

You'll use the SUM function to add the total take-home pay for the entire year in Diane's proposed budget.

To insert the SUM function:

1. Click cell **F9** to select it.
2. Click the **Formulas** tab on the Ribbon.
3. In the Function Library group on the Formulas tab, click the **Math & Trig** button. A list displays all of the math and trigonometry functions arranged in alphabetical order.
4. Scroll down the list, and then click **SUM**. The Function Arguments dialog box opens.

The Function Arguments dialog box lists all of the arguments associated with the SUM function. Required arguments are in bold type; optional arguments are in normal type. Excel tries to "anticipate" the values for the different arguments based on the location of the cell containing the formula and the data contained in other cells of the worksheet. In this case, the range reference F5:F8, which is the range that contains the couple's take-home pay for the summer months and is the range of numbers closest to the cell in which you are entering the SUM function, already appears for the first argument. Because you want to calculate the total take-home pay for the year, you'll replace this range reference with the reference D21:O21.

To enter the argument for the SUM function:

1. Click in the worksheet, and then select the range **D21:O21**. The range reference appears as the value of the Number1 argument. See Figure 3-8.

Figure 3-8 — Function Arguments dialog box

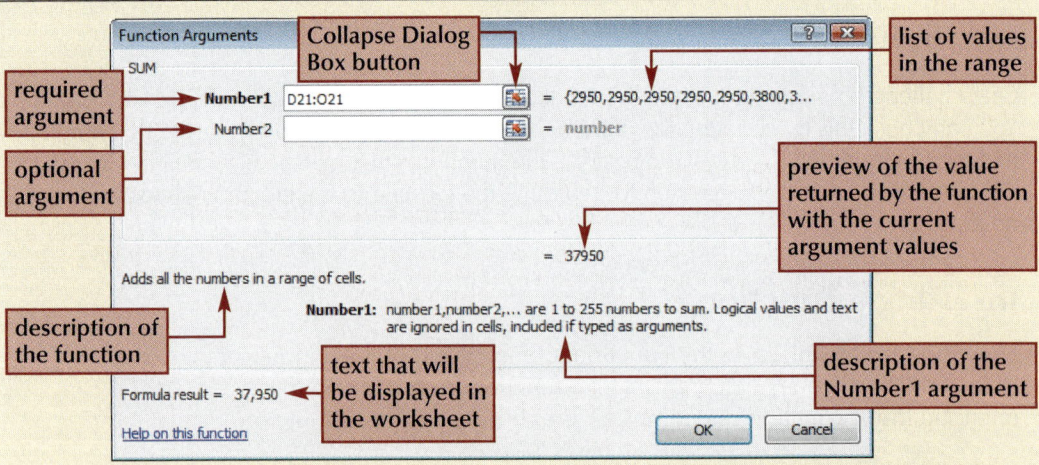

Tip

You can click the Collapse Dialog Box button to shrink the Function Arguments dialog box to see more of the worksheet, select the range, and then click the Expand Dialog Box button to restore the dialog box.

2. Click the **OK** button. The formula =SUM(D21:O21) is inserted into cell F9, which displays the value 37,950. This represents the total take-home pay for the year from both Diane and Glenn.

Diane also wants to know how this value compares to the total expenses for the year.

3. Click cell **F13**. This is where you want to enter the second SUM function.
4. In the Function Library group on the Formulas tab, click the **Math & Trig** button, and then click **SUM**. The Function Arguments dialog box opens. You'll enter the monthly expenses stored in the range D32:O32 for the argument.

▶ **5.** Select the range **D32:O32** in the worksheet, and then click the **OK** button in the Function Arguments dialog box. The formula =SUM(D32:O32) is inserted in cell F13, which displays the value 35,840. This represents the total projected expenses for the upcoming year. See Figure 3-9.

SUM functions entered | Figure 3-9

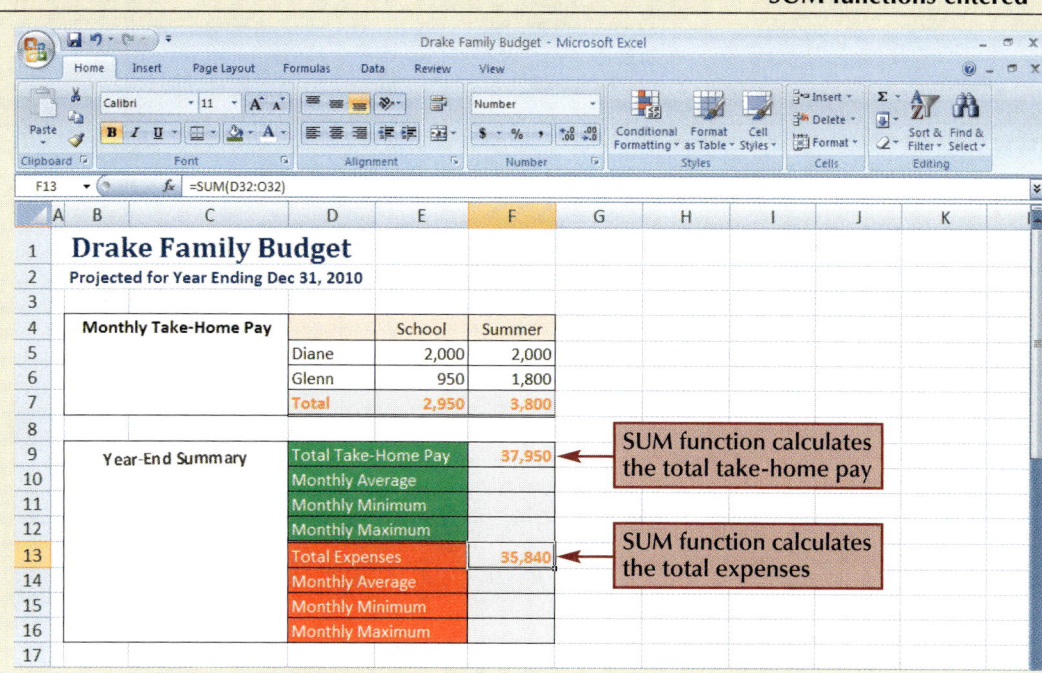

Diane projects that she and Glenn will earn roughly $2,000 more than they will spend throughout the year. It's easier for Diane to plan her budget if she knows how much, on average, the couple takes home and spends each month. You can use the AVERAGE function to do this calculation using the same method you used for the SUM function; but what if you weren't sure of the function's name or its function category? You can use the Insert Function dialog box. The **Insert Function dialog box** organizes all of the functions by category and allows you to search for functions that perform particular calculations.

To insert the AVERAGE function to calculate the average take-home pay:

▶ **1.** Click cell **F10**.

▶ **2.** In the Function Library group on the Formulas tab, click the **Insert Function** button. The Insert Function dialog box opens.

▶ **3.** Type **Calculate an average value** in the Search for a function box, and then click the **Go** button. Functions for calculating an average appear in the Select a function box. See Figure 3-10.

Figure 3-10 | Insert Function dialog box

Tip
You can also open the Insert Function dialog box by clicking the Insert Function button on the formula bar.

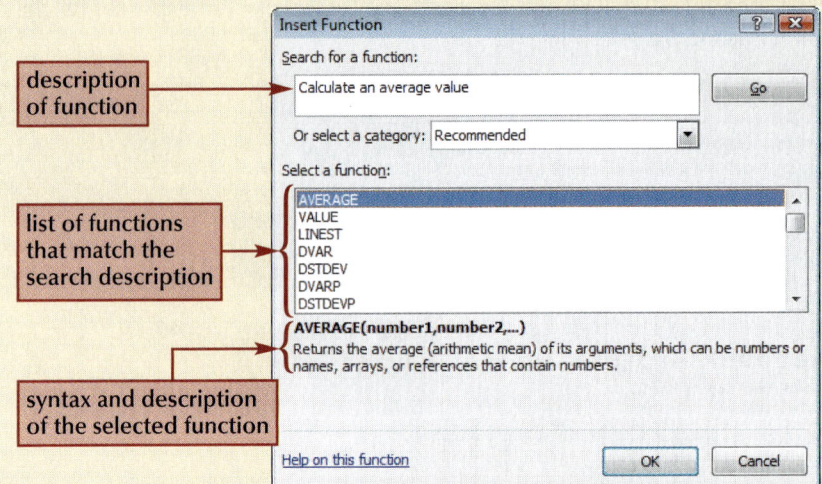

- description of function
- list of functions that match the search description
- syntax and description of the selected function

▶ 4. Verify that **AVERAGE** is selected in the Select a function box, and then click the **OK** button. The Function Arguments dialog box opens with the arguments for the AVERAGE function. As before, a range reference for cells directly above this cell already appears for the Number1 argument.

▶ 5. Select the range reference in the Number1 argument box, and then select the range **D21:O21** in the worksheet.

▶ 6. Click the **OK** button. The dialog box closes, and the formula =AVERAGE(D21:O21) is entered in cell F10, displaying the value 3,163, the average take-home pay.

Although the exact average take-home pay is 3,162.50, you see the value 3,163 in the cell because Diane formatted the worksheet to display currency values to the nearest dollar.

How does the couple's average take-home pay compare to their average expenses? To find out, you'll use the AVERAGE function again. Because the function has already been used in your workbook, you can select it from a list of recently used functions.

To calculate the average monthly expenses:

▶ 1. Click cell **F14**, and then click the **Insert Function** button *fx* on the formula bar. The Insert Function dialog box opens.

▶ 2. If necessary, click the **Or select a category** arrow, and then click **Most Recently Used**. The most recently used functions, sorted in order of recent use, appear in the Select a function box. The AVERAGE function is at the top followed by the SUM function.

▶ 3. Verify that **AVERAGE** is selected in the Select a function box, and then click the **OK** button.

▶ 4. Select the range **D32:O32** to insert the range reference D32:O32 in the Number1 box.

▶ 5. Click the **OK** button. The formula =AVERAGE(D32:O32) is inserted into cell F14, displaying the value 2,987. This represents the average expenses per month under Diane's budget. See Figure 3-11.

Figure 3-11 Average take-home pay and expenses

[Screenshot of Excel spreadsheet "Drake Family Budget" showing:
- Cell F14 with formula =AVERAGE(D32:O32)
- AVERAGE function label pointing to formula bar
- Drake Family Budget, Projected for Year Ending Dec 31, 2010
- Monthly Take-Home Pay table: Diane 2,000/2,000; Glenn 950/1,800; Total 2,950/3,800 (School/Summer)
- Year-End Summary: Total Take-Home Pay 37,950; Monthly Average 3,163 (labeled "average take-home pay per month"); Monthly Minimum; Monthly Maximum; Total Expenses 35,840; Monthly Average 2,987 (labeled "average expenses per month"); Monthly Minimum; Monthly Maximum]

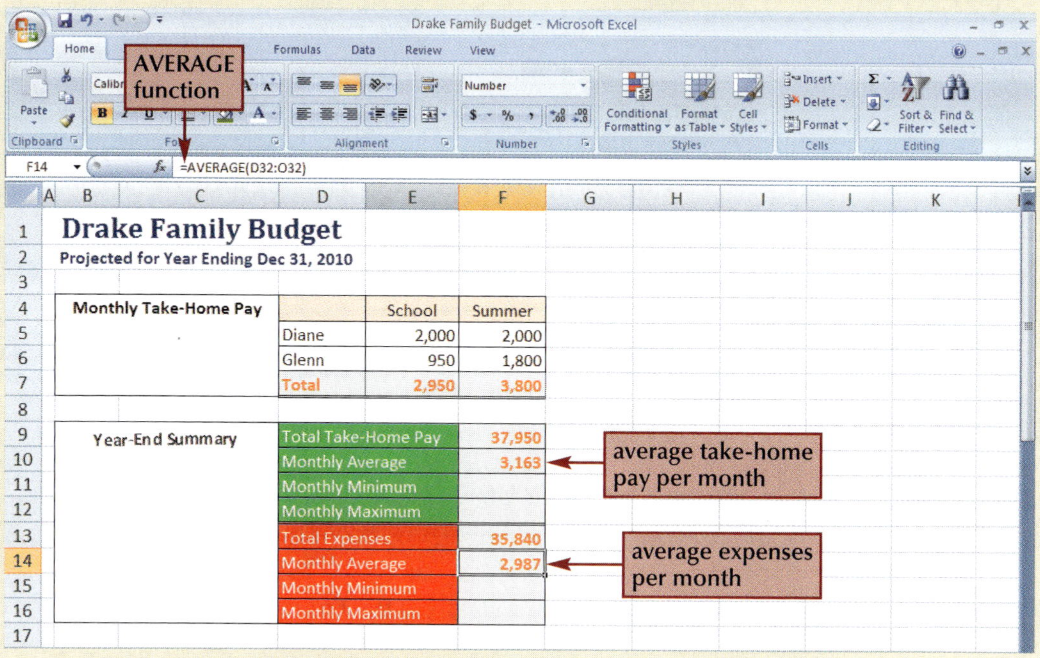

From the two averages, Diane sees that the couple will bring in about $200 more than they spend each month. That is not much, so Diane wants to know how much variation is in the budget. What is the most money she could expect to take home during a single month in the upcoming year? What is the least? And what are the largest and smallest values for the monthly expenses? You'll use the MAX and MIN functions to calculate those values.

Typing a Function

After you become more familiar with functions, it is often faster to type the functions directly in cells rather than using the Insert Function dialog box or the Function Library. As you begin to type a function name within a formula, a list of functions that begin with the letters you typed appears. For example, when you type *S*, the list shows all of the functions starting with the letter *S*; when you type *SU*, the list shows only those functions starting with the letters *SU*, and so forth. This helps to ensure that you're entering a legitimate Excel function name.

You'll type the formulas to calculate the minimum monthly take-home pay and expenses under Diane's proposed budget.

To calculate the minimum values for monthly take-home pay and expenses:

1. Click cell **F11**. This is the cell in which you want to enter the minimum take-home pay.
2. Type **=M**. As you type a formula, a list with function names starting with *M* opens.
3. Type **I**. The list shows only those functions starting with *MI*. See Figure 3-12. As soon as the function you want appears in the list, you can double-click its name to enter it in the cell without typing the rest of its name.

Figure 3-12 | Typing a function

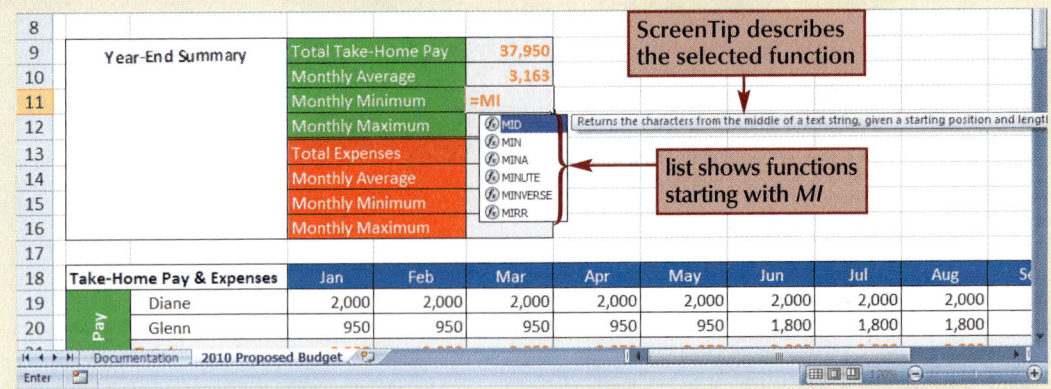

4. Double-click **MIN** in the list box. The MIN function with its opening parenthesis is inserted into cell F11 and a ScreenTip shows the syntax for the function. At this point, you can either type in the range reference or select the range with your mouse. To avoid typing errors, it's often better to use your mouse to enter range references.

5. Select the range **D21:O21**, type **)**, and then press the **Enter** key. The formula =MIN(D21:O21) is inserted in cell F11, displaying the value 2,950. This is the minimum amount that Diane expects the couple to bring home in a single month for the upcoming year.

   Next, you'll calculate the minimum monthly expense projected for the year.

6. Click cell **F15**, and then follow Steps 2 through 5 to enter the formula **=MIN(D32:O32)** in cell F15. The cell displays the value 2,265, which is the least amount that Diane expects to spend in a single month in the upcoming year.

The final piece of the year-end summary is the maximum monthly value for both take-home pay and expenses. Maximum values are calculated using the MAX function.

To calculate the maximum values for monthly take-home pay and expenses:

1. Click cell **F12**, and then enter the formula **=MAX(D21:O21)**. The value 3,800 appears in cell F12, indicating that the maximum take-home pay the couple can expect in a single month is $3,800.

   Trouble? If #NAME? appears in the cell, you probably mistyped the function name. Edit the formula to correct the misspelling.

2. Click cell **F16**, and then enter the formula **=MAX(D32:O32)**. The value 5,170 appears in cell F16, indicating that the maximum expenses for a single month are projected to be $5,170. See Figure 3-13.

Figure 3-13 Year-end summary values

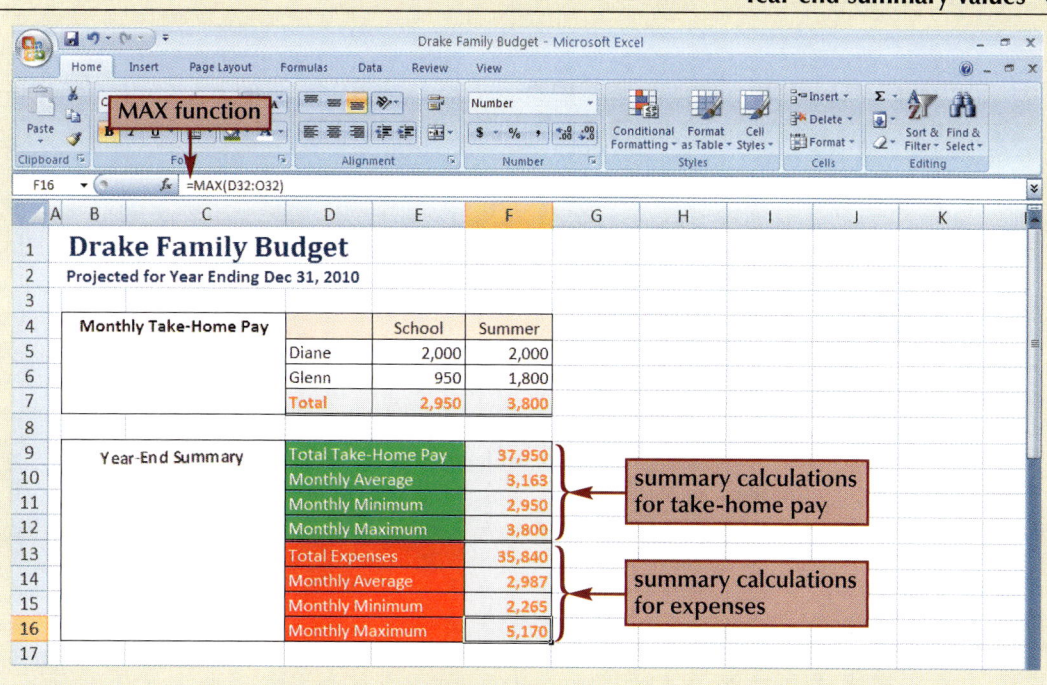

Based on the year-end summary, Diane and Glenn's monthly take-home pay will range from a minimum of $2,950 to a maximum of $3,800 with an average of about $3,163. Monthly expenses, on the other hand, range from a minimum of $2,265 to a maximum of $5,170 with an average of $2,987. Clearly, the Drake family budget does not have a lot of wiggle room.

Diane has just been promoted at work. Her take-home pay will increase from $2,000 per month to $2,500 per month. She wants to know how this affects the year-end summary.

To modify Diane's estimates of her take-home pay:

1. In cell E5, enter the value **2500**.

2. In cell F5, enter the value **2500**. Figure 3-14 shows the updated calculations for the couple's take-home pay for the entire year as well as the monthly average, minimum, and maximum values.

Figure 3-14 | **Revised salary values**

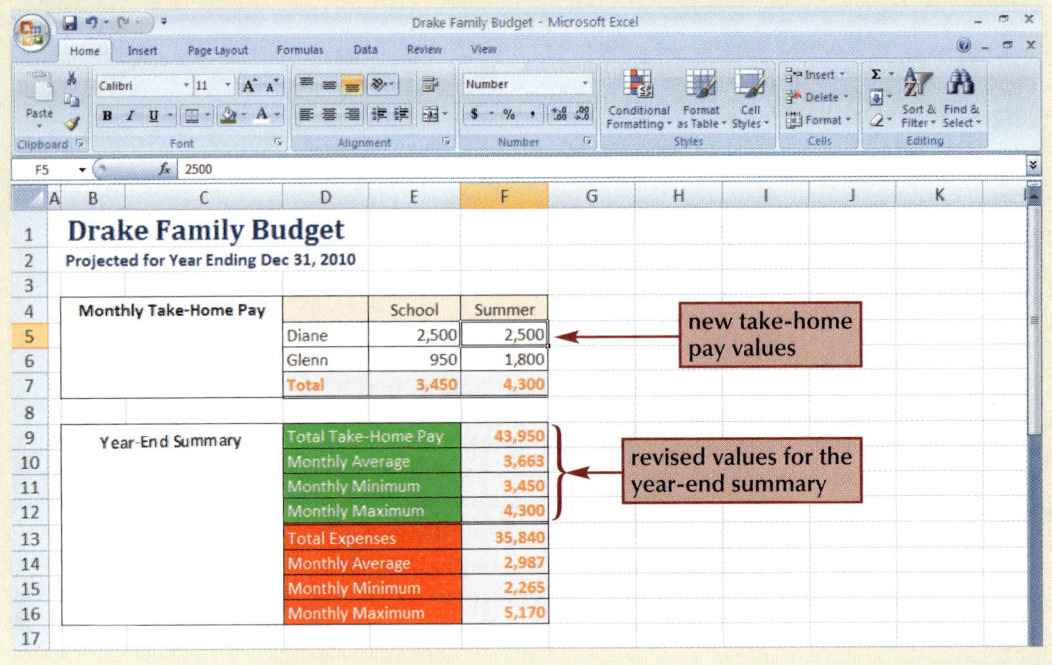

With Diane's new position, the couple's annual take-home pay increases from $37,950 to $43,950 and the monthly average increases from $3,163 to $3,663. The couple's take-home pay should exceed their expenses by an average of $700 per month. The monthly take-home pay now ranges from a minimum of $3,450 up to a maximum of $4,300. The raise has brightened the couple's financial picture quite a bit.

Diane now has a better picture of the family's finances for the upcoming year, and she's more confident about how to manage the couple's budget. She and Glenn hope to save enough for a down payment on a house in a few years. With the promotion, this seems like a real possibility. In the next session, you'll help Diane explore the couple's options in planning for a purchase of a house.

Review | Session 3.1 Quick Check

1. What is the absolute cell reference for cell B21? What are the two mixed references?
2. Cell B10 contains the formula =B1+B2. What formula is entered if this formula is copied and pasted into cell C20?
3. Cell B10 contains the formula =$B1+B$2. What formula is entered if this formula is copied and pasted into cell C20?
4. Cell B10 contains the formula =AVERAGE($A1:$A5). What formula is entered if this formula is copied and pasted into cell C20?
5. What are optional arguments? What happens if you do not include an optional argument in a function?
6. What formula should you enter to add the numbers in the range B1:B10?
7. The range of a set of values is defined as the maximum value minus the minimum value. What formula would you enter to calculate the range of the values in B1:B10?
8. What formula would you enter to calculate the ratio of the maximum value in the range B1:B10 to the minimum value?

Session 3.2

Working with AutoFill

Diane and Glenn hope to purchase a home in the next three years. Currently, the couple has $4,000 in their savings account, and they plan to start putting money into a home savings account. Diane wants to see what impact her proposed budget will have on their savings. To do that, you'll enter the current account information at the top of the worksheet. You'll include the current savings balance and the expected balance at the end of the next year under Diane's proposed budget.

To produce the results Diane wants, you will use a feature known as **AutoFill**, which copies content and formats from a cell or range into an adjacent cell or range. You'll begin by copying the formatting from the Monthly Take-Home Pay section to the range where you'll enter this new Savings section.

To format the range and insert data about the couple's savings account:

1. If you took a break after the previous session, make sure the Drake Family Budget workbook is open and the 2010 Proposed Budget worksheet is active.

2. Select the range **B4:F7**, and then, in the Clipboard group on the Home tab, click the **Format Painter** button to copy the formatting for the new section.

3. Select the range **H4:L7** to paste the selected format to this range.

4. Referring to Figure 3-15, enter the labels and data shown in the range H4:L7. In cell K7, enter a formula to add the values in the range K5:K6. In cell L7, enter a formula to add the values in the range L5:L6.

Figure 3-15   Initial savings data

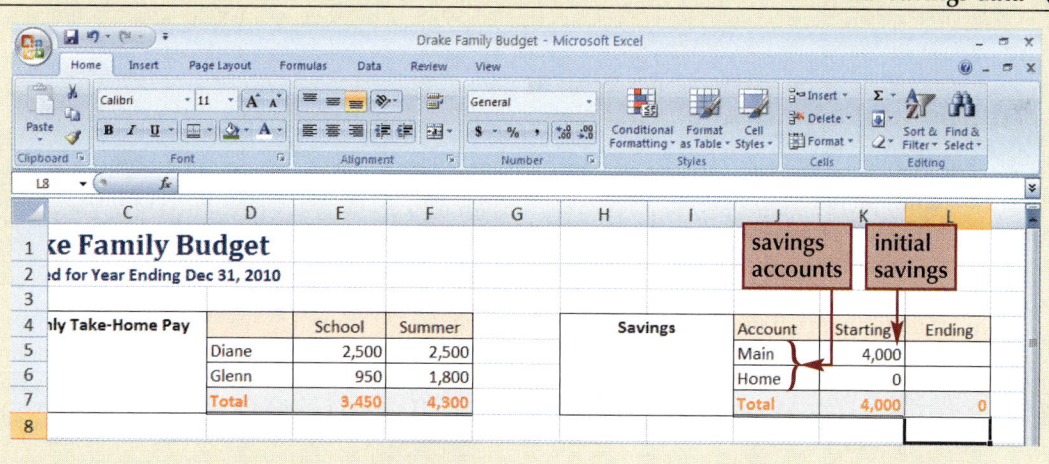

Diane wants to learn how much the couple could save each month. To find out, you must first determine the couple's monthly net cash flow, which is equal to their take-home pay minus their expenses. You'll start by formatting the cells where you'll enter this data and calculating the net cash flow during the month of January.

To format the range and calculate the net cash flow for January:

1. Click cell **B18**, and then, in the Clipboard group on the Home tab, click the **Format Painter** button.

2. Select the range **B33:C33**. The formatting from cell B18 is pasted into the range, merging the two cells.

3. In cell B33, type **Net Cash Flow**, and then right-align the contents of the cell.
4. In cell D33, enter the formula **=D21−D32**. This formula subtracts total expenses from total take-home pay for the month of January. The value −1,590 is displayed, indicating a projected shortfall of $1,590 for the month of January. Next, you'll format cell D33 to distinguish net cash flow amount from the other values.
5. Click cell **D33**.
6. In the Styles group, click the **Cell Styles** button, and then click the **60% – Accent6** style. See Figure 3-16.

Figure 3-16 | January net cash flow

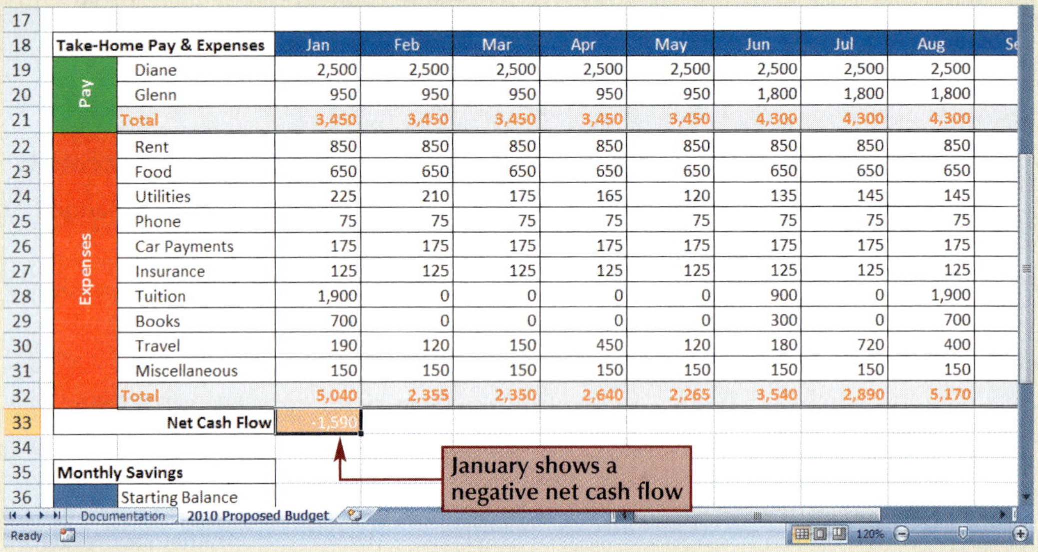

	Take-Home Pay & Expenses	Jan	Feb	Mar	Apr	May	Jun	Jul	Aug
18									
19	Diane	2,500	2,500	2,500	2,500	2,500	2,500	2,500	2,500
20	Glenn	950	950	950	950	950	1,800	1,800	1,800
21	Total	3,450	3,450	3,450	3,450	3,450	4,300	4,300	4,300
22	Rent	850	850	850	850	850	850	850	850
23	Food	650	650	650	650	650	650	650	650
24	Utilities	225	210	175	165	120	135	145	145
25	Phone	75	75	75	75	75	75	75	75
26	Car Payments	175	175	175	175	175	175	175	175
27	Insurance	125	125	125	125	125	125	125	125
28	Tuition	1,900	0	0	0	0	900	0	1,900
29	Books	700	0	0	0	0	300	0	700
30	Travel	190	120	150	450	120	180	720	400
31	Miscellaneous	150	150	150	150	150	150	150	150
32	Total	5,040	2,355	2,350	2,640	2,265	3,540	2,890	5,170
33	Net Cash Flow	-1,590							
34									
35	Monthly Savings								
36	Starting Balance								

January shows a negative net cash flow

AutoFilling a Formula

You could copy and paste the formula and format from cell D33 into the rest of the row to calculate the net cash flow for the other months, as you've done before, but AutoFill is faster. The small black square in the lower-right corner of a selected cell or range is called the **fill handle**. When you drag the fill handle over an adjacent range, Excel copies the formulas and formats from the original cell into the adjacent range. This process is more efficient than the two-step process of copying and pasting.

Reference Window | Copying Formulas and Formats with AutoFill

- Select the cell or range that contains the formula or formulas you want to copy.
- Drag the fill handle in the direction you want to copy the formula(s) and then release the mouse button.
- To copy only the formats or only the formulas, click the AutoFill Options button and select the appropriate option.

or

- Select the cell or range that contains the formula or formulas you want to copy.
- In the Editing group on the Home tab, click the Fill button.
- Select the appropriate fill direction and fill type (or click Series, enter the desired fill series options, and then click the OK button).

You'll use AutoFill to fill in the cash flow values for the remaining months of the year.

To copy the formulas and formats using AutoFill:

1. Click cell **D33**, if necessary. The fill handle appears in the lower-right corner of the cell.
2. Position the pointer over the fill handle until the pointer changes to ✛.
3. Drag the fill handle over the range **E33:O33**. A solid outline appears around the selected range as you move the pointer.
4. Release the mouse button. The selected range is filled in with the formula and format from cell D33, and the AutoFill Options button appears in the lower-right corner of the selected cells. See Figure 3-17.

Tip
With AutoFill, it's easy to copy formulas into the wrong range; if that happens, click the Undo button and try again.

Figure 3-17 Formulas and formats copied with AutoFill

	Mar	Apr	May	Jun	Jul	Aug	Sep	Oct	Nov	Dec
18										
19	2,500	2,500	2,500	2,500	2,500	2,500	2,500	2,500	2,500	2,500
20	950	950	950	1,800	1,800	1,800	950	950	950	950
21	3,450	3,450	3,450	4,300	4,300	4,300	3,450	3,450	3,450	3,450
22	850	850	850	850	850	850	850	850	850	850
23	650	650	650	650	650	650	650	650	650	650
24	175	165	120	135	145	145	140	140	170	210
25	75	75	75	75	75	75	75	75	75	75
26	175	175	175	175	175	175	175	175	175	175
27	125	125	125	125	125	125	125	125	125	125
28	0	0	0	900	0	1,900	0	0	0	0
29	0	0	0	300	0	700	0	0	0	0
30	150	450	120	180	720	400	130	150	250	300
31	150	150	150	150	150	150	150	150	150	150
32	2,350	2,640	2,265	3,540	2,890	5,170	2,295	2,315	2,445	2,535
33	1,100	810	1,185	760	1,410	-870	1,155	1,135	1,005	915

formula and formats copied to the selected range

AutoFill Options button

fill handle

Average: 676 Count: 12 Sum: 8,110

5. Review the monthly net cash flows to confirm that AutoFill correctly copied the formula into the selected range.

These calculations provide Diane with a better picture of how the couple's net cash flow varies from month to month. Only in January and August do the couple's expenses exceed their take-home pay. In most months, their take-home pay exceeds expenses by at least $1,000, and in July, it exceeds expenses by $1,410.

Using the AutoFill Options Button

By default, AutoFill copies both the formulas and the formats of the original range to the selected range. However, sometimes you might want to copy only the formulas or only the formatting. You can specify what is copied by using the AutoFill Options button that appears after you release the mouse button. As shown in Figure 3-18, clicking this button provides a list of AutoFill options. The Copy Cells option, which is the default, copies both the formulas and the formatting. The Fill Formatting Only option copies the formatting into the selected cells but not any formulas. The Fill Without Formatting option copies the formulas but not the formatting.

Figure 3-18 AutoFill options

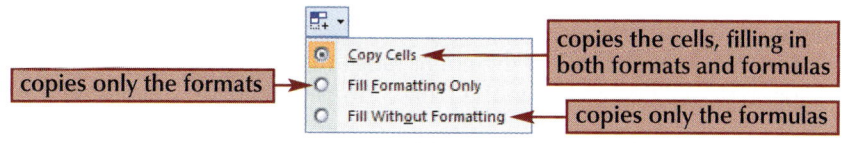

copies only the formats
copies the cells, filling in both formats and formulas
copies only the formulas

Filling a Series

AutoFill can also be used to create a series of numbers, dates, or text based on a pattern. To create a series of numbers, you enter the initial values in the series in a selected range and then use AutoFill to complete the series. Figure 3-19 shows how AutoFill can be used to insert the numbers from 1 to 10 in a selected range. You enter the first few numbers in the range A1:A3 to establish the pattern for AutoFill to use. Then, you select the range and drag the fill handle over the cells where you want the pattern continued. In Figure 3-19, the fill handle is dragged over the range A4:A10 and the rest of the series is filled in.

Figure 3-19   AutoFill extends a numeric sequence

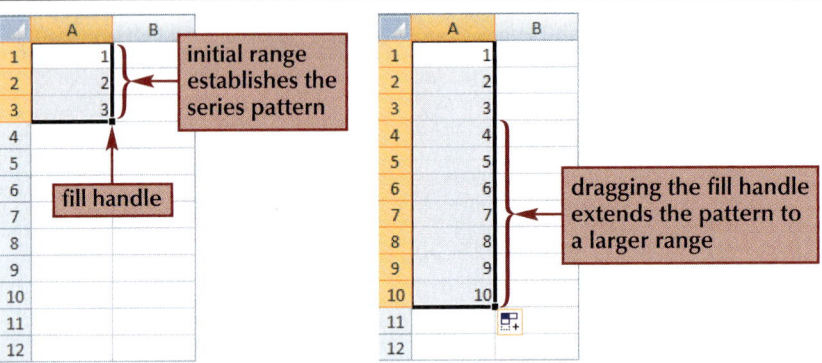

AutoFill can fill in a wide variety of series, including dates and times and text. Figure 3-20 shows examples of some series that AutoFill can generate. In each case, you must provide enough information for AutoFill to identify the pattern. AutoFill can recognize some patterns from only a single value, such as Jan or January to create a series of month abbreviations or names, or Mon or Monday to create a series of the days of the week.

Figure 3-20   AutoFill applied to different series

Type	Initial Entry	Extended Series
Values	1, 2, 3	4, 5, 6, ...
	2, 4, 6	8, 10, 12, ...
Dates and Times	Jan	Feb, Mar, Apr, ...
	January	February, March, April, ...
	15-Jan, 15-Feb	15-Mar, 15-Apr, 15-May, ...
	12/30/2010	12/31/2010, 1/1/2011, 1/2/2011, ...
	12/31/2010, 1/31/2011	2/28/2011, 3/31/2011, 4/30/2011, ...
	Mon	Tue, Wed, Thu, ...
	Monday	Tuesday, Wednesday, Thursday, ...
	11:00AM	12:00PM, 1:00PM, 2:00PM, ...
Patterned Text	1st period	2nd period, 3rd period, 4th period, ...
	Region 1	Region 2, Region 3, Region 4, ...
	Quarter 3	Quarter 4, Quarter 1, Quarter 2, ...
	Qtr3	Qtr4, Qtr1, Qtr2, ...

For more complex patterns, you can use the Series dialog box. Enter the first value of the series in a worksheet cell, select the entire range that will contain the series, click the Fill button in the Editing group on the Home tab, and then click Series. The Series dialog box opens. You then choose how a series grows, set how fast the series grows and its stopping value, and decide whether to use existing values in the selected range as the basis for the series trend.

Reference Window | Creating a Series with AutoFill

- Enter the first few values of the series into a range.
- Select the range, and then drag the fill handle of the selected range over the cells you want to fill.

or

- Enter the first few values of the series into a range.
- Select the entire range into which you want to extend the series.
- In the Editing group on the Home tab, click the Fill button, and then click Down, Right, Up, Left, Series, or Justify to set the direction you want to extend the series.

Diane wants to see how the monthly balances in her savings account are affected by the couple's changing expenses and take-home pay. She wants to make sure that the balance doesn't drop too low after months with particularly high expenses—such as January and August when Glenn's tuition payments are due. You'll add data to the worksheet to display the monthly savings balance. Diane already entered titles for the couple's different savings accounts. You'll use AutoFill to enter the month titles.

To use AutoFill to enter a series of months:

1. In cell **D35**, enter **Jan**. This is the first value in the series. Because Jan is a common abbreviation for January, Excel recognizes it as a month and you don't need to type Feb for the next month in the series.

2. Click cell **D35**, center the text, format it using the **Accent1** cell style, and then add a single border around the cell. This is the formatting you want to use for all the month abbreviations.

3. Position the pointer over the fill handle in cell D35 until the pointer changes to ✚.

4. Drag the fill handle over the range **E35:O35**. As you drag the fill handle, Screen-Tips show the month abbreviations. When you release the mouse button, AutoFill enters the remaining three-letter abbreviations for each month of the year with the formatting you applied to cell D35. See Figure 3-21.

Figure 3-21   Formatted month titles

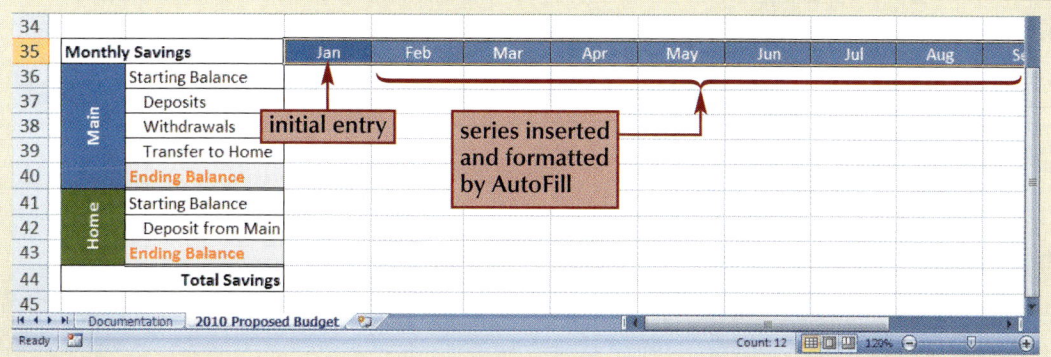

Next, you'll enter formulas to calculate the changing balance in the couple's main savings account and their home savings account. The main savings account balance is determined by four factors: the initial balance, the amount of money they deposit, the amount of money they withdraw, and the amount of money they transfer into their home savings account. The amount Diane and Glenn deposit will always equal their take-home pay, and the amount they withdraw will always equal their expenses. For now, you'll assume that the couple won't transfer any money from their main savings account into their home savings account.

To calculate the initial balances in the savings accounts:

1. In cell D36, enter the formula **=$K$5**. The formula uses an absolute reference to set the starting balance in the main savings account (cell D36) equal to the starting balance for the year (cell K5), which is already entered at the top of the worksheet. The absolute reference ensures that the copied formula always refers to the correct cell.

2. In cell D37, enter **=D21** to retrieve the couple's take-home pay for January.

3. In cell D38, enter **=D32** to retrieve the January expenses. You'll leave cell D39 blank because, at this point, you won't assume that any money will be transferred from the main savings account to the home savings account.

4. In cell D40, enter **=D36+D37−D38−D39**. This formula calculates the ending balance for the main savings account, which is equal to the starting balance plus any deposits minus the withdrawals and transfers. Cell D40 displays the value 2,410, representing the balance in the main savings account at the end of January.

5. In cell D41, enter the formula **=$K$6**. The formula sets the starting balance for the home savings account equal to the starting balance for the year. Again, you used an absolute reference to ensure that the formula won't change when copied.

6. In cell D42, enter the formula **=D39**. Any deposits in the home savings account will be the result of transfers from the main savings account.

7. In cell D43, enter the formula **=D41+D42**. The ending balance in the home savings account will be equal to the starting balance plus any deposits.

8. In cell D44, enter the formula **=D40+D43**. The total savings is equal to the amount in both accounts at the end of the month.

9. Add borders around the cells in the range D36:D43.

10. Use the Format Painter to copy the formats from cell D32 into cells D40 and D43, and then use the Format Painter to copy the formats from cell D33 into cell D44. See Figure 3-22.

Figure 3-22   Formatted savings account values for January

		Jan	Feb	Mar	Apr	May	Jun	Jul	Aug
Monthly Savings									
Main	Starting Balance	4,000							
	Deposits	3,450							
	Withdrawals	5,040							
	Transfer to Home								
	Ending Balance	2,410							
Home	Starting Balance	0							
	Deposit from Main	0							
	Ending Balance	0							
	Total Savings	2,410							

January savings

At this point, the couple's projected savings at the end of January will be $2,410, which is $1,590 less than their starting balance of $4,000 at the beginning of the year. The savings formulas for the remaining months are the same as for January except that their starting balances are based on the ending balance of the previous month.

To calculate the remaining balances in the savings accounts:

1. Copy the range **D36:D44**, and then paste it into the range **E36:E44**.

2. Change the formula in cell E36 to **=D40** so that the February starting balance for the main savings account equals the January ending balance.

3. Change the formula in cell E41 to **=D43** so that the starting February balance in the home savings account is equal to the ending January balance.

   Next, you'll use AutoFill to copy the February formulas into the remaining months of the year.

4. Select the range **E36:E44**, and then drag the fill handle over the range **F36:O44**. All of the formulas and formatting for the rest of the year are filled in. See Figure 3-23.

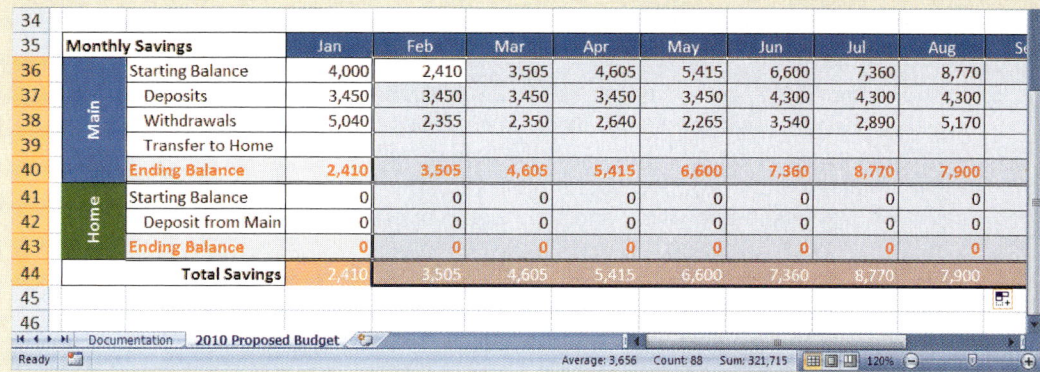

Figure 3-23 Savings values for the remaining months

Diane wants to see the ending balances for the two savings accounts without scrolling, so you'll add the ending balances at the top of the worksheet.

5. In cell L5, enter the formula **=$O$40**. You used an absolute reference so that the formula won't change if you later copy it to another cell. The ending balance of the main savings account in December—12,110—appears in cell L5.

6. In cell L6, enter the formula **=$O$43**. Again, you used an absolute reference to ensure the formula won't change if you later copy it to another cell. The ending balance of the home savings account in December—0—appears in cell L6.

Developing a Savings Plan

Under her current budget projections, Diane expects to have $12,110 in the main savings account at the end of the next year but nothing in the home savings account. Diane wants to transfer some money into the home savings account each month. Because the home savings account is used for longer-term savings, Diane cannot withdraw money from it without penalty. So, she wants to make sure the main savings account always has enough money to meet monthly expenses and any unexpected bills without relying on money from the home savings account.

Diane needs to balance two things in her savings plan: a desire to keep a reasonable amount in the main savings account and the desire to save enough for a future down payment on a home mortgage. To achieve this balance, she needs to determine her overall savings goal and how soon she and Glenn want to meet that goal.

To help Diane determine an overall savings goal, you'll create a new worksheet with calculations for different savings plans. Diane wants to know how much money the couple can save if they put $500 to $1,000 into the home savings account each month for the next three years. You'll create a worksheet that shows the total amount saved in one, two, and three years from deposits starting at $500 that increase in $100 increments through $1,000.

To create the savings plan:

1. Insert a new worksheet named **Home Savings Plan** at the end of the workbook.

2. In cell A1, enter **Home Savings Projections**, and then format the title using the **Title** cell style.

3. Merge and center the range **B3:G3**, enter **Savings Deposit per Month** in the merged cell, and then format the merged cell using the **Heading 2** cell style.

4. In cell A4, enter **Months**, format the cell in bold.

5. In cell B4, enter **500**; in cell C4, enter **600**; select the range **B4:C4**; and then drag the fill handle to cell **G4**. The values entered in the series—500, 600, 700, 800, 900, and 1,000—are the different amounts the couple might transfer into their home savings account each month.

6. In the range A5:A7, enter the values **12**, **24**, and **36**. These monthly values are equal to one year, two years, and three years, respectively. You entered the years in months because Diane and Glenn plan to deposit money into their home savings account each month. So, they would make 12 deposits in one year, they would make 24 deposits in two years, and they would make 36 deposits in three years.

7. Format the range B4:G4;A5:A7 with the **Input** cell style.

   Next, you'll use mixed cell references to calculate the amount of money saved under each plan. The amount saved is equal to the number of months of savings multiplied by the deposit per month.

8. In cell **B5**, enter **=$A5*B$4**. This formula uses mixed references to calculate the amount of savings generated by saving $500 per month for 12 months. The first mixed reference in the formula, $A5, has a fixed column reference and a relative row reference. When you copy the formula across row 5, the reference to cell A5 remains unchanged. When you copy the formula down column B, the reference to cell A5 changes to cell A6 in row 6 and cell A7 in row 7, which references the correct number of months of savings in the formula. The second mixed cell reference, B$4, has a relative column reference and a fixed row reference. When you copy the formula down column B, the reference to cell B4 remains unchanged. When you copy the formula across row 5, the reference to cell B4 changes to cell C4 in column C, cell D4 in column D, and so forth, which references the correct deposit per month in the formula.

9. Copy cell **B5** and paste the formula into the range **B5:G7**. The formula results show the projected savings based on different combinations of monthly deposits and lengths of time. Notice that the mixed references in each cell always reference a monthly deposit value from the range B4:G4 and a time length from the range A5:A7. The mixed references enable you to copy and paste the correct formulas quickly.

10. Format the values in the range B5:G7 using a thousands separator with no digits to the right of the decimal point, and add a single border around each cell in the range. Figure 3-24 shows the completed and formatted values.

Savings from monthly deposits — Figure 3-24

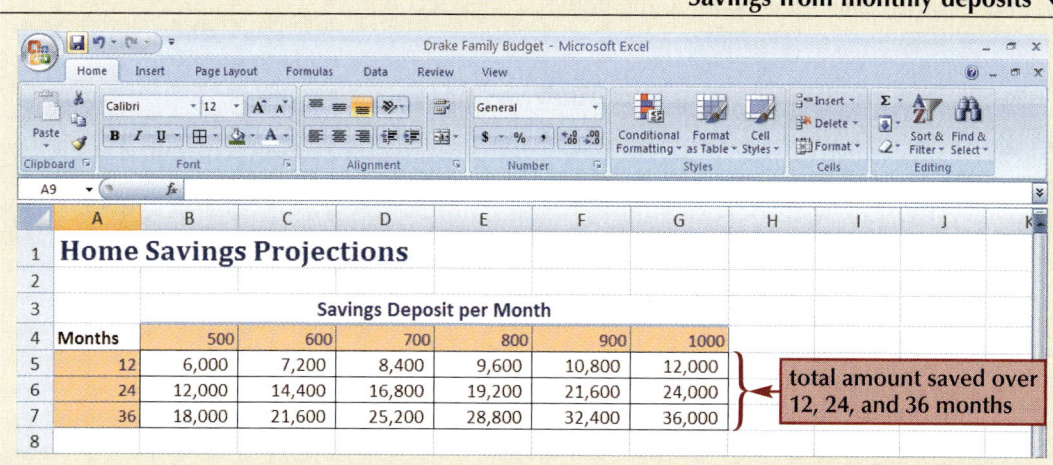

The data shows how increasing the amount that Diane and Glenn save toward their home each month quickly adds up. For example, if they save $800 per month, at the end of three years (36 months), they would have saved $28,800. This is just a little less than the $30,000 they want to save for the down payment. Diane asks you to enter in the budget projections the transfer of $800 from the main savings account to the home savings account each month.

To enter and format the home savings plan section:

1. Switch to the **2010 Proposed Budget** worksheet.
2. In cell H9, enter **Home Savings Plan**, and then format the cell in bold.
3. In cell H10, enter **Monthly Transfer to Home Acct**, and then, in cell K10, enter **800**.
4. Merge the range **H10:J10**, left-align the merged cell, and then format the cell using the **20% – Accent6** cell style.
5. Add a border around cell H10 and cell K10. See Figure 3-25.

Formatted savings plan — Figure 3-25

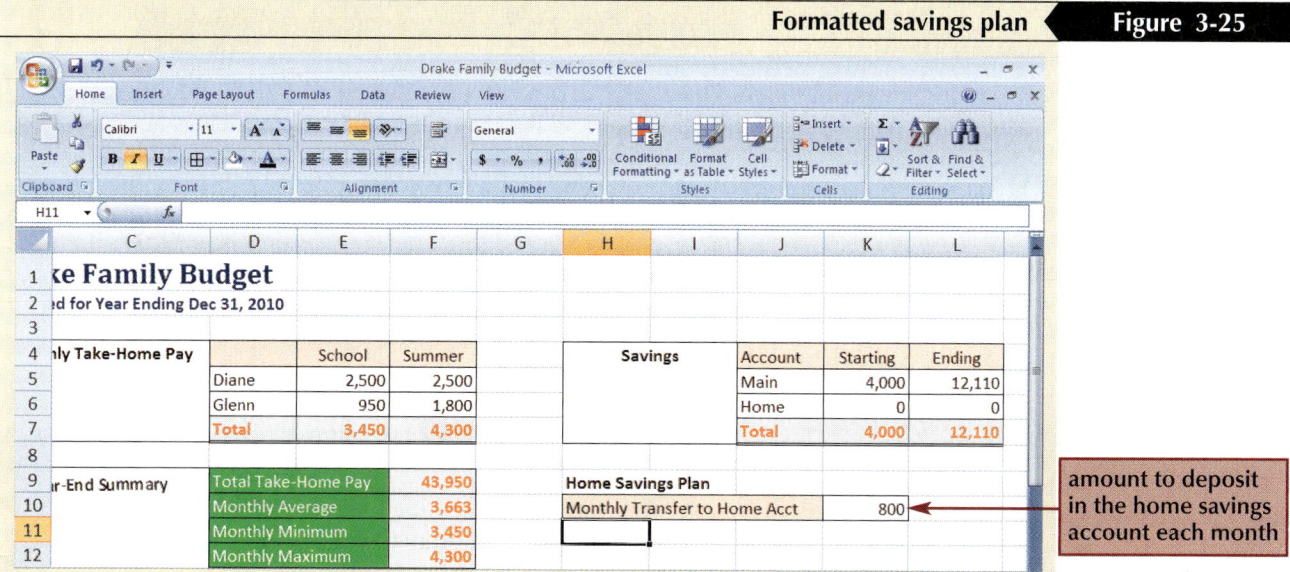

Next, you'll apply this $800 per month deposit value to the monthly transfer of funds from the main savings account to the home savings account.

To project the new savings account balances:

1. In cell **D39**, enter the formula **=$K$10**. You used an absolute value in this formula because the amount to transfer to the home savings account each month is always in cell K10 and you don't want the cell reference to change when you copy the formula to the rest of the months. The value 800 is displayed in the cell, indicating that for the month of January, $800 will be transferred from the couple's main savings account into the home savings account. The ending balance of the home savings account is now $800.

2. Copy cell **D39** and paste it into the range **E39:O39**. The value 800 is pasted into the rest of the row, indicating that each month the couple will transfer $800 into the home savings account. See Figure 3-26.

Figure 3-26 Monthly savings balance

		Jan	Feb	Mar	Apr	May	Jun	Jul	Aug
35	**Monthly Savings**								
36	Starting Balance	4,000	1,610	1,905	2,205	2,215	2,600	2,560	3,170
37	Deposits	3,450	3,450	3,450	3,450	3,450	4,300	4,300	4,300
38	Withdrawals	5,040	2,355	2,350	2,640	2,265	3,540	2,890	5,170
39	Transfer to Home	800	800	800	800	800	800	800	800
40	Ending Balance	1,610	1,905	2,205	2,215	2,600	2,560	3,170	1,500
41	Starting Balance	0	800	1,600	2,400	3,200	4,000	4,800	5,600
42	Deposit from Main	800	800	800	800	800	800	800	800
43	Ending Balance	800	1,600	2,400	3,200	4,000	4,800	5,600	6,400
44	Total Savings	2,410	3,505	4,605	5,415	6,600	7,360	8,770	7,900

amount transferred to the home savings account each month

balance in the home savings account

3. Examine the monthly balance in both the main savings account and the home savings account under Diane's proposed savings plan. Notice that the ending balance in the main savings account falls below $2,000 some months.

4. Scroll to the top of the worksheet and verify that the value displayed in cell L5 is 2,510 and the value displayed in cell L6 is 9,600.

Under this savings plan, Diane and Glenn will have deposited $9,600 into the home savings account by the end of the year and the balance in their main savings account will be down to $2,510. Although Diane is pleased that $9,600 will be moved into the home savings account in the next year, she's concerned about the amount of money left in the main savings account. Even more troubling are the month-to-month balances in that account. For example, the balance in the main savings account will be $1,500 at the end of August and will remain below $2,000 for several months of the year. Recall that Diane does not want to have a savings plan that will leave the couple with insufficient funds in the main savings account to handle unforeseen expenses.

Part of the problem is that the couple's net cash flow is negative during several months of the year. If they continue to transfer $800 into the home savings account during those months, the main savings account might fall below an acceptable level. Diane wants to modify her savings plan so that money is not transferred into the home savings account during months of negative cash flow. You need a formula that can "choose" whether to transfer the funds. You can build this kind of decision-making capability into a formula through the use of a logical function.

Working with Logical Functions

A **logical function** is a function that works with values that are either true or false. If it seems strange to think of a value as being true or false, consider a statement such as "Today is Monday." If today is Monday, that statement is true or has a true value. If today isn't Monday, the statement has a value of false. In Excel, you usually will not work with statements regarding days of the week (unless you're creating a calendar application), but instead you'll examine statements such as "Is cell A5 equal to 3?" or "Is cell B10 greater than cell C10?"

Using the IF Function

You can use the IF function to evaluate a statement such as "Is cell A5 equal to 3?" The **IF function** is a logical function that returns one value if the statement is true and returns a different value if the statement is false. The syntax of the IF function is as follows:

```
IF(logical_test, value_if_true, [value_if_false])
```

In this function, *logical_test* is a statement that is either true or false, *value_if_true* is the value returned by the IF function if the statement is true, and *value_if_false* is the value returned by the function if the statement is false. Although the *value_if_false* argument is optional, you should usually include this argument so that the IF function covers both possibilities.

The statement in the *logical_test* argument of the IF function always includes a comparison operator. A **comparison operator** is a symbol that indicates the relationship between two values. Figure 3-27 describes the different comparison operators. The most common comparison operator is the equal sign.

Figure 3-27 Comparison operators

Operator	Statement	Tests whether
=	A1 = B1	the value in cell A1 *is equal to* the value in cell B1
>	A1 > B1	the value in cell A1 *is greater than* the value in cell B1
<	A1 < B1	the value in cell A1 *is less than* the value in cell B1
>=	A1 >= B1	the value in cell A1 *is greater than or equal to* the value in cell B1
<=	A1 <= B1	the value in cell A1 *is less than or equal to* the value in cell B1
<>	A1 <> B1	the value in cell A1 *is not equal to* the value in cell B1

For example, you might want a formula that compares the values in cells A1 and B1. If they're equal, you want to return a value of 100; if they're not equal, you want to return a value of 50. The IF function to perform this test is as follows:

```
=IF(A1=B1, 100, 50)
```

In many cases, however, you will not use values directly in the IF function. The following formula uses cell references, returning the value of cell C1 if A1 equals B1; otherwise, it returns the value of cell C2.

```
=IF(A1=B1, C1, C2)
```

The IF function also works with text. For example, consider the following formula:

=IF(A1="YES", "DONE", "RESTART")

This formula tests whether the value of cell A1 is equal to YES. If it is, the formula returns the text DONE; otherwise, it returns the text RESTART. Also, you can nest other functions inside an IF statement. Consider the following formula:

=IF(A1="MAXIMUM", MAX(B1:B10), MIN(B1:B10))

This function first tests whether cell A1 contains the text MAXIMUM. If it does, the formula uses the MAX function to return the maximum of the values in the range B1:B10. If it doesn't, the formula uses the MIN function to return the minimum of the values in that range.

Diane wants the IF function to test whether the net cash flow for the current month is greater than zero. If it is, the couple has increased their savings and she wants to transfer some of it into the home savings account. On the other hand, if the net cash flow is negative, the couple has not saved any money and Diane doesn't want to transfer any funds to the home savings account. For the month of January, the formula to determine how much money is transferred is as follows:

=IF(D33>0, $K$10, 0)

Recall that cell D33 contains the net cash flow for the month of January and cell K10 contains the amount of money that Diane wants to transfer when she can. So, this function tests whether the net cash flow for the month of January (cell D33) is positive (greater than zero). If it is, the formula returns $800 (the value in cell K10) as the amount to transfer from the main savings account into the home savings account; otherwise, it returns 0 and no money will be transferred that month. You'll delete the formula currently in cell D39, and then insert this function.

To insert the IF function:

▶ 1. Right-click cell **D39**, and then click **Clear Contents** on the shortcut menu. The cell's contents are erased.

▶ 2. In the Function Library group on the Formulas tab, click the **Logical** button, and then click **IF** in the list of logical functions. The Function Arguments dialog box opens.

▶ 3. Enter **D33>0** in the Logical_test argument box. This tests whether the net cash flow for January is positive (greater than zero).

▶ 4. Enter **$K$10** in the Value_if_true argument box. If the value in cell D33 is greater than zero (the net cash flow for the month is positive), then the formula returns the value in cell K10, which is the amount of money to transfer from the main savings account into the home savings account. You used an absolute reference because you don't want the cell reference to change when you copy the formula to the other months.

▶ 5. Enter the value **0** in the Value_if_false argument box. If the value in cell D33 is less than zero (the net cash flow for the month is negative), the formula returns the value 0 and no money will be transferred from the main savings account into the home savings account that month. See Figure 3-28.

Figure 3-28 Function arguments for the IF function

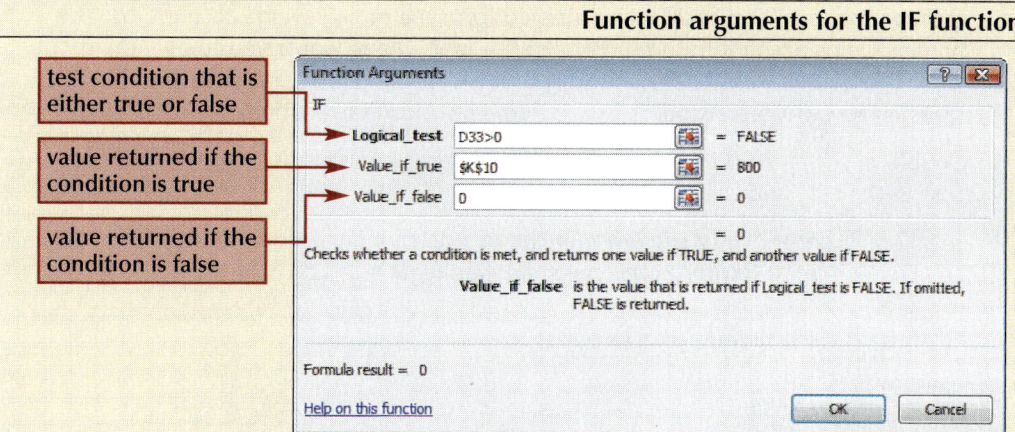

- test condition that is either true or false
- value returned if the condition is true
- value returned if the condition is false

▶ 6. Click the **OK** button. A value of 0 is displayed in cell D39. Because the net cash flow for January is –1,590, no money will be transferred from the main savings account into the home savings account. You'll copy this formula into the remaining months of Diane's proposed budget.

▶ 7. Click cell **D39**, and then drag the fill handle over the range **E39:O39**. The remaining values are filled in, as shown in Figure 3-29. Examine the monthly balance in both savings accounts.

Figure 3-29 Amount to transfer to the home savings account each month

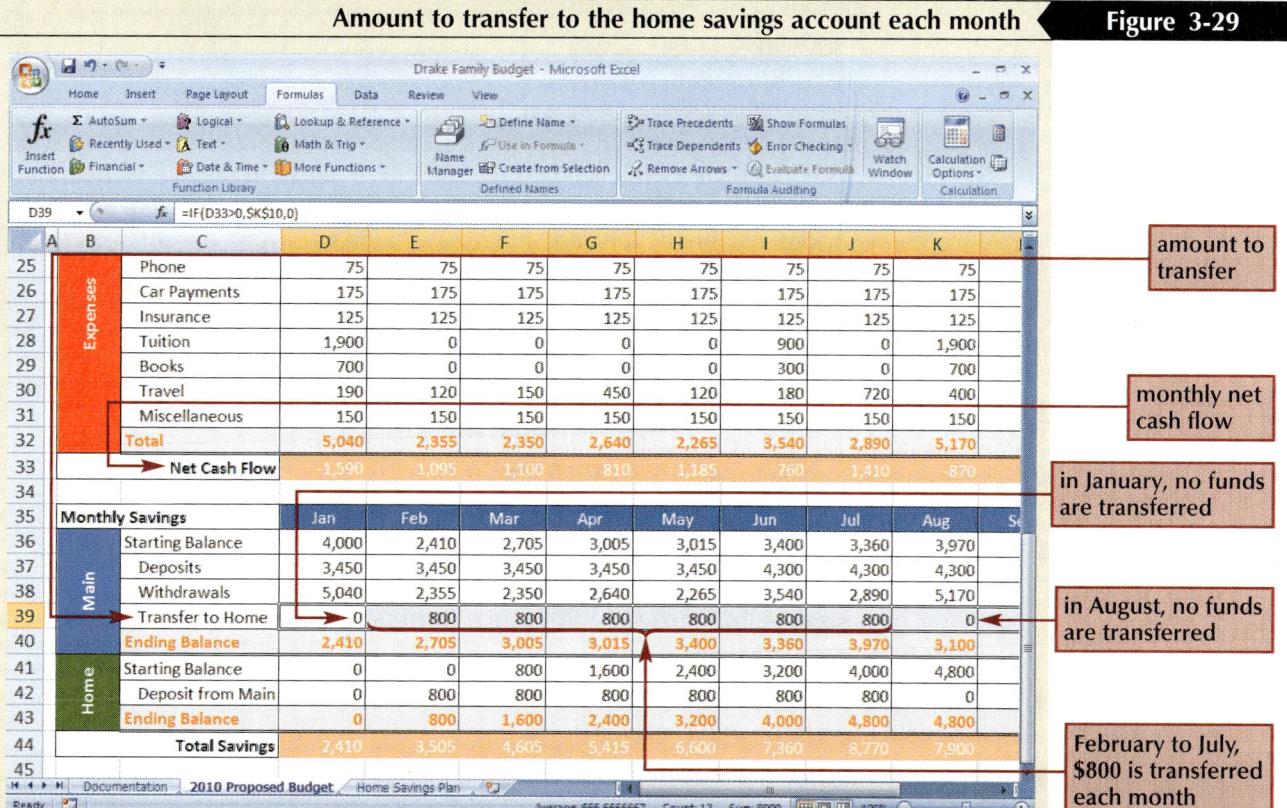

- amount to transfer
- monthly net cash flow
- in January, no funds are transferred
- in August, no funds are transferred
- February to July, $800 is transferred each month

The monthly ending balance in the main savings account remains above $3,000 for most of the year, and $800 is transferred from the main savings account into the home savings account in ten months of the year. Diane wants you to document what the formula results are showing. You'll enter text that clarifies when funds are transferred between accounts in the Home Savings Plan section.

8. Double-click cell **H10** to enter editing mode, type an asterisk (*****) at the end of the text in the cell, and then press the **Enter** key.

9. In cell H11, enter ***Only during months of positive cash flow**, and then format cell H11 using the **Explanatory** cell style. See Figure 3-30.

Figure 3-30 Results of the revised savings plan

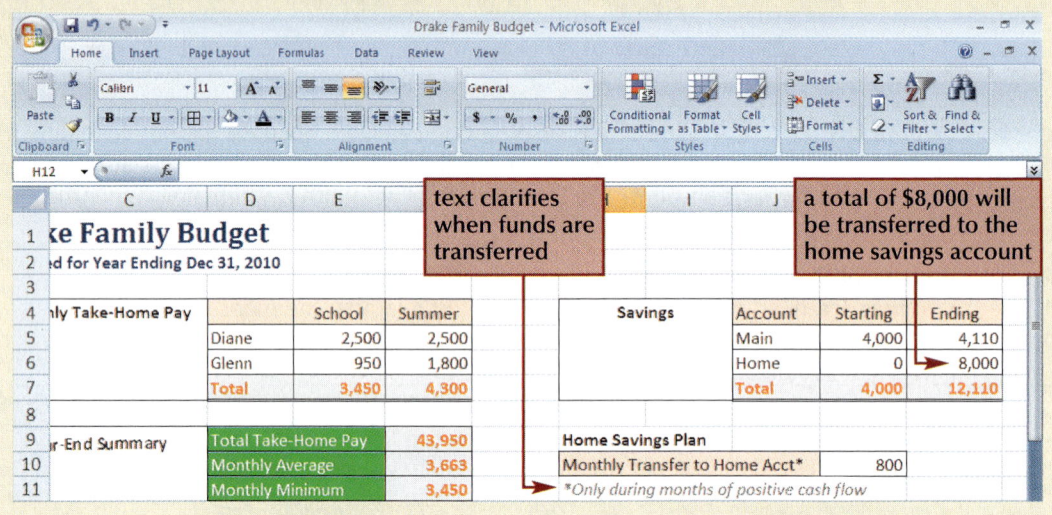

Based on this savings plan, Diane can transfer $800 from the main savings account to the home savings account in all but two months of the year, depositing a total of $8,000 into the home savings account by the end of the year. The main savings account balance stays above $3,000 for most of the year. Diane feels this is adequate, but wants to explore what would happen if she increases the monthly transfer from $800 to $1,000. How would that affect the monthly balance of the main savings account?

To change the amount transferred per month:

1. Change the value in cell K10 to **1000**. The total in the home savings account at the end of the year increases to $10,000.

2. Scroll down the worksheet and examine how the monthly balance in the main savings account changes throughout the year. Under this scenario, the balance in the main savings account drops to $1,900 in the month of August. This is a little too low for Diane.

3. Change the value in cell K10 to **900**. With this savings plan, the couple will save $9,000 toward the purchase of a home.

4. Scroll through the worksheet, examining the monthly balances of the two savings accounts. The balance in their savings account stays above $2,500 for most of the year. This seems like a good compromise to Diane, and she decides to adopt it as a model budget for the upcoming year.

Working with Date Functions

Diane's budget is just the start of her financial planning. To be effective, budgets need to be monitored and updated as conditions change. In the upcoming year, Diane plans to use this workbook to enter the actual salaries, expenses, and savings. This will enable her to track how well her projected values match the actual values. Because Diane will be updating the workbook throughout the year, she wants the worksheet to always display the current date so she can tell how far she is into her budget projections. You can accomplish this using a **date function**. Seven of the date functions supported by Excel are described in Figure 3-31. You can use these functions to help with scheduling or to determine on what days of the week certain dates occur.

Figure 3-31   Date functions

Function	Description
DATE(*year, month, day*)	Creates a date value for the date represented by the *year*, *month*, and *day* arguments
DAY(*date*)	Extracts the day of the month from the *date* value
MONTH(*date*)	Extracts the month number from the *date* value where 1=January, 2=February, and so forth
YEAR(*date*)	Extracts the year number from the *date* value
WEEKDAY(*date*, [*return_type*])	Calculates the day of the week from the *date* value, where 1=Sunday, 2=Monday, and so forth; to choose a different numbering scheme, set the optional *return_type* value to "1" (1=Sunday, 2=Monday, ...), "2" (1=Monday, 2=Tuesday, ...), or "3" (0=Monday, 1=Tuesday, ...)
NOW( )	Displays the current date and time
TODAY( )	Displays the current date

Perhaps the most commonly used date function is the TODAY function, which returns the current date. The syntax of the TODAY function is as follows:

`=TODAY()`

The TODAY function doesn't have any arguments. Neither does the NOW function, which returns both the current date and current time. The values returned by the TODAY and NOW functions are updated automatically whenever you reopen the workbook or enter a new calculation. If you don't want the date and time to change, you must enter the date and time value directly in the cell.

Diane wants the 2010 Proposed Budget workbook to display the current date.

To enter the TODAY function to display the current date:

1. In cell J1, enter **Current Date**.
2. Merge cells **J1** and **K1**, right-align the merged cell, and then apply the **20% – Accent6** cell style.
3. Click cell **L1**. You'll enter the TODAY function in this cell.
4. In the Function Library group on the Formulas tab, click the **Date & Time** button, and then click **TODAY** in the date functions list. The Function Arguments dialog box opens, but there are no arguments for the TODAY function.

> **5.** Click the **OK** button. The Function Arguments dialog box closes, and the current date appears in cell L1. See Figure 3-32.

Figure 3-32 — TODAY function displays the current date

Tip
You can also enter the TODAY function by typing =TODAY() directly in a cell.

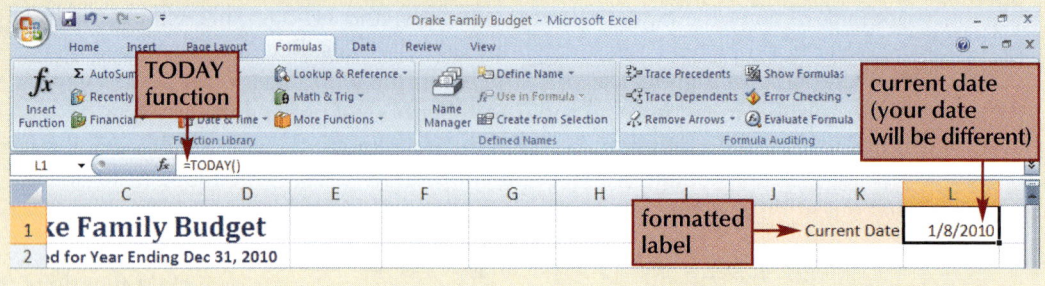

Working with Financial Functions

Diane wants to estimate how much monthly mortgage payments for a house might be. You can use the **PMT function** to calculate the payments for any type of loan.

The PMT function is one of many **financial functions** in Excel that calculate values from loans and investments. Figure 3-33 describes this and some of the other financial functions often used to develop budgets. These financial functions are the same as those widely used in business and accounting to perform various financial calculations, such as depreciation of an asset, the amount of interest paid on an investment, and the present value of an investment.

Figure 3-33 — Financial functions for loans and investments

Function	Description
FV(rate, nper, pmt, [pv=0] [,type=0])	Returns the future value of an investment, where *rate* is the interest rate per period, *nper* is the total number of periods, *pmt* is the payment in each period, *pv* is the present value of the investment, and *type* indicates whether payments should be made at the end of the period (0) or the beginning of the period (1)
PMT(rate, nper, pv, [fv=0] [,type=0])	Calculates the payments required each period on a loan or investment
IPMT(rate, per, nper, pv, [fv=0] [,type=0])	Calculates the amount of a loan payment devoted to paying the loan interest, where *per* is the number of the payment period
PPMT(rate, per, nper, pv, [fv=0] [,type=0])	Calculates the amount of a loan payment devoted to paying off the principal of a loan, where *per* is the number of the payment period
PV(rate, nper, pmt, [fv=0] [,type=0])	Calculates the present value of a loan or investment based on periodic, constant payments
NPER(rate, pmt, pv, [fv=0] [,type=0])	Calculates the number of periods required to pay off a loan or investment
RATE(nper, pmt, pv, [fv=0] [,type=0])	Calculates the interest rate of a loan or investment based on periodic, constant payments

For expensive items, such as cars and houses, people often borrow money from a bank to make the purchase. Every loan has two main components: the principal and the interest. **Principal** is the amount of money being loaned, and **interest** is the amount charged for lending the money. You can think of interest as a kind of "user fee" because the borrower is paying for the right to use the lender's money for a period of time. The more money borrowed and the longer time for which it's borrowed, the higher the user fee. A few years ago, Diane and Glenn borrowed money to buy a second car and are still repaying the principal and interest on that loan.

Interest is calculated either as simple interest or as compound interest. In **simple interest**, the interest paid is equal to a percentage of principal for each period that the money has been lent. For example, if Diane and Glenn deposit $1,000 in an account that pays simple interest at a rate of 5% per year, they'll receive $50 in interest each year that the money is deposited. More often, interest is calculated as **compound interest** in which the interest paid is calculated on the principal and any previous interest payments that have been added to that principal. For example, the interest payment for a $1,000 deposit at a 5% interest that is compounded every year is $50. If the interest is left in the account, the interest payment for the second year is calculated on $1,050 (the original principal plus the previous year's interest), resulting in an interest payment for the second year of $52.50. With compound interest, the borrower always pays more money to the lender the following year. Most banks and financial institutions use compound interest in their financial transactions.

Using Functions to Manage Personal Finances | InSight

Excel has many financial functions you can use to manage your personal finances. The following list can help you determine which function to use for the most common personal finance problems:

- To determine how much an investment will be worth after a series of monthly payments at some future time, use the FV (future value) function.
- To determine how much you have to spend each month to repay a loan or mortgage within a set period of time, use the PMT (payment) function.
- To determine how much of your monthly loan payment is used to pay the interest, use the IPMT (interest payment) function.
- To determine how much of your monthly loan payment is used for repaying the principal, use the PPMT (principal payment) function.
- To determine the largest loan or mortgage you can afford at present, given a set monthly payment, use the PV (present value) function.
- To determine how long it will take to pay off a loan with constant monthly payments, use the NPER (number of periods) function.

In each case, you usually need to enter the annual interest rate divided by the number of times the interest is compounded during the year. If interest is compounded monthly, divide the annual interest rate by 12; if interest is compounded quarterly, divide the annual rate by 4. You must also convert the length of the loan or investment to the number of interest payments per year. If you will make payments monthly, multiply the number of years of the loan or investment by 12.

Using the PMT Function to Determine a Monthly Loan Payment

You'll use the PMT function to calculate the potential monthly loan payment for Diane and Glenn. For loan or investment calculations, you need to know the following information:

- The annual interest rate
- The payment period, or how often payments are due and interest is compounded (usually monthly for mortgages)

- The length of the loan in terms of the number of payment periods
- The amount being borrowed or invested

In Diane and Glenn's neighborhood, starter homes are selling for about $200,000. If Diane and Glenn can keep to their savings plan, they will have saved $9,000 by the end of the year (as shown in cell L6 in the Proposed Budget 2010 worksheet). If they save this same amount for the next three years, they will have at least $27,000 in their home savings account to put toward the down payment. Based on this, Diane estimates that she and Glenn will need a home loan of about $170,000. To calculate how much it would cost to repay such a loan, you can use the PMT (payment) function. The PMT function has the following syntax:

```
PMT(rate, nper, pv, [fv=0] [type=0])
```

In this function, *rate* is the interest rate for each payment period, *nper* is the total number of payment periods required to pay off the loan, and *pv* is the present value of the loan or the amount that needs to be borrowed. For Diane and Glenn, the present value of the loan is $170,000.

The PMT function has two optional arguments: *fv* and *type*. The *fv* argument is the future value of the loan. Because the intent with most loans is to pay them off completely, the future value is equal to 0 by default. The *type* argument specifies when the interest is charged on the loan, either at the end of the period (*type*=0), which is the default, or at the beginning of the period (*type*=1).

For most loans, the payment period is one month. This means that Diane and Glenn must make a payment on the loan every month, and interest on the loan is compounded every month. The annual interest rate on home loans in Diane and Glenn's area is 6.5%. To determine the interest rate per month, you divide the annual interest rate by 12. For Diane and Glenn, the interest rate each month or payment period is 6.5% divided by 12, or about 0.541% per month.

Diane and Glenn want to pay off their home loan in 20 years, which is a payment period of 240 months (20 years multiplied by 12 payment periods each year). Putting all of this information together, you can calculate the monthly payment for the couple's home loan with the following formula:

```
=PMT(0.065/12, 20*12, 170000)
```

This formula returns a value of –$1,267.47. The value is negative because the payment is considered an expense, or a negative cash flow. If you want to display this value as a positive number in a worksheet, enter a minus symbol directly before the PMT function as follows:

```
=-PMT(0.065/12, 20*12, 170000)
```

Based on these calculations, Diane and Glenn would have to pay the bank $1,267.47 every month for 20 years before the loan and the interest are completely paid. Right now, the couple is spending about $850 per month on rent. So this home loan is a significant increase over their current expenses. Diane asks you to calculate the monthly payment for a home loan of $160,000. You'll make that calculation in another worksheet.

To set up the monthly loan payment calculation:

1. Insert a new worksheet named **Loan Analysis** at the end of the workbook.

2. In cell A1, enter **Home Loan**, format cell A1 using the **Title** cell style, and then increase the width of column A to **25** characters.

3. In the range A3:A9;B3:B8, enter the labels and components of the home loan shown in Figure 3-34. In cell B5, enter **=B3/B4** to calculate the interest rate per period by dividing the annual interest rate by the number of payments per year. In cell B7, enter **=B4*B6** to calculate the number of loan payments per year by multiplying the number of payments per year (12) by the number of years of the loan (20).

Loan Analysis worksheet | **Figure 3-34**

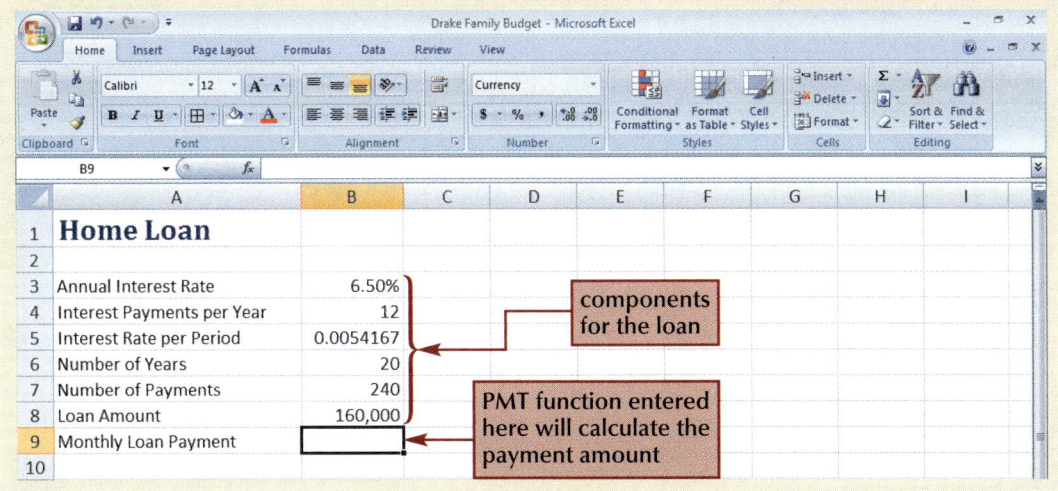

Next, you'll enter the PMT function to calculate the monthly payment for the $160,000 home loan.

To enter the PMT function to calculate the monthly payment:

▸ 1. Apply the **Calculation** cell style to cell B9 to distingish the monthly loan payment amount from the loan components.

▸ 2. In the Function Library group on the Formulas tab, click the **Financial** button, and then click **PMT** in the list of financial functions. The Function Arguments dialog box opens.

▸ 3. For the Rate argument, enter the cell reference **B5**, which is the cell with the interest rate per payment period.

▸ 4. For the Nper argument, enter the cell reference **B7**, which is the cell with the total number of payments.

▸ 5. For the Pv argument enter the cell reference **B8**, which is the cell with the present value of the loan. See Figure 3-35.

Function Arguments dialog box for the PMT function | **Figure 3-35**

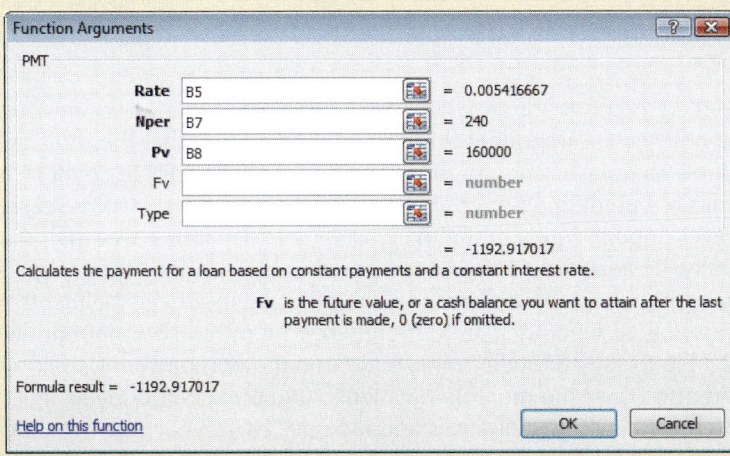

▸ 6. Click the **OK** button. The value $1,192.92 is displayed in parentheses in cell B9 to indicate a negative currency value.

▶ 7. Double-click cell **B9**, type **–** (minus symbol) between = and PMT, and then press the **Enter** key. The value $1,192.92 is displayed as a positive currency value. See Figure 3-36.

| Figure 3-36 | Monthly payment for a $160,000 loan |

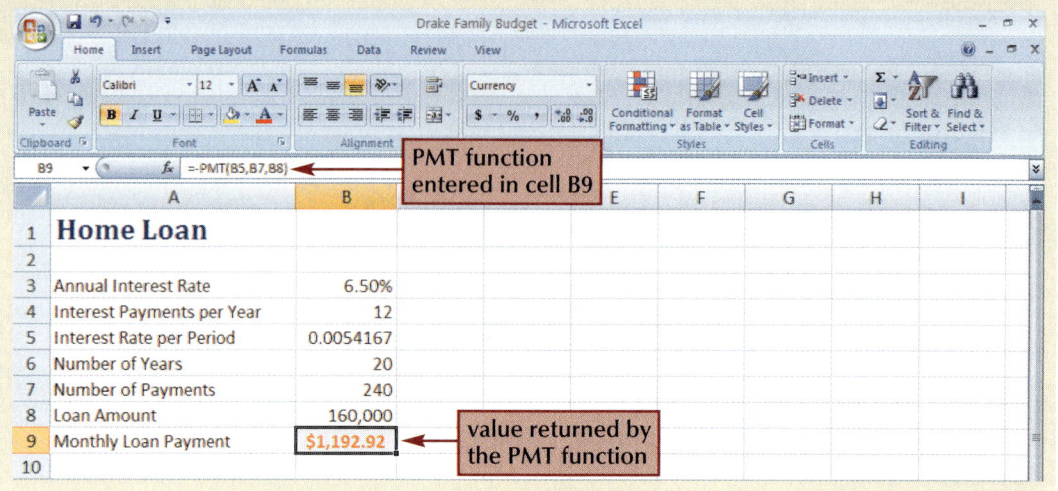

Diane and Glenn would have to pay about $1,193 per month for 20 years to repay a $160,000 loan at 6.5% interest. Diane is interested in other loan possibilities. Because you already set up the worksheet, you can quickly try other scenarios without having to reenter any formulas. Diane wonders whether extending the length of the loan would reduce the monthly payment by a sizeable margin. She asks you to calculate the monthly payment for a 30-year loan.

To calculate other loan options:

▶ 1. In cell B6, change the value to **30**. The amount of the monthly payment drops to $1,011.31, which is $180 less per month. Next, Diane wants to see the monthly payments for a $150,000 loan with these same conditions.

▶ 2. In cell B8, change the value to **150,000**. For this smaller home loan, the monthly payment drops even further to $948.10 per month. This is only about $100 more than the couple is currently paying in rent.

▶ 3. Save your changes to the workbook, and then close it.

You've completed your work on Diane and Glenn's budget. Based on your analysis, Diane has learned several important things. She's discovered that the projected budget allows the couple to transfer enough money to the home savings account to make a down payment on a home in about three years. The savings plan seems reasonable to Diane and leaves enough funds in the main savings account to cover their monthly expenses. Finally, by analyzing some of the possible loan options they might encounter when they buy a home, Diane realizes that the monthly mortgage payments will not be substantially more than what they are currently paying in rent. So, not only will Diane and Glenn be able to save enough to make the initial down payment, their monthly income should also cover the monthly payments. Of course, all budgets must be revised periodically to meet changing expenses and income. However, your work has given Diane and Glenn enough information to make informed choices about their immediate financial future.

Session 3.2 Quick Check | Review

1. How do you use AutoFill to copy a set of cell values, but not the formatting?
2. The first three selected values in a series are 3, 6, and 9. What are the next three values that will be inserted using AutoFill?
3. Cell A5 contains the text Mon. If you select the cell and drag the fill handle over the range A6:A8, what text will be entered into those cells?
4. If cell A3 is greater than cell A4, you want to display the text "OK"; otherwise, you want to display the text string "RETRY". What formula accomplishes this?
5. What formula do you use to display the current date?
6. What formula do you use to display the current date and time?
7. You want to take out a loan for $130,000. The interest on the loan is 5% compounded monthly. You intend to pay back the loan in 20 years. What formula do you enter to calculate the monthly payment required to pay off the loan under those conditions?
8. What financial function do you use to determine how payment periods are required to pay off a loan?

Tutorial Summary | Review

In this tutorial, you learned how to work with Excel functions and formulas. First, you learned about relative, absolute, and mixed cell references and under what conditions you would use each. Then, you looked at function syntax, entered a function using the Insert Function dialog box, and then you entered a function directly into the worksheet to calculate sums, counts, averages, maximums, and minimums. You also searched for a function that matched search criteria. Next, you used AutoFill to quickly copy formulas and formatting and to extend a series of numbers, text, or dates. Then, you used logical functions to return different values based on conditions in the worksheet, and then you entered a date function. Finally, you examined financial functions and used the PMT function to calculate the monthly payments to repay a loan within a set interval of time.

Key Terms

absolute reference	financial function	nested
argument	IF function	optional argument
AutoFill	Insert Function dialog box	PMT function
comparison operator	interest	principal
compound interest	logical function	relative reference
date function	median	simple interest
F4 key	mixed reference	syntax
fill handle	mode	

Practice | Review Assignments

Practice the skills you learned in the tutorial using the same case scenario.

Data File needed for the Review Assignments: Timov.xlsx

Diane and Glenn appreciate the work you did on their budget. Their friends, Sergei and Ava Timov, ask you to create a similar workbook for their family budget. The Timovs want to purchase a new home. They are considering two houses with different mortgages. They want the budget worksheet you create to display the impact of monthly mortgage payments on the couple's cash flow. The couple has already designed the workbook and entered estimates of their take-home pay and expenses for the upcoming year. They want you to set up the formulas.

Complete the following:

1. Open the **Timov** workbook located in the Tutorial.03\Review folder included with your Data Files, and then save the workbook as **Timov Family Budget** in the same folder.
2. In the Documentation sheet, enter your name in cell B3 and the date in cell B4.
3. In the Family Budget worksheet, in the range C17:N17, use AutoFill to enter the month names **January** through **December**.
4. In the range C20:N20, calculate the family's take-home pay. In the range C26:N26, calculate the monthly expenses. In the range C27:N27, calculate the monthly net cash flow (equal to the monthly take-home pay minus the expenses).
5. In cell C6, enter a formula to calculate the sum of Sergei's monthly salary for the entire year. In cell D6, calculate Sergei's average take-home pay each month. In cell E6, calculate Sergei's maximum monthly take-home pay. In cell F6, calculate Sergei's minimum monthly take-home pay.
6. Select the range C6:F6, and then use AutoFill to copy the formula in the C6:F6 range into the C7:F15 range. Use the AutoFill Options button to copy only the formulas into the selected range and not both the formulas and formats. (*Hint:* Because you haven't yet entered any mortgage payment values, cell D13 will show the value #DIV/0!, indicating that Excel cannot calculate the average mortgage payment. You'll correct that problem shortly.)
7. In the range J5:J12, enter the following loan and loan conditions of the first mortgage:
   - The loan amount (or value of the principal) is **$315,000**.
   - The annual interest rate is **6.7%**.
   - The interest rate is compounded **12** times a year (or monthly).
   - The mortgage will last **30** years.

   The monthly rate is equal to the annual interest rate divided by how often the interest rate is compounded. The number of payments is equal to the number of years the mortgage will last multiplied by 12.
8. In cell J11, enter the PMT function to calculate the monthly payment required to repay this loan. The *rate* argument is equal to the monthly rate, the *nper* argument is equal to the number of payments, and the *pv* argument is equal to the value of the principal.
9. In cell J11, enter a minus symbol between = and PMT to make the value positive.
10. In the range N5:N12, enter the following loan and loan conditions of the second mortgage:
    - The loan amount (or value of the principal) is **$218,000**.
    - The annual interest rate is **6.7%**.
    - The interest rate is compounded **12** times a year (or monthly).
    - The mortgage will last **20** years.

11. In cell N11, enter the PMT function to calculate the monthly payment needed to pay off this loan, and then make the PMT value positive.
12. Sergei and Ava want to be able to view their monthly cash flow under both mortgage possibilities. The mortgage being applied to the budget will be determined by whether 1 or 2 is entered into cell C3. To switch from one mortgage to another, do the following:
    - In cell C25, enter an IF function that tests whether cell C3 equals 1. If it does, display the value from cell J11; otherwise, display the value from cell N11. Use absolute cell references in the formula.
    - Use AutoFill to copy the formula in cell C25 into the range D25:N25.
    - Verify that the values in the range C25:N25 match the monthly payment for the first mortgage condition.
13. In cell C3, edit the value from 1 to **2**. Verify that the monthly payment for the second mortgage appears in the range C25:N25.
14. Sergei and Ava want to maintain an average net cash flow of at least $1,000 per month. Under which mortgage is this achieved?
15. Save and close the workbook, and then submit the finished workbook to your instructor, either in printed or electronic form, as requested.

Apply | Case Problem 1

Use the skills you learned to create a grading sheet for a chemistry course.

Data File needed for this Case Problem: Chemistry.xlsx

Chemistry 303   Karen Raul is a professor of chemistry at a community college in Shawnee, Kansas. She has started using Excel to calculate the final grade for students in her Chemistry 303 course. The final score is a weighted average of the scores given for three exams and the final exam. Karen wants your help in creating the formulas to calculate the final score and to summarize the class scores on all exams. One way to calculate a weighted average is by multiplying each student's exam score by the weight given to the exam, and then totaling the results. For example, consider the following four exam scores:

- Exam 1 = 84
- Exam 2 = 80
- Exam 3 = 83
- Final Exam = 72

If the first three exams are each given a weight of 20% and the final exam is given a weight of 40%, the weighted average of the four scores is:

84*0.2 + 80*0.2 + 83*0.2 + 72*0.4 = 78.2

Karen already entered the scores for her students and formatted much of the workbook. She wants you to enter the final formulas and highlight the top 10 overall scores in her class. Figure 3-37 shows the worksheet you'll create.

Figure 3-37

	A	B	C	D	E	F	G	H
1	**Chemistry 303**							
2	First Semester Scores							
3	Posted 12/20/2010							
4								
5	Students	36						
6								
7		Exam	Weight	Median	Maximum	Minimum	Range	
8	Class Summary	Exam 1	20%	86.0	99.0	52.0	47.0	
9		Exam 2	20%	80.0	99.0	53.0	46.0	
10		Exam 3	20%	83.0	98.0	50.0	48.0	
11		Final Exam	40%	81.5	99.0	51.0	48.0	
12		Overall	100%	80.5	96.8	55.8	41.0	
13								
14								
15	**Student Scores**				Top Ten Overall Scores			
16	Student ID	Exam 1	Exam 2	Exam 3	Final Exam	Overall		
17	390-120-2	84.0	80.0	83.0	72.0	78.2		
18	390-267-4	98.0	92.0	91.0	99.0	95.8		
19	390-299-8	54.0	56.0	51.0	65.0	58.2		
20	390-354-3	98.0	95.0	90.0	94.0	94.2		

Complete the following:

1. Open the **Chemistry** workbook located in the Tutorial.03\Case1 folder included with your Data Files, and then save the workbook as **Chemistry 303 Final Scores** in the same folder.
2. In the Documentation sheet, enter your name in cell B3 and enter the date in cell B4.
3. In the First Semester Scores worksheet, in cell F17, enter a formula to calculate the weighted average of the first student's four exams. Use the weights found in the range C8:C11, matching each weight with the corresponding exam score. Use absolute cell references for the four weights.
4. Use AutoFill to copy the formula in cell F17 into the range F18:F52.
5. In cell B5, enter a formula to count the number of final scores in the range F17:F52.

EXPLORE

6. In cell D8, use the MEDIAN function to calculate the median or middle score for the first exam.
7. In cell E8, calculate the maximum score for the first exam.
8. In cell F8, calculate the minimum score for the first exam.
9. In cell G8, calculate the range of scores for the first exam, which is equal to the difference between the maximum and minimum score.
10. Repeat Steps 6 through 9 for each of the other two exams, the final exam, and the overall weighted score.
11. Use conditional formatting to highlight the top 10 scores in the range F17:F52 in a light red fill with dark red text.
12. Insert a page break at cell A14, repeat the first three rows of the worksheet in any printout, and verify that the worksheet is in portrait orientation.
13. Save and close the workbook, and then submit the finished workbook to your instructor, either in printed or electronic form, as requested.

Apply | Case Problem 2

Use the skills you learned to create an order form for a fireworks company.

Data File needed for this Case Problem: Wizard.xlsx

WizardWorks Andrew Howe owns and operates WizardWorks, an online seller of fireworks based in Franklin, Tennessee. Andrew wants you to help him use Excel to develop an order form for his business. The form needs to contain formulas to calculate the charge for each order. The total charge is based on the quantity and type of items ordered plus the shipping charge and the 5% sales tax. Orders can be shipped using standard 3 to 5 day shipping for $4.99 or overnight for $12.99. Andrew is also offering a 3% discount for orders that exceed $200. Both the shipping option and the discount need to be calculated using formulas based on values entered into the worksheet. Figure 3-38 shows a preview of a sample order.

Figure 3-38

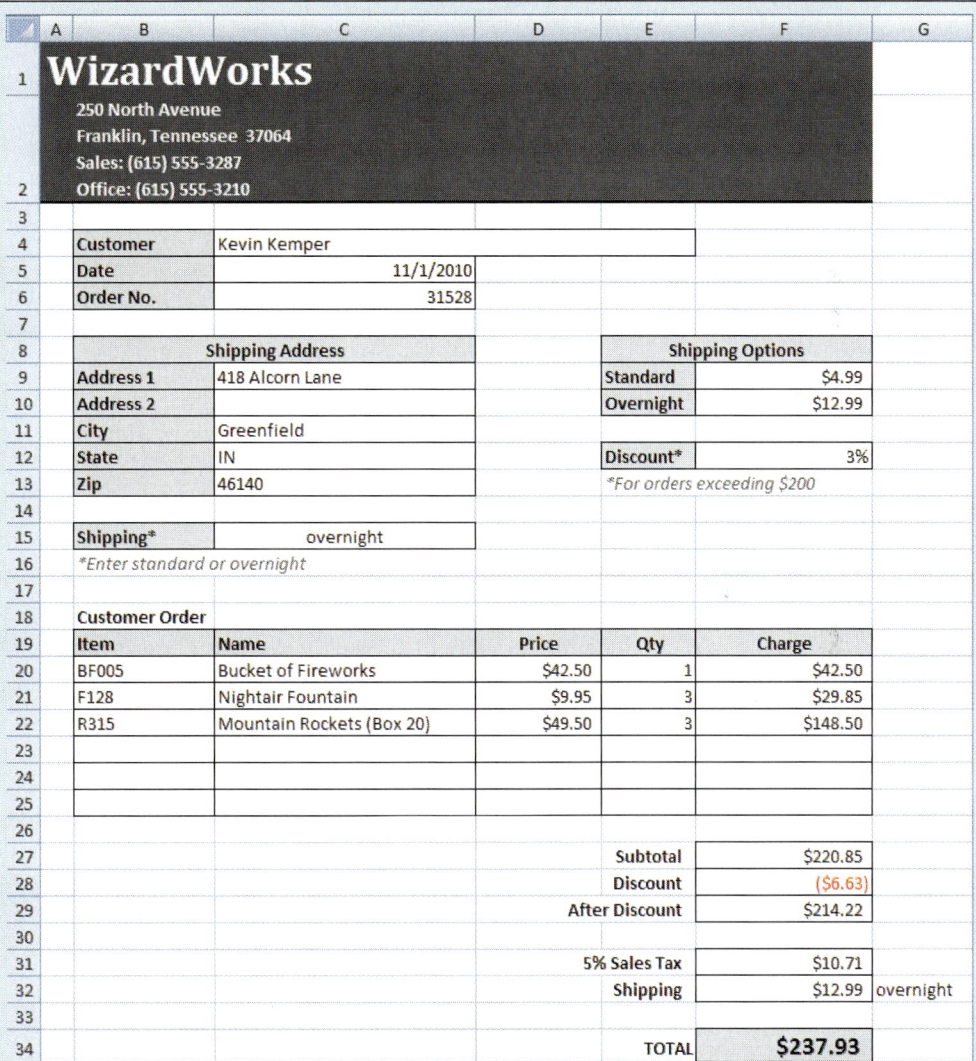

Complete the following:

1. Open the **Wizard** workbook located in the Tutorial.03\Case2 folder included with your Data Files, and then save the workbook as **WizardWorks Order Form** in the same folder.
2. In the Documentation sheet, enter your name in cell B3 and enter the date in cell B4.

3. In the Order Form worksheet, in cell C4, enter the customer name, **Kevin Kemper**. In cell C6, enter the order number, **31528**. In the range C9:C13, enter the following address:

   Address 1:   **418 Alcorn Lane**
   City: **Greenfield**
   State: **IN**
   Zip: **46140**

EXPLORE

4. In cell C5, enter a function that displays the current date.
5. In the range B20:E22, enter the following orders:

Item	Name	Price	Qty
BF005	Bucket of Fireworks	$42.50	1
F128	Nightair Fountain	$9.95	3
R315	Mountain Rockets (Box 20)	$49.50	3

6. In cell C15, enter **overnight** to ship this order overnight.

EXPLORE

7. In cell F20, enter an IF function that tests whether the order quantity in cell E20 is greater than 0 (zero). If it is, return the value of E20 multiplied by D20; otherwise, return no text by entering "". AutoFill this formula into the range F21:F25.
8. In cell F27, calculate the sum of the values in the range F20:F25.
9. In cell F28, enter an IF function that tests whether cell F27 is greater than 200. If it is, return the negative value of F27 multiplied by the discount percentage in cell F12; otherwise, return the value 0 (zero).
10. In cell F29, add the subtotal from cell F27 and the discount value from cell F28.
11. In cell F31, calculate the sales tax by multiplying the after discount value in cell F29 by the sales tax percentage, 0.05.
12. In cell F32, determine the shipping charge by entering an IF function that tests whether cell C15 equals "standard". If it does, return the value in cell F9; otherwise, return the value in cell F10.
13. In cell G32, display the value of cell C15.
14. In cell F34, calculate the total of the after discount value, the sales tax, and the shipping fee.
15. Scale the order form so that it will print on a single page.
16. Reduce the quantity of Mountain Rockets boxes from 3 to **2**, and then verify that the discount is changed to 0 for the order. Change the shipping option from overnight to **standard**, and then verify that the shipping fee is changed to the fee for standard shipping.
17. Save and close the workbook, and then submit the finished workbook to your instructor, either in printed or electronic form, as requested.

Challenge | Case Problem 3

Explore how to use relative and absolute references and the PMT function to create a loan table.

Data File needed for this Case Problem: Loan.xlsx

Eason Financial Services Jesse Buchmann is a finance officer at Eason Financial Services in Meridian, Idaho. She works with people who are looking for home mortgages. Most clients want mortgages they can afford, and affordability is determined by the size of the monthly payment. The monthly payment is determined by the interest rate, the total number of payments, and the size of the home loan. Jesse can't change the interest rate, but homebuyers can reduce their monthly payments by increasing the number of years to repay the loan. Jesse wants to give her clients a grid that displays combinations of loan amounts and payment periods so that they can select a loan that best meets their needs and budget. Figure 3-39 shows a preview of the grid that Jesse has in mind.

Figure 3-39

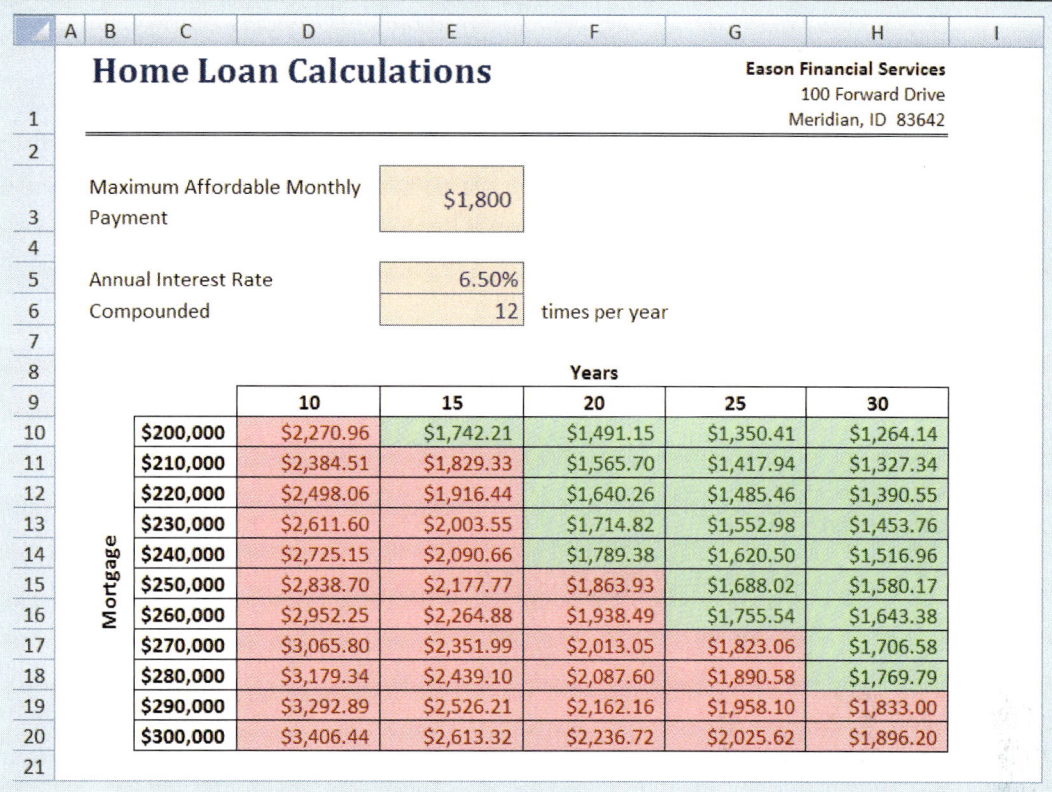

Jesse already entered much of the layout and formatting for the worksheet containing the loan payment grid. She needs your help in entering the PMT function.

Complete the following:

1. Open the **Loan** workbook located in the Tutorial.03\Case3 folder included with your Data Files, and then save the workbook as **Loan Grid** in the same folder.
2. In the Documentation sheet, enter your name and the date.
3. In the Loan Calculation worksheet, in cell E3, enter a monthly payment of **$2,200**.
4. In cell E5, enter the annual interest rate of **6.5%**. In cell E6, enter **12** to indicate that the interest payment is compounded 12 times a year, or monthly.
5. In the range C10:C20, use AutoFill to enter the currency values **$200,000** through **$300,000** in increments of $10,000. In the range D9:H9, use AutoFill to enter the year values **10** through **30** in increments of 5 years.

EXPLORE
6. In cell D10, use the PMT function to calculate the monthly payment required to repay a **$200,000** loan in **10** years at **6.5%** interest compounded monthly. Use absolute references to cells E5 and E6 to enter the annual interest rate and number of payments per year. Use the mixed references D$9 and $C10 to cells D9 and C10, respectively, to reference the number of years to repay the loan and the loan amount. Place a minus symbol before the PMT function so that the value returned by the function is positive rather than negative.

EXPLORE
7. Using AutoFill, copy the formula in cell D10 into the range D11:H10, and then copy that range of formulas into the range D11:H20. Verify that the values entered in those cells match the values shown in Figure 3-39.

EXPLORE 8. Conditionally format the range D10:H20 to highlight all of the values in the range that are less than the value in cell E3 in a dark green font on a green fill.

9. Add a second conditional format to the range D10:H20 to highlight all of the values in the range that are greater than the value in cell E3 in a dark red font on a red fill.

EXPLORE 10. Change the value in cell E3 from $2,200 to **$1,800**. If this represents the maximum affordable monthly payment, use the values in the grid to determine the largest mortgage for payment schedules lasting 15 through 30 years. Can any of the home loan values displayed in the grid be repaid in 10 years at $1,800 per month?

11. Save and close the workbook, and then submit the finished workbook to your instructor, either in printed or electronic form, as requested.

| Create | **Case Problem 4** |

Create a workbook that automatically grades a driving exam.

Data File needed for this Case Problem: V6.xlsx

V-6 Driving Academy Sebastian Villanueva owns and operates the V-6 Driving Academy, a driving school located in Pine Hills, Florida. In addition to driving, students must take multiple-choice tests offered by the Florida Department of Motor Vehicles. Students must answer at least 80% of the questions correctly to pass each test. Sebastian has to grade these tests himself. Sebastian realizes that he can save a lot of time if the test questions were in a workbook and Excel totaled the test results. He asks you to help create the workbook.

Sebastian already entered a 20-question test into a workbook. He needs you to format this workbook and insert the necessary functions and formulas to grade a student's answers.

Complete the following:

1. Open the **V6** workbook located in the Tutorial.03\Case4 folder included with your Data Files, and then save the workbook as **V6 Driving Test** in the same folder.

2. In the Documentation sheet, enter your name in cell B3 and enter the date in cell B4.

3. In the Exam1 worksheet, format the questions and possible answers so that the worksheet is easy to read. The format is up to you. At the top of the worksheet, enter a title that describes the exam and then enter a function that returns the current date.

4. Add a section somewhere on the Exam1 worksheet where Sebastian can enter the student's name and answers to each question.

EXPLORE 5. The answers for the 20 questions are listed below. Use this information to write functions that will grade each answer, giving 1 point for a correct answer and 0 otherwise. Assume that all answers are in lowercase letters; therefore, the function that tests the answer to the first question should check for a "c" rather than a "C".

Question	Answer	Question	Answer	Question	Answer
1	c	8	a	15	b
2	a	9	c	16	b
3	b	10	b	17	b
4	a	11	c	18	b
5	c	12	b	19	b
6	b	13	b	20	c
7	c	14	a		

6. At the top of the worksheet, insert a formula to calculate the total number of correct answers.
7. Insert another formula that divides the total number of correct answers by the total number of exam questions on the worksheet. Display this value as a percentage.
8. Enter a logical function that displays the message "PASS" on the exam if the percentage of correct answers is greater than or equal to 80%; otherwise, the logical function displays the message "FAIL".

Test your worksheet on the following student exams. Which students passed and which failed? What score did each student receive on the exam?

Juan Marquez

Question	Answer	Question	Answer	Question	Answer
1	b	8	a	15	b
2	a	9	c	16	b
3	b	10	b	17	a
4	a	11	c	18	b
5	c	12	c	19	b
6	b	13	b	20	a
7	c	14	a		

Kurt Bessette

Question	Answer	Question	Answer	Question	Answer
1	c	8	b	15	c
2	c	9	c	16	b
3	b	10	b	17	a
4	a	11	c	18	b
5	c	12	a	19	b
6	b	13	b	20	b
7	c	14	a		

Rebecca Pena

Question	Answer	Question	Answer	Question	Answer
1	c	8	a	15	b
2	a	9	c	16	c
3	b	10	a	17	b
4	a	11	c	18	b
5	c	12	b	19	b
6	b	13	b	20	c
7	c	14	a		

9. Save and close the workbook, and then submit the finished workbook to your instructor, either in printed or electronic form, as requested.

Research | Internet Assignments

Use the Internet to find and work with data related to the topics presented in this tutorial.

The purpose of the Internet Assignments is to challenge you to find information on the Internet that you can use to work effectively with this software. The actual assignments are updated and maintained on the Course Technology Web site. Log on to the Internet and use your Web browser to go to the Student Online Companion for New Perspectives Office 2007 at **www.course.com/np/office2007**. Then navigate to the Internet Assignments for this tutorial.

Assess | SAM Assessment and Training

If you have a SAM user profile, you may have access to hands-on instruction, practice, and assessment of the skills covered in this tutorial. Log in to your SAM account (**http://sam2007.course.com**) to launch any assigned training activities or exams that relate to the skills covered in this tutorial.

Review | Quick Check Answers

Session 3.1

1. Absolute cell reference is $B$21. Mixed cell references are $B21 and B$21.
2. =C11+C12
3. =$B11+C$2
4. =AVERAGE($A11:$A15)
5. Optional arguments are not required in a function. If not included, Excel assumes a default value for the argument.
6. =SUM(B1:B10)
7. =MAX(B1:B10)–MIN(B1:B10)
8. =MAX(B1:B10)/MIN(B1:B10)

Session 3.2

1. Drag the fill handle over the selected range, click the AutoFill Options button, and then click Fill Without Formatting.
2. 12, 15, 18
3. Cell A6 displays the text Tue, cell A7 displays Wed, and cell A8 displays Thu.
4. =IF(A3 > A4, "OK", "RETRY")
5. =TODAY()
6. =NOW()
7. =PMT(0.05/12, 12*20, 130000)
8. NPER

Ending Data Files

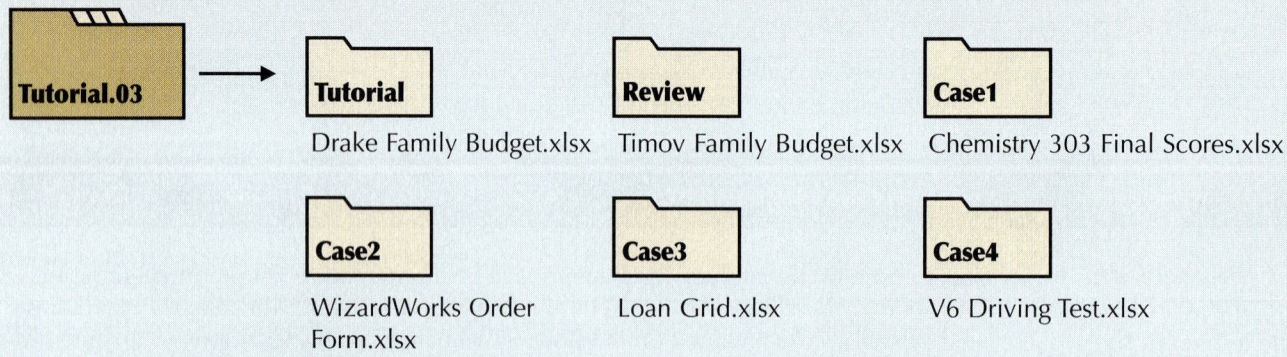

Tutorial 4

Excel EX 161

Objectives

Session 4.1
- Create an embedded chart
- Work with chart titles and legends
- Create and format a pie chart
- Work with 3D charts
- Create and format a column chart

Session 4.2
- Create and format a line chart
- Use custom formatting with chart axes
- Work with tick marks and scale values
- Create and format a combined chart
- Insert and format a graphic shape
- Create a chart sheet

Working with Charts and Graphics

Charting Financial Data

Case | Seaborg Group

Ajita Jindal is a financial assistant for the Seaborg Group, a financial consulting agency located in Providence, Rhode Island. One of her duties is to prepare financial reports on the investments the Seaborg Group makes for its clients. These reports go into a binder containing the financial status of the client's different investments. The client receives the binder at annual meetings with his or her financial advisor, and receives updates on the status of the investments periodically throughout the year.

Many of the company's clients invest in the New Century Fund, a large growth/large risk mutual fund that has been operating for the past 10 years. Ajita needs to create a one-page report that summarizes the fund's financial holdings as well as its 10-year performance record. She already entered the financial data into an Excel workbook, but needs some help in finishing the report. Because many clients are overwhelmed by tables of numbers, Ajita wants to include charts and graphs in the report that display the current and past performance of the New Century Fund. She asks you to help create these charts.

Starting Data Files

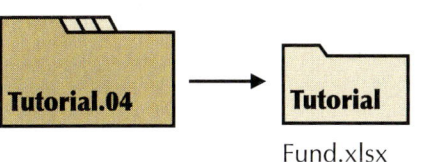
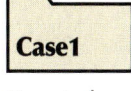

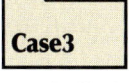

Tutorial.04 → Tutorial: Fund.xlsx | Review: Crockett.xlsx | Case1: Kenai.xlsx | Case2: Cloud.jpg, Tornado.xlsx | Case3: Mitchell.xlsx | Case4: Basketball.xlsx

Session 4.1

Creating Charts

Ajita already created a workbook in which she entered and formatted data that describes the New Century Fund. You'll begin by opening this workbook.

To open Ajita's workbook:

1. Open the **Fund** workbook located in the **Tutorial.04\Tutorial** folder included with your Data Files, and then save the workbook as **New Century Fund** in the same folder.

2. In the Documentation sheet, enter your name in cell B3 and the date in cell B4.

3. Review the contents of the workbook.

Ajita's workbook contains the following four worksheets in addition to the Documentation sheet:

- The Summary Report worksheet includes summary data and facts about the New Century Fund.
- The Assets worksheet lists the assets of the New Century Fund grouped by investment categories.
- The Sector Weightings worksheet shows the economic sectors in which the New Century Fund invests.
- The Performance History worksheet provides a table that shows how well the New Century Fund performed over the past 10 years compared to two similar funds.

Ajita wants financial data from the Assets, Sector Weightings, and Performance History worksheets placed in the Summary Report worksheet as charts, or graphs. A **chart**, or **graph**, is a visual representation of a set of data. Charts show trends or relationships in data that are more difficult to see by simply looking at numbers, such as the range of months in which the New Century Fund performed exceptionally well.

Figure 4-1 shows Ajita's sketch of how she wants the final Summary Report worksheet to look. In the summary report, she wants one chart that shows the performance of the New Century Fund compared to two similar funds, and she wants two charts that show how money in the New Century Fund is currently invested. The final Summary Report worksheet will be a single page that includes all of the information Ajita wants her clients to see.

Tutorial 4 Working with Charts and Graphics | Excel EX 163

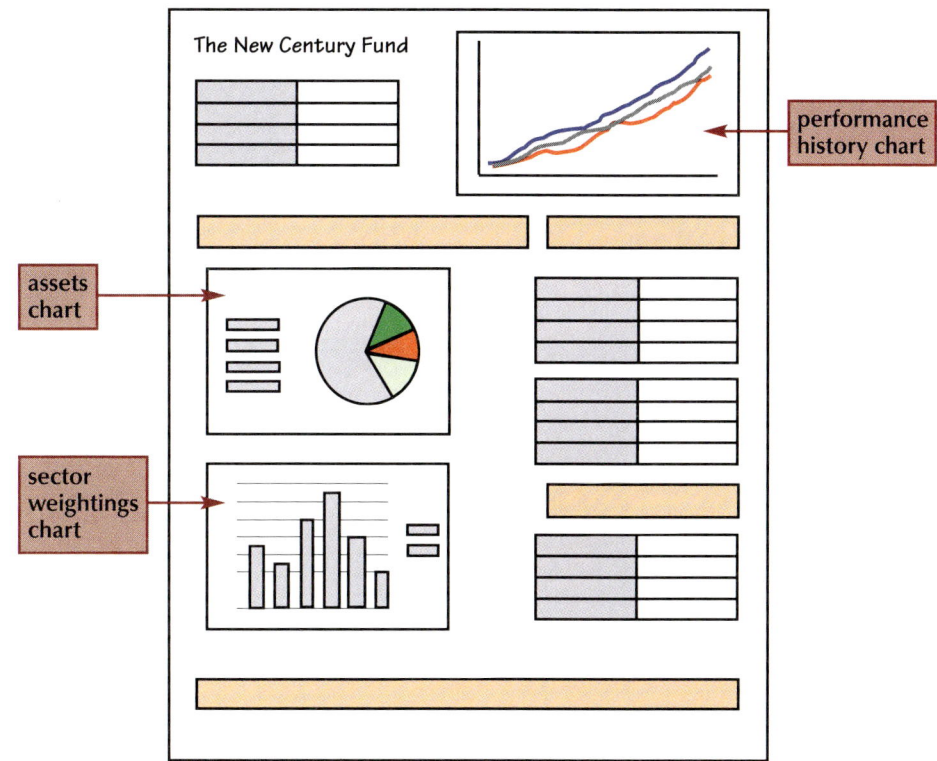

Figure 4-1 Ajita's proposed summary report

Inserting a Chart | Reference Window

- Select the data source with the range of data you want to chart.
- In the Charts group on the Insert tab, click a chart type, and then click a chart subtype in the Chart gallery.
- In the Location group on the Chart Tools Design tab, click the Move Chart button to place the chart in a chart sheet or embed it into a worksheet.

Selecting a Data Source

Each chart must have a data source. The **data source** is the range that contains the data you want to display in the chart. Each data source is a collection of one or more data series, where each **data series** is a range of values that is plotted as a single unit on the chart. Each data series has three components: the **series name** identifies the data series, the **series values** are the actual data displayed in the chart, and the **category values** are the groups or categories that the series values belong to. After you select the data source, Excel determines the series name, series values, and category values based on that data source. Sometimes, you might need to edit the data series Excel selects.

You'll select the data source for the chart that shows how the money in the New Century Fund is divided among investment categories. This data is located on the Assets worksheet.

To select the data source for the assets chart:

1. Click the **Assets** sheet tab to make the Assets worksheet active. You'll select one data series that shows the assets for five investment categories.

2. Select the range **A3:B8**. See Figure 4-2.

Figure 4-2   Data source selected for the assets chart

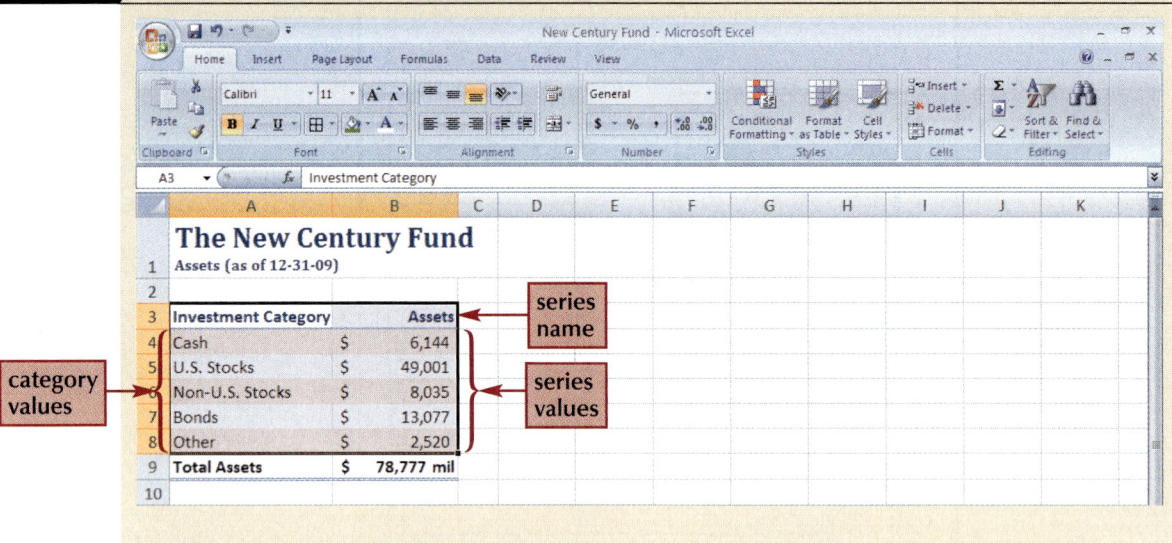

The range you selected for the data source, A3:B8, has a single data series. Excel uses the first row of the selected range as the series name, the first column as the category values, and the remaining columns as the series values. This data source has only one data series, the Assets data series. Its category values in the range A4:A8 list the different asset categories, and its series values in the range B4:B8 contain the data.

If the data source is organized in rows rather than in columns, the first row contains the category values, the remaining rows contain the data values for each data series, and the first column of each series row contains the series names. If your data is organized differently, you can specify a layout for the data source. You'll look at the tools to do this later in this tutorial.

Selecting a Chart Type

Next, you select the type of chart you want to create. Excel supports 73 built-in charts organized into 11 categories. Figure 4-3 describes the different chart type categories. You can also create custom chart types based on the built-in charts.

Figure 4-3 Categories of Excel chart types

Chart Type	Description
Column	Compares values from different categories. Values are indicated by the height of the columns.
Line	Compares values from different categories. Values are indicated by the height of the line. Often used to show trends and changes over time.
Pie	Compares relative values of different categories to the whole. Values are indicated by the areas of the pie slices.
Bar	Compares values from different categories. Values are indicated by the length of the bars.
Area	Compares values from different categories. Similar to the line chart except that areas under the lines contain a fill color.
XY (Scatter)	Shows the patterns or relationship between two or more sets of values. Often used in scientific studies and statistical analyses.
Stock	Displays stock market data, including the high, low, opening, and closing prices of a stock.
Surface	Compares three sets of values in a three-dimensional chart.
Doughnut	Compares relative values of different categories to the whole. Similar to the pie chart except that it can display multiple sets of data.
Bubble	Shows the patterns or relationship between two or more sets of values. Similar to the XY (Scatter) chart except the size of the data marker is determined by a third value.
Radar	Compares a collection of values from several different data sets.

Ajita wants you to create a pie chart of the assets data. A **pie chart** is a chart in the shape of a circle (like a pie) that shows data values as a percentage of the whole. Each value in the data series represents a slice of the pie. The larger the value, the larger the pie slice. For the assets data, each slice will represent the percentage of the total assets from each investment category in the New Century Fund.

Pie charts are most effective with six or fewer slices, and when each slice is large enough to view. The pie chart you are creating for Ajita has five large slices, representing each of the five asset categories—Cash, U.S. Stocks, Non-U.S. Stocks, Bonds, and Other. Notice in Figure 4-2 that you did not select the Total Assets row. The Total Assets row is not an asset category and should not be included in a pie chart.

Tip

Do not include a totals row or column in the data source for a pie chart. Only select the rows or columns that contain the data values and the individual categories.

To insert a pie chart:

1. Click the **Insert** tab on the Ribbon. The Ribbon displays the insert options.

2. In the Charts group, click the **Pie** button to open the Charts gallery, and then click **Pie** (the first pie chart) in the 2-D Pie section. The pie chart is inserted in the Assets sheet, and three new tabs appear on the Ribbon with a label identifying them as Chart Tools contextual tabs. See Figure 4-4.

Figure 4-4 Pie chart inserted in the Assets sheet

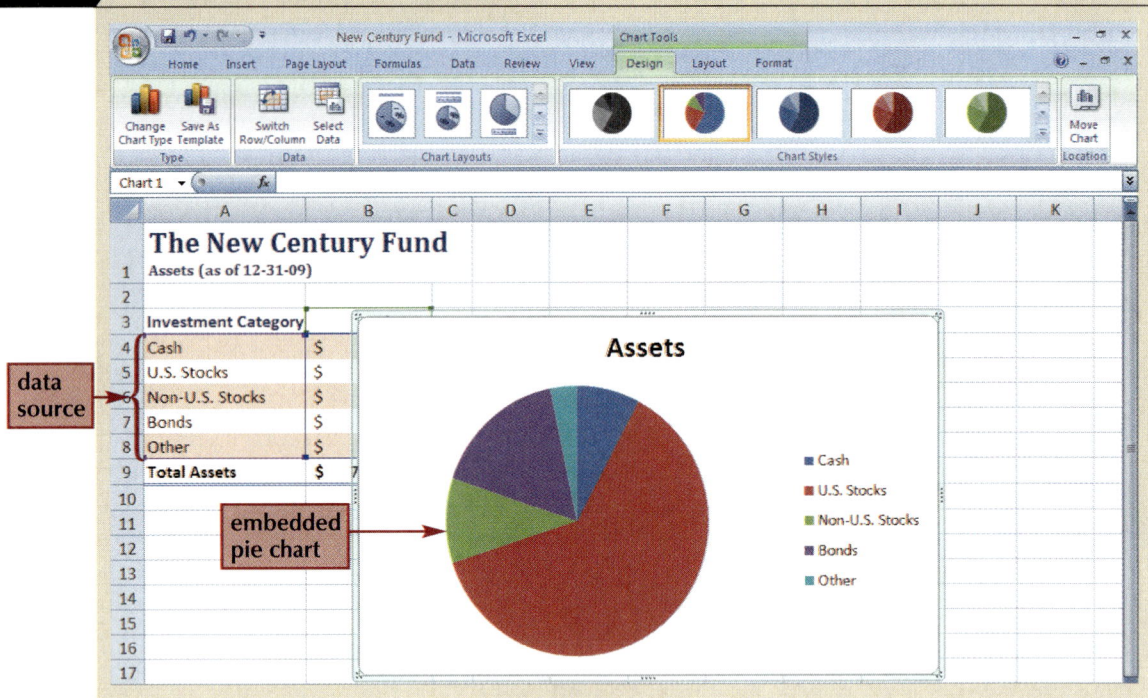

Each slice in the pie chart you just created is a different size based on its value in the data series. The biggest slice of the pie represents the U.S. stocks, because that category has the largest value in the data series. The smallest slice of pie represents the Other category, which has the smallest value in the data series.

When you create or select a chart, three Chart Tools contextual tabs appear on the Ribbon. The Design, Layout, and Format tabs provide additional commands to work with the chart's content and appearance. On the Design tab, you set the chart's overall design. On the Layout tab, you work with individual elements of the chart, such as the chart's title. On the Format tab, you format graphic shapes found in the chart, such as the chart's border or markers placed in the chart. When you select a worksheet cell or another object that is not a chart, the Chart Tools contextual tabs disappear until you reselect the chart.

Moving and Resizing Charts

By default, a chart is inserted as an **embedded chart**, which means the chart is placed in a worksheet next to its data source. The advantage of an embedded chart is that you can display the chart alongside any text or figures that can explain the chart's meaning and purpose. An embedded chart covers worksheet cells, which might contain data and formulas.

You can also place a chart in a **chart sheet**, so that the entire sheet contains only the chart and no worksheet cells. Chart sheets are helpful for detailed charts that need more space to be seen clearly or when you want to show a chart without any worksheet text or data. For now, you'll leave Ajita's pie chart as an embedded chart. You'll work with chart sheets later in this tutorial.

Right now, the pie chart is embedded in the Assets worksheet. However, Ajita wants the chart embedded in the Summary Report worksheet. You can move an embedded chart to a different worksheet in the workbook or you can move it into a chart sheet. Likewise, you can move a chart from a chart sheet and embed it in any worksheet you select. The Move Chart dialog box provides options for moving charts between worksheets and chart sheets. You can also cut and paste a chart to a new location in the workbook.

To move the embedded pie chart to the Summary Report worksheet:

▶ 1. In the Location group on the Chart Tools Design tab, click the **Move Chart** button. The Move Chart dialog box opens.

   Trouble? If you don't see the Chart Tools Design tab on the Ribbon, the chart is probably not selected. Click the chart in the Assets sheet to select it, and then repeat Step 1.

▶ 2. Click the **Object in** arrow to display a list of worksheets in the active workbook, and then click **Summary Report**. See Figure 4-5.

Move Chart dialog box — Figure 4-5

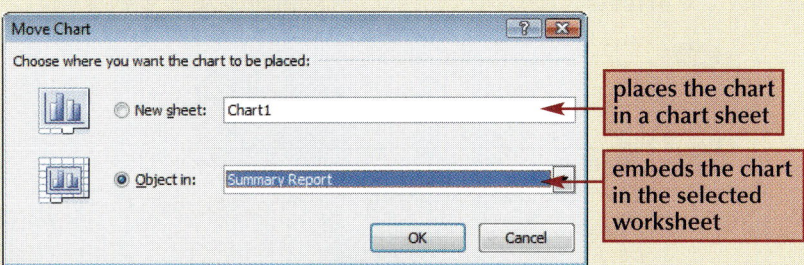

- places the chart in a chart sheet
- embeds the chart in the selected worksheet

▶ 3. Click the **OK** button. The embedded pie chart moves from the Assets worksheet to the Summary Report worksheet, and remains selected.

The pie chart is now in the correct worksheet, but its location and size obscures other content in the Summary Report worksheet. You move or resize an embedded chart by first selecting the chart, which displays a **selection box** around the chart, and then dragging the selection box to a new location in the worksheet. You can also drag a **resizing handle** on the selection box to change the chart's width and height.

To move and resize the pie chart:

▶ 1. Move the pointer over an empty area of the selected chart until the pointer changes to ✥ and you see the ScreenTip "Chart Area."

▶ 2. Drag the chart so its upper-left corner is within cell **A13**, and then release the mouse button. The chart's upper-left corner is in cell A13, but it still overlaps some data.

   Trouble? If the pie chart resizes or does not move to the new location, you probably didn't drag the chart from the chart area. Press the Ctrl+Z keys to undo your last action, and then repeat Steps 1 and 2, being sure to drag the pie chart from the chart area.

▶ 3. Move the pointer over the resizing handle in the lower-right corner of the chart until the pointer changes to ⤡, and then drag the resizing handle up to cell **E21**. The chart resizes to cover the range A13:E21 and remains selected. See Figure 4-6.

Figure 4-6 | Moved and resized pie chart

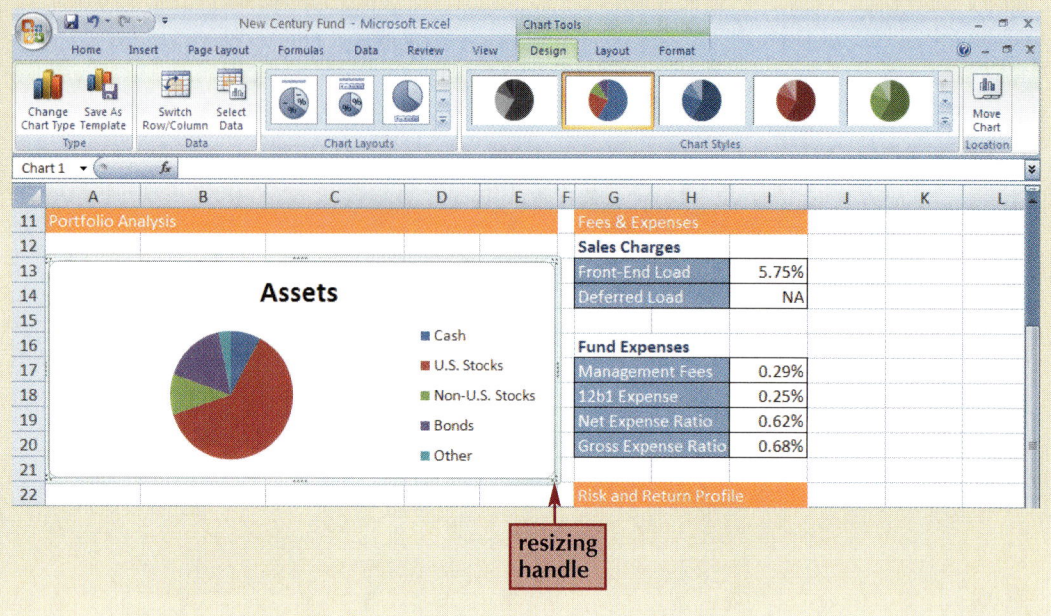

Working on Chart Design

The assets pie chart you have just resized includes a lot of empty space. Also, it's unclear how the different asset categories are related. For example, you can easily see that the largest slice represents the U.S. Stocks category, but it's difficult to tell whether the non-U.S. stocks slice is bigger than the Cash slice. To clarify the relationship between the pie slices, Ajita wants each slice to display its percentage of the whole. She also wants less empty space within the chart.

Selecting Chart Elements

Pie charts have five elements that are common to most charts. The **chart area** is the rectangular box containing the chart and all of the other chart elements. The **chart title** is a descriptive label or name for the chart, and usually appears at the top of the chart area. The **plot area** is the part of the chart that contains the graphical representation of all the data series in the chart. Each data value or data series is represented by a **data marker**. For pie charts, the data markers are the individual pie slices, which represent the data values. The **legend** is a rectangular area that labels the markers or symbols used in the chart. If the chart contains several data series, the legend identifies the markers used for each series. Pie charts, having only one data series, use the legend to identify the different pie slices. Figure 4-7 identifies each of these elements on the pie chart you just created for the assets data.

Figure 4-7 Common chart elements

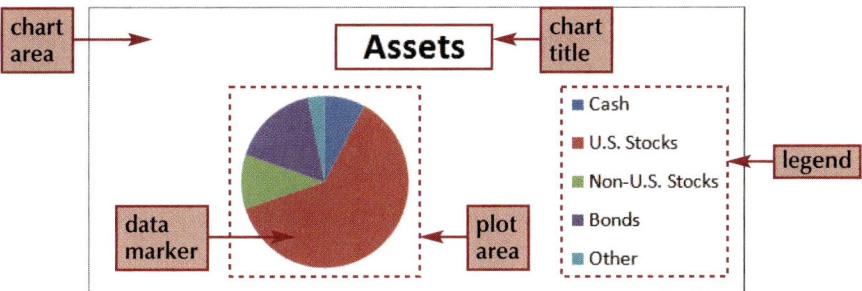

You can select and format any chart element individually or you can apply a built-in style or chart layout to format all of these elements at once. To select a chart element, you click that element or select it from a list of chart elements on the Chart Tools Layout tab. As you move your pointer over a chart element, its name appears in a ScreenTip. When you click that element, its name appears in the Chart Elements button in the Current Selection group on the Chart Tools Layout tab.

To select elements of the pie chart:

▶ 1. Move your pointer over the chart title until you see the ScreenTip "Chart Title," and then click the chart title. A selection box appears around the chart title.

▶ 2. Click the **Chart Tools Layout** tab on the Ribbon. The Ribbon displays the layout options for charts.

▶ 3. In the Current Selection group, click the **Chart Elements arrow** to display an alphabetical list of all the chart elements in the active chart. In this case, the Chart Elements box shows "Chart Title," indicating that this element is currently selected.

▶ 4. Click **Legend**. The legend is selected in the chart.

▶ 5. In the Current Selection group, click the **Chart Elements arrow**, and then click **Plot Area**. The chart's plot area is selected.

▶ 6. Click the chart area in the chart. The chart area is selected.

Choosing a Chart Style and Layout

The assets pie chart uses the default style for the different slices. A chart style is similar to a cell style or a table style in that it formats several chart elements at one time. You can change the color and appearance of the slices by selecting a different chart style from the Chart Styles gallery on the Chart Tools Design tab. Ajita wants a chart style that gives the slices a rounded, shaded look.

To apply a different chart style to the assets pie chart:

▶ 1. Click the **Chart Tools Design** tab on the Ribbon. The Ribbon displays the design options for charts.

▶ 2. In the Chart Styles group, click the **More** button to open the Chart Styles gallery, and then click **Style 26** (the fourth row, second column). Each pie slice now has a rounded, raised look. See Figure 4-8.

| Figure 4-8 | Style 26 chart style applied |

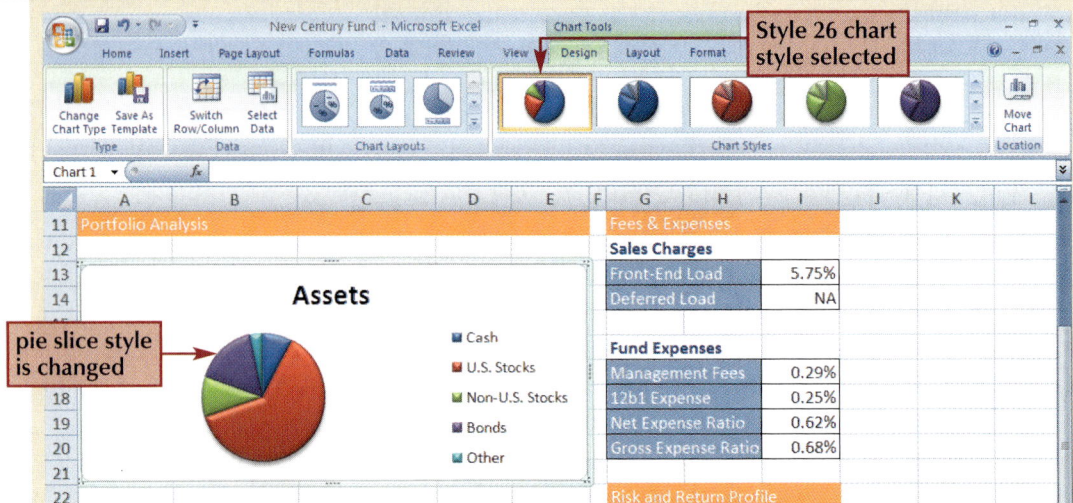

Trouble? If a dialog box opens, indicating that complex formatting applied to the selected chart may take awhile to display, click the Yes button to continue using the formatting.

You can also use a chart layout to choose which chart elements are displayed and how they are formatted. The chart layouts include some of the most common ways of displaying different charts. Each chart type has its own collection of layouts. Figure 4-9 shows the available layouts for pie charts. Depending on the pie chart layout you choose, you can hide or display the chart title, display a chart legend or place legend labels in the pie slices, and add percentages to the pie slices.

| Figure 4-9 | Pie chart layouts |

Layout	Name	Pie chart with
	Layout 1	Chart title, labels, and percentages
	Layout 2	Chart title, percentages, and legend above the pie
	Layout 3	Legend below the pie
	Layout 4	Labels in pie slices
	Layout 5	Chart title and labels in pie slices
	Layout 6	Chart title, percentages, and legend to the right of the pie
	Layout 7	Legend to the right of the pie

Ajita wants you to apply a layout that shows percentages for the pie slices so her clients can tell exactly how large each asset category is relative to the whole. She also wants to the chart title to remain displayed above the chart and the legend to remain displayed to the side of the chart. Layout 6 does all of these things.

To apply Layout 6 to the assets pie chart:

1. In the Chart Layouts group on the Chart Tools Design tab, click the **More** button to open the Chart Layouts gallery.

2. Click **Layout 6** in the second row, third column. Percentages appear on or next to the slices in the pie chart. See Figure 4-10.

Figure 4-10 Layout 6 chart layout applied

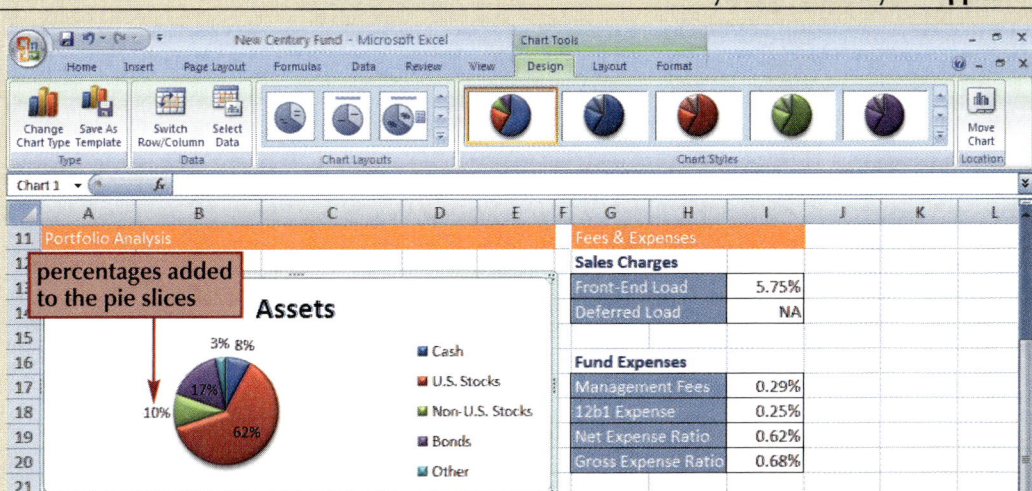

Tip
Percentages appear on pie slices large enough to fit the number; otherwise, percentages appear next to the slices in the chart area.

Trouble? Depending on your monitor size and resolution, your chart might look different from that shown in Figure 4-10. This does not affect your work with the pie chart.

The percentages on the pie chart will enable clients to quickly see how the assets of the New Century Fund are allocated. For example, 62% of the New Century Fund is invested in U.S. stocks and 10% in non-U.S. stocks. To fit the percentages, Excel reduced the size of the pie chart in the plot area. Ajita wants the pie chart larger, so you'll format some of the other chart elements smaller to make more space for the pie.

Working with the Chart Title

Ajita thinks that the chart title is too large and not descriptive enough. The chart title uses the heading from the column of asset values in the Assets worksheet. You'll change the title to "Allocation of Assets" and reduce its font size to 12 points.

To format the chart title:

1. Click the chart title to select it. A selection box appears around the chart title.

2. Type **Allocation of Assets**, and then press the **Enter** key. The chart title is updated with your typed entry, and remains selected.

3. Click the **Home** tab on the Ribbon.

Tip
You can revise the title text rather than replace it by double-clicking the chart title to place the insertion point in the text, and then editing the text as needed.

4. In the Font group, click the **Font Size arrow**, and then click **12**. The chart title shrinks from 18 points to 12 points, and the pie chart increases in size to fill in the extra space. See Figure 4-11.

Figure 4-11 | **Chart title updated and formatted**

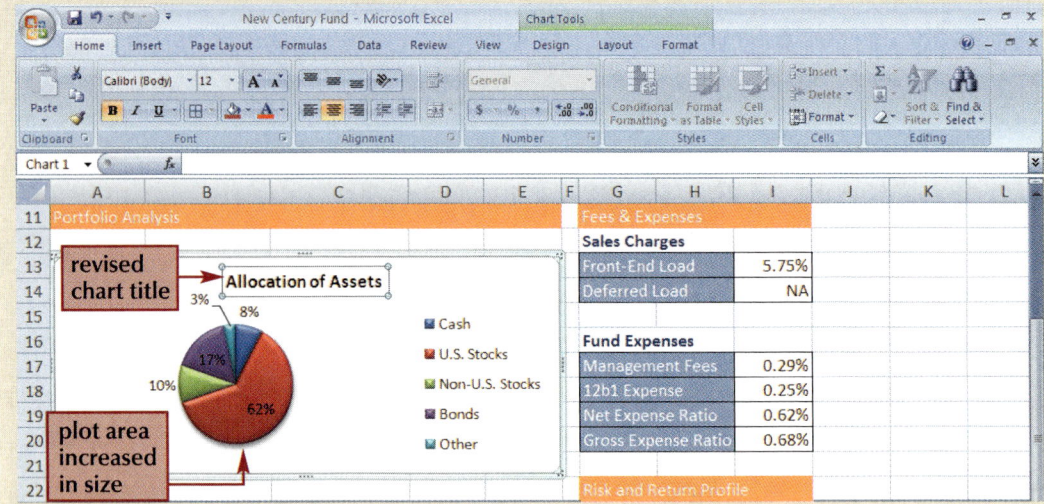

Trouble? Depending on your monitor size and resolution, your chart might look slightly different from that shown in Figure 4-11. This does not affect your work with the pie chart.

Working with the Chart Legend

Ajita wants the legend moved to the left side of the chart and an orange border added around the legend text to distinguish it from the rest of the chart. You'll use the tools on the Chart Tools Layout tab to format the legend.

To format the chart legend:

1. Click the **Chart Tools Layout** tab on the Ribbon.

2. In the Labels group, click the **Legend** button, and then click **Show Legend at Left**. The legend moves to the left side of the chart.

3. In the Labels group, click the **Legend** button, and then click **More Legend Options**. The Format Legend dialog box opens. Every chart element has a corresponding dialog box from which you can select more advanced options to format the element's appearance.

4. Click **Border Color** in the list on the left side of the dialog box. The Border Color options appear on the right side of the dialog box.

5. Click the **Solid line** option button. Two more options related to border colors appear.

6. Click the **Color** button to open the color palette, and then click **Orange, Accent 6, Lighter 40%** (the fourth row, last column) in the Theme Colors section. See Figure 4-12.

Figure 4-12 Border Color options set in the Format Legend dialog box

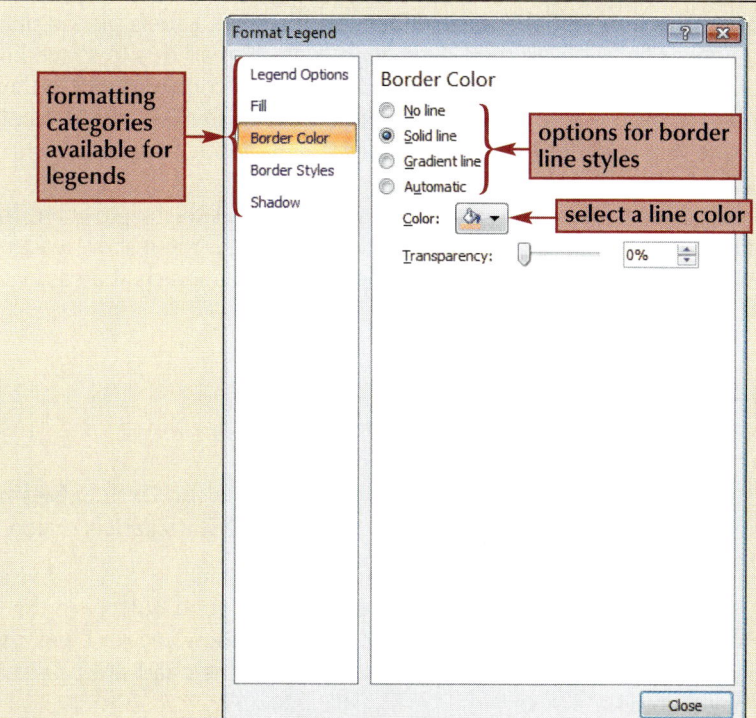

▶ 7. Click the **Close** button, and then click cell **A23** to deselect the chart. The legend now has a light orange border. See Figure 4-13.

Figure 4-13 Chart legend moved and formatted

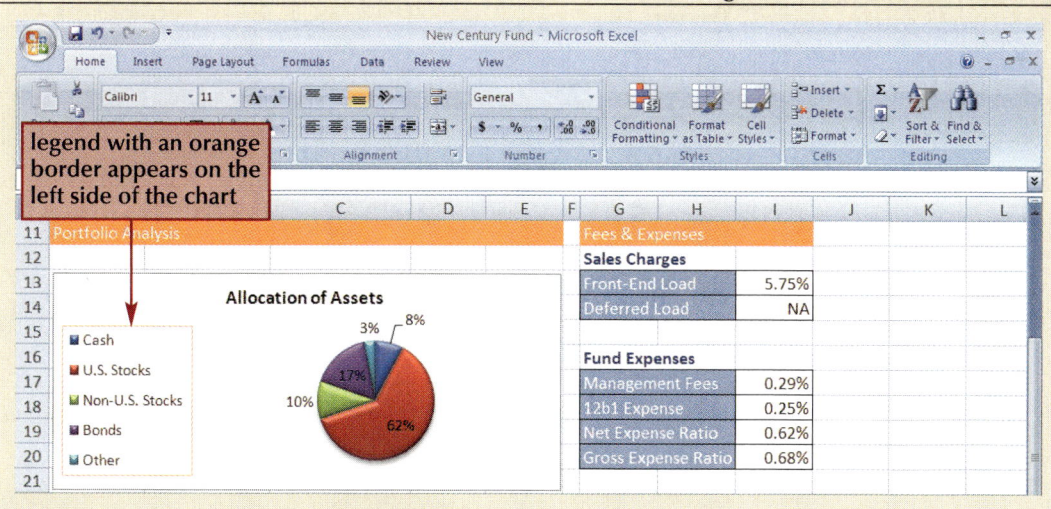

Formatting a Pie Chart

Chart titles and legends are common to almost all types of charts. Another common element is a **data label**, which is text associated with a data value. In pie charts, data labels are added to the slices. You already created data labels for the assets chart when you selected Layout 6 to add percentages to the slices. These labels were placed where they best fit in relation to the pie slices. For some asset categories, the label appears within the pie slice; for others, the label appears alongside the slice. Labels placed outside of the pie might appear farther from their slices than is easily read due to space limitations. In those cases, **leader lines** might be added to the labels to connect them to their corresponding slices. For example, a leader line connects the Cash slice and its label in Figure 4-13. Note that a leader line will disappear when enough space exists in the pie chart to place a label next to its slice.

For consistency, Ajita wants all the data labels to appear outside the pie chart. This will make the text for the dark blue and red pie slices easier to read. You'll show leader lines for the labels, which means the leader lines will appear only when the chart area does not have enough space for the labels to appear close to their pie slices.

To format the pie chart's data labels:

1. Click the chart to select it.

2. In the Labels group on the Chart Tools Layout tab, click the **Data Labels** button, and then click **More Data Label Options**. The Format Data Labels dialog box opens with the the Label Options displayed.

3. In the Label Position section, click the **Outside End** option button. In the Label Contains section, the Percentage check box and the Show Leader Lines check box are already checked because these were included in the chart layout you applied earlier. See Figure 4-14.

Figure 4-14   **Label Options in the Format Data Labels dialog box**

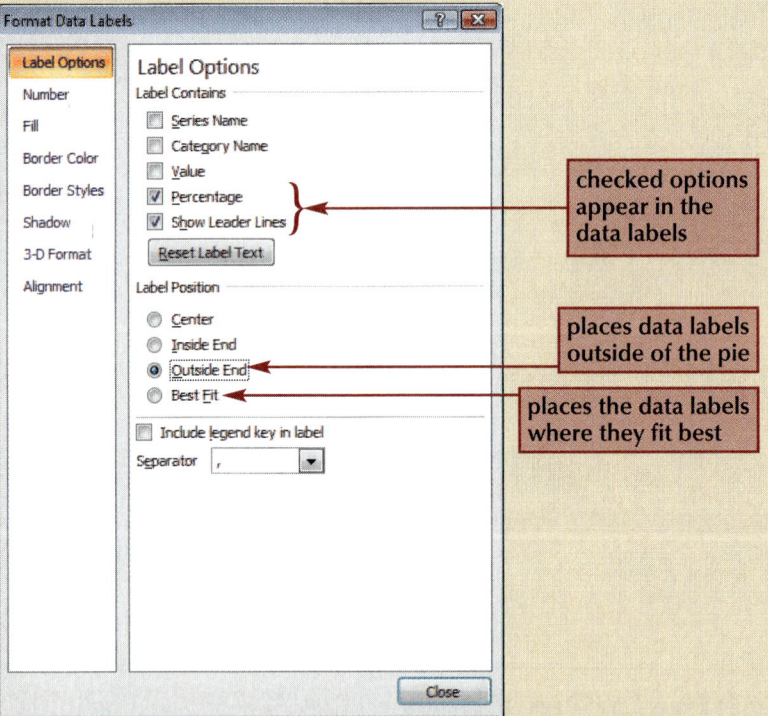

These options set the data labels to display percentages outside the pie chart and use leader lines when needed to connect the labels with their corresponding pie slices. Next, you'll change the percentage values to show two decimal places for more accuracy.

▶ 4. Click **Number** in the list on the left side of the dialog box.

▶ 5. Click **Percentage** in the Category list, and then verify that **2** appears in the Decimal places box.

▶ 6. Click the **Close** button to close the Format Data Labels dialog box, and then click cell **A23** to deselect the chart. See Figure 4-15. Leader lines don't appear in the pie chart shown in Figure 4-15 because the chart area has enough space to place the labels close to their slices.

Pie chart data labels formatted   Figure 4-15

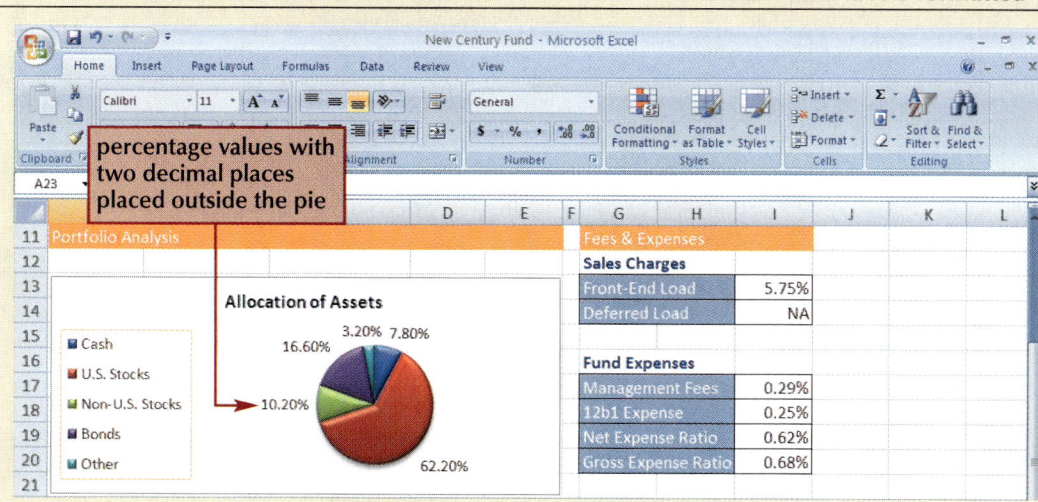

Setting the Pie Slice Colors

The pie slices for Cash, Bonds, and Other have similar colors. Depending on the printer quality or the monitor resolution, these slices might be difficult to distinguish in the final report. In pie charts with legends, it's best to make the slice colors as distinct as possible to avoid confusion, especially slices adjacent to each other in the pie. You'll change the fill color of the Other slice to yellow and the Cash slice to light blue. Because each slice represents a different value in the series, you must format each slice rather than the entire data series.

To select and format pie slices in the assets pie chart:

▶ 1. Click the pie to select the entire data series.

▶ 2. Click the light blue **Other** slice, which represents 3.20% of the pie. Only that value, or slice, is selected.

▶ 3. Click the **Home** tab on the Ribbon.

▶ 4. In the Font group, click the **Fill Color button arrow**, and then click **Yellow**, the fourth color in the Standard Colors section. The Other slice and legend marker change to yellow.

▶ 5. Click the dark blue **Cash** slice, which covers 7.80% of the pie.

▶ 6. In the Font group, click the **Fill Color button arrow**, and then click **Light Blue**, the seventh color in the Standard Colors section. The Cash slice and legend marker change to light blue. Each slice of the pie is now a distinct color. See Figure 4-16.

Figure 4-16 Pie slices with new colors

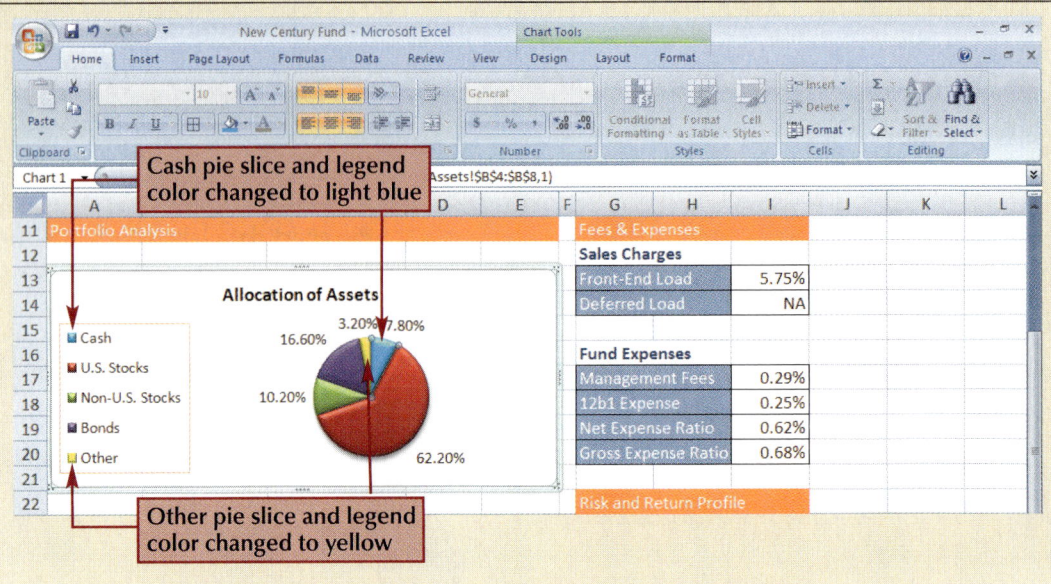

Pie slices do not need to be fixed in place. An **exploded pie chart** moves one slice away from the pie as if someone were taking the piece out of the pie. To explode a pie slice, select that slice and then drag it away from the pie. To explode all of the slices, select the entire pie and drag the pointer away from the center of the pie. Exploded pie charts are useful when you want to emphasize one category above all of the others. Although you can explode more than one slice, the resulting pie chart is rarely effective.

Creating a 3D Pie Chart

Ajita thinks the pie chart will look better as a three-dimensional (3D) figure. Although 3D charts are visually attractive, they can obscure the relationship between the values in the chart. For example, it is unclear which slice—red or yellow—is bigger in the pie chart shown in Figure 4-17. Actually, they are the same size, each representing 20% of the whole. The yellow slice appears bigger because the 3D effect brings that slice closer to the viewer.

Figure 4-17 Misleading 3D pie chart

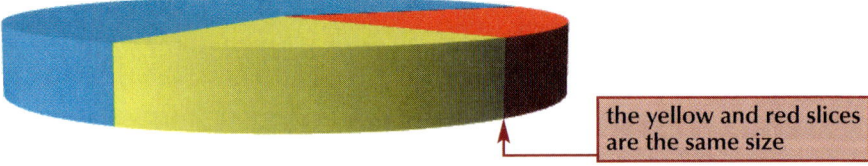

Because you already added data labels to the assets pie chart, Ajita thinks her clients will not misinterpret a 3D pie chart. She thinks that making the assets pie chart 3D will provide visual interest to the report while maintaining the pie chart's effectiveness.

To change the assets pie chart to 3D:

1. Click the chart area to select the chart, and then click the **Chart Tools Design** tab on the Ribbon.

2. In the Type group, click the **Change Chart Type** button. The Change Chart Type dialog box opens.

3. Click **Pie in 3-D** (the second chart type in the Pie section).

4. Click the **OK** button. The pie chart is now a 3D chart.

Creating Effective 3D Charts | InSight

Because of the visual distortion that can result with 3D representations, you should include data labels with all 3D charts. Also, try to avoid extreme viewing angles that elongate the chart and misrepresent the data. Although 3D charts can be eye-catching, do not use this effect if it overrides the main purpose of a chart, which is data interpretation.

Working with 3D Options

The 3D pie chart does not look very different from the 2D version because you are looking straight down on the chart from "above." To increase the 3D effect, you need to rotate the chart. You can rotate the chart in two directions: horizontally along the x-axis and vertically along the y-axis. Increasing the rotation along the x-axis spins the chart clockwise. Increasing the rotation along the y-axis raises the viewpoint higher above the chart. All 3D charts have a third axis that corresponds to the depth of the chart. Depth values can range from 0 to 2000. The larger the value, the thicker the chart appears. You can also change the chart's **perspective**, which controls how fast the chart appears to recede from the viewer's eye. Perspective values range from 0° to 90°. A 90° perspective value exaggerates the 3D effect, making distant objects appear very small, whereas perspective values near 0° minimize this effect. Try different values for depth and perspective to determine which work best for your chart.

You'll orient the pie chart so that the viewer's eye level is slightly above the chart. You'll also rotate the chart along the horizontal axis so that the largest slice is on the left side of the pie. Often you'll need to experiment to find the right angles for a 3D chart by rotating the chart in different directions until it looks correct without distorting the data. In this case, you'll rotate the chart 90° along the horizontal axis and place the viewer's eye at an angle of 20° above the chart. You will not change the chart's perspective or depth.

To rotate the 3D pie chart:

1. Click the **Chart Tools Layout** tab on the Ribbon, and then, in the Background group, click the **3-D Rotation** button. The Format Chart Area dialog box opens with the 3-D Rotation options displayed.

2. In the Rotation section, type **90** in the X box and type **20** in the Y box. See Figure 4-18.

| Figure 4-18 | **Format Chart Area dialog box** |

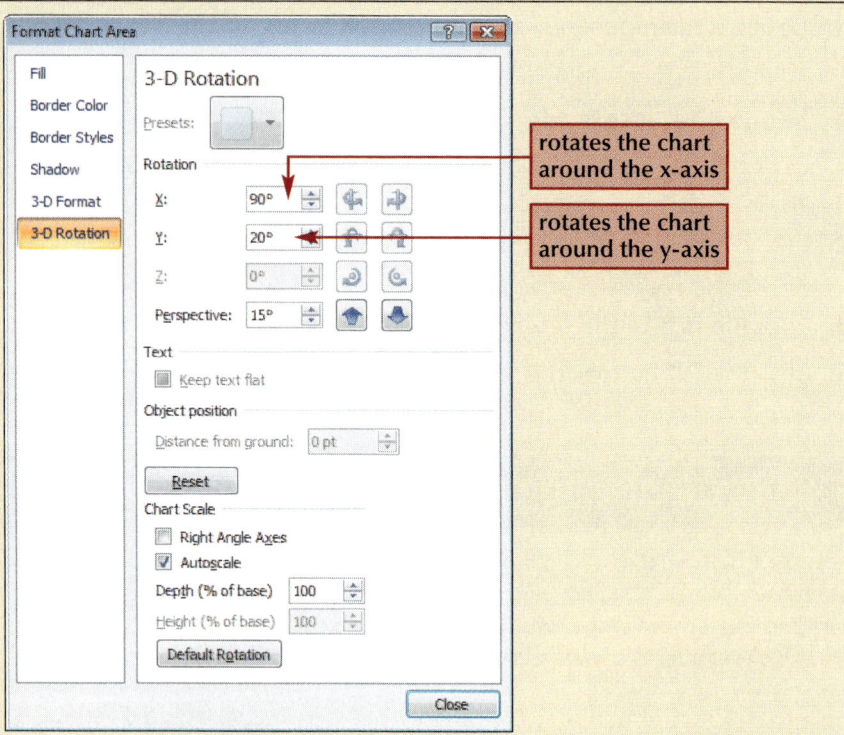

▶ 3. Click the **Close** button. The pie chart rotates based on the new x-axis and y-axis values. See Figure 4-19.

| Figure 4-19 | **3D assets pie chart** |

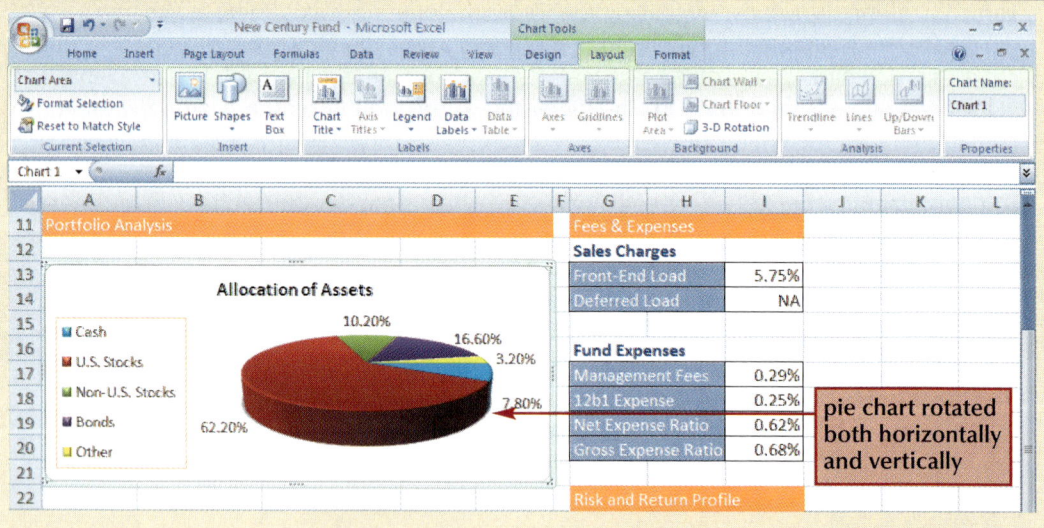

The new x-axis and y-axis values have a significant impact on the way the chart looks. The new x-axis value shifted the pie chart clockwise one quarter of the way around the circle so the largest slice, the red U.S Stocks slice, is in the front. The new y-axis value turned the pie chart so the viewer is looking down on the chart. Ajita is pleased with the 3D effect you added.

The Format Chart Area dialog box shown in Figure 4-18 also includes options to change the 3-D Format of the chart. These options allow you to add drop shadows, raised or beveled corners, and textured surfaces that give the illusion of light reflecting off the chart elements. You saw an example of such a surface in Figure 4-13 when you added a shaded, rounded chart style to the pie chart. You will not use the 3-D Format options for the assets pie chart.

Editing Chart Data

Charts remain linked or connected to their data sources, even if they appear in different worksheets. If you change any values or labels in the data source, the chart is automatically updated to show the new content. For example, if the Other assets increase from $2,520 to $4,520 and the remaining assets are unchanged, the Other slice becomes bigger to reflect its larger percentage of the whole and the remaining slices shrink to reflect their smaller percentage of the whole.

Ajita wants you to edit the data source for the assets pie chart. She thinks the Other category would be better titled as Other Assets and she wants you to correct the assets value for that category. You'll make both of these changes to the data in the Assets worksheet.

To edit the data source for the assets pie chart:

1. Click the **Assets** sheet tab to make it the active worksheet.

2. Edit the text in cell A8 to **Other Assets**, and then change the value in cell B8 to **4520**.

3. Click the **Summary Report** sheet tab, and then verify that the pie chart was updated with the new data value and category name. See Figure 4-20. Note that the percentage values for each category are recalculated based on the new data. As a result, the Other Assets slice increased in size to reflect its larger percentage of the whole, and the remaining slices decreased in size.

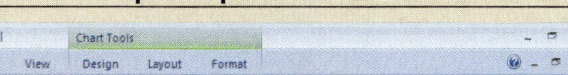

Updated pie chart based on revised data — Figure 4-20

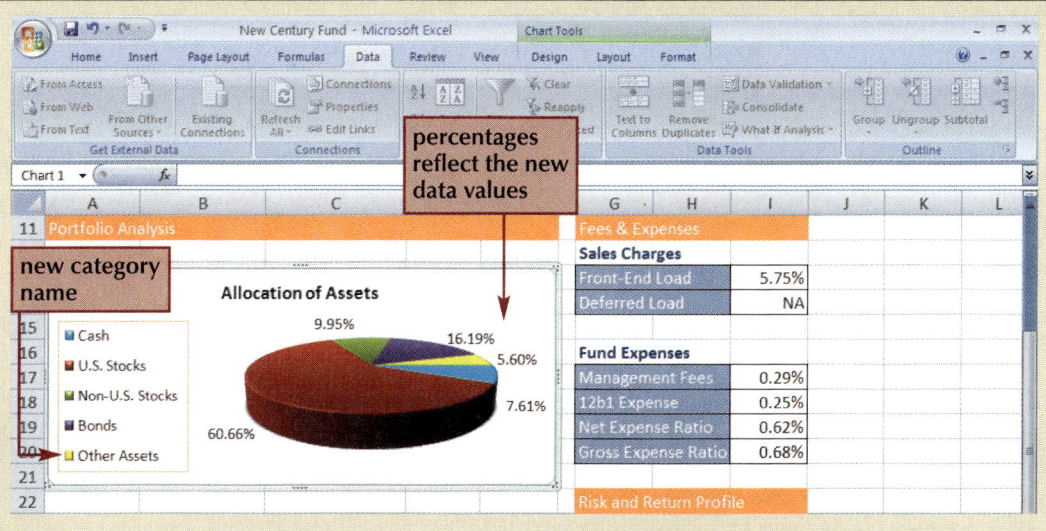

Occasionally, you will not want a chart to reflect new values in the data source, such as when a chart shows a "snapshot" of the data at a certain time. You can do this by copying and pasting the chart as a picture. Select the chart, copy it as usual, click the Paste button arrow, point to As Picture, and then click Paste as Picture. The chart is pasted as a picture without any connection to its data source and cannot be edited or formatted in any way.

Working with Column Charts

The pie chart in the summary report clearly shows that most assets of the New Century Fund are allocated toward U.S. stocks. The next part of the summary report lists the type of stocks being purchased by the fund. Each mutual fund invests in different kinds of stocks. Some funds are heavily invested in information technology, others in the service industry, and still others in manufacturing. Diversification (the distribution of investments among a variety of companies or sectors to limit losses in the event one company or sector has an economic downturn) is important, so all funds are invested to some degree in multiple economic sectors. The New Century Fund is invested in 12 different economic sectors, organized into categories of information, services, and manufacturing.

Creating a Column Chart

Twelve categories are too many for an effective pie chart, so Ajita wants you to create a column chart to display this economic sector data. A **column chart** displays values in different categories as columns; the height of each column is based on its value. Related to the column chart is the **bar chart**, which is a column chart turned on its side, so each bar length is based on its value.

Column and bar charts are superior to pie charts when the number of categories is large or the categories are close in value. It is easier to compare height or length than area. Figure 4-21 displays the same data as a pie chart and a column chart. As you can see, it's difficult to determine which pie slice has the largest area and by how much. This is much simpler to determine in the column chart.

Figure 4-21   Same data displayed as a pie chart and a column chart

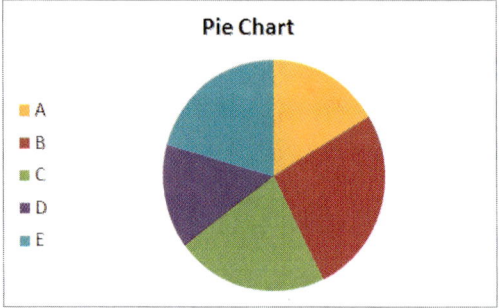
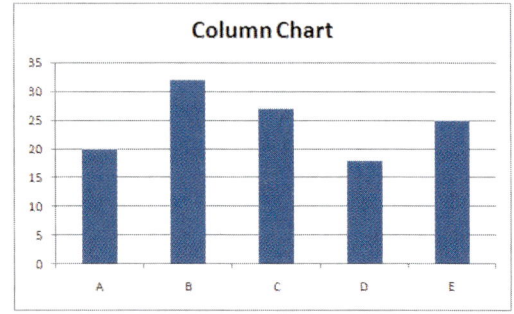

Column and bar charts can also be applied to a wider range of data than pie charts. For example, you can demonstrate how a set of values changes over time, such as the value of the New Century Fund over several years. You can also include several data series in a column or bar chart, such as the value of three funds over several years. The values from different data series are displayed in columns side by side. Pie charts usually show only one data series.

Ajita wants you to create a column chart that shows how the the New Century Fund is distributed among the 12 sectors in which it is invested. The columns will represent only one data series, so you'll use the 2D Clustered Columns chart type. A clustered columns chart uses vertical rectangles to compare values across categories.

To create a column chart from the sector data:

1. Click the **Sector Weightings** sheet tab, and then select the range **A3:C15**.

2. Click the **Insert** tab on the Ribbon.

3. In the Charts group, click the **Column** button, and then click the **Clustered Column** chart, the first chart in the 2-D Column section. The column chart is inserted in the Sector Weightings worksheet, and the Chart Tools Design tab on the Ribbon is selected.

4. In the Location group on the Chart Tools Design tab, click the **Move Chart** button. The Move Chart dialog box opens. You'll move the chart to the Summary Report worksheet.

5. Click the **Object in** arrow, click **Summary Report**, and then click the **OK** button. The column chart moves to the Summary Report worksheet.

6. In the Summary Report worksheet, click a blank spot in the chart area of the column chart, and then drag the chart down so its upper-left corner is in cell **A23**.

7. Drag the resizing handle in the lower-right corner of the chart until the chart covers the range **A23:E37**. See Figure 4-22.

Figure 4-22 Column chart moved and resized in the Summary Report worksheet

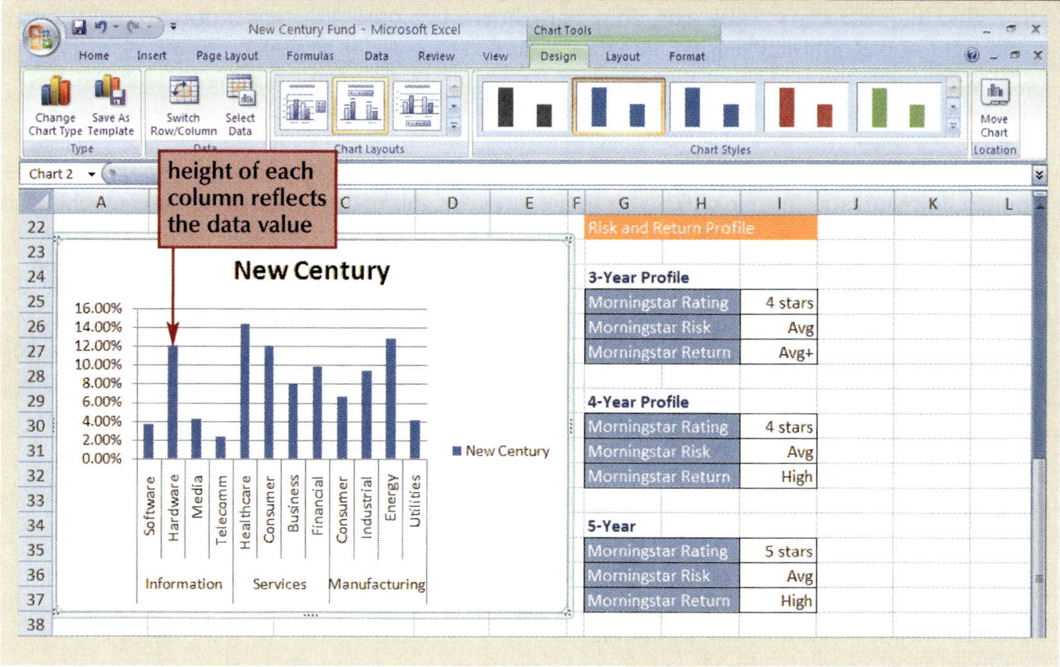

The column chart shows that the New Century Fund is most heavily invested in health care and consumer services, hardware information technology, and energy manufacturing. On the other hand, the fund does not invest much in telecommunications, software, and media.

Formatting Column Chart Elements

Similar to the pie chart, the column chart has a chart title and a legend that identifies different data series rather than values within a data series. Because this column chart contains only one data series, the sector weightings of the New Century Fund, the legend has only one entry. The column chart also has a few new elements, which are identified in Figure 4-23.

Figure 4-23 — Elements of the column chart

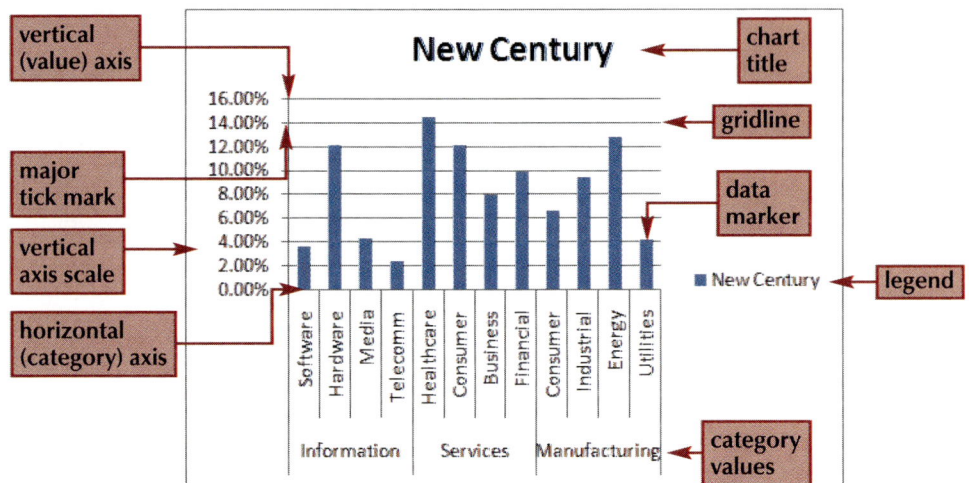

The **vertical**, or **value, axis** displays the values associated with the heights of each column. You can use two value axes to plot different types of data on a chart, such as the number of units sold and the revenue generated from the sale of a group of products. One axis (usually the axis on the left) is called the **primary value axis**, and the other axis is called the **secondary value axis**. The chart shown in Figure 4-23 has a primary value axis but not the optional secondary value axis.

Excel selects the scale that best displays the values in the chart. A **scale** is a range of values that spans the vertical axis, which is 0% to 16% in Figure 4-23. Each value has a **major tick mark** that acts like the lines on a ruler, making it easier to read the scale. In Figure 4-23, major tick marks appear every 2% along the scale. Some axes also use **minor tick marks** to further divide the space between the major tick marks. Figure 4-23 does not display minor tick marks.

Many charts use **gridlines** to extend the tick marks across the plot area. As you can see in Figure 4-23, gridlines make it easier to determine the value of a column. For example, little more than 14% of the stocks from the New Century Fund are invested in healthcare services. A chart can also have vertical gridlines, though none are shown here.

The **horizontal**, or **category, axis** displays the categories associated with each data value. This column chart has two levels of category values: one for the sector category and one for the sector name. You can include as many levels as you need to clearly define the category values; Excel will fit as many as possible below the category axis. In this chart, Excel rotated the sector names to fit them in the space. You can format the axes text, rotate and align the text entries, or select which entries to display in the chart.

The data markers in the column chart are the individual columns. The same data marker (a column) is used for an entire data series; only the columns' heights differ from one data value to another. When a chart has only one data series—such as the column chart you just created—the chart title and legend are redundant. Ajita asks you to remove the legend, and then edit and format the chart title.

To format the legend and chart title of the column chart:

1. Click the **Chart Tools Layout** tab on the Ribbon.
2. In the Labels group, click the **Legend** button, and then click **None**. The chart legend no longer appears in the chart, and the column chart is resized to fill the available space.
3. Click the chart title to select it, and then click the **Home** tab on the Ribbon.
4. In the Font group, click the **Font Size arrow**, and then click **12**. The chart title is reduced to 12 points, and remains selected.

▶ 5. Type **Sector Weightings** as the new chart title, and then press the **Enter** key.

Formatting the Chart Axes

Ajita thinks that the font used in both the value axis and the category axis is too large, and that the value axis scale looks crowded. She asks you to reduce the font size of the axes, place the major tick marks at 5% intervals, and display the percentages without any decimal places.

To format the chart axes:

▶ 1. Click the **category axis** to select it.

▶ 2. In the Font group on the Home tab, click the **Font Size arrow**, and then click **8**. The category axis labels are smaller.

▶ 3. Click the **value axis** to select it, and repeat Step 2 to change the axis font size to **8** points.

▶ 4. Click the **Chart Tools Layout** tab on the Ribbon.

▶ 5. In the Axes group, click the **Axes** button, point to **Primary Vertical Axis**, and then click **More Primary Vertical Axis Options**. The Format Axis dialog box opens with the Axis Options displayed. The value axis options are set to Auto, which tells Excel to set the values. You'll modify these so that the major tick marks appear at 5% intervals on the vertical axis to make the chart less cluttered and easier to read.

▶ 6. Click the **Major unit Fixed** option button, press the **Tab** key, and then type **0.05** for the size of the major tick mark. Major tick marks will now appear on the value axis in 5% increments. See Figure 4-24.

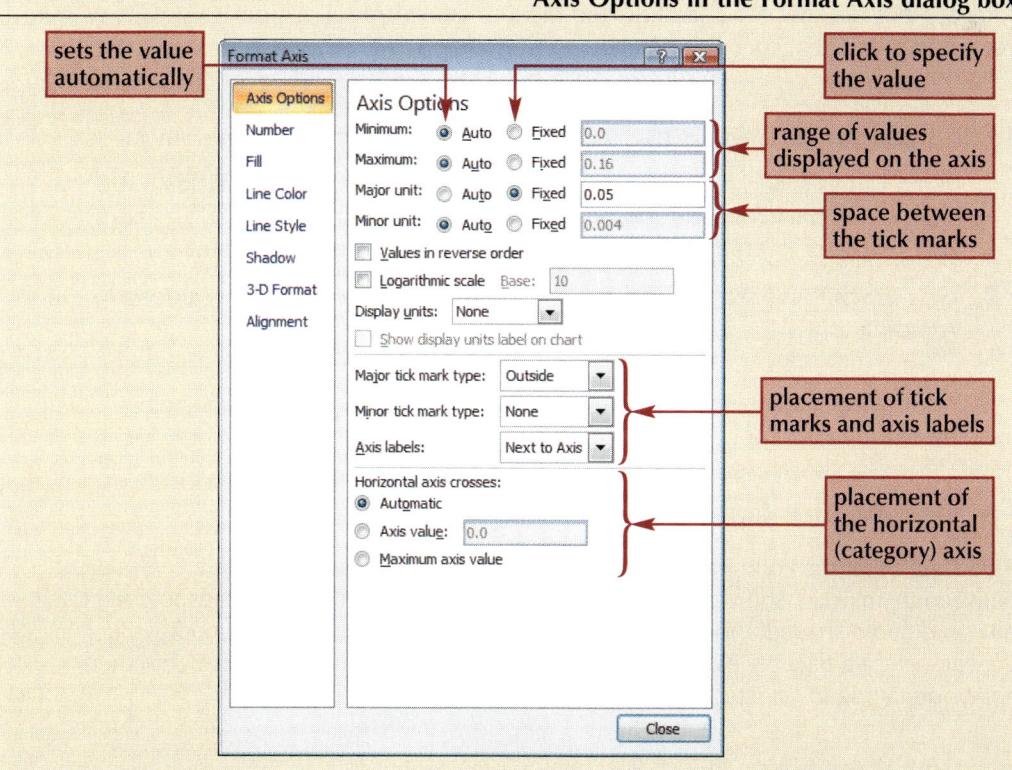

Figure 4-24 Axis Options in the Format Axis dialog box

7. Click **Number** on the left side of the dialog box, type **0** in the Decimal places box, and then click the **Close** button. The percentages on the value axis show no decimal places. See Figure 4-25.

Figure 4-25 **Formatted chart axes**

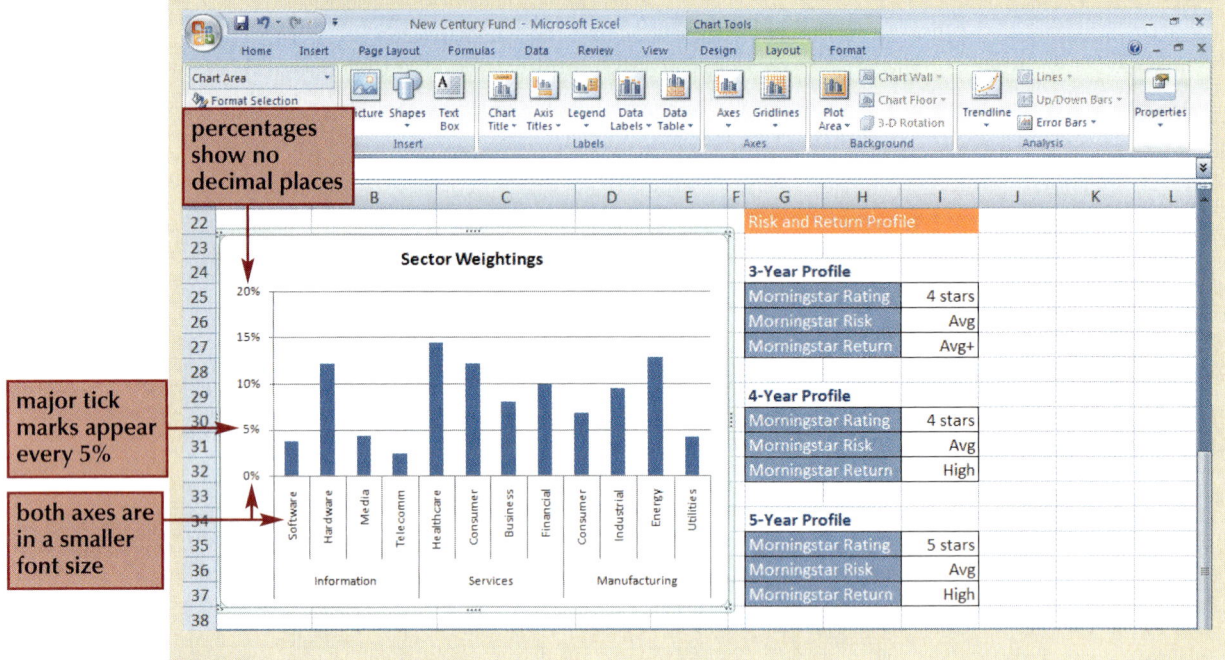

The value axis now ranges from 0% to 20% rather than 16%, and the percentages no longer show any decimal places. These changes make the value axis easier to read. Also, the smaller font size used for the value and category axes left more room for the data series. No titles appear next to the value and category axes. This isn't a problem for the category axis because the chart title and the axis labels are self-explanatory. Ajita wants you to add the title "Stock Percentages" to the value axis and rotate it to save space.

To add a rotated title to the value axis:

1. In the Labels group on the Chart Tools Layout tab, click the **Axis Titles** button, point to **Primary Vertical Axis Title**, and then click **Rotated Title**. The text "Axis Title" appears rotated to the left of the vertical axis in a selection box.

2. Type **Stock Percentages**, and then press the **Enter** key. The title is added to the vertical axis.

As with other chart text in the chart, you can format an axis title. Ajita is pleased with the current format of the vertical axis title, so no further changes are needed.

Formatting the Chart Columns

Ajita thinks that the columns are spaced too widely and wants you to reduce the gap between them. Also, she wants you to change the fill color of the columns to a lighter blue and add a shaded appearance to make the columns stand out. To modify the appearance of a data series, you first select the data markers for that series and then apply formatting to selected markers.

To format the chart columns:

1. Click any column in the Sector Weightings chart. A selection box surrounds each column in the chart, indicating that the entire series is selected.

   Trouble? If only the column you clicked is selected, you selected only a single data value rather than the entire data series. Click a blank spot in the chart area, and then repeat Step 1 to select the entire series.

2. In the Current Selection group on the Chart Tools Layout tab, click **Format Selection**. The Format Data Series dialog box opens with the Series Options displayed.

3. Drag the Gap width slider to **50%** to reduce the gap between adjacent columns. The columns become wider to fill the space.

   Trouble? If you cannot drag the Gap width slider to exactly 50%, type the value 50 in the Gap width box below the slider.

4. Click **Fill** on the left side of the dialog box, and then click the **Gradient fill** option button to fill the columns with a gradually changing mix of colors.

5. Click the **Direction** button to open a gallery of fill directions, and then click **Linear Right** (the fourth fill direction in the first row). The columns have a gradient fill that blends to the right. See Figure 4-26.

> **Tip**
> You can also highlight a data value by formatting one column in a column chart; select the data series and then click the column you want to format. Any formatting applies only to that data marker.

Figure 4-26   Fill options set in the Format Data Series dialog box

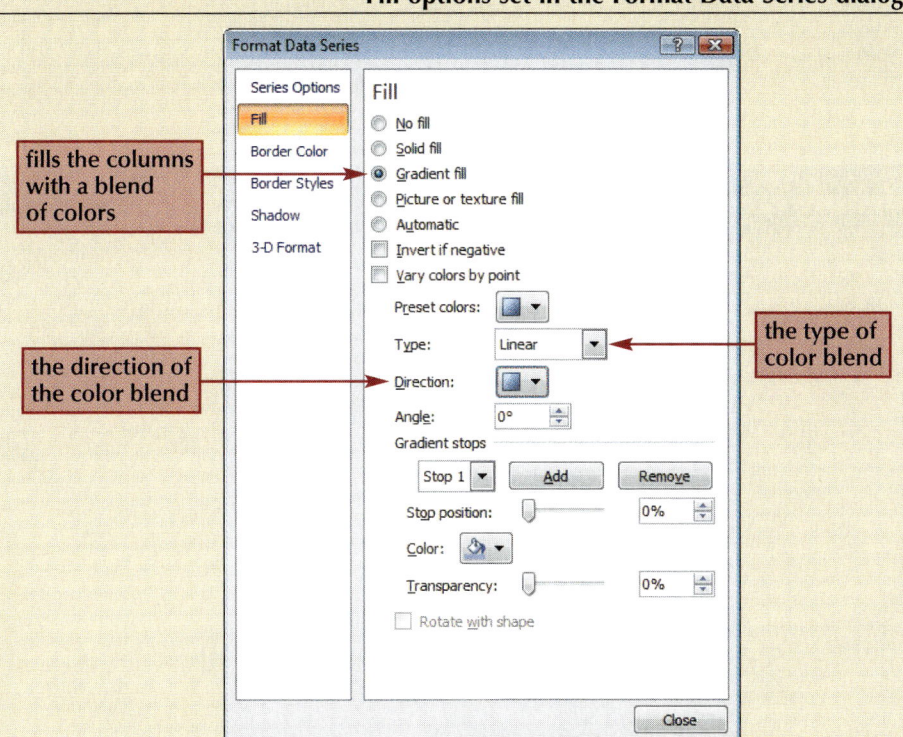

6. Click the **Close** button, and then click cell **A38** to deselect the chart. See Figure 4-27.

Figure 4-27 Formatted chart columns

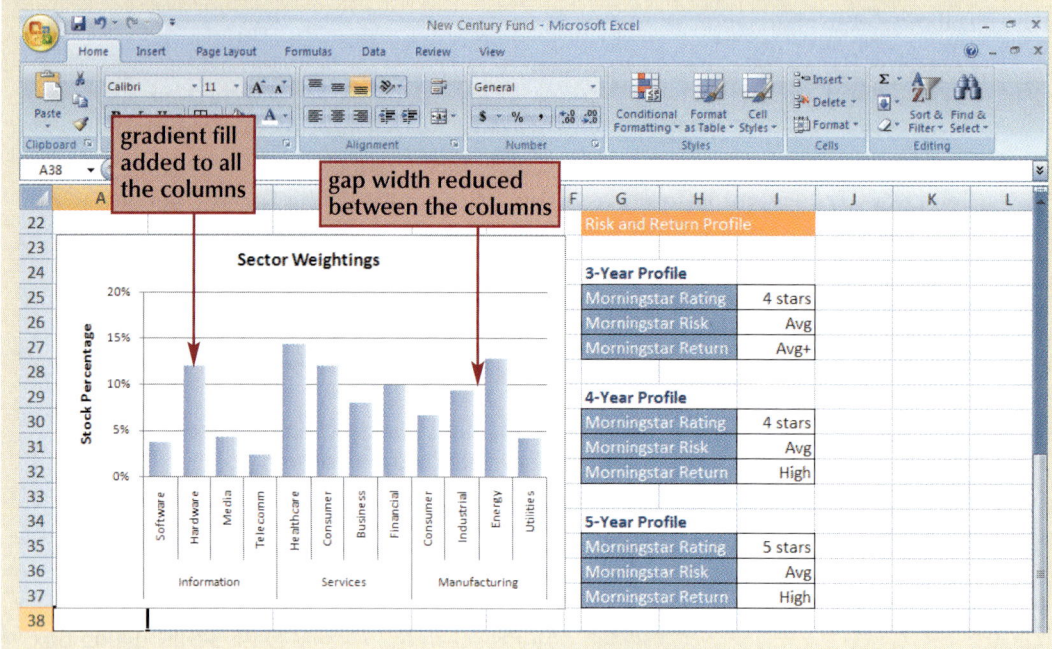

Ajita is pleased with the two charts you've created for the Summary Report worksheet. In the next session, you'll add a chart that describes the performance of the New Century Fund over the past 10 years and work with drawing objects.

InSight | Designing Effective Charts

A well-designed chart can illuminate facts that might be hidden by viewing only the numbers. However, poorly designed charts can mislead readers and make it more difficult to interpret data. Keep in mind the following tips for creating more effective and useful charts:

- Keep it simple. Do not clutter a chart with too many graphic elements. Focus attention on the data rather than on decorative elements that do not inform.
- Limit the number of data series used in the chart. Line charts and column charts should display no more than three or four data series. Pie charts should have no more than six slices.
- Use gridlines in moderation. Gridlines should be used to provide only approximate values for the data markers. Too many gridlines can obscure the data being graphed.
- Choose colors carefully. Display different data series in contrasting colors to make it easier to distinguish one series from another. Do not always accept the default color choices. When printing charts, make sure the colors are distinct in the printed copy.
- Limit the use of different text styles to no more than two. Too many text styles in one chart can distract attention from the data.
- Analyze whether you need a chart in the first place. Remember, not all data is meant to be charted. Some data is presented more effectively in a table or as part of a narrative.

Session 4.1 Quick Check | Review

1. What are the three components of a data series?
2. In what two locations can a chart be placed?
3. What is the difference between the chart area and the plot area?
4. A data series contains values divided into 10 categories. Which chart would be better for displaying this data: a pie chart or a column chart? Why?
5. Explain how 3D charts can lead to a false interpretation of the data. What can you do to correct this problem?
6. What are major tick marks, minor tick marks, and gridlines?
7. What is a bar chart?
8. How do you rescale a chart axis?

Session 4.2

Creating a Line Chart

Ajita will include the performance history of the New Century Fund in the summary report because her clients always want to know how well their investments are doing. Clients also want to compare different investments, so Ajita has other data that provides a standard of comparison, or benchmark, to the performance of the New Century Fund. One benchmark is the average performance of other large growth funds, and the other benchmark is the S&P 500 (or Standard and Poor's 500, which is an index of 500 blue chip stocks that is commonly used to measure the performance of stocks and funds).

Ajita entered this data in the Performance History worksheet. She calculated the quarterly returns for the past 10 years from an initial investment of $10,000. Because there are 40 data points for each of the three data series, you'll create a line chart. A **line chart** compares values from several categories with a sequential order, such as dates and times that occur at evenly spaced intervals. The values are indicated by the height of the line. In this case, you'll plot the quarterly value of each investment on the vertical axis and the date on the horizontal axis.

To create the line chart:

1. If you took a break after the previous session, make sure the New Century Fund workbook located in the Tutorial.04\Tutorial folder is open.

2. Click the **Performance History** sheet tab to make it the active worksheet, and then select the range **A4:D44**. This range contains the data for the value of the New Century Fund, the average value of large growth funds, and the value of the S&P 500 for each quarter of 2000 through 2009.

3. Click the **Insert** tab on the Ribbon.

4. In the Charts group, click the **Line** button, and then click the **Line** chart (the first chart in the 2-D Line section). A line chart is embedded in the Performance History worksheet.

5. In the Location group on the Chart Tools Design tab, click the **Move Chart** button to open the Move Chart dialog box, click **Summary Report** in the Object in list, and then click the **OK** button. The line chart moves to the Summary Report worksheet.

6. Move and resize the chart to cover the range **D1:I9**. See Figure 4-28.

| Figure 4-28 | Moved and resized line chart |

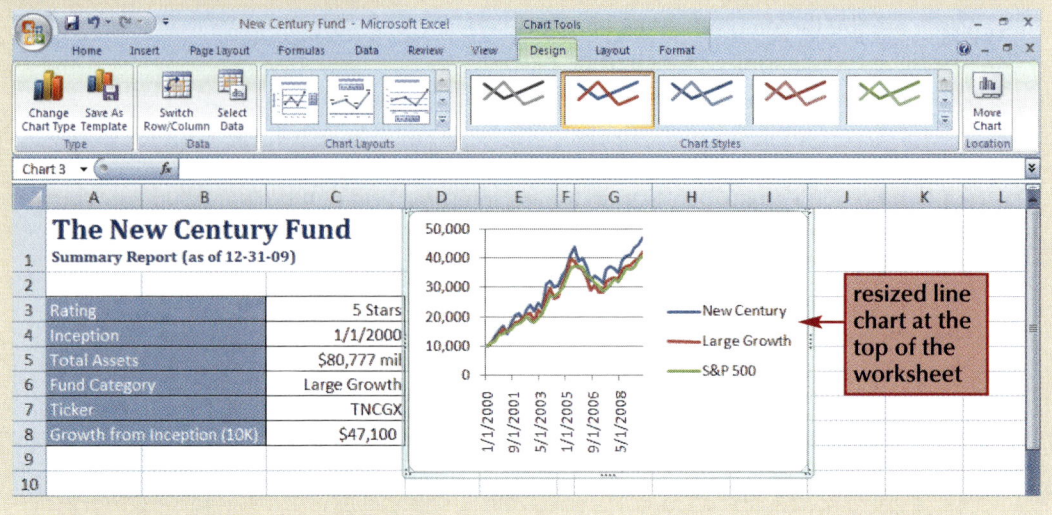

This chart includes three data series—the New Century Fund, the average of large growth funds, and the S&P 500. Each series has a different line color, which is identified in the legend on the right side of the chart area. However, the line chart has little blank space in the chart area and seems crowded by the legend and the date labels on the category axis. You'll reduce the font size of the axis and legend labels, and then add a chart title that clearly identifies the chart's content—the growth of $10,000 for the New Century Fund and the two benchmarks.

To edit the line chart:

1. Click the **Chart Tools Layout** tab on the Ribbon.

2. In the Labels group, click the **Chart Title** button, and then click **Above Chart**. A chart title appears above the line chart surrounded by a selection box.

3. Type **Growth of $10,000** and then press the **Enter** key. The new, descriptive title appears above the chart.

4. Click the **Home** tab on the Ribbon.

5. In the Font group, click the **Font Size arrow**, and then click **10**. The chart title is reduced to 10 points.

6. Click the **value axis** to select it, and then set its font size to **8** points.

7. Click the **category axis** to select it, and then set its font size to **8** points.

8. Click the **chart legend** to select it, and then set its font size to **8** points. The line chart resizes to fill the space left by the smaller chart titles, axes, and chart legend.

Formatting Date Labels

Reducing the font size of the different chart elements helps the layout, but the chart still needs work. The most awkward part of the chart is the list of dates. Ajita is more interested in the general trend from year to year, than the exact date on which the different fund values were calculated. She wants the labels to show only years. You can save space by showing the labels only every other year. To do this, you have to set the major tick marks to appear at two-year intervals. You'll also set the minor tick marks to appear at one-year intervals, even though you won't display the minor tick marks on the chart until later.

To format the category axis labels:

1. Click the **Chart Tools Layout** tab on the Ribbon.

2. In the Axes group, click the **Axes** button, point to **Primary Horizontal Axis**, and then click **More Primary Horizontal Axis Options**. The Format Axis dialog box opens with the Axis Options displayed.

   Because the horizontal axis contains date values, its scale is based on dates rather than on numbers. This means you can set the tick mark intervals in terms of months and years. You'll display the major tick marks (and their labels) every two years. You'll set the interval for minor tick marks to one year.

3. Click the **Major unit Fixed** option button, type **2** in the box, press the **Tab** key, select **Years** in the list. The major tick marks are set to every two years.

4. Click the **Minor unit Fixed** option button, verify that **1** is entered in the box, select **Years** in the list, and then press the **Tab** key. The minor tick marks are set to every year. See Figure 4-29.

Figure 4-29 Date intervals for tick marks

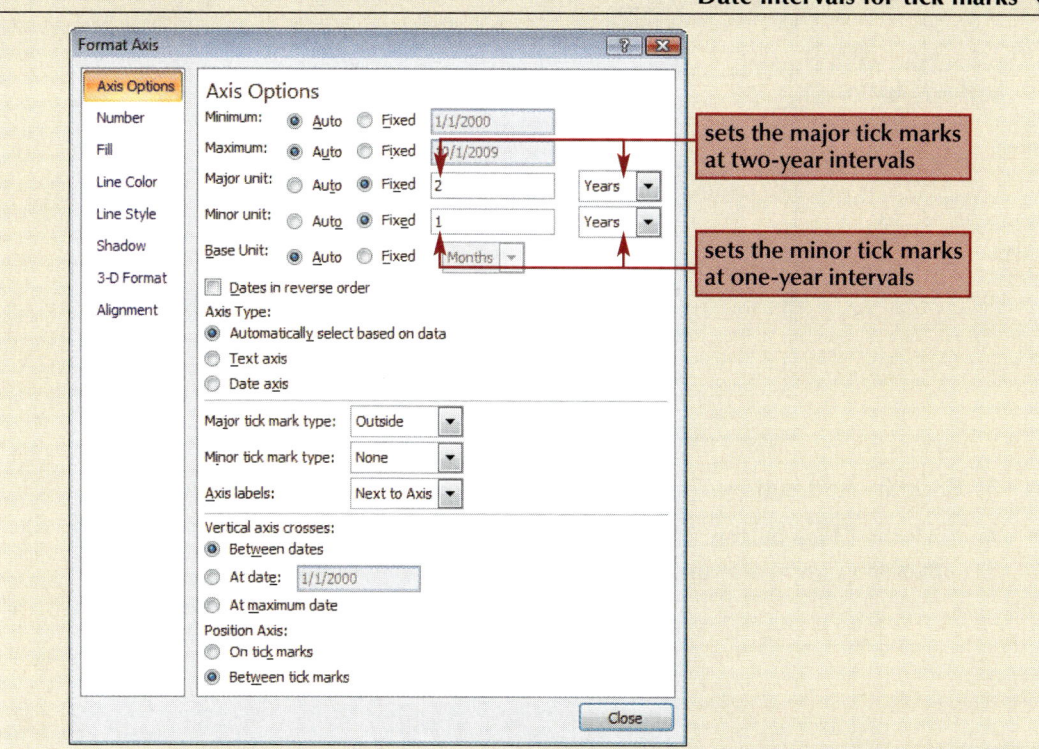

Next, you'll format the category labels to show the four-digit year value rather than the complete date. Excel does not have a built-in format to display four-digit year values, but you can create a custom format. Custom date formats use combinations of the letters *m*, *d*, and *y* for months, days, and years. The number of each letter controls how Excel displays the date. Use *m* or *mm* to display the month number, *mmm* to display the month's three-letter abbreviation, and *mmmm* to display the month's full name. For days, use *dd* to display a two-digit day value and *dddd* to display the day's full name. For example, a custom format of *mmm-dd* shows a three-letter month abbreviation followed by a hyphen and a two-digit day number (such as Apr-05). If you don't want to display the month or day but only the year, use the custom format *yy* for a two-digit year or *yyyy* for a four-digit year.

To create a custom format for the four-digit year:

▶ 1. Click **Number** on the left side of the Format Axis dialog box.

▶ 2. Type **yyyy** in the Format Code box, which is the code for displaying only years. See Figure 4-30.

Figure 4-30 | Number options

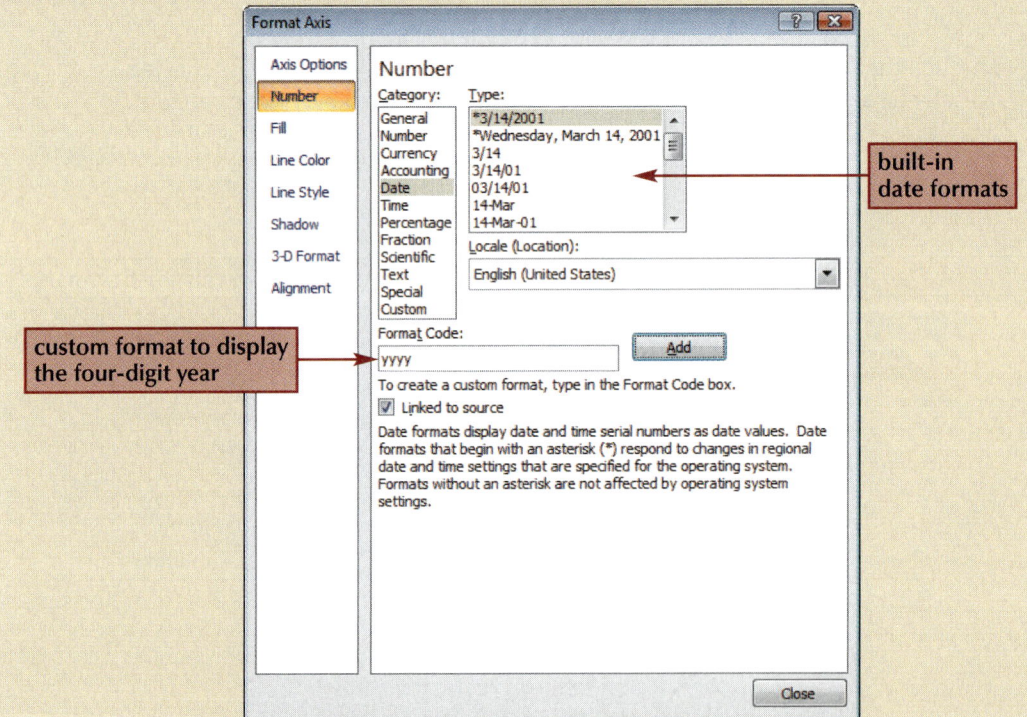

▶ 3. Click the **Add** button. This format code is added to the list of custom formats.

▶ 4. Click the **Close** button. The Format Axis dialog box closes and the category axis labels show values for every other year on the major tick marks. See Figure 4-31.

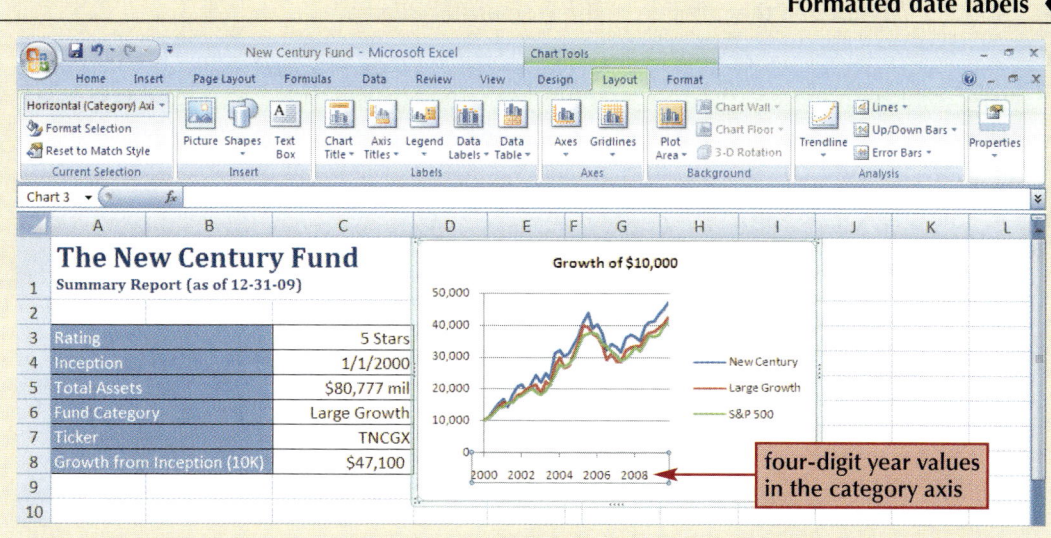

Formatted date labels | **Figure 4-31**

The category axis shows four-digit year values for 2000, 2002, 2004, 2006, and 2008. Because fewer years are included on the axis, there is enough room to display the labels horizontally instead of rotated.

Setting Label Units

Changing the format and tick mark intervals for the category axis has made the text easier to read. Ajita wants you to do something similar for value axis labels. Rather than displaying a large value such as "20,000," she wants to save space by displaying numbers in units of one thousand.

To format the value axis labels:

▶ 1. In the Axes group on the Chart Tools Layout tab, click the **Axes** button, point to **Primary Vertical Axis**, and then click **More Primary Vertical Axis Options**. The Format Axis dialog box opens, displaying the Axis Options.

▶ 2. Click the **Display units** arrow, click **Thousands**, and then move the dialog box so you can see the chart. The scale of the value axis changes from 10,000 to 50,000 in intervals of 10,000 to 0 through 50 in intervals of 10. The title "Thousands" is added to the axis to indicate that the values are expressed in units of one thousand. To save space, you'll remove this title from the chart.

▶ 3. Click the **Show display units label on chart** check box to remove the check mark.

Without the Thousands title, there is no indication what the numbers of the value axis mean. Ajita suggests you add the letter *k* to each number, displaying the numbers as 10k, 20k, and so forth. To do this, you need to create another custom format. In this custom format, you specify the text you want to appear at the end of number. The text must be placed in quotation marks. So, to display the letter *k* after the number you use the custom format #,##0"k". The first part of the custom format specifies that the number should include a thousands separator, and the second part indicates that the number should be followed by the the letter *k*. Next, you'll create the custom format to add the letter *k* after the number.

To create a custom format showing the thousandths unit:

1. Click **Number** on the left side of the Format Axis dialog box.
2. Click in the Format Code box after the number format, and then type **"k"** to make the format code #,##0"k". The quotation marks surround the text you want to add after the number, which, in this case, is the letter *k*.
3. Click the **Add** button. This format code is added to the list of custom formats.
4. Click the **Close** button. The Format Axis dialog box closes, and the value axis labels are revised. See Figure 4-32.

Figure 4-32   Formatted labels in the vertical axis

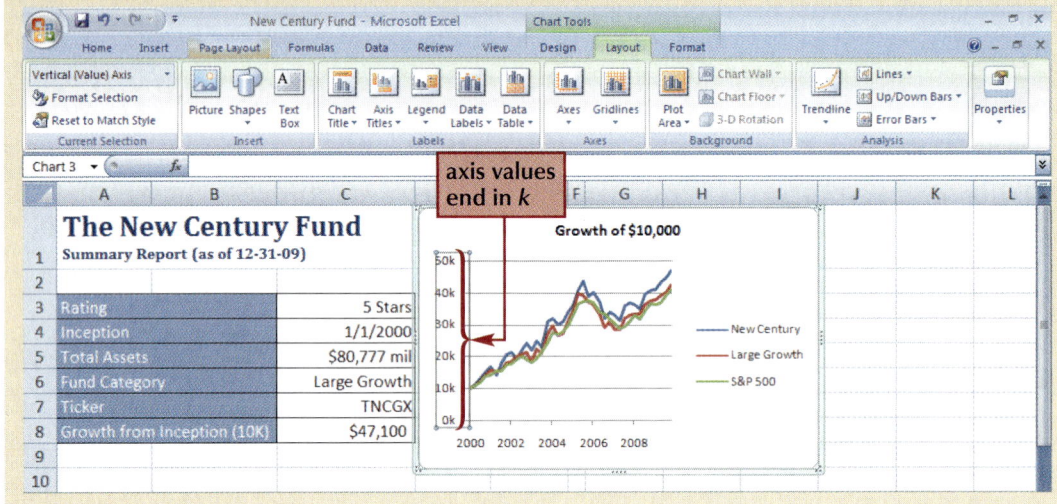

Overlaying a Legend

The modified value axis labels freed space in the chart area. The only other place where you can save space is the chart legend. Rather than displaying the chart legend on the right, you can overlay the legend. There seems to be enough space in the lower-right corner for a legend that will not obscure any of the data lines in the chart.

You can also overlay chart titles on surrounding chart elements to save space, but be aware that overlapping elements might obscure some of the chart content.

Tip

You can also resize a chart legend by selecting the legend, and then dragging a resizing handle.

To format and overlay the chart legend:

1. In the Labels group on the Chart Tools Layout tab, click the **Legend** button, and then click **More Legend Options**. The Format Legend dialog box opens, displaying Legend Options.
2. Click the **Show the legend without overlapping the chart** check box to remove the check mark. The legend moves left, overlaying the chart. Because the plot and the legend now intersect, you'll add a fill color and border to the legend to make it easier to read.
3. Click **Fill** on the left side of the Format Legend dialog box, and then click the **Solid fill** option button.
4. Click the **Color** button, and then click **white** (the first color) in the Theme Colors section.

Tutorial 4 Working with Charts and Graphics | Excel | EX 193

▸ 5. Click **Border Color** on the left side of the Format Legend dialog box, and then click the **Solid line** option button.

▸ 6. Click the **Color** button, and then click **Blue** (the eighth color) in the Standard Colors section.

▸ 7. Click the **Close** button. The Format Legend dialog box closes, and the reformatted legend overlays the chart.

An overlaid chart element floats in the chart area and is not fixed to a particular position. This means you can drag the chart element to a new location. You'll drag the overlaid legend down a bit so it doesn't obscure any of the data in the line chart.

To move the chart legend:

▸ 1. Position the pointer over a blank spot in the chart legend so the pointer changes to and "Legend" appears in a ScreenTip.

▸ 2. Drag the legend to the lower-right corner of the plot area so the bottom of the legend is on the horizontal axis. The legend no longer covers the data lines.

The chart has many horizontal lines from the horizontal gridlines and the chart legend; the chart would look better with vertical gridlines at each minor tick mark.

▸ 3. In the Axes group on the Chart Tools Layout tab, click the **Gridlines** button, point to **Primary Vertical Gridlines**, and then click **Minor Gridlines**. Vertical gridlines appear on the chart at each minor tick mark (recall that minor tick marks appear every year).

▸ 4. Click cell **J2** to deselect the chart. See Figure 4-33.

Final line chart — Figure 4-33

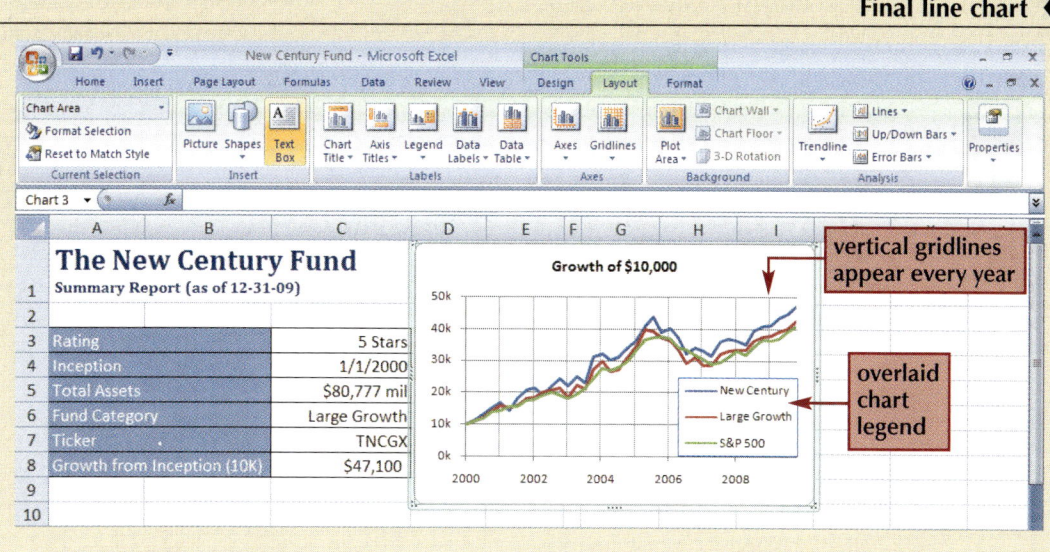

Ajita is pleased with the final version of the line chart. It's easier to read than the unformatted version, and it highlights how well the New Century Fund has performed in the past 10 years compared to the two benchmarks.

Adding a Data Series to an Existing Chart

Ajita wonders how the distribution of stocks owned by the New Century Fund compares to the S&P 500. For example, does the New Century Fund invest more in the information sector, and is that why it outperformed the S&P 500 for the past 10 years? Ajita researched the sector weightings for the S&P 500. She wants you to enter this data in the Sector Weightings worksheet and then add it to the Sector Weightings column chart you already created.

To enter data on the S&P 500 to the Sector Weightings worksheet:

▶ 1. Click the **Sector Weightings** sheet tab to make that the active worksheet, and then select the range **C3:C15**. You'll copy these formats from the New Century Fund data and paste them in column D for the S&P 500 data.

▶ 2. Click the **Home** tab on the Ribbon, and then, in the Clipboard group, click the **Format Painter** button.

▶ 3. Select the range **D3:D15** to paste the formats. Now, you'll enter the S&P data in the range you just formatted.

▶ 4. In the range **D3:D15**, enter the data shown in Figure 4-34.

Figure 4-34   Sector weightings for the S&P 500

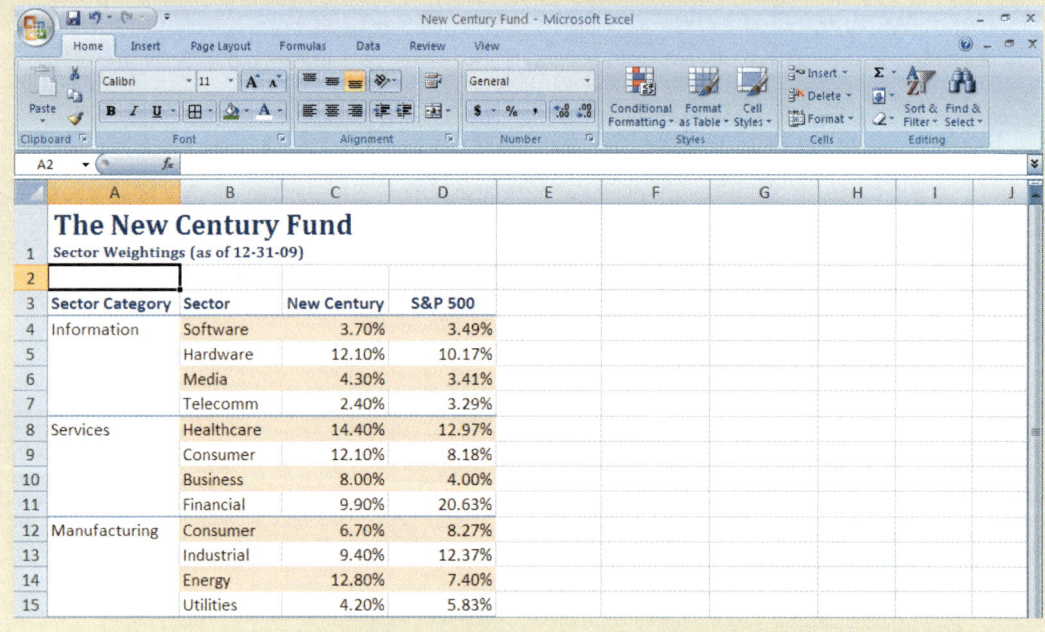

Adding the data to the table in the Sector Weightings worksheet does not add the data to the chart you already created. You must explicitly add the new data series to the chart. A new data series will have the same style and format as the existing data series in the chart.

Reference Window | Adding a Data Series to a Chart

- Select the chart to which you want to add a data series.
- In the Data group on the Chart Tools Design tab, click the Select Data button.
- Click the Add button in the Select Data Source dialog box.
- Select the range with the series name and series values you want for the new data series.
- Click the OK button in each dialog box.

You'll add the sector weightings data for the S&P 500 to the column chart in the Summary Report worksheet.

To add a data series to the existing column chart:

1. Click the **Summary Report** sheet tab, and then click the chart area of the column chart to select it.

2. Click the **Chart Tools Design** tab on the Ribbon, and then, in the Data group, click the **Select Data** button. The Select Data Source dialog box opens. The left side lists all of the data series displayed in the chart. The right side lists the category axis labels associated with each data series. You can add, edit, or remove any of these data series from the chart.

3. Click the **Add** button. The Edit Series dialog box opens. In this dialog box, you specify the name of the new data series and its range of data values.

4. With the insertion point in the Series name box, click the **Sector Weightings** sheet tab, click cell **D3**, and then press the **Tab** key. The cell with the series name is entered and the insertion point is in the Series values box.

5. Click the **Sector Weightings** sheet tab, and then select the range **D4:D15**. See Figure 4-35.

Figure 4-35 | Edit Series dialog box

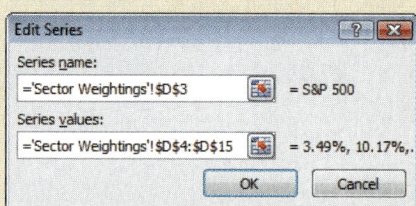

6. Click the **OK** button. In the Select Data Source dialog box, you can see that the S&P 500 data is added to the list of data series in the chart. See Figure 4-36.

Figure 4-36 | Select Data Source dialog box

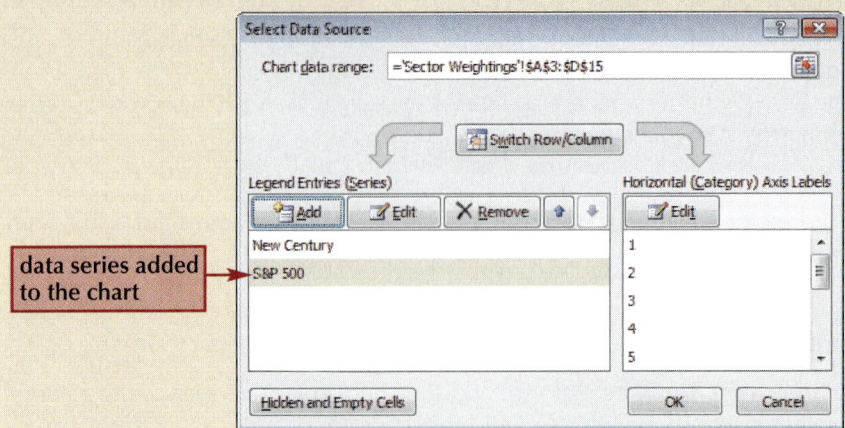

data series added to the chart

▶ 7. Click the **OK** button. The S&P 500 sector values appear as red columns in the chart. See Figure 4-37.

Figure 4-37 | Column chart with added series

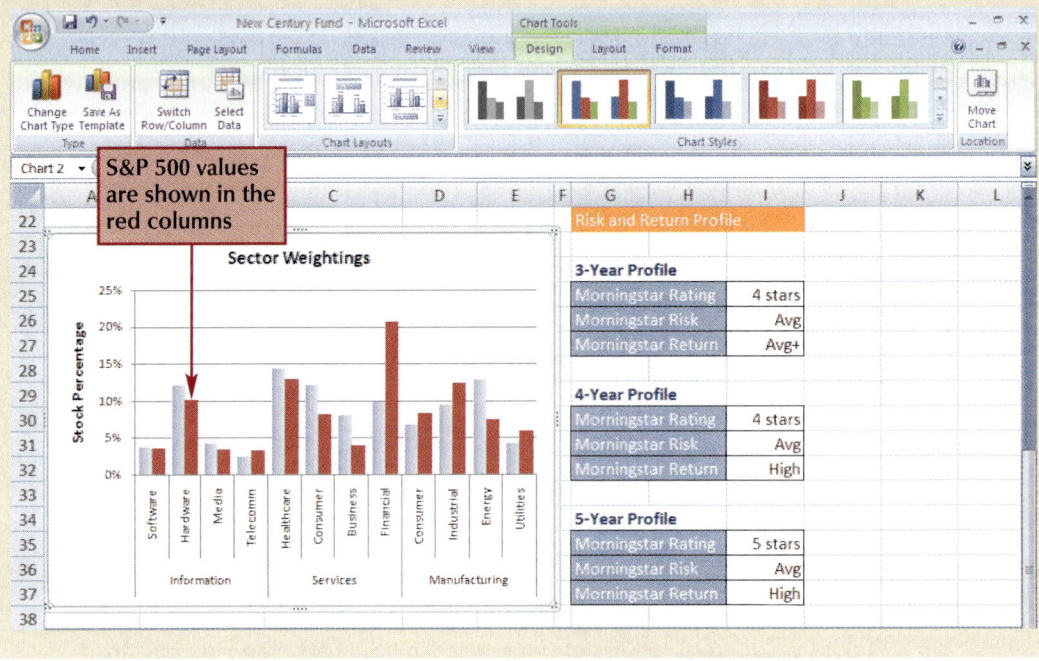

S&P 500 values are shown in the red columns

With so many columns, the data is difficult to read and interpret. Ajita suggests you separate the S&P 500 values from the New Century Fund values by plotting them as lines rather than columns.

Creating a Combination Chart

Tip

Combination charts can only be two-dimensional. You cannot create 3-D combination charts.

The type of chart that Ajita wants you to create is a **combination chart**, which is a chart that combines two or more chart types in a single graph. To create a combination chart, you select a data series in an existing chart, and then apply a new chart type to that series, leaving the other data series in its original format.

Tutorial 4 Working with Charts and Graphics | Excel **EX 197**

Creating a Combination Chart | Reference Window

- Select a data series in an existing chart that you want to appear as another chart type.
- In the Type group on the Chart Tools Design tab, click the Change Chart Type button, and then click the chart type you want.
- Click the OK button.

You'll display the S&P 500 values as a line chart so that it's easier to distinguish between the two data series.

To apply the line chart type to a data series:

1. Click any red column to select the entire S&P 500 data series.
2. In the Type group on the Chart Tools Design tab, click the **Change Chart Type** button. The Change Chart Type dialog box opens.
3. In the Line section, click **Line with Markers** (the fourth Line chart type).
4. Click the **OK** button. The S&P 500 values change to a line chart with markers. See Figure 4-38.

Figure 4-38 — Combination chart

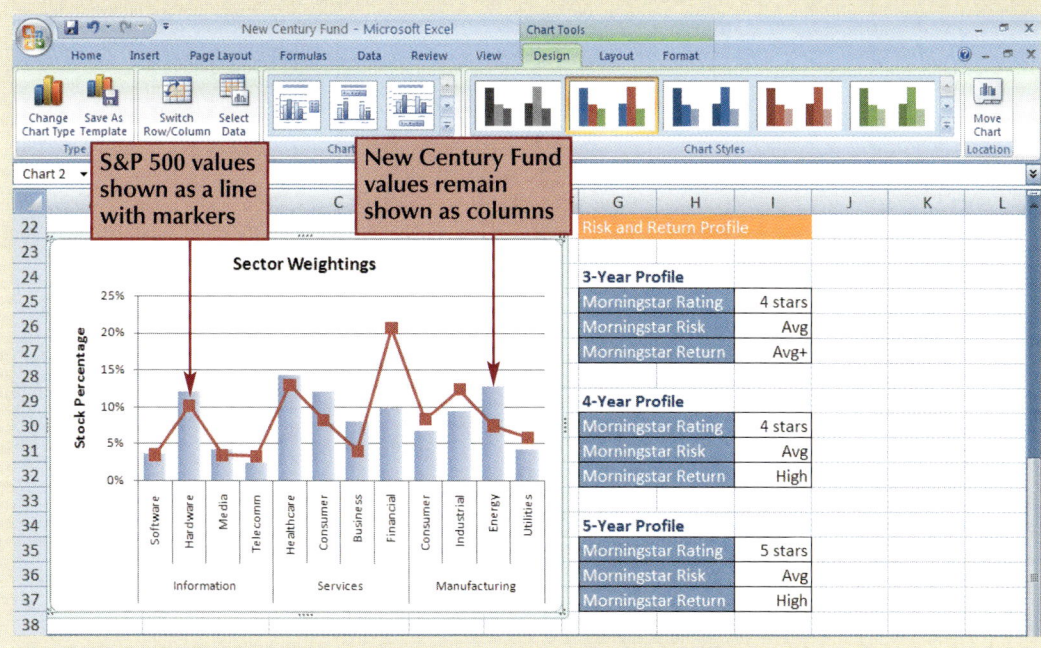

S&P 500 values shown as a line with markers

New Century Fund values remain shown as columns

As noted earlier, line charts are best for categories that follow some sequential order, such as the performance history chart in which the categories represented dates. In this case, the sector categories do not have a sequential order and the lines between sectors have no meaning. You'll remove these lines from the chart to avoid confusing Ajita's clients. Also, you'll change the square markers to horizontal line markers at each data point.

To remove the lines and edit the markers in the line chart:

1. Click the red line in the S&P 500 line chart to select it.
2. Click the **Chart Tools Layout** tab on the Ribbon, and then, in the Current Selection group, click **Format Selection**. The Format Data Series dialog box opens.
3. Click **Line Color** on the left side of the dialog box, and then click the **No line** option button to remove the line from the line chart.
4. Click **Marker Options** on the left side of the dialog box, and then click the **Built-in** option button.
5. Click the **Type** arrow and click the horizontal line marker (the seventh marker in the list), and then click the **Size** up arrow until **10** appears in the box. See Figure 4-39.

Figure 4-39 — Marker Options in the Format Data Series dialog box

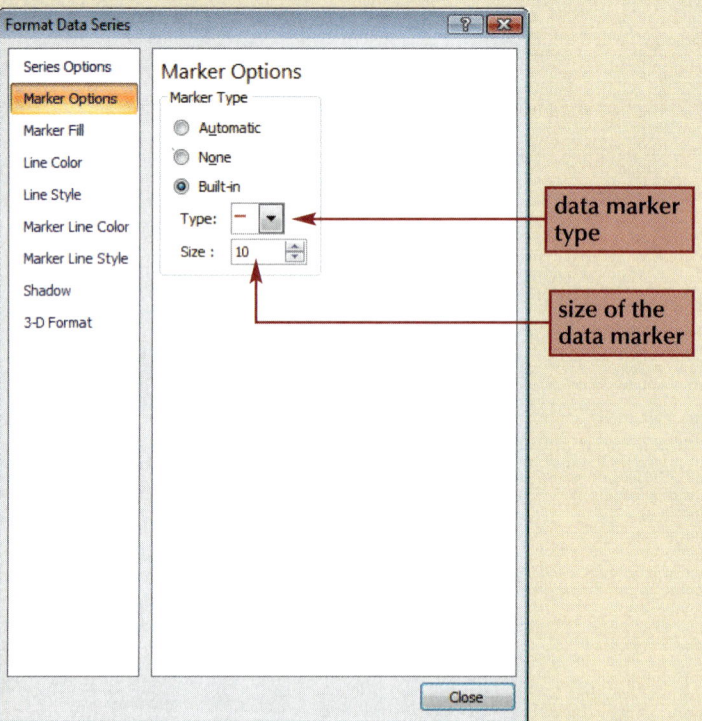

6. Click the **Close** button. The S&P 500 values appear only as data markers.

   Because the chart now has two data series, you'll add a legend to the top of the chart to identify them.

7. In the Labels group, click the **Legend** button, and then click **Show Legend at Top**. The legend appears above the chart.
8. Click the **legend** to select it, click the **Home** tab on the Ribbon, and then reduce the font size of the legend to **8** points.
9. Click cell **A38** to deselect the chart. See Figure 4-40.

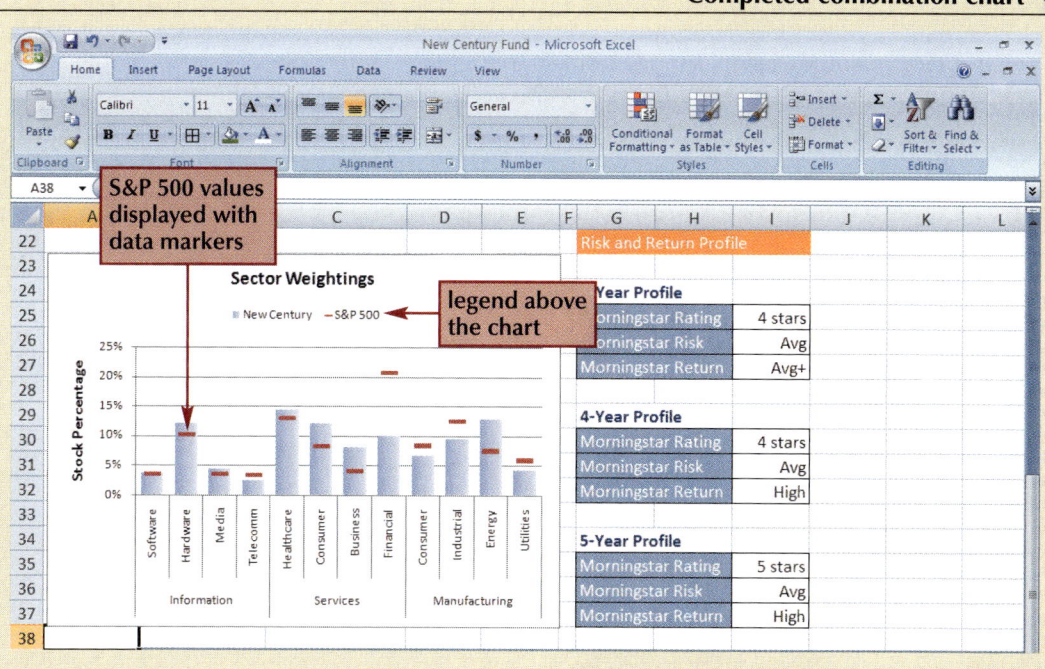

Figure 4-40 Completed combination chart

The combination chart effectively shows that the New Century Fund invests less than the S&P 500 in sectors from the financial service industry, and invests more in other sectors such as energy, consumer services, and hardware. This might account for the higher performance of the New Century Fund.

Choosing the Right Type of Chart | InSight

How do you know which type of chart to use with your data? In general, pie charts should be used only when the number of categories is small and the relative sizes of the different slices can be easily determined. If you have several categories, use a column or bar chart.

Line charts are best for categories that follow a sequential order. Be aware, however, that the time intervals must be a constant length if used in a line chart. Line charts will distort data that occurs in irregular time intervals, making it appear that the data values occurred at regular intervals when they did not.

Pie, column, bar, and line charts assume that numbers are plotted against categories. In science and engineering applications, you will often want to plot two numeric values against one another. For that data, use **XY scatter charts**, which show the patterns or relationship between two or more sets of values. XY scatter charts are also good for data recorded at irregular time intervals.

If you still can't find the right chart to meet your needs, you can create a custom chart based on the built-in chart types. Third-party vendors also sell software to allow Excel to create charts not built into the software.

Working with Shapes

Financial analysts give the New Century Fund a five-star rating based on its performance history. In cell C3, Ajita entered this rating as text. She wants you to replace the text with five stars.

Inserting a Shape

Tip

You can add text to a shape by selecting the shape, and then typing the text you want to insert.

Excel, like all Office programs, includes a gallery of 160 different shapes organized into eight categories. These shapes range from simple squares and circles to more complex objects such as flowchart symbols, block arrows, and banners. After you insert a shape into a chart or worksheet, you can resize and move it, set its fill color and border color, and apply 3D effects to make it stand out on the page.

You'll add the first star shape to the Summary Report worksheet.

To insert a star shape in cell C3:

1. Right-click cell **C3**, and then click **Clear Contents** on the shortcut menu. The text "5 Stars" is erased from the cell.

2. Click the **Insert** tab on the Ribbon.

3. In the Illustrations group, click the **Shapes** button to display the Shapes gallery, and then click **5-Point Star** (the fourth star) in the Stars and Banners section. The pointer changes to ✛.

4. Drag the pointer over cell C3 to create a star shape. The embedded star shape is selected and the Format tab appears on the Ribbon with a label identifying it as Drawing Tools. The Drawing Tools Format tab appears whenever you select a shape. See Figure 4-41.

Figure 4-41   Star shape embedded in cell C3

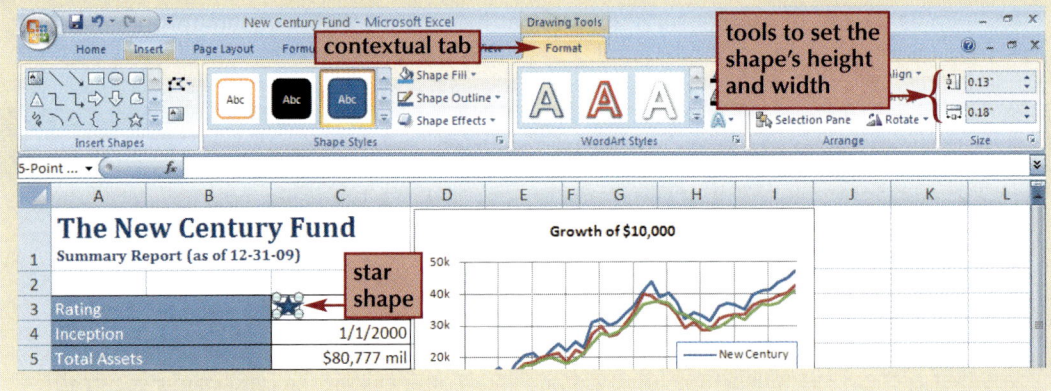

Resizing, Moving, and Copying a Shape

Shapes, like embedded charts, are objects you can move and resize. To set a shape's size more exactly, you enter the width and height you want in the Size group on the Drawing Tools Format tab. You'll match the star's height and width to the cell's height and width so it fills the cell.

Tip

You can move an embedded shape more precisely by selecting the shape, and then pressing the arrow keys on your keyboard in the direction you want the shape to move.

To resize the star shape:

1. In the Size group on the Drawing Tools Format tab, click the **Shape Height** down arrow to set the height to **0.1"**.

2. In the Size group, click the **Shape Width** down arrow to set the width to **0.1"**.

3. Drag the star to the left edge of cell C3 and center it within the height of the cell.

The first star is embedded and positioned in cell C3. Next, you'll copy the star shape and paste four copies into cell C3 so that the contains a total of five stars.

To copy and paste the star shape:

▶ 1. With the star selected, click the **Home** tab on the Ribbon, and then, in the Clipboard group, click the **Copy** button.

▶ 2. In the Clipboard group, click the **Paste** button to paste the star shape. The new star shape is pasted to the lower-right of the first star.

▶ 3. Drag the star to the right of the star already in cell C3.

▶ 4. Repeat Steps 2 and 3 until you have five stars next to each other in cell C3. The stars do not have to align exactly. You'll align them next.

Aligning and Grouping Shapes

Placing shapes by dragging is inexact and can be frustrating. Instead of dragging and dropping shapes, you can line them up neatly using the tools on the Drawing Tools Format tab. You can horizontally align selected shapes in several ways: by their tops, by their bottoms, or by their middles. If you're aligning the shapes vertically, you can align them along their left edges, their right edges, or their centers. In this case, you'll line up the stars by their middles, and then distribute them horizontally so that they are evenly spaced from each other.

To horizontally and vertically align the five star shapes:

▶ 1. Click the first star in cell C3 to select it.

▶ 2. Hold down the **Shift** key, click each of the four remaining stars, and then release the **Shift** key. Each star you click is added to the selected shapes.

▶ 3. Click the **Drawing Tools Format** tab on the Ribbon.

▶ 4. In the Arrange group, click the **Align** button, and then click **Align Middle**. The stars align along their middles. You also want the stars evenly spaced in the cell.

▶ 5. In the Arrange group, click the **Align** button and then click **Distribute Horizontally**. The five stars are evenly spaced within the cell.

When you have several shapes that you want to treat as one unit, you can **group** them. You can move and resize grouped shapes as one, which makes it easier to develop interesting graphical shapes composed of several smaller parts. It also frees you from having to realign and redistribute the shapes if you move or copy them to a new location in the worksheet. You'll group the five stars in cell C3 so that they always remain together and aligned properly.

To group several shapes into a single unit:

▶ 1. With all five stars selected, in the Arrange group on the Drawing Tools Format tab, click the **Group** button, and then click **Group**. A single selection box surrounds the five stars, indicating that they are grouped. The grouped stars can be moved together if needed without losing their relative alignment.

▶ 2. Click cell **A2** to deselect the group of stars. See Figure 4-42.

| Figure 4-42 | Grouped and aligned star shapes |

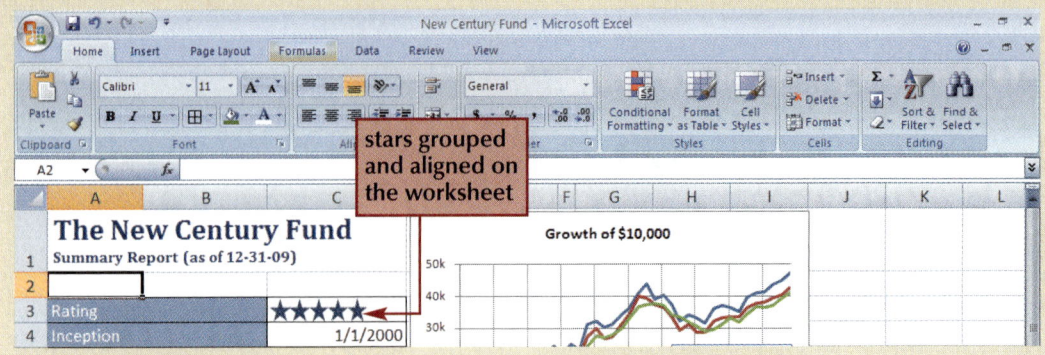

Creating a Chart Sheet

Tip

A chart sheet can contain embedded charts, enabling you to display several charts at once within a single sheet.

Ajita asks you to create a cover sheet for the workbook that shows a 3D image of the performance of the New Century Fund over the past 10 years. Because this chart is purely decorative, you can make a visually interesting chart without concern about easily reading its data. The cover sheet will contain only the chart and no other data or text, so you'll create a chart sheet. Recall that chart sheets show only charts and no worksheet data.

To create a chart sheet:

1. Click the **Performance History** sheet tab, and then select the range **A4:B44**, if necessary. This range contains the data you want to use in the chart.

2. Click the **Insert** tab on the Ribbon.

3. In the Charts group, click the **Line** button, and then click the **3-D Line** chart type. The 3D line chart is embedded in the Performance History worksheet. You'll move this chart to its own chart sheet.

4. In the Location group on the Chart Tools Design tab, click the **Move Chart** button. The Move Chart dialog box opens.

5. Click the **New sheet** option button, type **Cover Sheet** in the box, and then click the **OK** button. A chart sheet named "Cover Sheet" that contains the 3D line chart is inserted in the workbook.

6. Drag the **Cover Sheet** sheet tab to the right of the Documentation sheet tab. See Figure 4-43.

Chart sheet with the 3D line chart Figure 4-43

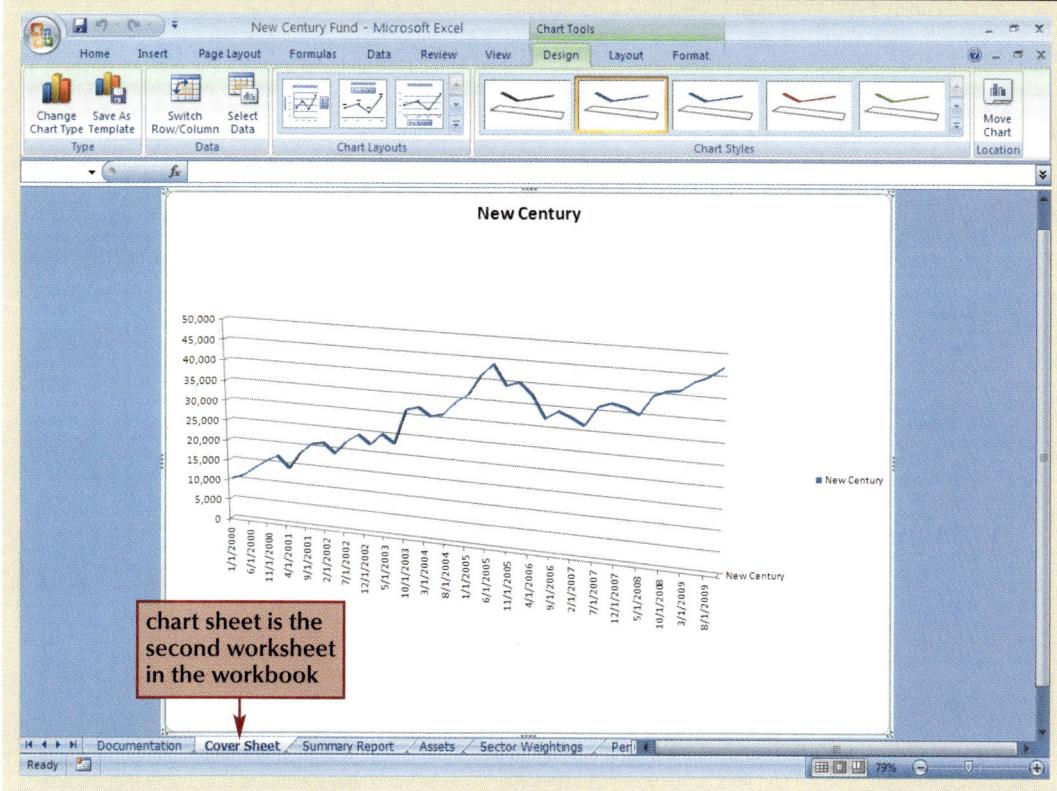

The Cover Sheet appears before Summary Report worksheet and the worksheets that contain the detailed data used to create the summary report. Next, you'll remove the axes labels and legend from the chart and rotate the chart in three dimensions. To increase the 3D effect, you'll widen the chart's base from 100 to 1000 points.

To format the chart sheet:

1. If necessary, click the chart area to select it.

2. In the Chart Styles group on the Chart Tools Design tab, click the **More** button, and then click **Style 40** (the fifth row, last column) of the Chart Styles gallery.

3. Click the **Chart Tools Layout** tab on the Ribbon.

4. In the Labels group, click the **Legend** button, and then click **None** to turn off the legend.

5. In the Axes group, click the **Axes** button, point to **Primary Horizontal Axis**, and then click **None** to remove the horizontal axis.

6. In the Axes group, click the **Axes** button, point to **Primary Vertical Axis**, and then click **None** to remove the vertical axis from the chart.

7. In the Axes group, click the **Axes** button, point to **Depth Axis**, and then click **None** to remove the depth axis.

8. In the Background section, click the **3-D Rotation** button. The Format Chart Area dialog box opens, displaying the 3-D Rotation options.

9. In the Rotation section, set X to **60°**, Y to **20°**, and Perspective to **80°**, and then, in the Chart Scale section, set the Depth (% of base) to **1000**.

These settings rotate the chart, exaggerate the 3D effect, and make the chart appear thicker. Next, you'll change the background color of the chart area to a gradient fill.

▶ 10. Click **Fill** on the left side of the dialog box, and then click the **Gradient fill** option button.

▶ 11. Click the **Preset colors** button, and then click **Daybreak**, the fourth color in the first row.

▶ 12. Click the **Direction** button, and then click **Linear Down**, the second direction in the first row.

▶ 13. Click the **Close** button. See Figure 4-44.

Figure 4-44   **Formatted chart sheet**

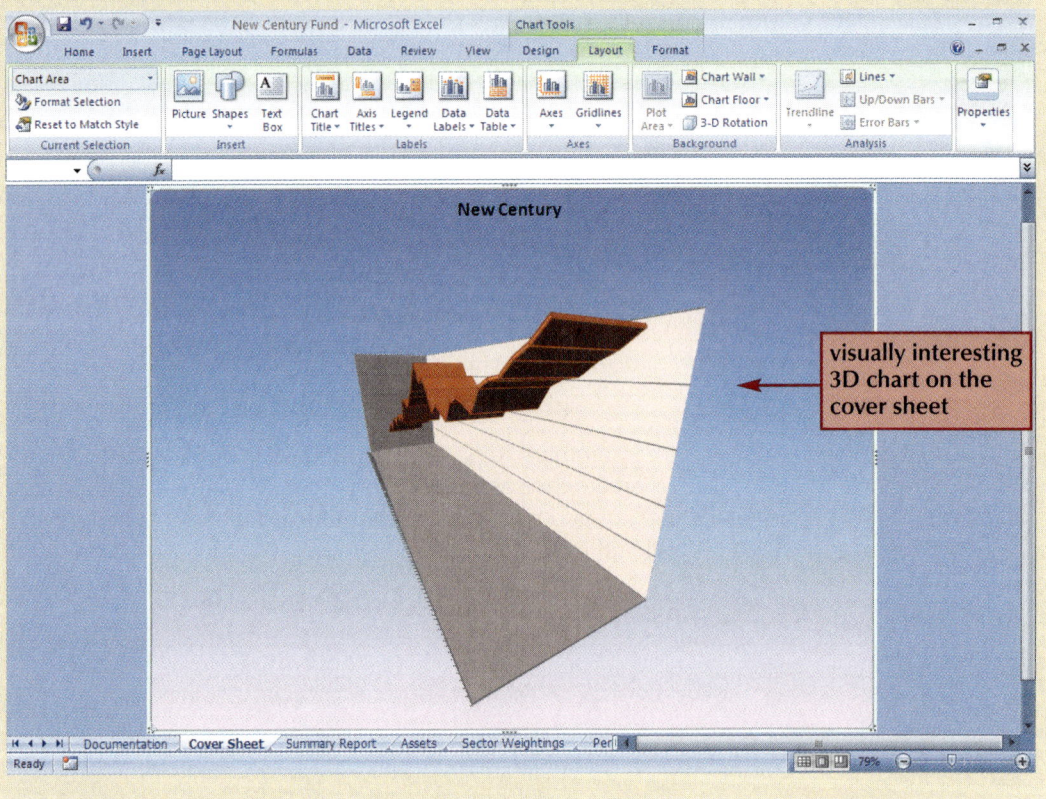

To complete the chart sheet, you'll overlay the chart title "The New Century Fund," and format it in a 48-point white font.

To overlay and format the chart title:

▶ 1. In the Labels group on the Chart Tools Layout tab, click the **Chart Title** button, and then click **Centered Overlay Title**. The chart title is overlaid above the chart.

▶ 2. Type **The New Century Fund**, and then press the **Enter** key. The new title is entered.

▶ 3. Click the **Home** tab on the Ribbon, and then set the font size to **48** points and the font color to **white**.

▶ 4. Click outside of the chart to deselect it. The cover sheet is final. See Figure 4-45.

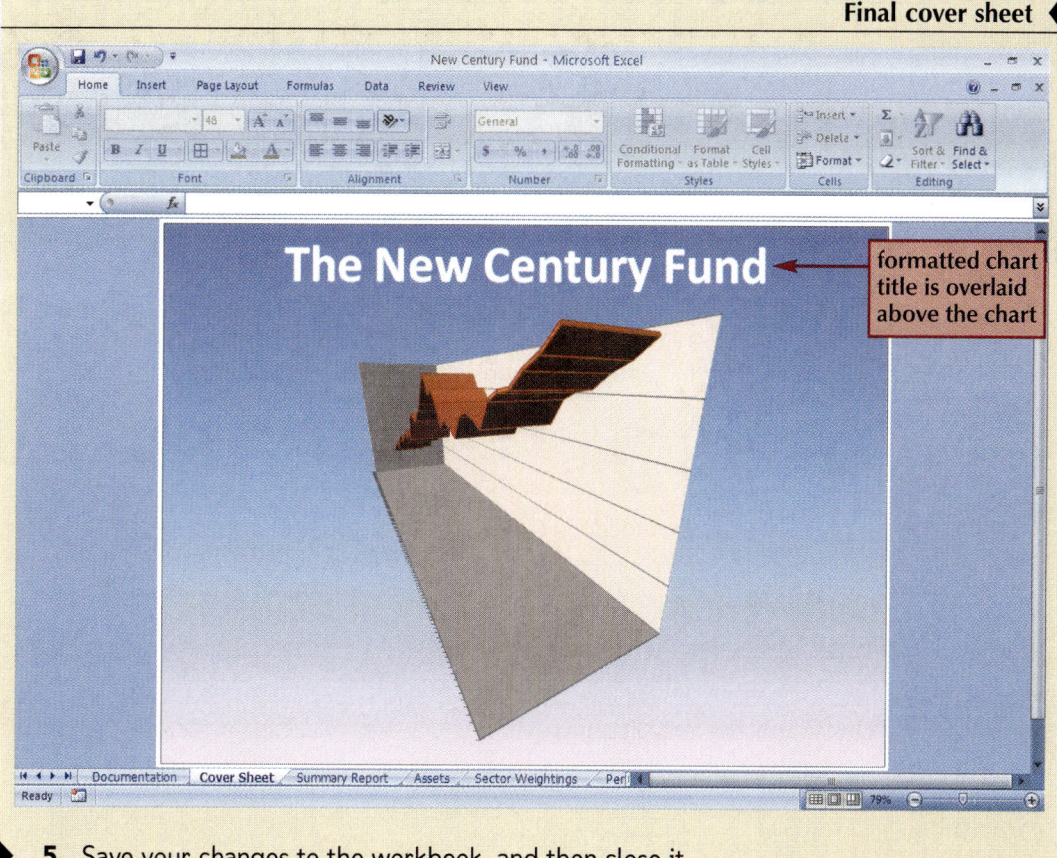

Figure 4-45 Final cover sheet

formatted chart title is overlaid above the chart

▶ 5. Save your changes to the workbook, and then close it.

You show the final version of the cover sheet and the workbook to Ajita. She is pleased with the work you've done adding charts and graphics to the workbook. Ajita will present the Summary Report worksheet, with the embedded charts, to her clients to provide them a concise report on the performance of the New Century Fund. The cover sheet you've created adds visual interest to the report.

Session 4.2 Quick Check | Review

1. When should you use a line chart in place of a column chart?
2. How do you overlay a chart legend?
3. How do you add a data series to an already existing chart?
4. What is a combination chart? Describe how you create a combination chart.
5. How do you insert a shape into a worksheet?
6. Describe how to set the exact height and width of a shape.
7. Describe how to horizontally align the tops of three shapes in Excel.
8. How do you create a chart sheet?

Review | Tutorial Summary

In this tutorial, you learned how to work with charts and graphics. You reviewed the different parts of a chart and the relationship between charts and data sources. Then, you inserted an embedded chart and reviewed the different types of chart, chart layouts, and chart styles supported by Excel. The first chart you created was a pie chart. You worked with the pie chart legend and formatted individual slices. Next, you made the pie chart a 3D chart and learned about some limitations of 3D charts. The second chart you created and formatted was a column chart. The third chart you created and formatted was a line chart. You also learned when line charts are preferable to column charts. The fourth chart you created was a combination chart that combined the column and line charts. You then inserted shapes into a worksheet, and aligned and grouped them. Finally, you created a chart sheet as a cover sheet for the entire workbook.

Key Terms

bar chart	embedded chart	pie chart
category values	exploded pie chart	plot area
chart	graph	primary value axis
chart area	gridlines	resizing handle
chart sheet	group	scale
chart title	horizontal (category) axis	secondary value axis
column chart	leader line	selection box
combination chart	legend	series name
data label	line chart	series values
data marker	major tick mark	vertical (value) axis
data series	minor tick mark	XY scatter chart
data source	perspective	

Practice | Review Assignments

Practice the skills you learned in the tutorial using the same case scenario.

Data File needed for the Review Assignments: Crockett.xlsx

Ajita asks you to help on a new project. She has to create a report on the investment portfolio for Brian and Tammy Crockett. She wants to add charts that display where the couple's money is currently being invested and how their portfolio has performed in recent years. She's already entered the data. She needs you to complete the report by adding the charts and a decorative cover sheet.

Complete the following:

1. Open the **Crockett** workbook located in the Tutorial.04\Review folder included with your Data Files, and then save the workbook as **Crockett Portfolio** in the same folder. In the Documentation sheet, enter your name in cell B3 and the date in cell B4.
2. In the Composition worksheet, select the range A3:B8, and then insert a 2D pie chart. Move and resize the embedded pie chart to cover the range D1:G9 in the Portfolio Report worksheet.
3. Move the legend to the left side of the chart area. Change the chart title to **Composition** and set its font size to 12 points. Change the fill color of the Cash slice to yellow. Add data labels that show the percentage of each pie slice to two decimal places outside of the pie chart, and then set the font size of the labels to 8 points.
4. Change the pie chart to a 3D pie chart and set the 3D rotation of the x-axis to 230° and the y-axis to 40°.
5. In the Sector Weightings worksheet, select the range A3:D15, and then insert a 2D clustered column chart. Move and resize the embedded chart to cover the range A12:D25 in the Portfolio Report worksheet.
6. Change the font size of the axis labels and legend to 8 points. Insert the chart title **Sector Weightings** over the plot and set its font size to 12 points. Change the format of the percentages in the vertical axis to display no decimal places. Overlay the legend at the top of the chart, and then change its fill color to white and insert a solid border around the legend.
7. Change the chart type of the S&P 500 series to a line chart, remove the line connecting the markers in the chart, and then change the marker type to a solid horizontal line of size 10.
8. Change the fill color of the columns for the Portfolio data series to the theme color Purple, Accent 4, Lighter 60%. Set the gap width of the columns in the Portfolio data series to 30%.
9. In the Portfolio Value worksheet, select the range A3:B127, and then insert a 2D area chart. Move and resize the chart to cover the range D28:G42 in the Portfolio Report worksheet. (*Hint:* You will need to scroll down the Portfolio Report worksheet to locate the chart when you move it from the Portfolio Value worksheet.)
10. Remove the chart legend. Set the font size of the chart title to 11 points, and then set the font size of the axis labels to 8 points. Change the fill color of the data series to the theme color Purple, Accent 4, Lighter 60%.
11. Modify the category axis so that the vertical axis crosses the maximum date. (*Hint:* Use the Axis Options in the Format Axis dialog box.)
12. Set the major tick mark interval at two years and the minor tick mark interval at one year. Use a custom format that displays the category axis date values as four-digit year values. Insert vertical gridlines for the minor tick marks.

13. In the Portfolio Value worksheet, select the range A3:B127, and insert a 3D area chart. Move the embedded chart into a new chart sheet named **Cover Sheet**. Move the Cover Sheet worksheet directly after the Documentation sheet.
14. Change the chart style to Style 34, located in the fifth row and second column of the Chart Styles gallery. Remove the display of the horizontal, vertical, and depth axes. Remove the chart legend.
15. For the 3D rotation, set the x-axis to 60°, the y-axis to 10°, the perspective to 40°, and the depth of the base to 2000.
16. Change the chart title to **Crockett Family Portfolio**. Set the font size of the chart title to 40 points.
17. Insert two 5-pointed stars, one directly to the left and the other directly to the right of the chart title. Set the height and width of each star to 0.3". Align the middle of the two stars and then group them into a single object.
18. Save and close your workbook, and then submit the finished workbook to your instructor, either in printed or electronic form, as requested.

Apply | Case Problem 1

Use the skills you learned to create 3D charts of usage data for a national park.

Data File needed for this Case Problem: Kenai.xlsx

Kenai Fjords National Park Maria Sanford is the chief of interpretation at Kenai Fjords National Park. Part of her job is to report on park usage at each visitor center and all visitor centers. She has recorded last year's usage data in an Excel workbook. She asks you to present this data in a 3D column chart for an upcoming meeting with her supervisor. She wants the chart to show the monthly usage totals organized by visitor center. Figure 4-46 shows a preview of the 3D column chart you'll create for Maria.

Figure 4-46

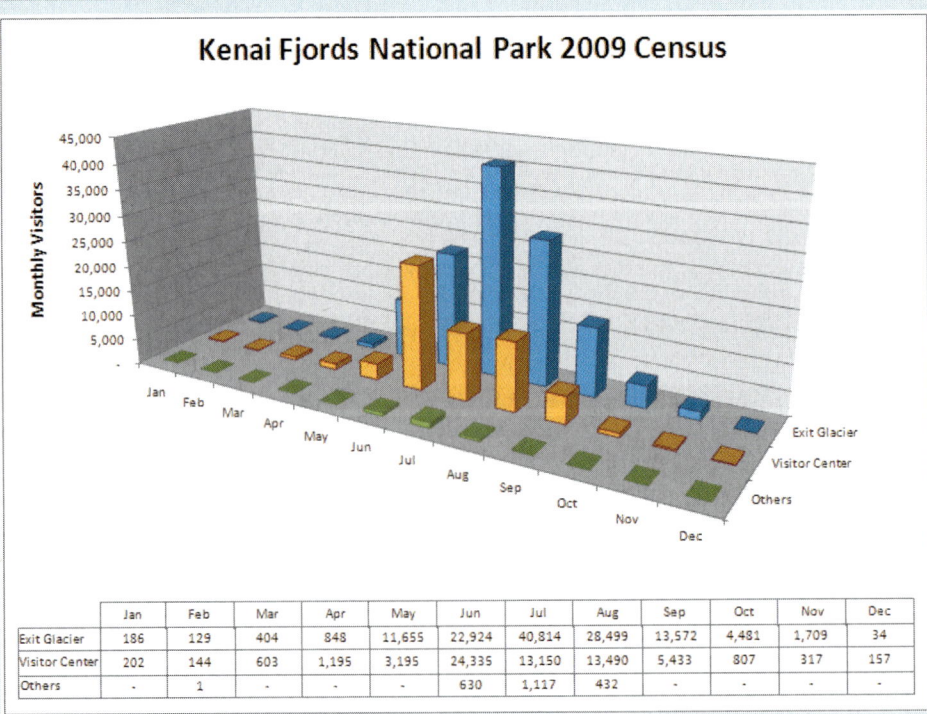

Complete the following:

1. Open the **Kenai** workbook located in the Tutorial.04\Case1 folder included with your Data Files, and then save the workbook as **Kenai Fjords Park** in the folder. In the Documentation sheet, enter your name in cell B3 and the date in cell B4.
2. In the Park Usage Data worksheet, select the range A4:D16, and then insert the 3-D Column chart (the last chart in the 3-D Column section in the Charts gallery).
3. Move the chart to a chart sheet named **Monthly Visits**. Place the Monthly Visits chart sheet directly after the Documentation sheet.
4. Change the style of the chart to Style 34 (the fifth style in the second column in the Chart Styles gallery).
5. Insert the chart title **Kenai Fjords National Park 2009 Census** at the top of the chart area, and then set its font size to 24 points. Remove the legend from the chart.
6. Add the title **Monthly Visitors** to the vertical axis. Rotate the title 90° and set the font size to 14 points.
7. Rotate the 3D chart using the following parameters: x-axis rotation 30°, y-axis rotation 20°, perspective 25°, and base width 130. Modify the depth axis so that the values are displayed in reverse order.

EXPLORE

8. Insert a data table without legend keys below the 3-D chart to provide data values so that the reader is not confused about the relative sizes of the different columns. (*Hint:* Use the Data Table button in the Labels group on the Chart Tools Layout tab.)
9. Change the fill color of the Exit Glacier series to light blue. Change the fill color of the Visitor Center series to orange.
10. In the Park Usage Data worksheet, select the range B4:D4;B17:D17, and then insert a 3D pie chart. Move the embedded chart to a chart sheet named **Center Visits**. Place the Center Visits sheet directly after the Monthly Visits chart sheet.
11. Insert the chart title **Kenai Fjords National Park: Visits by Center** above the pie chart, and set its font size to 24 points.
12. Move the chart legend below the pie chart, and change its font size to 18 points.
13. Change the fill color of the Exit Glacier slice to light blue. Change the fill color of the Visitor Center slice to orange.
14. Add data labels to the outside end of the pie chart showing the values (not percentages) of each slice. Set the font size of the labels to 18 points.
15. Save and close your workbook, and then submit the finished workbook to your instructor, either in printed or electronic form, as requested.

Apply | Case Problem 2

Use the skills you learned to create a combination chart describing the occurrence of tornados in the twentieth century.

Data Files needed for this Case Problem: Cloud.jpg, Tornado.xlsx

Midwest Tornado Institute Joyce Bishop is a meteorologist at the Midwest Tornado Institute located in Decatur, Illinois. Joyce is preparing for a talk she is giving to a local civic group on the possible effects of global warming on tornados. She's collected data on minor, moderate, and major tornado sightings in five-year periods during the second half of the twentieth century and wants to create a graph for her talk showing her data. She's already entered her data into an Excel workbook; she needs your help in creating the chart. Figure 4-47 shows a preview of the chart you'll create for Joyce.

Figure 4-47

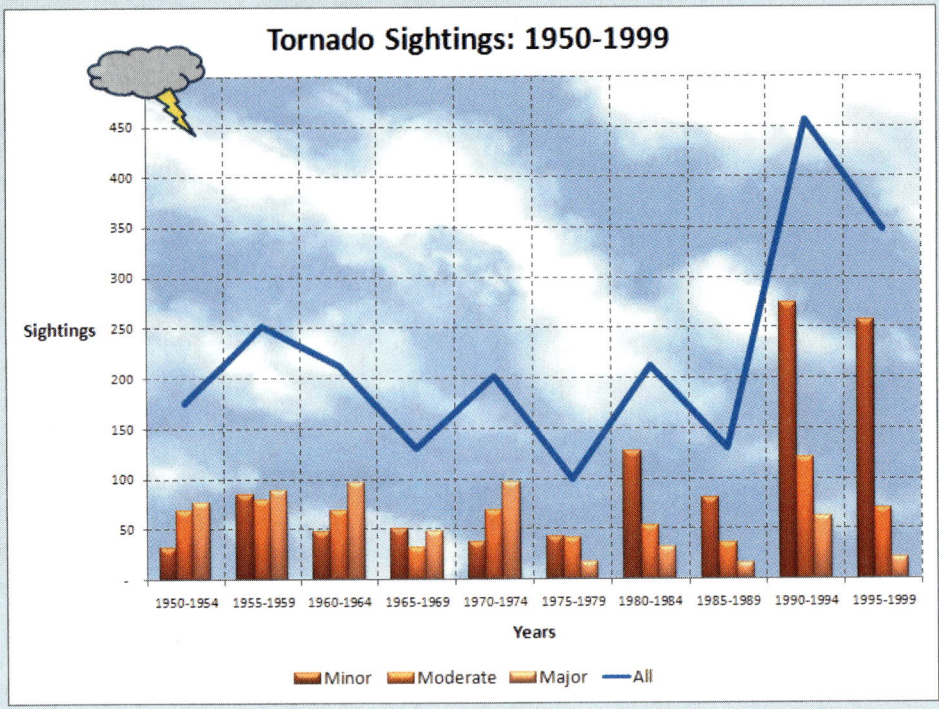

Complete the following:

1. Open the **Tornado** workbook located in the Tutorial.04\Case2 folder included with your Data Files, and then save the workbook as **Tornado Sightings** in the same folder. In the Documentation sheet, enter your name in cell B3 and the date in cell B4.
2. In the Sightings History worksheet, select the range A3:E13, and then insert a 2D clustered column chart. Move the embedded chart to a chart sheet named **Sightings Chart**.
3. Change the chart style to Style 32 (the last chart style in the fourth row of the Chart Styles gallery).
4. Insert the chart title **Tornado Sightings: 1950 – 1999** at the top of the chart in a 24-point font.
5. Add the vertical axis title **Sightings** in a 14-point font with horizontal orientation. Add the horizontal axis title **Years** in a 14-point font.
6. Move the legend to the bottom of the chart, and then set its font size to 14 points.

7. Change the line style of the horizontal gridline from a solid line to a dashed line. (*Hint:* Use the Dash type list in the Line Style group in the Format Major Gridlines dialog box.)
8. Add vertical gridlines to the major tick marks in the chart. Display the gridlines as dashed lines.
9. Change the chart type of the All data series from a column chart to a 2D line chart. Change the color of the line to a standard blue.
10. In the upper-left corner of the chart, insert a cloud shape. Set the width of the cloud to 1.2". Set the height to 0.5". Set the fill color of the cloud shape to a light gray.
11. Adjacent to the cloud shape, insert a lightning bolt shape with a height of 0.48" and a width of 0.42". Set the fill color of the shape to yellow.
12. Group the cloud and lightning bolt shapes.

EXPLORE

13. Select the plot area and change the fill to a picture fill, using the **Cloud.jpg** file located in the Tutorial.04\Case2 folder included with your Data Files. (*Hint:* Click the Shape Fill button in the Shape Styles group on the Drawing Tools Format tab, click Picture, and then locate and select the picture file.)

14. Save and close your workbook, and then submit the finished workbook to your instructor, either in printed or electronic form, as requested.

| Challenge | Case Problem 3 |

Explore how to use Excel to chart stock market data.

Data File needed for this Case Problem: Mitchell.xlsx

Hardin Financial   Kurt Lee is a financial analyst for Hardin Financial, a consulting firm in Owatonna, Minnesota. As part of his job, he records stock market activity in Excel workbooks. One of his workbooks contains the recent stock market activity of Mitchell Oil. He wants your help in creating a chart displaying the stock values. The chart should display the stock's opening, high, low, and closing values and number of shares traded for each day of the past few weeks. The volume of shares traded should be expressed in terms of millions of shares.

Excel includes several chart types specially designed for displaying stock market activity. A preview of the chart you'll create for Kurt is shown in Figure 4-48.

Figure 4-48

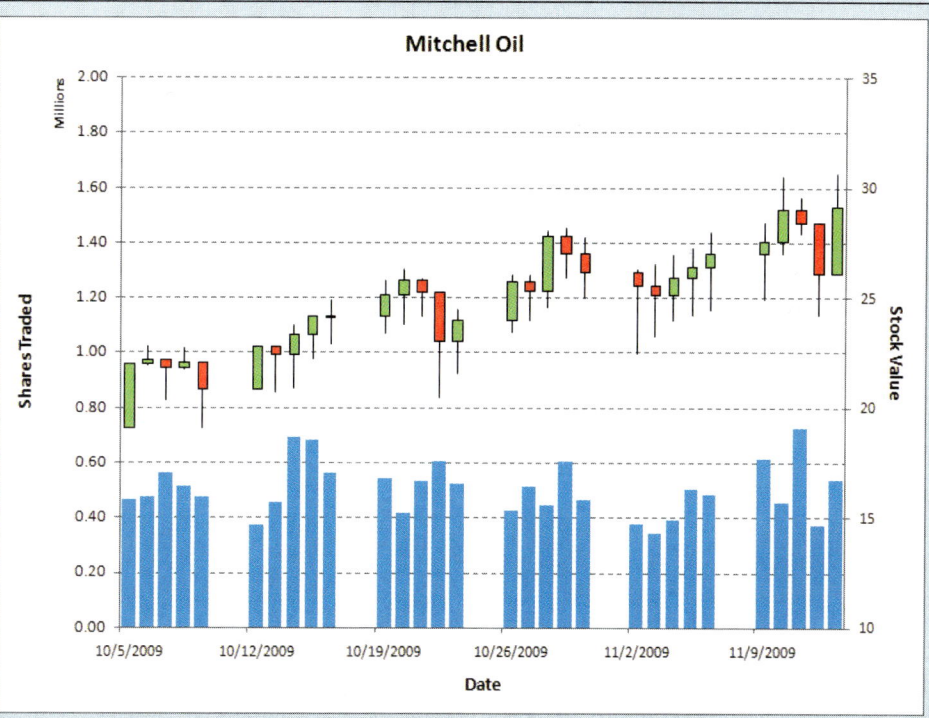

Complete the following:

1. Open the **Mitchell** workbook located in the Tutorial.04\Case3 folder included with your Data Files, and then save the workbook as **Mitchell Oil** in the same folder. In the Documentation sheet, enter your name and the date.

EXPLORE 2. In the Stock Values worksheet, select the range A3:F33, and then insert a Volume-Open-High-Low-Close stock chart. Move the embedded chart to the chart sheet named **Stock History**.

3. Insert the chart title **Mitchell Oil** above the plot area. Remove the chart legend.

4. Add the title **Date** to the primary horizontal axis, and then set its font size to 14 points. Add the title **Shares Traded** to the primary vertical axis, set its font size to 14 points, and then rotate the title 270°, as shown in Figure 4-48.

EXPLORE 5. Add the title **Stock Value** to the secondary vertical axis, set its font size to 14 points, and rotate the title 90°, as shown in Figure 4-48. (*Hint:* Open the Format Axis Title dialog box for the secondary vertical axis and use the Text Direction button found in the Alignment category.)

6. Set the font size of all of the axes values to 12 points.

7. Display the horizontal gridlines using a dashed line style. Set the interval between major tick marks on the primary horizontal axis to 7 days.

8. For the primary vertical axis, display the values in units of one million, change the number format to two decimal place accuracy, and then set the maximum value of the axis scale to 2,000,000.

9. For the secondary vertical axis, set the minimum value of the scale to 10.

10. Decrease the gap width between the columns in the plot to 30% and change the fill color to light blue.

EXPLORE 11. In a stock market chart, the daily chart values will either show an increase or a decrease from the previous day. Increases are shown with an up bar displayed in white and decreases are shown in a down bar displayed in black. Select the data series for the up bars and change their fill colors to light green. Select the data series for the down bars and change their fill colors to red.

12. Save and close your workbook, and then submit the finished workbook to your instructor, either in printed or electronic form, as requested.

Create | **Case Problem 4**

Create an Excel workbook to provide a graphical report on a sporting event.

Data File needed for this Case Problem: Basketball.xlsx

Blowout Sports Steve Eagan is the owner and operator of Blowout Sports, a sports information and scouting company located in Lexington, Kentucky. One of Steve's jobs is to provide detailed graphical reports and analysis of college basketball games for the media, coaches, and interested fans. Steve has been placing box score data and game logs into an Excel workbook. He wants to summarize this data in one worksheet using charts and graphs. He's asked you to help develop the workbook. Steve has a sample workbook containing the results of a recent basketball game for you to work on.

Complete the following:

1. Open the **Basketball** workbook located in the Tutorial.04\Case4 folder included with your Data Files, and then save the workbook as **Basketball Report** in the same folder. In the Documentation sheet, enter your name and the date.

2. The Game Report worksheet contains some basic information about a recent basketball game. Supplement this information with charts and graphs. The final format of the sheet is up to you and you may insert additional information if you desire.

3. The Game Log worksheet contains the minute-by-minute score of the game. Use the data in this worksheet to create a line chart describing the ebb and flow of the game that is embedded in the Game Report worksheet. The format of the chart is up to you, but should include titles for the chart and the axes, a chart legend overlay, vertical gridlines spaced at 4-minute intervals, and horizontal gridlines at 5-point intervals. (*Hint:* To display vertical gridlines at 4-minute intervals, you must turn off the multi-level category labels.)

4. The Box Score worksheet contains statistical summaries of the game. Use the data in this worksheet to create two column charts describing the points scored by each player on the two teams. Embed the charts in the Game Report worksheet. The format of the charts is up to you, but should include titles for the chart and axes and fill colors for the columns that employ a fill gradient.

5. The Box Score worksheet also contains team statistics. Use this data to create several pie charts that compare the two teams. Embed the pie charts in the Game Report worksheet. The final pie charts should include data labels for the pie slices and slice colors that match the team's colors (red for Wisconsin, gold for Iowa).

6. Create a chart sheet for the report that will be a cover sheet. The cover sheet should include a 3D chart from some of the data in the workbook. The format of the chart and chart sheet is up to you.

7. Save and close your workbook, and then submit the finished workbook to your instructor, either in printed or electronic form, as requested.

| Research | **Internet Assignments** |

Use the Internet to find and work with data related to the topics presented in this tutorial.

The purpose of the Internet Assignments is to challenge you to find information on the Internet that you can use to work effectively with this software. The actual assignments are updated and maintained on the Course Technology Web site. Log on to the Internet and use your Web browser to go to the Student Online Companion for New Perspectives Office 2007 at **www.course.com/np/office2007**. Then navigate to the Internet Assignments for this tutorial.

| Assess | **SAM Assessment and Training** |

If you have a SAM user profile, you may have access to hands-on instruction, practice, and assessment of the skills covered in this tutorial. Log in to your SAM account (**http://sam2007.course.com**) to launch any assigned training activities or exams that relate to the skills covered in this tutorial.

| Review | **Quick Check Answers** |

Session 4.1

1. the series name, series values, and category values
2. in a chart sheet or embedded in a worksheet
3. The chart area contains the entire chart, including the plot area. The plot area contains the region of the chart in which the data values are plotted.
4. A column chart is more appropriate because there are so many categories; pie charts make it difficult to compare one category to another.

5. Objects that are rendered as more distant from the eye will appear smaller, reducing their significance in the chart. To avoid confusion, 3D charts should include data labels explicitly identifying the values associated with different data markers.
6. A major tick mark matches each entry on the chart axis. Minor tick marks further divide the space between the major tick marks. Gridlines extend the tick marks into the plot area.
7. A bar chart is similar to a column chart except that the length of the bars, rather than the height of the columns, is used to indicate the data value.
8. Click the Axes button in the Axes group on the Chart Tools Layout tab, select the axis you want to rescale, and then click the More Options button. Enter the new axis scale in the Axis Options of the Format Axis dialog box, specifying the minimum and maximum value of the new scale and the space between the minor and major tick marks.

Session 4.2

1. Use line charts in place of column charts when the number of categories is so large that the columns will be forced to be too small to read, and the categories have a natural, sequential order (such as time and dates) that you want to show in the chart.
2. Click the Legend button in the Labels group on the Chart Tools Layout tab and select one of the overlay options, or open the Format Legend dialog box and deselect the check box to show the legend without overlaying the chart.
3. Click the Select Date button in the Date group on the Data tab. Click the Add button in the Select Data Source dialog box and select the range with the new data series.
4. A combination chart combines two or more of the Excel chart types. To create a combination chart, select a data series from the chart and apply a chart type to that series.
5. Click the Shapes button in the Illustrations group on the Insert tab, and then select a shape from the gallery.
6. Select the shape, and then enter the exact height and width in the Shape Height and Shape Width boxes in the Size group on the Drawing Tools Format tab.
7. Select all of the shapes by holding down the Shift key and clicking each of the shapes. Click the Align button in the Arrange group on the Drawing Tools Format tab, and then click Align Top.
8. Select a chart, and then click the Move Chart button in the Location group on the Chart Tools Design tab. Specify the name of the chart sheet in the Move Chart dialog box.

Ending Data Files

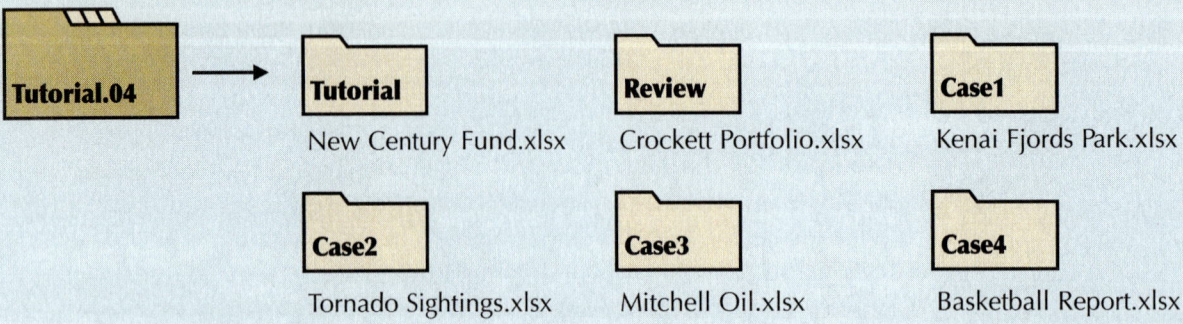

Reality Check

Excel is valuable to a wide audience of users: from accountants of *Fortune 500* companies to homeowners managing their budgets. An Excel workbook can be complex, recording data from thousands of financial transactions, or it can simply track a few monthly expenses. Everyone who has to balance a budget, track expenses, or project future income can make use of the financial tools in Excel. In this exercise, you'll use Excel to create a sample budget workbook that will contain information of your choice, using Excel skills and features presented in Tutorials 1 through 4. Use the following steps as a guide to completing your workbook.

Note: Please be sure *not* to include any personal information of a sensitive nature in any workbooks you create to be submitted to your instructor for this exercise. Later, you can update the workbooks with such information for your personal use.

1. Create a new workbook for the sample financial data. Use the first worksheet as a documentation sheet that includes your name, the date on which you start creating the workbook, and a brief description of the workbook's purpose.
2. In a second worksheet, enter realistic monthly earnings for each month of the year. Use formulas to calculate the total earnings each month, the average monthly earnings, and the total earnings for the entire year.
3. On the same worksheet, enter realistic personal expenses for each month. Divide the expenses into at least three categories, providing subtotals for each category and a grand total of all the monthly expenses. Calculate the average monthly expenses and total expenses for the year.
4. Calculate the monthly net cash flow (the value of total income minus total expenses).
5. Use the cash flow values to track the savings throughout the year. Use a realistic amount for savings at the beginning of the year. Use the monthly net cash flow values to add or subtract from this value. Project the end-of-year balance in the savings account under your proposed budget.
6. Format the worksheet's contents using appropriate text and number formats. Add colors and line borders to make the content easier to read and interpret. Use cell styles and themes to provide your worksheet with a uniform appearance.
7. Use conditional formatting to automatically highlight negative net cash flow calculated in Step 4.
8. Insert a pie chart that compares the monthly expenses for the categories.
9. Insert a column chart that charts all of the monthly expenses regardless of the category.
10. Insert a line chart that shows the change in the savings balance throughout the 12 months of the year.
11. Insert new rows at the top of the worksheet and enter titles that describe the worksheet's contents.

12. Think of a major purchase you might want to make—for example, a car. Determine the amount of the purchase and the current annual interest rate charged by your local bank. Provide a reasonable length of time to repay the loan, such as five years for a car loan or 20 to 30 years for a home loan. Use the PMT function to determine how much you would have to spend each month on the payments for your purchase. Add this information to your monthly budget. If the payment exceeds your budget, reduce the estimated price of the item you're thinking of purchasing until you determine the monthly payment you can afford under the conditions of the loan.
13. Format the worksheets for your printer. Include headers and footers that display the filename of your workbook, the workbook's author, and the date on which the report is printed. If the report extends across several pages, repeat appropriate print titles on all of the pages and include page numbers and the total number of pages on every printed page.
14. Save and close your workbook, and then submit the completed workbook to your instructor, in printed or electronic form, as requested.

Excel EX 217

Tutorial 5

Objectives

Session 5.1
- Explore a structured range of data
- Freeze rows and columns
- Plan and create an Excel table
- Rename and format an Excel table
- Add, edit, and delete records in an Excel table
- Sort data

Session 5.2
- Filter data
- Insert a Total row to summarize an Excel table
- Insert subtotals into a range of data
- Use the Outline buttons to show or hide details

Session 5.3
- Create and modify a PivotTable
- Apply PivotTable styles and formatting
- Filter and sort a PivotTable
- Group PivotTable items
- Create a PivotChart

Working with Excel Tables, PivotTables, and PivotCharts

Tracking Museum Art Objects

Case | LaFouch Museum

Henry LaFouch, a rancher in Missoula, Montana, amassed a huge collection of North American art, particularly art of the West. Henry was a well-respected, active member of the community, and he often donated art to the town. Similarly, he loaned the town artwork to place in public locations and community centers. Upon his death, Henry donated his art collection to the town of Missoula and its people. They established an art museum in his name.

Mary Littlefield was recently hired as the curator and director of the LaFouch Museum. She is responsible for assessing the current holdings and using the endowment set aside by Henry to purchase additional art in keeping with his vision for the collection. One of Mary's first tasks was to establish an accurate inventory of the museum's holdings. For each piece of artwork, she identified the title, the artist, the date acquired, the type of art, and other pertinent facts such as its location in the museum, its condition, and its appraised value. Then, she entered all this data in an Excel worksheet.

Mary asks you to help her maintain this data so she can provide current and accurate information to the administration and board of directors about the art objects. You'll work with the data using Excel table features. You will sort the data and add, modify, and delete the data to ensure it is current. You'll also filter the information to display only data that meets certain criteria. Finally, you'll summarize the data using a PivotTable and a PivotChart.

Starting Data Files

Tutorial.05

Tutorial
Museum.xlsx

Review
Art.xlsx

Case1
Pledges.xlsx

Case2
Ring.xlsx

Case3
CustLoans.xlsx

Case4
Bowls.xlsx

Session 5.1

Planning a Structured Range of Data

One of the more common uses of a worksheet is to manage data, such as lists of clients, products, and transactions. Using Excel, you can store and update data, sort data, search for and retrieve subsets of data, summarize data, and create reports. In Excel, a collection of similar data can be structured in a range of rows and columns. Each column in the range represents a **field** that describes some attribute or characteristic of a person, place, or thing, such as a last name, address, city, or state. Each row in the range represents a **record**, or a collection of related fields that are grouped together. The first row of the range contains column headers that describe the data fields in each column. Figure 5-1 shows a portion of the data Mary compiled for the LaFouch Museum's art objects. In this data, the ArtID, Artist, and Title columns are the first three fields. Each row is a record that stores the data for each art object—art ID, artist name, title, date acquired, category, condition, location, and appraised value. All the art object records make up the structured range of data. A structured range of data is commonly referred to as a list or table.

Figure 5-1 LaFouch Museum art objects data

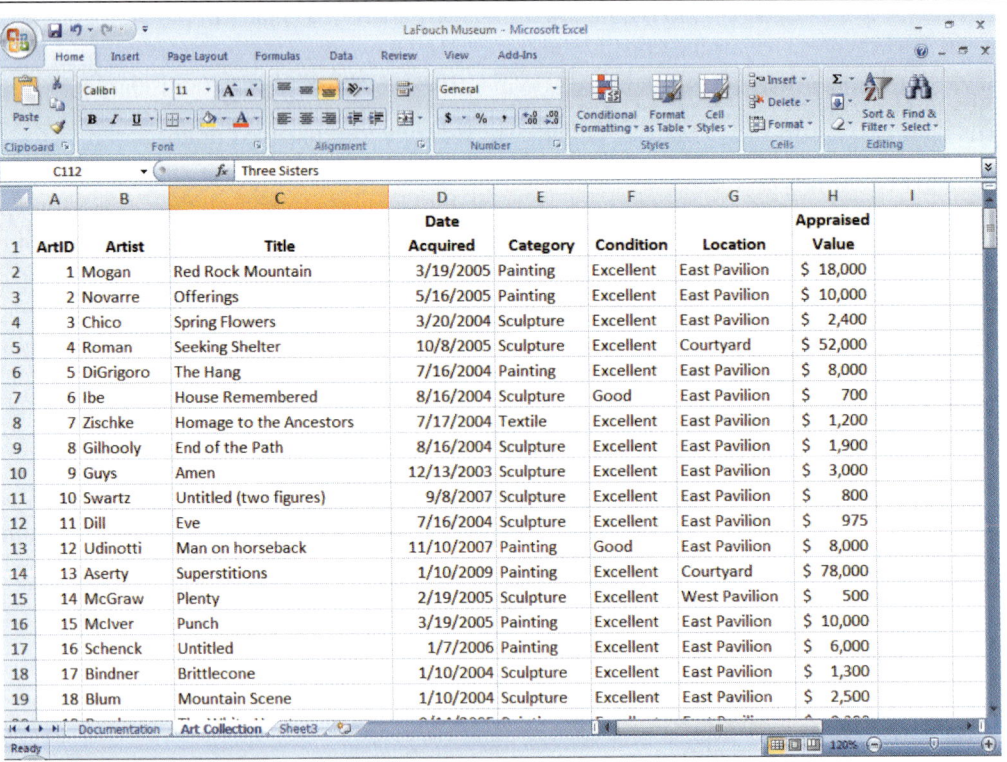

InSight | The Importance of Planning

Before you create a structured range of data, you should do some planning. Spend time thinking about how you will use the data. Consider what reports you want to create for different audiences (supervisors, customers, directors, and so forth) and the fields needed to produce those reports. Also consider the various questions, or queries, you want answered and the fields needed to create these results. The end results you want to achieve will help you determine the kind of data to include in each record and how to divide that data into fields. Careful and thorough planning will help to prevent having to redesign a structured range of data later on.

Before creating the list of art objects, Mary carefully planned what information she needs and how she wants to use it. Mary plans to use the data to track where each art object is located in the museum, its condition, the date it was acquired, its art category, and its appraised value. She wants to be able to create reports that show specific lists of art objects, such as all the objects by a specific artist or all the objects that are paintings. Based on her needs, Mary developed a **data definition table**, which is documentation that lists the fields to be maintained for each record (in this case, each art object) and a description of the information each field will include. Figure 5-2 shows Mary's completed data definition table.

Figure 5-2 — Data definition table for the art objects

Field	Description
ArtID	Unique number
Artist	Name of artist
Title	Title of art object
Date Acquired	Date of purchase or donation of art object
Category	Painting, Sculpture, Installation, Textile
Condition	Excellent, Good, Fair, Poor
Location	Location of art object
Appraised Value	Appraised value of art object

After you determine the fields and records you need, you can enter the data in a blank worksheet or use a range of data that is already entered in a worksheet. You can then work with the data in many ways. The following is a list of common operations you can perform on a structured range of data:

- Add, edit, and delete data in the range
- Sort the data range
- Filter to display only rows that meet specified criteria
- Insert formulas to calculate subtotals
- Create summary tables based on the data in the range (usually with PivotTables)
- Add data validation to ensure the integrity of the data
- Apply conditional formatting

You'll perform many of these operations on the art objects data.

| InSight | **Creating an Effective Structured Range of Data** |

For a range of data to be used effectively, it must have the same structure throughout. Keep in mind the following guidelines:
- Enter field names in the top row of the range. A **field name** (also called a **column header**) is a unique label that describes the contents of the data in that column. The row of field names is called the **header row**. Although the header row often is row 1, it can be any row.
- Use short, descriptive field names. Shorter field names are easier to remember and enable more fields to appear in the workbook window at once.
- Format field names to distinguish the header row from the data. For example, apply bold, color, and a different font size.
- Enter the same kind of data for a field in each record.
- Separate the data from other information in the worksheet by *at least* one blank row and one blank column. The blank row and column enable Excel to accurately determine the range of the data.

You'll open the workbook in which Mary entered the art objects data according to the data definition table.

To open and review the Museum workbook:

1. Open the **Museum** workbook located in the **Tutorial.05\Tutorial** folder included with your Data Files, and then save the workbook as **LaFouch Museum** in the same folder.

2. In the Documentation worksheet, enter your name in cell B3 and the current date in cell B4.

3. Switch to the **Art Collection** worksheet. This worksheet (which is shown in Figure 5-1) contains data about the museum's art objects. Currently, the worksheet lists 115 art objects. Each art object record is a separate row (rows 2 through 116) and contains eight fields (columns A through H). The top row, the header row, contains labels that describe the data in each column. The field names are boldface to make it easier to distinguish them from the data.

4. Scroll the worksheet to row 116, the last record. The column headers, in the top row, are no longer visible.

5. Press the **Ctrl+Home** keys to return to cell A1.

Freezing Rows and Columns

You want to see the column headers as you scroll the art objects data. Without the column headers visible, it is difficult to know what the data entered in each column represents. You can select rows and columns to remain visible in the workbook window as you scroll around the worksheet. **Freezing** a row or column lets you keep headings visible as you work with the data in a large worksheet. To freeze a row or column, you select the cell immediately below the row(s) and to the right of the column(s) you want to freeze. For example, if you want to keep only the column headers in the top row displayed on the screen, you click cell A2 (first column, second row), and then freeze the panes. As you scroll the data, the first row remains on the screen so the column headers are visible, making it easier to identify the data in each record.

You'll freeze the first row, which contains the column headers, so that they remain on the screen as you scroll the data.

To freeze the top row in the worksheet:

1. Click the **View** tab on the Ribbon. The Ribbon changes to display the View options.
2. In the Window group, click the **Freeze Panes** button, and then click **Freeze Top Row**. A dark, horizontal line appears below the column headers to indicate which row is frozen.
3. Scroll the worksheet to row 116. This time, the column headers remain visible as you scroll. See Figure 5-3.

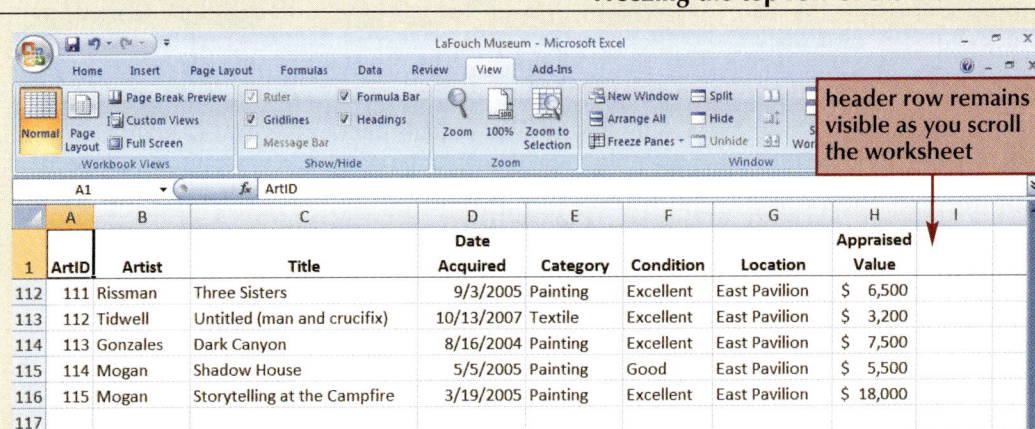

Figure 5-3 Freezing the top row of the worksheet

4. Press the **Ctrl+Home** keys to return to cell A2, the cell directly below the frozen row.

After you freeze panes, the first option on the Freeze Panes menu changes to Unfreeze Panes. This option unlocks all the rows and columns so you can scroll the entire worksheet. You will use a different method to keep the column headers visible, so you will unfreeze the top row of the worksheet.

To unfreeze the top row of the worksheet:

1. In the Window group on the View tab, click the **Freeze Panes** button. The first Freeze Panes option is now Unfreeze Panes.
2. Click **Unfreeze Panes**. The dark, horizontal line below the column headers is removed, and you can scroll all the rows and columns in the worksheet.

Creating an Excel Table

You can convert a structured range of data, such as the art objects data in the range A1:H116, to an Excel table. Recall that an Excel table is a range of related data that is managed independently from the data in other rows and columns in the worksheet. An Excel table uses features designed to make it easier to identify, manage, and analyze the groups of related data. You can create more than one Excel table in a worksheet.

InSight | Saving Time with Excel Table Features

Excel tables provide many advantages to structured ranges of data. When you create an Excel table, you can perform the same operations as you can for a structured range of data. In addition, you can do the following:

- Format the Excel table quickly using a table style.
- Add new rows and columns to the Excel table that automatically expand the range.
- Add a Total row to calculate the summary function you select, such as SUM, AVERAGE, COUNT, MIN, and MAX.
- Enter a formula in one table cell that is automatically copied to all other cells in that table column.
- Create formulas that reference cells in a table by using table and column names instead of cell addresses.

These Excel table features let you focus on analyzing and understanding the data, letting the program perform the more time-consuming tasks. You will use these Excel table features in this and other tutorials.

Next, you'll create an Excel table from the art objects data in the Art Collection worksheet. By doing so, you'll be able to take advantage of the many features and tools for working with Excel tables to analyze data effectively.

Tip
If your data does not contain column headers, Excel adds headers with the default names Column1, Column2, and so forth to the table.

To create an Excel table from the art objects data:

1. Verify that the active cell is cell **A2**, which is in the range of art objects data.
2. Click the **Insert** tab on the Ribbon, and then, in the Tables group, click the **Table** button. The Create Table dialog box opens. The range of data for the table is entered in the dialog box. See Figure 5-4.

Figure 5-4   Create Table dialog box

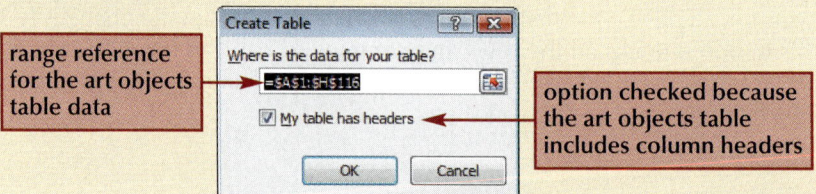

3. Click the **OK** button. The dialog box closes, and the range of data is converted to an Excel table. Filter arrows appear in the header row, the table is formatted with a predefined table style, and the Table Tools Design contextual tab appears on the Ribbon. See Figure 5-5.

Tutorial 5 Working with Excel Tables, PivotTables, and PivotCharts

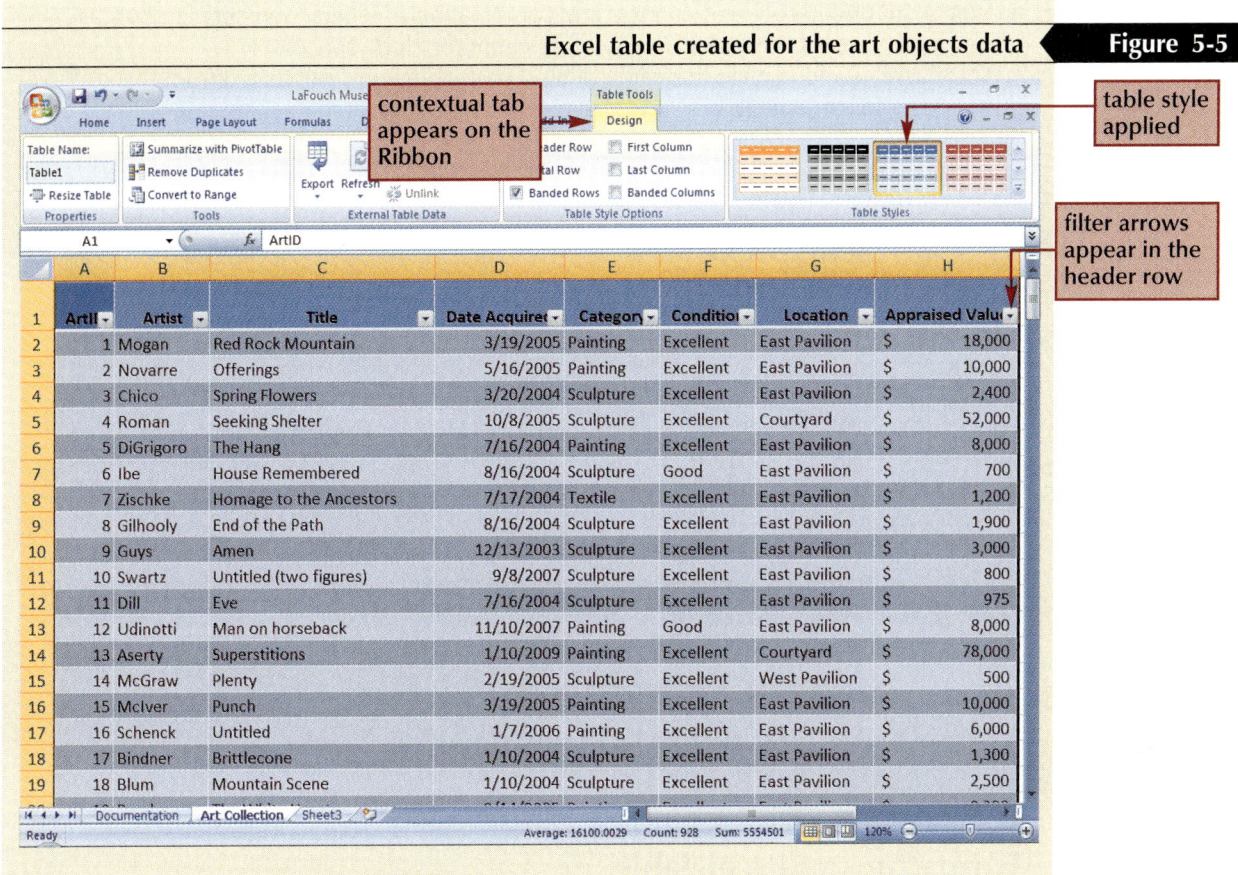

Figure 5-5   Excel table created for the art objects data

4. Scroll the table down. The text of the header row replaces the standard lettered column headings (A, B, C, and so on) as you scroll so that you don't need to freeze panes to keep the header row visible. See Figure 5-6.

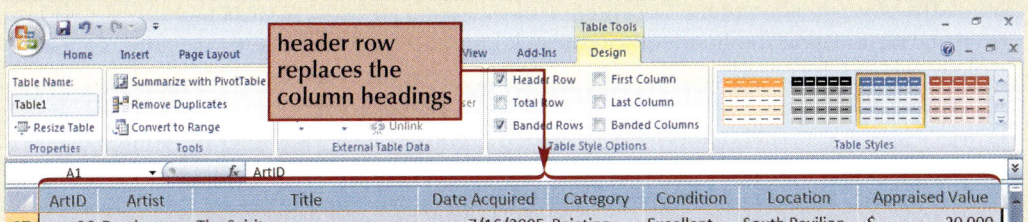

Figure 5-6   Art objects table scrolled

5. Press the **Ctrl+Home** keys to make cell A1 active. The column headings return to the standard display, and the header row scrolls back into view as row 1.

Renaming an Excel Table

Excel assigns the name Table1 to the first Excel table created in a workbook. Any additional Excel tables you create in the workbook are named consecutively, Table2, Table3, and so forth. You can assign a more descriptive name to a table, which makes it easier to identify a particular table by its content. Descriptive names are especially useful when you create more than one Excel table in the same workbook. Table names must start with a letter or an underscore and can use any combination of letters, numbers, and underscores for the rest of the name. Table names cannot include spaces.

Mary asks you to change the name of the Excel table you just created from the art objects data to ArtObjects.

To rename the Table1 table:

▶ 1. In the Properties group on the Table Tools Design tab, select **Table1** in the Table Name box. See Figure 5-7.

Figure 5-7   Table Name box

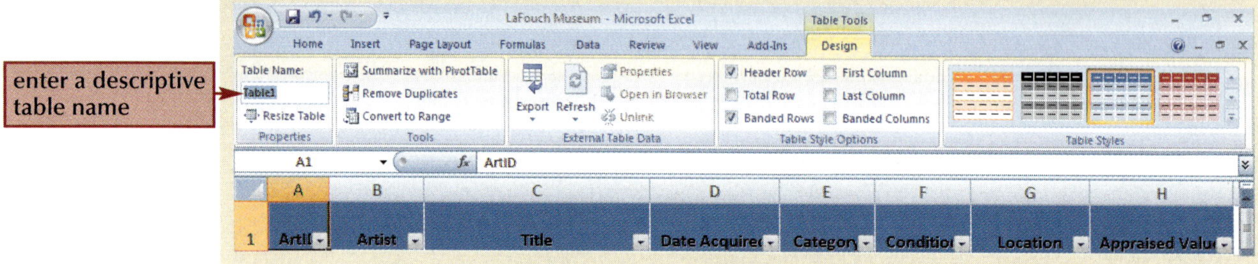

enter a descriptive table name

▶ 2. Type **ArtObjects**, and then press the **Enter** key. The Excel table is renamed ArtObjects.

Formatting an Excel Table

Refer to Figure 5-7 and note the check boxes in the Table Style Options group on the Table Tools Design tab. These check boxes enable you to quickly and easily add or remove table elements or change the format of the table elements. For example, you can choose to remove the header row in a table by deselecting the Header Row check box; you can easily toggle back to display the header row by clicking to select this check box. Similarly, you can change the appearance of a table from banded rows to banded columns by deselecting the Banded Rows check box and then clicking to select the Banded Columns check box. With these options readily available on the Table Tools Design tab, it's easy to achieve the exact content and look for a table.

Mary likes the default table style applied to the Excel table, but asks you to make a few modifications to improve the table's appearance. She wants the ArtID values in the first column of the table highlighted for emphasis. She also wants the width in the Date Acquired and Appraised Value columns reduced to better fit the values.

To format the ArtObjects table:

▶ 1. In the Table Style Options group on the Table Tools Design tab, click the **First Column** check box to insert a check mark. The text in the ArtID column is bold, and the fill color is the same as the header row.

▶ 2. Change the width of column D to **12**. The Date Acquired column width better fits the dates.

▶ 3. Change the width of column H to **12**. The Appraised Value column better fits the monetary values.

▶ 4. Click cell **A1**, if necessary.

Maintaining an Excel Table

Mary has several changes that need to be reflected in the ArtObjects table. First, the museum acquired a new painting and received a sculpture from an anonymous donor; both art objects need to be added to the table. Second, Mary just learned that the Moonlight painting needs to be repaired as its condition has deteriorated; the condition of this art object needs to be changed from Fair to Poor. Finally, one of the paintings has been sold to raise money for new acquisitions; the record for this art object needs to be deleted from the table. Mary asks you to update the ArtObjects table to reflect these changes.

Adding Records

As you maintain an Excel table, you often need to add new records. You add a record to an Excel table in a blank row. The simplest and most convenient way to add a record to an Excel table is to enter the data in the first blank row below the last record. You can then sort the data to arrange the table in the order you want. You can also insert a row within the table for the new record, if you want the record in a specific location.

| Adding a Record to an Excel Table | Reference Window |

- Click in the row below the last row of the Excel table.
- Type the values for the new record, pressing the Tab key to move from field to field.
- Press the Tab key to create another new record, or press the Enter key if this is the last record.

Next, you'll add records for the new painting and sculpture to the ArtObjects table.

To add two records to the ArtObjects table:

1. Press the **End+↓** keys to make cell A116 the active cell. This cell is in the last row of the table.

2. Press the **↓** key to move the active cell to cell A117. This is the first blank row below the table.

3. Type **116** in cell A117, and then press the **Tab** key. Cell B117 in the Artist column becomes the active cell. The table expands to include a new row in the table structure with the same formatting as the rest of the table. The AutoCorrect Options button appears so you can undo the table formatting if you hadn't intended the new data to be part of the existing table. The sizing handle in the lower-right corner of the table indicates the last row and column in the table. You can use the sizing handle to add columns or rows to the Excel table to expand it or remove them to make the table smaller. See Figure 5-8.

New row added to the ArtObjects table — Figure 5-8

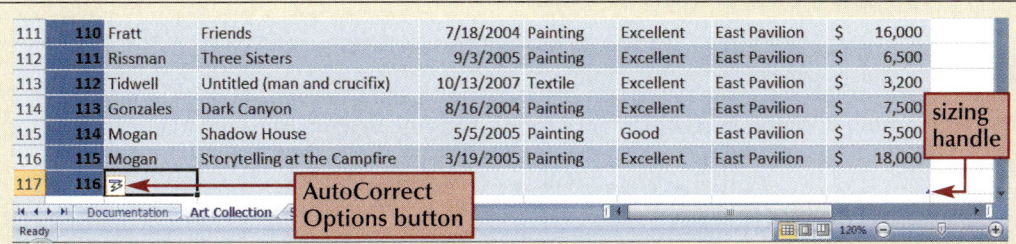

Tip

As you type in a cell, AutoComplete displays any existing entry in the column that matches the characters you typed. Press the Tab key to accept the entry or continue typing to replace it.

Trouble? If cell A118 is the active cell, you probably pressed the Enter key instead of the Tab key. Click cell B117 and then continue entering the data in Step 4.

4. In the range B117:H117, enter **Giama**, **Starry Night**, **4/3/2010**, **Painting**, **Excellent**, **South Pavilion**, and **8500** for the Artist, Title, Date Acquired, Category, Condition, Location, and Appraised Value fields, pressing the **Tab** key to move from cell to cell, and pressing the **Tab** key after you enter all the data for the record. Cell A118 becomes the active cell and the table expands to incorporate row 118.

   Next, you'll enter the second record.

5. In the range A118:H118, enter **117**, **Higgins**, **Apache Warrior**, **4/5/2010**, **Sculpture**, **Excellent**, **Garden**, and **23000**, and then click cell **A119** after the last entry. The record for the sculpture is added to the table. See Figure 5-9.

Figure 5-9 | Two records added to the ArtObjects table

two new records

Trouble? If a new row is added to the table, you probably pressed the Tab key instead of the Enter key after the last entry in the record. On the Quick Access Toolbar, click the Undo button to remove the extra row.

Finding and Editing Records

You need to update the condition for the art object with the title Moonlight. Although you can manually scroll through the table to find a specific record, a quicker and more accurate way to locate a record is to use the Find command. You edit the data in a field the same way as you edit data in a worksheet cell. You'll use the Find command to locate the record for the Moonlight painting, which has deteriorated to poor condition. Then, you'll edit the record in the table to change the condition to "Poor."

To find and edit the record for the Moonlight painting:

1. Press the **Ctrl+Home** keys to move to the top of the worksheet, and then click cell **C2** to make it the active cell.

2. In the Editing group on the Home tab, click the **Find & Select** button, and then click **Find**. The Find and Replace dialog box opens.

3. Type **Moonlight** in the Find what box, and then click the **Find Next** button. Cell C69, which contains the title Moonlight, is selected. This is the record you want. If it weren't, you would click the Find Next button again to display the next record that meets the search criteria.

4. Click the **Close** button. The Find and Replace dialog box closes.

5. Press the **Tab** key three times to move the active cell to the Condition column, and then type **P**. AutoComplete displays Poor in the cell, which is the condition text you want to enter.

▶ 6. Press the **Tab** key to enter the AutoComplete entry. The painting's condition is changed in the table.

▶ 7. Press the **Ctrl+Home** keys to make cell A1 active.

Deleting a Record

The final update you need to make to the ArtObjects table is to delete the record for the Trappers painting (art ID 90), which is the art object that was sold. You'll use the Find command to locate the painting's record. Then, you'll delete the record from the table.

To find and delete the Trappers painting record:

▶ 1. In the Editing group on the Home tab, click the **Find & Select** button, and then click **Find**. The Find and Replace dialog box opens.

▶ 2. Type **90** in the Find what box, and then click the **Find Next** button. Because Excel searches the entire worksheet (not just the current column), and because it finds the search value even if it is part of another value, the appraised value $1,900 is selected. This is not the record you want to delete.

▶ 3. Click the **Find Next** button to highlight the appraised value $1,900 for a different record, and then click the **Find Next** button again to highlight the value 90 in the ArtID column. This is the record you need to delete.

▶ 4. Click the **Close** button. The Find and Replace dialog box closes.

Next, you'll delete the record for the Trappers painting.

▶ 5. In the Cells group on the Home tab, click the **Delete button arrow**, and then click **Delete Table Rows**. The record for the Trappers painting is deleted from the table.

Trouble? If a different record was deleted, the active cell was not in the record for the Trappers painting. On the Quick Access Toolbar, click the Undo button to restore the record, and then repeat Steps 1 through 5.

▶ 6. Press the **Ctrl+Home** keys to make cell A1 active.

> **Tip**
> You can find fields whose contents match a value (such as 90) exactly by clicking the Options button in the Find & Replace dialog box, and checking the Match entire cell contents check box.

> **Tip**
> Be sure to verify that you select the correct record to delete, because a dialog box does not open for you to confirm the delete operation.

Sorting Data

The records in the ArtObjects table appear in the order that Mary entered them. As you work with tables, however, you'll want to view the same records in a different order, such as by the artist name or by the art object's location in the museum. You can rearrange, or **sort**, the records in a table or range based on the data in one or more fields. The fields you use to order the data are called **sort fields**. For example, to arrange the art objects by artist name, you can sort the data using the Artist column as the sort field.

You can sort data in ascending or descending order. **Ascending order** arranges text alphabetically from A to Z, numbers from smallest to largest, and dates from oldest to newest. **Descending order** arranges text in reverse alphabetical order from Z to A, numbers from largest to smallest, and dates from newest to oldest. In both ascending and descending order, blank fields are placed at the end of the table.

Sorting One Column Using the Sort Buttons

The simplest way to sort data with one sort field is to use the ![A-Z] or ![Z-A] button. Mary wants you to sort the art objects in ascending order by the artist. This will rearrange the table data so that the records appear in alphabetical order by the artist name.

To sort the art objects table in ascending order by the artist name:

> **Tip**
> You can also access the Sort buttons in the Editing group on the Home tab by clicking the Sort & Filter button and clicking a sort option.

1. Click any cell in the Artist column. You do not need to select the entire ArtObjects table, which consists of the range A1:H117. Excel determines the table's range when you click any cell in the table.

2. Click the **Data** tab on the Ribbon, and then, in the Sort & Filter group, click the **Sort A to Z** button ![A-Z]. The data is sorted in ascending order by Artist. The Artist filter arrow indicates the data is sorted by that column. See Figure 5-10.

Figure 5-10   ArtObjects table sorted by Artist

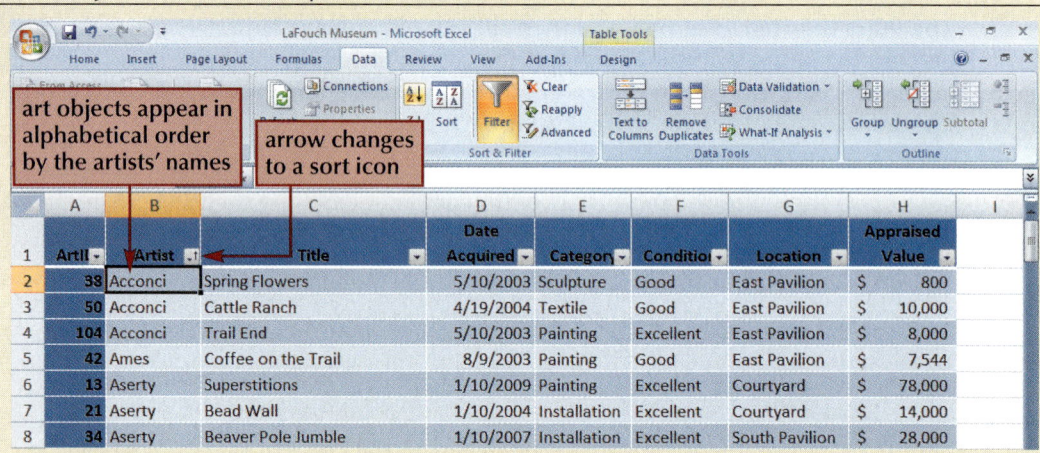

Trouble? If the data is sorted in the wrong order, you might have clicked in a different column than the Artist column. Repeat Steps 1 and 2.

Sorting Multiple Columns Using the Sort Dialog Box

Sometimes, sorting by one sort field is not adequate for your needs. For example, Mary wants you to arrange the ArtObjects table so that all the art objects in each location are together, and then all the objects for each artist within each location are together, and then each artist's work is arranged by the date acquired. You must sort on more than one column to accomplish this. The first sort field is called the **primary sort field**, the second sort field is called the **secondary sort field**, and so forth. You can use up to 64 sort fields in a single sort. In this case, the Location field is the primary sort field, the Artist field is the secondary sort field, and the Date Acquired field is the tertiary sort field. When you have more than one sort field, you should use the Sort dialog box to specify the sort criteria.

| Reference Window

Sorting Data Using Multiple Sort Fields

- Click any cell in a table or range.
- In the Sort & Filter group on the Data tab, click the Sort button to open the Sort dialog box.
- If the Sort by row exists, modify the primary sort by selections; otherwise, click the Add Level button to insert the Sort by row.
- Click the Sort by arrow, select the column heading that you want to specify as the primary sort field, click the Sort On arrow to select the type of data, and then click the Order arrow to select the sort order.
- To sort by a second column, click the Add Level button to add the first Then by row. Click the Sort by arrow, select the column heading that you want to specify as the secondary sort field, click the Sort On arrow to select the type of data, and then click the Order arrow to select the sort order.
- To sort by additional columns, click the Add Level button and select appropriate Then by, Sort On, and Order values.
- Click the OK button.

Mary wants you to sort the art objects by location, and then within location by artist, and then within artist by date acquired with the most recently acquired objects for the artist appearing before the older ones. This will make it faster for her to find information about the location and the creator of the art objects in each location.

To sort the art objects table by location, then by artist, and then by date acquired:

1. Click cell **A1** in the ArtObjects table. Cell A1 is the active cell, although you can click any cell in the table to sort the table data.

2. In the Sort & Filter group on the Data tab, click the **Sort** button. The Sort dialog box opens. Any sort specifications (sort field, type of data sorted on, and sort order) from the last sort appear in the dialog box.

   You'll set the primary sort field—Location.

3. Click the **Sort by** arrow to display the list of the column headers in the ArtObjects table, and then click **Location**.

4. If necessary, click the **Sort On** arrow to display the type of sort, and then click **Values**. Typically, you want to sort by the numbers, text, or dates stored in the cells, which are all values. However, you can also sort by formats, such as cell color, font color, and cell icon (a graphic that appears in a cell as a result of applying a conditional format).

5. If necessary, click the **Order** arrow to display sort order options, and then click **A to Z**. The sort order is set to ascending.

   The specification for the primary sort field are complete. Next, you will specify the secondary sort field—Artist. First, you need to insert a blank sort level.

6. Click the **Add Level** button. A Then by row is added below the primary sort field.

7. Click the **Then by** arrow and click **Artist**, and then verify that **Values** appears in the Sort On box and **A to Z** appears in the Order box.

   The second sort field is specified. You'll add the third sort field—Date Acquired.

8. Click the **Add Level** button to add a second Then by row.

▶ 9. Click the second **Then by** arrow and click **Date Acquired**, verify that **Values** appears in the Sort On box, click the **Order** arrow, and then click **Newest to Oldest** to specify a descending sort order for the Date Acquired values. See Figure 5-11.

Figure 5-11 | Sort dialog box with complete sort specifications

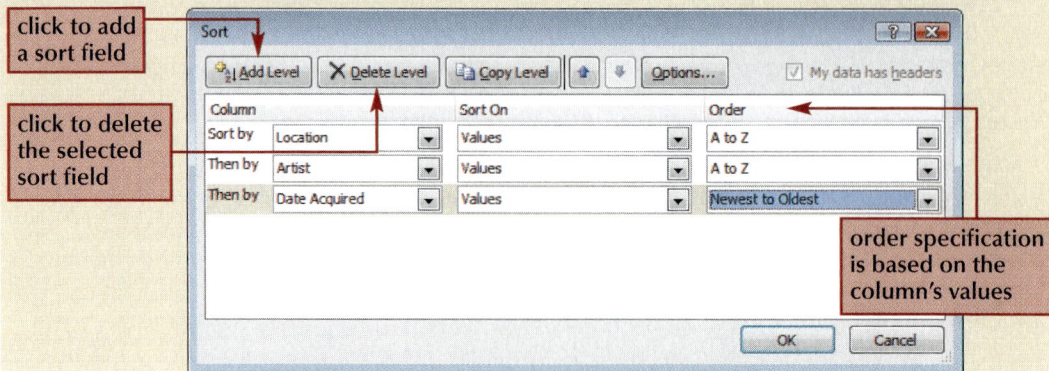

▶ 10. Click the **OK** button. Excel sorts the table records first in ascending order by Location, then within each location by Artist (again, in ascending order), and then within each artist by Date Acquired. For example, notice the three works by Acconci located in the East Pavilion; the works are arranged in descending order by the value in the Date Acquired column, so that the newer works appear before the older works. See Figure 5-12.

Figure 5-12 | Art objects sorted by Location, then by Artist, and then by Date Acquired

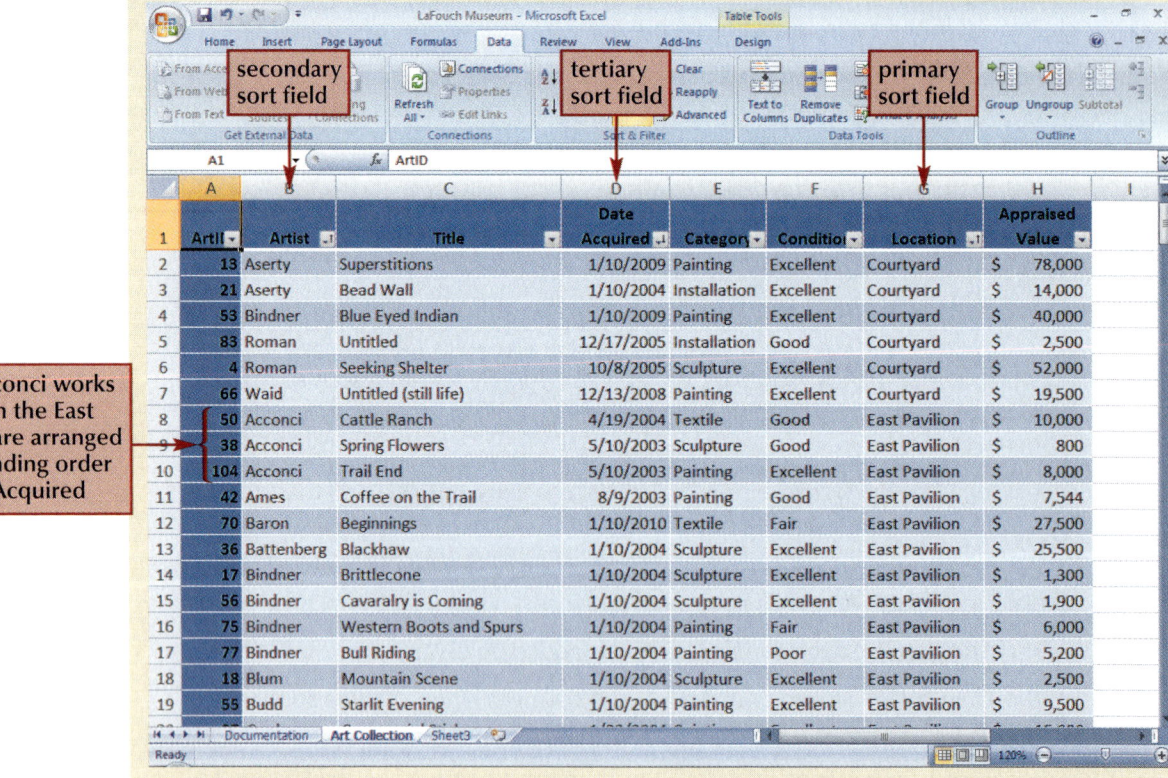

▶ 11. Scroll the table to view the sorted table data.

Mary wants to review the condition of each art object to determine how many objects need repairs. To do this more easily, she asks you to sort the objects by Condition. Because she wants to sort by only one field, you'll use the Sort A to Z button.

To sort the table by condition:

1. Click any cell in the **Condition** column.
2. In the Sort & Filter group on the Data tab, click the **Sort A to Z** button. The previous sort is removed and the art objects are now sorted in ascending order by Condition.
3. Scroll the table to see the reordered art objects.

As Mary reviews the sorted table, she realizes that the data is sorted in alphabetical order by the condition of the art objects: Excellent, Fair, Good, and Poor. This default sort order for fields with text values is not appropriate for the condition ratings. Instead, Mary wants you to base the sort on quality ranking rather than alphabetical. You'll use a custom sort list to set up the sort order Mary wants.

Sorting Using a Custom List

Text is sorted in ascending or descending alphabetical order unless you specify a different order using a custom list. A **custom list** indicates the sequence in which you want data ordered. Excel provides four predefined custom sort lists. Two days-of-the-week custom lists (Sun, Mon, Tues, ... and Sunday, Monday, Tuesday, ...) and two months-of-the-year custom lists (Jan, Feb, Mar, Apr, ... and January, February, March, April, ...). If a column consists of day or month labels, you can sort them in their correct chronological order using one of these predefined custom lists. You can also create custom lists to sort records in a sequence you define. In this case, you want to create a custom list to arrange the art objects based on their condition, with the top-quality condition appearing first, as follows: Excellent, Good, Fair, Poor.

Creating a Custom List | Reference Window

- In the Sort & Filter group on the Data tab, click the Sort button.
- Click the Order arrow, and then click Custom List.
- In the List entries box, type each entry for the custom list, pressing the Enter key after each entry.
- Click the Add button.
- Click the OK button.

You'll create a custom list that Mary can use to sort the records by the Condition field.

To create the custom list based on the Condition field:

1. Make sure the active cell is in the table, and then, in the Sort & Filter group on the Data tab, click the **Sort** button. The Sort dialog box opens, showing the sort specifications from the previous sort.
2. Click the **Sort by** arrow, click **Condition** to select the sort field (if necessary), and then verify that **Values** appears in the Sort On box.

▸ 3. Click the **Order** arrow to display the sort order options, and then click **Custom List**. The Custom Lists dialog box opens.

▸ 4. Click **NEW LIST** in the Custom lists box to place the insertion point in the List entries box.

   Next, you'll enter the condition values in the order you want them sorted. You must press the Enter key after each entry.

▸ 5. Type **Excellent**, press the **Enter** key to move the insertion point to the next line, type **Good**, press the **Enter** key, type **Fair**, press the **Enter** key, type **Poor**, and then press the **Enter** key. The four items appear in the List entries box.

▸ 6. Click the **Add** button. The custom list entries are added to the Custom lists box. See Figure 5-13.

Figure 5-13 | Custom Lists dialog box with custom list defined

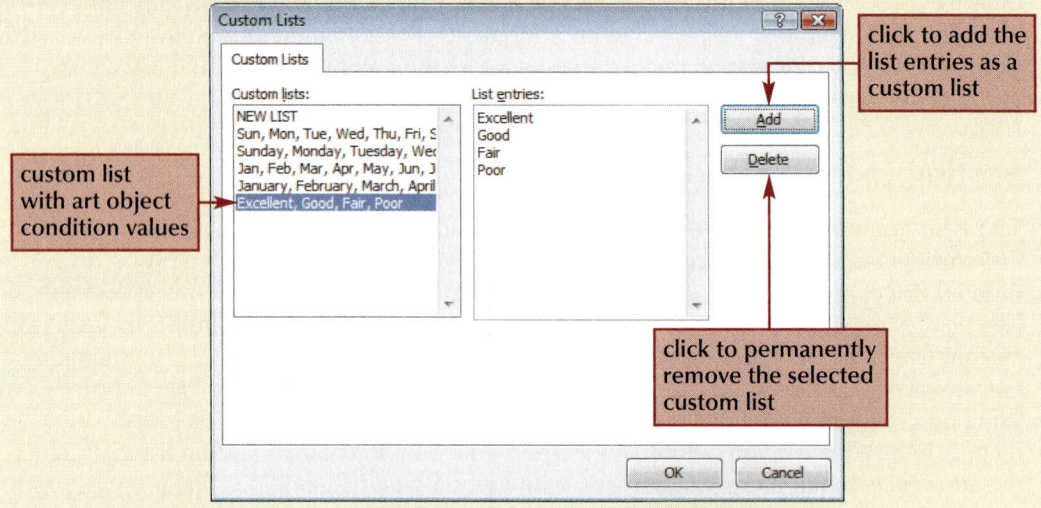

▸ 7. Click the **OK** button to return to the Sort dialog box. The custom sort list—Excellent, Good, Fair, Poor—appears in the Order box.

▸ 8. Click the **OK** button. The table is sorted based on the custom list.

▸ 9. Scroll the sorted table to verify that the art objects are sorted by their condition rankings: Excellent, Good, Fair, and Poor. Note that there are six art objects in poor condition.

In this session, you created an Excel table for the art objects, and then named and formatted the table. Next, you updated the table by adding records, editing a record, and deleting a record. You sorted the records by one field and then by three fields. Finally, you created a custom list to sort the Condition field by its quality ratings. In the next session, you will filter the ArtObjects table to retrieve specific information on some of the art objects.

Review | Session 5.1 Quick Check

1. What is the purpose of the Freeze Panes button in the Window group on the View tab? Why is this feature helpful?
2. What three elements indicate an Excel table has been created in the worksheet?

3. What fields do you use to order data?
4. An Excel table of college students tracks each student's first name, last name, major, and year of graduation. How can you order the table so students graduating the same year appear together in alphabetical order by the student's last name?
5. How do you enter a new record in an Excel table?
6. An Excel table of faculty data includes the Rank field with the values Full, Associate, Assistant, and Instructor. How can you sort the data by rank in the following order: Full, Associate, Assistant, and Instructor?
7. If you sort table data from the most recent purchase date to the oldest purchase date, in what order have you sorted the data?

Session 5.2

Filtering Data

Mary is working on her budget for the upcoming year. She needs to determine which art objects the museum can afford to repair this year. She asks you to prepare a list of all paintings in poor condition. Mary will then examine these paintings, estimate the repair costs, and decide which ones to place on the upcoming year's repairs list.

Although you could sort the list of paintings by condition to group those in poor condition, you are still working with the entire table. A better solution is to display only the specific records you want. The process of displaying a subset of rows in the table that meets the criteria you specify is called **filtering**. Filtering, rather than rearranging the data as sorting does, temporarily hides any records that do not meet the specified criteria. After data is filtered, you can sort, copy, format, chart, and print it.

Filtering Using One Column

When you create an Excel table, filter arrows appear in each of the column headers. You can see these filter arrows in the ArtObjects table you created for Mary. You click a filter arrow to open the Filter menu for that field. You can use options on the Filter menu to create three types of filters. You can filter a column of data by its cell colors or font colors; by a specific text, number, or date filter, although the specific choices depend on the type of data in the column; or by selecting one or more of the exact values by which you want to filter in the column. After you filter a column, the Clear Filter command becomes available so you can remove the filter and redisplay all the records.

Mary wants to see only paintings in poor condition. First, you need to filter the ArtObjects table to show only those records with the value "Paintings" in the Category column. Remember, filtering the data only hides some of the records.

> **Tip**
>
> You can display or hide filter arrows for an Excel table or a range of data by using the Filter button in the Sort & Filter group on the Data tab.

To filter the ArtObjects table to show only paintings:

▶ 1. If you took a break after the previous session, make sure the LaFouch Museum workbook is open, the Art Collection worksheet is active, and the ArtObjects table is active.

▶ 2. Click the **Category filter arrow**. The Filter menu opens, as shown in Figure 5-14, listing the unique entries in the Category column: Installation, Painting, Sculpture, and Textile. Initially, all the items are selected, but you can select which items you want to use to filter the data. In this case, you want to select the Painting item.

Figure 5-14 — Filter menu for the Category column

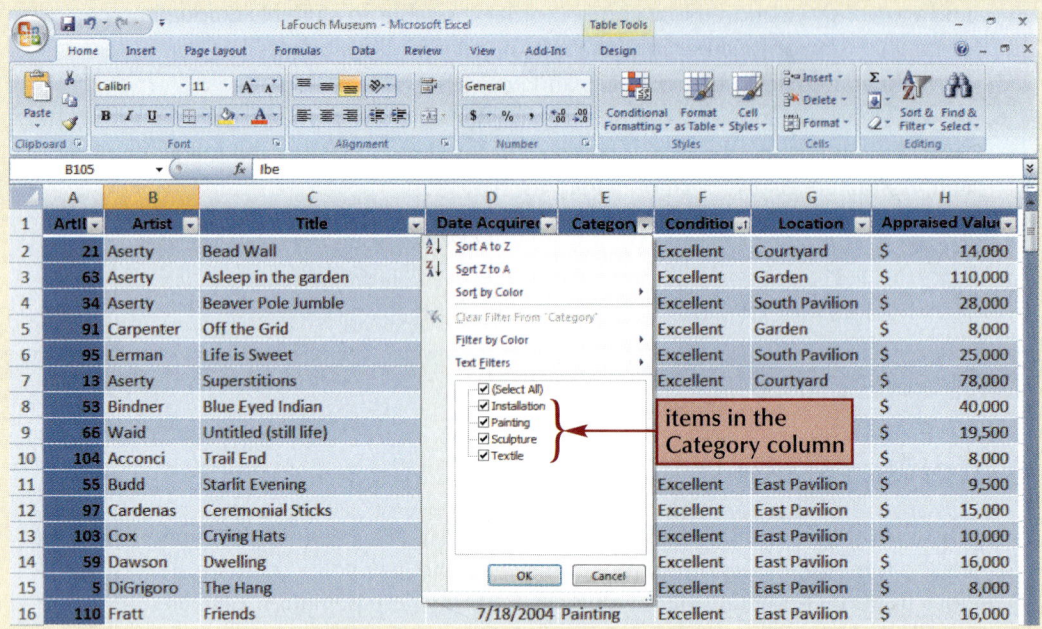

Notice the **Sort by Color** and **Filter by Color** options in the filter menu. These options enable you to filter and sort data using color, one of many cell attributes. Suppose that Mary used specific cell background colors for certain works of art in the ArtObjects table. For example, she might want to highlight those works given to the museum by its two most generous donors, using yellow for one and red for the other. So, the cells in the Title column for the two donors would be formatted with these colors. You could then click the Sort by Color option in the filter menu to display a list of available colors by which to sort, and then click the specific color so that all the records for the first donor (formatted with yellow) would appear together, and all the records for the second donor (formatted with red) would appear together. Similarly, you could click the Filter by Color option to display a submenu with the available colors by which to filter, and then click a color. In this example, if you selected yellow, only the records for the first donor would be displayed in the table, allowing you to focus on just those records.

▶ 3. Click the **(Select All)** check box to remove the check marks from all the Category items, and then click the **Painting** check box to insert a check mark. The filter will show only those records that match the checked item and hide records that contain the unchecked items.

▶ 4. Click the **OK** button. The filter is applied. The status bar lists the number of paintings found in the entire table. Fifty-seven of the 116 records in the table are displayed. See Figure 5-15.

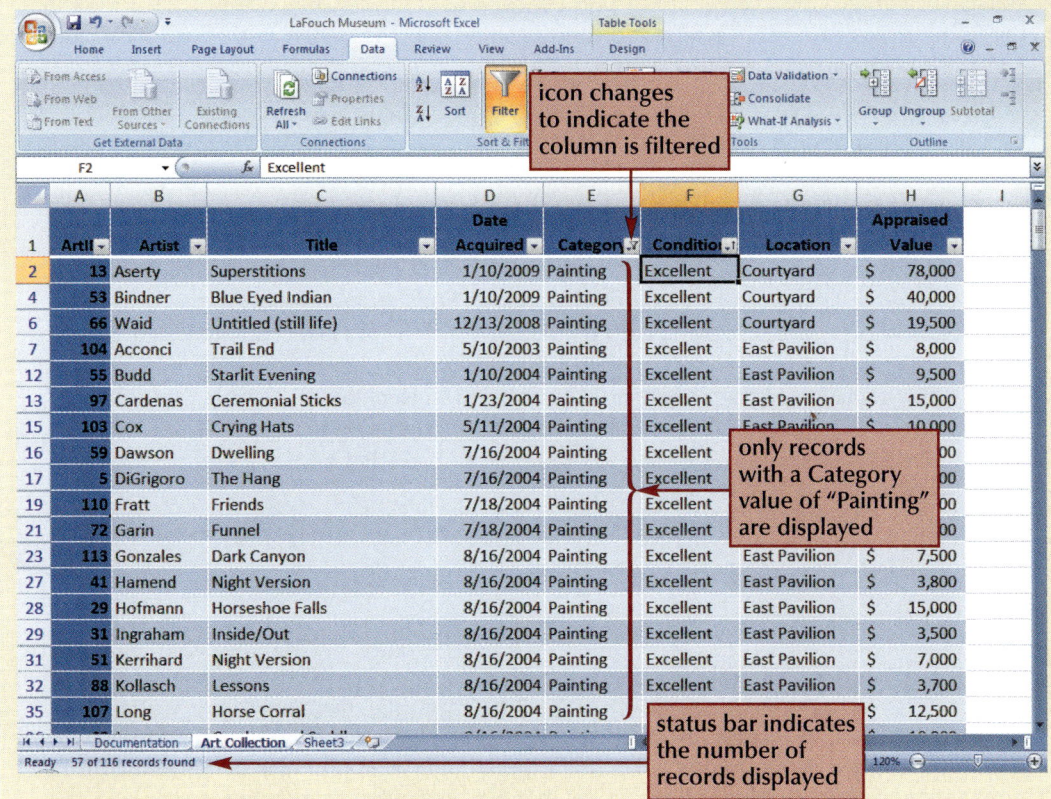

Figure 5-15 ArtObjects table filtered to show only paintings

5. Review the records to verify that only records with a value equal to Painting in the Category column are visible. All records that do not have the value Painting in this column are hidden. Notice the gaps in the row numbers in the worksheet. As a reminder that the records are filtered, the row numbers of the filtered records are blue and the Category filter arrow changes to indicate that this column is being used to filter the table.

6. Point to the **Category filter arrow**. A ScreenTip—Category: Equals "Painting"—describes the filter applied to the column.

InSight | Exploring Text Filters

You can use different text filters to display the records you want. If you know only part of a text value or want to match a certain pattern, you can use the Begins With, Ends With, and Contains operators to filter a text field to match the pattern you specify.

The following examples are based on a student directory table that includes First Name, Last Name, Address, City, State, and Zip fields:

- To find a student named Smith, Smithe, or Smythe, create a text filter using the Begins With operator. In this example, use Begins With *Sm* to display all records that have *Sm* at the beginning of the text value.
- To Find anyone whose Last Name ends in "son" (such as Robertson, Anderson, Dawson, Gibson, and so forth), create a text filter using the Ends With operator. In this example, use Ends With *son* to display all records that have *son* as the last characters in the text value.
- To find anyone whose street address includes *Central* (such as 101 Central Ave, 1024 Central Road, or 457 Avenue De Central), create a text filter using the Contains operator. In this example, use Contains *Central* to display all records that have *Central* anywhere in the text value.

When you create a text filter, think about the results you want. Then, consider what text filter you can use to best achieve those results.

Filtering Using Multiple Columns

If you need to further restrict the records that appear in a filtered table, you can filter by one or more of the other columns. Each additional filter is applied to the currently filtered data and further reduces the records that are displayed. Mary wants to see only paintings that are in poor condition, rather than all the paintings in the ArtObjects table. To do this, you need to filter the paintings records to display only those with the value "Poor" in the Condition column. You'll use the filter arrow in the Condition column to add this second filter criterion to the filtered data.

To filter the painting records to show only those in poor condition:

1. Click the **Condition filter arrow**. The Filter menu opens.
2. Click the **Excellent**, **Good**, and **Fair** check boxes to remove the check marks. The Poor check box remains checked, so only paintings in poor condition will be displayed.
3. Click the **OK** button. The ArtObjects table is further filtered and shows the three paintings that are in poor condition. See Figure 5-16.

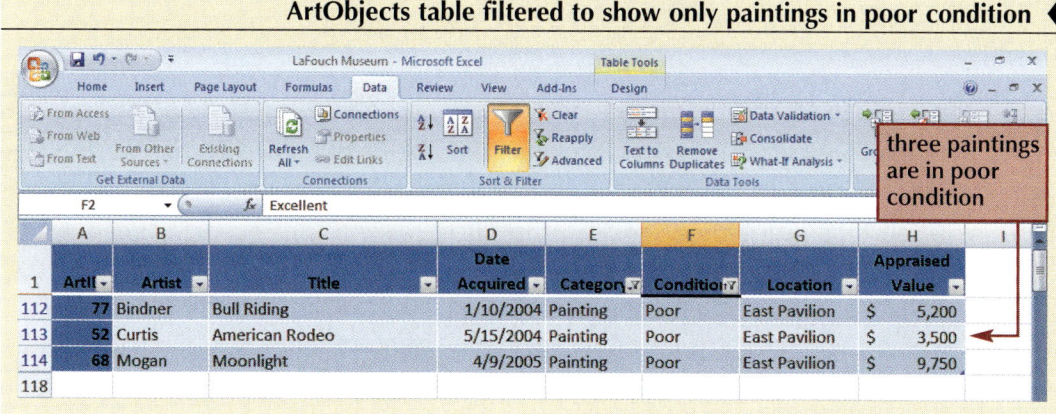

Figure 5-16 ArtObjects table filtered to show only paintings in poor condition

Clearing Filters

When you want to see all the data in a filtered table, you can **clear** (or remove) the filters. When you clear a filter from a column, any other filters are still applied. For example, in the ArtObjects table, you would see all the paintings in the table if you cleared the filter from the Condition field, or you would see all the art objects in poor condition if you cleared the filter from the Category field. To redisplay all the art objects in the table, you need to clear both the Condition filter and the Category filter. You will do this now to restore the entire table of art objects.

To clear the filters to show all the records in the ArtObjects table:

1. Click the **Condition filter arrow**, and then click **Clear Filter From "Condition"**. The Condition filter is removed from the table. The table shows only paintings because the Category filter is still in effect.

2. Click the **Category filter arrow**, and then click **Clear Filter From "Category"**. The Category condition is removed, and all the records in the ArtObjects table are displayed again.

Selecting Multiple Filter Items

You can often find the information you need by selecting a single filter item from a list of filter items. Sometimes, however, you need to specify a more complex set of criteria to find the records you want. Earlier, you selected one filter item for the Category column and one filter item for the Condition column to display the records whose Category field value equals Painting AND whose Condition field value equals Poor. The records had to have both values to be displayed. The AND condition requires that all of the selected criteria be true for the record to be displayed. Now you want to select two filter items for the Category column to display records whose Category field value equals Installation OR whose Category field value equals Sculpture. The records must have at least one of these values to be displayed. A filter that selects more than one item from the list of items uses the OR condition, which requires that only one of the selected criteria be true for a record to be displayed. For example, if you check the Installation and Sculpture check boxes in the Category filter items, you create the filter condition *"Category equal to installation"* OR *"Category equal to sculpture."*

The museum's board of directors wants a list of all installations or sculptures valued above $20,000. Mary asks you to create a list of these holdings.

> **To select multiple filter items:**
>
> ▶ 1. Click the **Category filter arrow**, and then click the **Painting** and **Textile** check boxes to remove the check marks.
>
> ▶ 2. Verify that the **Installation** and **Sculpture** check boxes remain checked. When you select more than one item, you create a multiselect filter.
>
> ▶ 3. Click the **OK** button. The ArtObjects table is filtered, and the status bar indicates that 51 out of 116 records are either an installation or a sculpture.

Creating Criteria Filters to Specify More Complex Criteria

Filter items enable you to filter a range of data or an Excel table based on exact values in a column. However, many times you need broader criteria. **Criteria filters** enable you to specify various conditions in addition to those that are based on an "equals" criterion. For example, you might want to find all art objects with an appraised value greater than $20,000 or acquired after 7/1/2009. You use criteria filters to create these conditions.

The type of criteria filters available change depending on whether the data in a column contains text, numbers, or dates. Figure 5-17 shows some of the options for text, number, and date criteria filters.

Figure 5-17 ▶ Options for text, number, and date criteria filters

Filter	Criteria	Records displayed
Text	Equals	Exactly match the specified text string
	Does Not Equal	Do not exactly match the specified text string
	Begins With	Begin with the specified text spring
	Ends With	End with the specified text string
	Contains	Have the specified text string anywhere
	Does Not Contain	Do not have the specified text string anywhere
Number	Equals	Exactly match the specified number
	Greater Than or Equal to	Are greater than or equal to the specified number
	Less Than	Are less than the specified number
	Between	Are greater than or equal to *and* less than or equal to the specified numbers
	Top 10	Are the top or bottom 10 (or the specified number)
	Above Average	Are greater than the average
Date	Today	Have the current date
	Last Week	Are in the prior week
	Next Month	Are in the month following the current month
	Last Quarter	Are in the previous quarter of the year (quarters defined Jan, Feb, Mar; Apr, May, June; and so on)
	Year to Date	Are since January 1 of the current year to the current date
	Last Year	Are in the previous year (based on the current date)

You will modify the filtered ArtObjects table to add a criteria filter that includes only objects valued greater than $20,000.

To create a number criteria filter:

▸ 1. Click the **Appraised Value filter arrow**, and then point to **Number Filters**. A menu opens displaying the comparison operators available for columns of numbers.

▸ 2. Click **Greater Than**. The Custom AutoFilter dialog box opens. The upper-left box lists *is greater than*, the comparison operator you want to use to filter the Appraised Value column. You enter the value you want to use for the filter criteria in the upper-right box, which, in this case, is 20,000.

▸ 3. Type **20000** in the upper-right box. See Figure 5-18. You use the lower set of boxes if you want the filter to meet a second condition. You click the And option button to display rows that meet both criteria. You click the Or option button to display rows that meet either of the two criteria. You only want to set one criteria for this filter, so you'll leave the lower boxes empty.

Custom AutoFilter dialog box   Figure 5-18

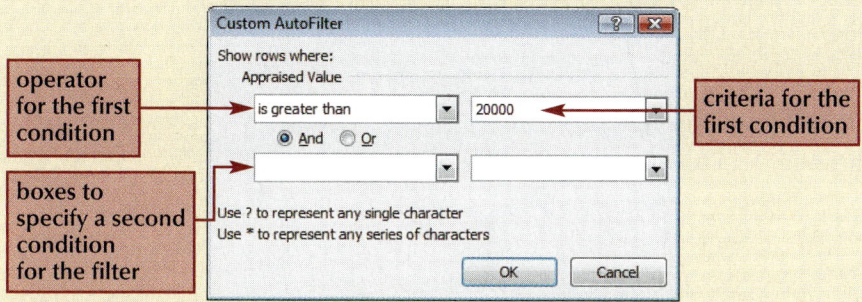

▸ 4. Click the **OK** button. The status bar indicates that 7 of 116 records were found. The seven records that appear in the ArtObjects table are either installations or sculptures and have an appraised value greater than $20,000.

Before Mary sends this list to the board of directors, you'll sort the filtered data to show the largest appraised value first. Although you can sort the data using Sort buttons, as you did earlier, these sort options are also available on the Filter menu for your convenience. If you want to perform a more complex sort, you still need to use the Sort dialog box.

To sort the filtered table data:

▸ 1. Click the **Appraised Value filter arrow**. The Filter menu opens. The sort options are at the top of the menu.

▸ 2. Click **Sort Largest to Smallest**. The filtered table now displays installations and sculptures with an appraised valued above $20,000 sorted in descending order. See Figure 5-19.

Figure 5-19 — Filtered ArtObjects table

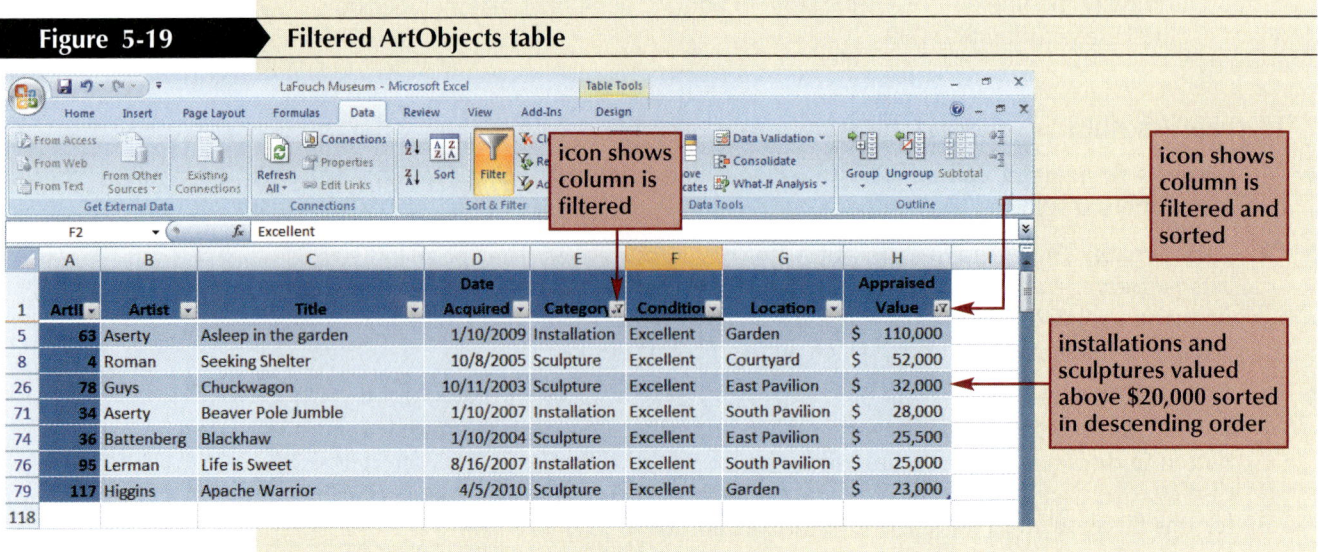

Mary will send this list to the board of directors. You need to restore the entire table of art objects, which you can do by clearing all the filters at one time.

To clear all the filters from the ArtObjects table:

▶ 1. Click the **Data** tab on the Ribbon, if necessary.

▶ 2. In the Sort & Filter group, click the **Clear** button. All the records appear in the table.

Using the Total Row to Calculate Summary Statistics

You can calculate summary statistics (including sum, average, count, maximum, and minimum) on all the columns in an Excel table or on a filtered table in a Total row. A **Total row**, which you can display at the end of the table, is used to calculate summary statistics for the columns in an Excel table. When you click in each cell in the Total row, an arrow appears that you can click to open a list of the most commonly used functions.

Mary is creating a brochure for an upcoming fund-raising event, and wants to know the number and value of the items in the current museum collection, excluding art objects in poor condition. She asks you to filter the table to display art objects that are in excellent, good, and fair condition. Then, you will display the Total row for the ArtObjects table to count the number of art objects and add their total appraised value.

To add a Total row and select summary statistics:

▶ 1. Click the **Condition filter arrow**, click the **Poor** check box to remove the check mark, and then click the **OK** button. The ArtObjects table displays objects that are in excellent, good, or fair condition. The status bar indicates that 110 of 116 records remain in the filtered table.

Next, you will display the Total row.

▶ 2. Click the **Table Tools Design** tab on the Ribbon, and then, in the Table Style Options group, click the **Total Row** check box to insert a check mark.

▶ **3.** Scroll to the end of the table. The Total row is the last row of the table, the word "Total" appears in the leftmost cell, and the total appraised value $1,118,723 appears in the rightmost cell. By default, the Total row adds the numbers in the last column of the Excel table or counts the number of records if the data in the last column contains text. See Figure 5-20.

Figure 5-20   Total row added to the ArtObjects table

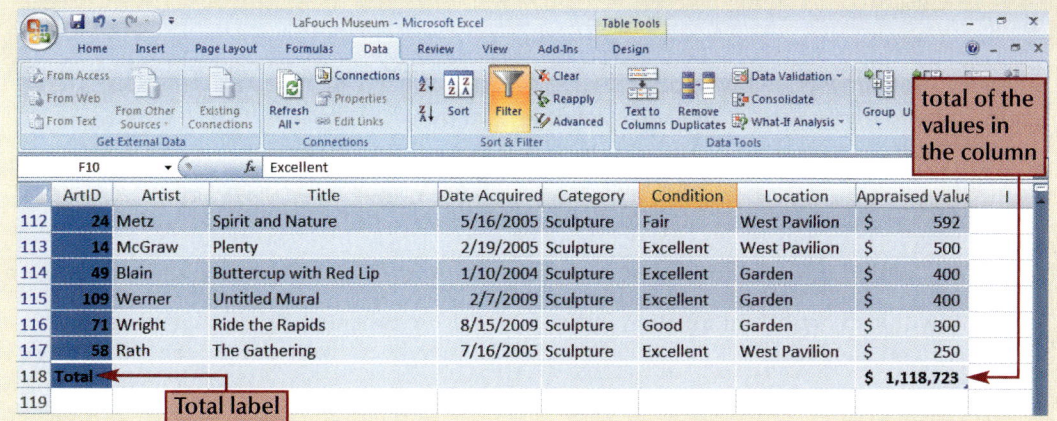

In the Artist cell of the Total row, you want to count the number of records whose Appraised Values were added in the last column.

▶ **4.** Click cell **B118** (the Artist cell in the Total row), and then click the **arrow button** to display a list of functions. None is the default function in all columns except the last column. See Figure 5-21.

Figure 5-21   Total row functions

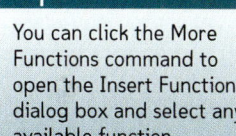

Tip

You can click the More Functions command to open the Insert Function dialog box and select any available function.

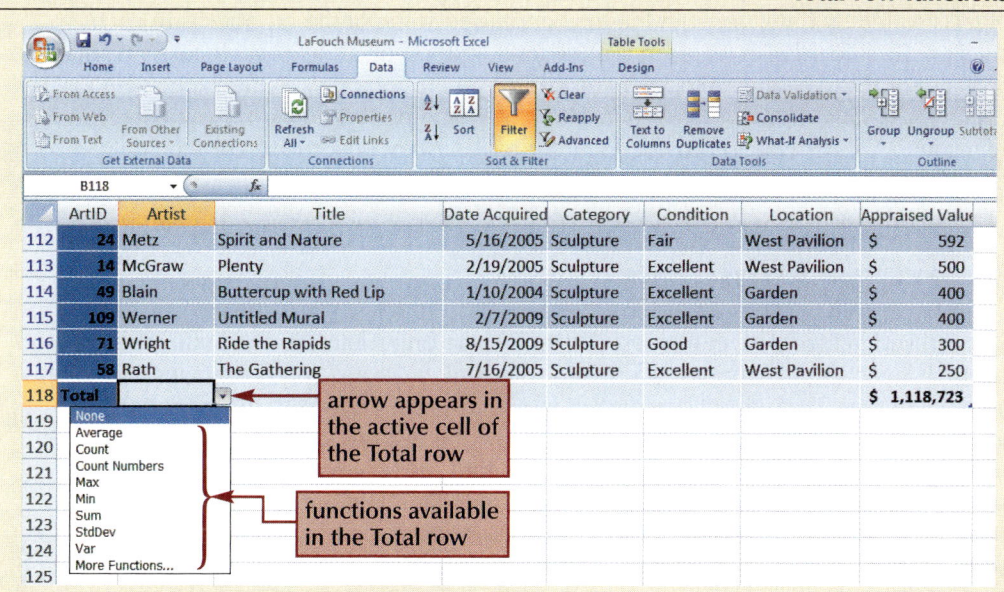

▶ **5.** Click **Count**. The number 110 appears in the cell, which is the number of records in the filtered ArtObjects table. See Figure 5-22.

Figure 5-22 Count of records in the filtered table

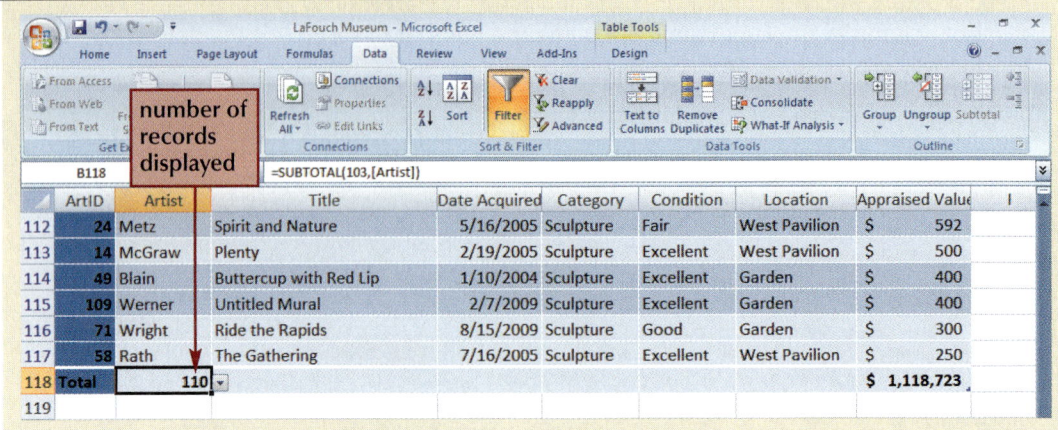

Mary will include this information in her fund-raising brochure. You will remove the Total row and clear the filter.

Tip
If you redisplay the Total row, the functions you last used will appear even after you save, close, and then reopen the file.

To remove the Total row and clear the filter from the ArtObjects table:

1. In the Table Style Options group on the Table Tools Design tab, click the **Total Row** check box to remove the check mark. The Total row is no longer visible.

2. Scroll to the top of the table, click the **Condition filter arrow**, and then click **Clear Filter From "Condition"**. The ArtObjects table displays all the art objects.

The board of directors asked Mary to create a report that shows all the museum's art objects sorted by Category with the total appraised value of the art objects in each category. The board also wants to see the total appraised value for each category after the last item of that category. Although you could use the Total row in the Excel table to calculate the results, you would need to filter, total, and print the data for each category separately. A faster way to provide the information Mary needs is to use the Subtotal command.

Inserting Subtotals

You can summarize data in a range of data by inserting subtotals. The Subtotal command offers many kinds of summary information, including counts, sums, averages, minimums, and maximums. The Subtotal command inserts a subtotal row into the range for each group of data and adds a grand total row below the last row of data. Because Excel inserts subtotals whenever the value in a specified field changes, you need to sort the data so that records with the same value in a specified field are grouped together *before* you use the Subtotal command. The Subtotal command cannot be used in an Excel table, so you must first convert the Excel table to a range.

Tutorial 5 Working with Excel Tables, PivotTables, and PivotCharts | Excel EX 243

Calculating Subtotals for a Range of Data | Reference Window

- Sort the data by the column for which you want a subtotal.
- If the data is in an Excel table, in the Tools group on the Table Tools Design tab, click the Convert to Range button, and then click the Yes button to convert the Excel table to a range.
- In the Outline group on the Data tab, click the Subtotal button.
- Click the At each change in arrow, and then click the column that contains the group you want to subtotal.
- Click the Use function arrow, and then click the function you want to use to summarize the data.
- In the Add subtotal to box, click the check box for each column that contains the values you want to summarize.
- To calculate another category of subtotals, click the Replace current subtotals check box to remove the check mark, and then repeat the previous three steps.
- Click the OK button.

To produce the results Mary needs, you will sort the art objects by category and calculate subtotals in the Appraised Value column for each category grouping.

To calculate appraised values subtotals for each category of art object:

1. Click the **Category filter** arrow, and then click **Sort A to Z** on the Filter menu. The ArtObjects table is sorted in ascending order by the Category field. This ensures one subtotal is created for each category.

2. In the Tools group on the Table Tools Design tab, click the **Convert to Range** button. A dialog box opens, asking if you want to convert the table to a normal range.

3. Click the **Yes** button. The Excel table is converted to a range. You can tell this because the filter arrows and the Table Tools Design tab disappear, and the Home tab on the Ribbon is selected.

   Next, you'll calculate the subtotals. The active cell needs to be in the header row so you can select the correct column.

4. Press the **Ctrl+Home** keys to make cell A1 the active cell, click the **Data** tab on the Ribbon, and then, in the Outline group, click the **Subtotal** button. The Subtotal dialog box opens. See Figure 5-23.

Subtotal dialog box | Figure 5-23

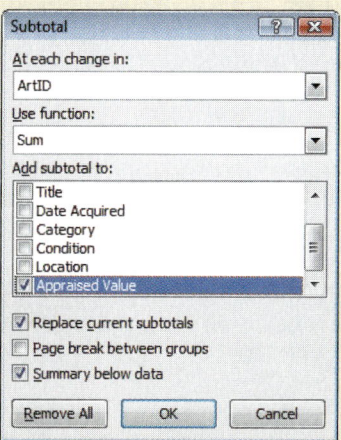

5. Click the **At each change in** arrow, and then click **Category**. This is the column you want Excel to use to determine where to insert the subtotals; it's the column you sorted. A subtotal will be calculated at every change in the Category value.

6. If necessary, click the **Use function** arrow, and then click **Sum**. The Use function list provides several options for subtotaling data, including counts, averages, minimums, maximums, and products.

7. In the Add subtotal to list box, make sure only the **Appraised Value** check box is checked. This specifies the Appraised Value field as the field to be subtotaled. If the data already included subtotals, you would check the Replace current subtotals check box to replace the existing subtotals or uncheck the option to display the new subtotals on separate rows above the existing subtotals. Because the data has no subtotals, it makes no difference whether you select this option.

8. Make sure the **Summary below data** check box is checked. This option places the subtotals below each group of data, instead of above the first entry in each group, and places the grand total at the end of the data, instead of at the top of the column just below the row of column headings.

9. Click the **OK** button to insert subtotals into the data. Excel inserts rows below each category group and displays the subtotals for the appraised value of each art category. A series of Outline buttons appears to the left of the worksheet so you can display or hide the detail rows within each subtotal.

   Trouble? If each item has a subtotal following it, you probably forgot to sort the data by Category. Repeat Steps 1 through 9.

10. Scroll through the data to see the subtotals below each category and the grand total at the end of the data. See Figure 5-24.

Figure 5-24 — Subtotals and grand total added to the art objects data

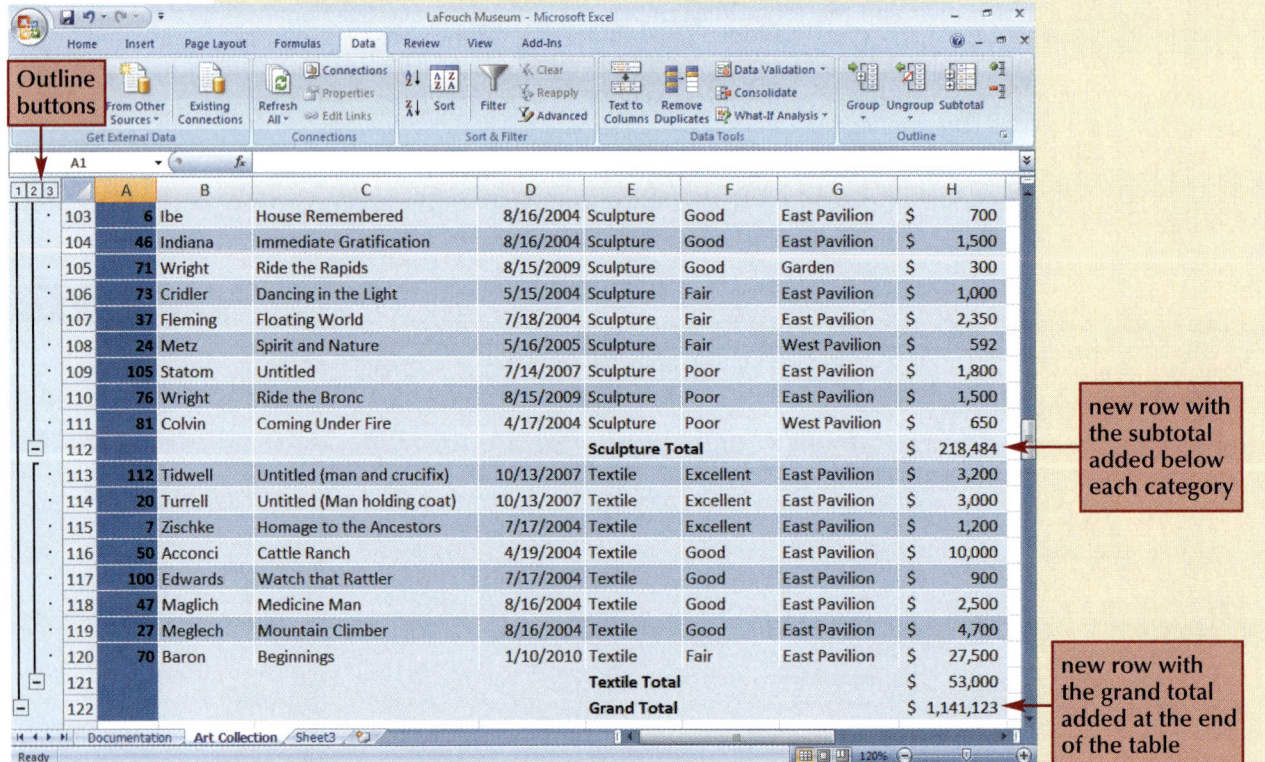

Trouble? If necessary, increase the column width so you can view the subtotal values.

Using the Subtotal Outline View

In addition to displaying subtotals, the Subtotal feature "outlines" your worksheet so you can control the level of detail that is displayed. The three Outline buttons at the top of the outline area, as shown in Figure 5-24, allow you to show or hide different levels of detail in the worksheet. By default, the highest level is active, in this case, Level 3. Level 3 displays the most detail—the individual art object records, the subtotals, and the grand total. Level 2 displays the subtotals and the grand total, but not the individual records. Level 1 displays only the grand total.

The subtotals are useful, but Mary wants you to isolate the different subtotal sections so that she can focus on them individually. You will use the Outline buttons to prepare a report for Mary that includes only subtotals and the grand total.

To use the Outline buttons to hide records:

▶ 1. Click the **Level 2 Outline** button. The individual art object records are hidden, and you see only the subtotals for each category and the grand total. See Figure 5-25.

Figure 5-25 Table displaying only subtotals and grand total

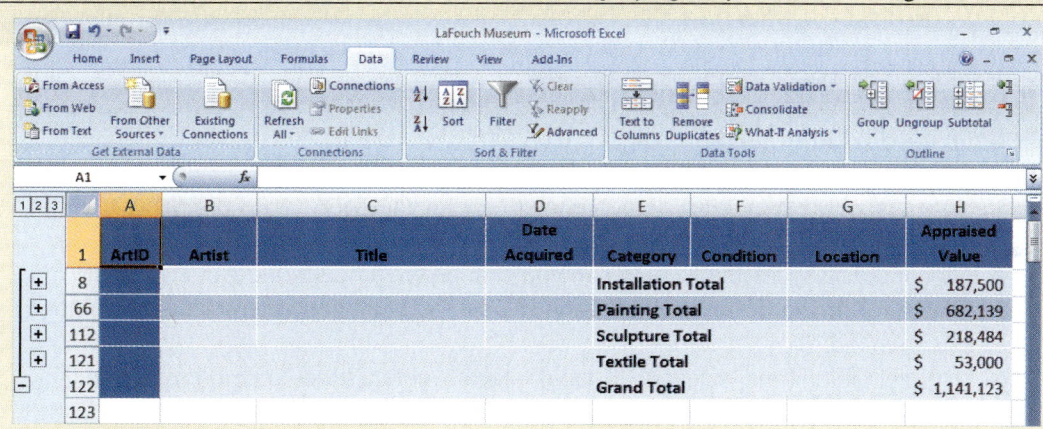

Trouble? If necessary, scroll the worksheet up to see the complete Level 2 list.

▶ 2. Click the **Level 1 Outline** button. The individual art object records and the subtotals for each category are hidden. Only the grand total remains visible.

▶ 3. Click the **Level 3 Outline** button. All the records along with the subtotals and the grand total are visible.

Mary has all the information she needs for her meeting with the board to review financial plans for the next fiscal cycle. So you can remove the subtotals from the data.

To remove the subtotals from the art objects data:

▶ 1. In the Outline group on the Data tab, click the **Subtotal** button. The Subtotal dialog box opens.

▶ 2. Click the **Remove All** button to remove the subtotals from the data. Only the records appear in the worksheet.

   You'll reset the art objects data as an Excel table.

▶ 3. Make sure the active cell is a cell within the structured range of data.

▶ 4. Click the **Insert** tab on the Ribbon, and then, in the Tables group, click the **Table** button. The Create Table dialog box opens.

▶ 5. Click the **OK** button to create the Excel table, and then click any cell in the table. The table structure is active.

   You need to rename the table as ArtObjects.

▶ 6. In the Properties group on the Table Tools Design tab, type **ArtObjects** in the Table Name box, and then press the **Enter** key. The Excel table is again named ArtObjects.

Mary needs to generate some information for a meeting with the budget director to review financial plans for the next fiscal cycle. You will work with the art objects data in the next session to gather the information she needs for that meeting.

Review | Session 5.2 Quick Check

1. Explain the relationship between the Sort and Subtotal commands.
2. An Excel table includes records for 500 employees. What can you use to calculate the average salary of employees in the finance department?
3. How can you display a list of marketing majors with a GPA of 3.0 or greater from an Excel table with records for 300 students?
4. After you display subtotals, how can you change the amount of detail displayed?
5. True or False: The Count function is a valid subtotal function when using the Subtotal command.
6. An Excel table of major league baseball players includes the column Position (pitchers, catchers, infielders, outfielders, and so forth). What feature can you use to display only pitchers and catchers in the table?
7. If you have a list of employees that includes fields for gender and salary, among others, how can you determine the average salary for females using the Total row feature?

Session 5.3

Analyzing Data with PivotTables

An Excel table can contain a wealth of information, but the large amounts of detailed data often make it difficult to form a clear, overall view of that information. You can use a PivotTable to help organize the data into a meaningful summary. A **PivotTable** is an interactive table that enables you to group and summarize either a range of data or an Excel table into a concise, tabular format for easier reporting and analysis. A PivotTable summarizes data into categories using functions such as COUNT, SUM, AVERAGE, MAX, and MIN. For example, Mary is preparing a presentation for the museum's board of directors that will include a report of the appraised value of the museum's art objects by location, category, and condition. A PivotTable can generate the information she needs.

To create a PivotTable report, you need to specify which fields in your data source you want to summarize. In the ArtObjects table, the Appraised Value field is the most likely field to summarize. In other applications, fields such as salaries, sales, and costs are frequently summarized fields for PivotTables. In PivotTable terminology, the fields that contain summary data are known as **value fields**. **Category fields** group the values in a PivotTable by fields, such as condition, location, and year acquired. Category fields appear in PivotTables as row labels, column labels, and report filters, which allows you to focus on a subset of the PivotTable by displaying one, several, or all items. Figure 5-26 shows the PivotTable you will create.

Figure 5-26 Sample PivotTable

	A	B	C	D	E	F
1	Location	(All)				
2						
3	Sum of Appraised Value	Column Labels				
4	Row Labels	Excellent	Good	Fair	Poor	Grand Total
5	Installation	$185,000	$2,500			$187,500
6	Painting	$611,520	$41,669	$10,500	$18,450	$682,139
7	Sculpture	$194,292	$16,300	$3,942	$3,950	$218,484
8	Textile		$7,400	$18,100	$27,500	$53,000
9	Grand Total	$998,212	$78,569	$41,942	$22,400	$1,141,123

You can easily rearrange, hide, and display different category fields in the PivotTable to provide alternative views of the data. This ability to "pivot" the table—for example, change row headings to column positions and vice versa—gives the PivotTable its name and makes it a powerful analytical tool. The PivotTable in Figure 5-26 could be rearranged so that the Condition items appear as row labels and the Category items appear as column labels.

To conceptualize the layout of a PivotTable and convey your ideas to others who might implement them, a useful first step in creating a PivotTable is to sketch its layout. Mary's sketch, shown in Figure 5-27, illustrates the PivotTable you will create to show the appraised value of the art objects organized by location, category, and condition.

Figure 5-27 PivotTable sketch

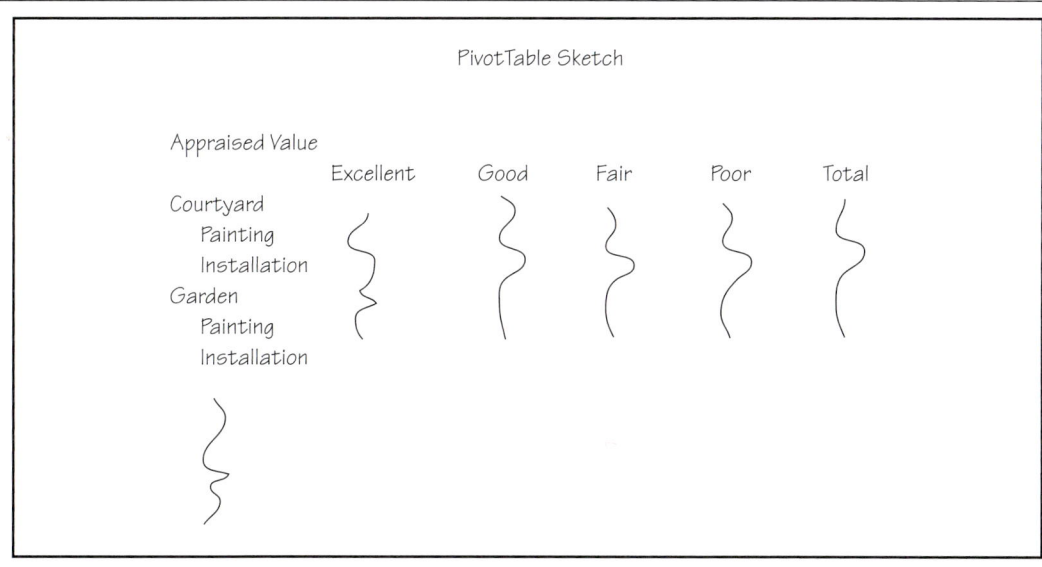

You are ready to create a PivotTable summarizing the total appraised value of art objects by location, category, and condition.

> **InSight | Creating a Professional Report with PivotTables**
>
> PivotTables are a great way to summarize data in a professional looking report when you do not want to see detailed data and you have many variables you want to summarize.
>
> Although PivotTables most frequently show results using the SUM function, you can use many other functions to summarize the data, including COUNT, AVERAGE, MIN, MAX, PRODUCT, COUNT NUMBERS, STDEV, STDEVP, VAR, and VARP.
>
> You can also display the values of a PivotTable in different views. If you want to compare one item to another item in the PivotTable, you can show the values as a percentage of a total. You can display the data in each row as a percentage of the total for the row. You can display the data in each column as a percentage of the total for the column. You can display the data as a percentage of the grand total of all the data in the PivotTable. Viewing data as a percentage of total is useful for analyses such as comparing product sales with total sales within a region or expense categories compared to total expenses for the year.

Creating a PivotTable

To create the PivotTable that will provide Mary with the information she needs, you will use the PivotTable dialog box to select the data to analyze and the location of the PivotTable report. Often when creating a PivotTable, you begin with data stored in a worksheet, although a PivotTable can also be created using data stored in an external database file, such as one in Access. In this case, you will use the ArtObjects table to create the PivotTable and place the PivotTable in a new worksheet.

> **Reference Window | Creating a PivotTable**
>
> - Click in the Excel table or select the range of data for the PivotTable.
> - In the Tables group on the Insert tab, click the PivotTable button.
> - Click the Select a table or range option button and verify the reference in the Table/Range box.
> - Click the New Worksheet option button or click the Existing Worksheet option button and specify a cell.
> - Click the OK button.
> - Click the check boxes for the fields you want to add to the PivotTable (or drag fields to the appropriate box in the layout section).
> - If needed, drag fields to different boxes in the layout section.

To create a PivotTable using the ArtObjects table:

▶ 1. If you took a break after the previous session, make sure the LaFouch Museum workbook is open, the Art Collection worksheet is active, and the Excel table is active.

▶ 2. Click the **Insert** tab on the Ribbon, and then, in the Tables group, click the **PivotTable** button. The Create PivotTable dialog box opens. See Figure 5-28.

Figure 5-28   Create PivotTable dialog box

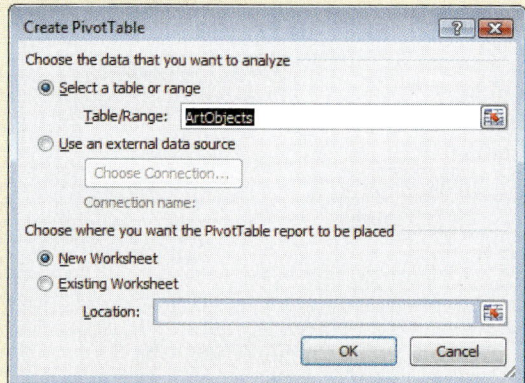

In this dialog box, you specify where to find the data for the PivotTable. The data can be an Excel table or range in the current workbook or an external data source such as an Access database file. You also specify whether to place the PivotTable in a new or existing worksheet. If you place the PivotTable in an existing worksheet, you must also specify the cell in which you want the upper-left corner of the PivotTable to appear. For the appraised value PivotTable report, you will use the ArtObjects table and place the PivotTable in a new worksheet.

> **Tip**
>
> You can also create a PivotTable by clicking the Summarize with PivotTable button in the Tools group on the Table Tools Design tab.

▶ 3. Make sure the **Select a table or range** option button is selected and **ArtObjects** appears in the Table/Range box.

▶ 4. Click the **New Worksheet** option button, if necessary. This sets the PivotTable report to be placed in a new worksheet.

▶ 5. Click the **OK** button. A new worksheet, Sheet1, is inserted to the left of the Art Collection worksheet and the PivotTable Tools contextual tabs appear on the Ribbon. The left side of Sheet1 shows an empty PivotTable report area, which is where the finished PivotTable will be placed. On the right is the PivotTable Field List, which you use to build the PivotTable by adding, removing, and arranging fields, or columns. See Figure 5-29.

Figure 5-29 PivotTable report area and PivotTable Field List

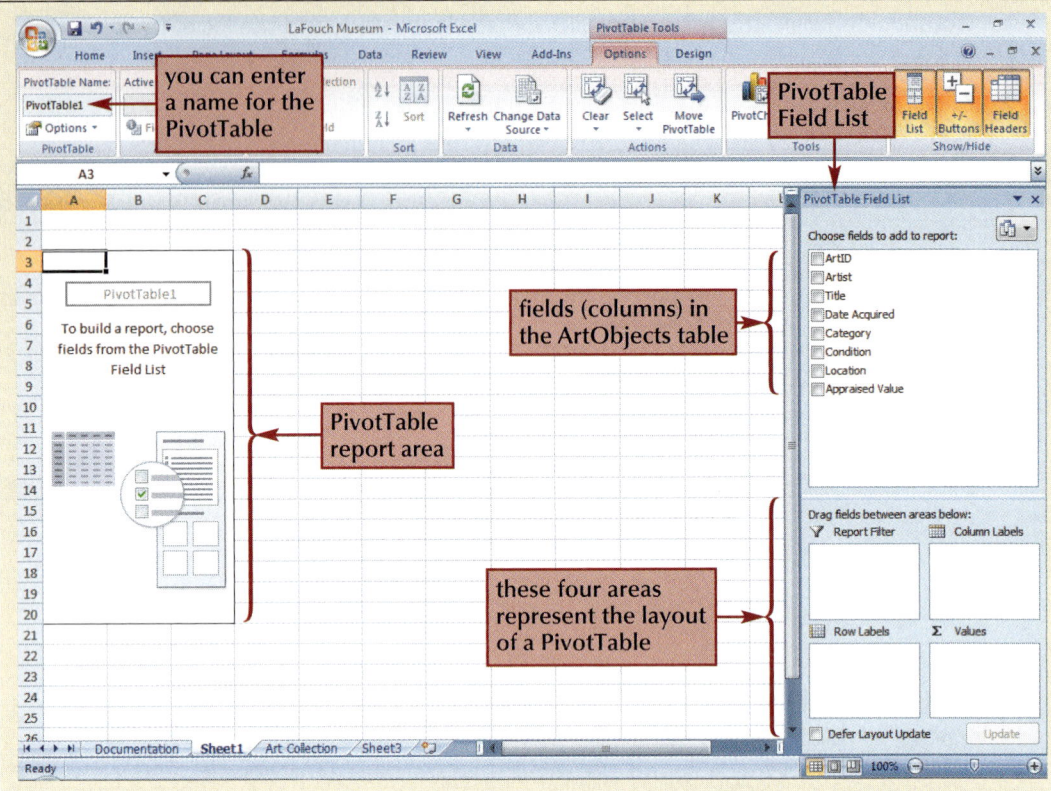

The PivotTable Field List is divided into two sections. The upper field list section displays the names of each field in the ArtObjects table. You check a field check box to add that field to the PivotTable. The lower layout section includes boxes for the four areas in which you can place fields: Report Filter, Row Labels, Column Labels, and Values. Figure 5-30 describes the function of each area.

Figure 5-30 Layout areas for a PivotTable

Layout Area	Description
Row Labels	The fields you want to display as the rows in the PivotTable. One row is displayed for each unique item in this area. You can have nested row fields.
Column Labels	The fields you want to display as columns at the top of the PivotTable. One column is displayed for each unique item in this area. You can have nested column fields.
Report Filter	A field used to filter the report by selecting one or more items, enabling you to display a subset of data in a PivotTable report.
Values	The fields you want to summarize.

Initially, selected fields with numeric data are placed in the Values area and the SUM function is used to summarize the PivotTable. Fields with nonnumeric data are placed in the Row Labels area. You can always change these default placements of fields in the PivotTable by dragging them to other layout areas to better suit your needs.

Adding Fields to a PivotTable

You need to calculate the total appraised value of art objects by location, within location by category, and within category by condition. In the PivotTable, you'll begin by adding the Location, Category, and Condition fields to appear as row labels, and the data in the Appraised Value field to be summarized. First, you will create a PivotTable summarizing Appraised Value by Location. Then, you'll expand the PivotTable report by adding the Category and Condition fields.

To add fields to the PivotTable:

1. In the PivotTable Field List, click the **Location** check box. The Location field is added to the Row Labels box and the unique values in the Location field—Courtyard, East Pavilion, Garden, South Pavilion, and West Pavilion—appear in the PivotTable report area. See Figure 5-31.

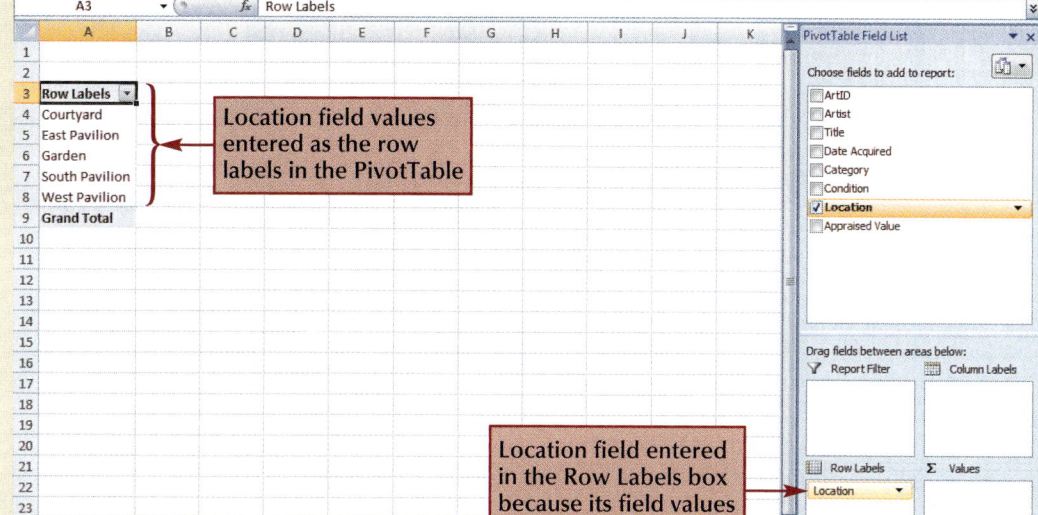

Figure 5-31 PivotTable with the Location field items as row labels

2. Click the **Appraised Value** check box in the PivotTable Field List. The Sum of Appraised Value button appears in the Values box. The PivotTable groups the items from the ArtObjects table by Location, and calculates the total appraised value for each location. The grand total appears at the bottom of the PivotTable. See Figure 5-32.

Figure 5-32 — PivotTable of the appraised value of art objects by location

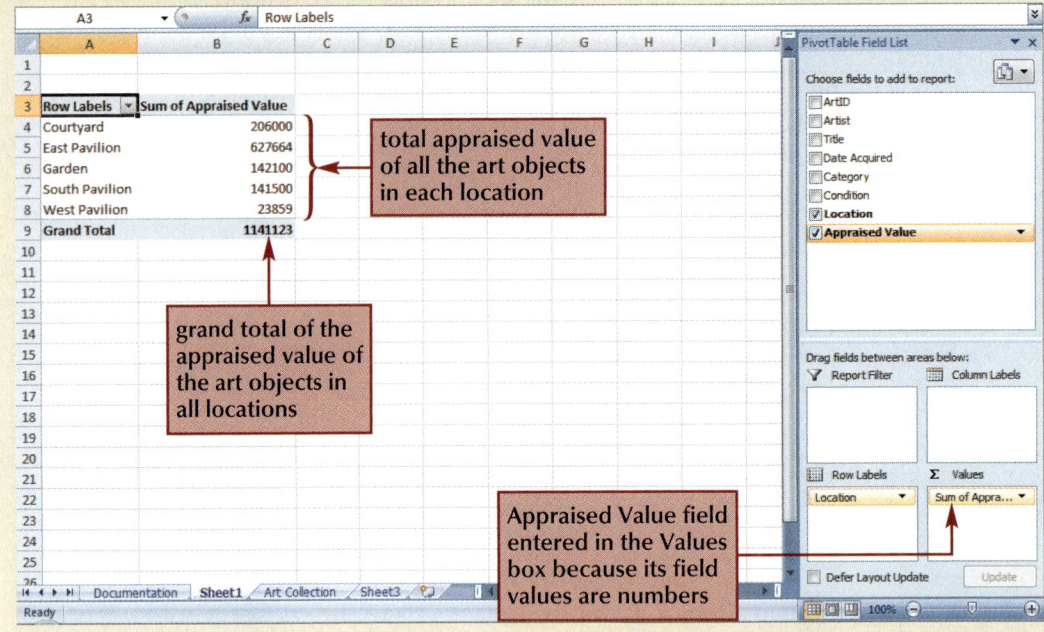

3. Rename the worksheet as **Appraised Value Summary**.

By default, the PivotTable report uses the SUM function for numbers in the Values area and the COUNT function for text and other nonnumeric values. If you want a different summary function, such as average, maximum, or minimum, click the appropriate button in the Values box (in this case, the button is called Sum of Appraised Value) in the Pivot-Table Field List, and then click Value Field Settings. The Value Field Settings dialog box opens. You can then select the type of calculation you want from the list of available functions, and then click the OK button.

Next, you'll add the Category and Condition fields to the PivotTable.

To add the Category and Condition fields to the PivotTable:

1. In the PivotTable Field List, click the **Category** check box. The Category field appears in the Row Labels box below the Location field and the unique items in the Category field are indented below each location field item in the PivotTable.

2. In the PivotTable Field List, click the **Condition** check box. The Condition field appears in the Row Labels box below the Category field and its unique items are indented below the Location and Category fields already in the PivotTable. See Figure 5-33.

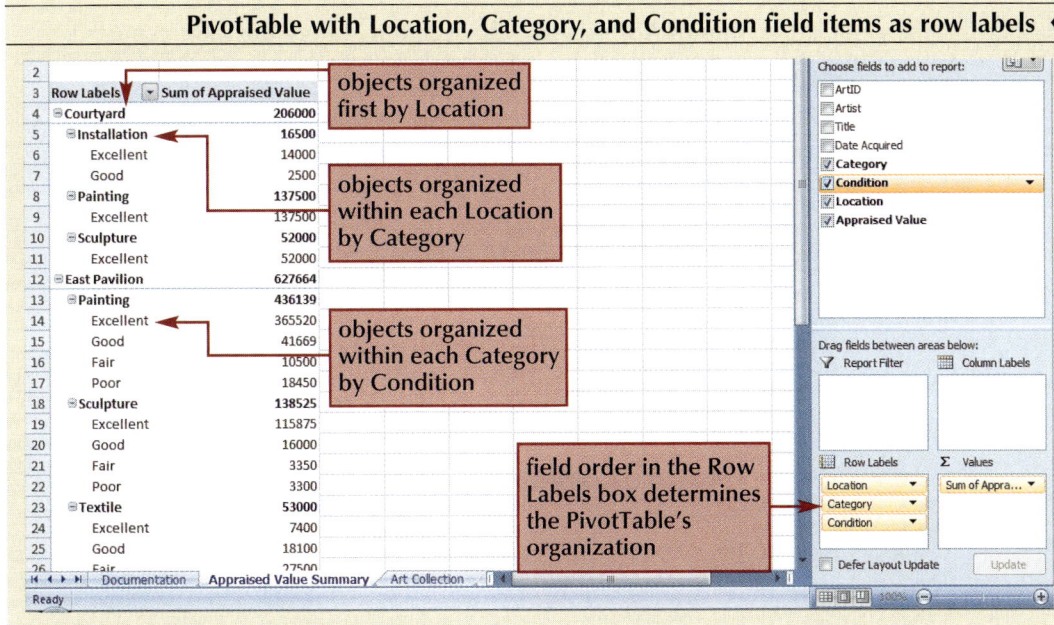

Figure 5-33 PivotTable with Location, Category, and Condition field items as row labels

Applying PivotTable Styles

As with worksheet cells and Excel tables, you can quickly format a PivotTable report using a preset style. You can choose from a gallery of PivotTable styles similar to Table styles. Remember that you can point to any style in the gallery to see a Live Preview of the PivotTable with that style applied. You also can modify the appearance of PivotTables using PivotTable Style Options by adding or removing Banded Rows, Banded Columns, Row Headers, and Column Headers.

Mary wants you to apply the Medium 3 Style, which makes each group in the PivotTable stand out and subtotals in the report easier to find.

To apply a PivotTable style to the PivotTable report:

1. Make sure the active cell is in the PivotTable, and then click the **PivotTable Tools Design** tab on the Ribbon.

2. In the PivotTable Styles group, click the **More** button to open the PivotTable Styles gallery.

3. Move the pointer over each style to preview the PivotTable report with that style.

4. Click the **Pivot Style Medium 3** style (the third style in the Medium section). The style is applied to the PivotTable.

Formatting PivotTable Value Fields

Applying PivotTable styles does not change the numeric formatting in the PivotTable. Mary wants the numbers in the PivotTable to be quickly recognized as currency. You can format cells in a PivotTable the same way as you do cells in the worksheet. You'll change the total appraised values in the PivotTable to Currency style.

To format the appraised value numbers in the PivotTable:

1. Click any cell in the **Sum of Appraised Value** column of the PivotTable report.

2. Click the **PivotTable Tools Options** tab on the Ribbon, and then, in the Active Field group, click the **Field Settings** button. The Value Field Settings dialog box opens. See Figure 5-34.

Figure 5-34   Value Field Settings dialog box

> **Tip**
> You can use the Summarize by tab to change the SUM function to a different summary function, such as AVERAGE. The name in the PivotTable is updated to reflect your selection.

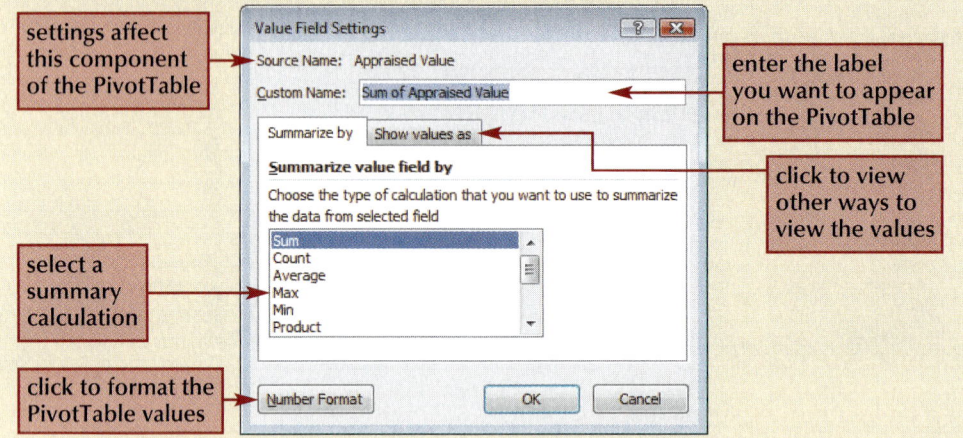

If you want to change "Sum of Appraised Value" (cell B3), the name used to describe the calculations in the PivotTable report, use the Custom Name box in the Value Field Settings dialog box.

3. Click the **Number Format** button. The Format Cells dialog box opens. This is the same dialog box you've used before to format numbers in worksheet cells.

4. Click **Currency** in the Category list, and then type **0** in the Decimal places box.

5. Click the **OK** button in each dialog box. The numbers in the PivotTable are formatted as currency with no decimal places.

With the style applied and the numbers formatted as currency, the data in the PivotTable is much easier to interpret.

Rearranging a PivotTable

Although you cannot change the values within a PivotTable, you can add, remove, and rearrange fields to change the PivotTable's layout. Recall that the benefit of a PivotTable is that it summarizes large amounts of data into a readable format. After you create a PivotTable, you can view the same data in different ways. The PivotTable Field List enables you to change, or pivot, the view of the data in the PivotTable by dragging the field buttons to different areas in the layout section.

Refer back to Mary's PivotTable sketch in Figure 5-27. As illustrated in the sketch, the Condition field items should be positioned as column labels instead of row labels in the PivotTable. You'll move the Condition field now to produce the format Mary wants.

To move the Condition field:

1. In the layout section of the PivotTable Field List, drag the **Condition** field button from the Row Labels box to the Column Labels box. The PivotTable is rearranged so that the Condition field is a column label instead of a row label. See Figure 5-35. Each time you make a change in the PivotTable Field List, the PivotTable layout is rearranged.

Figure 5-35   PivotTable rearranged with Condition as a column label

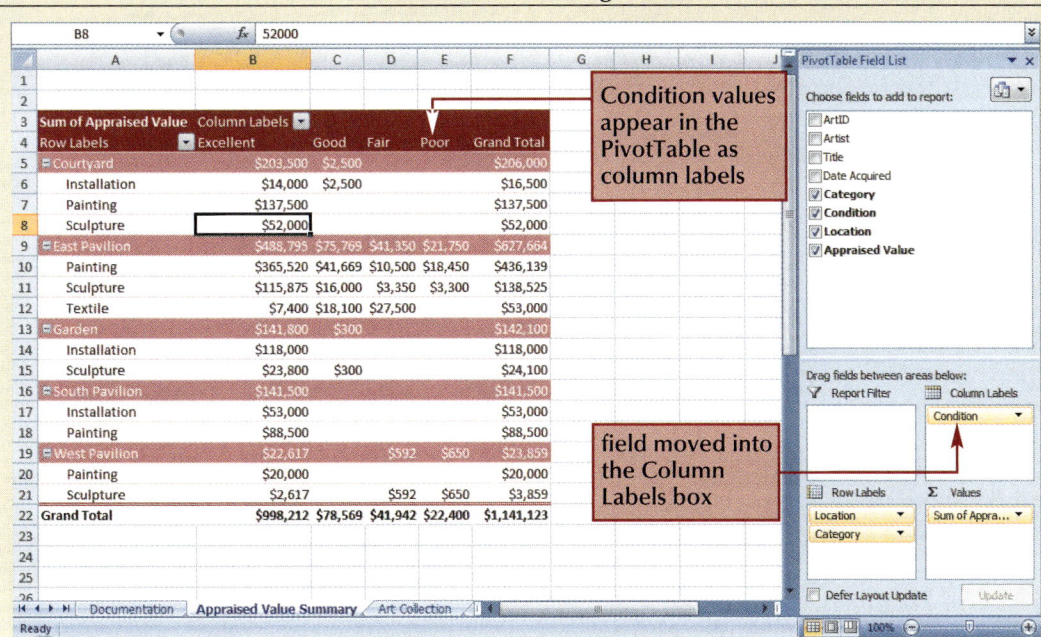

Changing the PivotTable Report Layout Options

The Compact report layout, shown in Figure 5-35, places all fields from the row area in a single column and indents the items from each field below the outer fields. This is the default layout for PivotTable reports. You can choose two other layouts. In the Outline report layout, each field in the row area takes a column in the PivotTable. By default, the outline form shows the subtotals for each group at the top of every group. The Tabular report layout displays one column for each field and leaves space for column headers. A total for each group appears at the bottom of each group. You can find these report layout options on the PivotTable Tools Design tab in the Layout group. Mary asks you to show her how the PivotTable looks in these alternative layouts so she can select the one she prefers.

To display the PivotTable in Outline and Tabular layouts:

1. Click the **PivotTable Tools Design** tab on the Ribbon.
2. In the Layout group, click the **Report Layout** button, and then click **Show in Outline Form**. The PivotTable layout changes. See Figure 5-36.

Figure 5-36   Outline PivotTable report layout

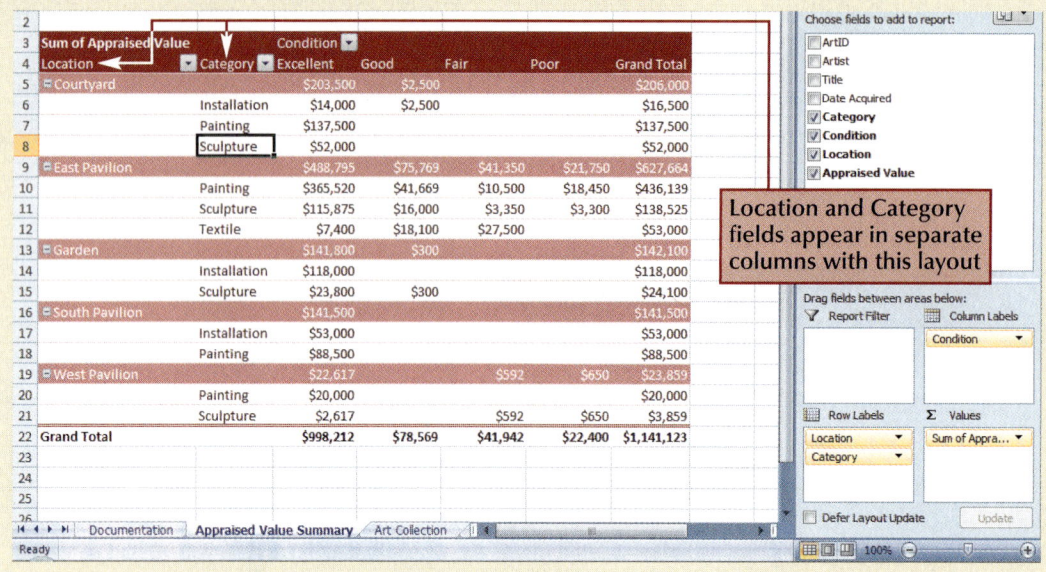

Next, you'll review the Tabular report layout.

▶ 3. In the Layout group, click the **Report Layout** button, and then click **Show in Tabular Form**. The PivotTable layout changes. See Figure 5-37.

Figure 5-37   Tabular PivotTable report layout

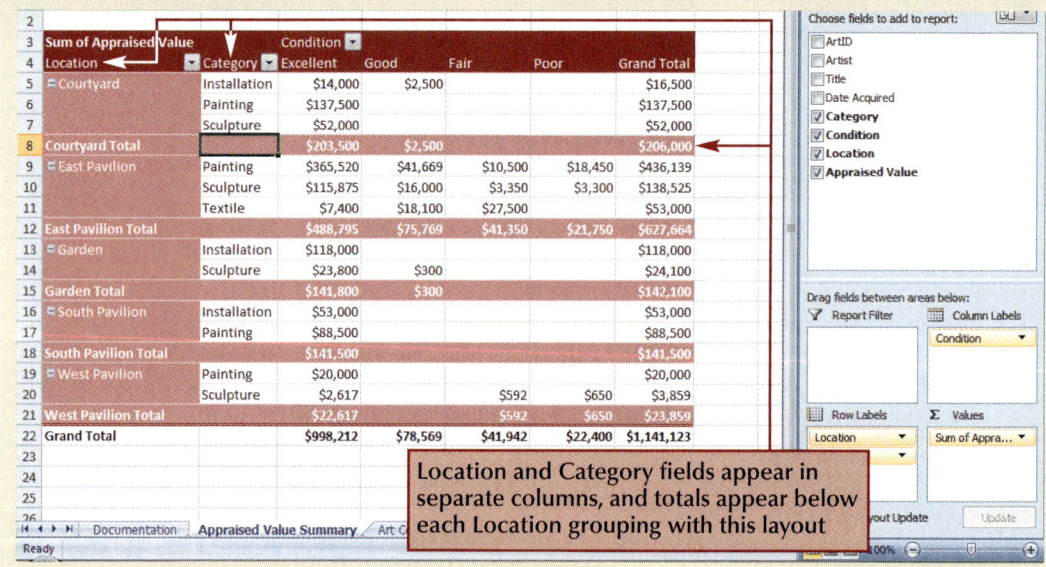

Mary prefers the original layout, the Compact form.

▶ 4. In the Layout group, click the **Report Layout** button, and then click **Show in Compact Form**.

Adding a Report Filter to a PivotTable

You can drag a field to the Report Filter area to create a filtered view of the PivotTable report. A **report filter** allows you to filter the PivotTable to display summarized data for one or more field items or all field items in the Report Filter area. For example, creating a report filter for the Location field allows you to view or print the total appraised value for all locations or for specific locations such as the Courtyard.

You will add a report filter for the Location field to see if displaying the information in this way adds value to the report.

To add a report filter for the Location field:

1. Drag the **Location** button from the Row Labels box to the Report Filter box. The Report Filter field item shows All to indicate that the PivotTable report displays all the summarized data associated with the Location field. See Figure 5-38.

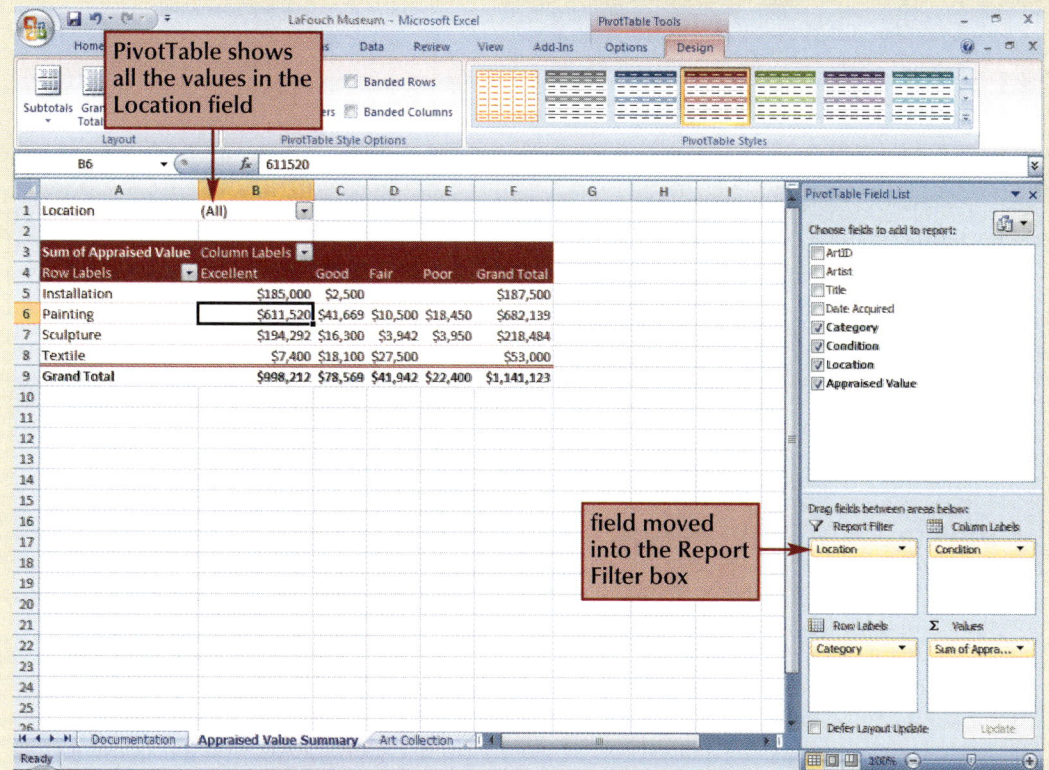

Figure 5-38 PivotTable with the Location report filter applied

Next, you'll change the summarized report to show only art objects in the East Pavilion.

> **Tip**
> If you want to filter more than one location at a time, you can click the Select Multiple Items check box to add a check box next to each item. You could then choose multiple items from the list.

▶ 2. Click the **report filter arrow** in cell B1. A filter menu opens, showing the field items displayed.

   Mary wants you to filter by a single item.

▶ 3. Click **East Pavilion** in the filter menu, and then click the **OK** button. The PivotTable displays the total appraised value of art objects located in the East Pavilion only. The report filter arrow changes to an icon to indicate the PivotTable is currently filtered. See Figure 5-39.

Figure 5-39 Report filter view for art objects in the East Pavilion

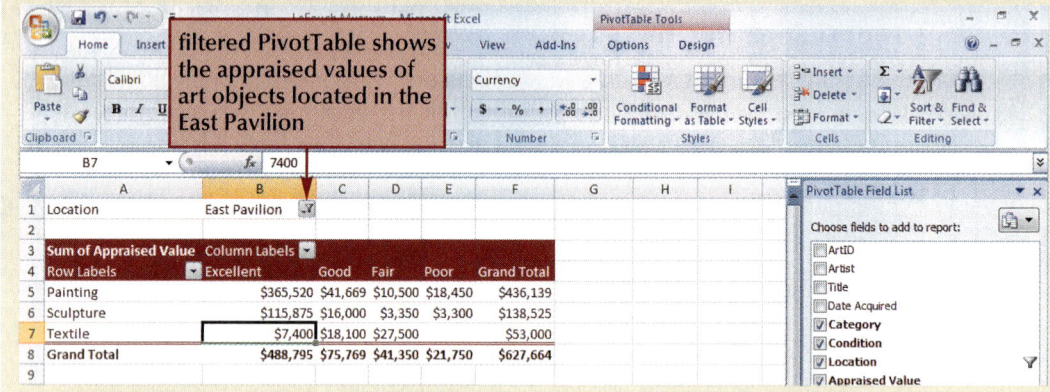

After reviewing the PivotTable, Mary decides she prefers the previous layout.

▶ 4. In the PivotTable Field List, drag the **Location** button from the Report Filter box to the top of the Row Labels box. The Location field is positioned above the Category field, and the PivotTable returns to its previous layout.

   Trouble? If the PivotTable report is arranged differently, the Location field is not the top field in the Row Labels box. Drag the Location button in the Row Labels box above the Category button.

Filtering PivotTable Fields

Filtering a field lets you focus on a subset of items in that field. You can filter field items in the PivotTable by clicking the field arrow button in the PivotTable that represents the data you want to hide and then uncheck the check box for each item you want to hide. To show hidden items, you click the field arrow button and check the check box for the item you want to show.

Mary wants to focus her analysis on art objects in excellent, good, and fair condition. She asks you to remove art objects in poor condition from the PivotTable. You will hide the art objects in poor condition from the PivotTable report.

To filter the Condition field items from the PivotTable:

▶ 1. In the PivotTable, click the **Column Labels filter arrow**. The Filter menu displays the list of items in the Condition field.

▶ 2. Click the **Poor** check box to remove the check mark. The Select All check box is deselected as well.

▶ 3. Click the **OK** button. The Poor column is removed from the PivotTable. The PivotTable includes only art objects in excellent, good, and fair condition. See Figure 5-40.

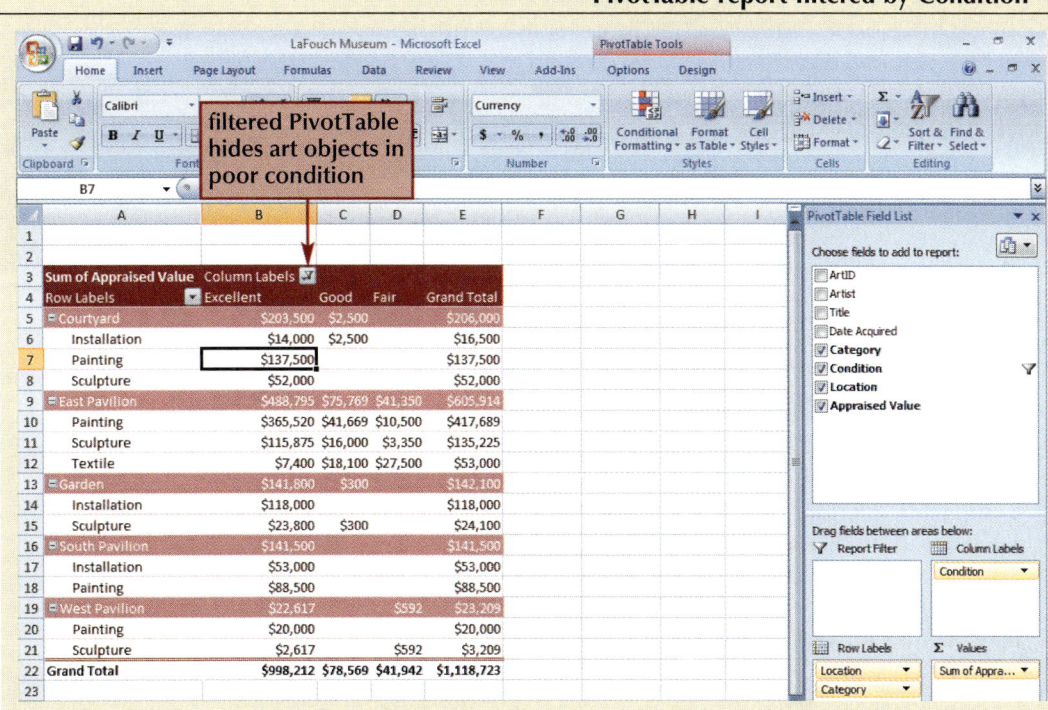

Figure 5-40 PivotTable report filtered by Condition

The report contains the art objects data Mary wants to review. Although the art objects in poor condition are hidden, you can show them again by clicking the Column Labels arrow and checking the Poor check box.

Collapsing and Expanding Items

You can expand and collapse items in the row labels of the PivotTable to view fields at different levels of detail. The Expand and Collapse buttons identify where more details exist. The Expand button indicates you can show more details for that item, and the Collapse button indicates you can hide details for that item. The lowest level of the hierarchy does not have Expand and Collapse buttons because there is no data to expand or collapse. These buttons are helpful when you have complex PivotTables where you want to switch quickly between a detailed view and an overview.

Mary wants to see the total appraised value for each location without the Category items in the PivotTable. She asks you to collapse the level of detail so that only the Location items are showing. Currently, all items are expanded.

To collapse the Courtyard items in the PivotTable:

1. Point to the **Collapse** button ⊟ next to Courtyard until the pointer changes to ⇖, and then click the **Collapse** button ⊟ next to Courtyard. The detail items below Courtyard are hidden, and the Collapse button changes to an Expand button.

2. Click the **Collapse** button ⊟ next to East Pavilion, Garden, South Pavilion, and West Pavilion. The details for these four locations are hidden, and only the Location items are displayed. The PivotTable provides a higher level summary without displaying the Category details. See Figure 5-41.

| Figure 5-41 | PivotTable with all locations collapsed and categories hidden |

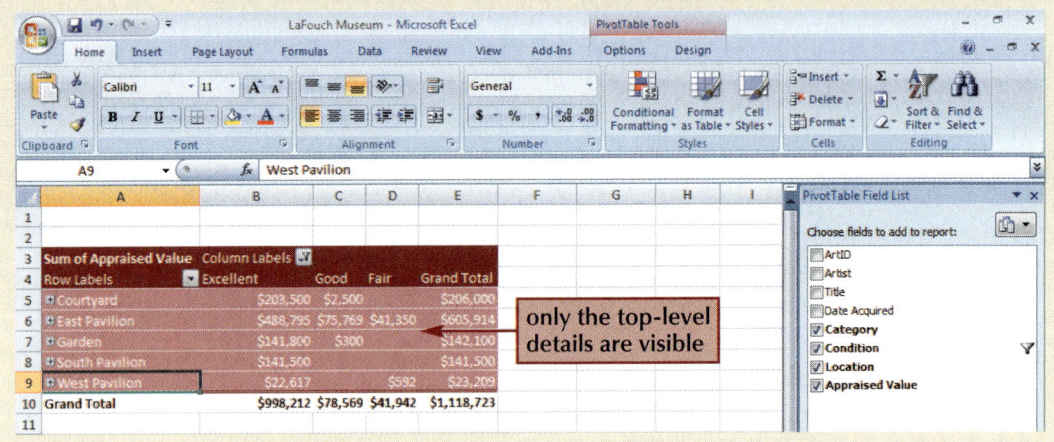

You can collapse or expand all level of detail in a PivotTable at one time. You'll do this to return to the original level of detail.

To expand all items in the PivotTable:

▶ 1. Click the **PivotTable Tools Options** tab on the Ribbon. The Active Field group has buttons for expanding or collapsing all the details at one time.

▶ 2. In the Active Field group, click the **Expand Entire Field** button. The detail items for all levels reappear. The lowest level of the hierarchy does not have Expand and Collapse buttons.

Sorting PivotTable Fields

Mary thinks the PivotTable would be more informative if the appraised values in each location were sorted in descending order. You can sort a PivotTable field either by its own items, for example alphabetizing fields such as Location and Category, or on the values in the body of the PivotTable. To sort a PivotTable field, you can use any of the Sort buttons on the Options tab to sort the information in a PivotTable report. These options are similar to the sort options you used earlier in the tutorial.

Mary wants you to sort the PivotTable so that the location with the highest total appraised value is displayed first. You need to sort the PivotTable values in descending order.

To sort the PivotTable to display the Location values in descending order based on their total appraised value amounts:

▶ 1. Click cell **E5**, which contains the Grand Total for Courtyard. This is the field total you want to sort.

2. In the Sort group on the PivotTable Tools Options tab, click the **Sort Largest to Smallest** button. The Location field is sorted based on the total appraised value for each location. Note, for example, that the East Pavilion location appears first in the PivotTable because it has the highest total appraised value, $605,914. The Courtyard location appears next because it has the second highest total appraised value, $206,000, and so on. See Figure 5-42.

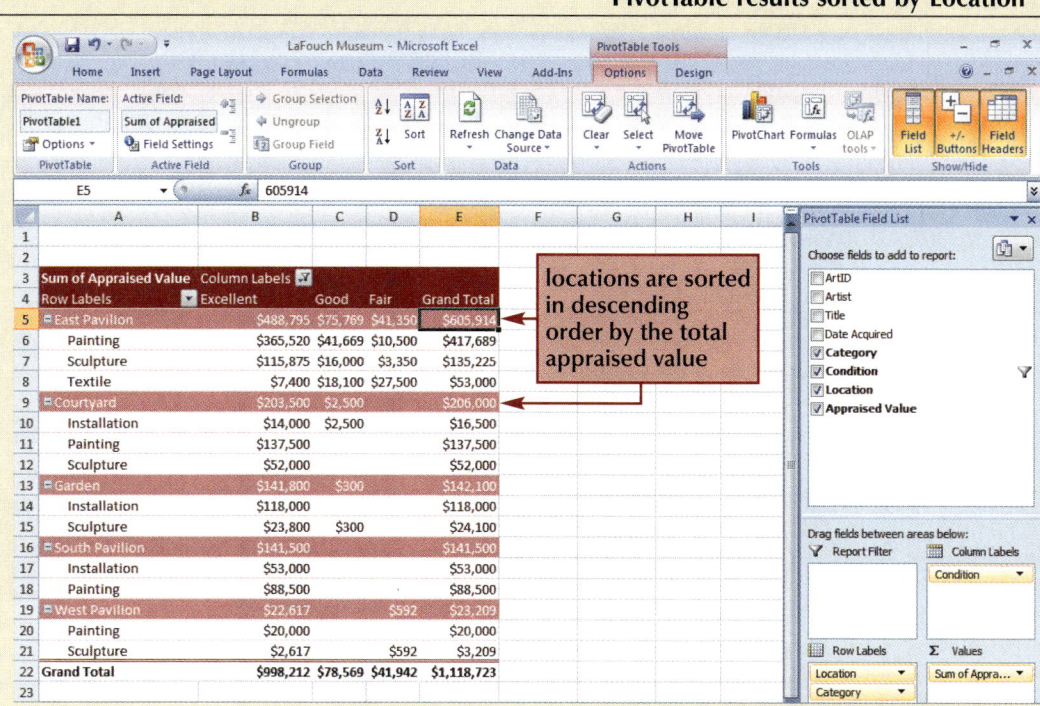

Figure 5-42 PivotTable results sorted by Location

Adding a Second Value Field to a PivotTable

You can expand a PivotTable to create a more informative table by adding fields to the Values layout area. For example, Mary believes that a more accurate presentation of the art objects would include the number of objects corresponding to the total value in each cell of the PivotTable. Adding the Title field to the Values box would count the number of art objects in each location-category-condition combination (because the title is a nonnumeric field). Mary thinks the additional information will be useful during her meeting with the board of directors. You will add the Title field to the PivotTable.

To drag and drop the Title field to the Values box:

1. In the PivotTable Field List, drag **Title** from the field list to immediately below the Sum of Appraised Value button in the Values box. The PivotTable displays the number of art objects as well as the total appraised value. The Values box in the layout area includes a second button, Count of Title, and fields from the Values box are added to the Column Labels box. See Figure 5-43.

Figure 5-43 — Count of art objects added to the PivotTable

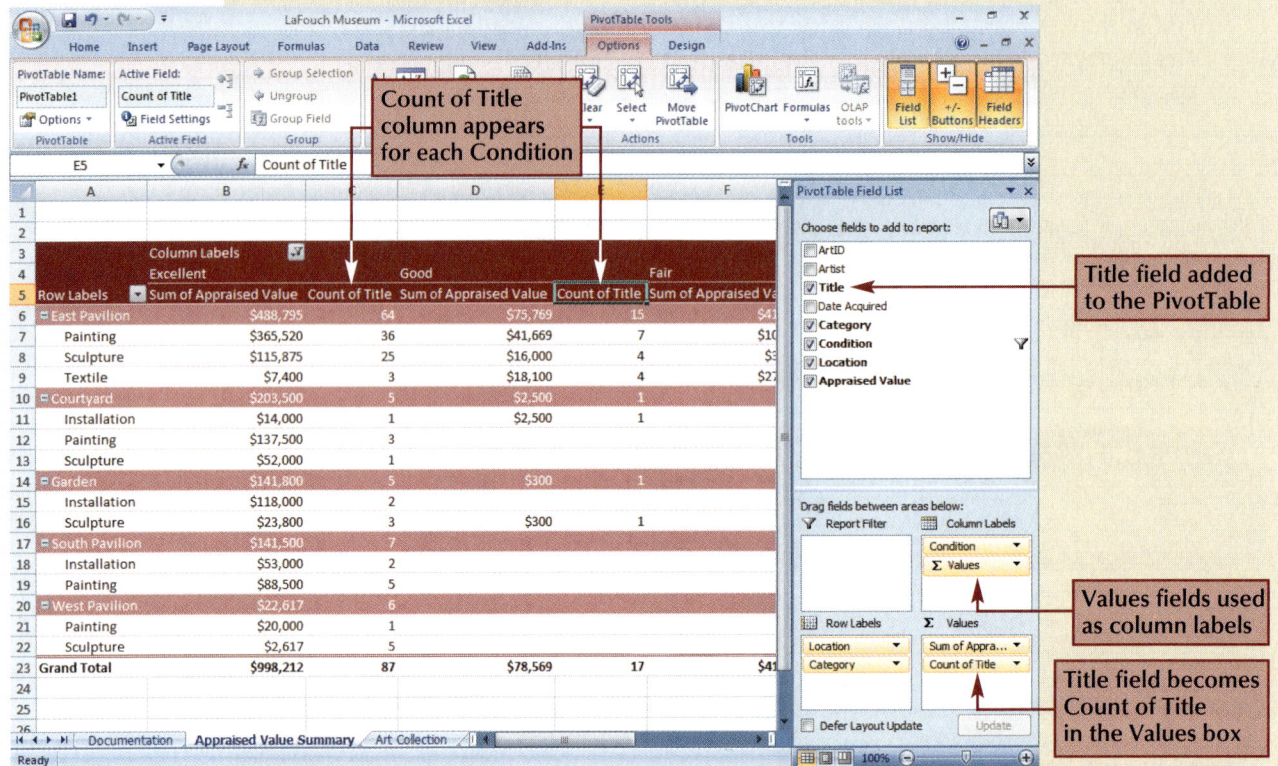

Part of the PivotTable is hidden behind the PivotTable Field List. You'll hide the PivotTable Field List so you can view more of the PivotTable.

▶ **2.** In the Show/Hide group on the PivotTable Tools Options tab, click the **Field List** button. The PivotTable Field List disappears.

Next, you'll change the "Count of Title" label to "Count."

▶ **3.** In the PivotTable, click any of the **Count of Title** labels.

▶ **4.** In the Active Field group on the PivotTable Tools Options tab, click the **Field Settings** button. The Value Field Settings dialog box opens.

▶ **5.** In the Custom Name box, type **Count**, and then click the **OK** button. The Count label appears in the PivotTable instead of Count of Title.

Tip

You can also rename a value label by typing the new text directly in any cell where the value label appears in the PivotTable.

Removing a Field from a PivotTable

The PivotTable report with the Count looks cluttered and is difficult to read. Mary asks you to remove the Count field. If you want to remove a field from a PivotTable, you click the field's check box in the PivotTable Field List. Removing a field from the PivotTable has no effect on the underlying Excel table. You will remove the Title field from the PivotTable.

To remove the Title field from the PivotTable:

▸ 1. In the Show/Hide Group on the PivotTable Tools Options tab, click the **Field List** button. The PivotTable Field List is displayed.

▸ 2. Click the **Title** check box in the field area. The Count column is removed from the PivotTable, which returns to its previous layout. The Title field is still in the ArtObjects table.

The PivotTable is almost complete. Mary asks you to improve the appearance of the PivotTable by removing the field headers (Row Labels and Column Labels) and hiding the Expand/Collapse buttons.

To hide field headers and the Expand/Collapse buttons from the PivotTable:

▸ 1. In the Show/Hide group on the PivotTable Tools Options tab, click the **+/- Buttons** button. The Expand/Collapse buttons disappear from the PivotTable.

▸ 2. In the Show/Hide group, click the **Field Headers** button. The headers Column Labels and Row Labels are hidden. See Figure 5-44.

Figure 5-44   PivotTable without field headers and Expand/Collapse buttons

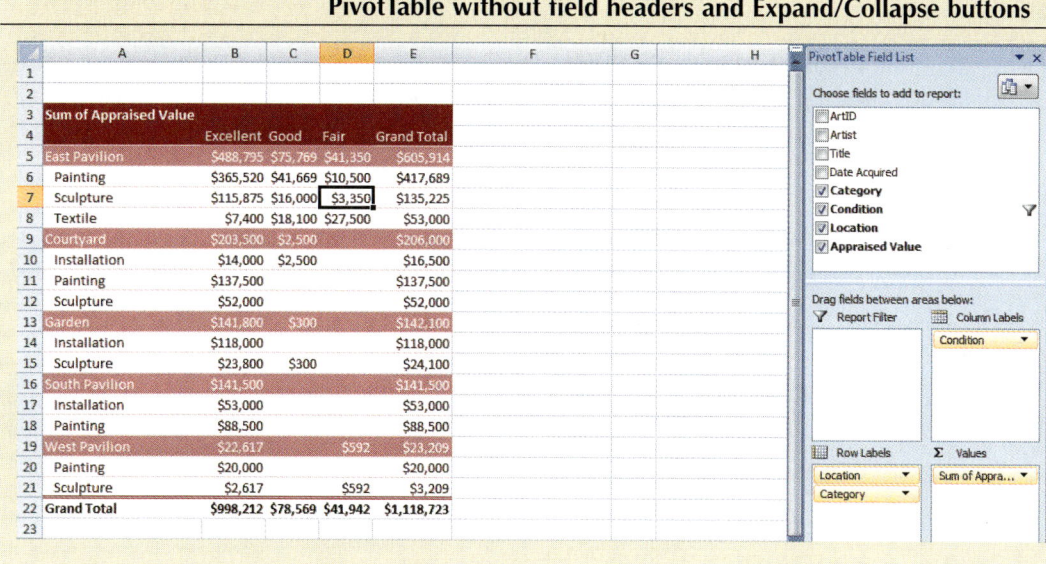

Refreshing a PivotTable

Mary just learned that the art object Dancing in the Light by Cridler has been reappraised and its value is now $4,000 (its value is currently listed as $1,000). You cannot change the data directly in the PivotTable. Instead, you must edit the Excel table, and then **refresh**, or update, the PivotTable to reflect the current state of the art objects list.

You'll edit the record for Dancing in the Light in the ArtObjects table. This sculpture is located in the East Pavilion and is in fair condition. This one change will affect the Pivot-Table in several locations. For example, currently the Total value of objects in the East Pavilion is $605,914; the sculptures in the East Pavilion are valued at $135,225; and sculptures in the East Pavilion in fair condition are valued at $3,350. After you update the appraised value of this art object in the Excel table, all these values in the PivotTable will increase by $3,000.

To update the ArtObjects table:

1. Switch to the **Art Collection** worksheet, and then find **Cridler, Dancing in the Light** (ArtID 73).

2. Click the record's Appraised Value cell, and then enter **4000**. The sculpture's value is updated in the table. You'll return to the PivotTable report to see the effect of this change on its values.

3. Switch to the **Appraised Value Summary** worksheet. The appraised value totals for the East Pavilion are still $605,914, $135,225, and $3,350, respectively.

   The PivotTable is not updated when the data in its source table is updated, so you need to refresh the PivotTable manually.

4. Click any cell in the PivotTable.

5. Click the **PivotTable Tools Options** tab on the Ribbon, and then, in the Data group, click the **Refresh** button. The PivotTable report is updated. The appraised value totals are now $608,914, $138,225, and $6,350. See Figure 5-45.

Figure 5-45   Refreshed PivotTable

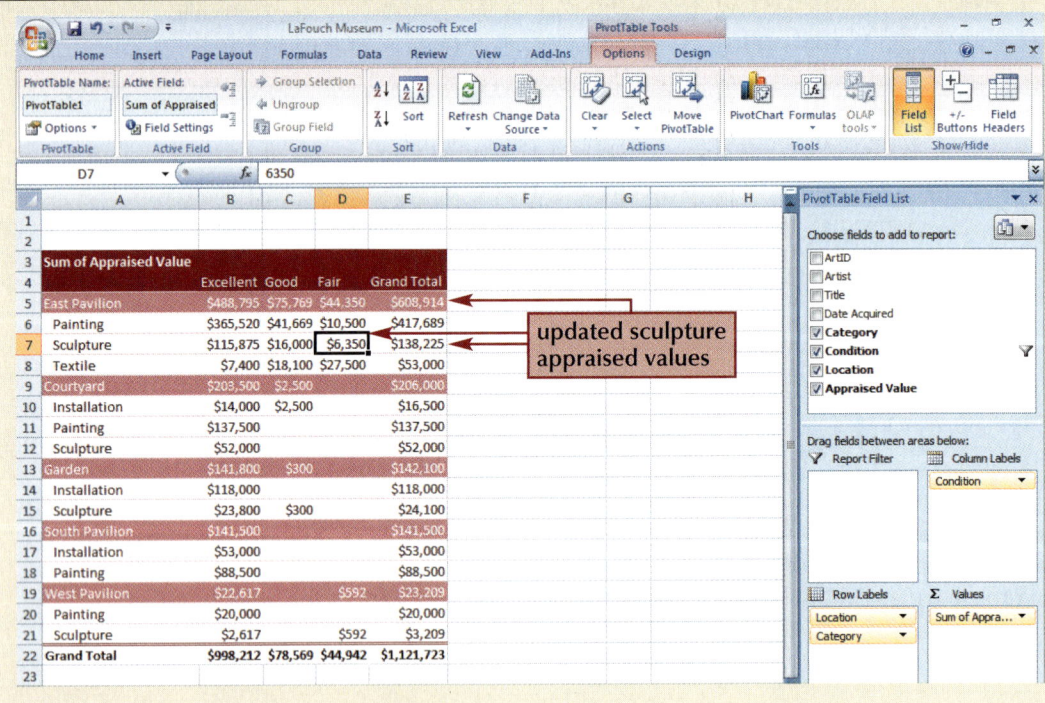

Mary is satisfied with the final version of the PivotTable report.

Grouping PivotTable Items

When a field contains numbers, dates, or times, you can combine items in the rows of a PivotTable and combine them into groups automatically. Mary thinks another PivotTable, one displaying the number of objects acquired each year, would be of interest to the board of directors. This report involves using the Date Acquired field as a row label and ArtID (or other field) as the value field. When using a date field as a row label in a PivotTable, each date initially appears as a separate item. Typically, you want to analyze date data by month, quarter, or year. To do that, you need to group the data in the Date Acquired field. Grouping items combines dates into larger groups such as months, quarters, or years, so that the PivotTable can include the desired level of summarization. You can also group numeric items, typically into equal ranges. For example, you can calculate the number of art objects in appraised value groups based on increments of any amount you specify (for example, 1–25,000, 25,001–50,000, and so on).

You'll add a second PivotTable in a new worksheet.

To create the PivotTable based on the Date Acquired field:

1. Switch to the **Art Collection** worksheet, and then click any cell in the Excel table. The table is active.

2. Click the **Insert** tab on the Ribbon, and then, in the Tables group, click the **PivotTable** button. The Create PivotTable dialog box opens.

3. Verify that the Table/Range box shows **ArtObjects** and the **New Worksheet** option button is selected, and then click the **OK** button. The PivotTable report area and PivotTable Field List appear in a new worksheet.

4. In the PivotTable Field List, click the **Date Acquired** check box. The Date Acquired field appears in the Row Labels box. Each unique date appears in the PivotTable report area. Mary wants each year to appear as a row label. You will correct that shortly.

   Next, you'll add the ArtID field to the PivotTable.

5. Click the **ArtID** check box in the PivotTable Field List. The Sum of ArtID appears in the Values box in the layout area, because the ArtID field contains numeric data. See Figure 5-46.

Figure 5-46   PivotTable with Sum of ArtID for each date

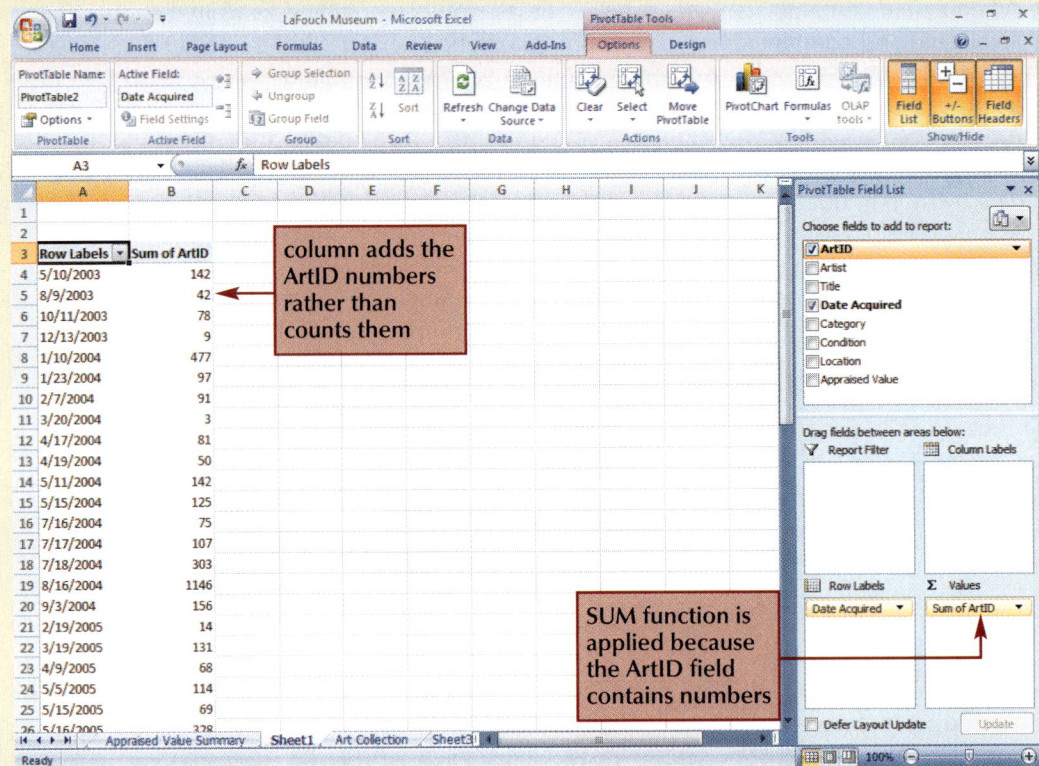

The PivotTable includes the sum of ArtIDs instead of a count of art objects, as Mary requested. This occurs because fields that contain numbers placed in the Values area are summed. Adding all the ArtIDs together to get a total is meaningless; you need to count the number of ArtIDs in each year. To do this, you need to change the SUM function to the COUNT function so Excel will *count* the number of objects in each group.

▶ 6. Click any value in the **Sum of ArtID** column, and then, in the Active Field group on the PivotTable Tools Options tab, click the **Field Settings** button. The Value Field Settings dialog box opens.

▶ 7. Click **Count** in the Summarize value field by box, and then type **Count** in the Custom Name box. The label indicating the type of summary in the PivotTable will be changed to Count.

▶ 8. Click the **OK** button. The dialog box closes and the PivotTable report displays the number of art objects acquired by date. See Figure 5-47.

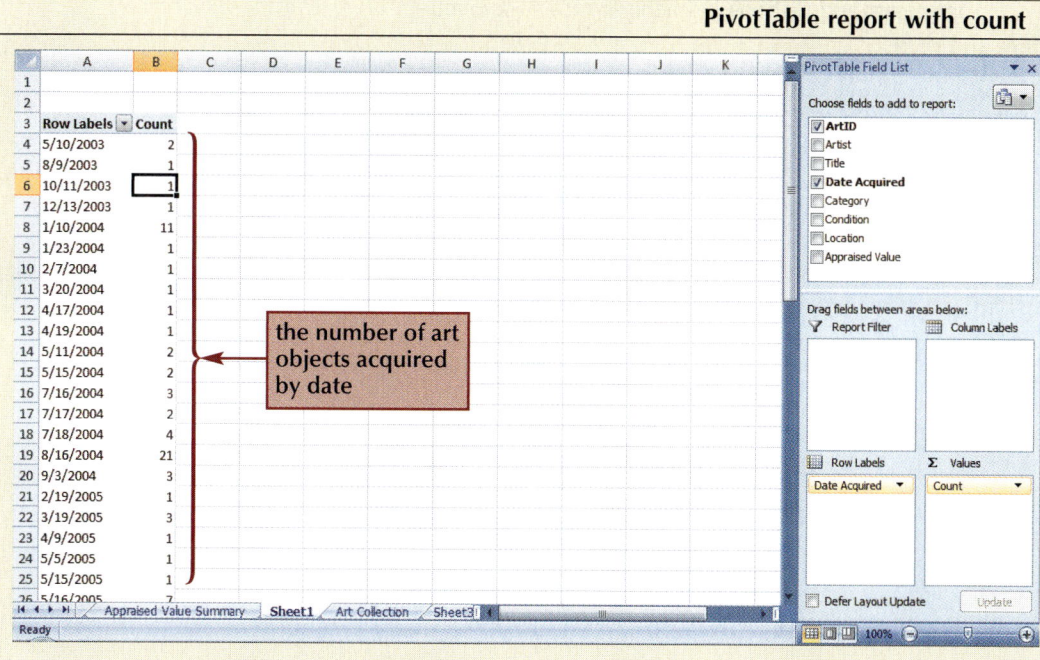

Figure 5-47 PivotTable report with count

Grouping Date Fields

The layout of this PivotTable is not what Mary would like. Mary wants a count of acquisitions by year, not by date. You can group a range of dates into periods such as months, quarters, or years using the Group Fields command. Mary wants to group the Date Acquired dates by year.

To group Date Acquired by year:

1. Click any date value in the Row Labels column of the PivotTable, and then, in the Group group on the PivotTable Tools Options tab, click the **Group Field** button. The Grouping dialog box opens.

2. Click **Months** to deselect it, and then click **Years** to select it. See Figure 5-48.

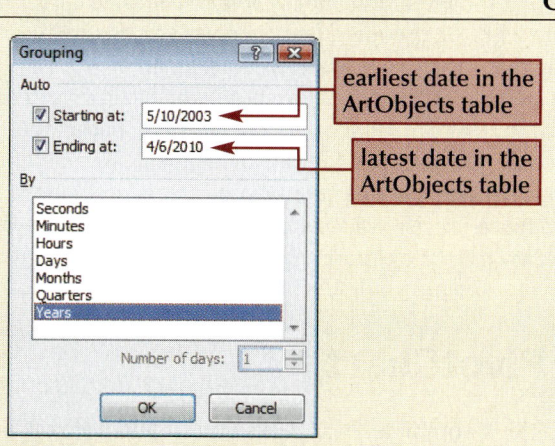

Figure 5-48 Grouping dialog box

▶ 3. Click the **OK** button. The PivotTable report is grouped by year, displaying the number of art acquisitions in each year. See Figure 5-49.

Figure 5-49 | **PivotTable report of annual acquisitions**

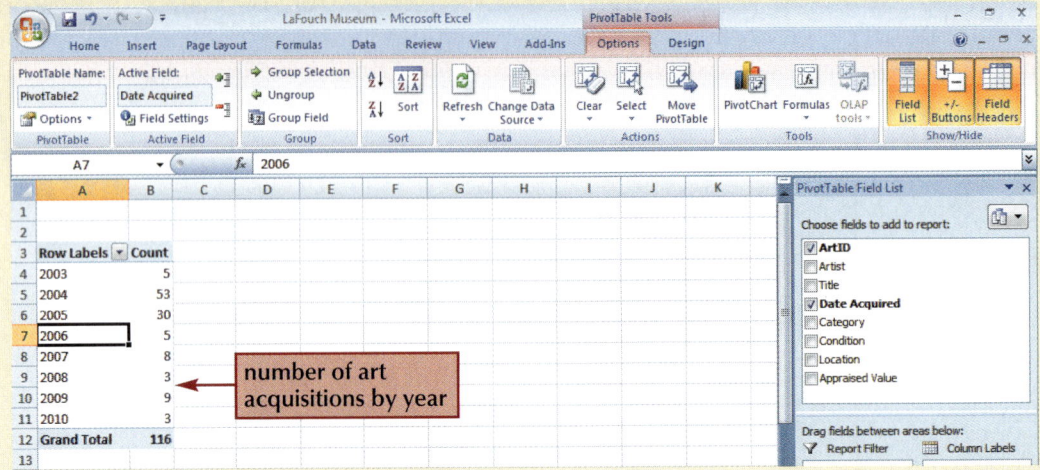

▶ 4. Rename the worksheet as **Acquired By Year**.

InSight | Creating Different Types of PivotTable Reports

This tutorial only touched the surface of the variety of PivotTable reports you can create. Here are a few more examples:

- Most PivotTable summaries are based on numeric data, but PivotTables can also contain only nonnumeric data. You cannot add nonnumeric data, so you must use the COUNT function to produce summaries. For example, you could count the number of art objects by Location and Category.
- You can use PivotTables to combine items into groups. Items that appear as row labels or column labels can be grouped. If items are numbers or dates, they can be grouped automatically using the Grouping dialog box or manually using the Ctrl key to select items in a group and choosing Group from the shortcut menu. For example, you can manually combine the Courtyard and Garden locations into an Outdoor group and combine the three pavilion locations into an Indoor group and then provide counts or total appraised values by these groups within the PivotTable. Being able to combine categories that aren't part of your original data with the grouping feature gives you flexibility to summarize your PivotTables in a way that meets your analysis requirements.
- You can develop PivotTables using the value filter, which allows you to filter one of your row or column fields in the PivotTable based on numbers that appear in the Values area of the PivotTable. For example, a PivotTable can show the total value of art objects for each artist and be filtered to display only artists whose total is greater than $25,000. Filtering provides you with a more precise way to view the PivotTable results by enabling you to include or remove data from the report.

Creating a PivotChart

Now that the PivotTable is complete, Mary asks you to add a PivotChart next to the PivotTable. A **PivotChart** is a graphical representation of the data in a PivotTable. A

PivotChart allows you to interactively add, remove, filter, and refresh data fields in the PivotChart similar to working with a PivotTable. PivotCharts can have all the same formatting as other charts, including layouts and styles. You can move and resize chart elements, or change formatting of individual data points.

Mary asks you to prepare a clustered column chart next to the new PivotTable report. You can create a PivotChart from the PivotTable.

To create the PivotChart:

1. Click any cell in the PivotTable, and then, in the Tools group on the PivotTable Tools Options tab, click the **PivotChart** button. The Insert Chart dialog box opens.

2. Click the **Clustered Column** chart (the first chart in the first row of the Column section), if necessary, and then click the **OK** button. A PivotChart appears next to the PivotTable along with the PivotChart Filter Pane, which you use to filter the data shown in the PivotChart.

3. Close the PivotTable Field List, and then move the PivotChart Filter Pane to the right of the PivotChart.

   Because the PivotChart has only one series, you do not need a legend.

4. In the PivotChart, click the **legend** to select it, and then press the **Delete** key. The legend is removed from the PivotChart.

   Next, you'll modify the chart title.

5. Right-click the **chart title**, and then click **Edit Text**. The insertion point appears in the title so you can edit it.

6. Select the title, type **Number Acquired By Year** as the new title, and then click the **chart area** to deselect the title.

7. Move the PivotChart so its upper-left corner is in cell D3. The PivotChart is aligned with the PivotTable. See Figure 5-50.

> **Tip**
> You can also create a PivotChart based directly on the Excel table, in which case both a PivotTable and a PivotChart are created.

Figure 5-50   PivotChart added to the PivotTable report

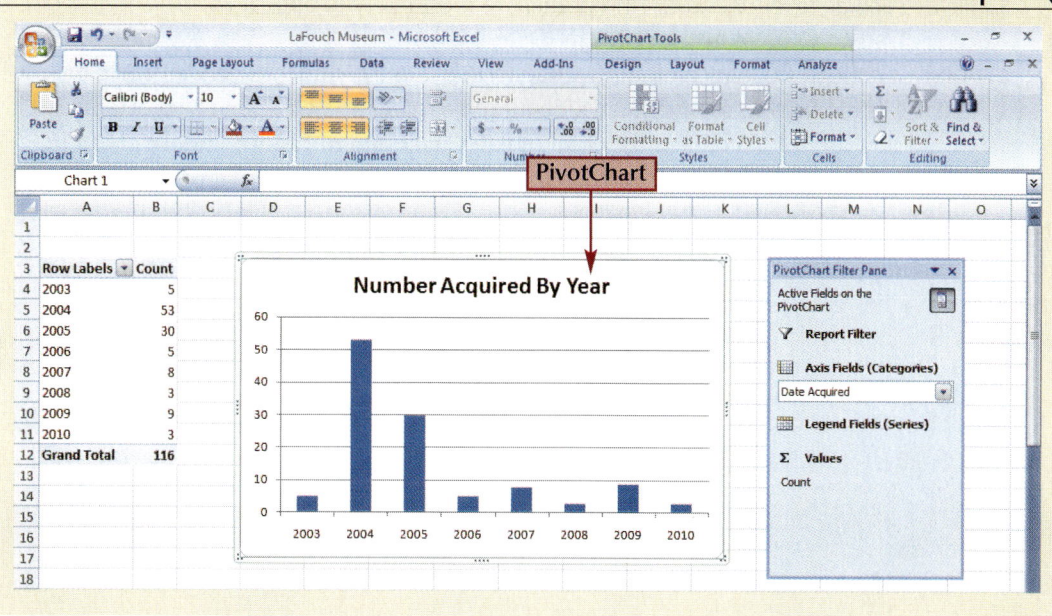

The PivotChart Tools contextual tabs enable you to manipulate and format the selected PivotChart the same way as an ordinary chart. A PivotChart and its associated PivotTable are linked. When you modify one, the other also changes. Mary asks you to display only art acquisitions after 2004.

To filter items in the PivotChart:

1. Make sure the PivotChart is selected, and then, in the PivotChart Filter Pane, click the **Axis Fields (Categories) filter arrow**. The filter menu opens.

2. Click the **<5/10/2003**, **2003**, and **2004** check boxes to remove the check marks.

3. Click the **OK** button. The PivotChart displays only art objects acquired after 2004. The PivotTable is also filtered to display the same results.

   You have completed your work on the LaFouch Museum workbook.

4. Save your changes to the workbook, and then close it.

Mary is pleased with the PivotTable and PivotChart. Both show the number of art objects acquired by year, which will be important information for her upcoming board meeting.

Review | Session 5.3 Quick Check

1. What is the default summary function for numeric data in a PivotTable?
2. When creating a PivotTable, what do you use to lay out the fields in the PivotTable report?
3. After you update data in an Excel table, what must you do to a PivotTable based on that table?
4. Fields such as region, state, and country are most likely to appear as _____ in a PivotTable.
5. Fields such as revenue, costs, and profits are most likely to appear as _____ in a PivotTable.
6. A list of college students includes a code to indicate the student's gender (male or female) and a field to identify the student's major. Which tool, Filter or PivotTable, would you use to (a) create a list of all females majoring in history, and (b) count the number of males and females in each major?

Tutorial Summary | Review

In this tutorial, you learned how to create an Excel table, enter, edit, and delete data in the table, and then sort data. You filtered the Excel table to display only data that meets certain criteria. You used the Total row to display detailed rows along with summary results for a filtered table. You inserted subtotals into a structured range of data. Finally, you summarized a table using a PivotTable and PivotChart.

Key Terms

ascending order	field	record
category field	field name	refresh
clear	filter	report filter
column header	freeze	secondary sort field
criteria filter	header row	sort
custom list	PivotChart	sort field
data definition table	PivotTable	Total row
descending order	primary sort field	value field

Practice | Review Assignments

Practice the skills you learned in the tutorial using the same case scenario.

Data File needed for the Review Assignments: Art.xlsx

Mary has another art object that needs to be entered in the art objects list. To further understand the information in the workbook, she wants to sort the data by date acquired. She wants to filter data to retrieve all art with the word *cowboy* in the title. She wants to use a PivotTable to determine the average value of artwork for each artist. Mary has asked you to gather the information she needs for further analysis of the museum's art objects.

Complete the following:

1. Open the **Art** workbook located in the Tutorial.05\Review folder included with your Data Files, and then save the workbook as **Art Museum** in the same folder.
2. In the Documentation sheet, enter your name and the date, and then switch to the Art Collection worksheet.
3. Create an Excel table for the art objects data. Change the table style to Medium 25.
4. Rename the Excel table as **Collection**.
5. Sort the art objects by Date Acquired to display the newest objects first. Make a copy of the Art Collection worksheet, rename the copied worksheet as **Q5** (for "Question 5"), and then return to the Art Collection worksheet. (*Hint*: Ctrl + drag the sheet tab to make a copy of the worksheet.)
6. Sort art objects by Category (Z to A), Location (A to Z), Artist (A to Z) in ascending order, and by Date Acquired (showing the oldest first). Make a copy of the Art Collection worksheet, rename the copied worksheet as **Q6** (for "Question 6"), and then return to the Art Collection worksheet.
7. Filter the Collection table to produce a list of art objects with the word *Cowboy* in the title, and then redisplay all the art objects. Make a copy of the Art Collection worksheet, rename the copied worksheet as **Q7**, and then return to the Art Collection worksheet. Display all records.
8. Use the Total row to calculate the average value of objects acquired between 2006 and 2010. Change the label in the Total row from Total to **Average**. Make a copy of the Art Collection worksheet, rename the copied worksheet as **Q8**, and then return to the Art Collection worksheet. Remove the Total row.
9. Use the Subtotal command to count how many art objects there are in each Location, displaying the count in the ArtID column. Make a copy of the Art Collection worksheet, rename the copied worksheet as **Q9**, and then return to the Art Collection worksheet. Remove the subtotals.
10. Create a PivotTable to show the average value of art objects by artist. Format the Value column.
11. Sort the PivotTable showing the artist with highest average value first.
12. Rename the PivotTable sheet as **Q10-15 Artist Summary**.
13. Modify the PivotTable to include Category as a Report filter field, and then filter the report so the average by Artist is based on Paintings.
14. Insert a new record in the Collection Excel table, and then enter the following data:
    ArtID #: **118**   Category: **Painting**
    Artist: **Abonti**   Condition: **Excellent**
    Title: **Trouble Ahead**   Location: **Garden**
    Date Acquired: **4/15/2010**   Appraised Value: **1200**
15. Refresh the PivotTable.
16. Save and close the workbook. Submit the finished workbook to your instructor, either in printed or electronic form, as requested.

Tutorial 5 Working with Excel Tables, PivotTables, and PivotCharts | Excel | EX 273

Apply | **Case Problem 1**

Use the skills you learned to analyze and summarize donation data for a zoo.

Data File needed for this Case Problem: Pledges.xlsx

Hewart Zoo Marvis Chennard is the director of fund-raising for the Hewart Zoo. The zoo relies on donations to fund operations, temporary exhibits, and special programs. Marvis created an Excel table to track information about donors and their pledges. Marvis asks you to analyze the data in the list.

Complete the following:

1. Open the **Pledges** workbook located in the Tutorial.05\Case1 folder included with your Data Files, and then save the workbook as **Zoo Pledges** in the same folder.
2. In the Documentation worksheet, enter the date and your name, and then switch to the Pledges worksheet.
3. Create an Excel table, and then rename the table as **PledgeData**.
4. Sort the data in ascending order by Donor Type and Fund Name, and in descending order by Amt Pledged (largest first). Make a copy of the Pledges worksheet, rename the copied worksheet as **Q4** (for "Question 4"), and then return to the Pledges worksheet. (*Hint*: Ctrl + drag the sheet tab to make a copy of the worksheet.)
5. Filter the data to display Individual donors whose Amt Owed is over zero. Sort the filtered data by Pledge Date, with the oldest date displayed first. Make a copy of the Pledges worksheet, rename the copied worksheet as **Q5** (for "Question 5"), and then return to the Pledges worksheet. Display all records.
6. Filter the data to display records that have a Pledge Date in October through December. Sort the filtered data by Amt Pledged (largest first). Make a copy of the Pledges worksheet, rename the copied worksheet as **Q6**, and then return to the Pledges worksheet. Display all records.
7. Filter the data to display only records with Amt Received greater than zero. Then use the Subtotal command (SUM) to display the total Amt Received by Fund Name. Make a copy of the Pledges worksheet, rename the copied worksheet as **Q7**, and then return to the Pledges worksheet. Remove the subtotals.
8. Create a PivotTable that displays the total and average Amt Owed by each Donor Type and Fund Name. Place the PivotTable in a new worksheet. Select an appropriate report layout and format, and rename the worksheet with a descriptive name.
9. Using Figure 5-51 as a guide, create a PivotTable on a new worksheet that shows the Amt Pledged by month and Fund Name. Format the PivotTable appropriately, and then rename the worksheet with a descriptive name. Print the PivotTable report.

Figure 5-51

Sum of Amt Pledged	Column Labels				
Row Labels	Bird Sanctuary	General Support	Kids Zoo	ZooMobile	Grand Total
Jan		$1,000	$100		$1,100
Feb			$1,100	$150	$1,250
Mar			$100	$1,000	$1,100
Apr	$75	$500	$425		$1,000
Jun			$1,000	$50	$1,050
Jul	$1,000	$1,000			$2,000
Sep	$100	$25	$250	$150	$525
Oct	$200	$200			$400
Nov		$250			$250
Dec			$150	$750	$900
Grand Total	$1,375	$2,975	$3,125	$2,100	$9,575

10. Add the following data to the Pledge table, and then update the PivotTable you created in Step 9.

Pledge #	Donor Name	Donor Type	Fund Name	Pledge Date	Amt Pledged
2129	Elliot Anderson	Individual	Kids Zoo	12/31/2010	1000

11. Save and close the workbook. Submit the finished workbook to your instructor, either in printed or electronic form, as requested.

Apply | Case Problem 2

Use the skills you learned to analyze and summarize expenditure data for a farm.

Data File needed for this Case Problem: Ring.xlsx

Ring Family Farm Fred and Alesia Ring own a small family farm just outside Abita Springs, Louisiana. The couple wants to better organize their financial records for their accountant. They created an Excel workbook to record the various expenses associated with farming. Typical expenses include those associated with hay production (seed, fertilizer, and irrigation), animal husbandry, fence maintenance, veterinary services, self-administered medicines, vehicles and maintenance, and so forth. The workbook includes categories associated with these expenses as well as an area to record how much is spent, the purpose of the expenditure, the check number, and the date paid.

Complete the following:

1. Open the **Ring** workbook located in the Tutorial.05\Case2 folder included with your Data Files, and then save the workbook as **Ring Farm** in the same folder.
2. Insert a new worksheet. Enter the company name, your name, the date, and a purpose statement in the worksheet, and then rename the worksheet as **Documentation**.
3. Create an Excel table in the Expenditures worksheet, and then rename the table as **Checkbook**.
4. Replace the Category code Farm in each record with the more descriptive Category code **Payroll**.
5. Sort the Checkbook table in ascending order by Category, then by Description, and then by Date Paid (newest first). Make a copy of the Expenditures worksheet, rename the copied worksheet as **Q5** (for "Question 5"), and then return to the Expenditures worksheet. (*Hint*: Ctrl + drag the sheet tab to make a copy of the worksheet.)
6. Filter the Checkbook table to display all expenditures for Equipment and Repairs in December, and then sort by Amount (smallest first). Make a copy of the Expenditures worksheet, rename the copied worksheet as **Q6** (for "Question 6"), and then return to the Expenditures worksheet. Display all records.
7. Filter the Checkbook table to display all checks that include the word **vet** in the description. Include the total Amount at the bottom of the table. Make a copy of the Expenditures worksheet, rename the copied worksheet as **Q7**, and then return to the Expenditures worksheet. Remove the filter and totals.
8. Use conditional formatting to apply a Yellow Fill with Dark Yellow text to all Outstanding checks. (*Hint*: "Yes" appears in the Outstanding column.) Make a copy of the Expenditures worksheet, rename the copied worksheet as **Q8**, and then return to the Expenditures worksheet.
9. Use the Subtotal command to display total Amount for each Category, displaying the subtotal in the Amount column. Make a copy of the Expenditures worksheet, rename the copied worksheet as **Q9**, and then return to the Expenditures worksheet. Remove all subtotals.

Tutorial 5 Working with Excel Tables, PivotTables, and PivotCharts Excel **EX 275**

10. Create a PivotTable that summarizes expenditures by Category and month. Place the PivotTable in a new worksheet. Format the PivotTable appropriately, choose a layout, and then rename the worksheet with a descriptive name.
11. Insert a PivotChart with the Clustered Column chart type on the same sheet as the PivotTable.

12. Create the PivotTable shown in Figure 5-52 in a new worksheet. Sort the Amount column in descending order. (*Hint:* Check the Show values as tab in the Value Field Setting dialog box to calculate percent of total.)

Figure 5-52

	A	B	C
1			
2			
3		Values	
4	Row Labels	Sum of Amount	Pct of Total
5	Equipment	$6,575.00	37.0%
6	Payroll	$2,638.27	14.9%
7	Vet	$2,320.57	13.1%
8	Repairs	$2,003.44	11.3%
9	Feed	$2,002.24	11.3%
10	Medicine	$1,249.32	7.0%
11	Administration	$958.09	5.4%
12	Grand Total	$17,746.93	100.0%

13. Save and close the workbook. Submit the finished workbook to your instructor, either in printed or electronic form, as requested.

Apply | Case Problem 3

Use the skills you learned to analyze and summarize loan data for a bank.

Data File needed for this Case Problem: CustLoans.xlsx

High Desert Bank Eleanor Chimayo, loan manager for High Desert Bank, is getting ready for the bank's quarterly meeting. Eleanor is expected to present data on the status of different types of loans within three New Mexican cities. Eleanor asks you to summarize and analyze the data for her presentation.

Complete the following:

1. Open the **CustLoans** workbook located in the Tutorial.05\Case3 folder included with your Data Files, and then save the workbook as **High Desert Bank** in the same folder.
2. In the Documentation sheet, enter the date and your name.
3. In the Loans worksheet, create an Excel table, and then rename the table as **LoanData**.
4. Format the Amount and Interest Rate fields so it is clear that these fields contain dollars and percentages.
5. Change the table style to one of your choice.
6. To the right of the Type column, insert a new column named **Monthly Payment**. Use the PMT function to calculate the monthly payment for each loan. Adjust the formula so each loan is displayed as a positive amount and improve the formatting.
7. Sort the loan data in ascending order by Type, within Type by City, and within City by Last Name.

8. Use conditional formatting to display loans above average using a format that highlights these loans. Make a copy of the Loans worksheet, rename the copied worksheet as **Q3–8**, for ("Question 3–8"), and then return to the Loans worksheet. (*Hint*: Ctrl + drag the sheet tab to make a copy of the worksheet.)

9. Filter the LoanData table to display loans made during March and April of 2010. Include the number of loans, total amount of loans, and average monthly payment for the filtered data at the bottom of the table. Make a copy of the Loans worksheet, rename the copied worksheet as **Q9**, for ("Question 9"), and then return to the Loans worksheet. Then remove the total loans and show all records.

10. Sort the loans in ascending order by City; then by Type of loan; and then by Amount of loan (largest loan first). Insert subtotals (Average) for loan Amount and Monthly Payment by City. Include your name in a custom footer. Make a copy of the Loans worksheet, rename the copied worksheet as **Q10**, and then return to the Loans worksheet. Remove the subtotals.

11. Create a PivotTable that displays the number (Count) and average loan by Type and City. Place the PivotTable in a new worksheet. Remove the Other loan type from the PivotTable. Format the PivotTable appropriately. Rename the PivotTable worksheet as **Q11 Loans-Type And City**.

EXPLORE 12. Create a second PivotTable, shown in Figure 5-53, in a new worksheet. The PivotTable shows three calculations: Number of Loans, total loans (Loan Amount), and total monthly payments (Payment) categorized by Type of loan. Insert a report filter based on Loan Date, grouped so you can filter by month. Filter the PivotTable report for March and April. Rename the PivotTable worksheet as **Q12 Loans-Type and Loan Date**.

Figure 5-53

	A	B	C	D
1	Loan Date	(Multiple Items)		
2				
3		Number of Loans	Loan Amount	Payment
4	Car	5	$157,000	$3,681.77
5	Mortgage	5	$929,000	$7,890.77
6	Other	2	$35,000	$860.49
7	Grand Total	12	$1,121,000	$12,433.03

13. Save and close the workbook. Submit the finished workbook to your instructor, either in printed or electronic form, as requested.

Challenge | Case Problem 4

Explore how to summarize data from a department store by creating more complex subtotals, PivotTables, and PivotCharts.

Data File needed for this Case Problem: Bowls.xlsx

Bowls Department Stores Bowls Department Stores, with corporate headquarters in Portland, Oregon, operates department stores in midsize towns in selected northwestern areas. Although the organization maintains a large computer system for its accounting operations, the sales department often downloads data to complete additional analysis of its operations. Daniel Partner, analyst for the corporate sales department, regularly downloads data by territories and product areas including automotive, electronics, garden centers, and sporting goods. He often presents reports based on his analysis of sales by product areas and territory, best and worst performing product group-periods, and total sales for certain regions and product groups. He asks you to help him compile and summarize the data.

Complete the following:

1. Open the **Bowls** workbook located in the Tutorial.05\Case4 folder included with your Data Files, and then save the workbook as **Bowls Stores** in the same folder.
2. In the Documentation sheet, enter the date and your name and an appropriate purpose statement.
3. In the SalesData worksheet, create an Excel table. Rename the table as **ProductSales**. Format the Sales column in the Currency number format with no decimal places.
4. Sort the table in ascending order by Territories, then by Product Group, then by Year, and then by Month. Month should be sorted in Jan, Feb, Mar, ... order, not alphabetically. Make a copy of the SalesData worksheet, rename the copied worksheet as **Q4**, for ("Question 4"), and then return to the SalesData worksheet. (*Hint*: Ctrl + drag the sheet tab to make a copy of the worksheet.)

EXPLORE 5. Display records for Automotive and Electronic products in 2010, excluding sales in Vancouver. Sort this data by Sales in descending order. Add a Total row and calculate the average sales for the filtered data. Change the label in the Total row to **Average**. Insert a new worksheet and copy this filtered data to the new worksheet. Split the worksheet into two panes. The top pane displays all the rows but the last row on your screen. The bottom pane displays the Total row. (*Hint*: Click the Split button in the Window group on the View tab.) Rename the new worksheet as **Q5 Auto Electronic**. Return to the SalesData worksheet, remove the Total row, and display all the records.

EXPLORE 6. Display subtotals for sales (Sum) by Year, Month (Jan, Feb, Mar, ...), and Territory. Make a copy of the SalesData worksheet, rename the copied worksheet as **Q6**, for ("Question 6"), and then return to the SalesData worksheet. Remove the subtotals.

7. Display the five lowest periods based on sales. Assume each row represents a period. Sort the Sales so lowest sales appears first. Insert a new worksheet and copy this filtered data to the new worksheet. Rename the new worksheet as **Q7 Lowest Periods**. Return to the SalesData worksheet, and then display all the records.

EXPLORE 8. Create a PivotTable similar to the one shown in Figure 5-54, displaying percentage of sales by Product Group, Territories, and Year. Omit the columnar grand totals. Use a tabular layout, inserting subtotals at the bottom of each Product Group and excluding the Sporting product group. Rename the worksheet as **Q8 Percent of Sales**.

Figure 5-54

	A	B	C	D
1				
2				
3	Pct of Sales		Year	
4	Product Group	Territories	2009	2010
5	Automotive	Oregon	10.05%	8.85%
6		Vancouver	7.32%	9.71%
7		Washington	6.88%	9.94%
8	Automotive Total		24.25%	28.50%
9	Electronics	Oregon	7.53%	8.67%
10		Vancouver	7.61%	6.88%
11		Washington	8.05%	9.22%
12	Electronics Total		23.20%	24.78%
13	Gardening	Oregon	8.19%	6.85%
14		Vancouver	8.46%	5.89%
15		Washington	9.77%	9.91%
16	Gardening Total		26.42%	22.66%
17	Houseware	Oregon	6.86%	5.01%
18		Vancouver	8.20%	7.67%
19		Washington	11.07%	11.39%
20	Houseware Total		26.14%	24.07%
21	Grand Total		100.00%	100.00%

EXPLORE

9. Using Figure 5-55 as a guide, create a PivotChart of total Sales By Product Group. Create a second PivotChart of total Sales By Territory in the same worksheet. Include only the PivotCharts in the worksheet. Rename the worksheet as **Q9 PivotCharts**.

Figure 5-55

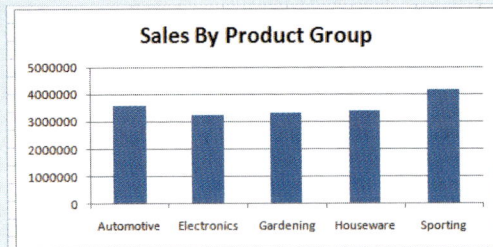 

10. Using Figure 5-56 as a guide, create a PivotTable to show four calculations: minimum, maximum, average, and total Sales categorized by Territories and Product Group and filtered by Year. Display the results for 2010. Rename the worksheet as **Q10 Statistical Summary**.

Figure 5-56

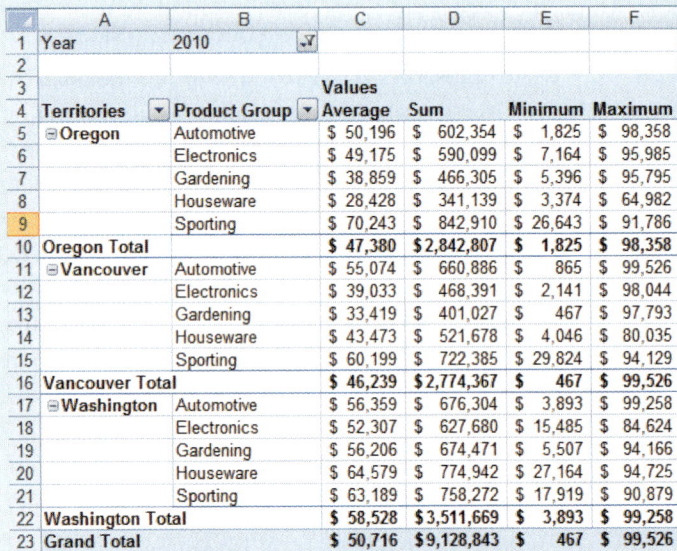

11. Save and close the workbook. Submit the finished workbook to your instructor, either in printed or electronic form, as requested.

Research | Internet Assignments

Use the Internet to find and work with data related to the topics presented in this tutorial.

The purpose of the Internet Assignments is to challenge you to find information on the Internet that you can use to work effectively with this software. The actual assignments are updated and maintained on the Course Technology Web site. Log on to the Internet and use your Web browser to go to the Student Online Companion for New Perspectives Office 2007 at **www.course.com/np/office2007**. Then navigate to the Internet Assignments for this tutorial.

Assess | SAM Assessment and Training

If you have a SAM user profile, you may have access to hands-on instruction, practice, and assessment of the skills covered in this tutorial. Log in to your SAM account (**http://sam2007.course.com**) to launch any assigned training activities or exams that relate to the skills covered in this tutorial.

Review | Quick Check Answers

Session 5.1

1. To keep, or freeze, rows and columns so that they don't scroll out of view as you move around the worksheet. Freezing the rows and columns that contain headings makes understanding the data in each record easier.
2. Filter arrows appear in the column headers, a table style format is applied to the table, and the Table Tools Design contextual tab appears on the Ribbon.
3. sort fields
4. Sort by year of graduation and then by last name.
5. Enter the data for the new record in the row immediately following the last row of data in the table.
6. Create a custom list.
7. descending (Newest to Oldest)

Session 5.2

1. You must first sort the data for which you want to calculate subtotals, because subtotals are inserted whenever the value in the specified field changes.
2. Filter the table to show only the finance department, and then use the AVERAGE function in the Total row.
3. Click the Major filter arrow, and then check only the Accounting and Finance check boxes. Click the GPA filter arrow, point to Number Filters, click Greater Than, and then enter the value 3.0 in the Greater Than dialog box to specify the condition for a GPA greater than 3.0.

4. Click the Level Outline buttons.
5. True
6. Multiselect
7. Click the Gender filter arrow, and check only the Female check box. Insert the Total row, click the arrow that appears to the right of the total for the Salary column, and then click Average in the list of functions.

Session 5.3

1. SUM
2. PivotTable Field List box
3. refresh the PivotTable
4. rows labels, column labels, or report filters
5. values
6. (a) Filter; (b) PivotTable

Ending Data Files

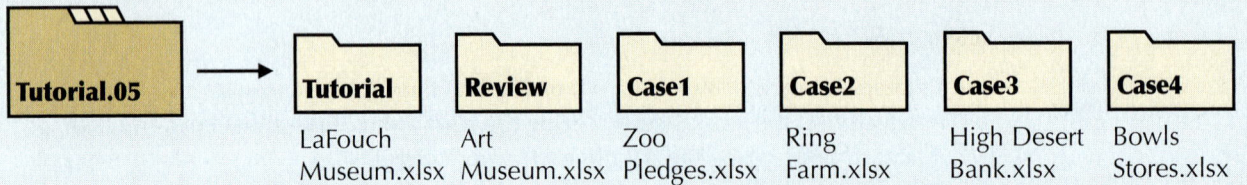

Tutorial.05 → Tutorial: LaFouch Museum.xlsx | Review: Art Museum.xlsx | Case1: Zoo Pledges.xlsx | Case2: Ring Farm.xlsx | Case3: High Desert Bank.xlsx | Case4: Bowls Stores.xlsx

Excel | EX 281

Tutorial 6

Objectives

Session 6.1
- Format and edit multiple worksheets at once
- Create cell references to other worksheets
- Consolidate information from multiple worksheets using 3-D references
- Create and print a worksheet group

Session 6.2
- Create a link to data in another workbook
- Create a workbook reference
- Learn how to edit links
- Create and use an Excel workspace

Session 6.3
- Insert a hyperlink in a cell
- Create a custom template
- Create a Web page

Managing Multiple Worksheets and Workbooks

Summarizing Ticket Sales

Case | Global Travel

Global Travel, a member-owned organization, provides a variety of services ranging from travel assistance to insurance programs to discounted vacation packages. Global Travel also offers special services and discounts to one-time entertainment events. Global Travel purchases tickets to selected theme and amusement parks to resell to its members, particularly those with families. Each local office of Global Travel markets and sells these tickets to its members. Theme and amusement park sales account for more than 10 percent of Global Travel's sales. Rhohit Gupta, accountant for Global Travel in New Mexico, is responsible for tracking ticket sales within the state and preparing an analysis for the corporate controller. Rhohit asks you to create a summary report that shows the quarterly sales in New Mexico for the past year. He already entered each quarter's values in separate worksheets, but wants you to "roll up" all the information in the four quarterly worksheets into one summary worksheet.

Rhohit reports to Alvin Alton, controller for Global Travel. Alvin already received workbooks from Colorado and Utah. After Alvin receives the New Mexico workbook, he will create a workbook that summarizes the annual totals from each state workbook in the Southwest region. He asks for your help with this.

Starting Data Files

Tutorial.06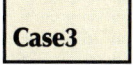

Tutorial
Colorado.xlsx
NM.xlsx
Sales 2010.docx
TravelTotals.xlsx
Utah.xlsx

Review
Idaho.xlsx
NW Totals 2010.xlsx
NW Travel.xltx
OR.xlsx
Washington.xlsx

Case1
Cafe.xlsx

Case2
Carson.xlsx
Reno.xlsx
Vegas.xlsx

Case3
InBurger.xlsx

Case4
Europe.xlsx
North America.xlsx
Pluto Template.xltx
South America.xlsx

Session 6.1

Using Multiple Worksheets

Workbook data is often placed in several worksheets. Using multiple worksheets makes it easier to group and summarize data. For example, a company such as Global Travel with branches in different geographic regions can place sales information for each region in separate worksheets. Rather than scrolling through one large and complex worksheet that contains data for all regions, users can access sales information for a specific region simply by clicking a sheet tab in the workbook.

Multiple worksheets enable you to place summarized data first. Managers interested only in an overall picture can view the first worksheet of summary data without looking at the details available in the other worksheets. Others, of course, might want to view the supporting data in the individual worksheets that follow the summary worksheet. In the case of Global Travel, Rhohit used separate worksheets to summarize the number of tickets sold and sales in dollars for the New Mexico branch offices for each quarter of the 2010 fiscal year. You will open Rhohit's workbook and review the current information.

To open and review the Global Travel workbook:

1. Open the **NM** workbook located in the **Tutorial.06\Tutorial** folder included with your Data Files, and then save the workbook as **New Mexico** in the same folder.

2. In the **Documentation** worksheet, enter your name and the current date.

3. Switch to the **Quarter 1** worksheet, and then view the number of tickets sold and sales for the first quarter of the year. See Figure 6-1.

Figure 6-1   Quarter 1 worksheet for Global Travel—New Mexico

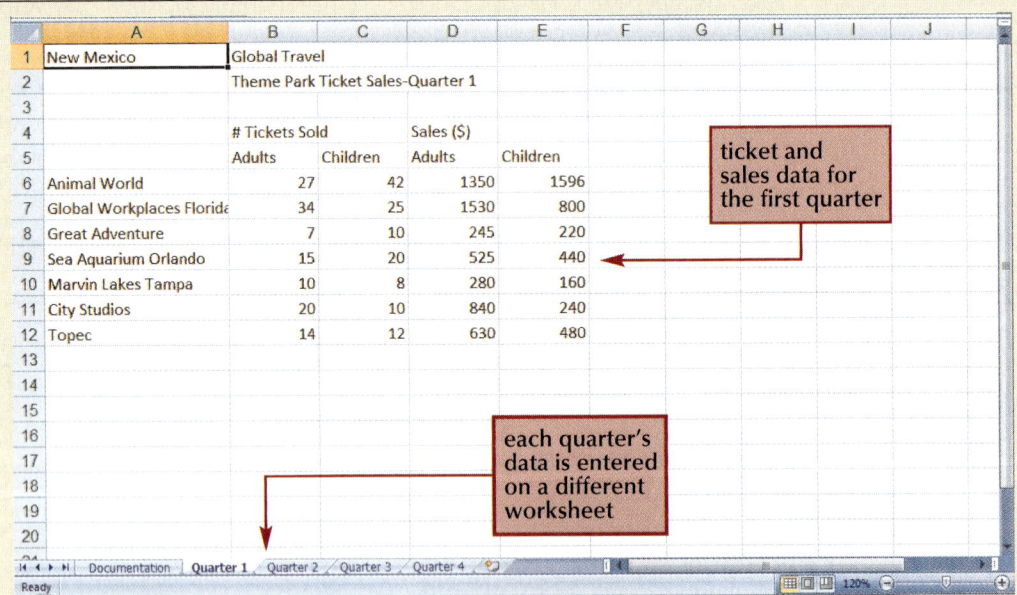

4. Review the **Quarter 2**, **Quarter 3**, and **Quarter 4** worksheets. The layout for all four worksheets is identical.

Grouping Worksheets

Rhohit didn't enter any formulas in the workbook. You need to enter formulas to calculate the total number of tickets and sales for each column (B through E) in all four worksheets. Rather than retyping the formulas in each worksheet, you can enter them all at once by creating a worksheet group. A **worksheet group** is a collection of two or more selected worksheets. When worksheets are grouped, everything you do to the active worksheet also affects the other worksheets in the group. For example, you can:

- Enter data and formulas in cells in one worksheet to enter the data and formulas in the same cells in all the worksheets in the group.
- Apply formatting to the active worksheet to format all the worksheets in the group, including changing row heights or column widths and applying conditional formatting.
- Edit data or formulas in one worksheet to edit the data and formulas in the same cells in all the worksheets in the group. Commands such as insert rows and columns, delete rows and columns, and find and replace can also be used with a worksheet group.
- Set the page layout options in one worksheet to apply the settings to all the worksheets in the group, such as orientation, scaling to fit, and inserting headers and footers.
- Apply view options such as zooming, showing and hiding worksheets, and so forth to all worksheets in the group.
- Print all the worksheets in the worksheet group at the same time.

Worksheet groups save you time because you can perform an action once, yet affect multiple worksheets. A worksheet group, like a range, can contain adjacent or nonadjacent worksheets.

Tip
If a worksheet group includes all the worksheets in a workbook, you can edit only the active worksheet.

Grouping and Ungrouping Worksheets | Reference Window

- To select an adjacent group, click the sheet tab of the first worksheet in the group, press and hold the Shift key, and then click the sheet tab of the last worksheet in the group.
- To select a nonadjacent group, click the sheet tab of one worksheet in the group, press and hold the Ctrl key, and then click the sheet tabs of the remaining worksheets in the group.
- To ungroup the worksheets, click the sheet tab of a worksheet not in the group (or right-click the sheet tab of one worksheet in the group, and then click Ungroup Sheets on the shortcut menu).

Entering Formulas in a Worksheet Group

In the travel workbook, you'll select an adjacent range of worksheets: the Quarter 1 worksheet through the Quarter 4 worksheet.

To group the quarterly worksheets:

1. Click the **Quarter 1** sheet tab to make the worksheet active. This is the first worksheet you want to include in the group.
2. Press and hold the **Shift** key, and then click the **Quarter 4** sheet tab. This is the last worksheet you want to include in the group.
3. Release the **Shift** key. The sheet tabs for Quarter 1 through Quarter 4 are white, indicating they are all selected. The text *[Group]* appears in the title bar to remind you that a worksheet group is selected in the workbook. See Figure 6-2.

Tip
If you cannot see the sheet tab of a worksheet you want to include in a group, use the sheet navigation controls to display it.

Figure 6-2 Grouped worksheets

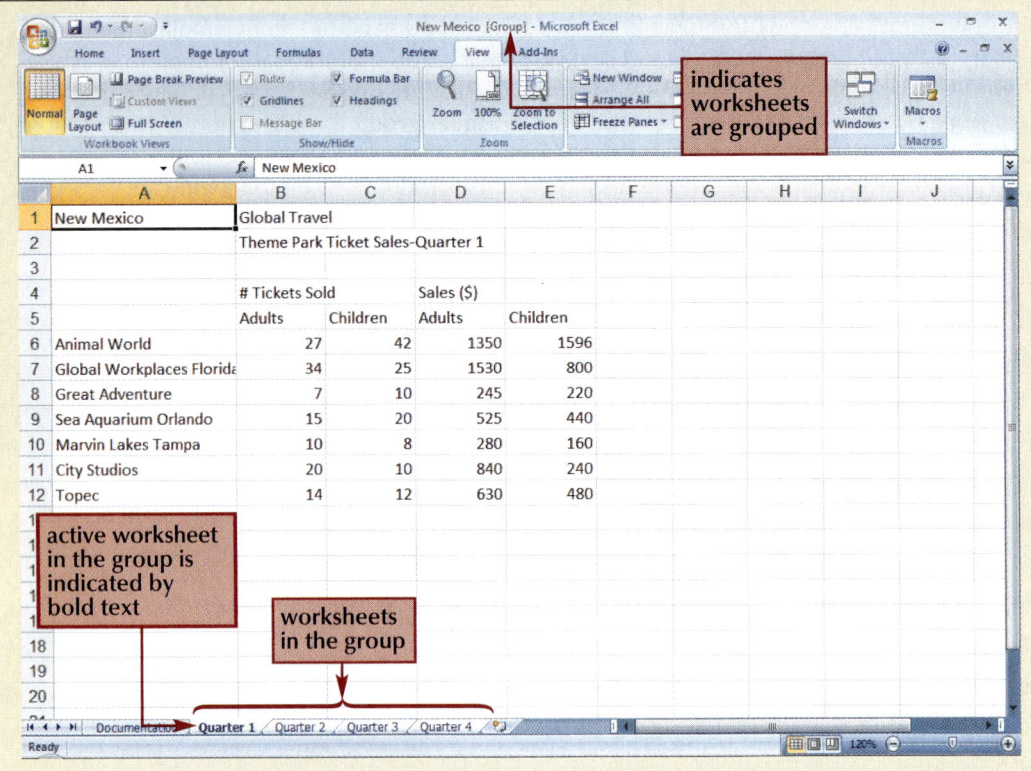

With the quarterly sheets grouped, you can enter the formulas to calculate the total number of tickets sold and total sales. When you enter a formula in the active worksheet (in this case, the Quarter 1 worksheet), the formula is entered in the same cells in all the worksheets in the group. The grouped worksheets must have the exact same organization and layout (rows and columns) for this to work. Otherwise, any formulas you enter in the active sheet will be incorrect in the other worksheets in the group and could overwrite existing data.

To enter the same formulas in all the worksheets in the group:

1. Click cell **B13**. You want to enter the formula in cell B13 in each of the four grouped worksheets.

2. In the Editing group on the Home tab, click the **Sum** button Σ, and then press the **Enter** key. The formula =SUM(B6:B12) is entered in the cell and adds the total number of adult tickets sold in the quarter, which is 127.

   You will copy the formula to add the total number of children's tickets sold, the total adult ticket sales, and the total children's ticket sales.

3. Copy the formula in cell B13 to the range **C13:E13**.

4. In cell A13, enter **Totals**, and then, in the Alignment group on the Home tab, click the **Increase Indent** button. The label shifts to the right.

   The formulas and label you entered in the Quarter 1 worksheet were entered in the Quarter 2, 3, and 4 worksheets at the same time.

5. Click the **Quarter 2** sheet tab, and then click cell **B13**. The value 174 appears in the cell and the formula =SUM(B6:B12), which adds the number of adult tickets sold in Quarter 2, appears in the formula bar.

6. Click the **Quarter 4** sheet tab, and then click cell **B13**. The value 177 appears in the cell, and the same formula used in cell B13 in the Quarter 1 and Quarter 2 worksheets appears in the formula bar. See Figure 6-3.

Figure 6-3 Formulas entered in all worksheets in the group

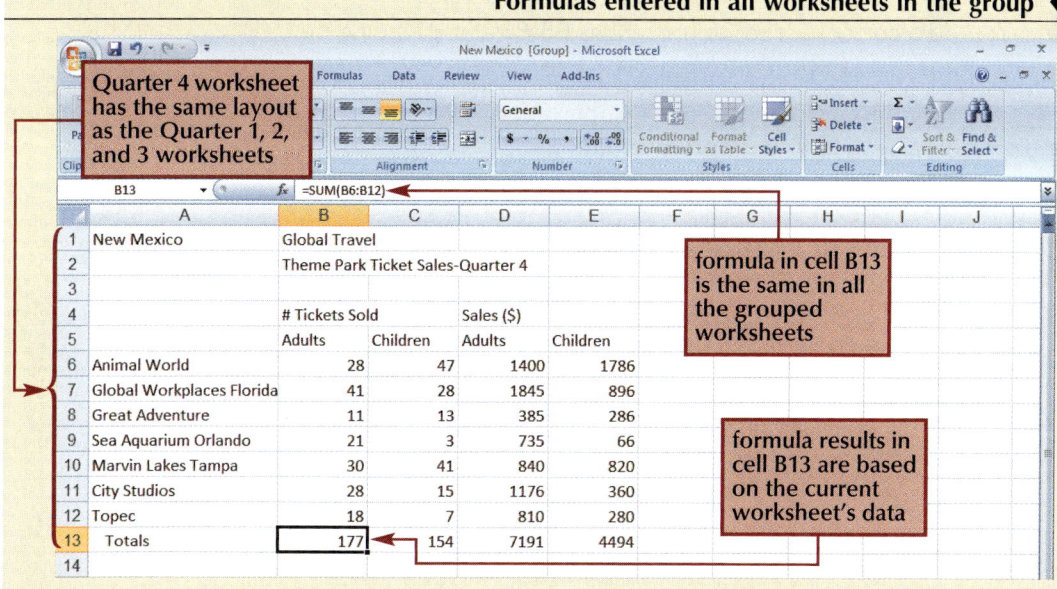

7. Click the **Quarter 1** sheet tab to redisplay the Quarter 1 results.

Editing Grouped Worksheets | InSight

When you enter, edit, or format cells in a worksheet group, the changes you make to one worksheet are automatically applied to the other worksheets in the group. For example, if you delete a value from one cell, the value in that cell in all the worksheets in the group is also deleted. Be cautious when editing the contents of a worksheet when it is part of a group. Also, remember to ungroup the worksheet group after you finish entering data, formulas, and formatting. Otherwise, changes you intend to make to a cell or range in one worksheet will be made to all the worksheets in the worksheet group, potentially producing incorrect results.

Formatting a Worksheet Group

Now that you've applied a common set of formulas to the quarterly worksheets, you can format them. As with inserting formulas and text, any formatting changes you make to a single sheet in a group are applied to all sheets.

To apply the same formatting to all the worksheets in the group:

1. Bold the text in the nonadjacent range **A1:B2;A6:A13;B4:E5**.
2. Increase the width of column A to **24**.
3. Merge and center each of the ranges **B1:E1**, **B2:E2**, **B4:C4**, and **D4:E4**.
4. Center the text in the range **B5:E5**.

5. Apply the **Comma Style** number format with no decimal places to the range **B6:C13**. No change is visible because all the numbers are less than 1000.

6. Apply the **Accounting** number format with no decimal places to the range **D6:E13** so the values appear with a dollar sign and no decimal places.

7. Add a bottom border to the ranges **B5:E5** and **B12:E12**.

8. Click cell **A1**. All the worksheets in the group are formatted. See Figure 6-4.

Figure 6-4   **Formatting applied to the worksheet group**

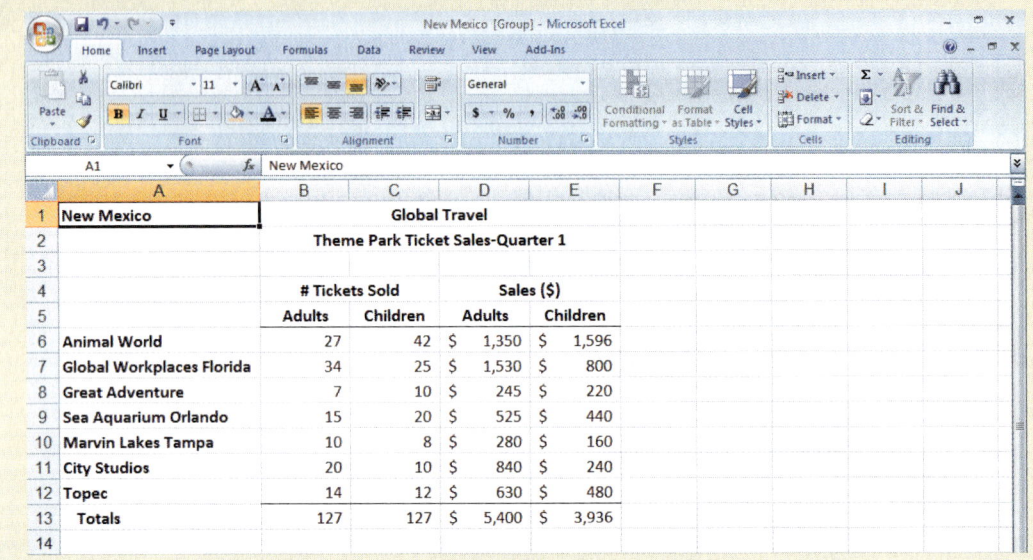

9. Click each sheet tab in the worksheet group to view the formatting changes, and then click the **Quarter 1** sheet tab.

Ungrouping Worksheets

You can ungroup the quarterly worksheets so you can work in each worksheet separately. When you ungroup the worksheets, each worksheet functions independently again. If you forget to ungroup the worksheets, any changes you make in one worksheet will be applied to all the worksheets in the group.

To ungroup the quarterly worksheets:

1. Click the **Documentation** sheet tab. The worksheets are ungrouped and the text *[Group]* is removed from the Excel title bar.

2. Verify that the worksheets are ungrouped and the word *[Group]* no longer appears in the title bar.

Tip

To ungroup worksheets, you can also right-click any sheet tab in the worksheet group, and then click Ungroup Sheets on the shortcut menu.

Copying Worksheets

Next, you'll create the Summary worksheet to provide an overall picture of the data included in the detailed quarterly worksheets. The Summary worksheet needs the same formatting and structure as the quarterly worksheets. To ensure consistency among worksheets, you will copy the Quarter 1 worksheet, and then modify its contents. The fastest way to copy an entire worksheet or worksheet group is to press and hold the Ctrl key as you drag and drop the sheet tab to another location in the workbook. A number in parentheses is added to the copy's sheet tab to distinguish it from the original worksheet. You will use this method to create the Summary worksheet.

Tip

To move a worksheet or worksheet group to another location in the same workbook, select the worksheets and then drag and drop them by the selected sheet tabs.

| Reference Window

Copying Worksheets to Another Workbook

- Select the sheet tabs of the worksheets you want to copy.
- Right-click the sheet tabs, and then click Move or Copy on the shortcut menu.
- In the Move or Copy dialog box, select the worksheets you want to move or copy to another workbook.
- Click the To book arrow, and then click an existing workbook name or (new book) to create a new workbook for the worksheets.
- Click the Create a copy check box to insert a check mark if you want to copy the worksheets to another workbook, leaving the originals in the current workbook; uncheck the Create a copy check box to move the worksheets.
- Click the OK button.

You'll copy the Quarter 1 worksheet to the beginning of the workbook, and then modify the new copy to create the Summary worksheet.

To copy the Quarter 1 worksheet and create the Summary worksheet:

1. Click the **Quarter 1** sheet tab, press and hold the **Ctrl** key, drag the worksheet to the left of the Documentation sheet, and then release the **Ctrl** key. An identical copy of the Quarter 1 worksheet appears in the new location. The sheet tab shows *Quarter 1 (2)* to indicate that this is the copied sheet.

2. Rename the copied worksheet as **Summary**.

3. Move the Summary worksheet between the Documentation worksheet and the Quarter 1 worksheet.

   You will modify the Summary worksheet.

4. In cell A2, enter **2010**. This is the year to which the summary refers.

5. In cell B2, enter **Theme Park Ticket Sales-Total**. The new title reflects this worksheet's content.

   The range B6:E12 should add the results for the entire year. You need to delete the Quarter 1 sales, which were copied from the Quarter 1 worksheet.

6. Select the range **B6:E12**, and then press the **Delete** key. The Quarter 1 sales data is removed, but the formatting remains intact and will apply to the sales data for all four quarters that you will enter shortly.

Referencing Cells and Ranges in Other Worksheets

The Summary worksheet will show the total sales for all four quarters, which are stored in separate worksheets. When you use multiple worksheets to organize related data, you can reference a cell or range in another worksheet in the same workbook. You'll do this to create the sales totals for the entire year.

To reference a cell or range in a different worksheet, you precede the cell or range reference with the worksheet name followed by an exclamation mark. The syntax is as follows:

```
=SheetName!CellRange
```

In this formula, *SheetName* is the worksheet's name as listed on the sheet tab and *CellRange* is the reference for the cell or range in that worksheet. An exclamation mark (!) separates the worksheet reference from the cell or range reference. For example, to enter a formula in the Summary worksheet that references cell D10 in the Quarter1 worksheet, you would enter the following formula:

```
=Quarter1!D10
```

If the worksheet name contains spaces, you must enclose the sheet name in single quotation marks. For example, the reference for the *Quarter 1* worksheet is *'Quarter 1'!D10*. You can use these references to create formulas that reference cells in different locations in different worksheets. For example, to add sales from two worksheets—cell E12 in the Quarter 1 worksheet and cell D12 in the Quarter 2 worksheet—you would enter the following formula:

```
='Quarter 1'!E12+'Quarter 2'!D12
```

Reference Window | Entering a Formula That References Another Worksheet

- Click the cell where you want to enter the formula.
- Type = and enter the formula. To insert a reference from another worksheet, click the sheet tab for the worksheet, and then click the cell or select the range you want to reference.
- When the formula is complete, press the Enter key.

Rhohit wants you to enter a formula in cell A2 in each quarterly worksheet that displays the fiscal year from cell A2 in the Summary worksheet. All four quarterly worksheets will use the formula *=Summary!A2* to reference the fiscal year in cell A2 of the Summary sheet. You could type the formula directly in the cell, but it is faster and more accurate to use the point-and-click method to enter references to other worksheets.

To enter a formula in the quarterly worksheets that references the Summary worksheet:

1. Click the **Quarter 1** sheet tab, press and hold the **Shift** key, and then click the **Quarter 4** worksheet. The Quarter 1 through Quarter 4 worksheets are grouped.

2. Click cell **A2**. This is the cell in which you want to enter the formula to display the fiscal year.

3. Type **=** to begin the formula, click the **Summary** sheet tab, click cell **A2**, and then press the **Enter** key. The reference to cell A2 in the Summary worksheet is entered in the formula in the grouped worksheets.

4. In the Quarter 1 worksheet, click cell **A2**. The formula *=Summary!A2* appears in the formula bar and 2010 appears in the cell. See Figure 6-5.

Figure 6-5 Formula with a worksheet reference

- cell displays the contents of cell A2 from the Summary worksheet
- formula references cell A2 in the Summary worksheet

A2 =Summary!A2

	A	B	C	D
1	New Mexico		Global Travel	
2	2010		Theme Park Ticket Sales-Quarter 1	
3				

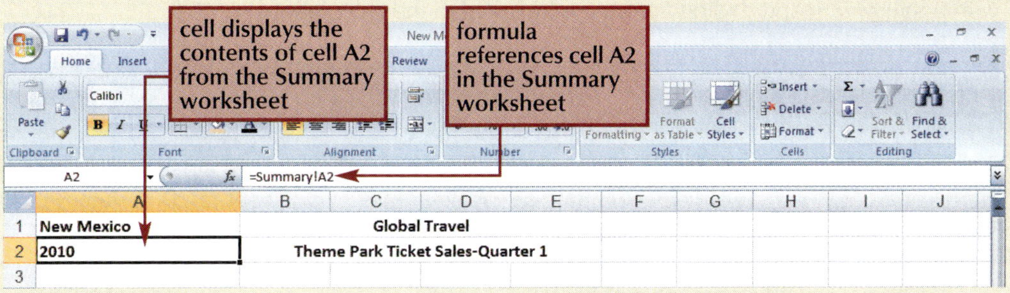

▸ **5.** In each worksheet, verify that the formula =*Summary!A2* appears in the formula bar and 2010 appears in cell A2.

Rhohit wants to use a more descriptive label in cell A2.

▸ **6.** Switch to the **Summary** worksheet. The quarterly worksheets are ungrouped.

▸ **7.** In cell A2, enter **Fiscal Year - 2010**.

▸ **8.** Verify that the label in cell A2 changed in the Quarter 1 through Quarter 4 worksheets.

Using 3-D References to Add Values Across Worksheets

You need to calculate the number of tickets sold and the total sales for each theme park for the year and display the totals for the fiscal year in the Summary worksheet. To calculate the totals for the year, you can add the results from each quarterly worksheet and place the sum in the Summary worksheet. For example, in cell B6 of the Summary worksheet, you can enter the formula:

```
='Quarter 1'!B6+'Quarter 2'!B6+'Quarter 3'!B6+'Quarter 4'!B6
```

This formula calculates the number of Adult tickets sold to Animal World by adding the values in cell B6 in each of the quarterly worksheets. Continuing this approach for the entire worksheet is time consuming and error prone. There is an easier way.

When two or more worksheets have *identical* row and column layouts, as do the quarterly worksheets in the New Mexico workbook, you can enter formulas with 3-D references to summarize those worksheets in another worksheet. A **3-D reference** refers to the *same* cell or range in multiple worksheets in the same workbook. The reference specifies not only the range of rows and columns, but also the range of worksheet names in which the cells appear. The general syntax of a 3-D cell reference is as follows:

```
WorksheetRange!CellRange
```

WorksheetRange is the range of worksheets you want to reference and is entered as *FirstSheetName:LastSheetName* with a colon separating the first and last worksheets in the worksheet range. *CellRange* is the same cell or range in each of those worksheets that you want to reference. An exclamation mark (!) separates the worksheet range from the cell or range.

For example, the formula *=SUM(Quarter1:Quarter4!E13)* adds the values in cell E13 in the worksheets between Quarter1 and Quarter4, including Quarter1 and Quarter4. If worksheets named *Quarter1, Quarter2, Quarter3,* and *Quarter4* are included in the workbook, the worksheet range *Quarter1:Quarter4* references all four worksheets. Although *Quarter2* and *Quarter3* aren't specifically mentioned in this 3-D reference, all worksheets positioned within the starting and ending names are included in the calculations.

> **InSight | Managing 3-D References**
>
> The results of a formula using a 3-D reference reflect the current worksheets in the worksheet range. If you move a worksheet outside the referenced worksheet range or remove a worksheet from the workbook, the formula results will change. For example, consider a workbook with four worksheets named *Quarter1, Quarter2, Quarter3, and Quarter4*. If you move the Quarter3 worksheet after the Quarter4 worksheet, the worksheet range *Quarter1:Quarter4* includes only the Quarter1, Quarter2, and Quarter4 worksheets. Similarly, if you insert a new worksheet or move an existing worksheet within the worksheet range, the formula results reflect the change. To continue the example, if you insert a Quarter5 worksheet before the Quarter4 worksheet, the 3-D reference *Quarter1:Quarter4* includes the Quarter5 worksheet.
>
> When you create a formula, make sure that the 3-D cell reference reflects the appropriate worksheets. Also, if you later insert or delete a worksheet within the 3-D reference, be aware of how doing so will affect the formula results.

3-D references are used in formulas that contain Excel functions, including SUM, AVERAGE, COUNT, MAX, MIN, STD, and VAR. You enter a 3-D reference either by typing the reference directly in the cell or by using your mouse to select first the sheet range, and then the cell or cell range.

> **Reference Window | Entering a Function That Contains a 3-D Reference**
>
> - Click the cell where you want to enter the formula.
> - Type = to begin the formula, type the name of the function, and then type (to indicate the beginning of the argument.
> - Click the sheet tab for the first worksheet in the worksheet range, press and hold the Shift key, and then click the tab for the last worksheet in the worksheet range.
> - Select the cell or range to reference, and then press the Enter key.

In the New Mexico workbook, you'll use 3-D references in the Summary worksheet to add the total number of tickets sold and sales for the year.

You will begin by entering a formula to add the number of tickets sold to adults for the Animal World theme park in all four quarters of the year. Then, you'll copy this formula to calculate the tickets sold to adults and children for each theme park as well as the sales generated.

To enter a formula with the 3-D reference to the quarterly worksheets:

▶ **1.** In the Summary sheet, click cell **B6**, and then type **=SUM(** to begin the formula. A ScreenTip shows the SUM function syntax.

You'll enter a 3-D reference to cell B6 in the four quarterly worksheets.

▶ **2.** Click the **Quarter 1** sheet tab, press and hold the **Shift** key, click the **Quarter 4** sheet tab, and then release the **Shift** key. The worksheet range is selected and added to the SUM function as *'Quarter 1:Quarter 4'*. Single quotation marks appear around the worksheet range because the worksheet names include spaces.

▶ 3. In the Quarter 1 worksheet, click cell **B6**. The cell is selected and added to the function. See Figure 6-6.

Figure 6-6   3-D reference added to the SUM function

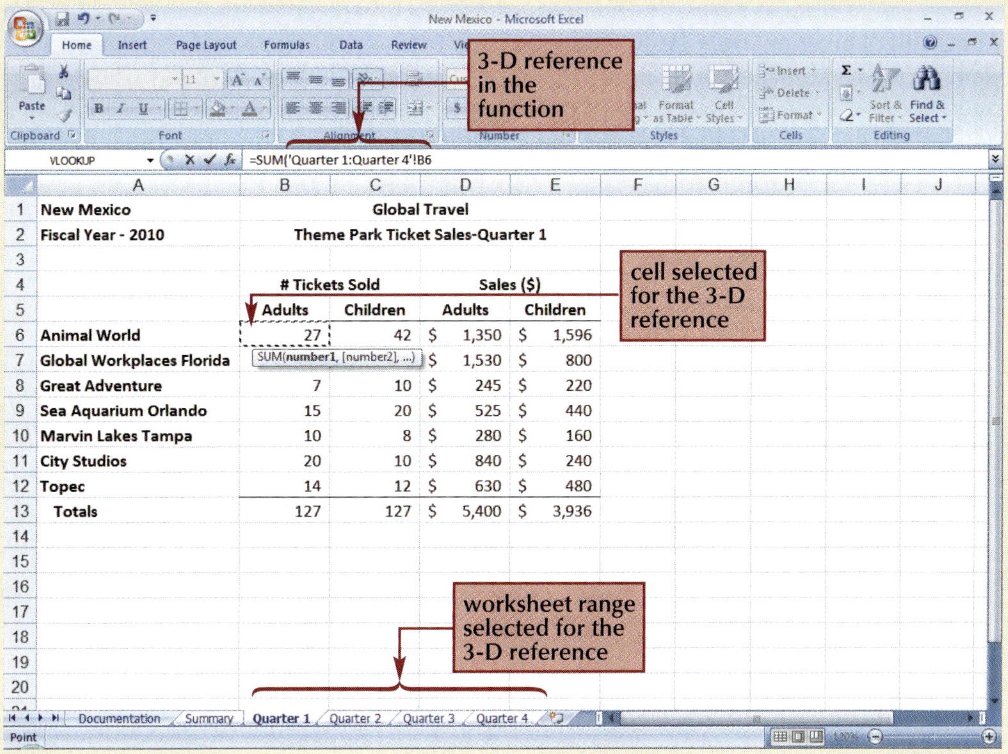

▶ 4. Press the **Enter** key to complete the formula, and then, in the Summary worksheet, click cell **B6**. The completed formula =SUM('Quarter 1:Quarter 4'!B6) appears in the formula bar, and 116—the total number of tickets for Animal World sold to adults in 2010—appears in cell B6.

You'll repeat the process to enter a 3-D reference in cell C6 that adds the total number of tickets sold to children for Animal World in 2010.

▶ 5. In the Summary worksheet, click cell **C6**, and then type **=SUM(** to begin the formula.

▶ 6. Click the **Quarter 1** sheet tab, press and hold the **Shift** key, click the **Quarter 4** sheet tab, and then release the **Shift** key. The quarterly worksheets are grouped.

▶ 7. In the Quarter 1 worksheet, click cell **C6** to select the cell, and then press the **Enter** key to complete the formula and return to the Summary worksheet.

▶ 8. In the Summary worksheet, click cell **C6**. The following formula appears in the formula bar: =SUM('Quarter 1:Quarter 4'!C6). Also, the value 175—the total number of tickets sold to children for Animal World in 2010—appears in cell C6.

In cells D6 and E6, you'll enter the SUM function with a 3-D reference to calculate the total revenue from tickets sales for Animal World.

▶ 9. In the Summary worksheet, click cell **D6**, type **=SUM(** to begin the formula, group the **Quarter 1** through **Quarter 4** worksheets, click cell **D6**, and then press the **Enter** key. The SUM function with a 3-D reference to cell D6 in the quarterly worksheets is entered. The completed formula is =SUM('Quarter 1:Quarter 4'!D6) and the total revenue from ticket sales to adults for Animal World in 2010 is $5,800.

10. In the Summary worksheet, click cell **E6**, then enter the SUM function formula with a 3-D reference to cell **E6** in the quarterly worksheets. The completed formula is =SUM('Quarter 1:Quarter 4'!E6) and the total revenue from ticket sales to children for Animal World in 2010 is $6,650.

Instead of entering the SUM function to create the totals for the remaining theme parks, you can copy the formulas to the rest of the range. You copy formulas with 3-D references the same way you copy other formulas—using copy and paste or AutoFill. You'll copy the formulas in the range B6:E6 to the range B7:E12 so you can calculate the total ticket sales and revenue in 2010 for the remaining theme parks.

To copy the formulas with 3-D cell references:

1. Select the range **B6:E6**. This range contains the SUM functions with the 3-D references you already entered.

2. Drag the fill handle down over the range **B7:E12**. The formulas are copied for the rest of the theme park rows. The Auto Fill Options button appears below the copied range.

3. Below cell E12, click the **Auto Fill Options** button, and then click the **Fill Without Formatting** option button. You don't want to copy the formatting in this case because you want to keep the bottom border formatting in the range B12:E12. The total values for the year appear in the range.

4. Click cell **B6** to deselect the range. See Figure 6-7.

Figure 6-7   Summary worksheet with all the 3-D reference formulas

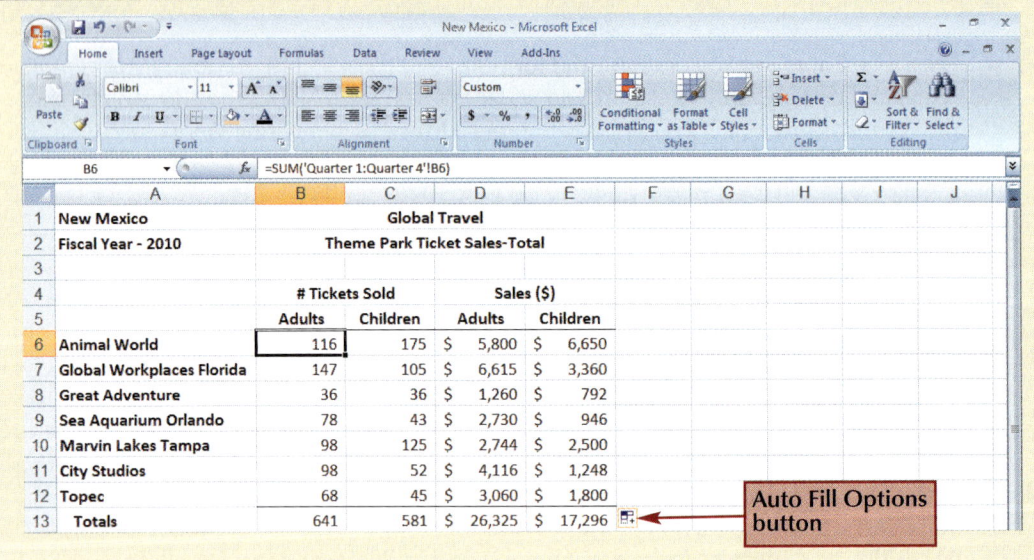

The Summary worksheet now shows the totals for the year 2010 in New Mexico for each theme park as well as statewide totals.

Rhohit discovered an error in the ticket sales data. Sea Aquarium Orlando sold 17 adult tickets in Quarter 1, not 15. One benefit of summarizing data using 3-D reference formulas, like any other formula, is that if you change the value in one worksheet, the results of formulas that reference that cell reflect the change. You will correct the number of tickets sold for Sea Aquarium Orlando in Quarter 1.

To change a value in the Quarter 1 worksheet:

1. In the Summary worksheet, note that 78 adult tickets were sold for Sea Aquarium Orlando in 2010 and 641 total adult tickets were sold.

2. Switch to the **Quarter 1** worksheet, and then, in cell B9, enter **17**. The total adult tickets sold in Quarter 1 is now 129.

   The results in the Summary worksheet are also updated because of the 3-D references in the formulas.

3. Switch to the **Summary** worksheet. The total number of tickets sold to adults for Sea Aquarium Orlando in 2010 is now 80, and the total number of tickets sold to adults for all theme parks in 2010 is now 643. See Figure 6-8.

Figure 6-8 Summary worksheet with updated ticket data

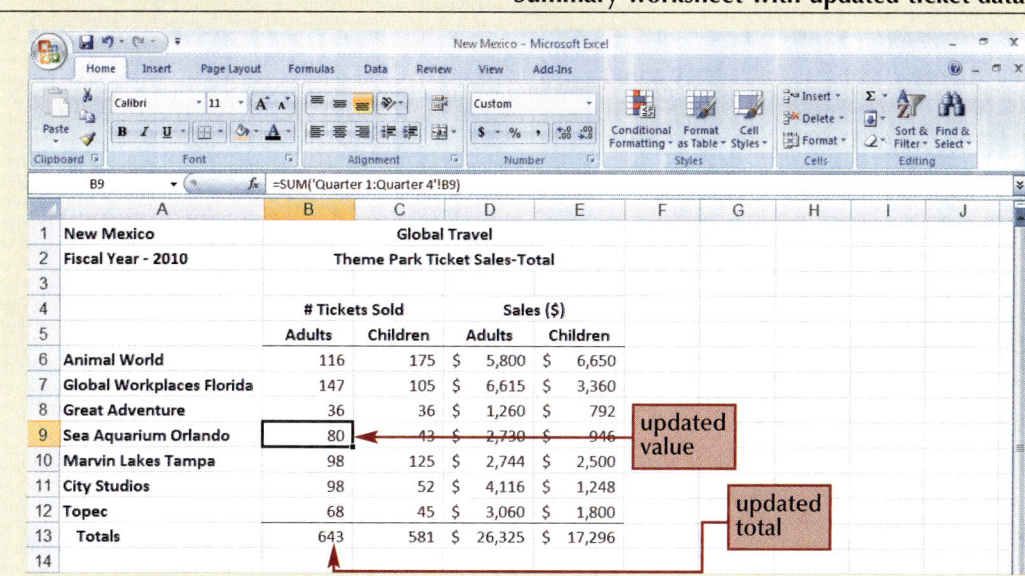

Printing a Worksheet Group

The Summary worksheet is complete and accurate. Rhohit asks you to print the five Ticket Sales worksheets to include in his report. He wants the same setup on each page. Recall that you set up the page layout and print area separately for each worksheet using the Page Layout tab on the Ribbon. Because the layout will be the same for all the quarterly worksheets in the New Mexico workbook, you can speed the page layout setup by creating a worksheet group before using the Page Setup dialog box. You will set up the worksheet group to print the report centered horizontally on the page with the name of the worksheet in the header and your name and the date in the footer.

To print the Summary and quarterly worksheets with a custom header and footer:

1. Select the **Summary** worksheet through the **Quarter 4** worksheet. The five worksheets are grouped.

2. Click the **Page Layout** tab on the Ribbon, and then, in the Page Setup group, click the Dialog Box Launcher. The Page Setup dialog box opens with the Page tab active.

3. Click the **Margins** tab, and then click the **Horizontally** check box to insert a check mark. The printed content will be centered horizontally on the page.

4. Click the **Header/Footer** tab, click the **Custom Header** button to open the Header dialog box, click in the **Center section** box, click the **Insert Sheet Name** button to add the code &[Tab] in the section box to insert the sheet tab name in the center section of the header, and then click the **OK** button. A preview of the header appears in the upper portion of the dialog box.

5. Click the **Custom Footer** button to open the Footer dialog box, type your name in the Left section box, click in the Right section box, click the **Insert Date** button to add the code &[Date] in the section box to insert the current date in the right section of the footer, and then click the **OK** button.

6. Click the **Print Preview** button. The Summary worksheet, the first worksheet in the group, appears in Print Preview. See Figure 6-9.

Figure 6-9   Print Preview of the worksheet group

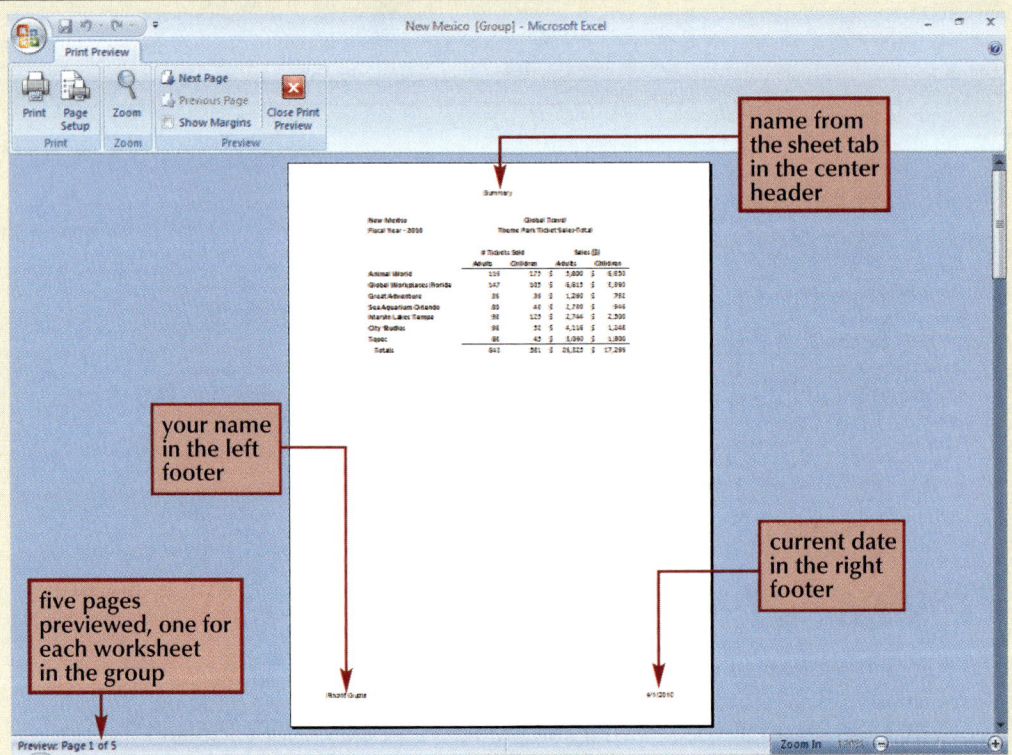

7. In the Preview group on the Print Preview tab, click the **Next Page** button four times to view the other four worksheets in the group. Each page has the same page layout but the header shows the sheet tab names.

   Trouble? If only one page appears in the Print Preview window, the worksheets are not grouped. Close the Print Preview window and repeat Steps 1 through 7.

8. In the Preview group on the Print Preview tab, click the **Close Print Preview** button to close the Print Preview window without printing the worksheet group, unless you are instructed to print. In that case, in the Print group on the Print Preview tab, click the **Print** button.

9. Switch to the **Documentation** sheet to ungroup the worksheets, and then switch to the **Summary** worksheet.

You have consolidated the data in Global Travel's New Mexico workbook in a Summary sheet, which will help Rhohit and the corporate controller to quickly see the totals for the theme park sales. Next, you will help the corporate controller to determine the annual totals for all of Global Travel's southwest locations—New Mexico, Utah, and Colorado.

Session 6.1 Quick Check | Review

1. What is a worksheet group?
2. How do you select an adjacent worksheet group? How do you select a nonadjacent worksheet group? How do you deselect a worksheet group?
3. What formula would you enter in the Summary worksheet to reference cell A10 in the Quarter 2 worksheet?
4. What is the 3-D cell reference to cell A10 in the adjacent Summary 1, Summary 2, and Summary 3 worksheets?
5. Explain what the formula *MAX(Sheet1:Sheet4!B1)* calculates.
6. If you insert a new worksheet (named *Sheet5*) after Sheet4, how would you change the formula in Question 5 to include Sheet5 in the calculation? How would you change the formula in Question 5 to include Sheet5 in the calculation if Sheet5 were positioned before Sheet4?
7. How do you apply the same printing page layout to all the worksheets in a workbook?

Session 6.2

Linking Workbooks

Alvin Alton, controller for Global Travel, has workbooks from the Colorado and Utah accountants similar to the one that you helped Rhohit prepare. Alvin now has three travel workbooks (named New Mexico, Colorado, and Utah), which contain the number of tickets sold and sales for the year 2010. Alvin wants to create a company-wide workbook that summarizes the annual totals from each state workbook.

If while creating formulas in one workbook you need to reference data located in one or more other workbooks, you must create a link between the workbooks. A **link** is a connection between the files that allows data to be transferred from one file to the other. When two files are linked, the **source file** is the workbook that contains the data, and the **destination file** (sometimes referred to as the *dependent* file) is the workbook that receives the data. In this case, as illustrated in Figure 6-10, the New Mexico, Utah, and Colorado workbooks are the *source* files because they contain the data from the three states. The Totals 2010 workbook is the *destination* file because it receives the data from the three state workbooks to calculate the company totals for 2010. Creating a link in the Totals 2010 workbook to the three state workbooks means the Totals 2010 workbook will always have access to the most recent information in the state workbooks, because it can be updated whenever any of the state workbook values change.

Figure 6-10 Source and destination files

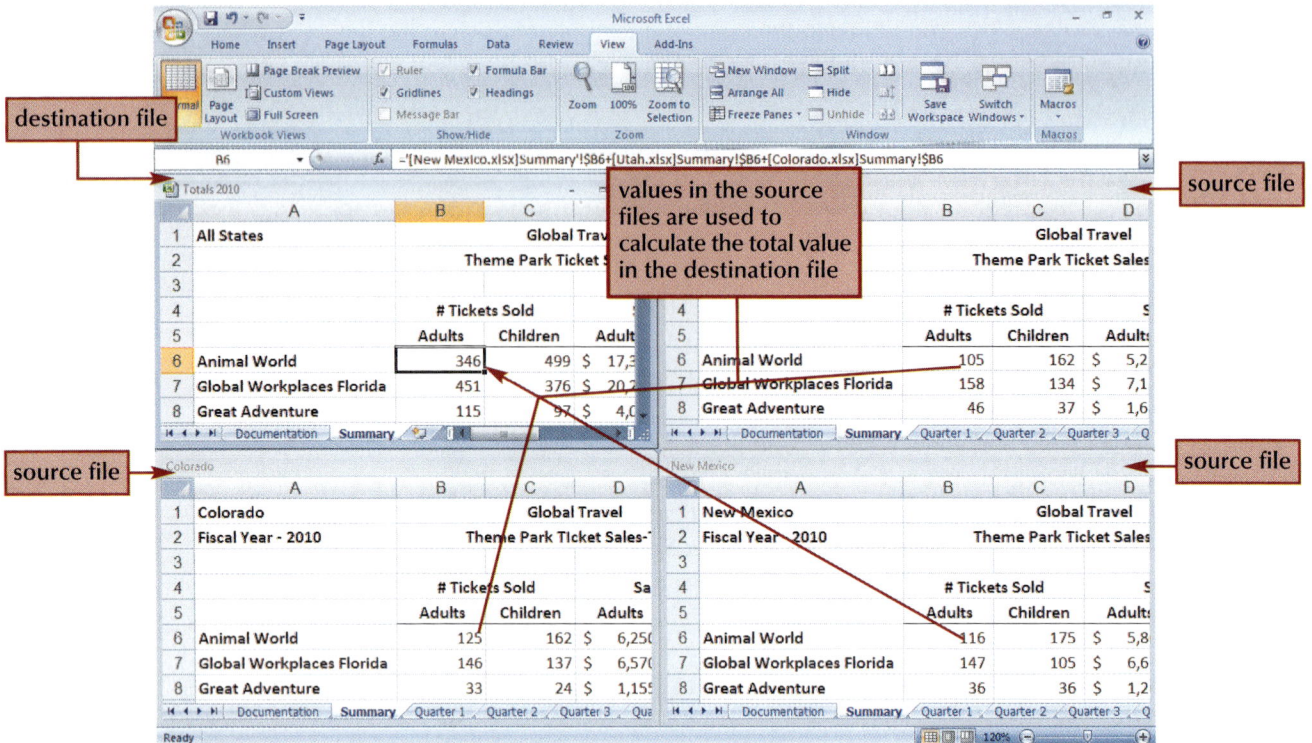

To create the link between destination and source files, you need to insert a formula in the Totals 2010 workbook that references a specific cell or range in the three state workbooks. Because the formula will contain a reference to a cell or range in a worksheet in another workbook, that reference is called an **external reference**. The syntax of an external reference is the following:

`[WorkbookName]WorksheetName!CellRange`

WorkbookName is the filename of the workbook (including the file extension) enclosed in square brackets. *WorksheetName* is the name of the worksheet that contains the data followed by an exclamation mark. *CellRange* is the cell or range that contains the data. For example, if you were to create a formula in one workbook to reference cell B6 in the Summary worksheet of the Colorado.xlsx workbook, you would enter the following formula:

`=[Colorado.xlsx]Summary!B6`

If the workbook name or the worksheet name contains one or more spaces, you must enclose the entire workbook name and worksheet name in single quotation marks. For example, to reference cell B6 in the Summary worksheet of the New Mexico.xlsx workbook, you would enter the following formula:

`='[New Mexico.xlsx]Summary'!B6`

Tip

When you use the point-and-click method to build formulas with external references, Excel enters all of the required punctuation, including quotation marks.

When the source and destination workbooks are stored in the same folder, you need to include only the workbook name in the external reference. However, when the source and destination workbooks are located in different folders, the workbook reference must include the file's complete location (also called the path). For example, if the destination file is stored in C:\TicketSales and the source file is stored in C:\TicketSales\Domestic Sales, the complete reference in the destination file would be:

='C:\TicketSales\Domestic Sales\[New Mexico.xlsx]Summary'!B6

The single quotation marks start at the beginning of the path and end immediately before the exclamation mark.

Understanding When to Link Workbooks | InSight

Linking workbooks is useful in many instances. The following are several examples of when to use linked workbooks:

- Separate workbooks have the same purpose and structure. For example, you can use related workbooks for different stores, branch offices, or departments with the same products or expenditure types and reporting periods (weekly, monthly, quarterly).
- A large worksheet has become unwieldy to use. You can break the large worksheet into smaller workbooks for each quarter, division, or product.
- A summary worksheet consolidates information from different workbook files. The linked workbooks enable you to more quickly and accurately summarize the information, and you know the summary worksheet contains the most current information if the information is later updated.
- Source workbooks you receive from another person or group are continually updated. With linked workbooks, you can replace an outdated source workbook and the destination workbook will then reflect the latest information without you having to modify the formulas.

Navigating and Arranging Multiple Workbooks

You'll combine the three state worksheets into one regional summary. You'll open all the workbooks you need to reference. Then, you'll switch between them to make each Summary worksheet the active sheet in preparation for creating the external references.

To open and switch between the workbooks needed to create the regional summary:

1. If you took a break after the previous session, make sure the New Mexico workbook is open and the Summary worksheet is active.

2. Open the **TravelTotals** workbook located in the **Tutorial.06\Tutorial** folder included with your Data Files, and then save the workbook as **Totals 2010** in the same folder.

3. Enter your name and the current date in the Documentation sheet, and then make the **Summary** worksheet active.

4. Open the **Utah** and **Colorado** workbooks located in the **Tutorial.06\Tutorial** folder included with your Data Files. Each open workbook has a button on the taskbar, but only one workbook is active.

5. Click the **View** tab on the Ribbon, and then, in the Window group, click the **Switch Windows** button to open a list of all the workbooks currently open.

6. Click **Utah** to make that the active workbook, and then make the **Summary** sheet active.

7. In the Window group on the View tab, click the **Switch Windows** button, click **Colorado** to switch to the Colorado workbook, and then make the **Summary** worksheet active.

8. Make the **Totals 2010** workbook the active workbook.

You'll need to move between open workbooks when you create the external reference formulas in the Totals 2010 workbook. Although you can use the Switch Windows button in the Window group on the View tab to change which workbook is active, you might find it easier to click the taskbar button for the workbook you want to make active.

Reference Window | **Arranging Workbooks**

- In the Window group on the View tab, click the Arrange All button.
- Select the desired option for arranging the workbook: Tiled, Horizontal, Vertical, or Cascade.
- When arranging multiple workbooks, uncheck the Windows of active workbook option unless you are arranging worksheets within one workbook.
- Click the OK button.

You might also want to display all the open workbooks on your screen at the same time. This way, you can easily click among the open workbooks to create links without having to continually change the active workbook. You can choose to arrange multiple open workbooks in one of four layouts:

- **Tiled** divides the open workbooks evenly on the screen.
- **Horizontal** divides the open workbooks into horizontal bands.
- **Vertical** divides the open workbooks into vertical bands.
- **Cascade** layers the open workbooks on the screen.

Currently, four workbooks are open but only one is visible. You'll arrange the workbooks using the tiled arrangement.

To tile the open workbooks:

1. In the Window group on the View tab, click the **Arrange All** button. The Arrange Windows dialog box opens so you can select the layout arrangement you want.

2. Click the **Tiled** option button, if necessary. The Tiled option arranges the four Global Travel workbooks evenly on the screen.

3. Click the **OK** button. The four open workbooks appear in a tiled layout. See Figure 6-11. Totals 2010 is the active workbook (you might have a different workbook active). In the tiled layout, the active workbook has darker text in the title bar and includes scroll bars.

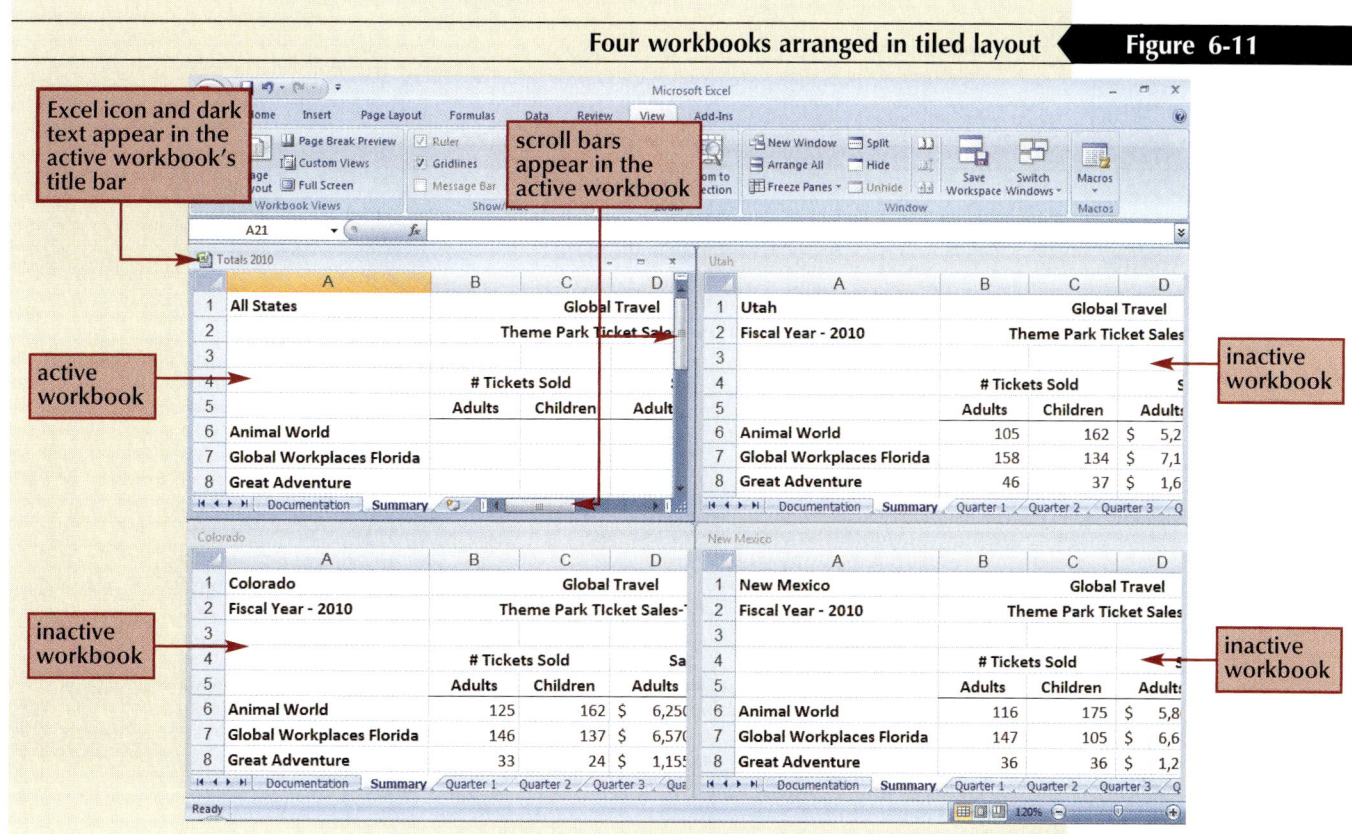

Figure 6-11 Four workbooks arranged in tiled layout

Creating External Reference Formulas

You need to enter the external reference formulas in the Totals 2010 workbook to create a set of linked workbooks and be able to summarize the states' totals into one workbook for Alvin. The process for entering a formula with an external reference is the same as entering any other formula using references within the same worksheet or workbook. You can enter the formulas by typing them or using the point-and-click method. In most situations, you will use the point-and-click method to switch between the source files and destination files so that Excel enters the references to the workbook, worksheet, and cell using the correct syntax.

You'll start by creating the formula that adds the total number of adult tickets to Animal World sold in New Mexico, Utah, and Colorado. You cannot use the SUM function with 3-D references here because you are referencing multiple workbooks.

To create the external reference formula to total adult tickets for Animal World:

1. In the Summary worksheet in the Totals 2010 workbook, click cell **B6**, and then type **=** to begin the formula.

2. Click anywhere in the **New Mexico** workbook, and then, in the Summary worksheet, click cell **B6**. The external reference to cell B6 in the Summary worksheet of the New Mexico workbook—'[New Mexico.xlsx]Summary'!$B$6—is added to the formula in the Totals 2010 workbook. See Figure 6-12.

Figure 6-12 — External reference entered in formula

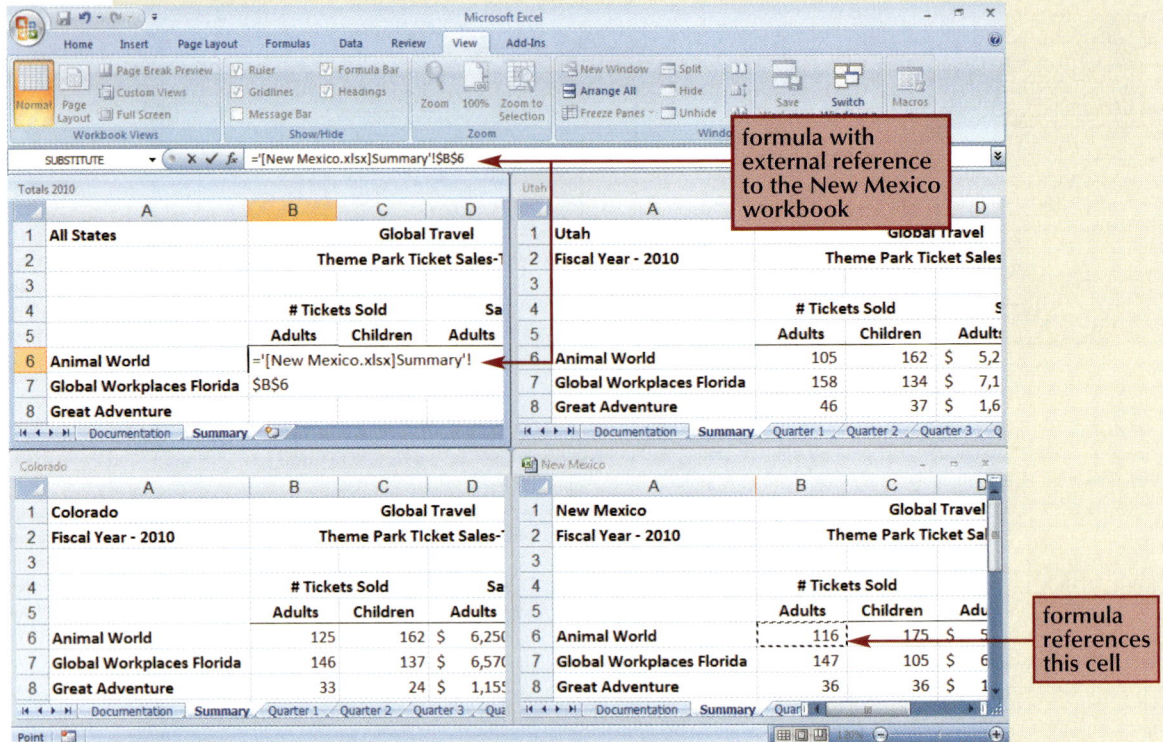

▶ 3. Type **+**. The Totals 2010 workbook becomes active and you can continue entering the formula. You need to create an external reference to the Utah workbook.

▶ 4. Click anywhere in the **Utah** workbook, click cell **B6** in the Summary worksheet, and then type **+**. The formula in the Totals 2010 workbook includes the external reference to the cell that has the total number of adult tickets to Animal World sold in Utah. The formula links two state workbooks to the Totals 2010 workbook.

Next, you'll create the external reference to the Colorado workbook.

▶ 5. Click anywhere in the **Colorado** workbook, click cell **B6** in the Summary worksheet, and then press the **Enter** key. The formula with three external references is entered in the Summary sheet in the Totals 2010 workbook.

▶ 6. In the Totals 2010 workbook, in the Summary sheet, click cell **B6**. The complete formula appears in the formula bar and the formula results appear in cell B6, showing that 346 adult tickets to Animal World were sold in the three states: 116 in New Mexico, 105 in Utah, and 125 in Colorado. See Figure 6-13.

Figure 6-13 Complete formula with external references

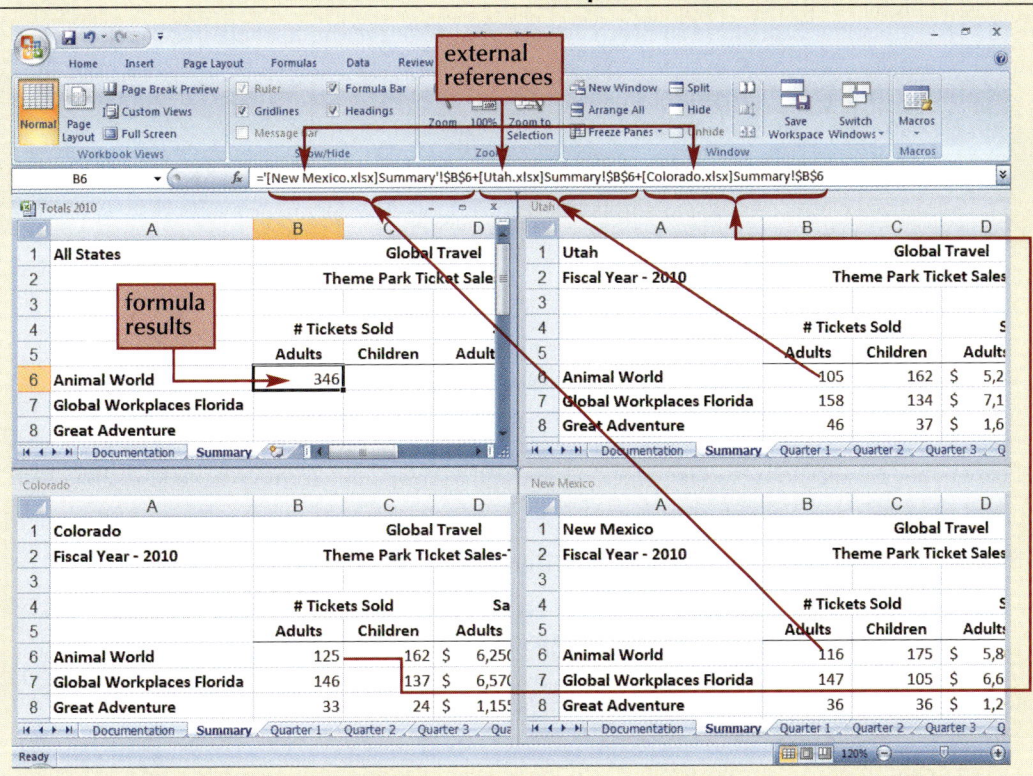

Trouble? If 346 doesn't appear in cell B6 in the Summary sheet in the Totals 2010 workbook, you might have clicked an incorrect cell for an external reference in the formula. Repeat Steps 1 through 6 to correct the formula.

You'll use the same process to enter the external reference formula for cell C6, which is the number of children's tickets to Animal World sold in the three states. Then you'll do the same to create the formulas to calculate the total sales from all three states.

To create the remaining external reference formulas:

1. In the Totals 2010 workbook, in the Summary worksheet, click cell **C6**, and then type **=** to begin the formula.

2. Click the **New Mexico** workbook, click cell **C6** in the Summary worksheet, and then type **+**. The formula in the Totals 2010 includes the external reference to cell C6 in the Summary worksheet in the New Mexico workbook.

3. Click the **Utah** workbook, click cell **C6** in the Summary worksheet, and then type **+**. The formula includes an external reference to cell C6 in the Summary worksheet in the Utah workbook.

4. Click the **Colorado** workbook, click cell **C6** in the Summary worksheet, and then press the **Enter** key. The external reference formula is complete.

5. In the Totals 2010 workbook, click cell **C6** in the Summary sheet. Cell C6 displays 499, the total children's tickets sold to Animal World, and the following formula appears in the formula bar: **='[New Mexico.xlsx]Summary'!$C$6+ [Utah.xlsx]Summary!$C$6+[Colorado.xlsx]Summary!$C$6.**

Next, you'll enter the external reference formulas in cells D6 and E6 to add the total sales from adult and children's tickets to Animal World.

6. Use the same procedure in Steps 1 through 4 to enter the formula in cell **D6** in the Summary worksheet in the Totals 2010 workbook. The formula results displayed in cell D6 are 17300—the total sales from adult tickets to Animal World in New Mexico, Utah, and Colorado.

7. Use the same procedure in Steps 1 through 4 to enter the formula in cell **E6** in the Summary worksheet in the Totals 2010 workbook. The formula results displayed in cell E6 are 18962—the total sales from children's tickets to Animal World in New Mexico, Utah, and Colorado.

You need to enter the remaining formulas for the six other theme parks (rows 7 to 12). Rather than creating the rest of the external reference formulas manually, you can copy the formulas in row 6 to rows 7 through 12. The formulas created using the point-and-click method contain absolute references. Before you copy the formula to other cells, you need to change the formulas to mixed references because the rows in the formula need to change.

To edit the external reference formulas to use mixed references:

1. Maximize the Totals 2010 workbook. The Totals 2010 workbook fills the program window. The other workbooks are still open but are not visible.

2. In the Summary worksheet, double-click cell **B6** to enter editing mode and display the formula in the cell.

3. Click in the first absolute reference in the formula, and then press the **F4** key twice to change the absolute reference $B$6 to the mixed reference $B6.

4. Edit the other two absolute references in the formula to be mixed references with absolute column references and relative row references.

5. Press the **Enter** key. The formula is updated to include mixed references, but the formula results aren't affected. Cell B6 still displays 346, which is correct.

6. Edit the formulas in cells C6, D6, and E6 to change the absolute references to the mixed references $C6, $D6, and $E6, respectively. The formulas are updated, but the cells in the range C6:D6 still correctly display 499, 17300, and 18962, respectively.

> **Tip**
> You can also create the mixed reference by deleting the $ from the row references in the formula.

With the formulas corrected to include mixed references, you can now copy the external reference formulas in cells B6:E6 to the other rows.

To copy the formulas to rows 7 through 12 and total the column values:

1. Select the range **B6:E6**, and then drag the fill handle to select the range **B7:E12**. The formulas are copied to the rest of the range B7:E12 and the formula results appear in the cells. The Auto Fill Options button appears in the lower-right corner of the selected range.

Next, you'll enter the SUM function to total the values in each column.

2. In cell B13, enter the SUM function to add the range **B6:B12**. A total of 2035 adult tickets were sold for all theme parks.

3. Copy the formula in cell B13 to the range **C13:E13**. The totals are 1855, 81889, and 55704, respectively.

4. Format cells D6:E13 with the **Accounting** number format with no decimal place.

5. Format the range **B12:E12** with a bottom border, and then click cell **A1** to deselect the range. See Figure 6-14.

Figure 6-14 Completed formulas in the Summary worksheet in the Totals 2010 workbook

	A	B	C	D	E
1	All States		Global Travel		
2			Theme Park Ticket Sales-Total		
3					
4		# Tickets Sold		Sales ($)	
5		Adults	Children	Adults	Children
6	Animal World	346	499	$ 17,300	$ 18,962
7	Global Workplaces Florida	451	376	$ 20,295	$ 12,032
8	Great Adventure	115	97	$ 4,025	$ 2,134
9	Sea Aquarium Orlando	202	100	$ 7,000	$ 2,200
10	Marvin Lakes Tampa	431	428	$ 12,068	$ 8,560
11	City Studios	283	149	$ 11,886	$ 3,576
12	Topec	207	206	$ 9,315	$ 8,240
13	Total	2035	1855	$ 81,889	$ 55,704

Alvin is pleased; the regional summary results match the executive team's expectations.

Managing Linked Workbooks | InSight

As you work with a linked workbook, you might need to replace a source file or change where you stored the source and destination files. However, replacing or moving a file can affect the linked workbook. Keep in mind the following guidelines to manage your linked workbooks. If you rename a source file, the destination workbook won't be able to find it. A dialog box opens, indicating "This workbook contains one or more links that cannot be updated." You click the Continue button to open the workbook with the most recent values, or you click the Change Source button in the Edit Links dialog box to specify the new name of that linked source file.

If you move a source file to a different folder, the link breaks between the destination and source files. Click the Change Source button in the Edit Links dialog box to specify the new location of the linked workbook.

If you receive a replacement source file, you can replace the original source file with the replacement file with no additional corrections.

If you receive a destination workbook but the source files are not included, Excel will not be able to find the source files, and a dialog box opens with the message "This workbook contains one or more links that cannot be updated." Click the Continue button to open the workbook with the most recent values, or click the Break button in the Edit Links dialog box to replace the external references with current values.

If you change the name of a destination file, you can open the destination file using a new name without making any corrections.

Updating Linked Workbooks

Rhohit calls Alvin to tell him of an incorrect value in the New Mexico workbook. The Animal World children's sales amount for Quarter 4 should be $2,786 not $1,786, which is currently in the file. Alvin asks you to change the value in the New Mexico workbook. How will a change to a value in any of the source workbooks affect the destination workbook?

When workbooks are linked, it is important that the data in the destination file accurately reflects the contents of the source file. When data in the source file changes, you want the destination file to reflect the changes. If both the source and destination files are open when you make a change, the destination file is updated automatically. If the destination file is closed when you make a change in the source file, you choose whether to update the link to display the current values when you open the destination file or continue to display the older values from the destination file.

You have both the source and destination files open. You will increase the value of Animal World children's sales for Quarter 4 in the New Mexico workbook by $1,000. This change will increase the amount in the Summary worksheet of the New Mexico workbook and the regional total in the Totals 2010 workbook.

To change the value in the source workbook with the destination file open:

▶ 1. Switch to the **New Mexico** workbook, and then make the **Quarter 4** worksheet active. You'll update the value of the Animal World children's dollar amount in this worksheet.

▶ 2. In cell E6, enter **2786**. The Animal World children's sales are updated.

▶ 3. Switch to the **Summary** worksheet in the New Mexico workbook, and then verify that the total Animal World children's sales is now $7,650.

Next, you'll check the regional total.

▶ 4. Switch to the **Totals 2010** workbook, and then, in the Summary worksheet, verify that the value in cell E6 is $19,962 and the total dollar amount from sales of children's tickets is $56,704, reflecting the new value you entered in the New Mexico workbook. Because both the destination and source files are open, Excel updated the destination file automatically.

▶ 5. Save the New Mexico and Totals 2010 workbooks, and then close the Utah, Colorado, and Totals 2010 workbooks. The New Mexico workbook remains open.

Opening Destination Workbooks with Source Workbooks Closed

When you save a workbook that contains external reference formulas, such as Totals 2010, Excel stores the most recent results of those formulas in the destination file. Source files, such as the New Mexico, Colorado, and Utah workbooks, are often updated while the destination file is closed. In that case, the values in the destination file are not updated at the same time the source files are updated. When you open the destination file again it contains the old values in the cells containing external reference formulas. Therefore, some of the values in the edited source workbooks are different from the values in the destination workbook. How do you update the destination workbook?

When you open a workbook with external reference formulas (the destination file), as part of the Excel security system that attempts to protect against malicious software, links to other workbooks cannot be updated without your permission. As a result, a Security Warning appears in the Message Bar immediately below the Ribbon, notifying you that the automatic update of links has been disabled. If you "trust" the provider of the source file(s), you can choose to "Enable this content," which allows the external reference formulas to function and updates the links in the destination workbook. If you do not "trust" the provider of the source files or do not want the destination file updated at that time, do not select "Enable this content." The old values in the destination workbook are displayed and the links to the source files remain disabled.

Tip

To change the default behavior of disabling automatic links, click the Office Button, click the Excel Options button, and then click Advanced. In the General section, uncheck the Ask to update automatic links check box, and then click the OK button.

Rhohit informs Alvin that the New Mexico workbook needs a second correction. Great Adventure adult sales in Quarter 4 are $435 not $385, which is the value currently in the New Mexico workbook. You will increase the amount of the Great Adventure adult sales in Quarter 4 by $50. As a result, sales in the Summary sheet of the New Mexico workbook and the regional total in the Totals 2010 workbook will both increase by $50.

Alvin asks you to open the New Mexico workbook, correct the value in the cell, and then save the workbook. You'll edit the source file, the New Mexico workbook, while the destination file is closed.

To update the source workbook with the destination file closed:

1. In the New Mexico workbook, make the **Quarter 4** worksheet active.

2. In cell D8, enter **435**. The total sales for adults in Quarter 4 increases to $7,241.

3. Switch to the **Summary** worksheet. The total sales for 2010 in cell D8 is $1,310 and total adult sales is $26,375. See Figure 6-15.

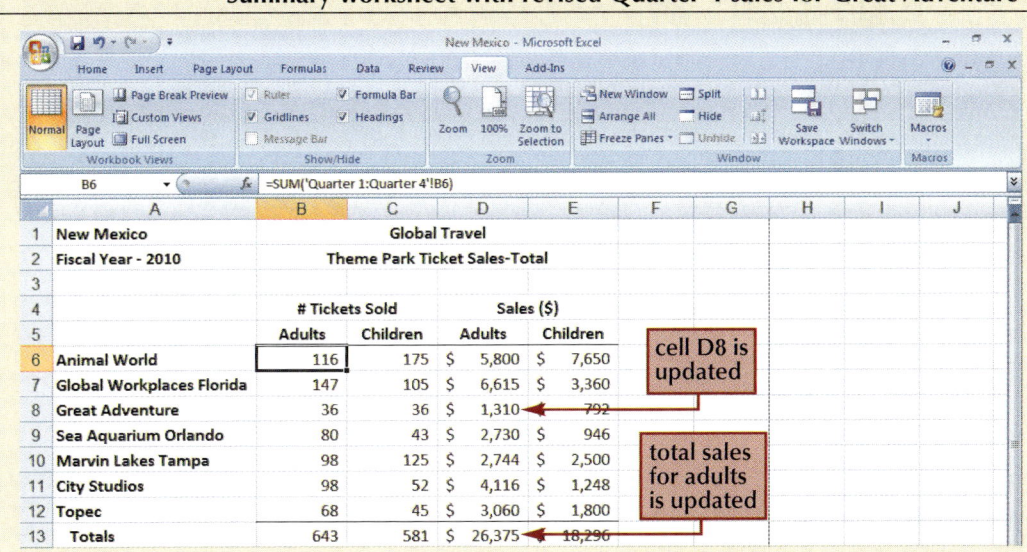

Figure 6-15 Summary worksheet with revised Quarter 4 sales for Great Adventure

4. Save and close the New Mexico workbook.

Now you'll open the destination file (the regional workbook) to see if the total is automatically updated.

5. Open the **Totals 2010** workbook, and then switch to the **Summary** worksheet. The value in cell D8 has *not* changed; it still is $4,025. A Security Warning message appears in the Message Bar, indicating that automatic update of links has been disabled. See Figure 6-16.

Tip

When the destination file is open and the source files are closed, the complete file path is included as part of the external reference formula that appears in the formula bar.

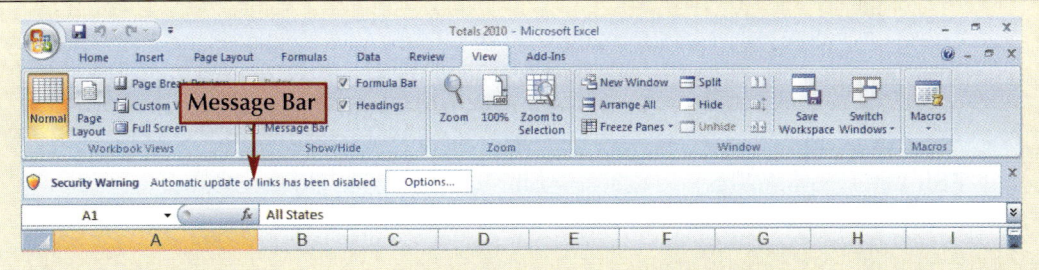

Figure 6-16 Security Warning in the Message Bar

You want the current values in the source files to appear in the destination workbook.

▶ 6. Click the **Options** button in the Message Bar. The Microsoft Office Security Options dialog box opens. See Figure 6-17.

Figure 6-17 | **Microsoft Office Security Options dialog box**

▶ 7. Click the **Enable this content** option button, and then click the **OK** button. The values in the destination file are updated. The sales in cell D8 of the Totals 2010 workbook increase to $4,075 and the total in cell D13 increases to $81,939.

▶ 8. Save the workbook.

Managing Links

After the fiscal year audit is completed and there are no more revisions to the source workbooks, Alvin will archive the summary workbook as part of his year-end backup process, and he'll move the files to an off-site storage location. He will make a copy of the Totals 2010 workbook and name it *Audited 2010*. Using the copy, he will break the links using the Break Links command in the Edit Links dialog box, which converts all external reference formulas to their most recent values.

To save a copy of the Totals 2010 workbook and open the Edit Links dialog box:

▶ 1. Click the **Office Button**, and then click **Save As**. The Save As dialog box opens.

▶ 2. Change the filename to **Audited 2010**, make sure the save location is the **Tutorial.06\Tutorial** folder included with your Data Files, and then click the **Save** button. The Totals 2010 workbook closes and the Audited 2010 workbook remains open.

▶ 3. Click the **Data** tab on the Ribbon, and then, in the Connections group, click the **Edit Links** button. The Edit Links dialog box opens. See Figure 6-18.

Tutorial 6 Managing Multiple Worksheets and Workbooks | Excel **EX 307**

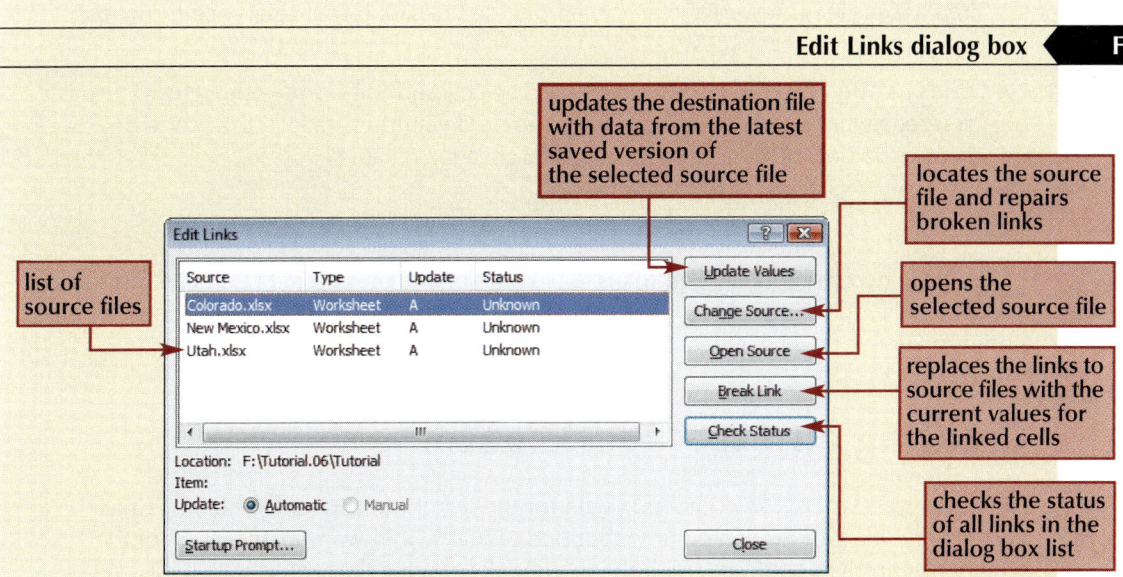

Figure 6-18 Edit Links dialog box

The Edit Links dialog box lists all of the files the destination workbook is linked to so that you can update, change, open, or remove the links. You can see that the destination workbook, Audited 2010, has links to the Colorado, New Mexico, and Utah workbooks. The dialog box shows the following information about each link:

- **Source**. The file the link points to. The Audited 2010 workbook contains three links pointing to the workbooks New Mexico.xlsx, Colorado.xlsx, and Utah.xlsx.
- **Type**. The type of each source file. In this case, the type is an Excel worksheet but it could also be a Word document, PowerPoint presentation, or some other type of file.
- **Update**. The way values are updated from the source file. The letter *A* indicates the link is updated automatically when you open the workbook or when both the source and destination files are open simultaneously. The letter *M* indicates the link must be updated manually by the user. You can set a link to update manually when you want to see the older data values before updating to the new data. Click the Update Values button in the Edit Links dialog box if the Update option is set to *M* and you want to see the new data values.
- **Status**. Whether Excel successfully accessed the link and updated the values from the source document (Status is OK), or Excel has not attempted to update the links in this session (Status is Unknown). The status of the three links in the Audited 2010 workbook is Unknown.

You'll break the links so the Audited 2010 workbook contains only the updated values (and is no longer affected by changes in the source files). Then you'll save the Audited 2010 workbook for Alvin to archive. This allows Alvin to store a "snapshot" of the data at the end of the fiscal year.

To convert all external reference formulas to their current values:

1. Click the **Break Link** button. A dialog box opens, alerting you that breaking links in the workbook permanently converts formulas and external references to their existing values.
2. Click the **Break Links** button. No links appear in the Edit Links dialog box.
3. Click the **Close** button. The Audited 2010 workbook now contains values instead of formulas with external references.

Tip

When you use the Break Link button, you cannot undo that action. To restore the links, you must reenter the external reference formulas.

You'll examine the worksheet to see how the links (external reference formulas) were converted to values.

4. Click cell **B6**. The value 346 appears in the cell and the formula bar; the external reference formula was replaced with the data value. All cells in the range B6:E12 contain values rather than external reference formulas.

5. Save and close the Audited 2010 workbook.

You have two workbooks. The Totals 2010 workbook has external reference formulas, and the Audited 2010 workbook has current values. The Audited 2010 workbook will be stored in Global Travel's off-site storage.

Creating an Excel Workspace

Alvin has four workbooks containing data for the ticket sales. Usually, he'll need to access only one workbook at a time, but occasionally he'll want to access all of the workbooks. If Alvin could open all the workbooks at once, he would save time, and, more important, not have to remember all the filenames and folder locations.

To open multiple workbooks at one time, you need to create a workspace. A **workspace** is an Excel file that saves information about all of the currently opened workbooks, such as their locations, window sizes, zoom magnifications, and other settings. The workspace does not contain the workbooks themselves—only information about them. To use that set of workbooks, you can open the workspace file. Excel then opens the workbooks and settings in the same configuration they were in when you saved the workspace file. Even if a workbook is included in a workspace file, you can still open that workbook separately.

You will create a workspace file for Alvin that includes the four workbooks in a cascade layout, which arranges the open workbooks so that they overlap each other with all the title bars visible. Alvin prefers this layout, because he can see more of the active workbook.

> **Tip**
>
> Because the workspace file contains only the location and name of each file, not the actual workbooks and worksheets, you cannot copy only the workspace file to another computer. Instead, you need to also copy the workbook files.

To create the Theme Parks workspace file:

1. Open the **Colorado**, **New Mexico**, **Utah**, and **Totals 2010** workbooks located in the **Tutorial.06\Tutorial** folder included with your Data Files. Four workbooks are open.

2. Make sure the **Summary** worksheet is the active worksheet in each workbook.

3. Switch to the **Totals 2010** workbook.

4. Click the **View** tab on the Ribbon, and then, in the Window group, click the **Arrange All** button. The Arrange Windows dialog box opens.

5. Click the **Cascade** option button, and then click the **OK** button. The four workbooks overlap each other, with the title bars visible. See Figure 6-19.

Workbooks arranged in the cascade layout | Figure 6-19

cascade arrangement (your workbook order might differ)

	A		# Tickets Sold		Sales ($)		E	F	G	H
1	All States		Global Travel							
2			Theme Park Ticket Sales-Total							
3										
4			# Tickets Sold		Sales ($)					
5			Adults	Children	Adults	Children				
6	Animal World		346	499	$ 17,300	$ 19,962				
7	Global Workplaces Florida		451	376	$ 20,295	$ 12,032				
8	Great Adventure		115	97	$ 4,075	$ 2,134				
9	Sea Aquarium Orlando		202	100	$ 7,000	$ 2,200				
10	Marvin Lakes Tampa		431	428	$ 12,068	$ 8,560				
11	City Studios		283	149	$ 11,886	$ 3,576				
12	Topec		207	206	$ 9,315	$ 8,240				
13	Total		2035	1855	$ 81,939	$ 56,704				

▶ 6. In the Window group on the View tab, click the **Save Workspace** button. The Save Workspace dialog box opens and functions similarly to the Save As dialog box.

▶ 7. Type **Theme Parks** in the File name box, verify that **Workspaces** is selected in the Save as type box, verify that the save location is the **Tutorial.06\Tutorial** folder, and then click the **Save** button. A dialog box might open, prompting you to save your changes to the open workbook files, if you haven't already done so.

▶ 8. If prompted to save changes, click the **Yes** button. The Theme Parks workspace file is saved. The workspace file has the file extension .xlw.

You will test the workspace file you created to make sure it opens all four Global Travel workbooks.

To test the Theme Parks workspace file:

▶ 1. Close all four workbooks.

▶ 2. Click the **Office Button**, and then click **Open**. The Open dialog box opens, displaying the Tutorial.06\Tutorial folder. The icon for the Theme Parks workspace file is different from the Excel workbook file icon.

▶ 3. Click **Theme Parks** in the list of files, and then click the **Open** button. The four travel workbooks open and are arranged in a cascade layout, the same layout in which you saved them. You can then work with the workbooks as usual

▶ 4. Click the **Colorado** workbook title bar to bring it to the front of the cascaded workbooks. Colorado is now the active workbook.

The workspace file provides a quick way to open a series of workbooks in a specific display. Because it doesn't actually contain the workbooks, you must close each workbook separately, saving as needed.

▶ 5. Close the New Mexico, Utah, Colorado, and Totals 2010 workbooks without saving any changes.

In this session, you worked with multiple worksheets and workbooks, summarizing data and linking workbooks. This ensures that the data in the summary workbook is accurate and remains updated with the latest data in the source files.

Review | Session 6.2 Quick Check

1. What is the external reference to the range A1:A10 in the Sales Info worksheet in the Product Report workbook located in the Reports folder on drive D?
2. What is a source file?
3. What is a destination file?
4. Name two ways to update a link in a workbook.
5. How would you determine to what workbooks a destination file is linked?
6. What is a workspace file?
7. Explain how workspace files can help you organize your work.

Session 6.3

Creating a Hyperlink

Alvin has written an executive memo summarizing the results for 2010. He wants to give members of the executive team at Global Travel easy access to the memo by including a hyperlink from his workbook to the memo.

Inserting a Hyperlink

You can insert a hyperlink directly in a workbook file. A **hyperlink** is a link in a file, such as a workbook, to information within that file or another file. The hyperlinks are usually represented by colored words with underlines or images. When you click a hyperlink, the computer switches to the file or portion of the file referenced by the hyperlink. Although hyperlinks are most often found on Web pages, they can also be placed in a worksheet and used to quickly jump to a specific cell or range within the active worksheet, another worksheet, or another workbook. Hyperlinks can also be used to jump to other files, such as a Word document or a PowerPoint presentation, or sites on the Web.

To use a hyperlink, you click the text inside the cell that contains the link. If you click white space in the cell or any text that flows into an adjacent cell, the hyperlink does not work.

Tutorial 6 Managing Multiple Worksheets and Workbooks | Excel | EX 311

| Inserting a Hyperlink | Reference Window

- Select the text, graphic, or cell in which you want to insert the hyperlink.
- In the Links group on the Insert tab, click the Hyperlink button.
- To link to a file or Web page, click Existing File or Web Page in the Link to list, and then select the file or Web page from the Look in box.
- To link to a location in the current workbook, click Place in This Document in the Link to list, and then select the worksheet, cell, or range in the current workbook.
- To link to a new document, click Create New Document in the Link to list, and then specify the filename and path of the new document.
- To link to an e-mail address, click E-mail Address in the Link to list, and then enter the e-mail address of the recipient and a subject line for the e-mail message.
- Click the OK button.

Alvin wrote a memo summarizing the sales results for New Mexico, Utah, and Colorado in 2010. He wants the Totals 2010 workbook to include a link to this memo that points to the Word document Sales 2010.docx located in the Tutorial.06\Tutorial folder included with your Data Files.

To insert a hyperlink into the Totals 2010 workbook:

1. Open the Totals 2010 workbook located in the **Tutorial.06\Tutorial** folder included with your Data Files.

2. Switch to the **Documentation** worksheet, and then click cell **A12**. You want to create the hyperlink in this cell.

3. Click the **Insert** tab on the Ribbon, and then, in the Links group, click the **Hyperlink** button. The Insert Hyperlink dialog box opens with the Existing File or Web Page button selected in the Link to bar and the Current Folder displayed in the Look in area. You use this dialog box to define the hyperlink. See Figure 6-20.

Figure 6-20 Insert Hyperlink dialog box

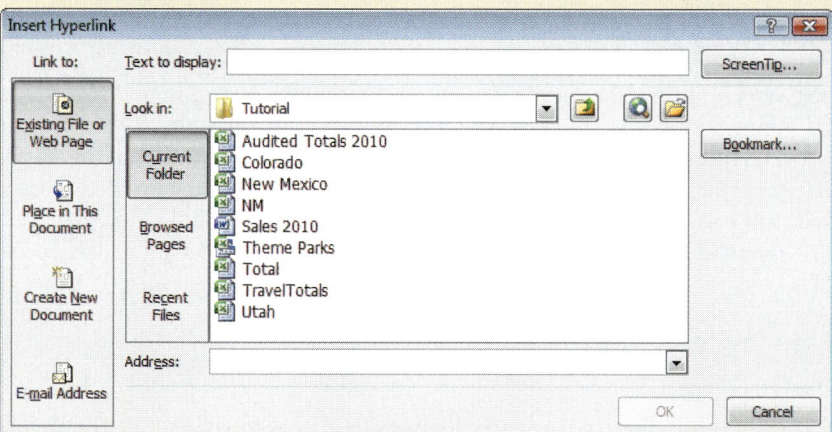

Trouble? If either the Existing File or Web Page option or the Current Folder option is not selected, select it before continuing.

4. Click the **Text to display** box, and then type **Click here to read Executive Memo**. This is the hyperlink text that will appear in cell A12 in the Documentation sheet.

5. Click the **Sales 2010** Word document in the list of files, and then click the **OK** button. As shown in Figure 6-21, the hyperlink text is in underlined blue font, indicating that the text within the cell is a hyperlink.

Figure 6-21 — Hyperlink to the Sales 2010 document

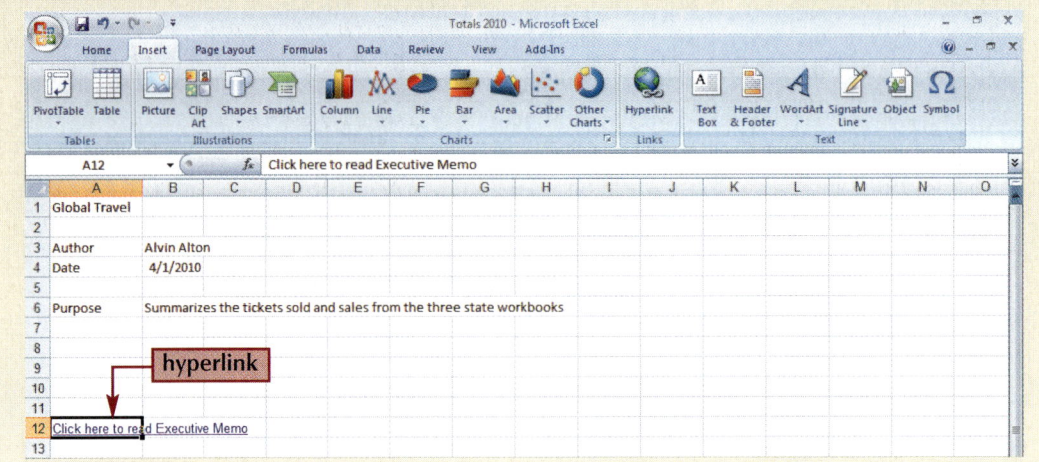

You will test the hyperlink that you just created to ensure it works correctly. To use a hyperlink, you click the text inside the cell that contains the link.

To jump to the hyperlink:

1. Point to cell **A12** until you see ♛, and then click the hyperlink. The Sales 2010 document opens in Word.

   Trouble? If the hyperlink doesn't work, you might have clicked the text that overflows cell A12. Point to the text within cell A12, and then click the hyperlink.

2. Click the **Close** button ⊠ on the Word title bar to close the document and exit Word. The Documentation sheet in the Totals 2010 workbook is active. The color of the hyperlink in cell A12 changed to indicate that you have used the link.

Editing a Hyperlink

ScreenTips, which appear whenever you place the pointer over a hyperlink, provide additional information about the target of the link. The default ScreenTip is the folder location and filename of the file you will link to. Alvin doesn't think that this is very helpful. He wants you to change the ScreenTip for the link you just created to be more descriptive. You can insert a ScreenTip when you create a hyperlink. However, because you've already created this hyperlink, you'll edit the hyperlink to change the ScreenTip.

To edit the hyperlink:

1. In the Documentation worksheet, right-click cell **A12**, and then click **Edit Hyperlink** on the shortcut menu. The Edit Hyperlink dialog box opens; it has the same layout and information as the Insert Hyperlink dialog box.

2. Click the **ScreenTip** button. The Set Hyperlink ScreenTip dialog box opens.

3. Type **Click to view sales analysis for 2010** in the ScreenTip text box, and then click the **OK** button.

4. Click the **OK** button to close the Edit Hyperlink dialog box.

5. Point to cell **A12**, confirm that the ScreenTip *Click to view sales analysis for 2010* appears just below the cell, and then save and close the Totals 2010 workbook.

Alvin agrees that the ScreenTip is a useful addition to the hyperlink. If you want to remove a hyperlink, right-click the cell containing the hyperlink and then click Clear Contents on the shortcut menu to delete the hyperlink and text.

> **Tip**
> You can keep the text of a hyperlink but remove the functioning link by clicking Remove Hyperlink on the shortcut menu.

Creating Templates

The three state workbooks for 2010 have the same format. Alvin wants to use this workbook format for data collection and analysis for next year. One approach to accomplish this goal is to open one of the state workbooks, save it with a new name, and then replace the 2010 values with blank cells. Alvin is reluctant to use that approach because he might forget to change the filename and inadvertently overwrite the previous year's figures with blank cells when he saves the workbook. A better alternative is to have an Excel workbook that Alvin can open with the labels, formats, and formulas already built into it. Such a workbook is called a **template**. You use the template workbook as a model from which you create new workbooks.

When you use a template to create a new workbook, a copy of the template opens that includes text (row and column labels), formatting, and formulas from the template. Any changes or additions you make to the new workbook do not affect the template file. The original template retains its formatting and formulas, and the next time you open a workbook based on the template, those original settings will still be present.

There are several advantages to creating and using templates:

- Templates save you time entering formulas and formatting when you need to create several workbooks with similar features.
- Templates help you standardize the appearance and content of workbooks.
- Templates prevent you from accidentally saving new data in an old file if you use the Save command instead of the Save As command when basing a new workbook on an existing workbook.

Using Excel Templates | InSight

Excel has many templates available. Some are automatically installed on your hard disk when you install Excel, and others are available from the Microsoft Office Online Web site. In fact, the blank Book1 workbook that opens when you start Excel is based on the **default template**. The default template contains no text or formulas, but it includes all the formatting available in every new workbook: General number format applied to numbers, Calibri 11-point font, labels aligned to the left side of a cell, values and the formula results aligned to the right side of a cell, column width set to 8.43 characters, three worksheets inserted in the workbook, and so forth.

You can also download templates from the Microsoft Office Online Web site. These templates provide commonly used worksheet formats, saving you from "reinventing the wheel." Some of the task-specific templates available from the Microsoft Office Online Web site include the following:

- **Family Budget**. This template builds projections and actual expenditures for items such as housing, transportation, and insurance.
- **Inventory List**. This template tracks the cost and quantity reorder levels of inventory.
- **Team Roster**. This template lists each player's name, phone number, e-mail address, and so forth.
- **Time sheet**. This template creates an online time card to track employees' work hours.

If you need to create the same type of workbook repeatedly, it's a good idea to use a template to both save time and to ensure consistency in the design and content of the workbooks you create.

Creating a Workbook Based on an Existing Template

To see how templates work, you'll create a new workbook based on one of the Excel templates provided by Microsoft.

Reference Window | Creating a Workbook Based on a Template

- Click the Office Button, and then click New.
- In the Templates pane, click a template category for the type of workbook you want to create.
- In the center pane, click the template you want to use, and then click the Download button.
- Click the Continue button to let Microsoft verify your software.
- Save the workbook with a new filename.

You'll download the Time card template. **Note:** You need an Internet connection to complete the following set of steps; if you don't have an Internet connection, you should read but not complete the steps involving creating and using the online template.

To create a workbook based on a Microsoft Office Online template:

1. Click the **Office Button**, and then click **New**. The New Workbook dialog box opens. The left pane lists the Microsoft Office Online template categories.

2. Click **Time sheets**. A gallery of Time sheet templates appears in the center pane. The right pane shows a preview of the selected template.

3. Scroll down the center pane until you see Time card, and then click the **Time card** thumbnail image. A preview of the worksheet based on the template appears in the right pane. See Figure 6-22.

Figure 6-22   Preview of the Time card template

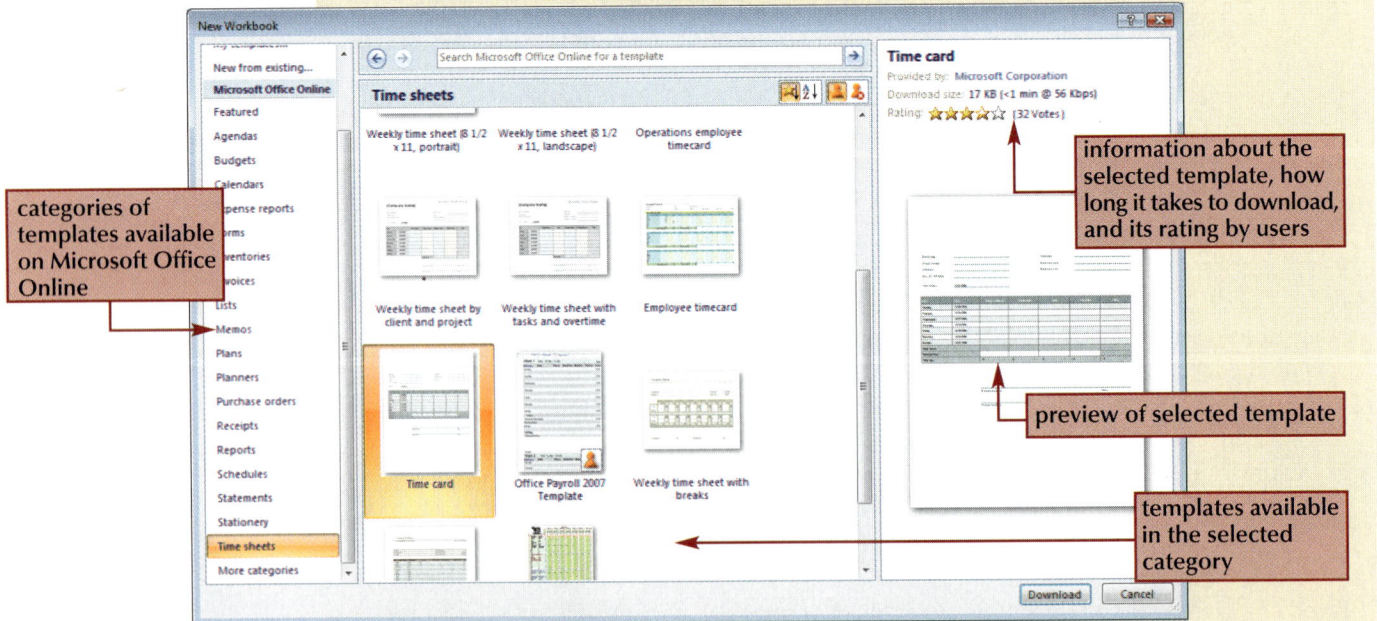

▶ 4. Click the **Download** button. The Microsoft Office Genuine Advantage dialog box opens. Before you can access the templates on Microsoft Office Online, Microsoft verifies that you have an authentic copy of the software.

▶ 5. Click the **Continue** button to verify the copy of Microsoft Office on your computer. The Time card template opens. See Figure 6-23.

Figure 6-23 Workbook created from the Time card template

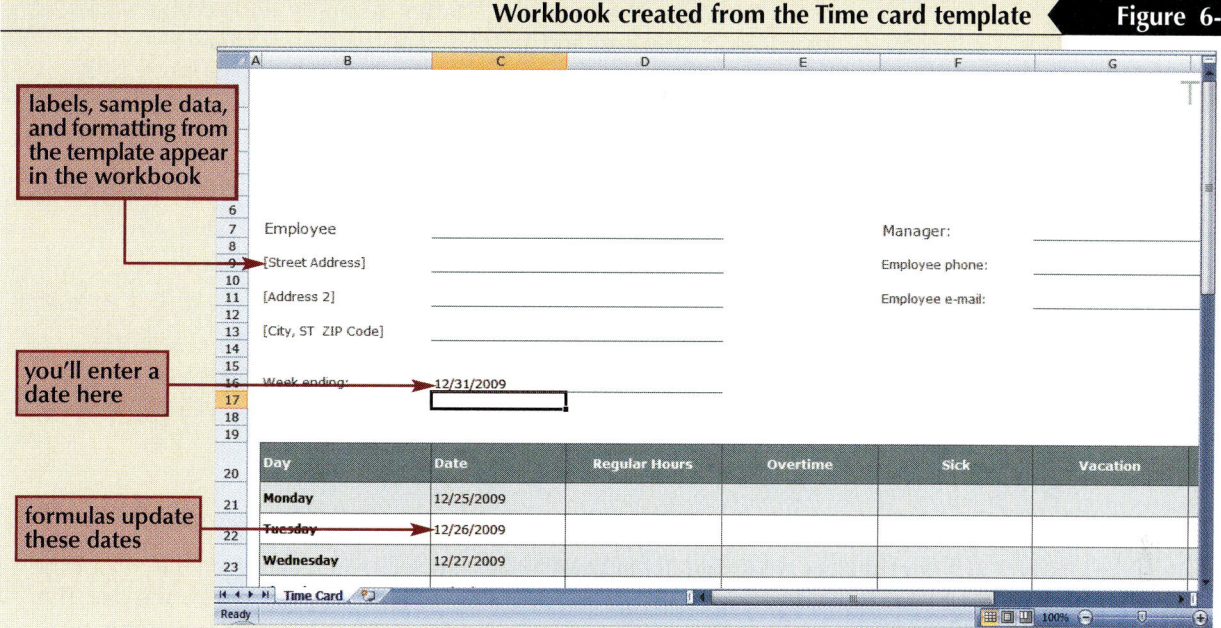

Trouble? If the Microsoft Office Genuine Advantage dialog box indicates that the software installed on your computer is not genuine, then Microsoft was not able to validate your software. Click the Resolve Later button, and ask your instructor or technical support person for help.

The workbook based on the Time card template shows the name *Time card1* in the title bar, not *Time card*. Just as a blank workbook that you open is named sequentially, *Book1*, *Book2*, and so forth, a workbook based on a specific template always displays the name of the template followed by a sequential number. Any changes or additions to data, formatting, or formulas you make in this workbook affect only the new workbook you are creating and not the template (in this case, the Time card template). If you want to save your changes, you must save the workbook in the same way as you would save any new workbook.

Look at the labels and formatting already included in the Time Card worksheet. Some cells have descriptive labels, others are blank so you can enter data in them, and still other cells contain formulas where calculations for total hours worked each day and pay category will be automatically displayed as data is entered.

You'll enter data for Ed Hoot, the student assisting Alvin, in the worksheet based on the Time card template.

To enter data in the workbook based on the Time card template:

▶ 1. In cell C7, enter **Ed Hoot**.

▶ 2. In cell C16, enter **3/21/2010**. The dates in cells C21:C27 are automatically updated to reflect the week you specify.

▶ 3. In cell D21, enter **8**. This is the total regular hours Ed worked on Monday. Totals appear in cells H21, D28, and H28 because formulas are already entered into these cells. Cell H21 shows 8 hours worked that day, cell D28 shows 8 regular hours worked that week, and cell H28 shows 8 hours total worked that week.

▶ 4. In cell D22, enter **8** as the total regular hours Ed worked on Tuesday, and then, in cell E22, enter **2** as the total overtime hours Ed worked on Tuesday. The totals are updated to show 10 hours worked that day, 16 regular hours worked that week, 2 overtime hours worked that week, and 18 total hours worked that week.

Next, you'll enter the regular hourly pay rate.

▶ 5. In cell D29, enter **10**. The Total pay amounts in cells D30 and H30 are updated to show $160 total pay.

Next, you'll enter the overtime hourly pay rate.

▶ 6. In cell E29, enter **15**. The Total pay amounts are updated to show $160 total pay for regular hours, $30 total pay for overtime hours, and $190 total pay for the week ending 3/21/2010.

▶ 7. Save the workbook as **Hoot Time Card** in the **Tutorial.06\Tutorial** folder included with your Data Files. The Hoot Time Card workbook, like any other workbook, is saved with the .xlsx file extension. It does not overwrite the template file.

▶ 8. Close the workbook.

Each day Ed Hoot works at Global Travel, he or his supervisor can open the Hoot Time Card workbook just like any other workbook and enter his hours worked for the day. The total hours and pay are automatically updated. You can see how useful templates with formulas to produce a weekly time card that is fully formatted.

Having completed the New Mexico workbook according to Alvin's specifications, you have the basis for a template that can be used for similar projects. Instead of using one of the Excel templates, you can use the New Mexico workbook to create your own template file. Then, Alvin can create new workbooks based on that template and distribute them to the accountants preparing the state workbooks.

Creating a Custom Workbook Template

A **custom template** is a workbook template you create that is ready to run with the formulas for all calculations included as well as all formatting. Usually, the template is set up so a user enters the data and sees results immediately. A template can use any Excel feature, including formulas, charts, data validation, cell protection, macros, and so forth. In other words, a template includes everything but the data.

To create a template from an existing workbook, you need to be sure that all the formulas work as intended, the numbers and text are entered correctly, and the worksheet is formatted appropriately. Next, you need to remove any values and text that will change in each workbook created from the custom template. Be careful not to delete the formulas. Finally, you need to save the workbook using the Excel template file format. You can store template files in any folder, although if you store the file in the Templates folder, your custom templates are available when you click Templates in the New Workbook dialog box. If you don't save the template to the Templates folder, you can save it to another location.

> **Tip**
> You might find it helpful to replace variable data values with spaces, and apply a background color to cells in which you want data entered to differentiate them from other cells in the worksheet.

| Reference Window

Creating a Custom Template

- Prepare the workbook: enter values, text, and formulas as needed; apply formatting; and replace data values with zeros or blank cells.
- Click the Office Button, and then click Save As.
- In the File name box, enter the template name.
- Click the Save as type button, and then click Excel Template.
- Save the file in the Templates folder or select an alternative folder location.
- Click the Save button.

Alvin wants you to use the New Mexico workbook as the basis for creating a custom template. You'll reopen the workbook and clear the data values in the worksheets, leaving all of the formulas intact. After completing these modifications, you will save the workbook as a template.

To replace the data values in the New Mexico workbook:

1. Open the **New Mexico** workbook located in the **Tutorial.06\Tutorial** folder included with your Data Files.

2. Group the **Quarter 1** through **Quarter 4** worksheets. All the worksheets are grouped except the Summary and Documentation worksheets.

3. Select the range **B6:E12**. This range includes the specific ticket and sales data for each theme park. You want to delete these values.

4. Click the **Home** tab on the Ribbon, in the Editing Group click the **Clear** button, and then click **Clear Contents**. The data values are cleared from the selected range in each of the quarterly worksheets, but the formulas and formatting remain intact. The cleared cells are blank. The range B13:E13 displays dashes, representing zeros, where there are formulas.

   You'll apply a color to the range where you want users to enter data, the range B6:E12.

5. In the Font group on the Home tab, click the **Fill Color button arrow**, and then click **Orange** (the third color in the Standard Colors section of the Fill Color gallery). The selected range has an orange fill to indicate where to enter quarterly data for the number of tickets sold and the sales amount.

6. In cell A1, enter **=Summary!A1**. This formula inserts the contents of cell A1 in the Summary worksheet into cell A1 in the quarterly worksheets. The text "New Mexico" is still displayed because that's the text currently in cell A1 in the Summary worksheet.

7. Switch to the **Summary** worksheet. The quarterly worksheets are ungrouped, and dashes, representing zeros, appear in the cells in the range B6:E13, which contain formulas.

8. In cell A1, enter **Enter state name here**, and then, in cell A2, enter **Enter Fiscal Year – yyyy**. This text will remind users to enter the correct state name and year. See Figure 6-24.

Figure 6-24 — Worksheet with formatting and formulas but no data

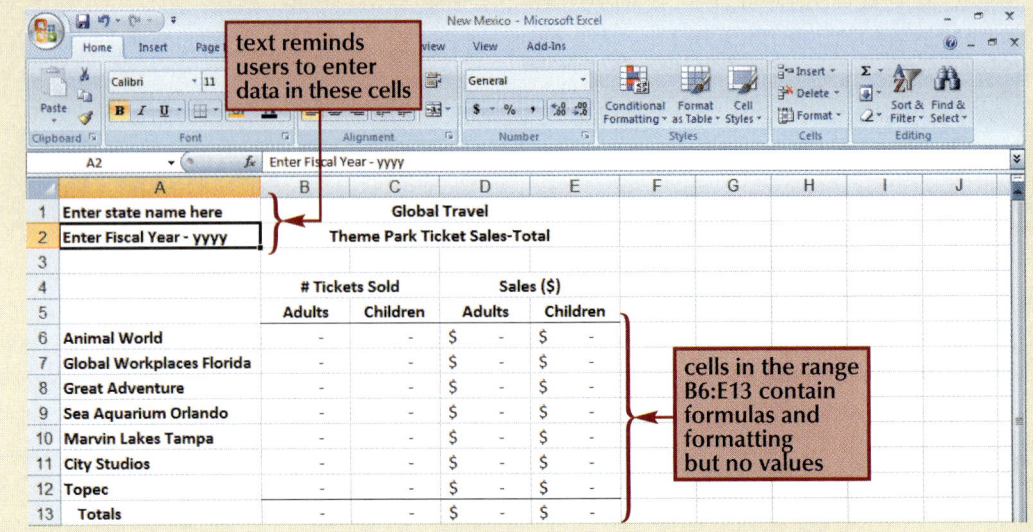

9. Switch to the **Documentation** worksheet, delete your name and the date from the range **B3:B4**, enter **Theme park ticket sales** in cell B6, and then click cell **A1**. The Documentation sheet is updated to reflect the purpose of the workbook.

The workbook is ready to save in template format. It no longer contains any specific data, but the formulas and formatting will still be in effect when new data is entered.

To save the workbook as a template:

1. Click the **Office Button**, and then click **Save As**. The Save As dialog box opens.
2. Type **Travel Template** in the File name box.
3. Click the **Save as type** button, and then click **Excel Template**. The Address bar displays the Templates folder, which is where custom template files are often stored. Excel, by default, looks for template files in this folder. However, you can store templates in other folders as well. Because you might not have access to the Templates folder, you will save the template file with your other Data Files.
4. Navigate to the **Tutorial.06\Tutorial** folder included with your Data Files, and then click the **Save** button.
5. Close the Travel Template workbook template.

Alvin will use the Travel Template file to create the workbooks to track next year's sales for each state and then distribute the workbooks via e-mail to each accountant. By basing these new workbooks on the template file, he has a standard workbook with identical formatting and formulas for each accountant to use. He also avoids the risk of accidentally changing the workbook containing the 2010 data when preparing for 2011. All template files have the .xltx extension. This extension differentiates template files from workbook files, which have the .xlsx extension. After you have saved a workbook in a template format, you can make the template accessible to other users.

Creating a New Workbook from a Template

After you have saved a template in the Templates folder, you open the New Workbook dialog box and go to the My Templates folder to select the template you want to use. If you don't save the template to the Templates folder, the New from existing button enables you to create a new workbook from a template, much like creating a workbook based on a template found in the Templates folder.

You will use the latter approach to create a workbook from the Travel Template file because you saved the template in your Tutorial.06\Tutorial folder. Alvin asks you to test the process of creating the workbook before the state workbooks are distributed to the accountants.

To create a new workbook based on the Travel Template template:

1. Click the **Office Button**, and then click **New**. The New Workbook dialog box opens.

2. Click **New from existing** in the Templates pane. The New from Existing Workbook dialog box opens, with All Excel Files displayed. This dialog box differs from the Open dialog box in two ways. First, instead of opening the actual workbook, it opens a copy of it. Second, when you save the workbook, it adds a number to the end of the filename and opens the Save As dialog box, which makes it very difficult to overwrite the original file.

3. Click **Travel Template** in the **Tutorial.06\Tutorial** folder included with your Data Files, and then click the **Create New** button. A copy of the Travel Template workbook opens named *Travel Template1* to indicate this is the first copy of the Travel Template workbook created during the current Excel session.

4. Click the **Summary** sheet tab, and then, in cell **A1**, enter **New Mexico** and in cell **A2**, enter **Fiscal Year - 2011**.

5. Switch to the **Quarter 1** worksheet. The text "New Mexico" appears in cell A1, and the text "Fiscal Year - 2011" appears in cell A2.

   You'll enter test data in the data area (which has an orange background fill color).

6. Click cell **B6**, type **120**, click cell **C6**, type **150**, click **D6**, type **3000**, click **E6**, type **2850**, and then press the **Enter** key. The range B13:E13 shows the totals of each column because these cells contain formulas to sum each column.

7. Click cell **B7**, type **180**, click cell **C7**, type **200**, click **D7**, type **3500**, click **E7**, type **3150**, and then press the **Enter** key. The range B13:E13 is updated because these cells contain formulas to sum each column. See Figure 6-25.

> **Tip**
> The worksheet that is active when you create, save, and close a template workbook is the active worksheet when you create a new workbook based on the template. In this case, the Documentation sheet is active.

Figure 6-25 — New workbook based on Travel Template

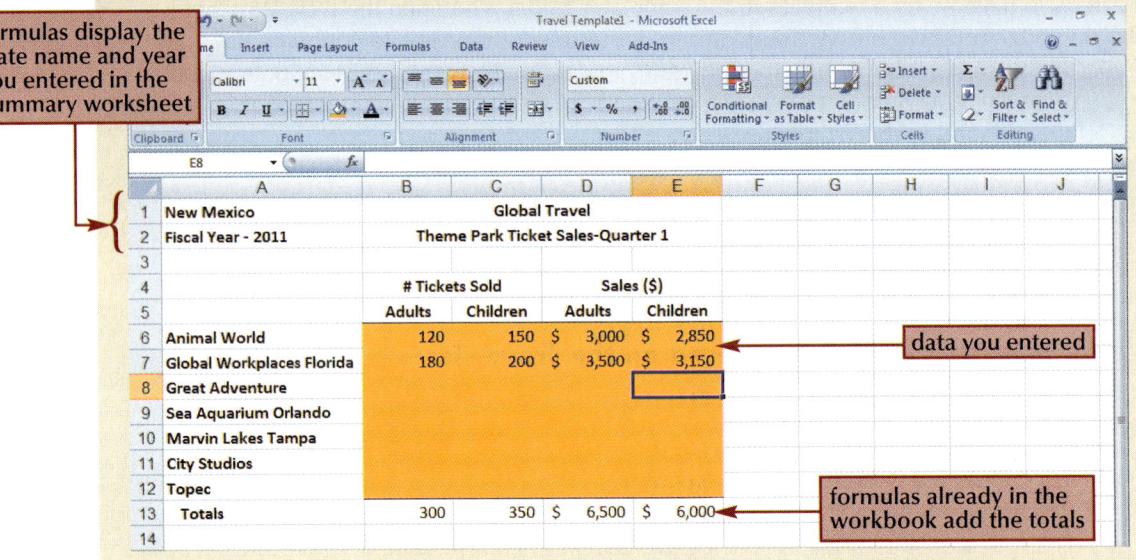

8. Switch to the **Summary** worksheet. Totals appear in the ranges B6:E7 and B13:E13 as a result of the formulas in this worksheet. See Figure 6-26.

Figure 6-26 — Summary worksheet after data is entered

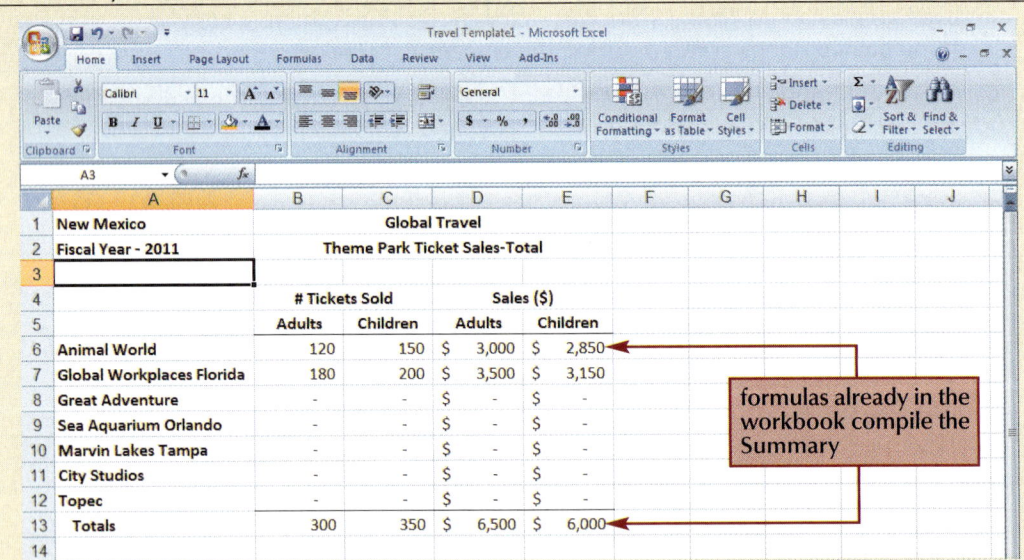

9. Save the workbook as **New Mexico 2011** in the **Tutorial.06\Tutorial** folder included with your Data Files. The copy of the template is saved as a workbook with the .xlsx extension. The original template file is not changed.

10. Close the workbook.

Alvin asks you to add data to the Quarter 2, Quarter 3, and Quarter 4 worksheets to verify that the Summary worksheet is correctly adding numbers from the four worksheets.

To test the New Mexico 2011 workbook:

1. Open the **New Mexico 2011** workbook located in the **Tutorial.06\Tutorial** folder included with your Data Files.

2. Group the **Quarter 2**, **Quarter 3**, and **Quarter 4** worksheets. You'll enter test values in the range B6:C6 so that each quarterly worksheet contains data.

3. In cell B6, enter **120**, and then, in cell C6, enter **150**.

4. Switch to the **Summary** worksheet. The total in cell B6 is 480 and the total in cell C6 is 600. The formulas in the Summary worksheet correctly add values from all the quarterly worksheets. So, Alvin knows that the template workbook is functioning as intended.

5. Save and close the workbook.

Alvin will use the custom template to create and distribute new state workbooks to each accountant for the next fiscal year.

Saving a Workbook as a Web Page

Alvin wants you to store the summary of the annual company-wide Theme Park Ticket Sales report you helped him create on the company's intranet which is a computer network, based on Internet technology, that is designed to meet the internal needs for sharing information within an organization.

You can convert Excel workbooks, worksheets, or ranges into Web pages that can be placed on the Web to be viewed by others. Excel allows you to create a Web page where users can scroll through the contents of an Excel workbook and switch between worksheets, but cannot make any changes to the data or formatting displayed on the Web page. When you save a worksheet as a Web page, Excel converts the contents of the worksheet into **HTML** (Hypertext Markup Language), which is a language used to write Web pages.

You can save an Excel workbook, a worksheet, or an item in a worksheet as a Web page and make it available to viewers via the Internet or an intranet. Alvin wants to make the company-wide results available to the executive team, so he needs you to create a Web page of the Totals 2010 Summary worksheet.

You use the Save As dialog box to create a Web page based on a workbook, a single worksheet, or a range within a worksheet. When you save a workbook as a Web page, you can save the workbook in one of two formats. The Web Page format saves the worksheet as an HTML file and creates a folder that stores the supporting files, such as a file for each graphic and worksheet that is included on the Web page. The Single File Web Page format saves all the elements of the Web page including text and graphics into a single file in the MHTML (Multipurpose Internet Mail Extension HTML) format.

Accessing Workbooks on the Web Interactively | InSight

In Excel 2007, if you want to publish interactive versions of your workbook or items from the worksheet as a Web page with spreadsheet functionality, you need to use a component of Microsoft Office Share-Point Server called Excel Services. This component lets users access all or part of the workbook in browsers interactively. Users can sort and filter an Excel table, use PivotTables for data analysis, and perform what-if analysis from a Web browser. To learn more, search the Excel Help system for "publish a workbook to Excel Services."

| Reference Window | **Saving a Workbook, Worksheet, or Range as a Web Page**

- Click the Office Button, and then click Save As.
- Click the Save as type button, and then click Web Page or Single File Web Page.
- Click the Publish button.
- Click the Choose arrow, and select which portion of the workbook you want to publish as a Web page.
- Click the Change button to change the title of the Web page.
- Click the Browse button to change the filename and location for the Web page.
- Check or clear the AutoRepublish every time this workbook is saved check box.
- Check or clear the Open published web page in browser check box.
- Click the Publish button.

First, you will create and test the Web page on your hard drive. You will open the Save As dialog box, and then choose the Web Page file format, because it is the standard format the company uses for its Web pages, to create the Web page for the regional 2010 results.

After previewing your work offline, Alvin will "publish" the Web page by putting all of the files (both HTML files and graphic files) on the Web server that hosts the Global Travel site.

To start creating the Web page:

1. Open the **Totals 2010** workbook located in the **Tutorial.06\Tutorial** folder included with your Data Files.

2. Click the **Office button**, and then click **Save As**. The Save As dialog box opens.

3. Click the **Save as type** button, and then click **Web Page**. The area below the Save as type box expands to display several Web-based options. See Figure 6-27.

| Figure 6-27 | **Expanded Save As dialog box**

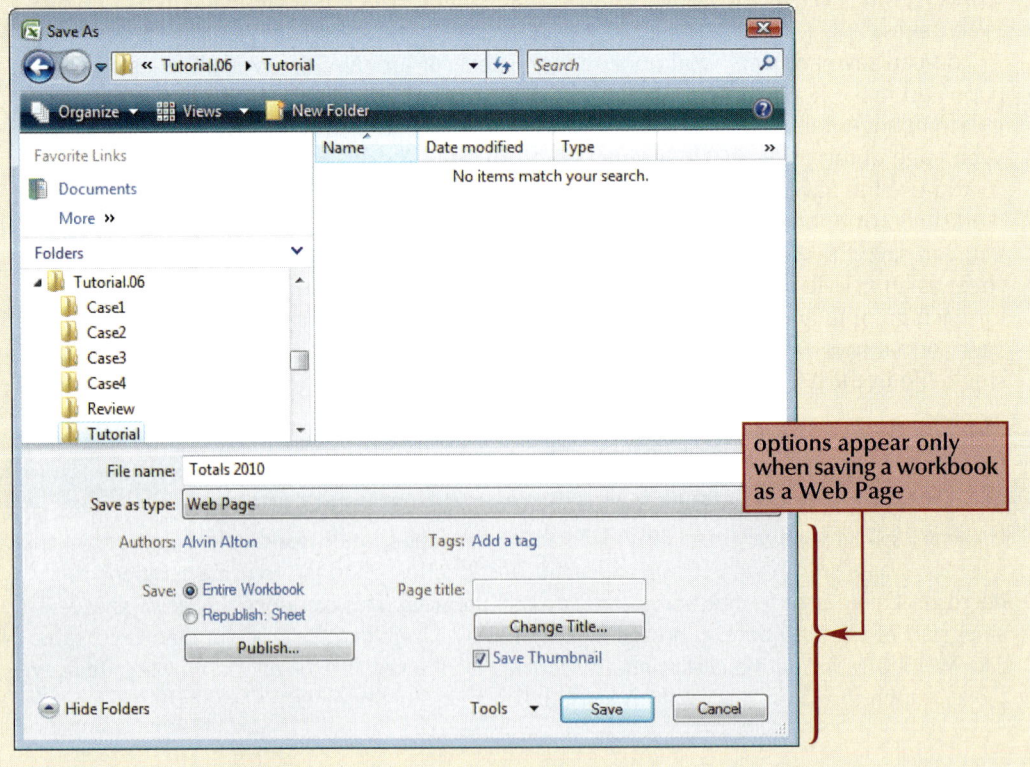

Setting the Page Title

Web pages usually have a page title that appears in the title bar of the Web browser. If a page title is not entered, the browser will display the page's file path and filename. Alvin wants the Web page title to clearly indicate to the executive team the purpose of the report. You'll enter a descriptive page title.

To specify the page title:

1. Click the **Change Title** button. The Set Page Title dialog box opens.

2. Type **Global Travel Theme Park Ticket Sales - 2010** in the Page title text box, and then click the **OK** button. The page title you just typed appears in the Page title box at the bottom of the Save As dialog box.

The next step in setting up the page for publishing on the Web is to choose which elements of the workbook to include in the Web page.

Setting the Web Page Options

You can specify which elements to include as part of the Web page. You can select the entire workbook, a specific worksheet in the workbook, a range of cells, or previously published items (which are items already on the Web server) that you are modifying. In this case, Alvin wants to include only the contents of the Summary worksheet.

To select the Summary worksheet for the Web page:

1. In the Save As dialog box, click the **Publish** button. The Publish as Web Page dialog box opens. See Figure 6-28.

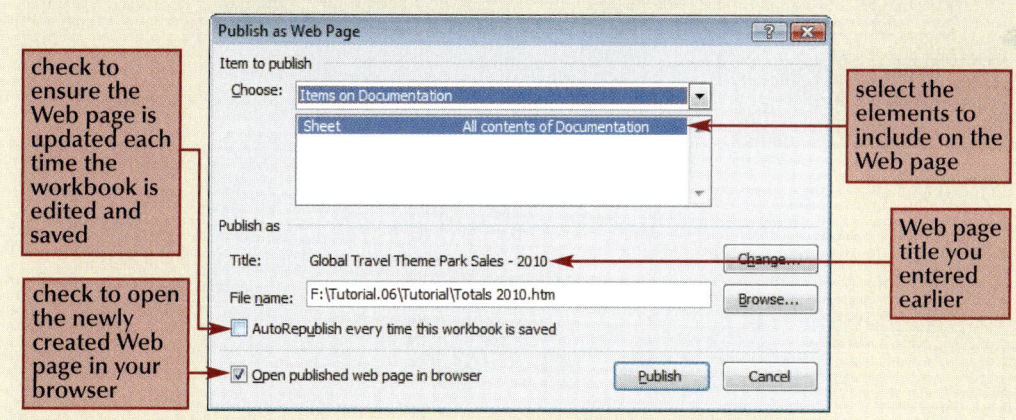

Figure 6-28 Publish as Web Page dialog box

- check to ensure the Web page is updated each time the workbook is edited and saved
- select the elements to include on the Web page
- Web page title you entered earlier
- check to open the newly created Web page in your browser

You'll specify the Summary worksheet as the item to include on the Web page.

2. Click the **Choose** arrow, and then click **Items on Summary**. Items on Summary appears in the Choose box and the Summary worksheet is the active sheet in the workbook behind the dialog box.

In the Publish as section of the Publish as Web Page dialog box, you can also change the Web page title, browse to find the folder where you want to publish the Web page and assign or change the filename, enable automatic republishing of the Web page every time a change is saved to the workbook so the Web page always matches the source workbook, and immediately view the Web page in a browser.

The default filename for a Web page is based on the workbook's filename, which, in this case, is *Totals 2010.htm*. Alvin wants the name to conform to the company style. For consistency in naming company-related Web pages, he will name the file *Web Totals 2010.htm*. The extension .htm refers to an HTML file. You will change the filename.

To specify a filename for the Web page:

1. Click the **Browse** button. The Publish As dialog box opens.

2. Verify that the **Tutorial.06\Tutorial** folder is selected, and then type **Web Totals 2010** in the File name box.

3. Click the **OK** button. The filename appears in the Publish as Web Page dialog box.

4. Make sure the **Open published web page in browser** check box is checked so the Web page will open in a browser as soon as you complete these steps.

5. Click the **Publish** button. Excel creates the Web page based on the contents of the Summary worksheet and opens the page in your browser. You don't need an Internet connection to see the Web page, because the HTML file is stored locally on your computer. The page title *Global Travel Theme Park Sales - 2010* appears in the browser's title bar, tab, and as a heading above the information from the worksheet. See Figure 6-29.

Figure 6-29   **Web page based on the Summary worksheet**

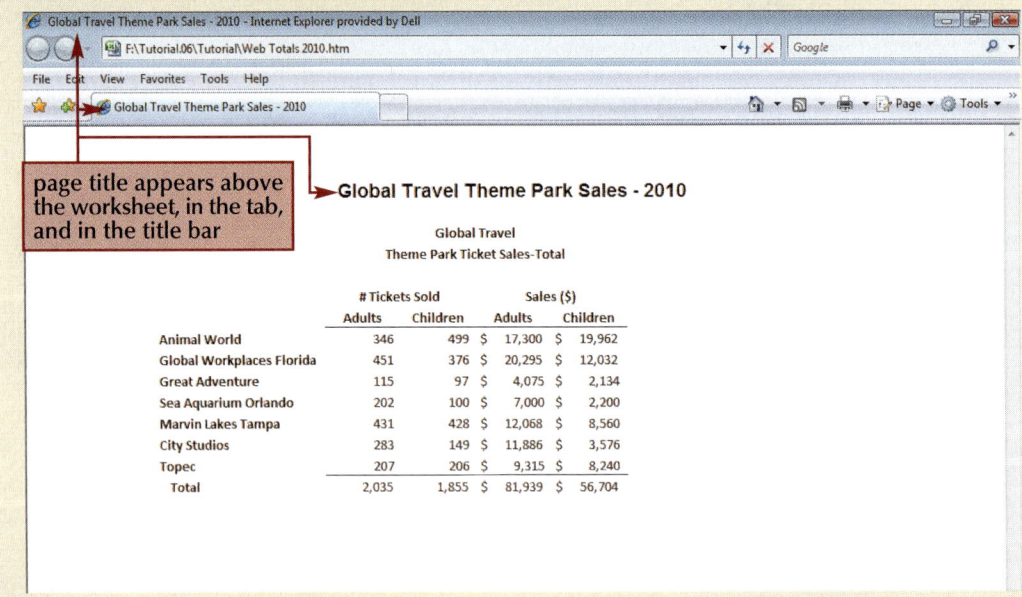

6. Close your Web browser, and then close the Totals 2010 workbook without saving.

The Web page provides a concise summary of the Global Travel ticket sales. Alvin will complete the process by uploading the Web page you created to the company's intranet later on.

Session 6.3 Quick Check | Review

1. How do you insert a hyperlink into a worksheet cell?
2. True or False? A hyperlink in a worksheet cell can be used to jump to another worksheet in the same workbook.
3. What is a template?
4. What is an advantage of using a custom template rather than simply using the original workbook file to create a new workbook?
5. How do you save a file as a template?
6. What are the two different types of Web page file formats available?

Tutorial Summary | Review

In this tutorial, you worked with multiple worksheets and workbooks. You learned how to create a worksheet group and then edit multiple worksheets at once. You consolidated information in multiple worksheets using 3-D references. You also set up grouped worksheets for printing. You linked workbooks using external references. You created an Excel workspace file and explored the advantages of using workspace files when you need to work with multiple workbooks that are related to one project or goal. You added a hyperlink to a worksheet. You learned about Excel templates and created a custom template from an existing worksheet. Finally, you converted a worksheet into a Web page.

Key Terms

3-D reference
custom template
default template
destination file
external reference
HTML (Hypertext Markup Language)

hyperlink
link
ScreenTip
source file

template
worksheet group
workspace

Practice | Review Assignments

Practice the skills you learned in the tutorial using the same case scenario.

Data Files needed for the Review Assignments: OR.xlsx, Idaho.xlsx, Washington.xlsx, NW Totals 2010.xlsx, NW Travel.xltx

Elaine Dennerson, accountant for Global Travel in Oregon, needs your help. Global Travel has added Oregon to the Northwest territory, which already includes Washington and Idaho. She asks you to complete the Summary worksheet in the Oregon workbook and enter the formulas in the regional workbook, NW Totals 2010, to summarize the Northwest states' totals into one workbook.

Complete the following:

1. Open the **OR** workbook located in the Tutorial.06\Review folder included with your Data Files, and then save the workbook as **Oregon** in the same folder.
2. In the Documentation sheet, enter your name and the current date, and then review the worksheets in the workbook.
3. Create a worksheet group that contains the Qtr 1 through Qtr 4 worksheets.
4. In the worksheet group, insert formulas to total each column. Format each worksheet to match other state quarterly workbooks. Bold the range A1:B2;A6:A13;B4:E5. Merge and center the ranges B1:E1, B2:E2, B4:C4, and D4:E4. Format the range A6:A12 in italic. Add a top and double bottom border to the range B13:E13. Add a fill color to the range B1:E2 using the Orange theme color. Apply the Accounting number format with no decimal places to the range D6:E13. Ungroup the worksheets.
5. Make a copy of the Qtr 1 worksheet, name it **Summary**, and place it immediately after the Documentation worksheet. Remove the data from the range B6:E12. Change the heading in cell B2 to **Theme Park Ticket Sales-Total**. In cell A2, enter the label **Fiscal Year – 2010**.
6. In worksheets Qtr 1 through Qtr 4, enter formulas to reference the labels in cells A1 and A2 of the Summary worksheet.
7. In the Summary worksheet, create 3-D reference formulas to calculate annual totals for theme park tickets sold and sales.
8. Prepare all worksheets except the Documentation sheet for printing. Display the name of the workbook and the name of the worksheet on separate lines in the right section of the header. Display your name and the date on separate lines in the right section of the footer. Preview the worksheets.
9. Ungroup the worksheets and save the workbook.
10. Open the regional **NW Totals 2010** workbook located in the Tutorial.06\Review folder included with your Data Files, and then enter the external reference formulas in the NW Totals 2010 workbook to create a set of linked workbooks to summarize the states' totals into one workbook.
11. In the NW Totals 2010 workbook, switch to the Documentation sheet. In the range A10:A12, enter the name of each state. Create hyperlinks from each state label to the corresponding workbook (Idaho, Oregon, and Washington). Test each hyperlink.
12. Create a workspace with the following four workbooks in a tiled layout: Idaho, Oregon, Washington, and NW Totals 2010. Make the Summary worksheet in each workbook the active worksheet, and make the NW Totals 2010 workbook the active workbook. Save the workspace as **NW Workspace**.

13. Create a new workbook based on the **NW Travel** template, which is located in the Tutorial.06\Review folder included with your Data Files. Save the workbook as **Oregon 2011** in the same folder. In the Summary worksheet, enter **Oregon** in cell A1 and **Fiscal Year – 2011** in cell A2. In the Qtr 1 worksheet, enter **1000** in each cell of the range B6:C12. In the Qtr 2 worksheet, enter **2000** in each cell of the range B6:C12. Confirm that the values entered in this step were correctly totaled in the Summary worksheet. Save the Oregon 2011 workbook.
14. Create a Web page of the entire Oregon workbook, which you created in Steps 2 through 9. Add a title. Include all worksheets in the workbook. Use the Web Page format and name the Web page as **Web Oregon 2010**.
15. Close all the workbooks. Submit the finished workbooks to your instructor, either in printed or electronic form, as requested.

Apply | Case Problem 1

Use the skills you learned to summarize quarterly sales data for a coffee retailer.

Data File needed for this Case Problem: Cafe.xlsx

Java Café Java Café currently has three stores in the Southwest: Tempe, Arizona; Las Cruces, New Mexico; and Austin, Texas. Jayne Mitchell manages the three stores and uses Excel to summarize sales data from these stores. She asks you to total the sales by product group and store for each quarter and then format each worksheet. Jayne also needs you to add another worksheet to calculate Summary sales for the stores and product groups.

Complete the following:

1. Open the **Cafe** workbook located in the Tutorial.06\Case1 folder included with your Data Files, and then save the workbook as **Java Cafe** in the same folder.
2. In the Documentation sheet, enter your name and the current date, and then switch to the Quarter 1 worksheet.
3. For each quarter, calculate the total sales for each product group and store, and then improve the formatting of the quarterly worksheets using the formatting of your choice.
4. Insert a new worksheet between the Documentation and Quarter 1 worksheets. Rename this as worksheet **Summary Sales**. Its appearance should be identical to the quarterly worksheets.
5. In the range B5:E7 of the Summary Sales worksheet, insert the formulas that add the sales in the corresponding cells of the four quarterly worksheets. Calculate the totals for each product group and store.
6. Set up the Summary Sales and four quarterly worksheets for printing. Each worksheet should be centered horizontally with the name of the worksheet centered in the header, and your name and the date placed on separate lines in the right section of the footer.
7. Save the Java Cafe workbook, and then remove the sales data, but not the formulas, from each of the quarterly worksheets.
8. Return to cell A1 of the Documentation sheet, and then save the workbook as an Excel template with the name **Java Template** in the Tutorial.06\Case1 folder included with your Data Files.
9. Use the Java Template template you created to create a new workbook. Name the workbook as **Java Cafe 2011**. In the range B5:E7 of all four quarterly worksheets, enter **1**. Save the workbook.

10. Create a Web page of the **Java Cafe** workbook in the Web Page format with the filename **Web Java**. Add an appropriate title. Include all worksheets in the workbook. Preview the file in your Web browser, and then close it.
11. Close the workbook. Submit the finished workbooks to your instructor, either in printed or electronic form, as requested.

Create | Case Problem 2

Create linked workbooks to summarize sales data for a car dealership.

Data Files needed for this Case Problem: Carson.xlsx, Reno.xlsx, Vegas.xlsx

Ute Auto Sales & Services Hardy Ute is founder and operator of Ute Auto Sales & Services with dealerships in Las Vegas, Reno, and Carson City, Nevada. His dealerships sell new and used cars, SUVs, minivans, and trucks as well as service customers' vehicles. To analyze sales and service at each of his three dealerships, Hardy asks his staff to prepare a regular report. Hardy wants the report to show the unit and dollar sales of new and used vehicles by type. In addition, he wants to see if his service business is bringing in the revenue that he anticipates.

Complete the following:

1. Open the **Carson** workbook located in the Tutorial.06\Case2 folder included with your Data Files, and then save the workbook as **UTE Carson City** in the same folder.
2. In the Documentation sheet, enter your name and the current date, and then switch to the Quarter 1 worksheet.
3. For each quarter, calculate the totals in the range B10:G10, and then improve the formatting of the quarterly worksheets using the formatting of your choice.
4. Insert a new worksheet between the Documentation and Quarter 1 worksheets. Rename this worksheet **Summary**. Format the worksheet identically to any of the quarterly worksheets except leave the range B6:G9 blank.
5. In the range B6:G9 of the Summary worksheet, insert the formulas that add the sales in the corresponding cells of the four quarterly worksheets.
6. Prepare the five sales worksheets for printing. Page setup should include the following: centered horizontally, the name of the worksheet centered in the header, and your name and the date placed on separate lines in the right section of the footer.
7. Save your changes to the workbook and close the workbook.
8. Open the **Reno** workbook located in the Tutorial.06\Case2 folder included with your Data Files, and then save the workbook as **UTE Reno**. Repeat Steps 2 through 7 for this workbook.
9. Open the **Vegas** workbook located in the Tutorial.06\Case2 folder, and then save the workbook as **UTE Vegas**. Repeat Steps 2 through 7 for this workbook.
10. Create a new workbook and use Figure 6-30 as a guide as you summarize the three dealerships' workbooks. Save the workbook as **UTE Summary**.

Figure 6-30

	A	B	C	D	E	F	G
1			Ute Auto Sales & Services				
2			Sales - All Dealers				
3							
4			New		Pre-owned		Service
5			Units	Sales ($)	Units	Sales ($)	Units	Sales ($)
6	Cars		733	$ 14,940,828	203	$ 1,476,397	5405	$ 1,058,958
7	SUVs		288	$ 7,979,268	76	$ 478,632	1798	$ 492,525
8	Vans		166	$ 3,928,990	87	$ 750,758	1007	$ 328,662
9	Trucks		113	$ 1,639,386	64	$ 341,907	691	$ 117,874
10	Totals		1300	$ 28,488,472	430	$ 3,047,694	8901	$ 1,998,019

11. Use the Web Page format to create a Web page based on the Summary worksheet in the UTE Summary workbook. Change the page title to **UTE Auto Sales & Services**. Open the Web page using your browser. Name the file **UTE Web Page**.
12. Use the UTE Carson City workbook to create an Excel template with the name **UTE Template** in the Tutorial.06\Case2 folder included with your Data Files. Add appropriate formatting of your choice.
13. Create a new workbook using the UTE Template. Add appropriate test data for Quarter 1. Save the workbook as **Carson City 2011** in the Tutorial.06\Case2 folder included with your Data Files.
14. Close the workbook. Submit the finished workbooks to your instructor, either in printed or electronic form, as requested.

| Create | **Case Problem 3** |

Create linked workbooks to summarize sales data for a specialty soft drink producer.

Data File needed for this Case Problem: InBurger.xlsx

Infusion Blend Micki Goldstein, a sales representative for a specialty soft drink producer, Infusion Blend, has Florida as her territory where she is based out of Tampa. Her job takes her around the state where she meets and presents her product offerings to store managers from major supermarket chains to the small mom-and-pop corner markets. Although she does not personally make the deliveries, she often works closely with the delivery staff to assure quality service to her customers.

Micki must report her sales progress to her regional manager in Atlanta, Georgia. These reports include the overall sales volume, the types of products sold, locations, and stores into which the products were delivered. For the larger markets, she must prepare a separate workbook for each chain store.

Complete the following:

1. Open the **InBurger** workbook located in the Tutorial.06\Case3 folder included with your Data Files, and then save the workbook as **InBurger 2010** in the same folder.
2. In the Documentation sheet, enter your name and the current date, and then switch to the January worksheet.
3. For each month (January through December), enter formulas to calculate the total sales for each product and store, and then improve the formatting of the monthly worksheets using the formatting of your choice.

4. Insert a new worksheet between the Documentation and January worksheets. Rename this worksheet **YTD Summary**. Format this worksheet identically to the monthly worksheets except leave the range B6:G11 blank.
5. Use 3-D reference formulas to add the cases sold from January through December. For example, in cell B6, the product Popgo sold in the Elteron store equals 1335 cases.
6. Insert formulas that add the total cases sold by product in column G and total cases sold by store in row 12. Calculate the Summary total for all products.

EXPLORE
7. Insert a new worksheet following the Documentation worksheet. Rename this worksheet as **Annual Recap**. Using Figure 6-31 as a guide, create three separate summaries on this worksheet: by Products, Store, and Month.
   a. Insert formulas that add the total cases sold of each product in the range C7:C12 (column G in the monthly worksheets). Calculate totals for all products.
   b. Insert formulas that add the total cases sold at each store in the range G7:G11 (row 12 in the monthly worksheets). Calculate totals for all stores.
   c. Insert formulas that add the total cases sold each month in the range K7:K18 (cell G12 in each worksheet). Calculate totals for all months.

Figure 6-31

	A	B	C	D	E	F	G	H	I	J	K	L
1					In Burger's Sales by Store and Product							
2							Cases Sold					
3												
4												
5			Breakdown by Products				Breakdown by Store				Breakdown by Month	
6		Products	Cases Sold	Percent		Store	Cases Sold	Percent		Store	Cases Sold	Percent
7		Popgo	7,065	31%		Elteron	4,700	20%		January	8,975	39%
8		Diet Popgo	4,760	21%		Mesa	4,600	20%		February	7,120	31%
9		Mt. Spring	3,360	15%		Franklin	4,700	20%		March	3,905	17%
10		Red Burst	1,675	7%		Grant	4,625	20%		April	2,980	13%
11		Dr Selsa	3,135	14%		Grover	4,355	19%		May	0	0%
12		Sun Maid	2,985	13%		Totals	22,980			June	0	0%
13		Totals	22,980							July	0	0%
14										August	0	0%
15										September	0	0%
16										October	0	0%
17										November	0	0%
18										December	0	0%
19										Totals	22,980	

8. Insert formulas in columns D, H, and L to calculate the percentage of products, stores, and months, respectively.
9. Results for the month of May are shown in Figure 6-32. Enter this data into the May worksheet.

Figure 6-32

	A	B	C	D	E	F	G
1		In Burger's Sales by Store and Product					
2				Cases Sold			
3							
4				Stores			
5	Products	Elteron	Mesa	Franklin	Grant	Grover	Totals
6	Popgo	515	545	560	670	510	2,800
7	Diet Popgo	435	445	435	430	410	2,155
8	Mt. Spring	235	275	240	240	205	1,195
9	Red Burst	125	125	150	150	325	875
10	Dr Selsa	160	145	150	160	125	740
11	Sun Maid	325	240	175	245	225	1,210
12	Totals	1,795	1,775	1,710	1,895	1,800	8,975

10. In the Documentation sheet, in the range A8:A19, type the months **January** through **December**. Create hyperlinks from each cell to its corresponding worksheet. Test the hyperlinks.
11. Save and close the workbook. Submit the finished workbook to your instructor, either in printed or electronic form, as requested.

Challenge | Case Problem 4

Explore using worksheet groups, 3-D references, external references, workspaces, and templates to summarize data for a pharmaceutical manufacturer.

Data Files needed for this Case Problem: Europe.xlsx, North America.xlsx, South America.xlsx, PlutoTemplate.xltx

Pluto Pharmaceuticals Pluto Pharmaceuticals is a multinational manufacturer of healthcare products. The chief financial analyst, Kevin Cross, asks you to prepare the first quarter revenue summary for three global regions based on workbooks from the regions of North America, South America, and Europe. Each workbook has monthly worksheets displaying forecasted and actual revenues of the major product groups for the first quarter. Kevin wants you to calculate the difference between forecasted and actual sales (Difference) and the percent change between forecasted and actual sales (% Change). He also wants you to summarize each workbook, reporting the quarterly forecasted and actual totals for revenues in a new worksheet. After you have added this information to each workbook, Kevin wants you to consolidate the information from the three regional workbooks, reporting in a single workbook the summarized information for each region.

Complete the following:

1. Open the **Europe**, **North America**, and **South America** regional revenue workbooks located in the Tutorial.06\Case4 folder included with your Data Files. Save the Europe workbook as **PlutoEU**, the North America workbook as **PlutoNA**, and the South America workbook as **PlutoSA** in the same folder. In the Documentation sheet in each regional revenue workbook, enter your name and the date.

2. Each regional workbook contains a Documentation sheet, a first quarter summary worksheet, and three monthly worksheets. Complete the monthly worksheets in each region's workbook by doing the following:
   - Calculate the difference for each product group: Actual–Forecast.
   - Calculate the % change for each product group: Difference/Forecast.
   - Calculate the total revenue for the Forecast, Actual, and Difference columns, and then calculate the total % Change.
   - Format the numbers to improve the appearance of the worksheets.
3. In each workbook, complete the Quarter 1 worksheet by first summarizing the forecasted and actual totals for product groups for the first three months of the year, then calculating the difference and the % change, and, finally, summarizing the forecasted, actual, difference, and % change values for the quarter. (*Hint:* The Total Revenue % change (cell E10) is not the sum of the column; it is the percent change between the forecasted and actual totals.) Use Figure 6-33 as a guide as you complete the worksheet.

Figure 6-33

	A	B	C	D	E
1		Pluto Pharmaceuticals-North America			
2		Revenue - Quarter 1			
3					
4	Product Group	Forecast	Actual	Difference	% Change
5	Healthcare	$ 2,295,600	$ 2,363,891	$ 68,291	3.0%
6	Consumer Healthcare	$ 340,500	$ 363,536	$ 23,036	6.8%
7	Animal Healthcare	$ 2,079,100	$ 2,101,693	$ 22,593	1.1%
8	Prescription Medicine	$ 522,300	$ 526,672	$ 4,372	0.8%
9	Over-the-Counter Medicine	$ 1,006,200	$ 976,096	$ (30,104)	-3.0%
10	Total Revenue	$ 6,243,700	$ 6,331,888	$ 88,188	1.4%

4. Format the Quarter 1 sheet for each regional workbook with the same formatting used for the monthly worksheets, and then save the workbooks.
5. Create a new workbook, and save it as **Pluto Summary** in the Tutorial.06\Case4 folder included with your Data Files. Rename the Sheet1 worksheet as **Documentation**, and in column A enter the same labels used in the Documentation sheets in the other workbooks. In column B, enter **Corporate** as the region, enter your name as the author and the current date as the date created, and then enter **To report on revenue for all regions** as the purpose. Format the Documentation sheet to match the Documentation worksheet formatting in the PlutoNA, PlutoSA, and PlutoEU workbooks.
6. Switch to the Sheet2 worksheet, and then use Figure 6-34 as a guide to enter the text shown. Enter formulas to total the forecasted and actual revenue for each product group. Compute the difference and % change for each product group. Include the totals for the Forecast, Actual, and Difference columns, and calculate the % Change for the total revenue for the quarter. Rename the worksheet as **Quarter 1**.

Figure 6-34

	A	B	C	D	E
1	Pluto Pharmaceuticals-Corporate				
2	Revenue - Quarter 1				
3					
4	Product Group	Forecast	Actual	Difference	% Change
5	Healthcare	$ 5,670,800	$ 5,913,673	$ 242,873	4.3%
6	Consumer Healthcare	$ 1,210,500	$ 1,250,000	$ 39,500	3.3%
7	Animal Healthcare	$ 4,632,300	$ 4,662,070	$ 29,770	0.6%
8	Prescription Medicine	$ 1,432,900	$ 1,507,357	$ 74,457	5.2%
9	Over-the-Counter Medicine	$ 2,707,600	$ 2,657,288	$ (50,312)	-1.9%
10	Total Revenue	$ 15,654,100	$ 15,990,388	$ 336,288	2.1%

EXPLORE 7. Insert a bar chart that compares the actual and forecast sales by product group. The chart is similar to Figure 6-35. Place the chart beneath the data you entered in the Quarter 1 worksheet. Change the axis so the sales are displayed in millions of dollars.

Figure 6-35

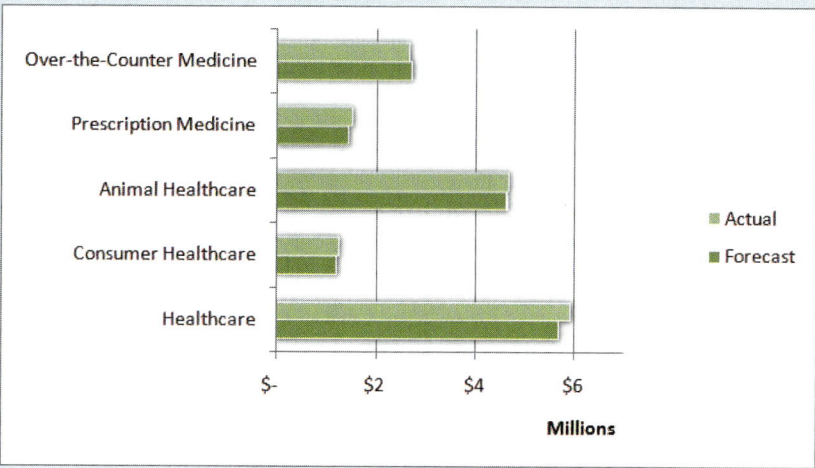

8. Prepare the three regional and corporate workbooks for printing. On each page, include the worksheet name in the center section of the header and your name in the left section of the footer.

9. Create a workspace that opens with the Quarter 1 worksheet active in each workbook using a horizontal layout for the four workbooks, and then save it as **Quarter1 Files** in the Tutorial.06\Case4 folder included with your Data Files.

10. Open the **Pluto Summary** workbook located in the Tutorial.06\Case4 folder included with your Data Files, and then save the workbook as **Pluto Yearend** in the same folder. For year-end backup, break the links in the Pluto Yearend workbook.

EXPLORE 11. You receive a new source file to substitute for the original source file. The new source file has a different name.
   a. Open the **Pluto Summary** workbook, and then save the workbook as **Pluto Summary Test**. Close the workbook.

b. Open the **PlutoNA** workbook, and then save the workbook as **PlutoNorth**. In the PlutoNorth workbook in the March worksheet, change the actual healthcare revenue in cell C5 to **$863,298**. Save and close the PlutoNorth workbook.

c. Open the **Pluto Summary Test** workbook, and change the link to the source workbook from PlutoNA to **PlutoNorth**. (*Hint:* Use the Edit Links dialog box.) Save and close the Pluto Summary Test workbook.

EXPLORE 12. Update the source program but not the destination file.

a. Open the **PlutoEU** workbook, and then save the workbook as **PlutoEurope**.

b. Open the **Pluto Summary Test** workbook, and change the link to the source workbook from PlutoEU to **PlutoEurope**. Note the actual total revenue in the Quarter 1 worksheet (cell C10). Close the Pluto Summary Test workbook.

c. In the PlutoEurope workbook, switch to the March worksheet and change the actual animal healthcare revenue in cell C7 to **$275,569**. Save and close the PlutoEurope workbook.

d. Open the **Pluto Summary Test** workbook but keep the automatic update of the links disabled. How does this affect the Quarter 1 total actual revenue (cell C10) in the Pluto Summary Test workbook (compare the current value to the value you noted in Step b)?

e. Use the Edit Links dialog box to update the Pluto Summary Test workbook. How does this affect the Quarter 1 total actual revenue (cell C10) in the Pluto Summary Test workbook (compare the current value to the value you noted in Step d)?

EXPLORE 13. Modify the template named **PlutoTemplate** located in the Tutorial.06\Case4 folder. Make the following two changes to the template, and then save the modified template as **PlutoTemplateRevised**.

a. Instead of column E displaying #DIV/0! in all sheets, change the formula in column E to display 0% when no values are entered in column B (Forecast).

b. Apply a fill color of your choice to the range B5:C9 in the monthly worksheets to identify where to enter data.

14. Create a new workbook from the modified PlutoTemplateRevised template. Enter **$500,000** in the range B5:B9 of each monthly worksheet. Enter **$550,000** in the range C5:C9 of each monthly worksheet. Save the workbook as **Pluto2011**.

15. Save and close all the workbooks. Submit the finished workbooks to your instructor, either in printed or electronic form, as requested.

| Research | **Internet Assignments** |

Use the Internet to find and work with data related to the topics presented in this tutorial.

The purpose of the Internet Assignments is to challenge you to find information on the Internet that you can use to work effectively with this software. The actual assignments are updated and maintained on the Course Technology Web site. Log on to the Internet and use your Web browser to go to the Student Online Companion for New Perspectives Office 2007 at **www.course.com/np/office2007**. Then navigate to the Internet Assignments for this tutorial.

Assess | SAM Assessment and Training

If you have a SAM user profile, you may have access to hands-on instruction, practice, and assessment of the skills covered in this tutorial. Log in to your SAM account (**http://sam2007.course.com**) to launch any assigned training activities or exams that relate to the skills covered in this tutorial.

Review | Quick Check Answers

Session 6.1

1. A worksheet group is a collection of two or more worksheets that have been selected.
2. To select an adjacent group of worksheets, click the first sheet tab, press and hold the Shift key, and then click the sheet tab of the last worksheet in the range. To select a nonadjacent group of worksheets, click the sheet tab of one of the worksheets in the group, press and hold the Ctrl key, and then click the sheet tabs of the remaining worksheets in the group. Deselect a worksheet group by either clicking the sheet tab of a worksheet not in the group or right-clicking one of the sheet tabs in the group and clicking Ungroup Sheets on the shortcut menu.
3. ='Quarter 2'!A10
4. 'Summary 1:Summary 3'!A10
5. the maximum value found in cell B1 of all worksheets from Sheet1 to Sheet4
6. MAX(Sheet1:Sheet5!B1); if Sheet5 were positioned before Sheet4, then MAX(Sheet1:Sheet4!B1) includes Sheet5.
7. Select a worksheet group that consists of all sheets in the workbook, click the Page Layout tab, and then select the page layout specification that you want to apply to all worksheets in the group.

Session 6.2

1. 'D:\Reports\[Product Report]Sales Info'!A1:A10
2. The source file is the file that contains the data values you want to link to.
3. The destination file receives the value(s) from the source file.
4. If both the destination and source files are open, Excel will update the link automatically when you update a value in the source file; when you open the destination file, click the Options button in the Message Bar, click the Enable this content option button, and then click the OK button.
5. In the Connections group on the Data tab, click the Edit Links button to open the Edit Links dialog box. The linked workbooks are listed in the dialog box.
6. A workspace file is a file containing information about all opened workbooks, including their locations, window sizes, and screen positions.
7. By opening a workspace file, you open all workbooks defined in the workspace. Using a workspace helps you organize projects that might involve several workbooks.

Session 6.3

1. Click the cell in which you want to insert the hyperlink, and then in the Links group on the Insert tab, click the Hyperlink button. Type the hyperlink text in the Insert Hyperlink dialog box.
2. True
3. A template is a workbook that contains specific content and formatting that you can use as a model for other similar workbooks.
4. A user can modify the contents of a workbook based on a template without changing the template file itself. The next time a new workbook is created based on a template, the workbook opens with all the original properties intact. If you use the workbook file to create a new workbook, you first must delete the values from cells that you want to change and then use the Save As dialog box to assign a new filename to the workbook.
5. Click the Office Button, click Save As, click the Save as type button, click Template, type a filename for the template, and then click the Save button.
6. Web Page; Single File Web Page

Ending Data Files

Tutorial.06 →

Tutorial
Audited 2010.xlsx
Colorado.xlsx
Hoot Time Card.xlsx
New Mexico.xlsx
New Mexico 2011.xlsx
Sales 2010.docx
Theme Parks.xlw
Totals 2010.xlsx
Travel Template.xltx
Utah.xlsx
Web Totals 2010.htm

Review
Idaho.xlsx
NW Totals 2010.xlsx
NW Travel.xltx
NW Workspace.xlw
Oregon.xlsx
Oregon 2011.xlsx
Washington.xlsx
Web Oregon 2010.htm
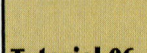 Web Oregon 2010_files

Case1
Java Cafe.xlsx
Java Cafe 2011.xlsx
Java Template.xltx
Web Java.htm

Case2
Carson City 2011.xlsx
UTE Carson City.xlsx
UTE Reno.xlsx
UTE Summary.xlsx
UTE Template.xltx
UTE Vegas.xlsx
UTE Web Page.htm

Case3
InBurger 2010.xlsx

Case4
Pluto 2011.xlsx
Pluto Summary.xlsx
Pluto Summary Test.xlsx
Pluto Yearend.xlsx
PlutoEU.xlsx
PlutoEurope.xlsx
PlutoNA.xlsx
PlutoNorth.xlsx
PlutoSA.xlxs
PlutoTemplateRevised.xltx
Quarter1 Files.xlw

Tutorial 7

Using Advanced Functions, Conditional Formatting, and Filtering

Reviewing Employee Data

Objectives

Session 7.1
- Evaluate a single condition using the IF function
- Evaluate multiple conditions using the AND function
- Calculate different series of outcomes by nesting IF functions
- Test whether one or more conditions are true with the OR function

Session 7.2
- Return values from a table with the VLOOKUP function
- Check for duplicate values using conditional formatting
- Check for data entry errors using the IFERROR function
- Summarize data using the COUNTIF, SUMIF, and AVERAGEIF functions
- Review the COUNTIFS, SUMIFS, and AVERAGEIFS functions

Session 7.3
- Use advanced filters
- Summarize data using Database functions

Case | Talent Tracs

Rita Corvales founded Talent Tracs, a software development company for the music and entertainment industry located in Austin, Texas. Talent Tracs sells EasyTracs, a software program that matches venues with artists and then schedules the performances. As the company's reputation grew, the business expanded rapidly. Today, Talent Tracs has nearly 100 employees, ranging from software developers to online customer relations staff. Rita uses Excel to track basic employee information such as each employee's name, gender, birth date, hire date, health plan, job status, pay type (hourly or salaried), pay grade, and annual salary.

Rita needs to review and manage the information about her company's employees on a regular basis. For example, she needs to track employee enrollment and costs in the benefit programs offered by the company. She also wants to calculate each employee's life insurance premium and how much the company contributes to each employee's 401(k) retirement account and health plan. And Rita needs to calculate the amount Talent Tracs spends on bonuses, which are based on employee pay grades and performance.

To provide Rita with the information she needs, you'll use a variety of Excel functions, filters, and conditional formatting.

Starting Data Files

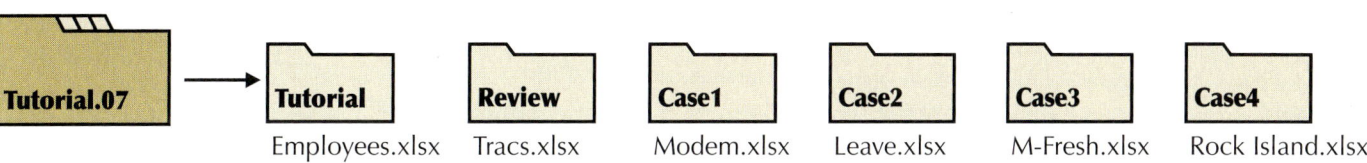

Session 7.1

Working with Logical Functions

The Talent Tracs compensation package includes salary, bonuses, and benefits. Right now, Rita wants to focus on three types of benefits: life insurance, retirement savings, and healthcare. Employees can choose to purchase additional supplemental life insurance coverage equal to their annual base salary times the insurance premium rate. The 401(k) retirement savings plan matches eligible employees' contributions, dollar for dollar, up to 3 percent of their salary. Employees can select a PPO or HMO health plan for families or individuals, or they can opt out of the health plan by providing evidence of other healthcare coverage.

Rita created a workbook that contains descriptive data for employees and their benefits. You will open this workbook now and review the employee information.

To open the Employees workbook:

1. Open the **Employees** workbook located in the **Tutorial.07\Tutorial** folder included with your Data Files, and then save the workbook as **Talent Tracs** in the same folder.

2. In the Documentation worksheet, enter your name and the current date.

3. Switch to the **Employee Data** worksheet. See Figure 7-1.

Figure 7-1 | **Employee Data worksheet**

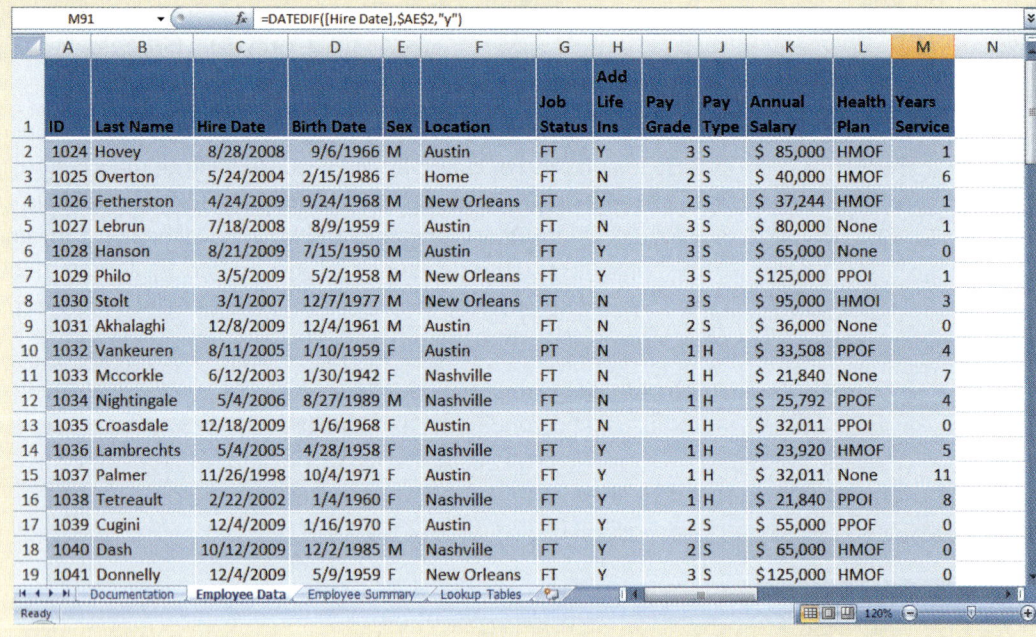

The Employee Data worksheet contains an Excel table of employee data. Rita entered each employee's ID, last name, hire date, birth date, gender, location, job status (FT for full-time, PT for part-time, or CN for paid consultant), additional life insurance coverage (Y for Yes, N for No), pay grade (1, 2, or 3), and pay type (S for Salaried, H for Hourly). The worksheet also includes the employee's annual salary, the type of health plan the employee selected (HMOF for HMO-Family, HMOI for HMO-Individual, PPOF for PPO-Family, PPOI for PPO-Individual, or None), and the number of years the employee has worked at Talent Tracs (Years Service). Rita stores the employees' additional personal information, including home address, phone numbers, Social Security numbers, and so forth, in another workbook.

Creating Fields in a Table | InSight

Keep the following guidelines in mind when creating fields in an Excel table:
- **Create fields that require the least maintenance.** For example, fields such as Hire Date and Birth Date require no maintenance because their values do not change, unlike fields such as Age and Years of Service, whose values change each year. If you need to track information such as the specific age or years of service, a best practice is to use calculations to determine these values based on values in the Hire Date and Birth Date fields.
- **Store the smallest unit of data possible in a field.** For example, use three separate fields for City, State, and Zip Code rather than one field. Using separate fields for each unit of data enables you to sort or filter each field. If you want to display data from two or more fields in one column, you can use a formula to reference the City, State, and Zip Code fields. For example, you can use the concatenation operator (the ampersand) to combine the city, state, and zip code in one cell as follows: =C2 & D2 & E2.
- **Apply a text format to fields with numerical text data.** For example, formatting fields such as Zip Code and Social Security Number as text ensures that leading zeros are stored as part of the data. Otherwise, the zip code 02892 is stored as a number and displayed as 2892, which is not the intended result.

Rita formatted the data as an Excel table to take advantage of the additional analysis and organization tools available for Excel tables. Rita asks you to replace the default name for the Excel table with a more descriptive name.

To rename the Excel table:

▶ 1. Make sure cell **A1** (the first cell in the Excel table) is the active cell, and then click the **Table Tools Design** tab on the Ribbon.

▶ 2. In the Properties group, select **Table1** in the Table Name box, type **Employee**, and then press the **Enter** key. The Excel table is now named *Employee*.

Next, you'll insert formulas that calculate each employee's additional life insurance premium (if any), 401(k) cost, health plan cost, and bonus amount. After you calculate those values, Rita wants you to summarize that information in the Employee Summary worksheet, so she can quickly see the impact of the compensation and benefits package on the company.

Whenever you enter a formula into an empty table column, Excel automatically fills the rest of that table column with the formula. This is referred to as a **calculated column**. If you need to modify the formula in a calculated column, you edit the formula in one cell of the column and the formulas in that table column are also modified. If you edit a cell in a calculated column so it is no longer consistent with the other formulas in the column (such as replacing a formula with a value), a green triangle appears in the upper-left corner of the cell, making the inconsistency easy to see. After a calculated column contains an inconsistency, any other edits you make to that column are no longer automatically applied to the rest of the cells in that column because Excel does not overwrite custom values.

Tip
Calculated columns work only in Excel tables. To achieve the same results in a range of data, you must copy and paste the formula or use the AutoFill feature.

You'll start by calculating the additional life insurance premiums. This amount depends on whether an employee has elected additional life insurance coverage. So, you'll need to enter a formula that includes the IF function to determine the amount of the premium.

Using the IF Function

In many situations, the value you store in a cell depends on certain conditions. Consider the following examples:

- An employee's gross pay depends on whether that employee worked overtime.
- An income tax rate depends on the taxpayer's adjusted taxable income.
- A shipping charge depends on the size of an order.

To evaluate these types of conditions in Excel, you use the IF function. Recall that the IF function is a logical function that evaluates a condition (a logical test), and then returns one value if the condition is true and another value if the condition is false. The IF function has the following syntax:

`IF(logical_test, value_if_true, [value_if_false])`

In this function, *logical_test* is a condition such as A5="Yes" that is either true or false, *value_if_true* is the value displayed in the cell if the logical test is true, and *value_if_false* is the value displayed in the cell if the logical test is not true. Although the *value_if_false* argument is optional, you should usually include it so the IF function covers both possibilities.

You use the IF function to create a conditional statement such as =IF(A5="Yes",C5+B5,B5–C5). The first argument, the *logical_test* A5="Yes", is always performed first and has a result that is either true or false. If the *logical_test* is true, the *value_if_true*, C5+B5, is calculated next and its value is displayed in the cell. If the *logical_test* is false, the *value_if_false*, B5–C5, is calculated next and its value is displayed in the cell. The IF function results in only one value—either the *value_if_true* or the *value_if_false*; the other is ignored.

Talent Tracs employees can purchase additional life insurance coverage equal to the employee's annual salary multiplied by the premium rate (.001). Rita created the flowchart shown in Figure 7-2, which illustrates the logic for calculating an employee's additional life insurance premium. The flowchart shows that if the employee elected additional life insurance (Add Life Ins = "Y" is True), then the premium is calculated using the formula Salary*.001. If the employee did not elect additional life insurance (Add Life Ins = "Y" is False), then the premium is 0.

Figure 7-2 Flowchart with logic for the additional life insurance premium

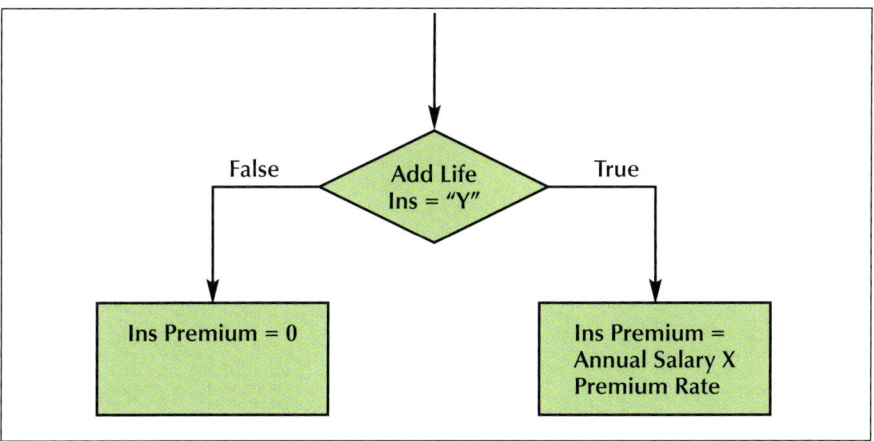

You will add a column in the Employee table to display the life insurance premium. Then, you'll enter a formula with an IF function to calculate the life insurance premium employees will pay if they select additional life insurance coverage.

To calculate the life insurance premium using an IF function:

▶ 1. In cell **N1**, enter **Life Ins Premium**. The Excel table expands to include this column and applies the table formatting to all the rows in the new column.

▶ 2. Make sure cell **N2** is the active cell, and then, on the formula bar, click the **Insert Function** button f_x. The Insert Function dialog box opens.

▶ 3. Click **Logical** in the Or select a category list, click **IF** in the Select a function box, and then click the **OK** button. The Function Arguments dialog box for the IF function opens. You will use this dialog box to enter the values for the IF function arguments.

▶ 4. In the Logical_test argument box, type **H2="Y"** and then press the **Tab** key. This sets the logical test to evaluate whether the employee wants additional life insurance, indicated by Y for Yes or N for No in cell H2. *TRUE* appears to the right of the Logical_test argument box, indicating the result for the employee in row 2 is true. That is, the employee wants additional life insurance.

> **Tip**
> Testing for text values is not case-sensitive. So the conditions H2="Y" and H2="y" return the same value.

▶ 5. In the Value_if_true argument box, type **K2*0.001**. This argument specifies that if the condition is true (the employee wants additional life insurance), the result of the employee's current salary (listed in cell K2) is multiplied by 0.1% and appears in cell N2. The value to the right of the Value_if_true argument box is 85, which is the premium the employee in row 2 will pay for additional life insurance if the condition is true.

▶ 6. In the Value_if_false argument box, type **0**. This argument specifies that if the condition is false (the employee does not want additional life insurance), 0 appears in cell N2. The value to the right of the Value_if_false argument box is 0, which is the value that appears in cell N2 if the condition is false. See Figure 7-3.

Figure 7-3   **Function Arguments dialog box for IF function**

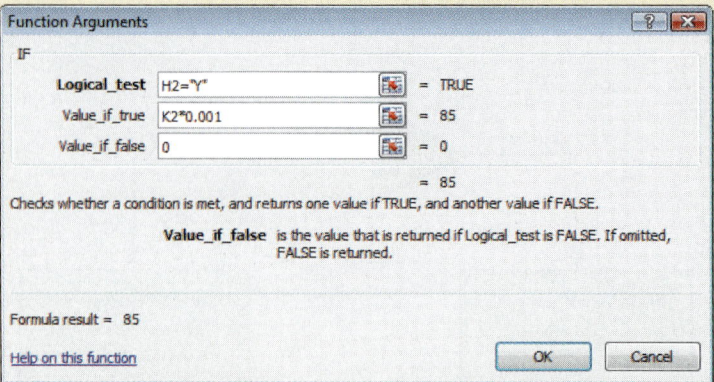

Tip

Click the top portion of the column header in an Excel table (not the worksheet column heading) to select the column data but not the header; double-click to select the entire column including the column header.

7. Click the **OK** button. The formula =IF(H2="Y",K2*0.001,0) appears in the formula bar, and the value 85 appears in cell N2 because the condition is true. The results are automatically copied to all rows in column N of the table.

8. Point to the top of cell **N1** until the pointer changes to ↓, and then click to select the range N2:N101. The data in the Life Ins Premium column is selected, but not the column header.

9. Format the selected range N2:N101 with the **Accounting** number format with **2** decimal places. The Life Ins Premium column shows the premiums employees will pay for additional life insurance, formatted as currency. See Figure 7-4.

Figure 7-4   **Life Ins Premium column added to the Employee table**

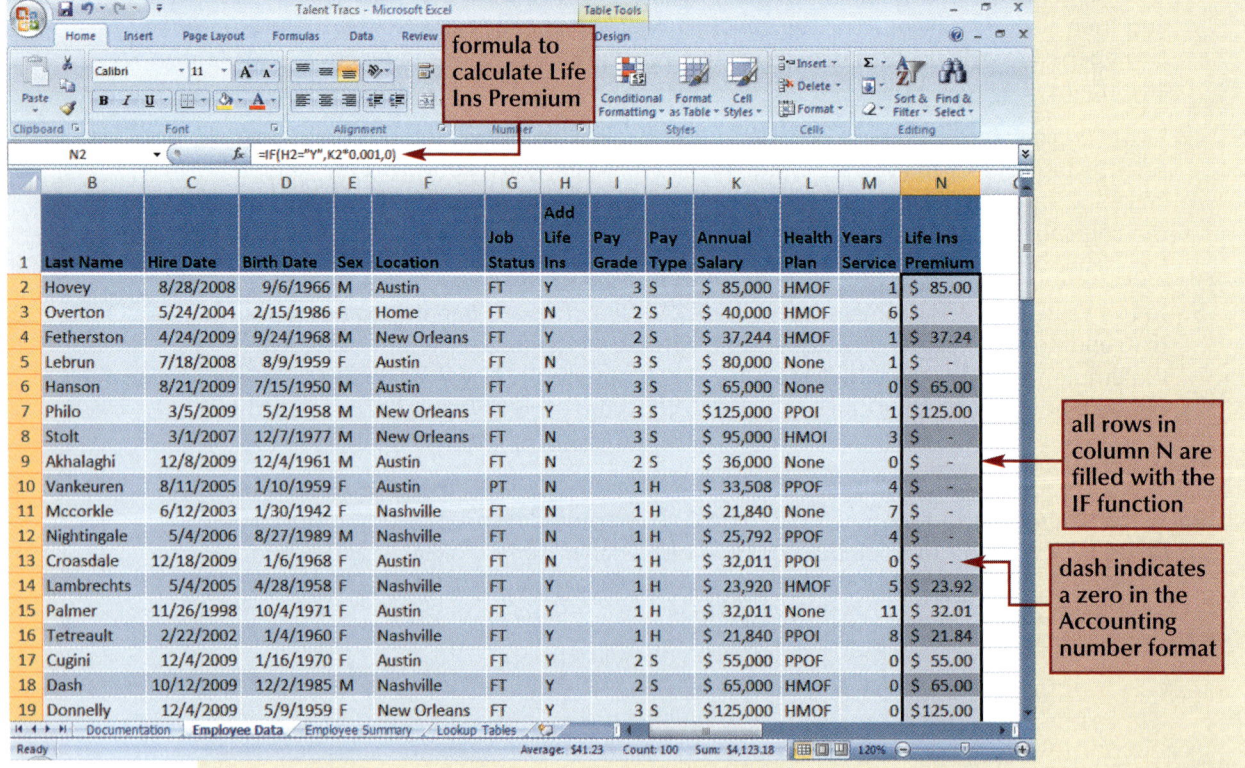

Using the And Function

Employees are eligible for the 401(k) benefit if they are full-time (FT in Job Status) *and* have worked for the company for one or more years (1 or greater in Years Service). As long as *both* conditions are true, the company contributes an amount equal to 3 percent of the employee's salary to the employee's 401(k). If neither condition is true or if only one condition is true, the employee is not eligible for the 401(k) benefit and the company's contribution is 0. Rita outlined these eligibility conditions in the flowchart shown in Figure 7-5.

Figure 7-5 Flowchart illustrating logic for the 401(k) benefit

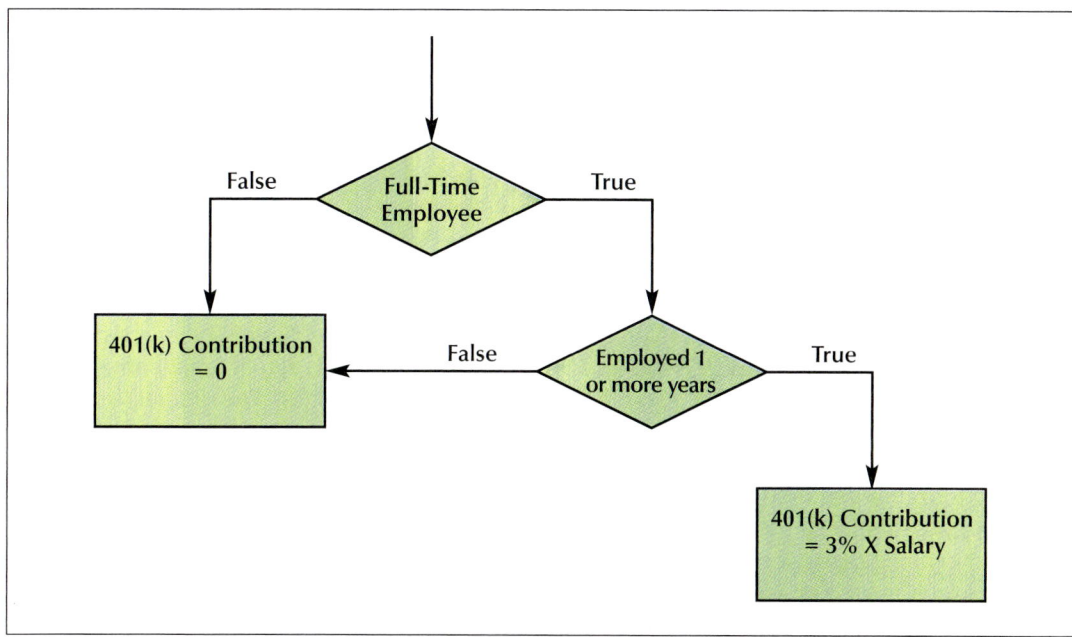

The IF function evaluates a single condition; however, you often need to test two or more conditions and determine whether *all* conditions are true. You can do this with the AND function. The **AND function** is a logical function that returns a TRUE value if all the logical conditions are true and a FALSE value if any or all of the logical conditions are false. The syntax of the AND function is as follows:

AND(*logical1* [,*logical2*]...)

In this function, *logical1* and *logical2* are conditions that can be either true or false. If all of the logical conditions are true, the AND function returns the logical value TRUE; otherwise, the function returns the logical value FALSE. You can include up to 255 logical conditions in the AND function, but keep in mind that *all* the logical conditions listed in the AND function must be true for the AND function to return a TRUE value.

To calculate the contribution amount for each employee to the 401(k) plan, you need to use the AND function along with the IF function. You use the AND function to test whether each employee in the Employee table fulfills the eligibility requirements, as shown in the following formula:

=AND(G2="FT",M2>=1)

This formula tests whether the value in cell G2 (the job status for the first employee) is equal to FT (the abbreviation for full-time) and whether the value in cell M2 (the years of service for the first employee) is greater than or equal to 1 (indicating one or more years of employment at Talent Tracs). Therefore, if the employee is a full-time employee (G2="FT") *and* has worked one or more years at Talent Tracs (M2>=1), the AND function returns the value TRUE; otherwise, the AND function returns the value FALSE.

The AND function, however, does not calculate how much Talent Tracs will contribute to the employee's 401(k) plan. To determine whether an employee is eligible *and* to calculate the amount of the 401(k) contribution, you need to insert the AND function within an IF function, as shown in the following formula:

```
=IF(AND(G2="FT",M2>=1),K2*0.03,0)
```

The first argument of the IF function, =IF(AND(G2="FT",M2>=1), uses the AND function to determine if the employee is eligible for a 401(k) contribution. If the employee is eligible, the logical test AND(G2="FT",M2>=1) returns the logical value TRUE and the formula in the value_if_true argument of the IF function multiplies the employee's annual salary by 0.03 (K2*0.03). If one or both conditions are false, the logical test AND(G2="FT",M2>=1) returns the logical value FALSE, and the IF function displays the value 0.

You'll insert a new column in the Employee table, and then enter the formula to calculate the 401(k) contribution using structured references.

Using Structured References with Excel Tables

When you create a formula that references all or parts of an Excel table, you can replace the specific cell or range address with a **structured reference**, the actual table name or column header. The table name is Table1, Table2, and so forth unless you entered a more descriptive table name, as you did for the Employee table. Column headers provide a description of the data entered in each column. Structured references make it easier to create formulas that use portions or all of an Excel table because the names or headers are usually simpler to identify than cell addresses. For example, in the Employee table, the table name *Employee* refers to the range A2:N101, which is the range of data in the table excluding the header row and Total row. When you want to reference an entire column of data in a table, you create a column qualifier, which has the following syntax:

```
Tablename[qualifier]
```

The *Tablename* is the name entered in the Table Name box in the Properties group on the Table Tools Design tab. The *qualifier* is the column header enclosed in square brackets. For example, the structured reference *Employee[Annual Salary]* references the annual salary data in the range K2:K101 of the Employee table. You use structured references in formulas, as shown in the following formula:

```
=SUM(Employee[Annual Salary])
```

This formula adds the annual salary data in the range K2:K101 of the Employee table. In this case, *[Annual Salary]* is the column qualifier.

When you create a calculated column, as you did to calculate life insurance premiums in the Employee table, you can use structured references to create the formula. A formula that includes a structured reference can be fully qualified or unqualified. In a fully qualified structured reference, the table name precedes the column qualifier. In an unqualified structured reference, only the column qualifier appears in the reference. For example, you could have used either of the following formulas with structured references to calculate Life Ins Premium in the calculated column you added to the Employee table (the first formula is unqualified, and the second is fully qualified):

```
=IF([Add Life Ins]="Y",[Annual Salary]*001,0)
=IF(Employee[Add Life Ins]="Y",Employee[Annual Salary]*.001,0)
```

> **Tip**
>
> If you are not sure of a table's name, click in the table, click the Table Tools Design tab on the Ribbon, and then check the Table Name box in the Properties group.

If you are creating a calculated column or formula within an Excel table, you can use the unqualified structured reference in the formula. If you use a structured reference outside the table or in another worksheet to reference an Excel table or portion of the table, you need to use a fully qualified reference.

In addition to referencing a specific column in a table by its column header, you can also reference other portions of a table, such as the header row or Total row. Figure 7-6 lists the special item qualifiers needed to reference these table portions in the formula.

Figure 7-6 Special item qualifiers for structured references

Qualifier	References	Example of Structured Reference
#All	The entire table, including column headers, data, and Total row if displayed	=Employee[#All]
#Data	The data in the table	=Employee[#Data]
#Headers	The header row in the table	=Employee[#Headers]
#Totals	The Total row in the table; if the Total row is hidden, then an error is returned	=Employee[#Totals]
#ThisRow	The current row in the specified column of the table	=Employee[[#ThisRow],[Column Header]]

You'll use structured references to calculate the 401(k) contributions for Talent Tracs.

To enter a formula with IF and AND functions to calculate 401(k) contributions:

1. In cell O1, enter **401(k)** as the column header. The Excel table expands to include the new column, and cell O2 is the active cell.

2. In cell O2, type **=I**. A list of valid function names opens scrolled to the I entries.

3. Double-click **IF**. The first part of the formula with the IF function, =IF(, appears in the cell and the formula bar with the insertion point placed directly after the opening parenthesis so you can continue typing the formula. The syntax of the IF function appears in a ScreenTip below cell O2. See Figure 7-7.

Tip

You can also insert the selected function in the list by pressing the Tab key.

Figure 7-7 IF function ScreenTip

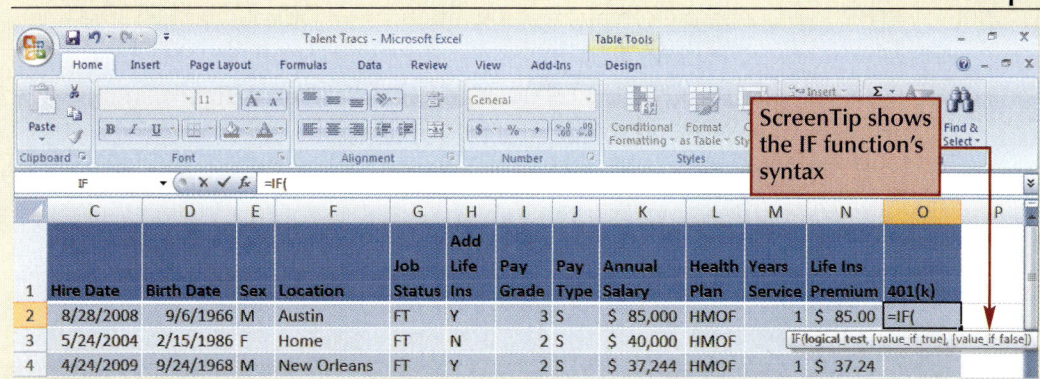

Next, you'll enter the AND function as the logical test for the IF function.

▶ 4. Type **A** to open the function list scrolled to the A entries, and then double-click **AND**. The first part of the AND function is added to the formula, and =IF(AND(appears in the cell and the formula bar. The syntax of the AND function appears in a ScreenTip below cell O2.

Trouble? If a function other than the AND function appears in cell O2, you probably double-clicked a different function name. Press the Backspace key to delete the incorrect function name and redisplay the list of function names. When you see the AND function, double-click the name.

You'll enter the logical conditions for the AND function using structured references.

▶ 5. Type **[** to display a list of all the column headers in the Employee table. You want to enter the Job Status column for the first logical condition. See Figure 7-8.

Figure 7-8   **List of column qualifiers**

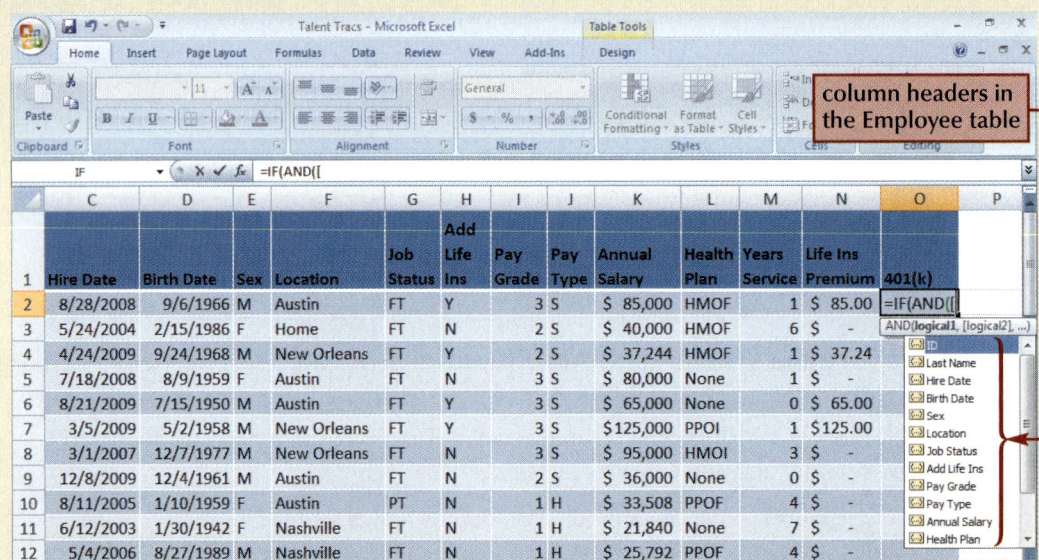

▶ 6. Double-click **Job Status**, and then type **]** to enter the structured reference for column G, which is the Job Status column. A blue box surrounds the Job Status data and [Job Status] is colored blue in the formula =IF(AND([Job Status] in the cell. This is the first part of the logical condition for the AND function, which is job status is full-time.

▶ 7. Type **="FT",** (including the comma) to complete the first logical condition. The first logical condition states that the content in the Job Status cell must equal FT.

▶ 8. Type **[** to begin the second logical condition, double-click **Years Service** in the list, and then type **]**. The structured reference for cell O2, which is years of service for the first employee, is entered in the formula. A green box surrounds the Years Service data and the structured reference is colored green in the formula.

▶ 9. Type **>=1),** to complete the second logical condition. The second logical condition states that the content in the Years Service cell must be greater than or equal to 1. The complete logical expression for the IF function, =IF(AND([Job Status]="FT",[Years Service]>=1), appears in the cell and the formula bar. The ScreenTip shows the syntax of the IF function again, because you are ready to enter the value_if_true argument and the value_if_false argument.

▶ 10. Type **[** to open the list of column headers, double-click **Annual Salary**, and then type **]*0.03,** to complete the value_if_true argument using a structured reference. The Annual Salary data appears in a purple box, and the structured reference in the formula is purple. If the employee is eligible for the 401(k) contribution, as determined by the AND function, then the amount in the Annual Salary cell for the employee is multiplied by 3%.

You'll complete the formula by entering the value_if_false argument.

▶ 11. Type **0)** for the value_if_false argument, and then press the **Enter** key. The formula is entered in cell O2 and copied to the rest of the 401(k) column in the table. If the employee is not eligible for the 401(k) contribution, as determined by the AND function, then 0 is entered in the 401(k) cell. In this case, cell O2 displays the value 2550, which is the result of multiplying the employee's annual salary of $85,000 by 3 percent, because the employee in row 2 meets both conditions of the logical test (job status is full-time and years of service is 1 year). See Figure 7-9.

Figure 7-9 Formula using IF and AND functions to calculate 401(k)

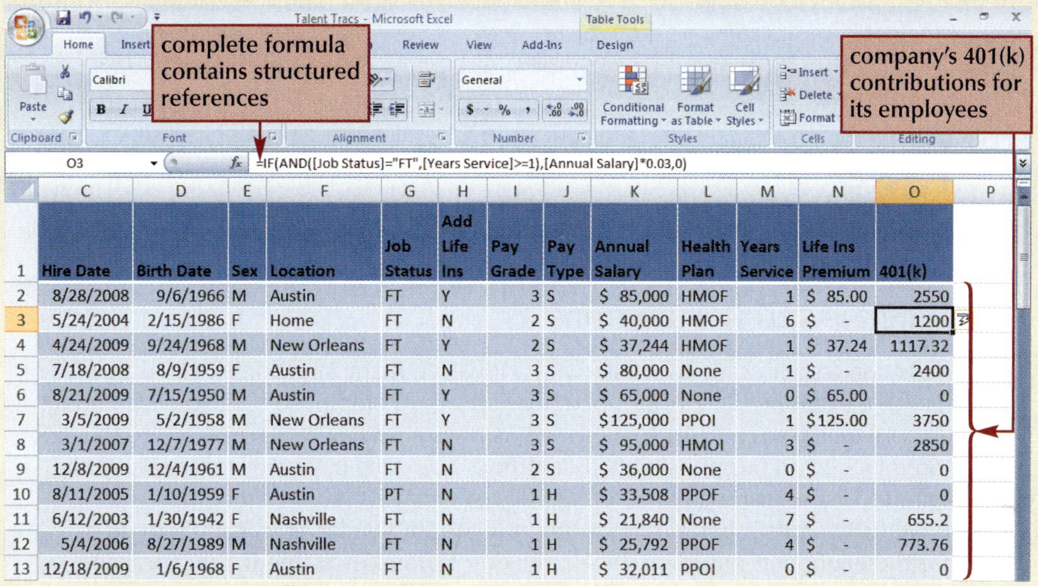

complete formula contains structured references

company's 401(k) contributions for its employees

=IF(AND([Job Status]="FT",[Years Service]>=1),[Annual Salary]*0.03,0)

	C	D	E	F	G	H	I	J	K	L	M	N	O
1	Hire Date	Birth Date	Sex	Location	Job Status	Add Life Ins	Pay Grade	Pay Type	Annual Salary	Health Plan	Years Service	Life Ins Premium	401(k)
2	8/28/2008	9/6/1966	M	Austin	FT	Y	3	S	$ 85,000	HMOF	1	$ 85.00	2550
3	5/24/2004	2/15/1986	F	Home	FT	N	2	S	$ 40,000	HMOF	6	$ -	1200
4	4/24/2009	9/24/1968	M	New Orleans	FT	Y	2	S	$ 37,244	HMOF	1	$ 37.24	1117.32
5	7/18/2008	8/9/1959	F	Austin	FT	N	3	S	$ 80,000	None	1	$ -	2400
6	8/21/2009	7/15/1950	M	Austin	FT	Y	3	S	$ 65,000	None	0	$ 65.00	0
7	3/5/2009	5/2/1958	M	New Orleans	FT	Y	3	S	$125,000	PPOI	1	$125.00	3750
8	3/1/2007	12/7/1977	M	New Orleans	FT	N	3	S	$ 95,000	HMOI	3	$ -	2850
9	12/8/2009	12/4/1961	M	Austin	FT	N	2	S	$ 36,000	None	0	$ -	0
10	8/11/2005	1/10/1959	F	Austin	PT	N	1	H	$ 33,508	PPOF	4	$ -	0
11	6/12/2003	1/30/1942	F	Nashville	FT	N	1	H	$ 21,840	None	7	$ -	655.2
12	5/4/2006	8/27/1989	M	Nashville	FT	N	1	H	$ 25,792	PPOF	4	$ -	773.76
13	12/18/2009	1/6/1968	F	Austin	FT	N	1	H	$ 32,011	PPOI	0	$ -	0

Trouble? If a dialog box opens, indicating that your formula contains an error, you might have omitted a comma, a square bracket, or a parenthesis. Edit the formula as needed to ensure the complete formula is =IF(AND([Job Status]="FT",[Years Service]>=1),[Annual Salary]*0.03,0), and then press the Enter key.

▶ 12. Point to the top of cell **O1** until the pointer changes to ↓, click to select the 401(k) data values, and then format the range using the **Accounting** number format with **2** decimal places.

| InSight | **Using the DATEDIF Function** |

The column Years Service was calculated using the DATEDIF function. The **DATEDIF function** calculates the difference between two dates and shows the result in months, days, or years. The DATEDIF function has the following syntax:

   DATEDIF(Date1,Date2,Interval)

In this function, *Date1* is the earliest date, *Date2* is the latest date, and *Interval* is the unit of time the DATEDIF function will use in the result. You specify the *Interval* with one of the following interval codes:

Interval Code	Meaning	Description
"m"	Months	The number of complete months between Date1 and Date2
"d"	Days	The number of complete days between Date1 and Date2
"y"	Years	The number of complete years between Date1 and Date2

Thus, the formula to calculate years of service at Talent Tracs in complete years is:

   =DATEDIF(C2,$AE$2,"y")

The earliest date is located in cell C2, the Hire Date. The latest date is in cell $AE$2, which shows the date used to compare against the Hire Date, the Years Service as of a cut-off date. The Interval is "y" to indicate you want to display the number of complete years between these two dates.

Note that the DATEDIF function is undocumented in Excel, but it has been available since Excel 97. If you want to learn more about this function, use your favorite search engine to search the Web for *DATEDIF function in Excel*.

Creating Nested IF Functions

The IF function tests for only two outcomes. However, many situations involve a series of outcomes. For example, Talent Tracs pays three levels of employee bonuses. Each bonus is based on the employee's pay grade, which is a system Talent Tracs uses to group jobs based on difficulty and responsibility. Talent Tracs has three pay grade codes (1, 2, and 3). Pay grade 1 has a starting bonus of $2,500, pay grade 2 has a starting bonus of $5,000, and pay grade 3 has a starting bonus of $7,500. Supervisors can increase or decrease these amounts based on the employee's performance. The IF function can choose between only two outcomes; it cannot choose between three outcomes. However, you can nest IF functions to allow for three or more outcomes. A **nested IF function** is when one IF function is placed inside another IF function to test an additional condition. You can nest more than one IF function. In this case, you need to nest three IF functions to calculate the different series of outcomes for the employee bonuses.

   Rita created a flowchart to illustrate the logic for determining bonus awards, shown in Figure 7-10. She used different colors to identify each nested IF function. The flowchart shows that if the employee has a pay grade equal to 1, then the bonus equals $2,500 and the IF function is finished (the green portion of the flowchart). If the pay grade is not equal to 1, then the second IF function (shown in blue) is evaluated. If the employee has a pay grade equal to 2, then the bonus equals $5,000 and the IF function is finished. If the pay grade is not equal to 2, then the third IF function (shown in gray) is evaluated. If the employee has a pay grade equal to 3, then the bonus equals $7,500 and the IF function is finished. If the pay grade is not equal to 3, then the message "Invalid pay grade" (shown in dark yellow) is entered in the cell.

Flowchart illustrating the logic to determine the bonus amount — Figure 7-10

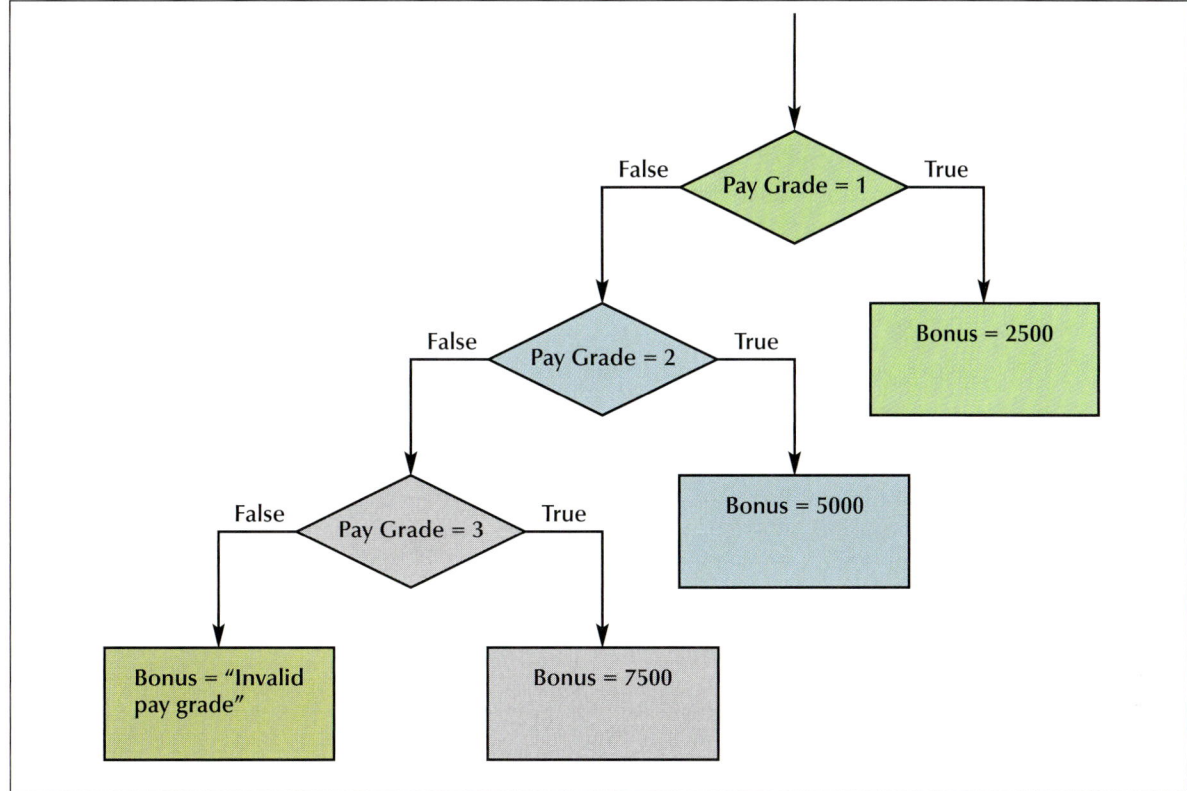

Next, you need to convert Rita's flowchart into a formula. The complete formula is as follows:

```
=IF([Pay Grade]=1,2500,IF([Pay Grade]=2,5000, IF([Pay Grade]=3,
7500,"Invalid pay grade")))
```

The first IF function (shown in green in the flowchart and the formula) tests whether the value in the current Pay Grade cell is equal to 1. If the condition ([Pay Grade]=1) is true, the formula enters 2500 in the Bonus cell. The second IF function (shown in blue in the flowchart and the formula) is executed only if Pay Grade is equal to 1 is false. If the value in the current Pay Grade cell is equal to 2, then the formula returns 5000 in the Bonus cell. The third IF function (shown in gray in the flowchart and the formula) is executed only if [Pay Grade]=2 is false. If the value in the current Pay Grade cell is equal to 3, then the formula returns 7500 in the Bonus cell. If the current value of Pay Grade is not equal to 3, then the message "Invalid pay grade" is entered in the Bonus cell (shown in dark yellow in the flowchart and the formula).

Next, you'll add a column to the Employee table to track the bonus and enter the formula to calculate the bonus amount. Rita mentions that the bonus amounts for each pay grade are not yet final. To make the bonus calculation more flexible, she stored the three bonus amounts (2500, 5000, 7500) in cells Y2, Y3, and Y4 of the Employee Data worksheet. You will reference these cells as you build the formula to calculate the employee bonus. This approach enables you to quickly update the calculated bonus amounts, by changing the values in cells Y2, Y3, and Y4, without having to edit the bonus formula.

To enter nested IFs to calculate employee bonuses:

▶ 1. In cell P1, enter **Bonus**. A new column with the column header Bonus is added to the Employee table, and cell P2 is the active cell.

▶ 2. In cell P2, type **=I**, and then double-click **IF**. The beginning of the formula =IF(appears in the cell and formula bar. The syntax of the IF function appears in a ScreenTip below cell P2.

▶ 3. Type **[** to open a list of all the column headers in the Employee table, double-click **Pay Grade**, type **]** to complete the column qualifier, and then type **=1,$Y$2,** to complete the first logical condition. This condition states that if the logical condition [Pay Grade]=1 is true, then the value stored in cell Y2 (which contains the 2500 bonus) is displayed.

Next, you'll nest a second IF function inside the first IF function.

▶ 4. Type **IF** and then press the **Tab** key to select the IF function.

▶ 5. Type **[p**, press the **Tab** key to enter Pay Grade for the structured reference, type **]** to complete the column qualifier, and then type **=2,$Y$3,** to enter the rest of the first nested IF function. The partial formula IF([Pay Grade]=1,$Y$2,IF([Pay Grade]=2,$Y$3 appears in the cell. The second IF function, IF([Pay Grade]=2,$Y$3, is complete and is executed if the logical condition [Pay Grade]=1 is false. If the condition [Pay Grade]=2 is true, the value stored in cell Y3 (which contains 5000) is displayed.

Next, you'll enter a third IF function inside the second IF function.

▶ 6. Type **IF([Pay Grade]=3, $Y$4,"Invalid pay grade")))**. The formula is complete. The third IF function is executed only if an employee's pay grade is neither 1 nor 2. If the condition [Pay Grade]=3 is true, the value stored in cell Y4 is displayed. If the Pay Grade cell is not equal to 3, then the message "Invalid pay grade" is displayed in the cell instead of the bonus amount.

▶ 7. Press the **Enter** key. The value 7500 appears in the cell because this employee has a pay grade of 3. The bonus formula is automatically copied to all other rows in the Bonus column. The references to cells Y2, Y3, and Y4 are absolute references and do not change as you move from cell to cell in the Bonus column.

Trouble? If a dialog box opens, indicating that the name you typed is invalid, you might have omitted a square bracket around [Pay Grade] or made a typing error. Click the OK button. The section of the formula that appears to have a problem is highlighted in the formula bar. Compare the formula you typed to =IF([Pay Grade]=1,$Y$2,IF([Pay Grade]=2,$Y$3, IF([Pay Grade]=3,$Y$4,"Invalid pay grade"))) and edit the formula as needed to correct the problem.

▶ 8. Format the Bonus values in the **Accounting** number format with no decimals. See Figure 7-11.

Tip

You can type an apostrophe to the left of the = sign to convert the formula to text, and then make the corrections to the text, saving you from retyping a long formula. After you correct the formula, delete the apostrophe to test the formula again.

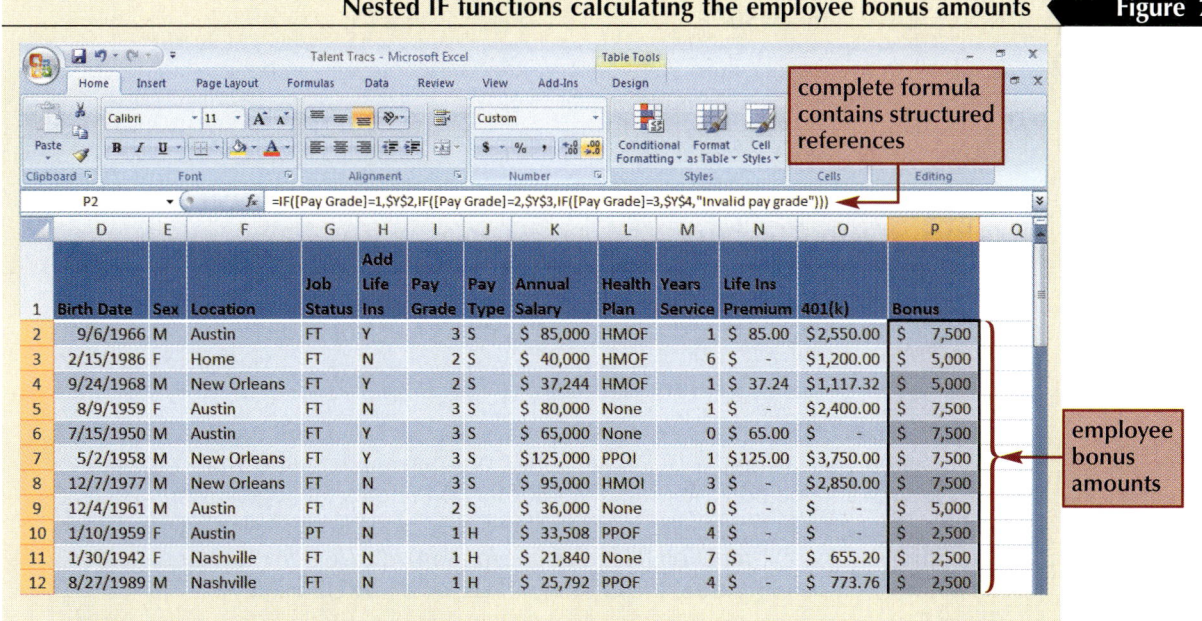

Figure 7-11 Nested IF functions calculating the employee bonus amounts

Checking Formulas for Matching Parentheses | InSight

You should verify that you enclosed the correct argument, function, or term within the parentheses of the formula you are creating. This is especially important when you develop a complex formula that includes many parentheses, because it's easy to lose track of how many closing parenthesis marks you need, particularly at the end of a complex formula. Excel color-codes the parentheses so you can quickly determine whether you have complete pairs of them. You can also verify that the formula includes matching pairs of parentheses by selecting the cell with the formula and then clicking in the formula bar. Press the right arrow key to move the insertion point through the formula one character at a time. When the insertion point moves across one parenthesis, its pair is also highlighted briefly. This color coding helps you make sure that all parentheses in a formula are part of a pair (opening and closing parentheses), which helps to ensure the accuracy of the formula and the results it produces.

You'll scroll the Bonus column to verify that all the bonus amounts were assigned correctly.

To check for invalid pay grade messages in the Employee table:

1. Scroll the Bonus column. Cell P31 displays the message, "Invalid pay grade." Rita tells you the correct pay grade for this employee is 3.

2. In cell I31 (row 31 of the Pay Grade column), enter **3**. The invalid pay grade code entry is removed and the correct bonus amount, $7,500, is displayed.

3. AutoFit the column width of the Bonus column.

The executive team increased the bonus for employees in pay grade 1 from $2,500 to $2,750. Rita asks you to update the bonus amount for pay grade 1 so the employee bonuses will be current.

To update the Bonus amount for pay grade 1:

▶ 1. In cell Y2, enter **2750**.

▶ 2. Scroll to the Bonus column and observe that all employees with a pay grade equal to 1 now show a bonus amount equal to $2,750.

Exploring the OR Function

The **OR function** is a logical function that returns a TRUE value if any of the logical conditions are true and a FALSE value if all the logical conditions are false. The syntax of the OR function is as follows:

```
OR(logical1 [,logical2,]...)
```

In this function, *logical1* and *logical2* are conditions that can be either true or false. If any of the logical conditions are true, the OR function returns the logical value TRUE; otherwise, the function returns the logical value FALSE. You can include up to 255 logical conditions in the OR function. However, keep in mind that *if any* logical condition listed in the OR function is true, the OR function returns a TRUE value.

Talent Tracs' executive team is considering changing the criteria to determine which employees receive a bonus. They are considering excluding employees who have worked at Talent Tracs for less than one year or employees who earn more than $100,000 and have other compensation packages.

The OR function can be nested within the IF function to determine employees who are not eligible for a bonus under the proposed criteria and assign a 0 bonus for those employees. The modified formula to calculate the bonus is as follows:

```
=IF(OR([Years Service]<1,[Annual Salary]>100000),0,IF([Pay Grade]=
1,$T$1,IF([Pay Grade]=2,$T$2, IF([Pay Grade]=3,$T$3,"Invalid pay
grade"))))
```

This formula uses the OR function to test whether the current cell for Years Service is less than 1 and also whether the current cell for Annual Salary is greater than 100,000 (shown in red). If either condition or both conditions are true, the OR function returns a TRUE value and 0 is entered in the Bonus cell. If both conditions are false, the OR function returns a FALSE value and determines the bonus for the employee using the nested IF functions you just entered to calculate bonuses based on the pay grade (shown in blue).

In this session, you used the IF and AND functions to calculate the additional life insurance premium and 401(k) benefits for Talent Tracss' employees. You also used nested IF functions to calculate the employee bonuses. Next, Rita needs to calculate health plan costs and the employee recognition award for each employee. She also wants to ensure the validity of data entered into the Employee table and then summarize the results in the Employee Summary worksheet. You'll complete these tasks in the next sessions.

Session 7.1 Quick Check | Review

1. What changes occur in an Excel table's appearance and size after you enter the new column header *Phone*?
2. What term describes the following behavior in Excel: Whenever you enter a formula in an empty column of an Excel table, Excel automatically fills the column with the same formula.
3. An Excel worksheet stores the cost per meal in cell C5, the number of attendees in cell C6, and the total cost of meals in cell C7. What IF function would you enter in cell C7 to calculate the total cost of meals (cost per meal times the number of attendees) with a minimum cost of $10,000?
4. True or False? The AND function is a logical function that returns a TRUE value if any of the logical conditions are true and a FALSE value if all of the logical conditions are false.
5. Write the formula that displays the label *Outstanding* if the amount owed (cell J5) is above 0 and the transaction date (cell D5) is before 3/15/2008, but otherwise leaves the cell blank.
6. When you create a formula that references all or part of an Excel table, you can replace the specific cell or range address with the actual table name or column header name. What are these references called?
7. What are you creating when you include one IF function inside another IF function?

Session 7.2

Using Lookup Tables and Functions

At Talent Tracs, all employees are eligible for the company's health plan. Employees can choose one of four health plans: an HMO for individuals (HMOI), an HMO for families (HMOF), a PPO for individuals (PPOI), and a PPO for families (PPOF). Each health plan has a different monthly premium, and Talent Tracs pays the entire amount. If an employee shows evidence of coverage elsewhere, there is no health plan cost. Figure 7-12 shows the HealthPlanRates table that Rita created with the cost per employee for the different available health plans.

Figure 7-12 HealthPlanRates table

	A	B	C	D
1				
2				
3		Plan	Monthly Premium	
4		HMOF	$ 1,500	
5		HMOI	$ 875	
6		PPOF	$ 1,650	
7		PPOI	$ 950	
8		None	$ -	
9				

Rita created a flowchart to explain the logic for determining health plan costs, as shown in Figure 7-13. The flowchart shows that if the employee chooses the HMO for Family health plan (Health Plan=HMOF), then Talent Tracs pays $1500 per month (Health Plan Cost=1500) and the IF function is finished. If the employee chooses the HMO for Individual health plan (Health Plan=HMOI), then Talent Tracs pays $875 per month (Health Plan Cost=875) and the IF function is finished. If the employee chooses the PPO for Family health plan (Health Plan=PPOF), then Talent Tracs pays $1650 per month (Health Plan Cost=1650) and the IF function is finished. If the employee chooses the PPO for Individual health plan (Health Plan=PPOI), then Talent Tracs pays $950 per month (Health Plan Cost=950) and the IF function is finished. If the employee chooses none of the health plans (Health Plan=None), then Talent Tracs pays $0 per month (Health Plan Cost=0), and the IF function is finished.

Figure 7-13 Flowchart illustrating the logic of calculating health plan costs

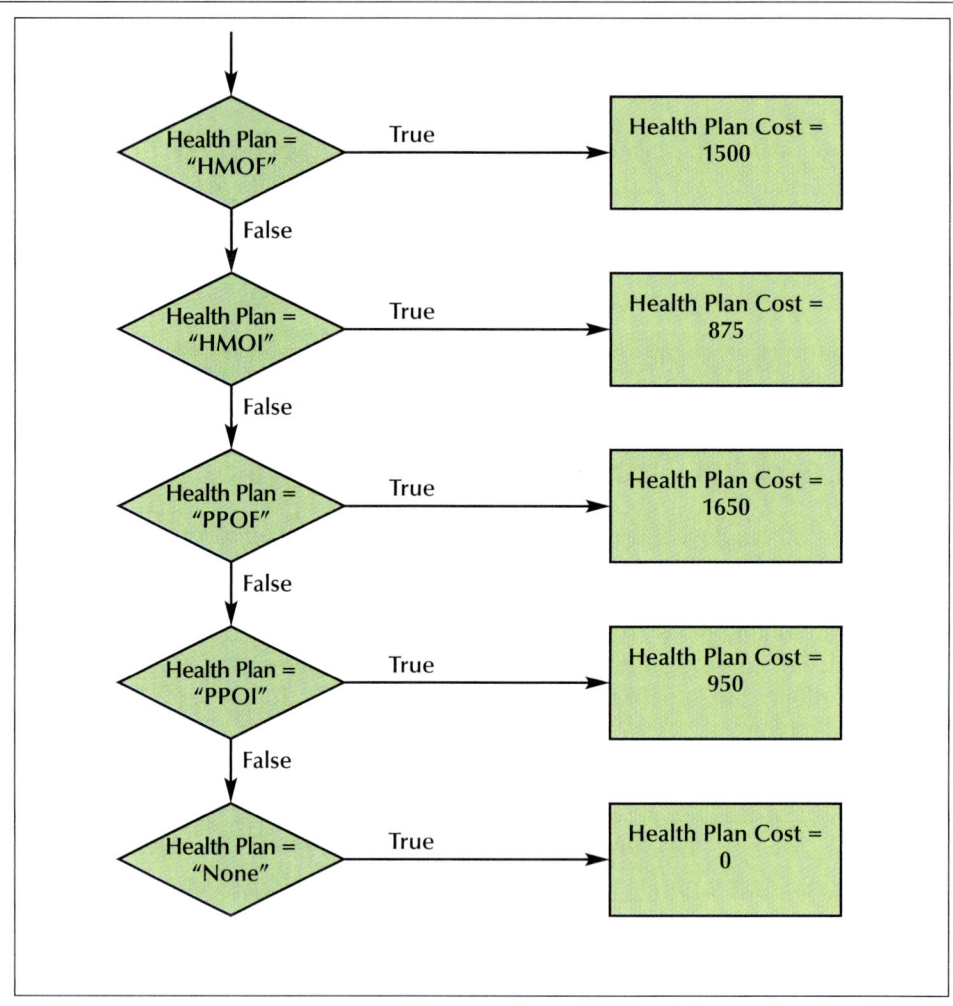

You could calculate these health plan costs using several nested IF functions. However, an easier approach is to use a lookup table. A **lookup table** is a table that organizes data you want to retrieve into different categories, such as each health plan code. The categories for the lookup table, called **compare values**, are located in the table's first column or row. To retrieve a particular value from the table, a **lookup value** (the value you are trying to find) needs to match the compare values. When the lookup value matches a particular compare value, a value from an appropriate column (or row) in the lookup table is returned to the cell in which the lookup formula is entered or used as part of a more complex formula.

You can use the HealthPlanRates table shown in Figure 7-12 that Rita created in the Lookup Tables worksheet as a lookup table. For example, the health plan cost for each eligible employee is based on the plan the employee selected. The lookup value is the employee's health plan code, which is entered in column L of the Employee table. The compare values come from the first column of the HealthPlanRates table, which is in the range B4:C8 in the Lookup Tables worksheet. To retrieve the monthly cost for an employee, Excel moves down the first column in the lookup table (HealthPlanRates) until it finds the health plan code that matches (is equal to) the lookup value. Then, it moves to the second column in the lookup table to locate the monthly cost, which is displayed in the cell where the lookup formula is entered or used as part of a calculation.

To retrieve correct values from the lookup table, you use either the VLOOKUP or HLOOKUP function. VLOOKUP and HLOOKUP functions search a lookup table and, based on what you entered, retrieve the appropriate value from that table. The **VLOOKUP** (vertical lookup) **function** searches vertically down the lookup table and is used when the compare values are stored in the first column of the lookup table. The **HLOOKUP** (horizontal lookup) **function** searches horizontally across the lookup table and is used when the compare values are stored in the first row of the lookup table.

The HealthPlanRates table's compare values are in the first column, so you will use the VLOOKUP function. The HLOOKUP function works similarly. The VLOOKUP function has the following syntax:

```
VLOOKUP(lookup_value, table_array, col_index_num, [range_lookup])
```

In this function, *lookup_value* is the value you want to use to search the first column of the lookup table; *table_array* is the cell reference of the lookup table or its table name, *col_index_num* is the number of the column in the lookup table that contains the value you want to return, and *range_lookup* indicates whether the compare values are a range of values (sometimes referred to as an approximate match) or an exact match. When you use a range of values (such as in a tax rate table), you set the *range_lookup* value to TRUE; when you want the *lookup_value* to exactly match a value in the first column of the *table_array* (such as in the HealthPlanRates table), you set the *range_lookup* value to FALSE. The *range_lookup* argument is optional; if you don't include a *range_lookup* value, the value is considered TRUE (an approximate match).

Looking Up an Exact Match

You'll use the VLOOKUP function to calculate the annual health plan cost for Talent Tracs. You'll use the VLOOKUP function because you want to search the values in the first column of the lookup table. You can use range references or structured references when you create the formula for the annual health plan cost for an employee from the HealthPlanRates table shown earlier in Figure 7-12, as follows (the first formula uses range references, and the second formula uses structured references):

```
=VLOOKUP(L2,'Lookup Tables'!$B$4:$C$8,2,FALSE)*12
=VLOOKUP([HealthPlan],HealthPlanRates,2,FALSE)*12
```

The formula uses the VLOOKUP function to search for the code in the Health Plan column (column L) of the Employee table in the first column of the lookup table (the HealthPlanRates table in the range B4:C8 in the Lookup Tables worksheet), and then return the value in the second column of the HealthPlanRates lookup table, which shows the monthly cost. This value is then multiplied by 12 to return the annual cost. The formula uses FALSE as the *range_lookup* argument because you want the lookup value to exactly match a value in the first column of the HealthPlanRates table.

To use the VLOOKUP function in the Employee table to find an exact match in the HealthPlanRates table:

1. If you took a break after the previous session, make sure the Talent Tracs workbook is open and the Employee Data worksheet is active.

2. In cell Q1, enter **Health Cost**. The table expands to include the new column and the table's formatting is applied to all rows in the new column.

3. Make sure cell **Q2** is the active cell, and then click the **Insert Function** button f_x on the formula bar. The Insert Function dialog box opens.

4. Click the **Or select a category** arrow, click **Lookup & Reference**, and then double-click **VLOOKUP** at the bottom of the function list. The Function Arguments dialog box opens.

5. Drag the Function Arguments dialog box below row 2 to make it easier to see the column headers.

6. In the Lookup_value argument box, enter **L2**. The *lookup_value* is the employee's health plan code, which is located in column L.

   Next, you'll enter the *table_array* argument, which is equal to the range containing the HealthPlanRates table located in the Lookup Tables worksheet.

7. Click the Table_array argument **Collapse** button to shrink the dialog box to show only the Table_array argument box, switch to the **Lookup Tables** worksheet, select the range **B4:C8** (the HealthPlanRates table), and then click the **Expand** button to return the dialog box to its full size. The table name *HealthPlanRates* appears in the Table_array argument box. If the HealthPlanRates data was entered in a range of cells instead of an Excel table, the table_array would be *'Lookup Tables'!B4:B8*, and you would need to change the range to absolute references *'Lookup Tables'!$B$4:$B$8* so the formula would copy correctly to other cells.

8. In the Col_index_num argument box, enter **2**. The number 2 indicates the monthly cost is stored in the second column of the HealthPlanRates lookup table. When entering the col_index_num value, be sure to enter the number that corresponds to the column's position within the lookup table, rather than its column letter.

9. In the Range_lookup argument box, enter **FALSE**. This sets the function to find an exact match in the lookup table. See Figure 7-14.

> **Tip**
>
> If you see #NAME? or #VALUE! as the result of a VLOOKUP formula, you might have entered a letter for the col_index_num instead of a number.

Figure 7-14
Function Arguments dialog box for the VLOOKUP function

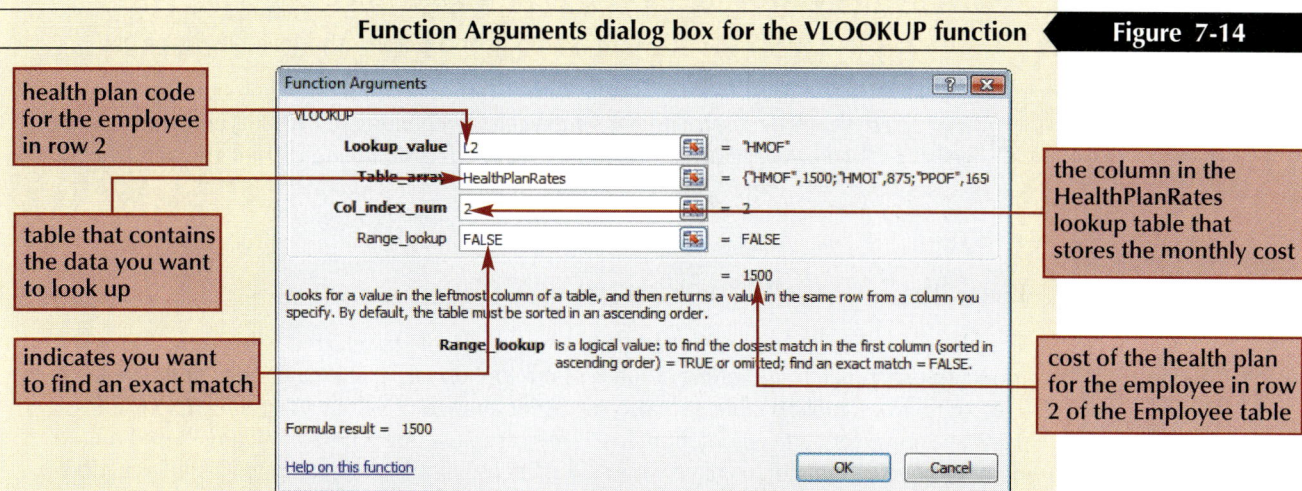

- health plan code for the employee in row 2
- table that contains the data you want to look up
- indicates you want to find an exact match
- the column in the HealthPlanRates lookup table that stores the monthly cost
- cost of the health plan for the employee in row 2 of the Employee table

▶ 10. Click the **OK** button. The dialog box closes and the result 1500 appears in cell Q2. The formula *VLOOKUP(L2,HealthPlanRates,2,FALSE)* appears in the formula bar. The remaining rows in the Health Cost column are filled with the VLOOKUP function. If a value in column L does not match a value in the first column of the HealthPlanRates table, there is not an exact match and #N/A appears in the cell, as you'll see shortly.

▶ 11. Format the Health Cost values in the **Accounting** number format with no decimal places. Recall that a dash indicates a 0 in the Accounting number format. See Figure 7-15.

Figure 7-15
Employee table with health plan costs calculated

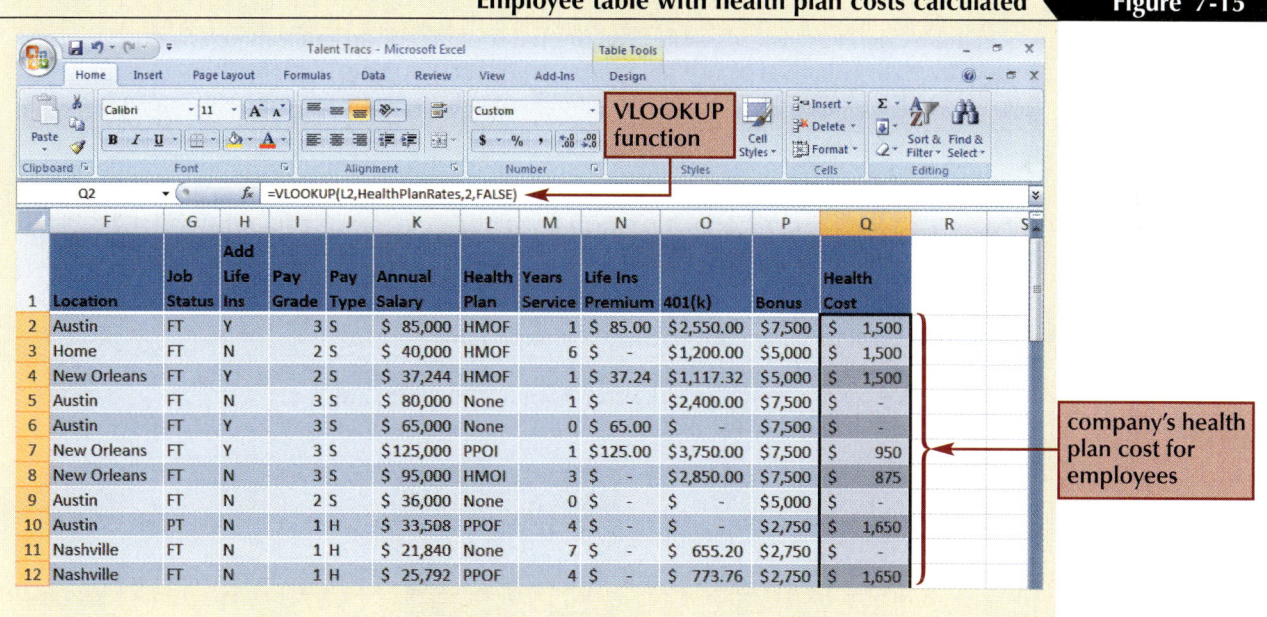

- VLOOKUP function
- company's health plan cost for employees

The health plan costs in the Employee table are monthly amounts rather than annual. You need to modify the formula in the Health Cost column to reflect the annual amounts. Because the formula is in a calculated table column, you need to make the change in only one cell and the change will automatically be copied to all the cells in the column.

> **To modify the VLOOKUP function in the calculated column:**
>
> ▸ 1. Double-click cell **Q2** to enter editing mode and display the formula in the cell.
>
> ▸ 2. Click at the end of the formula, type ***12** to multiply the monthly amount by 12, and then press the **Enter** key. The amount in cell Q2 changes to $18,000 and all the other cells in the column are updated with the revised formula and display the annual cost.

Looking Up an Approximate Match

The previous table lookup used the HealthPlanRates table to return a value only if Excel found an exact match in the first column of the lookup table. The categories in the first column or row of a lookup table can also represent a range of values. As part of Talent Tracs 10-year anniversary, management plans to give employee recognition awards based on the number of years individuals have worked for Talent Tracs. Rita developed the criteria shown in Figure 7-16 to summarize how the company plans to distribute the recognition award.

Figure 7-16   Recognition award distribution based on years of service

Years of Service	Award
>=0 years and < 1 year	0
>=1 year and <3 years	100
>=3 years and <5 years	200
>=5 years and <7 years	300
7 years or more	500

In the recognition awards table, you are not looking for an *exact match* for the lookup value. Instead, you need to use an *approximate match* lookup, which determines whether the lookup value falls within a range of values. You want to use the table lookup to determine what service range an employee falls into and then return the recognition award based on the appropriate row. To accomplish this, you must rearrange the first column of the lookup table so each compare value (row) in the table represents the low end of the category range. Rita followed this format when she created the Recognition lookup table as shown in Figure 7-17.

Figure 7-17   Recognition award table converted to a lookup table

	F	G	H	I
1				
2				
3		Years of Service	Recognition Award	
4		0	$ -	
5		1	$ 100	
6		3	$ 200	
7		5	$ 300	
8		7	$ 500	
9				

To determine whether a lookup value falls within a range of values in the revised lookup table, Excel searches the first column of the table until it locates the largest value that is still less than the lookup value. Then, Excel moves across the table to retrieve the appropriate row. For example, an employee working at Talent Tracs for six years would receive a $300 employee recognition award.

> ### Setting Up an Approximate Match Lookup Table | InSight
>
> When a lookup table is used with a range of values, the compare values must be sorted in alphabetical order if they are text, and low-to-high order if they are numbers. When the compare values are arranged in a different order, Excel cannot retrieve the correct results. In this case, the VLOOKUP function seems incorrect, but the real problem is how the lookup table is organized. The setup of the lookup table in an approximate match is critical for a VLOOKUP formula to work as intended.
>
> Consider the following example, in which an instructor uses Excel to calculate grades. The instructor assigns final grades based on the grading policy shown below, on the left. To set up the lookup table correctly, the leftmost column in the lookup table must represent the lower end of the range for each category *and* the lookup table must be sorted in ascending order based on the value in the first column. Otherwise, Excel cannot retrieve the correct result. Following this structure, the lookup table for the instructor's grading policy would be arranged as shown below, on the right.
>
> | Grading Policy | | Lookup Table | |
> |---|---|---|---|
> | Score | Grade | Score | Grade |
> | 90–100 | A | 0 | F |
> | 80–89 | B | 60 | D |
> | 70–79 | C | 70 | C |
> | 60–69 | D | 80 | B |
> | 0–59 | F | 90 | A |
>
> If a VLOOKUP or HLOOKUP function with an approximate match doesn't return the values you expected, first confirm that you entered the formula correctly. Then, verify that the lookup table has the proper arrangement.

You'll create the formula in the Employee table to determine the recognition award for each employee. You will use an approximate match VLOOKUP formula because the years of service in the lookup table has a range of values.

To insert an approximate match VLOOKUP formula:

▶ 1. In cell R1, enter **Award**. A new column is added to the table.

▶ 2. In cell R2, type **=V** and then double-click **VLOOKUP**. The start of the formula =VLOOKUP(appears in the cell and formula bar.

▶ 3. Type **[** to open a list of all the column headers in the Employee table, scroll down and double-click **Years Service**, and then type **],** to complete the entry for the first argument of the VLOOKUP function.

▶ 4. Type **R** and then double-click **Recognition** to enter the second argument, the lookup table. *Recognition* is the name of the Excel table in the range G4:H8 in the Lookup Tables worksheet.

▶ 5. Type **,2)** to complete the VLOOKUP formula. The number 2 indicates the column number in the Recognition lookup table where the award amount is stored. You did not enter the optional fourth argument in the VLOOKUP formula; Excel assumes the value to be TRUE and uses an approximate match table lookup.

> **Tip**
>
> You can also enter a column header in a formula by starting to type the name of the column header until it is highlighted in the list, and then pressing the Tab key.

▶ 6. Press the **Enter** key. Each cell in the calculated column Award is filled. The employee in row 2 has 1 year of service and will receive a recognition award of $100. The employee in row 3 has 6 years of service and will receive an award of $300. This second employee is a good illustration of the approximate match lookup, because 6 is not equal to a value in the first column of the lookup table. Instead, it falls within two values in the table. See Figure 7-18.

| Figure 7-18 | Recognition award column |

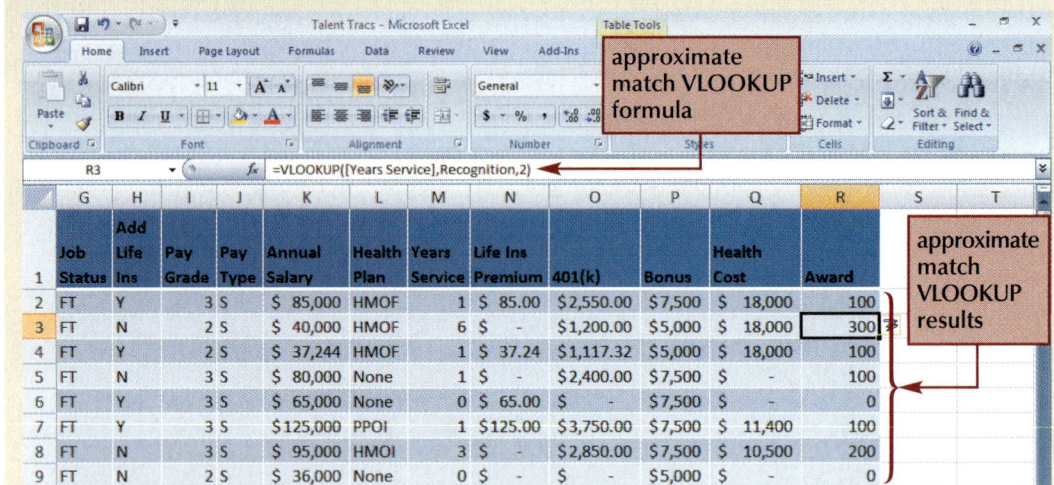

▶ 7. Format the Award values in the **Accounting** number format with no decimals places, and then AutoFit the column width.

Checking for Data Entry Errors

Rita believes the current data in the Employee table is accurate, but she is concerned that invalid data could be entered into the table. She wants to use conditional formatting and the IFERROR function to help reduce data entry errors.

| Reference Window | **Highlighting Duplicate Records with a Custom Format** |

- Select the column you want to search for duplicates.
- In the Styles group on the Home tab, click the Conditional Formatting button, point to Highlight Cells Rules, and then click Duplicate Values.
- Click the values with arrow, and then click Custom Format.
- In the Format Cells dialog box, set the formatting you want to use.
- Click the OK button in each dialog box.

Highlighting Duplicate Values with Conditional Formatting

Conditional formatting changes a cell's formatting when its contents match a specified condition. You've already used conditional formatting to add data bars that indicate the relative values in a range and to add highlights to cells based on their values for emphasis. Now you'll use conditional formatting to highlight duplicate values in a column of data. Duplicate value highlighting helps verify that columns of data have unique entries, such as the employee ID column in the Employee table. Rita wants you to change the background color of records that have duplicate employee IDs to red. This alert will help Rita ensure that each employee is entered in the table only once.

To highlight duplicate records in the Employee table:

1. Scroll to column A, point to the top of cell **A1** until the pointer changes to ↓, and then click the top of cell **A1** just below the column header. Rows 2 through 101 in the ID column are selected.

2. Click the **Home** tab on the Ribbon, and then, in the Styles group, click the **Conditional Formatting** button.

3. Point to **Highlight Cells Rules**, and then click **Duplicate Values**. The Duplicate Values dialog box opens.

4. Click the **values with** arrow to display a list of formatting options, and then click **Custom Format** to create a format that is not in the list. The Format Cells dialog box opens. You'll change the background fill color to red.

5. Click the **Fill** tab, and then, in the Background Color palette, click **Red** (the second color in the last row).

6. Click the **OK** button in the Format Cells dialog box, and then click the **OK** button in the Duplicate Values dialog box. Any duplicate values in the ID column are in a red cell.

7. Scroll the table to see if any duplicate values are found.

No duplicate records are found in the Employee table. You need to test the conditional format to make sure it works as intended. As you build a formula, you should test all situations to verify how the formula performs in each case. In this case, you should test the column both with duplicate values and without duplicate values. You'll intentionally change the ID of the last record from 1123 to 1024, which is the ID of the first employee, to confirm the duplicate IDs are formatted in red cells. Then, you will return the ID to its original value and confirm that the duplicate highlighting is removed.

To test that the duplicate value conditional format works correctly:

1. Click in the **Name** box, type **A101**, and then press the **Enter** key. The active cell moves to the last record in the Employee table.

2. In cell A101, enter **1024**. The ID changes from 1123 to 1024 and red fills this cell because it has a duplicate ID. See Figure 7-19.

Duplicate record highlighted — Figure 7-19

	A	B	C	D	E	F	G	H	I	J	K	L	M	N
99	1121	Winters	2/14/2002	3/1/1953	F	Nashville	FT	N	1	H	$ 33,800	PPOF	8	$ -
100	1122	Wang	8/24/1998	8/11/1966	F	Austin	FT	N	1	H	$ 35,048	PPOI	11	$ -
101	1024	Harrison	6/19/2009	11/25/1963	M	Austin	FT	N	2	S	$ 41,000	PPOF	1	$ -
102														
103														

duplicate value highlighted in red

▶ 3. Press the **Ctrl+Home** keys to move to the top of the table. Cell A2 also has a red background fill because it has the same ID you entered in cell A101. Excel identified the duplicate records.

InSight | Using a Formula to Conditionally Format Cells

Sometimes you might find that the built-in conditional formatting rules do not fit your needs. In these cases, you can create a conditional formatting rule based on a formula that uses a logical expression to describe the condition you want. For example, you can create a formula that uses conditional formatting to compare cells in different columns or to highlight an entire row.

When you create the formula, keep in mind the following guidelines:
- The formula must start with an equal sign.
- The formula must be in the form of a logical test that results in a true or false value.
- In most cases, the formula should use relative references and point to the first row of data in the table. If the formula references a cell or range outside the table, use an absolute reference.
- After you create the formula, enter test values to ensure the conditional formatting works in all situations that you intended.

For example, to use conditional formatting to highlight whether the Hire Date entered in column C is less than the Birth Date entered in column D (which would indicate a data entry error), you need to enter a formula that applies conditional formatting that compares cells in different columns of a table. Do the following:

1. Select the range you want to format (in this case, the Hire Date column).
2. Click the Conditional Formatting button in the Styles group on the Home tab, and then click New Rule.
3. In the Select a Rule Type box, click the "Use a formula to determine which cells to format" rule.
4. In the Format values where this formula is true box, enter the appropriate formula (in this case, =C2<D2).
5. Click the Format button to open the Format Cells dialog box, and select the formatting you want to apply.
6. Click the OK button in each dialog box.

Another example is to highlight the entire row if an employee has 10 or more years of service. In this case, you would select the range of data, such as A2:R101, and enter =M$2>10 in the Format values where this formula is true box. The other steps remain the same.

The red background fill makes the text difficult to read. Rita asks you to use yellow as the fill color to better contrast with the black text. After you apply a conditional format, you can modify it from the Conditional Formatting Rules Manager dialog box.

Using the Conditional Formatting Rules Manager

Each time you create a conditional format, you are defining a conditional formatting rule. A **rule** specifies the type of condition (such as formatting cells greater than a specified value), the type of formatting when that condition occurs (such as light red fill with dark red text), and the cell or range the formatting is applied to. You can edit existing conditional formatting rules from the Conditional Formatting Rules Manager dialog box. You'll use this dialog box to edit the rule that specifies the formatting applied to duplicate values in the ID column of the Employee table.

Tutorial 7 Using Advanced Functions, Conditional Formatting, and Filtering | Excel **EX 363**

To change the duplicate values background fill color to yellow:

▶ 1. In the Styles group on the Home tab, click the **Conditional Formatting** button, and then click **Manage Rules**. The Conditional Formatting Rules Manager dialog box opens, listing all the formatting rules for the current selection, which, in this case, is the Employee table.

▶ 2. Verify that the Show formatting rules for box displays **This Table**. All the rules currently in effect in the Employee table are displayed. You can add new rules and edit or delete existing rules. You also can control which formatting rules are displayed in the dialog box, such as all rules in a specific worksheet or table. See Figure 7-20.

Conditional Formatting Rules Manager dialog box — Figure 7-20

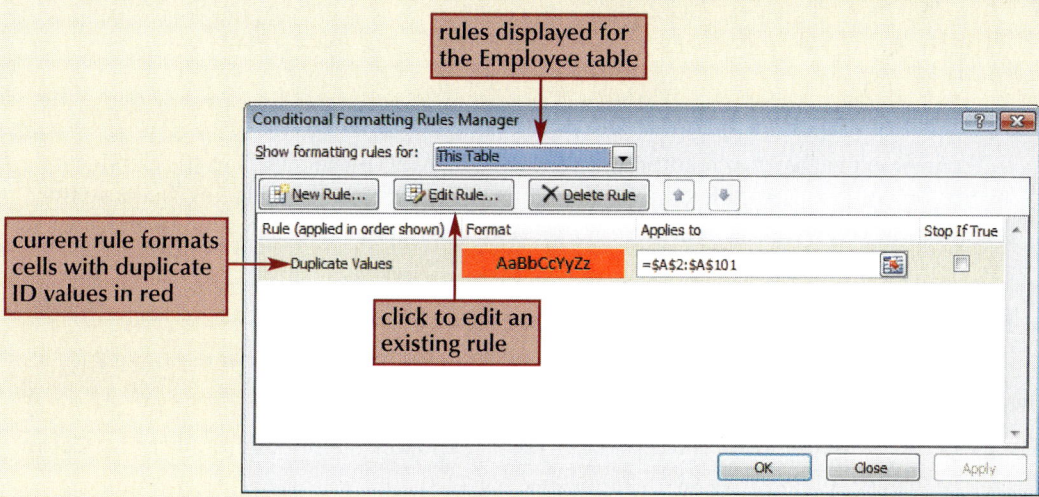

You want to change the Duplicate Values rule to use a yellow background fill color for duplicate entries in the ID column.

▶ 3. Click **Duplicate Values** in the Rule list to select the rule, and then click the **Edit Rule** button. The Edit Formatting Rule dialog box opens. See Figure 7-21.

Edit Formatting Rule dialog box — Figure 7-21

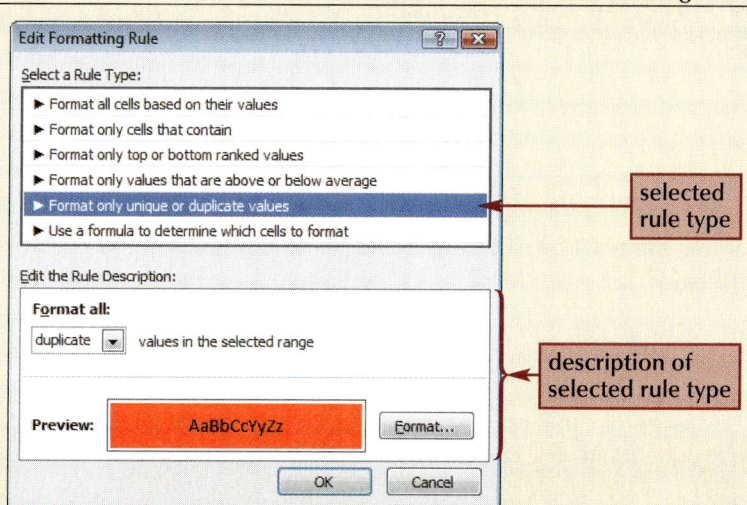

▶ 4. Click the **Format** button. The Format Cells dialog box opens.

▶ 5. Click the **Fill** tab, if necessary, and then click **Yellow** in the Background Color palette (the fourth color in the last row).

▶ **6.** Click the **OK** button in each dialog box. The duplicate records in the table are now formatted with a yellow background color. See Figure 7-22.

Figure 7-22 | **Revised conditional format for duplicate records**

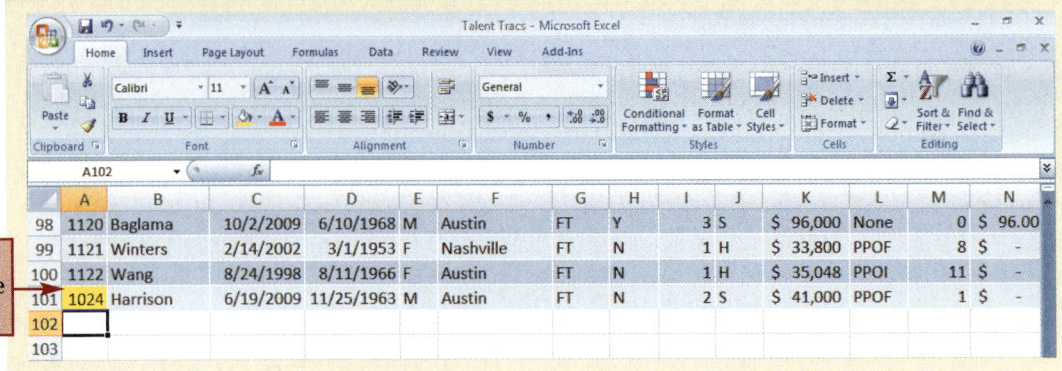

background color of duplicate value is yellow

The cell text is easier to read on the yellow background. You can filter the duplicate records by color. This enables you to view only records that are duplicates, because they are in the yellow background.

To filter duplicate records by color:

▶ **1.** Click the **Data** tab on the Ribbon, and then, in the Sort & Filter group, click the **Filter** button. Filter arrows appear on the column headers.

▶ **2.** Click the **ID** filter arrow to open the Filter menu, and then point to **Filter by Color** to display the Filter by Cell Color palette.

▶ **3.** Click the **yellow** color. The filter is applied and only records with a yellow cell color (duplicate records) are displayed.

You'll redisplay all records.

▶ **4.** Click the **ID** filter arrow to open the Filter menu, and then click **Clear Filter From "ID"**. The filter is removed and all of the records are displayed.

▶ **5.** In the Sort & Filter group on the Data tab, click the **Filter** button to remove the filter arrows from the column headers.

Tip

You can also sort records by color. Click the filter arrow to open the Filter menu, and then click Sort by Color.

You'll correct the duplicate ID in cell A101 by entering the employee's actual ID number.

To correct the duplicate ID:

▶ **1.** In cell A101, enter **1123**. The employee's ID is updated and the conditional formatting is removed because the value in the ID column is no longer a duplicate. However, the conditional formatting is still active. This rule will apply to any new records that Rita adds to the Employee table, which will help her to ensure that each employee has only one record in the table.

▶ **2.** Scroll to the top of the Employee table, and verify that the conditional formatting no longer appears in cell A2.

▶ **3.** Click cell **A1**.

The Duplicate Values rule enables you to verify that each entry in the ID column is unique, but it doesn't ensure that each unique value is accurate. Excel uses error values to help you find incorrectly entered data.

Using the IFERROR Function

Only five codes are used for the Health Plan column—PPOI, PPOF, HMOI, HMOF, and None. Rita wants to make sure that only these five valid codes are entered in the Health Plan column because the formula in the Health Cost column requires a valid health plan code. For instance, entering an inaccurate health plan code for an employee, such as HMOG instead of HMOF, would result in the error value (#N/A) in the Health Cost cell because the VLOOKUP function cannot find the invalid code in the HealthPlanRates lookup table.

Error values such as #DIV/0!, #N/A, and #VALUE! indicate that some element in a formula or a cell referenced in a formula is preventing Excel from returning a calculated value. An error value begins with a number sign (#) followed by an error name, which indicates the type of error. Figure 7-23 describes common error values you might see in workbooks.

Figure 7-23   Excel error values

Error Value	Description of Error
#DIV/0!	The formula or function contains a number divided by 0.
#NAME?	Excel doesn't recognize text in the formula or function, such as when the function name is misspelled.
#N/A	A value is not available to a function or formula, which can occur when an invalid value is specified in the LOOKUP function.
#NULL!	A formula or function requires two cell ranges to intersect, but they don't.
#NUM!	Invalid numbers are used in a formula or function, such as text entered in a function that requires a number.
#REF!	A cell reference used in a formula or function is no longer valid, which can occur when a cell used by the function was deleted from the worksheet.
#VALUE!	The wrong type of argument is used in a function or formula, which can occur when you supply a range of values to a function that requires a single value.

These error value messages are not particularly meaningful or helpful, so Rita wants you to display a more descriptive message when Excel detects an error value. If a record includes an invalid health plan code, #N/A appears in the corresponding Health Cost cell because the VLOOKUP function doesn't find a value in the first column of the lookup table and cannot return a value. The IFERROR function enables you to display a more descriptive message that helps users fix the problem rather than adding confusion, as error values often do. The **IFERROR function** can determine if a cell contains an error value and display the message you choose rather than the default error value. The IFERROR function has the following syntax:

`IFERROR(expression,valueIfError)`

In this function, *expression* is the formula you want to check for an error and *valueIfError* is the message you want displayed if Excel detects an error in the formula you are checking. If Excel does not detect an error, the result of the *expression* is displayed.

The IFERROR function enables you to easily find and handle formula errors. For example, you can enter the following formula to determine whether an invalid code was entered in the Health Plan column of the Employee table:

`=IFERROR(VLOOKUP(L2,HealthPlanRates,2,False)*12,"Invalid code")`

Based on this formula, if the value in cell L2 is HMOF, the result of the VLOOKUP formula is $1,500 (a value from the HealthPlanRates table), and then the first argument in the IFERROR function (shown in blue) is executed. On the other hand, if cell L2 has an invalid Health Plan code, such as HMOG, the VLOOKUP function returns the error value #N/A, and then the second argument in the IFERROR function (shown in red) is executed, and the message "Invalid code" is displayed. You will scan the Health Cost column to verify that all employees have been assigned a health cost to determine if the formula calculating the health costs is working correctly.

To check for an error value in the Health Cost column:

▸ 1. Scroll to row 54 of the Health Cost column to see the error value #N/A in cell Q54. See Figure 7-24.

Figure 7-24   **Error value in Health Cost column**

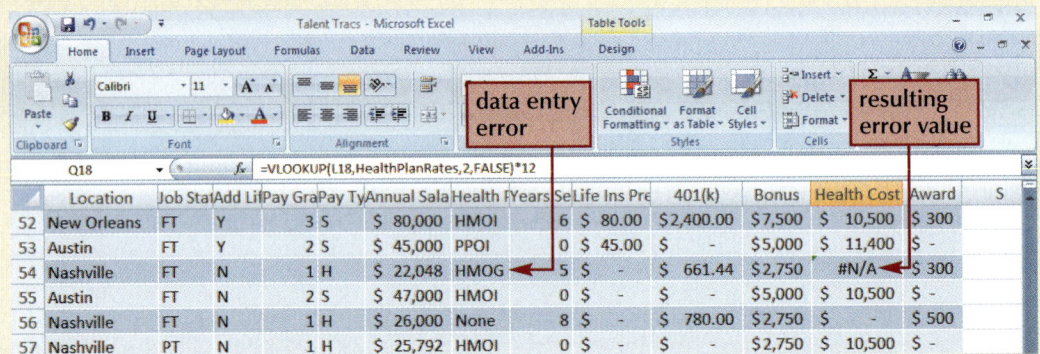

▸ 2. In row 54 in the Health Plan column, observe that the Health Plan code is HMOG, which is an invalid code.

Rita asks you to modify the formulas in the Health Cost column to display a more descriptive error message. She wants the message "Invalid code" to appear rather than the error value. The IFERROR function will check for errors in the formula, and display the error message you create rather than the error value if it finds an error.

You'll nest the VLOOKUP function within the IFERROR function to display the message "Invalid code" in the Health Cost column if Excel detects an error value.

To nest the VLOOKUP function within the IFERROR function:

▸ 1. Double-click cell **Q54** to enter editing mode. The formula =VLOOKUP(L54, HealthPlanRates,2,FALSE)*12 appears in the cell and the formula bar.

You'll nest this formula within the IFERROR function.

▸ 2. Click to the right of = (the equal sign), and then type **IFERROR(** to begin entering the IFERROR function. The first argument in the IFERROR function is the formula you want to use if no error value is found; this is the VLOOKUP formula already entered in the cell.

▸ 3. Move the insertion point to the right of the VLOOKUP formula, and then type **,"Invalid code")** to add the text you want to display if an error is found.

▸ 4. Press the **Enter** key, and then click cell **Q54**. The error message "Invalid code" appears in cell Q54, and the revised formula is automatically copied to all cells in the column. See Figure 7-25.

Figure 7-25 Invalid code message in the Health Cost column

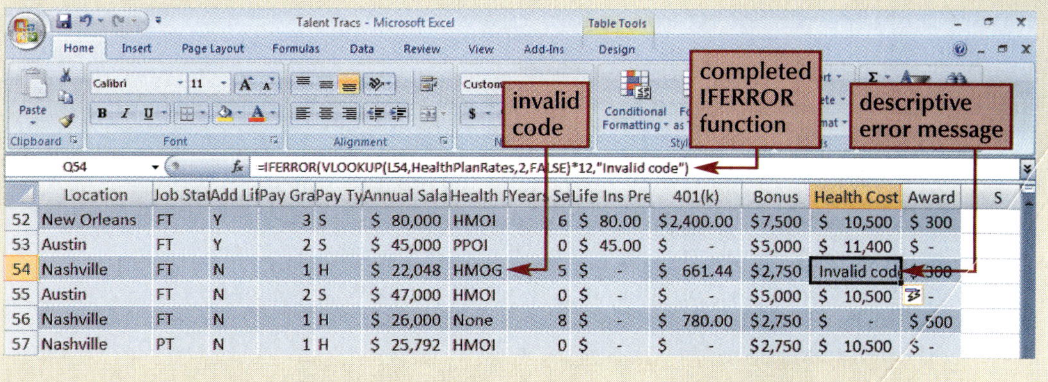

[Screenshot of Excel showing table with invalid code, completed IFERROR function, and descriptive error message callouts. Formula bar shows: =IFERROR(VLOOKUP(L54,HealthPlanRates,2,FALSE)*12,"Invalid code")]

▶ 5. In cell L54 (Health Plan), enter **HMOF**. You entered a valid Health Plan code, so the Health Cost value $18,000 appears in cell Q54.

▶ 6. Scroll to the top of the table, click cell **Q2**, and observe in the formula bar that the IFERROR formula was copied to this cell.

> **Tip**
> You can change a formula in any row of an Excel table (it doesn't have to be the first row) and all values in the column will be updated with the new formula.

Summarizing Data Conditionally

The COUNT function tallies the number of data values in a range, the SUM function adds the values in a range, and the AVERAGE function calculates the average of the values in a range. However, sometimes you need to calculate a conditional count, sum, or average using only those cells that meet a particular condition. In those cases, you need to use the COUNTIF, SUMIF, and AVERAGEIF functions. Rita wants you to create a report that shows the number, total, and average salaries for employees in Austin, New Orleans, and Nashville as well as for employees who work from home.

Using the COUNTIF Function

You can calculate the number of cells in a range that match criteria you specify using the **COUNTIF function**, which is sometimes referred to as a **conditional count**. The COUNTIF function has the following syntax:

COUNTIF(*range*,*criteria*)

In this function, *range* is the range of cells you want to count and *criteria* is an expression that defines which cells to count. Rita wants to know how many employees are located in Austin. You can use the COUNTIF function to find this answer, because you want a conditional count (a count of employees who meet a specified criterion; in this case, "employees located in Austin"). The location information is stored in column F of the Employee table. To count the number of employees in Austin, you can use either one of the following formulas (the first uses cell references, and the second uses fully qualified structured references):

=COUNTIF('Employee Data'!F2:F101,"Austin")
=COUNTIF(Employee[Location],"Austin")

With either formula, Excel counts all the cells in the Location column of the Employee table that contain the text "Austin". Because Austin is a text string, you must enclose it within quotation marks. Numeric criteria are not enclosed in quotes. You will enter this formula using the COUNTIF function in the Employee Summary worksheet.

> **Tip**
> You can use structured references or cell and range addresses to reference cells within an Excel table. If an Excel table has not been created for a range of data, you must use cell and range addresses.

To use the COUNTIF function to count employees located in Austin:

1. Switch to the **Employee Summary** worksheet. You will enter a formula using worksheet and range references to calculate the number of employees who work in Austin.

2. Click cell **C4**, type **=COU**, and then double-click **COUNTIF**. The beginning of the formula, =COUNTIF(, appears in the cell and the formula bar.

3. Type **'Employee Data'!F2:F101,** to enter the range to search. In this case, 'Employee Data'!F2:F101 refers to all data values in the range F2:F101 (Location column) of the Employee Data worksheet.

4. Type **B4)** to finish the formula. Cell B4, which contains the value Austin, is the criteria. The formula =COUNTIF('Employee Data'!F2:F101,B4) appears in the cell and the formula bar.

5. Press the **Enter** key. The value 57 appears in cell C4, indicating the company has 57 employees in Austin.

You will enter a similar formula using structured references to calculate the number of employees who work from home.

To use structured references to enter the COUNTIF function:

1. In cell C5, type **=COU**, and then double-click **COUNTIF**. The beginning of the formula, =COUNTIF(, appears in the cell and the formula bar.

2. Type **E** and then double-click **Employee**.

3. Type **[** to open the list of column headers, double-click **Location**, and then type **]**, to complete the first argument of the COUNTIF function. In this formula, the structured reference Employee [Location] refers to the data values in the Location column (F2:F101) of the Employee table.

4. Type **B5)**. Cell B5 stores the value Home, which is the criterion. The formula =COUNTIF(Employee[Location],B5) appears in the cell and formula bar.

5. Press the **Enter** key. The formula results indicate that 7 employees work from home.

Next, you'll copy the formula in cell C5 to cells C6 and C7.

To copy the COUNTIF function:

1. Copy the formula in cell **C5** and then paste the formula in cells **C6** and **C7** to calculate the number of employees for Nashville (cell B6) and New Orleans (cell B7). The formula results show that Talent Tracs has 21 employees working in Nashville and 15 employees working in New Orleans.

2. In cell C8, enter a formula with the SUM function to calculate the total number of employees working at Talent Tracs. The formula results show that Talent Tracs has a total of 100 employees.

Using the SUMIF Function

The SUMIF function is similar to the COUNTIF function. You can add the values in a range that meet criteria you specify using the **SUMIF function**, which is also called a **conditional sum**. The syntax of the SUMIF function is:

SUMIF(range,criteria[,sum_range])

In this formula, *range* is the range of cells that you want to filter before calculating a sum, *criteria* is the condition used in the range to filter the table, and *sum_range* is the range of cells that you want to add. The *sum_range* argument is optional; if you omit it, Excel will add the values specified in the *range* argument. For example, if you want to add the salaries for all employees with salaries greater than $50,000, you do not use the optional third argument.

Rita wants to know the total salaries paid to employees at each location. She can use the SUMIF function to do this, because she wants to conditionally add salaries of employees at a specified location. Each employee's location is recorded in column F of the Employee Data worksheet, and the salary data is stored in column K. The formula to calculate this value is as follows (the first uses cell references, and the second uses fully qualified structured references):

=SUMIF('Employee Data'!F2:F101,"Austin",'Employee Data'!K2:K101)
=SUMIF(Employee[Location],"Austin",Employee[Annual Salary])

This formula states that employees whose location is "Austin" will have their salary values added to the total. You will insert this formula using the SUMIF function into the Employee Summary worksheet.

To use the SUMIF function:

▸ 1. In cell D4, enter **=SUMIF('Employee Data'!F2:F101,B4,'Employee Data'!K2:K101)**. The value $3,969,426—the total salaries paid to employees in Austin—appears in cell D4. The first argument specifies to use the range F2:F101 from the Employee Data worksheet (Location column) to filter the employee data. The second argument specifies that the criterion is equal to the value in cell B4 (Austin). The third argument indicates that the Annual Salary column, the range K2:K101 in the Employee Data worksheet, is used to add the filtered rows.

You will enter the formula to calculate the total salaries for employees working from home using structured references.

▸ 2. In cell D5, enter **=SUMIF(Employee[Location],B5,Employee[Annual Salary])**. Talent Tracs pays $236,313 per year to employees working from home. The first argument uses the structured reference Employee[Location] to specify you want to use the cells in the Location column to filter the employee data. The second argument specifies that the criterion is equal to the value in cell B5 (Home). The third argument uses the structured reference Employee[Annual Salary] to indicate that the Annual Salary column will be used to add the filtered rows.

▸ 3. Copy the SUMIF formula in cell D5 to the range **D6:D7**. The total salaries per year for employees working in Nashville (from cell B6) is $587,833. The total salaries per year for employees working in New Orleans (from cell B7) is $1,570,994.

▸ 4. In cell D8, use the SUM function to calculate the total of all salaries. The total salaries of all Talent Tracs employees is $6,364,566.

▶ **5.** If necessary, format the range D4:D8 in the **Accounting** number format with no decimal places.

Using the AVERAGEIF Function

The AVERAGEIF function works in the same way as the SUMIF function. You use the **AVERAGEIF function** to calculate the average of values in a range that meet criteria you specify. The syntax of the AVERAGEIF function is:

AVERAGEIF(range,criteria[,average_range])

In this function, *range* is the range of cells that you want to filter before calculating the average, *criteria* is the condition used in the range to filter the table, and *average_range* is the range of cells that you want to average. The *average_range* argument is optional; if you omit it, Excel will average the values specified in the *range* argument.

Rita wants to know the average salaries paid to employees at each location. Each employee's location is recorded in column F of the Employee Data worksheet, and the salary data is stored in column K. The formula to calculate this value is as follows (the first formula uses cell references, and the second uses fully qualified structured references):

=AVERAGEIF('Employee Data'!F2:F101,"Austin",'Employee Data'!K2:K101)
=AVERAGEIF(Employee[Location],"Austin",Employee[Annual Salary])

This formula states that any employee whose location is "Austin" will have his or her salary included in the average. You will enter this formula using the AVERAGEIF function into the Employee Summary worksheet.

To use the AVERAGEIF function:

▶ **1.** In cell E4, enter **=AVERAGEIF(Employee[Location],B4,Employee[Annual Salary])**. The value 69,639—the average salary paid to employees in Austin—appears in the cell. The first argument indicates that you want to use the cells in the Location column to filter the employee data. The second argument specifies that the criterion to filter the location column is equal to the value in cell D4 (Austin). The third argument indicates that the Annual Salary column will be used to average the filtered rows.

You will enter the formula to calculate the average salaries for employees working at Home, Nashville, and New Orleans.

▶ **2.** Copy the formula in cell E4 to the range **E5:E7**. Talent Tracs pays an average of $33,759 to employees working at home, $27,992 to employees working in Nashville, and $104,733 to employees working in New Orleans.

Next, you will calculate the average salary at Talent Tracs by dividing the total salaries at Talent Tracs by the number of employees at the company.

▶ **3.** In cell E8, enter **=D8/C8**. The average salary for all employees is $63,646.

▶ **4.** If necessary, format the range E4:E8 in the **Accounting** number format with no decimal places.

▶ **5.** Add a bottom border to the range C7:E7. See Figure 7-26.

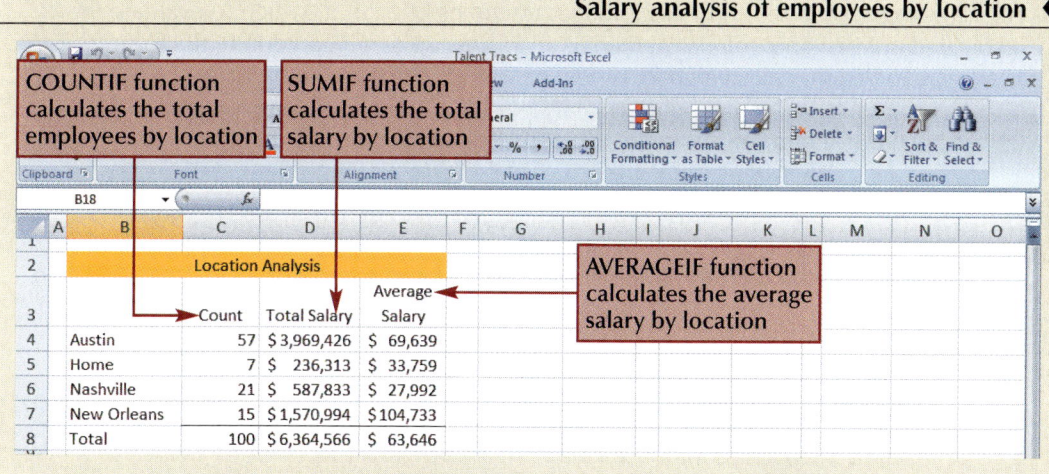

Figure 7-26 Salary analysis of employees by location

As Rita enters new employees or edits the location or annual salary values of current employees, the values in the Employee Summary worksheet will be automatically updated because the formulas reference the Employee table.

Summarizing Data Using the COUNTIFS, SUMIFS, and AVERAGEIFS Functions

The COUNTIFS, SUMIFS, and AVERAGEIFS functions are similar to the COUNTIF, SUMIF, and AVERAGEIF functions except with the latter functions you can specify only one condition to summarize the data, whereas the former functions enable you to summarize the data using several conditions.

The **COUNTIFS function** counts the number of cells within a range that meet multiple criteria. Its syntax is as follows:

```
COUNTIFS(criteria_range1,criteria1[,criteria_range2,criteria2...])
```

In this function, *criteria_range1, criteria_range2*, represents up to 127 ranges (columns of data) in which to evaluate the associated criteria, and *criteria1, criteria2* and up to 127 criteria in the form of a number, expression, cell reference, or text define which cells will be counted. Criteria can be expressed as a number such as 50 to find a number equal to 50, ">10000" to find an amount greater than 10000, "FT" to find a text value equal to FT, or B4 to find the value equal to the value stored in cell B4. Each cell in a range is counted only if all of the corresponding criteria specified in the COUNTIFS function are true.

For example, to count the number of full-time employees (FT) who are female (F) and earn more than $50,000, you can use the following function:

```
=COUNTIFS(Employee[Job Status],"FT",Employee[SEX],"F",Employee
[Annual Salary],">50000")
```

This function counts the full-time employees using the argument combination Employee [Job Status],"FT", that are female using the arguments Employee[Sex],"F", and have a salary greater than 50,000 using the arguments Employee[Annual Salary],">50000".

The SUMIFS and AVERAGEIFS functions have a slightly different syntax. The **SUMIFS function** adds values in a range that meet multiple criteria using the following syntax:

```
SUMIFS(sum_range,criteria_range1,criteria1[,criteria_range2,
criteria2...])
```

In the SUMIFS function, *sum_range* is the range you want to add; *criteria_range1*, *criteria_range2*, represent up to 127 ranges (columns of data) in which to evaluate the associated criteria; and *criteria1*, *criteria2* and so on up to 127 criteria in the form of a number, expression, cell reference, or text define which cells will be added.

For example, to calculate the total salary paid to full-time (FT) employees hired after 2007 who are living in Austin, you can use the following SUMIFS function:

```
=SUMIFS(Employee[Annual Salary],Employee[Location],"Austin",
Employee[Hire Date],">=1/1/2008",Employee[Job Status],"FT")
```

This function adds the salaries (Employee[Annual Salary]) of employees located in Austin using the argument combination Employee[Location],"Austin", having a hire date on or later than 1/1/2008 using the arguments Employee[Hire Date],">=1/1/2008", and are full-time employees using arguments Employee [Job Status],"FT".

The **AVERAGEIFS function** calculates the average of values within a range of cells that meet multiple conditions. Its syntax is as follows:

```
AVERAGEIFS(average_range,criteria_range1,criteria1[,criteria_range2,
criteria2...])
```

In this function, *average_range* is the range to average; *criteria_range1*, *criteria_range2*, represent up to 127 ranges in which to evaluate the associated criteria; and *criteria1*, *criteria2* and so on up to 127 criteria in the form of a number, expression, cell reference, or text define which cells will be averaged.

For example, to calculate the average salary paid to males (M) who have worked at Talent Tracs for more than 5 years, you can use the following AVERAGEIFS function:

```
=AVERAGEIFS(Employee[Annual Salary],Employee[Sex],"M", Employee[Years
Service],">5")
```

This function averages the salaries (Employee[Annual Salary]) of male employees using the arguments Employee[Sex],"M", having more than 5 years of service using the arguments Employee[Years Service],">5".

In this session, you used the VLOOKUP function to calculate the health plan cost and employee recognition award. You used conditional formatting to identify duplicate employee IDs and the IFERROR function to help you correct errors. You used functions and features that deal with conditional situations. In the next session, you will use advanced filtering techniques to find potential candidates for a new full-time position and Database functions to prepare a report on the number of employees in each health plan who are classified as salaried and hourly.

Review | Session 7.2 Quick Check

1. Explain the difference between an exact match and approximate match table lookup.
2. A customers table includes name, street address, city, state abbreviation, and zip code. A second table includes state abbreviations and state names from all 50 states. You need to add a new column to the customers table with the state name. What is the most appropriate function to use to display the state name in this new column?
3. Would you apply the duplicate value conditional formatting rule to a table column of last names? Why or why not?

4. In cell D5, the error value #DIV/0! is displayed when you divide by 0. Use the IFERROR function with the formula =C5/C25 so instead of the error value #DIV/0!, you display the message "Dividing by 0" in the cell.
5. Explain what the formula =COUNTIF(Employee[SEX],"F") calculates.
6. Explain what the formula =AVERAGEIF(Employee[Pay Type],"H",(Employee[Salary]) calculates.
7. If you receive a worksheet that includes conditional formatting, which dialog box would you use to find out the criteria for the formatting?

Session 7.3

Using Advanced Filtering

Talent Tracs is growing rapidly and management plans to hire additional full-time employees. Rita wants to give first preference to part-time employees and consultants currently working for the company. She asks you to create a list of individuals who meet the following criteria:

- Consultants who have worked for Talents Tracs for more than three years earning less than $55,000

  or

- Part-time employees who have worked for Talent Tracs for two or more years

You need to use advanced filtering features to retrieve the list of individuals Rita wants. Advanced filtering enables you to perform OR conditions across multiple fields, such as the criteria Rita wants you to use to find eligible candidates within the company for the new full-time positions. You can also use advanced filtering to create complex criteria using functions and formulas. For example, if Rita wants to find all female salaried employees whose salary falls below the median salary for all employees, she could use advanced filtering.

Advanced filtering, similar to filtering, displays a subset of the rows in a table or range of data. The primary difference is that you specify criteria in a range outside the data you want to filter. So, before you can use advanced filters, you need to create a criteria range. The **criteria range** is an area in a worksheet, separate from the range of data or Excel table, used to specify the criteria for the data to be displayed after the filter is applied to the table. The criteria range consists of a header row that lists one or more field names from the table's header row and at least one row of the specific filtering criteria for each field. A criteria range must include at least two rows. The first row must contain field names (column headers). All other rows consist of the criteria. Figure 7-27 shows the criteria range you will create to display the eligible candidates within the company for the new full-time positions.

Figure 7-27   Criteria range above Excel table

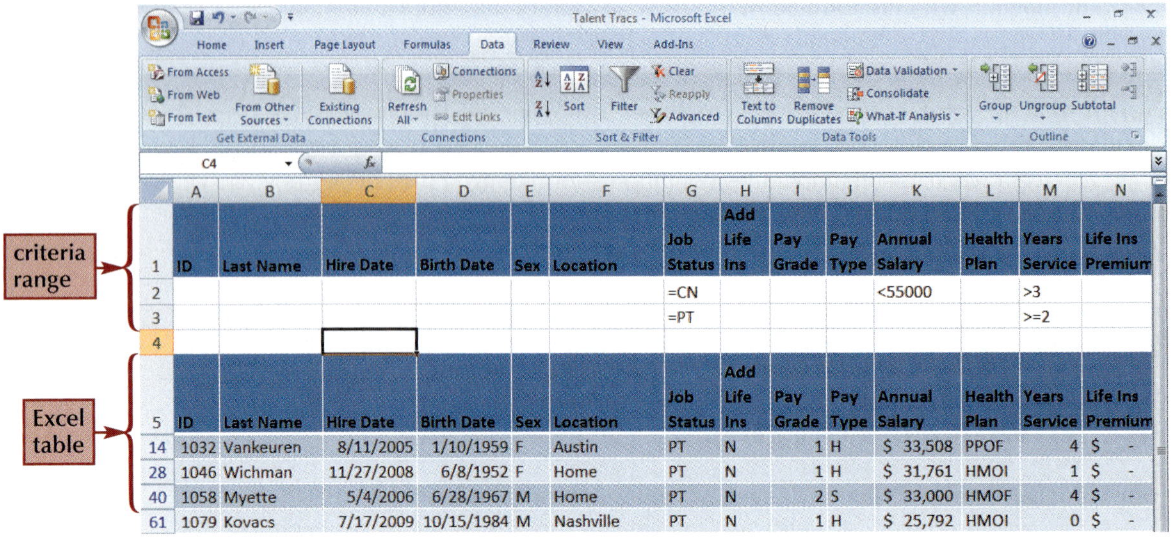

criteria range (rows 1–4) and *Excel table* (rows 5+) shown in an Excel screenshot with columns: ID, Last Name, Hire Date, Birth Date, Sex, Location, Job Status, Add Life Ins, Pay Grade, Pay Type, Annual Salary, Health Plan, Years Service, Life Ins Premium.

Criteria range values:
- Row 2: Job Status =CN, Annual Salary <55000, Years Service >3
- Row 3: Job Status =PT, Years Service >=2

Excel table sample rows:
Row	ID	Last Name	Hire Date	Birth Date	Sex	Location	Job Status	Add Life Ins	Pay Grade	Pay Type	Annual Salary	Health Plan	Years Service	Life Ins Premium
14	1032	Vankeuren	8/11/2005	1/10/1959	F	Austin	PT	N	1	H	$33,508	PPOF	4	$ -
28	1046	Wichman	11/27/2008	6/8/1952	F	Home	PT	N	1	H	$31,761	HMOI	1	$ -
40	1058	Myette	5/4/2006	6/28/1967	M	Home	PT	N	2	S	$33,000	HMOF	4	$ -
61	1079	Kovacs	7/17/2009	10/15/1984	M	Nashville	PT	N	1	H	$25,792	HMOI	0	$ -

To create a criteria range, you need to specify the condition for each criterion. Text, numeric, and date conditions each use different syntax. Figure 7-28 lists the type of condition, corresponding syntax, and an example for each criterion. For example, to develop a criteria range to filter employees whose annual salaries (numeric data) are greater than (condition) 50,000, the top row of the criteria range contains the column header from the Employee table, Annual Salary, and the second row contains the criterion >50000.

Figure 7-28   Types of conditions

Condition	Text Data		Numeric Data		Date Data	
	Syntax	Sample Last Name	Syntax	Sample Annual Salary	Syntax	Sample Hire Date
Exact match	="=text string"	="=Stolt"	value	50000	mm/dd/yyyy	1/3/2010
Begins with	text string	S	does not apply		does not apply	
Greater than	>text string	>S	>value	>50000	>mm/dd/yyyy	>12/31/2009
Greater than or equal to	>=text string	>=S	>=value	>=50000	>= mm/dd/yyyy	>=1/1/2010
Less than	< text string	<S	<value	<50000	<mm/dd/yyyy	<1/1/2010
Less than or equal to	<= text string	<=S	<=value	<=50000	<=mm/dd/yyyy	<=12/31/2009
Between (beginning and ending points must be in separate cells)	>=beginning text string	>=Sa	>= beginning value	>=50000	> beginning mm/dd/yyyy	>=4/1/2010
	<=ending text string	<=Sm	<= ending value	<=60000	< ending mm/dd/yyyy	<=4/30/2010

Understanding Criteria Ranges

The criteria range specifies which records from the Excel table will be included in the filtered data. The following examples illustrate multiple criteria conditions. Criteria placed on the same row are considered connected with the logical operator AND. That means all criteria in the same row must be met before a record is included in the filtered table. Figure 7-29 shows an AND criteria range to retrieve all employees from Nashville who are earning more than $55,000.

Example of AND criteria range — **Figure 7-29**

	F	G	H	I	J	K
1	Location	Job Status	Add Life Ins	Pay Grade	Pay Type	Annual Salary
2	="=Nashville"					>55000
3						

Specifying the equality comparison operator (exact match) for a text string in the criteria range, as in the Location field in Figure 7-29, is not intuitive. When you type a formula in a cell, the equal sign indicates that a formula follows. If you want to indicate the equality comparison operator within the criteria range, you must type the criteria using the following syntax:

`="=entry"`

In this syntax, *entry* is the text or value you want to find.

Criteria placed on separate rows are treated as the logical operator OR. That means records that meet all the criteria on either row in the criteria range will be displayed. Figure 7-30 shows the criteria range to retrieve female employees or employees who are working in Austin.

Example of OR criteria range — **Figure 7-30**

	E	F	G	H	I	J
1	Sex	Location	Job Status	Add Life Ins	Pay Grade	Pay Type
2	="=F"					
3		="=Austin"				
4						

To specify criteria between a range of values in the same field, you use the same field name repeated in separate cells within the same row to match a range of values (BETWEEN criteria). Figure 7-31 shows the criteria range to retrieve all employees who were hired between 1/1/2005 and 12/31/2008.

Example of BETWEEN criteria range — **Figure 7-31**

	B	C	D	E	F	G
1	Hire Date	Hire Date	Birth Date	Sex	Location	Job Status
2	>=1/1/2005	<=12/31/2008				
3						

You can also set up criteria to find records that begin with a group of characters. Figure 7-32 shows the criteria range that retrieves all records with a location that begin with *Home*. This criteria range would retrieve Talent Tracs employees working in Homewood, Illinois, along with those working from Home. If you want more precise results, you need to use the exact match criteria. The exact match criteria would be entered as ="=Home" and only employees working from Home would be retrieved.

Figure 7-32 Example of BEGINS WITH criteria range

	F	G	H	I	J	K
1	Location	Job Status	Add Life Ins	Pay Grade	Pay Type	Annual Salary
2	Home					
3						

> **Tip**
> Because the field names in the criteria range must exactly match the field names in the Excel table or range except for capitalization, you should copy and paste the field names instead of retyping them.

Creating a Criteria Range

Typically, you place a criteria range above the Excel table to keep it separate from the table. If you place a criteria range next to the Excel table, the criteria might be hidden when the advanced filtering cause rows to be hidden. You can also place a criteria range in a separate worksheet, particularly if you need to enter several criteria ranges in different cells to perform calculations based on various sets of filtered records.

You will place the criteria range in rows 1 to 4 of the Employee Data worksheet to make it easier to locate.

To create the criteria range to find eligible candidates for full-time positions:

1. Switch to the **Employee Data** worksheet, and then click cell **A1**.

   You'll insert four blank rows above the Excel table in which to place the criteria range.

2. Select rows **1** through **4**, right-click the selected row headings, and then click **Insert** on the shortcut menu. Four rows are added at the top of the worksheet.

   Next, you'll copy the column headers from the Excel table into row 1.

3. Point to the left side of cell **A5** until the pointer changes to ➡, and then click the mouse button. The column headers in row 5 are selected.

4. Click the **Home** tab on the Ribbon, if necessary, and then, in the Clipboard group, click the **Copy** button. The field names are copied to the Clipboard.

5. Click cell **A1**, and then, in the Clipboard group on the Home tab, click the **Paste** button. The field names for the criteria range appear in row 1.

   In row 2, you will enter an AND criteria range with the criteria for consultants (code CN) who earn less than $55,000 and have worked at Talent Tracs for more than three years.

6. In cell G2, enter **="=CN"**. The condition =CN is displayed, which specifies the criteria to retrieve all consultants, employees with Pay Status code equal to CN.

7. In cell K2, enter **<55000**. This condition specifies the criteria to retrieve all employees who have salaries less than $55,000.

8. In cell M2, enter **>3**. This condition specifies the criteria to retrieve all employees with more than three years of service.

   The criteria in row 2 selects all employees who are consultants and who earn less than $55,000 and have more than three years service at Talent Tracs. Next, you will enter the criteria for part-time employees working more than two years.

9. In cell **G3**, enter **="=PT"**; and then, in cell **M3**, enter **>=2**. The criteria in row 3 selects all employees who are part-time (Job Status is equal to PT) and who have two or more years service at Talent Tracs (Years Service is greater than or equal to 2). See Figure 7-33.

Figure 7-33 Criteria range

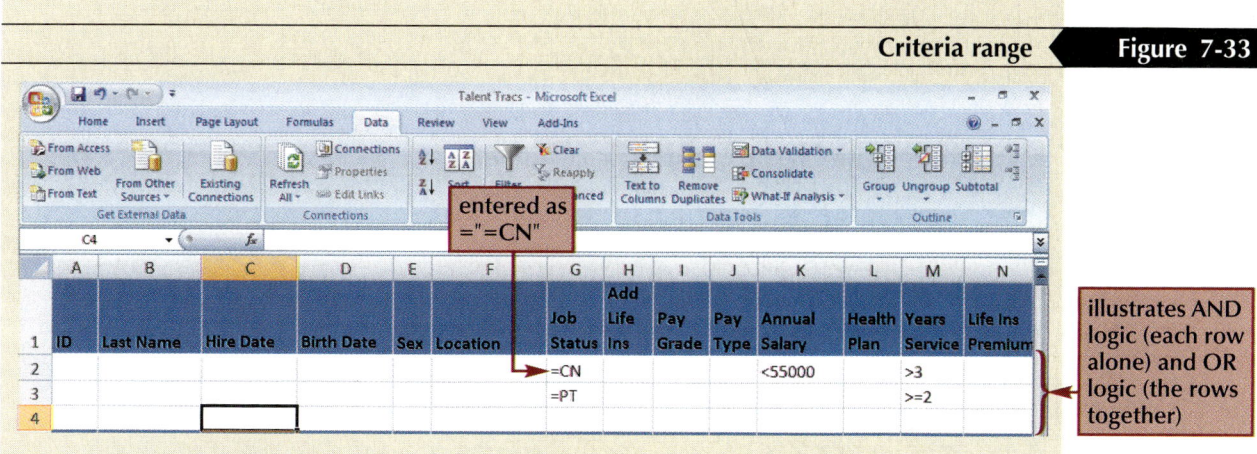

Now that the criteria range is established, you can use the Advanced Filter command to filter the Employee table. You can filter the records in their current location by hiding rows that don't match your criteria, as you have done with the Filter command. Or, you can copy the records that match your criteria to another location in the worksheet. Rita wants you to filter the records in their current location.

To filter the Employee table in its current location:

1. Click any cell in the Employee table to make the table active.

2. Click the **Data** tab on the Ribbon, and then, in the Sort & Filter group, click the **Advanced** button. The Advanced Filter dialog box opens.

3. Make sure the **Filter the list, in-place** option button is selected and the range **$A$5:$R$105** appears in the List range box. The range $A$5:$R$105 is the current location of the Employee table, which is the table you want to filter.

   Trouble? If the List range displays $A$5:$L$105, you need to edit the range to $A$5:$R$105 to include the entire table.

4. Type **$A$1:$R$3** in the Criteria range box. This is the range in which you entered the criteria range. See Figure 7-34.

Figure 7-34 Advanced Filter dialog box

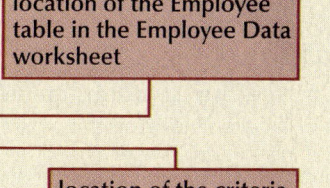

5. Click the **OK** button, and then scroll to the top of the worksheet. The list is filtered in its current location, and nine employee records match the criteria, as indicated in the status bar. See Figure 7-35.

Figure 7-35 | Filtered Employee table

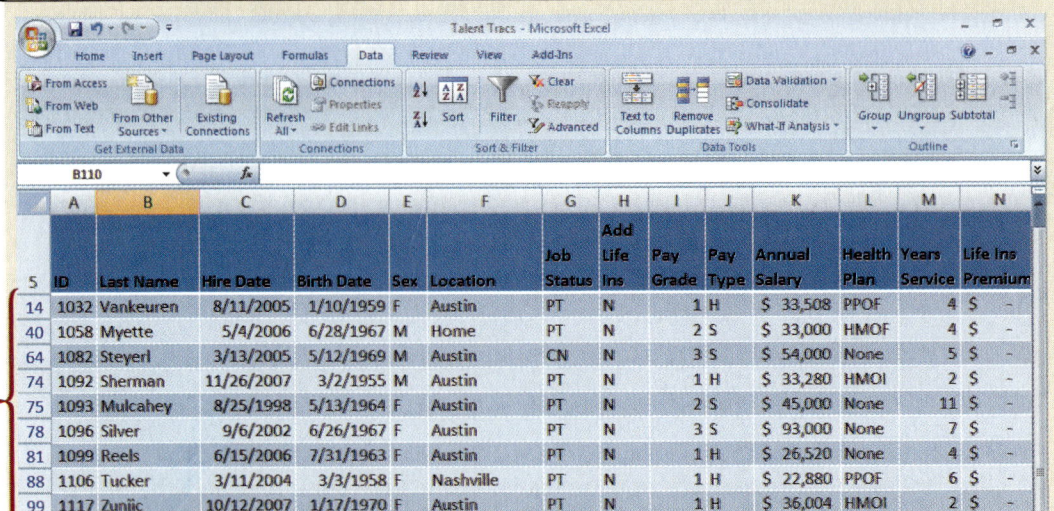

nine employees are eligible to apply for the full-time positions

Trouble? If no records appear in the filtered table, the list range or criteria range might be incorrect. Click the Clear button in the Sort & Filter group on the Data tab, and then repeat Steps 1 through 5, making sure the list range is $A$5:$R$105 and the criteria range is $A$1:$R$3 in the Advanced Filter dialog box.

After providing the list of eligible employees to Rita, you remove the filter to display all the records in the Employee table.

To show all the records in the Employee table:

1. In the Sort & Filter group on the Data tab, click the **Clear** button. All the records in the Employee table reappear.

InSight | Copying Filtered Records to a New Location

The Advanced Filtering command does more than filter data in a range or an Excel table. You can also copy data in a table to another worksheet location. If you want to filter the data and then copy the filtered data to a different location, you select the Copy to another location option button in the Action section of the Advanced Filter dialog box and specify the first cell of the range where you want to copy the filtered records in the Copy to box. Excel copies the filtered records to the location beginning at the cell you specified in the Copy to box. All cells below this cell will be cleared when the Advanced Filter is applied.

The Advanced Filtering command offers many advantages, allowing you to copy the following:

- All the columns from the original table in their current order to another worksheet location.
- A subset of columns from the original table to another worksheet location.
- A subset or all the columns from the original table and change the sequence of columns in the new worksheet location.
- A unique list of values from the original table into another worksheet location. For example, you can obtain a unique list of customer names from a table of invoices where customer names are repeated many times.

Using Database Functions to Summarize Data

Functions that perform summary data analysis (SUM, AVERAGE, COUNT, and so on) on a table of values based on criteria that you set are called the **Database functions**, or **Dfunctions**. Figure 7-36 lists the Database functions. Although the SUMIF, AVERAGEIF and COUNTIF functions, the Total row feature of an Excel table, and PivotTables often can achieve the same results as Database functions and are considered simpler to use, some situations call for Database functions. For example, the type of summary analysis, the placement of the summary results, or the complexity of the criteria might require that you use Database functions.

Figure 7-36   Database functions

Function Name	Description
DAVERAGE	Returns the average of the values that meet specified criteria
DCOUNT	Returns the number of cells containing numbers that meet specified criteria
DCOUNTA	Returns the number of nonblank cells that meets specified criteria
DMAX	Returns the maximum value in search column that meets specified criteria
DMIN	Returns the minimum value in search column that meets specified criteria
DSTDEV	Returns the estimate of standard deviation based on a sample of entries that meet the specified criteria
DSUM	Returns the sum of the values in the summary column that meets specified criteria

Rita wants you to provide a report summarizing the number of salaried and hourly workers by health plan. Rita's request combines the HMOF and HMOI codes into one group on the report and the PPOF and PPOI codes into another group. You must set up a criteria range to retrieve the appropriate records for each calculation. As a result, a Dfunction becomes a good approach for solving Rita's request.

Dfunctions use a criteria range to specify the records to summarize. In a Dfunction, the criteria range is used as one of the arguments of the function. Any Dfunction has the following general syntax:

```
DfunctionName(table range, column to summarize, criteria range)
```

In this syntax, *table range* refers to the cells where the data to summarize is located, including the column header, *column to summarize* is the column name of the field you want to summarize, and *criteria range* is the range where the criteria that determines which records are used in the calculation is specified.

You will use Dfunctions to complete the Employee Summary worksheet, summarizing the number of salaried and hourly employees covered by HMO and PPO health plans. First, you will set up a separate criteria range for each cell in the report, excluding totals for rows and columns. Although the criteria range often includes all fields from the table, even those that are not needed to select records, you do not have to include all field names from the table when setting up a criteria range. In setting up the criteria range to use with the Database functions, you will use only the fields needed to specify the criteria.

You will create six criteria ranges to complete the Health Plan Count report.

To establish criteria ranges for the Health Plan Count report:

1. Switch to the **Employee Summary** worksheet. The column headers for the criteria range have already been copied from the Employee Data worksheet.

You'll set up the criteria for salaried employees who have selected HMOs, PPOs, and No Plan.

2. In cell G15, enter **HMO**, and then, in cell H15, enter **S**. You entered *begins with* criteria (HMO) to find all HMOs (HMOI and HMOF). The code for salaried employees is S and because only S or H codes are used in the Pay Type column, you used the *begins with* criteria to find salaried employees. The criteria range for salaried employees electing either HMO plan is complete.

3. In cell J15, enter **PPO** as the *begins with* criteria to find all PPOs (PPOI and PPOF), and then, in cell K15, enter the *begins with* criteria **S** to find salaried employees. The criteria range for salaried employees electing either PPO plan is complete.

4. In cell M15, enter the *begins with* criteria **None**, and then, in cell N15, enter the *begins with* criteria **S** to find salaried employees. The criteria range for salaried employees with no plan is complete.

You'll set up the criteria for Hourly HMOs, Hourly PPOs, and Hourly No Plan.

5. In cell G20, enter the *begins with* criteria **HMO** to find all HMOs (HMOI and HMOF), and then, in cell H20, enter the *begins with* criteria **H** to find hourly employees. The criteria range for hourly employees electing an HMO plan is complete.

6. In cell J20, enter the *begins with* criteria **PPO** to find all PPOs (PPOI and PPOF), and then, in cell K20, enter the *begins with* criteria **H** to find hourly employees. The criteria range for hourly employees electing a PPO plan is complete.

7. In cell M20, enter the *begins with* criteria **None**, and then, in cell N20, enter the *begins with* criteria **H** to find hourly employees. The criteria range for hourly employees with no plan is complete. See Figure 7-37.

Figure 7-37   **Criteria range for report**

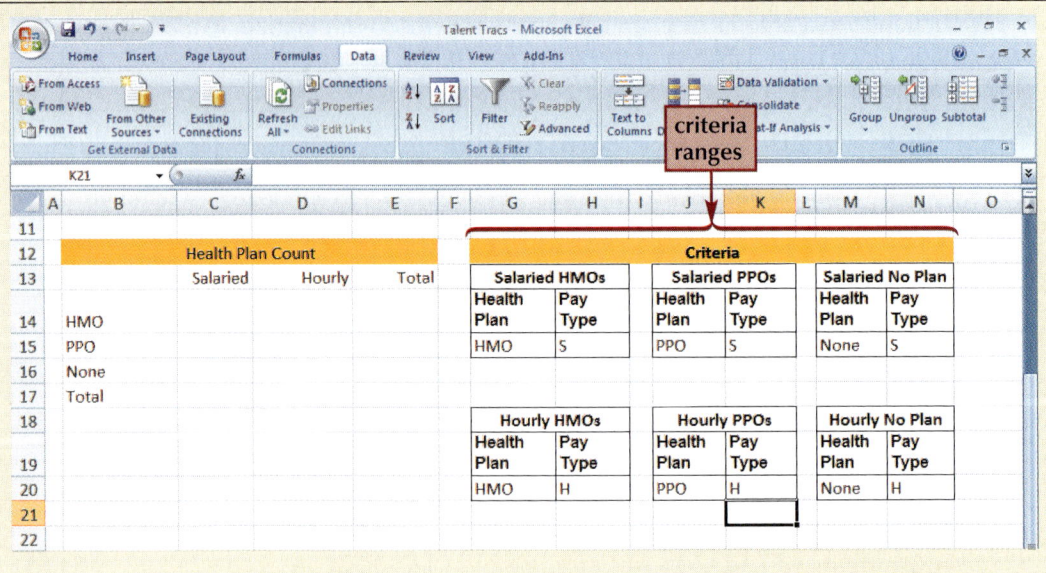

The criteria ranges are complete, so you can enter the formulas to finish the Health Plan Count report for Rita. You will enter the DCOUNT function six times. In each function, the first two arguments are identical. The third argument, the criteria range, is different for each function so that you can count a different subset of employees each time.

To enter the first DCOUNT function:

▶ 1. In cell C14, type **=D** and double-click **DCOUNT**. The beginning of the formula, =DCOUNT(, appears in the cell and the formula bar.

▶ 2. Type **Em** and then press the **Tab** key to enter Employee in the first argument. Employee references only the data in the Employee table.

▶ 3. Type **[#** to open the list of special Item qualifiers, press the **Tab** key to enter #All, and then type **],** to complete the first argument, Employee[#All],. The special qualifier [#All] indicates you want to reference the column headers as well as the data.

▶ 4. Type **"ID",** to specify the field in the Employee table that you want to count. The second argument, ID, shows the column whose cells will be counted. The field name must be within quotation marks.

▶ 5. Type **G14:H15)** to complete the formula. The third argument G14:H15 references the criteria range that determines which cells in the ID column to count.

▶ 6. Press the **Enter** key, and then click cell **C14**. There are 32 salaried employees electing either HMO plan. The formula =DCOUNT(Employee[#All],"ID",G14:H15) appears in the formula bar.

You'll repeat this process to finish the Health Plan Count report. The DCOUNT function is the same for each of the remaining counts, except the third argument reflects the appropriate criteria range that you entered in the Employee Summary worksheet.

To enter the remaining DCOUNT functions for the Health Plan Count report:

▶ 1. In cell C15, enter **=DCOUNT(Employee[#All],"ID",J14:K15)**. This DCOUNT function calculates the number of salaried employees electing either PPO plan. The formula is identical to the first DCOUNT function you entered except the criteria range J14:K15 specifies the criteria to retrieve salaried employees electing either PPO plan. There are 15 in this category.

▶ 2. In cell C16, enter **=DCOUNT(Employee[#All],"ID",M14:N15)**. This DCOUNT function calculates the number of salaried employees with no health plan. Again, the formula is identical to the other DCOUNT functions you entered except the criteria range M14:N15 specifies the criteria to retrieve salaried employees with no health plan. There are 18 employees in this category.

▶ 3. In cell D14, enter **=DCOUNT(Employee[#All],"ID",G19:H20)** to calculate the number of hourly HMO employees. The formula is identical to the other DCOUNT functions you entered except the criteria range G19:H20 specifies the criteria to retrieve hourly employees electing either HMO plan. There are 13 in this category.

▶ 4. In cell D15, enter **=DCOUNT(Employee[#All],"ID",J19:K20)** to calculate the number of hourly PPO employees. The criteria range references the criteria range J19:K20, which retrieves hourly workers electing either PPO plan. There are 14 employees in this category.

▶ 5. In cell D16, enter **=DCOUNT(Employee[#All],"ID",M19:N20)** to calculate the number of hourly employees with no plan. The criteria range references the range M19:N20, which retrieves hourly workers with no health plan. There are 8 in this category.

▶ 6. In cells C17 and D17, enter the SUM function to calculate totals for each column.

▶ 7. In the range E14:E17, use the SUM function to total each row.

8. Add a bottom border to the range C16:E16, and then click cell **C18** to deselect the report. See Figure 7-38.

Figure 7-38   Health Plan Count report

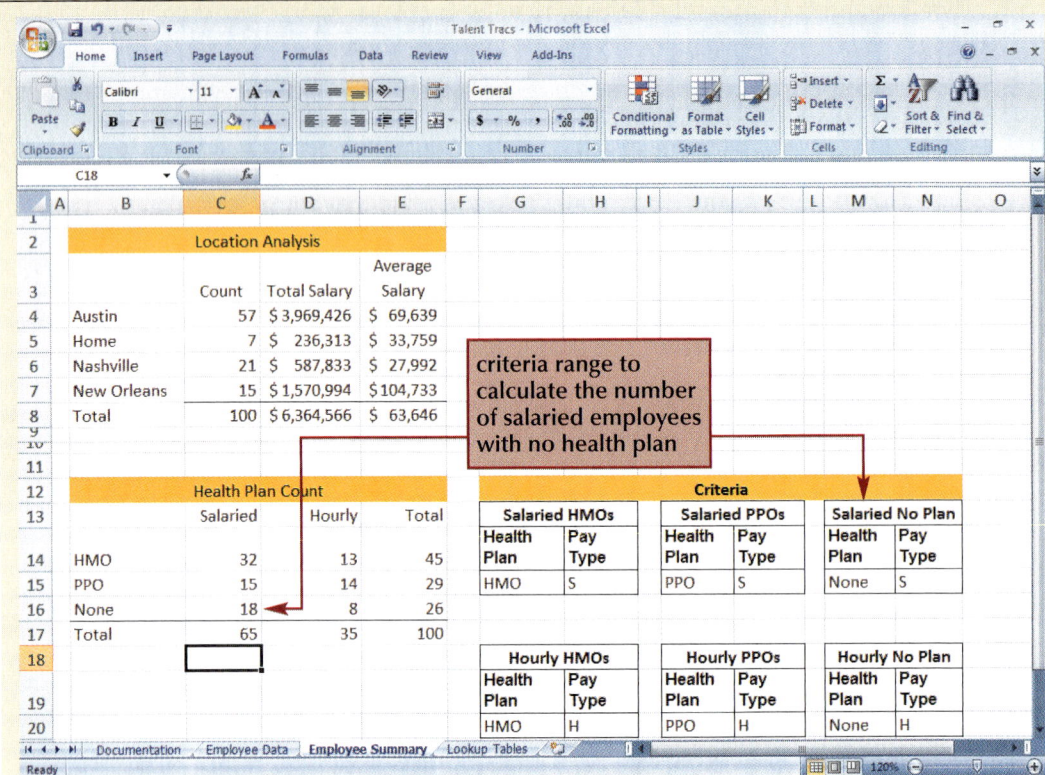

9. Save the workbook, and then close it.

The Health Plan Count report provides Rita with useful information as she goes into a meeting to plan Talent Tracs' healthcare coverage for future years.

Session 7.3 Quick Check | Review

1. Describe in words the following criteria range:

Sex	Salary Class
="=M"	="=H"

2. Create a criteria range to retrieve employees located in either Austin or New Orleans. The column name is Location.
3. Describe in words the following criteria range:

Annual Salary	Annual Salary
<25000	
	>=100000

4. After an Advanced Filter command has filtered records, how do you redisplay all the records in the table?
5. Explain the function: =DSUM(Employee[#All],"Annual Salary",T1:U2)

   The following criteria range appears in the range T1:U2:

Sex	Hire Date
M	>=1/1/2010

6. Why would you use the structured reference Employee[#All] in Quick Check 5 instead of Employee?
7. Rewrite the DSUM function in Quick Check 5 using range addresses instead of structured references. The employee data is found in the Employee Data worksheet in the range A5:R105. The DSUM function is entered in the Employee Summary worksheet.

Tutorial Summary | Review

In this tutorial, you used the Logical functions IF, AND, and OR, and you nested one IF function inside another IF function. You used the VLOOKUP function to look up data in a table. You used conditional formatting and the IFERROR function to locate and fix data entry errors. You also used the COUNTIF, SUMIF, and AVERAGEIF functions to calculate counts, sums, and averages based on search criteria. You filtered a table using more advanced filtering criteria. Finally, you used Database functions to summarize a table based on specified criteria.

Key Terms

AND function
AVERAGEIF function
AVERAGEIFS function
calculated column
compare value
conditional count
conditional sum
COUNTIF function
COUNTIFS function

criteria range
Database function
DATEDIF function
Dfunction
error value
HLOOKUP function
IFERROR function
lookup table
lookup value

nested IF function
OR function
rule
structured reference
SUMIF function
SUMIFS function
VLOOKUP function

Practice | Review Assignments

Practice the skills you learned by using the Employee Data worksheet to test alternative calculations.

Data File needed for the Review Assignments: Tracs.xlsx

Rita suggests you try some alternative calculations for bonuses and benefits. Complete the following:

1. Open the **Tracs** workbook located in the Tutorial.07\Review folder included with your Data Files, save the workbook as **Tracs Employees** in the same folder, and then, in the Documentation sheet, enter the date and your name.
2. In the Employee Data worksheet, rename the Excel table as **EmpData**.
3. Employees who want additional coverage (Add Life Ins) pay 0.1% premium rate times annual salary. For employees who do not elect additional coverage, enter 0 in the Life Ins Premium column. The life insurance premiums are entered in cell Z9. Calculate the life insurance premiums using an IF function and include a reference to cell Z9 to obtain the life insurance rate.
4. All full-time (Job Status) employees over the age of 30 (Age in column N) are eligible for the 401(k) benefit. Use the IF and AND functions to calculate the 401(k) benefit as 3% of annual salary. If the employee is not eligible, enter 0. In the formula you create, include a reference to cell Z10 to obtain the 401(k) matching percent rate (3%).
5. Calculate Bonus assuming it is available to all employees with 1 or more years of service (Years Service). Employees with pay grade 1 receive $3,000 (cell Z6), pay grade 2 receive $6,000 (cell Z7), and pay grade 3 receive $8,000 (cell Z8). For employees not eligible for a bonus, display the label **NE**. For pay grades not equal to 1, 2, or 3, display the message **Invalid pay grade**. Use nested IF functions to calculate the bonus.
6. Change the format color of the duplicate value conditional formatting rule to Green (sixth color in the last row of the color palette) using the Conditional Formatting Rules Manager dialog box.
7. Calculate the health plan cost using the HLOOKUP function to do an exact match lookup. The layout of Health Plan Rates data ($B$2:$F$3) in the Lookup Tables worksheet has been revised to work with the HLOOKUP function. Use the range address reference in the HLOOKUP function to reference Health Plan Rates data.
8. Modify the calculation of the recognition award (Award) to incorporate the IFERROR function. Display the message **Invalid hire date**.
9. Change the hire date in cell C12 from 3/1/2007 to **#/1//2007** (note that you are entering a date with an intentional error). Insert a comment in cell S12 describing what appears in row 12 of the Years Service, Bonus, and Award columns. After entering the comment, change the date in cell C12 to **3/1/2007**.
10. Complete the criteria range located in the range A1:S3 of the Employee Data worksheet so you can use advanced filtering to display all part-time (PT) employees working in Austin as well as full-time (FT) employees working at home and earning $40,000 or more.
11. Use the COUNTIF count and AVERAGEIF functions to complete the Gender Summary report in the range B4:D5 of the Reports worksheet.
12. Use the Database function to calculate the average salary by Sex (F or M) and Pay Type (S or H). Enter the criteria in the ranges J12:K12, M12:N12, J17:K17, and M17:N17 in the Reports worksheet, and then use the DAVERAGE function to complete the report found in the range B11:D13 of the Reports worksheet.
13. Save and close the workbook. Submit the finished workbook to your instructor, either in printed or electronic form, as requested.

Apply | Case Problem 1

Apply the skills you learned to analyze and summarize monthly sales data for a computer supply store.

Data File needed for this Case Problem: Modem.xlsx

PC-Market Distribution Linda Klaussen works for PC-Market Distribution, a computer supply store. She needs your help in designing an Excel workbook to enter purchase order information. She has already entered the product information on PC-Market's line of modems. She wants you to insert a lookup function to look up data from the product table. The company also supports three shipping options that vary in price. She wants the purchase order worksheet to be able to calculate the total cost of the order, including the type of shipping the customer requests. She also wants to use advanced filtering to copy data on all modems under $50 to a new worksheet to review prices of the inexpensive items. Finally, she wants to calculate average prices for each category of modems using a Database function.

Complete the following:

1. Open the **Modem** workbook located in the Tutorial.07\Case1 folder included with your Data Files, save the workbook as **PC Modem** in the same folder, and then, in the Documentation worksheet, enter the date and your name.
2. In the Purchase Order worksheet, Product ID numbers will be entered in cell B5. Create three lookup functions: the first to display the product type in cell C7, the second to display the model name in cell C8, and the third to display the price in cell C9. Product information is displayed in the Product List worksheet.
3. If an incorrect product ID number is entered in cell B5, then cells C7, C8, and C9 will display the #N/A error value. Linda wants these cells to display the message **Product ID not found** if the ID entered is not found.
4. Enter one of three shipping options offered by PC-Market (Standard, Express, Overnight) in cell B15. Set up an area in the range D40:E42 to store Standard shipping costs $9.50, Express shipping costs $14.50, and Overnight shipping costs $18.50. Use IF functions to display the costs of the shipping in cell C17. If an invalid shipping option is entered in cell B15, then **Invalid Shipping option** should appear in cell C17. If the Shipping option, cell B15, is blank, then cell C17 should be blank. (*Hint:* The IF functions should reference the cells in the range D40:E42.)
5. Display the total cost of the product (price times quantity) plus shipping in cell C19. If the cell equals an error value (#Value!), display the message **Check Product ID, Quantity, or Shipping option**.
6. Test the worksheet using a product ID number of **1050**, quantity **2**, and the **Express** shipping option.
7. On the Product List worksheet use advanced filtering to display all 56K Desktop modems (Type) with a price under $50 or Modem Card (Type) over $200. Make sure the values in all the columns are visible. Make a copy of the Product List worksheet, rename the copied worksheet **Q7 Advanced Filter** and then return to the Product List worksheet. Display all the records.
8. In the Summary worksheet, use appropriate functions to determine the average modem price and count for each modem type.
9. Save and close the workbook. Submit the finished workbook to your instructor, either in printed or electronic form, as requested.

Apply | Case Problem 2

Apply the skills you learned by creating a worksheet that tracks the amount of vacation time and family leave to which an employee is entitled.

Data File needed for this Case Problems: Leave.xlsx

Town of Baltic Administrative Office Alan Welton, HR Generalist, at the Town of Baltic Administrative Office in Baltic, Indiana, has a workbook that tracks the amount of vacation time and family leave used by each employee in the town. Alan needs to calculate how much vacation and family leave each employee is eligible for. Then, he can subtract the amount they have already used from that amount. He also wants to calculate the total number of vacation and family leave days used by all employees, as well as the total number of days remaining. The eligibility requirements for the different vacation and family leave plans are as follows:

For vacation:
- 15 days for full-time employees who have worked 4 or more years
- 10 days for full-time employees who have worked 2 years but less than 4 years
- 5 days for full-time employees who have worked 1 year but less than 2 years
- 0 days for everyone else

For family leave:
- 5 days for full-time employees who have worked 1 or more years
- 3 days for full-time employees who have worked less than 1 year or for part-time employees who have worked more than 1.5 years
- 0 days for everyone else

Use these eligibility requirements to calculate the available vacation and family leave time for each employee.

Complete the following:

1. Open the workbook **Leave** located in the Tutorial.07\Case2 folder included with your Data Files, save the workbook as **Baltic Leave** in the same folder, and then enter the date and your name in the Documentation worksheet.

2. In the LeaveData worksheet, create an Excel table from the range A5:J107, name the Excel table as **Leave**, and then remove the filter arrows. Set the column width for columns B through J to **10**.

3. Calculate Years Employed in column D. Use Date Hired and current date (assume 7/1/2010, which is stored in cell Z6) and express length of time employed in years. Use the formula (current date – date hired)/365.

4. In column E, enter a formula using nested IF and AND functions to determine the number of vacation days (based on the vacation rules described previously) each employee is eligible for based on the employee's job status in column B and on the Length of Time Employed in column D.

5. Subtract the amount of vacation used from the available vacation time, displaying the remaining vacation time in column G for all employees.

EXPLORE 6. In column H, enter a formula to determine each employee's total family leave time (based on the family leave rules described previously). (*Hint*: Use nested IF, AND, and OR functions.)

7. To determine the remaining family time, subtract the used portion of the family leave from their total family leave and display the results in column J.

8. In the Leave Summary worksheet, use a function to calculate the total number of employees eligible for the different vacation leave plan. (*Hint*: An employee who is eligible for the 15-day vacation leave will have the value 15 in column E of the Leave Data worksheet.)

9. Enter formulas in the Vacation Leave Summary report to calculate the total number of vacation days and days remaining for each vacation plan.

10. Calculate the total number of employees, total days, and days remaining in row 8 of the report you started in Step 9.

11. Use advanced filtering to display all full-time employees with five remaining family leave days as well as all part-time employees with three remaining family leave days. Make a copy of the Leave Data worksheet, rename the copied worksheet **Q11 Advanced Filter**, and then return to the Leave Data worksheet. Clear the filter.

12. Save and close the workbook. Submit the finished workbook to your instructor, either in printed or electronic form, as requested.

Challenge | Case Problem 3

Create reports for a water company based on different billing plans.

Data File needed for this Case Problem: M-Fresh.xlsx

M-Fresh Water Company A small independent water company in Miami, Oklahoma, M-Fresh Water Company provides water to its commercial customers throughout the region, delivering the supply of water through pipelines, on-demand storage tanks, and bottles. Customers of M-Fresh Water range from government offices to nonprofit organizations to commercial retail shops and markets. Town regulations indicate that the latter group of commercial customers is taxed on their usage, whereas nonprofit and government offices are not. Furthermore, M-Fresh Water will, from time to time, choose to waive a water bill based on its charitable giving policy.

Dawes Cado is in charge of the billing system that must take into account these business rules and ensure accurate and on-time billing, which is completed each quarter. Complete the following:

1. Open the **M-Fresh** workbook located in the Tutorial.07\Case3 folder included with your Data Files, save the workbook as **Water Bills** in the same folder, and then enter the date and your name in the Documentation worksheet.

2. In the Quarterly Data worksheet, create an Excel table for the range A1:G73. Name the table as **WaterData**. Remove the filter arrows. Format the Gal Used data in the Comma Style number format with no decimal places. Add the following three columns to the table: **Water Bill**, **Tax**, and **Total Bill**.

3. Calculate the Water Bill based on the following rules:
   - If a customer's bill is waived, place 0 in the Water Bill column.
   - Gal Used (gallons used) must be greater than 25,000 gallons during the quarter; otherwise, the water bill is 0.
   - For all other accounts, the billing rate varies based on the type of customer. The billing rate is $3, $2, or $1.50 per *thousand* gallons used depending on the type of customer (see the Billing Rate worksheet). For example, a commercial customer using 75,000 gallons has a water bill of $225(75×$3), whereas a government customer using 100,000 gallons pays $150(100×$1.50). A commercial customer using 15,000 gallons has a water bill of 0.

4. Calculate Tax based on the following rule: If a customer is taxable, then multiply the water bill times 3.5%; otherwise, the tax is 0. (Tax rate is stored in cell T1.)

5. Calculate the Total Bill amount using the following formula: *Water Bill + Tax*.
6. Improve the formatting of the number fields, and then insert totals for GalUsed (average) and Total bill (sum). Make a copy of the Quarterly Data worksheet, rename the copied worksheet **Q2-6** and then return to the Quarterly Data worksheet.
7. Use conditional formatting to highlight the top 15% of customers based on the total bill. Use appropriate formatting. Filter the bills so only the top 15% are displayed. Sort the largest first. Make a copy of the Quarterly Data worksheet, rename the copied worksheet **Q7** and then return to the Quarterly Data worksheet. Display all records.
8. Insert a new worksheet and then create the Water Usage and Billing By Type of Customer report (shown in Figure 7-39). Rename the worksheet as **Q8 Billing Summary**. Use conditional IF functions to prepare the report.

Figure 7-39

	A	B	C	D	E	F
1						
2						
3						
4		Customer Type	Nbr Customers	Avg Gals Used	Total Billed	
5		Commercial	37	322,437	$ 37,043.12	
6		Non-profit	11	87,661	$ 224.18	
7		Government	24	774,532	$ 27,901.44	
8		Total	72	437,267	$ 65,168.74	
9						
10						

EXPLORE 9. Make a copy of the Quarterly Data worksheet, rename the copied worksheet **Q9-10**. Management is considering eliminating the 25,000 gallon cutoff and bill waivers. In the Quarterly Data worksheet use advanced filtering to copy all data for waived customers or customers using 25,000 gallons or less to row 101 in the Q9-10 worksheet.

EXPLORE 10. Use the data you retrieved from Step 9 to calculate the lost revenue from waived bills and customers with water usage below 25,000. Assume for the purposes of the analysis that all water usage (25,000 gallon cutoff no longer exists) will be billed. Prepare a report.

EXPLORE 11. You want to know how many businesses are either churches, schools, or clinics. Use the COUNTIF function to complete the report in a new worksheet named **Q11 Type Institution**. (*Hint:* Use Help to research using the wildcard characters as part of your criteria.)

12. Save and close the workbook. Submit the finished workbook to your instructor, either in printed or electronic form, as requested.

Tutorial 7 Using Advanced Functions, Conditional Formatting, and Filtering

Create | Case Problem 4

Create a worksheet that compiles and summarizes reports for a newspaper.

Data File needed for this Case Problem: Rock Island.xlsx

Rock Island Home Sales   Tim Derkson, reporter for Rock Island Times, in Rock Island, Illinois, is compiling a quarterly real estate sales analysis for his newspaper. He obtained data on home sales from the local real estate association and county records. He asked you to help design a worksheet that will display summary information on the home sales in Rock Island. Tim has already set up and formatted a workbook, but he wants you to insert the correct formulas. Tim stored the housing data in the Home Data worksheet. He wants to use the Home Summary worksheet to search for information about the homes.

Complete the following:

1. Open the **Rock Island** workbook located in the Tutorial.07\Case4 folder included with your Data Files, save the workbook as **Home Sales** in the same folder, and then, in the Documentation worksheet, enter the date and your name.
2. In the Home Sales Data worksheet, create an Excel table in the range A6:K123. Remove the filter arrows. Name the Excel table as **SalesData**.
3. Using the Date Sold and Date Listed columns, add a calculated column named **Days on Market**, which is the difference between these two dates. (*Hint:* You might need to format this column in the General number format.)

EXPLORE
4. Use conditional formatting to highlight records where the sales price was above the asking price. Add appropriate formatting. (*Hint:* Create a new rule using the formula rule type and build a conditional statement to compare first data row between the two columns of interest.) Make a copy of the Home Sales Data worksheet, rename the copied worksheet **Q3-4**, and then return to the Home Sales Data worksheet.
5. Insert a new worksheet, and then rename it as **Q5-6 Sales Summary**. Create a report on Overall Home Sales based on Sales Price, using Figure 7-40 as a guide.

Figure 7-40

A	B	C	D	E	F	G
			Rock Island Home Sales			
			Overall Data			
		Number Sold	Average Sales Price	Highest Sales Price	Lowest Sales Price	
		117	$100,461.54	$ 215,000	$ 51,000	

EXPLORE
6. Below the report, create a report on Home Sales based on Sales Price and broken down by Type of Home. Figure 7-41 shows the output. Use conditional IF functions for Number Sold and Average Sales Price and database functions (DMAX and DMIN) to calculate the highest and lowest price.

Figure 7-41

	Type	Number Sold	Average Sales Price	Highest Sales Price	Lowest Sales Price
7		By Type of Home			
8					
9	Type	Number Sold	Average Sales Price	Highest Sales Price	Lowest Sales Price
10	Condo	23	$ 90,347.83	$ 182,500	$ 53,000
11	Ranch	46	$ 91,842.39	$ 193,500	$ 51,000
12	Victorian	48	$113,567.71	$ 215,000	$ 51,750
13					

7. In the Home Sales Data worksheet use Advanced Filtering to display all homes that were:
   - On the market more than 150 days and 25 or more years old

   OR

   - Have more than 2 bedrooms and 1.5 or more bathrooms

   Sort the filtered data by Days on Market in descending order. Make a copy of the Home Sales Data worksheet, rename the copied worksheet **Q7 Advanced Filter** and then return to the Home Sales Data worksheet. Display all records.

EXPLORE 8. Insert a new worksheet. Rename the worksheet as **Q8-9 DaysOnMarket**. Create a PivotTable to create a report with the information in Figure 7-42.

Figure 7-42

4		Values	
5	Days	Number Sold	Avg Sales Price
6	1-100	31	$ 94,451.61
7	101-200	27	$ 106,879.63
8	201-300	37	$ 103,939.19
9	301-400	22	$ 95,204.55
10	Grand Total	117	$ 100,461.54

EXPLORE 9. In a separate section of the same Q8-9 DaysOnMarket worksheet, use Database functions and complete the criteria ranges to create the report shown in Figure 7-43, which provides the same information as the report you created in Step 8.

Figure 7-43

	Days	Number Sold	Avg Sales Price
15	Days	Number Sold	Avg Sales Price
16	1-100	31	$ 94,451.61
17	101-200	27	$ 106,879.63
18	201-300	37	$ 103,939.19
19	301-400	22	$ 95,204.55
20	Total	117	$ 100,461.54

10. Display the Total row in the SalesData table. In this row, display a count of homes sold, average taxes, average asking price, average sales price, and average days on market. Make a copy of the Home Sales Data worksheet, rename the copied worksheet **Q10-11 Home Sales Data** and then return to the Home Sales worksheet.

EXPLORE 11. In the Q10-11 Home Sales Data worksheet, split the Home Sales Data worksheet so the top section shows all the Home Data table. The bottom section is the last one or two rows on your screen, which displays the Total row. (*Hint:* Use Excel Help to find information on how to split the window.)

12. Save and close the workbook. Submit the finished workbook to your instructor, either in printed or electronic form, as requested.

Research | Internet Assignments

Use the Internet to find and work with data related to the topics presented in this tutorial.

The purpose of the Internet Assignments is to challenge you to find information on the Internet that you can use to work effectively with this software. The actual assignments are updated and maintained on the Course Technology Web site. Log on to the Internet and use your Web browser to go to the Student Online Companion for New Perspectives Office 2007 at **www.course.com/np/office2007**. Then navigate to the Internet Assignments for this tutorial.

Assess | SAM Assessment and Training

If you have a SAM user profile, you may have access to hands-on instruction, practice, and assessment of the skills covered in this tutorial. Log in to your SAM account (**http://sam2007.course.com**) to launch any assigned training activities or exams that relate to the skills covered in this tutorial.

Review | Quick Check Answers

Session 7.1

1. The table style is applied to all rows in the new column; the range of the Excel table expands to include the new column (Phone). All features that apply to other columns in the table apply to the Phone column, too.
2. calculated column
3. In cell C7, enter = IF(C5*C6 > 10000,C5*C6,10000).
4. False
5. =IF(AND(J5>0,D5<3/15/2008),"Outstanding","")
6. structured references
7. nested IF

Session 7.2

1. An exact match compares the lookup value to the compare value. They must be equal for a value to be returned from the lookup table. An approximate match also compares the lookup value to the compare value. The two values do not have to be equal, just fall within a range of values for Excel to return a value from the lookup table.
2. VLOOKUP function
3. No, duplicate last names do not mean the data in the Last Name column is a duplicate.
4. =IFERROR(C5/C25,"Dividing by 0")
5. counts the number of females in the Employee table

6. Calculate the average salary for all hourly employees.
7. Conditional Formatting Rules Manager dialog box

Session 7.3

1. retrieve all male employees classified as hourly
2. Location
   ="=Austin"
   ="=New Orleans"
3. retrieve employees earning less than 25,000 or 100,000 or more in annual salary
4. Clear command
5. sum the annual salaries of all males hired on 1/1/2010 or later
6. The structured reference to Employee includes only the data in an Excel table, whereas Employee[#ALL] includes the header and total row. The DSUM function's first argument must reference the header row.
7. =DSUM('Employee Data'!A5:R105,"Annual Salary",T1:U2)

Ending Data Files

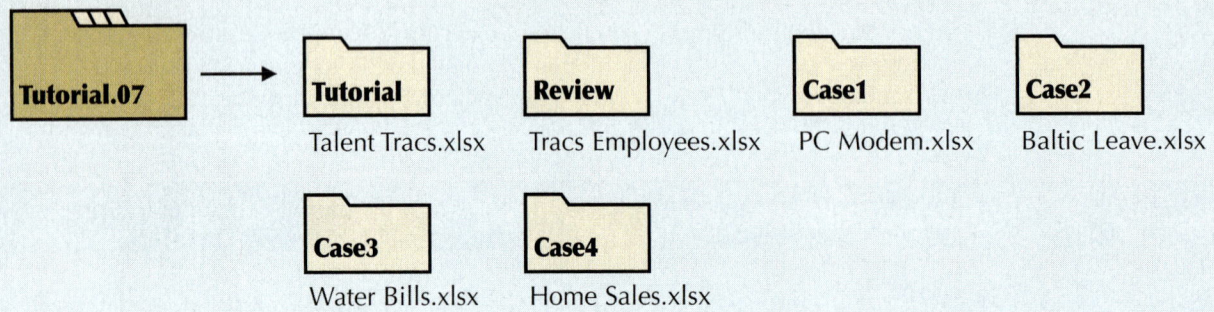

Tutorial.07 → Tutorial: Talent Tracs.xlsx
Review: Tracs Employees.xlsx
Case1: PC Modem.xlsx
Case2: Baltic Leave.xlsx
Case3: Water Bills.xlsx
Case4: Home Sales.xlsx

Excel | EX 393

Tutorial 8

Objectives

Session 8.1
- Create an application
- Create, edit, and delete defined names for cells and ranges
- Paste a list of defined names as documentation
- Use defined names in formulas
- Add defined names to existing formulas

Session 8.2
- Create validation rules for data entry
- Protect the contents of worksheets and workbooks
- Add, edit, and delete comments

Session 8.3
- Learn about macro viruses and Excel security features
- Create a macro using the macro recorder
- Edit a macro using the Visual Basic Editor
- Assign a macro to a keyboard shortcut and a button
- Save a workbook in macro enabled format
- Minimize the Ribbon

Developing an Excel Application

Creating an Invoice

Case | Eugene Community Theatre

Ellen Jefferson, business manager for the Eugene Community Theatre in Eugene, Oregon, is automating several processes for the theatre's business office. Each year, the theatre mails a brochure to patrons and other interested individuals showcasing the upcoming seasons' offerings. Then, theatre-goers make their selections and mail in the order form. Ellen wants to automate the process of invoicing, capturing the order, calculating the charges, and printing an invoice. She also wants the invoice system to reflect specific requests for tickets (number, series, and location in theatre).

Many of these tasks can be accomplished in Excel. But without validating data entry, protecting cells with formulas from accidental deletion, and reducing repetitious keystrokes and mouse clicks, Ellen realizes too many opportunities for errors exist. In addition, the theatre, as a nonprofit organization, relies on numerous volunteers who have varying degrees of computer experience and skill. To accommodate these varying skill levels and reduce potential errors, Ellen wants to create a custom interface for this project that does not rely exclusively on the Ribbon, galleries, and so forth. You'll help Ellen create a unique Excel application that can resolve these issues and help ensure accurate data entry.

Starting Data Files

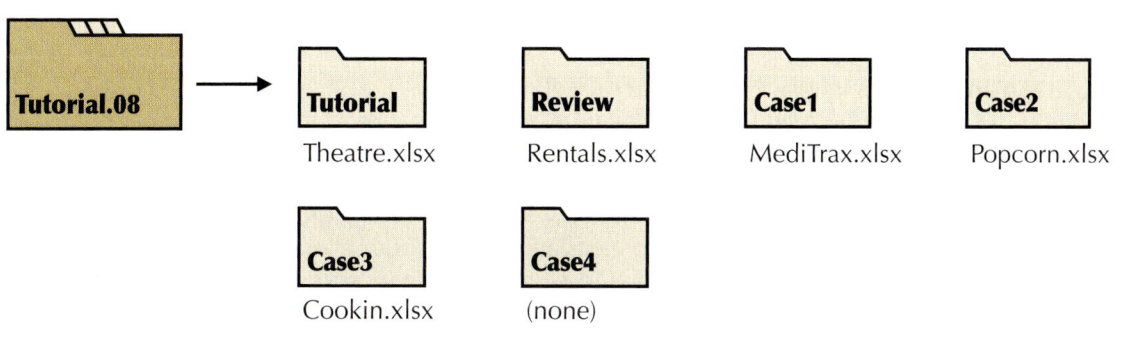

Session 8.1

Planning an Excel Application

An **Excel application** is a spreadsheet written or tailored to meet the user's specific needs. Applications typically include the following:

- Reports and/or charts designed to aid understanding and produce insights
- A way to enter and edit data, often controlling the type of values that can be entered and where data can be entered
- An interface that assists the user, ranging from buttons for executing specific tasks to customizing the entire Excel interface with custom tabs, menus, and toolbars
- Clearly written instructions and documentation

Ellen sketched the application she wants you to create, which is shown in Figure 8-1. She wants to be able to easily print the invoice and transfer the invoice items to another worksheet. In addition, she wants volunteers to be able to enter data for a season ticket in a specific area of the worksheet reserved for input. The application would use this data to automatically generate and print the invoice. To keep the process simple, she also wants users to be able to click buttons to print a single invoice, print the entire worksheet, and transfer the data from one worksheet to another.

Figure 8-1   Ellen's sketch of the Excel application for invoicing

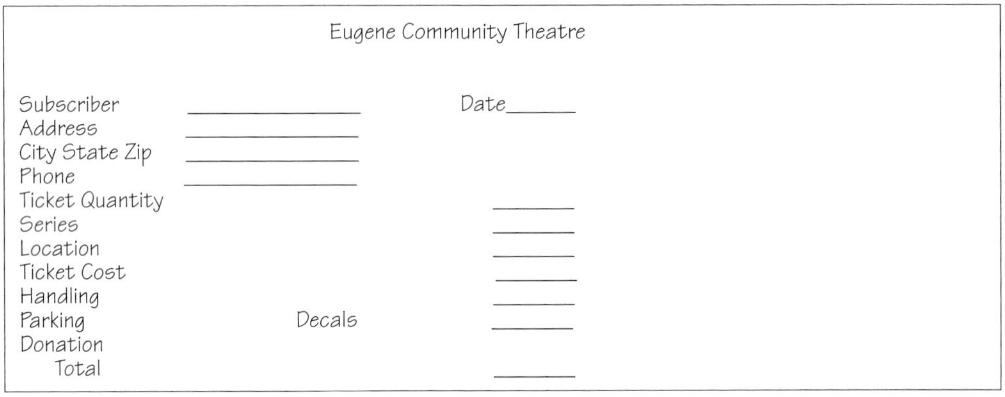

```
                        Eugene Community Theatre

    Subscriber      _____         Date_____
    Address         _____
    City State Zip  _____
    Phone           _____
    Ticket Quantity                    _____
    Series                             _____
    Location                           _____
    Ticket Cost                        _____
    Handling                           _____
    Parking         Decals             _____
    Donation                           _____
       Total                           _____
```

Application planning includes designing how the worksheet(s) will be organized. You can include different sections for each function, depending on the complexity of the project. For example, you could include separate sections to:

- Enter and edit data (even setting what types of values can be entered and where a user can enter data)
- Store data after it has been entered
- Use formulas to manipulate and perform calculations on data
- Prepare outputs, such as reports and charts

An application's interface helps others use it. For example, you can have separate sections for inputting data and displaying outputs. You can create special buttons for performing specific tasks. You can also change the entire Excel interface by adding custom menus, toolbars, and commands.

An application often includes internal documentation in a Documentation worksheet as well as comments to explain cell contents and provide instructions. It can also include a set of clearly written instructions. All of these help you and others use the workbook correctly and accurately.

You'll open the workbook Ellen created and complete the application.

To open and review the Theatre workbook:

1. Open the **Theatre** workbook located in the **Tutorial.08\Tutorial** folder included with your Data Files, and then save the workbook as **Community Theatre** in the same folder.

2. In the Documentation sheet, enter the current date and your name.

3. Review the contents of the workbook, and then switch to the **Invoice** worksheet. See Figure 8-2.

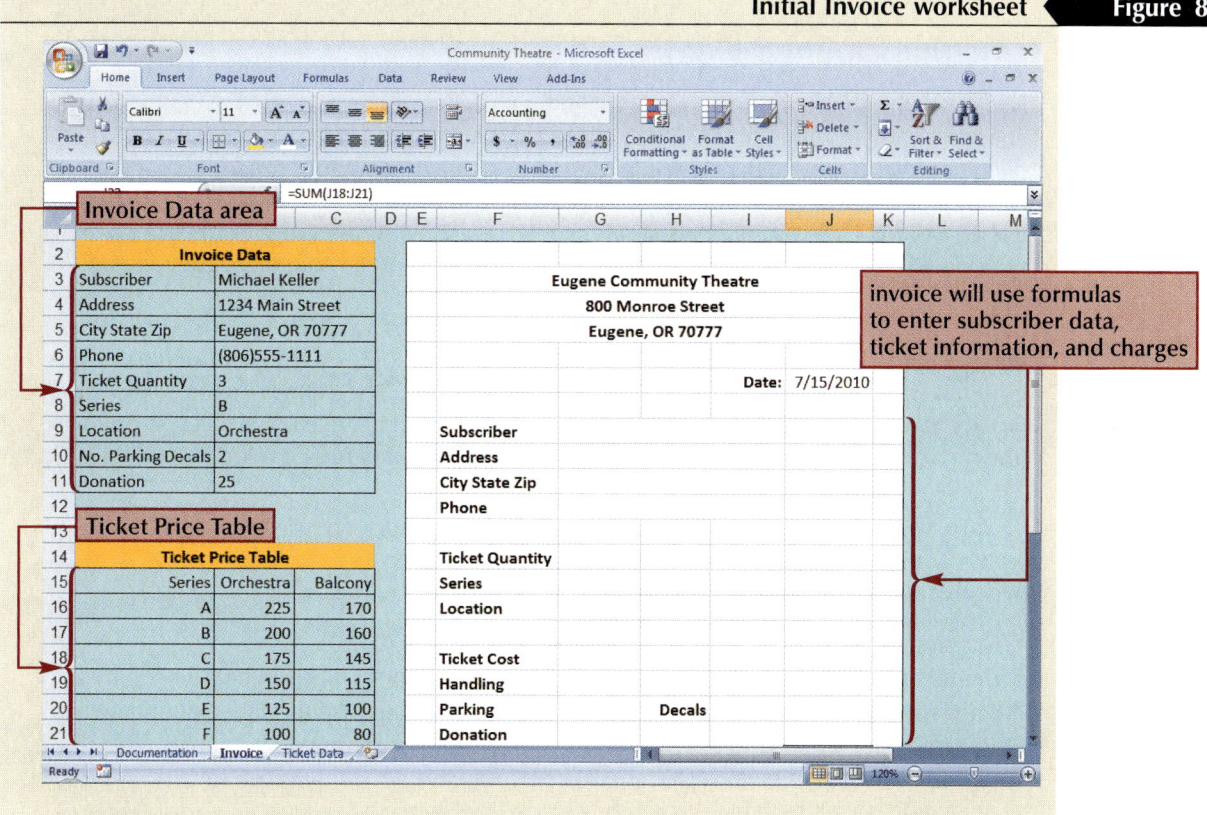

Figure 8-2   Initial Invoice worksheet

In addition to the Documentation worksheet, the Community Theatre workbook includes two other worksheets: Invoice and Ticket Data.

The Invoice worksheet contains input, output, and transfer data sections. The input section is divided into the following three areas:

- Invoice Data contains items that change for each request, such as the subscriber name, address, phone number, ticket quantity, series, location of seats, and so forth.
- Ticket Price Table contains the pricing table for all tickets for the upcoming season.
- Invoice Constants contains charges for items that will not change during the upcoming theatre season, such as the cost for parking ($15/decal) and the handling charge ($8/invoice).

The output section contains formulas and labels used to generate the invoice based on data in the input section. The invoice in the output section will be printed. The transfer data section gathers selected data from the invoice in one area before the data is transferred to the Ticket Data worksheet for storage. The transfer data section makes it simpler to move the data to the Ticket Data worksheet.

Tip

Larger and more complex applications often place the input and output sections in separate worksheets.

Naming Cells and Ranges

In the Invoice worksheet, the range B3:B11 contains the data values for each request for season tickets. As you can see, this range includes many variables. It will be simpler to remember where different data is stored by assigning a descriptive name to each cell or range rather than using its cell address. For example, the name *Customer* is easier to remember than cell B3. Assigning names to cells or ranges makes building an application more intuitive and easier to document. Ellen asks you to name the cells in the input section.

Creating Defined Names

So far, you have referred to a cell or range by its cell and range address except when you entered formulas within an Excel table. Cell and range references do not indicate what data is stored in those cells. Instead, you can assign a meaningful, descriptive name to a cell or range. A **defined name** (often called simply a **name**) is a word or string of characters associated with a single cell or a range. For example, if the range D1:D100 contains sales data for 100 transactions, you can define the name *Sales* to refer to the range of sales data.

You can use a defined name to quickly navigate within a workbook to the cell with defined name. You can also create more descriptive formulas by using defined names in formulas instead of cell or range references. For example, the defined name *Sales* can replace the range reference D1:D100 in a formula to calculate average sales, as follows (the first formula uses a range reference, the second formula uses a defined name):

=AVERAGE(D1:D100)
=AVERAGE(Sales)

When you define a name for a cell or range, keep in mind the following rules:

- The name must begin with a letter or _ (an underscore).
- The name can include letters and numbers as well as periods and underscores, but not other symbols or spaces. To distinguish multiword names, use an underscore between the words or capitalize the first letter of each word. For example, the names *Net_Income* or *NetIncome* are valid, but *Net Income* and *Net-Income* are not.
- The name cannot be a valid cell address (such as *FY2010*), function name, or reserved word (such as *Print_Area*).
- The name can include as many as 255 characters, although short, meaningful names of 5 to 15 characters are more practical.
- The name is not case-sensitive. For example, *Sales* and *SALES* are the same name and refer to the same cell or range.

Saving Time with Defined Names | InSight

Defined names have several advantages over cell references, especially as a worksheet becomes longer and more complex. Some advantages include:

- Names, such as *TaxRate* and *TotalSales*, are more descriptive than cell references, making it easier to remember a cell or range's content.
- Names can be used in formulas, making it easier for users to understand the calculations being performed. For example, =*GrossPay–Deductions* is more understandable than =*C15–C16*.
- When you move a named cell or range within a worksheet, its name moves with it. Any formulas that contain the name automatically reference the new location.
- In a formula, a named cell or range is the same as using the cell or range's absolute reference. So, if you move a formula that includes a defined name, the reference remains pointed to the correct cell or range.

By using defined names, you'll often save time and have a better understanding of what a formula is calculating.

Creating a Name for a Cell or Range | Reference Window

- Select the cell or range to which you want to assign a name.
- Click in the Name box on the formula bar, type the name, and then press the Enter key (or in the Defined Names group on the Formulas tab, click the Define Name button, type a name in the Name box, and then click the OK button).

or

- Select the range with labels and blank cells in the top row or first column to which you want to assign a name.
- In the Defined Names group on the Formulas tab, click the Create from Selection button.
- Specify whether to create the ranges based on the top row, bottom row, left column, or right column in the list.
- Click the OK button.

The fastest way to create a defined name is to use the Name box. You'll use the Name box to define names for the cells that contain the handling costs and the parking fee. Then, you'll define a name for the Ticket Price Table, which you will use in a formula later in the tutorial.

To use the Name box to name the invoice constants and the Ticket Price Table:

1. Click cell **B24** to make it active, and then click the **Name box**. The cell reference for the active cell, B24, is selected in the Name box.

2. Type **HandlingCost**, and then press the **Enter** key. Cell B24 remains active, and the name *HandlingCost* appears in the Name box instead of the cell reference.

   Trouble? If the label *HandlingCost* appears in cell B24, you probably did not click the Name box before typing the name. On the Quick Access Toolbar, click the Undo button, and then repeat Steps 1 and 2.

3. Click cell **B25** to make it active, click the **Name box** to select the cell reference, type **ParkingFee**, and then press the **Enter** key. Cell B25 remains active, and the name *ParkingFee* appears in the Name box instead of the cell reference. See Figure 8-3.

Figure 8-3   Defined name for cell B25

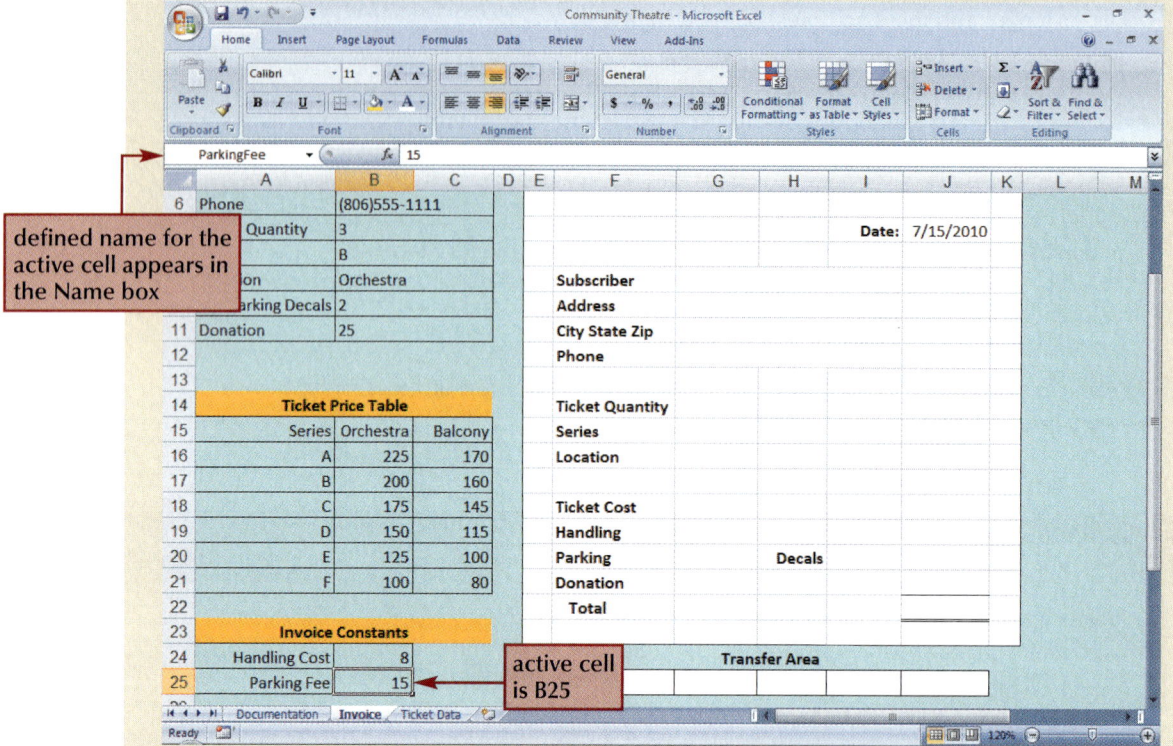

▶ 4. Select the range **A16:C21**. The cell reference for the active cell in the range appears in the Name box.

▶ 5. Click the **Name box**, type **TicketPrices**, and then press the **Enter** key. The name *TicketPrices* is assigned to the range A16:C21.

▶ 6. Select the range **F25:J25**, click the **Name box**, type **TransferArea**, and then press the **Enter** key. The name *TransferArea* is assigned to the range F25:J25.

The Name box, as the title implies, displays all of the names in a workbook. You can select a name in the Name box to quickly select the cell or range referenced by the name. You'll view the defined names you added to the workbook.

To select cells and ranges with the Name box:

▶ 1. Click the **Name box** arrow to open a list of defined names in the workbook. Four names appear in the list: *HandlingCost*, *ParkingFee*, *TicketPrices*, and *TransferArea*.

▶ 2. Click **ParkingFee**. The active cell moves to cell B25.

▶ 3. Click the **Name box** arrow, and then click **TicketPrices**. The range A16:C21 is selected in the worksheet, and cell A16 is the active cell.

Ellen wants to define names to each cell in the Invoice Data area. You can quickly define names without typing them if the data is organized in a tabular format with labels in the first or last column or top or bottom row. The names are based on the row or column labels. Any blanks or parentheses in the row or column labels are changed to an underscore (_) in the defined name.

You will create names for the Invoice Data area, using the labels in the range A3:A11.

To create defined names by selection for the Invoice Data area:

1. Select the range **A3:B11**. In this range, column A contains the labels you want to use as the defined names and column B contains the cells you want to name.

2. Click the **Formulas** tab on the Ribbon, and then, in the Defined Names group, click the **Create from Selection** button. The Create Names from Selection dialog box opens. See Figure 8-4.

Figure 8-4   Create Names from Selection dialog box

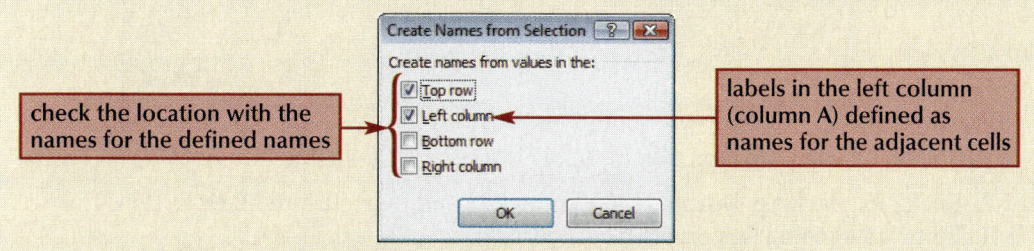

check the location with the names for the defined names

labels in the left column (column A) defined as names for the adjacent cells

3. Click the **Top row** check box to remove the check mark, and then verify that the **Left column** check box contains a check mark. The labels in the left column will be used to create the defined names.

4. Click the **OK** button. Each cell in the range B3:B11 is named based on its label in column A.

Although you can use the Name box to verify the names were created, the Name Manager dialog box lists all of the names currently defined in the workbook, including Excel table names. You can also use the Name Manager dialog box to a create new names, edit or delete existing names, and filter the list of names.

To use the Name Manager dialog box to edit and delete defined names:

1. In the Defined Names group on the Formulas tab, click the **Name Manager** button. The Name Manager dialog box opens, listing the nine defined names based on the labels in the range A3:A11 in the Invoice Data area as well as the four names you defined with the Name box. See Figure 8-5.

Tip

The Name Manager dialog box also lists Excel table names.

| Figure 8-5 | Name Manager dialog box |

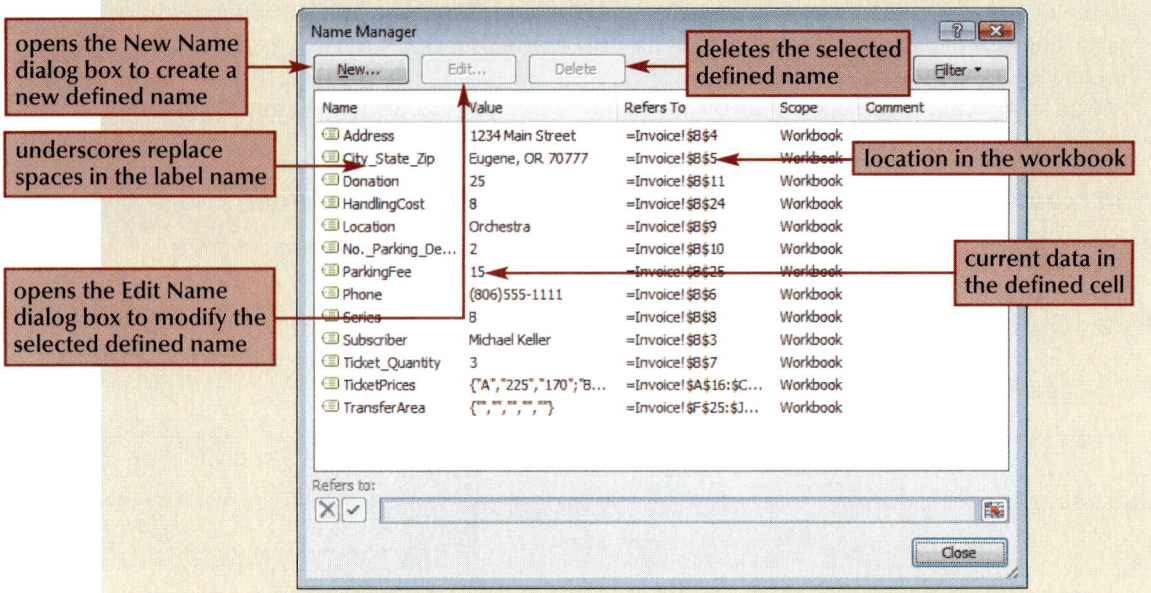

The name *No._Parking_Decals* is too long, so you'll change it to *Decals*.

▶ 2. Click **No._Parking_Decals** in the Name list, and then click the **Edit** button. The Edit Name dialog box opens. See Figure 8-6.

| Figure 8-6 | Edit Name dialog box |

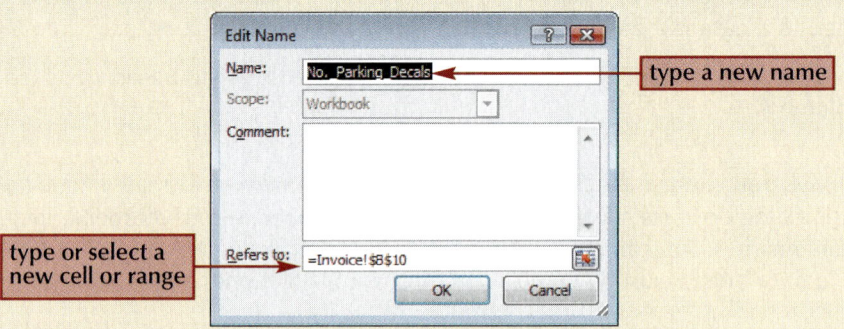

▶ 3. In the Name box, type **Decals**, and then click the **OK** button. The edited name appears in the list.

Ellen decides the name *TransferArea* is not needed.

▶ 4. Click **TransferArea**, and then click the **Delete** button. A dialog box opens, confirming that you want to delete the selected name.

▶ 5. Click the **OK** button. The name is removed from the list.

▶ 6. Click the **Close** button. The Name Manager dialog box closes.

When a workbook contains many defined names, it can be helpful to list all of the defined names and their corresponding cell addresses as part of the workbook's documentation. You can generate a list of names using the Paste Names command.

To create a list of defined names in the Documentation worksheet:

▶ 1. Switch to the **Documentation** worksheet.

▶ 2. Click in cell **A12**, type **Defined Names**, and then press the **Enter** key. The heading for the list of defined names appears in cell A12, and cell A13 is the active cell.

▶ 3. In the Defined Names group on the Formulas tab, click the **Use in Formula** button. The list includes all the defined names in the workbook followed by the Paste Names command.

▶ 4. Click **Paste Names**. The Paste Name dialog box opens. You can paste any selected name, or you can paste the entire list of names.

▶ 5. Click the **Paste List** button. The defined names and their associated cell references are pasted into the range A13:B24.

▶ 6. Adjust the column widths of columns A and B to display all the defined names data, if necessary, and then deselect the range. See Figure 8-7.

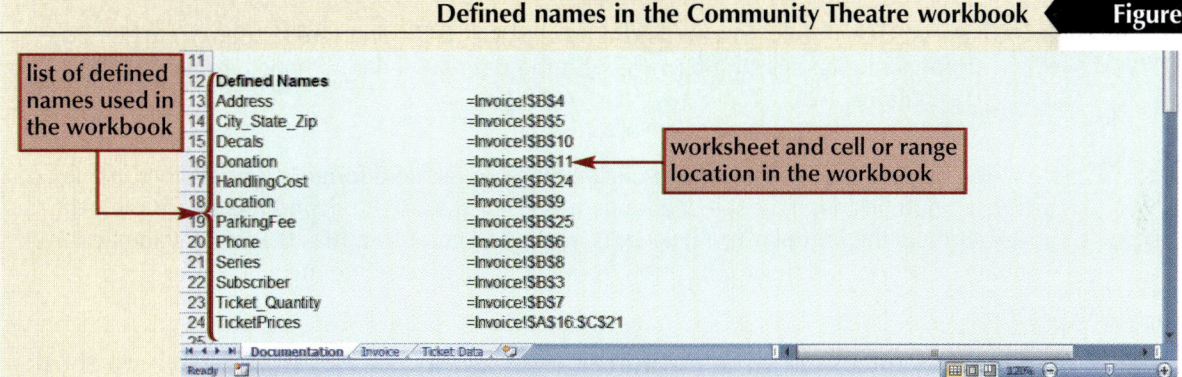

Figure 8-7 Defined names in the Community Theatre workbook

▶ 7. Switch to the **Invoice** worksheet.

If you edit a defined name or add a new defined name, the list of defined names and their addresses in the Documentation worksheet is not updated. You must paste the list again to update the names and locations. Usually, it is a good idea to wait until the workbook is complete before pasting defined names in the Documentation worksheet.

Entering Formulas with Defined Names

Ellen already entered the TODAY function in cell J7 to ensure the current date always appears on the invoice. You'll enter the remaining formulas needed to generate the invoice. You'll start by entering formulas to display the subscriber's name and address in the invoice. Ellen entered sample subscriber data in the input section of the Invoice worksheet so you can test the formulas as you enter them.

To enter formulas to display the subscriber's name and address:

▶ 1. In cell G9, enter **=B3**. Michael Keller, the subscriber's name in the sample data, appears in the cell.

▶ 2. In cell G10, enter **=B4**. The subscriber's address, 1234 Main Street, appears in the cell.

▶ 3. Click cell **G10**. The formula =B4 appears in the formula bar.

You entered these formulas using cell addresses rather than defined names. Although you defined names for cells B3 and B4, the names do not automatically replace the cell addresses in the formula. Because defined names make formulas simpler to enter and understand, you will use the named cells and ranges as you enter the remaining formulas.

As you type a defined name in a formula, the Formula AutoComplete box lists items that match the letters you typed. You can type the entire name, double-click the name in the Formula AutoComplete box, or press the Tab key to enter the selected name.

To type defined names in formulas:

▶ 1. In cell G11, enter **=City_State_Zip**.

▶ 2. Click cell **G11**. The data from cell B5 appears in the cell, and the formula with the defined name, =City_State_Zip, appears in the formula bar.

▶ 3. In cell G12, enter **=Phone**, and then click cell **G12**. The sample data from cell B6 appears in the cell, the formula with the defined name, =Phone, appears in the formula bar.

You can also use the point-and-click method to create a formula with defined names. When you click a cell or select a range, Excel substitutes the defined name for the cell reference in the formula. You'll use this method to enter formulas that display the ticket quantity, series, and theatre location from the input area in the invoice.

To enter formulas with defined names using the point-and-click method:

▶ 1. Click cell **I14**, type **=**, and then click cell **B7**. The formula uses the defined name *Ticket_Quantity* rather than the cell reference B7.

▶ 2. Press the **Enter** key. The number 3, indicating the number of tickets the subscriber ordered, appears in cell I14.

▶ 3. In cell I15, type **=**, and then click cell **B8**. The formula uses the defined name *Series* rather than the cell reference B8.

▶ 4. Press the **Enter** key. The letter B, indicating the series the subscriber selected, appears in cell I15.

Next, you'll move the subscriber's preferred location to the invoice.

▶ 5. In cell I16, type **=**, click **B9**, and then click the **Enter** button ✓ on the formula bar. Orchestra, the location the subscriber selected, appears in cell I16, and the formula with the defined name, =Location, appears in the formula bar. See Figure 8-8.

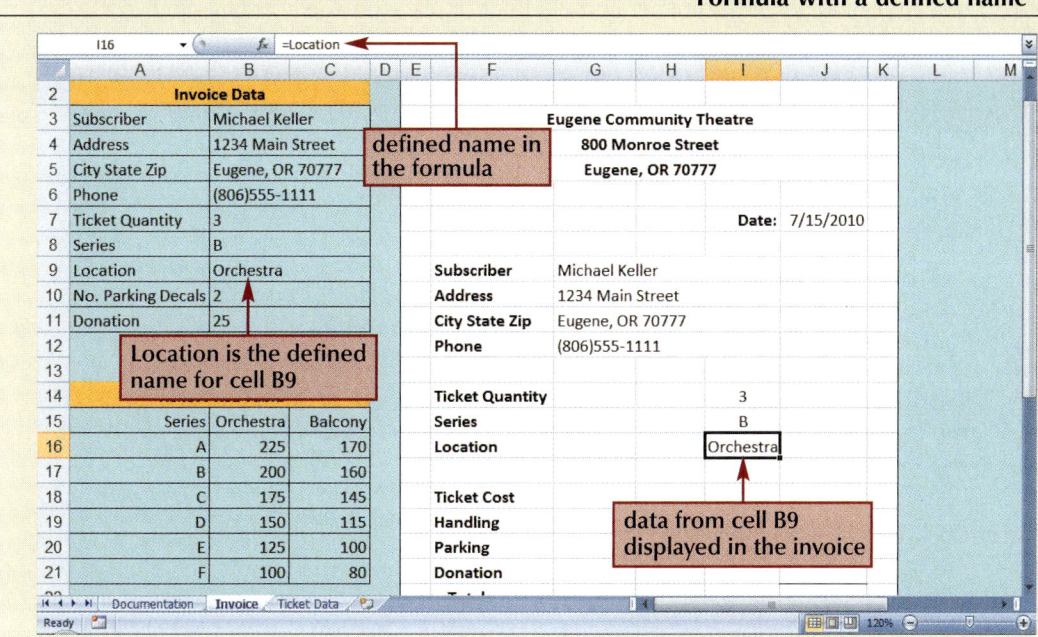

Figure 8-8 Formula with a defined name

Next, you will enter the formula to calculate the ticket cost to the subscriber. You need to combine two VLOOKUP functions within an IF function to create the formula to calculate ticket costs. The VLOOKUP functions will find the ticket price. The lookup value is the Series the subscriber selects (A, B, C, D, E, or F). Recall that the lookup value searches the first column of the lookup table to find the appropriate row. In this case, the lookup table is the Ticket Price Table (the range you earlier named *TicketPrices*) which has two columns of ticket prices. Column 2 of the table lists the prices for the Orchestra and column 3 of the table lists the prices for the Balcony. The column used to return the ticket prices depends on the Location the subscriber selected. You need to use an IF function to determine whether to search the second or third column for the ticket price.

To enter the formula to determine ticket cost:

1. In cell J18, enter **=IF(Location="Orchestra",VLOOKUP(Series,TicketPrices, 2,FALSE),VLOOKUP(Series,TicketPrices,3,FALSE))*Ticket_Quantity**. The ticket cost based on the sample subscriber data is $600. The first argument of the IF function, *Location="Orchestra"*, determines which VLOOKUP formula to use—the one returning a value from column 2 (Orchestra) in the TicketPrices table or the one returning a value from column 3 (Balcony) in the TicketPrices table. The second argument, *VLOOKUP(Series,TicketPrices,2,FALSE)*, uses the VLOOKUP function to find a ticket price for a seat in the Orchestra. The first argument of the VLOOKUP function, *Series*, is the defined name that stores the Series code (A, B, C, and so on) used to look up a value in the second argument, *TicketPrices* (range A16:C21). The third argument, *2*, returns a ticket price from the second column (Orchestra) of the TicketPrices table. The fourth argument, *FALSE*, indicates an exact match lookup. The second VLOOKUP function is identical except the third argument has a value of 3, which returns a ticket price from the third column (Balcony) of the TicketPrices table. The final part of the formula, **Ticket_Quantity*, multiplies the ticket price by the number of tickets to calculate the ticket cost.

   Trouble? If #Name? or #Value? appears in the cell J18, you might have entered the formula incorrectly. Click cell J18, compare the formula you entered with the formula in Step 1, and then edit the formula in the formula bar as needed. Also, make sure the references in your defined names are correct (see Figure 8-7).

2. Click cell **J18**, and then click the **Expand Formula Bar** button on the right side of the formula bar. The entire formula is visible in the expanded formula bar. The IF function determines which column in the TicketPrices range to use to return the ticket price. If Location in the invoice data area is Orchestra, then the condition Location="Orchestra" is TRUE and the VLOOKUP function returns a ticket price from column 2. If the subscriber requests the Balcony location, then the VLOOKUP function searches column 3 for the ticket price. The price for one ticket, as determined by the IF and VLOOKUP functions, is multiplied by the ticket quantity to calculate the total ticket cost for this transaction. See Figure 8-9.

Figure 8-9   Formula to calculate the ticket cost

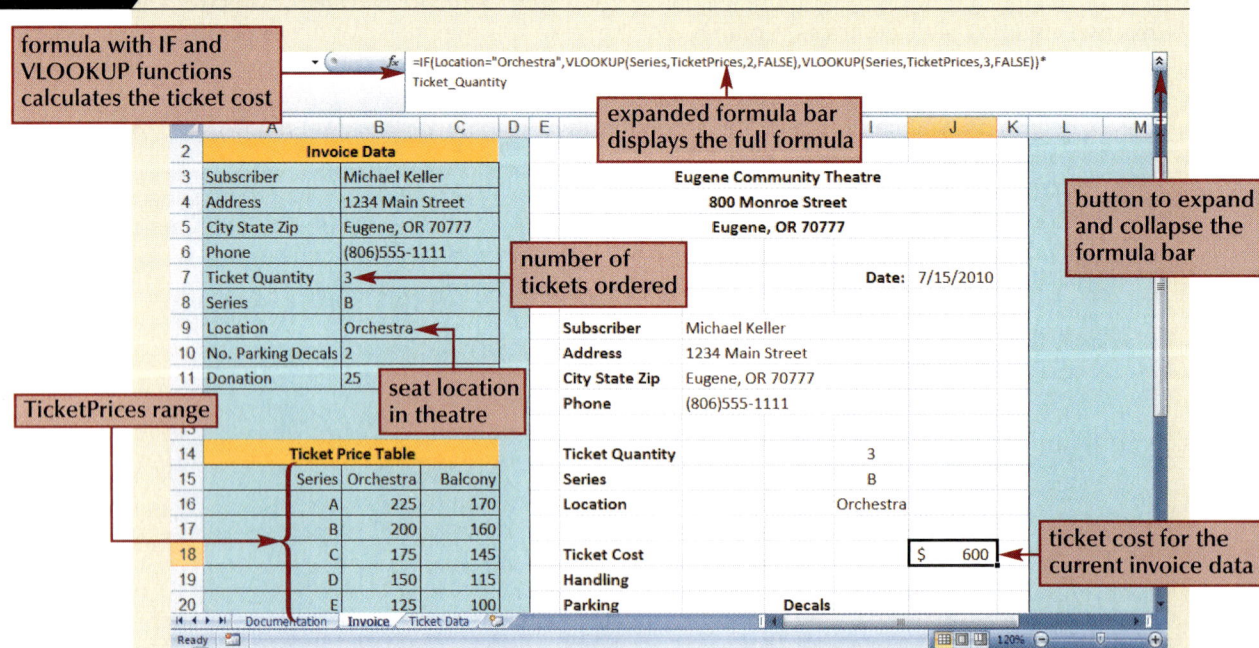

3. Click the **Collapse Formula Bar** button on the formula bar. The formula bar returns to its usual height.

You'll enter the remaining formulas needed to complete the invoice.

To enter the remaining formulas in the invoice:

1. In cell J19, enter **=HandlingCost**. The handling cost is $8, which is the amount in cell B24 in the Invoice Constants area.

2. In cell I20, enter **=Decals**. The number of parking decals ordered is 2, which is the number listed in cell B10 in the Invoice Data area.

3. In cell J20, enter **=Decals*ParkingFee**. The parking cost is $30, which is the number of decals listed in cell B10 multiplied by the parking fee in cell B25. You can see how the defined names make entering this calculation faster and the formula easier to understand.

4. In cell J21, enter **=Donation**. The donation amount is $25, which is listed in cell B11.

5. In cell J22, enter **=SUM(J18:J21)**. The SUM function adds all the costs to determine the total invoice amount of $663. See Figure 8-10.

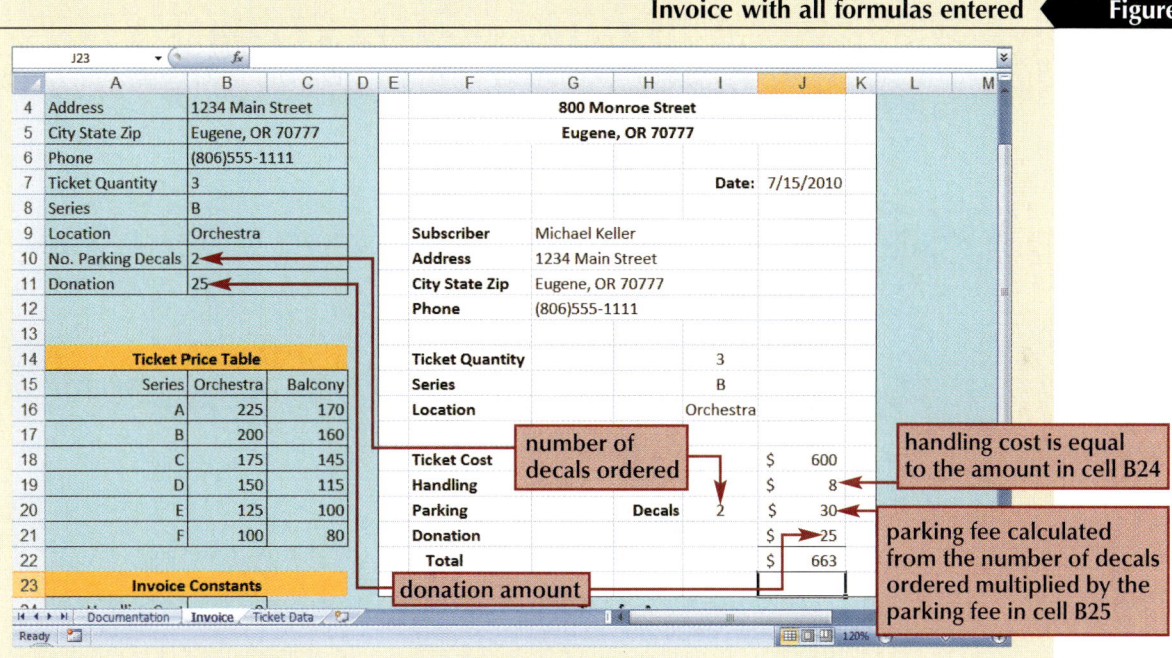

Figure 8-10 Invoice with all formulas entered

Adding Defined Names to Existing Formulas

Sometimes, you might name cells after creating formulas in the worksheet. Other times, you might not use the defined names when you create formulas (as with the first two formulas you created in the invoice for the subscriber name and address). Recall that defined names are not automatically substituted for the cell addresess in a formula. However, you can replace cell addresses in existing formulas with their defined names to make the formulas more understandable.

Tip

If a formula uses a defined name that doesn't exist, #NAME? appears in the cell. Verify the defined name is spelled correctly and that the name wasn't deleted from the worksheet.

Reference Window | Adding Defined Names to Existing Formulas

- In the Defined Names group on the Formulas tab, click the Define Name button arrow, and then click Apply Names (if the cell reference and defined name definition are in the same worksheet).
- In the Apply Names dialog box, select the names you want to apply, and then click the OK button.

or

- Edit the formula by selecting the cell reference and typing the defined name (or clicking the appropriate cell).

You'll change the two formulas you created to display the subscriber name and address in the invoice to use defined names instead of cell references.

To add defined names to existing formulas in the invoice:

1. In the Defined Names group on the Formulas tab, click the **Define Name** button arrow, and then click **Apply Names**. The Apply Names dialog box appears. See Figure 8-11.

Figure 8-11   Apply Names dialog box

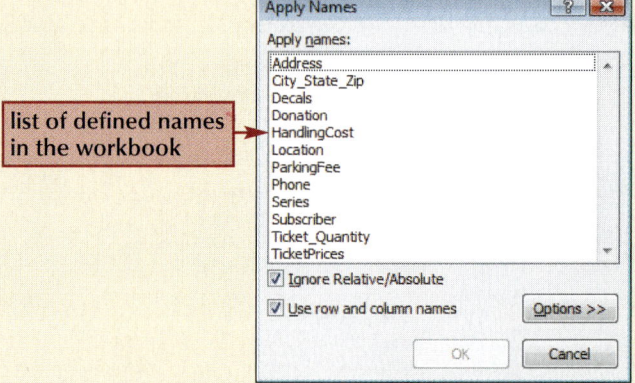

list of defined names in the workbook

You want to select only the two names you need for the existing formulas with cell references.

2. If any name is selected in the Apply names list, click that name to deselect it.

   Now that no names are selected in the Apply names list, you will select the names you want to apply to the formulas.

3. In the Apply names list, click **Address** and **Subscriber**. The two names are selected.

4. Click the **OK** button. The two selected names are applied to the formulas.

5. Click cell **G9** and verify that the formula changed to =Subscriber, and then click cell **G10** and verify that the formula changed to =Address.

Ellen wants to store the following items in the Ticket Data worksheet: subscriber name, transaction date, ticket quantity, ticket cost, and total amount owed from the invoice. Displaying these data items in the Transfer Area enables you to copy and paste all the items to the Ticket Data worksheet at once. You'll enter formulas to display the appropriate items in this section of the worksheet.

To enter formulas to display data in the Transfer Area:

1. In cell F25, enter **=Subscriber**. The formula displays the subscriber name in this cell.
2. In cell G25, enter **=J7**. The formula displays the current date.
3. In cell H25, enter **=I14**. The formula displays the number of tickets.
4. In cell I25, enter **=J18**. The formula displays the ticket cost.
5. In cell J25, enter **=J22**. The formula displays the total cost.

The worksheet contains all the formulas to create the invoice based on the subscriber information. Because Ellen relies on volunteers to enter season ticket requests into the worksheet and print invoices, she wants to be sure the values entered are correct. You will continue to work on Ellen's application by creating validation checks, which are designed to prevent users from inserting incorrect data values. You will also protect cells so that volunteers cannot accidentally overwrite or delete the formulas. You'll do both of these tasks in the next session.

Session 8.1 Quick Check | Review

1. What is a defined name? Give two advantages of using names in workbooks.
2. Describe three ways to create a name.
3. Which of the following is a valid defined name?
    a. Annual_Total
    b. 3rdQtr
    c. Annual total
4. How can you quickly select a cell or range using its name?
5. In the Report workbook, the Expenses name refers to a list of expenses stored in the range D2:D100. Currently the total expenses are calculated with the formula =SUM(D2:D100). Change this formula to use the defined name.
6. True or False? If you define names for a range referenced in an existing formula, you cannot change the formula to use the new name.

Session 8.2

Validating Data Entry

To ensure that correct data is entered and stored in a worksheet, you can use **data validation** to create a set of rules that determine what users can enter in a specific cell or range. Each **validation rule** defines criteria for the data that can be stored in a cell or range. You can specify the type of data allowed (for example, whole numbers, decimals, dates, time, text, and so forth) as well as a list or range of acceptable values (for example, the condition codes *Excellent*, *Good*, *Fair*, and *Poor*, or integers between 1 and 100).

You can also add messages for the user to that cell or range. An **input message** appears when the cell becomes active and can be used to specify the type of data the user should enter in that cell. An **error alert message** appears if a user tries to enter a value in the cell that does not meet the validation rule.

Reference Window | Validating Data

- In the Data Tools group on the Data tab, click the Data Validation button.
- Click the Settings tab.
- Click the Allow arrow, click the type of data allowed in the cell, and then enter the validation criteria for that data.
- Click the Input Message tab, and then enter a title and text for the input message.
- Click the Error Alert tab, and then, if necessary, click the Show error alert after invalid data is entered check box to insert a check mark.
- Select an alert style, and then enter the title and text for the error alert message.
- Click the OK button.

Specifying a Data Type and Acceptable Values

Ellen wants you to add three validation rules to the workbook to help ensure that volunteers enter the correct values in the designated range of the Invoice worksheet. These three rules are:

- The Ticket Quantity value in cell B7 should be between 1 and 19. In previous years, 19 was the maximum number of tickets purchased in any invoice transaction.
- The Series value in cell B8 is one of the following: A, B, C, D, E, or F.
- The Location value in cell B9 is either Orchestra or Balcony.

These validation rules will help ensure that the invoice is completed accurately.

Each of these rules specifies the type of values allowed and the validation criteria used when entering a value in a cell. For example, the first rule allows a range of numbers, the second and third rules allow only the values in a list. When you create a data validation rule, you specify what types of values you want to allow as well as the validation criteria. Figure 8-12 describes the types of values you can allow.

Tip

Each cell can have only one validation rule. Creating a second validation rule for a cell replaces the existing rule.

Figure 8-12   Allow options for the validation criteria

Value Type	Cell Accepts
Any value	Any number, text, or date; removes any existing data validation.
Whole number	Integers only; you can specify the range of acceptable integers.
Decimal	Any type of number; you can specify the range of acceptable numbers.
List	Any value in a range or entered in the Data Validation dialog box separated by commas.
Date	Dates only; you can specify the range of acceptable dates.
Time	Times only; you can specify the range of acceptable times.
Text length	Text limited to a specified number of characters.
Custom	Values based on the results of a logical formula.

You will define the validation rule for the number of season tickets.

To specify a whole number range validation rule for the number of tickets:

1. If you took a break after the previous session, make sure the Community Theatre workbook is open and the Invoice worksheet is active.

2. Click cell **B7**. This is the first cell for which you will enter a validation rule.

▶ 3. Click the **Data** tab on the Ribbon, and then, in the Data Tools group, click the **Data Validation** button. The Data Validation dialog box opens. It contains three tabs: Settings, Input Message, and Error Alert. You use the Settings tab to enter the validation rule for the active cell.

Cell B7, the number of tickets, requires an integer that is greater than 0 and less than 20.

▶ 4. On the Settings tab, click the **Allow** arrow, and then click **Whole number**. This option specifies that the number must be an integer. The Data Validation dialog box expands to display the options specific to whole numbers. The Ignore blank check box is checked, which means the validation rule is not applied when the cell is empty. If you uncheck the option, users are required to make an entry in the cell.

▶ 5. If necessary, click the **Data** arrow, and then click **between**. The dialog box reflects the selected criteria.

▶ 6. Click the **Minimum** box, and then type **1** to specify the smallest value a user can enter.

▶ 7. Press the **Tab** key to move to the Maximum box, and then type **19** to specify the largest value a user can enter. See Figure 8-13.

Settings tab in the Data Validation dialog box | Figure 8-13

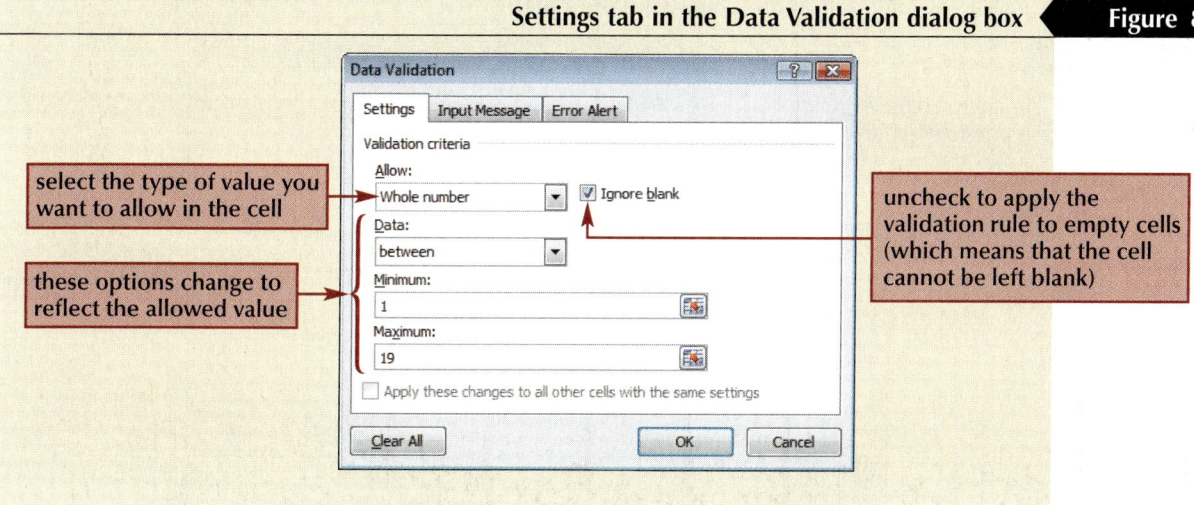

Validating Existing Data | InSight

Validation rules come into play only during data entry. If you add validation rules to a workbook that already contains data with erroneous values, Excel does not determine if any existing data is invalid. Instead, you can use the Circle Invalid Data command to help identify invalid data that is already in the workbook. (You'll learn about the Circle Invalid Data command later in this tutorial.)

Specifying an Input Message

One way to reduce the chance of a data-entry error is to display an input message when a user makes the cell active. An input message provides additional information about the type of data allowed for that cell. Input messages appear as ScreenTips next to the cell when the cell is selected. You can add an input message to a cell even if you don't set up a rule to validate the data in that cell.

Before a user enters values into the input section of the workbook, Ellen wants them to see the acceptable data values that can be entered in the cell. You will create an input message for cell B7, where users enter the ticket quantity. The input message will help minimize the chance of a volunteer entering an incorrect value.

To create an input message for the ticket quantity cell:

▶ 1. In the Data Validation dialog box, click the **Input Message** tab. You enter the input message title and text on this tab.

▶ 2. Verify that the **Show input message when cell is selected** check box contains a check mark. If you uncheck this option, you cannot enter a new input message and any existing input message will not be displayed.

▶ 3. Click in the **Title** box, and then type **Number of Tickets**. This title will appear in bold at the top of the ScreenTip above the text of the input message.

▶ 4. Press the **Tab** key to move the insertion point to the Input message box, and then type **Enter the number of tickets purchased**. This text will appear in the Screen-Tip when the cell becomes active. See Figure 8-14.

Figure 8-14   **Input Message tab in the Data Validation dialog box**

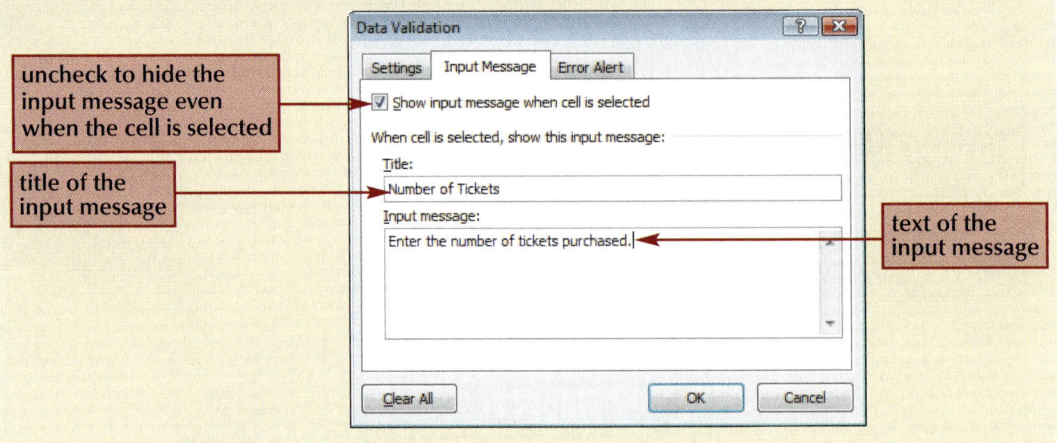

Specifying an Error Alert Style and Message

Ellen wants to display an error alert message if a volunteer enters data that violates the validation rule. The three error alert styles are Stop, Warning, and Information. The style of the error alert determines what happens after a user attempts to make an invalid entry. The Stop alert prevents the entry from being stored in the cell. The Warning alert prevents the entry from being stored in the cell, unless the user overrides the rejection and decides to continue using the data. The Information alert accepts the data value entered, but allows the user to choose to cancel the data entry.

Although ticket quantities between 1 and 19 are the norm for the theatre, occasionally a subscriber wants to purchase 20 or more tickets, and those entries should be allowed. To account for this possibility, you will create a Warning error alert that appears when a user enters a value greater than 20 or less than 1 for the number of tickets purchased. The user can verify the number entered. If the entry is correct, the user can accept the entry. If the entry is incorrect, the user can reenter a correct number.

You'll enter the Warning error alert message for the ticket quantity cell.

To create the Warning error alert message for the ticket quantity cell:

1. In the Data Validation dialog box, click the **Error Alert** tab. You use this tab to select the type of error alert and enter the message you want to appear.

2. Make sure that the **Show error alert after invalid data is entered** check box is checked. If unchecked, the error alert won't appear when an invalid value is entered in the cell.

3. Click the **Style** arrow, and then click **Warning**. This style allows the user to accept the invalid value, return to the cell and reenter a valid value, or cancel the data entry and restore the previous value to the cell.

4. Click in the **Title** box, and then type **Number of Tickets Invalid?**. This text will appear as the title of the error alert message box.

5. Press the **Tab** key to move the insertion point to the Error message box, and then type **You have entered a value less than 1 or greater than 19. Check the number you entered. If it is correct, click Yes. If it is incorrect, click No. If you are not sure, click Cancel.** (including the period). See Figure 8-15.

Tip
You might hide the input and error alert messages when only experienced users will enter data in the workbook. Because the messages are not deleted, you can show them again if a new user will enter data in the workbook.

Figure 8-15 Error Alert tab in the Data Validation dialog box

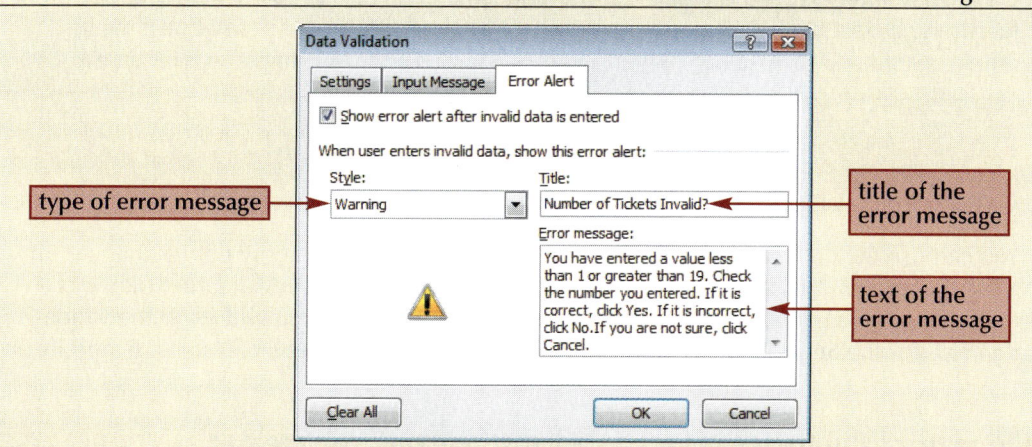

6. Click the **OK** button. The input message appears below cell B7. See Figure 8-16.

Figure 8-16 Input message for cell B7

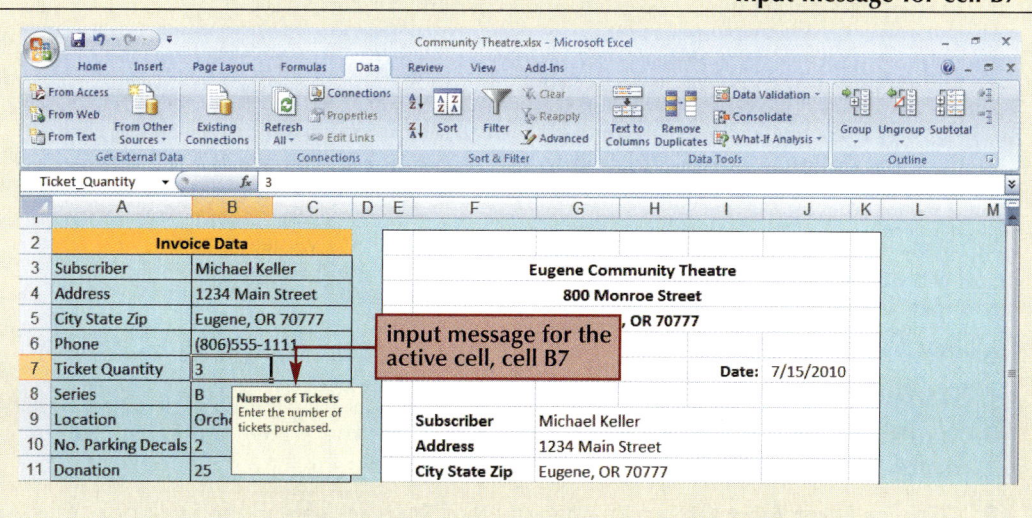

| InSight | Using Formulas to Define Complex Validation Criteria |

The built-in data validation rules are adequate for most simple needs. Sometimes, however, those rules just don't fit your specific worksheet. In those cases, you need to create a custom validation rule that includes a formula. To create a custom validation rule, open the Data Validation dialog box. On the Settings tab, click the Allow arrow, and then click Custom. You can then create the data validation formula.

The formula you specify must be in the form of a condition that returns either True or False. If True is returned, the data entered is considered valid and accepted. If False is returned, the entry is considered invalid and an error alert message is displayed. Consider the following two data validation examples.

The first example uses data validation to prevent the entry of dates that fall on Saturday or Sunday. The WEEKDAY function returns a number (1 to 7) for the date entered in the cell, and then you create a formula to display an error alert if values of 1 (Sunday) or 7 (Saturday) are detected. Assuming the date is entered in cell B2, the following formula returns False if either Saturday or Sunday is entered in cell B2:

```
=AND(WEEKDAY(B2)<>1,WEEKDAY(B2)<>7)
```

The second example uses data validation to ensure all product codes begin with the letter C. To prevent any letter except a C as the first character entered in cell A2, you would use the LEFT function to extract the first character in the cell. The following formula returns True if the first character entered in cell A2 begins with a C; otherwise, an error alert message is displayed:

```
=LEFT(A2,1) = "C"
```

Creating a List Validation Rule

You can use the data validation feature to restrict a cell to accept only entries that are on a list you create. You can create the list of valid entries in the Data Validation dialog box, or you can use a list of valid entries in a single column or row. You will enter the validation rule for the Series being requested, which is one of six values (A, B, C, D, E, and F).

To restrict the Series values to a list of entries you create:

1. Click cell **B8**. Users will enter the series data in this cell.

2. In the Data Tools group on the Data tab, click the **Data Validation** button to open the Data Validation dialog box, and then click the **Settings** tab.

3. Click the **Allow** arrow, and then click **List**. The dialog box expands to display the Source box. You can enter values directly in the Source box separated by commas, or you can select a range of valid entries in the worksheet.

4. Click the **Collapse** button next to the Source box so you can see the entire worksheet.

5. Select the range **A16:A21**, which lists the valid six entry values in a row, and then click the **Expand** button. The Data Validation dialog box returns to its full size. Next, you'll enter an input message.

6. Click the **Input Message** tab, click in the **Title** box, and then type **Series** to enter the title of the input message.

7. Click in the Input message box, and then type **Click the arrow and select one of the choices listed.** to enter the text of the input message.

8. Click the **Error Alert** tab, and then verify that **Stop** appears in the Style box. You want to prevent a user from entering a value that is not included in the list of values you specified.

▶ 9. In the Title text box, type **Invalid Series**, and then in the Error message box, type **An invalid series has been entered. Click Retry. Press the Esc key, and click the arrow to the right of cell B8. Select A, B, C, D, E, or F.** (including the period). This is the title and text for the error alert message.

▶ 10. Click the **OK** button. An arrow appears to the right of cell B8 and the input message appears in a ScreenTip.

You need to enter a third data validation rule for cell B9, which indicates the subscriber's choice of location. You will create another list validation rule that allows a user to select either Orchestra or Balcony. You will also create an error alert message.

To create a drop-down list for the Location field:

▶ 1. Click cell **B9**, and then, in the Data Tools group on the Data tab, click the **Data Validation** button. The Data Validation dialog box opens.

▶ 2. Click the **Settings** tab, select **List** in the Allow box, and then set the Source box for the range **B15:C15**. This range contain the two values you want to allow users to select for the location.

▶ 3. Click the **Input Message** tab, type **Location** in the Title box, and then type **Click the arrow and select Orchestra or Balcony** in the Input message box.

▶ 4. Click the **Error Alert** tab, verify that **Stop** is in the Style box, type **Invalid Location** in the Title box, and then type **An invalid location has been entered. Click Retry, press Esc, and click the arrow to the right of cell B9. Select Orchestra or Balcony.** (including the period) in the Error message box.

▶ 5. Click the **OK** button. The data validation rule is complete.

You will test the validation feature you've just created by entering incorrect values that violate the validation rules.

To test the data validation rules:

▶ 1. Click cell **B7**. The input message appears in a ScreenTip, indicating the type of data allowed in the cell. You will enter an invalid value to test the validation rule for the Ticket Quantity field.

▶ 2. Type **30**, and then press the **Tab** key. The Number of Tickets Invalid? message box opens, informing you that the value you entered might be incorrect. The entry 30 is incorrect; you'll enter a valid number.

▶ 3. Click the **No** button, type **3** in cell B7, and then press the **Enter** key. The data is entered in cell B7. Cell B8 is the active cell and the input message for Series appears.

You will select a value for the Series using the list.

▶ 4. Click the arrow to the right of cell B8, and then click **C**. The value is accepted.

The only way an error occurs in cells that have a list validation is if an incorrect entry is *typed* in the cell. You'll try that method.

▶ 5. In cell B8, enter **G**. The Invalid Series message box opens.

> 6. Click the **Retry** button to close the message box, press the **Esc** key to clear the current value from the cell, and then click the arrow to the right of cell B8 and select **B**. The value is accepted.
>
>   Next, you will enter the Location value. You should use the arrow to select an option but you'll intentionally type an invalid entry.
>
> 7. In cell B9, enter **Mezzanine**. The Invalid Location message box opens, indicating that the Location must be Orchestra or Balcony.
>
> 8. Click the **Retry** button, press the **Esc** key, click the arrow to the right of cell B9, and then click **Orchestra**. The value is accepted. The three validation rules you entered work as you intended.

Drawing Circles Around Invalid Data

Data validation prevents users from entering invalid data into a cell. It does not verify data that was already entered into a worksheet before the validation criteria were applied. To ensure the entire workbook contains valid data, you need to also verify any data previously entered in the workbook. You can use the Circle Invalid Data command to find and mark cells that contain invalid data. Red circles appear around any data that does not meet the validation criteria, making it simple to scan a worksheet for errors. After you correct the data in a cell, the circle disappears.

To display circles around invalid data, you must perform the following steps:

1. Apply validation rules to existing data.
2. In the Data Tools group on the Data tab, click the Data Validation button arrow, and then click Circle Invalid Data. Red circles appear around cells that contain invalid data.
3. To remove the circle from a single cell, enter valid data in the cell.
4. To hide all circles, in the Data Tools group on the Data tab, click the Data Validation button arow, and then click Clear Validation Circles.

To ensure an error-free workbook, you should use the Circle Invalid Data command to verify data entered before you set up the validation criteria or to verify data in a workbook you inherited from someone else, such as a coworker.

Protecting a Worksheet and Workbook

Another way to reduce data-entry errors is to limit access to certain parts of the workbook. When you **protect** a workbook, you limit the ability users have to make changes to the file. For example, you can prevent users from changing formulas in a worksheet, or you can keep users from deleting worksheets or inserting new ones. You can even keep users from viewing the formulas used in the workbook.

To further help the volunteers work error-free, Ellen wants to protect the contents of the Invoice and Ticket Data worksheets. She wants users to have access only to the range B3:B11, where new season request data are entered. She wants to prevent users from editing the contents of any cells in the Ticket Data worksheet.

Locking and Unlocking Cells

Every cell in a workbook has a **locked property** that determines whether changes can be made to that cell. The locked property has no impact as long as the worksheet is unprotected. However, after you protect a worksheet, the locked property controls whether the cell can be edited. You unlock a cell by turning off the locked property. By default, the locked property is turned on for each cell, and worksheet protection is turned off.

So, unless you unlock cells in a worksheet *before* protecting the worksheet, all of the cells in the worksheet will be locked, and you won't be able to make any changes in the worksheet. Usually, you will want to protect the worksheet, but leave some cells unlocked. For example, you might want to lock cells that contain formulas and formatting so they cannot be changed, but unlock cells in which you want to enter data.

To protect some—but not all—cells in a worksheet, you first turn off the locked property of cells in which data can be entered. Then, you protect the worksheet to activate the locked property for the remaining cells.

In the Invoice worksheet, you want users to be able to enter data in the range B3:B11 but not any other cell in the worksheet. To do this, you must unlock the cells in the range B3:B11.

To unlock the cells in the range B3:B11:

1. In the Invoice worksheet, select the range **B3:B11**. You want to unlock the cells in this range before you protect the worksheet.

2. Click the **Home** tab on the Ribbon, and then, in the Font group, click the **Dialog Box Launcher**. The Format Cells dialog box opens with the Font tab active.

3. Click the **Protection** tab, and then click the **Locked** check box to remove the check mark.

4. Click the **OK** button, and then click cell **A1** to deselect the highlighted cells. The cells in the range B3:B11 are unlocked.

Protecting a Worksheet

When you set up worksheet protection, you specify which actions are still available to users in the protected worksheet. For example, you can choose to allow users to insert new rows or columns or to delete rows and columns. You can limit the user to selecting only unlocked cells or allow the user to select any cell in the worksheet. These choices remain active as long as the worksheet is protected.

A protected worksheet can always be unprotected. You can also add a password to the protected worksheet that users must enter in order to turn off the protection. If you are concerned that users will turn off protection and make changes to formulas you should use a password; otherwise, it's probably best to not specify a password.

> **Tip**
>
> You can password-protect ranges of cells by selecting the ranges and clicking the Allow Users to Edit Ranges button in the Changes group on the Review tab. Specify a name for the selected cells and provide a password to protect the values in the range. Range passwords become active only when the worksheet is protected.

Protecting a Worksheet | Reference Window

- Select the cell or range you want to unlock.
- In the Font group on the Home tab, click the Dialog Box Launcher.
- In the Format Cells dialog box, click the Protection tab, click the Locked check box to remove the check mark, and then click the OK button.
- In the Changes group on the Review tab, click the Protect Sheet button.
- Enter a password (optional).
- Select all of the actions you want to allow users to take when the worksheet is protected.
- Click the OK button.

Ellen wants to protect the Invoice and Ticket Data worksheets, but she doesn't want a password specified. You will enable worksheet protection that will allow users to select any cell in those worksheets, but enter data only in the unlocked cells.

To protect the Invoice and Ticket Data worksheets:

1. Click the **Review** tab on the Ribbon, and then, in the Changes group, click the **Protect Sheet** button. The Protect Sheet dialog box opens, as shown in Figure 8-17.

Figure 8-17   **Protect Sheet dialog box**

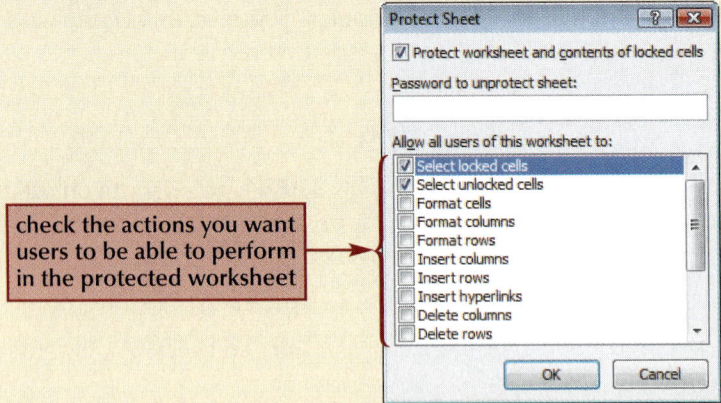

check the actions you want users to be able to perform in the protected worksheet

Tip

Keep passwords in a safe place. Remember, passwords are case sensitive. If you forget the password, it is very difficult to remove the worksheet protection.

You will leave the Password box blank because you do not want to use a password. By default, users can select locked and unlocked cells, which are all cells in the worksheet, but they can enter or edit values only in unlocked cells. Ellen wants the volunteers to be able to perform these actions.

2. Click the **OK** button. The Protect Sheet dialog box closes.

You'll test the protection by trying to edit a locked cell and then an unlocked cell in the Invoice worksheet.

3. Click cell **I14**, and then type **8**. As soon as you press any key, a dialog box opens, indicating that the cell is protected and cannot be modified.

4. Click the **OK** button.

5. Click cell **B7**, type **8**, and then press the **Enter** key. The ticket quantity is updated because you allowed editing in the range B3:B11. A user can enter and edit values in these cells. Although users can select any cell in the worksheet, they cannot make an entry in any other cell.

6. On the Quick Access Toolbar, click the **Undo** button to return the Ticket Quantity to 3.

Next, you will protect all of the cells in the Ticket Data worksheet.

7. Switch to the **Ticket Data** worksheet.

8. In the Changes group on the Review tab, click the **Protect Sheet** button to open the Protect Sheet dialog box, and then click the **OK** button to accept the default set of user actions.

You will test to see what would happen if someone tried to edit one of the cells in the Ticket Data worksheet.

▶ 9. Click cell **A2** and type **B**. A dialog box opens, indicating that the cell is protected and cannot be modified. All the cells in this worksheet are protected because no cells have been unlocked.

▶ 10. Click the **OK** button to close the dialog box.

Protecting a Workbook

The contents of the Invoice and Ticket Data worksheets, with the exception of the range B3:B11 in the Invoice worksheet, cannot be changed. However, worksheet protection applies only to the contents of the worksheet, not to the worksheet itself. So, a theatre volunteer could inadvertently rename or delete the protected worksheet. To keep the worksheets themselves from being modified, you need to protect the workbook.

You can protect both the structure and the windows of the workbook. Protecting the structure prohibits users from renaming, deleting, hiding, or inserting worksheets. Protecting the windows prohibits users from moving, resizing, closing, or hiding parts of the Excel window. The default is to protect only the structure of the workbook, not the windows used to display it. You can also add a password; however, the same guideline is true here as for protecting worksheets. Add a password only if you are concerned that others might unprotect the workbook and modify it. If you add a password, keep in mind that it is case sensitive and you cannot unprotect the workbook without it.

Protecting a Workbook | Reference Window

- In the Changes group on the Review tab, click the Protect Workbook button.
- Click the check boxes to indicate whether you want to protect the workbook's structure, windows, or both.
- Enter a password (optional).
- Click the OK button.

Ellen doesn't want users to be able to change the structure of the workbook, so you will set protection for the workbook structure, but not the window.

To protect a workbook:

▶ 1. In the Changes group on the Review tab, click the **Protect Workbook** button. The Protect Structure and Windows dialog box opens. You can choose to protect the structure, protect the windows, or both. See Figure 8-18.

Protect Structure and Windows dialog box   Figure 8-18

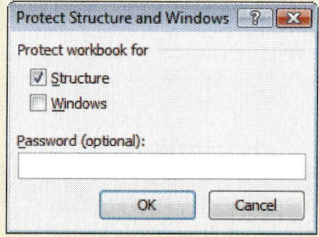

▶ 2. Make sure the **Structure** check box is checked, the Windows check box is unchecked, and the Password box is blank.

▶ 3. Click the **OK** button to protect the workbook without specifying a password.

▶ 4. Right-click the **Ticket Data** sheet tab, on the shortcut menu, notice that the Insert, Delete, Rename, Move or Copy, Tab Color, Hide, and Unhide commands are gray, indicating that the options that modify the worksheets are no longer available for the Ticket Data worksheet.

▶ 5. Press the **Esc** key to close the shortcut menu.

Unprotecting a Worksheet

Ellen is pleased with the different levels of protection that can be applied to the worksheet. At this point, you still have a lot of editing to do in the Invoice worksheet, so you'll turn off worksheet protection in that worksheet. Later, when you've completed your modifications, Ellen can turn worksheet protection back on.

To turn off worksheet protection for the Invoice worksheet:

Tip
You can also remove workbook protection; in the Changes group on the Review tab, click the Unprotect Workbook button.

▶ 1. Switch to the **Invoice** worksheet.

▶ 2. In the Changes group on the Review tab, click the **Unprotect Sheet** button. Worksheet protection is removed from the Invoice worksheet. The button changes back to the Protect Sheet button. If you had assigned a password when you protected the worksheet, you would have had to enter the password to remove worksheet protection.

Adding Worksheet Comments

Providing documentation is important for a successful application. In addition to including a documentation sheet that provides an overview of the workbook, you used defined names instead of cell addresses to make it easier to write and understand formulas and then you pasted a list of these names in the worksheet for you and others to see. You also used input messages to assist with data validation. Another source of documentation you can use in a workbook is comments. A **comment** is a text box that is attached to a specific cell in a worksheet. Comments are often used in workbooks to: (a) explain the contents of a particular cell, such as a complex formula, (b) provide instructions to users, and (c) share ideas and notes from several users collaborating on a project.

Reference Window | Inserting a Comment

- Click the cell to which you want to attach a comment.
- Right-click the cell, and then click Insert Comment on the shortcut menu (or in the Comments group on the Review tab, click the New Comment button).
- Type the comment into the comment box.

Ellen wants you to insert a brief note about entering data from the order form into the input section in cell A2 and a note explaining how the IF and VLOOKUP functions are used to determine the cost of theatre tickets in cell J18.

To insert comments in cells A2 and J18:

1. In the Invoice worksheet, right-click cell **A2**, and then click **Insert Comment** on the shortcut menu. A text box opens to the right of cell A2. The user name for your installation of Excel appears in bold at the top of the box. A small red triangle appears in the upper-right corner of the cell.

2. Type **Enter all data from the order form into cells B3 through B12** in the text box. An arrow points from the text box to cell A2 which contains the comment. Selection handles appear around the text box, which you can use to resize the box; you can drag the text box by its hatched border to move the comment to a new location in the worksheet. See Figure 8-19.

Comment added to cell A2   **Figure 8-19**

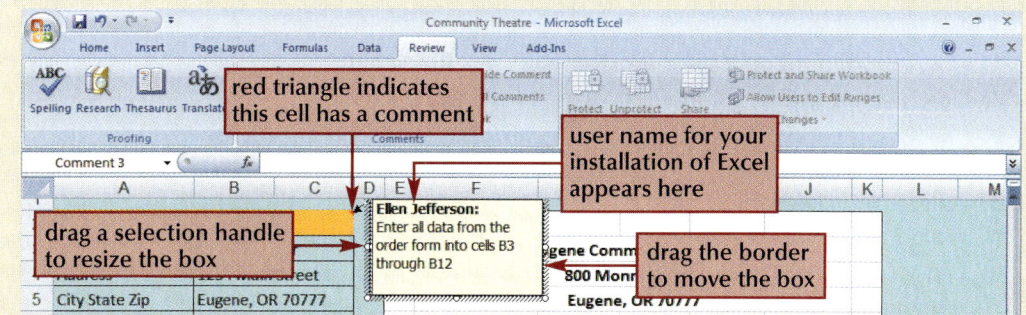

3. Click cell **B12** to hide the comment. The comment disappears. A small red triangle remains in the upper-right corner of cell A2 to indicate this cell contains a comment.

   The comment in cell A2 should reference the range B3:B11. You'll edit the comment.

4. Click cell **A2**, and then, in the Comments group on the Review tab, click the **Edit Comment** button. The text box appears with the insertion point at the end of the comment text.

5. In the text box, change B12 to **B11**.

6. Click any cell to hide the text box, and then point to cell **A2** to view the edited comment.

   Next, you'll add a comment to cell J18.

7. Click cell **J18**, and then, in the Comments group on the Review tab, click the **New Comment** button. A comment box opens to the right of cell J18.

8. Type **This IF function determines whether to use a VLOOKUP function referencing column 2 or 3 of the Ticket Price table** in the text box.

9. Drag the lower-right selection handle down to increase the size of the text box to fit the comment.

10. Click cell **I17** to hide the comment. A small red triangle remains in the upper-right corner of cell J18 to indicate it contains a comment.

11. Point to cell **J18** to see the comment.

    Ellen decides that the volunteers don't need to know how the ticket cost is calcuated. You'll delete the comment in cell J18.

Tip

To keep an active cell's comment on screen, in the Comments group on the Review tab, click the Show/Hide Comment button. Click the button again to hide the active cell's comment. To show or hide all the comments in a worksheet, click the Show All Comments button.

> 12. Click cell **J18**, and then, in the Comments group on the Review tab, click the **Delete** button. The comment is deleted, and the red triangle in the upper-right corner of cell J18 is removed.

In this session, you used data validation to help ensure that all values entered in the Invoice worksheet are accurate. You created validation rules that included input messages and error alert messages. You learned how to protect and unprotect both the worksheet and the workbook. In addition, you learned how to use comments to add notes to specific cells in the workbook. In the next session, you'll automate some of the steps in the application by recording macros.

Review | Session 8.2 Quick Check

1. How do you turn on data validation for a specified cell?
2. How do you specify an input message for a cell?
3. Describe the three types of error alert messages Excel can display when a user violates a validation rule.
4. What is a locked cell?
5. What is the difference between worksheet protection and workbook protection?
6. Can you rename a protected worksheet? Explain why or why not.
7. What are the steps for editing a comment?

Session 8.3

Working with Macros

Ellen needs to print the entire Invoice worksheet, which includes the input area, transfer area, and invoice, for her paper files. In addition, she needs to print only the invoice to send to the season subscriber. Each printout has different custom headers and footers. In addition, data from the invoice needs to be transferred to the Ticket Data worksheet. Ellen wants to simplify these tasks so volunteers don't need to repeat the same actions for each subscriber order and also to reduce the possibility of errors being introduced during the repetitive process.

You can automate any task you perform repeatedly with a macro. A **macro** is a series of stored commands that can be run whenever you need to perform the task. For example, you can create a macro to print a worksheet, insert a set of dates and values, or import data from a text file and store it in Excel. Macros perform repetitive tasks more quickly than you can. And, after the macro is created, you can be assured that no mistakes will occur from performing the same task over and over again.

To create and run macros, you need to use the Developer tab. By default, this tab is not displayed on the Ribbon, so you'll display it. The Developer tab has three groups: one for code, one for controls, and one for XML. You'll use the Code group when working with macros.

To display the Developer tab on the Ribbon:

> 1. If you took a break after the previous session, make sure the Community Theatre workbook is open and the Invoice worksheet is active.
>
> 2. Look for the **Developer** tab on the Ribbon. If you see the Developer tab, continue with Step 5. If you do not see the Developer tab, continue with Step 3.

3. Click the **Office Button**, and then click the **Excel Options** button. The Excel Options dialog box opens with the Popular options displayed. See Figure 8-20.

Popular category in the Excel Options dialog box **Figure 8-20**

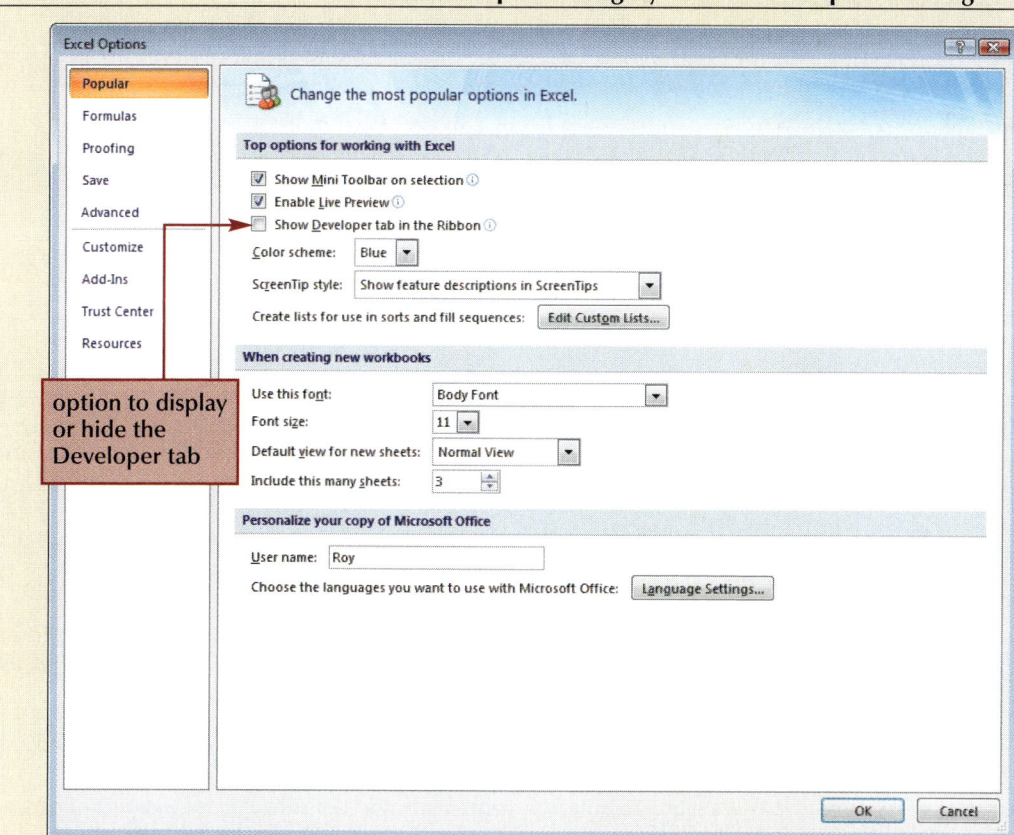

4. In the Top options for working with Excel section, click the **Show Developer tab in the Ribbon** check box to insert a check mark, and then click the **OK** button. The Developer tab appears on the Ribbon.

5. Click the **Developer** tab. See Figure 8-21.

Developer tab on the Ribbon **Figure 8-21**

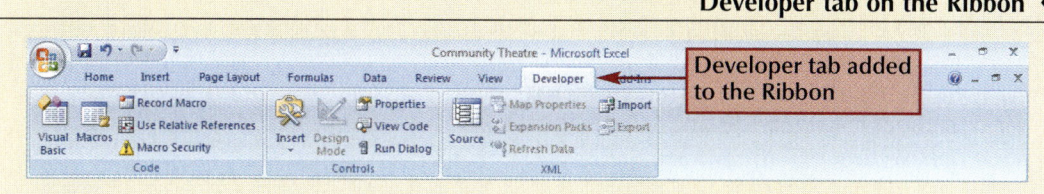

Protecting Against Macro Viruses

In recent years, viruses have been attached as macros to files created in Excel and other Office programs. When unsuspecting users opened these infected workbooks, Excel automatically ran the attached virus-infected macro. **Macro viruses** are a type of virus that uses a program's own macro programming language to distribute the virus. Most macro viruses are not harmful and do not affect data in any way. For example, one macro virus changed the title bar text from *Microsoft Excel* to *Microsofa Excel*. Occasionally, macro viruses are destructive and can modify or delete files that may not be recoverable. Because it is possible for a macro to contain a virus, Microsoft Office 2007 provides several options from which you can choose to set a security level you feel comfortable with.

Macro Security Settings

The **macro security settings** control what Excel will do about macros in a workbook when you open that workbook. For example, one user may choose to run macros only if they are "digitally signed" by a developer who is on a list of trusted sources. Another user might want to disable all macros in workbooks and see a notification when a workbook contains macros. The user can then elect to enable the macros. Excel has four macro security settings, as described in Figure 8-22.

Figure 8-22 — Macro security settings

Setting	Description
Disable all macros without notification	All macros in all workbooks are disabled and no security alerts about macros are displayed. Use this setting if you don't want macros to run.
Disable a macro with notification	All macros in all workbooks are disabled, but security alerts appear when the workbook contains a macro. Use this default setting to choose on a case-by-case basis whether to run a macro.
Disable all macros except digitally signed macros	The same as the *Disable a macro with notification* setting except any macro signed by a trusted publisher runs if you have already trusted the publisher. Otherwise, security alerts appear when a workbook contains a macro.
Enable all macros	All macros in all workbooks run. Use this setting temporarily in such cases as when developing an application that contains macros. This setting is not recommended for regular use.

You set macro security in the Trust Center using the Security dialog box. The **Trust Center** is a central location for all the security settings in Office 2007. By default, all potentially dangerous content, such as macros and workbooks with external links, is blocked without warning. If content is blocked, the Message Bar (also called the trust bar), located under the Ribbon, appears, notifying you that some content was disabled. You can click the Message Bar to open a dialog box with all of the disabled content and options for enabling or disabling that content.

In Office 2007 you can define a set of locations (file path) where you can place files you consider trustworthy. This feature is known as *Trusted Locations*. Any workbook opened from a trusted location is considered "safe" and content such as macros will work without having to respond to additional security questions to use the workbook.

Tutorial 8 Developing an Excel Application | Excel **EX 423**

Setting Macro Security in Excel | Reference Window

- In the Code group on the Developer tab, click the Macro Security button.
- Click the option button for the security setting you want.
- Click the OK button.

or

- Click the Office Button, and then click the Excel Options button.
- Click the Trust Center category, and then click the Trust Center Settings button.
- Click the Macro Settings category, and then select the option button for the security setting you want.
- Click the OK button.

Ellen wants some protection against macro viruses, so she suggests you set the security level to *Disable all macros with notification*. When you open a file with macros, the macros will be disabled and a security alert will appear, allowing you to activate the macros if you believe the workbook comes from a trusted source.

To set the macro security level:

1. In the Code group on the Developer tab, click the **Macro Security** button. The Trust Center dialog box opens with the Macro Settings category displayed.

2. In the Macro Settings section, click the **Disable all macros with notification** option button if it is not selected. See Figure 8-23.

Macro Settings in the Trust Center dialog box | Figure 8-23

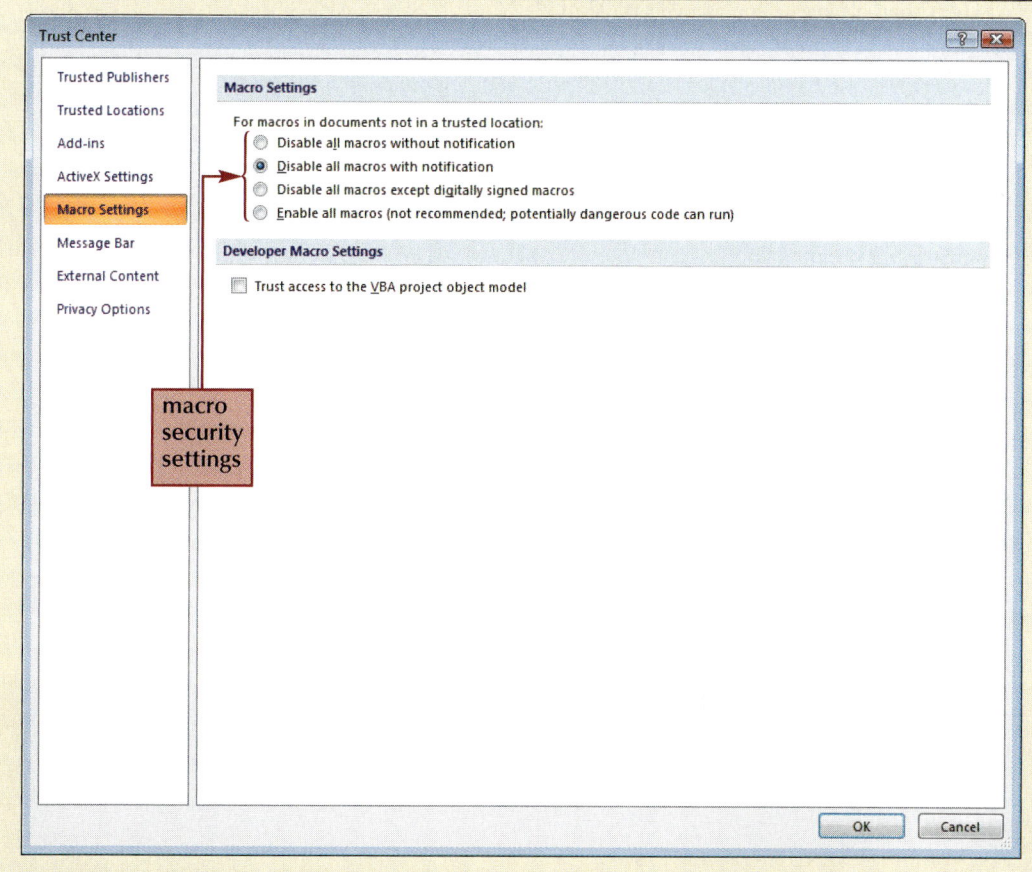

> 3. Click the **OK** button.

Each time you open a workbook that contains a macro that the Trust Center detects, the macro is disabled and a Message Bar appears below the Ribbon with the Security Warning that macros have been disabled. Click the Options button to open a security dialog box with the option to enable the macro or leave it disabled. If you developed the workbook or trust the person who sent you the workbook, click the Enable this content option button to run the macros in the workbook.

| InSight | **Using Digital Signatures with Macros** |

A **digital signature** is like a seal of approval. It's often used to identify the author of a workbook that contains macros. You add a digital signature as the last step before you distribute a file. Before you can add a digital signature to a workbook, you need to obtain a digital ID (also called a digital certificate) that proves your identity. Digital certificates are typically issued by a certificate authority. After you have a digital certificate, do the following to digitally sign a workbook:

1. Click the Office Button, point to Prepare, and then click Add a Digital Signature to open the Sign dialog box.
2. Click in the Purpose for signing this document box, and then type a reason why you are adding a digital signature to this workbook.
3. Click the Sign button. The invisible digital signature does not appear within the workbook, but users will see the Signatures button on the status bar.

By digitally signing a workbook that contains a macro you intend to publicly distribute, you assure others of two things: (1) the identity of the creator of the macro, and (2) the macro has not been altered since the digital signature was created.

When you open a digitally signed file, you can see who the author is and decide whether the information in the file is authentic and you trust that the macros in the workbook are safe to run.

The digital signature is removed any time a file is saved after the signature has been added to the file. Therefore, no one (including the original workbook author) can open a digitally signed file, make changes to the workbook, save the workbook, and then send the file to another user with the digital signature intact. The original author must digitally resign the modified workbook.

Recording a Macro

You can create an Excel macro in one of two ways: You can use the macro recorder to record keystrokes and mouse actions as you perform them, or you can enter a series of commands in the **Visual Basic for Applications (VBA)** programming language. The macro recorder can record only those actions you perform with the keyboard or mouse. The macro recorder is a good choice for creating simple macros. For more sophisticated macros, you might need to write VBA code directly in the Visual Basic Editor.

For Ellen's application, the tasks you need to perform can all be done with the keyboard and the mouse, so you will use the macro recorder to record the three macros. One macro will show the invoice in Print Preview, a second macro will show the entire Invoice worksheet in Print Preview, and a third macro will transfer data from the Invoice worksheet to the Ticket Data worksheet.

| InSight

Planning and Recording a Macro

Advance planning and practice help to ensure you create an error-free macro. First, decide what you want to accomplish. Then, consider the best way to achieve those results. Next, practice the keystrokes and mouse actions before you actually record the macro. This may seem like extra work, but it reduces the chance of error when you actually record the macro. As you set up the macro, consider the following:

- Choose a descriptive name that helps you recognize the macro's purpose.
- Weigh the benefits of selecting a shortcut key against its drawbacks. Although a shortcut key is an easy way to run a macro, you are limited to one-letter shortcuts, which can make it difficult to remember the purpose of each shortcut key. In addition, the macro shortcut keys will override the standard Office shortcuts for the workbook.
- Store the macro with the current workbook unless the macro can be used with other workbooks.
- Include a description that provides an overview of the macro and perhaps your name and contact information.

Ellen provides you with an outline of the actions needed for the macro to show the invoice in Print Preview. These are:

1. Set the print area (E2:J23).
2. Define the Page Layout setting with the custom heading I N V O I C E.
3. Display the invoice in Print Preview.
4. Close the Print Preview window.
5. Make cell B3 the active cell.

Each macro must have a unique name that begins with a letter. The macro name can be up to 255 characters, including letters, numbers, and the underscore symbol. The macro name cannot include spaces or special characters. It is helpful to use a descriptive name that describes the macro's purpose. You can assign a shortcut key to run the macro directly from the keyboard. You can also add a description of the macro. Finally, a macro needs to be stored somewhere. By default, the macro is stored in the current workbook, making the macro available in only that workbook when it is open. Another option is to store the macro in the **Personal Macro workbook**, a hidden workbook named *Personal.xlsb* that opens whenever you start Excel, making the macro available anytime you use Excel. The Personal Macro workbook stores commonly used macros that apply to many workbooks. It is most convenient for users on stand-alone computers. Finally, you can store the macro in a new workbook. Keep in mind, the new workbook must be open to use the macro. For example, an accountant might store a set of macros that help with end-of-the-month tasks in a separate workbook.

Recording a Macro | Reference Window

- In the Code group on the Developer tab, click the Record Macro button.
- Enter a name for the macro, and specify the location to store the macro.
- Specify a shortcut key (optional).
- Enter a description of the macro (optional).
- Click the OK button to start the macro recorder.
- Perform the tasks you want to automate.
- Click the Stop Recording button.

For Ellen's application, you'll record a macro named *PrintPreviewInvoice*, assigned a keyboard shortcut, with a description, stored in the Community Theatre workbook. Macro shortcut keys are used to run a macro. Assigning a shortcut key overrides the default Office shortcut for the open workbook. Therefore, pressing the Ctrl+p keys runs the PrintPreviewInvoice macro, overriding the default Office 2007 shortcut for printing a selected area. Some people find macro shortcut keys a quick way to run a macro; others dislike them because they lose the original function of the shortcut key. It's a personal preference.

You'll start the macro recorder.

To start the macro recorder:

▶ 1. In the Code group on the Developer tab, click the **Record Macro** button. The Record Macro dialog box opens. The Macro name box displays a default name for the macro that consists of the word *Macro* followed by a number that is one greater than the number of macros already recorded in the workbook during the current Excel session. See Figure 8-24.

Figure 8-24   **Record Macro dialog box**

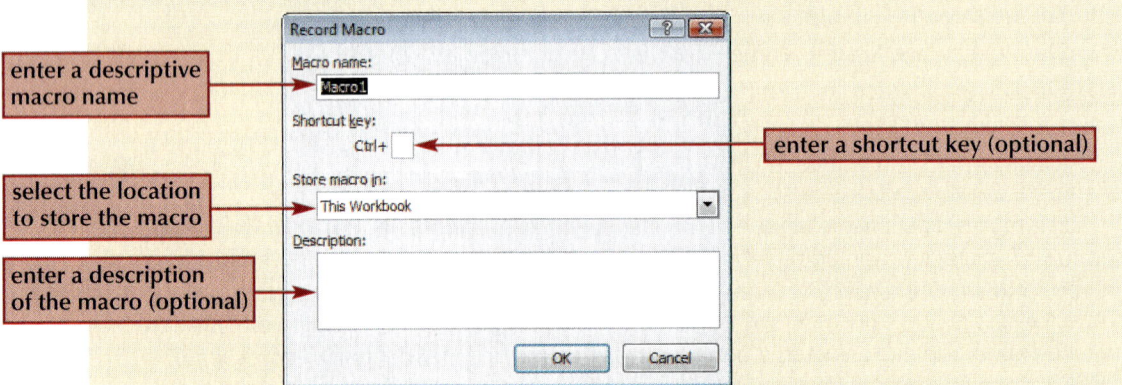

▶ 2. In the Macro name box, type **PrintPreviewInvoice** to change the default name to a more descriptive one, and then press the **Tab** key.

▶ 3. In the Shortcut key box, type **p** to set Ctrl+p as the shortcut to run the macro from the keyboard, and then press the **Tab** key.

▶ 4. Verify that **This Workbook** appears in the Store macro in box to store the macro in the Community Theatre workbook, and then press the **Tab** key.

▶ 5. In the Description box, type **Created 7/15/2010. Print Preview of invoice area: range E2:K23.** (including the period) to enter notes about the macro.

▶ 6. Click the **OK** button. The workbook enters macro record mode. The Record Macro button in the Code group on the Developer tab changes to the Stop Recording button, which also appears on the status bar.

From this point on, every mouse click and keystroke you perform will be recorded and stored as part of the PrintPreviewInvoice macro. For that reason, it's very important to follow the instructions in the next steps precisely. Take your time as you perform each step, reading the entire step carefully first. After you finish recording the keystrokes, you click the Stop Recording button to turn off the macro recorder.

To record the PrintPreviewInvoice macro:

▶ 1. Click the **Page Layout** tab on the Ribbon.

▶ 2. Click cell **E2**, press and hold the **Shift** key, click cell **K23**, and then release the Shift key to select the range E2:K23. This range contains the invoice area.

▶ 3. In the Page Setup group, click the **Print Area** button, and then click **Set Print Area**. The invoice area is set as the print area. Next, you'll insert a custom header.

▶ 4. In the Page Setup group, click the **Dialog Box Launcher** to open the Page Setup dialog box, click the **Header/Footer** tab, click the **Custom Header** button to open the Header dialog box, click in the **Center section** box, type **I N V O I C E**, and then click the **OK** button.

▶ 5. Click the **Margins** tab, verify that the **Horizontally** check box is checked to center the invoice on the page.

▶ 6. Click the **Print Preview** button. The invoice appears in Print Preview. Next, you will close the Print Preview window and set cell B3 as the active cell.

▶ 7. Click the **Close Print Preview** button to return to Normal view. Although this step is not intuitive, you need to close Print Preview before you can continue recording the macro or stop recording the macro. When you run the macro, Excel will automatically stop at the point where the Print Preview window opens to give the user the option of printing or closing Print Preview without printing.

▶ 8. In the Invoice worksheet, click cell **B3**. You've completed all the steps in the PrintPreviewInvoice macro. You'll turn off the macro recorder.

▶ 9. Click the **Stop Recording** button on the status bar. The button changes to the Record macro button.

   Trouble? If you made a mistake while recording the macro, close the Community Theatre workbook without saving your changes. Reopen the workbook, and then repeat all the steps beginning with the "To start the macro recorder" steps.

   Trouble? If you need to save your work before completing the tutorial, read pages EX 439–440 to learn how to save a workbook with macros.

> **Tip**
> You can also turn off the macro recorder by clicking the Stop Recording button in the Code group on the Developer tab.

Running a Macro

Next, you'll test the macro to ensure it works as intended. To run the macro you created, you can either use the shortcut key you specified or select the macro in the Macro dialog box and click the Run button.

Running a Macro | Reference Window

- Press the shortcut key assigned to the macro.
or
- In the Code group on the Developer tab, click the Macros button.
- Select the macro from the list of macros, and then click the Run button.

To run the PrintPreviewInvoice macro:

1. Click the **Developer** tab on the Ribbon, and then, in the Code group, click the **Macros** button. The Macro dialog box opens, as shown in Figure 8-25. This dialog box lists all of the macros in the open workbooks. You can select a macro, and then run it, edit the macro with VBA, run the macro one step at a time so you can determine in which step an error occurs, or delete it.

Figure 8-25 | Macro dialog box

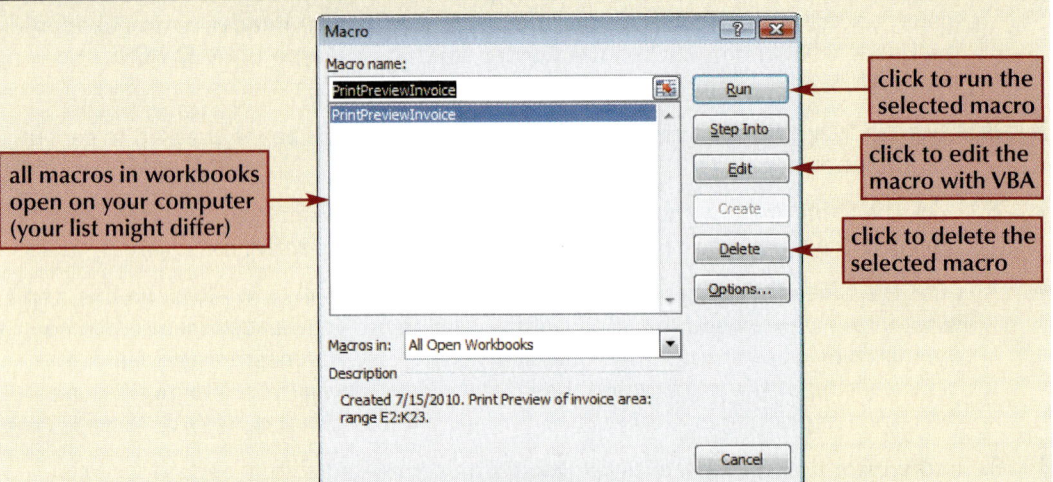

2. Verify that **PrintPreviewInvoice** is selected in the list, and then click the **Run** button. The PrintPreviewInvoice macro runs and the invoice appears in Print Preview. You can now print the invoice or close Print Preview without printing. Notice that the PrintPreviewInvoice macro did not run very quickly and caused some screen flicker. You will fix this later in the tutorial.

    Trouble? If the PrintPreviewInvoice macro did not run properly, you might have made a mistake in the steps while recording the macro. Click the Close Print Preview button in the Preview group on the Print Preview tab. Click the Developer tab, and then, in the Code group, click the Macros button. Select the PrintPreviewInvoice macro and then click the Delete button. Click the OK button to confirm the deletion, and then repeat all the steps beginning with the "To start the macro recorder" steps.

3. In the Preview group on the Print Preview tab, click the **Close Print Preview** button. The workbook returns to Normal view and cell B3 is the active cell. The macro works correctly. If you had printed the invoice, the Print Preview window would automatically close after the invoice printed.

    Next, you will test the shortcut keys you used for the PrintPreviewInvoice macro.

4. Press the **Ctrl+p** keys. The PrintPreviewInvoice macro runs. The invoice is displayed in the Print Preview window.

    You will not print the invoice.

5. In the Preview group, click the **Close Print Preview** button. The worksheet returns to Normal view and cell B3 is the active cell. As an alternative, you could select the Print command on the Print Preview tab to print the invoice. After printing the invoice, the worksheet would return to Normal view and cell B3 would be the active cell.

    Trouble? If your macro doesn't end on its own, you need to end it. Press the Ctrl+Break keys to stop the macro from running.

Tutorial 8 Developing an Excel Application | Excel **EX 429**

How Edits Can Affect Macros | InSight

Be careful when making seemingly small changes to your workbook, as these can have a great impact on your macros. If a runtime error (an error that occurs while running a macro) appears when you run a macro that has worked in the past, some part of the macro code no longer makes sense to Excel. For example, simply adding a space to a worksheet name can affect a macro that references the worksheet. If you recorded a macro that referenced a worksheet named *TicketData* (no spaces in the name) that you later changed to *Ticket Data* (space added to the name), the macro no longer works because the TicketData worksheet no longer exists. You can record the macro again, or you could edit the macro in VBA changing *TicketData* to *Ticket Data*.

Next, you'll record the macro to print the entire worksheet. The steps will be similar to the first macro, except that you'll set the print area to A1:K25, display *OFFICE COPY* as the custom header, display Ellen's name and title in the left section of the custom footer, and scale the worksheet to fit on one page. For this macro, you'll use the Ctrl+s shortcut keys.

To record the PrintPreviewEntireSheet macro:

1. On the status bar, click the **Record Macro** button. The Record Macro dialog box opens.

2. In the Macro name box, type **PrintPreviewEntireSheet** to enter a descriptive name, and then press the **Tab** key.

3. In the Shortcut key box, type **s**, and then press the **Tab** key twice. The This Workbook option appears in the Store macro in box.

4. In the Description box, type **Created 7/15/2010. Print Preview of entire worksheet area: range A1:K25**, and then click the **OK** button. The macro recorder is on.

5. Click the **Page Layout** tab on the Ribbon.

6. In the Invoice worksheet, select the range **A1:K25**, in the Page Setup group, click the **Print Area** button, and then click **Set Print Area**.

7. In the Page Setup group, click the **Dialog Box Launcher** to open the Page Setup dialog box, click the **Header/Footer** tab, click the **Custom Header** button, select the text in the Center section box, type **O F F I C E   C O P Y**, and then click the **OK** button.

8. Click the **Custom Footer** button, click in the **Left section** box, type **Ellen Jefferson, Business Manager**, and then click the **OK** button.

9. Click the **Page** tab in the Page Setup dialog box, in the Scaling section, click the **Fit To** option button, and then confirm that **1** appears in both Fit to boxes.

10. Click the **Print Preview** button to display the invoice in Print Preview.

11. Click the **Close Print Preview** button, and then click cell **B3**.

12. Click the **Stop Recording** button on the status bar. The button changes to the Record Macro button, and the macro recorder is turned off.

You'll use the shortcut key method to test both the PrintPreviewEntireSheet and PrintPreviewInvoice macros.

To test the PrintPreviewEntireSheet and PrintPreviewInvoice macros:

▶ 1. Press the **Ctrl+s** keys. The PrintPreviewEntireSheet macro runs.

▶ 2. In the Preview group on the Print Preview tab, click the **Close Print Preview** button. The worksheet returns to Normal view and cell B3 is the active cell. The PrintPreviewEntireSheet macro was successful.

   Trouble? If the PrintPreviewEntireSheet macro did not run properly, you might have made a mistake in the steps while recording it. Click the Close Print Preview button in the Preview group on the Print Preview tab. Click the Developer tab, and then, in the Code group, click the Macros button. Select the PrintPreviewEntireSheet macro, and then click the Delete button to remove the macro. Click the OK button to confirm the deletion, and then repeat all the steps beginning with the "To record the PrintPreviewEntireSheet macro" to record and test the macro again.

   Next, you'll run the PrintPreviewInvoice macro.

▶ 3. Press the **Ctrl+p** keys. The PrintPreviewInvoice macro runs.

▶ 4. In the Preview group on the Print Preview tab, click the **Close Print Preview** button.

Creating the TransferData Macro

You need to record one more macro. The data you entered earlier in the input section of the Invoice worksheet was never added to the Ticket Data worksheet. Ellen wants to add this data from the purchase of season tickets to the next available blank row in the Ticket Data worksheet. The macro that you'll create will fix that problem. The actions of this macro will be as follows:

- Switch to the Ticket Data worksheet.
- Turn off worksheet protection in the Ticket Data worksheet.
- Switch to the Invoice worksheet.
- Select and copy the Transfer Area to the Clipboard.
- Switch to the Ticket Data worksheet.
- Go to cell A1, and then go to last row in ticket data table.
- Turn on Relative References. The Relative Reference button controls how Excel records the act of selecting a range in the worksheet. By default, the macro will select the same cells regardless of which cell is first selected because the macro records a selection using absolute cell references. If you want a macro to select cells regardless of the position of the active cell when you run the macro, set the macro recorder to record relative cell references.
- Move down one row.
- Turn off Relative References.
- Paste values to the Ticket Data worksheet.
- Go to cell A1.
- Turn on worksheet protection.
- Switch to the Invoice worksheet, and go to cell A1.

Ellen wants you to name this new macro *TransferData*. You'll assign the Ctrl+t keys as the shortcut.

To record the TransferData macro:

1. Click the **Record Macro** button on the status bar to open the Record Macro dialog box, type **TransferData** in the Macro name box, type **t** in the Shortcut key box, type **Created 7/15/2010. Copy values in the transfer area in the Invoice worksheet to Ticket Data worksheet** in the Description box, and then click the **OK** button. The macro recorder is on.

2. Click the **Ticket Data** sheet tab, click the **Review** tab on the Ribbon, and then, in the Changes group, click the **Unprotect Sheet** button to turn off protection.

3. Click the **Invoice** sheet tab, and then select the range **F25:J25** in the Transfer Area.

4. Click the **Home** tab on the Ribbon, and then, in the Clipboard group, click the **Copy** button.

5. Click the **Ticket Data** sheet tab, click cell **A1**, and then press the **End+↓** keys to go to the last row with values.

6. Click the **Developer** tab on the Ribbon, and then, in the Code group, click the **Use Relative References** button. Relative references are on so you don't always go to row 5 in the Ticket Data worksheet

7. Click the **↓** key to move to the first blank cell in the worksheet.

8. In the Code group on the Developer tab, click the **Use Relative References** button. The Use Relative References button is toggled off.

9. Click the **Home** tab on the Ribbon, in the Clipboard group, click the **Paste button arrow**, and then click **Paste Values**. This option pastes the values in the transfer area to the data area rather than the formulas entered in the transfer area.

   Trouble? If #REF! appears in row 6 of the Ticket Data worksheet, you clicked the Paste button instead of the Paste Values button. Stop recording the macro. Delete the macro and begin recording the macro again.

10. Click cell **A1**, click the **Review** tab on the Ribbon, click the **Protect Sheet** button, and then click the **OK** button.

11. Click the **Invoice** sheet tab, and then click cell **B3**.

12. Click the **Stop Recording** button on the status bar. The macro recorder turns off.

You've completed recording the TransferData macro. Next, you'll test whether it works. Ellen has a new season ticket request to add to the worksheet. You'll enter this data as you test the TransferData macro.

To test the TransferData macro:

1. Enter the following data into the range B3:B11, pressing the **Enter** key after each entry.

   Kate Holland
   186 Pinetop Drive
   Eugene, OR 70777
   (888) 555–1234
   2 tickets, D series, Balcony
   1 decal, 40 donation

You'll print preview the invoice, and then you'll use the macro to transfer the data.

▶ 2. Press the **Ctrl+p** keys to display the invoice in Print Preview, and then in the Preview group on the Print Preview tab, click the **Close Print Preview** button.

▶ 3. Press the **Ctrl+t** keys. The TransferData macro runs and the data transfers to the Ticket Data worksheet.

▶ 4. Switch to the **Ticket Data** worksheet, verify the data for Kate Holland transferred, and then switch to the **Invoice** worksheet.

Fixing Macro Errors

If a macro does not work correctly, you can fix it. Sometimes, you'll find a mistake when you test a macro you just created. Other times, you might not discover that error until later. No matter when you find an error in a macro, you have the following options:

- Rerecord the macro using the same macro name.
- Delete the recorded macro, and then record the macro again.
- Run the macro one step at a time to locate the problem, and then use one of the previous methods to correct the problem.

You can delete or edit a macro by opening the Macro dialog box (shown earlier in Figure 8-25), selecting the macro from the list, and then clicking the appropriate button. To rerecord the macro, simply restart the macro recorder and enter the same macro name you used earlier. Excel overwrites the previous version of the macro.

Working with the Macro Editor

Ellen is concerned about the flickering screen activity that occurs when the PrintPreview-Invoice macro is running. She thinks that this might be disconcerting to some volunteers. Eric Dean, an Office application developer, says you can speed up the macro and eliminate the flicker using a simple VBA command.

| Reference Window | **Editing a Macro** |

- In the Code group on the Developer tab, click the Macros button, select the macro in the Macro name list, and then click the Edit button (or in the Code group on the Developer tab, click the Visual Basic button).
- Use the Visual Basic Editor to edit the macro code.
- Click File on the menu bar, and then click Close and Return to Microsoft Excel.

To view the code of the PrintPreviewInvoice macro, you need to open the **Visual Basic Editor**, which is a separate application that works with Excel and all of the Office programs to edit and manage VBA code. You can access the Visual Basic Editor through the Macro dialog box.

To view the code for the PrintPreviewInvoice macro:

▸ 1. Click the **Developer** tab on the Ribbon, and then, in the Code group, click the **Macros** button. The Macro dialog box opens.

▸ 2. Click **PrintPreviewInvoice** in the Macro name list, and then click the **Edit** button. The Visual Basic Editor opens as a separate program, consisting of several windows. The Code window contains the VBA code generated by the macro recorder. See Figure 8-26.

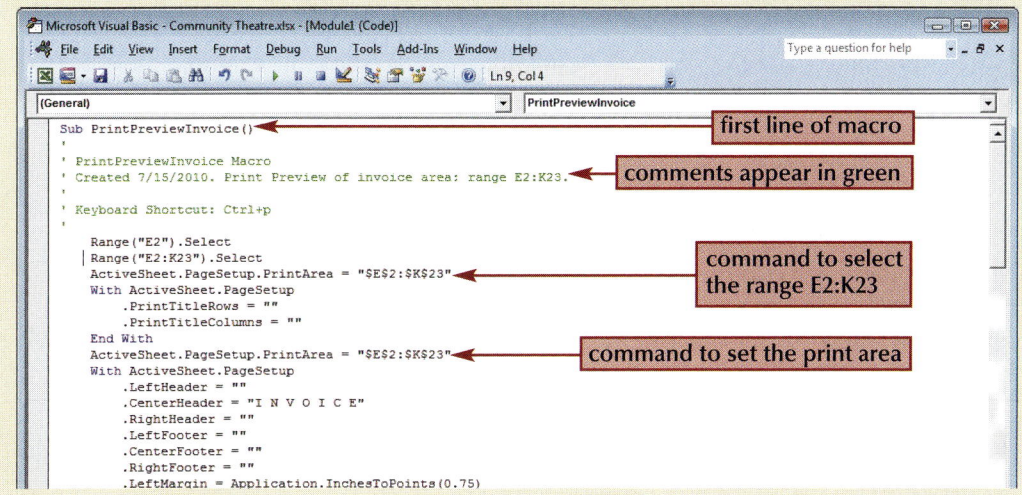

Figure 8-26 Code window in the Visual Basic Editor

Trouble? The number of windows and their contents will differ, depending on how your computer is configured. At this point, you can ignore all other windows aside from the Code window.

▸ 3. If the Code window is not maximized, click the **Maximize** button on the Code window title bar.

Understanding the Structure of Macros

The VBA code in the Code window lists all of the actions you performed when recording the PrintPreviewInvoice macro. In VBA, macros are called **sub procedures**. Each sub procedure begins with the keyword *Sub* followed by the name of the sub procedure and a set of parentheses. In this example, the code begins with:

```
Sub PrintPreviewInvoice()
```

which provides the name of this sub procedure, *PrintPreviewInvoice*—the name you gave the macro. The parentheses are used to include any arguments in the procedure. These arguments pass information to the sub procedure and have roughly the same purpose as the arguments in an Excel function. If you write your own VBA code, sub procedure arguments are an important part of the programming process, but they are not used when you create macros with the macro recorder.

   Following the Sub PrintPreviewInvoice() statement are comments about the macro, taken from the description you entered in the Record New Macro dialog box. Each line appears in green and is preceded by an apostrophe ('). The apostrophe indicates that the line is a comment and does not include any actions Excel needs to perform.

After the comments is the body of the macro, a listing of all of the commands performed by the PrintPreviewInvoice macro as written in the language of VBA. Your list of commands might look slightly different, depending on the exact actions you performed when recording the macro. Even though you might not know VBA, some of the commands are easy to interpret. Near the top of the PrintPreviewInvoice macro, you should see the command:

```
Range("E2:K23").Select
```

This command tells Excel to select the range E2:K23. The next command is:

```
ActiveSheet.PageSetup.PrintArea= $E$2:$K$23
```

This command sets the range E2:K23 as the print area. At the bottom of the macro is the statement:

```
End Sub
```

This statement indicates the end of the PrintPreviewInvoice sub procedure.

A Code window can contain several sub procedures, with each procedure separated from the others by the *Sub ProcedureName()* statement at the beginning, and the *End Sub* statement at the end. Sub procedures are organized into **modules**. As shown in Figure 8-26, all of the macros that have been recorded are stored in the Module1 module (your window may differ).

Writing a Macro Command

Eric wants you to insert two commands into the PrintPreviewInvoice sub procedure to hide the actions of the macro as it runs. The first command, which needs to be inserted directly after the *Sub PrintPreviewInvoice()* statement, is:

```
Application.ScreenUpdating = False
```

This command turns *off* Excel's screen updating, keeping any actions that run in the macro from being displayed on the screen. The second command, which needs to be inserted before the *End Sub* statement, is:

```
Application.ScreenUpdating = True
```

This command turns Excel's screen updating back on, enabling the user to see the final results of the macro after it has completed running.

You must enter these commands exactly. VBA will not be able to run a command if you mistype a word or omit part of the statement. The Visual Basic Editor provides tools to assist you in writing error-free code. As you type a command, the editor will provide pop-up windows and text to help you insert the correct code.

To insert the new commands into the macro:

1. At the top the Code window, click the end of the Sub PrintPreviewInvoice () statement and then press the **Enter** key. A new blank line appears under the statement.

2. Press the **Tab** key, and then type **Application.** (including the period, but no spaces). A list box opens with possible keywords you could type at this point in the command. You can either scroll down the list or continue typing the command yourself.

3. Type **ScreenUpdating =**. As you type the equal sign, another list box opens with two possible choices: True or False. This instruction eliminates the screen refreshing (updating) which causes the screen flickering.

4. Type **False** to turn off the screen updating feature of Excel, and then press the **Enter** key. Figure 8-27 shows the new command inserted into the sub procedure.

Command inserted in the PrintPreviewInvoice macro — Figure 8-27

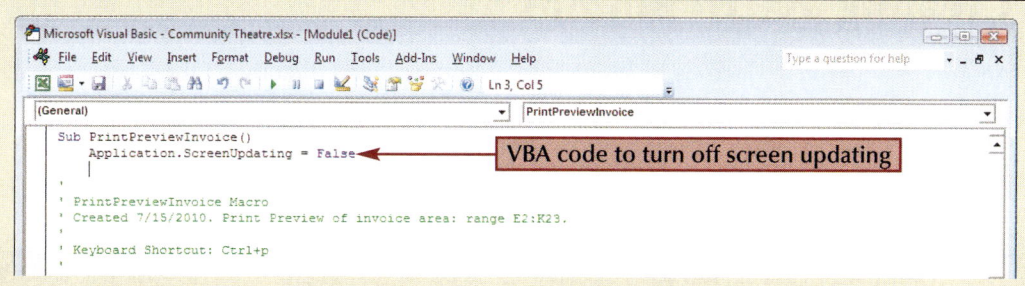

Next, you'll insert a command at the end of the sub procedure to turn screen updating back on.

5. Scroll down the Code window to view the end of the PrintPreviewInvoice sub procedure.

6. Click three lines above the End Sub statement at the end of the End With statement to position the insertion point, and then press the **Enter** key. A new blank line appears below the End With statement.

7. Type **Application.ScreenUpdating = True** and then press the **Enter** key. The command appears in the macro. See Figure 8-28.

Second command added to the PrintPreviewInvoice macro — Figure 8-28

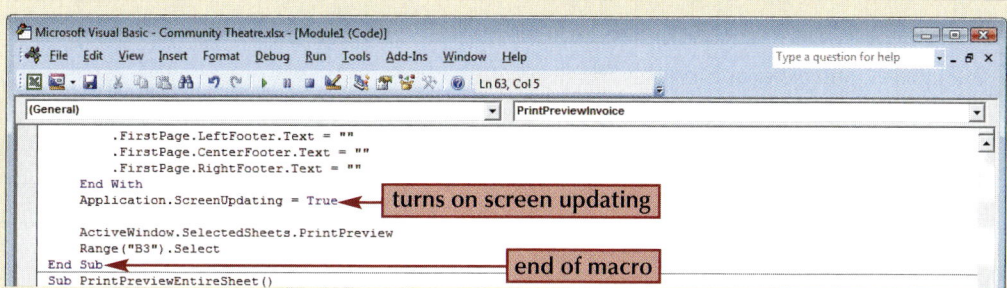

8. Click **File** on the menu bar, and then click **Close and Return to Microsoft Excel**. The Visual Basic Editor closes, and the Community Theatre workbook is redisplayed.

To return to the Visual Basic Editor, you can select a macro in the Macro dialog box and click the Edit button again, or you can click the Visual Basic button in the Code group on the Developer tab.

Eric suggests that you test the macro. You'll check to see whether the commands to turn off the screen updating feature make the macro run more smoothly.

To test the edited PrintPreviewInvoice macro:

1. Press the **Ctrl+p** keys. The PrintPreviewInvoice macro runs faster and without the flicker.

▶ **2.** In the Preview group on the Print Preview tab, click the **Close Print Preview** button. The worksheet returns to Normal view.

Ellen is pleased with the change you made to the macro. She thinks it runs more smoothly and will be less distracting to the theatre's volunteers.

Creating Macro Buttons

Another way to run a macro is to assign it to a button placed directly on the worksheet. Ellen wants you to add three macro buttons to the Invoice worksheet, one for each of the macros you've created. Macro buttons are often a better way to run macros than shortcut keys. Clicking a button (with a descriptive label) is often more intuitive and simpler for users than trying to remember different combinations of keystrokes.

Reference Window | Creating a Macro Button

- In the Controls group on the Developer tab, click the Insert button.
- In the Form Controls section, click the Button (Form Control) tool, click the worksheet where you want the macro button to be located, drag the pointer until the button is the size and shape you want, and then release the mouse button.
- In the Assign Macro dialog box, select the macro you want to assign to the button, and then, with the button still selected, type a new label.

You'll add the three macro buttons to the Invoice worksheet.

To insert a button on the worksheet:

▶ **1.** If necessary, scroll to the right so columns **L**, **M**, and **N** are completely visible.

▶ **2.** In the Controls group on the Developer tab, click the **Insert** button. The Form Controls appear, with a variety of objects that can be placed in the worksheet. You'll insert the Button form control. See Figure 8-29.

Figure 8-29 | Form Controls

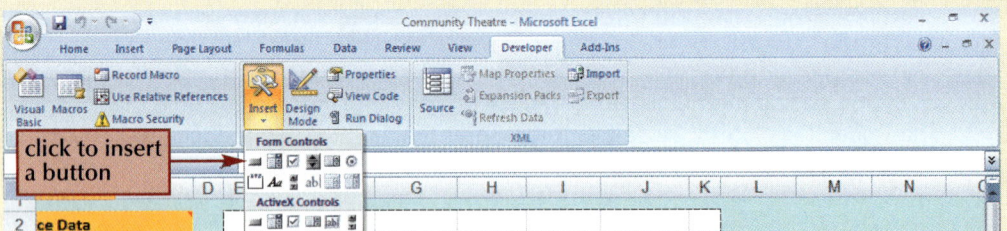

Trouble? If the Insert command is unavailable, the worksheet is protected. Click the Review tab on the Ribbon, in the Changes group, click the Unprotect Sheet button to unprotect the Invoice worksheet, and then repeat Step 2.

▶ **3.** In the Form Controls section, click the **Button (Form Control)** tool, and then point to cell **L3**. The pointer changes to $+$.

▶ **4.** Click and drag the pointer over the range **L3:M4**, and then release the mouse button. A button appears on the worksheet, and the Assign Macro dialog box opens with the button's default name in the Macro name box. See Figure 8-30.

Assign Macro dialog box — Figure 8-30

default macro name (yours might differ) → Button6_Click

click the macro you want to assign to the button → PrintPreviewInvoice

(Macro list: PrintPreviewEntireSheet, PrintPreviewInvoice, TransferData; Macros in: All Open Workbooks)

From the Assign Macro dialog box, you can assign a macro to the button. Ellen wants you to assign the PrintPreviewInvoice macro to this new button.

To assign a button to the PrintPreviewInvoice macro:

1. Click **PrintPreviewInvoice** in the list of macros, and then click the **OK** button. The PrintPreviewInvoice macro is assigned to the selected button.

   You will change the default label on the button to a descriptive one that indicates which macro will run when the button is clicked.

2. With the selection handles still displayed around the button, select the label text, and then type **Preview Invoice** (do not press the Enter key). The new label replaces the default label.

   Trouble? If no selection handles appear around the button, the button is not selected. Right-click the button, and then click Edit Text to place the insertion point within the button, and then repeat Step 2.

   Trouble? If you pressed the Enter key after entering the label on the button, you created a new line in the button. Press the Backspace key to delete the line, and then continue with Step 3.

3. Click any cell in the worksheet to deselect the macro button.

At this point, if you click the Preview Invoice button, the PrintPreviewInvoice macro will run. Before you test the Preview Invoice button, you will add the other buttons.

To add the remaining macro buttons to the Invoice worksheet:

1. In the Controls group on the Developer tab, click the **Insert** button to display the Form Controls, and then click the **Button (Form Control)** tool.

2. Point to cell **L6**, click and drag the pointer over the range **L6:M7**, and then release the mouse button. The Assign Macro dialog box opens.

3. Select **PrintPreviewEntireSheet** in the Macro name list, and then click the **OK** button. The selected macro button appears in the Invoice worksheet.

4. Select the label text in the button, type **Preview Worksheet** as the new label, and then click any cell to deselect the button.

Next, you'll insert the Transfer Data button.

5. In the Controls group on the Developer tab, click the **Insert** button, click the **Button (Form Control)** tool, and then drag the pointer over the range **L9:M10**.

6. Click **TransferData** in the Macro name list in the Assign Macro dialog box, and then click the **OK** button.

7. Type **Transfer Data** as the button label, and then click any cell in the worksheet to deselect the button. See Figure 8-31.

Figure 8-31   Macro buttons in the Invoice worksheet

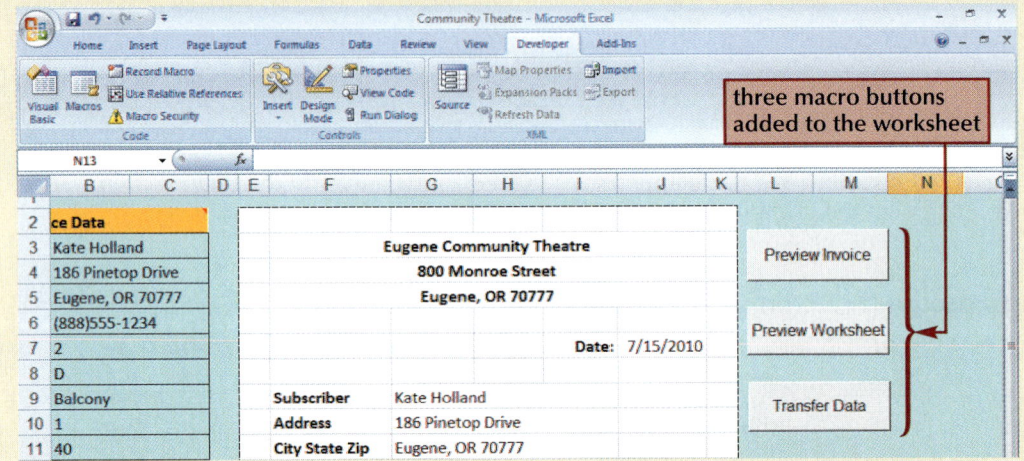

three macro buttons added to the worksheet

Tip

To move or resize a macro button, right-click the button to select it, press the Esc key to close the shortcut menu, and then drag a selection handle to resize the button or drag the selection border to move the button.

Trouble? If the macro buttons on your screen do not match the size and location of the buttons shown in the figure, right-click a button to select it, press the Esc key to close the shortcut menu, and then resize or reposition the button on the worksheet.

You have completed the application so you will reset worksheet protection.

8. Click the **Review** tab on the Ribbon, in the Changes group click the **Protect Sheet** button to open the Protect Sheet dialog box, and then click the **OK** button to turn on worksheet protection.

Next, you will test the macro buttons to verify that they run the macros. Ellen received another subscriber order. You will use the new macro buttons as you enter this data.

To test the macro buttons:

1. In the range **B3:B11**, enter the following subscriber order:

   George Zidane
   105 Central Ave.
   Eugene, OR 70777
   (808) 685–1111
   3 tickets, E series, Balcony
   2 parking decals, 30 donation

▶ 2. Click the **Preview Invoice** button to display the current invoice in Print Preview, and then close Print Preview to return to the Invoice worksheet.

▶ 3. Click the **Preview Worksheet** button to display the Invoice worksheet in Print Preview. The flickering occurs as this macro runs because you did not edit the code in the PrintPreviewEntireSheet macro.

▶ 4. Close Print Preview without printing.

▶ 5. Click the **Transfer Data** button to transfer data to the Ticket Data worksheet. Excel inserts the new transaction in the table.

▶ 6. Switch to the **Ticket Data** worksheet, and verify the data was transferred. See Figure 8-32.

Ticket Data worksheet with new transaction record   Figure 8-32

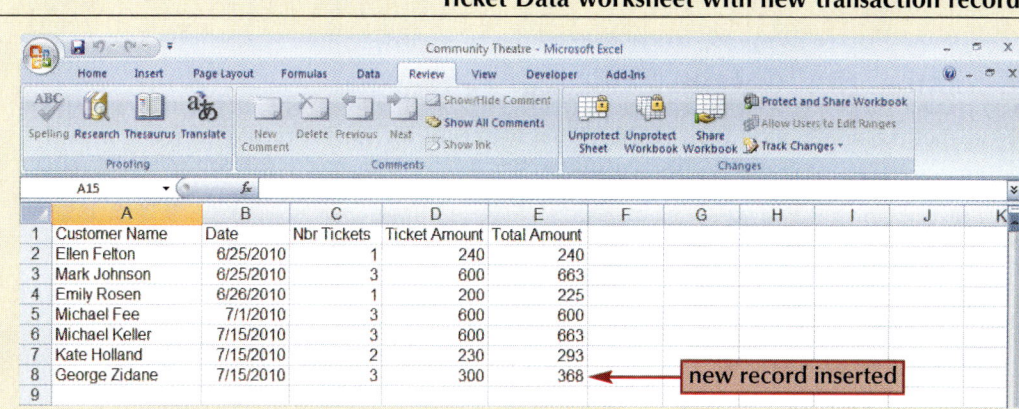

▶ 7. Switch to the **Documentation** sheet.

Saving Workbooks with Macros

You've completed your work on the Excel application, so you will save and close the workbook and then exit Excel.

To save a workbook with a macro:

▶ 1. On the Quick Access Toolbar, click the **Save** button. A dialog box opens, indicating that the workbook you are trying to save contains features that cannot be saved in a macro-free workbook. See Figure 8-33. The default Excel workbook (.xlsx file extension) does not allow macros to be stored as part of the file. If you click the Yes button, this workbook will be saved as a macro-free workbook, which means the macros you created will be lost.

Dialog box with macro warning   Figure 8-33

You want to include the macros in the file. To do this, you have to save the workbook as a new file; one that allows macros to be saved as part of the file.

▶ 2. Click the **No** button. The Save As dialog box opens.

▶ 3. In the File name box, type **Theatre With Macros** so you can easily determine which workbook contains macros.

The default Excel Workbook, which is a macro-free workbook, has the .xlsx file extension. You need to change this to a macro-enabled workbook, which has the .xlsm file extension.

▶ 4. Click the **Save as type** button, and then click **Excel Macro-Enabled Workbook**.

▶ 5. Click the **Save** button. The workbook is saved with the macros.

Minimize the Ribbon

Now that the application is complete, Ellen wants to provide more screen space for the input and output sections of the worksheet. You can minimize the Ribbon to make more space for the worksheet. When the Ribbon is minimized all that is displayed is the Quick Access Toolbar and the tab names. To access any command from the Ribbon, click the desired tab. The Ribbon expands to show all the groups and buttons on the tab.

To minimize the Ribbon:

▶ 1. Double-click any tab on the Ribbon. The Ribbon is minimized. See Figure 8-34.

Figure 8-34 | **Minimized Ribbon**

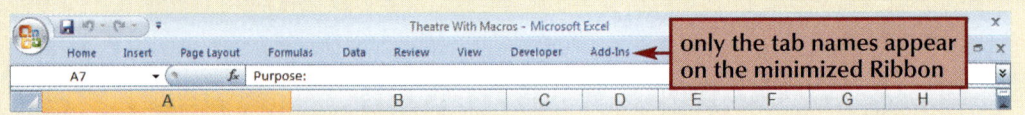

▶ 2. Click the **Home** tab to view all buttons and toolbars for this tab. You can click any other tabs on the Ribbon to display their options. After you click any button on the Ribbon or a cell in the worksheet, the Ribbon returns to its minimized state.

▶ 3. Close the workbook.

Opening a Workbook with Macros

What happens when you open a file with macros, Excel checks the opening workbook to see if it contains a macro. The response you see is based on the security level set on the computer. Ellen has disabled all macros with notification. So, all macros are disabled upon opening the workbook, but a security alert provides her with the option to enable the macros so they can be run or open the workbook with the macros disabled. If you know a workbook contains macros that you or a coworker created, you can enable them. You'll open the Theatre With Macros workbook.

To open the Community Theatre workbook that contains macros:

▶ 1. Open the **Theatre With Macros** workbook. The workbook opens, and a Message Bar appears below the Ribbon indicating the macros have been disabled. See Figure 8-35. Although the workbook is open you must complete one more step to use the macros.

Figure 8-35   Security alert appears when opening a workbook with macros

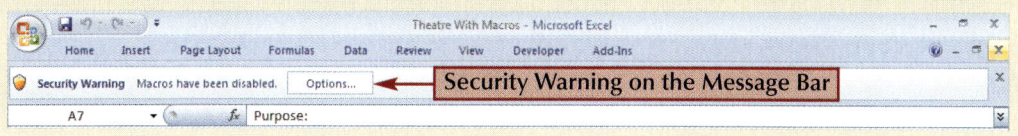

▶ 2. In the Message Bar, click the **Options** button to open the Microsoft Office Security Options dialog box. See Figure 8-36.

Figure 8-36   Microsoft Office Security Options dialog box

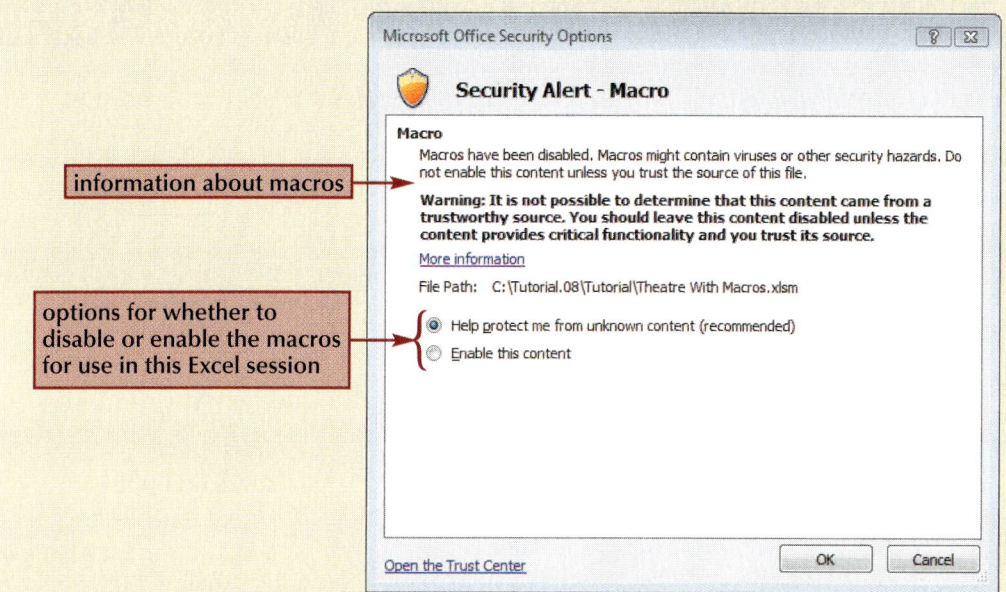

▶ 3. Click the **Enable this content** option button, and then click the **OK** button. The macros in the workbook are available for use. If you selected the recommended option, Help protect me from unknown content, the macros would remain disabled and unavailable during the current session. The other features of the workbook would still be available.

▶ 4. Click the **Invoice** sheet tab. The Ribbon is still minimized. It will remain minimized in Excel on this computer until you maximize the Ribbon.

▶ 5. Double-click any tab to maximize the Ribbon, and then close the workbook without saving the changes.

Finally, you'll remove the Developer tab from the Ribbon.

▶ 6. Click the **Office Button** 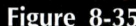, and then click the **Excel Options** button to open the Excel Options dialog box.

▶ 7. In the Popular section, click the **Show Developer tab in the Ribbon** check box to remove the check mark, and then click the **OK** button. The Developer tab is hidden from the Ribbon.

Ellen is pleased with the ease of the interface for the community theatre workbook. The workbook protection and macros will streamline the data entry process for the theatre volunteers.

Review | Session 8.3 Quick Check

1. Discuss two ways of creating a macro.
2. How do you identify a comment in the Visual Basic code?
3. What are the three places in which you can store a macro?
4. What are the steps you follow to delete a macro?
5. What are the steps you follow to edit a macro?
6. How do you insert a macro button into your worksheet?

Review | Tutorial Summary

In this tutorial, you learned how to create data validation rules that help guide users as they input data into a worksheet. You learned how to define names to make formulas easier to understand. You also learned how to protect the contents of worksheets, the worksheets themselves, and workbooks. Finally, you learned how to automate a series of actions by creating macros.

Key Terms

comment	locked property	protect worksheet
data validation	macro	sub procedure
defined name	macro security settings	Trust Center
digital signature	maco virus	validation rule
error alert message	module	Visual Basic Editor
Excel application	name	Visual Basic for Applications
input message	Personal Macro workbook	(VBA)

Practice | Review Assignments

Practice the skills you learned in the tutorial to create a workbook with macros for a car rental company.

Data File needed for the Review Assignments: Rentals.xlsx

Ellen's student intern, Mark, did such a good job helping her with the Community Theatre application that she recommended him to a friend who has a similar project. Ellen's friend needs to create an invoice system for his new car rental company, Eugene Discount Car Rental.

Complete the following:

1. Open the **Rentals** workbook located in the Tutorial.08\Review folder included with your Data Files, and then save the workbook as **Discount Rental** in the same folder.
2. Enter the current date and your name in the Documentation sheet.
3. In the Customer worksheet, define names for cells using the following information:

Cell	Defined Name	Cell	Defined Name
B4	Customer	H9	ChargePerDay
B5	TypeCar	H10	ChargePerMile
B6	DaysRented	A12:C16	RentalRates
B7	MilesDriven	B19	SalesTaxRate

4. Create the validation rules for cells B5, B6, and B7 shown in Figure 8-37.

Figure 8-37

Cell	Settings	Input Message	Error Alert
B5	List Source (A12:A16)	Enter an appropriate title and message	Style: Stop Title: Invalid Type Message: Enter an appropriate message
B6	Integers >0 and <30	Enter an appropriate title and message	Style: Warning Title: Warning Days Rented Message: Enter an appropriate message
B7	Integers >0 and <=5000	Enter an appropriate title and message	Style: Warning Title: Warning Miles Message: Enter an appropriate message

5. Enter the following formulas, using the defined names you created in Step 3, to calculate the Rental Bill:
   - Cell F6 is equal to the value in cell B4.
   - Cell F7 is equal to the value in cell B5.
   - Cell F9 is equal to the value in cell B6.
   - Cell F10 is equal to the value in cell B7.
   - Cell H9 is equal to charge per day, which depends on the type of car entered in cell B5 and the rate table. (*Hint:* Use the VLOOKUP function.)
   - Cell H10 is equal to the charge per mile, which depends on the type of car rented in cell B5 and the rate table. (*Hint:* Use the VLOOKUP function.)
   - Cell F12 is equal to the Rental Amount, which equals the days rented multiplied by the charge per day plus the miles driven multiplied by the charge per mile.
   - Cell F13 is equal to Sales Tax Rate times Rental Amount.
   - Cell F14 is equal to Rental Amount plus Sales Tax.
   - Use the IFERROR function in cells H9, H10, F12, F13, and F14 to test for an error value. If an error value is found, display a blank; otherwise, use the appropriate formula.

6. Test the worksheet using the data: **Myles Fast**, **Intermediate**, **4**, **450**.
7. Protect the worksheet so a user can enter data only in the range B4:B7. Do not use a password to enable protection. Save the workbook.

   Note: In the following steps, you'll be creating two macros. Save your workbook before recording each macro. That way, if you make a mistake in recording the macro, you can close the workbook without saving the changes, and then reopen the workbook and try again. Be sure to read the list of tasks before you begin recording them.
8. Remove worksheet protection from the Customer worksheet.
9. Create a macro named **PrintPreviewBill** with the shortcut key **Ctrl+p** that displays only the bill portion of the worksheet in the range E3:H15 in Print Preview, centers the bill horizontally on the page and shows your name in the right footer of the printout. Create a macro button, assign the PrintPreviewBill macro to the button, and then change the default label to **Preview Bill**.
10. Create a macro named **ClearInputs** with the shortcut key **Ctrl+c** that clears the data in the rental inputs section of the worksheet (range B4:B7). Create a macro button, assign the ClearInputs macro to the button, and then change the label to **Clear**.
11. Turn protection on in the Customer worksheet.
12. Test the macro using the data: **Eddie Elders**, **Intermediate**, **3** days, **2000** miles.
13. Use the Preview Bill macro button to preview the customer bill for Ed Elders.
14. Use the Clear macro button to remove the rental data.
15. In the Documentation worksheet, use the Paste List command to document the defined names and their locations.
16. Save the workbook with the name **Rentals With Macros** in the macro-enabled workbook format, and then close it. Submit the finished workbook to your instructor, either in printed or electronic form, as requested.

Apply | Case Problem 1

Apply the skills you learned to create, edit, and run macros to produce monthly reports.

Data File needed for this Case Problem: MediTrax.xlsx

MediTrax Controls MediTrax Controls, a U.S. subsidiary of a European multinational corporation, is testing an HVAC system designed to eliminate large temperature variances in its medical storage rooms. Lisa Goodman is a product tester for MediTrax, and each week, she records 25 temperature readings, five samples each day, in an Excel workbook. At the end of the month, Lisa sends the results to the parent company's Quality Department. Because many repetitive steps occur in developing the output requested by the parent company, Lisa asks you to create a macro to speed the creation of the report and reduce chances for error.

Complete the following:

1. Open the **MediTrax** workbook located in the Tutorial.08\Case1 folder included with your Data Files, and then save the workbook as **MediTrax Controls** in the same folder.
2. In the Documentation sheet, enter your name and the current date, and then review all the worksheets in the workbook. Make Week 1 the active worksheet.

3. Create a macro to convert the worksheet to the one shown in Figure 8-38. Name the macro **ConvertData** and assign the shortcut key **Ctrl+d** to run the macro. The macro performs the following steps:
   a. Formats the dates in the Date column using the date format type (3/14/2001).
   b. Formats the times in the Time column so they are displayed in 24-hour notation (format type 13:30).
   c. Types the title **Celsius** in cell D1.
   d. Converts the Fahrenheit temperatures to Celsius by entering the following formula in cell D2 and then copying down the column: **=5/9*(C2–32)**
   e. Formats the cells in column D using the Number format to 1 decimal place.
   f. Bolds the column heading and resizes the column to fully display "Fahrenheit."
   g. Places the label **Average** in cell A27, computes the average Celsius temperature for the week in cell D27 and bolds the row.
   h. Makes cell F1 the active cell.
   i. Uses Print Preview to view the results centered horizontally on the page with the worksheet name in the center header and your name in the right footer.
   j. Closes Print Preview.
   k. Stops recording the macro.

Figure 8-38

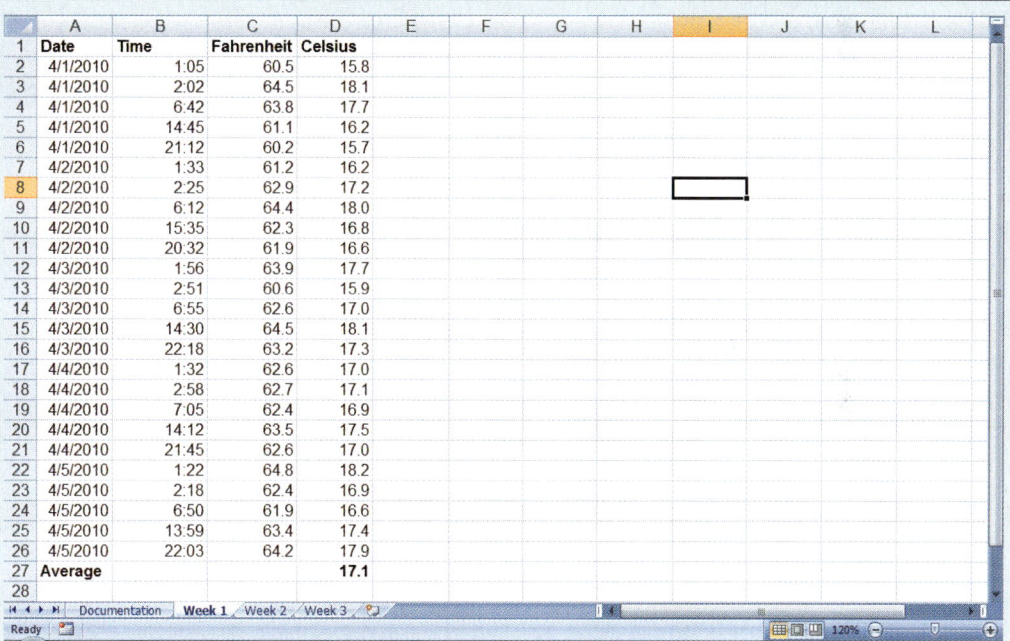

4. Switch to the Week 2 worksheet and test the macro using the shortcut key.
5. Edit the macro so screen updating is turned off while the macro is running and turned on when the macro ends.
6. Switch to the Week 3 worksheet and test the revised macro using the shortcut key.
7. Save the workbook as **MTC With Macros** as an Excel Macro-Enabled workbook, and then close it. Submit the finished workbook to your instructor, either in printed or electronic form, as requested.

Apply | Case Problem 2

Apply the skills you've learned to define data validation rules, name cells, set worksheet protection, and create macros in a profit analysis workbook.

Data File needed for this Case Problem: Popcorn.xlsx

Seattle Popcorn Seattle Popcorn is a small company located in Tacoma, Washington, that produces gourmet popcorn distributed in the Northwest. Steve Wilkes has developed a workbook that will allow him to perform a profit analysis for the company. Using this workbook, he wants to create formulas to determine the break-even point for the company—the sales volume needed so that revenues will match the anticipated monthly expenses. Three factors determine the break-even point: the sales price of each unit of Seattle Popcorn, the variable manufacturing cost to the company for each unit, and the fixed expenses (salaries, rent, insurance, and so on) that the company must pay each month. Steve wants to be able to explore a range of possible values for each of these factors, as follows:

- The sales price of each unit of Seattle Popcorn can vary from $5 to $15 (in whole numbers).
- The variable manufacturing cost of each unit can vary from $5 to $15 (in whole numbers).
- The fixed monthly expense for the company can vary from $15,000 to $30,000 (in whole numbers).

Figure 8-39 shows a preview of the application you'll create for Steve.

Figure 8-39

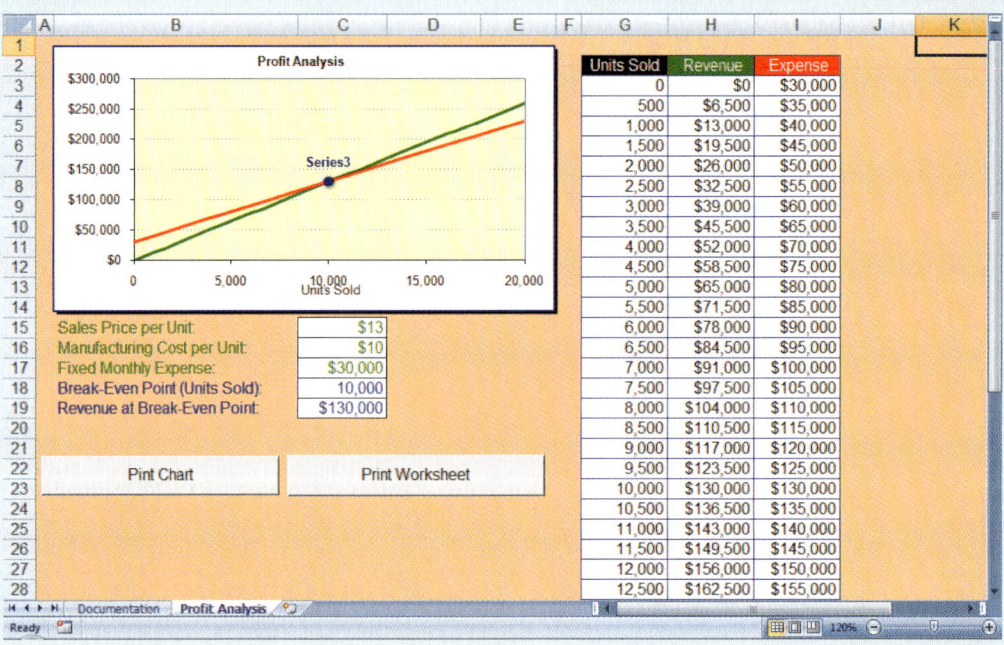

Complete the following:

1. Open the **Popcorn** workbook located in the Tutorial.08\Case2 folder included with your Data Files, and then save the workbook as **Seattle Popcorn** in the same folder. Enter the date and your name in the Documentation sheet.
2. Switch to the Profit Analysis worksheet, and then define the following names: in cell C15 **PricePerUnit**, in cell C16 **CostPerUnit**, and in cell C17 **MonthlyExpenses**.

3. In the range H3:H43, enter a formula using defined names to calculate the revenue, which is determined by the units sold multiplied by the price per unit. In the range I3:I43, enter a formula using defined names to calculate the expenses, which are determined by the units sold multiplied by the cost per unit plus the fixed monthly expense.
4. In cell C18, enter a formula to calculate the break-even point, which is determined by the fixed monthly expense divided by the difference between the price per unit and the cost per unit. Use the IFERROR function to display a blank cell instead of an error value.
5. In cell C19, enter a formula to calculate the revenue at the break-even point, which is determined by the break-even point multiplied by the sale price per unit. Use the IFERROR function to display a blank cell instead of an error value.
6. Create the validation rules for cells C15, C16, and C17, as shown in Figure 8-40.

Figure 8-40

Cell	Settings	Input Message	Error Alert
C15	Integers from 5 to 15	Enter an appropriate title and message	Title: Sales Price Warning Style: Warning Message: Enter an appropriate message
C16	Integers from 5 to 15	Enter an appropriate title and message	Title: Cost Warning Style: Warning Message: Enter an appropriate message
C17	Integers from 15000 to 30000	Enter an appropriate title and message	Title: Fixed Monthly Expense Warning Style: Warning Message: Enter an appropriate message

7. Protect the worksheet so the user can enter data only in cells C15, C16, and C17. Everything else in the worksheet should remain locked.
8. Enter the following values in the worksheet to determine how many units Seattle Popcorn must sell each month in order to break even:
   - Sales Price per Unit = **$13**
   - Manufacturing Cost per Unit = **$10**
   - Fixed Monthly Expense = **$30,000**

   Note: In the following steps, you'll create two macros. Save your workbook before recording each macro. That way, if you make a mistake while recording the macro, you can close the workbook without saving the changes, and then reopen it and try again. Also, read the list of tasks before you begin recording them.
9. Create a macro named **PrintChart** with the shortcut key **Ctrl+a** that performs the following tasks:
   a. Print Preview the chart and input/output area (range A1:E20) in landscape orientation, centered horizontally on the page, and with the text **Break-even Analysis** in the center header, and your name and date in the right footer.
   b. Closes Print Preview and then makes cell A1 the active cell.
10. Test the PrintChart macro by pressing the Ctrl+a keys. If the macro doesn't work, close the workbook without saving your changes, reopen the workbook, and record the macro again.
11. Create a button in the range A22:B23, assign the PrintChart macro to the button, and change the default label to a more descriptive one.
12. Edit the PrintChart macro so screen updating is turned off while the macro is running and turned on when the macro ends.

13. Run the PrintChart macro again to test the button and verify that screen updating is turned off while the macro is running and on when the macro ends.
14. Create a macro named **PrintWorksheet** with shortcut key **Ctrl+b** that performs the following tasks:
    a. Print Preview the entire worksheet on one page with text **Profit Analysis** in the center header and your name and date in the right footer.
    b. Closes Print Preview, and then makes cell A1 the active cell.
15. Test the PrintWorksheet macro by pressing the Crtl+b keys. If the macro doesn't work, close the workbook without saving your changes, reopen the workbook, and record the macro again.
16. Create a button in the range C22:E23, assign the PrintWorksheet macro to the button, and then change the default label to a more descriptive one.
17. Edit the macro so screen updating is turned off while the macro is running and turned on when the macro ends.
18. Run the PrintWorksheet macro again to test the button and verify that screen updating is turned off while the macro is running and on when the macro ends.
19. Save the workbook as **SP With Macros**, and then close it. Submit the finished workbook to your instructor, either in printed or electronic form, as requested.

| Apply | **Case Problem 3** |

Apply the skills you learned to design an Excel workbook for use as a data entry form.

Data File needed for this Case Problem: Cookin.xlsx

Cookin Good Cookin Good is a company that sells specialized home cooking products. The company employs individuals to organize "Cookin Good Parties" in which the company's products are sold. Cleo Benard is responsible for entering sales data from various Cookin Good Parties. She wants to design an Excel workbook to act as a data entry form. She has already created the workbook, but she needs your help in setting up data validation rules, creating a table lookup, and writing the macros to enter the data.

Complete the following:

1. Open the **Cookin** workbook located in the Tutorial.08\Case3 folder included with your Data Files, save the workbook as **Cookin Good** in the same folder. Enter your name and the date in the Documentation sheet, and then switch to the Sales Form worksheet.
2. Create appropriate defined names for each cell in the range C3:C8. Assign the name **ProductInfo** to the range E4:G15.
3. In the Sales Form worksheet, create the following validation rules:
    a. Cell C3 for which the criteria allows only one of five regions (represented by the numbers 1, 2, 3, 4, and 5) to be entered. Enter an appropriate input message and error alert.
    b. Cell C4 for which the criteria provides the list of 12 products (found in range E4:E15). Enter an appropriate input message and error alert.
    c. Cell C7 for which the criteria allows only positive numbers to be entered as the number of units sold. Enter an appropriate input message and error alert.
4. Use a Lookup function to have the product name and price automatically entered into the sales form when the ProductID is entered. (*Hint:* Cells should be blank if an error value appears in a cell.)

5. Enter a formula that automatically calculates the total sale for the order, which is determined by the number of units sold multiplied by the price of the product.
6. Prevent users from selecting any cell in the Sales Form worksheet other than cells C3, C4, and C7, and then protect all of the worksheets in the workbook, except for the Documentation sheet.
7. Test the data entry form by entering the following new record: Region = **1**, Product ID = **CW**, Units Sold = **5**.
8. Save the workbook, and then create a macro named **AddData** with the shortcut key **Ctrl+d** that performs the following tasks:
    a. In the Sales Form worksheet, copy the values in the range C3:C8. (*Hint:* You'll paste later in the macro.)
    b. Switch from the Sales Form worksheet to the Sales Record worksheet. Click cell A1.
    c. Turn on Relative References. Use the arrow keys to locate the last used row in the table.
    d. Use an arrow key to move to the next row. Turn off Relative References.
    e. Paste the copied values from Step A into the blank row. (*Hint:* Use the Paste Special command to paste transposed values, Values option, Transpose check box.)
    f. Switch to the Sales Table worksheet, click inside the PivotTable and refresh the contents of the PivotTable to include the new data.
    g. Switch to the Sales Form and clear the values in cells C3, C4, and C7 of the Sales Form worksheet. Make C3 the active cell.
    h. Stop Recording.
9. Create a button in the range C11:C12 on the Sales Form worksheet and assign the AddData macro to the button. Change the button label to **Transfer Sales Data**.
10. Test the data entry form and AddData macro by entering the following new records:

Region	Product ID	Units Sold
3	HR	7
4	OEG	3

11. Create a macro named **ViewTable** with the **Ctrl+t** shortcut key that displays the contents of the Sales Table worksheet.
12. Create a macro named **ViewChart** with the **Ctrl+c** shortcut key that displays the Sales Chart worksheet.
13. Create a macro named **ViewForm** with the **Ctrl+f** shortcut key that displays the Sales Form worksheet. Test each macro using its shortcut keys.
14. In the Documentation sheet, create three macro buttons to view the Sales Table (Step 11), the Sales Chart (Step 12), and the Sales Form (Step 13). Insert the macro buttons below row 9. Change the labels on the buttons to be more descriptive.

EXPLORE 15. Sales Table displays the Total product sales in each region. Change the display so the values in the cell are percentage of the total (Field Setting). You can return the original value by choosing Normal.
16. Save the workbook as **CG With Macros**, and then close it. Submit the finished workbook to your instructor, either in printed or electronic form, as requested.

EX 450 Excel | Tutorial 8 Developing an Excel Application

| Create | **Case Problem 4** |

Go beyond what you've learned to define names, apply worksheet protection, and create macros to prepare an invoice.

There are no Data Files needed for this Case Problem.

Alia's Senior Living Supplies Alia Moh for years had been touched by the needs of the senior population she was serving, thinking that if people had just a little help, they might not end up at her hospital. Ultimately, she left her job at a local hospital in Chicago to establish Alia's Senior Living Supplies, which supplies products and services designed for seniors. Products offered by Alia on her Web site range from safety step ladders, doorknob grippers, skid resistant surfaces, to wheelchair ponchos.

Finding these uniquely designed products a great help in their day-to-day lives, a large following of clients regularly purchase from Alia. To be sure her company stays in business, Alia must assure timely receipt of payments from her growing client base. She wants a billing/invoicing system to expedite that work. Figure 8-41 shows the finished application she asks you to create.

Figure 8-41

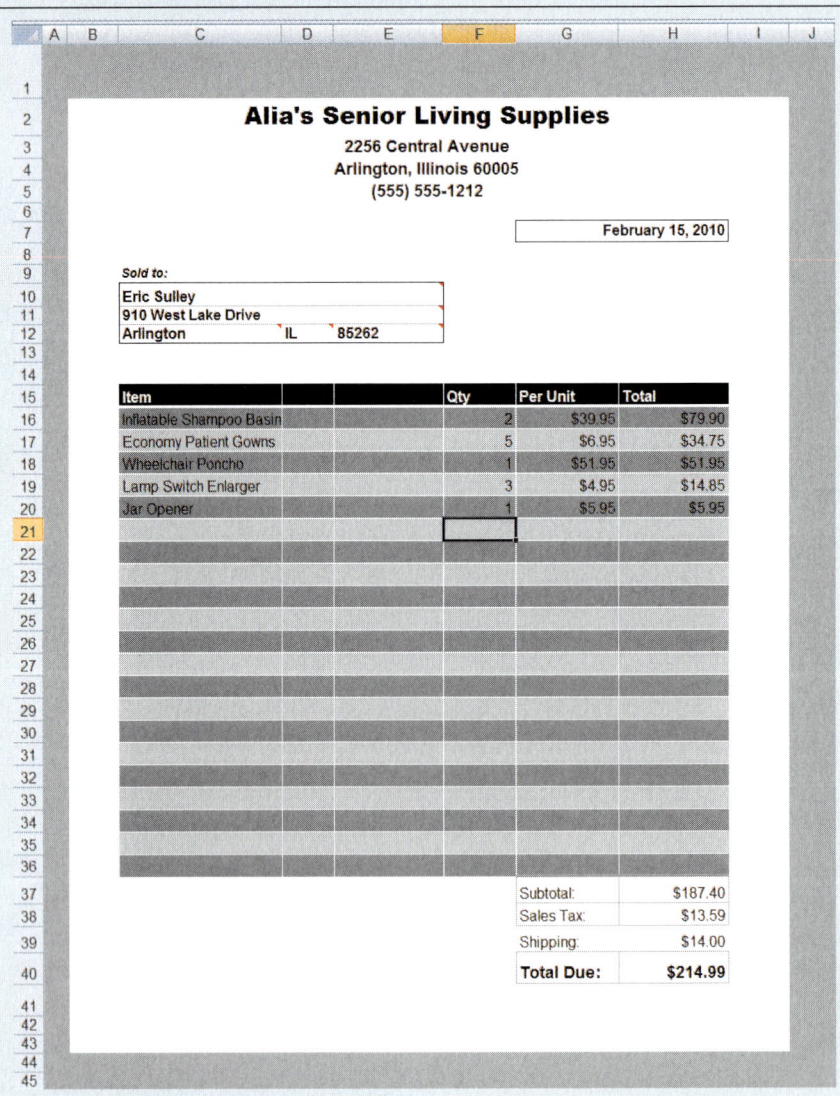

Complete the following:

1. Open a new workbook, and save it as **AliasSupplies** in the Tutorial.08\Case4 folder included with your Data Files.
2. Rename the first sheet **Documentation** and then enter the company name, your name, the current date, and a purpose statement. Rename the second sheet **Invoice**. Rename the third sheet **Product Pricing And Shipping**.
3. Review Figures 8-42 and 8-43, and the steps below before you begin to enter the tables, labels, and formulas to build the invoice. First, enter the data for Product Pricing (shown in Figure 8-42) and Shipping costs (shown in Figure 8-43) in the Product Pricing And Shipping worksheet. Next, follow Steps a through n and Figure 8-41 to build the invoice. Use defined names and structured referencing to assist in creating formulas.
   a. Current date in cell G7 (merged with H7).
   b. Insert comments as a reminder as to what data is to be entered in cells C10, C11, C12, D12, and E12.
   c. Adjust the column widths so column A is 2.57; column B is 6.14; column C is 20.86; Column D is 6.14; column E is 13.57; column F is 8.71; column G is 12.71; column H is 13.71; and column I is 7.29.
   d. Insert the column headers in row 15.
   e. Create an Excel table in the range C15:H36. Remove the filter arrows and format cells G7 and the range G40:H40 as bold.
   f. Use defined names wherever appropriate.
   g. Item column (the range C16:C36): User looks up Item using a list. Use the Product Pricing table, shown in Figure 8-42, for the Item.

Figure 8-42

	A	B
1	Product Pricing	
2		
3	Adjustable Home Bed Rail	89.95
4	Bed Cane	81.95
5	Doorknob Gripper	4.95
6	Easy Grip Utensils	32.95
7	Economy Patient Gowns	6.95
8	Full-page Magnifier	4.99
9	Giant TV Remote	34.95
10	Inflatable Shampoo Basin	39.95
11	Jar Opener	5.95
12	Lamp Switch Enlarger	4.95
13	Medication Dispenser	135.95
14	No Rinse Shampoo	34.95
15	Tilting Overbed Table	114.95
16	Trolley Walker	139.95
17	Wheelchair Poncho	51.95

   h. Qty column: User enters the quantity ordered. Issue an error alert warning message if the quantity is above 50.
   i. Per Unit column: Based on a table lookup in the Product Pricing table based on value selected in Item column (refer to Figure 8-42).
   j. Total column: Qty × Per Unit.
   k. Subtotal (cell H37): Sum of Total column. Format this cell appropriately.
   l. Sales tax: 7.25% of subtotal in cell H38 if the customer state is IL; otherwise, sales tax is 0. Format this cell appropriately.
   m. Shipping costs: If subtotal is $200 or more, no shipping cost; otherwise, look up shipping cost (refer to Figure 8-43) based on the subtotal in cell H37. Format this cell appropriately.

Figure 8-43

Subtotal amount	Shipping cost
0—54.99	5.95
55—99.99	8.25
100—149.99	11.50
150—199.99	14.00

    n. Total Due = Subtotal + Sales Tax + Shipping. Format this cell appropriately.

4. Protect the worksheet so a user can enter data in cells C10, C11, C12, D12, E12, items (C16:C36), and Qty (F16:F36) but not in any other cells. Do not use a password.
5. Create a macro named **PrintInvoice** that prints the Invoice. Assign the **Ctrl+p** shortcut key to this macro. Center the worksheet horizontally and fit it on 1 printed page. The heading has the label **I N V O I C E**. Attach a button and place it on the worksheet (column K) that is assigned to the PrintInvoice macro. Assign a descriptive name to the macro button.
6. Create a macro named **ClearInputs** that deletes the values from cells C10, C11, C12, D12, E12, items in the range C16:C36, and quantities in the range F16:F36. Assign the **Ctrl+c** shortcut key to this macro. Attach a button and place it on the worksheet (column K) that is assigned to the ClearInputs macro. Assign a descriptive name to the macro button.
7. In the Documentation sheet, paste a list of defined names with location, and list of macro names, shortcut keys, and purpose.
8. Test the worksheet using the data in Figure 8-40.
9. Use the PrintInvoice macro button to print the bill for the data you entered in Step 8, and then use the ClearInputs macro button to remove the input data.
10. Save the workbook as **Alia With Macros**, and then close it. Submit the finished workbook to your instructor, either in printed or electronic form, as requested.

Research | Internet Assignments

Use the Internet to find and work with data related to the topics presented in this tutorial.

The purpose of the Internet Assignments is to challenge you to find information on the Internet that you can use to work effectively with this software. The actual assignments are updated and maintained on the Course Technology Web site. Log on to the Internet and use your Web browser to go to the Student Online Companion for New Perspectives Office 2007 at **www.course.com/np/office2007**. Then navigate to the Internet Assignments for this tutorial.

Assess | SAM Assessment and Training

If you have a SAM user profile, you may have access to hands-on instruction, practice, and assessment of the skills covered in this tutorial. Log in to your SAM account (**http://sam2007.course.com**) to launch any assigned training activities or exams that relate to the skills covered in this tutorial.

Review | Quick Check Answers

Session 8.1

1. A descriptive word or characters assigned to a cell or range. Defined names make interpreting formulas easier. If you move a cell or range with a defined name to a different location, any formula using that named range reflects the new location.
2. any three of the following: Name box, New Name dialog box, Create Names from Selection dialog box, and Name Manager dialog box
3. (a) Annual_Total
4. Click Name box arrow, and then click the defined name
5. =SUM(Expenses)
6. False

Session 8.2

1. Select the cell, click the Data tab on the Ribbon, and then, in the Data Tools group, click the Data Validation button.
2. Select the cell, open the Data Validation dialog box, click the Input Message tab, and then enter the input message title and text.
3. The *Stop* alert prevents the user from storing the data in the cell; the *Warning* alert rejects the invalid data but allows the user to override the rejection; and the *Information* alert accepts the invalid data but allows the user to cancel the data entry.
4. A locked cell prohibits data entry when the worksheet is protected.
5. Worksheet protection controls the user's ability to edit cells within the worksheet. Workbook protection controls the user's ability to change the structure of the workbook (including worksheet names) and the format of the workbook window.
6. Yes, as long as the structure of the workbook is not protected.
7. Select the cell with a comment. In the Comments group on the Review tab, click the Edit Comment button, edit the comment in the text box, and then click any cell.

Session 8.3

1. Use the macro recorder to record the exact keystrokes and commands you want the macro to run, or write the macro code directly in the Visual Basic Editor with VBA macro language.
2. A line that begins with an apostrophe is treated as a comment; the line of a comment is green.
3. You can store a macro in the current workbook, in a new workbook, or in the Personal Macro workbook, which is available whenever you use Excel.
4. Click Developer tab, in the Code group click Macros to open the Macros dialog box, select the macro from the list of macros, and then click the Delete button.
5. Click the Developer tab on the Ribbon, in the Code group, click the Macros button to open the Macro dialog box, select the macro from the list of macros, and then click the Edit button.
6. If the worksheet is protected, unprotect the worksheet. In the Controls group on the Developer tab, click the Insert button to display the Form Controls toolbar. Click the Button (Form Control) tool, and then draw the button image on the worksheet. Assign a macro and label to the button.

Ending Data Files

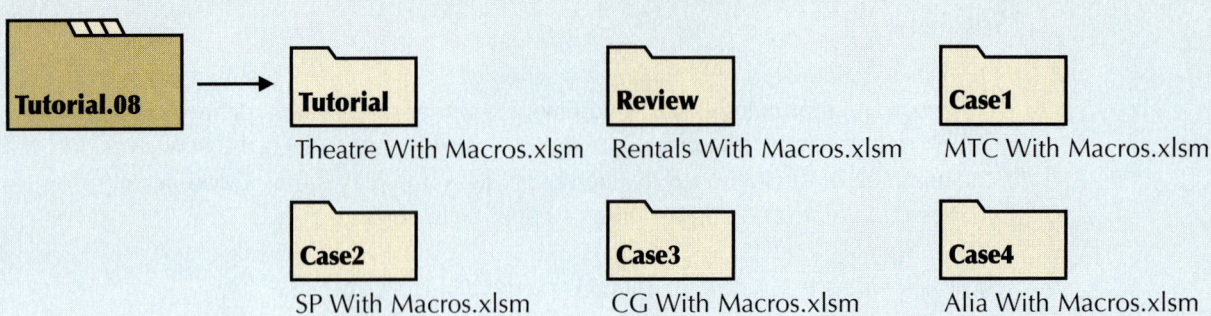

Reality Check

Excel can be a useful program for tracking information about many everyday activities, such as

- Organizations you belong to/participate in
- Collections
- Hobbies
- Community work
- Social events
- Sports records and statistics

In this exercise, you need to select an area that fits your interests and create an application in Excel to track information related to your area of interest, using the Excel skills and features presented in Tutorials 5 through 8.

Note: Please be sure *not* to include any personal information of a sensitive nature in any worksheets you create to submit to your instructor. Later, you can update the worksheets with such information for your own personal use.

1. Plan the organization of your workbook—what information related to your area of interest do you want to track; what fields do you need to enter; how will you organize the data; what calculations will you need to perform; how do you want to format the information, and so on.
2. Create a Documentation worksheet that includes your name, the date, and the purpose of your workbook. Format it appropriately.
3. Set up multiple worksheets to record your data on (for example, a budget for each event could be a separate worksheet). Use a worksheet group to enter labels and other nonvariable text, formatting, and formulas in the worksheets.
4. Apply validity checks to improve the accuracy of data entry.
5. Create a summary worksheet that consolidates the information from these worksheets.
6. Create an Excel table to track data. Enter an appropriate table name, column headers, and formulas. Format the table attractively. Add records to the table. Insert a Total row in the table with an appropriate summary calculation (SUM, COUNT, etc.).
7. Add a calculated column to the table with an appropriate function (such as an IF function, an AND function, and so on).
8. In a worksheet with a range of data, define names for cells and ranges. Convert the existing formulas in that worksheet to use the defined names.
9. Paste a list of defined names as documentation in the Documentation sheet.
10. Check for duplicate values using conditional formatting.
11. Check for data entry errors using the IFERROR function.
12. Sort the data as needed.
13. Use a filter to answer a specific question about the data. Add a comment to explain how the data was filtered and what question it answers.
14. Create an advanced filter using a criteria range, such as a filter to determine which events have food costs less than $100.

15. Use a PivotTable to analyze data in the workbook. Format, filter, and sort the PivotTable appropriately. Add a comment to explain what you learned from the PivotTable.
16. Plan and record an appropriate macro. Assign the macro to a button. Save the workbook in macro enabled format.
17. Prepare the workbook for printing. Include headers and footers that indicate the filename of your workbook, the workbook's author, and the date on which the workbook is printed. If a printed worksheet will extend across several pages, repeat appropriate print titles across all of the pages and include page numbers and the total number of pages on each printed page.
18. Save the workbook. Submit the completed workbook to your instructor, in printed or electronic form, as requested.

Excel EX A1

Appendix A

Objectives

- Open a workbook in Compatibility Mode
- Use the LEN function to determine the number of characters in a cell
- Use the LEFT function to extract a series of characters from a text string
- Use the Paste Values command
- Use the PROPER function to convert the case of a text string
- Use the Concatenation operator to join several text strings into one text string
- Use the Text to Columns command to separate multiple pieces of data in one column into separate columns
- USE the UPPER function to convert text to uppercase
- Use the SUBSTITUTE function to replace characters in a text string
- Use a special format for phone number
- Create custom formats for numbers and dates

Working with Text Functions and Creating Custom Formats

Cleaning Data in a Spreadsheet

Case | Zeus Engineering

Growth in the town of Bayville has strained the capacity of local roads. Traffic increases have created delays, vehicular hazards, and pedestrian safety concerns. To address these issues, the town has contracted Zeus Engineering to develop a Transportation Improvement Program (TIP).

Myron Londale, traffic analyst at Zeus Engineering, will analyze data on private homes and commercial buildings located along the route being analyzed. He received the data from the Bayville Assessor's office, which transferred the data to Excel. Before Myron begins his analysis, he needs to "clean" the data, and has asked for your help.

Starting Data Files

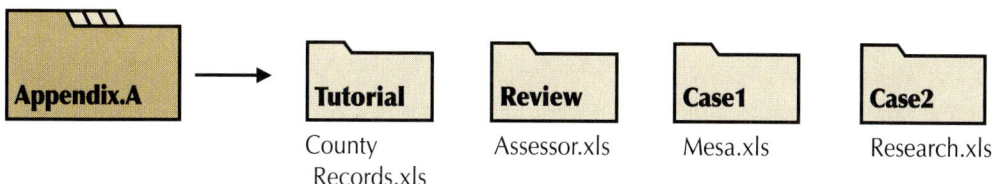

Opening and Saving Workbooks Created in Earlier Versions of Excel

The workbook Myron received from the Bayville Assessor's office was created in an earlier version of Excel. When you open a workbook that was created in an earlier version of Excel, Excel 2007 opens the workbook in **Compatibility Mode**. The words *[Compatibility Mode]* appear in the title bar, indicating the file is not in the latest Excel format. You can work in Compatibility Mode, which keeps the workbook in the older file format and makes the workbook accessible for users who do not have the current version of Excel installed. However, to have access to all the latest features and tools in Excel 2007, the workbook must be converted to the current file format, which has the file extension.xlsx. This is the file format you have used to save all workbooks in this book.

Myron wants to use Excel tables to manage and analyze the data. Because tables are a new feature in Excel 2007, Myron asks you to open the current workbook and convert it to the current file format. You can tell when a workbook has been saved in the current file format, because its file extension changes from .xls to .xlsx.

To save the County Records workbook in the Excel 2007 file format:

▶ 1. Open the **County Records** workbook located in the **Appendix.A\Tutorial** folder included with your Data Files. The workbook opens in Compatibility Mode, because the workbook was created in an earlier version of Excel. See Figure A-1.

Figure A-1 | **Workbook in Compatibility Mode**

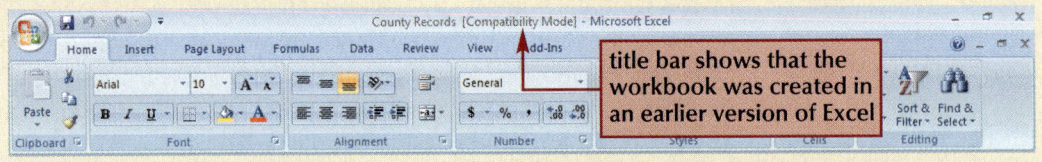

▶ 2. Click the **Office Button**, and then click **Save As**. The Save As dialog box opens.

▶ 3. Type **Bayville County** in the File name box.

The Save as type box shows that the current file format is Excel 97-2003 Workbook, which is the earlier file format. You'll change this to the latest file format.

▶ 4. Click the **Save as type** button, and then click **Excel Workbook**. This is the file format for Excel 2007.

▶ 5. Click the **Save** button. The workbook is saved with the new name and file type.

The workbook remains in Compatibility Mode, as you can see from the title bar. You can continue to work in Compatibility Mode, or you can close and then reopen the workbook in the new file format.

To open the Bayville County workbook in the Excel 2007 file format:

▶ 1. Close the Bayville County workbook.

▶ 2. Open the **Bayville County** workbook. The words *[Compatibly Mode]* no longer appear on the title bar, indicating the workbook is in the Excel 2007 file format.

▶ 3. In the Documentation sheet, enter your name and the current date.

The Data worksheet contains data obtained from the county assessor's office. Myron wants you to convert this data to an Excel table.

To create an Excel table from the county records:

1. Switch to the **Data** worksheet.
2. Click the **Insert** tab on the Ribbon, and then, in the Tables group, click the **Table** button. The Create Table dialog box opens with the data in the range A1:H51 selected.
3. Click the **OK** button to create the Excel table.
4. In the Properties group on the Table Tools Design tab, type **TIPData** in the Table Name box to rename the table.
5. Click the **Data** tab on the Ribbon, and then in the Sort & Filter group, click the **Filter** button. The filter arrows are removed from the column headers.
6. Click any cell in the Excel table.

Using Text Functions

If you receive a workbook from a coworker or obtain data from other software packages, you often have to edit (sometimes referred to as *clean* or *scrub*) and manipulate the data before it is ready to use. Many Text functions help users edit and correct the text values in their workbooks. Text values, also referred to as a *text string* or *string*, contain one or more characters and can include spaces, symbols, and numbers as well as uppercase and lowercase letters. For example, Text functions are used to return the number of characters, remove extra spaces, and change the case of text strings. Figure A-2 reviews some of the common Text functions available in Excel.

Figure A-2 Text functions

Function	Syntax	Description	Example
LEFT	LEFT(text,nbr chars)	Returns a specified number of characters at the left of the string	=LEFT("Michael",3) returns Mic
RIGHT	RIGHT(text,nbr chars)	Returns a specified number of characters at the right of the string	=RIGHT("Michael",3) returns ael
MID	MID(text,start nbr, nbr chars)	Returns a specified number of characters from a string, starting at a position you specify	=MID("Net Income"),5,3) returns Inc
UPPER	UPPER(text)	Converts all lowercase characters in a string to uppercase	=UPPER("kim") returns KIM
LOWER	LOWER(text)	Converts all uppercase characters in a string to lowercase	=LOWER("KIM") returns kim
PROPER	PROPER(text)	Capitalizes first letter of each word in a string	=PROPER("JASON BAKER") returns Jason Baker
LEN	LEN(text)	Returns the number of characters in a string	=LEN("Judith Tinker") returns 13
SEARCH	SEARCH(find_text, within_text, start_nbr)	Returns the number of the character at which the find_text is first found reading from left to right	=SEARCH("Main", "1234 Main St",1) returns 6
TEXT	TEXT((value, format_text_code)	Formats numbers within text using a specific number format	="Total Revenue" & TEXT(SUM(D5:D75),"$#,0.00")
TRIM	TRIM(text)	Remove all spaces from a string except for single spaces between words	=TRIM(" Mary Eck") returns Mary Eck

The Zip column includes zip codes in both 5-digit and 10-digit formats. Myron wants only the 5-digit component of the zip code. You will use the LEN and LEFT functions to convert all of the zip codes to the shorter format.

Using the LEN function

First, you need to determine how many characters are in each cell of the Zip column. The **LEN function** returns the number of characters (length) of the specified string. The syntax for the LEN function is:

LEN(*text*)

In this function, *text* is a string constant or cell address containing a text string. For example, cell D4 stores the text value *Narragansett, ri* so the formula =LEN(D4) returns the value 16, the number of characters, including spaces, in *Narragansett, ri*.

The LEN function will be nested inside an IF function to test whether the length of the zip code is equal to 10. If the length is equal to 10, you will use the LEFT function to display the first 5 digits of the zip code; otherwise, the entire contents of the cell will be displayed.

Using the LEFT Function

The **LEFT function** returns a specified number of characters from the beginning of the string. The syntax for the LEFT function is:

LEFT(*text, number of characters*)

In this function, *text* is a string constant or cell address, and *number of characters* indicates the number of characters from the beginning of the string that you want to return. For example, to extract the 5-digit zip code from the zip code 92975-0999 stored in cell G3, you use the following LEFT function to return 92975:

=LEFT(G3,5)

You can use the IF function to display a 5-digit zip code. The IF function uses the LEN function to test whether the zip code has 10 digits. If true (the zip code is 10 digits), the LEFT function displays the first 5 digits in the cell. If false (the code is not 10 digits), all the digits in the cell are displayed. You'll enter the following formula to display the first five digits from the Zip column:

=IF(LEN([Zip]) = 10, LEFT([Zip],5),[Zip])

You'll insert a new column to the left of the Phone column in which to display the results.

To extract the 5-digit zip code from the Zip column:

1. Click cell **F2**. You'll insert the table column to the left of this column.
2. Click the **Home** tab on Ribbon, in the Cells group, click the **Insert button arrow**, and then click **Insert Table Columns to the Left**. A new column named *Column1* is inserted with the same formatting as the column to its left. The new column is formatted in the Text number format, which is the same format as the Zip column (column E).

   You cannot enter a formula in a cell formatted as Text. You'll convert the new column to General number format.
3. Select the range **F2:F51**, and then, in the Number group on the Home tab, click the **Number Format** box arrow and click **General**.

   Now, you can insert the formula in cell F2.
4. Click cell **F2**, type **=I** and then double-click **IF** to start the formula.
5. Type **L** and then double-click **LEN**. The LEN function is nested in the IF function.

6. Type **[** to begin the column specifier, double-click **Zip**, and then type **])** to complete the LEN function.

7. Type **=10,** to complete the first argument of the IF function. The logical test *LEN([Zip])=10* tests whether the number of characters in the current cell of the Zip column equals 10.

8. Type **L** and double-click **LEFT** to begin the second argument of the IF function.

9. Type **[** to begin the column specifier, double-click **Zip**, and then type **],5),** to complete the second argument. If LEN([Zip])=10 is true, LEFT([ZIP],5) displays the first five characters from the value in the cell.

10. Type **[** to begin the column specifier, double-click **Zip**, and then type **])** to enter the third argument. If LEN([Zip])=10 is false, [Zip] displays all the characters from the value in the cell. The complete formula =IF(LEN([Zip])=10,LEFT([Zip],5),[Zip]) appears in the cell and formula bar.

11. Press the **Enter** key. Each cell in column F displays the 5-digit zip code. See Figure A-3.

Figure A-3 — Table column displays 5-digit zip codes

Parcel ID	First Name	Last Name	City State	Zip	Column1	Phone	Acquired	Market Value
11371432	GRAHAM	EATON	Carolina, ri	02975	02975	4017622349	5/3/2001	433500
12627149	ROXANA	UHLIG	Carolina, ri	02975-0999	02975	3017899520	3/8/1990	342000
135-15-509	DOLORES	FORRESTER	Narragansett, ri	02895	02895	2025493923	5/26/1990	206200
14000828	ELIZABETH	WHITNEY	Narragansett, ri	02895-1222	02895	4013643409	10/23/2006	474300
16410001	CHARLES	BULLOCK	Carolina, ri	02975	02975	4018840669		
17732304			ett, ri	02895-1225	02895	2074834659		
19869177				02975	02975	9784486934		
204-11-401	CYNTHIA	BEROUNSKY	Narragansett, ri	02895	02895	5084571235		
22502215	BARBARA	RICHMOND	Wakefield, ri	02079-1111	02079	4017897684	11/29/1990	413900
23980026	CHARLES	DEVINE	Wakefield, ri	02082-1001	02082	9414931055	10/29/1994	559500
24570875	DAWN	TORTOLANI	Narragansett, ri	02895	02895	8605641644	8/14/2004	444000
264-18-396	GEORGE	HOOPER	Wakefield, ri	02080	02080	7818435164	8/31/1992	440400

You now have two columns with zip codes (column E and F). You need to keep only the column that displays the 5-digit zip code. However, the data in column F is dependent on column E. If you delete column E, column F displays the error value #REF!. Therefore, before you delete column E, you need to convert the data in column F, which is based on a formula, to values. The easiest way to do that is to copy and paste the formula results, but not the actual formula, to a new column using the Paste Values command. Then, you can delete columns E and F.

To convert the 5-digit zip code formula results to values:

1. Click cell **G2**, in the Cells group on the Home tab, click the **Insert button arrow**, and then click **Insert Table Columns to the Left**. A new column named Column 2 is inserted to the left of the Phone column.

2. Select the range **F2:F51**, which contains the formula results you want to convert to values.

3. In the Clipboard group on the Home tab, click the **Copy** button.

4. Click cell **G2**, in the Clipboard group, click the **Paste button arrow**, and then click **Paste Values**. The values from Column 1 are pasted into Column 2.

5. Press the **Esc** key, and then click cell **F2**. The formula appears in the formula bar and the formula results appear in the cell.

> 6. Click cell **G2**. Both the formula bar and the cell display values because you pasted the range using the Paste Values command.
>
>   You no longer need columns E and F, so you will delete them.
>
> 7. Select columns E and F, right-click the selected columns, and then click **Delete**. The two columns are removed.
>
> 8. In cell E1, enter **Zip**. Column E, which stores the 5-digit zip code values, now has a descriptive column header.

Using the Proper Function

Myron wants to capitalize the first letter of each name in the First Name and Last Name columns. The **PROPER function** converts the first letter of each word in a text string to uppercase, capitalizes any letter in a text string that does not follow another letter, and changes all other letters to lowercase. The syntax of the PROPER function is:

PROPER(text)

In this function *text* is a string constant or contents of a cell. For example, the following formula changes the word *BOOTH* to *Booth*:

=PROPER("BOOTH")

Joining Text Using the Concatenation Operator

Myron wants to combine the First Name and Last Name columns into one column named Owner. You need to use the concatenation operator (&, an ampersand) to do this. **Concatenation** describes what happens when you join the contents of two or more cells. The syntax of the concatenation operator is as follows:

Value1 & Value2 [& Value3 …]

where & (the ampersand) operator joins (or concatenates) two or more string constants, cells, or expressions to produce a single string. For example, if cell B2 contains the last name *Eaton* and cell C2 contains the first name *Graham*, and you want to combine these cells' contents to display the full name in cell D2, you can use the following formula to join the contents of the two cells (last name and first name):

=B2 & C2

However, this formula returns *EatonGraham* in cell D2. To include a comma and a space between the two names, you must change the formula to the following:

=B2 & ", " & C2

This formula uses two concatenation operators and a string constant (a comma and a space enclosed in quotation marks) to display *Eaton, Graham*.

You need to combine the PROPER function and the concatenation operator as shown in the following formula:

=PROPER(B2) & ", " & PROPER(C2)

This formula capitalizes the first letter in the First Name and Last Name columns and combines them into one column named *Owner*.

Appendix A Working with Text Functions and Creating Custom Formats

To enter the formula to change the names to standard capitalization and combine them in one column:

1. Click cell **D2**, in the Cells group on the Home tab, click the **Insert button arrow**, and then click **Insert Table Columns to the Left**. A new column named *Column1* is inserted to the left of the City State column.

2. In cell D2, type **=PR**, and then double-click **PROPER**. The beginning of the formula, =PROPER(, appears in the cell and the formula bar.

3. Type **[** to begin the column specifier, double-click **Last Name**, and then type **])** to complete the PROPER function that converts the last name to upper and lowercase letters.

4. Type **& ", "** to join the contents of cell D2 with a comma and space.

5. Type **& PR** and then double-click **PROPER** to begin the second PROPER function.

6. Type **[** to begin the column specifier, double-click **First Name**, and then type **])** to complete the second PROPER function. The complete formula =PROPER([Last Name]) & ", " & PROPER([First Name]) appears in the cell and the formula bar.

7. Press the **Enter** key. Each cell in column D displays the owner's name in the form *Last name, First name* with the first letter of each name capitalized. See Figure A-4.

Figure A-4 Owner's names displayed in one column

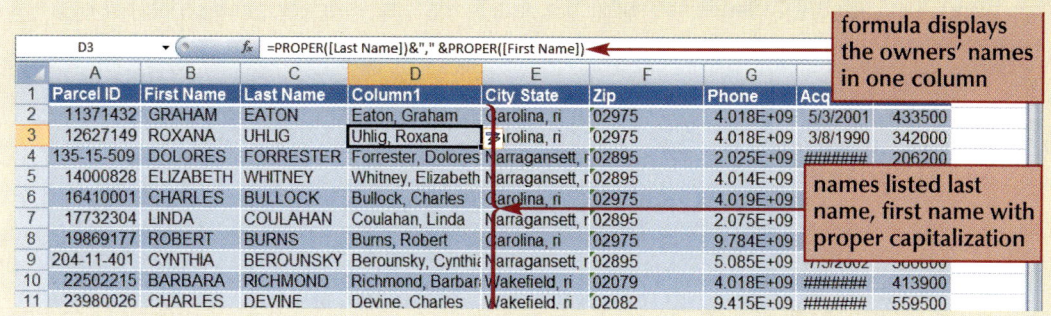

Now that the owners' names data is stored in column D, you no longer need the data in column B (Last Name) and column C (First Name). Because the results in column D are based on a formula, you need to convert the formula in column D to values before you delete columns B and C.

To paste the formula results as values and delete the original data:

1. Click cell **E2**, in the Cells group on the Home tab, click the **Insert button arrow**, and then click **Insert Table Columns to the Left**. A new column named *Column2* is added to the table.

2. Select the range **D2:D51**. You want to copy this range and paste the values to Column2.

3. In the Clipboard group on the Home tab, click the **Copy** button.

4. Click cell **E2**, in the Clipboard group, click the **Paste button arrow**, and then click **Paste Values**.

5. Press the **Esc** key, and then AutoFit column E so you can see the owners' full names.

6. In cell E1, enter **Owner** as the column header.

7. Select columns **B**, **C**, and **D**, right-click the selected columns, and then click **Delete** on the shortcut menu. The three columns are deleted. Column B, the Owner column, remains in the Excel table.

Using the Text to Columns Command

Myron wants you to split the city and state data into different columns. When multiple data is stored in one cell, you can separate each piece of data into a separate column using the Text to Columns command. You select what **delimits**, or separates, the data, such as a tab, a semicolon, a comma, or a space.

To split the city and state data into separate columns:

1. Click cell **D2**, in the Cells group on the Home tab, click the **Insert button arrow**, and then click **Insert Table Columns to the Left**. A new column named *Column1* is inserted to the left of the Zip column.

2. Select the range **C2:C51**. These cells contain the values you want to split.

3. Click the **Data** tab on the Ribbon, and then, in the Data Tools group, click the **Text to Columns** button. The Convert Text to Columns Wizard - Step 1 of 3 dialog box opens. You select how the data is organized in this step—delimited or a fixed width.

4. In the Original data type area, verify that the **Delimited** option button is selected, and then click the **Next** button. The Convert Text to Columns Wizard - Step 2 of 3 dialog box opens. You select the delimiter character in this step.

5. Click any check box with a check mark in the Delimiters section to remove the check mark, and then click the **Comma** check box. The data in the City State column is separated by a comma. The Data preview box shows the City and State data in separate columns. See Figure A-5.

Figure A-5   Convert Text to Columns Wizard - Step 2 of 3 dialog box

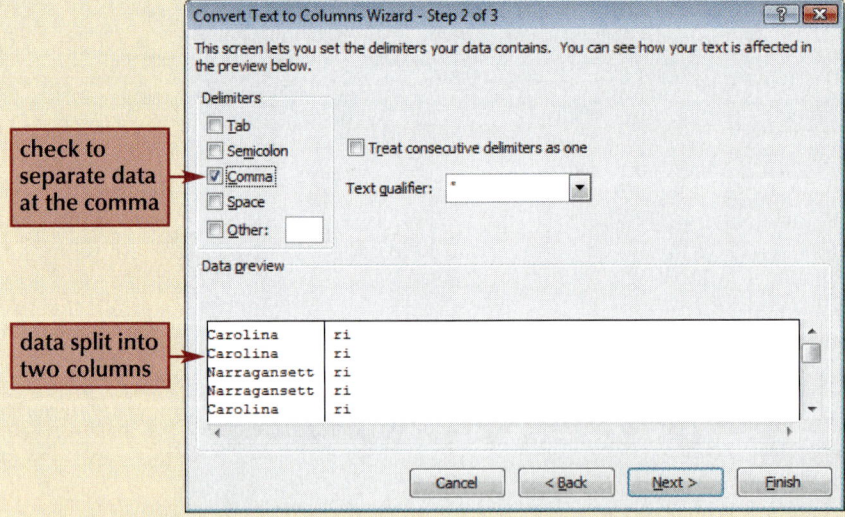

6. Click the **Next** button. The Convert Text to Columns Wizard - Step 3 of 3 dialog box opens so you can set the data format for each column. The Data preview box shows that each column is set to the General number format. You'll leave this format.

7. Click the **Finish** button. The cities remain in column C and the states move to column D.

8. In cell C1, enter **City**. In cell D1, enter **State**. See Figure A-6.

Appendix A Working with Text Functions and Creating Custom Formats | Excel | EX A9

City and state in separate columns | Figure A-6

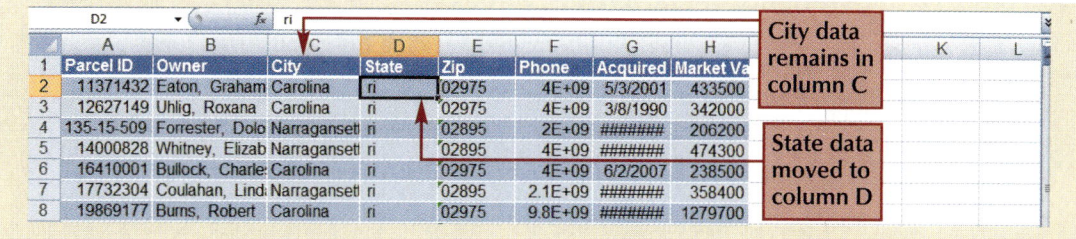

Using the UPPER Function to Convert Case

The state abbreviations in column D are all lowercase. Myron wants to capitalize them. The **UPPER function** converts all letters of each word in a text string to uppercase. The syntax of the UPPER function is:

UPPER(text)

In this function, *text* is a string constant or contents of a cell. For example, the following formula returns RI:

=UPPER("ri")

You'll enter the UPPER function now.

Tip
You can convert cell contents to all lowercase by using the LOWER function.

To enter the UPPER function to capitalize the state abbreviations:

1. Click cell **E2**, and then click the **Home** tab on Ribbon.
2. In the Cells group, click the **Insert button arrow**, and then click **Insert Table Columns to the Left**. A new column named *Column1* is inserted to the left of the Zip column.
3. In cell E2, type **=U**, and then double-click **UPPER**. The beginning of the formula, =UPPER(, appears in the cell and the formula bar.
4. Type **[** to begin the column specifier, double-click **State**, and then type**])**. The formula =UPPER([STATE]) appears in the formula bar.
5. Press the **Enter** key. The state abbreviation appears in all uppercase in column E. See Figure A-7.

UPPER function converts the state abbreviations to uppercase | Figure A-7

You need to keep only the data in column E. Because the results of column E are based on a formula, you again need to convert the formula in column E to values before you delete columns D and E.

To paste the state abbreviations as values:

1. Click cell **F2**. In the Cells group on the Home tab, click the **Insert button arrow**, and then click **Insert Table Columns to the Left**. A new column named Column2 is inserted to the left of column E.

2. Select the range **E2:E51**. You want to copy and paste these values to Column2.

3. In the Clipboard group on the Home tab, click the **Copy** button.

4. Click cell **F2**, in the Clipboard group, click the **Paste button arrow**, and then click **Paste Values**.

5. Select columns **D** and **E**, right-click the selected columns, and then click **Delete** on the shortcut menu. The two columns are deleted. Column D remains in the Excel table.

6. In cell D1, enter **State**. The column is renamed with a more descriptive header.

Using the SUBSTITUTE Function

The entries in Parcel ID, column A, are inconsistent. Sometimes they are an 8-digit value, other times hyphens separate the components of the Parcel (Book No., Map No., and Parcel No.). Myron wants you to remove the hyphens from the Parcel ID. The **SUBSTITUTE function** replaces existing text with new text in a text string. The SUBSTITUTE function has the following syntax:

SUBSTITUTE (*text,old_text,new_text,instance_num*)

In this function, *text* is a string constant or reference to a cell containing text you want to replace, *old_text* is the existing text you want to replace, *new_text* is the text you want to replace *old_text* with, and *instance_num* specifies which occurrence of *old_text* you want to replace. If you omit *instance_num*, every instance of *old_text* is replaced. For example, the following formula returns 16445890:

=SUBSTITUTE("164-45-890","-","").

You'll enter the formula to remove the hyphens from the Parcel ID data.

To remove hyphens from the Parcel ID data:

1. Click cell **B2**. In the Cells group on the Home tab, click the **Insert button arrow**, and then click **Insert Table Columns to the Left**. A new column named Column1 is inserted to the left of the Owner column.

2. Click the **Insert Function** button on the formula bar. The Insert Function dialog box opens.

3. Click the **Or select a category** arrow, click **Text** to display the Text functions, and then double-click **SUBSTITUTE** in the Select a function box. The Function Arguments dialog box opens.

4. In the Text argument box, type **A2**. The text in cell A2 is displayed.

5. In the Old_text argument box, type **"-"**. The hyphen is the text you want to remove.

6. In the New_text argument box, type **""**. You want to replace the old text with nothing. You do not need to enter anything in the Instance_num argument box because you want to replace every instance of a hyphen.

Appendix A Working with Text Functions and Creating Custom Formats | Excel EX A11

7. Click the **OK** button. All of the Parcel IDs are changed to 8-digit numbers. The hyphens were replaced with an empty string (a blank or nothing). See Figure A-8.

Figure A-8 SUBSTITUTE function removed hyphens from the Parcel IDs

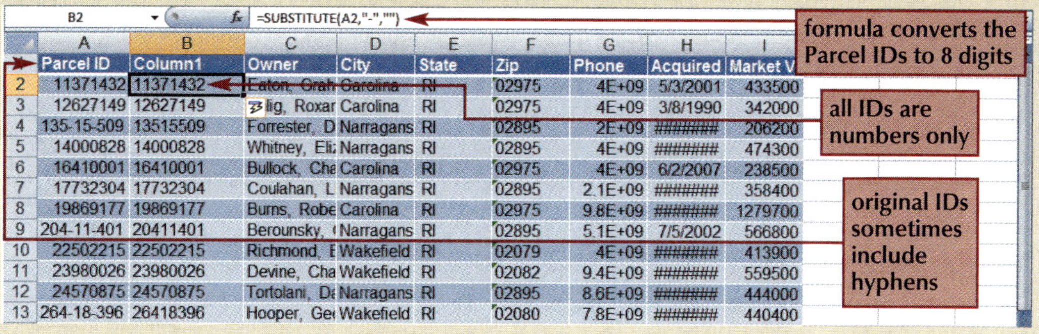

	A	B	C	D	E	F	G	H	I
	Parcel ID	Column1	Owner	City	State	Zip	Phone	Acquired	Market V
2	11371432	11371432	Eaton, Grah	Carolina	RI	02975	4E+09	5/3/2001	433500
3	12627149	12627149	lig, Roxar	Carolina	RI	02975	4E+09	3/8/1990	342000
4	135-15-509	13515509	Forrester, D	Narragans	RI	02895	2E+09	######	206200
5	14000828	14000828	Whitney, Eli	Narragans	RI	02895	4E+09	######	474300
6	16410001	16410001	Bullock, Cha	Carolina	RI	02975	4E+09	6/2/2007	238500
7	17732304	17732304	Coulahan, L	Narragans	RI	02895	2.1E+09	######	358400
8	19869177	19869177	Burns, Robe	Carolina	RI	02975	9.8E+09	######	1279700
9	204-11-401	20411401	Berounsky,	Narragans	RI	02895	5.1E+09	7/5/2002	566800
10	22502215	22502215	Richmond, E	Wakefield	RI	02079	4E+09	######	413900
11	23980026	23980026	Devine, Cha	Wakefield	RI	02082	9.4E+09	######	559500
12	24570875	24570875	Tortolani, D	Narragans	RI	02895	8.6E+09	######	444000
13	264-18-396	26418396	Hooper, Ge	Wakefield	RI	02080	7.8E+09	######	440400

formula converts the Parcel IDs to 8 digits

all IDs are numbers only

original IDs sometimes include hyphens

After you convert the formula in column B to values, you can delete columns A and B.

To paste the Parcel ID column as values:

1. Click cell **C2**. In the Cells group on the Home tab, click the **Insert button arrow**, and then click **Insert Table Columns to the Left**. A new column named *Column2* is inserted to the left of the Owner column.

2. Select the range **B2:B51**. You want to copy this range and paste the values in Column2.

3. In the Clipboard group on the Home tab, click the **Copy** button.

4. Click cell **C2**. In the Clipboard group, click the **Paste button arrow**, and click **Paste Values**.

5. Select columns **A** and **B**, right-click the selected columns, and then click **Delete** on the shortcut menu. The two columns are deleted. Column A, the Parcel ID column, remains in the Excel table.

6. In cell A1, enter **Parcel ID**.

7. AutoFit the Parcel ID, Owner, State, City, Zip, Phone, Acquired, and Market Value columns.

You have cleaned all of the data in the worksheet. Myron can more easily work with the data in this arrangement.

Adding Special and Custom Formatting

Now that the data in the workbook is clean, Myron wants you to apply the following formatting to the data:

- Display the phone number using the common format of area code in parentheses and a hyphen between the prefix and the last four digits.
- Display the market values in thousands, so that a value such as 456600 is displayed as 457.
- Display the acquired date with the name of the month followed by the year (for example, 6/12/2005 is displayed as June, 2005).

These formatting changes will make the data easier to understand and use.

Using Special Formats

Four commonly used formats, referred to as Special formats, are available. They include two zip code formats (5-digit and 10-digit), a phone number format (with area code in parentheses and hyphen between the prefix and the last four digits), and a social security number format. Using these Special formats allows you to type a number without punctuation, yet still display that number in its common format.

> **To format the phone number with the Phone Number format:**
> 1. Select the range **F2:F51**.
> 2. In the Numbers group on the Home tab, click the **Dialog Box Launcher**. The Format Cells dialog box opens with the Number tab active.
> 3. In the Category list, click **Special**. Four special formats appear in the Type list: Zip Code, Zip Code + 4, Phone Number, and Social Security Number.
> 4. In the Type list, click **Phone Number**, and then click the **OK** button. The phone numbers are formatted in a standard phone number format.

Creating Custom Formats

Excel supplies a generous collection of formats and styles to improve the appearance and readability of your documents. However, sometimes you still will not be able to find formats and styles to accommodate a specific requirement. In these cases, you can create your own formats, called **custom formats**. Custom formats use **format codes**, a series of symbols, to describe exactly how Excel should display a number, date, time, or text string. You can use format codes to display text strings and spaces, and determine how many decimal places to display in a cell.

Working with Numeric Format Codes

Each number is composed of digits. In displaying these digits, Excel makes special note of **insignificant zeros**, which are zeros whose omission from the number does not change the number's value. For example, the number 0.1 is displayed in the General number format but changes to 0.10 when the cell is formatted as a number. To format a value, Excel uses the **placeholders** shown in Figure A-9 to represent individual digits.

Description of digit placeholders — Figure A-9

Placeholder	Description
#	Displays only significant digits; insignificant zeros are omitted.
0 (zero)	Displays significant digits as well as insignificant zeros.
?	Replaces insignificant zeros with spaces on either side of the decimal point so that decimal points align when formatted with a fixed-width font, such as Courier.

A custom format can use combinations of these placeholders. For example, the custom format #.00 displays the value 8.9 as 8.90. If a value has more digits than placeholders in the custom format, Excel rounds the value to match the number of placeholders. Thus, the value 8.938 formatted with the custom format #.## is displayed as 8.94. Figure A-10 shows how the same series of numbers appear with different custom number formats.

Examples of digit placeholders — **Figure A-10**

Value in Cell	Custom Formats			
	#.##	0.00	?.??	#.#0
0.57	.57	0.57	.57	.57
123.4	123.4	123.40	123.4	123.40
3.45	3.45	3.45	3.45	3.45
7.891	7.89	7.89	7.89	7.89
5.248	5.25	5.25	5.25	5.25

In addition to digit placeholders, number formats also include separators, such as the decimal point separator (.), the thousands separator (,), and the fraction separator (/). The thousands separator can be used to separate the number in groups of one thousand, but it can also be used to scale a number by a multiple of one thousand.

The fraction separator displays decimal values as fractions. The general syntax is *placeholder/placeholder*, where *placeholder* is one or more of the custom format placeholders discussed above. Excel displays the fraction that best approximates the decimal value. You can also specify the denominator for the fraction to convert the decimals to halves, quarters, and so forth. Figure A-11 provides examples of the thousands separator and the fraction separator.

Examples of thousands separator and fraction separator — **Figure A-11**

Value in Cell	Custom Format	Appearance
12000	#,###	12,000
12000	#,	12
12200000	0.0,,	12.2
5.4	# #/#	5 2/5

All of the numeric format codes can be combined in a single custom format, providing you with great control over data's appearance. If you don't specify a numeric code for data values, Excel uses the General format code, which applies a general numeric format to the data values. The General format hides all insignificant zeros.

Myron wants you to display the market value of the properties to the nearest thousand. You will create the custom format #,###, to display the market values to the nearest thousands.

To create a custom format for the market values to the nearest thousands:

▶ 1. Select the range **H2:H51**.

▶ 2. In the Number group on the Home tab, click the **Dialog Box Launcher**. The Format Cells dialog box opens with the Number tab active.

You will enter a custom format to display the numbers to the nearest thousand.

▶ 3. Click **Custom** in the Category box.

▶ 4. In the Type box, double-click **General** to select it, and then type **#,###,** as the custom format code. See Figure A-12.

| Figure A-12 | Custom category on the Number tab |

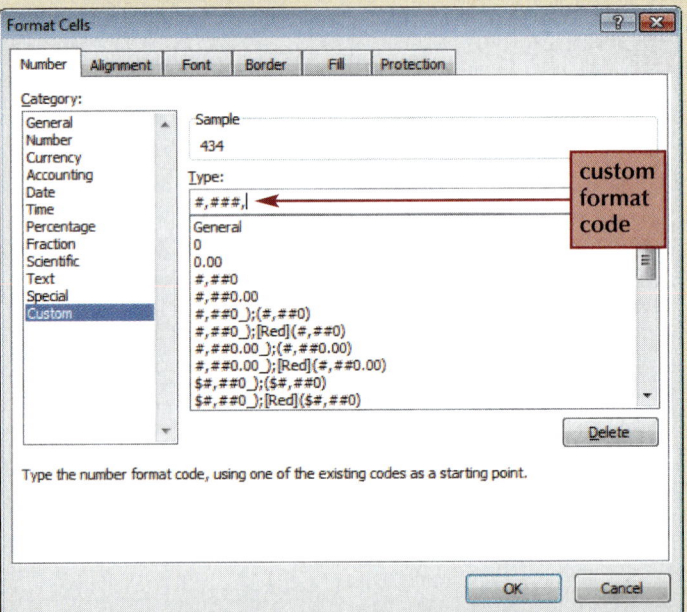

▶ 5. Click the **OK** button. The market values are displayed to the nearest thousand.

Next, you'll enter a comment in cell H1 to explain how the values are displayed.

▶ 6. Right-click cell **H1**, and then click **Insert Comment** on the shortcut menu. A comment box appears next to the cell.

▶ 7. Type **market values are rounded to nearest thousand**, and then click any cell to close the comment box.

▶ 8. Point to cell **H1**. The comment appears.

Formatting Dates

When you have dates, times, or both in a workbook, you can use a predefined date and time format to display this information in a readable format. Although the predefined time and date formats are usually fine, you can also create your own custom date formats. Figure A-13 describes the format codes used for dates and times.

Figure A-13 Date and Time format codes

Symbol	To Display
m	Months as 1 through 12
mm	Months as 01 through 12
mmm	Months as Jan through Dec
mmmm	Months as January through December
d	Days as 1 through 31
dd	Days as 01 through 31
ddd	Days as Sun through Sat
dddd	Days as Sunday through Saturday
yy	Years as 00 through 99
yyyy	Years as 1900 through 9999
h	Hours as 1 through 24
mm	Minutes as 01 through 60 (when immediately following h, mm signifies minutes; otherwise, months)
ss	Seconds as 01 through 60

Myron wants the date values in the Acquired column to show the name of the month followed by the year (for example, July, 2010). You need to apply the custom format code *mmmm, yyyy* to do this.

To apply a custom date format to the Acquisition dates:

1. Select the range **G2:G51**.
2. In the Number group on the Home tab, click the **Dialog Box Launcher**. The Format Cells dialog box opens with the Number tab active.
3. Click **Custom** in the Category box.
4. In the Type box, select the current format, and then type **mmmm, yyyy**. The Sample box shows an example of the custom format you entered.
5. Click the **OK** button, and then click cell **A1** to deselect the range. See Figure A-14.

Figure A-14 Final formatted workbook

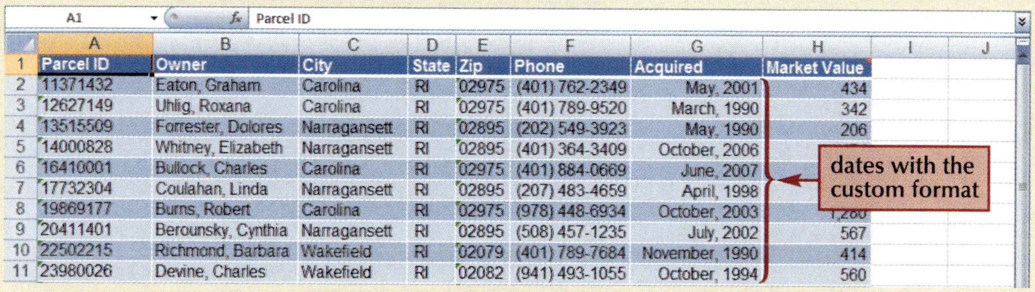

	A	B	C	D	E	F	G	H
1	Parcel ID	Owner	City	State	Zip	Phone	Acquired	Market Value
2	11371432	Eaton, Graham	Carolina	RI	02975	(401) 762-2349	May, 2001	434
3	12627149	Uhlig, Roxana	Carolina	RI	02975	(401) 789-9520	March, 1990	342
4	13515509	Forrester, Dolores	Narragansett	RI	02895	(202) 549-3923	May, 1990	206
5	14000828	Whitney, Elizabeth	Narragansett	RI	02895	(401) 364-3409	October, 2006	
6	16410001	Bullock, Charles	Carolina	RI	02975	(401) 884-0669	June, 2007	
7	17732304	Coulahan, Linda	Narragansett	RI	02895	(207) 483-4659	April, 1998	
8	19869177	Burns, Robert	Carolina	RI	02975	(978) 448-6934	October, 2003	1,260
9	20411401	Berounsky, Cynthia	Narragansett	RI	02895	(508) 457-1235	July, 2002	567
10	22502215	Richmond, Barbara	Wakefield	RI	02079	(401) 789-7684	November, 1990	414
11	23980026	Devine, Charles	Wakefield	RI	02082	(941) 493-1055	October, 1994	560

dates with the custom format

6. Save the workbook.

Any custom format you create is stored in the workbook, and you can apply the custom format to any other cell or range in the workbook. However, you can use a custom format only in the workbook in which it was created. If you want to use the custom formats you created for the Bayville County workbook in another workbook, you need to reenter them.

InSight | Storing Dates and Time in Excel

Excel stores dates and times as a number representing the number of days since January 0, 1900 plus a fractional portion of a 24-hour day. This is called a **serial date**, or serial date-time.

Dates The integer portion of the number is the number of days since January 0, 1900. For example, the date 1/1/2010 is stored as 40,179, because 40,179 days have passed since January 0, 1900. The number 1 is the serial date for 1/1/1900.

Times The decimal portion of the number is the fraction of a 24-hour day that has passed. For example, 6:00 AM is stored as 0.25, which is 25% of a 24-hour day. Similarly, 6 PM is stored as 0.75, which is 75% of a 24-hour day.

Any date and time can be stored as the sum of the date and the time. For example, 3 PM on 1/1/2010 is stored in Excel as 40,179.625.

As an experiment, enter 1/1/2010 in cell A1 of a new worksheet. Change the format in the cell to General. The value appears as 40179. Change the format to a Short Date format to see the value displayed as 1/1/2010.

Using the Compatibility Checker

Myron needs to travel to Seattle while continuing to work on this project. Although all of the desktop computers at Zeus Engineering have Excel 2007 installed, Myron's notebook computer hasn't yet been upgraded. Myron asks you to make a copy of the current workbook, converting it to a format Excel 2003 can read. When you save an Excel 2007 formatted workbook to an earlier format, the **Compatibility Checker** alerts you to any features that are not supported by earlier versions of Excel.

To convert an Excel 2007 workbook to an earlier Excel file format:

1. Click the **Office Button**, and then click **Save As**. The Save As dialog box opens.
2. In the File Name box, change the filename to **Bayville County 2003**.
3. Click the **Save as type** button, and then click **Excel 97-2003 Workbook**. This is the earlier Excel file format you want to use.
4. Click the **Save** button. The Microsoft Office Excel – Compatibility Checker dialog box opens, alerting you to features not supported by earlier versions of Excel. See Figure A-15.

Figure A-15 | **Compatibility Checker**

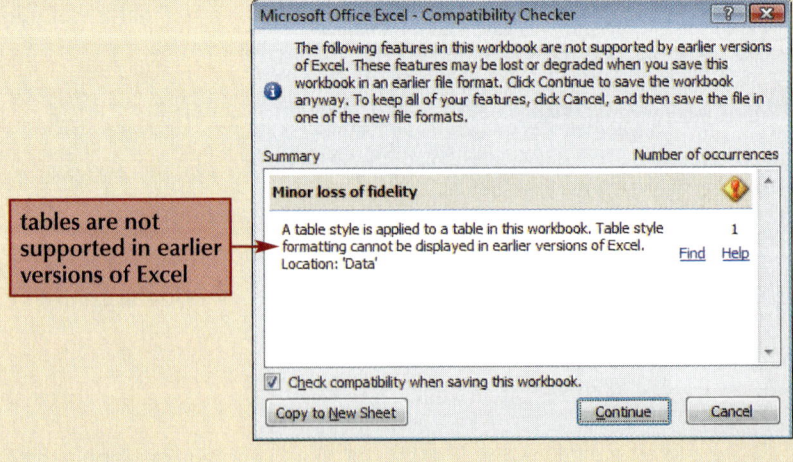

tables are not supported in earlier versions of Excel

> 5. Read the message, and then click the **Continue** button. The workbook is saved in the earlier file format with the file extension .xls.
>
> 6. Close the workbook.

The workbook data is clean and formatted in the best way for Myron. He'll analyze this data as he comes up with a proposal to address Bayville's traffic concerns.

Appendix Summary | Review

In this appendix, you used a variety of Text functions, the concatenation operator, and the Text to Column command. You created a custom format to round numbers to the nearest thousands. Finally, you created a custom format code to display dates as a month and year.

Key Terms

Compatibility Checker	format code	PROPER function
Compatibility Mode	insignificant zero	serial date (or serial date-time)
concatenation	LEFT function	
custom format	LEN function	SUBSTITUTE function
delimit	placeholder	UPPER function

Practice

Practice the skills you learned in the appendix using the same case scenario.

Review Assignments

Data File needed for the Review Assignments: Assessor.xls

As part of the Transportation Improvement Program (TIP) study, Myron Londale, traffic analyst at Zeus Engineering, obtained a second workbook from the Bayville Assessor's Office containing data on private homes and commercial buildings located along the route being reviewed. The assessor's office was able to transfer the data requested by Zeus Engineering to Excel. Before Myron begins his analysis, he asks you to clean and format the data.

Complete the following:

1. Open the **Assessor** workbook located in the Appendix.A\Review folder included with your Data Files, and then save the workbook in the Excel 2007 format as **Owners** in the same folder.
2. Insert a new worksheet. Enter your name, the date, and a purpose statement in the worksheet, and then rename the worksheet as **Documentation**.
3. Create an Excel table for the data in the range A1:G5.
4. Use the Text to Columns command to split the Owner column into two columns named **Last Name** and **First Name**. Insert a blank column to the left of column C to store the first name and leave the last name in column B.
5. In cell I1, enter the column header **Status**. In the Status column, use the IF and LEFT functions to display the word **Discard** if the address is a PO Box; otherwise, leave the cell blank.
6. In cell J1, enter the column header **Twn**. In cell J2, enter a formula to convert the data in the Town column to proper case.
7. In cell K1, enter the column header **St**. In column K, enter a formula to convert the data in the State column to uppercase.
8. In cell L1, enter the column header **Town State**. In column L, combine the town and state data into one column using the format *town, state*.
9. Format the data in the SSN column (column A) with the special Social Security number format.
10. Save and close the workbook. Submit the finished workbook to your instructor, either in printed or electronic form, as requested.

Apply

Apply the skills you learned to clean and format membership data.

Case Problem 1

Data File needed for this Case Problem: Mesa.xls

Mesa Senior Center Elliot Turner, director of the Mesa Senior Center, has begun compiling a list of its members. He's asked you to clean and format the data in the worksheet before he continues working on the project.

Complete the following:

1. Open the **Mesa** workbook located in the Appendix.A\Case1 folder included with your Data Files, and then save the workbook as **Senior Center** in the same folder.
2. Insert a new worksheet. Enter your name and the date in the worksheet, and then rename the worksheet as **Documentation**.

3. In the Members worksheet, apply the special Social Security Number format to the data in the SSN column.
4. Split the Name data into two columns. Store the first name in column B and the last name in column C. Change the column headers to **First Name** (column B) and **Last Name** (column C).
5. Insert two columns to the left of the City column. In column D, apply the proper case to the first name data, and change the column header to **F Name**. In column E, apply the proper case to the last name data, and change the column header to **L Name**.
6. In the Member Since column, apply a custom format that displays only the year.
7. Split the CSZ column into three columns named **City**, **State**, and **Zip**.
8. Sort the data by City and then within City by L Name.
9. Name column J as **UniqueID**. Instead of using Social Security numbers as the unique identifier, the senior center is considering using an ID of the first three letters of the last name (L Name) followed by the first letter of first name (F Name). If the last name is fewer than three characters, the letter Z replaces each missing character. Use the LEN and LEFT functions and the concatenation operator to display the proposed Unique ID.
10. Save the workbook. Submit the finished workbook to your instructor, either in printed or electronic form, as requested.

| Apply | Case Problem 2 |

Apply the skills you learned to calculate overhead allocation.

Data File needed for this Case Problem: Research.xls

Steuben Institute Every two weeks Elli Pjster processes payroll information for employees whose salaries are paid fully or partially from research grants. She downloads an Excel workbook from the Institute's Research and Grant Accounting system to calculate overhead. The overhead rate varies depending on the research grant. Overhead is calculated by multiplying the employee salary by the overhead rate of the grant that funds the employee. She asks you to clean and format the data in the worksheet.

Complete the following:

1. Open the **Research** workbook located in the Appendix.A\Case2 folder included with your Data Files, and then save the workbook in the Excel 2007 file format as **Grants** in the same folder.
2. Insert a new worksheet, enter the company name, your name, the date, and a purpose statement in the worksheet, and then rename the worksheet as **Documentation**.
3. In the Pay Period worksheet, create an Excel table for the data in the range A1:C51. Hide the filter arrows.
4. Split the data in column A into separate columns for the first name and the last name. Change the column headers to **First Name** and **Last Name**. AutoFit the two columns, and then sort the table by the Last Name data.

EXPLORE
5. Use the MID function to extract the grant number from the ChartString column and display it in column E. Name the new column **Grant Nbr**. The Grant Nbr is a four-digit number that begins in position ten of the ChartString column. (*Hint:* Research the MID function in the Help system.)

6. In the column to the right of the Grant Nbr column (column F), enter a VLOOKUP function to find the grant number in the lookup table in the Overhead Rates worksheet and display the grant name from column 2. Name the column header in cell F1 **Grant Name**. AutoFit the column.

7. In column G enter the formula to calculate overhead, which is the Overhead Rate located in the third column of the Overhead Rates worksheet multiplied by Salary. You need to use a VLOOKUP function to find the correct overhead rate for the grant. Name the column **Overhead**.

8. Format the Salary and Overhead columns in the Accounting number format with two decimals place.

9. Save and close the workbook. Submit the finished workbook to your instructor, either in printed or electronic form, as requested.

Ending Data Files

Appendix.A → Tutorial
Bayville County.xlsx
Bayville County 2003.xls

Review
Owners.xlsx

Case1
Senior Center.xlsx

Case2
Grants.xlsx

Integrating Excel with Other Windows Programs

Creating Integrated Documents

Objectives

- Learn about methods of integration using Office programs
- Link an Excel worksheet to a Word document
- Update a linked object
- Embed an object
- Modify an embedded object

Case | Metro Zoo

Marvin Hall is the director of Metro Zoo. Each year, he sends out a financial report to the zoo's supporters and contributors. Marvin stores the financial data in an Excel workbook, and he uses Word to create a letter that includes data from Excel. Marvin wants to be able to copy the Excel data and insert it directly into the Word document. He also wants to tie the two documents together, so that if he updates the financial information in the Excel workbook, the report in the Word document will be automatically updated as well.

Marvin asks you to help him integrate his Excel data into his Word document and link the files, so that the data in the report is automatically updated each time Marvin modifies the workbook.

Starting Data Files

→ Tutorial
MZoo.xlsx
Zoo Letter.docx

Review
Sales Memo.docx
State Sales.xlsx

Case1
Event.docx
Quote.xlsx

Case2
Request.docx
Usage.xlsx

Methods of Integration

Excel is part of a suite of programs called Microsoft Office. In addition to Excel, the Office programs include Word, a word-processing program; Access, a database management program; PowerPoint, a presentation and slide show program; Outlook, a personal information manager; and Publisher, a program for creating desktop publishing projects. All of these programs share a common interface and can read each other's file formats.

Occasionally, you will create a file that relies on data from more than one program. This type of file is called a **compound file**. The **source file** (or files) supplies the data to be shared. The **destination file** (or files) displays the data from the source file (or files). Compound files are easy to create in Office because of the tight integration of the Office programs. At Metro Zoo, Marvin needs to create a letter using Word that incorporates information from an Excel workbook that contains financial data as well as a chart.

There are three ways to insert data from one program into another program: copying and pasting, linking, and embedding. Each of these techniques can be used to create a compound file. Figure B-1 describes each of these methods, and provides examples of when each method is appropriate.

Figure B-1: Integration methods

Method	Description	Use When
Copying and pasting	Inserts an object into a file	You want to exchange the data between the two files only once, and it doesn't matter if the data changes.
Linking	Displays an object in the destination file but doesn't store it there—only the location of the source file is stored in the destination file	You want to use the same data in more than one file, and you need to ensure that the data will be current and identical in each file. Any changes you make to the source file will be reflected in the destination file(s).
Embedding	Displays and stores an object in the destination file	You want the source data to become a permanent part of the destination file, or the source data will no longer be available to the destination file. Any changes you make to either the destination file or the source file do not affect the other.

Copying and Pasting Data

You can copy text, values, cells and ranges, or even charts and graphics from one program and paste it in another program using the Windows copy and paste features. The item being copied and pasted is referred to as an **object**. When you paste an object from the source file into the destination file, you are inserting the object so that it is part of the destination file. The **pasted object** is static, having no connection to the source file. If you want to change the pasted object, you must do so in the destination file. For example, a range of cells pasted into a Word document can be edited only within the Word document. Any changes made in the original Excel workbook have no impact on the Word document. For this reason, pasting is used only for one-time exchanges of information.

Object Linking and Embedding

If you want to create a live connection between two files, so that changes in the source file are automatically reflected in the destination file, you must use object linking and embedding. **Object linking and embedding (OLE)** refers to the technology that allows you to copy and paste objects, such as graphic files, cell and ranges, or charts, so that information about the program that created the object is included with the object itself.

The objects are inserted into the destination file as either linked objects or embedded objects. A **linked object** is actually a separate file that is linked to the source file. If you make a change to the source file, the destination file can automatically reflect the change. On the other hand, an **embedded object** is stored in the destination file (Word, in this example) and is no longer part of the source file. In the case of Office programs, embedded objects include their Ribbon, tabs, and buttons. This means you can edit an Excel worksheet or chart embedded in a Word document using Excel tools and commands to modify the worksheet or chart content. Because embedded objects have no link to the source file, changes made to the embedded object are not reflected in the source file.

Thus, the main difference between linked and embedded objects lies in where the data is stored and how the data is updated after being inserted into the destination file. Figure B-2 illustrates the difference between linking and embedding.

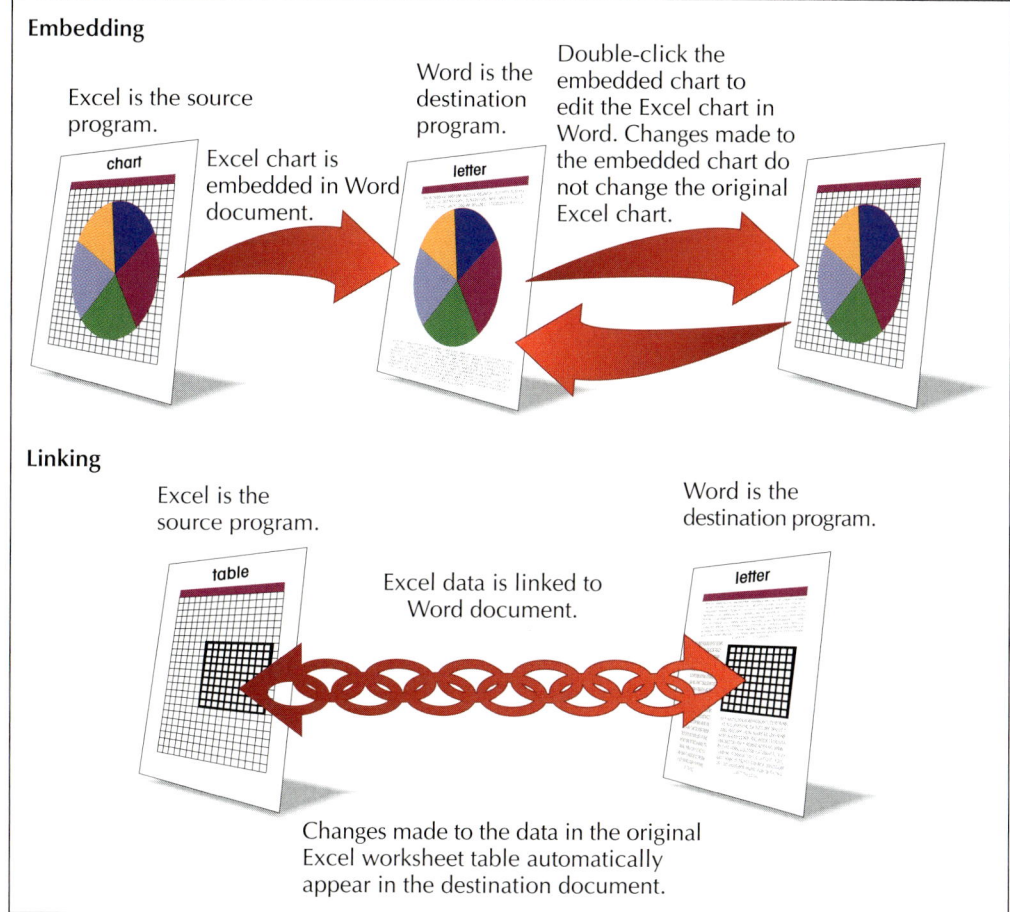

Figure B-2 Embedding contrasted with linking

Linking Excel and Word Files

Marvin asks you to insert the financial data stored in a workbook into a letter he has been writing to Metro Zoo's supporters. He is still working on the details of the financial report, and he might need to edit some of the values in the workbook. Rather than pasting the data each time he modifies the report, Marvin wants you to create a link between his Excel workbook and his Word document, so that any changes he makes to the workbook are automatically reflected in the letter. You will open both files and link the Excel data to the Word document.

To open Marvin's two files:

1. Open the **MZoo** Excel workbook located in the **Appendix.B\Tutorial** folder included with your Data Files, and then save the workbook as **Metro Zoo** in the same folder.
2. In the Documentation sheet, enter your name and the current date.
3. Open the **Zoo Letter** Word document located in the **Appendix.B\Tutorial** folder included with your Data Files, and then save the document as **Metro Zoo Ltr** in the same folder.
4. Return to the **Metro Zoo** workbook, and then switch to the **Financial Summary** worksheet.

The financial data Marvin wants to display in his letter is stored in the range A2:D17 of the Financial Summary worksheet. To transfer that data, you'll copy the range in the workbook and then paste the data as a link in the Word document.

To copy and paste a link:

1. Select the range **A2:D17**.
2. In the Clipboard group on the Home tab, click the **Copy** button.
3. Return to the **Metro Zoo Ltr** document, and then click the paragraph mark below the letter's second paragraph (below the sentence that reads "Below are Metro Zoo's revenues and expenses for the past two years"). See Figure B-3.

Figure B-3 Metro Letter document

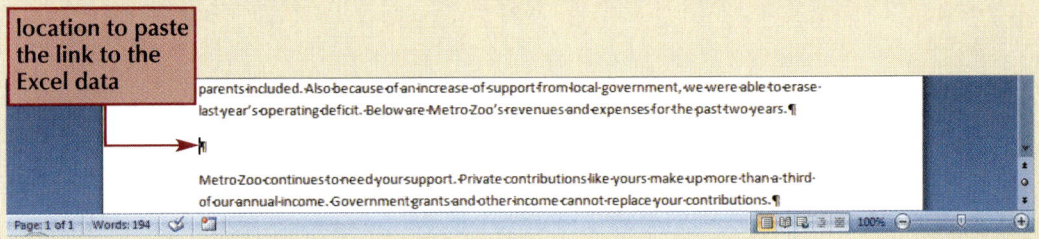

location to paste the link to the Excel data

Trouble? If your document does not show paragraph marks at the end of each paragraph, you need to show the nonprinting characters. In the Paragraph group on the Home tab, click the Show/Hide button.

4. In the Clipboard group on the Home tab, click the **Paste button arrow**, and then click **Paste Special**. The Paste Special dialog box opens. The Paste link option enables you to paste data in several different formats. The default format is to insert the data as a Word table using HTML (Hypertext Markup Language). You could also paste the data as a graphic image, unformatted text, or an embedded worksheet object. See Figure B-4.

Appendix B Integrating Excel with Other Windows Programs

Figure B-4: Paste Special dialog box

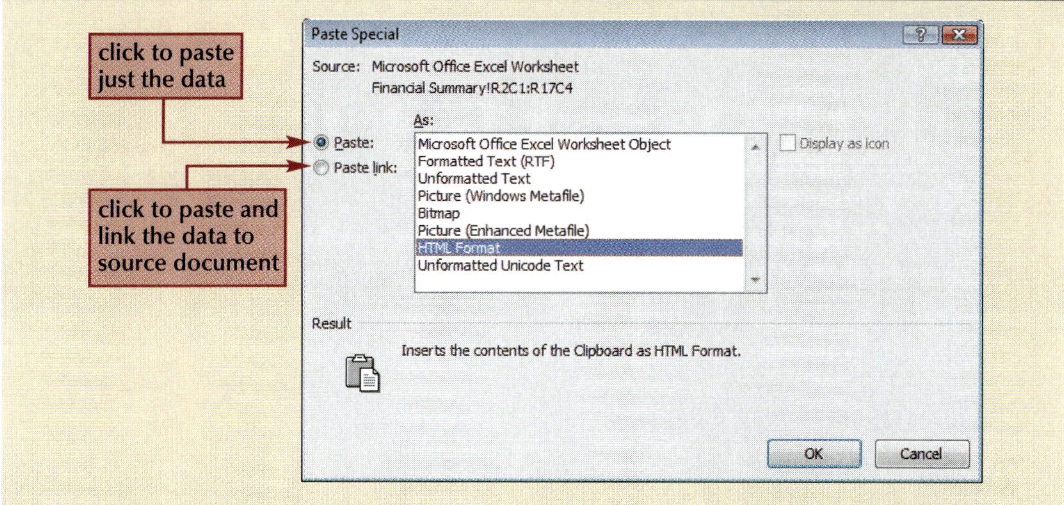

- click to paste just the data
- click to paste and link the data to source document

▶ 5. Click the **Paste link** option button, and then click **Microsoft Office Excel Worksheet Object**.

▶ 6. Click the **OK** button. Word places a link (the location of the source file) to the Excel object within the Word document so the financial data is linked to the Excel workbook. A representation of the financial data is displayed in the Word document, as shown in Figure B-5.

Figure B-5: Financial data pasted into the Metro Zoo Ltr document

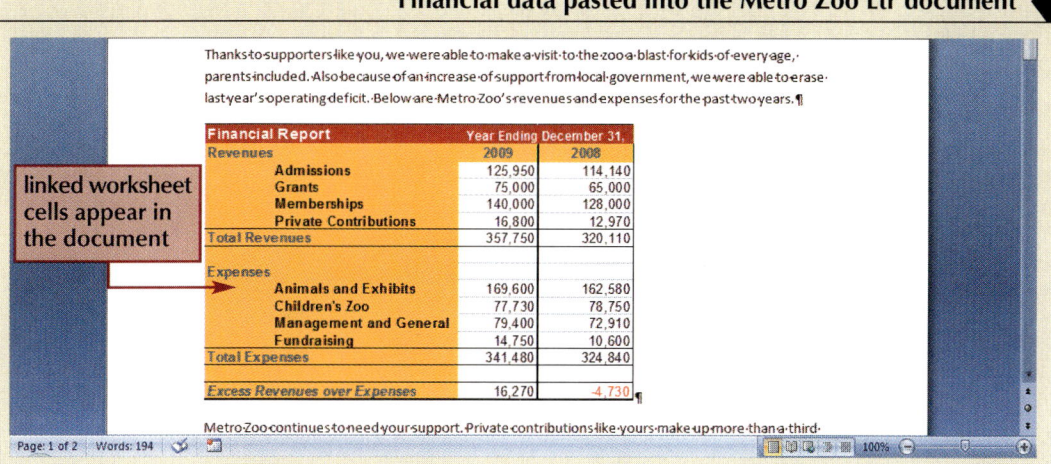

- linked worksheet cells appear in the document

Tip
You can edit and format this table using any of the Word formatting features.

Updating a Linked Object

When an object is linked, the linked objects are updated automatically. This means that Word updates the linked information every time you open the Word document or any time the Excel source file changes while the Word document is open.

Marvin finished reviewing the financial summary in the Metro Zoo workbook. He finds a data-entry error in the report. A $2500 overstatement of a government grant to Metro Zoo was entered in error. You need to correct the total amounts of grants. You can update the linked data without having to paste the data again.

To update the linked data:

1. Return to the **Metro Zoo** workbook, and then press the **Esc** key to deselect the range A2:D17.
2. In cell C5 enter **72500**. The correct value for the government grants is inserted.
3. Switch to the **Metro Zoo Ltr** document to verify that the value of the grant changed, reflecting the current value in the Metro Zoo workbook.

   Trouble? If the link doesn't update automatically, right-click the table and click Update Link on the shortcut menu.

> **Tip**
> You can also double-click the Excel object in Word to return to Excel and edit the Excel worksheet. The linked object in Word is automatically updated.

Embedding an Object

Marvin also wants the letter to include the pie chart in the Metro Zoo workbook that details the source of Metro Zoo's revenue. Marvin is confident that the financial summary is correct and requires no further edits. Therefore, you don't need to create a link between Marvin's letter and the workbook's chart. Instead, Marvin wants to embed the chart in the letter. Then, he will be able to use the Excel chart-editing tools directly from the Word document, if he chooses to modify the chart's appearance before printing the letter. You will embed the Revenue chart in the document.

To embed an Excel chart in a Word document:

1. Switch to the **Metro Zoo** workbook, and then click the **Revenues** chart to select it.
2. In the Clipboard group on the Home tab, click the **Copy** button.
3. Switch to the **Metro Zoo Ltr** document, and then click the paragraph mark above the letter's next to last paragraph (above the sentence that reads "If you would like to learn more about the Metro Zoo...").
4. In the Clipboard group on the Home tab, click the **Paste button arrow**, and then click **Paste Special**. The Paste Special dialog box opens, displaying two format options for charts in the As box. You can choose to paste the chart as an Excel chart object; or you can choose to paste the chart as a graphic object. Marvin wants to be able to use the Excel chart-editing tools, so you'll choose the first option.
5. Verify that the **Paste** option button is selected, click **Microsoft Office Excel Chart Object**, and then click the **OK** button. Excel places a copy of the chart as an embedded object into the letter. See Figure B-6.

Figure B-6 — Chart embedded in the Metro Zoo Letter document

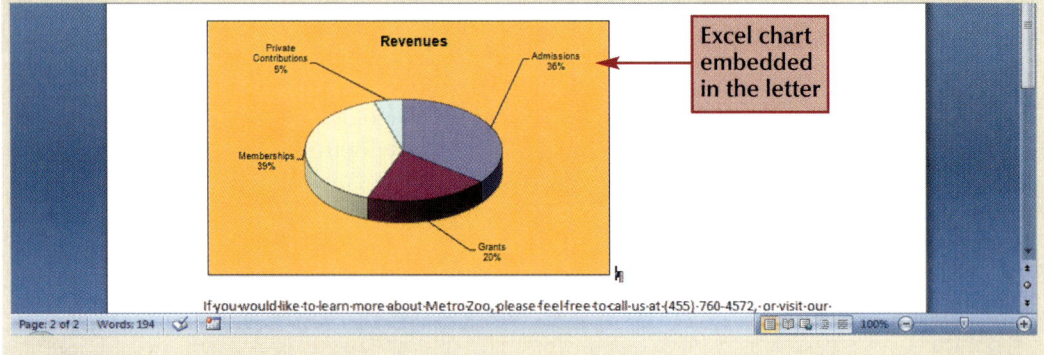

Modifying an Embedded Object

Embedded objects such as the chart become part of the Word document after they are inserted; they are no longer linked to the source file. For example, if you change the chart in the source file, the embedded object in Word does not change. Conversely, if you change the embedded object in Word, the source file is not modified.

After viewing the contents of the chart, Marvin wants you to change the chart's title from "Revenues" to "Revenues for 2009." You can do this by editing the chart within Word. Recall that when you make changes to an embedded object, those changes will not be reflected in the object in the source file. You will change the title of the chart that is embedded in the letter.

To edit the embedded chart:

1. Double-click the embedded chart in the Metro Zoo Letter document, and then click anywhere within the chart. The hatch-marked border appears around the chart, and the embedded object appears in an Excel workbook window, as shown in Figure B-7. Also, notice that the Ribbon shows the Excel tabs and buttons.

Figure B-7 Embedded chart selected for editing

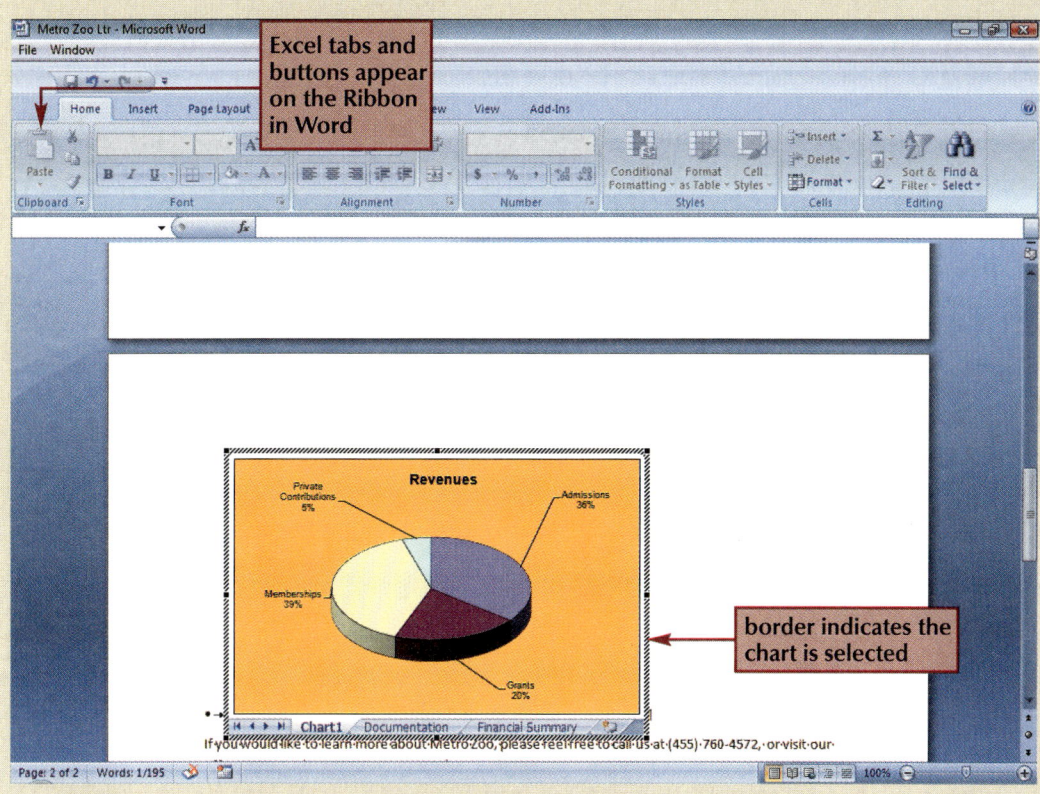

You can edit the object using the Excel chart-editing tools within Word.

2. Click the **Title object** and change the title to **Revenues for 2009**. The chart title is updated.

3. Click outside the chart to deselect it. See Figure B-8.

Figure B-8 Embedded chart updated with new chart title

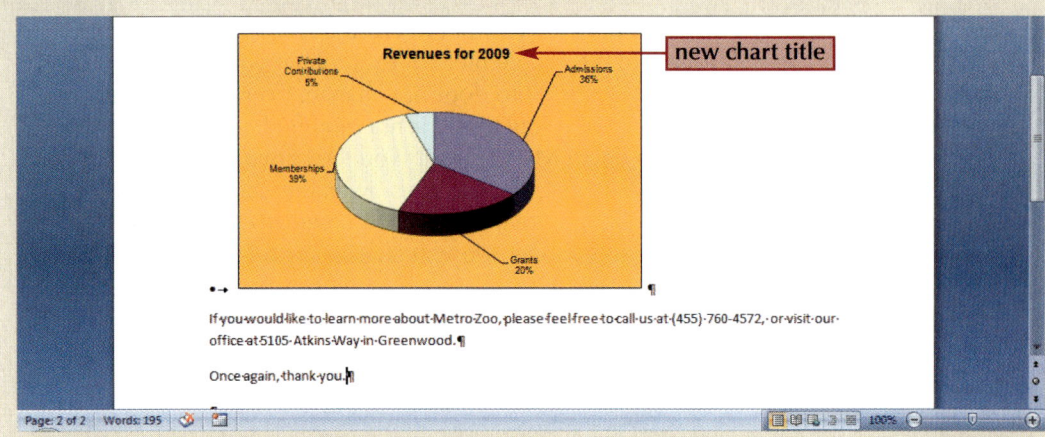

Your work on both the Metro Zoo workbook and the Metro Zoo Letter document are complete. You can save your changes and then exit the programs.

4. Save and close the Metro Zoo Ltr document, and then exit Word.

5. Return to the **Metro Zoo** workbook, and verify that the revenue chart title remains *Revenues*. The title was not updated to *Revenues for 2009* because you edited the embedded chart, which is not linked to the Excel workbook.

6. Save and close the Metro Zoo workbook, and then exit Excel.

You may have noticed in Figure B-8 that the embedded object included not just the chart sheet for the revenue statement, but also the other worksheets in the workbook. You could have selected one of the other worksheets in the workbook and displayed that information in place of the chart. This highlights one disadvantage of embedded objects: They tend to greatly increase the size of the destination file. The Metro Zoo Letter document now contains both the original letter and the Metro Zoo workbook. For this reason, you should embed objects only when file size is not an issue.

Appendix Summary | Review

In this appendix, you examined the different methods for sharing data between Office programs. You learned how to copy data from Excel to Word using pasting and linking. You saw how changes to the data in an Excel workbook are updated automatically in a linked Word document. You also learned how to embed an Excel chart within a Word document, making Excel tools available in Word.

Key Terms

compound file
destination file
embedded object
linked object
object
object linking and
    embedding (OLE)
pasted object
source file

Practice

Practice the skills you learned in the appendix.

Review Assignments

Data Files needed for the Review Assignments: State Sales.xlsx, Sales Memo.docx

Happy Morning Farms Cassie Meyers is product manager for a line of breakfast cereals at Happy Morning Farms. Cassie is waiting for one number to complete her sales report for next week's Operations Management Team (OMT) meeting. As she is working on the report, she receives an urgent call from the Chicago sales representative, asking her to come to Chicago immediately to deal with a customer problem that requires management attention. Cassie plans to complete her sales report while she is in Chicago. After she finishes the report, she will e-mail it to John Styles, a colleague, who will represent her at the meeting.

Complete the following:

1. Open the **State Sales** workbook located in the Appendix.B\Review folder included with your Data Files, and then save the workbook as **State Sales Embed** in the same folder.
2. In the Documentation sheet, enter the date and your name, and then switch to the Sales Data worksheet.
3. Open the **Sales Memo** document located in the Appendix.B\Review folder, and then save the document as **Sales Memo Embed** in the same folder.
4. Return to the State Sales Embed workbook, and then copy the range A1:C24 in the Sales Data worksheet.
5. Return to the Sales Memo Embed document, and embed the worksheet data you copied at the end of the memo.
6. Save the Sales Memo Embed document. Close the State Sales Embed workbook.
7. Update the Word document by entering the Iowa sales for this month, which are $42.1 (omit the 000). Do not open the Excel workbook.
8. Save and close the Sales Memo Embed document.
9. Open the **State Sales** workbook located in the Appendix.B\Review folder included with your Data Files, and then save the workbook as **State Sales Link** in the same folder.
10. In the Documentation sheet, enter the date and your name, and then switch to the Sales Data worksheet.
11. Open the **St Memo** document located in the Appendix.B\Review folder, and then save the document as **Sales Memo Link** in the same folder.
12. Return to the State Sales Link workbook, and then copy the range A1:C24 in the Sales Data worksheet.
13. Return to the Sales Memo Link document, and then paste the selected range as a link at the end of the memo. Save the Word document.
14. Update the State Sales Link workbook by entering the Iowa sales for this month, which are $42.1 (omit the 000).
15. Save and close the Sales Memo Link document.
16. Open both the **State Sales Embed** and **State Sales Link** workbooks. Scroll to cell C10, sales for Iowa, in each worksheet. Using the results in these cells, explain the differences between object linking and embedding.
17. Close all files. Submit the finished workbooks and documents to your instructor, either in printed or electronic form, as requested.

Apply | Case Problem 1

Apply the skills you learned by inserting Excel objects into a Word document.

Data Files needed for this Case Problem: Quote.xlsx, Event.docx

Kirk Harbor Inn Ellen Felton is events coordinator at Kirk Harbor Inn, which is located on Cape Cod. She schedules weddings, conferences, engagements, and so forth at this waterfront Victorian inn. She constantly is sending quotes to potential clients and asks you to assist her in linking the workbook she developed to the letter she sends to potential clients.

Complete the following:

1. Open the **Quote** workbook located in the Appendix.B\Case1 folder included with your Data Files, and then save the workbook as **Harbor Quote** in the same folder.
2. In the Documentation sheet, enter the date and your name, and then switch to the Quote worksheet.
3. Open the **Event** document located in the Appendix.B\Case1 folder, and then save the document as **Event Planner** in the same folder.
4. Return to the Harbor Quote workbook, and then copy the range B2:H20 in the Quote worksheet.
5. Return to the Event Planner document, and then paste the selected range as a link below the sentence "Here are the details."
6. Ellen's client requests two changes: move the wedding to the Salon room and change the number of guests to 160. Make these changes in the Harbor Quote workbook, and then verify that the Harbor Quote document is updated. (*Hint*: You might need to right-click the mouse and click Update Link.)
7. Save and close the Harbor Quote and Event Planner files. Submit the finished workbook and document to your instructor, either in printed or electronic form, as requested.

Apply | Case Problem 2

Apply the skills you learned by inserting Excel objects into a Word document.

Data Files needed for this Case Problem: Usage.xlsx, Request.docx

Bright Light Peter Skinner is writing a letter to the state government to report on the Shelter and meal programs used at Bright Light. He has data in an Excel workbook and needs to incorporate the data into the letter he is composing in Word. Because the report will also include projections for the upcoming year, which he might modify, Peter wants to create a link between the information in the Excel workbook and the Word document. He also wants to embed in the Word document a chart that he has created in his workbook. He asked you to help link the two files.

Complete the following:

1. Open the **Usage** workbook located in the Appendix.B\Case2 folder included with your Data Files, and then save the workbook as **Bright Usage** in the same folder.
2. In the Documentation sheet, enter the date and your name, and then switch to the Shelter Usage worksheet.
3. Open the **Request** document located in the Appendix.B\Case2 folder, and then save the document as **Bright Request** in the same folder.
4. Return to the Bright Usage workbook, and then copy the range A2:G9 in the Shelter Usage worksheet.
5. Return to the Bright Request document, and then paste the selected range as a link below the first paragraph of Peter's letter. (*Hint*: If necessary, display the paragraph marks in the Word document.)

EXPLORE

6. Peter discovered that the number of client days in the domestic abuse shelter in December 2010 was actually 75, not 72. Make this change in the Bright Usage workbook, and then verify that the Bright Request document is automatically updated. (*Hint*: If necessary, use the Update Link command on the shortcut menu to see the change.)
7. Copy the Projected Usage chart from the Shelter Usage worksheet, and then embed the chart below the second paragraph in Peter's letter (do not link the chart).
8. Edit the embedded chart, changing the background color of the plot area from yellow to white.
9. Save and close the Bright Request and Bright Usage files. Submit the finished workbook and document to your instructor, either in printed or electronic form, as requested.

Ending Data Files

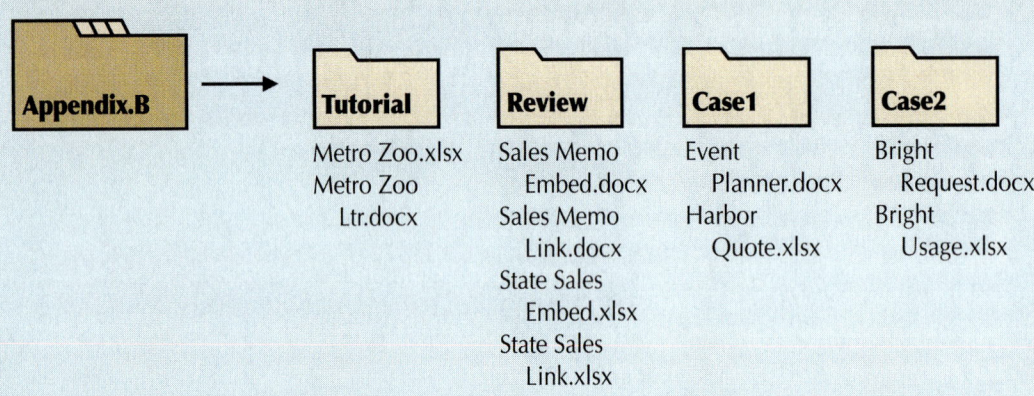

Appendix.B → **Tutorial**
Metro Zoo.xlsx
Metro Zoo
Ltr.docx

Review
Sales Memo
  Embed.docx
Sales Memo
  Link.docx
State Sales
  Embed.xlsx
State Sales
  Link.xlsx

Case1
Event
  Planner.docx
Harbor
  Quote.xlsx

Case2
Bright
  Request.docx
Bright
  Usage.xlsx

APPENDIX A

Introduction to Microsoft Windows 7

This appendix introduces you to the new Microsoft Windows 7 operating system. In this appendix, you'll find a complete tutorial, "Exploring the Basics of Microsoft Windows 7," which covers fundamental Windows concepts and skills, including:

- Exploring the desktop and Start menu
- Running software programs and switching between them
- Navigating your computer using Windows Explorer and the Computer window
- Getting Help with Windows tasks

In addition, this appendix highlights some of the exciting advances in Windows 7, including the updated taskbar, the simplified Navigation pane, and the innovative library feature for easier file management.

This appendix also offers a preview of the new design elements you'll find in the upcoming Microsoft Windows 7 and Microsoft Office 2010 texts being produced by the *New Perspectives Series*:

- New *Visual Overviews* at the beginning of each session include colorful, enlarged screenshots with numerous callouts and key term definitions, giving you a comprehensive preview of the topics to be presented as well as a handy study guide.
- New *ProSkills boxes* provide guidance for how to use the software in real-world, professional situations, with relevant information on one or more of the following soft skills: decision making, problem solving, teamwork, verbal communication, and written communication.

Exploring the Basics of Microsoft Windows 7

Investigating the Windows 7 Operating System

OBJECTIVES

Session 1
- Start Windows 7 and tour the desktop
- Explore the Start menu
- Run software programs, switch between them, and close them
- Identify and use the controls in windows and dialog boxes

Session 2
- Navigate your computer using Windows Explorer and the Computer window
- Change the view of the items in your computer
- Get help with Windows 7 tasks
- Turn off Windows

Case | Back to Work

Back to Work is a nonprofit agency in Minneapolis, Minnesota, that helps people who want to develop skills for the contemporary workforce, such as retirees and parents who are returning to careers after raising a family. Back to Work creates customized plans for people preparing for full- or part-time work. Elena Varney, the director of the agency, coordinates training sessions on developing a wide range of computer skills.

Elena recently hired you to teach some introductory computer classes. Your first class on using the Microsoft Windows 7 operating system meets next week. To help you prepare for your class, Elena offers to walk you through the curriculum, from starting the computer and opening and closing programs to shutting down the computer. In this tutorial, you will start Windows 7 and practice some fundamental computer skills. Then, you'll learn how to navigate using the Computer window and Windows Explorer. Finally, you'll use the Windows 7 Help system and turn off Windows 7.

STARTING DATA FILES

There are no starting Data Files needed for this tutorial.

SESSION 1 VISUAL OVERVIEW

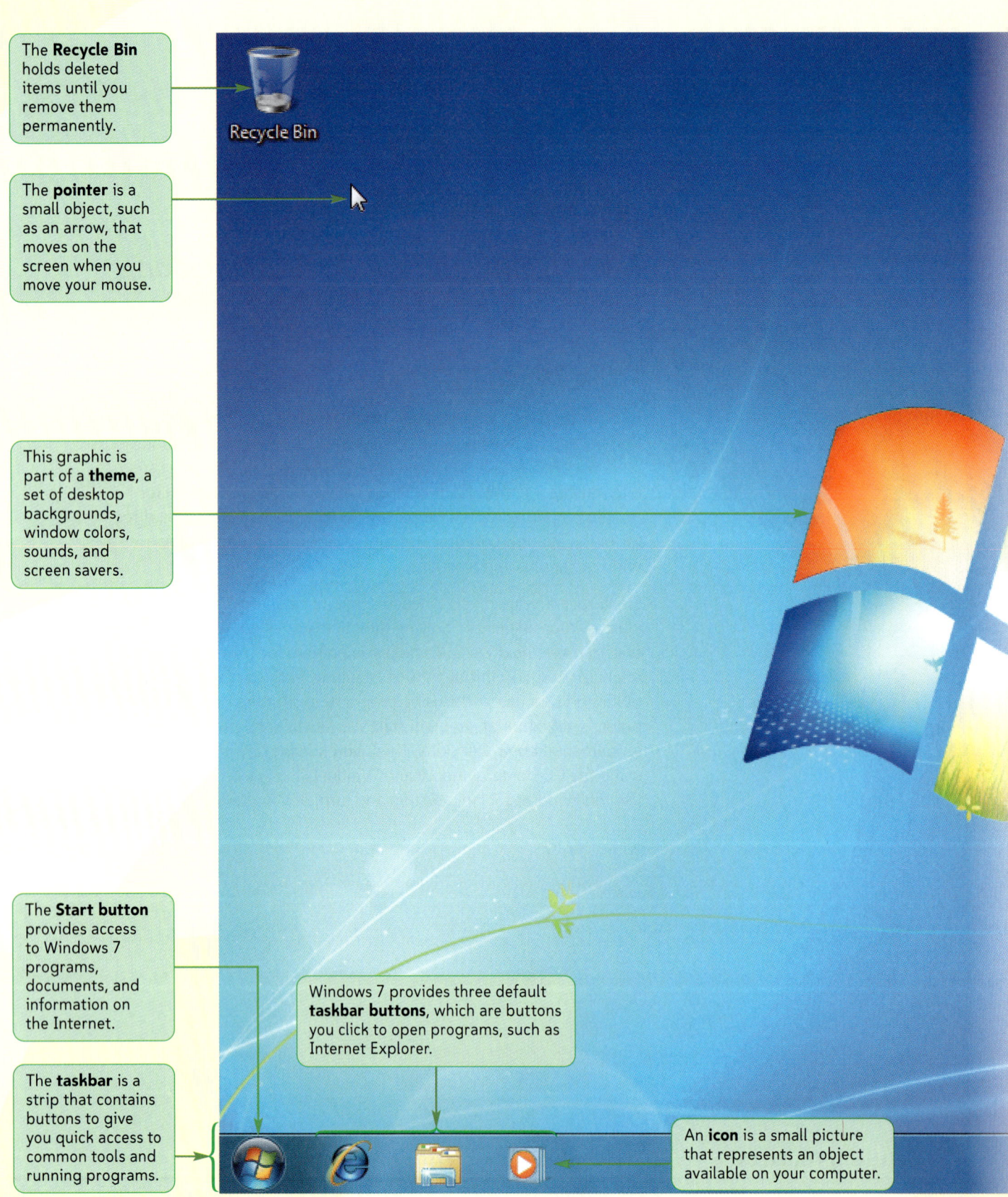

The **Recycle Bin** holds deleted items until you remove them permanently.

The **pointer** is a small object, such as an arrow, that moves on the screen when you move your mouse.

This graphic is part of a **theme**, a set of desktop backgrounds, window colors, sounds, and screen savers.

The **Start button** provides access to Windows 7 programs, documents, and information on the Internet.

The **taskbar** is a strip that contains buttons to give you quick access to common tools and running programs.

Windows 7 provides three default **taskbar buttons**, which are buttons you click to open programs, such as Internet Explorer.

An **icon** is a small picture that represents an object available on your computer.

THE WINDOWS 7 DESKTOP

The Windows 7 **desktop** is your workspace on the screen.

The **notification area** displays icons corresponding to services running in the background, such as an Internet connection.

The **Date/Time control** is an element that shows the current date and time and lets you set the clock.

Starting Windows 7

The **operating system** is software that manages and coordinates activities on the computer and helps the computer perform essential tasks, such as displaying information on the computer screen and saving data on disks. (The term *software* refers to the **programs**, or **applications**, that a computer uses to complete tasks.) Your computer uses the **Microsoft Windows 7** operating system—**Windows 7** for short. *Windows* is the name of the operating system, and *7* indicates the version you are using.

Much of the software created for the Windows 7 operating system shares the same look and works the same way. This similarity in design means that after you learn how to use one Windows 7 program, you are well on your way to understanding how to use others. Windows 7 allows you to use more than one program at a time, so you can easily switch between your word-processing program and your appointment book program, for example. It also makes it easy to access the **Internet**, a worldwide collection of computers connected to one another to enable communication.

Windows 7 starts automatically when you turn on your computer. After completing some necessary start-up tasks, Windows 7 displays a Welcome screen, which lists all the users for the computer. Before you start working with Windows 7, you might need to click your **user name** (a unique name that identifies you to Windows 7) and type a **password** (a confidential series of characters) before you can work with Windows 7. After you provide this information, the Windows 7 desktop appears.

To begin your review of Windows 7, Elena asks you to start Windows 7.

To start Windows 7:

1. Turn on your computer. After a moment, Windows 7 starts and the Welcome screen appears.

   Trouble? If you are asked to select an operating system, do not take action. Windows 7 should start automatically after a designated number of seconds. If it does not, ask your instructor or technical support person for help.

2. On the Welcome screen, click your user name and enter your password, if necessary. The Windows 7 desktop appears, as shown in the Session 1 Visual Overview. Your desktop might look different.

   Trouble? If your user name does not appear on the Welcome screen, first try pressing the Ctrl+Alt+Del keys to enter it. If necessary, ask your instructor or technical support person for further assistance.

   Trouble? If you need to enter a user name and a password, type your assigned user name, press the Tab key, type your password, and then click the Continue button or press the Enter key to continue.

   Trouble? If a blank screen or an animated design replaces the Windows 7 desktop, your computer might be set to use a **screen saver**, a program that causes a monitor to go blank or to display an animated design after a specified amount of idle time. Press any key or move your mouse to restore the Windows 7 desktop.

The Windows 7 desktop uses a **graphical user interface** (**GUI**, pronounced *gooey*), which uses graphics to represent items stored on your computer, such as programs and files. A computer **file** is a collection of related information; typical types of files include text documents, spreadsheets, digital pictures, and songs. Your computer displays files as icons, which are pictures of familiar objects, such as file folders and documents. Windows 7 gets its name from the rectangular work areas, called windows, that appear on your screen as you work, such as those shown in Figure 1.

Figure 1 Two windows open on the desktop

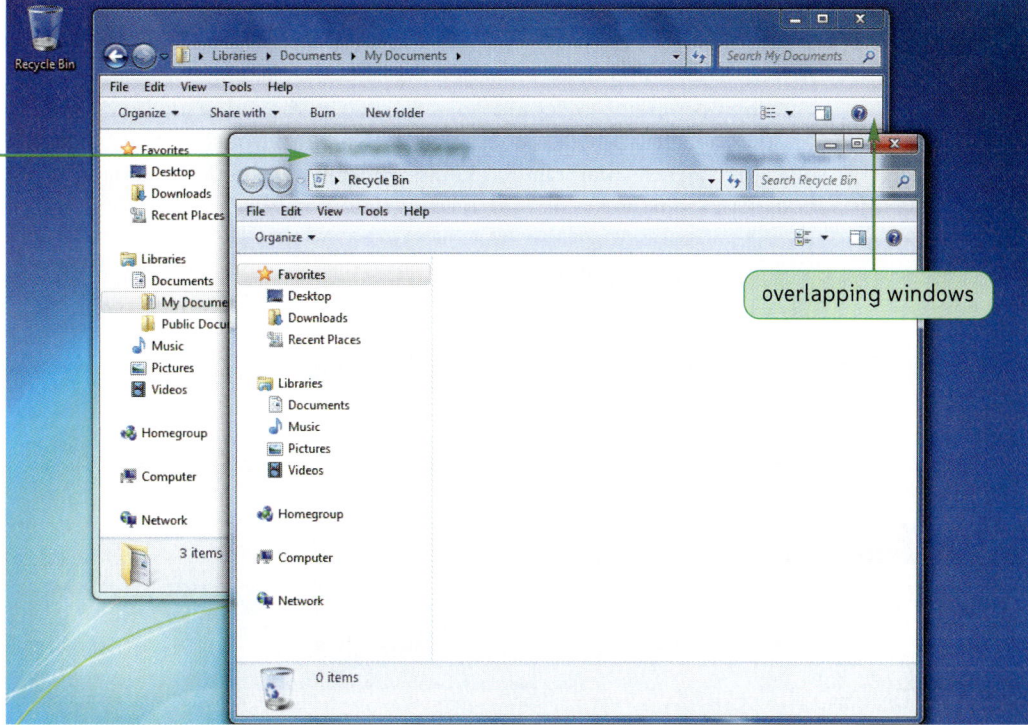

translucent color is characteristic of the Aero experience

overlapping windows

INSIGHT

Windows 7 and the Aero Desktop Experience

Windows 7 provides themes, which are sets of desktop backgrounds, window colors, sounds, and screen savers that allow you to personalize the Aero desktop experience. The themes that take advantage of Aero's rich three-dimensional appearance are called Aero themes. You can use an Aero theme only if your computer hardware and version of Windows 7 support it. (The Microsoft Web site at *www.microsoft.com* provides detailed information about the requirements for using Aero themes.) Otherwise, your computer is set by default to use a desktop theme called Windows 7 Basic, which provides most of the same elements as the enhanced experience, including windows and icons, but not the same graphic effects. In this appendix, the figures show the Windows 7 Aero theme. If you are using Windows 7 Basic or a high contrast theme, the images on your screen will vary slightly from the figures and some features will not be available. (These are noted throughout the appendix.)

Touring the Windows 7 Desktop

In Windows terminology, the desktop is a workspace for projects and the tools that you need to manipulate your projects. When you first start a computer, it uses **default settings**, those Windows 7 has already set. The default desktop you see after you first install Windows 7, for example, displays a blue background with a four-color Windows logo. However, Microsoft designed Windows 7 so that you can easily change the appearance of the desktop. You can, for example, change images or add patterns and text to the desktop.

Interacting with the Desktop

To interact with the objects on your desktop, you use a **pointing device**. The most common type is called a **mouse**, so this book uses that term. If you are using a different pointing device, such as a trackball or touchpad, substitute that device whenever you see the term *mouse*.

You use a pointing device to move the mouse pointer over objects on the desktop, or to **point** to them. The pointer is usually shaped like an arrow, although it changes shape depending on the pointer's location on the screen and the tasks you are performing. As you move the mouse on a surface, such as a mouse pad, the pointer on the screen moves in a corresponding direction.

When you point to certain objects, such as the icons on the taskbar, a **ScreenTip** appears near the object to tell you the name or purpose of that object.

Elena suggests that you acquaint students with the desktop by viewing a couple of ScreenTips.

To view ScreenTips:

1. Use the mouse to point to the **Start** button on the taskbar. After a few seconds, you see a ScreenTip identifying the button, as shown in Figure 2.

   Trouble? If you don't see the ScreenTip, make sure you are holding the mouse still for a few seconds.

Figure 2 — Viewing a ScreenTip

2. Point to the time and date displayed at the right side of the taskbar. A ScreenTip showing today's date (or the date to which your computer's calendar is set) appears in a long format, such as Monday, December 2, 2013.

Clicking refers to pressing a mouse button and immediately releasing it. Clicking sends a signal to your computer that you want to perform an action on the object you click. In Windows 7, you perform most actions with the left mouse button. If you are told to click an object, position the pointer on that object and click the left mouse button, unless instructed otherwise.

When you click the Start button, the Start menu opens. A **menu** is a group or list of commands, and a **menu command** is text that you can click to complete tasks. If a right-pointing arrow follows a menu command, you can point to the command to open a **submenu**, which is a list of additional choices related to the command. The **Start menu** provides access to programs, documents, and much more.

To open the Start menu:

1. Point to the **Start** button on the taskbar.
2. Click the left mouse button. The Start menu opens. An arrow points to the All Programs command on the Start menu, indicating that you can view additional choices by navigating to a submenu.
3. Click the **Start** button on the taskbar to close the Start menu.

You need to select an item, or object, before you can work with it. To **select** an object in Windows 7, you usually point to and then click that object. Sometimes you can select menu commands simply by pointing to them. Windows 7 shows you which object is selected by highlighting it, usually by changing the object's color, putting a box around it, or making the object appear to be pushed in.

Appendix A Exploring the Basics of Microsoft Windows 7 | Windows

To select a menu command:

1. Click the **Start** button on the taskbar.
2. Point to **All Programs** on the Start menu. The All Programs command is highlighted to indicate it is selected. After a short pause, the All Programs list opens. See Figure 3.

Figure 3   All Programs list

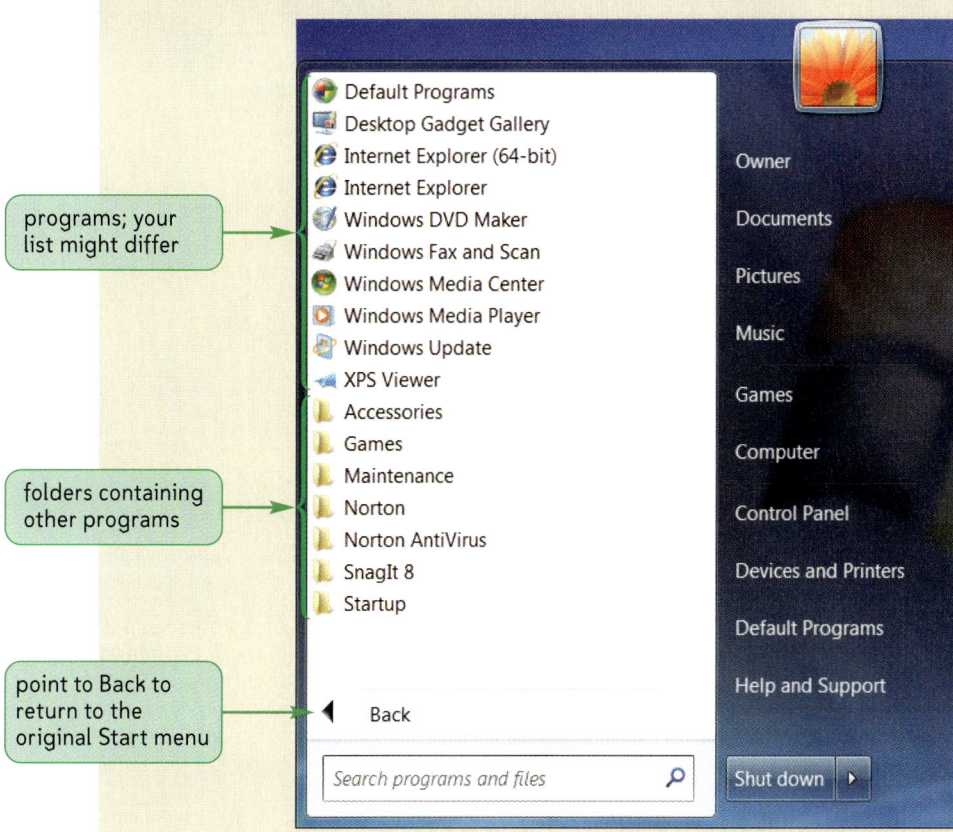

3. Click the **Start** button on the taskbar to close the Start menu.

In addition to clicking an object to select it, you can double-click an object to open or start the item associated with it. For example, you can double-click a folder icon to open the folder and see its contents. (A **folder** is a container that helps to organize the contents of your computer, such as files and folders.) Or you can double-click a program icon to start the program. **Double-clicking** means clicking the left mouse button twice in quick succession.

Elena suggests that you have students practice double-clicking by opening the Recycle Bin. The Recycle Bin holds deleted items until you remove them permanently.

To view the contents of the Recycle Bin:

1. Click the **desktop** to clear any selections, and then point to the **Recycle Bin** icon on the desktop. A ScreenTip appears that describes the Recycle Bin.
2. Click the left mouse button twice quickly to double-click the **Recycle Bin** icon. The Recycle Bin window opens, as shown in Figure 4.

Figure 4 Contents of the Recycle Bin

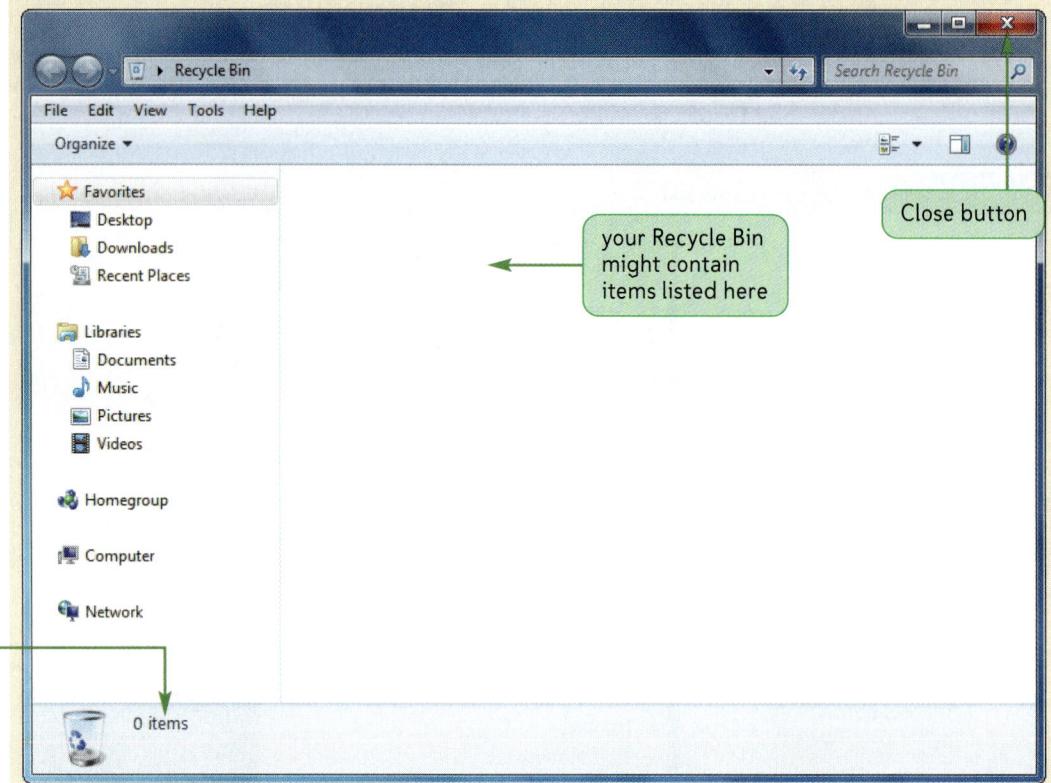

Trouble? If the Recycle Bin window does not open, and you see only the Recycle Bin name highlighted below the icon, you double-clicked too slowly. Double-click the icon again more quickly.

3. Click the **Close** button in the upper-right corner of the Recycle Bin window.

You'll learn more about opening and closing windows later in this session.

Your mouse has more than one button. In addition to the left button, the mouse has a right button that you can use to perform certain actions in Windows 7. However, the term *clicking* continues to refer to the left button; clicking an object with the right button is called **right-clicking**.

In Windows 7, right-clicking selects an object and opens its **shortcut menu**, which lists actions you can take with that object. You can right-click practically any object—the Start button, a desktop icon, the taskbar, and even the desktop itself—to view commands associated with that object. Elena reminds you that you clicked the Start button with the left mouse button to open the Start menu. Now you can right-click the Start button to open the shortcut menu for the Start button.

To right-click an object:

1. Position the pointer over the **Start** button on the taskbar.
2. Right-click the **Start** button to open its shortcut menu. This menu offers a list of actions you can take with the Start button. See Figure 5.

Appendix A Exploring the Basics of Microsoft Windows 7 | Windows   WIN7 11

Figure 5 — Start button shortcut menu

- right-click the Start button
- shortcut menu; yours might differ

Trouble? If the shortcut menu does not open and you are using a trackball or a mouse with a wheel, make sure you click the button on the far right, not the one in the middle.

Trouble? If your menu looks slightly different from the one in Figure 5, it is still the correct Start button shortcut menu. Its commands often vary by computer.

3. Press the **Esc** key to close the shortcut menu.

After opening the Start menu and its shortcut menu, you're ready to explore its contents.

Exploring the Start Menu

Recall that the Start menu is the central point for accessing programs, documents, and other resources on your computer. The Start menu is organized into two **panes**, which are separate areas of a menu or window. Each pane lists items you can point to or click. See Figure 6.

Figure 6 — Start menu

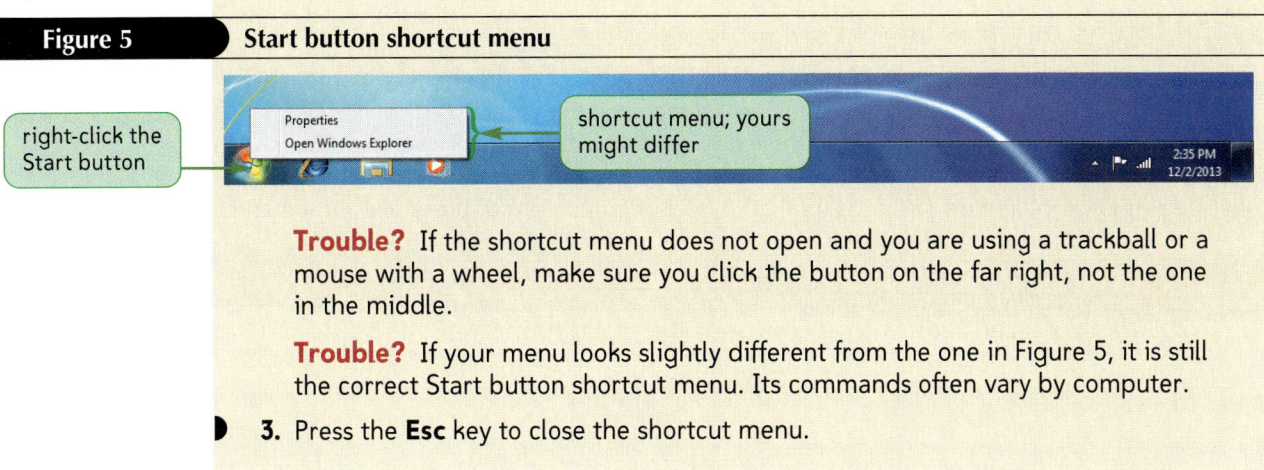

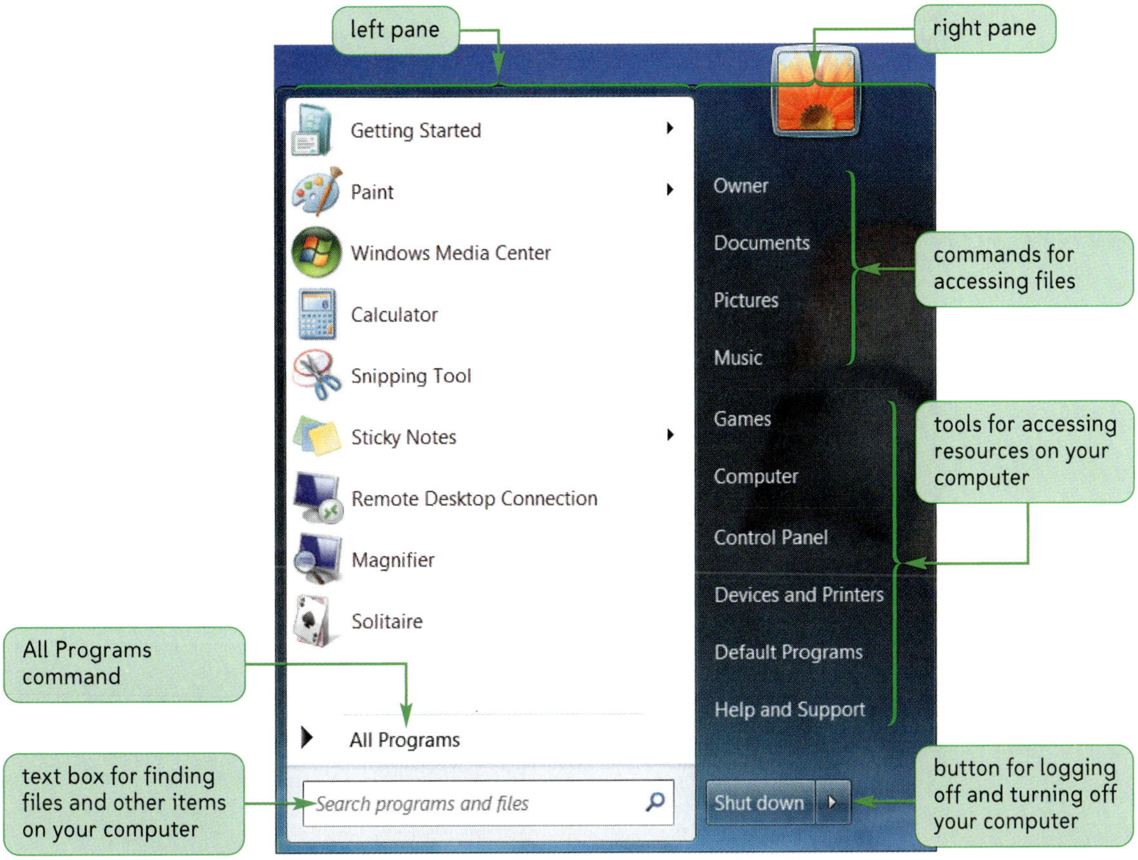

- left pane
- right pane
- commands for accessing files
- tools for accessing resources on your computer
- All Programs command
- text box for finding files and other items on your computer
- button for logging off and turning off your computer

The left pane organizes programs for easy access. When you first install Windows 7, the left pane contains a short list of programs on your computer. After you use a program, Windows 7 adds it to this list so you can quickly find it the next time you want to use it. The Start menu can list only a certain number of programs—after that, the programs you have not opened recently are replaced by the programs you used last.

Near the bottom of the left pane is the All Programs command, which you have already used to display the All Programs list. The All Programs list provides access to the programs currently installed on your computer. You'll use the All Programs list shortly to start a program.

The **Search programs and files box** helps you quickly find anything stored on your computer, including programs, documents, pictures, music, videos, Web pages, and e-mail messages. When you want to use the Search programs and files box, you open the Start menu and type one or more words related to what you want to find. For example, if you want to find and play the Happy Birthday song stored on your computer, you could type *birthday* in the Search programs and files box. Windows 7 searches your computer for that song and displays it and any other search results in the Start menu, where you can click the song to play it.

From the right pane of the Start menu, you can access common locations and tools on your computer. For example, the **Computer window** is a tool that you use to view, organize, and access the programs, files, and drives on your computer.

From the bottom section of the right pane, you can open windows that help you effectively work with Windows 7, including the **Control Panel**, which contains specialized tools that help you change the way Windows 7 looks and behaves, and **Help and Support**, which provides articles, video demonstrations, and steps for performing tasks in Windows 7. You also turn off your computer from the Start menu.

> **TIP**
>
> When the Start menu displays search results, it organizes them into groups, such as programs and files.

REFERENCE

Starting a Program

- Click the Start button on the taskbar, and then click the name of the program you want to start.

or

- Click the Start button on the taskbar, and then point to All Programs.
- If necessary, click the folder that contains the program you want to start.
- Click the name of the program you want to start.

Windows 7 includes an easy-to-use word-processing program called WordPad, which you can use to write a letter or report. To start WordPad, you open the Start menu and then navigate to the Accessories folder in the All Programs list.

To start the WordPad program from the Start menu:

1. Click the **Start** button on the taskbar to open the Start menu.
2. Point to **All Programs**, and then click **Accessories**. The Accessories folder opens. See Figure 7.

   Trouble? If a different folder opens, point to Back to return to the initial Start menu, point to All Programs, and then click Accessories.

Appendix A Exploring the Basics of Microsoft Windows 7 | Windows   WIN7 13

| Figure 7 | Accessories folder open on the Start menu |

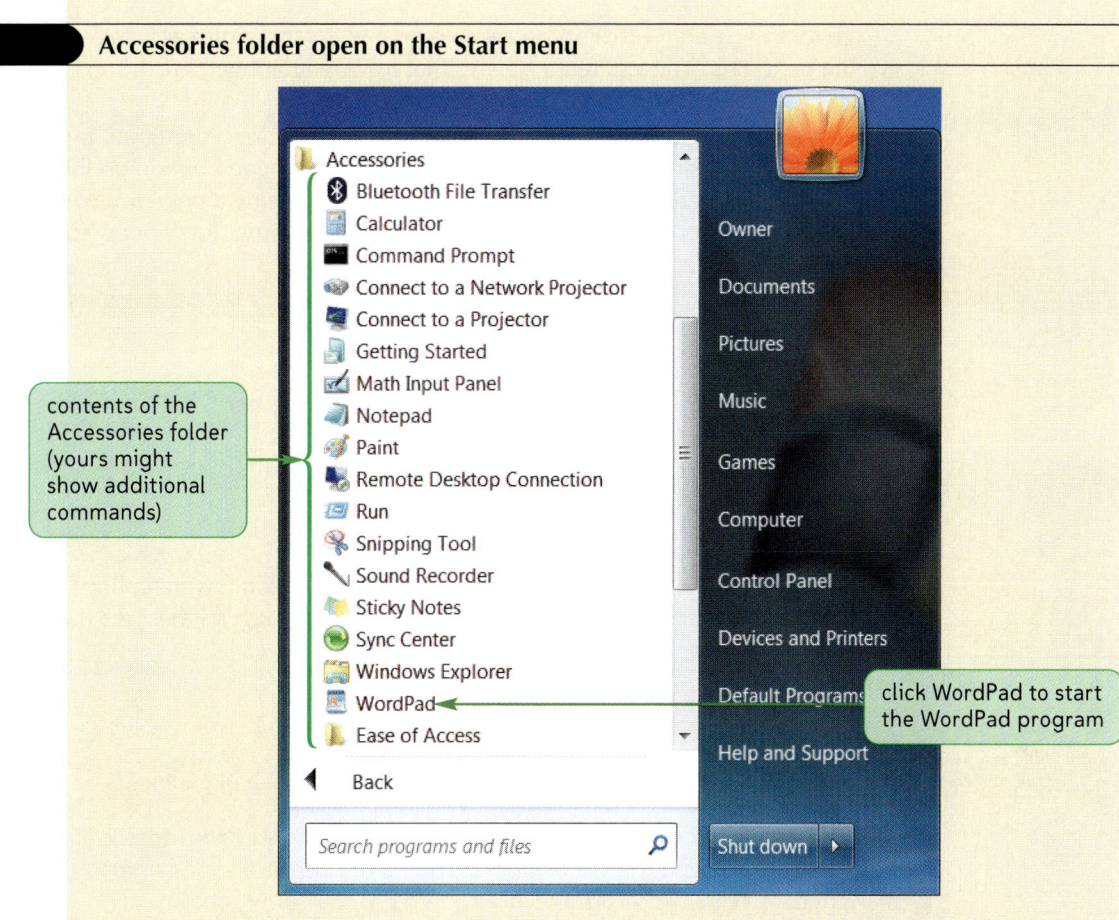

3. Click **WordPad**. The WordPad program window opens, as shown in Figure 8.

| Figure 8 | WordPad program window |

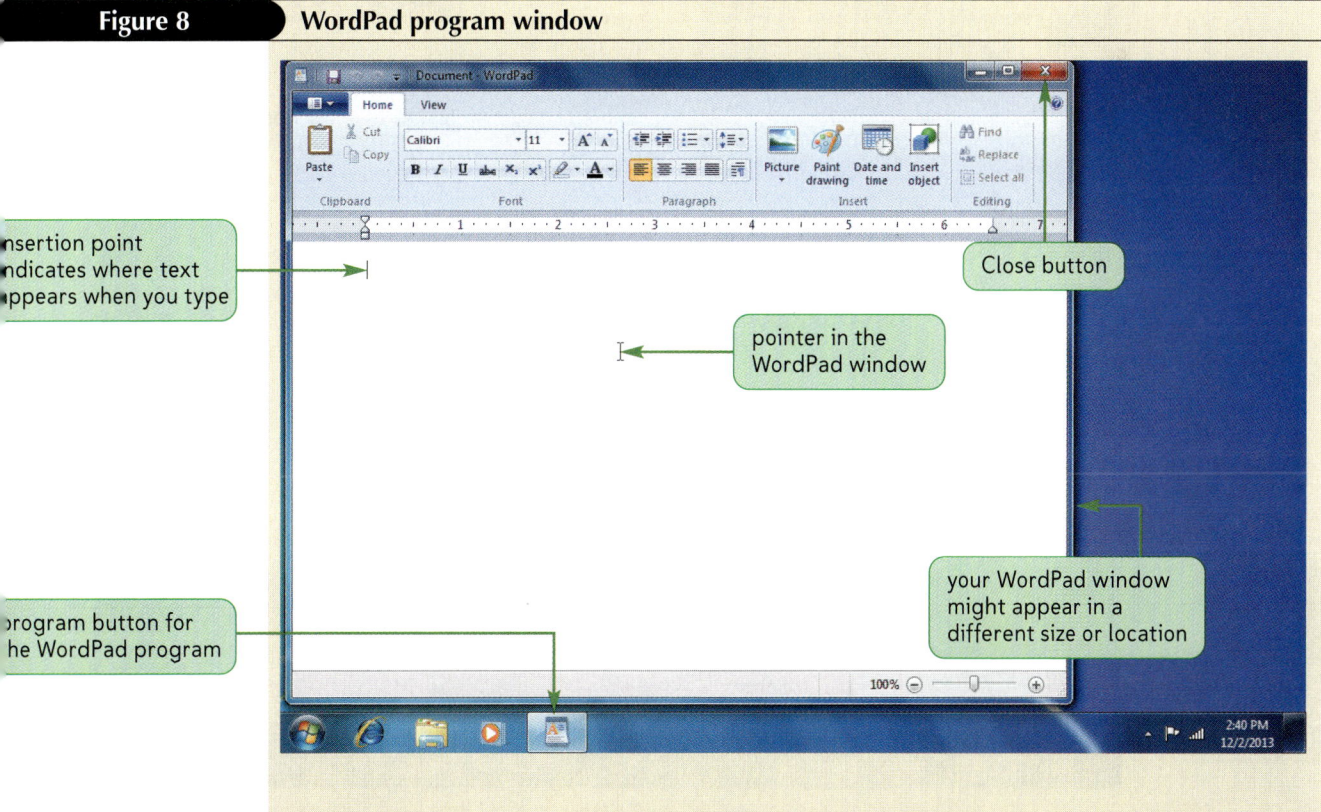

Trouble? If the WordPad program window fills the entire screen, continue with the next step. You will learn how to manipulate windows shortly.

When a program is started, it is said to be open or running. A **program button** appears on the taskbar for each open program. You can click a program button on the taskbar to switch between open programs. When you are finished using a program, you can click the Close button located in the upper-right corner of the program window to **exit**, or close, that program.

To exit the WordPad program:

1. Click the **Close** button on the WordPad title bar. The WordPad program closes and you return to the desktop.

Running Multiple Programs

One of the most useful features of Windows 7 is **multitasking**, which allows you to work on more than one task at a time. To demonstrate, Elena suggests that you start WordPad and leave it running while you start the Paint program.

To run WordPad and Paint at the same time:

1. Start WordPad again.
2. Click the **Start** button on the taskbar, point to **All Programs**, click **Accessories**, and then click **Paint**. The Paint program window opens, as shown in Figure 9. Now two programs are running at the same time.

Figure 9   Two programs open

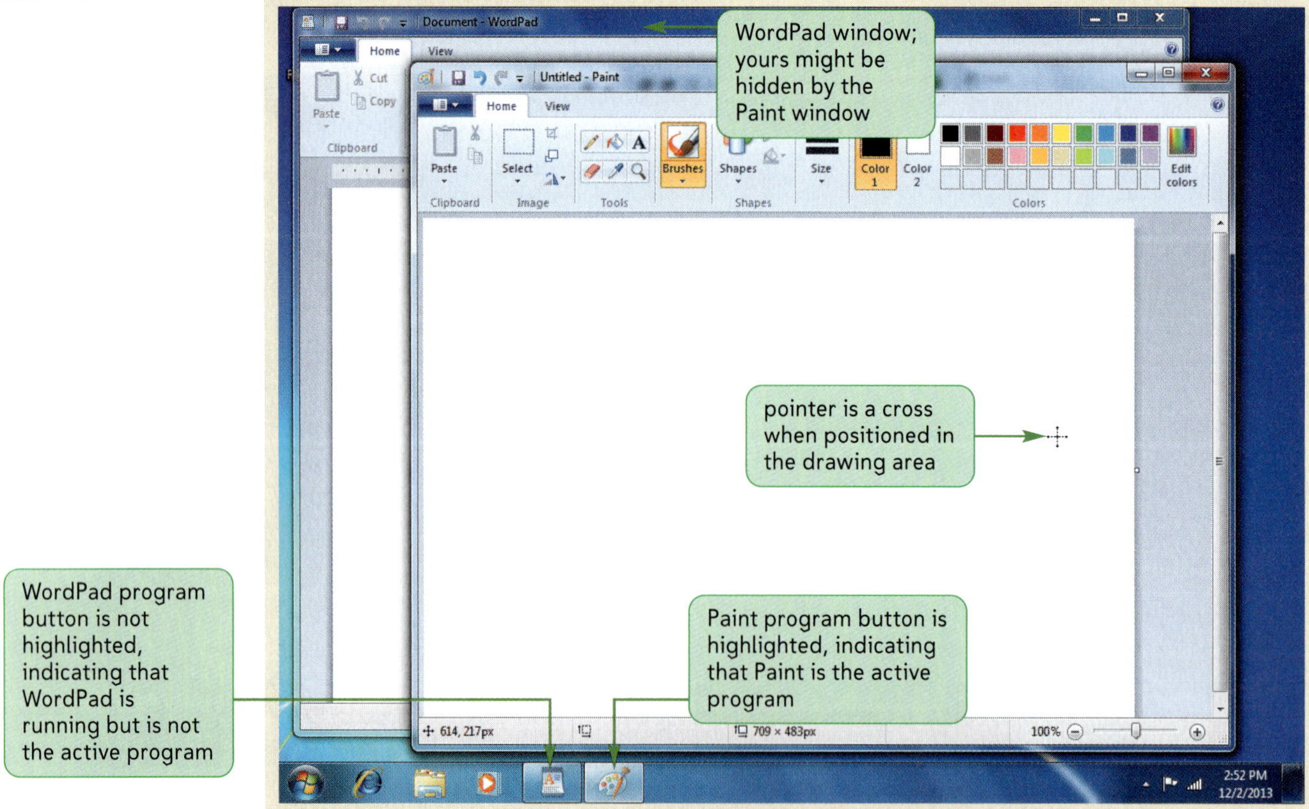

WordPad window; yours might be hidden by the Paint window

pointer is a cross when positioned in the drawing area

WordPad program button is not highlighted, indicating that WordPad is running but is not the active program

Paint program button is highlighted, indicating that Paint is the active program

Appendix A Exploring the Basics of Microsoft Windows 7 | Windows

Trouble? If the Paint program fills the entire screen, continue with the next set of steps. You will learn how to manipulate windows shortly.

The **active program** is the one you are working with—Windows 7 applies your next keystroke or command to the active program. Paint is the active program because it is the one you are currently using. The WordPad program button is still on the taskbar, indicating that WordPad is still running even if you can't see its program window.

> **TIP**
> When more than one window is open, the active program appears on top of all other open windows.

Switching Between Programs

Because only one program is active at a time, you need to switch between programs if you want to work in one or the other. The easiest way to switch between programs is to use the program buttons on the taskbar.

To switch between WordPad and Paint:

1. Click the **WordPad** program button on the taskbar. The WordPad program window moves to the front, and the WordPad program button appears highlighted, indicating that WordPad is the active program.

2. Click the **Paint** program button on the taskbar to switch to the Paint program. The Paint program is again the active program.

> **TIP**
> The Windows key displays the Windows logo, which is a curved, four-part window, and is usually located in the lower-left part of the keyboard.

You can also bypass the taskbar and use keyboard shortcuts to switch from one open window to another. A **keyboard shortcut** is a key or combination of keys that perform a command. If you are using an Aero theme, you can press and hold the Windows key and then press the Tab key to activate **Aero Flip 3D** (often shortened to *Flip 3D*), which displays all your open windows in a three-dimensional stack so you can see the windows from the side, the way you view the spine of a book. See Figure 10. To flip through the stack, you press the Tab key or scroll the wheel on your mouse while continuing to hold down the Windows button. When you release the Windows and Tab keys, you close Flip 3D and the window at the top of the stack becomes the active window.

Figure 10

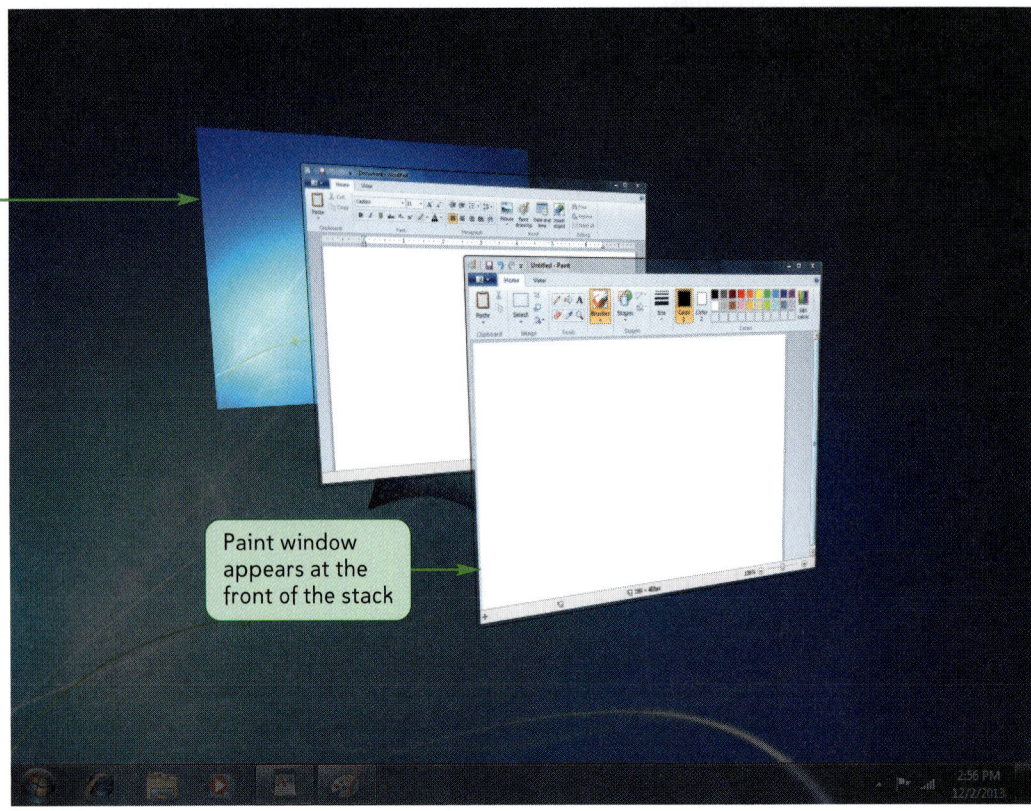

two windows and the desktop image are flipped and stacked

Paint window appears at the front of the stack

You can use another Aero keyboard shortcut called Windows Flip to switch from one window to another. When you hold down the Alt key and press the Tab key once, Windows Flip displays thumbnails (miniature versions) of your open windows. See Figure 1-11. The thumbnails display the exact contents of the open windows instead of generic icons so you can easily identify the windows. While continuing to hold down the Alt key, you can press the Tab key to select the thumbnail for the program you want; you release the Alt key to close Windows Flip.

Figure 11

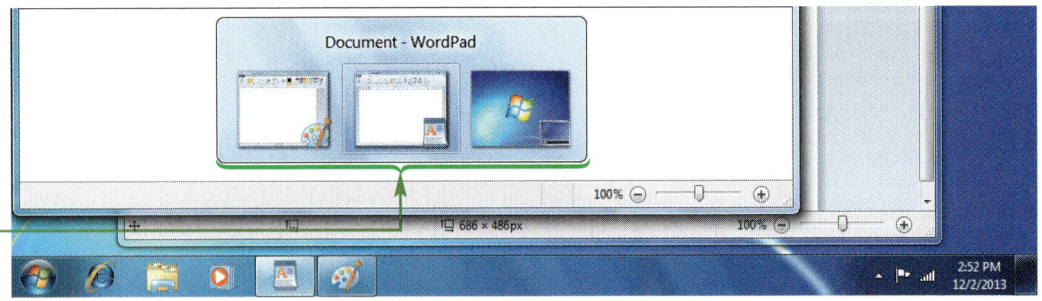

thumbnails of the Paint window, WordPad window, and desktop

To switch between program windows using Aero Flip 3D:

1. Press and hold the **Windows** key and then press the **Tab** key. Windows arranges the Paint and WordPad windows and the desktop in a stack, with the Paint window at the top of the stack.

> **Trouble?** If a task switcher window displaying generic program icons opens when you press the Windows+Tab keys, you are not using an Aero theme. Click outside the task switcher window and then read, but do not perform, the remaining steps.
>
> 2. Press the **Tab** key to flip the WordPad window to the front of the stack. The Paint window moves to the back of the stack.
> 3. Press the **Tab** key to flip the desktop to the front of the stack, and then press the **Tab** key again to flip the Paint window to the front of the stack.
> 4. Release the **Windows** key to turn off Flip 3D and make Paint the active program.

In addition to using the taskbar to switch between open programs, you can close programs from the taskbar.

Closing Programs from the Taskbar

You should always close a program when you are finished using it. Each program uses computer resources, such as memory, so Windows 7 works more efficiently when only the programs you need are open. Elena reminds you that you've already closed an open program using the Close button on the title bar of the program window. You can also close a program, whether active or inactive, by using the shortcut menu associated with the program button on the taskbar.

> **To close WordPad and Paint using the program button shortcut menus:**
>
> 1. Right-click the **Paint** program button 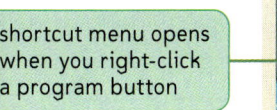 on the taskbar. The shortcut menu for the Paint program button opens. See Figure 12.

Figure 12 Program button shortcut menu

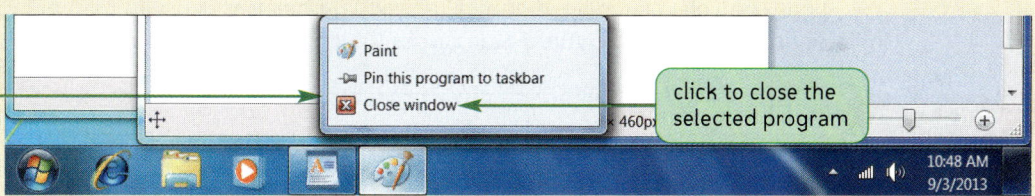

> 2. Click **Close window** on the shortcut menu. The Paint program closes and its program button no longer appears on the taskbar.
>
> **Trouble?** If a message appears asking if you want to save changes, click the Don't Save button.
>
> 3. Right-click the **WordPad** program button on the taskbar, and then click **Close window** on the shortcut menu. The WordPad program closes, and its program button no longer appears on the taskbar.

PROSKILLS

Problem Solving: Working Efficiently on the Desktop

When you work with Windows and its programs, especially on a complicated project, you often start and run more than one program and open many windows. This can lead to two common problems that affect your productivity: having too many windows open can make it difficult to find the information you need, and running too many programs can slow the performance of your computer.

Deciding how many windows to open and how to arrange them on the desktop depends on your personal preference. Some people like to maximize all their open windows and use the taskbar to switch from one window to another. Other people like to size and arrange each window so it is visible on the desktop, even if that means having some small and overlapping windows. Keep in mind that a clean and organized desktop increases your productivity. Find an arrangement that works for you without cluttering your desktop.

If you find that your computer responds to your keystrokes and mouse actions more slowly than usual, you might have too many programs running at the same time. Closing the programs you are not using frees up system resources, which makes your computer faster and more responsive and can solve performance problems.

Using Windows and Dialog Boxes

When you run a program in Windows 7, the program appears in a **window**, a rectangular area of the screen that contains a program, text, or other data. A window also contains **controls**, which are graphical or textual objects you use to manipulate the window or use the program. Figure 13 describes the controls you see in most windows.

Figure 13 Window controls

Control	Description
Program menu button	Lists commands for common program tasks, such as creating, opening, and saving documents
Quick Access Toolbar	Contains buttons for performing tasks, such as saving a document
Ribbon	Provides access to the main set of commands organized by task into tabs and groups
Sizing button	Lets you enlarge, shrink, or close a window
Status bar	Displays information or messages about the task you are performing
Tab	Organizes commands on the Ribbon related to similar tasks
Title bar	Contains the window title and basic window control buttons
Window title	Identifies the program and document contained in the window
Workspace	Includes the part of the window where you manipulate your work—enter text, draw pictures, and set up calculations, for example
Zoom controls	Magnify or shrink the content displayed in the workspace

Elena suggests that you start WordPad and identify its window controls.

To look at the window controls in WordPad:

▸ 1. Start WordPad. On your screen, identify the controls that are labeled in Figure 14.

Figure 14 | WordPad window controls

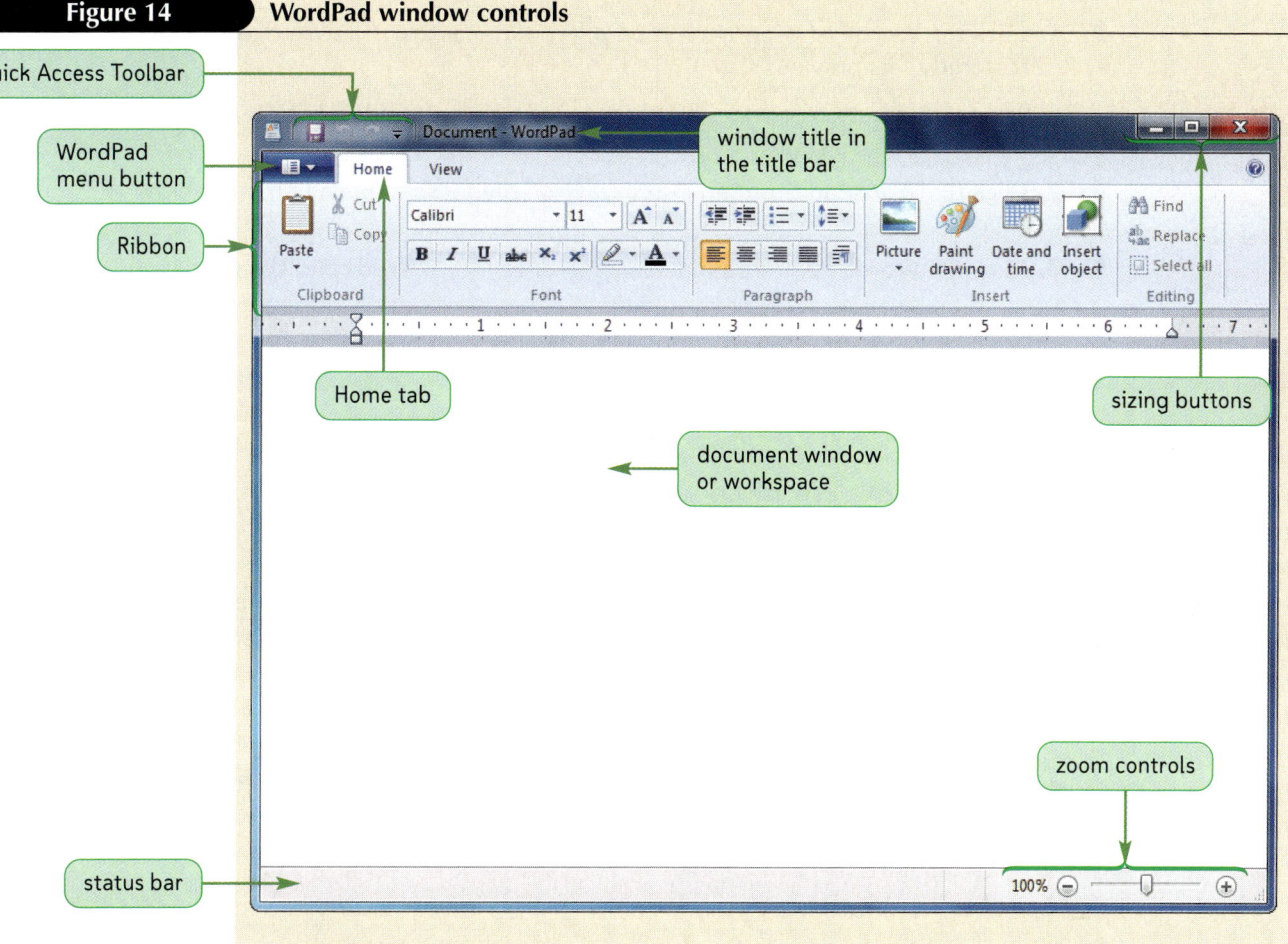

After you open a window, you can manipulate it by changing its size and position.

Manipulating Windows

In most windows, three buttons appear on the right side of the title bar. The first button is the Minimize button, which hides a window so that only its program button is visible on the taskbar. Depending on the status of the window, the middle button either maximizes the window or restores it to a predefined size. You are already familiar with the last button—the Close button. You can use the Minimize button when you want to temporarily hide a window but keep the program running.

To minimize the WordPad window:

▸ 1. Click the **Minimize** button on the WordPad title bar. The WordPad window shrinks so that only the WordPad program button on the taskbar is visible.

Trouble? If the WordPad program window closed, you accidentally clicked the Close button. Use the Start button to start WordPad again, and then repeat Step 1. If you accidentally clicked the Maximize button or the Restore Down button, repeat Step 1.

You can redisplay a minimized window by clicking the program's button on the taskbar. When you redisplay a window, it becomes the active window.

To redisplay the WordPad window:

1. Click the **WordPad** program button on the taskbar. The WordPad window is restored to its previous size.

   The taskbar button provides another way to switch a window between its minimized and active states.

2. Click the **WordPad** program button on the taskbar again to minimize the window.

3. Click the **WordPad** program button once more to redisplay the window.

The Maximize button enlarges a window so that it fills the entire screen. Use maximized windows when you need to see more of the program and your data.

To maximize the WordPad window:

1. Click the **Maximize** button on the WordPad title bar.

   Trouble? If the window is already maximized, it fills the entire screen, and the Maximize button does not appear. Instead, you see the Restore Down button. Skip this step.

The Restore Down button reduces the window so that it is smaller than the entire screen. This feature is useful if you want to see more than one window at a time, move the window to another location on the screen, or change the dimensions of the window.

To restore a window:

1. Click the **Restore Down** button on the WordPad title bar. After a window is restored, the Restore Down button changes to the Maximize button.

You can use the mouse to move a window to a new position on the screen. When you click an object and then press and hold down the mouse button while moving the mouse, you are **dragging** the object. You can move objects on the screen by dragging them to a new location. If you want to move a window, you drag the window by its title bar. You cannot move a maximized window.

To drag the restored WordPad window to a new location:

1. Position the mouse pointer on the WordPad title bar.
2. Press and hold down the left mouse button, and then move the mouse up or down a little to drag the window. The window moves as you move the mouse.

> **3.** Position the window anywhere on the desktop, and then release the left mouse button. The WordPad window stays in the new location.
>
> **4.** Drag the WordPad window to the upper-left corner of the desktop.
>
> **Trouble?** If the WordPad window is maximized when you drag it near the upper part of the desktop, click the Restore Down button before performing the next steps.

You can also use the mouse to change the size of a window. When you point to an edge or corner of a window, the pointer changes to a double-headed arrow, similar to. Use this resize pointer to drag an edge or corner of the window and change the size of the window.

To change the size of the WordPad window:

> **1.** Position the pointer over the lower-right corner of the WordPad window. The pointer changes to. See Figure 15.

Figure 15   Preparing to resize a window

> **2.** Press and hold down the mouse button, and then drag the corner down and to the right.
>
> **3.** Release the mouse button. Now the window is larger.

You can also use the resize pointer to drag any of the other three corners of the window to change its size. To change a window's size in any one direction, drag the left, right, top, or bottom window borders left, right, up, or down.

Using the Ribbon

TIP

By default, the Ribbon displays the Home tab when you start WordPad. To display the contents of the View tab, you click the View tab on the Ribbon.

Many Windows 7 programs use a Ribbon to organize the program's features and commands. The **Ribbon** is located at the top of the program window, immediately below the title bar, and is organized into tabs. Each **tab** contains commands that perform a variety of related tasks. For example, the Home tab has commands for tasks you perform frequently, such as changing the appearance of a document. You use the commands on the View tab to change your view of the WordPad window.

To select a command and perform an action, you use a button or other type of control on the Ribbon. Controls for related actions are organized on a tab in **groups**. For example, to enter bold text in a WordPad document, you click the Bold button in the Font group on the Home tab. Figure 16 shows examples of Ribbon controls.

| Figure 16 | Examples of Ribbon controls |

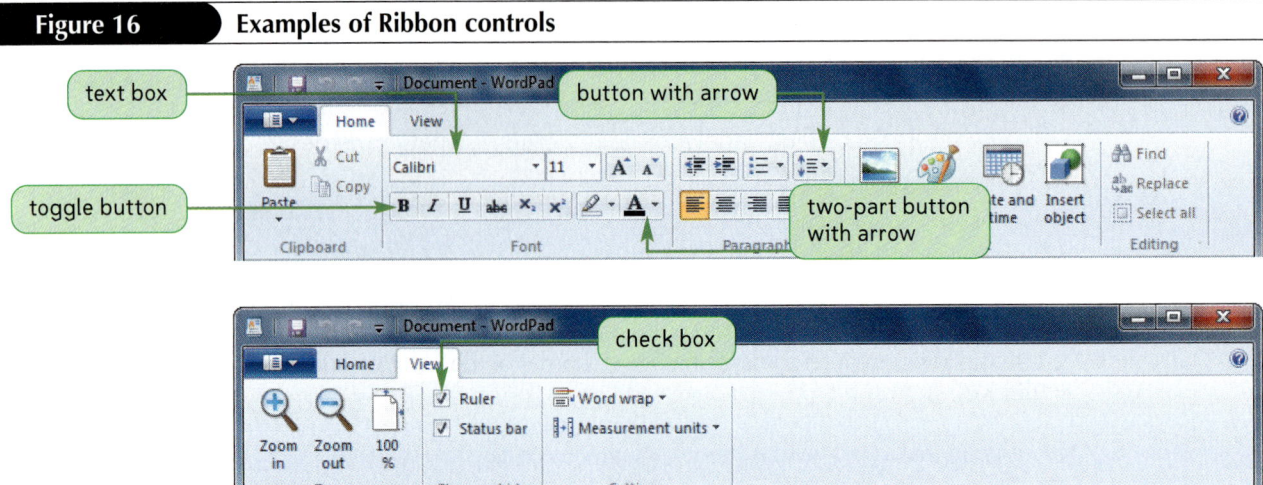

Figure 17 describes the Ribbon controls.

| Figure 17 | Types of controls on the Ribbon |

Control	How to Use	Example
Button with arrow	Click the button to display a menu of related commands.	
Check box	Click to insert a check mark and select the option, or click to remove the check mark and deselect the option.	
Text box	Click the text box and type an entry, or click the arrow button to select an item from the list.	
Toggle button	Click the button to turn on or apply a setting, and then click the button again to turn off the setting. When a toggle button is turned on, it is highlighted.	
Two-part button with arrow	If an arrow is displayed on a separate part of the button, click the arrow to display a menu of commands. Click the button itself to apply the current selection.	

Elena suggests exploring the buttons on the WordPad Ribbon by viewing their ScreenTips.

To determine the names and descriptions of the buttons on the WordPad Ribbon:

1. On the Home tab of the WordPad Ribbon, position the pointer over the **Bold** button in the Font group to display its ScreenTip.
2. Move the pointer over each remaining button on the Home tab to display its name.

Most Windows 7 programs, including WordPad and Paint, include a **Quick Access Toolbar**, which is a row of buttons on the title bar that let you perform common tasks such as saving a file and undoing an action. You can display the name of each button on the Quick Access Toolbar in a ScreenTip by pointing to the button, just as you do for buttons on the Ribbon. You also can select a button on the Quick Access Toolbar or the Ribbon by clicking the button, which performs the associated command. One of the buttons you pointed to on the WordPad Ribbon is the Bold button, which you click to bold selected text. On the Quick Access Toolbar, you can click the Undo button to reverse the effects of your last action. Elena says you can see how both buttons work by typing some bold text, and then clicking the Undo button to remove that text.

To use buttons on the WordPad Ribbon and Quick Access Toolbar:

1. Click the **Bold** button B in the Font group on the Home tab of the WordPad Ribbon. Now any text you type will appear as bold text.
2. Type your full name in the WordPad window.
3. Click the **Undo** button on the Quick Access Toolbar. WordPad reverses your last action by removing your name from the WordPad window.

Using List Boxes

As you might guess from the name, a **list box** displays a list of available choices from which you can select one item. For example, to select a font size in WordPad, you use the Font size list box on the Home tab. A list box is helpful because it only includes options that are appropriate for your current task, such as selecting a font size. Some lists might not include every possible option, so you can type the option you want to select. In most cases, the right side of the list box includes an arrow. You can click the list box arrow to view all the options and then select one or type appropriate text.

Buttons can also have arrows. The arrow indicates that the button has more than one option. Rather than crowding the window with a lot of buttons, one for each possible option, including an arrow on a button organizes its options logically and compactly into a list. Ribbon tabs often include list boxes and buttons with arrows. For example, the Font size button list box on the Home tab includes an arrow. Elena suggests you select a different font size using the arrow on the Font size button list box.

To select a new font size in the Font size button list box:

1. In the Font group on the Home tab, click the **Font size button arrow** 11.
2. Click **18**. The Font size list closes, and the font size you selected appears in the list box.
3. Type your full name to test the new font size, and then press the **Enter** key.
4. Click the **Font size button arrow** 11 on the Home tab again, and then click **12**.
5. Type your full name again to test this type size. Your name appears in 12-point font.

List boxes sometimes include a vertical scroll bar, which appears when the list of available options is too long or wide to fit in the list box. The scroll bar includes an up and down arrow and a scroll box that you use to scroll the list. Horizontal and vertical scroll bars are more common in windows and dialog boxes. You'll examine a typical dialog box next.

Working with Dialog Boxes

A **dialog box** is a special kind of window in which you enter or choose settings for how you want to perform a task. Dialog boxes can include tabs, option buttons, check boxes, and other controls to collect information about how you want to perform a task. Figure 18 displays examples of common dialog box controls.

Figure 18 Examples of dialog box controls

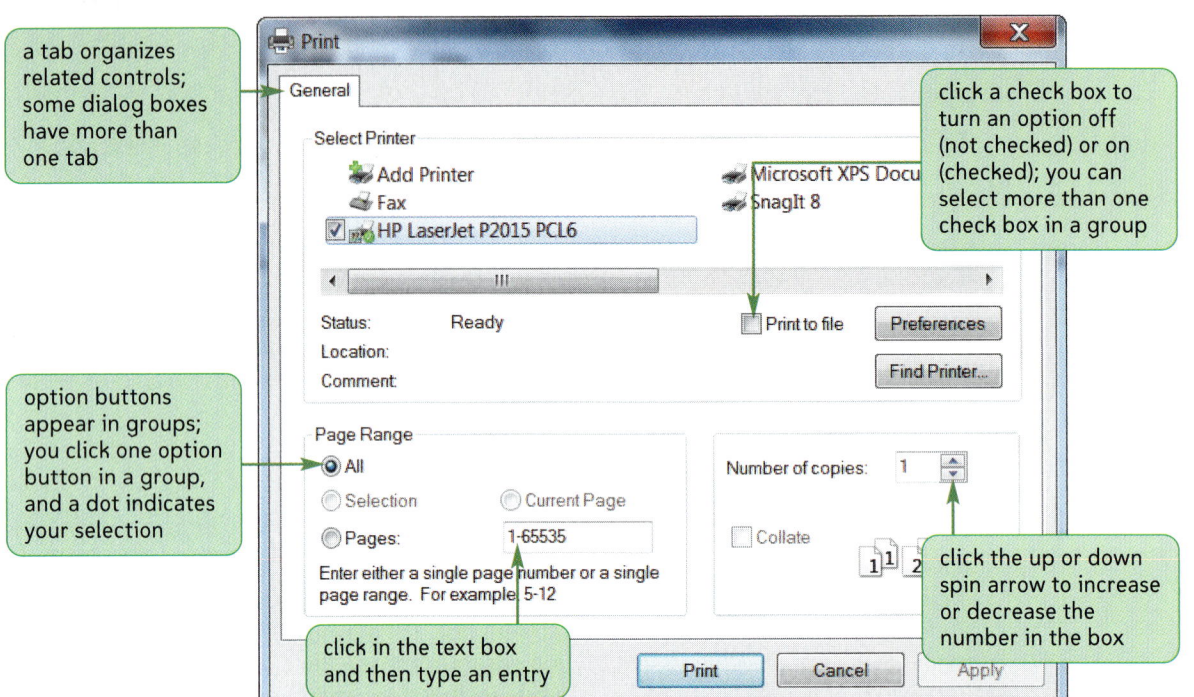

Besides using buttons on Ribbon tabs, you can also open dialog boxes by selecting a command on the WordPad button menu. The WordPad menu button appears in the upper-left corner of the WordPad window. You click the WordPad menu button to display a list of commands, such as Open, Save, and Print. To open a dialog box, such as the Print dialog box, you click the appropriate command, such as Print. If you point to certain commands on the WordPad button menu, a submenu appears listing related commands. A right-pointing arrow indicates that a command has a submenu. For example, when you point to the Print command, a submenu appears listing the Print, Quick print, and Print preview commands.

A good way to learn how dialog box controls work is to open a typical Windows 7 dialog box in WordPad, such as the Page Setup dialog box. You use this dialog box to determine how text appears on a page by specifying margins, page numbers, orientation, and other settings. Before selecting options in the Page Setup dialog box, you can switch to Print Preview using the WordPad menu button to see exactly how your selections affect the WordPad document containing two copies of your name.

Appendix A Exploring the Basics of Microsoft Windows 7 | Windows   WIN7 25

To work with a typical Windows 7 dialog box:

1. Click the **WordPad menu** button in the upper-left corner of the WordPad window, point to **Print**, and then click **Print preview**. The current document appears as it will when printed. Note that the page appears in portrait orientation, which is longer than it is wide. A page number might also appear at the bottom of the page. The Ribbon now contains only one tab—the Print preview tab.

2. In the Print group on the Print preview tab, click the **Page setup** button. The Page Setup dialog box opens.

3. Click the **Landscape** option button to change the orientation of the page.

4. If a check mark appears in the Print Page Numbers check box, click the **Print Page Numbers** check box to remove the check mark. This means no page numbers will appear in the document.

5. Click the **OK** button. WordPad accepts your changes and closes the Page Setup dialog box. Now the page appears in landscape orientation, so it is wider than it is long, and no page number appears at the bottom of the page.

Now that you're finished exploring dialog boxes, you can close Print Preview and exit WordPad. Besides using the Close button in the upper-right corner of the title bar, you can exit a program by clicking the program menu button and then clicking Exit.

To close Print Preview and exit WordPad:

1. In the Close group on the Print preview tab, click the **Close print preview** button. The WordPad window appears in its original view, including the Home and View tabs.

2. Click the **WordPad menu** button, and then click **Exit**. A WordPad dialog box opens asking if you want to save the document.

3. Click the **Don't Save** button to close WordPad without saving the document.

In this session, you started Windows 7 and toured the desktop, learning how to interact with the items on the desktop and on the Start menu. You also started two Windows programs, manipulated windows, and learned how to select options from a Ribbon, toolbar, menu, and dialog box.

REVIEW

Session 1 Quick Check

1. What does the operating system do for your computer?
2. A(n) _____ is a confidential series of characters.
3. True or False. Your computer represents files with icons, which are pictures of familiar objects, such as file folders and documents.
4. What happens when you point to the Start button with a mouse? What happens when you click the Start button with the left mouse button?
5. In Windows 7, right-clicking selects an object and opens its _____.
6. When more than one window is open, the _____ appears on top of all other open windows.
7. Why should you close each program when you are finished using it?

SESSION 2 VISUAL OVERVIEW

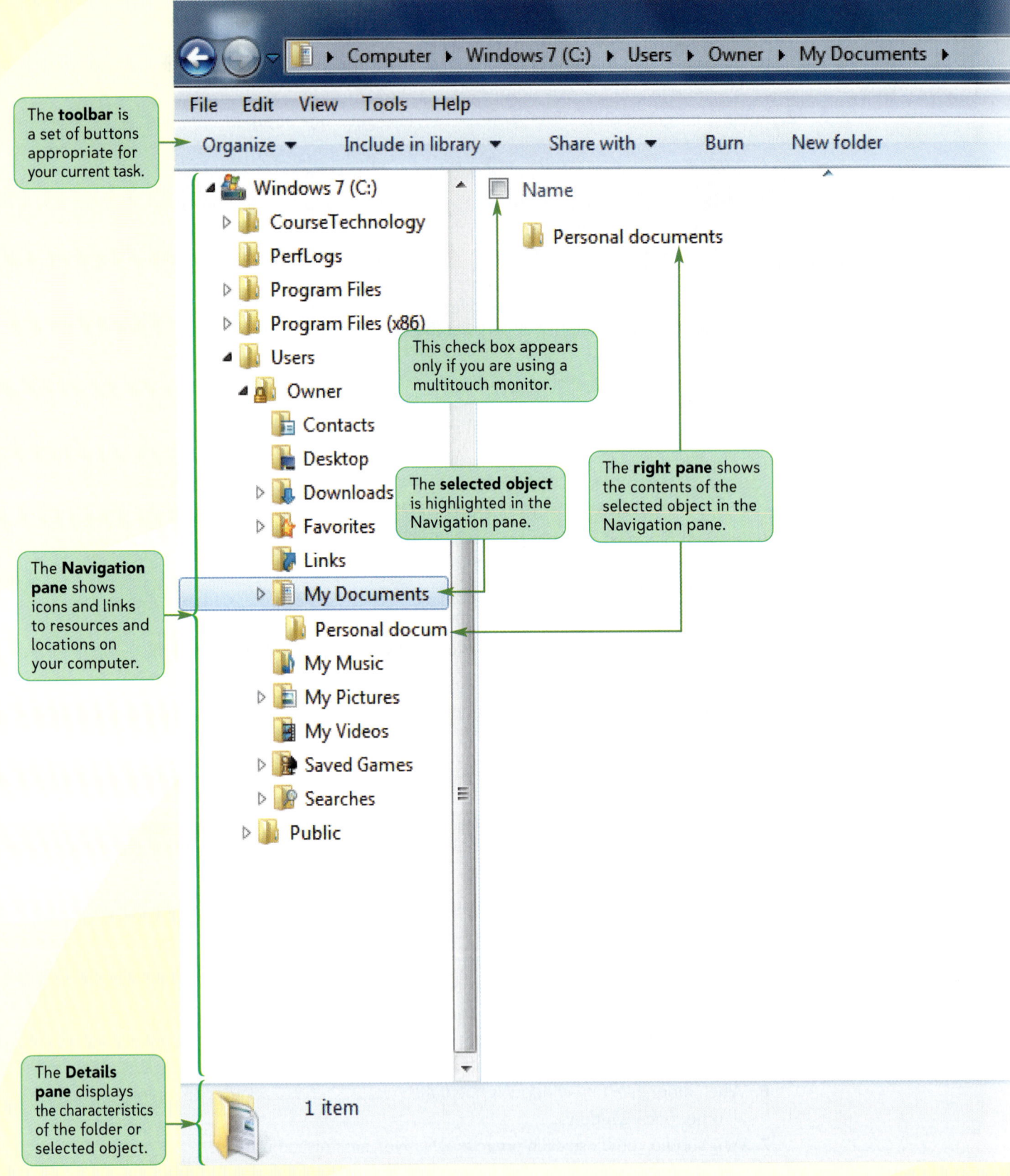

THE COMPUTER WINDOW

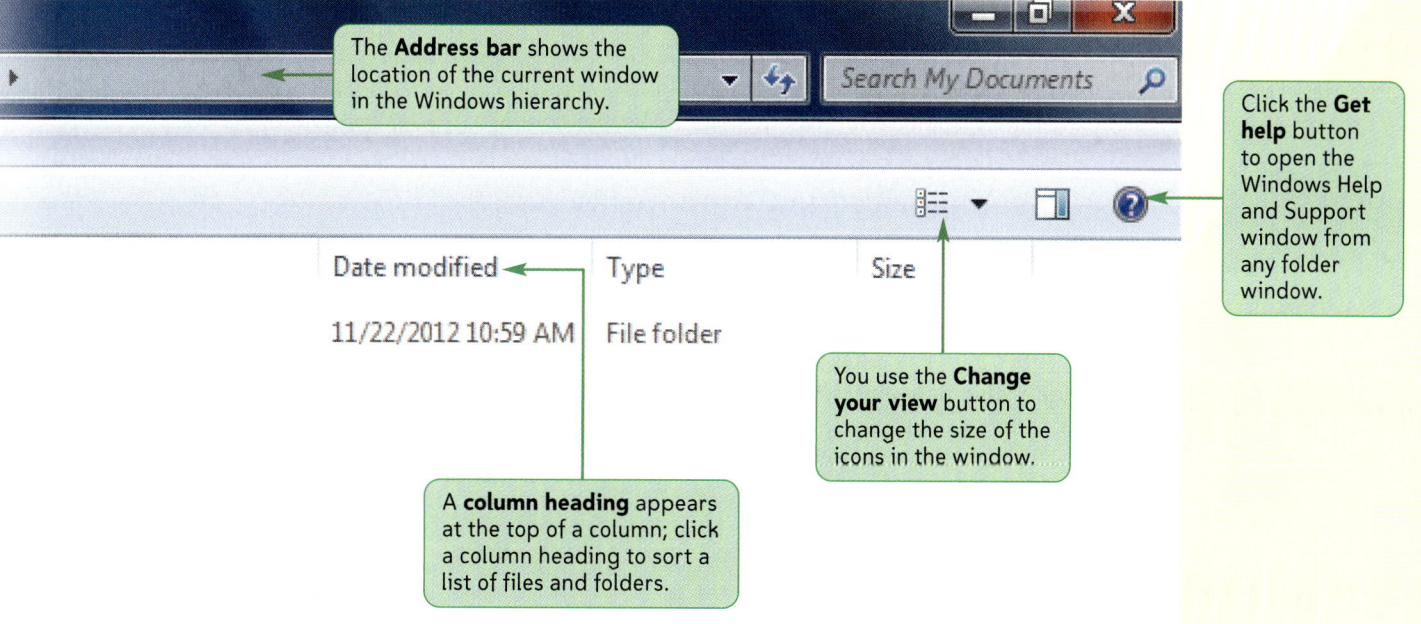

Exploring Your Computer

To discover the contents and resources on your computer, you explore, or navigate, it. **Navigating**, in this context, means to move from one location to another on your computer, such as from one window to another. Windows 7 provides two ways to navigate, view, and work with the contents and resources on your computer—the Computer window (shown in the Session 2 Visual Overview) and Windows Explorer. Both are examples of **folder windows**, which display the contents of your computer.

Navigating with the Computer Window

The Computer window represents your computer, its storage devices, and other objects. The icons for each of these objects appear in the right pane of the Computer window. See Figure 19.

Figure 19   Relationship between your computer and the Computer window

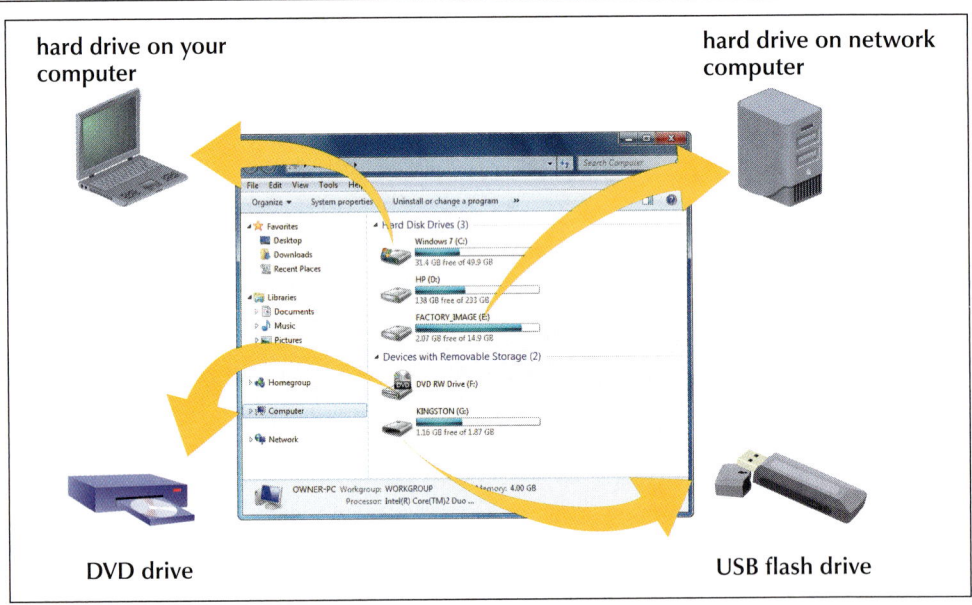

The Computer window also has a left pane, called the Navigation pane, which shows icons and links to other resources your computer can access. This window also contains a toolbar with buttons that let you perform common tasks, and a Details pane that displays the characteristics of an object you select in the Computer window.

Each storage device you can access on your computer is associated with a letter. The first hard drive is usually drive C (if you add other hard drives, they are usually designated D, E, and so on). If you have a CD or DVD drive or a USB flash drive plugged in to a USB port, it usually has the next letter in the alphabetic sequence. If you can access hard drives on other computers in a network, those drives sometimes (although not always) have letters associated with them as well. In the example shown in Figure 19, the network drive has the drive letter Z.

You can use any folder window, including the Computer window, to explore your computer and organize your files. In this session, you explore the contents of your hard disk, which is assumed to be drive C. If you use a different drive on your computer, such as drive E, substitute its letter for C throughout this session.

Elena suggests you explore the Music library, which is a convenient location for storing your music files. (A **library** is a central place to view and organize files and folders stored anywhere that your computer can access, such as those on your hard disk, removable drives, and network.) Even if you store some music files on your hard disk and

Appendix A Exploring the Basics of Microsoft Windows 7 | Windows   WIN7 29

others on an external drive, such as a digital music player attached to your computer, they are all displayed in the Music library. Many digital music players use this location by default when you rip, download, play, and burn music.

The computer Elena provides for you has a multitouch monitor, which lets you interact with objects on the screen using your finger instead of a mouse. If you have a multitouch monitor, a feature in Windows 7 called Windows Touch lets you perform tasks such as selecting icons, opening folders, and starting programs using your finger as a pointing device. To make it easier to select objects and identify which ones are selected, Windows Touch displays a check box next to objects such as files and icons on the desktop and in folder windows. For example, you could touch the check box shown in Figure 20 to select all the folders in the Music library. If you are not using a multitouch monitor, these check boxes do not appear in your folder windows or on the desktop.

To explore the contents of your computer using the Computer window:

1. If you took a break after the previous session, make sure that your computer is on and Windows 7 is running.

2. Click the **Start** button on the taskbar, and then click **Computer** in the right pane of the Start menu. The Computer window opens.

3. In the Navigation pane, click the **Music** link. The right pane displays the contents of the Music library. See Figure 20.

| Figure 20 | Contents of the Music library |

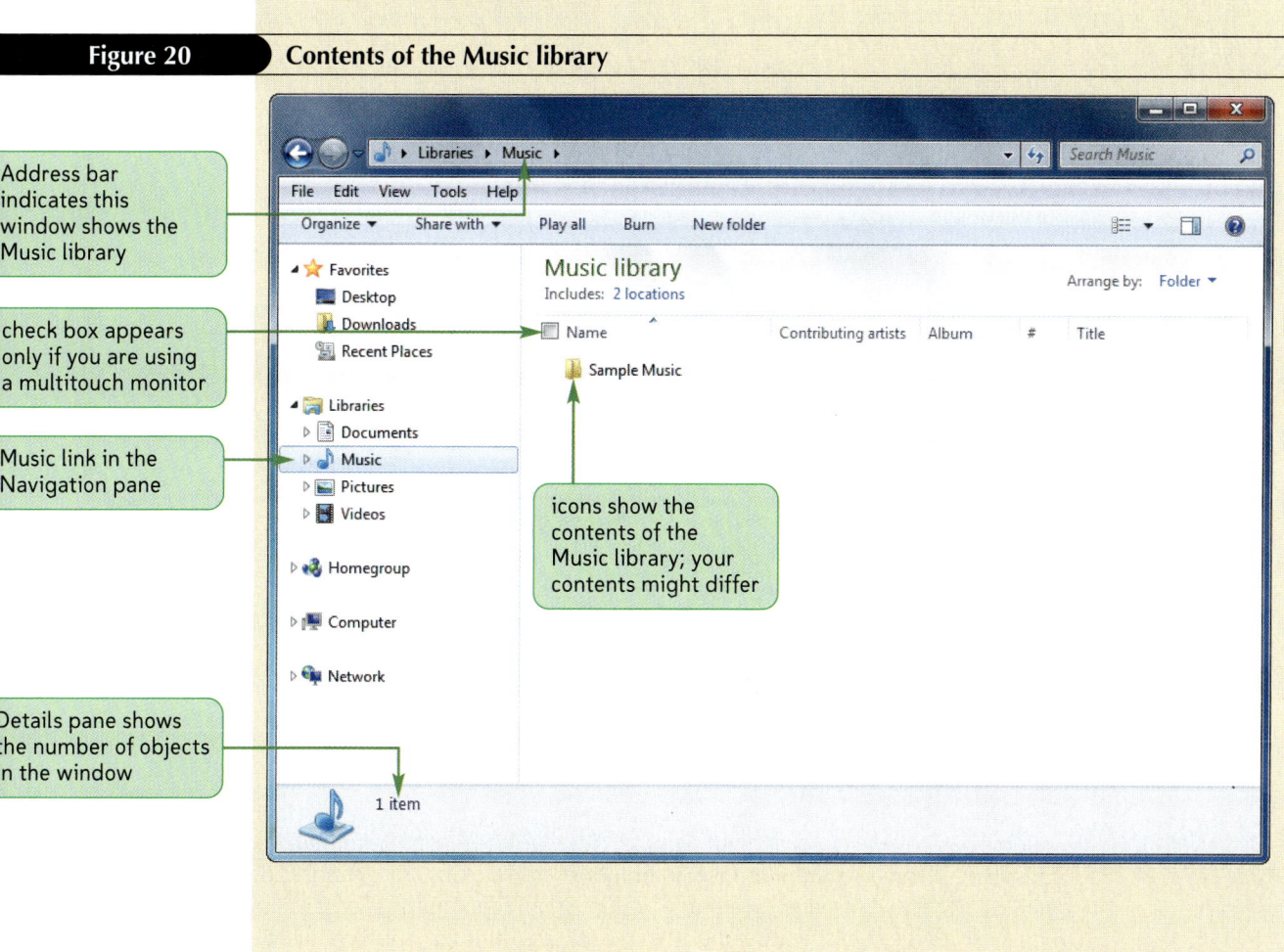

Address bar indicates this window shows the Music library

check box appears only if you are using a multitouch monitor

Music link in the Navigation pane

icons show the contents of the Music library; your contents might differ

Details pane shows the number of objects in the window

TIP

The Address bar displays your current location as a series of links separated by arrows. Click a folder name in the Address bar to display the contents of that folder.

Trouble? If your window looks different from Figure 20, you can still perform the rest of the steps. For example, your window might contain a different number of folders and files.

4. In the right pane, double-click the **Sample Music** icon to open the Sample Music folder. The right pane of the window shows the contents of the folder you double-clicked. You can learn more about the contents of a folder by selecting one or more of its files.

5. Click the first file listed in the Sample Music folder to select it. See Figure 21. (Your files might appear in a different order.)

Figure 21 Viewing files in a folder window

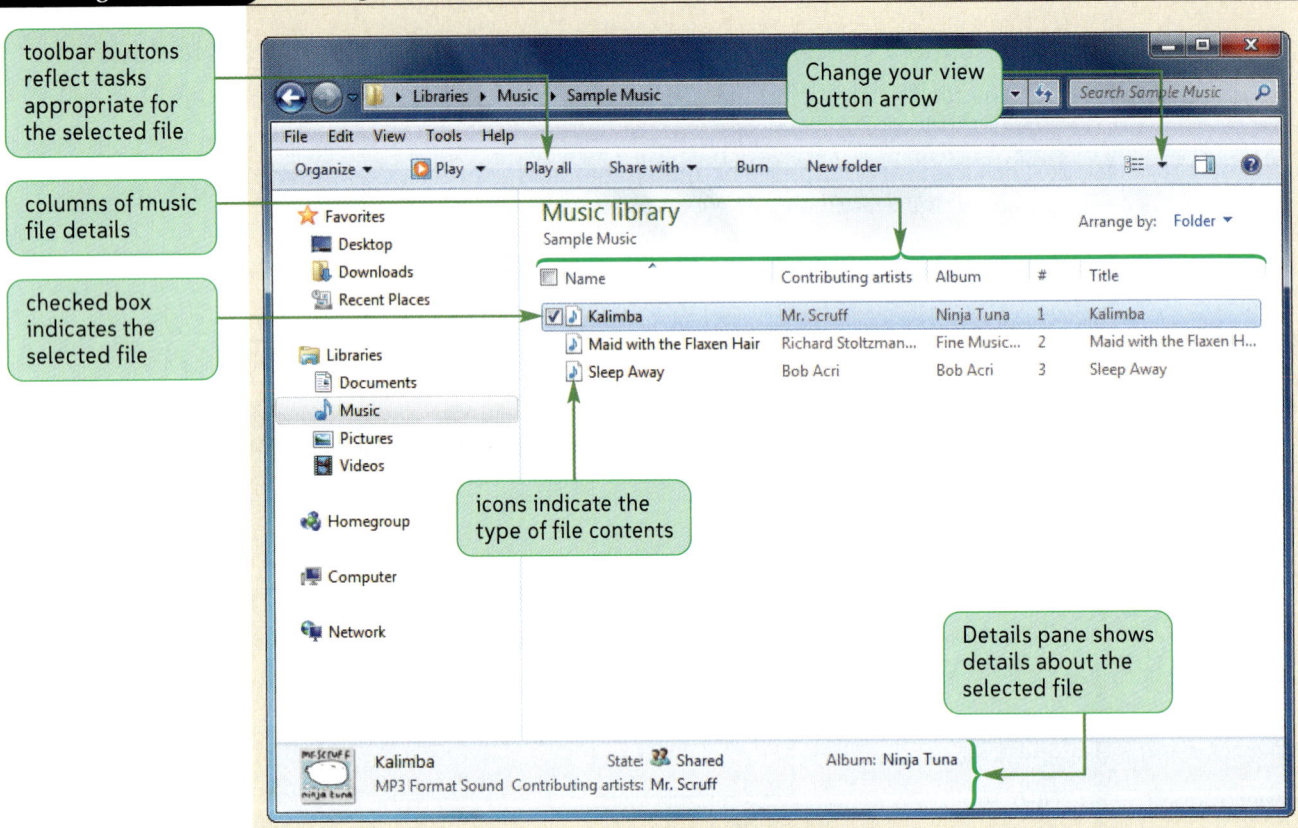

As you open folders and navigate with the Computer window, the contents of the toolbar change so that they are appropriate for your current task. In Figure 21, the toolbar lists actions to take with the selected music file, such as Play all and Burn.

Elena mentions that you can change the appearance of folder windows to suit your preferences, which you'll do next.

Changing the View

Windows 7 provides at least eight ways to view the contents of a folder—Extra Large Icons, Large Icons, Medium Icons, Small Icons, List, Details, Tiles, and Content. The default view is Details view, which displays a small icon and lists details about each file. The icon provides a visual cue about the file type. Although only Details view lists all file details, such as the contributing artists and album title for music files, you can see these details in any other view by pointing to an icon to display a ScreenTip.

To practice switching from one view to another, Elena says you can display the contents of the Sample Music folder in Tiles view. To do so, you'll use the Change your view button on the toolbar.

To view files in Tiles view:

1. In the Sample Music folder window, click the **Change your view button arrow** on the toolbar. See Figure 22.

   Trouble? If you click the Change your view button instead of the arrow, you cycle through the views. Click the Change your view button arrow, and then continue with Step 2.

Figure 22 Preparing to change views

TIP

To change the appearance of the icons using the Change your view button, you can also drag the slider to select an icon size or set a size somewhere between the predefined views.

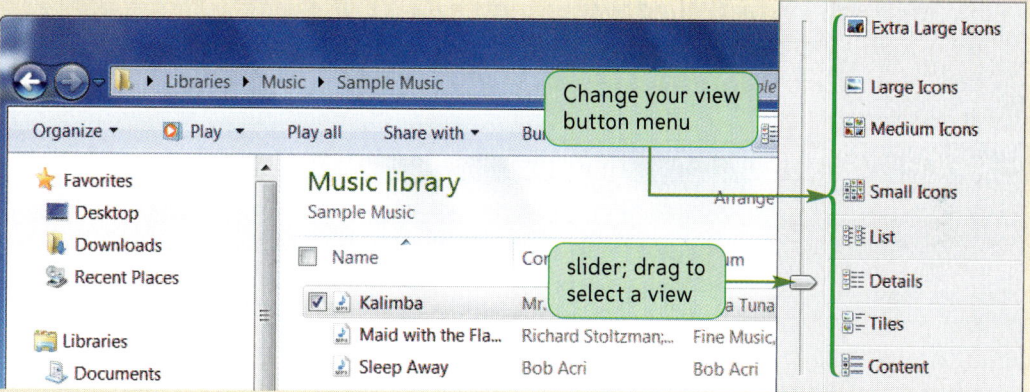

2. Click **Tiles**. The window shows the same files, but with larger icons than in Details view.

3. Click the **Change your view button arrow** on the toolbar, and then click Details to return to **Details** view.

No matter which view you use, you can sort the file list by filename or another detail, such as size, type, or date. If you're viewing music files, you can sort by details such as contributing artists or album title; and if you're viewing picture files, you can sort by details such as date taken or size. Sorting helps you find a particular file in a long file listing. For example, suppose you want to listen to a song on a certain album, but you can't remember the song title. You can sort the music file list in alphabetic order by album to find the song you want.

To sort the music file list by album:

1. Click the **Album** button at the top of the list of files. The up-pointing arrow in the upper-middle part of the Album button indicates that the files are sorted in ascending (A–Z) alphabetic order by album name.

2. Click the **Album** button again. The down-pointing arrow on the Album button indicates that the sort order is reversed, with the albums listed in descending (Z–A) alphabetic order.

3. Click the **Close** button to close the Sample Music window.

Now Elena says you can compare the Computer window to Windows Explorer, another navigation tool.

Navigating with Windows Explorer

Like the Computer window, Windows Explorer also lets you easily navigate the resources on your computer. All of the techniques you use with the Computer window apply to Windows Explorer—and vice versa. Both let you display and work with files and folders. The only difference is the initial view each tool provides. By default, when you open the Computer window, it shows the drives and devices on your computer. When you start Windows Explorer, it displays the Libraries folder, which lets you access resources such as documents, music, pictures, and videos.

Elena suggests you use both tools to navigate to folders people work with frequently. She also mentions that because people use Windows Explorer often, Windows 7 provides its button on the taskbar for easy access.

To start Windows Explorer:

1. Click the **Windows Explorer** button on the taskbar. The Windows Explorer window opens, displaying the contents of the Libraries folder, as shown in Figure 23.

Figure 23 — Windows Explorer window

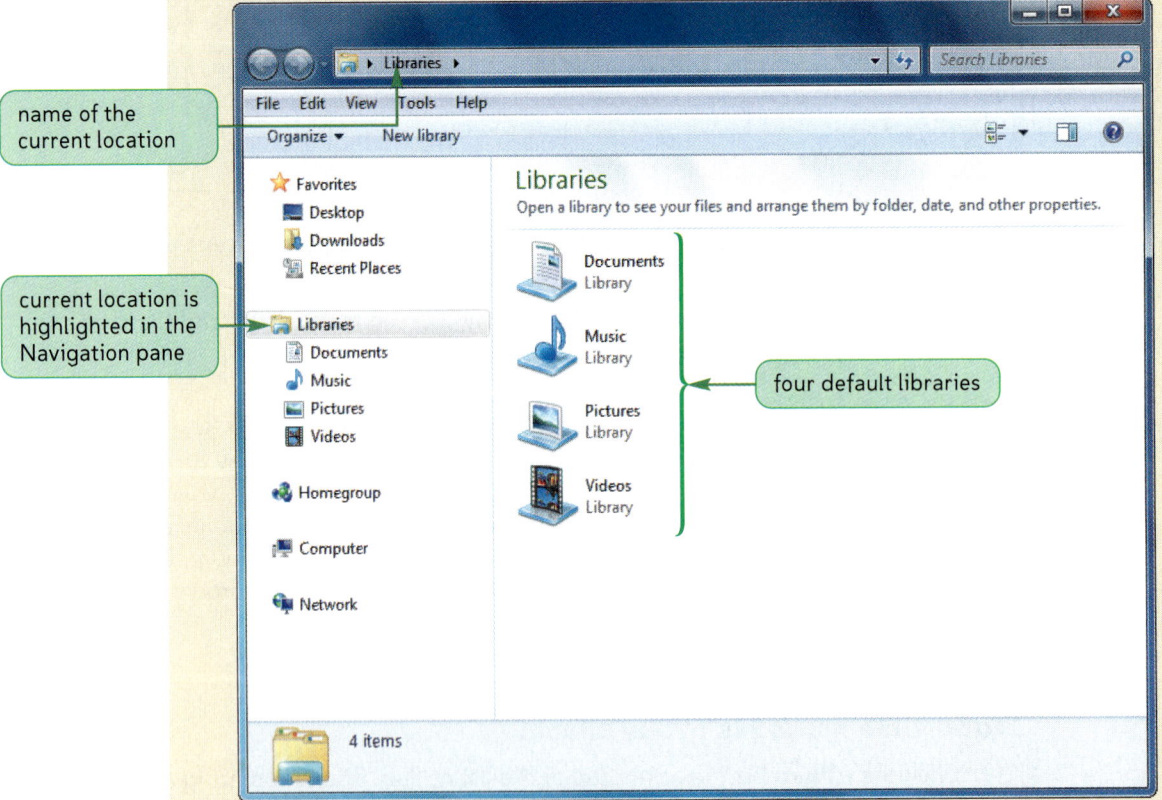

Trouble? If your Windows Explorer window looks slightly different from the one displayed in Figure 23, the configuration of your computer probably differs from the computer used in this figure.

Windows Explorer has the same tools and features you used in the Computer window: the Navigation pane, toolbar, Details pane, and file list in the right pane. The Navigation pane organizes resources into five categories: Favorites (for locations you access frequently), Libraries (for the Windows default libraries), Homegroup (for your shared home network, if any), Computer (for the drives and devices on your computer), and Network (for network locations your computer can access).

When you move the pointer into the Navigation pane, triangles appear next to some icons. An open triangle, or expand icon, ▷ indicates that a folder contains other folders that are not currently displayed in the Navigation pane. Click the triangle to expand the folder and display its subfolders. A filled triangle, or collapse icon, ◢ indicates the folder is expanded, and its subfolders are listed below the folder name. As you saw when working with the Computer window, you can click a folder in the Navigation pane to navigate directly to that folder and display its contents in the right pane.

INSIGHT

Exploring with the Navigation Pane

Using the Navigation pane to explore your computer usually involves clicking expand icons to expand objects and find the folder you want, and then clicking that folder to display its contents in the right pane. To display a list of all the folders on a drive, expand the Computer icon in the Navigation pane, and then expand the icon for the drive, such as Local Disk (C:). The folders list shows the hierarchy of folders on the drive, so you can use it to find and manage your files and folders.

Now you're ready to use the Navigation pane to find and open a folder people use often—the My Documents folder, which is a convenient place to store your documents and other work. The My Documents folder is stored in the Documents library by default.

To open the My Documents folder:

1. If necessary, click the **expand** icon ▷ next to Libraries in the Navigation pane to display the four built-in library folders for Documents, Music, Pictures, and Videos. (Your computer might include additional library folders.)

   Trouble? If the expand icon ▷ does not appear next to Libraries in the Navigation pane, the Libraries folder is already expanded. Skip step 1.

2. Click the **expand** icon ▷ next to Documents to display the folders in the Documents library. See Figure 24.

Figure 24 — Folders in the Documents library

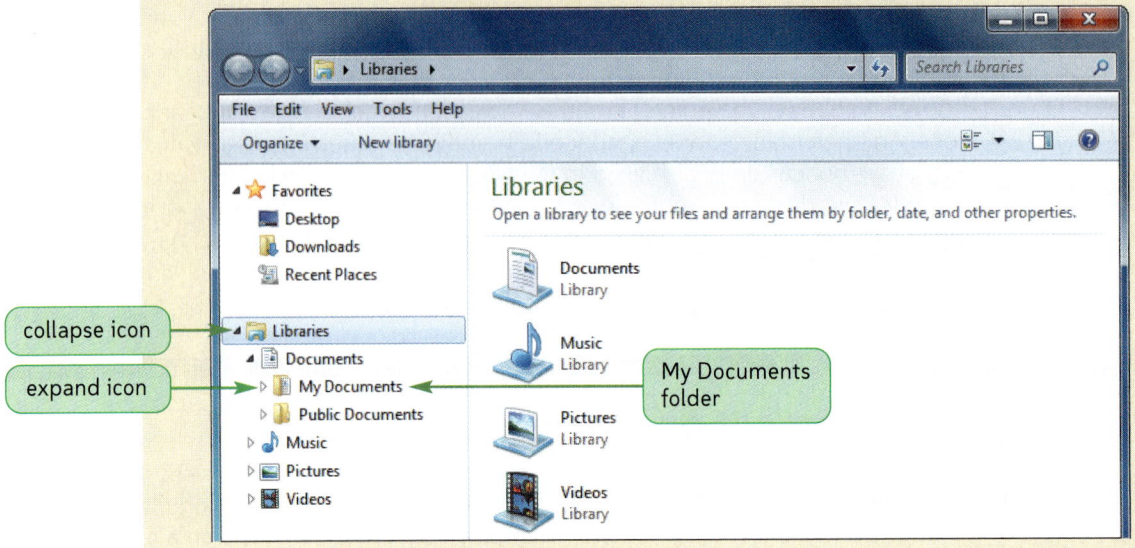

3. Click the **My Documents** folder to display its contents in the right pane. (Your My Documents folder might not contain any files or folders.)
4. Close the folder window.

Getting Help

Windows 7 Help and Support provides on-screen information about the program you are using. Help for the Windows 7 operating system is available by clicking the Start button and then clicking Help and Support on the Start menu.

REFERENCE

Starting Windows Help and Support

- Click the Start button on the taskbar.
- Click Help and Support.

or

- Click the Help button on any folder window.

When you start Help for Windows 7, a Windows Help and Support window opens, which gives you access to Help files stored on your computer as well as Help information stored on the Microsoft Web site. If you are not connected to the Web, you only have access to the Help files stored on your computer.

Appendix A Exploring the Basics of Microsoft Windows 7 | Windows   WIN7 35

To start Windows 7 Help:

1. Click the **Start** button on the taskbar.

2. Click **Help and Support** in the right pane of the Start menu. The home page of Windows Help and Support opens. See Figure 25. The contents of the home page differ depending on whether you are connected to the Internet.

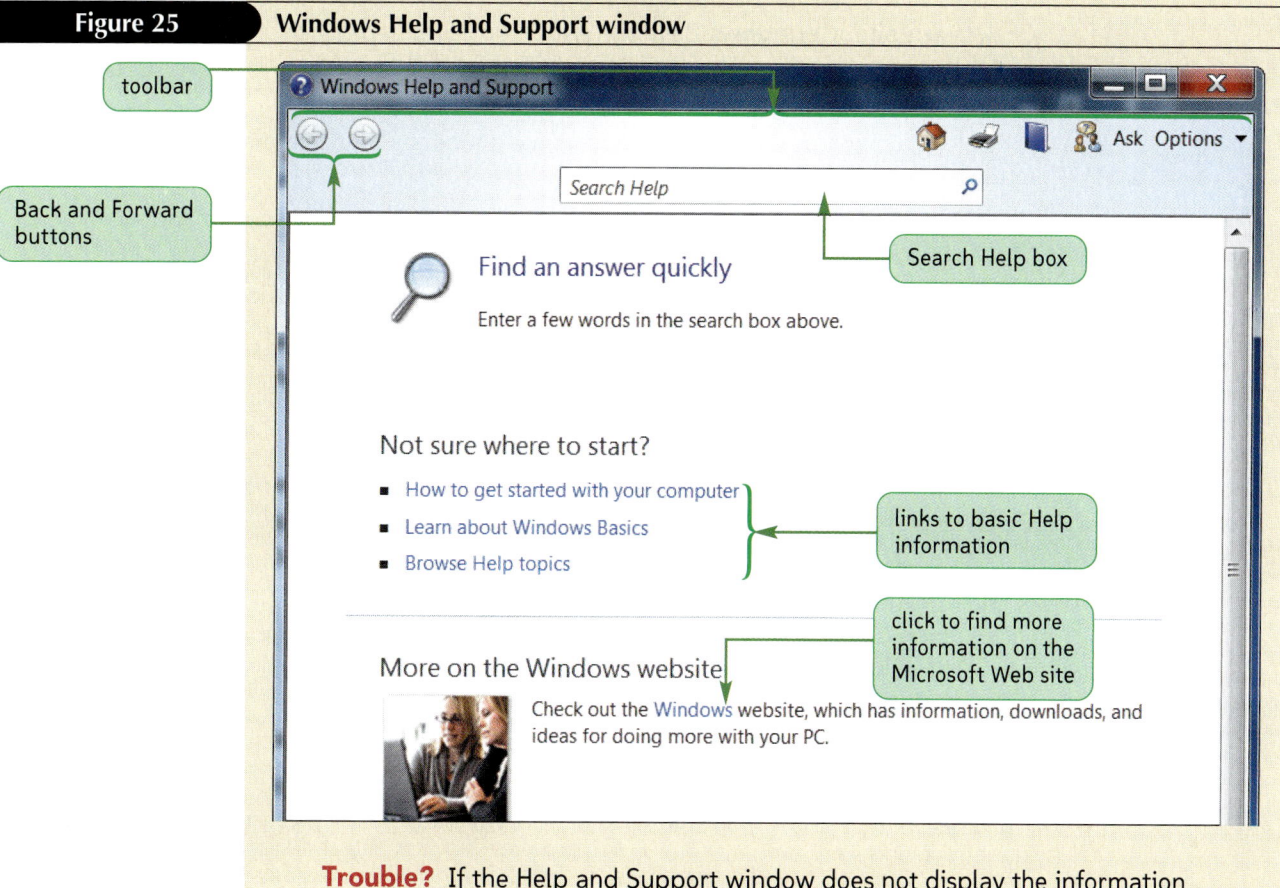

Figure 25 Windows Help and Support window

Trouble? If the Help and Support window does not display the information you see in Figure 25, click the Help and Support home button on the toolbar at the top of the window to view Help contents.

TIP

You can also start Windows 7 Help and Support from a folder window by clicking the Help button on the toolbar.

The home page in Windows Help and Support provides tools for finding answers and other information about Windows 7. To view popular topics, you click a link in the *Find an answer quickly* section of the Windows Help and Support home page. Click a topic to open an article providing detailed information about that topic or instructions for performing a task. You can also use the toolbar to navigate Windows Help and Support. For example, click the Help and Support home button to return to the home page. In addition to buttons providing quick access to pages in Windows Help and Support, you can use the Back button to return to the previous page you viewed. By doing so, you activate the Forward button, which you can click to go to the next page of those you've opened.

Viewing Windows Basics Topics

Windows Help and Support includes instructions on using Help itself. You can learn how to find a Help topic by using the *Learn about Windows Basics* link on the Windows Help and Support home page.

To view Windows Basics topics:

1. Click **Learn about Windows Basics**. A list of topics related to using Windows 7 appears in the Windows Help and Support window.
2. Scroll down to the *Help and support* heading, and then click **Getting help**. An article explaining how to get help appears, with the headings in the article listed in the *In this article* section on the right.
3. Click **Getting help with dialog boxes and windows**. The Windows Help and Support window scrolls to that heading in the article.
4. Click the **Back** button on the toolbar. You return to the previous page you visited, which is the Windows Basics: all topics page. The Forward button is now active.

You can access the full complement of Help pages by using the Contents list.

Selecting a Topic from the Contents List

The Contents list logically organizes all of the topics in Windows Help and Support into topics and categories. In the Contents list, you can click a category to display the titles of related topics. Click a topic to get help about a particular task or feature. For example, you can use the Contents list to learn more about files and folders.

To find a Help topic using the Contents list:

1. Click the **Help and Support home** button on the toolbar to return to the home page for Windows Help and Support.
2. Click the **Browse Help** button on the toolbar. A list of categories appears in the Windows Help and Support window.
3. Click **Files, folders, and libraries** to display the list of topics and other categories related to files, folders, and libraries.
4. Click the topic **Working with files and folders**. The Windows Help and Support window displays information about that topic.
5. In the first paragraph below the *Working with files and folders* heading, click the word **icons**, which is green by default. A ScreenTip shows the definition of *icons*.
6. Click a blank area of the Windows Help and Support window to close the ScreenTip.

Another Help tool is the Search Help box, a popular way to find answers to your Windows 7 questions.

Searching the Help Pages

If you can't find the topic you need by clicking a link or using the toolbar, or if you want to quickly find Help pages related to a particular topic, you can use the Search Help box. Elena provides a typical example. Suppose you want to know how to exit Windows 7, but you don't know if Windows refers to this as exiting, quitting, closing, or shutting down. You can search the Help pages to find just the right topic.

To search the Help pages for information on exiting Windows 7:

1. Click in the Search Help box. A blinking insertion point appears.
2. Type **shut down** and then press the **Enter** key. A list of Help pages containing the words *shut down* appears in the Windows Help and Support window. See Figure 26. (Your results might differ.)

Figure 26 Search Help results

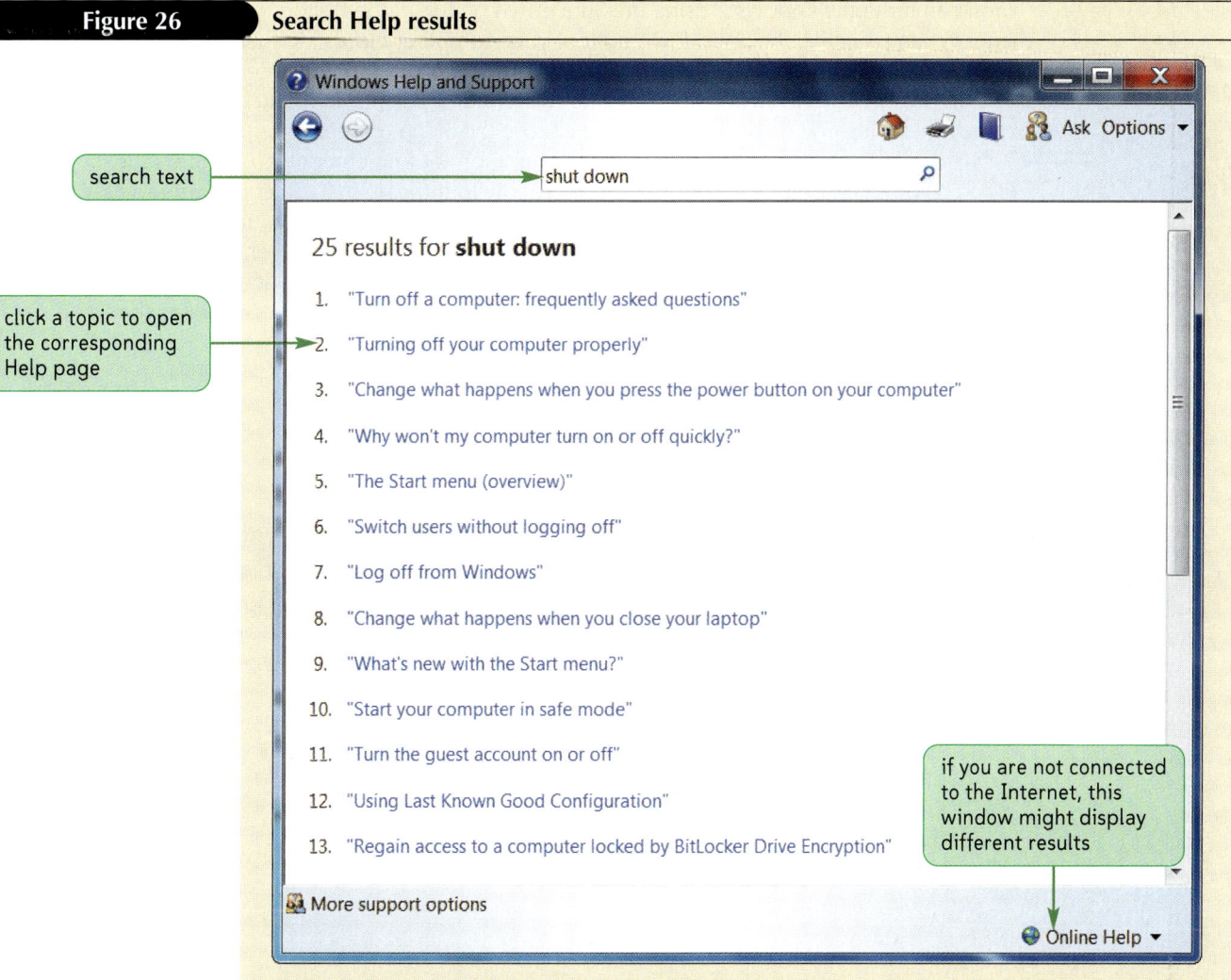

3. Click the **Turning off your computer properly** topic. The article appears in the Windows Help and Support window.

   Trouble? If a *Topic not found* message appears in the window instead of a Help topic, click the Back button on the toolbar, and then click a different link in the Windows Help and Support window, such as *Turn off a computer: frequently asked questions*.

If this article did not answer your question, you could click the Ask button on the toolbar. Doing so opens a page listing other ways to get Help information.

4. Click the **Close** button on the title bar to close the Windows Help and Support window.

Now that you know how Windows 7 Help works, Elena reminds you to use it when you need to perform a new task or when you forget how to complete a procedure.

Turning Off Windows 7

You should always shut down Windows 7 before you turn off your computer. Doing so saves energy, preserves your data and settings, and makes sure your computer starts quickly the next time you use it.

You can turn off Windows 7 using the Shut down button at the bottom of the Start menu. When you click the Shut down button, your computer closes all open programs, including Windows itself, and then completely turns off your computer. For greater flexibility, you can click the arrow on the Shut down button to display a menu of shut down options, including Log off and Sleep. If you choose the Sleep option, Windows saves your work and then turns down the power to your monitor and computer. A light on the outside of your computer case blinks or turns yellow to indicate that the computer is sleeping. Because Windows saves your work, you do not need to close your programs or files before putting your computer to sleep. To wake a desktop computer, you press any key or move the mouse. To wake a notebook computer, you might need to press the hardware power button on your computer case instead. After you wake a computer, the screen looks exactly as it did when you turned off your computer.

TIP

Shutting down does not automatically save your work, so be sure to save your files before clicking the Shut down button.

To turn off Windows 7:

1. Click the **Start** button on the taskbar.
2. Click **Shut down**. Windows 7 displays a message that it is shutting down, and then turns off your computer.

   Trouble? If you are supposed to log off rather than shut down, skip Step 2, click the More Options button instead, click Log off, and follow your school's logoff procedure.

PROSKILLS

Decision Making: Log Off, Sleep, or Shut Down?

If you are using a computer on the job, your organization probably has a policy about what to do when you're finished working on the computer. If it does not, deciding on the best approach depends on who uses the computer and how long it will be idle. Keep the following guidelines in mind as you make your decision:

- Log off: This command closes all programs and logs you off of Windows 7 but leaves the computer turned on. If another person might use your computer shortly, log off Windows to protect your data and prepare the computer for someone else to use.
- Sleep: By default, Windows 7 is set to sleep after 15–30 minutes of idle time, depending on whether you are using a notebook or desktop computer. Sleep is a low-power state in which Windows saves your work and then turns down the power to your monitor and computer. If you will be away from the computer for more than 15 minutes but less than a day, you can generally let the computer go to sleep on its own.
- Shut down: If your computer is plugged in to a power outlet and you don't plan to use the computer for more than a day, you save wear and tear on your electronic components and conserve energy by shutting down, which ends your Windows 7 session and turns off your computer off. You should also turn off the computer when it is susceptible to electrical damage, such as during a lightning storm, and when you need to install new hardware or disconnect the computer from a power source. If your notebook computer is running on battery power only and you don't plan to use it for more than a few hours, you should also turn it off to save your battery charge.

In this session, you learned how to start and close programs and how to use multiple programs at the same time. You learned how to work with windows and the controls they provide. Finally, you learned how to get help when you need it and how to turn off Windows 7. With Elena's help, you should feel comfortable with the basics of Windows 7 and be prepared to teach Back to Work clients the fundamentals of using this operating system.

REVIEW

Session 2 Quick Check

1. The left pane in a folder window is called the _____, which shows icons and links to other resources your computer can access.
2. True or False. The Music library is a convenient location that Windows provides for storing your music files.
3. Describe two ways to change the view in a folder window.
4. In the Windows Explorer window, what appears in the right pane when you click a folder icon in the left pane?
5. How can you view file details, such as size or date modified, in Large Icons view?
6. The _____ list logically organizes all of the topics in Windows Help and Support into books and pages.
7. How can you quickly find Help pages related to a particular topic in the Windows Help and Support window?
8. Describe what happens when you choose the Sleep option on the Shut down button menu.

Appendix A Exploring the Basics of Microsoft Windows 7 | Windows

Practice the skills you learned in the tutorial using the same case scenario.

PRACTICE

Review Assignments

There are no Data Files needed for the Review Assignments.

The day before your first class teaching Back to Work clients the basics of using Windows 7, Elena Varney offers to observe your tour of the operating system. You'll start working on the Windows 7 desktop, with no windows opened or minimized. Complete the following steps, recording your answers to any questions according to your instructor's preferences:

1. Start Windows 7 and log on, if necessary.
2. Use the mouse to point to each object on your desktop. Record the names and descriptions of each object as they appear in the ScreenTips.
3. Click the Start button. How many menu items or commands are on the Start menu?
4. Start WordPad. How many program buttons are now on the taskbar? (Don't count toolbar buttons, items in the notification area, or the three default taskbar buttons to the right of the Start button.)
5. Start Paint and maximize the Paint window. How many programs are running now?
6. Switch to WordPad. What are two visual cues that tell you that WordPad is the active program?
7. Close WordPad and then click the Restore Down button in the Paint window.
8. Open the Recycle Bin window. Record the number of items it contains. Drag the Recycle Bin window so that you can see it and the Paint window.
9. Close the Paint window from the taskbar. What command did you use?
10. Click the Organize button on the toolbar in the Recycle Bin window. Write down the commands on the menu. Point to Layout, and then click Menu bar to display the menu bar.
11. Use any menu on the Recycle Bin menu bar to open a dialog box. What steps did you perform? What dialog box did you open? For what do you think you use this dialog box? Click Cancel to close the dialog box. Close the Recycle Bin window.
12. Open a folder window, and then open the Public Documents folder from the Navigation pane. Explain how you navigated to this folder.
13. Open a folder in the Videos library and then describe its contents.
14. Change the view of the folder window. What view did you select? Describe the icon(s) in the folder window.
15. Close the folder window, and then open Windows Help and Support.
16. Use the *Learn about Windows Basics* link to learn something new about the Windows 7 desktop. What did you learn? How did you find this topic?
17. Return to the Home page, and then browse Help topics to find information about customizing your computer. How many topics are listed? (*Hint*: Don't include Help categories.) Use the Search Help box to find information about customizing your computer. How many topics are listed?
18. Close Help, and then close any other open windows.
19. Turn off Windows 7 by using the Sleep command, shutting down, or logging off.
20. Submit your answers to the preceding questions to your instructor, either in printed or electronic form, as requested.

Use your skills to explore the contents of a computer for a small electronics business.

APPLY

Case Problem 1

There are no Data Files needed for this Case Problem.

First Call Electronics First Call Electronics is a small business in Atlanta, Georgia, that provides training and repair services for electronic devices, including computers, cell phones, cameras, and portable music players. Antoine Guillaume runs the training department and has hired you to conduct one-on-one training sessions with new computer users. You are preparing for a visit to a client who wants to determine the contents of his new Windows 7 computer, including sample media files and related programs already provided in folders or menus.

Some of the following steps instruct you to list the contents of windows. Refer to the instructions in the ProSkills exercise at the end of this tutorial if you want to print images of these windows instead. Complete the following steps:

1. Start Windows 7 and log on, if necessary.
2. Open a folder window.
3. List the names of the drives on the computer.
4. Click the Pictures link in the Navigation pane. Does the Pictures library contain any folders? If so, what are the names of the folders?
5. In the Navigation pane, expand the hard disk, such as Local Disk (C:), to display its contents. Navigate the folders on your computer to find the folder displayed in the Pictures library. Where is that folder located in the folder structure of your computer?
6. Open any folder in the Pictures library that contains images. View the files as Extra Large Icons.
7. Navigate to a folder that contains other types of media files, such as music, videos, or recorded TV. Point to a file to display the ScreenTip. What type of file did you select? What details are provided in the ScreenTip?
8. Use the Start menu to display the contents of the Accessories folder in the All Programs list, and then click Getting Started. Describe the contents of the Getting Started window.
9. Close all open windows, and then use the Start menu to open a program that you could use with DVDs. What program did you start?
10. Use the Start menu to open any program you might use with music or sound files. What program did you start?
11. Open Windows Help and Support, and then find and read topics that explain how to use a program you started in a previous step. Explain the purpose of one of the programs.
12. Close all open windows.
13. Submit your answers to the preceding questions to your instructor, either in printed or electronic form, as requested.

Work with Windows 7 on a computer for a catering business.

APPLY

Case Problem 2

There are no Data Files needed for this Case Problem.

East End Catering After completing culinary school and working as a sous chef for restaurants in Santa Fe, New Mexico, Felicia Makos started a catering company called East End Catering that specializes in dishes that contain organic, locally grown ingredients. So that she can concentrate on cooking and marketing, she hired you to help her perform office tasks as her business grows. She asks you to start by teaching her the basics of using her computer, which runs Windows 7. She especially wants to know which programs are installed on her computer and what they do.

Some of the following steps instruct you to list the contents of windows and menus. Refer to the instructions in the ProSkills exercise at the end of this tutorial if you want to print images of these windows instead. Complete the following steps:

1. Open the Start menu and write down the programs listed in the left pane.
2. Start one of the programs in the left pane and then describe what it does. Close the program.
3. Open the Start menu, display the All Programs list, and then open the Accessories folder. Examine the list of programs in the Accessories folder and its subfolders, and then close the Start menu.

EXPLORE
4. Click the Start button, and then start typing the name of a program you noted in a previous step. Describe what happens.
5. Use Windows Help and Support to research one of the programs you examined in the previous step, such as Calculator or Notepad. Describe the purpose of the program and how to perform a task using that program.
6. Use the Search Help box in Windows Help and Support to list all the Help topics related to the program you researched in the previous step. How many topics are displayed in the results?

EXPLORE
7. Start the program you researched. Click the Help button on the program's menu bar, and then explore the Help topics. Open and read a Help topic in the program.
8. Find a similar topic in Windows Help and Support, and then read that topic. Compare these topics to the ones included in the Windows Help and Support window.
9. Close all open windows.
10. Submit your answers to the preceding questions to your instructor, either in printed or electronic form, as requested.

Extend what you've learned to customize folder windows.

CHALLENGE

Case Problem 3

There are no Data Files needed for this Case Problem.

Friedman Alternatives Warren Friedman recently started his own small firm called Friedman Alternatives, which analyzes and recommends sources of alternative energy for various manufacturing businesses. Most of these businesses want to cut their expenses related to energy, and are interested in helping to conserve fuel and preserve the environment. Warren typically uses the Windows Explorer window to work with his files, but suspects he is not taking full advantage of its features. As his new special-projects employee, he asks you to show him around the Windows 7 folder windows and demonstrate how to customize their appearance. Complete the following steps:

1. Start Windows Explorer. Click the Organize button on the Windows Explorer toolbar, and write down any commands that seem related to changing the appearance of the window.

EXPLORE 2. Select a command that lays out the Windows Explorer window so that it displays a single pane for viewing files. What command did you select? Restore the window to its original condition.

3. Navigate to the Pictures library and display its contents. Double-click the Sample Pictures folder to open it. (If your computer does not contain a Sample Pictures folder, open any folder that displays pictures.) Display the icons using Large Icons view.

4. Change the view to Content view. Describe the differences between Large Icons and Content view.

EXPLORE 5. Click the Slide show button on the toolbar. Describe what happens, and then press the Esc key.

6. With the Details pane open, click a picture file. Describe the contents of the Details pane. Also identify the buttons on the toolbar.

EXPLORE 7. Repeatedly click the Change your view button to cycle from one view to another. Describe the changes in the window.

8. Display the window in Details view.

EXPLORE 9. On the Organize button menu, click Folder and search options to open the Folder Options dialog box. Select the option that shows all folders in the Navigation pane, and then click the OK button. Describe the changes in the Sample Pictures window.

EXPLORE 10. Open the Folder Options dialog box again, click the Restore Defaults button, and then click the OK button.

11. Open the Windows Help and Support window and search for information about folder options. Find a topic explaining how to show hidden files. Explain how to do so.

12. Close all open windows.

13. Submit the results of the preceding steps to your instructor, either in printed or electronic form, as requested.

RESEARCH

Use the Internet to provide information to an import/export company.

Case Problem 4

There are no Data Files needed for this Case Problem.

Majolica Imports   After moving from southern France to New York City, Marie and Bruno Tattinger decided to start a company that imports hand-painted French and Italian ceramics. Both Marie and Bruno travel frequently, and they use laptop computers running Windows 7 to manage their business when they are on the move. They have hired you as a consultant to help them use and maintain their computers. Marie asks you to help her research wireless networks so she can set up a wireless network at home and in their office. You suggest starting with Windows Help and Support, and then expanding to the Internet to search for the latest information. Complete the following steps:

1. In Windows Help and Support, find information about the hardware Marie needs to set up a wireless network.
2. Use the Ask button to visit the Microsoft Web site to obtain more information about wireless networks.
3. Choose a topic that describes how to set up a wireless network for a home or small office, and then read the topic thoroughly.
4. On the Microsoft Web site, search for information about adding a Bluetooth device to the network.
5. Write one to two pages for Marie and Bruno explaining what equipment they need to set up a wireless network and the steps they should perform. Also explain how they can add their Bluetooth mobile phones to the network.
6. Submit the results of the preceding steps to your instructor, either in printed or electronic form, as requested.

ENDING DATA FILES

There are no ending Data Files needed for this tutorial.

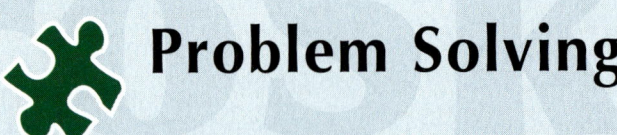

Problem Solving

Gathering Information to Solve Potential Computer Problems

When you solve problems, you work through a series of stages to gather information about the problem and its possible solutions. Problem solving in general involves the following tasks:

1. Recognize and define the problem.
2. Determine possible courses of action.
3. Collect information needed to evaluate alternative courses of action.
4. Evaluate each alternative's merits and drawbacks.
5. Select an alternative.
6. Implement the decision.
7. Monitor and evaluate performance to provide feedback and take corrective action.

If you are involved in solving a complex problem with many possible causes, you perform all seven steps in the process. If you are solving a simpler problem or have limited time to explore solutions, you can condense the steps. For example, you might recognize the problem in one step, determine possible actions, evaluate and select an alternative in the next step, and then implement and evaluate your decision in another step.

Recognize and Define the Problem

A problem is an obstacle that prevents you from reaching a goal. This definition is especially fitting for work with a computer. For example, suppose your goal is to create a report containing text and graphics, but you don't know which program to use. In this case, your lack of familiarity with the programs on your computer is an obstacle preventing you from reaching your goal of efficiently creating a report with text and graphics.

After identifying a simple problem such as which computer program to use, you can focus on solutions. Start by considering any possible solution. For example, start each program on your computer related to text and graphics and examine its features. Next, compare and evaluate those alternatives. Which programs help you meet your goal most effectively? Select the best solution and then try it, observing the results to make sure it actually solves the problem. Can you efficiently create the report with the program you selected? If not, try a different program until you find the best possible solution.

Anticipate Computer Problems

Even if you are familiar with some features of Windows 7 or regularly use your computer for certain tasks, such as accessing Web sites or exchanging e-mail, take some time to explore the basics of Windows 7 on your computer. To solve system problems that might occur later, you should capture and save images of your current desktop, the Start menu, and other resources on your computer. You can save these images for reference if you experience problems with your computer later or want to restore these settings.

To save screen images:

1. Start Paint, and then minimize the program window.
2. Open the window you want to preserve or arrange the desktop as you want it. If you want to capture a window, make sure that window is the active window.
3. Hold down the Alt key and press the Print Screen key. (The Print Screen key might be labeled *PrtScn* or something similar on your keyboard.) Pressing this key combination captures an image of the active window. To capture an image of everything shown on the screen, press the Print Screen key without holding down the Alt key.
4. Restore the Paint program window, and then press the Ctrl+V keys to paste the image in the Paint program window.
5. Click the Save button on the Quick Access Toolbar to open the Save As dialog box. By default, Paint saves images in the My Pictures folder in the Pictures library. Use the Navigation pane to navigate to a different folder, if necessary. Type a filename, and then press the Save button to save the screen image.
6. To print the screen images, click the Paint menu button, and then click Print to open the Print dialog box. Select your printer and other settings, and then click the Print button.
7. To open a new window for the next screen image, click the Paint menu button, and then click New.

Now you can explore Windows 7 on your computer and preserve screen images, which will help you solve computer problems:

1. Start Windows 7 and log on, if necessary.
2. Save and print images of your current desktop, the Start menu, the Computer window showing the drives on your computer, and your Documents folder.
3. Open a folder in the Documents library that you are likely to use often. Make sure the Navigation pane shows the location of this folder on your computer. Capture and save an image of this window.
4. To learn more about the programs that are included with Windows 7 and how they can help you solve problems, start at least two accessory programs that are new to you. Open a menu in each program, and then capture and save the image of each program window.
5. Using the Ribbon, toolbar, or menu bar in the new programs, find a dialog box in each program that you are likely to use. Capture and save images of the dialog boxes.

6. Explore both programs to determine how they might help you solve problems related to using your computer, completing your school work, or performing on the job.
7. Use Windows Help and Support to find information about a feature in one program that can help you solve problems. Choose an appropriate topic. Print an image of the Windows Help and Support window displaying information about this topic.
8. Close all open windows, and then shut down or log off Windows.

Glossary/Index

Note: Boldface entries include definitions.

Special Characters

\> (greater than symbol), EX 141
< (less than symbol), EX 141
<> (not equal to symbol), EX 141
(hash mark), EX 13
* (asterisk), EX 28
+ (plus sign), EX 28
– (minus sign), EX 28
/ (slash), EX 28f
= (equal sign), EX 141
^ (caret), EX 28
≥ (greater than or equal to symbol), EX 141
≤ (less than or equal to symbol), EX 141

A

absolute reference Cell reference that points to a specific cell and does not change when copied; appears with a dollar sign ($) before each column and row designation. EX 116–118, EX 119
accent A variation on an. Excel theme color. EX 61
Access. *See* Microsoft Office Access 2007
active cell The selected cell in the worksheet; indicated with a dark border. EX 4, EX 5
    changing, EX 6
active sheet The worksheet currently displayed in the workbook window. EX 5, EX 319
    changing, EX 7–8
active workbook The workbook you are currently using. EX 4
active workbook window The window displaying the active workbook. EX 4
addition operator (+), EX 28
adjacent range A single rectangular block that includes a group of contiguous cells. EX 21
    selecting, EX 22
alignment
    cell content, EX 67–68
    shapes, EX 203
AND criteria range, EX 375
AND function A logical function that returns a TRUE value if all the logical conditions are true and a FALSE value if any or all of the logical conditions are false. EX 343–344
application. *See*. Excel application
application settings The most common program options. OFF 18
Apply Names dialog box, EX 406
area chart, EX 167
argument Specifies the numbers, text, or cell references used by the function to calculate a value. EX 121
arithmetic operator A symbol, such as +, -, *, or /, used in a formula to perform arithmetic calculations. EX 27–28

ascending order Sorts text alphabetically from A to Z, numbers from smallest to largest, and dates from oldest to newest. EX 227
Assign Macro dialog box, EX 437
asterisk (*), multiplication operator, EX 28
AutoComplete (Excel) The feature that helps make entering repetitive text easier. As you enter text in a worksheet, text that begins with the same letters as a previous entry in the same column is displayed. EX 12
AutoFill An. Excel tool that enables you to copy the contents of the selected cells by dragging the fill handle over another adjacent cell or range of cells rather than using the Copy and Paste commands. EX 131–137
    copying formulas and formats, EX 132–133
    filling series, EX 134–137
    options, EX 133
autofit To eliminate empty space by matching the column width to the longest cell entry or the row height to the tallest cell entry. EX 17
automatic color A color option that uses the Windows default text and background color values. EX 61
AutoSum A button that quickly inserts. Excel functions that summarize all the values in a column or row using a single statistic—SUM, AVERAGE, COUNT, MIN or MAX. EX 33
AVERAGE function, EX 122, EX 123, EX 125–126
AVERAGEIF function A function that calculates the average of values in a range that meet criteria you specify. EX 370–371
AVERAGEIFS function A function that calculates the average of values within a range of cells that meet multiple conditions. EX 372
axis
    formatting, EX 185–186
    horizontal (category), EX 184
    setting label units, EX 193–194
    vertical (value), EX 184

B

background image, worksheets, EX 63–64
banded rows In an. Excel table, rows of alternating colors that make data easier to read. EX 82–83
bar chart A column chart turned on its side, so each bar length is based on its value. EX 167, EX 182
Begins with criteria range, EX 376
BETWEEN criteria range, EX 375
border A line that prints along the side of a table cell or around the outside of selected text. EX 71–72
bubble chart, EX 167
button An icon you click to initiate an action. OFF 10–12. *See also specific buttons*
    adding to Quick Access Toolbar, OFF 18
    macros, creating, EX 436–439

C

calculated column A column in an. Excel table that. Excel automatically fills with a formula after you enter or edit a formula in one cell of that column. EX 339

caret (^), exponentiation operator, EX 28
cascade layout, EX 298
case converting, EX A 9–10
category axis. *See* horizontal (category) axis
category field A field used to group the values in a PivotTable. EX 247
category value The group or category to which a series value belongs. EX 165
cell The intersection of a column and row in a worksheet. EX 5
    defined names, EX 396–407
    entering dates, EX 13
    entering multiple lines of text, EX 12–13
    entering numbers, EX 13–15
    entering text, EX 10–12
    formatting. *See* formatting worksheet cells
    highlighting, EX 90–94
    locking and unlocking, EX 414–415
    merging, EX 69–70
    number exceeding size, EX 13
    password-protecting ranges, EX 415
    referencing cells in other worksheets, EX 288–289
cell range. *See* range
cell reference The address of a cell indicating its column and row location. EX 5
    absolute, EX 116–118, EX 119
    copying formulas, EX 114–120
    entering using mouse, EX 30
    mixed, EX 118–120
    relative, EX 115–116, EX 119
    tables, EX 367
    3-D references, EX 289–293
chart Graph that provides a visual representation of the workbook data. EX 164–201
    axes, EX 184, EX 185–186
    choosing right type, EX 201
    column. *See* column chart
    combination, EX 198–201
    editing chart data, EX 181–182
    effective, designing, EX 188
    elements, EX 170–171
    embedded, EX 168–170
    existing, adding data series, EX 196–198
    gridlines, EX 184
    inserting, EX 165
    legend, EX 170, EX 174–175
    line. *See* line chart
    moving, EX 168–170
    pie chart. *See* pie chart
    PivotChart, EX 268–270
    resizing, EX 168–170
    scale, EX 184
    selecting chart type, EX 166–168
    selecting data source, EX 165–166
    style and layout, EX 171–173
    title, EX 173–174
chart area The entire chart and all the elements contained in the chart or graph, such as the title and legend. EX 170

chart sheet A new sheet that is automatically inserted into the workbook, occupies the entire document window, and provides more space and details for the chart. EX 4, EX 168, EX 204–207
    formatting, EX 205–206

chart title Term that appears above the plot area and describes the contents of the plot area and the data series. EX 170, EX 173–174

clear To remove. EX 20, EX 237
    clearing conditional formats, EX 89–90
    data but leave the basic structure of the worksheet unchanged. EX 20
    filters, EX 237

closing files, OFF 21

Collapse button, EX 259–260

color
    automatic, EX 61
    custom, EX 60–61
    fill, EX 61–62
    fill, worksheets, EX 61–62
    fonts, EX 61–62
    pie chart slices, EX 177–178
    standard, EX 60
    theme, EX 60
    worksheets, EX 60–64

column
    calculated, EX 339
    changing width, EX 15–17
    clearing, EX 20
    deleting, EX 20
    filtering using multiple columns, EX 236–237
    freezing, EX 220
    inserting, EX 18–19

column chart A type of chart that displays values in different categories as columns; the height of each column is based on its value. EX 167, EX 182–188
    creating, EX 182–183
    formatting axes, EX 185–186
    formatting columns, EX 186–188
    formatting elements, EX 183–185

column header. *See* field name.

column heading The part of a worksheet that identifies each column by a different letter. EX 4–5

combination chart A chart that combines two or more chart types in a single graph. EX 198–201

comment A text box that is attached to a specific cell in a worksheet; used for documentation or notes. EX 418–420

compare value A category for a lookup table that is located in the table's first column or row. EX 355

comparison operator Symbol that indicates the relationship between two values. EX 141–142

Compatibility Checker The dialog box that, when you save an Excel 2007 workbook to an earlier format, alerts you to features that are not supported by the earlier version of. Excel. EX A 16

Compatibility Mode The mode in which you can work with a workbook file that is an older, Excel file format. EX A 2

compound file A file that relies on data from more than one program. EX B 2

compound interest An amount for which the interest paid is calculated on the principal and any previous interest payments that have been added to that principal. EX 147

Computer window A tool that you use to view, organize, and access the programs, files, and drives on your computer. WIN 7 12

concatenation The joining of the contents of two or more cells. EX A 6–7

conditional count. *See* COUNTNIF function

conditional formatting A setting that applies formatting only when a cell's value meets a specified condition. EX 86–94
    clearing formats, EX 89–90
    data bars, EX 87–89
    effective use, EX 94
    highlighting cells, EX 90–94
    highlighting duplicate values, EX 360–362
    Rules Manager, EX 362–364

Conditional Formatting Rules Manager dialog box, EX 362–364

conditional sum. *See* SUMIF function

contextual tab A Ribbon tab that contains commands related to the selected object so you can manipulate, edit, and format that object OFF 15

copying
    cell ranges, EX 25–26
    filtered records to new location, EX 378
    formats. *See* copying formats
    formulas with AutoFill, EX 132–233
    grouped worksheets, EX 287
    shapes, EX 203
    worksheets, EX 36

copying and pasting, EX B 2
    formulas, EX 30–31

copying formats
    AutoFill, EX 132–233
    Format Painter, EX 74–75
    Paste Options button, EX 75
    Paste Special, EX 76

COUNT function, EX 122

COUNTA function, EX 122

COUNTIF function A function that calculates the number of cells in a range that match criteria you specify; also called a conditional count. EX 367–368

COUNTIFS function A function that counts the number of cells within a range that meet multiple criteria. EX 371

Create Names from Selection dialog box, EX 399

Create PivotTable dialog box, EX 249

Create Table dialog box, EX 222

criteria filter Conditions you specify for a filter. EX 238–240

criteria range An area in a worksheet, separate from the range of data or, Excel table, used to specify the criteria for the data to be displayed after the filter is applied to the table. EX 373–378
    creating, EX 376–378

Cube functions, EX 122

Custom AutoFilter dialog box, EX 239

custom color A color you specify as a mixture of red, blue, and green color values, which makes available 16.7 million custom colors—more colors than the human eye can distinguish. EX 60–61

custom format A format code you specify to indicate exactly how. Excel should display a number, date, time, or text string. EX A 12–14
    numeric format codes, EX A 12–14

custom list The sequence you specify to sort data. EX 231

Custom Lists dialog box, EX 232

custom template A workbook template you create that is ready to run with the formulas for all calculations included as well as all formatting. EX 316–321

cut To remove data from a cell and place it on the Office Clipboard. EX 25–26

cutting and pasting cell ranges, EX 25–26

D

data
    charts, editing, EX 181–182
    formatting in worksheets, EX 64–67
    hiding in worksheets, EX 94–95
    highlighting data values, EX 187
    invalid, drawing circles around, EX 414
    structured ranges of, planning, EX 218–221

data bar A horizontal bar added to the background of a cell whose length reflects the cell's value. EX 87–89

data definition table Documentation that lists the fields to be maintained for each record and a description of the information each field will include. EX 219

data entry errors, checking for, EX 360–367
    conditional formatting, EX 360–364
    IFERROR function, EX 365–367

data label Text associated with a data value. EX 175–177

data marker The graphical representation of the values in the data series of a chart, including items such as each column in a column chart, the pie slices in pie charts, and the points used in XY (scatter) charts. EX 170

data series The Chart Wizard organizes data sources into a collection, where each data series is a range of data values that is plotted as a unit on the chart. EX 165
    adding to existing chart, EX 196–198

data source The variable information that is contained in a data source, which can be a Word table, an Access database, or some other source. EX 165–166

data validation A set of rules that determine what users can enter in a specific cell or range. EX 407–414
    drawing circles around invalid data, EX 414
    error alert style and message, EX 410–412
    existing data, EX 409
    input message, EX 409–410
    list validation rules, EX 412–414
    specifying data type and acceptable values, EX 408–409

Data Validation dialog box, EX 410, EX 411

database A collection of related tables stored in the same file. OFF 2

Database function (Dfunction) A function that performs summary data analysis (SUM, AVERAGE, COUNT, and so on) on a table of values based on criteria that you set. EX 122, EX 379
    summarizing data using, EX 379–382

date
    formatting, EX A 14–16, EX 66–67
    international audiences, EX 67
    storing, EX A 16
Date & Time functions, EX 122
date data A value in a recognized date format. EX 9
    entering in cells, EX 13
DATE function, EX 145
date function A category of. Excel functions that store and calculate dates as numeric values, representing the number of days since January 1, 1900. EX 145–146
DATEDIF function A function that calculates the difference between two dates and shows the result in months, days, or years. EX 348
DAVERAGE function, EX 379
DAY function, EX 145
DCOUNT function, EX 379, EX 380–382
DCOUNTA function, EX 379
default A setting that is preset by the operating system or program OFF 8
default template A template that creates the blank Book1 workbook that opens when you start. Excel. The default template contains no text or formulas, but it includes all the formatting available in every new workbook. EX 313
defined name (name) A word or string of characters associated with a single cell or a range. EX 396–407
    adding to existing formulas, EX 405–407
    advantages, EX 397
    creating, EX 396–401
    entering formulas, EX 401–405
delete To remove a cell or cells from a worksheet, shifting the remaining worksheet cells into the space previously occupied by the deleted cell or cells; also to remove a worksheet entirely from a workbook. EX 20
    cell ranges, EX 26, EX 27
    records, EX 227
    rows and columns, EX 20
delimit To separate. EX A 8
descending order Sorts text in reverse alphabetical order from Z to A, numbers from largest to smallest, and dates from newest to oldest. EX 227
desktop Your workspace on the screen for projects and the tools that you need to manipulate them. WIN7 5
destination file The workbook that receives the data when two files are linked; sometimes referred to as the dependent file. EX 295, EX 296, EX B 2
    opening destination workbooks with source workbooks closed, EX 304–308
Dfunction. *See* Database function
dialog box A special kind of window where you enter or choose settings for how you want to perform a task. OFF 13–14
Dialog Box Launcher A button you click to open a task pane or dialog box that provides more advanced functionality for a group of tasks OFF 13
digital signature Authentication of digital information to assure the signer's authenticity, the integrity of the data, and the origin of the signed content. EX 424
division operator (/), EX 28
DMAX function, EX 379
DMIN function, EX 379

document A collection of data that has a name and is stored in a computer; also called a file. OFF 2
documentation sheet, EX 9
doughnut chart, EX 167
drag and drop To move an item (either text or a graphic) by selecting it and then dragging it with the mouse. EX 24–25
DSTDEV function, EX 379
DSUM function, EX 379
duplicate values, highlighting with conditional formatting, EX 360–362

E

Edit Formatting Rule dialog box, EX 363
Edit Links dialog box, EX 307
Edit Name dialog box, EX 400
editing
    chart data, EX 181–182
    hyperlinks, EX 312–313
    macros, EX 432–436
    records, EX 226–227
    workbooks, effects on macros, EX 429
    worksheet groups, EX 285
    worksheets, EX 36–40
editing mode A mode in which you can edit part of an entry rather than the entire contents of a cell. EX 36–37
embedded chart A chart that is displayed within a worksheet and one that you can place alongside the data source, giving context to the chart. EX 168–170
embedded object An object that is stored in the destination file and is no longer part of the source file. EX B 3
embedded shape, EX 202
embedding, EX B 2, EX B 6
    modifying embedded objects, EX B 7–8
Engineering functions, EX 122
equal to operator (=), EX 141
error
    data validation to prevent. *See* data validation
    macros, fixing, EX 432
    protecting worksheets and workbooks, EX 414–418
error alert message A message that appears if a user tries to enter a value in a cell that does not meet its validation rule. EX 407
    specifying, EX 410–412
error value Text displayed in a cell indicate that some element in a formula or a cell referenced in that formula is preventing. Excel from returning a calculated value; common error values are #DIV/0!, #N/A, and #VALUE!. EX 365
Excel. *See* Microsoft Office. Excel 2007
Excel application A spreadsheet written or tailored to meet the user's specific needs; usually includes specially designed reports and/or charts, data entry cells, custom interface, and documentation. EX 393–442
    macros. *See* macro
    naming cells and ranges, EX 396–407
    planning, EX 394–395
    protecting worksheets and workbooks, EX 414–418
    validating data entry, EX 407–414
    worksheet comments, EX 418–420
Excel Options dialog box, EX 421

Excel table A range of data you can treat as a distinct object in a worksheet. EX 82
    styles, EX 82
Excel window
    elements, EX 4–5
    opening, EX 3–4
exiting programs, OFF 28–29
Expand button, EX 259, EX 260
exploded pie chart A pie chart with one slice moved away from the pie as if someone were taking the piece out of the pie. EX 178
exponentiation operator (^), EX 28
external reference A reference to a cell or range in a worksheet in another workbook. EX 296
    converting external reference formulas to current values, EX 307–308
    formulas, EX 299–303

F

field An attribute or characteristic of a person, place, or thing (such as a last name, address, city, or state); in. Excel, each column represents a field. EX 218
    creating, EX 339
    PivotTables. *See* PivotTable
    sort, EX 227, EX 228–229
field name A unique label that describes the contents of the data in a column; also called a column header. EX 220
    entering in formulas, EX 360
file
    closing, OFF 21
    earlier versions of Office, OFF 19
    new, creating, OFF 22
    open, switching between, OFF 5
    opening, OFF 21–22
    printing, OFF 27–28
    saving, OFF 18–21
file extension A multi-character code that Office appends to a filename to identify the program in which that file was created. The default file extensions are .docx for Word, .xlsx for. Excel, .pptx for PowerPoint, and .accdb for Access. OFF, 19
filename The name you provide when you save a file and the name you associate with that file. OFF 19
fill color, worksheets, EX 61–62
fill handle A small black square in the lower-right corner of a selected cell or cell range that you drag to copy the contents of the selected cells to adjacent cells. EX 132
filter The process of temporarily hiding records that do not meet the specified criteria. EX 233–240
    clearing filters, EX 237
    copying filtered records to new location, EX 378
    criteria filters, EX 238–240
    criteria ranges, EX 373–378
    multiple columns, EX 236–237
    multiple items, EX 258
    PivotTable fields, EX 258–259
    selecting multiple filter items, EX 237–238
    text filters, EX 236
    using one column, EX 233–235
financial function A category of. Excel functions that calculate values from loans and investments. EX 122, EX 146–150

Find The command to locate specific letters and numbers in a workbook. EX 38–39

finding and replacing items in worksheets, EX 38–39

finding records, EX 226–227

flowchart, EX 353–354

folder A container for your files. OFF 19, WIN7 9

font A set of characters that uses the same typeface, style, and size. EX 59
- color in worksheets, EX 61–62
- nontheme, EX 59
- sans serif, EX 59
- serif, EX 59
- theme, EX 59

font size Determined by point size, which is a unit of measurement equal approximately to 1/72 of an inch. EX 59, EX 60

font style Various ways that fonts can be displayed, such as regular, italic, bold, or bold italic; a special attribute applied to the characters of a font. EX 59

footer Text that appears at the bottom of every page in a document or at the bottom of every slide in a presentation. EX 98–100

format To change the appearance, not the data, of your workbook. EX 58. *See also* formatting worksheet cells; formatting worksheets
- chart columns, EX 186–188
- chart sheets, EX 205–206
- column chart elements, EX 183–185
- conditional. *See* conditional formatting
- copying formats. *See* copying formats
- custom formats, EX A 11, EX A 12–14
- date labels in line chart, EX 190–193
- dates, EX A 14–16
- pie charts, EX 175–181
- special formats, EX A 11, EX A 12
- tables, EX 224
- value fields, EX 253–254
- worksheet cells. *See* formatting worksheet cells
- worksheet groups, EX 285–286
- worksheets. *See* formatting worksheets; formatting worksheets for printing

Format Cells dialog box, EX 72–74

format code A series of symbols. EX A 12

Format Painter A button on the Ribbon that, when selected, copies a format from one cell range to another. EX 74–75

formatting worksheet cells, EX 67–74
- adding cell borders, EX 71–72
- aligning cell content, EX 67–68
- Format Cells dialog box, EX 72–74
- indenting cell content, EX 68–69
- merging cells, EX 69–70
- rotating cell content, EX 70–71

formatting worksheets, EX 58–100
- cells. *See* formatting worksheet cells
- color, EX 60–64
- conditional formats, EX 86–94
- copying formats with Format Painter, EX 74–75
- copying formats with Paste Options button, EX 75
- copying formats with Paste Special, EX 76
- data, EX 64–67
- data bars, EX 87–89
- dates and times, EX 66–67

defining print area, EX 96
headers and footers, EX 98–100
hiding worksheet data, EX 94–95
highlighting cells, EX 90–94
numbers, EX 65–66
page breaks, EX 96–97
print titles, EX 98
for printing, EX 95–100
styles, EX 76–78, EX 80
table styles, EX 82–86
text, EX 58–60
themes, EX 78–80
titles, EX 81–82

formatting worksheets for printing, EX 95–100
- defining print area, EX 96
- headers and footers, EX 98–100
- page breaks, EX 96–97
- print titles, EX 98

formula A mathematical expression that calculates a value; all. Excel formulas always begin with an equal sign (=) followed by an expression that describes the calculation to be done. EX 27–31
- adding, EX 27–30
- adding defined names to existing formulas, EX 405–407
- arithmetic operators, EX 27–28
- cell references. *See* cell reference
- checking for matching formulas, EX 351
- conditionally formatting cells using, EX 362
- converting external reference formulas to current values, EX 307–308
- converting to text, EX 350
- copying and pasting, EX 30–31
- copying with AutoFill, EX 27–31EX 132–233
- defining complex validation criteria, EX 412
- entering, EX 29
- entering cell references using mouse, EX 30
- entering column headers, EX 360
- entering in worksheet groups, EX 283–285
- entering with defined names, EX 401–405
- external references, EX 299–303
- order of precedence rules, EX 28
- point-and-click method of building, EX 296
- referencing another worksheet, EX 288
- 3-D references, EX 290–292
- viewing, EX 29–30

formula bar The bar located above the workbook window in which the contents of a cell are displayed. EX 4, EX 5, EX 9

Formula view. Excel view in which cell formulas are displayed, rather than the values returned by the formulas. EX 44

freeze The process of keeping rows and/or columns you select visible in the workbook window as you scroll the worksheet. EX 220–221

function A predefined formula that performs calculations using specific values called arguments. EX 31–34, EX 120–130
- effective, EX 34
- entering, EX 32
- entering with AutoSum, EX 33–34
- horizontal scroll bar, EX 4, EX 5
- inserting, EX 123–127
- managing personal finances, EX 147–150

syntax, EX 121–123
3-D references, EX 290
typing, EX 127–130

Function Arguments dialog box, EX 342, EX 357

FV function, EX 146

G

gallery A grid or menu that shows a visual representation of the options available for a command. OFF 12–13

General number format Default number format that automatically displays numbers, for the most part, the same way you enter them. EX 65

graph. *See* chart

greater than or equal to symbol ($\geq$), EX 141

greater than symbol (>), EX 141

gridline A line that extends across the plot area indicating the location of tick marks on the chart's horizontal or vertical axes. EX 184

group A collection of buttons for related commands on the Ribbon. OFF 11

grouping
- date fields, EX 267–268
- PivotTable items, EX 265–268
- shapes, EX 203–204
- worksheets. *See* worksheet group

H

header Text that appears at the top of every page in a document or every slide in a presentation. EX 98–100

header row The row of field names. EX 220

Help Information in Office that you can use to find out how to perform a task or obtain more information about a feature. OFF 23–27
- ScreenTips, OFF 12, OFF 23

Help window A window that provides access to all the Help topics, templates, and training installed on your computer with Office and available on Microsoft Office Online. OFF 23–27

hiding worksheet data, EX 94–95

highlighting
- cells, EX 90–94
- data values, EX 187
- duplicate values with conditional formatting, EX 360–362

HLOOKUP function A function that searches horizontally across a lookup table to retrieve a value from that table; used when the compare values are stored in the first row of the lookup table. EX 355

horizontal (category) axis On the horizontal axis, or x-axis, are the data series' category values, or x values. EX 184

horizontal layout, EX 298

HTML (Hypertext Markup Language) A language used to write Web pages. EX 321

hyperlink A link in a file, such as a workbook, to information within that file or another file that, when clicked, switches to the file or portion of the file referenced by the hyperlink. EX 310–312
- editing, EX 312–313
- inserting, EX 311–312
- removing while keeping text, EX 313

I

icon set, EX 87

IF function A logical function that returns one value if the statement is true and returns a different value if the statement is false. EX 141–144, EX 340–342
    nested IF functions, EX 348–352

IFERROR function The function used to determine if a cell contains an error value and displays the message you choose rather than the default error value. EX 365–367

image, background, EX 63–64

indenting cell content, EX 68–69

Information functions, EX 122

input message A message that appears when a user clicks a cell; can be used to specify the type of data to enter in the cell. EX 407
    specifying, EX 409–410, EX 411

insignificant zero A zero whose omission from the number does not change the number's value. EX A 12

INT function, EX 122

integrating, Excel with other Windows programs, EX B 1–9
    embedding objects, EX B 6
    linking, Excel and Word files, EX B 3–5
    methods, EX B 2–3
    modifying embedded objects, EX B 7–8
    updating linked objects, EX B 5–6

integration The ability to share information between programs through OLE. OFF 3

interest The amount charged for lending money. EX 147

IPMT function, EX 146

K

keyboard shortcut A combination of keys you press to perform a command. OFF 12

L

landscape orientation A type of page orientation in which the page is wider than it is tall, so that text spans the widest part of the page. EX 42–43, EX 96

layout
    charts, EX 171–173
    multiple workbooks, EX 298–299
    PivotTables, EX 250, EX 255–256
    worksheet, EX 41

leader line In a pie chart, a line that connects a data label outside of a pie slice to its corresponding label when space limitations force. Excel to place a data label far from its slice. EX 176

LEFT function The function that returns a specified number of characters from the beginning of the string. EX A 3, EX A 4–6

legend Used to identify the format of the data marker used for each series in a chart. Used if the chart contains more than one data series. EX 93–94, EX 170, EX 174–175
    moving, EX 195
    overlaying, EX 194–195
    resizing, EX 194

LEN function The function that returns the number of characters (length) of the specified string. EX A 3, EX A 4

less than or equal to symbol (≤), EX 141

less than symbol (<), EX 141

line chart A chart that compares values from several categories with a sequential order, such as dates and times that occur at evenly spaced intervals. The values are indicated by the height of the line. EX 167, EX 189–195
    editing, EX 190
    formatting date labels, EX 190–193
    overlaying legends, EX 194–195
    setting label units, EX 193–194

link A connection between the files that allows data to be transferred from one file to the other. EX 295
    automatic, disabling, EX 304
    breaking
    managing, EX 307
    managing, EX 306–308

linked object An object inserted into a destination file as a separate file that is linked to the source file, changes to the linked object in the source file are reflected in the destination file, and vice versa. EX B 3
    updating, EX B 5–6

linking, EX B 2
    Excel and Word files, EX B 3–5
    updating linked objects, EX B 5–6
    workbooks. *See* linking workbooks

linking workbooks, EX 295–308
    arranging workbooks, EX 297–298
    external reference formulas, EX 299–303
    managing linked workbooks, EX 303
    navigating, EX 297–298
    opening destination workbooks with source workbooks closed, EX 304–308
    updating linked workbooks, EX 303–304
    when to use linked workbooks, EX 297

list, custom, EX 231

Live Preview An Office feature that shows the results you would achieve in your file, such as the effects of formatting options on a document's appearance, if you click the option to which you are pointing. EX 58, OFF 13

loan payment, determining using PMT function, EX 147–150

locked property A setting that determines whether changes can be made to a cell. EX 414–415

logical functions A category of. Excel functions that test, or evaluate, whether a condition, usually entered as an expression, is true or false. EX 122, EX 141–144, EX 338–352
    DATEDIF function, EX 348
    AND function, EX 343–344
    IF function, EX 141–144, EX 340–342
    OR function, EX 352
    structured references, EX 344–347

Lookup & Reference functions, EX 122

lookup table A table that organizes data you want to retrieve into different categories. EX 355
    approximate matches, EX 358–360
    exact matches, EX 355–358

lookup value The value you are trying to find or retrieve from a lookup table. EX 355

LOWER function, EX A 3

M

macro A series of stored commands that can be run whenever you need to perform the recorded task. EX 420–441
    buttons, EX 436–439
    commands, writing, EX 434–436
    digital signatures, EX 424
    editing, EX 432–436
    fixing errors, EX 432
    opening workbooks with, EX 440–441
    planning, EX 425
    protecting against macro viruses, EX 421–424
    recording, EX 424–427
    running, EX 427–432
    saving workbooks with, EX 439–440
    security settings, EX 422–424
    structure, EX 433–434
    workbook edits, EX 429

Macro dialog box, EX 428

macro security settings The settings that control what. Excel will do about macros in a workbook when you open that workbook. EX 422–424

macro virus A type of virus that uses a program's own macro programming language to distribute the virus. EX 421
    protecting against, EX 421–424

major tick mark The indication of the major units of increment on the x- or y-axis. EX 184

manual page break A page break you insert anywhere on a page. EX 96–97

margin The space between the page content and the edges of the page. EX 98

Math & Trig functions, EX 122

MAX function, EX 122

median The middle value in data. EX 121

MEDIAN function, EX 122

merge To combine the main document with a data source. EX 69–70

Microsoft Office 2007 A collection of the most popular Microsoft programs: Word, Excel, PowerPoint, Access, and Outlook. OFF 2
    common window elements, OFF 6–10
    contextual tools, OFF 15–17
    files. *See* file
    Help. *See* Help
    integrating programs, OFF 3
    Ribbon, OFF 10–14
    starting programs, OFF 3–5
    switching between programs and files, OFF 5

Microsoft Office Access 2007 A database program you use to enter, organize, display, and retrieve related information. OFF 2

Microsoft Office. Excel 2007 A spreadsheet program you use to display, organize, and analyze numerical data. EX 1, EX 3–4, OFF 2
    starting, EX 3–4

Microsoft Office Help button, OFF 6

Microsoft Office Online A Web site maintained by Microsoft that provides access to the latest information and additional Help resources. OFF 23

Microsoft Office Outlook 2007 An information management program you use to send, receive, and organize e-mail; plan your schedule; arrange meetings; organize contacts; create a to-do list; and jot down notes. You can also use Outlook to print schedules, task lists, and other documents. OFF 2

Microsoft Office PowerPoint 2007 A presentation program you use to create a presentation in the form of on-screen slides, a slide presentation in a Web site, or overheads; the slides can contain text, charts, and pictures. OFF 2

Microsoft Office Security Options dialog box, EX 306

Microsoft Office Word 2007 A word-processing program you use to create text documents. OFF 2
    linking, Excel and Word files, EX B 3–5

Microsoft Windows 7 A recent version of the Windows operating system. WIN7 6

MID function, EX A 3

MIN function, EX 122

Mini toolbar A toolbar that appears next to the pointer whenever you select text and contains buttons for the most commonly used formatting commands, such as font, font size, styles, color, alignment, and indents that may appear in different groups or tabs on the Ribbon. EX 62, OFF 15–16

minor tick mark The indication of the minor units of increment on the x- or y-axis. EX 184

minus sign (-), EX 28

mixed reference Cell reference that contains both relative and absolute references, for example, B$4. EX 118–120
    external reference formulas, EX 302

mode The most common value in data. EX 121

module In VBA, a collection of sub procedures. EX 434

MONTH function, EX 145

mouse, entering cell references in formulas, EX 30

moving
    cell ranges, EX 24–25
    chart legends, EX 195
    grouped worksheets, EX 287
    macro buttons, EX 438
    worksheets, EX 36

multiple worksheets. *See* worksheet group

multiplication operator (*), EX 28

N

name. *See* defined name

Name box The box located on the far left of the Formula bar in which the cell reference to the active cell is also displayed. EX 5

Name Manager dialog box, EX 399–400

navigation
    multiple workbooks, EX 297–298
    worksheets, EX 6–7

nested Functions or other parts of a formula placed inside another function. EX 123

nested IF function One IF function placed inside another IF function to test an additional condition. EX 348–352

nonadjacent range Cell range that is comprised of two or more separate adjacent ranges. EX 21
    selecting, EX 22

nontheme font In. Excel, a font that can be used no matter what theme the workbook has. EX 59

Normal view The view that renders the workbook and worksheets for the computer screen. EX 41

not equal to operator (<>), EX 141

NOW function, EX 145

NPER function, EX 146

number data A numerical value that can be used in a mathematical calculation. EX 9
    entering in cells, EX 13–15
    formatting in worksheets, EX 65–66

numeric format codes, EX A 12–14

O

object Anything that can be manipulated independently as a whole, such as a chart, table, picture, video, or sound clip. OFF 15, EX B 2
    embedding, EX B 6–8
    linked, EX B 3, EX B 5–6
    pasted, EX B 2

object linking and embedding (OLE) The technology that allows you to copy and paste objects, such as graphic files, cell and ranges, or charts, so that information about the program that created the object is included with the object itself. EX B 2–3

Office. *See* Microsoft Office 2007

Office Button A button that provides access to document-level features, such as creating new files; opening, saving, printing, and closing files; as well as the most common program options. OFF 18
    Excel, EX 4, EX 5
    Office programs, OFF 6

opening
    dialog boxes, OFF 13–14, WIN7 24
    files, OFF 21–22
    workbooks, EX 220
    workbooks created in earlier versions of. Excel, EX A 2–3
    workbooks with macros, EX 440–441

operator A mathematical symbol that you use to combine values and then return a single value. EX 27–28
    arithmetic, EX 27–28
    comparison, EX 141–142

optional argument An argument that is not necessary for the function to calculate a value (if an optional argument is not included, Excel assumes a default value for it). EX 121

OR criteria range, EX 375

OR function A logical function that returns a TRUE value if any of the logical conditions are true and a FALSE value if all the logical conditions are false. EX 352

order of precedence A set of predefined rules that. Excel follows to unambiguously calculate a formula by determining which operator is applied first, which operator is applied second, and so forth. EX 28

Outline buttons
    subtotals, EX 245

Outlook. *See* Microsoft Office Outlook 2007

P

page break Location in a worksheet that determines where a new page begins. EX 96–97

Page Break Preview view In. Excel, a view that displays the worksheet as it is divided up into pages. Anything outside of the print area is grayed out. EX 41–42

Page Layout view In. Excel, a view that shows how the worksheet will be laid out on the pages sent to the printer. EX 41

page orientation, EX 42–43, EX 96

parentheses, matching, checking for, EX 351

password
    cell ranges, EX 415
    protecting, EX 416

Paste Options button, copying formats, EX 75

Paste Special command, copying formats, EX 76

Paste Special dialog box, EX B 5

pasted object An object inserted as part of the destination file, which has no connection to the source file. EX B 2

pasting. *See* copying and pasting; cutting and pasting

payment on loan, determining using PMT function, EX 147–150

personal finances, using functions to manage, EX 147–150

Personal Macro workbook A hidden workbook named Personal.xlsb that opens whenever you start. Excel that stores commonly used macros. EX 425

perspective The illusion that some parts of the 3-D chart are farther away from you than others. EX 179

pie chart A chart in the shape of a circle (like a pie) that shows data values as percentage of the whole. EX 167–168, EX 175–181
    colors, EX 177–178
    exploded, EX 178
    formatting data labels, EX 176–177
    3D, EX 178–181

PivotChart A graphical representation of the data in a PivotTable in which you can interactively add, remove, filter, and refresh data fields. EX 268–270

PivotTable An interactive table that enables you to group and summarize either a range of data or an. Excel table into a concise, tabular format for easier reporting and analysis. EX 246–268
    adding fields, EX 251–253
    adding value fields, EX 261–262
    category fields, EX 247
    collapsing and expanding items, EX 259–260
    creating, EX 248–250
    filtering fields, EX 258–259
    formatting value fields, EX 253–254
    grouping items, EX 265–268
    layout areas, EX 250
    layout options, EX 255–256
    rearranging, EX 254–255
    refreshing, EX 263–264
    removing fields, EX 262–263
    report filters, EX 257–258
    sorting fields, EX 260–261
    styles, EX 253
    types of reports, EX 268
    value fields, EX 247

pixel A colored dot that, when combined with other pixels, forms a picture or graphics display; stands for picture element. EX 15

placeholder Symbols that represent individual digits. EX A 12–13

planning
    Excel applications, EX 394–395
    macros, EX 425
    structured ranges of data, EX 218–221
    workbooks, EX 8–9

planning analysis sheet A worksheet that includes questions to help you define the purpose and objectives of a workbook. EX 8–9

plot area A rectangular area containing a graphical representation of the values in the data series. EX 170

plus sign (+), EX 28

PMT function, EX 146, EX 147–150

point The unit used to measure the size of the characters in a font. EX 15, EX 59, EX 60

portrait orientation A type of page orientation in which the page is taller than it is wide (like a typical business letter). EX 42

PowerPoint. *See* Microsoft Office PowerPoint 2007

PPMT function, EX 146

presentation The file you create in PowerPoint. OFF 2

previewing worksheets, EX 40–43

primary sort field The first sort field. EX 228

primary value axis The axis in a column chart that displays the primary values associated with the heights of each column. EX 184

principal The amount of money being loaned. EX 147

print area Selected portion of a worksheet to be printed. EX 96

print title In. Excel, information that prints on each page. EX 98

printing
    files, OFF 27–28
    worksheet groups, EX 293–294
    worksheets, EX 43

program. *See also specific programs*
    exiting, OFF 28–29
    open, switching between, OFF 5, WIN7 15–17

program button A button that appears on the taskbar for each open program. WIN7 14

PROPER function The function that converts the first letter of each word in a text string to uppercase, capitalizes any letter in a text string that does not follow another letter, and changes all other letters to lowercase. EX A 3, EX A 6

protect To limit user access to certain parts of a workbook and the ability to make changes in the workbook to reduce data-entry errors. EX 414–418
    locking and unlocking cells, EX 414–415
    macro viruses, EX 421–424
    unprotecting worksheets, EX 418
    workbooks, EX 417–418
    worksheets, EX 415–417

Protect Sheet dialog box, EX 416

Protect Structure and Windows dialog box, EX 417

PV function, EX 146

Q

Quick Access Toolbar A collection of buttons that provide one-click access to commonly used commands, such as Save, Undo, and Repeat. OFF 18
    Excel, EX 4, EX 5
    Office programs, OFF 6

R

radar chart, EX 167

RAND() function, EX 122

range A group of worksheet cells, which can be adjacent or nonadjacent; also called a cell range. EX 21–27
    adjacent, EX 21, EX 22
    copying, EX 25–26
    defined names, EX 396–407
    deleting, EX 26, EX 27
    inserting, EX 26, EX 27
    moving, EX 24–25
    nonadjacent, EX 21, EX 22
    password-protecting, EX 415
    referencing ranges in other worksheets, EX 288–289
    selecting, EX 22–23

range reference Identification of a cell range using the upper-left and lower-right corners of the rectangular selection of cells. EX 22

range reference Identification of a cell range using the upper-left and lower-right corners of the rectangular selection of the cells.
    inserting, EX 32
    tables, EX 367
    3-D references
    inserting, EX 289–293

RATE function, EX 146

record A collection of related fields that are grouped together; in. Excel, each row represents a record. EX 218
    adding to tables, EX 225–227
    copying filtered records to new location, EX 378
    deleting, EX 227
    editing, EX 226–227
    finding, EX 226–227

Record Macro dialog box, EX 426

recording macros, EX 414–417

redoing actions, worksheets, EX 38

refresh To update. EX 263–264

relative reference In a formula, the address of a cell range based on the relative position of the cell that contains the formula and the cell the formula refers to. If you copy the formula, the relative reference is adjusted to reflect the new location of the cell containing the formula. EX 115–116, EX 119

removing fields from PivotTables, EX 262–263

renaming worksheets, EX 35–36

Replace The command to overwrite letters and numbers in a workbook with another entry. EX 38–39

report, PivotTable, EX 268

report filter Filters the PivotTable to display summarized data for one or more field items or all field items in the Report Filter area. EX 257–258

resizing
    macro buttons, EX 438
    shapes, EX 202–203

window, OFF 6–7
workspace, OFF 6–7

resizing handle A square or dot on a selection box that lets you change an object's width and height. EX 169

Ribbon The main set of commands in Office that you click to execute tasks. OFF 10–14, WIN7 18
    clicking button icons, OFF 10–12
    Excel, EX 4, EX 5
    galleries, OFF 12–13
    key tips, OFF 12
    keyboard shortcuts, OFF 12
    Live Preview, OFF 13
    opening dialog boxes and task panes, OFF 13–14
    reducing and redisplaying, OFF 10
    tabs, OFF 10

RIGHT function, EX A 3

rotating
    cell content, EX 70–71
    3D pie charts, EX 179–180

ROUND function, EX 122

row
    changing height, EX 15, EX 18
    clearing, EX 20
    deleting, EX 20
    freezing, EX 220
    inserting, EX 18–20

row heading In Excel, the part of a worksheet that identifies each row by a different number. EX 4, EX 5

rule A statement that specifies the type of condition (such as formatting cells greater than a specified value), the type of formatting when that condition occurs (such as light red fill with dark red text), and the cell or range the formatting is applied to. EX 362–364

running macros, EX 427–432

S

sans serif font A font that does not have the small horizontal lines (called serifs) at the tops and bottoms of letters. EX 59

saving
    files, OFF 18–21
    workbooks, EX 21
    workbooks created in earlier versions of. Excel, EX A 2–3
    workbooks with macros, EX 439–440

savings plan, creating, EX 137–140

scale (n.) The range of values that spans along an axis. EX 184

scale (v.) To change the size of a graphic to make it fit into a document. EX 44

scatter chart. *See* XY scatter chart

ScreenTip Onscreen text that appears when you position the mouse pointer over certain objects. ScreenTips tell you the purpose or function of the object. OFF 12, OFF 23, EX 312

scrolling worksheets, EX 7

SEARCH function, EX A 3

secondary sort field The second sort field. EX 228

secondary value axis The axis in a column chart that displays the secondary values associated with the heights of each column. EX 184

Select All button, EX 4, EX 5
selecting
  cell ranges, EX 22–23
  multiple filter items, EX 237–238
selection box A box surrounding an object that lets you move or resize the object. EX 169
serial date (or serial date-time) A date and/or time that is stored as a number representing the number of days since January 0, 1900 plus a fractional portion of a 24-hour day. EX A 16
series, filling with AutoFill, EX 134–137
series name The name of the data series. EX 165
series value The actual data displayed in a chart. EX 165
serif font A font that includes small horizontal lines (called serifs) at the tops and bottoms of letters. EX 59
shape, EX 201–204
  adding text, EX 202
  aligning, EX 203
  copying, EX 203
  grouping, EX 203–204
  inserting, EX 202
  inserting in cells, EX 202
  resizing, EX 202
sharing styles and themes, EX 80
sheet. *See* chart sheet; worksheet
sheet tab The area at the bottom of a worksheet that identifies the worksheet; clicking a sheet tab makes the worksheet active. EX 4, EX 5
sheet tab scrolling button, EX 4, EX 5
shortcut menu A list of commands directly related to the object that you right-clicked. OFF 17, WIN7 18
signature, digital, EX 424
simple interest The type of interest in which the interest paid is equal to a percentage of principal for each period that the money has been lent. EX 147
sizing buttons, Office programs, OFF 6, WIN7 18
slash (/), division operator, EX 28
sort The process of rearranging data in a certain order, such as ascending or descending. EX 227–232
  custom lists, EX 231–232
  multiple columns, EX 228–231
  PivotTable fields, EX 260–261
  single column, EX 228
  sort buttons, EX 228
  Sort dialog box, EX 228–231
Sort dialog box, EX 228–231
sort field A field you use to order data. EX 227
source file The workbook that contains the data when two files are linked. EX 295, EX 296, B2
  opening destination workbooks with source workbooks closed, EX 304–308
spelling checker A feature that checks the the words in a document against the program's built-in dictionary and helps you avoid typographical errors. EX 39–40
spreadsheet A tool used in business for budgeting, inventory management, and decision making for analyzing and reporting information. EX 2–3
standard color A color that is always available regardless of the workbook's theme. EX 60
starting Office programs, OFF 3–5

Statistical functions, EX 122
status bar An area at the bottom of the program window that contains information about the open file or the current task on which you are working.
  getting information, OFF 7–8, WIN7 18
  Office programs, OFF 6
stock chart, EX 167
structured reference The. Excel table name or table column header that you can use in a formula in place of its cell or range reference. EX 344–347
  qualifiers, EX 345, EX 346
  tables, EX 367
style A saved collection of formatting options—number formats, text alignment, font sizes and colors, borders, and background fills—that can be applied to cells in a worksheet. EX 76–78, EX 253
  applying, EX 77–78
  charts, EX 171–173
  sharing, EX 80
  table. *See* table style
sub procedure In VBA, a macro. EX 433
SUBSTITUTE function The function that replaces existing text with new text in a text string. EX A 10–11
subtotal, EX 242–246
  Outline buttons, EX 245–246
  Subtotal command, EX 242–245
Subtotal dialog box, EX 243
subtraction operator (-), EX 28
SUM function, EX 122, EX 124–125
SUMIF function A function that adds the values in a range that meet criteria you specify; also called a conditional sum. EX 369–370
SUMIFS function A function that adds values in a range that meet multiple criteria. EX 371–372
summarizing data conditionally, EX 367–372
  AVERAGEIF function, EX 370–371
  AVERAGEIFS function, EX 372
  COUNTIF function, EX 367–368
  COUNTIFS function, EX 371
  SUMIF function, EX 369–370
  SUMIFS function, EX 371–372
summarizing data using database functions, EX 379–382
surface chart, EX 167
switching
  between open programs and files, OFF 5
  views, OFF 8
syntax Rules that specify how a function should be written; the general syntax of all. Excel functions is FUNCTION(argument1, argument2, ..). EX 121–123

T

tab Part of the Ribbon that includes commands related to particular activities. OFF 10, WIN7 18
  contextual, OFF 15
table
  adding records, EX 225–227
  calculated columns, EX 339
  calculating summary statistics, EX 240–242
  cell references, EX 367
  creating, EX 221–224
  creating fields, EX 339
  data definition. *See* data definition table

  deleting records, EX 227
  features, EX 222
  filtering data. *See* filter
  finding and editing records, EX 226–227
  formatting, EX 224
  lookup. *See* lookup table
  PivotTables. *See* PivotTable
  range references, EX 367
  renaming, EX 223–224, EX 339
  sorting data. *See* sort
  structured references, EX 344–347, EX 367
  subtotals. *See* subtotal
Table Name box, EX 224
table style An. Excel setting that applies styles to four table elements (header row, first column, last column, and totals row). EX 82–86
  applying to existing table, EX 82–84
  selecting options, EX 84–86
task pane A window that provides access to commands for common tasks you'll perform in Office programs. OFF 13
template A workbook that you can open with labels, formats, and formulas already built into it from which you create new workbooks. EX 313–321
  automatically installed with. Excel, EX 313
  based on existing template, creating, EX 314–316
  creating new workbook from, EX 319–321
  custom, creating, EX 316–321
  default, EX 313
  downloading, EX 313
text
  adding to shapes, EX 202
  formatting in worksheets, EX 58–60
  selections, formatting, EX 62
text data A combination of letters, numbers, and some symbols. EX 9
  entering in cells, EX 10–12
  entering multiple lines in cells, EX 12–13
text filters, EX 236
TEXT function, EX A 3
text functions, EX A 3–11, EX 122
  concatenation operator, EX A 6–7
  LEFT function, EX A 4–6
  LEN function, EX A 4
  PROPER function, EX A 6
  SUBSTITUTE function, EX A 10–11
  Text to Columns command, EX A 8–9
  UPPER function, EX A 9–10
text string Two or more text characters. EX 9
Text to Columns command, EX A 8–9
theme A designed collection of formatting options that include colors, graphics, and background images. EX 58, EX 78–80
theme color The 12 colors that belong to a workbook's theme. EX 60
theme font A font associated with a particular design theme and used for headings and body text. EX 59
3D pie chart, EX 178–181
  rotating, EX 179–180
3-D reference The same cell or range in multiple worksheets in the same workbook. EX 289–293
  tiled layout, EX 298

time
  formatting, EX A 14–16
  storing, EX A 16
time data A value in a recognized time format. EX 9
  formatting in worksheets, EX 66–67
title
  charts, EX 170, EX 173–174
  Web pages, EX 323
title bar
  Excel, EX 4, EX 5
  Office programs, OFF 6
TODAY function, EX 145–146
Total row A row at the end of an. Excel table that is used to calculate summary statistics for the columns in the table. EX 240–242
TRIM function, EX A 3
truncate To cut off, or hide, the part of an entry that does not fit in a cell. EX 9
Trust Center A central location for all the security settings in Office 2007. EX 422
typeface The specific design of a set of printed characters, including letters, numbers, punctuation marks, and symbols. EX 58

U

undoing actions in worksheets, EX 37–38
ungrouping worksheets, EX 286
unprotecting worksheets, EX 418
updating, EX 263–264
  linked objects, EX B 5–6
  linked workbooks, EX 303–304
UPPER function The function that converts all letters of each word in a text string to uppercase. EX A 3, EX A 9–10

V

validation rule A statement that defines criteria for the data that can be stored in a cell or range; you can specify the type of data allowed as well as a list or range of acceptable values. EX 407, EX 408–409
  complex, formulas to define, EX 412
  list, EX 412–414
value axis. *See* vertical (value) axis
value field In a PivotTable, a field that contains summary data. EX 247
  formatting, EX 253–254
  second, adding to PivotTable, EX 261–262
Value Field Settings dialog box, EX 254
vertical (value) axis The y-axis where, for example, data values, such as sales values, are plotted. EX 184
vertical layout, EX 298
vertical scroll bar, EX 4, EX 5
view, switching, OFF 8
view shortcuts, EX 4, EX 5, OFF 6
virus, macro, EX 421
  protecting against, EX 421–424

Visual Basic Editor A separate program that works with. Excel and all of the Office products to edit and manage VBA code. EX 432–436
Visual Basic for Applications (VBA) A programming language. EX 424
VLOOKUP function A function that searches vertically down a lookup table to retrieve a value from that table; used when the compare values are stored in the first column of the lookup table. EX 355
  approximate matches, EX 358–360
  exact matches, EX 355–358
  nesting within IFERROR function, EX 366–367

W

Web page
  saving workbook as, EX 321–324
  setting options, EX 3230324
  setting page title, EX 323
WEEKDAY function, EX 145
what-if analysis An approach using an electronic spreadsheet in which you change one or more of the values in the worksheet and then examine the recalculated values to determine the effect of the change. EX 2
window A rectangular work area on the screen that contains a program, text, graphics, or data. WIN7 18–25
  resizing, OFF 6–7
window element, common, OFF 6–10
Windows Explorer
  navigating using, WIN7 32–34
Windows Flip, WIN7 16–17
Windows key, WIN7 15
Word. *See* Microsoft Office Word 2007
workbook The file in which. Excel stores an electronic spreadsheet. EX 4, EX 220, OFF 2
  accessing on Web interactively, EX 321
  created in earlier versions of. Excel, opening and saving, EX A 2–3
  edits, effects on macros, EX 429
  effective, EX 8
  formatting, EX 58. *See also* formatting worksheet cells; formatting worksheets
  linking. *See* linking workbooks
  opening with macros, EX 440–441
  planning, EX 8–9
  protecting, EX 417–418
  saving, EX 21
  saving as Web page, EX 321–324
  saving with macros, EX 439–440
  templates. *See* template
workbook window Window in which a workbook is displayed; also called worksheet window. EX 4, EX 5
worksheet Each workbook is made up of individual worksheets, or sheets containing formulas, functions, values, text, and graphics. EX 4, EX 35–46
  active. *See* active sheet
  changing view, EX 41–42
  comments, EX 418–420
  copying, EX 36

  deleting, EX 35
  editing, EX 36–40
  finding and replacing items, EX 38–39
  formatting. *See* formatting worksheet cells; formatting worksheets
  formulas. *See* formulas
  functions. *See* functions
  inserting, EX 35
  moving, EX 36
  multiple. *See* multiple worksheets
  navigating, EX 6–7
  page orientation, EX 42–43
  previewing, EX 40–43
  printing, EX 43
  protecting, EX 415–417
  redoing actions, EX 38
  renaming, EX 35–36
  scrolling, EX 7
  spell checking, EX 39–40
  undoing actions, EX 37–38
  unprotecting, EX 418
worksheet group A collection of two or more selected worksheets in which everything you do to the active worksheet also affects the other worksheets in the group. EX 283–286
  copying, EX 287
  editing, EX 285
  entering formulas, EX 283–285
  formatting, EX 285–286
  printing, EX 293–294
  referencing cells and ranges in other worksheets, EX 288–289
  3-D references to add values across worksheets, EX 289–293
  ungrouping, EX 286
workspace (Excel) An. Excel file that saves information about all of the currently opened workbooks, such as their locations, window sizes, zoom magnifications, and other settings. EX 308–310
workspace (Office)
  resizing, OFF 6–7
  zooming, OFF 8–10

X

XY scatter chart A chart that shows the patterns or relationship between two or more sets of values. EX 167, EX 201
YEAR function, EX 145

Z

zoom To magnify or shrink your view of a window. OFF 8–10
zoom controls
  Excel, EX 4, EX 5
  Office programs, OFF 6

Task Reference

TASK	PAGE #	RECOMMENDED METHOD
3-D reference, use	EX 290	See Reference Window: Entering a Function That contains a 3-D Reference
Absolute reference, change to relative	EX 119	See Reference Window: Entering Relative, Absolute, and Mixed References
Action, redo	EX 38	Click
Action, undo	EX 38	Click
AutoFill, copy formulas	EX 132	See Reference Window: Copying Formulas and Formats with AutoFill
AutoFill, create series	EX 135	See Reference Window: Creating a Series with AutoFill
Background color, apply	EX 61	Select range, in Font group on Home tab click , click color
Border, create	EX 71	Select range, in Font group on Home tab click , click border
Cell reference, change	EX 119	See Reference Window: Entering Relative, Absolute, and Mixed References
Cell, clear contents of	EX 20	Right-click cell, click Clear Contents
Cell, edit	EX 37	Double-click cell, enter changes
Cells, delete	EX 20	Select range, click Delete button in Cells group on Home tab
Cells, insert	EX 19	See Reference Window: Inserting a Column or Row
Cells, lock or unlock	EX 415	Select cell or range, in Font group on the Home tab, click Dialog Box Launcher, click Protection tab, check or uncheck Locked check box, click OK
Cells, merge and center	EX 70	Select adjacent cells, in Alignment group on Home tab click
Cell or range name, create	EX 397	See Reference Window: Creating a Name for a Cell or Range
Cell or range, select by name	EX 398	Click Name box arrow, click defined name
Cells, reference in other worksheets	EX 288	Enter reference in the following format: =SheetName!CellRange
Chart axis title, add or edit	EX 184	Select chart, in Labels group on Chart Tools Layout tab click Axis Titles button
Chart title, edit	EX 171	Double-click chart title, edit text of title
Chart, add data label	EX 174	Click chart, in Labels group on Chart Tools Layout tab click Data Labels button, select options
Chart, add data series	EX 195	See Reference Window: Adding a Data Series to a Chart
Chart, add gridline	EX 193	Click chart, in Axes group on Chart Tools Layout tab click Gridlines button
Chart, change location	EX 167	Select chart, in Location group on Chart Tools Design tab click Move Chart button
Chart, change to 3D	EX 177	Select chart, in Type group on Chart Tools Design tab click Change Chart Type button, select 3D chart type
Chart, format data marker	EX 185	Click data marker, in Current Selection group on Chart Tools Layout tab click Format Selection
Chart, move	EX 167	Select chart, drag to new location
Chart, resize	EX 167	Select chart, drag resizing handle
Chart, select	EX 167	Move pointer over a blank area of the chart, and then click
Chart, update	EX 179	Enter new values for chart's data source
Column, change width	EX 16	See Reference Window: Changing the Column Width or Row Height

Microsoft Office Excel 2007—Introductory

TASK	PAGE #	RECOMMENDED METHOD
Column, insert	EX 19	See Reference Window: Inserting a Column or Row
Column, select	EX 19	Click column heading; to select a range of columns, click the first column heading in the range, hold down Shift and click the last column heading
Combination chart, create	EX 197	See Reference Window: Creating a Combination Chart
Comment, delete	EX 420	Click cell with comment, in Comments group on the Review tab, click the Delete button
Comment, insert	EX 418	See Reference Window: Inserting a Comment
Comment, show or hide	EX 419	Click cell with comment, in the Comments group on the Review tab, click the Show/Hide Comment button
Comments, show or hide all	EX 419	In the Comments group on the Review tab, click the Show All Comments button
Computer window, open	WIN7 29	Click , click Computer
Conditional format, apply	EX 87	See Reference Window: Applying Conditional Formats (Data Bars and Highlights)
Conditional Formatting Rules Manager, use	EX 363	In the Styles group on the Home tab, click the Conditional Formatting button, click Manage Rules
Criteria filters, specify complex criteria	EX 239	Click filter arrow, point to Number Filters, Text Filters, or Date Filters, specify filter criteria, click OK as needed
Custom formats, create	EX A13	In the Number group on the Home tab, click the Dialog Box Launcher, on Number tab, click Custom in the Category box, enter format codes in the Type box, click OK
Data, create error alert message	EX 408	See Reference Window: Validating Data
Data, create input message	EX 408	See Reference Window: Validating Data
Data, create validation rule	EX 408	See Reference Window: Validating Data
Data series, add to chart	EX 195	See Reference Window: Adding a Data Series to a Chart
Date, insert current	EX 145	Insert TODAY() or NOW() function
Dates, fill in using AutoFill	EX 135	See Reference Window: Creating a Series with AutoFill
Developer tab, display or hide on the Ribbon	EX 420	Click , click Excel Options button, check or uncheck the Show Developer tab in the Ribbon check box, click OK
Duplicate records, highlight	EX 361	In the Styles group on the Home tab, click Conditional Formatting button, point to Highlight Cells Rules, click Duplicate Values
Embedded object, create	EX B5	Copy selection, place insertion point where you want to place the object, in the Clipboard group on the Home tab, click the Paste button arrow, click Paste Special, click Paste option button, select object type, click OK
Embedded object, edit	EX B6	Double-click the embedded object, make edits, deselect object
Excel, start	EX 3	Click , click All Programs, click Microsoft Office, click Microsoft Office Excel 2007
Excel table, add record	EX 225	See Reference Window: Adding a Record to an Excel table
Excel table, create	EX 222	On Insert tab, in Tables group, click Table button, verify range of data, click OK
Excel table, format	EX 224	In Table Style Options group on Table Tools Design tab, click an option
Excel table, rename	EX 224	Click in table, in Properties group on Table Tools Design tab, select name in Table Name box, type name

TASK	PAGE #	RECOMMENDED METHOD
External reference formula, create	EX 299	Click cell in destination file, type=, click cell in source file, complete formula as usual
File, close	OFF 21	Click , click Close
File, open	OFF 22	See Reference Window: Opening an Existing File or Creating a New File
File, print	OFF 27	See Reference Window: Printing a File
File, save	OFF 18	See Reference Window: Saving a File
Filter, clear from column	EX 237	Click column filter arrow, click Clear Filter command
Filter, clear from entire table	EX 240	In Sort & Filter group on Data tab, click the Clear button
Filter, select multiple items in a column	EX 238	Click filter arrow, check two or more items, click OK
Filter, use multiple columns	EX 236	Filter for one column, then repeat to filter for additional columns
Filter, use one column	EX 233	Click the column's filter arrow, check item to filter by, click OK
Filter arrows, display or hide	EX 233	In Sort & Filter group on Data tab, click Filter button
Filter by color, apply	EX 364	Click filter arrow, point to Filter by Color, click a color in the palette
Folder, sort files in	WIN7 31	In a folder window, click a column heading (button)
Folder list, expand	WIN7 33	Click ▷
Font, change color	EX 61	In Font group on Home tab, click **A**, click color
Font, change size	EX 60	In Font group on Home tab, click Font Size arrow, click point size
Font, change style	EX 60	In Font group on Home tab, click **B**, click *I*, or click U
Font, change typeface	EX 59	In Font group on Home tab, click Font arrow, click font
Format, apply Accounting Style, Percent Style, or Comma Style	EX 65–66	In Number group on Home tab, click $, click %, or click ,
Format, copy using Format Painter	EX 75	Select range, in Clipboard group on Home tab click , click range
Format, decrease decimal places	EX 66	In Number group on Home tab, click
Format, find and replace	EX 38	In Editing group on Home tab, click Find & Select, click Replace
Format, increase decimal places	EX 66	In Number group on Home tab, click
Format Cells dialog box, open	EX 72	In Number group on Home tab, click Dialog Box Launcher
Formula, copy	EX 24	See Reference Window: Moving or Copying a Cell or Range
Formula, copy using the fill handle	EX 132	See Reference Window: Copying Formulas and Formats with AutoFill
Formula, enter	EX 29	See Reference Window: Entering a Formula
Formula, reference another worksheet	EX 288	See Reference Window: Entering a Formula That References Another Worksheet
Formula results, copy and paste as values	EX A8	Copy range with formula results, click first cell in paste location, in the Clipboard group on the Home tab, click the Paste button arrow, click Paste Values
Formulas, add names to existing	EX 406	See Reference Window: Adding Defined Names to Existing Formulas
Formulas, view	EX 44	Click , press Ctrl+`
Function, insert	EX 123	See Reference Window: Inserting a Function
Header/footer, create	EX 99	In Page Layout view, click header or footer section, type text or click button in Header & Footer Elements group on Design tab
Help, find topic in Windows 7	WIN7 35	Click , click Help and Support, click in the Search Help box, type a word or phrase, press Enter

Microsoft Office Excel 2007—Introductory | REF 13

TASK	PAGE #	RECOMMENDED METHOD
Help task pane, use	OFF 24	*See* Reference Window: Getting Help
Hyperlink, create	EX 311	*See* Reference Window: Inserting a Hyperlink
Hyperlink, edit	EX 312	Right-click cell with hyperlink, click Edit Hyperlink, make edits in Edit Hyperlink dialog box, click OK
Input message, create	EX 408	*See* Reference Window: Validating Data
Invalid data, circle	EX 414	In the Data Tools group on the Data tab, click the Data Validation button arrow, click Circle Invalid Data
Linked object, edit	EX B5	Edit as usual in source file, or double-click the linked object in the destination file, make edits, deselect object
Linked object, paste to another file	EX B4	Copy selection, place insertion point where you want to place the link, in the Clipboard group on the Home tab, click the Paste button arrow, click Paste Special, click Paste link option button, select object type, click OK
Linked workbooks, update	EX 304	Click in source file and edit as usual
Links, manage	EX 306	In the Connections group on the Data tab, click the Edit Links button, select desired option, click OK
Macro, edit	EX 432	*See* Reference Window: Editing a Macro
Macro, record	EX 425	*See* Reference Window: Recording a Macro
Macro, run	EX 427	*See* Reference Window: Running a Macro
Macro, set security level for	EX 423	*See* Reference Window: Setting Macro Security in Excel
Macro, view code	EX 432	*See* Reference Window: Editing a Macro
Macro button, create	EX 436	*See* Reference Window: Creating a Macro Button
Macro button, move	EX 438	Right-click the button, press Esc, drag the button by its selection border to a new location
Macro button, resize	EX 438	Right-click the button, press Esc, drag a selection handle
Music library, open	WIN7 29	In a folder window, click Music in the Navigation pane
My Documents folder, open	WIN7 32	In a folder window, click ▷ next to Libraries, click ▷ next to Documents, click My Documents
Name, add to existing formulas	EX 406	*See* Reference Window: Adding Defined Names to Existing Formulas
Name, create for cell or range	EX 397	*See* Reference Window: Creating a Name for a Cell or Range
Office program, start	OFF 3	*See* Reference Window: Starting Office Programs
Page, change orientation	EX 96	Click Page Layout tab, click Orientation button in Page Setup group, choose orientation type
Page break, set	EX 97	*See* Reference Window: Setting and Removing Page Breaks
Page break preview, switch to	EX 96	Click
Pie chart, 3D, rotate	EX 177	Select chart, in Background group on Chart Tools Layout tab, click 3-D Rotation button
Pie chart, create	EX 165	Select data values to chart, click Insert tab, click Pie button in Charts group, select a chart to sub-type
PivotChart, create	EX 269	In the Tools group on the PivotTable Tools Options tab, click the PivotChart button, complete the Insert Chart dialog box, click OK
PivotTable, create	EX 248	*See* Reference Window: Creating a PivotTable
PivotTable, rearrange	EX 255	Drag field buttons in the PivotTable Field List

TASK	PAGE #	RECOMMENDED METHOD
PivotTable, refresh	EX 264	In the Data group on the PivotTable Tools Options tab, click the Refresh button
PivotTable field, remove	EX 263	In PivotTable Field List, uncheck items in the field area
PivotTable fields, filter	EX 258	Click the field arrow button in the PivotTable for the data you want to filter, then check and uncheck items
PivotTable items, group	EX 267	In the Group group on the PivotTable Tools Options tab, click the Group Field button, select options in the Grouping dialog box, click OK
PivotTable report layout, change	EX 255	In the Layout group on the PivotTable Tools Design tab, click the Report Layout button, click a layout
PivotTable style, apply	EX 253	In the PivotTable Styles group on the PivotTable Tools Design tab, click More button, click a style
PivotTable value fields, format	EX 254	Click cell in PivotTable, in the Active Field group on the PivotTable Tools Options tab, click Field Settings button, click Number Format button, select format, click OK
Print area, define	EX 96	Select range, click Page Layout tab, click Print Area button in Page Setup group, click Set Print Area
Program, Office, exit	OFF 28	Click X on the title bar
Program, start in Windows 7	WIN7 12	See Reference box: Starting a Program
Programs, Office, open	OFF 3	See Reference Window: Starting Office Programs
Range, copy	EX 24	See Reference Window: Moving or Copying a Cell or Range
Range, move	EX 24	See Reference Window: Moving or Copying a Cell or Range
Range, select adjacent	EX 22	See Reference Window: Selecting Cell Ranges
Range, select nonadjacent	EX 22	See Reference Window: Selecting Cell Ranges
Record, delete from Excel table	EX 227	Select the record, in Cells group on Home tab, click Delete button arrow, and then click Delete Table Rows
Records, find and replace in Excel table	EX 226	Click in table, in Editing group on Home tab, click the Find & Select button, use Find and Replace dialog box as usual
Relative reference, change to absolute	EX 119	See Reference Window: Entering Relative, Absolute, and Mixed References
Report filter, add to a PivotTable	EX 257	In the PivotTable Field List, drag a field button to the Report Filter box
Report filter, modify	EX 257	Click the report filter arrow, click filter items
Ribbon, minimize or maximize	EX 440	Double-click any tab
Row, change height	EX 16	See Reference Window: Changing the Column Width or Row Height
Row, delete from Excel table	EX 27	See Reference Window: Inserting or Deleting a Cell Range
Row, hide	EX 95	In Cells group on Home tab, click Format button, point to Hide & Unhide, click Hide Rows
Row, insert	EX 19	See Reference Window: Inserting a Column or Row
Row, select	EX 19	Click row heading; to select a range of rows, click the first row heading in the range, hold down Shift and click the last row in the range
Row, unhide	EX 95	Select rows above and below hidden rows, in Cells group on Home tab click Format button, point to Hide & Unhide, click Unhide Rows
Rows, repeat in printout	EX 98	Click Page Layout tab, click Print Titles button in Page Setup group, click Rows to repeat at top

TASK	PAGE #	RECOMMENDED METHOD
Row(s) and column(s), freeze	EX 221	Click cell below and to right of row(s) and column(s) to freeze. On View tab, in Window group, click Freeze Panes button, click option
Row(s) and column(s), unfreeze	EX 221	On View tab, in Window group, click Freeze Panes button, click Unfreeze Panes
Shape, insert	EX 200	Click Insert tab, click Shapes button in Illustrations group, click desired shape, drag pointer to create shape
Sort, create a custom list	EX 231	See Reference Window: Creating a Custom List
Sort, multiple columns	EX 229	See Reference Window: Sorting Data Using Multiple Sort Fields
Sort, one column	EX 228	Click [A-Z] or [Z-A]
Special formats, use	EX A12	In the Number group on the Home tab, click the Dialog Box Launcher, on Number tab, click Special in the Category box, select a format, click OK
Spelling, check in worksheet	EX 40	Click Review tab, click Spelling in Proofing group
Style, apply	EX 77	See Reference Window: Applying Styles
Subtotal Outline view, use	EX 245	Click an outline button to show or hide the selected outline level
Subtotals, insert	EX 243	See Reference Window: Calculating Subtotals for a Range of Data
Subtotals, remove	EX 246	In Outline group on the Data tab, click Subtotal button, click Remove All button, click OK
Sum function, apply	EX 33	Click cell, in Editing group on Home tab, click Σ
Template, create custom	EX 317	See Reference Window: Creating a Custom Template
Text, align within a cell	EX 68	In Alignment group on Home tab, click [icon], click [icon], or click [icon]
Text, enter into cell	EX 10	Click the cell, type text entry, press Enter
Text, enter multiple lines in a cell	EX 12	See Reference Window: Entering Multiple Lines of Text Within a Cell
Text, increase or decrease indent of	EX 68	In Alignment group on Home tab, click [icon] or [icon]
Total row, add or remove from Excel table	EX 240	In Table Style Options group on the Table Tools Design tab, check or uncheck Total Row check box
Total row, select summary statistics	EX 240	Click arrow button in Total row cell, click summary function
Validation circles, clear all	EX 414	In the Data Tools group on the Data tab, click the Data Validation button, click Clear Validation Circles
Validation circles, clear from a cell	EX 414	Enter valid data
Validation circles, create	EX 414	In the Data Tools group on the Data tab, click the Data Validation button, click Circle Invalid Data
Validation rule, create	EX 408	See Reference Window: Validating Data
VBA code, view	EX 432	See Reference Window: Editing a Macro
VBA, insert a command	EX 434	Open the Visual Basic Editor, display the macro in the Code window, click at the end of a VBA command, press Enter, type the new command
View, change in a folder window	WIN7 30	Click [icon], click the view to change to
Visual Basic Editor, open or close	EX 432	See Reference Window: Editing a Macro
Web page, create from a workbook, worksheet, or range	EX 326	See Reference Window: Saving a Workbook, Worksheet, or Range as a Web Page
Window, close	OFF 6	Click [icon] or click [icon]
Window, maximize	OFF 7	Click [icon] or click [icon]
Window, minimize	OFF 7	Click [icon] or click [icon]

TASK	PAGE #	RECOMMENDED METHOD
Window, restore	OFF 7	Click ⧉ or click ▢
Windows, switch between using Aero Flip 3D	WIN7 16	Press and hold the Windows key and press Tab
Windows Explorer, open in Windows 7	WIN7 32	Click 📁 on the taskbar
Windows 7, log off	WIN7 39	Click ⊕, point to ▸, click Log off
Windows 7, turn off	WIN7 39	Click ⊕, click Shut down
Workbook, create from template	EX 314	See Reference Window: Creating a Workbook Based on a Template
Workbook, preview	EX 43	Click ⊕, click Print, click Print Preview
Workbook, print	EX 43	Click ⊕, click Print, click Print, click OK
Workbook, protect	EX 417	See Reference Window: Protecting a Workbook
Workbook, save	EX 21	On Quick Access Toolbar, click 💾
Workbook, save as a Web page	EX 326	See Reference Window: Saving a Workbook, Worksheet, or Range as a Web Page
Workbook, save earlier version in Excel 2007 file format	EX A2	In Save As dialog box, select save location, enter filename, click the the Save as type button, click Excel Workbook, click Save
Workbook, save in earlier Excel file format	EX A17	In Save As dialog box, change filename, select save location, click the Save as type button, click Excel 97-2003 Workbook, click Save
Workbook, save with macros	EX 440	In Save As dialog box, select save location, enter filename, click the Save as type button, click Excel Macro-Enabled Workbook, click Save
Workbooks, arrange	EX 298	See Reference Window: Arranging Workbooks
Workbooks, link	EX 296	Enter a formula in the following form: =[WorkbookName]WorksheetName!CellRange
Workbooks, switch	EX 297	In the Window group on the View tab, click the Switch Windows button, click the workbook to make active
Worksheet group, print	EX 293	Select worksheet group, set up worksheets and print as usual
Worksheet, add background image	EX 63	Click Page Layout tab, click Background button in Page Setup group, click image file, click Insert
Worksheet, delete	EX 35	Right-click sheet tab, click Delete
Worksheet, insert	EX 35	Click 🗒
Worksheet, move	EX 36	Drag sheet tab to new location
Worksheet, protect	EX 415	See Reference Window: Protecting a Worksheet
Worksheet, rename	EX 36	Double-click sheet tab, type new name, press Enter
Worksheet, unprotect	EX 418	Make worksheet active, in Changes group on the Review tab, click the Unprotect Sheet button
Worksheets, copy to another workbook	EX 287	See Reference Window: Copying Worksheets to Another Workbook
Worksheets, group or ungroup	EX 283	See Reference Window: Grouping and Ungrouping Worksheets
Worksheets, move between	EX 7	Click sheet tab; or click a tab scrolling button and then click the sheet tab
Workspace, create	EX 309	Open and arrange workbooks as desired, in the Window group on the View tab, click the Save Workspace button, type a filename, select save location, click Save
Workspace, zoom	OFF 8	See Reference Window: Zooming the Workspace